THE
WORLD'S
HISTORY

THIRD EDITION

COMBINED VOLUME

THE WORLD'S HISTORY

THIRD EDITION

COMBINED VOLUME

HOWARD SPODEK

PEARSON

Prentice Hall

Upper Saddle River, N.J. 07458

Editorial Director: Charlyce Jones Owen
Executive Editor: Charles Cavaliere
Development Editor: Elaine Silverstein
Editorial Assistant: Shannon Corliss
Executive Marketing Manager: Heather Shelstad

Credits and acknowledgments borrowed from other sources and reproduced, with
permission, in this textbook appear on pages xix–xxii.

Pearson Prentice Hall™ is a trademark of Pearson Education, Inc.
Pearson® is a registered trademark of Pearson plc.
Prentice Hall® is a registered trademark of Pearson Education, Inc.

Pearson Education LTD.
Pearson Education Australia PTY, Limited
Pearson Education Singapore, Pte. Ltd
Pearson Education North Asia Ltd
Pearson Education, Canada, Ltd
Pearson Educación de Mexico, S.A. de C.V.
Pearson Education–Japan
Pearson Education Malaysia, Pte. Ltd

*Advanced Placement and AP are registered trademarks of the College Entrance
Examination, which was not involved in the production of this product and does
not endorse it.

This book was designed and produced by
Laurence King Publishing Ltd, London
www.laurenceking.co.uk
Every effort has been made to contact the copyright holders, but should there be
any errors or omissions, Laurence King Publishing Ltd would be pleased to insert
the appropriate acknowledgment in any subsequent printing of this publication.

Editor: Richard Mason
Picture Researcher: Emma Brown
Design: Newton Harris Design Partnership

Front cover: *Iksander at Sea*, from the *Khamsa (Five Poems)* of Nizami, 1505. Miniature
painting. British Library, London.

10 9 8 7 6 5 4 3
ISBN 0-13-192868-6

BRIEF CONTENTS

CONTENTS

Part 3
Empire and Imperialism

2000 B.C.E.–1100 C.E.

What are Empires and Why are they Important? **122**

5 DAWN OF THE EMPIRES

2000 B.C.E.–300 B.C.E.

6 ROME AND THE BARBARIANS

750 B.C.E.–500 C.E.

Part 7

Exploding Technologies

19 METHODS OF MASS PRODUCTION AND DESTRUCTION

20 WORLD WAR II AND THE COLD WAR

21 COLD WAR AND NEW NATIONS

MAPS

AT A GLANCE

CHARTS

PICTURE CREDITS

I-6 British Library, London
I-11 Novosti (London)
3 (top) © Jonathan Blair/Corbis
3 (bottom) © Jonathan Blair/Corbis
4 © Paul A. Souders/Corbis
9 © Museum of Fine Arts, Houston, Texas, USA/Bridgeman Art Library
10 By permission of the Syndics of Cambridge University Library (DAR140.4)
14 Science Photo Library/John Reader
15 Natural History Museum, London
16 © Sygma Collection/Corbis
17 Natural History Museum, London
19 Natural History Museum, London
25 Royal Geographic Society/Bridgeman Art Library
27 Musée National de Préhistoire, Les Eyzies de Tayac, France
28 (top) Natural History Museum, London
28 (bottom) Jean Vertut, Issy-les-Molineaux
30 (top) Yan, Toulouse
31 J. Clottes, Ministère de la Culture et la Communication–Direction du Patrimonie, sous Direction de l'Archéologie
36 Howard Spodek
37 (top) Musée Guimet, Paris, France/Bridgeman Art Library
38 Photo courtesy of Science Museum of Minnesota
40–41 Bridgeman Art Library
42 © Dean Conger/Corbis
48 AKG Images/Erich Lessing
49 Hilprecht Collection, Friedrich-Schiller University, Jena
50 British Museum, London
53 (top) Hirmer Verlag, München
53 (bottom) University of Pennsylvania Museum
54 British Museum, London
55 British Museum, London
58 © Photo RMN
59 © Photo RMN
64 AKG Images
66 British Museum, London
68 British Museum, London
71 © Photo RMN
72 Egyptian Museum, Cairo
73 British Museum, London
74 AKG Images
78 Egyptian Museum, Cairo
82 (top) National Museum of India, New Delhi
82 (bottom) National Museum of Pakistan, Karachi
85 James Blair
90 Institute of Archaeology, Beijing
91 East Asian Library, Columbia University
93 Historical Museum, Beijing
95 Academia Sinica, Taipei
100 Museo Regional de Veracruz, Jalapa, Mexico
102 South American Pictures
103 British Museum, London

104 University of Pennsylvania Museum
110 South American Pictures
113 AKG Images
114 National Museum, Lagos, Nigeria
115 Private Collection
118 Museum of Anatolian Civilizations, Ankara, Turkey/Bridgeman Art Library
119 © Bettman/Corbis
120 Art Archive/Musée du Louvre, Paris
121 AKG Images
123 Stapleton Collection/Bridgeman Art Library
124 Art Archive/Dagli Orti
128 Photo Scala, Florence
131 British Museum, London
132 Robert Harding Picture Library
137 Giraudon/Bridgeman Art Library
141 National Archaeological Museum, Athens
144 (top) Staatliche Museen, Berlin
147 Alison Frantz, Princeton, N.J.
149 Acropolis Museum, Athens
151 British Museum, London
156 © Fotografica Foglia, Naples
158 Museo Capitolino, Rome
162 AKG Images
164 Museo Capitolino, Rome
169 (top) Photo Scala, Florence
169 (bottom) Art Archive
172 Photo Scala, Florence
174 Werner Forman Archive
176 Leonard von Matt
177 Alinari, Florence
179 Musei Vaticani, Rome
185 A.F. Kersting, London
186 Fototeca Unione, Rome
187 Alinari, Florence
193 Württembergisches Landesmuseum, Stuttgart
199 G.E. Kidder-Smith
204 Spectrum, London
206 Spectrum, London
215 Robert Harding Picture Library
219 British Library, London
221 British Museum, London
225 Werner Forman Archive
227 (top) Topham Picturepoint
227 (bottom) Idemitsu Museum of Arts, Tokyo
228 (top) Xinhua News Agency
228 (bottom) AKG Images/Jürgen Sorges
233 Werner Forman Archive
240 © Charles & Josette Lenars/CORBIS
245 Oriental & India Office, London
246 Oriental & India Office, London
249 Hulton Deutsch
250 (top) Boudot-Lamotte, Paris
250 (bottom) British Museum, London
251 (left) British Museum, London
252 British Museum, London
253 Robert Harding Picture Library
255 British Museum, London
258 Robert Harding Picture Library
259 Robert Harding Picture Library

264 AKG Images
265 Bridgeman Art Library
266 Mary Evans Picture Library
267 Alinari, Florence
269 AKG Images
270 AKG Images/Jean-Louis Nou
277 Hutchison Library/Nancy Durrell McKenna
280 © Lindsay Hebberd/Corbis
282 (left) Metropolitan Museum of Art, New York
282 (right) Boudot-Lamotte, Paris
283 Boudot-Lamotte, Paris
286 Archaeological Museum, Sarnath
288 Robert Harding Picture Library
289 Bridgeman Art Library
292 Anne and Bury Peerless
293 Nelson Atkins Museum of Art, Kansas City, Missouri. Purchase: Nelson Trust (34–10)
296 (top) British Library, London
296 (bottom) University of Pennsylvania Museum
306 © Domkapitel Aachen. Photo: Ann Münchow
311 Israel Museum, Jerusalem
313 Sonia Halliday Photographs
314 A.S.A.P. Tel Aviv
316 National Archaeological Museum, Damascus, Syria
318 AKG Images/Erich Lessing
319 Alinari, Florence
322 (right) Historiska Museet, Stockholm
331 AKG Images
334 Shimon Lev
338 (left) Musée des Antiquités, St.-Germain-en-Laye, France/Photo RMN
338 (right) © Photo RMN
340 © Angelo Hornak
344 Metropolitan Museum of Art, New York, 39.20
347 Bridgeman Art Library
348 Bibliothèque Nationale de France
353 Bibliothèque Nationale de France
356 Spectrum, London
358 Edinburgh University Library
362 Bibliothèque Nationale de France
371 Courtesy Institute Amattler d'Art Hispànic, Barcelona
374 Werner Forman Archive
375 A.F. Kersting
378 British Library, London
379 Spectrum, London
385 AKG Images
386 Stapleton Collection/Bridgeman Art Library
386 AKG Images
387 Courtesy Shri Swaminarayan Madir, Neasden, London
389 Bodleian Library, Oxford
390 Bridgeman Art Library/Bibliothèque Nationale de France

394 South American Pictures
399 © Comstock 1997/Georg Gerster
400 Seattle Art Museum
401 British Library, London
403 Bridgeman Art Library
408 Bibliothèque Nationale de France
409 Victoria and Albert Museum, London
412 National Palace Museu, Taiwan
417 Bibliothèque Nationale de France
424 Service Historique de l'Armée de Terre, France/Bridgeman Art Library
427 British Library, London/Bridgeman Art Library
431 Museo Correr, Venice
433 Bridgeman Art Library
436 British Museum, London
437 Bibliothèque Nationale de France
439 (left) Photo Scala, Florence
439 (right) National Gallery, London
440 (left) Bridgeman Art Library
440 (right) Bridgeman Art Library
441 AKG Images
442 AKG Images
444 Bridgeman Art Library
450 British Library, London
454 (top) The Granger Collection, New York
454 (bottom) Werner Forman Archive
457 South American Pictures
460 The Granger Collection, New York
464 Fotomas Index
467 Bridgeman Art Library/Johnny van Haeften Gallery, London
469 Werner Forman Archive
474 Hulton Getty
475 Bridgeman Art Library/Hermitage, St Petersburg
478 Werner Forman Archive
484 Graphische Sammlung Albertina, Vienna
487 © 1990 Photo Scala, Florence. Courtesy of the Ministero Beni e Att. Culturali
489 R.Higginson
492 Bridgeman Art Library
493 Werner Forman Archive
494 Bridgeman Art Library/Alexander Turnbull Library, New Zealand
497 AKG Images/ Bibliothèque Nationale, Paris
504 Chester Beatty Library, Dublin
506 V&A Images
507 Historiographical Institute, University of Tokyo
509 Ancient Art & Architecture Collection
516 (top) © Corbis/Bettmann
516 (bottom) © Corbis
517 (top left) Mary Evans Picture Library
517 (top right) © Hulton Deutsch Collection/Corbis
517 (bottom left) © Corbis
517 (bottom right) © British Library
519 Prado, Madrid
520 Bridgeman Art Library/Bibliothèque Nationale, Paris

525 Bridgeman Art Library
527 Art Archive
530 Art Archive
534 Bibliothèque Nationale, Paris
536 Capitol Collection, Washington D.C.
537 AKG Images/Yale University Art Gallery
541 Musée Carnavalet, Paris
542 The Granger Collection, New York
544 AKG Images/Bibliothèque Nationale, Paris
545 Giraudon/Bridgeman Art Library
548 The Granger Collection, New York
552 © Christie's Images/Corbis
554 AKG Images/Bibliothèque Nationale, Paris
560 © Hulton Deutsch Collection/Corbis
564 (top) AKG Images/Stedelijk Museum, Leiden
564 (bottom) Mary Evans Picture Library
565 Ann Ronan at Image Select
568 Ann Ronan at Image Select
570 Bridgeman Art Library/Guildhall Library, Corporation of London
571 Coo-ee Historical Picture Library
573 Brown Brothers
576 Art Archive
577 Brown Brothers
579 Hulton Getty
580 Mary Evans Picture Library
581 Hulton Getty
585 Museum Folkwang, Essen
589 Hulton Getty
590 Musée Marmottan, Paris
592 Brown Brothers
596 Bridgeman Art Library/V&A
602 (top) Mary Evans/Douglas McCarthy
602 (bottom) Werner Forman Archive
609 Brown Brothers
614 D.O.D. & U.S.A.F.
616 © Todd Gipstein/Corbis
617 Library of Congress, Washington D.C.
620 © Punch Ltd.
623 Bridgeman/Taylor Gallery, London
629 Hulton Getty
630 Mark Azavedo Photo Library
635 Mary Evans Picture Library
636 Victoria Hyde
638 Old Japan Picture Library
644 (top) © Stapleton Collection/Corbis
644 (bottom) © Underwood & Underwood/Corbis
645 (top left) © Bettmann/Corbis
645 (top right) Angelo Hornak Picture Library
645 (bottom) © Bettmann/Corbis
647 © Bettmann/U.P.I.
648 © Corbis
650 Hulton Getty
652 The Curie and Joliot-Curie Association, Paris
656 Bridgeman Art Library
659 Brown Brothers
660 (top) South American Pictures
660 (bottom) South American Pictures

665 Imperial War Museum, London
670 © Bettmann/Corbis
672 David King Collection
674 Art Archive
675 David King Collection
678 David King Collection
679 Art Archive
684 © Corbis
687 © Corbis
689 The National Archives
691 © Schenectady Museum; Hall of Electrical History Foundation/Corbis
692 Hulton Getty
694 © Succession Picasso/DACS 2004
698 © Bettmann/Corbis
700 D.O.D.
702 Imperial War Museum, London
703 (top) © Bettmann/Corbis
703 (bottom) D.O.D. & U.S.A.F.
706 The Granger Collection
708 (top) Camera Press
708 (bottom) © Bettmann/U.P.I.
711 © Richard Kalvar/Magnum Photos
717 © Bettmann/Corbis
718 © Yevgeny Khaldei/Corbis
724 © Bettmann/Corbis
726 © Corbis
728 N.A.S.A.
731 Rex Features
733 © Burt Glinn/Magnum
735 © Bettmann/U.P.I.
736 © Bettmann/U.P.I.
737 © Bettmann/Corbis
738 Topham Picturepoint
740 Topham Picturepoint
741 © Nicolas Tikhomiroff/Magnum Photos
747 South American Pictures
748 Camera Press/Romuald Meigneux
753 © Bettmann/Corbis
757 Rex Features
766 © Bettmann/Corbis
771 David King Collection
773 Courtesy of Peabody Essex Museum, Salem
777 © Bettmann/Corbis
778 © Magnum Photos/Cartier-Bresson
779 © Associated Press
780 (top) The National Archives
780 (bottom) © Xinhua/Sovfoto
785 Hulton Getty
789 Popperfoto
791 Topham Picturepoint
793 © Bettmann/Corbis
802 (left) © Bettmann/Corbis
802 (right) © Stephanie Maze/Corbis
803 (top) © Neal Preston/Corbis
803 (bottom left) © Greg Martin/Corbis/Sygma
803 (middle right) © Antoine Serra/In Visu/Corbis
805 © Associated Press/Greg Baker
806 © Paul Lowe/Panos Pictures

LITERARY CREDITS

Every effort has been made to obtain permission from all copyright holders, but in some cases this has not proved possible. The publishers therefore wish to thank all authors or copyright holders who are included without acknowledgement. Prentice Hall and Laurence King Publishing apologizes for any errors or omissions in this list and would be grateful to be notified of any corrections that should be incorporated in the next edition.

Cambridge University Press: *The Journals of Captain James Cook on His Voyages of Discovery* by James Cook, edited by J. C. Beaglehole, 2 vols. (Cambridge University Press, for the Hakluyt Society, 1955, 1961).

Columbia University Press: *Sources of Indian Tradition: Volume 1*, edited by Ainslee Embree (Columbia University Press, 1988), © 1988 Columbia University Press; *Roman Civilization: Selected Readings: The Republic and the Augustan Age; Volume II: The Empire*, edited by Naphtali Lewis and Meyer Reinhold (Columbia University Press, 1990); *Sources of Chinese Tradition: Volume 1*. Second Edition, edited by William Theodore de Bary and Irene Bloom (Columbia University Press, 1999); *The Selected Poems of Du Fu*, translated by Burton Watson (Columbia University Press, 2002); *Poems of Love and War: From the Eight Anthologies and the Ten Long Poems of Classical Tamil*, translated by A. K. Ramanujan (Columbia University Press, 1985), © 1985 by Columbia University Press; *Introduction to Contemporary Civilization in the West*, 2 vols. (Columbia University Press, 1954); *Sources of Chinese Tradition: From 1600 Through The Twentieth Century*, vol. 2, edited by William Theodore de Bary and Richard Lufrano (Columbia University Press, 2000).

Faber & Faber Ltd.: 'The Waste Land', *Collected Poems 1909–1962* by T. S. Eliot (Harcourt Brace Jovanovich, 1936).

Farrar, Straus & Giroux: Homer's *Odyssey*, translated by Robert Fitzgerald (Farrar, Straus & Giroux, 1998).

Grove/Atlantic Inc.: *The Wonder That Was India* by A. L. Basham (Grove Press, 1954); *The Gandhi Reader*, edited by Homer Jack (Grove Press, 1956).

The Hakluyt Society: *Travels in Asia and Africa, 1325–1354* by Ibn Battuta, edited by H. A. R. Gibb (The Hakluyt Society, 1958), by permission of David Higham Associates.

Harcourt Brace Inc.: 'The Century's Decline', *View with a Grain of Sand* by Wislawa Szymborska (Harcourt Brace, 1995).

HarperCollins Publishers: *The Faith and Practice of al-Ghazalli*, translated by W. Montgomery Watt (George Allen & Unwin, 1953), by permission of the publisher; *A Forest of Kings: The Untold Story of the Ancient Maya* by Linda Schele and David Freidel (William Morrow, 1990), © 1990 by Linda Schele and David Freidel, by permission of the publisher; *Three Chinese Poets: Translations of Poems by Wang Wei, Li Bai, and Du Fu* by Vikram Seth (HarperCollins Publishers, 1993); *Capitalism and Material Life, 1400-1800* by Fernand Braudel, translated by Miriam Kochan (Harper & Row, 1973).

Hodder Murray Publishers: *Ibn Khaldun, An Arab Philosophy of History* by Ibn Khaldun, translated by Charles Issawi (John Murray, 1950).

Houghton Mifflin Company: *The Human Record: Sources of Global History*, vol. 2, edited by Alfred J. Andrea and James H. Overfield (Houghton Mifflin, 3rd edition, 1998).

Jawaharlal Nehru Memorial Fund: *Glimpses of World History* by Jawaharlal Nehru (Oxford University Press India, 1982); *Hind Swaraj or Indian Home Rule* by Mohandas Karamchand Gandhi (Navajivan Press, 1938).

The New Press: *Truth and Lies: Stories from the Truth and Reconciliation Commission in South Africa* by Jillian Edelstein (The New Press, 2001).

Oxford University Press Inc.: *Historian Records* by Sima Qian, translated by Raymond Dawson (Oxford University Press, 1994).

Oxford University Press India: *Asoka and the Decline of the Mauryas* by Romila Thapar (Oxford University Press India, 1963), by permission of the publisher.

Penguin Group (UK): *The Epic of Gilgamesh*, translated by N. K. Sandars (Penguin Classics, 1960, Third Edition 1972), © N. K. Sandars, 1960, 1964, 1972; *The History of the Peloponnesian War* by Thucydides, translated by Rex Warner (Penguin Classics, 1954), translation © Rex Warner, 1954; *Two Lives of Charlemagne* by Einhard and Notker the Stammerer, translated by Professor Lewis Thorpe (Penguin Classics, 1969), translation © Professor Lewis Thorpe, 1969; *The Travels of Marco Polo*, translated by

Ronald Latham (Penguin Classics, 1958), all by permission of Penguin Books Ltd.

Princeton University Press: *Ancient Near Eastern Texts Relating to the Old Testament*, edited by James B. Pritchard (Princeton University Press, 1969); *The Collected Dialogues of Plato*, edited by Edith Hamilton and Huntington Cairns, translated by B. Jowett (Princeton University Press, 1975).

Random House Inc.: *Bhagavad-Gita*, translated by Barbara Stoler Miller (Bantam Books, 1986), © 1986 by Barbara Stoler Miller, by permission of Bantam Books, a Division of Random House, Inc.; *A Higher Kind of Loyalty* by Liu Binyan (Pantheon Books, 1990).

Simon & Schuster Inc.: *Popul Vuh*, translated by Dennis Tedlock (Pocket Books, 1985), © 1985 by Dennis Tedlock, by permission of Simon & Schuster Adult Publishing Group; *Virgil's Aeneid*, translated by Rolfe Humphries (Charles Scribner's Sons, 1951), © 1951 by Charles Scribner's Sons, by permission of Scribner, a Division of Simon & Schuster Adult Publishing Group; *Chinese Civilization: A Sourcebook*, Second Edition, edited by Patricia Buckley Ebrey (The Free Press, 1993), © 1993 by Patricia Buckley Ebrey, by permission of The Free Press, a Division of Simon & Schuster Adult Publishing Group.

Stanford University Press: *The Pattern of the Chinese Past* by Mark Elvin (Stanford University Press, 1973), © 1973 by Mark Elvin, by permission of the publisher.

University of California Press: *Canto General* by Pablo Neruda, translated by Jack Schmitt (University of California Press, 1991).

The University of Chicago Press: *The Islamic World*, edited by William H. McNeill and Marilyn Robinson Waldman (University of Chicago Press, 1983).

University of Texas Press: *Ancient Egyptian Literature: An Anthology*, translated by John L. Foster (University of Texas Press, 2001), © 2001 John L. Foster, by permission of the author and publisher.

A. P. Watt Ltd.: 'The White Man's Burden', *Rudyard Kipling: Selected Poems*, edited by Peter Keating (Penguin Twentieth-Century Classics, 1993); 'The Second Coming' by W. B. Yeats, cited in *Literature of the Western World*, edited by Brian Wilkie and James Hurt (Macmillan, 1984).

SUPPLEMENTS

The World's History comes with an extensive package of supplementary print and multimedia materials for both instructors and students, many of which are available free to qualified adopters.

FOR THE INSTRUCTOR

- The *Instructor's Manual/Test-Item File* includes chapter outlines, overviews, key concepts, discussion questions, suggestions for useful audiovisual resources, and approximately 1500 test items (essay, multiple choice, true/false, and matching).

- The *Instructor Resource CDROM*, compatible with both Windows and Macintosh environments, provides instructors with such essential teaching tools as hundreds of digitized images and maps for classroom presentations, PowerPoint lectures, and other instructional material. The assets on the IRCDROM can be easily exported into online courses, such as WebCT and Blackboard.

- *Test Manager* is a computerized test management program for Windows and Macintosh environments. The program allows instructors to select items from the test-item file to create tests. It also allows online testing.

- The *Transparency Package* provides instructors with full color transparency acetates of all the maps, charts, and graphs in the text for use in the classroom.

- A *Correlation Guide to the Advanced Placement Exam* provides strategies and suggestions for using *The World's History* in AP World History courses.

FOR THE STUDENT

- *History Notes* (Volumes I and II) provides practice tests, essay questions, and map exercises to help reinforce key concepts.

- *Documents in World History* (Volumes I and II) is a collection of 200 primary source documents in global history. Questions accompanying the documents can be used for discussion or as writing assignments.

- Produced in collaboration with Dorling Kindersley, the world's most respected cartography publisher, *The Prentice Hall Atlas of World History* includes approximately 100 maps fundamental to the study of world history—from early hominids to the twenty-first century.

- *World History: An Atlas and Study Guide* is a four-color map workbook that includes over 100 maps with exercises, activities, and questions that help students learn both geography and history.

- *Reading Critically About History* is a brief guide to reading effectively that provides students with helpful strategies for reading a history textbook.

- *Understanding and Answering Essay Questions* suggests helpful analytical tools for understanding different types of essay questions, and provides precise guidelines for preparing well-crafted essay answers.

- Prentice Hall is pleased to provide adopters of *The World's History* with an opportunity to receive significant discounts when copies of the text are bundled with Penguin Classics titles in world history. Contact your local Prentice Hall representative for details.

MEDIA RESOURCES

- Prentice Hall's New Online Resource **OneKey** lets instructors and students in to the best teaching and learning resources—all in one place. This all-inclusive online resource is designed to help you minimize class preparation and maximize teaching time. Conveniently organized by chapter, OneKey for *The World's History, Third Edition* reinforces what students have learned in class and from the text. Among the student resources available for each chapter are: a complete, media-rich, interactive e-book version of *The World's History, Third Edition*; quizzes organized by the main subtopics of each chapter; over 200 primary-source documents; and interactive map quizzes.

  For instructors, OneKey includes images and maps from *The World's History, Third Edition*; instructional material; hundreds of primary-source documents; and PowerPoint presentations.

- *Prentice Hall OneSearch with Research Navigator: History 2005* This brief guide focuses on developing critical-thinking skills necessary for evaluating and using online sources. It provides a brief introduction to navigating the Internet with specific references to History web sites. It also provides an access code and instruction on using Research Navigator, a powerful research tool that provides access to three exclusive databases of reliable source material: ContentSelect Academic Journal Database, the New York Times Search by Subject Archive, and Link Library.

- The *Companion Website™* (www.prenhall.com/spodek) works in tandem with the text and features objectives, study questions, web links to related Internet resources, document exercises, interactive maps, and map labelling exercises.

- *Prentice Hall World History Image Library* Bringing together hundreds of images—many of which have never before been digitized—this innovative new CDROM organizes images of fine art, culture, photographs, posters, cartoons, and manuscripts from around the world into thematic units, allowing instructors to efficiently export the material into customized PowerPoint lectures or other presentation platforms. In addition, interactive global maps showing change over time allow instructors to visually portray the large patterns of world history.

- *World History Documents CD-ROM* Bound into every new copy of this textbook is a free World History Documents CD-ROM. This is a powerful resource for research and additional reading that contains more than 200 primary source documents central to World History. Each document provides essay questions that are linked directly to a website where short-essay answers can be submitted online or printed out. A complete list of documents on the CD-ROM is found at the end of the text.

PREFACE

Why History?

The professional historian and the student of an introductory course often seem to pass each other on different tracks. For the professional, nothing is more fascinating than history. For the student, particularly one in a compulsory course, the whole enterprise often seems a bore. This introductory text is designed to help the student understand and share the fascination of the historian. It will also remind professors of their original attraction to history, before they began the specialization that has almost certainly marked their later careers. Furthermore, it encourages student and professor to explore together the history of the world and the significance of this study.

Professional historians love their field for many reasons. History offers perspective and guidance in forming a personal view of human development. It teaches the necessity of seeing many sides of issues. It explores the complexity and interrelationship of events and makes possible the search for patterns and meaning in human life.

Historians also love to debate. They love the challenge of demonstrating that their interpretations of the pattern and significance of events are the most accurate and the most satisfying in their fit between the available data and theory. Historians also love the detective work of the profession, whether it is researching through old archives, uncovering and using new sources of information, or reinterpreting long-ignored sources. In recent years historians have turned, for example, to oral history, old church records, files of photographs, cave paintings, individual census records, and reinterpretations of mythology.

Historical records are not simply lists of events, however. They are the means by which historians develop their interpretations of those events. Because interpretations differ, there is no single historical record, but various narrations of events each told from a different perspective. Therefore the study of history is intimately linked to the study of values, the values of the historical actors, the historians who have written about them, and of the students engaged in learning about them.

Professional historians consider history to be the king of disciplines. Synthesizing the concepts of fellow social scientists in economics, politics, anthropology, sociology, and geography, historians create a more integrated and comprehensive interpretation of the past. Joining with their colleagues in the humanities, historians delight in hearing and telling exciting stories that recall heroes and villains, the low born and the high, the wisdom and the folly of days gone by. This fusion of all the social sciences and humanities gives the study of history its range, depth, significance, and pleasure. Training in historical thinking provides an excellent introduction to understanding change and continuity in our own day as well as in the past.

Why World History?

Why specifically world history? Why should we teach and study world history, and what should be the content of such a course?

First, world history is a good place to begin for it is a new field for professor and student alike. Neither its content nor its pedagogy is yet fixed. Many of the existing textbooks on the market still have their origins in the study of western Europe, with segments added to cover the rest of the world. World history as the study of the inter-relationships of all regions of the world, seen from the many perspectives of the different peoples of the earth, is still virgin territory.

Second, for citizens of multicultural, multiethnic nations such as the United States, Canada, South Africa, and India, and for those of the many other countries such as the United Kingdom and Australia which are moving in that direction, a world history course offers the opportunity to gain an appreciation of the national and cultural origins of all their diverse citizens. In this way, the study of world history may help to strengthen the bonds of national citizenship.

Third, as the entire world becomes a single unit for interaction, it becomes an increasingly appropriate subject for historical study. The noted historian E.H. Carr explained that history "is an unending dialogue between the present and the past". The new reality of global interaction in communication, business, politics, religion, culture, and ecology has helped to generate the new academic subject of world history.

Organization and Approach

The text, like the year-long course, links *chronology*, *themes*, and *geography* in eight units, or parts of study. The parts move progressively along a time line from the emergence of early humans to the present day. Each part emphasizes a single theme—for example, urbanization or religion or trade —and students learn to use all eight themes to analyze historical events and to develop a grasp of the chronology of human development. Geographically, each part cover the entire globe, although specific topics place greater emphasis on specific regions.

REVISIONS TO THE THIRD EDITION

Readers of the first and second editions will find that this third edition builds on the strengths of the first two while adding new materials and new perspectives. Every aspect of the book's program has been exhaustively reviewed and revised. The pedagogical features were carefully examined. Revised and new, more useful elements were added including Review Questions, Key Topics, a running in-text glossary, up-to-date, annotated bibliographies, interactive maps, and Turning Point essays, which use visual sources to help the reader move from the themes of one part to the new themes of the next. The text has been reworked extensively to produce a narrative with improved coverage of gender issues, trade, technology and capitalism, the Islamic world and its influence, Africa and Latin America.

ORGANIZATIONAL CHANGES

Theme and Chronology

One of the most important organizational principles of this text from the beginning has been its emphasis on a thematic introduction to world history. Readers generally applauded this approach, but warned that sometimes it led us to neglect chronology. As in the first two editions, one theme is highlighted in each of the eight parts of the textbook, and the parts trace major chronological eras in the world's history, from the evolution of humans to the early 21st century. In this edition we have addressed much more effectively the problem of keeping chronology clear even as we continue to concentrate on themes. Readers should find this attention to consistent chronology—with much less of the moving back and forth in time periods that characterized earlier editions —also an important improvement.

Reorganization and New Materials

Readers familiar with the earlier editions will notice revisions and reorganization throughout the text, from beginning to end. The most striking difference appears in the final unit. It has been entirely reorganized, divided into two separate parts. The first of these looks at the world from the early twentieth century until about 1980, following much of the structure of the original and continuing to use the theme of "The Human Uses of Technology." A new unit has then been added that analyzes issues since about 1980 analyzed through the new theme of "Identity." Arguing that human action comes, in part, out of the sense of who we are, it examines new issues of religious, national, gender, and age identity. In each case it asks how new technologies, especially of communication, have affected these identities, and how these identities have affected technology. The final chapter will examine these new identity issues in several different regions of the world. Another major change is the addition of a new chapter, number 13, which examines European Visions 1000–1776. This chapter, along with Chapter 12 now forms a bridge between the pre-modern and modern worlds, and between volumes 1 and 2 in the paperback edition.

Historiography

A fundamental principal of the first two editions was the emphasis on the three questions: "What Do We Know?" "How Do We Know It?" and "What Difference Does It Make?" Teachers and students, both at the university level and, increasingly, in Advanced Placement courses appreciated the attention to these three historiographical issues, but they often found them cluttering the text. Discussions of the work and arguments of various historians appeared frequently, but inconsistently. In this edition each feature has been given a clearer place so that faculty and students can use them more effectively. In general, the main narrative conveys the "What Do We Know?" materials. Separate, color-coded, boxed features—usually two in every chapter—carry the "How Do We Know?" materials, demonstrating how historians sift through source materials and debate their interpretation. Questions accompany each of these "How Do We Know?" features to encourage students to appreci-ate the work of the historians in producing the records we have today. Additional color-coded boxed features in each chapter will introduce relevant primary sources for further analysis. Finally, each chapter ends with a discussion of "What Difference Does It Make?: Legacies to the Future." In another new feature, a set of questions end each chapter to guide students in their analyses of the material.

New Layout and Design

Readers will also see immediately a streamlined, cleaner design. A larger format provides for a more aesthetically-pleasing presentation, while the abundance of special feature boxes that filled the earlier editions have been reduced. More importantly, the basic material of many of the boxes has been incorporated into the narrative text. The text is now set in single-column, which allows for a more spacious layout. Each chapter now opens with a two-page spread that features an illustration embodying the core theme of each chapter.

CONTENT CHANGES

Within each part, materials have been updated, revised, and added. Examples of some of the more notable changes and additions include: a discussion of the fossils of early hominids discovered in Chad; additional materials on early urbanization in India and Africa; new evaluations for the decline of the Roman empire; consideration of the Gnostic gospels and their significance in understanding early Christianity; the assimilation of Islam into African empires in the

10th through the fifteenth centuries. Part Five, on world trade, 1000 to 1776 and Part Six, on migration and demography, 1200–1750, have been restructured into a single unit on the movement of goods, ideas, and people. The Scientific Revolution of the sixteenth, seventeenth, and eighteenth century gets more coverage. The Industrial Revolution has been placed into a wider context, more clearly setting the stage for the events that began to unfold in late eighteenth-century England. As noted, the twentieth century is now given expanded coverage, and divided into two chronological periods, each with its own theme. The region-by-region analysis presented in the closing chapters of the first two editions has been replaced by a more thematic consideration of global issues in the late twentieth century, more in keeping with the thematic approach of the rest of the text. Throughout the book increased prominence has been given to issues of gender.

In updating the book to cover most recent events, new materials have been added to reflect new developments, for example: the increasing importance of China in world trade; of religious/cultural militancy in India; of economic recovery in Southeast Asia and decline in parts of Latin America; of the global economy; of responses to the global AIDS epidemic, especially in Africa; of breakthroughs and cautions in cloning and applications of genome research; of the attacks on America of September 11, 2001, the American response; and global reactions to both the attacks and the American responses.

Chapter-by-Chapter Revisions

Chapter 1 incorporates the results of the most recent archaeological research, and new information on the discovery of a fossil skull in Chad that may extend hominid evolution 2.5 million years back in time

Chapter 2 includes improved coverage on the Sumerians and their contributions to the development of early civilizations.

Chapter 3 has been dramatically reorganized to treat various aspects of ancient Egyptian history to fit the thematic trajectory of the chapters. It contains new material on daily life and an extended analysis of gender roles in society. Much of the material previously included in this chapter has been moved to Chapter 5 on the rise of empires.

Chapter 4 has been revised to better connect themes within the Parts. In keeping with the overall desire to improve coverage of gender issues, more information is supplied on women in Chinese societies. The chapter now also contains more information on the Zhou.

Chapter 5 has been reorganized to include the Egyptian empire as among the early empires. The section on Alexander the Great has been brought up-to-date and expanded. In addition the coverage of gender has been improved.

Chapter 6 has been revised for improved readability and also includes a more detailed discussion of gender in the ancient world. It also includes fresh material on the decline of the Roman Empire.

Chapter 7 has been reorganized to present a clear discussion of China's earliest ideologists. It also has improved coverage of gender.

Chapter 8 contains a much clearer discussion of Indian culture, and includes additional thoughts on the comparison of different imperial systems.

Chapter 10 adds new materials on the controversial Gnostic gospels and their significance for the interpretation of Christianity.

Chapter 11 clarifies the chronology of the early caliphate and the wars of succession. It includes a reorganized and expanded section on Islam, which more clearly highlights gender issues in Islam and compares them with other religions.

Chapter 12 has been thoroughly revised. It is far more comprehensive on trade networks, and their significance, especially sea-borne networks.

Chapter 13 has been thoroughly revised to examine more fully the background to European overseas expansion. Medieval European history has been moved here and conceptually placed in a global context, including the decline of Mediterranean trade and the rise of Atlantic exploration. It also looks at the Medieval European revival of trade and its relationship to Renaissance ideas, and new worldviews in general.

Chapter 14 has been completely revised, with more attention to the nation-state and fuller discussion of "the great divergence," analyzing the economic restructuring of the world in which western Europe rose to prominence over China.

Chapter 15 has been restructured for greater clarity and clearer comparison of the various kinds of population movements, free, indentured, enslaved, settler, and conquest.

Chapter 16 adds more extensive coverage of the scientific revolution and clarifies issues of comparison among the several major political revolutions of the time.

Chapter 17 expands the discussion of the historical background to the industrial revolution, adds information on indentured labor, reorders the material for greater clarity and stronger indication of the connection among economic, political, and social relationships.

Chapter 18 has been restructured and updated for more careful consideration of the relationships between capitalism, the industrial revolution, imperialism, and responses to the imperial outreach.

Chapter 19 has been extensively revised and contains an enhanced discussion of the contests over the uses of technology. Greatly expanded coverage of World War I and the global depression, and their significance. The chronology has been restructured for greater clarity.

Chapter 20 includes extensive revisions to cover the ideologies of the combatants in World War II, the war and its consequences, including the early confrontations of the cold war.

Chapter 21 has been thoroughly revised to cover the cold war, the end of colonialism, the rise of newly independent nations, and the creation of a third world bloc.

Chapter 22 contains additional materials on Mao's planning, on Gandhi's work on behalf of industrial unions, and on problems and hazards of technology.

Chapter 23 is a new thematically-based chapter covering key identity issues of the late-twentieth and early twenty-first centuries, especially those created by the end of the cold war and the increasing network of economic globalization, but also considering the cultural identities that are emerging as a result of these changes.

Chapter 24 is a new chapter of brief case studies of contemporary themes in five geographical areas: the integration of the European Union, the dissolution of Yugoslavia, continuing warfare between Israelis and Palestinians, the Truth and Reconciliation Commission in South Africa, and the economic revival of contemporary China. Also coverage of global criminal networks.

PEDAGOGICAL ENHANCEMENTS

This edition retains many of the pedagogical features of the previous editions, including source boxes and timelines. We have introduced several new pedagogical features including a list of key topics at the beginning of each chapter, chapter review questions at the end of each chapter, one–two interactive maps per chapter, a running glossary of items highlighted in the text that appears in the margins as well as at the back of the book, and "Turning Points" essays at the end of each part use visual sources to highlight the key themes in each part. Each of these features is designed to make the text more accessible to students. Collectively, these materials provide a rich, comprehensive and challenging introduction to the study of world history and the methods and key interpretations of its historians.

- Substantially revised, the **Introduction** describes the key themes of the text and the methods historians use to practice their craft.
- The timelines have been completely redesigned to make the information easier to read and are now called **At a Glance**.
- New **Turning Points** essays illustrate visually the connections between one part and the next. In some cases, the **Turning Points** tell their own story as well, notably in the bridge into the twentieth century that uses the modern Olympic Games to illustrate and introduce many of the issues that are to follow.
- The **How Do We Know?** features have been separated from the text and placed in color-coded boxes. There are usually two in every chapter. Each **How Do We Know?** feature aims to help the student examine primary source materials, and each one ends with pertinent, thought-provoking questions.
- Each chapter ends with a discussion of legacies to the future, namely, **What Difference Does It Make?**
- This edition also continues the emphasis on the use of **Primary Sources**, for these are the kinds of materials from which the historical record is argued and fashioned. Each chapter usually has two primary sources, clearly highlighted in color-coded feature boxes.
- The **Bibliography** for each chapter has been thoroughly revised and up-dated to reflect current scholarship. In addition, each item in the bibliography is now annotated to direct students with their reading.
- Each chapter begins with a list of **Key Topics** that provide an overview of the chapter.
- Each chapter now ends with **Review Questions** to help students to re-examine the material. The questions are also useful for classroom debates and could serve as essay topics.
- The introduction to each of the eight **Parts** now includes more specific key references to the chapters that follow.
- **World History Documents CD-ROM.** Bound into every new copy of this textbook is a free World History Documents CD-ROM. This is a powerful resource for research and additional reading that contains more than 200 primary source documents central to World History. Each document provides essay questions that are linked directly to a website where short-essay answers can be submitted online or printed out. A complete list of documents on the CD-ROM is found at the end of the text.

Maps and Illustrations

To aid the student, extensive, clear and informative charts and maps represent information graphically and geographically. Several new maps have been added to provide better geographical context in the narrative. New to this edition one map in most chapter is now interactive. A wide range of illustrations, many in color, supplement the written word. For the third edition we have added more than 130 new illustrations.

One element that has not changed in this new edition is the mental image I keep before me of my own children—albeit at a younger age, since by now their knowledge in so many fields surpasses my own—and of my students. I write for them.

ACKNOWLEDGEMENTS FOR THE THIRD EDITION

Prentice Hall has taken an active role in the preparation of this edition. The wise interventions of Charlyce Jones-Owen, Editorial Director; the copy-editing of Marty Green and Elaine Silverstein, Developmental Editors; the content editing of Nancy Fitch, Professor of History at California State University, Fullerton; and the advice compiled from many external reviews by Charles Cavaliere, Executive Editor, have all resulted in many of the improvements evident in this edition. Laurence King Publishers in London continue to provide the excellent work in the production of the text and I am deeply indebted to them. Lee Ripley Greenfield, Director of College and Fine Arts, has assured that this transoceanic venture has proceeded reasonably smoothly, aided by Lesley Henderson, Senior Editor, Richard Mason, Senior Managing Editor, Nick Newton, Designer, and Emma Brown, Picture Researcher. Without them, there would be no third edition, and I am grateful for their patient and firm guidance and wise diplomacy. I have also benefited immensely from the kindness of many teachers and students who have used this book and took time to write to me with their advice and suggestions. I thank them and hope that they will see the benefits of their experience and wisdom in this edition.

Grateful acknowledgments are also extended to the following reviewers of the third edition: Wayne Ackerson, Salisbury University; Ewa Bacon, Lewis University, Illinois; Maurice Borrero, St. John's University; Stuart Borsch, Assumption College; Kenneth M. Chauvin, Appalachian State University; Jorge Cañizares-Esguerra, State University of New York, Buffalo; Nupur Chaudhuri, Texas Southern University; Mark Gunn, Meridian Community College; Phyllis Jestice, University of Southern Mississippi; Frank Karpiel, College of Charleston; David Kenley, Marshall University; Ane Lintvedt, McDonogh School; Angus Lockyer, Wake Forest University; John Langdon, University of Alberta; Louis McDermott, California Maritime Academy; Susan Maneck, Jackson State University; Michael Pavkovic, Hawaii Pacific University.

ABOUT THE AUTHOR

Howard Spodek received his B.A. degree from Columbia University (1963), majoring in history and specializing in Columbia's newly designed program in Asian Studies. He received his M.A. (1966) and Ph.D. (1972) from the University of Chicago, majoring in history and specializing in India. His first trip to India was on a Fulbright Fellowship, 1964–66, and he has spent a total of some seven years studying and teaching in India. He has also traveled widely throughout the United States, Latin America, Asia, Africa, and Europe. He has been a faculty member at Temple University since 1972, appointed Full Professor in 1984. He was awarded Temple's Great Teacher award in 1993.

Spodek's work in world history began in 1988 when he became Academic Director of a comprehensive, innovative program working with teachers in the School District of Philadelphia to improve their knowledge base in world history and facilitate a rewriting of the world history program in the schools. Immediately following this program, he became principal investigator of a program that brought college professors and high school teachers together to reconsider, revise, and, in many cases, initiate the teaching of world history in several of the colleges and universities in the Philadelphia metropolitan area. Those projects led directly to the writing of the first edition of the current text (1997).

Howard Spodek has published extensively on India, including *Urban-Rural Integration in Regional Development* (1976); *Urban Form and Meaning in South-East Asia* (editor, with Doris Srinivasan, 1993); and a wide array of articles, especially on urbanization—and on women's development issues—in India. He has written on his experiences with world history faculty at the college and high school levels in articles in The History Teacher (1992, 1995). In addition he wrote and produced the documentary film, *Ahmedabad* (1983). He has received funding for his research, writing, teaching, and film from Fulbright, the National Endowment for the Humanities, the National Science Foundation, the American Institute of Indian Studies, and the Smithsonian Institution.

INTRODUCTION: THE WORLD THROUGH HISTORIANS' EYES

THEMES AND TURNING POINTS

Most readers of this textbook have probably not taken many courses in history. Few are (thus far) planning to major in history, much less become professional historians. A lot therefore rides on this single text. It must present a general introduction to world history that interests, engages, and even fascinates the reader through its subject matter, its narrative, and its analysis. It must open the eyes, minds, and hearts of students who come to this course believing that history is only about the past, and mostly a matter of learning names, dates, and places. It must introduce them to the methods and "habits of mind" of the historian. It must demonstrate how knowledge of the contents and methods of world history—and of this book in particular—will broaden their horizons and also have practical usefulness.

"Usefulness" is not always associated with the study of history. Indeed, in everyday conversation, the phrase "that's history" means that an event is no longer significant. It may once have been important, but it is not now. From this point of view, "history" is a record of people and events that are dead and gone. For the historian, however, the opposite is true. The past has made us who we are, and continues to influence who we are becoming. In this sense, the past is not dead, just as people whom we have known personally and who have influenced our lives are not "dead," even though they may no longer be with us. This text will highlight ways in which the past continues to have profound effects on the present and future. It will help us understand who we have become.

History does not provide specific answers to today's problems, but it does provide examples and case studies that help us improve our thinking. Generals study past wars to understand how modern battles may be fought; economists study past periods of growth and recession to understand how we can encourage the former and avoid the latter. Understanding the ways in which families and relationships have functioned in the past helps us find ways to make our own families and relationships more satisfying today.

World history gives us the largest possible canvas on which to carry out these studies. We cannot, however, study everything that ever happened. We must choose what to include and what to exclude. We must choose strategies that maximize our ability to understand our lives today in the context of the whole range of human experience.

In this text we choose two fundamental organizing principles as our framework for the study and teaching of world history. First, we choose a series of eight chronological turning points, each of which changed the patterns of human life. Second, we explain the importance of each of these changes in terms of the new themes they introduced into human experience. These two elements—chronological turning points and interpretive themes—go together.

This text is organized around eight turning points and themes. Others might also have been chosen, but these turning points represent eight of the most important transformations in human life. The thematic analysis of these turning points encourages students to grapple with the origins and continuing presence of eight of the most significant themes in life: the biological and cultural qualities that make humans the special creatures that we are; the settlements we create and live in; the political power that we assemble and sometimes oppose; the religious systems through which many people find meaning in their individual lives and communities; the movement of trade and people that has linked the peoples of the world ever more closely, sometimes in cooperation, sometimes in competition, and sometimes in conflict; the political, industrial, and social revolutions, especially of the seventeenth through the twentieth centuries; the continuing technological developments that continue to re-shape our world; and the quest for personal and group identity, so prevalent in our own times.

Because real life does not fit neatly into exact chronological periods, there will be significant overlap among the turning points. Readers may argue that the themes are also not limited to single chronological periods. For example, political regimes, religious systems, and economic organizations appear at all times in history. This argument is, of course, correct: "everything is related to everything else," and in reality each chronological period will include several themes. We have chosen, however, to highlight particular themes in particular historical periods so that students will understand these themes more thoroughly and learn to employ them as tools of analysis in forming their own understanding of our world.

CHRONOLOGICAL TURNING POINTS AND PART THEMES

PART ONE. TURNING POINT: The emergence of the first humans. Biological and early cultural evolution, 5 million B.C.E. to 10,000 B.C.E.
THEME: Historians and anthropologists search for and interpret artifacts and records to determine what is human about humans.

PART TWO. TURNING POINT: Creating settlements, first agricultural villages and, later, cities. 10,000 B.C.E. to 1000 C.E.
THEME: Settlements—villages, towns, and cities—are created to meet community needs.

PART THREE. TURNING POINT: The creation of early empires, 2000 B.C.E. to 1100 C.E., from Sargon of Assyria through Alexander the Great, Qin and Han China, Republican and Imperial Rome, and India of the Mauryas and Guptas.
THEME: Imperial political power is generated, increased, consolidated, and resisted.

PART FOUR. TURNING POINT: The creation and diffusion of global religions: Judaism, Christianity, Islam, Hinduism, and Buddhism. 2500 B.C.E. to 1500 C.E.
THEME: Spiritual feelings are mobilized into powerful religious systems, some of which attain global scope.

PART FIVE. Global movement of goods and people, and the linking of continents; 1000–1776.
THEME: The flows of goods and people are channeled into global networks.

PART SIX. TURNING POINT: Revolutions, both political and industrial, 1640–1914.
THEME: Vast, abrupt changes in political and economic systems create new social values and systems affecting individuals, families, and communities.

PART SEVEN. TURNING POINT: Technological change and its human control; 1914 to 1980.
THEME: New technological systems—both simple and complex—are instituted to improve or threaten human life.

PART EIGHT. TURNING POINT: The formation of new identities; global, national, regional, cultural, and personal, 1975 to the present.
THEME: Increasingly tight-knit webs of communication, trade, and power bring diverse individuals and groups into contact, forcing them to constantly reconsider their identities.

Global Scope

The scope of this text, and of each turning point and theme within it, is global. For example, the study of the industrial revolution in Europe includes its funding—in part—from the wealth that poured into Europe from its New World conquests of people, land, gold, and silver, and from African slave labor; its global extensions in the form of imperialism in Asia, Africa, Australia, and Latin America; and the interactions of colonizers and colonized in response to the new opportunities and challenges.

SOCIAL SCIENCE METHODS, COMPARATIVE HISTORY, AND THE STUDY OF VALUES

Comparative History and the Methods of the Social Sciences

The global, interactive, and comparative format of this text provides also an introduction to social science methodology. The methods of the social sciences are embedded in the structure of the book. Because each part is built on comparisons among different regions of the world, the reader will become accustomed to posing hypotheses based on general principles and to testing them against comparative data from around the world.

This method of moving back and forth between general theory and specific case study, testing the degree to which the general theory and the specific data fit each other, is at the heart of the social sciences. For example, in Part 2 we will explore the general characteristics of cities, and then examine how well the generalizations hold up through case studies of various cities around the world. In Part 3 we will seek general theories of the rise and fall of early empires based on comparisons of China, Rome, and India. In Part 4 we will search for commonalities among religious systems through a survey of five world religions. In Part 8 we begin with an analysis of new issues of political and cultural identity and then examine their significance in a series of six brief case studies in different regions of the world. These comparisons enable us more clearly to think about and to understand the workings of cities, empires, and religions not only of the past, but also of our own time and place.

Multiple Perspectives

The text highlights the importance of multiple perspectives in studying and interpreting history. The answers we get—the narrative histories we write—are based on the questions we ask. Each part suggests a variety of questions that can be asked about the historical event that is being studied and a variety of interpretations that can emerge in the process of answering them. Often there is more than one "correct" way of understanding change over time and its significance. Different questions will trigger very different research and very different answers. For example, in Part 5 we ask about the stages and processes by which Western commercial power began to surpass that of Asia. This question presupposes the fact that at earlier times Asian power had been superior and raises the additional questions why it declined and why European power advanced. In Part 7 we ask how the industrial revolution affected and changed relationships between men and women; this question will yield different research and a different narrative from questions about, for example, women's contributions to industrialization, which is a useful question, but a different one.

Through the systematic study of the past in this thematic, comparative framework, students will gain tools for understanding and making their own place in the world today. They will not only learn how the peoples of the world have gotten to where we are, but also consider the possibility of setting out in new directions for new goals.

Evaluating Values

This form of analysis will also introduce a study of values. In order to understand the choices made by people in the past, we must attempt to understand the values that informed their thinking and actions. These values may be similar to, or quite different from, our own. In order to understand the interpretations introduced by later historians, we must understand the historians' values as well. These, too, may be similar to, or different from, our own. Historians usually had personal perspectives from which they viewed the past, and these perspectives influenced their interpretations. Finally, in order for student-readers to form their own understanding of the past, and to make it more useful in their own lives, they must also see how their own values influence their evaluation of past events.

For most of the past century, social scientists spoke of creating "value free" disciplines. Today, most scholars believe that this is impossible. We cannot be "value free." On the contrary, we must attempt to understand the values that have inspired historical actors, previous historians, and ourselves. Coming to an understanding of the values of others – historical actors and historians who have studied them – will help readers to recognize and formulate their own values, a central part of a liberal arts education.

HISTORY AND IDENTITY

History is among the most passionate and bitterly contentious of disciplines because most people and groups locate a large part of their identity in their history. Americans may take pride in their nationality, for example, for having created a representative, constitutional democracy that has endured for over 200 years (see Part 7). Yet they may be saddened, shamed, or perhaps incensed by the existence of 250 years of slavery followed by inequalities in race relations continuing to the present (see Part 6). Christians may take pride in two thousand years of missions of compassion toward the poor and downtrodden, yet they may be saddened, shamed, or even incensed by an almost equally long record of religious warfare and of persecution of those whose beliefs differed from their own (see Part 4).

As various ethnic, religious, class, and gender groups represent themselves in public political life, they seek not only to understand the history that has made them what they are, but also to persuade others to understand that history in the same way, to create a new consciousness. Feminist historians, for example, find in their reading of history that patriarchy, a system of male-created and male-dominated institutions, has subordinated women. From available data and their interpretation of them, they attempt to weave a persuasive argument that will win over others to their position.

Some will not be persuaded. They may not even agree that women have been subordinated to men, but argue that both genders have shared in a great deal of suffering (and joy) throughout history (see Parts 1 and 7). The historical debates over the origins and evolution of gender relationships evoke strong emotions because people's self-image, the image of their group, and the perceptions others hold of them are all at stake. And the stakes can be high.

CONTROL OF HISTORICAL RECORDS

From earliest times, control over the historical records and their interpretation has been fundamental to control over people's thoughts. The first emperor of China, Qin

Shihuang (r. 221–207 B.C.E.), the man who built the concept of a united China that has lasted until today attempted to destroy all knowledge of the past:

> He then abolished the ways of ancient sage kings and put to the torch the writings of the Hundred Schools in an attempt to keep the people in ignorance. He demolished the walls of major cities and put to death men of fame and talent. (deBary, I: 229).

Lenin addressing troops in Sverdlov Square, Moscow, May 5, 1920. The leaders of the Russian Communist revolution crudely refashioned the historical record to suit the wishes of the winners. After Lenin's death in 1924, his second-in-command Leon Trotsky (pictured sitting on the podium in the left-hand picture) lost to Josef Stalin the bitter power struggle that ensued. Not only was Trotsky banished from the Soviet Union, but so was his appearance in the official archives (see doctored picture below).

So wrote Jia Yi (201–168? B.C.E.), poet and statesman of the succeeding Han dynasty. Shihuang wished that only his interpretation of China's past, and his place in it, be preserved. Later intellectuals condemned his actions—but the lost records were irretrievable (see Part 3).

In similar fashion, the first great historian of the Christian Church, Eusebius of Caesarea (c. 260–339) in his accounts of the early Christians in the Roman Empire, chose carefully to include elements that he considered of "profit" to his mission, and to exclude those that were not.

> It is not for us to describe their miserable vicissitudes [in persecution] … just as it is not a part of our task to leave on record their faction-fights and their unnatural conduct towards each other, prior to the persecution. That is why we have decided to say no more about them than suffices for us to justify God's Judgment … We shall rather set forth in our whole narrative only what may be of profit, first, to our own times, and then to later times. (MacMullen, p. 6).

Historical Revision

Interpretations of events may become highly contested and revised even after several centuries have passed. Colonial governments seeking to control subject peoples sometimes argued that the conquered people were so backward that they benefited from the conquest. Later historians, with more distance and more detachment, were often less kind to the colonizers. Some 1900 years ago the historian Tacitus was writing bitterly of the ancient Romans in their conquest of England: "Robbery, butchery, rapine, the liars call Empire; they create a desolation and call it peace" (*Agricola*, 30)

In our own era, the many nations that have won their freedom from colonialism echo similar resentments against their foreign rulers and set out to revise the historical record in keeping with their newly won political freedom. Jawaharlal Nehru, the first prime minister of independent India (1947–64), wrote in 1944 from the prison cell in which he had been imprisoned for his leadership of his country's independence movement:

> British accounts of India's history, more especially of what is called the British period, are bitterly resented. History is almost always written by the victors and conquerors and gives their viewpoint; or, at any rate, the victors' version is given prominence and holds the field. (Nehru, p. 289)

Philip Curtin, historian of Africa and of slavery, elaborates an equally critical view of European colonial accounts of Africa's history:

> African history was seriously neglected until the 1950s … The colonial period in Africa left an intellectual legacy to be overcome, just as it had in other parts of the world. … The colonial imprint on historical knowledge emerged in the nineteenth and early twentieth centuries as a false perspective, a Eurocentric view of world history created at a time of European domination … Even where Europeans never ruled, European knowledge was often accepted as modern knowledge, including aspects of the Eurocentric historiography. (Curtin, p. 54)

Instead, Curtin continues, a proper historiography must:

> show the African past from an African point of view … For Africans, to know about the past of their own societies is a form of self-knowledge crucial to a sense of identity in a diverse and rapidly changing world. A recovery of African history has been an important part of African development over recent decades. (p. 54)

Religious and ethnic groups, too, may seek to control historical records. In 1542, the Roman Catholic Church established an Index of Prohibited Books to ban writings it considered heretical. (The Spanish Inquisition, ironically, stored away many records that later scholars used to recreate its history and the history of those it persecuted.) More recently, despite all the evidence of the Holocaust, the murder of 6 million Jews by the Nazi government of Germany during World War II, a few people have claimed that the murders never took place. They deny the existence of such racial and religious hatred and of its consequences, and ignore deep-seated problems in the relationships between majority and minority populations.

The significance of the voyages of Columbus was once celebrated uncritically in the United States in tribute both to "the Admiral of the Ocean Sea" himself and to the courage and enterprise of the European explorers and early settlers who brought their civilizations to the Americas. In South America, however, where Native American Indians are more numerous and people of European ancestry often form a smaller proportion of the population, the celebrations have been far more ambivalent, muted, and meditative.

In 1992, on the 500th anniversary of Columbus' first voyage to the Americas, altogether new and more sobering elements entered the commemoration ceremonies, even in the United States. The negative consequences of Columbus' voyages, previously ignored, were now recalled and emphasized: the death of up to 90 percent of the Native American Indian population in the century after the arrival of Europeans; the Atlantic slave trade, initiated by trade in Indian slaves; and the exploitation of the natural resources of a continent until then little touched by humans. The ecological consequences, which are only now beginning to receive more attention, were not all negative, however. They included the fruitful exchange of natural products between the hemispheres. Horses, wheat, and sheep were introduced to the Americas; potatoes, tomatoes, and corn to Afro-Eurasia. Unfortunately, the spread of syphilis was one of

Indians giving Hernán Cortés a headband, from Diego Duran's *Historia de las Indias*, 1547. Bent on conquest and plunder, the bearded Spaniard Cortés arrived on the Atlantic coast of Mexico in 1519. His forces sacked the ancient city of Tenochtitlán, decimated the Aztec people and imprisoned their chief, Montezuma, before proclaiming the Aztec Empire "New Spain." By stark contrast, this bland Spanish watercolor shows local tribesmen respectfully paying homage to the invader as if he were a god; in ignoring the brutality exercised in the colonization of South America, the artist is, in effect, "rewriting" history. (*Biblioteca National, Madrid*)

the consequences of the exchange; scholars disagree on who transmitted this disease to whom (see Part 5).

Thugs sometimes gain control of national histories. George Orwell's satirical novel *Animal Farm* (published in 1945) presented an allegory in which pigs come to rule a farm. Among their many acts of domination, the pigs seize control of the historical records of the farm animals' failed experiment in equality and impose their own official interpretation, which justifies their own rule. The rewriting of history and suppression of alternative records by the Communist Party of the former Soviet Union between 1917 and 1989 reveals the bitter truth underlying Orwell's satire (see Part 8).

Although the American experience is much different, in the United States, too, records have been suppressed. Scholars are still trying to use the Freedom of Information Act to pry open sealed diplomatic archives. (Most official archives everywhere have twenty-, thirty-, or forty-year rules governing the waiting period before certain sensitive records are opened to the public. These rules, which are designed to protect living people and contemporary policies from excessive scrutiny, are the general rule everywhere.)

WHAT DO WE KNOW? HOW DO WE KNOW IT? WHAT DIFFERENCE DOES IT MAKE:

So, historical records are not simply lists of events. They are the means by which individuals and groups develop their interpretations of these events. All people develop their own interpretations of past events; historians do it professionally. Because interpretations differ, there is no single historical record, but various narrations of events, each told from a different perspective. Therefore the study of history is intimately linked to the study of values.

To construct their interpretations, historians examine the values—the motives, wishes, desires, visions—of people of the past. In interpreting those values, historians must confront and engage their own values, comparing and contrasting these values with those of people in the past. For example, they ask how various people viewed slavery, or child labor, or education, or art and music in societies of the past. In the back of their minds they compare and contrast those older values with values held by various people today and especially with their own personal values. They ask: How and why have values changed or remained the same through the passage of time? Why, and in what ways, do my values compare and contrast with values of the past? By learning to pose such questions, students will be better equipped to discover and create their own place in the continuing movement of human history. This text, therefore consistently addresses three fundamental questions:

> What Do We Know?
> How Do We Know It?
> What Difference Does It Make?

Even when historians agree on which events are most significant, they may differ in evaluating why the events are significant. One historian's interpretation of events may be diametrically opposed to another's. For example, virtually all historians agree that part of the significance of World War II lay in its new policies and technologies of destruction: nuclear weapons in battle and genocide behind the lines. In terms of interpretation, pessimists might stress the continuing menace of these legacies of terror, while optimists might argue that the very violence of the war and the Holocaust triggered a search for limits on nuclear arms and greater tolerance for minorities. With each success in nuclear arms limitation and in toleration, the optimists seem more persuasive; with each spread of nuclear weapons and each outbreak of genocide, the pessimists seem to win.

The study of history is thus an interpretation of significance as well as an investigation of facts. The significance of events is determined by their consequences. Sometimes we do not know what the consequences are; or the consequences may not have run their course; or we may differ in our assessments of the consequences. This play between past events and their current consequences is what historian E.H. Carr had in mind in his famous description of history as "an unending dialogue between the present and the past" (Carr, p. 30).

TOOLS

The study of history requires many tools, and this text includes most of the principal ones:

- Primary sources are accounts that were produced at the time an event occurred. Those who produced them were eyewitnesses with direct knowledge of what happened. The core of historical study is an encounter with primary materials, usually documents, but including other artifacts—for example, letters, diaries, newspaper accounts, photographs, and artwork. Every chapter in this text includes representative primary materials.
- Visual images, a strong feature of this book, complement the written text, offering non-verbal "texts" of the time. These are often central pieces of evidence. For example, in Chapter 9 we illustrate the influence of Hinduism and Buddhism in Southeast Asia through the temple architecture of the region.
- Maps place events in space and in geographical relationship to one another.
- Chronological timelines situate events in time and sequence.
- Brief charts supply summaries as well as contextual information on topics such as religion, science, and trade.

Review Questions

- Please review the eight themes and turning points selected here. From what you already know of world history, do these seem well-chosen? Would you select different or additional themes and turning points for your account? If so, which ones and why?
- Examine how one of the values in which you believe has come from historical experience, either your own experience or that of relatives and friends, or the experience of groups to which you belong.
- When you tell other people about yourself, what "records" from your past do you highlight? Which ones do you leave out of the story, or even conceal? Are there any that you would like to destroy? Can you destroy them? How does the audience you are speaking to affect your choice of "records"?

Suggested Readings

BASIC, COMPREHENSIVE, INTRODUCTORY MATERIALS

Carr, E.H. *What Is History?* (Harmondsworth, Middlesex: Penguin Books, 1964). A classic introduction to the study of history and historiography from the point of view of a master.

Tosh, John. *The Pursuit of History: Aims, Methods, and New Directions in the Study of Modern History*, 2nd ed. (London: Longman, 1991). Excellent, comprehensive introduction to the study of history, with discussions of many different kinds of historical study, their methods and purposes.

MORE SPECIALIZED MATERIALS

Bennett, Judith M. "Medieval Women, Modern Women: Across the Great Divide," in David Aers, ed., *Culture and History, 1350–1600: Essays on English Communities, Identities, and Writing* (New York: Harvester Wheatsheaf, 1992), 147–75. Discusses continuity, in contrast to change, in women's history.

Curtin, Philip D. "Recent Trends in African Historiography and Their Contribution to History in General," in Joseph Ki-Zerbo, ed., *General History of Africa, Vol. I: Methodology and African Pre-History* (Berkeley: University of California Press, 1981), 54–71. An excellent introduction to this fine series commissioned by the United Nations.

deBary, William Theodore, et al., comps. *Sources of Chinese Tradition.* 2nd ed. 2 vols. (New York: Columbia University Press, 1999, 2000). THE anthology of materials on the subject.

Lerner, Gerda. *The Creation of Patriarchy* (New York: Oxford University Press, 1986). A controversial study of patriarchy in ancient Mesopotamia by a distinguished historian of the United States. Lerner re-tooled to study this fundamental feminist question.

MacMullen, Ramsay. *Christianizing the Roman Empire (A.D. 100–400)* (New Haven: Yale University Press, 1984). Excellent analysis of the factors leading to Christianity's success in the Roman Empire. Gives major role to government support.

Nehru, Jawaharlal. *The Discovery of India* (Delhi: Oxford University Press, 1989). A history of his country, written in jail during the freedom struggle by the man who became India's first prime minister.

Orwell, George. *Animal Farm* (New York: Harcourt, Brace, 1946). A classic satire on government by thugs; aimed at the USSR.

Tacitus, Cornelius. *Tacitus' Agricola, Germany, and Dialogue on Orators*, trans. Herbert W. Benario (Norman: University of Oklahoma Press, 1991). One of ancient Rome's great historians who understood the cruelty underlying the power of empire.

THE WORLD'S HISTORY

THIRD EDITION

PART 1

Human Origins and Human Cultures

5 million B.C.E. –10,000 B.C.E.

BUILDING AN INTERPRETIVE FRAMEWORK: WHAT DO WE KNOW AND HOW DO WE KNOW IT?

Historians ask some very big questions. Of course, the stereotype of the historian as a person who searches in dusty archives for tiny, concrete bits of data is often correct. Detail and accuracy are important. Beneath this search for details, however, lie profound questions of fundamental importance. In this chapter we address some of the biggest questions of all: Where did humans come from? How did our collective life on earth begin? How are we similar to other living species, and how are we unique?

Many historians would consider such questions to relate to prehistory, for no written records exist to answer them. We choose, however, to include prehistory as part of our search, for we historians are eclectic in our methods; we begin with questions about the past and our relationship to it, and then choose whatever methods help us to find answers. In this chapter we find that until the mid-nineteenth century, stories, often religious narratives, provided the answers to our questions about human origins. Then a re-evaluation of religious and narrative traditions invited a search for additional answers with a scientific basis. About the same time, new techniques of archaeology developed to provide those answers.

What does it mean to be human? This profound question turns most historians and prehistorians to the study of human creativity. Humans are what humans do. We travel and migrate, often out of sheer curiosity as well as to find food and shelter. As we shall see, by about 15,000 B.C.E., humans had traveled, mostly over land, and established themselves on all the continents of the earth except Antarctica. We also create and invent tools. Our account begins with the simplest stone tools dating back millions of years and continues up to the invention of pottery and of sedentary farming some 10,000 years ago. Finally, we humans also express our feelings and ideas in art, music, dance, ritual, and literature. In this chapter we examine early evidence of this creativity in the forms of sculptures and cave paintings from 20,000 years ago.

For time periods more recent than 20,000 years ago, we usually adopt the notation "B.C.E." (Before the Common Era) and "C.E." (Common Era). These designations correspond exactly to the more familiar "B.C." (Before Christ) and "A.D." (Anno Domini, "in the year of our Lord"), but remove the specific reference to a single religion. For dates more than 20,000 years ago, "B.P." (Before the Present) is sometimes used.

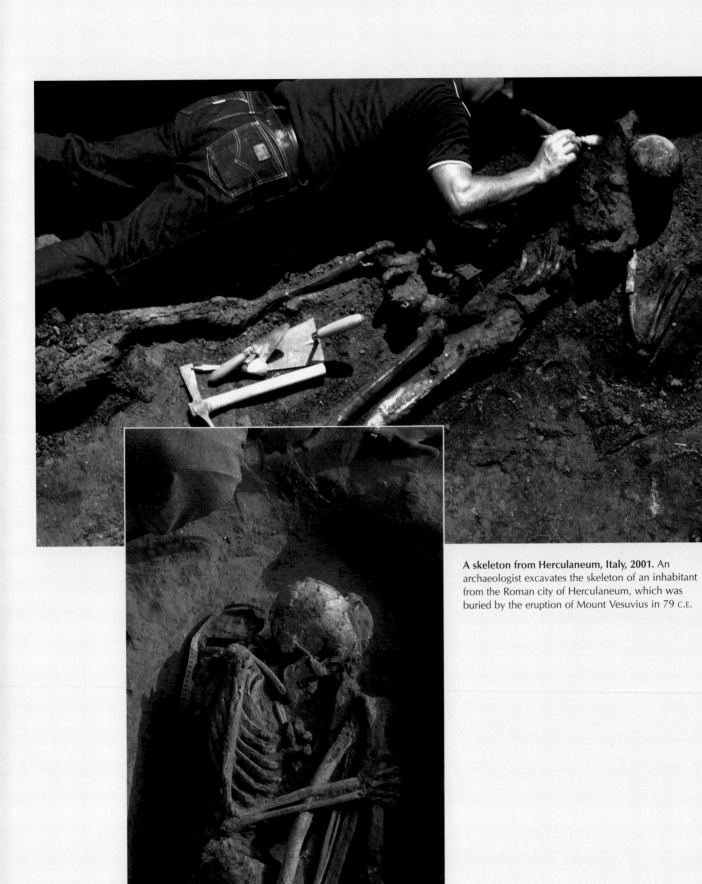

A skeleton from Herculaneum, Italy, 2001. An archaeologist excavates the skeleton of an inhabitant from the Roman city of Herculaneum, which was buried by the eruption of Mount Vesuvius in 79 C.E.

THE DRY BONES SPEAK

5 million B.C.E.–10,000 B.C.E.

KEY TOPICS
- Human Origins in Myth and History
- Fossils and Fossil Hunters
- Humans Create Culture

HUMAN ORIGINS IN MYTH AND HISTORY

Where did we come from? How did humans come to inhabit the earth? These questions are difficult to answer because the earliest human beings left no written records or obvious oral traditions. For more than a century, we have sought the answer to these questions in the earth, in the records of the fossils that archaeologists and **paleoanthropologists** (students of the earliest humans) have discovered and interpreted. But before the diggers came with their interpretations, human societies from many parts of the world developed stories based on popular beliefs to explain our origins. Passed from generation to generation as folk wisdom, these stories gave meaning to human existence. They not only tell *how* humans came to inhabit the earth, they also suggest *why*. Some of these stories, especially those that have been incorporated into religious texts such as the Bible, still inspire the imaginations and govern the behavior of hundreds of millions of people around the world.

paleoanthropologist A student of the earliest humans and the setting in which they lived.

Early Myths

As professional history developed, many historians considered that these stories were of limited value in the study of history and dismissed them as **myth**, an imaginative construction that cannot be verified with the kinds of records historians usually use. Nonetheless, myth and history are closely related, and many historians and anthropologists now accept myths as important commentaries that help us to understand how various societies have interpreted the origins of the human world. Myth and history share a common purpose—trying to explain how the world came to be as it is. Though there are limitations to mythical evidence, myths often contain important truths, and they can have powerful effects on people's values and behavior. Shared myths give cohesion to social relationships and bring them into a sense of shared community.

myth An interpretive story of the past that cannot be verified historically but has a deep moral message.

For thousands of years various creation stories have presented people with explanations of their place in the world and of their relationship to the gods, to the rest of creation, and to one another. The narratives have similarities, but also significant differences. Some portray humans as the exalted crown of creation, others as reconfigured parasites; some depict humans as partners with the gods, others as their servants; some suggest the equality of all humans, others stress a variety of caste, race, and gender hierarchies. To some degree, surely, people transmitted the stories as quaint tales told for enjoyment only, but they also provided guidance on how people should understand and live their lives.

One of the earliest known stories is the *Enuma Elish* epic of the people of Akkad in Mesopotamia. This account probably dates back to almost 2000 B.C.E. The goddess Tiamat and her consort Kingu revolt against the existing gods of Mesopotamia. These gods call on Marduk, a young, strong god, who defends the old order by defeating, killing, and dismembering the rebellious deities.

According to the *Enuma Elish*, the victorious gods created humans out of the blood of the defeated and slain leader of the rebels. The humans were to devote themselves

Opposite **A skeleton from Herculaneum, Italy, 2001.** An archaeologist excavates the skeleton of an inhabitant from Herculaneum.

to the service of the victors. In the context of the violent city-states of Mesopotamia at the time the epic was written down, this myth gave meaning and direction to human life and affirmed the authority of the powerful priestly class.

India, vast and diverse, has many different stories about the origin of humans. Two of the most widespread and powerful illustrate two principal dimensions of the thought and practice of Hindu religious traditions (see Chapter 9). The ancient epic *Rigveda*, which dates from about 1000 B.C.E., emphasizes the mystical, unknowable qualities of life and its origins:

> Who verily knows and who can here declare it, whence it was born and whence comes this creation?
>
> The Gods are later than this world's production. Who knows then whence it first came into being?
>
> He, the first origin of this creation, whether he formed it all or did not form it, whose eye controls this world in highest heaven, he verily knows it or perhaps he knows not.

In contrast to this reverent but puzzled view of creation, another of the most famous hymns of the *Rigveda*, the Purusha-sakta, describes the creation of the world by the gods' sacrifice and dismemberment of a giant man, Purusha:

> His mouth became the Brahmin; his arms were made into the Warrior, his thighs the People, and from his feet the Servants were born.
>
> The moon was born from his mind; from his eye the sun was born. Indra and Agni came from his mouth, and from his vital breath the Wind was born. (Ch. 10; v. 129)

AT A GLANCE: EARLY HUMANS AND THEIR ANCESTORS

DATE	PERIOD	HOMINID EVOLUTION	MATERIAL CULTURE
5 million	■ Pliocene	■ Fragments found in northern Kenya; possibly *Australopithecus*	
3.75 million	■ Pleistocene	■ *Australopithecus* genus, inc. Lucy (east and southern Africa) ■ *Homo habilis* (eastern and southern Africa) ■ *Homo erectus* (Africa) ■ *Homo erectus* thought to have moved from Africa into Eurasia	■ Tools ■ Stone artifacts ■ Use of fire
500,000		■ *Homo sapiens* (archaic form) ■ Remains of Peking Man (*Sinanthropus*) found at Zhoukoudian	
130,000–80,000		■ *Homo sapiens* (Africa and western Asia)	■ Stone artifacts
100,000–33,000		■ Neanderthals (Europe and western Asia)	
40,000	■ Aurignacian		■ Tools include long blades ■ First passage from Siberia to Alaska
30,000	■ Gravettian	■ Human remains of the Upper Paleolithic type, *Homo sapiens sapiens* (25,000) found in China	■ Venus figures (25,000–12,000)
20,000	■ Solutrean		■ Chauvet cave, France (18,000)
17,000	■ Magdalenian		■ Lascaux cave paintings (c. 15,000) ■ Altamira cave paintings (c. 13,550)

In this account, humans are part of nature, subject to the laws of the universe, but they are not born equal among themselves. Several groups are created with different qualities, in different **castes** or social, economic, and ritual positions inherited at birth. This myth of creation supported the hierarchical organization of India's historic caste system.

Perhaps the most widely known creation story is told in the Book of Genesis in the Hebrew Bible. Beginning from nothing, in five days God created heaven and earth; created light and separated it from darkness; created water and separated it from dry land; and created flora, birds, and fishes, and the sun, moon, and stars. God began the sixth day by creating larger land animals and reptiles, and then humans "in his own image."

The Book of Genesis assigns humans a unique and privileged place as the final crown and master of creation. Humans are specially created in God's own image, with dominion over all other living creatures. When the creation of humans and the charge to them are complete, God proclaims the whole process and product of creation as "good." Here humans hold an exalted position within, but also above, the rest of creation.

Until the late eighteenth century, these kinds of story were the only accounts we had of the origins of humans. No other explanations seemed necessary. In any case, no one expected to find actual physical evidence for the processes by which humans came to exist.

caste A hierarchical ordering of people into groups, fixed from birth, based on their inherited ritual status and determining whom they may marry and with whom they may eat.

The Evolutionary Explanation

During the eighteenth century some philosophers and natural scientists in Europe, who were most familiar with the creation story told in the Bible, began to challenge its belief in the individual, special creation of each life form. They saw so many similarities among different species that they could not believe that each had been created separately, but they could not demonstrate the processes through which these similarities and differences had developed. They saw some creatures changing forms during their lifecycle, such as the metamorphosis of the caterpillar into the moth, or the tadpole into the frog, but they could not establish the processes by which one species metamorphosed into another. They also knew the processes of breeding by which farmers encouraged the development of particular strains in the farm animals and plants, but they lacked the conception of a timeframe of millions of years that would allow for the natural evolution of a new species from an existing one.

Challenging the authority of the biblical account required a new method of inquiry, a new system for organizing knowledge. By the mid-eighteenth century, a new intellectual environment had begun to emerge (see Chapter 15). Scientific method called for the direct observation of nature, the recording and analysis of observation, and the discussion and debate of findings throughout an international community of scholars. It rejected the authority of religious texts that asserted truths without presenting substantiating evidence.

Charles Darwin (1809–82) and Alfred Russel Wallace (1823–1913), separately, formulated the modern theory of

Shiva Nataraja, Indian School, 13th century. Bronze. The cosmic dance of the Hindu Lord Shiva brings about a destruction that crushes evil underfoot and prepares the way for rebirth in the cycle of existence.

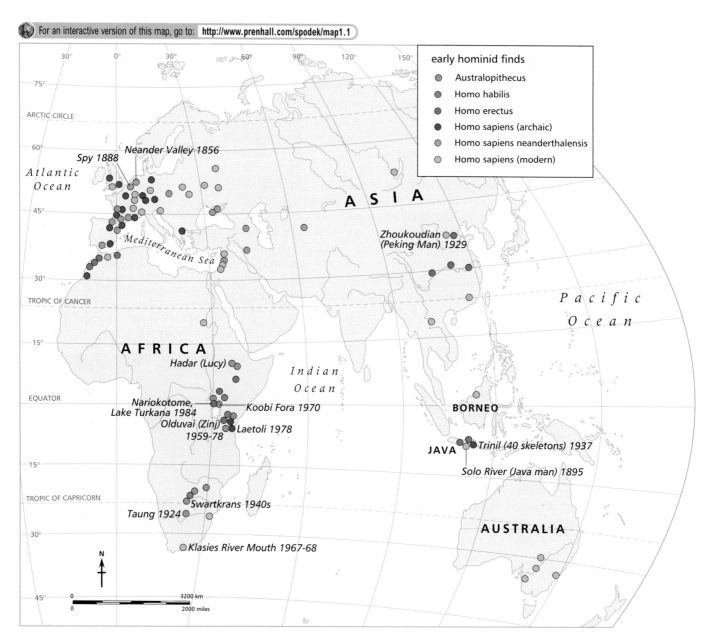

For an interactive version of this map, go to: http://www.prenhall.com/spodek/map1.1

early hominid finds

- Australopithecus
- Homo habilis
- Homo erectus
- Homo sapiens (archaic)
- Homo sapiens neanderthalensis
- Homo sapiens (modern)

Spy 1888
Neander Valley 1856

Atlantic Ocean

Mediterranean Sea

ASIA

Zhoukoudian
(Peking Man) 1929

Pacific Ocean

AFRICA

Hadar (Lucy)

Indian Ocean

Nariokotome,
Lake Turkana 1984   Koobi Fora 1970
Olduvai (Zinj)   Laetoli 1978
1959-78

BORNEO

JAVA   Trinil (40 skeletons) 1937

Solo River (Java man) 1895

Swartkrans 1940s
Taung 1924

AUSTRALIA

Klasies River Mouth 1967-68

ARCTIC CIRCLE

TROPIC OF CANCER

EQUATOR

TROPIC OF CAPRICORN

N

0   3200 km
0   2000 miles

Human ancestors. Fossil remains of the earliest direct human ancestors, *Australopithecus* and *Homo habilis*, dating from 1 million to 5 million years ago, have been found only in tropical Africa. The unique soil and climatic conditions there have preserved the fossils. *Homo erectus* remains, from 1.5 million years ago, are the earliest to be found outside Africa. They, along with *Homo sapiens*, have been found throughout Eurasia.

the biological evolution of species. They also saw the mounting evidence of biological similarities among related species; they understood that these similar species were, in fact, related to one another, not separate creations, and they allowed a timeframe adequate for major transformations of species to take place. They then went on to demonstrate the method by which small differences within a species were transmitted from generation to generation, increasing the differentiation until new forms were produced.

Both Darwin and Wallace reached their conclusions as a result of extensive travel overseas. Darwin carried out his observations on a scientific voyage around the world in 1831–6 aboard the British warship *Beagle*, and especially during his stay in the Galapagos Islands off the equatorial west coast of South America. Wallace traveled for many years in the islands of southeast Asia. In 1855 he published a paper suggesting a common ancestor for primates and man. In 1858 Wallace and Darwin published a joint paper on the basic concepts of evolution.

In the isolated Galapagos Islands, Darwin had found various kinds of finches, all of which were similar to each other except in their beaks. He rejected the idea that each kind of finch had been separately created. Rather, he argued, there must have been an ancestor common to them all throughout the islands. Because each island offered slightly different food sources, different beaks were better suited to each separate island. The different ecological niches on each separate island to which the birds had immigrated had evoked slightly different evolutionary development. So from a single, common ancestor, new species evolved over time on the different islands.

Darwin compared natural selection to the selection process practiced by humans in breeding animals. Farmers know that specific traits among their animals can be exaggerated through breeding. Horses, for example, can be bred either for speed or for power by selecting those horses in which the desired trait appears. In nature the act of selection occurs spontaneously, if more slowly, as plants and animals that have traits more appropriate to an environment survive and reproduce while others do not.

In 1859 Darwin published his findings and conclusions in *On the Origin of Species by Means of Natural Selection*, a book that challenged humankind's conception of life on earth and of our place in the universe. Darwin explained that the pressure for each organism to compete, survive, and reproduce created a kind of natural selection. The population of each species increased until its ecological niche was filled to capacity. In the face of this population pressure, the species that were better adapted to the niche survived; the rest were crowded out and tended toward extinction. Small differences always appeared within a species: some members were taller, some shorter; some more brightly colored, others less radiant; some with more flexible hands and feet, others less manipulable. Those members with differences that aided survival in any given ecological setting tended to live on and to transmit their differences to their descendants. Others died out. Darwin called this process "natural selection" or "survival of the fittest."

The New Challenges. Darwin's argument challenged two prevailing stories of creation, especially the biblical views. First, the process of natural selection had no goal beyond survival and reproduction. Unlike many existing creation myths, especially biblical stories, evolutionary theory postulated no **teleology**, no ethical or moral goals and purposes of life. Second, the theory of natural selection described the evolution of ever more "fit" organisms, better adapted to their environment, evolving from existing ones. The special, separate creation of each species was not necessary.

For Darwin, the process of natural selection of more complex, better adapted forms also explained the evolution of humans from simpler, less well-adapted organisms. Perhaps this was "the Creator's" method. Darwin concluded *On the Origin of Species*:

> Thus, from the war of nature, from famine and death, the most exalted object which we are capable of conceiving, namely, the production of the higher animals, directly follows. There is grandeur in this view of life, with its several powers, having been originally breathed by the Creator into a few forms or into one; and that, whilst this planet has gone cycling on according to the fixed law of gravity, from so simple a beginning endless forms most beautiful and most wonderful have been, and are being, evolved.

"That Troubles Our Monkey Again." **Cartoon of Charles Darwin from** *Fun,* **November 16, 1872.** As scientists and theologians struggled to come to terms with the implications of evolutionary theory, popular reaction was often hostile and derisive. In this cartoon from a contemporary British weekly, Darwin is caricatured as an ape checking the pulse of a woman—or, as the cartoonist ironically refers to her, a "female descendant of marine ascidian" (a tiny invertebrate).

teleology The philosophical study of final causes or purposes. Teleology refers especially to any system that interprets nature or the universe as having design or purpose. It has been used to provide evidence for the existence of God.

Note, however, that the words "by the Creator" did not appear in the first edition. Darwin added them later, perhaps in response to criticisms raised by more conventional Christian religious thinkers, who continued to find the biblical story a credible explanation for the origins of human beings.

Within a decade, Darwin's ideas had won over the scientific community. In 1871, Darwin published *The Descent of Man*, which extended his argument to the evolution of humans, concluding explicitly that "man is descended from some lowly organized form."

The search now began for evidence of the "missing link" between humans and apes, for some creature, alive or dead, that stood at an intermediate point in the evolutionary process. In this search archaeology flourished, and the adjunct field of paleo-anthropology, which explores the nature of early humans in their environment, developed. We shall now investigate the findings of these disciplines and the disputes they have engendered.

FOSSILS AND FOSSIL HUNTERS

The search for the "missing link" began in Europe, because that is where the major scientific researchers lived and worked, and that is where the discovery of Neanderthal skeletons in 1856 whetted their appetites for still more evidence. Later, the search led to Java, Indonesia, and Beijing, China. Still more recently, Africa has yielded the earliest specimens of the human species, *Homo sapiens sapiens*, fulfilling Darwin's prediction of an African origin of human evolution, based on the abundance of non-human primates—apes and chimpanzees—living on that continent.

As archaeologists discovered a variety of kinds of hominids—creatures that exhibited some characteristics of *Homo sapiens* but others of earlier primates—they concluded that there was no single missing link, but rather a variety of evolutionary paths that led to the emergence of humans. Our discussion will now follow the search for the missing link that ultimately led to this new understanding of the pattern of evolution. Readers who wish to know immediately the composite picture that has emerged from this research may now turn to the chart on pages 16–17.

The Puzzling Neanderthals

In August 1856, workers quarrying for limestone in a cave in the Neander Valley near Düsseldorf, Germany, found a thick skullcap with a sloping forehead and several skeletal bones of limbs. Some speculated that it was a deformed human. Others thought it was a soldier lost in a previous war. Other, similar, skeletal remains had been found, but without any clearer understanding of their meaning.

In 1863, Thomas Henry Huxley (1829–95), a leading advocate of Darwin's theory of evolution, argued that the skull was part of a primitive human being who stood between non-human primates and *Homo sapiens*, our own species. (The term *Homo sapiens* means "human, wise.") He claimed that it was the "missing link." In 1864, scholars gave the fossil a name that signified this intermediate position: *Homo neanderthalensis*.

One of the first questions archaeologists asked themselves was: What did *Homo neanderthalensis* look like? Reconstructing the appearance of Neanderthals was difficult, because soft tissue—hair, flesh, and cartilage—does not survive as fossils. Scientists had to use their imaginations.

The earliest efforts to picture Neanderthals showed them walking like apes, with a spine that had no curves, and hunchbacked, with their heads pushed forward on top

Diorama of "bovine" Neanderthals. Displayed for decades in the Field Museum of Natural History in Chicago, this reconstruction suggests that Neanderthals were unintelligent and clumsy. More recent interpretations portray a more intelligent, more graceful creature.

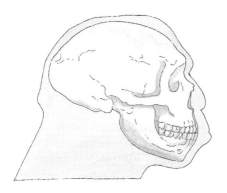 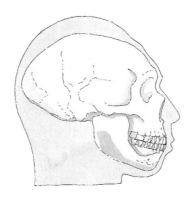

Alternate reconstructions from Neanderthal skull. Because soft tissues—hair, flesh, cartilage—don't survive as fossils, archaeologists must use their imaginations in adding these elements to the solid bone of excavated skeletons.

of their spines. Muscular but clumsy-looking, with heavy jaws and low, sloping foreheads, these pictures strongly suggested that *Homo neanderthalensis* was brutish and lacking in intelligence. For many years this interpretation, and others similar to it, carried great weight. Museum representations carried the message to the general public. Over the years, however, archaeologists have discovered more about Neanderthals' ability to make tools and survive in challenging environments. Impressed with these accomplishments, anthropologists now create reconstructions that show Neanderthals looking much less "primitive" and more like modern humans.

Moving beyond the individual skeleton in isolation, teams of experts from disciplines such as biology, geology, and climatology cooperate to reconstruct the natural setting of human and hominid development. As Neanderthal skeletons have been found from northern Europe to Africa, from Gibraltar to Iran, these natural settings vary greatly. Remains from caves near Gibraltar suggest that Neanderthals in that area lived in a nuclear family. Elsewhere, evidence shows that many Neanderthals lived in larger bands of up to twenty to thirty individuals.

One recent discovery suggests that at least some Neanderthals were cannibals. The evidence comes from a cave in southern France. A total of seventy-eight bones from at least two adults, two teenagers, and two children aged about seven show that the flesh from all parts of the bodies was carefully removed. Bones were smashed with rocks to get at the inside marrow and skulls were broken open. The Neanderthal bones and the bones of deer were tossed together into a heap and show similar marks from the same stone tools. On the other hand, there are many other examples of Neanderthals burying their dead carefully, suggesting that their cultural behavior differed from group to group.

While Neanderthals appeared to be *a* link between apes and humans, continuing excavations demonstrated that they were not *the* link. As researchers have continued to find additional examples of early hominids all over the world, it has become increasingly clear that there is no single link. There is no single chain leading directly from apes to humans. Rather, anthropologists now believe that many hominids contributed to a formation better described as a "bush" of various hominids with many branches. From the various interbreedings of these hominids, *Homo sapiens sapiens*, our species, evolved. All of the other intervening species died out and are no longer to be found

LANDMARKS IN EARLY LIFE

Years ago (millions)	Geological period	Life form
2500	Archaean	earliest living things
590	Cambrian	first fossils
505	Ordovician	first fish
438	Silurian	first land plants
408	Devonian	first amphibians
360	Carboniferous	first reptiles
286	Permian	reptiles expanded
248	Triassic	first mammals and dinosaurs
213	Jurassic	first birds
144	Cretaceous	heyday of dinosaurs
65	Cretaceous	mammals flourished; dinosaurs extinct
25	Tertiary	first hominoid (ancestor of apes and humans)
5	Tertiary	first hominid (human ancestor)
0.01	Quaternary	modern humans appeared

walking the earth. So it might appear that first there were apes and then, in a direct chain, there were humans. But the fossils of many different species in-between show that the evolutionary path was not so simple.

Homo erectus: A Worldwide Wanderer

Homo erectus The most widespread of all prehistoric hominids, and the most similar to humans. Evolved about 2 million years ago and became extinct 100,000 years ago.

The next of these prehistoric hominid species to be unearthed—the most widespread, and the closest to modern humans—was *Homo erectus* (the upright human). Examples of this species were discovered in widely dispersed locations throughout the eastern hemisphere and first named according to the locations in which they were found. Later, anthropologists recognized the similarities among them, named them collectively *Homo erectus*, and traced their migration patterns from their earliest home in Africa to new habitats across Asia.

In 1891, Eugène Dubois (1858–1940), a surgeon in the Dutch army in Java, Indonesia, was exploring for fossils. Employing the labor of convicts in Dutch prisons, along the bank of the Solo River, he discovered a cranium with a brain capacity of 900 cubic centimeters (compared to the modern human average of 1400 cc), a molar, and a femur. Dubois claimed to have discovered "pithecanthropus," ape-man. This find, widely referred to as Java Man, was the first early hominid discovered outside Europe. Dubois' Java Man forced scholars to consider the theories of the evolution of humans more seriously and to understand the process in a global context.

In 1929, in the vast Zhoukoudian cave 30 miles from Beijing, Chinese archaeologists discovered a 500,000-year-old skullcap. In the next few years, in this fossil-rich cave, they discovered fourteen more fossil skulls and the remains of some forty individuals, whom they dated from 600,000 to 200,000 years ago. The cave seems to have been the home of a band of hunters, who lived in a forested, grassy, riverine area and who ate plants as well as animals, such as bison and deer. Remaining bones and ash indicate their ability to use fire for light and cooking. With a brain capacity ranging from 775 to 1300 cubic centimeters and a height up to 5 feet 6 inches, anatomically Peking (Beijing) Man was almost identical to Java Man. About a decade later, further excavations in Java turned up the nearly complete skull of one hominid and the skeletons of some forty others who had lived some 100,000 to 900,000 years ago. Anthropologists soon recognized similarities between Java Man and Beijing Man and classified them collectively under the name *Homo erectus*. The forty skeletons from Java represent one-third of all the *Homo erectus* skeletons uncovered to this day in the entire world. Those in the Zhoukoudian cave represent another third. The most complete skeleton that we have of *Homo erectus* was discovered, however, in Africa, in 1984, on the shores of Lake Turkana, Kenya, by Richard Leakey. These fossils were later grouped as *Homo erectus*. The key problem was that the names were proliferating with no understanding of the relationships, and each discoverer considered his find to be a separate species.

The Search Shifts to Africa

In 1924, a medical student in South Africa called the attention of his professor, Raymond Dart, to some fossils in a quarry near Taung. Dart investigated and proclaimed the Taung skull to be *Australopithecus africanus*, "southern apelike creature of Africa," a 2-million-year-old ancestor of humans. Another medical doctor, Robert Broom, discovered additional hominid fossils including some of *Homo erectus*, similar to those discovered in Java and China. Between 1945 and 1955, Dart and his colleagues began to discover bone tools among the hominid fossils as well as evidence of the first controlled use of fire, about 1 million years ago. Their research extended beyond the archaeology of individual hominid skeletons to paleoanthropology, the study of the entire environment in which these hominids had lived. Their ecological analyses included, for example, the fossils of hundreds of animals discovered nearby the hominids.

Archaeologist Louis Leakey (1903–72) began his excavations in East Africa in the 1930s, although his most important discoveries were achieved with his wife Mary (1913–96) after 1959 in the Olduvai Gorge, where the Great Rift Valley cuts through northern Tanzania.

The Great Rift Valley runs from the Jordan River valley and the Dead Sea southward through the Red Sea, Ethiopia, Kenya, Tanzania, and Mozambique. The Rift is a fossil-hunter's delight. From at least 7 million years ago until perhaps 100,000 years ago, it was a fertile, populated region; it is geologically still shifting and, therefore, has covered and uncovered its deposits over time. Rivers that run through the Rift Valley further the process of uncovering the fossils, and it is volcanic, generating lava and ash that preserve the fossils caught within it and provide the material for relatively accurate dating.

At Olduvai in 1959, the Leakeys discovered a hominid they called *Zinjanthropus boisei*, soon nicknamed Zinj. At first they hoped that Zinj might be an early specimen of *Homo*, but its skull was too small, its teeth were too large, its arms were too long, and its face was too much like an ape's. Zinj, who was 1,750,000 years old, was another *Australopithecus*, a hominid closer to apes than to modern humans. The *Australopithecus* clan was thus extended to include a new cousin, *Australopithecus boisei*. The australopithecine family tree—or "bush"—by now showed a number of branches, although the relationship among them and to us is not always clear. The chart on page 16 represents these branches and relationships.

Louis and Mary Leakey examining the palate of the Zinj skull, 1959. This husband-and-wife team revolutionized our understanding of anthropology. Their excavations in the Olduvai Gorge in East Africa led to the generally accepted belief that hominids originally evolved in Africa.

Homo habilis. The Leakeys' continued excavations at Olduvai turned up skull fragments of creatures with brain capacities of 650 cubic centimeters, between the 400–500 cc of australopithecines and the 1400 cc of modern humans. The Leakeys named this new type of hominid *Homo habilis*, "handy person," because of the stone tools they made and used in scavenging, hunting, and butchering food. Dating suggested that *Homo habilis* lived at about the same time as Zinj, demonstrating that *Homo* and *Australopithecus* had lived side by side about 2 million years ago.

The Leakeys' discoveries at Olduvai furthered the search for the ancestors of modern humans in several directions: they pushed back the date of the earliest known representative of the genus *Homo* to 1.5–2 million years ago; they indicated the extent of the tool-using capacity of these early *Homo* representatives; and they reconstructed the ecology of the region 2.5–1.5 million years ago, placing *Homo habilis* within it as hunter and scavenger. Together with earlier discoveries, the findings enabled the Leakeys to identify Africa as the home of the earliest hominids and the earliest representatives of the genus *Homo*.

In the 1970s, Louis and Mary's son, Richard Leakey (1944–), discovered additional bones of the species *Homo habilis* at Koobi Fora on the east side of Lake Turkana in Kenya. The finds confirmed the size of its brain at about 650 cc; its opposable thumb, which allowed it to grip objects powerfully and manipulate them precisely, and thus to make tools; and its upright, bipedal (two-legged) walk, evident from the form of its thigh and leg bones.

Australopithecus afarensis. In 1974, at Hadar, Ethiopia, near the Awash River, Donald Johanson (1943–) discovered "Lucy," the first known representative of *Australopithecus afarensis*, named for the local Afar people. (Lucy herself was named for the popular Beatles song "Lucy in the Sky with Diamonds," which was playing on a tape recorder just as the Johanson team was realizing the importance of their find.) This discovery pushed back the date of the earliest known hominid to about 3.2 million years ago.

Lucy's overall height was between 3 feet 6 inches and 4 feet, and Johanson and his team estimated her weight as 60 pounds. The archaeologists were able to uncover about 40 percent of her total skeleton, making Lucy the earliest and most complete hominid skeleton known at the time. She had humanlike hands, but there is no evidence that she made or used tools, and her sturdy, curved arms are still consistent with tree-climbing. Later excavations at Hadar revealed numerous additional skeletons of *Australopithecus afarensis*, including the first complete skull, discovered by Johanson in 1992.

The cranial capacity of Lucy and her fellow *Australopithecus afarensis* was only 400 cubic centimeters, too small for her to be a *Homo*. Her pelvis was too small to allow the birth of offspring with a larger skull, but the form of that pelvis and the fit of her knee joints characterized Lucy as a two-legged hominid. Lucy had walked upright. She was a kind of bipedal ape, and, in her bipedalism, an ancestor of modern humans.

Further evidence of the bipedalism of these apelike creatures came from Laetoli, Tanzania. There, in 1978, Mary Leakey discovered the footprints of two *Australopithecus afarensis* walking side by side. In volcanic ash, she found seventy footprints walking a distance of 80 feet. The ash provided material for dating the prints; they were 3.5 million years old. The tracks suggest that *Australopithecus afarensis* had a slower, more rolling gait than modern man, although the prints reveal well-defined feet. Mary Leakey saw in them a slight sideward turn, a hesitation in direction, which she interpreted as the first evidence of human doubt.

In 1994, seventeen fossils of a new genus, *Ardipithecus ramidus*, "ground ape," were discovered in Aramis, Ethiopia, in the bed of the Awash River not far from the Lucy find. An international team of archaeologists analyzed them. Ten of the fossils were teeth, two were cranial fragments, and the remainder were bones from the left arm. Later, the team recovered about 80 percent of an *Ardipithecus ramidus* skeleton. It dated to 4.4 million years, pushing back the date of the earliest ape-like hominid by a half million years.

Then, in 2001, a team working in Chad, Africa, under the French paleoanthropologist Michel Brunet discovered a 6- to 7-million-year-old skull, nicknamed "Toumai," which means "hope of life" in the Goran language (see p. 19). Toumai is at least 2.5 million years older than any previously discovered hominid skull, and, remarkably, it is nearly complete. On the cusp between ape and human, its human characteristics include a relatively thick and continuous brow ridge, a relatively flat nose and face, and canine teeth which are shorter and more thickly enameled than those of chimpanzees. On the other hand, its cranial capacity is about the size of a chimp's, about one-fourth of a modern human's. It is not clear if Toumai was bipedal, but its spine entered its cranium in a pathway consistent with bipedalism. "Toumai" fits the dominant theories of

Hominid footprints, Laetoli, Northern Tanzania. These footprints in ash at Laetoli confirmed that hominids were walking upright 3.5 million years ago. The tracks suggest that *Australopithecus afarensis* had a slower, more rolling gait than modern man, although the prints reveal well-defined feet. Mary Leakey (pictured), who discovered the prints, saw in them a slight sideward turn, a hesitation in direction, which she interpreted as the first evidence of human doubt.

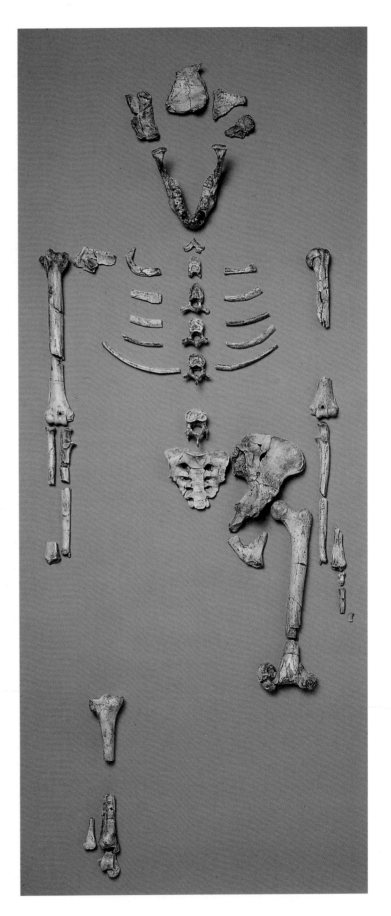

"Lucy" skeleton, *Australopithecus afarensis*, found at Hadar, Ethiopia. "Lucy" is thought to have lived about 3.2 million years ago and was at the time of her discovery in 1974 the earliest known hominid ancestor of modern man. She had humanlike hands and could walk upright; however, there is no evidence that she made or used tools, and her sturdy, curved arms are still consistent with tree-climbing. Until the discovery of Ardipithecus in 1994, Lucy was the most complete hominid skeleton from the period before 2 million years ago. (*Natural History Museum, London*)

evolution as to the time at which and the pattern by which the hominid line of evolution separated from the chimpanzee line, taking on its own distinct characteristics. It challenges most current beliefs, however, in suggesting that hominids evolved not only in the difficult, harsh, arid climate of the Rift Valley, where all the earlier hominids had been uncovered, but also in the more accommodating lush forests that covered western Chad 6 million years ago.

As paleoanthropologists assembled this record of the earliest human ancestors, they also found more recent skeletons that more closely resemble our own. The earliest known anatomically modern *Homo sapiens* fossil also appeared in Africa. It was discovered in 1967–8 in caves at the Klasies River Mouth on the coast of South Africa. These fossil remains of the oldest known example of the species *Homo sapiens* date to 75,000 to 115,000 years ago. They include lower and upper jaws, skull fragments, teeth, and bones of limbs. With them fossil-hunters found thousands of stone quartzite tools, an abundance of bones from numerous land mammals, and the remains of hundreds of thousands of shellfish, suggesting a diet rich in meat and seafood. The Klasies River Mouth discovery raised most provocatively the question of where the first *Homo sapiens* emerged and how they spread.

The Debate over African Origins

Almost all paleoanthropologists and archaeologists now believe that *Homo erectus* appeared first in Africa and spread from there to Asia and, perhaps, to Europe between 1 and 2 million years ago. But then the scholars split into two camps: the "multiregionalists" and the "out-of-Africa" camp.

The multiregionalists argue that *Homo erectus* evolved into *Homo sapiens* in each region of migration. Their thesis is often called the "candelabra" theory, since it sees the evolutionary branches beginning far back in history in many different locations.

The out-of-Africa group argues that *Homo erectus* evolved into *Homo sapiens* only once—in Africa. Then, about 100,000 years ago, the new humans emigrated to the rest of the world from Africa. This idea is often designated the "Noah's Ark" theory, since it proposes a much more recent common ancestry in Africa (see diagram, p. 18).

Both groups of scholars agree that the varieties of racial development—differences in physical characteristics such as skin color, characteristics of hair, bone structure, and minor genetic modification—are responses to different ecological niches. They differ, however, on the time and place of the development. If the evolution from *Homo erectus* to *Homo sapiens* began in several different locations up to 2 million years ago, then

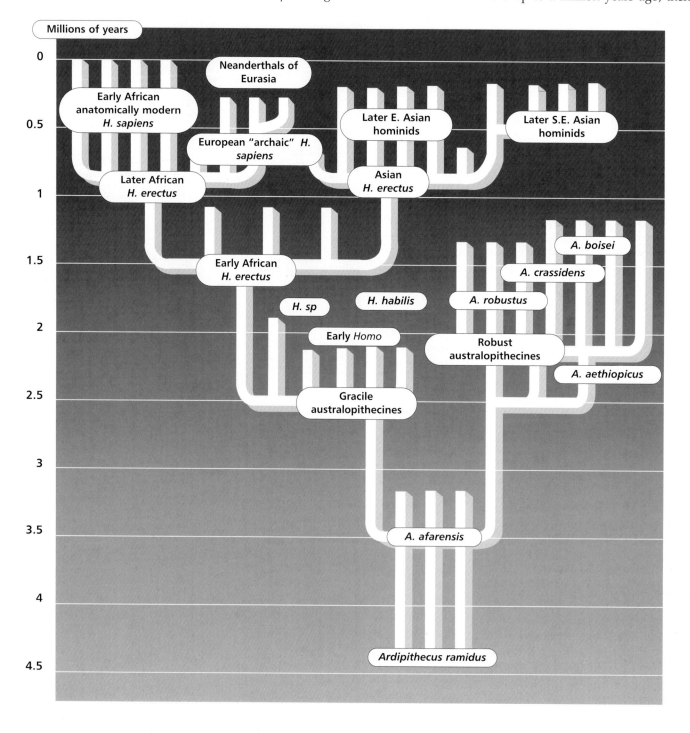

Skull reconstructions of some of the ancestors of modern man in chronological order. The generalized dates attached to each species imply that one followed the other, but actually some earlier species lived on for some time alongside more recent ones. By about 35,000 B.C.E., however, all except *Homo sapiens* were extinct.

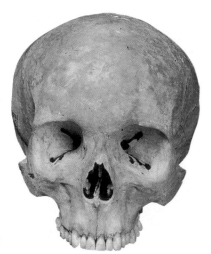

Homo sapiens sapiens
present day

Homo sapiens (Neanderthal)
50,000 B.P.

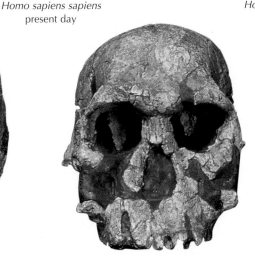

Homo erectus
1.4 million B.P.

Homo habilis
1.8 million B.P.

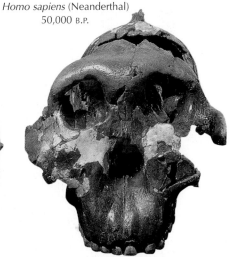

Australopithecus boisei
1.9 million B.P.

Opposite **The human "bush."** Popular thought usually imagines a straight-line development from apes to humans, but anthropologists speak of a human "bush," a variety of interacting and interbreeding species that finally produced *Homo sapiens*. Most anthropological models see *Ardipithecus ramidus* and *Australopithecus afarensis* as the first steps in the branching-apart of humans from apes about 5 million years ago. One line of further evolution led toward modern *Homo sapiens*. All the other hominid forms, those in our own line and those in other lines, subsequently became extinct.

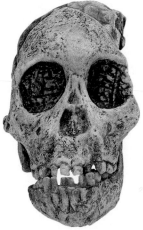

Australopithecus africanus
2.7 million B.P.

racial differentiation is very old. Even so, the groups did not remain entirely separate from one another, and over time substantial interbreeding took place among the different regional groups despite their geographic distances. No race remained "pure." If, according to the alternative theory, all modern *Homo sapiens* share a common origin until just 100,000 years ago, and began to differentiate by race only after emigrating from Africa to new locations, then these differences are much more recent and even more superficial.

At present, the supporters of the "out-of-Africa" theory are in the majority. They point out that it is more common for just one branch of any particular species to evolve into another and ultimately to displace all the other branches than for all of the different branches to evolve simultaneously. They minimize the biological significance of race based on skin color as a relatively recent, and only "skin-deep," difference among the peoples of the earth. The advocates of both the multiregional and the out-of-Africa schools of thought agree that at deeper levels, such as blood types and the ability to interbreed, race has no significance.

Reading the Genetic Record

In the search for the time and place of the origins of *Homo sapiens*, a different kind of discovery, based on genetics rather than fossils, on laboratory research rather than field excavations, emerged about thirty years ago. Scientists began to study the DNA record of human and animal genes. DNA is each cell's chemical code of instructions

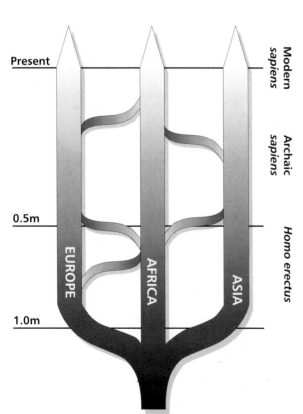

The candelabra, or multiregional, model. This suggests that *Homo erectus* emigrated from Africa throughout Europe and Asia and developed into *Homo sapiens* separately in all three regions. Some interbreeding did take place.

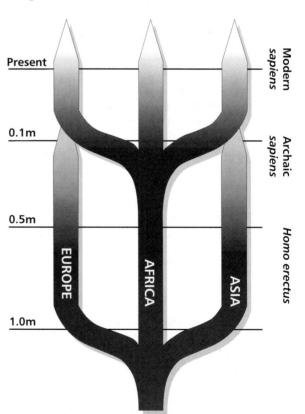

The Noah's Ark model. This suggests that *Homo erectus* did emigrate from Africa, but then died out everywhere else. The evolution to *Homo sapiens* took place only among those that remained in Africa—who later emigrated to Europe and Asia.

for building proteins, and the DNA research reveals the degrees of similarity and difference among the creatures studied.

Differences and similarities in the proteins and DNA of animals (including humans) living today suggest the date up to which they might have shared common ancestors before separating into different streams of evolution. In 1970, for example, biochemists first analyzed the protein albumin and the DNA of apes and humans and found that, genetically, modern humans are 97 percent the same as chimpanzees and 96 percent the same as gorillas. These data suggest that chimpanzees, gorillas, and humans shared common ancestors until 5–7 million years ago when evolutionary separation occurred. This genetic dating matches and reinforces the fossil record.

Extending the method further, researchers have used mitochondrial DNA (genetic material found outside the cell nucleus) to hypothesize that *Homo sapiens* emerged solely from Africa around 100,000 years ago. This confirmation of the "out-of-Africa" theory, however, remains controversial—and debate continues to rage. The journal *Nature* frequently carries these debates.

The Theory of Scientific Revolution

We have given a lengthy introduction to various explanations for the emergence of the first humans. Many historians would choose to move more quickly toward the present, although, of course, in covering 6 million years in one chapter we *are* moving swiftly! Some historians would be more comfortable covering "historic" times and places—that is, times and places with written records—but we have chosen to elaborate this account not only for its intrinsic interest but also because it helps to demonstrate most clearly our concern with "how we know" as well as with "what we know," since we believe that historians and paleoanthropologists share in the traditions of social science.

Paleoanthropologists maintain a lively debate about each of their findings and interpretations. They present their views and situate them within the ongoing debates in their field. This admirable procedure should inform all historical research and presentation, showing the historical record as an ongoing search and argument. Existing data may be re-evaluated; new data may be added; interpretations may be revised; new questions may arise. The historical record is never complete.

Amendments to the historical record, however, are usually minor additions to, or revisions of, a pattern already well known. Thomas Kuhn, in his pathbreaking study of the history of science, *The Structure of Scientific Revolutions*, wrote that

> normal science [like history] … is a highly cumulative enterprise, eminently successful in its aim, the steady extension of the scope and precision of scientific knowledge. Normal science does not aim at novelties of fact or theory and, when successful, finds none. (Kuhn, p. 52)

The history of the evolution of hominids usually follows this pattern of "normal science." Thus the discoveries of 4.5 million-year-old *Ardipithecus ramidus* in 1994 and of 6–7-million-year-old Toumai in 2001 did not surprise paleoanthropologists. The new fossils fit neatly into the expected

"Toumai," the oldest pre-human fossil, Chad, Africa, 2001. This skull was discovered by an international team of paleoanthropologists in Chad. It is from the earliest member of the pre-human family so far discovered, dating back 6–7 million years. "Toumai" is the name in Chad given to children born near the dry season.

paradigm A model of reality representing
one viewpoint.

timeframe for the process of evolution from apes to hominids (although the geo-graphical location of Toumai in Chad was unexpected). This was normal science filling in an existing model, or **paradigm**, with new detail.

Sometimes, however, new discoveries challenge existing paradigms. At first the new discoveries are discounted as exceptions to the rule. But when the exceptions increase, scientists seek new explanatory paradigms. Darwin's breakthrough followed this second pattern of scientific revolution. His discoveries on the voyage of the *Beagle* and his subsequent analyses of his findings challenged the existing concepts of creation that were based on biblical narratives. Darwin provided a radically different scientific explanation of the mechanisms of evolution that displaced the biblical paradigm. Both Darwin's scientific analysis and the Book of Genesis in the Bible, however, postulate the creation of an entire cosmos and world, replete with flora and fauna, before humans achieve their place in the universe and begin to name the other species.

Major revisions of the historical record often follow this trajectory. A general pattern of explanation is followed, until new research raises new questions and new theoretical paradigms provide more fitting explanations for all the available data and information. Throughout this text we shall continue to see changes in historical explanation over time. A "paradigm shift" may occur not only as a result of the discovery of new data, or of new interpretations better fitting the available data, but also as a response to new questions being raised that may not have been asked before. The historical record, like the scientific record on evolution, is always subject to re-evaluation.

HUMANS CREATE CULTURE

Biological Evolution and Cultural Creativity

Until now we have been examining biological evolution, "natural selection." Those organisms best able to survive did survive. By the time of *Homo habilis*, however, the *Homo* biological genus began creating simple tools through which it could shape nature to meet its needs. *Homo habilis* were already sculpting stone tools of increasing sophistication. They apparently hunted, scavenged, and gathered in groups and shared their booty. Throughout the intervening 2 million years up to our own day, *Homo* has continued to increase its sophistication in creating tools, art, rituals, settlements, concepts, and language, and in domesticating plants and animals—the basic elements of what anthropologists call culture. By the time that *Homo sapiens* had evolved, cultural creativity had superseded biology as the principal method by which humans coped with nature. Humans were no longer content to exist in nature. They sought to control it.

The cultural evolution seems to have been encouraged by biological evolution. As the *Homo* brain continued to develop and get bigger, it became impossible for the genus *Homo* to give birth through a relatively narrow birth canal to a child with a fully formed brain in a fully formed cranium. The brain capacity of human young must continue to develop for some time after birth. The brain of a newborn human weighs about 14 ounces, doubles to 35 ounces in about one year, and reaches its adult size of 45 ounces only by the age of six or seven. Within the genus *Homo*, therefore, parents must devote significant time to nurturing and teaching their young children. In addition, in female *Homo sapiens* the oestrus cycle, the alternating period of fertility and infertility, occurs each month rather than seasonally, allowing them to bear children more frequently than other primates. Increased childbearing further increases the time and energy devoted to nurturing the young. Because of the increased attention to nurturing, cultural life could flourish—and it did.

Since the earliest known appearance of *Homo sapiens* in the archaeological record about 120,000 years ago our species *Homo sapiens* has not changed anatomically. The skeletons unearthed at the Klasies River Mouth are no different from our own.

About 100,000 years ago, however, a new creativity appeared in the cultural and social life of *Homo sapiens*, perhaps the result of a modification in the internal structure of the brain. The people who lived before this development are called "archaic" *Homo sapiens*; those with the new cultural capabilities are considered a new subspecies, *Homo sapiens sapiens* (wise, wise human). They are us. Unlike their predecessors, *Homo sapiens sapiens* developed forms of symbolic expression, apparently spiritual and cultural in nature, including burial rituals and artwork that is sometimes stunningly beautiful and creative.

The remainder of this chapter presents seven creative behaviors that mark the arrival of *Homo sapiens sapiens*. First, we persisted. We are the lone survivor from among all the hominids of the last 6 million years. Second, we continued to spread to all parts of the globe in waves of migration that had begun even earlier. Third, we built small, temporary settlements to serve as base camps for hunting and gathering. Fourth, we continued to craft more sophisticated tools. Fifth, by about 25,000 B.C.E., on cave walls and in stone, we began to paint and sculpt magnificent

Two Aurignacian implements, France, Mesolithic era (c. 30,000 B.P.). Stone Age cultures first appeared in western Europe in 33,000 B.P. and underwent constant changes in technology—implying a gradual evolution in human behavior. By the Aurignacian era, flint-end scrapers (right) were employed in processing skins, woodworking, and carving artifacts like this bone spearpoint (left). (*Natural History Museum, London*)

KEY STAGES IN HUMAN DEVELOPMENT

4.5 m B.P.	First appearance of bipedalism. (*first clear appearance; Toumai of Chad, 6 m. B.C.E. was apparently bipedal*)
2 m B.P.	Change in structure of forelimbs— bipedalism is perfected. Gradual expansion and reorganization of the brain. Hunting, scavenging, and gathering cultures stimulate production of stone tools.
500,000 B.P.	Rapid brain growth.
200,000 B.P.	First forms of *Homo sapiens*. Early speech development. Fire now in use.
40,000 B.P.	Interglacial period. Existence of modern humans, with fully developed brain and speech. Tools constructed from component parts.
c. 25,000 B.P.	Cave art and portable art in Europe. Human migration begins from Asia into America.
10,000 B.C.E.	Invention of bow and arrows. Domestication of reindeer and dog (N. Eurasia). Settled food production.
8000–4000 B.C.E.	Increase of human population by 1500 percent. Domestication of sheep and goats (Near East). Earliest pottery (Japan). Farming spreads to W. Europe. Rice cultivation starts in Asia.
3000 B.C.E.	Writing, metals.

HOW DO WE KNOW?

Dating Archaeological Finds

Continuous improvements in dating techniques have changed our understanding of the relationships among the early Homo sapiens, and even among the earlier hominids, and their relationships to their environment. The most common technique, since its discovery in 1949, is **radiocarbon dating***, sometimes called the carbon 14 (C14) method. Living organisms breathe in air, and so they contain the same percentage of atoms of radioactive carbon as the earth's atmosphere. When an organism dies, its radiocarbon atoms disintegrate at a steady, known rate. By measuring the amount of radiocarbon remaining in a fossil skeleton, scientists can calculate backward to the date of death. Because the total amount of radiocarbon in any organism is small, little is left after 40,000 years, and the method does not work at all beyond 70,000 years into the past.*

For a broader spectrum of dates, scientists use a technique called **thermoluminescence***, developed in 1987. This technique was applied to burned flints discovered in the caves where early humans had lived. Radioactivity occurring in nature releases electrons in flint and clay, but they can finally escape only when the substance is heated. When the flints were first burned by the people of the caves, the electrons freed up to that time were released. Reheating the flints in the laboratory today releases the electrons stored up since the first burning. Scientists calculate the date of the first burning by measuring the light of those electrons. This technique works not only for burnt flint of 50,000–300,000 years of age, but also for burnt clay, enabling scientists to date pottery from the last 10,000 years.*

For much earlier dates, like those of the earliest hominid fossils that go back as much as 6 million years, scientists measure the decay of the radioactive element potassium 40 into argon 40, a process that takes place in volcanic rocks and soils. Potassium-argon dating, in use *since the 1950s, was invaluable in estimating the age of the soil in which stone tools and hominid remains were found in the Olduvai Gorge. This dating method was the clue to determining the deep antiquity of these fossils, and in shifting the search for the earliest hominids to Africa.*

- *Biochemists and physicists have their contribution to make in understanding—and dating—the evolution of the earliest humans. What have been the contributions of other academic specialists encountered in this book?*
- *What are the similarities between radiocarbon, thermoluminescence, and potassium-argon dating? Why is each limited to a particular time period?*
- *Which of these methods directly dates fossil remains? Which dates the soil in which fossils are found? What might be the problems with dating fossils by the soil in which they are found?*

radiocarbon dating A method of dating artifacts by measuring their radioactive carbon. Useful for objects 40,000–70,000 years old.

thermoluminescence A method of dating burnt flint by measuring electrons in it from 50,000–300,000 years ago, or of burnt pottery from the last 10,000 years.

works of art and symbolism. Sixth, we elaborated more sophisticated use of language. Seventh, by 10,000–15,000 B.C.E., we began to domesticate plants and animals, introducing the art and science of agriculture.

How Did We Survive?

From about 120,000 years ago, when we first appear in the archaeological record, until about 35,000 years ago, anatomically modern *Homo sapiens sapiens* seem to have coexisted alongside archaic *Homo sapiens* in several sites. The best studied of these places are caves in the area of Mount Carmel near Haifa, Israel. These caves have revealed skeletons and tools of both Neanderthals and modern humans. The fossils from the Tabun, Amud, and Kebara caves seem to be Neanderthals; those from Skhul and Qafzeh appear more modern.

The oldest Neanderthal, from Tabun, dated to 120,000–100,000 years ago; the two *Homo sapiens sapiens* at Qafzeh and Skhul were almost equally old, at 92,000 years ago; the two Neanderthal specimens at Kebara and Amud are 60,000–50,000 years old. One can only conclude, therefore, that Neanderthals and modern humans coexisted in the area of modern Israel for tens of thousands of years. Moreover, they shared similar types of tools. Neanderthals seem to have used slightly simpler, smaller Mousterian stone tools (named for the village of Le Moustier in southwestern France where they have been most clearly documented). Their modern human neighbors used the thinner, longer, more precisely crafted Aurignacian tools (named for another hunter-gatherer site in southern France). The differences were marked but not huge.

How, then, did modern *Homo sapiens sapiens* eventually displace all other hominids?

Three principal interpretations, in various combinations, have been suggested. The first is that modern humans defeated all the other hominids through aggression, warfare, and murder. This theory suggests a violent streak in the earliest humans. The second theory suggests that processes of mating and reproduction among the species bred the new human. In other words, our immediate ancestors made love not war, and we contain a Neanderthal heritage. Finally, it has been proposed that modern humans successfully filled up the ecological niche available, outcompeting archaic *Homo sapiens* for the available resources. According to this third theory, modern humans did not directly confront the archaic forms but displaced them—in a sense, we ate them out of house and home.

Global Migration

Homo sapiens sapiens appeared in Africa no later than 120,000 years ago, evolving from *Homo erectus*. Within 30,000 years the species began to appear throughout Europe and Asia. Anthropologists suspect that early human migrations were not just aimless wanderings, but were purposeful and specific. From earliest prehistory, people weighed their choices and opportunities and then chose appropriate actions. Global migration was the ultimate outcome.

Early humans in the Ice Age. By 20,000 years ago, when ice covered much of Europe and much of Canada, virtually the whole world (except Polynesia) had been colonized. Early humans were able to spread north because water frozen into ice sheets reduced sea levels so much that land bridges appeared, linking most major areas. The cold was intense, and the migrants' survival depended on their ability to stitch together animal hides into primitive clothing, control fire, and hunt large mammals.

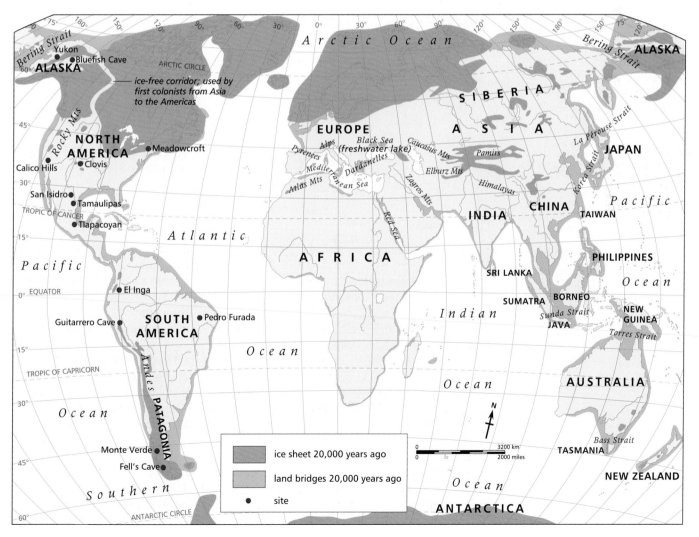

Changes in climate may have been one of the main reasons for migration. The Sahara, now a desert, provides one example. Until about 90,000 years ago, when the earth was in a warm, wet stage, the Sahara region was fertile and attractive to human settlement. People and animals from southern Africa migrated there. But then began an "ice age," one of the periods of global cooling that have affected the earth's climate over millions of years. Much of the earth's water froze. The Sahara dried up, turning the land to desert, and people and animals emigrated. Some may have turned back to southern Africa; some may have journeyed toward the North African coast; still others may have followed the Nile valley corridor into western Asia. So began one wave in a global process of migration.

To reach the most distant areas, such as Australia, the islands of the Pacific, and the Americas, took tens of thousands of years. These migrations required changes in

The colonization of the Pacific. The land bridges of the last Ice Age enabled early humans to spread south from China to Java and Borneo. There some knowledge of navigation was required to cross the Banda Sea to New Guinea and Australia. The most spectacular voyages were undertaken by the Polynesians, who journeyed hundreds and thousands of miles by canoe into the uncharted Pacific waters.

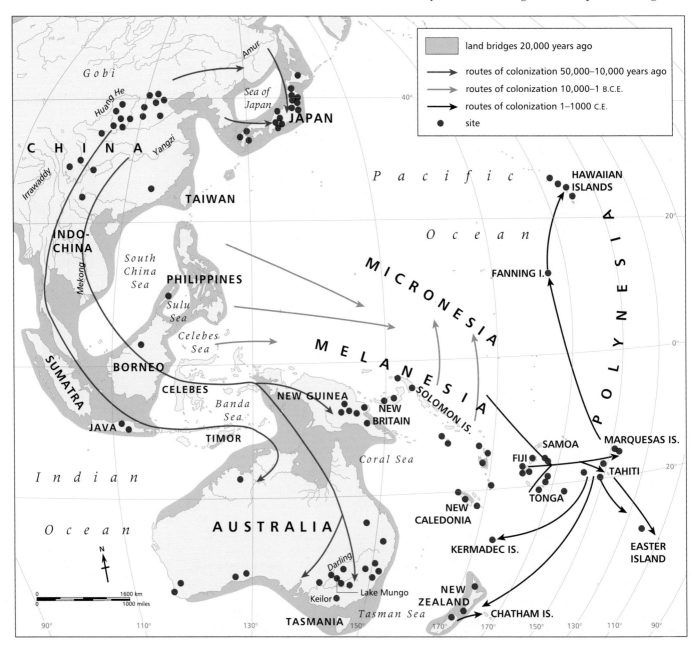

Charles Alexandre Lesueur, *Navigation in Van Diemen's Land*, pl. 14 from "Voyage of Discovery to Australian Lands," 1807. Engraving. When Europeans began settling Van Diemen's Land, now called Tasmania, in Australia, they found people who had arrived there some 40,000 years before, having crossed over from southeastern China. *(Royal Geographical Society, London)*

climate as well as in the skills of *Homo sapiens sapiens*. The successive ice ages of 90,000–10,000 years ago froze much of the water of the seas, reducing sea levels, extending the coasts of the continents, and creating land bridges that linked modern China with Japan, southeast Asia with the Philippines and Indonesia, and Siberia with Alaska. As long as the ice ages continued and the waters of seas and oceans were in frozen retreat, people could migrate across land passages.

There were exceptions. The Pacific islands known as Polynesia were not connected by land bridges to anywhere. As a result, they were peopled much later in history than most other regions. Only in 1000 B.C.E. did New Guineans, performing extraordinary feats of navigation in simple canoes, colonize Polynesia.

Increased Population and New Settlements

Gradually, as human population expanded, so, too, did the number of human groups and the closeness or "density" of their relationships to one another. Such increasing density and population pressure became a staple of human history. Frequently, the result was conflict among groups for the best lands and resources. Some groups chose to stand and fight for their territory, others reached accommodation with newcomers, and yet others emigrated, either by choice or by force, following losses in battle. These patterns, too, have repeated themselves for tens of thousands of years, and today there are some 20 million refugees in the world.

How large were these groups? They had to include enough members to provide security in defense and cooperation in work, yet be small enough to be able to subsist on the natural resources available and to resolve the interpersonal frictions that threatened the cohesion of the group and the safety of its members.

Calculated from the experience of modern hunter-gatherers, such as the Khoisan of the African Kalahari Desert, and theoretical mathematical models of group process, a five-family group of twenty-five persons seems the ideal balance. Mating and marriage rules might well have required, as they often do today, choosing a mate from outside the immediate band. For such an **exogamous** or external marriage pattern to function, a tribe would theoretically require at least nineteen bands of twenty-five members each, a total of 475 people, a figure reasonably close to the actual 500 found in modern hunter-gatherer societies.

How much territory did such bands require to support themselves? Anthropologists have calculated that an individual using the technology of Upper Paleolithic

exogamy The practice by which a person is compelled to choose a marital partner from outside his or her own group or clan, the opposite of endogamy, the choice of partner from within the group. Often the outside group from which the partner is to be chosen is specified.

times (150,000–12,000 years ago) would have required 77 square miles of relatively unproductive land or 7–8 square miles of fertile land to meet survival needs. At such densities, the area of the United States (excluding Alaska and Hawaii) might have supported a maximum of 600,000 people; the entire world, 10 million at most, although actual populations were less. As populations grew, bands began to stake out their own territories, and to mark out boundaries. They began to work out formal relationships with the occupants of neighboring areas.

Groups began to establish small settlements. The Neanderthals had occupied upland sites, but the later Cro-Magnon *Homo sapiens sapiens* (named for the region in France where this subspecies was originally discovered) moved down into the more valuable valleys and riverbeds. About half of their sites are within 1100 yards of a river, and all of them are near fords or shallows. These sites not only allow for easy crossing, but they are also at the points of animal crossings and therefore good for hunting. Tools took on regional patterns both in processes of manufacture and in styles of aesthetic appearance. These local patterns differentiated each group from its neighbors. Each group may have begun to develop a language, or a dialect, of its own.

HOW DO WE KNOW?

Man the Hunter or Woman the Gatherer?

In 1971 anthropologist Sally Slocum, writing under the pseudonym of Sally Linton, published one of the first feminist critiques of the current understanding of hominid evolution. She was responding to a set of papers published in 1968 entitled Man the Hunter. One of the papers asserted: "The biology, psychology, and customs that separate us from the apes—all these we owe to the hunters of time past." This argument, Slocum replied, put too much emphasis on aggressive behavior, the tools and organized planning required for hunting, the importance of fresh meat in the hominid diet, and male activities generally.

In "Woman the Gatherer: Male Bias in Anthropology," Slocum pointed out that gathering contributed more to group nutrition than hunting, as studies of modern hunter-gatherers showed. She also pointed out that tools usually linked to hunting might have been used for gathering instead, and she urged anthropologists to look afresh at the whole idea of tools:

Bones, sticks, and hand-axes could be used for digging up tubers or roots, or to

pulverize tough vegetable matter for easier eating. If, however, instead of thinking in terms of tools and weapons, we think in terms of cultural inventions, a new aspect is presented. I suggest that two of the earliest and most important cultural inventions were containers to hold the products of gathering, and some sort of sling or net to carry babies.

Further, Slocum argued, the skills of raising and nurturing young children, usually women's tasks, evoked more innovation and perhaps more development of the brain than did hunting:

I suggest that longer periods of infant dependency, more difficult births, and longer gestation periods also demanded more skills in social organization and communication—creating selective pressure for increased brain size without looking to hunting as an explanation. The need to organize for feeding after weaning, learning to handle the more complex social–emotional bonds that were developing, the new skills and cultural inventions surrounding more extensive gathering—all would demand larger brains. Too much attention has been given to the skills required by hunting, and too little to the skills required for gathering and the raising of dependent young.

Slocum concluded that anthropologists needed to confront their own assumptions about male dominance. As she put it, "The basis of any discipline is not the answers it gets, but the questions it asks."

- Sally Slocum suggests that our historical searches are determined by the questions we ask. Are there questions about the paleoanthropological record that you want to ask that have not been addressed thus far? Can you suggest methods to find answers to these questions?
- Sally Slocum wrote of "Male Bias in Anthropology." Do you think that the different experiences of men and women influence the questions that they ask in historical time as well as in prehistory? Give examples. Keep this list at hand as you read this book to determine whether you seem to be correct.
- How do the resources available for answering questions—such as stone tools as compared with fibers and cloths, or tools for hunting compared with tools for child-raising— determine the agendas for scholarly research?

Changes in the Toolkit

Even as the pace of exploration, migration, and trade increased, the clearest changes in human development appeared in our stone toolkits. The steady improvements in tool technology give this period its archaeological names. The entire period is called the Old Stone Age or Paleolithic. Tools show a slow progression from the Lower Paleolithic, ending about 150,000 years ago, to the Upper Paleolithic, which continued to about 10,000 B.C.E. (The Mesolithic and Neolithic—Middle and New Stone Ages, 8000–6000 B.C.E. and 6000–3000 B.C.E., respectively—will be explored in Chapter 2.)

From about 2.5 million years ago until about 150,000 years ago, the dominant technology of *Homo erectus* had been Acheulian hand-held axes and cleavers made of stone (named for St. Acheul in northern France, but actually developed first in Africa and only later throughout Europe and Asia).

About 250,000 years ago some sites reveal a more sophisticated technique, the Levallois (named for a suburb in Paris where the first examples were discovered). This Levallois technique produced more precise tools, including side scrapers and backed knives, fashioned by more consistent patterns of preparing flakes from the stone, and a more standardized final shape and size. This technique marked the emergence of archaic *Homo sapiens*.

The technology of *Homo sapiens sapiens* developed much more rapidly. By about 40,000 years ago, Aurignacian tools were being produced in or near a cave near the present-day village of Aurignac in the Pyrenees. This technology included narrow blades of stone as well as tools crafted from bone, ivory, and antler. Gravettian styles followed, about 30,000 to about 20,000 B.P. Then came Solutrean styles, 20,000–17,000 years ago, which included the production of the first known needles. Magdalenian tools, about 17,000–12,000 years ago, included barbed harpoons carved from antlers. Finally Azilian, 12,000–8000 B.C.E., completed the Paleolithic sequence. Each location and time period had its own aesthetic style, and each produced an increasing variety of tools.

THE EARLIEST TOOL KITS

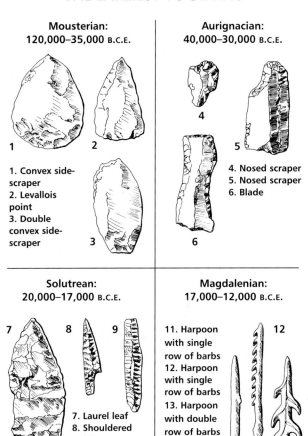

Mousterian: 120,000–35,000 B.C.E.

1. Convex side-scraper
2. Levallois point
3. Double convex side-scraper

Aurignacian: 40,000–30,000 B.C.E.

4. Nosed scraper
5. Nosed scraper
6. Blade

Solutrean: 20,000–17,000 B.C.E.

7. Laurel leaf
8. Shouldered point
9. Willow leaf
10. Unifacial point (worked on one side only)

Magdalenian: 17,000–12,000 B.C.E.

11. Harpoon with single row of barbs
12. Harpoon with single row of barbs
13. Harpoon with double row of barbs

Many of the earliest human tools were crafted from stone and show increasing sophistication. The "tool kits" shown here are named for the four different locations in which they were found. At first, humans simply chipped away at stone until edges and points were exposed. Later they began to carve the stone to meet more specific needs. The development took 100,000 years.

Bone flute, found in the Dordogne, France, c. 35,000 B.P. Simple wind instruments like this 4½ inch-long flute were made from the hollowed-out bones of birds, reindeer, and bears. They date back to as long ago as 35,000 B.P. (*Musée National de Préhistoire, Les Eyzies de Tayac, France*)

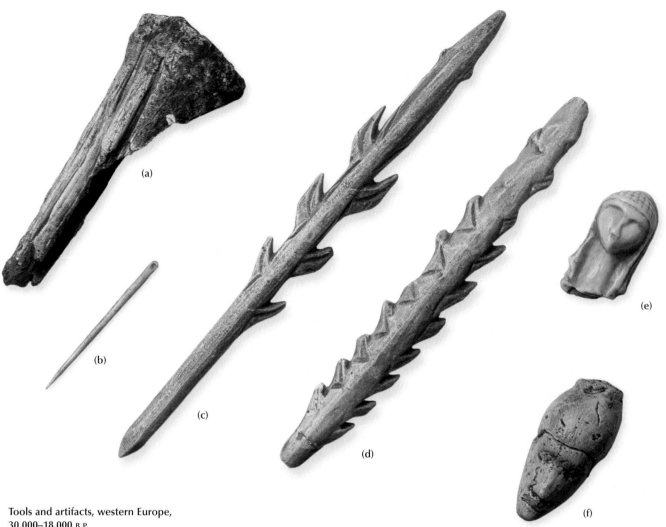

Tools and artifacts, western Europe, 30,000–18,000 B.P.
(a) Bone used to make needle blanks;
(b) Bone needle;
(c & d) Harpoon head and barbed point carved from antler;
(e & f) Two heads carved in mammoth ivory.
(*Natural History Museum, London*)

Spearthrower, Montastruc, France, 12,000 B.C.E. More than 14,000 years ago, beauty played an integral part in purely functional objects. Spearthrowers allowed hunters to propel their missiles with a surer aim and added leverage, as is symbolized by the streamlined and powerful figure of this leaping horse. Did the shape of the bone suggest the animal, or did the artist search for a bone to match his (or her) preconceived idea?

Tool patterns began to differ increasingly from one region to another, suggesting the formation of new communities among small hunter-gatherer bands, and a greater sense of separation and distinction between groups.

Not all tools were directly related to food production, nor even to work. As early as 35,000 B.P., flutes made from the bones of birds, reindeer, and bears suggest that creating and performing instrumental music had already become part of the human repertoire. Aesthetics and play already had their roles.

The tools we have found represent only a small fraction of the daily objects that early humans probably made and used. Tools made of stone have endured, those made of wood have not. Those made from natural fibers have, of course, disintegrated, which means we know little about clothing or basketry or food preparation. In most hunter-gatherer societies, making clothing and preparing food are usually women's work. So a whole area of technological development, most likely in the hands of women, was long overlooked through the focus on stone tools.

Language and Communication

Language is an intangible innovation, invisible in the archaeological record. It must be inferred from more solid evidence: global migration, fixed settlement sites, new tools and new materials, regional differences in production, trade across long distances, social hierarchies often marked by personal adornment and ritual burials, and the creation of art and instrumental music. Many of these activities would have been difficult, if not impossible, without some kind of language.

Exactly when a system of spoken language emerged is much debated, especially because we can only infer the answer from circumstantial evidence. The craniums of archaic *Homo sapiens* were as large as, or even larger than, our own, and they seem to have indentations indicating the presence of areas in the brain that influence speech capacity. Archaic *Homo sapiens* probably possessed a larynx that had descended sufficiently low in the throat to produce the sounds of modern human language.

The dispute arises here. Some anthropologists believe that with this biological equipment, humans began to develop modern language and speech slowly through cultural evolution. Others, notably linguist Noam Chomsky, believe that a change took place within the organization of the brain that gave humans a new capacity for language. Chomsky draws his conclusion from analyzing similarities in the "deep structure" of languages around the world. These universal similarities suggest that the rules of syntax of human language are embedded in the brain. Chomsky argues that just as humans are born to walk so they are born to talk. Just as bipedalism is not a learned cultural capacity, but has evolved biologically, so talking is not culturally learned but has biologically evolved. The use of individual languages is, of course, culturally specific.

Modern language provided the ability to communicate with others on an individual basis. It also allowed for increasingly elaborate social structures and greater complexity in human relationships. It facilitated deliberation over ethical principles of conduct for guiding and regulating those relationships. Moreover, it allowed for increasingly sophisticated internal thought and reflection. We could become more introspective as well as more communicative with others. The sophisticated psychological and social relationships that make us human became possible only with the development of language.

Cave Art and Portable Art

Cave paintings and portable art suggest both individual creativity and group process. They may represent the sharing of information, hope, and feelings, and serve as a means of transmitting them to subsequent generations. Finds of artwork from before 35,000 B.P., such as beads, pendants, and incised animal bones, are rare and disputed. Cave paintings and statuettes came later, and they appeared in numerous sites around the world. At Kundusi, Tanzania, Mary Leakey discovered stylized ocher paintings of human beings dating back perhaps 25,000 years. On the southern coast of Australia, in the Koonalda Cave, a flint mine at least 20,000 years old, a crisscross of abstract finger patterns was engraved into the soft limestone. In eastern Australia at about the same time, people were stenciling images of a hand and a pipe and stem onto the walls of Kenniff Cave. And at Kakadu, in northern Australia, a series of rock paintings begin about 20,000 B.P. Local peoples continued to paint new ones almost to the present.

Clay bison, from Tuc d'Audoubert, Ariège, France, after 15,000 B.C.E. Most cave art owes its survival to the very particular atmospheric conditions formed in the limestone caves in which they were sealed thousands of years ago. Only a very small number of sculptures have survived. The one reproduced here—in high relief—shows a female being pursued by a male bison.

In Europe, the artwork begins with some figurines and some wall painting as early as 30,000 B.P. and climaxes about 17,000–12,000 B.C.E. More than 200 decorated caves and more than 10,000 decorated objects (portable art) have been discovered in Europe, 85 percent of them in southern France and northern Spain. Many of the tools from the Magdalenian period (17,000–12,000 B.C.E.), as noted above, were fashioned to be beautiful as well as practical. Many of the figurines include delicately carved features, such as the face and hair on the figurine from about 22,000 B.P. discovered at Brassempouy, France, and only about 1½ inches high (see p. 28e). Many others pay scant attention to face and personal features, but accentuate and exaggerate sexual organs and buttocks, such as the 25,000-year-old figurine discovered at Dolní Vestonice, Moravia. The portable art represents a desire to create and enjoy beautiful objects. The exaggerated forms of the female, "Venus" objects that appear throughout Europe and in northwestern Asia suggest also a desire for human fertility.

The first of the cave art was rediscovered only in 1868, at Altamira, Spain. Although the painting was 14,000 years old, it was not recognized as prehistoric until 1902. By now, 200 caves decorated with artworks have been discovered in Europe, most of them in the river valleys of southwest France and the adjacent Pyrenees and the Cantabrian Mountains of northern Spain. The most recent discoveries, stunning in the variety of animal life depicted and the artistry employed, have been the Cosquer Cave in 1991 and the Chauvet Cave in 1994.

The painters used natural pigments, like ocher, that produced reds, browns, and yellows, and manganese oxides that made black and violet. Blues and greens have not been found. Human figures are rare in the European caves. The usual representations are of large animals, such as bison, deer, wild oxen, and horses. Occasionally there are mammoths, lions, and even fish. Fantasy figures, such as unicorns, also appear. At caves such as Le Tuc d'Audoubert, France, sculptures of clay bison have been found. In many caves, the outlines of human hands have been stenciled onto cave walls by projecting pigment around

"Venus" figurine, found at Dolní Vestonice, Moravia, c. 23,000 B.P. Several hundred early female figures have been recovered, but no male figures. This seems to support the thesis that these statuettes were created, not so much as representations of ideal feminine beauty, but as fertility charms—notice how the breasts, buttocks, and thighs are emphasized to the exclusion of any individualizing facial traits.

the hands. No one knows how the pigments were applied, but the most common guess is that they were chewed and then either spat directly or blown through a pipe onto the walls.

Some of the cave art was abstract, some representational, some painted, some in relief. This rich artistic tradition did not continue past the Magdalenian period, about 12,000 B.C.E. Many of the techniques of the cave paintings, such as perspective and the feeling of movement, did not reappear in Western art until the Renaissance, about 1400 C.E.

Ever since the cave art was rediscovered, people have wondered about its function and meaning. The first interpretation to gain widespread acceptance argued that the paintings represented a kind of magic designed to bring good fortune to the hunters of the animals represented on the cave walls. The seemingly abstract geometrical patterns, some said, represented hunting equipment, such as traps, snares, and weapons. The mural paintings of animals may represent a hope for their fertility so that the hunters might find abundant prey. Another interpretation suggested that the caves were meeting grounds to which neighboring bands of people returned each year to arrange marriages and to cement political and social alliances. The different styles of paintings in each cave represent the artistic production of many different groups.

The art is often located not at the mouth of the cave, where it would have been on daily view of the campsites, but deep in the inner recesses. Why were so many images—about one-third of the total—painted so deep inside the caves? Some scholars of prehistoric art have suggested that they were not just decorative, but were links

Chauvet Cave, Rhône-Alpes region, France, 18,000 B.C.E. On Christmas Day 1994, a team of archaeologists led by Jean-Marie Chauvet discovered a cave 1640 feet deep in the Ardèche River Canyon. The cave's 300-plus Paleolithic wall paintings of horses, buffalo, and lions are the earliest examples anywhere in the world.

shaman In the religious beliefs of some Asian and American tribal societies, a person capable of entering into trances and believed to be endowed with supernatural powers, with the ability to cure the sick, find lost or stolen property, predict the future, and protect the community from evil spirits. A shaman may act as judge or ruler, and as a priest a shaman directs communal sacrifices and escorts the souls of the dead to the next world.

to ancient spirits, which were remembered and invoked in the dark depths of the cave through shamanistic rituals. Among the San people of the Kalahari desert, **shamans** are thought to communicate with spirits through trances induced through the use of drugs, breathing exercises, singing, dancing, and rhythmic clapping. They enter into trance states of increasing intensity in which they "see" first geometric patterns, then images from nature, and finally creatures not found in nature at all. Sometimes they see these various images as projections on the wall. Supporters of this theory believe that the Upper Paleolithic cave paintings represent such shamanistic hallucinations or visions from trance states.

The cave art and the portable art of 25,000–10,000 B.P. begin the known record of human aesthetic creation. For the first time we have examples of what humans regarded as beautiful and therefore worth creating and preserving. From this time onward, the desire to create and appreciate beauty is part of the human story. The cave creations also give us insight into their creators' search for meaning and purpose in life. Our art gives outward expression to our understanding of, and our deepest feelings about, our place in the world. In our art we express our fears and our hopes for ourselves, our loved ones, our communities, our world. Through our art we attempt to connect with larger forces in the world and to communicate with one another. By studying the form and meaning of ancient art, historians attempt to understand the external aesthetics and the inner world of the people who produced it.

Agriculture: From Hunter-gatherer to Farmer

Some hunter-gatherers began to stay for longer periods at their temporary campsites. They noted the patterns of growth of the wild grains they gathered and the migration habits of the animals they hunted. They began to experiment in planting the seeds of the largest, most nutritious cereals in the Middle East and Europe, maize in the Americas, and rootcrops in southeast Asia. In addition to pursuing animals as prey, people may have tried to restrict their movements to particular locations. Or hunters may have built their own campsites at points frequented by the animals, adjusting human movements to those of the animals. They learned to domesticate dogs, and domesticated dogs may have accompanied the first Americans on their travels across Beringia. In the Middle East, the sheep was the first species to be domesticated, perhaps 10,000 years ago.

By 15,000–10,000 B.C.E., humans had the biological and cultural capacity to farm and raise animals. But first they had to want to do so. Otherwise why give up hunting and gathering? Why settle down? Perhaps the transformation took place at sites with especially valuable and accessible natural resources, such as the fishing sites of the Jomon people of Japan, or the quarries of obsidian stone, used for making sharp cutting tools, around Çatal Hüyük in modern Turkey. A permanent source of food to eat or materials to trade might have outweighed the desire to shift with the seasons and travel with the herds.

Perhaps rising population pressures left humans no alternative. The press of neighbors may have restricted scope for travel. On limited land, hunter-gatherers found that planting their own crops and domesticating their own animals could provide them with more food than hunting and gathering. Despite the risks of weather and of plant and animal diseases that left agricultural settlements vulnerable, some groups began to settle. Ten thousand years ago, almost all humans lived by hunting and gathering. Two thousand years ago, most were farmers or herders. This transformation created not only the first agricultural villages, but cities as well. Cities grew up as the central administrative, economic, and religious centers of their regions. A new era was beginning. It is the subject of the next chapter and Part 2.

THE STORY OF PREHISTORY
WHAT DIFFERENCE DOES IT MAKE?

The materials of this chapter, which are largely based on the research of paleoanthropologists, make us more aware of different ways of knowing and their different kinds of usefulness. They lead us to be open-minded, yet skeptical, for example, of the uses of creation stories as a way of explaining the significance of human life, and to note that different myths and stories encourage different behaviors. Myths that are widely accepted within a society are not merely quaint stories, they are powerful explanatory messages that speak deeply to people's understanding of the world.

Similarly, they lead us to be open-minded, yet skeptical, of the powers of science to explain the world, noting, for example, that the process of evolution was not immediately evident until scientists began asking the right questions; the role of women in cultural evolution was not considered until feminist researchers began asking questions that had not been asked before; Africa as a location for the earliest hominids and humans was ignored until racial prejudices were put aside. Scientific enquiry is an enormously powerful tool in unlocking the mysteries of the world, but it addresses only those questions that we ask it to.

We have also learned to distinguish between "ordinary" science, which builds on what is already known and accepted, and revolutionary science, which puzzles over new information and anomalies, elements that do not fit into already existing patterns, until it may create "paradigm shifts," new ways of understanding the world.

We have seen that from the very earliest times human behavior has been characterized by migration, the creation of tools, the formation of ever-larger groups, which nevertheless apparently create distinctions between members and "others," communication through language, self-expression through art, and oscillation between accepting nature as it is and trying to control it as a means of advancing our own agendas. These are the principal legacies of the earliest hominids and humans to us, and the record of our successes in finding methods of understanding our world more clearly through historiography and through paleoanthropology.

Review Questions

- Most historians work with written documents, while paleoanthropologists work with different kinds of fossil materials. Nevertheless, many of their concerns in exploring the past are similar. Do you agree or disagree? Why?
- What are the images of humankind represented in the creation stories cited here from the *Enuma Elish*, the *Rigveda*, and the Book of Genesis? To what degree is the place of humankind in the world similar in each of the stories? To what degree is it different?
- In what sense did the work of Charles Darwin make the work of paleoanthropology possible?
- Would you like to participate in an archaeological dig in Africa seeking to discover further examples of early hominids? What elements of the work appeal to you? What elements do not?
- What is the difference between "normal science" and "revolutionary science"? What examples of revolutionary science appear in this chapter?
- To what degree is the creation of art a major step forward in cultural creativity? How do discoveries of art help us understand the lives of early *Homo sapiens sapiens*?

Suggested Readings

PRINCIPAL SOURCES

Bahn, Paul G., ed. *Archaeology* (Cambridge: Cambridge University Press, 1996).

Barber, Elizabeth Wayland. *Women's Work: The First 20,000 Years: Women, Cloth, and Society in Early Times* (New York: W.W. Norton & Co., 1994). Fascinating account of the earliest known production of cloth, and women's role in producing it.

Constable, George and the Editors of Time-Life Books. *The Neanderthals* (New York: Time-Life Books, 1973).

Darwin, Charles. *Darwin*, ed. Philip Appleman (New York: W.W. Norton & Co., 2nd ed., 1979). Excellent anthology of works by and about Darwin.

Fagan, Brian M. *People of the Earth* (Upper Saddle River, NJ: Prentice Hall: 10th ed., 2000). Outstanding textbook introduction to prehistoric human life around the globe.

Johanson, Donald, Lenora Johanson, and Blake Edgar. *Ancestors: In Search of Human Origins* (New York: Villard Books, 1994). One of the greatest paleoanthropologists tells of his work and its significance.

Leakey, Richard and Roger Lewin. *Origins Reconsidered* (New York: Doubleday, 1992). A great paleoanthropologist, continuing and expanding the accomplishments of his even more famous parents, presents his account of the fossil record of evolution.

Lewin, Roger. *The Origin of Modern Humans* (New York: Scientific American Library, 1993). Remarkably lucid presentation of the story of evolution and early humans.

Past Worlds: The (London) Times Atlas of Archaeology (London: Times Books Ltd., 1988). Text, maps, pictures are all superb on all aspects of archaeological understanding and accomplishment.

Scientific American, Special Edition, "New Look at Human Evolution," August 25, 2003.

ADDITIONAL SOURCES

Brown, Judith. "Note on the Division of Labor by Sex," *American Anthropologist* LXXII (1970), 1075–6. Argues that historically women's work has been compatible with child-care responsibilities.

Chauvet, Jean-Marie, Eliette Brunel Deschamps, and Christian Hillaire. *Dawn of Art: The Chauvet Cave, the Oldest Known Paintings in the World* (New York: Abrams, 1996). Gorgeous presentation of this recently discovered cave art.

Clottes, Jean and Jean Courtin. *The Cave Beneath the Sea: Paleolithic Images at Cosquer* (New York: Abrams, 1996). Another prehistoric artistic treasure in a magnificent presentation.

Conkey, Margaret W. *Art and Design in the Old Stone Age* (San Francisco, CA: Freeman, 1982). Analysis and presentation of early portable art.

Darwin, Charles. *The Origin of Species by Means of Natural Selection or the Preservation of Favored Races in the Struggle for Life*, reprinted from the Sixth Edition, ed. Edmund B. Wilson (New York: Macmillan Company, 1927). The classic, revolutionary work.

Darwin, Charles. *The Works of Charles Darwin*, ed. Paul H. Barrett and R.B. Freeman, Vol. XV *On the Origin of Species* 1859 (New York: New York University Press, 1988). The first edition, without mention of "the creator."

Defleur, Alban, Tim White *et al.* "Neanderthal Cannibalism at Moula-Guercy, Ardèche, France," *Science* (October 1, 1999), 286:128–131. Recent scientific finds concerning the Neanderthal diet.

Fagan, Brian M. *The Journey from Eden* (London: Thames and Hudson, 1990). A very readable, comprehensive account of biological and cultural evolution by an anthropologist with superb writing skills.

Fedigan, Linda. "The Changing Role of Women in Models of Human Evolution," *Annual Review of Anthropology* XV (1986), 22–66. Comprehensive introduction to feminist perspectives on evolution.

Gamble, Clive. *Timewalkers: The Prehistory of Global Colonization* (Cambridge, MA: Harvard University Press, 1994). Gamble ponders the migrations of humans from earliest times to all corners of the earth.

Gould, Stephen Jay. *Ever Since Darwin: Reflections in Natural History* (New York: W.W. Norton & Co., 1977). Lucid account of the Darwinian position and later amendments to it.

Gould, Stephen Jay. *The Structure of Evolutionary Theory* (Cambridge, MA: Harvard University Press, 2002). A comprehensive summary of all that we know of evolution today, by a master scholar-writer, published just months before his death.

Holm, Jean, with John Bowker, eds. *Myth and History* (London: Pinter Publishers, 1994). Analysis of the functions of myth and of history in human understanding.

Lewis-Williams, David. *The Mind in the Cave: Consciousness and the Origins of Art* (London: Thames and Hudson, 2002). Argues that in prehistoric caves "image-making," religion, and social discriminations were a "package deal," as humans realized a new capability for higher-order thought.

Linton, Sally (pseud. for Sally Slocum). "Woman the Gatherer: Male Bias in Anthropology," in Sue-Ellen Jacobs, ed. *Women in Perspective: A*

Guide for Cross-Cultural Studies (Urbana: University of Illinois Press, 1971). Asking new questions from a feminist perspective, Linton demonstrates a much-enhanced role of women in early cultural evolution.

McNeill, William H. *Mythistory and Other Essays* (Chicago, IL: University of Chicago Press, 1986). A master historian discusses the difference between myth and the professional study of history, and how the two perspectives intersect in the public mind.

Mellars, Paul and Chris Stringer, eds. *The Human Revolution: Behavioural and Biological Perspectives on the Origins of Modern Humans* (Princeton, NJ: Princeton University Press, 1989). Papers of a 1987 multidisciplinary conference at Cambridge on human origins and early behavior patterns.

Morell, Virginia. *Ancestral Passions: The Leakey Family and the Quest for Humankind's Beginnings* (New York: Simon & Schuster, 1995). The internal dynamics of the Leakey family, as down-to-earth as their excavations.

Nature. Interdisciplinary scientific journal related to biological concerns. Volume 418 (2002) contained numerous articles on the discovery of Toumai, and reprinted several classic articles on earlier archaeological discoveries, from Dart's in 1925 to the present.

The New English Bible (New York: Oxford University Press, 1976). For clarity and simple, basic annotation, my favorite edition.

Pfeiffer, John. *The Creative Explosion* (Ithaca, NY: Cornell University Press, 1982). Argues for a dramatic leap in human intellectual and artistic capacities about 35,000 years ago in Europe. Very well written. Now more controversial than ever.

Scott, Joan W. "Gender: A Useful Category of Historical Analysis," *American Historical Review* XCI (1986), 1053–76. A classic article in helping to bring feminist perspectives into mainstream historical research.

White, Tim D., Berhane Asfaw, and Gen Suwa. "Ardipithecus ramidus, A Root Species for Australopithecus," in F. Facchini ed. *The First Humans and Their Cultural Manifestations* (Forli, Italy: A.B.A.C.O., 1996), 15–23. Early reports on the archaeological find.

Wood, Bernard. "The Oldest Hominid Yet," *Nature* Vol. 371 (Sept. 22, 1994), 280–81. Another early report on *Ardipithecus ramidus*, including evaluation of its significance.

The Agricultural Village

The evolution of maize from the rather stunted cob of wild corn from the valley of Mexico about 5000 B.C.E. through to the more productive and nutritious plant of about 1 B.C.E. reveals the key reason for the creation of agricultural villages. (See Richard MacNeish, "The Origins of New World Civilization," *Scientific American*, November 1964.) Settled agriculture could greatly increase both the quantity and quality of the food supply. As human populations grew, the produce brought by hunting and gathering became insufficient to feed their numbers. People had to travel ever greater distances, and this became dangerous because it brought them into direct conflict with their neighbors—who were also hard pushed to find adequate food and were also expanding. Settled agriculture was the solution. Increased population made it necessary; the end of the most recent ice age made it possible. Careful attention to plant and animal patterns on the part of hunter-gatherers had already set the stage.

As they settled down, humans began to domesticate not only food crops but also animals, which served for food, for power and energy in carrying goods and pulling plows, and for products such as milk, wool, fur, and leather. Village dwellers produced tools that were increasingly

Model reconstruction of Ban Po.

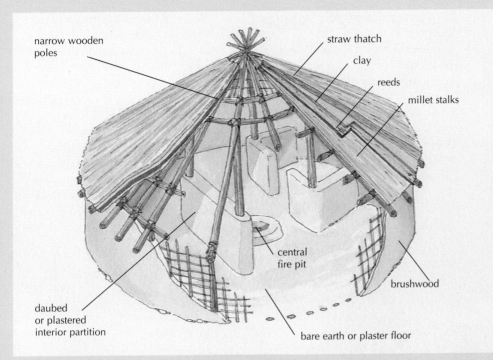

narrow wooden poles

straw thatch

clay

reeds

millet stalks

central fire pit

brushwood

daubed or plastered interior partition

bare earth or plaster floor

Typical Ban Po dwelling.

sophisticated in terms of both usefulness and aesthetic beauty. Some of these tools were made of organic materials, such as bone and fiber, but many were made of stone. Village dwellers became skilled at grinding and polishing the stone tools, and this era is called the Neolithic or New Stone Age.

Settled agriculture began in the fertile crescent—that is, Mesopotamia, the valley between the Tigris and Euphrates Rivers—and the Nile valley, both about 12,000 years ago. One of the best preserved early villages was discovered, however, in China in 1953, at Ban Po, near Xian. The residents cultivated millet and domesticated pigs and dogs. They practiced slash-and-burn agriculture, and pollen samples show distinct alternating periods of cultivation and fallow. The most ancient layers of the excavation, which date to about 6000 B.C.E., give a very clear idea of the

Jomon vase, Kanto province, Japan. Earthenware. (*Musée Guimet, Paris*)

physical form of an early agricultural village.

Immediately adjacent to the excavation, archaeologists have reconstructed a model of the entire prehistoric village. It represents Ban Po's three housing styles: square, round, and an oblong, split level, part underground and part above. Ban Po villagers stored their grain in some 200 underground pits, which were dug throughout the village. A moat surrounds the entire residential settlement.

North of the village was a pottery production center with six kilns, and next to them was a public cemetery where some 250 graves have been excavated. The bodies of children were placed in urns and buried in the main residential area. Archaeologists found seventy-six such burial urns, and no one knows why adults and children were buried separately.

In the center of the settlement was a large square building. What was its function? Presumably it had political and social significance for the entire

Obsidian blades, Çatal Hüyük, c. 3000 B.C.E.

village. Was it a ruler's palace? A priest's shrine? The official posting on the excavation identifies this central structure as "a place for the Ban Po inhabitants to discuss public affairs." This assertion about the politics of the village is consistent with the general belief of archaeologists that villages were more or less egalitarian places. This viewpoint is especially consistent with the Marxist philosophy that relatively egalitarian villages preceded more hierarchical cities, an ideology held by the communist government of China. In fact, however, we cannot be sure of the function of this central structure nor of the political structure of the village as a whole.

Although agriculture was the basis of most early villages, there were exceptions. In southern Japan, the Jomon people created villages that supported themselves by fishing and hunting deer and wild boar with bows and arrows, and by gathering and storing acorns, nuts, and seeds. Some of the Jomon lived in caves, but others built villages with individual pit-houses and central, communal buildings. They may have also cultivated rootcrops and cereals, but they were not primarily agricultural. They created stone tools but are most famous for their distinctive pottery, some of the world's earliest and most beautiful pottery which dates to as early as 10,500 B.C.E. It was made by forming clay into cords and wrapping the cords by hand into pots. At first the cords were simply allowed to dry without firing in kilns. For sedentary peoples, pottery is a useful means of storage. Often, however, as with the Jomon people, it is also valued as an artistic medium of self-expression.

Jomon culture spread throughout Japan, from the southern island of Kyushu, reaching Hokkaido by 6500 B.C.E. The Jomon people began to build wooden houses with elaborate hearths and to practice settled agriculture. In all, 30,000 Jomon sites

are known, dating from about 10,500 B.C.E. to about 300 B.C.E., most of them on the central island of Honshu.

Another non-agricultural development in villages occurred in eastern Anatolia (modern Turkey), around the shores of Lake Van. The presence of volcanic obsidian stone gave villagers a substance they could craft into blades of extraordinary sharpness, and they used these blades themselves and also traded them to villages hundreds of miles away on the eastern shores of the Mediterranean and the Persian Gulf. For most of these Anatolian villages,

the trade in obsidian was complementary to agriculture. But one site, Çatal Hüyük, grew into a 32-acre town, based on the manufacture and trade of obsidian tools. The manufacture and trade in obsidian tools enriched Çatal Hüyük and improved the productivity of villagers who traded their agricultural produce for the valued tools. In the context of the villages surrounding it, Çatal Hüyük stands out as a village that became a new kind of settlement, combining agriculture with industry and trade. It was a transitional form in the development of early cities.

Farming in China. Evidence of the earliest established agriculture in east Asia is found in the arid but fertile regions of north central China, along the central reaches of the Huang He (Yellow River). Villages such as Ban Po grew up on the floodplain, rich in alluvial and loess deposits, where drought-resistant plants such as millet could be cultivated.

QUESTIONS

1. Why was the development of agriculture essential to the growth of the city?
2. What is the difference between a village and a city?
3. In what ways did settling down and abandoning nomadism change people's lives?

PART 2

Settling Down

10,000 B.C.E. –1000 C.E.

THE FIRST CITIES AND WHY THEY MATTER: DIGS, TEXTS, AND INTERPRETATIONS

T he establishment of urban settlements introduced a new era in many parts of the world. The physical construction of the new cities, with their impressive buildings and crowds of inhabitants, most clearly marks the transformation, but many equally significant, though less tangible, developments also contributed to a revolution in human settlement patterns. Cities were nodes in the regional networks of exchange of goods and culture, and they encouraged the production of sophisticated arts, the specialization of labor, and the elaboration of a social hierarchy. Most significantly, cities signaled the emergence of a state organization for guiding and administering the city and its surrounding area. The new state, hand-in-glove with the new city, provided leadership, organization, and official control of armed power. It governed the people of the city, sometimes with their consent, often without it. The state enforced and helped to create the conditions of inequality that emerged among the people of the new cities. In all these characteristics, the ancient city reminds us of our own.

Northeastern façade of Ziggurat, Ur, present-day Iraq, c. 2100 B.C.E.
Sacred buildings and temples dominated the center of Ur and this three-story-high ziggurat was the most famous of them. Each major Mesopotamian city had a ziggurat dedicated to its deity. Ur's was dedicated to Nanna, the moon God (see p. 51).

Unlike modern cities, however, almost all early cities were relatively small. The largest contained perhaps 100,000 people in 8 square miles; most had only a few thousand inhabitants. Until the industrial revolution in the late nineteenth century, a few thousand people concentrated in 100 acres might have constituted a city, for cities held only a tiny percentage of the total population of any region.

Most of the world's population were farmers or hunter-gatherers when the first cities developed. The multiplication of cities and urban residents that we see today took place only after the industrial revolution created new urban factories, transportation hubs, and mass labor forces. Moreover, many of the early cities, although small, were centers of independent city-states; most cities today are single points in much larger national and even international networks. Finally, the earliest cities emerged in each of seven regions around the world. Mostly, they took root along great river banks in Africa and Asia, reflecting the importance of water, irrigation, and agriculture to their development. The world's earliest cities emerged between the Tigris and Euphrates Rivers in what is now modern Iraq. They developed along the Nile River in Egypt and in the Indus valley of modern Pakistan. In China the earliest cities flourished in the flood plain of the Yellow River. Finally, early cities appeared in West Africa near the great bed of the Niger River. The Americas provide some exceptions with the growth of great civilizations in the valleys and jungles of Mexico and on the heights of the Andes mountains.

Many of these early cities were dedicated to gods and were built on the foundations of existing shrine centers. As the cities grew, the shrines grew with them, providing a more profound meaning to the lives of their inhabitants by linking their mundane existence to transcendent and powerful supernatural forces.

FROM VILLAGE COMMUNITY TO CITY-STATE

FOOD FIRST: THE AGRICULTURAL VILLAGE
10,000 B.C.E.–750 B.C.E.

KEY TOPICS
- The Agricultural Village
- The First Cities
- Sumer: The Birth of the City
- The Growth of the City-State

Until about 12,000 years ago humans hunted and gathered their food, following the migrations of animals and the seasonal cycles of the crops. They established temporary base camps for their activities, and caves served them for homes and meeting-places, but they had not established permanent settlements. They had begun to domesticate some animals, especially the dog and the sheep, but they had not yet begun the systematic practice of agriculture. Then, about 10,000 B.C.E., people began to settle down, constructing the first agricultural villages.

Why did they do it? Is food production through agriculture easier than hunting and gathering? Surprisingly, the answer seems to be "no." Research suggests that, with the technology available at that time, adult farmers had to work an equivalent of 1000–1300 hours a year for their food, while hunter-gatherers needed only 800–1000 hours. Moreover, agricultural work was more difficult.

Why did they change? An appealing, although unproved, answer is that increasing population pressure, perhaps accompanied by worsening climatic conditions, forced people to take on the more productive methods of agriculture. Scientists estimate that even in a lush tropical environment, 0.4 square miles of land could support only nine persons through hunting and gathering; under organized, sedentary agricultural techniques, the same area could support 200–400 people. In the less fertile, sub-tropical and temperate climates into which the expanding populations were moving at the end of the last ice age, after about 13,000 B.C.E., hunting and gathering were even less productive. To survive, sedentary agriculture became a necessity.

The memory of this transition survives in myth. For example, the myth of Shen Nung, whom the ancient Chinese honored as the inventor of agriculture and its wooden tools (and of poetry), captures the transformation:

> The people of old ate the meat of animals and birds. But in the time of Shen Nung, there were so many people that there were no longer enough animals and birds to supply their needs. So it was that Shen Nung taught the people how to cultivate the earth. (Bairoch, p. 6)

In addition to increasing agricultural productivity, villages facilitated an increase in creativity of all kinds. It may have taken longer to raise food than to hunt and gather it, but the sedentary farmers did not stop work when they had secured their food supply. In their villages they went on to produce textiles, pottery, metallurgy, architecture, tools, and objects of great beauty, especially in sculpture and painting. Did the

Opposite **Sumerian ruins, Uruk, present-day Iraq, c. 2100 B.C.E.** A man and child stand amid what is left of the ancient city of Uruk.

AT A GLANCE: VILLAGE COMMUNITIES AND CITY-STATES

DATE	POLITICAL	RELIGION AND CULTURE	SOCIAL DEVELOPMENT
4500 B.C.E.	■ Ubaid people in Mesopotamia		
3500 B.C.E.	■ Sumerians (3300–2350) ■ Ziggurats built	■ Cuneiform writing ■ Sumerian pantheon	■ Urbanization in Mesopotamia
3000 B.C.E.	■ Hereditary kings emerge		■ Invention of the wheel ■ Bronze casting ■ Sumerian city-states (2800–1850)
2500 B.C.E.	■ Ur, First Dynasty (2500–2350) ■ Akkadian kingdoms (2350–2150); Sargon of Akkad (2334–2279) ■ 3rd Dynasty of Ur (c. 2112–2004)	■ Akkadian language used in Sumer ■ Epic of Gilgamesh (c. 2113–1991)	■ Sumerian Laws
2000 B.C.E.	■ Semitic rulers gain control of Mesopotamia ■ 1st dynasty of Babylon (c. 1894–1595) ■ Hammurabi (1792–1750) ■ Hittites in Asia Minor		■ Mycenaean traders in Aegean 1800–1000 B.C.E. ■ Hammurabi's Code of Law
1500 B.C.E.	■ Hittite Empire (c. 1460–1200)	■ "Golden age" of Ugarit	
1000 B.C.E.	■ Assyrian Empire (900–612)	■ Hebrew Scriptures recorded	
750 B.C.E.	■ Sargon II (d. 705) ■ Sennacherib (c. 705–681) ■ Ashurbanipal (d. 627) ■ Fall of Nineveh (imperial capital) (612) ■ Nebuchadnezzar (605–562)	■ Gilgamesh (complete version) ■ Homer (fl. 8th century) ■ Hesiod (fl. 700)	
600 B.C.E.	■ Neo–Babylonian Empire	■ Library at Nineveh	
500 B.C.E.	■ Persian Empire in control of Mesopotamia		

agriculturists work comparatively harder than the hunter-gatherers simply to survive under greater population pressure, or because they craved the added rewards of their extra labor, or both? We can never know for sure, but the agricultural village opened new possibilities for economic, social, political, and artistic creativity—while closing others. It changed forever humanity's concepts of life's necessities and potentials.

THE AGRICULTURAL VILLAGE

The first agricultural villages that archaeologists have discovered date to about 10,000 B.C.E. They are located in the "fertile crescent," which curves from the Persian Gulf and the Zagros Mountains in the east and south, on the border of today's Iraq and Iran, northwest into Anatolia, present-day Turkey, and then turns south and west through present-day Syria, Lebanon, and Israel on the Mediterranean Sea. In this region, wild grasses—the ancestors of modern wheat and barley—provided the basic grains, first for gathering, and later for cultivation. By 8000 B.C.E. the Natufians, named for their valley in northern Israel, and the peoples immediately to the south, in the Jordan River valley near Jericho, were growing fully domesticated cereals. Peas and lentils and other pulses and legumes followed. The peoples of the fertile crescent hunted gazelles and goats. Later, they domesticated the goat and the sheep. In Turkey they added pigs; around the Mediterranean, there were cattle.

In other parts of the world, agriculture and animal domestication focused on other varieties. In the western hemisphere, these included maize, especially in Mesoamerica, and rootcrops such as manioc and sweet potatoes in South America. Amerindians domesticated the llama, the guinea pig, and the turkey. Domesticated dogs probably accompanied their migrant masters across the Bering Straits about 15,000 years ago. Perhaps the process of domestication was then repeated with the dogs found in the Americas.

In southeast Asia and in tropical Africa, wild roots and tubers, including yams, were the staple crops. In the Vindhya Mountain areas of central India, rice was among the first crops to be cultivated, about 5000 B.C.E. Anthropologists are uncertain when rice was first cultivated, rather than just being harvested from the wild, in southeast and east Asia, but a date similar to India's seems likely. From earliest times, as today, China's agriculture seems to have favored rice in the south and millet in the north. Some crops, including cotton and gourds, were brought under cultivation in many locations around the globe.

Our knowledge of early agriculture continues to grow as the archaeological record is expanded and revised. European sedentary agriculture, for example, that was once thought to have been borrowed from the Near East, may have been a local response to changing climate conditions.

The era in which villages took form is usually called **Neolithic**, or New Stone Age, named for its tools rather than its crops. Farming called for a different toolkit from hunting and gathering. For cutting, grinding, chopping, scraping, piercing, and digging, village artisans fashioned new tools from stone. Archaeological digs from Neolithic villages abound with blades, knives, sickles, adzes, arrows, daggers, spears, fish hooks and harpoons, mortars and pestles, and rudimentary plows and hoes.

As villages expanded their economic base these stone tools often became valued as items of trade. Obsidian—a kind of volcanic glass with very sharp edges—was traded from Anatolia and is found in hundreds of digs from central Turkey to Syria and the Jordan valley. Among other items of trade, recognized by their appearance in digs a long distance away from their point of origin, are seashells, jade, turquoise, and ceramics.

Although ceramics occasionally appear among nomadic populations, the weight and fragility of clay make pottery essentially a creation of the more established Neolithic village. As a vessel for storage, pottery further reflected the sedentary character of the new village life. The fine designs and colors decorating its pottery became the most distinctive identifying mark of the Neolithic village, and archaeologists often designate eras, locations, and groups of people by descriptions of their pottery—the "grayware," the "red glazed," or the "cord-marked," for example.

Simple pottery is easy to make and accessible to anyone, but specialized craftspeople developed ceramics into a medium of artistic creativity. Fine ceramic jewelry, statuary, and figurines attained great beauty and were frequently used in religious rituals.

Historical change, however, does not proceed in a uniform, straight line. Historians must be alert not only to general patterns, but also to exceptions. Some villages did form on an economic base of hunting-and-gathering. In southern Japan, for example, a non-agricultural village society appeared among the Jomon people along with some of the earliest and most beautiful of

Neolithic "New Stone Age"—the last division of the Stone Age, immediately preceding the development of metallurgy and corresponding to the ninth–fifth millennia B.C.E. It was characterized by the increasing domestication of animals and cultivation of crops, established agricultural communities, and the appearance of such crafts as pottery and weaving.

The Fertile Crescent. The Tigris and Euphrates rivers gave life to the first known agricultural villages, about 10,000 years ago, and the first known cities in human history, about 5000 years ago. Fertile land extended to the Mediterranean and some contact apparently continued on to the Nile Valley. Its borders were defined to the south by arid regions receiving less than 10 inches of rainfall per year, and to the north by mountains and semi-arid plateaux.

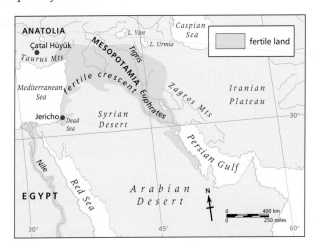

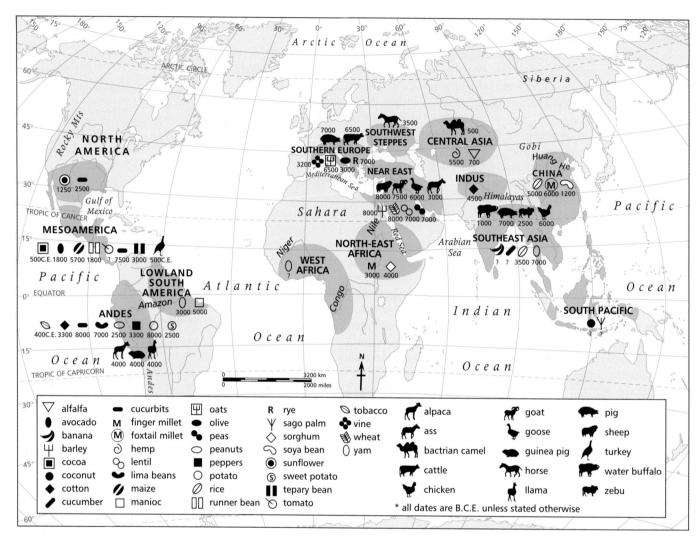

The origins of agriculture and domestic animals. The development of agriculture and the domestication of animals took place independently in different parts of the world, but the Near East, Mesoamerica, southeast Asia, and China were among the first and most significant regions.

pottery. Jomon pottery, which is marked by distinctive cord lines, dates back to 10,500 B.C.E. and spread from the southern island of Kyushu, northward through Honshu, reaching Hokkaido by 6500 B.C.E. The Jomon villagers supported themselves from fishing, hunting deer and wild boar, and gathering and storing nuts. They created stone tools and lived in caves and in pit-houses in settled villages with central, communal buildings. Yet the Japanese did not develop agricultural cultivation for another several thousand years.

THE FIRST CITIES

The first cities were constructed on the economic base of sedentary village agricultural communities. In excavating these earliest cities around the globe, archaeologists ask which city forms were invented indigenously, by their own inhabitants, and which were borrowed from earlier examples or, perhaps, imposed from outside on local rural populations. Technically, the question is one of **innovation** versus **diffusion**. Thus far, most experts agree that innovative primary urbanization, not borrowed or imposed from outside, took place in seven places: five river valleys in the eastern hemisphere—Mesopotamia, the Nile, the Indus, the Huang He, and the Niger—and, in the western

innovation The explanation that similar cultural traits, techniques, or objects found among different groups of people were invented independently rather than spread from one group to another.

diffusion The spread of ideas, objects, or traits from one culture to another.

hemisphere, in Mexico and in the Andes Mountains. The birth of primary urbanization took place in these seven locations at very different times, with Mesopotamia the oldest at about 3300 B.C.E. and the Niger the most recent at about 400 C.E.

Cities transform human life. The physical form of the early cities tells the story vividly. Even today we can trace on the surface of the earth the 5500-year-old designs of the first cities and the irrigation systems that supported them. Remnants of walls and fragments of monuments of these first cities still rise from their sites. From under the surface archaeologists salvage artifacts: bricks; pottery; tools of wood, bone, stone, and metal; jewelry; and skeletons of citizens and slaves. The technology of the early cities included new means of transportation; we find the remains of wheeled vehicles and of sailboats. The earliest city dwellers advanced their skills in metallurgy, and products of their craftsmanship in copper, tin, and their alloys abound in the archaeological excavations. In recognition of these technological breakthroughs we often call the era of the first cities the Bronze Age.

But cities are more than bricks and mortar, metal and artifacts. They require institutions for their larger scale of organization and administration. As society and economy became more complex, new class hierarchies emerged. Professional administrators, skilled artisans, long-distance traders, local merchants, and priests and kings enriched the diversity and sophistication of the growing cities. External relations with other cities required skilled negotiations, and a diplomatic corps emerged. Armies mobilized for defense and attack. In short, with the growth of the city the early state was also born, with its specialized organization, centralized rule, and powerful armies.

THE EARLIEST URBAN SETTLEMENTS

3500 B.C.E.	Rise of Sumer, southern Mesopotamia.
3100	Emergence of Egyptian state; new capital at Memphis.
2500	Development of Mohenjo-Daro, urban civilization on the Indus plain.
2500	City-states in northern Mesopotamia and the Levant, dominated by palace complexes.
1800	Urban growth after Shang dynasty established in northeast China.
1200	Formative period in Mesoamerica, marked by first shrine centers, especially the Olmec.
c. 400 B.C.E.	City-states in Mesoamerica and South America.
400 C.E.	Urbanization of Jenne-jeno, Nigeria, sub-Saharan Africa.

The spread of civilizations. The first civilizations developed where unique local climatic and soil conditions, favorable to settled agriculture, occurred, mostly in major river basins. With the development of an agricultural surplus came the growth of urban centers, trade, and population. Related civilizations tended to develop in regions adjacent to these heartlands, or along trade routes between them.

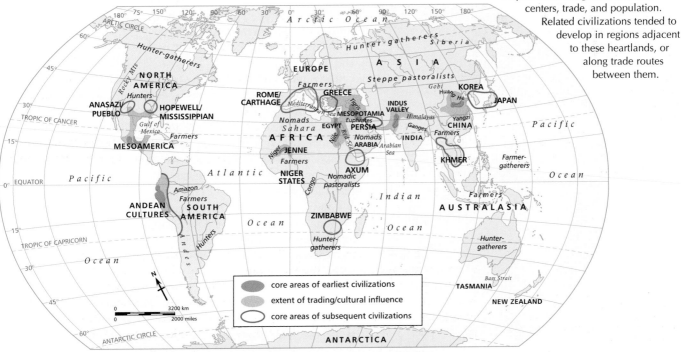

For an interactive version of this map, go to: http://www.prenhall.com/spodek/map2.3

To keep track of business transactions and administrative orders, the proclamations of rulers and the rituals of priests, the legends of gods and the histories of the city, new methods of record keeping were developed. At first these were tokens, pictures, seals, personalized markings, and, in the Andes, *quipu*, knots made in special lengths of string. By about 3300 B.C.E., in Sumer, which is geographically equivalent to today's southern Iraq, the world's first system of writing had evolved. This was one of the most revolutionary inventions in human history. The prestigious occupation of scribe was born, and schoolteachers soon followed.

From earliest times, city dwellers and analysts understood and commented on the significance of the first urban revolution. Today, we have more reason than ever to value and to evaluate its 5000-year-old heritage, for in modern times we are living through two new urban revolutions. By 1800 the industrial revolution opened a new era of urban development that re-invented the cities of western Europe and North America (see Chapter 17). In the twentieth century peasants streamed by the millions and tens of millions from rural villages to mammoth cities, creating massive, unprecedented urban environments around the globe (see Part 5). So we search humanity's earliest experiences with cities not only to understand our ancestors but also to understand ourselves.

SUMER: THE BIRTH OF THE CITY

A people called the Sumerians pioneered the world's first urban revolution in Mesopotamia, literally "between the rivers"—that is, the region between the Tigris and Euphrates Rivers, approximately modern Iraq. They migrated into southern Mesopotamia about 4000 B.C.E., perhaps from around the Caspian Sea, but no one knows for sure. They faced uncertain odds. While the area between the Tigris and Euphrates Rivers became known as the fertile crescent for its high agricultural productivity, high temperatures and unpredictable floods constantly challenged the Sumerians. To succeed in building cities in the region, peoples had to construct irrigation ditches and intricate canals.

The Sumerians were not the first to inhabit this land. Archaeological excavations of pottery show the earlier presence in Mesopotamia of the Ubaids, a Semitic-speaking people, beginning about 4500 B.C.E. The Ubaidians drained marshes and developed an early irrigation system. Although the language the Sumerians spoke was not Semitic, their use of Semitic word forms and names also suggests that Semitic-speaking people may have preceded them in the area.

Gradually, the Sumerians began to dominate the region, supplanting the Semitic-speaking populations. They dug better canals for irrigation, improved roads, and expanded urban developments. For a millennium, from 3300 B.C.E. until 2350 B.C.E., the Sumerians lived in warring city-states—Kish, Uruk, Ur, Nippur, Lagash, Umma, and dozens of smaller ones. Each of these city-states included a central city with a temple and the agricultural region surrounding it. The city controlled and protected the fields of grain, orchards, and land for livestock, which, in turn, provided enough food to support the cities' growing populations.

Stone tower and wall, Jericho, c. 8000 B.C.E. Before Sumer, a Neolithic community based at Jericho in the Jordan valley, Palestine, was the first to develop cereals of a fully domesticated type. In 8000 B.C.E these farmers, keen to secure their settlement in the arid environment, constructed a stone perimeter wall 10 feet thick that was strengthened at one point by a circular stone tower over 30 feet high. This wall is one of the earliest such defenses known.

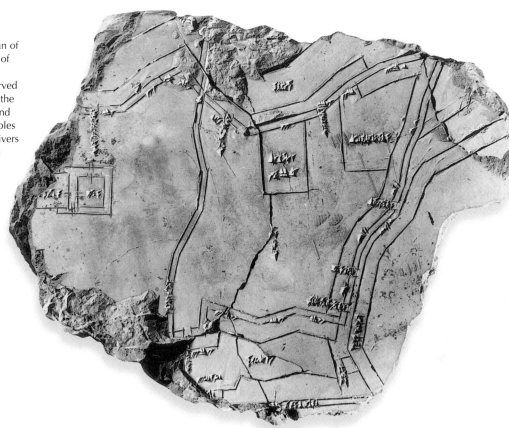

Map of Nippur, 1500 B.C.E. This plan of Nippur, the ancient cultural center of Sumer, is the oldest known city map. Inscribed in a well-preserved clay tablet, 8¼ by 7 inches in size, the map is drawn accurately to scale and shows several of the city's key temples and buildings, its central park, its rivers and canals, and especially its walls and gates. The script is mostly Sumerian with a few words of Akkadian, the language of the Semitic people who eventually conquered the Sumerians. (*Hilprecht Collection, Friederich-Schiller University, Jena*)

With the city-states constantly at war with each other, their leaders began to think in terms of conquering others to create large empires. In *c.* 2350 B.C.E., Sargon, king of the city of Akkad, conquered the Sumerian cities one by one, allowing the Semitic-speaking Akkadians to overshadow the Sumerians. Calling himself the "king of Sumer and Akkad," Sargon was the first to unite the city-states under a single, powerful ruler. After some 200 years under Akkadian rule, the Mesopotamian city-states regained their independence under the third dynasty of Ur (2112–2004 B.C.E.), but they resumed their inter-urban warfare, which weakened them. Eventually, Hammurabi (1792–1750 B.C.E.), king of "Old Babylonia," launched a series of aggressive military campaigns. He extended his control over much of Mesopotamia, including Sumer and Akkad, and Sumerian influence waned. The cities they had built died out, having fought each other to exhaustion. A series of foreign powers—Hittites, Assyrians, Babylonians again, Achaeminid Persians, and Greeks under Alexander the Great—variously conquered and controlled Mesopotamia. The Sumerian cultural legacy lived on, however, assimilated into their conquerors' literature, philosophy, religion, law, and patterns of urbanization.

THE GROWTH OF THE CITY-STATE

What were the characteristics of the urban revolution in Mesopotamia? How did its cities differ from the earlier villages? The most obvious feature was that the scale of the city-state—its physical size, population, and territorial control—was much greater than that of the village.

The Neolithic village housed a few dozen or a few hundred residents on a few acres. The largest Neolithic site in the Near East, Çatal Hüyük in Anatolia, grew by 5500 B.C.E.

Standard of Ur, from Iraq. Sumerian, Early Dynastic II. *c.* **2800–2400 B.C.E.** In Sumer the city-state was created as strong kings came to rule over walled cities and the surrounding countryside. This banqueting scene, found in a tomb in the royal cemetery at Ur, shows the court drinking to the health of the king. The boxlike "standard" is thought to have rested on top of a long pole during festive processions. (*British Museum, London*)

to occupy slightly more than 30 acres. It became a town. By comparison, the first cities of Mesopotamia were ten times larger, accommodating about 5000 people.

Over time, the larger cities reached populations of 35,000–40,000 and covered more than 1000 acres or 1½ square miles. The major cities were walled. The ramparts of Uruk (modern Warka, biblical Erech), the city of the king-god-hero Gilgamesh, stretched to a circumference of 6 miles, engirdling a population of 50,000 by 2700 B.C.E. By 2500 B.C.E. the region of Sumer held 500,000 people, four-fifths of them in its cities and villages! Urbanism in Sumer became a way of life.

To support these growing urban populations, the range of control of the Sumerian cities over the surrounding countryside, and its agricultural and raw material resources, continued to expand. For example, the total sway of Lagash, one of the major cities, probably extended over 1200 square miles. The king, priests, and private citizens controlled the fields of this area.

Networks of irrigation canals supported agriculture in this arid region and expanded Sumerian control over the land and its productivity. Irrigation permitted settlement to extend southward to central Mesopotamia, where cities would later emerge about 3300 B.C.E. The construction and maintenance of the canals required larger gangs of workers than the work teams that were based on family and clan alone. Loyalties that had been limited to blood relatives now extended beyond kinship to civic identity. In organizing these public works projects, a sense of citizenship, based on a shared space rather than on blood kinship, was born. It was enshrined in legal principles that made geographical residence the basis of citizenship. These new loyalties and laws marked the beginning of city life.

Organizing the canal systems required more powerful leaders than villages had known. At first, this leadership appears to have been exercised by councils of aristocratic elders, who worked closely with religious leaders. In times of crisis, especially during warfare with other cities, the council appointed a temporary single leader, but after about 2800 B.C.E., these men began to assume the position of hereditary kings and to rule in conjunction with temple priests. Political power and organization were both centralized and sanctified. Thus was the state born and consolidated.

Religion: The Priesthood and the City

Considerable power rested with the priests of the many deities of Sumer, because residents believed that their survival in the harsh environment of ancient Mesopotamia depended partly on the will of the gods. In contrast to modern patterns, in which the countryside is often considered more religious than the secular city, the authority of the ancient temple community gave the religious establishment enormous prestige and power in the city, and urban ritual practice was more fully elaborated than was its rural counterpart.

To consolidate their temporal and supernatural influences, the city priests built great temples, called **ziggurats**. Found throughout the region, ziggurats were a form of stepped temple built on a square or rectangular platform of small, locally produced, sun-baked bricks. The baked bricks were covered by glazed bricks, which may have had religious significance. A small sanctuary rested atop the structure, which could reach as many as ten stories high. The ziggurat lacked any internal chambers, and worshipers probably reached the sanctuary via external ramps. The walls themselves were more than 7 feet thick to support the weight of the massive edifice. (Ziggurats are probably the model for the Bible's Tower of Babel, which was depicted as a challenge to the power of the God Jehovah.) The ziggurats dominated the fields that the priests controlled and farmed, rented out, or turned over to their servants and favorites. As their power increased, the priests built the ziggurats taller and more massive. From within these vast temple complexes, they controlled huge retinues, including artisans and administrators, and retained gangs of field workers to farm the temple's estates. Temples employed and fed multitudes. The chief temple in the city of Lagash in Mesopotamia, for example, provided daily food and drink (ale) to some 1200 people by about 3000 B.C.E. The leading temples became virtual cities within cities.

Rituals, especially those of the priests and kings, suggest further the significance of religious thought in the minds of Sumerians. On New Year's day the king of Ur in Sumer proceeded to the top of the city's major ziggurat, where he was symbolically married to the goddess of fertility, Inanna. The entire population witnessed this affirmation of his divinity.

Royal burials also asserted the divinity and authority of the king. Royal tombs were elegant. Their arches, vaults, and domes suggesting new levels of architectural skill, were built of brick and stone, and many of the funeral objects interred with the dead were of gold and silver. As in the other ancient civilizations we shall encounter in later chapters, some of the royal dead were accompanied by attendants who might have been sacrificed for the purpose and were buried nearby. They, too, were adorned with jewelry of gold and silver. The British archaeologist Sir Leonard Woolley described the death pit adjacent to the royal burial place in Ur, which he excavated in the 1920s:

> Six men servants carrying knives or axes lay near the entrance lined up against the wall; in front of them stood a great copper basin, and by it were the bodies of four women harpists, one with her hands still on the strings of her instrument. Over the rest of the pit's area there lay in ordered rows the bodies of sixty-four ladies of the court. All of them wore some sort of ceremonial dress … Clearly these people were not wretched slaves killed as oxen might be killed, but persons held in honor, wearing their robes of office, and coming, one hopes, voluntarily to a rite which would in their belief be but a passing from one world to another, from the service of a god on earth to that of the same god in another place. (pp. 70–2)

ziggurat A temple tower of ancient Mesopotamia, constructed of square or rectangular terraces of diminishing size, usually with a shrine on top built of blue enamel bricks, the color of the sky.

In contrast to these elaborate royal burials, most common people were buried in small brick vaults in basement chambers of their own houses, and some were interred in cemeteries outside the city walls.

Occupational Specialization and Class Structure

The priests and the political-military rulers were only the most powerful of the new classes of specialists that emerged in the complex, large cities. Managers, surveyors, artisans, astronomers, brewers, warriors, traders, and scribes—all in addition to the farmers working their own fields and those of the temples and landowners—gave the cities a far more sophisticated hierarchical class structure than villages possessed.

Arts and Invention. Creativity flourished. Artisans crafted works of art in terra cotta, copper, clay, and colors surpassing village standards in their beauty and technical skill. Cylinder seals (small cylinders of stone engraved with designs for stamping clay tablets and sealing jars) became a common form of practical art in Sumer and spread as far as Anatolia and Greece. Astronomers established an accurate calendar based on lunar months that enabled them to predict the onset of seasons and to prepare properly for each year's planting and harvesting. Musicians created, designed, and played the lyre and composed and chanted songs, often dedicated to gods. Designers and architects, supervising armies of workers, built the canals of the countryside and the monuments of the cities.

Sumerians apparently invented the first wheels, the potter's wheel for ceramics and wagon wheels for transportation. They dramatically improved the plow, learning how to harness it to oxen. Metallurgists, smelting their new alloy of copper and tin, ushered in the Bronze Age. From the new metal they fashioned tips for the plow and an array of new tools: hoes, axes, chisels, knives, and saws. They turned their attention to

Mesopotamian trade. The Sumerian trading network, revealed by the wide range of valuable and exotic materials used by Mesopotamian craftsmen, was both extensive and sophisticated, drawing on resources often well over 2000 miles distant. Egyptian tomb paintings show Semitic merchants with donkey caravans, while some of the earliest writing is found on Sumerian clay tablets recording commercial transactions.

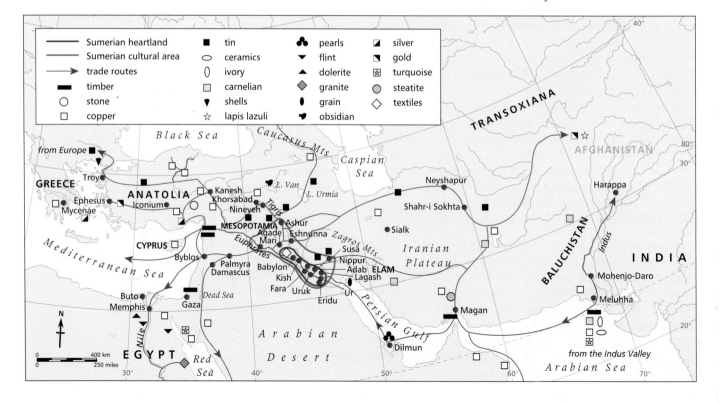

Engraved cylinder seal (left) and impression (right). Seals were first used as signatures before the invention of writing. The cylinders produce continuous patterns that are repetitive, but the figures themselves are remarkably naturalistic.

Lady Pu-abi's headdress (below). The splendor of this gold ornament, discovered in the 1920s in the royal burial place of Ur, reflects the wealth of this Mesopotamian urban society, the skill of its craftsmen, the hierarchy of its people, and the anticipation of some form of future life. (*University of Pennsylvania Museum*)

weapons and produced lance points and arrowheads, swords, daggers, and harpoons. They made bronze vessels and containers, as well as smaller items such as nails, pins, rings, and mirrors.

Trade and Markets: Wheeled Cart and Sailboat. Trade was central to urban life. Sumerian traders carried merchandise by land, river, and sea, in the world's first wheeled carts and sailboats, as well as by donkey caravan. Rich in agricultural commodities and artisan production but poor in raw materials, Sumerians traded with the inhabitants of hilly areas to the north for wood, stone, and metal. They sailed into the Persian Gulf to find copper and tin and then continued along the Arabian Sea coast as far east as the Indus valley for ivory and ceramics. They traveled east overland through the passes of the Zagros Mountains to bring back carnelian beads from Elam. Shells from the Mediterranean coast that have been found in Sumer indicate trade westward, probably overland, as well.

In the city marketplace, merchants sold locally produced foodstuffs, including vegetables, onions, lentils and beans, more than fifty varieties of fish taken from the Tigris and Euphrates Rivers, milk, cheese, butter, yogurt, dates, meat—mostly mutton—and ale. In vats in their homes, women, especially, brewed up to 40 percent of the barley and wheat harvest into ale for home use and for sale. For taste, effect, and storage purposes the Sumerians preferred ale to grain. (Hops had not yet been introduced to enable the processing of ale into beer.)

Thus, from king and priest through professionals, artisans, craftsmen, farmers, and laborers, specialization and division of labor and a hierarchical class structure marked the city's social and economic life as far more complex than that of the smaller, simpler village.

Monumental Architecture and Adornment

For the Sumerians, the size and elegance of their cities and monuments were a source of great pride. The earliest introduction to Gilgamesh, hero of the greatest surviving Sumerian epic, proclaims his excellence as city builder: "In Uruk he built walls, a great rampart, and the temple of blessed Eanna for the god of the firmament Anu, and for Ishtar the goddess of love. Look at it still today: the outer wall where the cornice runs, it shines with the brilliance of copper; and the inner wall, it has no equal."

Artwork adorned the city, especially the temple precincts. Sculptures, murals, mosaics, and especially stone **bas reliefs** (see p. 56) provided not only beauty and elegance, but represented pictorially key scenes in the history of the cities and their rulers. The magnificence of this monumental architecture and art defined the city's image, impressing residents and giving warning to enemies.

Writing

The Sumerians invented writing, thereby altering human history. Indeed historians so value writing as a means of communication and of recording events that they often call all the events prior to the invention of writing prehistory. For these historians, only when events are recorded in writing can they be called history since without writing we cannot know directly what people thought and said.

He-Goat and Flowering Tree. Offering stand for fertility god. Sumerian, from Ur, c. 2500 B.C.E. This offering stand was created with a magical as well as a functional purpose in mind, being intended to work as a fertility charm too. The goat, an ancient symbol of male sexuality, is shown rearing up against a flowering tree, emblem of nature's fecundity. (*British Museum, London*)

Pictographic c. 3000 B.C.E.										
Early cuneiform representation c. 2400 B.C.E.										
Late Assyrian c. 650 B.C.E.										
Sumerian phonetic equivalent and meaning	k eat	mŭsen bird	sag head	gu⁴ ox	še barley	ud day	sŭ hand	ku⁶ fish	a water	b cow

The earliest Sumerian scribes first used writing, beginning about 3300 B.C.E., for business purposes, to note the contents of commercial packages, the names of their owners, and to catalog this information into lists. They employed styluses made of bone or of hollow reed stems to incise **pictograms** (see p. 56), picture representations of the objects of their writing, onto clay tablets. By 3000 B.C.E. they were representing the key features of the pictures in wedge-shaped signs that we call **cuneiform** (see p. 56). Some cuneiform signs represented whole words, but others represented individual phonetic sounds based on words.

As the cuneiform became more sophisticated, so too did the subject matter, and by c. 2400 B.C.E. Sumerian writing began to transmit stories, proclaim political and military victories, sing the poetry of lovers, praise the glories of gods, and lament the fall of cities. Written literature took form and flourished. Archaeologists have excavated tens of thousands of Sumerian clay tablets, containing literature as well as business notations, and transferred them to research institutions around the world.

Many later peoples in the region—Elamites, Babylonians, Assyrians, and Akkadians—adopted cuneiform to write their own languages. The conquests of Alexander the Great in the fourth century B.C.E., however, helped to introduce alphabetic writing—of the Aramaic language—and cuneiform died out. The last known cuneiform text was written in 75 C.E.

Although some of the earliest town dwellers in other parts of the world—the settlers of the Niger valley of West Africa, the Olmec and Teotihuacanos of Mesoamerica, and the Chavin and Inca of the Andes Mountains of South America—achieved urban form and size without the use of any form of writing, most of the earliest cities did invent some system of recording. As in Sumer, these systems moved "from token to tablet"—that is, from a simple recording of business transactions and registration of ownership through designated tokens, often marked with individual notations, through picture writing, to **ideograms** (see p. 56), and finally to phonetic, alphabetical writing.

As we shall see in Chapters 3 to 5, not all civilizations followed this sequence. In China, for example, the first writing seems to have been symbols inscribed on oracle bones. They seem to have been an attempt to divine the future. Chinese as a written language has only recently been transliterated into a phonetic alphabet; its basic script is still ideographic. The Chavin and Inca developed a form of

Writing was invented in west Asia in the fourth millennium B.C.E. and developed from the need to keep a record of business transactions. From the wedge-shaped marks formed by a hollow-shaped reed, or stylus, cuneiform script evolved gradually. In this pictographic script, stylized drawings are used to represent words; each pictograph stands for a syllable, and abstract concepts are conveyed by using concrete notions that are close in meaning (e.g. "open mouth" for "eat").

Clay tablet with cuneiform, Jemdet Nasr, Iraq, 3000 B.C.E. This example of writing from Mesopotamia is among the earliest known anywhere in the world.

HOW DO WE KNOW?

Decoding Sumerian Writing

The Sumerians wrote no historical interpretive accounts of their accomplishments, but at least five kinds of written materials help us to reconstruct their past. King lists give us not only the names and dates of many of the principal kings of the major cities but also some chronology of their continuing warfare. Royal correspondence with officials illuminates relations with neighbors. Epics transmit Sumerian values and their sense of the heroic, and lamentations recount the continuing devastation wrought by their inter-city religious warfare. Finally, legal codes suggest the principles and hierarchies of their everyday life.

Despite Sumerian accomplishments, historians lost access to the Sumerians and their literature for at least 2000 years. The locations of even the grandest of the historic sites passed from memory. Biblical scholars, however, kept alive an interest in the region, searching for locations mentioned in Scripture, and British officials arriving with the British East India Company's outpost in Baghdad revived this interest. They began to investigate the ruins of Babylon and its

artifacts, and they dispatched artifacts, including written tablets, back to London. Still, no one knew what the wedge-shaped symbols meant.

Then, in the 1830s and 1840s, at Behistun, near Kermanshah, Persia, a British army officer began to copy a huge inscription that had been incised into a 300 foot high cliff to announce the military victories of the Persian king Darius I about 500 B.C.E. The officer, H. C. Rawlinson, had a scaffolding constructed so that he could reach the ancient writing, sometimes while hanging suspended from a rope 300 feet high above the surface of the earth. Rawlinson and other scholars found that the inscription actually included three scripts that represented different, but related languages: Old Persian, Babylonian, and Elamite. Old Persian and the Elamite were written in cuneiform scripts; the Babylonian in alphabetic script. The stone had probably been prepared to publicize Darius's triumphs in three of the major languages of his empire. The three inscriptions were translations of one another, enabling linguists who could already read the alphabetic script to crack the cuneiform—although it took several

generations before scholars completed this task.

Later archaeological digs in Mesopotamia uncovered tens of thousands of tablets and fragments, One especially rich cache was the royal library of the Assyrian king Ashurbanipal (r. 668–627 B.C.E.) at Nineveh. Through texts and digs, scholars resurrected the Sumerian economy, belief systems, and culture. Most of the texts deal with practical, everyday business transactions and administration. One contains the first known recipe for the ale that Sumerians enjoyed so much. Others recorded the world's first written literature.

- Why do you think the ancient language and literature of Sumer, like those of Egypt, were lost for 2000 years?
- How might the written records, once deciphered, complement the archaeological record known from excavations?
- How do the five kinds of records discovered in Sumerian writing differ from "historical interpretive accounts"? How do they contribute to an understanding of history even though they themselves may not be "historical interpretive accounts"?

bas relief In sculpture, relief is a term for any work in which the forms stand out from the background. In bas (or low) relief, the design projects only slightly from the background and the outlines are not undercut.

pictogram (alternative: pictograph) A pictorial symbol or sign representing an object or concept.

cuneiform A writing system in use in the ancient Near East from around the end of the fourth millennium to the first century B.C.E. The earliest examples are in Sumerian. The name derives from the wedge-shaped marks (Latin: *cuneus*, a wedge) made by pressing the slanted edge of a stylus into soft clay.

ideogram (alternative: ideograph) A character or figure in a writing system in which the idea of a thing is represented rather than its name. Languages such as Chinese use ideograms.

recording transactions and chronology through knots made in strings called *quipu*, but they did not develop an independent system of writing. Nor did the people of the Niger valley.

Writing facilitated communication, commerce, administration, religious ritual, and, later, the recording and transmission of literature. It enabled society to enlarge to a scale never seen before and it encouraged a self-consciousness and historical analysis previously unknown. It created a "knowledge industry," transmitted through systems of formal education and headed by scribes. By 2500 B.C.E., Sumerians had apparently established a number of schools where students could master the skill of writing. In a sense, this textbook had its origins in Sumer some 5000 years ago.

Achievements in Literature and Law

Much of what we know about the ancient Sumerian imagination and world vision comes from its literary works. *The Epic of Gilgamesh,* the most famous of the remaining literature, weaves together a series of tales about the hero Gilgamesh. Its most complete version comes from various shorter stories found in the library at Nineveh from about 750 B.C.E., but earlier fragments in the Sumerian excavations corroborate the antiquity of the core legends going back to the time when Gilgamesh ruled Uruk, about 2600 B.C.E.

SOURCE

The Epic of Gilgamesh

Like all epics, Gilgamesh *recounts the deeds of a larger-than-life hero. The Sumerian epic introduces the first hero in written literature:*

I will proclaim to the world the deeds of Gilgamesh. This was the man to whom all things were known; this was the king who knew the countries of the world. He was wise, he saw mysteries and knew secret things. … When the gods created Gilgamesh they gave him a perfect body. Shamash the glorious sun endowed him with beauty, Adad the god of the storm endowed him with courage, the great gods made his beauty perfect, surpassing all others, terrifying like a great wild bull. Two-thirds they made him god and one-third man.

Aruru, the goddess of Uruk, who had also created Gilgamesh, created Enkidu, a forest dweller, who became Gilgamesh's friend and played a central role in the epic. Gilgamesh *highlights the suggestive myth of Enkidu's seduction by an urban harlot who lures him from the wilderness to the pleasures of the city as well as to his wrestling match with Gilgamesh. The implication is that sexuality is experienced very differently in the city—more intensely and in more sophisticated fashion—than in the countryside. So, too, is friendship:*

the harlot and the trapper sat facing one another and waited for the game to come … on the third day the herds came; they came down to drink and Enkidu was with them … The trapper spoke to her: "There he is. Now, woman, make your breasts bare, have no shame, do not delay but welcome his love. Let him see you naked, let him possess your body. When he comes near uncover yourself and lie with him; teach him, the savage man, your woman's art, for when he murmurs love to you the wild beasts that shared his life in the hills will reject him." She was not afraid to take him, she made herself naked and welcomed his eagerness; as he lay on her murmuring love she taught him the woman's art.

For six days and seven nights they lay together, for Enkidu had forgotten his home in the hills; but when he was satisfied he went back to the wild beasts. Then, when the gazelle saw him, they fled. Enkidu would have followed, but his body was bound as though with a cord, his knees gave way when he started to run, his swiftness was gone. And now the wild creatures had all fled away; Enkidu was grown weak, for wisdom was in him, and the thoughts of a man were in his heart. So he returned and sat down at the woman's feet, and listened intently to what she said. "You are wise, Enkidu, and now you have become like a god. Why do you want to run wild with the beasts in the hills? Come with me. I will take you to the strong-walled Uruk, to the blessed temple of Ishtar and of Anu, of love and of heaven: there Gilgamesh lives, who is very strong, and like a wild bull he lords it over men." When she had spoken Enkidu was pleased; he longed for a comrade, for one who would understand his heart. "Come, woman, and take me to that holy temple, to the house of Anu and of Ishtar, and to the place where Gilgamesh lords it over the people. I will challenge him boldly."

With Enkidu's first encounter with Gilgamesh in the city, the epic also recounts the first example of male bonding, forged through a test of physical strength. When Gilgamesh and Enkidu first meet, they engage in a mighty wrestling match:

They broke the doorposts and the walls shook, they snorted like bulls locked together. They shattered the doorposts and the walls shook. Gilgamesh bent his knee with his foot planted on the ground and with a turn Enkidu was thrown. Then immediately his fury died … So Enkidu and Gilgamesh embraced and their friendship was sealed.

The epic also unveils the hero's driving ambition for fame and glory, both for himself and for his city, as Gilgamesh courageously chooses to enter the strongholds of Humbaba, guardian of the forest, and, with Enkidu, to fight him.

I will go to the country where the cedar is cut. I will set up my name where the names of famous men are written; and where no man's name is written I will raise a monument to the gods … I, Gilgamesh, go to see that creature of whom such things are spoken, the rumour of whose name fills the world. I will conquer him in his cedar wood and show the strength of the sons of Uruk, all the world shall know of it.

The importance of metallurgy and metals, especially for weapons, is highlighted:

He went to the forge and said, "I will give orders to the armorers: they shall cast us our weapons while we watch them." So they gave orders to the armorers and the craftsmen sat down in conference. They went into the groves of the plain and cut willow and box-wood; they cast for them axes of nine score pounds, and great swords they cast with blades of six score pounds each one, with pommels and hilts of thirty pounds. They cast for Gilgamesh the axe "Might of Heroes" and the bow of Anshan; and Gilgamesh was armed and Enkidu; and the weight of the arms they carried was thirty score pounds.

The victory of Gilgamesh and Enkidu over Humbaba parallels the massive assault by urbanites on the natural resources of the world, turning the products of nature into objects of trade and commerce, and using them to build cities.

Now the mountains were moved and all the hills, for the guardian of the forest was killed. They attacked the cedars, the seven splendours of Humbaba were extinguished. So they pressed on into the forest … and while Gilgamesh felled the first of the trees of the forest Enkidu cleared their roots as far as the banks of Euphrates.

Lower Mesopotamia has no stone, wood, or metal. To get these raw materials, Sumerians had to send parties over long distances to quarry, cut, and dig; to trade; and to conquer. The mixed responses of the gods to the murder of Humbaba suggest the deep ambivalence of the Sumerians to their own increasing power:

[Gilgamesh and Enkidu] set [the corpse of] Humbaba before the gods, before Enlil; they kissed the ground and dropped the shroud and set the head before him. When he saw the head of Humbaba, Enlil raged at them, "Why did you do this thing? From henceforth may the fire be on your faces, may it eat the bread that you eat, may it drink where you drink."

SUMER: KEY EVENTS AND PEOPLE

c. **3300** (B.C.E.)	Sumerians invent writing.
c. **3000** (B.C.E.)	Sumerians become dominant power in southern Mesopotamia.
c. **2800–2340**	Sumerian city-states: early dynastic period sees spread of Mesopotamian culture to the north.
c. **2350**	Sargon captures Sumer and establishes Semitic dynasty at Akkad, the new capital.
c. **2112–2004**	Third dynasty of Ur.
c. **1900**	Ammorites at Babylon.
1792–1750	Reign of Hammurabi; Babylon is the new capital of Mesopotamia.
c. **1600**	Invasion by Hittites and Kassites, destroying Hammurabi's dynasty.

The Epic of Gilgamesh presents a world of many gods before whom humans are passive and frightened subjects. Gilgamesh, however, defers neither to human nor to god. Devastated by the death of his closest friend Enkidu, he sets off to the underworld in search of eternal life. Along the way he encounters the Sumerian prototype of Noah. This man, Utnapishtim, tells him of a flood that destroyed all human life except his family. A god who counseled him to build a boat had saved them. In the bleak underworld of the dead, Gilgamesh obtains a plant that will give eternal youth, but on his return voyage a snake rises from the water and snatches it from him. Gilgamesh recognizes a fundamental truth: Misery and sorrow are unavoidable parts of human life. Resigned to his losses, Gilgamesh returns to Uruk. Finally, he dies at a ripe old age, honored and mourned by his fellow citizens.

A second form of written document that marks the evolution to a more complex society is the legal code. Archaeologists discovered at Ur fragments of a legal code that dates to the twenty-first century B.C.E., and legal systems must have already existed even before this. Legal systems remained crucial for all Mesopotamian urban societies. The post-Sumerian code of the

The stele of vultures. This limestone tablet, or stele, depicts in bas relief Lagash's victory over Umma, in about 2450 B.C.E. Some 3600 of the enemy were slaughtered by King Eannatum of Lagash and his soldiers, who are seen here marching into battle. (*Louvre, Paris*)

SOURCE

The Code of Hammurabi

As states grew larger, formal, written law codes replaced the customs and traditions of the farming villages. Around 1750 B.C.E., the Babylonian ruler Hammurabi conquered Mesopotamia, uniting the warring city-states under his rule. To reinforce that unity he set forth a code of laws that covered many aspects of daily life and business.

The code provides a marvelous insight into the problems and nature of urban life at the time. It provides a detailed insight into property rights and urban crime, as well as the social and gender divisions in the society. Finally, it gives students and scholars some idea of how justice was perceived in Hammurabi's world. The code is a list of 282 laws; only some of them are represented here. In the original list, they are not particularly organized so we have reorganized them here.

Property

Property laws incorporated laws of consumer protection for house buyers, boat renters, contractors for services. In one case, a brutal punishment for faulty workmanship indicates that common people, too, were viewed as commodities. The sins of the fathers may be taken out on the children. Some of the specific laws included:

- If [the collapse of a building] has caused the death of a son of the owner of the house, they shall put the son of that builder to death.
- If any one steal the property of a temple or of the court, he shall be put to death, and also the one who receives the stolen thing from him shall be put to death.

Stele of Hammurabi, from Susa, Iran, c. 1760 B.C.E. Hammurabi, the great king of Babylon, is the first known ruler to have created a detailed legal code; other societies with unknown rulers developed much earlier codes. On this commemorative stone slab, he is shown receiving the Babylonian laws from the sun-god Shamash. The laws themselves are inscribed below on the stele. (*Louvre, Paris*)

Urban Crime

Many laws provided for punishment for robbery and for personal injuries. Many of the latter varied according to the social class of the person inflicting the injury as well as the person suffering the injury:

- If any one is committing a robbery and is caught, then he shall be but to death.
- If a gentleman has destroyed the eye of a member of the aristocracy, they shall destroy his eye.
- If he has broken another gentleman's bone, they shall break his bone.
- If he has destroyed the eye of a commoner or broken the bone of a commoner, he shall pay one mina of silver.
- If he has destroyed the eye of a gentleman's slave or broken the bone of a gentleman's slave, he shall pay one half his value.

Gender in Ancient Babylonia

Numerous laws governed marriage, bride price, dowry, adultery, and incest. Although women did own the dowries given them, their rights of ownership were limited. Marriage is presented in large part as a commercial transaction, in which the groom's family pays a bride-price to the bride's father, while the bride's father gives her a dowry. Childlessness is grounds for divorce but the husband must return his wife's dowry. Behavioral restraints in marriage are unequal: if the husband "has been going out and disparaging her greatly," the wife may leave, taking her dowry; if the wife is "a gadabout, thus neglecting her house (and) humiliating her husband," he may have her drowned.

- If a woman quarrels with her husband, and says: "You are not congenial to me," the reasons for her prejudice must be presented. If she is guiltless, and there is not fault on her part, but he leaves and neglects her, then no guilt attaches to this woman, she shall take her dowry and go back to her father's house.
- If she is not innocent, but leaves her husband, and ruins her house, neglecting her husband, this woman shall be cast into the water.

HOW DO WE KNOW?

Some Modern Critiques of Early Urbanization

Sumer's city-states had many accomplishments to their credit, but some historians have pointed out that their civilization came at the cost of increasing warfare, growing social inequality, and the oppression of women. These modern critiques reflect the importance of studying the past in order to understand the present more fully.

Politically, each of the major cities of Sumer was also a state, ruling over the contiguous agricultural areas and often in conflict with neighboring city-states. The artwork of the city-states often depicts royal armies, military expeditions, conquests, and a general appreciation, even an exaltation, of warfare. The fighting seems to have been frequent, and the main combatants were the largest of the city-states. Battles were fought hand-to-hand and also from donkey-drawn chariots.

The warfare was especially destructive because the kings and soldiers believed that they were upholding the honor of their gods. When cities are sacred, conflicts between them mean holy war, fights to the finish. The "Lamentation over the Destruction of Ur," which was addressed to Ningal, goddess of the Ekushnugal Temple, describes that city's utter destruction after the Elamites sacked it, exiled its ruler, and destroyed the temple c. 1950 B.C.E.:

> After your city had been destroyed, how now can you exist!
> After your house had been destroyed, how has your heart led you on!
> Your city has become a strange city; how now can you exist!
> Your house has become a house of tears, how has your heart led you on!
> Your city which has been made into ruins—you are no longer its mistress!
> Your righteous house which has been given over to the pickax—you no longer inhabit it,
> Your people have been led to slaughter—you are no longer their queen. (Kramer, The Sumerians, p. 142)

Lewis Mumford, one of the most respected modern commentators on the history of cities, regarded this early union of power, religion, and continuous warfare as a permanent curse of urban life. He wrote, "even when it is disguised by seemingly hardheaded economic demands, uniformly turns into a religious performance; nothing less than a wholesale ritual sacrifice."

The first Sumerian cities fostered division of labor into occupational categories. We have noted the roles of kings, priests, landowners, architects, scribes, long-distance traders, local merchants, artisans, cooks, farmers, soldiers, laborers—the whole panoply of occupational categories absent in villages but forming the backbone of a sophisticated urban economy and society. Priests and kings held great wealth and power and largely controlled the means of production, but it is not clear that they formed an exclusive category of "haves" versus "have nots." The spectrum seems to have been more varied, including a substantial group of middle classes. But there is, nevertheless, much evidence of the enormous power of the aristocracy.

At the bottom of the economic hierarchy were slaves. People entered slavery in four ways: some were captured in battle; some were sentenced to slavery as punishment for crimes; some sold themselves (or their family members) into slavery to cope with poverty and debt; and some were born into slavery. We have no record of the number or proportion of slaves in the general population of Sumer and its cities. The law codes' extensive regulations of slaves and slavery suggest, however, their widespread existence.

The socialist philosopher-historian Karl Marx argued that the rise of cities brought about "the division of the population into two great classes." Marx's formulation was too stark, ignoring the broad range of classes in the city, but he does force us to think about the class structure in our own cities, including the relationship between rich and poor, and its implications for the health of society.

Finally, the transformation of society from a rural, egalitarian, kin base to an urban, hierarchical, territorial, and class base may have provided the entering wedge for the subordination of women. Some women in Sumer had great power. Several seem to have held independent high administrative posts in major temples controlling large land holdings. The high status of Lady Pu-abi (c. 2500 B.C.E.) was revealed in her burial. She was adorned with gold and buried with several other bodies, presumably servants, suggesting a woman of high rank, perhaps a queen. Shagshag, wife of King Uruinimgina (also known as Urukagina), c. 2300 B.C.E., held great powers in the name of her husband.

Women in Sumer generally had certain basic rights, including the rights to hold property, engage in business, and serve as legal witness. Nevertheless, it is clear that women's legal rights were limited by their husbands. Even powerful women were often only pawns in the power struggles of men.

Feminist historian Gerda Lerner argues that before the evolution of city-states, with their warfare and hierarchical class structures, the status of women had been more equal. Kin groups had been the basic economic units of society, and women had had more power in these family groups than they did in the city-states that displaced them. Lerner claims that inequalities between men and women are not products of unchanging biological differences. Rather, the inequalities have been created by humans—and they can be altered by humans.

- What did Lewis Mumford learn about warfare from his study of ancient cities? How did this affect his view of modern warfare?
- What did Karl Marx learn about class relations from his study of ancient cities? How did this affect his view of class relationships in modern (nineteenth-century) cities?
- What did Gerda Lerner learn about gender relationships from her study of ancient cities?

Babylonian King Hammurabi, formulated *c.* 1750 B.C.E. (but rediscovered only in 1901–2), seems to have been built on the earlier concepts.

The modern critiques of Mumford, Marx, and Lerner remind us how seriously the past, and our preconceptions—or myths—about it, have influenced our thinking. They urge us to rethink the past in order to redirect our future from repeating some terrible mistake—for example, making warfare into a religious obligation, isolating city from countryside, establishing oppressive class distinctions, and institutionalizing patriarchal suppression of women.

Underlying these warnings, however, is yet another myth. The pre-urban agricultural village, it is widely believed, was more egalitarian, less warlike, and more integrated into nature. We do not know if this was so. Pre-urban villagers produced no written records, and their artifactual remains are thin, inconclusive, and subject to widely divergent interpretation. Scholars draw many of their conclusions concerning pre-urban life from observing isolated groups in today's world, such as the !Kung people of the African Kalahari desert of a generation ago. But here, too, both observations and interpretations differ.

THE FIRST CITIES
WHAT DIFFERENCE DO THEY MAKE?

We do know that early cities facilitated some of the accomplishments that people then and now considered vitally important: increases in human population (a questionable asset under today's conditions, but not then); economic growth; effective organization for common tasks; creative breakthroughs in technology, art, and, perhaps most significantly, in writing and literature; the inauguration of a rule of law; and the formation of a non-kin-based community with a sense of purpose and humanity.

They did not always succeed, however. The city-states could not work out a system of government and regulation that would enable them to live in peace. At the same time powerful and vulnerable, oscillating between psalms of victory and lamentations of defeat, they seemed to fall into one of two painful alternatives: inter-state warfare or conquest by imperial rulers. Their shortcomings cost them dearly. As long as each political entity was a law unto itself—as were the city-states of Sumer, pre-Han China, classical Greece, medieval Europe, and of India during much of its history—war was the likely result. This problem of warfare among competitive states persists to our own day, although the scale has escalated from the city-state to the independent nation-state.

The evolution of the large, complex city implies the evolution of a state capable of organizing and administering it. In aristocratic and monarchical Sumer, much depended on the disposition of the king. Even the legendary Gilgamesh ended his royal career devoted to, and honored by, his people, but his career had begun differently. The epic tells us that in Gilgamesh's youth, "the men of Uruk muttered in their houses" about his faults:

> his arrogance has no bounds by day or night. No son is left with his father, for Gilgamesh takes them all, even the children … his lust leaves no virgin to her lover, neither the warrior's daughter nor the wife of the noble.

They realized that it should have been different—"The king should be a shepherd to his people"—but they apparently had to submit. The only recourse they saw was muttering in their houses and praying to their gods.

This question of the proper organization of the state became the key question of urbanization. Two thousand years after Gilgamesh might have ruled—and two thousand years before our own day—in the city-states of ancient Greece, the philosopher Aristotle summed up the issue:

> When several villages are united in a single complete community, large enough to be nearly or quite self-sufficing, the state comes into existence, originating in the bare needs of life, and continuing in existence for the sake of a good life ... man is by nature a political animal [a creature of the polis or city-state] ... the association of living beings who have this sense makes a family and a state ... justice is the bond of men in states, for the administration of justice, which is the determination of what is just, is the principle of order in political society.

polis The city-state of ancient Greece. It comprised not only the town, which was usually walled with a citadel (acropolis) and a market place (**agora**), but also the surrounding countryside. Ideally, the *polis* comprised the citizens, who could reside in either town or country.

From the time of Sumer, the political questions, the questions of how to organize and administer the **polis** or city-state to achieve a good life, have been central to the process of urbanization. In Sumer the answers depended on the edicts of the king and the priests. In the next two chapters, we shall see how these questions and answers evolved in other primary cities and city-states around the world.

Review Questions

- Why did people create the earliest cities? Note that several of the reasons that are usually given are disputed. Which of the reasons seems to be most convincing to you? Why?
- Why did Sumer become the site of the first cities? Why did the Nile and Indus valleys become the next two sites?
- What is the connection between the creation of the first cities and the creation of the first states?
- What was the importance of writing to the creation of the first cities? Please consider all the uses of writing in your answer. Later we will encounter cities that had no writing. What do you think that they will lack in comparison to the cities of the fertile crescent that did have it?
- When ancient cities were defeated in warfare, lamentations were often composed over their loss. What was the nature of the losses that were lamented?
- In what ways are our modern cities like the ancient cities of Sumer? In what ways are they different?

Suggested Readings

PRINCIPAL SOURCES

Fagan, Brian M. *People of the Earth: An Introduction to World Prehistory* (Upper Saddle River, NJ: Prentice Hall, 2000). Excellent general textbook introduction to prehistory.

Gilgamesh, The Epic of, trans. and ed. N.K. Sandars (Harmondsworth, Middlesex: Penguin Books, 1972). Very readable edition of the classic epic.

Kramer, Samuel Noah. *History Begins at Sumer: Thirty-Nine "Firsts" in Recorded History* (New York: Doubleday and Co., Inc., 1959). One of the greatest scholars in the field presents Sumer's pioneering accomplishments.

Kramer, Samuel Noah. *The Sumerians: Their History, Culture, and Character* (Chicago, IL: University of Chicago Press, 1963). A masterful, accessible summary by one of the greatest scholars in the field.

Lerner, Gerda. *The Creation of Patriarchy* (New York: Oxford University Press, 1986). Lerner brings a critical feminist perspective to studies of Sumer, although many scholars have criticized her scholarship here; her main field is American history.

Past Worlds: The Times Atlas of Archaeology (Maplewood, NJ: Hammond Inc., 1988). Excellent for its maps, pictures, time lines, brief discussions, and generally attractive presentation. Slightly dated.

Pritchard, James B., ed. *Ancient Near Eastern Texts Relating to the Old Testament* (Princeton, NJ:

Princeton University Press, 3rd ed. with supplement, 1969). Excellent compendium of primary source materials. Presentation is very scholarly and painstaking.

Roaf, Michael. *Cultural Atlas of Mesopotamia and the Ancient Near East* (New York: Facts on File, 1996). Another in the excellent Facts on File series, copiously supplied with maps and pictures as well as readable, scholarly, introductory text materials.

ADDITIONAL SOURCES

Aristotle. *Basic Works*, trans. and ed. Richard McKeon. (New York: Random House, 1941). Aristotle's *Politics*, in particular, presents very early, very thoughtful concepts of urban governance.

Bairoch, Paul. *Cities and Economic Development: From the Dawn of History to the Present*, trans. Christopher Braider (Chicago, IL: University of Chicago Press, 1988). Comprehensive presentation of the importance of cities in economic history. Europe is the main focus.

Cohen, Mark. *The Food Crisis in Prehistory* (New Haven, CT: Yale University Press, 1977). Asks why people began to settle into farming and continue it.

Hudson, M. and B. Levine, *Privatization in the Ancient Near East and the Classical World* (Cambridge, MA: Peabody Museum of Archaeology and Ethnology, 1996).

Marx, Karl. *Capital: A Critique of Political Economy*, trans. Ben Foulkes (New York: Vintage Books, 1977). Writing at the height of the industrial revolution in Western Europe, Marx explores the history of urbanization as part of his larger work.

Marx, Karl and Friedrich Engels. *The German Ideology* (New York: International Publishers, 1939). Includes a critical examination of the capitalist city.

Moore, Andrew M.T. "The Development of Neolithic Societies in the Near East," *Advances in World Archaeology*. Vol. 4., ed. Fred Wendorf and Angela E. Close (Orlando, FL: Academic Press, Inc., 1985). A fine, brief introduction.

Mumford, Lewis. *The City in History* (New York: Harcourt, Brace and World, Inc., 1961). The master examines the history of all cities, urging his readers to see the importance of social life and community as the key to the good city.

Oppenheim, A. Leo. *Ancient Mesopotamia. Portrait of a Dead Civilization* (Chicago, IL: University of Chicago Press, 1964). Scholarly articles covering a wide range of aspects of early Mesopotamian civilization, especially Babylonians and Assyrians.

Postgate, Nicholas. *The First Empires* (Oxford: Elsevier Phaidon, 1977). Comparative presentation of early city-states that preceded empires.

Redman, Charles L. *The Rise of Civilization: From Early Farmers to Urban Society in the Ancient Near East* (San Francisco, CA: W.H. Freeman and Co., 1978). Anthropologist's analysis of the basis of early cities, stresses ecological conditions and irrigation.

Sjoberg, Gideon. "The Origin and Evolution of Cities," *Scientific American*. (September 1965), 19–27. A sociologist, Sjoberg stresses the differences in political life and technological sophistication between pre- and post-industrial cities in this general introduction.

Wheatley, Paul. *The Pivot of the Four Quarters* (Chicago, IL: Aldine Publishing Company, 1971). For this enormously learned geographer, early cities were primarily concerned with their relationship with the gods and the cosmos, as reflected in their structure and leadership.

Woolley, C. Leonard. *Excavations at Ur* (London: Ernest Benn, Ltd., 1954). One of the greatest of the excavators describes his expeditions and their results. Well illustrated and very accessible.

World History Documents CD-ROM

1.1 Lugal Sulgi: Role Model for Mesopotamian Royalty
1.2 The Nippur Murder Trial and the "Silent Wife"
1.4 *The Epic of Gilgamesh*

RIVER VALLEY CIVILIZATIONS

THE NILE AND THE INDUS 7000 B.C.E.–750 B.C.E.

KEY TOPICS
- Egypt: the Gift of the Nile
- The Indus Valley Civilization and its Mysteries

Two other urban civilizations flanked Mesopotamia: the Nile valley to the southwest and the Indus valley to the southeast. Scholarly opinion is divided as to whether these two cultures learned to build cities and states from the Mesopotamian example or invented them independently. Whatever the source of inspiration, the peoples of these three river valleys created separate and distinct patterns of urbanization and political life.

In Mesopotamia's Tigris–Euphrates valley, development of the physical city and the institutional state went hand-in-hand. In the Nile valley, the creation of the Egyptian state had greater significance than the growth of individual cities. In the Indus valley, we have extensive archaeological information on the cities, but we know next to nothing about the formation of the state. Until scholars learn to decipher the script and language of the Indus civilization, our knowledge of its institutional development will remain limited.

EGYPT: THE GIFT OF THE NILE

Egypt has often been called the "Gift of the Nile" because outside the valley of that great river the country is a desert. An immense, flowing ribbon of water, the Nile spans the length of the country from south to north, branching finally into an extraordinary delta as it approaches the Mediterranean. The river provides natural irrigation along its banks and invites further man-made irrigation to extend its waters to the east and west. Unlike the unpredictable floods of Mesopotamia, from prehistoric times until the mid-twentieth century C.E. a more-or-less predictable flood of water poured through the Nile valley every July, August, and September, not only providing natural irrigation, but also carrying nutrient-rich silt that fertilized the land. (As we shall see in Chapter 18, twentieth-century dam construction brought more control over the annual flood, and hydroelectric power, but also stopped the flow of silt.) Meanwhile, increased population filled in marshlands adjacent to the river bed.

The vital significance of the Nile appears in this 4000-year-old Egyptian poem:

Food bringer, rich with provisions,
  himself the author of all his good things,
Awe-striking master, yet sweet the aromas rising about him
  and, how he satisfies when he returns! –
Transforming the dust to pastures for cattle,
  bringing forth for each god his sacrifice.
He dwells in the underworld, yet heaven and earth are his to command,
  and the Two Lands he takes for his own,
Filling the storerooms, heaping the grainsheds,
  giving his gifts to the poor. (Foster, p. 113)

Opposite **Mohenjo-Daro, present-day Pakistan, c. 2600–1800 B.C.E.** When it flourished, Mohenjo-Daro held some 40,000 inhabitants in its carefully laid-out precincts and it continued to exercise an attraction for thousands of years. The round *stupa*, or burial mound, that now crowns the settlement was built as part of a Buddhist monastery some two thousand years after Mohenjo-Daro had ceased being a city.

AT A GLANCE : **ANCIENT EGYPT**

DATE	POLITICAL	RELIGION AND CULTURE	SOCIAL DEVELOPMENT
4000–3600 B.C.E.	■ Nagada I		
3500 B.C.E.		■ Hieroglyphics in use	■ Villages in Nile valley
3000 B.C.E.	■ Early Dynasty (c. 3000–2700)	■ Ruler of Egypt becoming godlike	■ First use of stone in building
2500 B.C.E.	■ Old Kingdom (c. 2700–2181)	■ Step pyramid at Saqqara ■ Pyramids at Giza, including Great Pyramid (of Khufu)	■ Irrigation programs along Nile
2000 B.C.E.	■ First Intermediate Period (c. 2200–2050) ■ Middle Kingdom (c. 2050–1750) ■ Second Intermediate Period (c. 1750–1550)	■ Golden age of art and craftwork (1991–1786)	■ Social order upset; few monuments built (2181–1991) ■ Country divided into principalities (1786–1567)

hieroglyphs The characters in a writing system based on the use of **pictograms** or **ideograms**. In ancient Egypt, hieroglyphics were largely used for monumental inscriptions. The symbols depict people, animals, and objects, which represent words, syllables, or sounds.

Figurine of bone and ivory, "Nagada I" period, c. 4000–3600 B.C.E. Egypt's rise to a mighty empire had modest roots: a string of loosely affiliated villages lining the Nile. This attractive figurine, whose eyes are inlaid with lapis lazuli, was unearthed from a tomb of this early, predynastic age. (*British Museum, London*)

The desert flanking the Nile valley protected Egypt from external invasion from the east and west; cataracts—precipitous, impassable waterfalls in the river—provided a buffer against Nubia to the south; and the Mediterranean provided a defensible northern border. As a result, for the first half of its 5000 years of recorded history, Egypt was usually ruled by indigenous dynasties. The rule of the kings began about 3100 B.C.E. and continued with few exceptions for nearly 2600 years, an unparalleled stretch of cultural and political continuity. These kings later were called pharaohs during the New Kingdom (see Chapter 5) after the palaces they constructed, and gradually, pharaoh became the generic name of all Egyptian kings.

Monumental structures—like the pyramids and Sphinx at Giza near modern Cairo in the north of Egypt, the temples at Karnak and Thebes in the south, and the pharaohs' tombs nearby in the Valley of the Kings—make clear the wealth, skills, and organizational capacity of ancient Egypt. Nevertheless, we know less about the physical form of Egypt's ancient cities than about those of Mesopotamia. The Nile has washed away many ancient structures and eroded their foundations. On the other hand, we know much more about the Egyptian state than almost any other. The written records of ancient Egypt, once they were deciphered, provided the institutional information.

Earliest Egypt: Before the Kings

In Egypt, as in Mesopotamia, agriculture provided the underlying sustenance for city life. By 12,000 B.C.E., residents of Nubia and Upper Egypt were using stones to grind local wild grasses into food, and by 8000 B.C.E. flour was being prepared from their seeds. (Upper or southern Egypt and Lower or northern Egypt derived their names from the flow of the Nile River. The river rises south of Egypt and flows north to the Mediterranean Sea.) By 6000 B.C.E. the first traces appear of the cultivation of wheat and barley, grasses and cereals, and of the domestication of sheep and goats. To the west, the Sahara was becoming drier and some of its inhabitants may have moved to the Nile valley bringing with them more advanced methods of cultivation.

By 3600 B.C.E. a string of villages lined the Nile River, at intervals of every 20 miles or so. The village economies were based on cereal agriculture. They were linked by trade along the river, although, since they mostly produced the same basic food-stuffs, trade was not central to their economy. The villages show little evidence of social stratification. These settlements characterized the "Nagada I" period (*c.* 3500 B.C.E.).

Gradually, population increased, as did the size of villages, and by 3300 B.C.E. the first walled towns appeared in the upper Nile, at Nagada and Hierakonpolis. Tombs for rulers and elites were built nearby, suggesting new levels of social stratification.

The Written Record

Writing began early in Egypt, almost simultaneously with ancient Mesopotamia, about 3500–3000 B.C.E. Egyptians may have learned the concept of writing from Mesopotamia, but in place of cuneiform, they developed their own script based on tiny pictographs called **hieroglyphs**, a word based on the Greek for "sacred carvings." Some scholars believe that hiero-glyphic writing in Egypt was completely independent of the Mesopotamian invention, and possibly preceded it.

Scribes, an important and highly regarded occupational group in ancient Egypt as in Mesopotamia, later invented two shorthand transcriptions of hieroglyphs, first, hieratic script, later, the even more abbreviated form of demotic script. They wrote on stone tablets, on limestone flakes, on pottery, and on papyrus—a kind of paper—made by laying crossways the inner piths of the stalk of papyrus plants and pressing them until they formed into sheets.

As in Mesopotamia, some of the earliest Egyptian writing is notation for business and administration. Over the millennia it grew into a rich literature, including chronological lists of kings, religious inscriptions, spells to protect the dead, biogra-phies and autobiographies, stories, wisdom texts of moral instruction, love poems, hymns to gods, prayers, and mathe-matical, astronomical, and medical texts. From this literature, scholars have reconstructed a substantial picture of the history of Egypt.

For the earliest 500 to 1000 years, until about 2400 B.C.E., the written records are thin. They do, however, provide a list of *nomes*, or administrative districts, suggesting the geographical organization of the Egyptian state as early as 2900 B.C.E. They also provide lists of the earliest kings of Egypt.

King lists written on stone about 2400 B.C.E., and on papyrus about 1200 B.C.E., combined with lists compiled by the Greek historian Manetho in the third century B.C.E., give the names of the entire sequence of Egypt's kings from about 3100 B.C.E, all

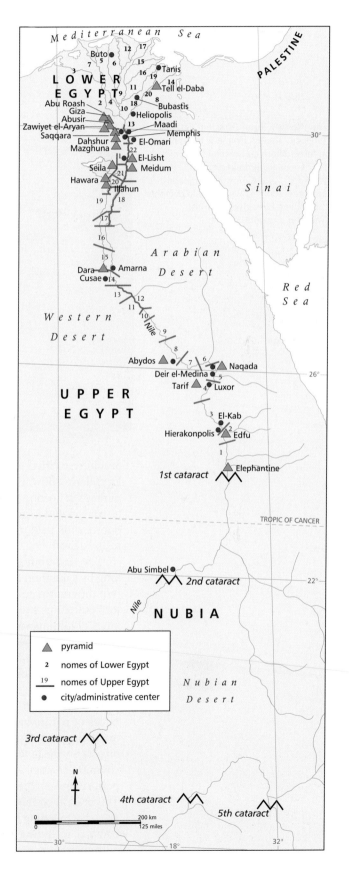

Land of the Nile. Stretching over 1000 miles along the Nile River, ancient Egyptian civilization depended on a strong government. The kingdom was divided into Lower and Upper Egypt, and further subdivided into *nomes* (tax districts).

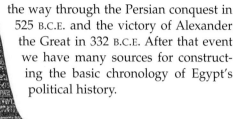

The **"Rosetta Stone,"** ancient Egyptian, **196 B.C.E.** The inscription is transcribed in three different forms: hieroglyphics, a later Egyptian shorthand called "demotic," and Greek. By comparing the three, scholars were able to decipher the ancient hieroglyphs. (*British Museum, London*)

the way through the Persian conquest in 525 B.C.E. and the victory of Alexander the Great in 332 B.C.E. After that event we have many sources for constructing the basic chronology of Egypt's political history.

Unification and the Rule of the Kings

The king lists, records of the *nomes* (administrative units) of Upper Egypt, and inscriptions and designs on pottery suggest strongly that Egyptian national life and history began with the unification of the kingdom about the year 3100 B.C.E. This unity was forged from the diversity of peoples who came to inhabit Egypt. Semites from the desert to the east, Phoenicians from the sea coast, Blacks from Nubia and the heart of Africa, and Europeans from across the Mediterranean immigrated and amalgamated into a common national stock. They recognized each other and intermarried without apparent reference to race or ethnicity. Paintings of ancient Egyptians show them sometimes pale in color, sometimes black, very often red, perhaps reflecting their mixed ethnicity. Many historians believe that the colors may also be related to gender—women, mostly relegated to household chores, were usually depicted as pale; men, assumed to be outside of the household, were often painted much darker.

Who first unified the upper and lower Nile into the single kingdom of Egypt? Most king lists mention Menes, but some cite Narmer. Some scholars believe that these were two different names for the same person. The event took place about 3100 B.C.E., but tombs of kings excavated at Abydos predate it by about 200 years. Perhaps these were kings of local regions, or perhaps unification was actually accomplished under a "pre-dynastic" king before Menes, or unification may have been a long process and "Menes" simply symbolizes the whole process.

As Egypt became unified, the kings grew steadily more powerful, finally gaining a position as gods, who lived on earth and were responsible for maintaining *ma'at*, justice and order, throughout the kingdom. They were responsible for keeping the forces of nature balanced and for inviting the annual flooding of the Nile River that made Egyptian agriculture possible. An increase in monumental tombs and funerary objects suggests an increasing hierarchy and an uneven distribution of wealth, two common characteristics of state building. A more or less unified artistic style in both pottery and architecture after that time mirrors the unification of Egyptian politics. This era, called the Early Dynastic period, lasted about 400 years, from *c.* 3100 to *c.* 2686 B.C.E. By this time Egypt exhibited the cultural complexity associated with early civilizations, including a national religious ideology and the centralized control of political administration and even of artistic productivity.

The Gods, the Unification of Egypt, and the Afterlife

Egyptian religious mythology gives great prominence to the political unification of the country. The triumph of Isis, Osiris, and their son Horus—three of Egypt's most important gods—over disorder and evil represents in mythic terms the significance of the unification of Egypt. Osiris represented order (*ma'at*) and virtue; his brother, Seth, disorder and evil. Seth tricked Osiris into lying down inside a box that was to be his coffin, sealed it, and set it floating down the Nile. Isis, Osiris' wife and sister, found the box and brought Osiris back home. Seth, however, re-captured the body and cut it into fourteen separate pieces, which he scattered throughout Egypt and the eastern Mediterranean. Isis tracked down all the parts, brought them back to Egypt, re-attached them, and briefly restored life to them. From the restored body, she conceived a son, Horus. Horus defeated Seth in battle and gave Osiris new life, this time as king and principal god of the underworld. In some representations Horus and Seth are seen in reconciliation, binding Egypt into a single state. Seth represents southern areas around Nagada and Thebes; Horus, less specifically, represents the north.

Horus became the patron god of the Egyptian kings, the first Egyptian god to be worshiped nationally. In painting and sculpture he is often depicted in the form of a falcon, sometimes perched on the head or shoulder of the king, sometimes atop the double crown that symbolized the unity of Upper and Lower Egypt. The kings

HOW DO WE KNOW?

Written Texts and Archaeological Excavations

Few modern Egyptian scholars had been interested in recovering the ancient past of their country, apparently because its pharaonic, polytheistic culture did not connect with their own monotheistic Islamic and Christian cultures. In Europe, however, scholars and researchers were attempting to understand the early history of this civilization. The interest in this scholarship was so great that when Napoleon Bonaparte led a French military invasion of Egypt in 1798 he brought along with his armies a contingent of scientists, literary scholars, and artists.

In 1799 one of Napoleon's officers working at a fort on the western, Rosetta branch of the Nile delta, discovered a large, black, basalt stone slab. This "Rosetta Stone" (see p. 68) carried an inscription from the year 196 B.C.E. issued by the Greek ruler of Egypt and written in three languages: the most ancient Egyptian script, hieroglyphs, at the top; demotic Egyptian, a simplified script based on the hieroglyphs, in the middle; and Greek at the bottom. The French

dispatched copies of the inscription back to Europe, where scholars were working on deciphering the Egyptian hieroglyphs. Until this time, their efforts had not been successful because they mistakenly believed that all of the hieroglyphs were ideographs, a kind of picture writing in which each symbol stood for a word or a concept. Now, however, a young French scholar of linguistics, Jean-François Champollion (1790–1832), using the Rosetta Stone to compare the ancient Egyptian forms with the Greek, which he knew, recognized that hieroglyphic writing combined several forms— ideographic, syllabic, and alphabetic. Once he made this discovery, he was prepared to crack the script. In 1822, after fourteen years of research, which he had begun at eighteen, he published the results of his work.

Champollion himself made only one trip to Egypt, in 1828–9. With an Italian student, he produced the first systematic survey of the history and geography of Egypt as revealed in its monuments and inscriptions. He earned the informal title of "Father of Egyptology," and in 1831 a chair in Egyptian history and archaeology was created for him at the College de France.

Archaeological excavations, primarily in search of monumental objects, began in 1858, although tomb robbing and the theft of ancient artifacts had been continuous from earliest times. The annual expeditions of British Egyptologist W.M. Flinders Petrie, beginning in 1880, introduced more scientific archaeological studies of Egypt and of Nubia, immediately to the south. By about 1900 scholars had identified the basic outlines of Egypt's history from 3600 B.C.E. to their own time. Working with both text and artifacts they could produce a doubly-rich historical record.

- *Why were modern Egyptian scholars no longer interested in the ancient past of their own country? Do you find this surprising? Why or why not?*
- *The earliest known alphabetic writing dates to about 1900 B.C.E. Its use in place of hieroglyphic writing has been described as revolutionary, "comparable to the invention of the printing press much later." Why?*
- *How do written accounts and monumental architecture complement each other in giving us a more complete understanding of ancient civilizations?*

believed that if they lived proper, ordered lives they would be united with Osiris after they died.

This belief in the afterlife inspired the mummification of the dead—at least of those who could afford it—and the construction of Egypt's most spectacular monuments, the pyramids, as a final resting place for the dead kings until their soul and life force emerged for their journey through the afterworld. After passing through the ordeal of judgment in the next world, the souls might also revisit these elaborate tombs.

At first believed to be a preserve of the kings alone, later the afterworld was seen as a destination also for important officials and, still later, for a larger proportion of the population. The belief in a utopian afterlife seems to have made optimists out of most Egyptians. Even those who may not have shared in this belief were urged to enjoy life in this world to the full, as this 3100-year-old song suggests:

All who come into being as flesh
    pass on, and have since God walked the earth;
       and young blood mounts to their places.
The busy fluttering souls and bright transfigured spirits
    who people the world below
       and those who shine in the stars with Orion,
They built their mansions, they built their tombs—
    And all men rest in the grave. . . .
So, seize the day! Hold holiday!
    Be unwearied, unceasing, alive,
       you and your own true love;
Let not your heart be troubled during your sojourn on earth,
    but seize the day as it passes! . . .
Grieve not your heart, whatever comes;
    let sweet music play before you;
Recall not the evil, loathsome to God,
    but have joy, joy, joy, and pleasure!

             (Foster, pp. 181–2)

Cities of the Dead

Burial sites, shrines, and sometimes towns were based on the need to provide final, collective, resting places for the bodies of the most prominent Egyptians. As early as 3100 B.C.E., kings and members of the court were buried at Abydos, a 300-mile boat trip upriver, south of Memphis. Their tombs, called *mastabas*, were made of sun-baked mud bricks, with flat roof and sloping sides, designed to last forever. Inside the structure were the food, weapons, tools, and furniture that the king might need in the afterlife. His body was mummified and buried in an underground chamber. Abydos later became the center for the worship of Osiris.

Another group of high officials was buried in the north, close to Memphis, near Saqqara, in mud-brick tombs. Their funerary goods included copper objects and stone vessels. Over the centuries a series of burial sites grew up nearby, stretching some 45 miles along the Nile. At the beginning of the second dynasty, 2770 B.C.E., the royal necropolis, the city of tombs, was sited at Saqqara itself.

GODS OF THE EGYPTIANS

Belief in one god (Aten, represented by the sun) was promoted during the reign of Akhenaten (r. 1353–1335), when the capital of Egypt was moved from Thebes to Amarna. At other times, the Egyptians worshiped a pantheon, whose main gods and goddesses are listed below:

Amon-Re	The universal god, depicted as ram-headed
Anubis	Jackal-headed god of funerals, son of Nephthus and Osiris. He supervised the weighing of souls at judgment
Hathor	The goddess of love, represented either as a woman with a cow's horns or as a cow with a solar disk
Horus	The falcon-headed god of light
Isis	Goddess of magic and fertility; sister and wife of Osiris; as mother of Horus, she was mother goddess of all Egypt
Nephthus	Sister of Isis, this funerary goddess befriended dead mortals at judgment
Osiris	Ruler of the underworld and chief judge of the dead, Osiris is normally depicted mummified or as a bearded man wearing the crown of Upper Egypt and with a flail and crook in his hands
Ptah	Magician and patron of the arts and crafts, Ptah later became judge of the dead. Normally represented as a mummy or holding an ankh (looped cross)
Seth	The god of evil and the murderer of Osiris
Thoth	The supreme scribe, depicted either with the head of an ibis or as a dog-headed baboon

Stele from the tomb of Djet (the "Serpent King"), Abydos, c. 3000 B.C.E. Horus, in the form of a falcon, is pictured above a serpent representing Djet, the "Serpent King," and the façade of a palace (*pharaoh* literally meant "great house" or "palace"). (*Louvre, Paris*)

Women of elite families were usually buried in simple pyramid tombs, but recently the more elaborate pyramid-tomb of Ankhesenpepi II was uncovered at Saqqara and explored. She was the wife of two Egyptian kings—first Pepi I (*c.* 2289–*c.* 2255), then his nephew Merenra (*c.* 2255–*c.* 2246)—and the mother of a third, Pepi II (*c.* 2246–*c.* 2152). Although her name means "she lives for Pepi," Ankhesenpepi II seems to have gained power also for herself . She is the first female known to have a magical, biographical, hieroglyphic text—a format found frequently in the tombs of kings—inscribed in her tomb to facilitate her access to the afterlife.

Adjacent to the burial sites were the towns of the workers who built the increasingly elaborate tombs for the kings and aristocrats. Several of these workers' towns have been excavated, most notably Deir el-Medina, in the south of Egypt, near the Valley of the Queens, opposite Thebes, although it dates to a later period. Mummification was also carried out in workshops in these towns.

The Growth of Cities

Unlike Mesopotamia, Egypt has almost no existing record of independent city-states. In Egypt, thousands of small, generally self-sufficient communities seem to have persisted under a national monarchy, but within a generally decentralized economy for the local production and consumption of food and basic commodities. The village economies were based on cereal agriculture, and they were linked by trade along the river, although, since they mostly produced the same basic foodstuffs, these villages traded only a little among themselves. They reveal little evidence of social stratification. These settlements characterized the "Nagada I" period (c. 3500 B.C.E.). Gradually, among the villages along the Nile, somewhat larger market towns must have grown up. Because administration, business, and transportation require some centralization, some of the villages began to house those functions. These selected villages, spaced strategically at larger intervals in the landscape, grew into larger settlements, and perhaps even into full-fledged cities.

In early dynastic Egypt, the siting of the administrative headquarters of the *nomes* would have given just such a boost to the towns in which they were located. Some settlements also hosted additional functions, including irrigation control and religious observance. The consolidation of villages into towns and towns into cities marks the beginning of "Nagada II" culture (c. 3300 B.C.E.) and the development of the site of Hierakonpolis along the Nile in Upper Egypt illustrates the process. Stretching for three miles along the banks of the Nile, Hierakonpolis ("Nekhen" in ancient Egyptian) did not have the form of a compact city, but it exercised many urban functions.

Archaeological excavations showed that the population of Hierakonpolis grew from a few hundred in 3800 B.C.E. to 10,500 by 3500 B.C.E. At least two cemeteries served the city, one for common people, another for the wealthier traders and more powerful administrators.

What precipitated the population growth, occupational specialization, and social hierarchy? One possibility is that local leaders introduced and implemented irrigation systems that saved agriculture and even enriched it during a period of severe drought. These changes enhanced the economy of the region and created subsequent growth and change. Indeed, Hierakonpolis seems to have been the capital from which King Menes, or Narmer, unified Egypt. The Narmer palette, a slate tablet illustrating this unification, was discovered here.

Political/administrative leaders continued to create irrigation systems along the Nile. These projects began in Old Kingdom Egypt, c. 2700–2200 B.C.E. They were expanded with the development of the Fayyum Lake region and the transfer of population to it during the Middle Kingdom, c. 2050–1750 B.C.E. New technology arose during the New Kingdom, c. 1550–1050 B.C.E., with the beginning of shaduf irrigation, which used buckets attached to a huge, turning wheel to dip into the river, bringing up water that then poured into man-made irrigation channels. The general predictability of the Nile's constant flow and annual flood meant that Egypt had fewer problems with its water supply than did Mesopotamia, but even here control of water resources influenced the formation of cities and the state.

Egypt's cities, like those of other early civilizations, had a religious base as well as an administrative one. Hierakonpolis, for example, housed a temple and prominent tombs as well as a ruler's palace. Perhaps the city flourished because its temple community and worship became especially attractive to surrounding villages. The combination of irrigation, administration, and worship built the city.

Earlier archaeological reports seemed to suggest that after unification under a single king Egyptian cities were not usually walled. The central government may have suppressed the kind of inter-city warfare that characterized Mesopotamia, rendering defensive walls unnecessary. Also, although invasions occurred from time

The Palette of King Narmer, c. 3200 B.C.E. This slate palette, used for ritual purposes, shows the power of King Narmer, who had just united Upper and Lower Egypt. In the top register, Narmer (left) inspects the bodies of dead enemies (right); at the bottom, the strength of the king is symbolized by the bull shown destroying the walls of a city. (*Egyptian Museum, Cairo*)

Wooden model of a sailing boat from Meir, Egypt, c. 2000 B.C.E. The presence of a mummy on board this Twelfth-dynasty model boat indicates that it was intended as a funerary artifact, used to symbolize the journey of the dead into the afterlife. We can glean important details about early Egyptian vessels—from the large central sail to the figures on deck, representing the pilot, the owner, and sailors working the halyards. (*British Museum, London*)

to time and required defensive precautions, the desert to the east and west of the Nile valley usually provided an adequate natural shield.

More recent excavations, however, question this view of open cities. The walls of some cities have been uncovered, and archaeologists are beginning to suspect that walls of other cities may have been removed and the materials used for other purposes. Excavations at El-Kab, across the Nile from Hierakonpolis, revealed a city enclosed in a wall, 1600 feet square, dating to 1788–1580 B.C.E. This wall, in turn, seems to have intersected a more primitive town, of circular or oval shape surrounded by a double wall.

Largest of all the Nile towns, presumably, were the political capitals, first in the north at Memphis, later in the south at Thebes, and occasionally at other locations. Most of the spectacular temples and monuments at Thebes today, for example, date only to the eighteenth and nineteenth dynasties, 1550–1196 B.C.E. This was a period of substantial population growth in Egypt, rising from 1.5 million to between 2.5 and 5 million people. Archaeologists cannot excavate below these monuments to reach older urban levels, and the residential buildings of that older city are probably below the current water table. They are irrecoverable.

Other types of cities completed the urban network. Trade cities, especially in the Nile delta, linked Egypt internally and to the outside world. As early as 3650 B.C.E., the city of Buto in the Nile delta near the Mediterranean served as the port of landing for shipping from the Levant (modern Syria, Lebanon, and Israel) and Mesopotamia. Further south but still in the delta, at El-Omari, many goods imported from the Mediterranean coast have also been found. In these ports, goods must have been off-loaded for transshipment in smaller boats or by donkey caravans to Maadi, near Memphis. Maadi was the trade link between the delta and Upper Egypt.

Monumental Architecture of the Old Kingdom: Pyramids and Fortresses

As in Mesopotamia, the increasing power of the Egyptian state inspired the construction of monumental architecture. In the third dynasty, 2649–2575 B.C.E., King Djoser's architect, Imhotep, elaborated the rather simple mastaba into a series of stepped stone slabs, one on top of the next, built to house the king's remains at death. This forerunner of the pyramids demonstrated an astonishing royal control over labor, finances, and architectural and building techniques. The administrative organization and economic productivity of government continued to increase, until, by the end of this dynasty, Egypt had extended its control of the Nile valley as far south as the first cataract, its classical southern frontier. At the same time, Egypt's artistic genius continued to develop the sculpture of its tombs and the sophistication of its script. The Old Kingdom had been established and Old Kingdom rulers spent fortunes constructing pyramid tombs to preserve their mummified bodies for the afterlife.

Within a half century, architects realized the beauty of filling in the steps of the multi-storied mastaba to create the simple, elegant, triangular form of the true pyramid. Kings of the fourth dynasty, 2575–2465 B.C.E., supervised the construction of the greatest pyramids in history. The 450-foot-high pyramids of Khufu (Cheops; r. 2551–2528 B.C.E.) and of Khefren (r. 2520–2494 B.C.E.), and the smaller pyramid of Menkaure (r. 2490–2472 B.C.E.), all arranged in a cluster with the Sphinx, proclaim creative vision, organizational power, and aspirations to immortality. The sculpture, reliefs, paintings, and inscriptions in the pyramids and in the many tombs of court officials and other powerful men of the time express the highest artistic achievements of the era. Tombs of queens and officials are situated in proximity to the kings' pyramids in accordance with their inhabitants' power and rank. (Tomb robbing was, however, so common that we have no idea how long any of them lay undisturbed in their tombs.) Following Menkaure, whose pyramid was already smaller than those of Khufu and Khefren, the building of such enormous monuments diminished, which may reflect a lessening of Egyptian power generally.

The Great Sphinx and the Pyramid of Khefren, Giza. The greatest of all the pyramids, the burial tombs of the kings, are at Giza, near modern Cairo, and date to around 2600–2500 B.C.E. The face of the sphinx—a mythological creature with a lion's body and a human head—is thought to be a likeness of King Khafre, who ruled Egypt some time after 2600 B.C.E.

Step pyramid of King Djoser, Saqqara, Egypt, c. 2700 B.C.E. This step pyramid, forerunner to the ancient architectural masterpieces at Giza, developed from the *mastaba*, a low rectangular benchlike structure that covered a grave. The purpose of this early pyramid, effectively a 200-foot-high ziggurat without a temple on top, was to mark and protect the underground tomb chamber 90 feet below.

Cutaway of Great Pyramid of Khufu, Giza. The rectangular plan and stepped form of Djoser's pyramid were gradually modified to become the colossal, smooth-faced monuments with which we are familiar. This pyramid is some 450 feet high on a square base occupying 13 acres and was built using forced labor.

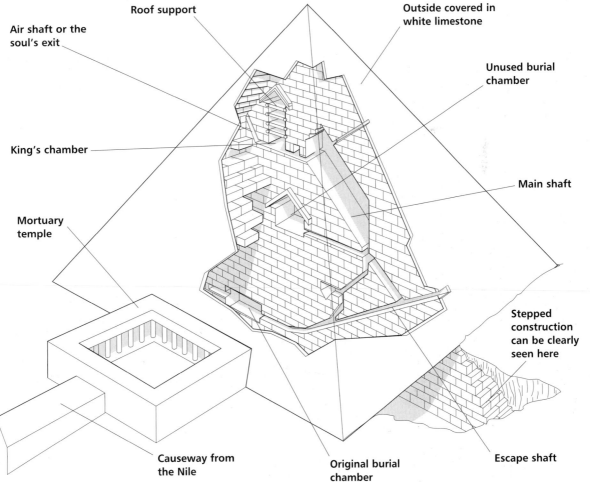

Roof support

Outside covered in
white limestone

Air shaft or the
soul's exit

Unused burial
chamber

King's chamber

Main shaft

Mortuary
temple

Stepped
construction
can be clearly
seen here

Causeway from
the Nile

Original burial
chamber

Escape shaft

At the height of the Old Kingdom, Egyptian trading, raiding, and mining initiatives began to extend southward into Nubia, above the first cataract of the Nile. These expeditions were protected and consolidated through the construction of the Buhen fortress at the second cataract, probably at about the time of the building of the great pyramids. That fortress, too, seems to have declined after about 2400 B.C.E., although trading and raiding expeditions continued. All of these architectural, spiritual, political, and military accomplishments date to the millennium we now call the pre-dynastic, early dynastic, and Old Kingdom.

The Disintegration of the Old Kingdom

Central authority weakened and provincial officials in each *nome*, called nomarchs, asserted their powers. They collected and kept the taxes for themselves, and their private armies ruled locally. Based on the size and records of cemeteries, the death rates seem to have increased at this time. Famine was prevalent. Apparently the Nile did not reach optimal flood heights for agriculture, and weak rulers could not create adequate irrigation works to compensate for the shortfall.

In 2181 B.C.E. the Old Kingdom fell. At first, several nomarchs held independent local power. Then two separate centers began to stand out in the contest for power: Herakleopolis in the north and Thebes in the south. This period of disunity, known as the First Intermediate Period, lasted for about a century.

SOURCE

The Egyptian Book of the Dead and the "Negative Confession"

Many ancient Egyptian texts concern the attempt to secure eternal happiness after death. A selection from these mortuary texts has been collected by modern scholars and titled The Book of the Dead. *A segment of these texts presents the "negative confession" of a deceased person in the court of judgment of the dead protesting his innocence of evil and crime:*

I have not committed evil against men.
I have not mistreated cattle.
I have not committed sin in the place of truth.
I have not tried to learn that which is not meant for mortals.
I have not blasphemed a god.
I have not done violence to a poor man.
I have not done that which the gods abominate.
I have not defamed a slave to his superiors.
I have not made anyone sick.
I have not made anyone weep.
I have not killed.
I have given no order to a killer.
I have not caused anyone suffering.
I have not cut down on the food or income in the temples.
I have not damaged the bread of the gods.
I have not taken the loaves of the blessed dead.
I have not had sexual relations with a boy.
I have not defiled myself.
I have neither increased or diminished the grain measure.
I have not diminished the measure of land.
I have not falsified the land records.
I have not added to the weight of the balance.
I have not weakened the plummet of the scales.

I have not taken milk from the mouths of children.
I have not driven cattle away from their pasturage.
I have not snared the birds of the gods.
I have not caught fish in their marshes.
I have not held up the water in its season.
I have not built a dam against running water.
I have not quenched a fire at its proper time.
I have not neglected the appointed times and their meat-offerings.
I have not driven away the cattle of the god's property.
I have not stopped a god on his procession.
I am pure: I am pure: I am pure: I am pure. ...

Behold me—I have come to you without sin, without guilt, without evil, without a witness against me, without one against whom I have taken action. I live on truth, and I eat of truth. I have done that which men said and that with which gods are content. I have satisfied a god with that which he desires. I have given bread to the hungry, water to the thirsty, clothing to the naked, and a ferry-boat to him who was marooned. I have provided divine offerings for the gods and mortuary offerings for the dead. So rescue me, you; protect me, you.

(Pritchard, pp. 34–6)

SOURCE

The Autobiography of Si-nuhe and the Glorification of Court and Capital

Si-nuhe, a high-ranking official and royal attendant, fled from the Egyptian court when a new king came to the throne. Apparently he feared that his loyalty to the new ruler was suspect and his safety endangered. A skilled warrior and administrator, even in self-imposed exile he earned high positions in several Asian kingdoms. In Si-nuhe's old age, however, the king of Egypt and his family invited him back to the court so that he could spend his last years "at home" in comfort and be buried with appropriate rites.

This personal tale of reconciliation is almost certainly based on reality. Its glorification of Egypt over other countries, of the city over the countryside, and especially of the royal capital and the royal court represented the beliefs of the Egyptian elite. This account of the career and the moral personality of a court official, and of the excellence of the reigning king is an outstanding example of the autobiographies inscribed in ancient Egyptian tombs. Si-nuhe's story became one of the most popular classics of Egyptian literature, and manuscripts that include it began to appear about 1800 B.C.E. and continued to about 1000 B.C.E. One modern scholar refers to it as "the crown jewel of Middle Egyptian literature." (Lichtheim, I, 11)

Si-nuhe returned to the capital, then in the city of Lisht, near the Faiyum Lake.

So I went forth from the midst of the inner chambers, with the royal children giving me their hands. Thereafter we went to the Great Double Door. I was put into the house of a royal son, in which were splendid things. A cool room was in it, and images of the horizon. Costly things of the Treasury were in it. Clothing of royal linen, myrrh, and prime oil of the king and of the nobles whom he loves were in every room. Every butler was busy at his duties. Years were made to pass away from my body. I was plucked, and my hair was combed. A load of dirt was given to the desert, and my clothes to the Sand-Crossers. I was clad in fine linen and anointed with prime oil.

I slept on a bed. I gave up the sand to them who are in it, and wood oil to him who is anointed with it. I was given a house which had a garden, which had been in the possession of a courtier. Many craftsmen built it, and all its woodwork was newly restored. Meals were brought to me from the palace three or four times a day, apart from that which the royal children gave, without ceasing a moment.

There was constructed for me a pyramid-tomb of stone in the midst of the pyramid-tombs. The stone-masons who hew a pyramid-tomb took over its ground-area. The outline-draftsmen designed in it; the chief sculptors carved in it; and the overseers of works who are in the necropolis made it their concern. Its necessary materials were made from all the outfittings which are placed at a tomb-shaft. Mortuary priests were given to me. There was made for me a necropolis garden, with fields in it formerly extending as far as the town, like that which is done for a chief courtier. My statue was overlaid with gold, and its skirt was of fine gold. It was his majesty who had it made. There is no poor man for whom like has been done.

(Pritchard, pp. 18–22)

The Rise and Fall of the Middle Kingdom

Finally, about 2050 B.C.E., King Mentuhotpe of Thebes defeated his rivals in the north and reunited the kingdom, initiating the Middle Kingdom, *c.* 2050–1750 B.C.E. Trade revived, with two patterns achieving special prominence. One was the local caravan trade in spices, resins, and minerals between the Nile Delta and Palestine, across the northern Sinai desert. The other—the long distance trade carried by ship throughout the eastern Mediterranean—was commanded by royal families to bring in timber and resins, lapis lazuli, copper, and ivory for official construction and for adornment.

The fine arts and literature flourished. Among the finest literary gems of the Middle Kingdom was "The Autobiography of Si-nuhe," the narrative of a high-ranking court official who went into self-exile until, in his old age, he was recalled to the capital and awarded great honors. The story reveals not only the intrigues of the court and the royal family, but also the sharp contrast between the life of the elites of the capital and the harsh rigors of the surrounding desert.

Most important, the Middle Kingdom saw the state develop more organization and power than ever before. Egypt was administered efficiently and spread its power into Nubia and into the Middle East more aggressively than before. Egypt became an empire, ruling over more distant, foreign peoples. From this time onward, Egypt's fate would be intertwined with the fate of its empire. The Middle Kingdom ended in part because the Nubians drove out their Egyptian conquerors, but more importantly because of the invasions of the Hyksos, or "princes of the foreign lands," who spoke a Semitic language and probably came from the north and east of the Sinai desert. The New Kingdom (*c.* 1550–1050 B.C.E.) would rise again as an empire by once again asserting its authority over Nubia and over large regions of Palestine and adjoining segments of Syria. These issues of empire and its significance for Egypt are discussed in Chapter 5, "Dawn of the Empires." One fascinating event from the New Kingdom period—the construction and destruction of the city Akhetaten—belongs here, however, because it highlights the symbolic importance of capital cities.

Akhetaten, Capital City of King Akhenaten

Sandstone statue of Akhenaten, Amarna period. Akhenaten worshiped one God, the god of the setting sun, which was represented by a winged solar disk. (*Egyptian Museum, Cairo*)

Modern excavations at Amarna on the east bank of the Nile unearthed the ruins of an ancient Egyptian capital that owed its entire existence to the idiosyncratic vision of one ruler—King Amenhotep IV, better known as Akhenaten.

Within a few years of coming to the throne, King Amenhotep IV (r. 1353–35 B.C.E.) challenged the order of ancient Egypt by adopting a new monotheistic religion. Instead of worshiping a whole pantheon of gods, he offered his devotion to a single deity—Aten, god of the solar disk (or sun). Amenhotep appointed himself mediator between his people and the god. Symbolically, he abandoned his official dynastic name in favor of Akhenaten ("he who serves Aten"). The name of Amon, principal god of the old religion, was swiftly erased from inscriptions throughout Egypt, as were the words "all gods" in certain texts.

To bolster the new order and escape the power of the hostile priesthood, Akhenaten moved his capital 200 miles north from the established center of Thebes to an untouched site in the desert. The city that he built was named Akhetaten ("horizon of Aten"; present-day Amarna) and it was here that Akhenaten, the Great Royal Wife Queen Nefertiti, and their six daughters practiced the new religion.

The eccentricity of Akhetaten's ruler was reflected in the city's architecture, sculpture, and wall painting. Solid statements of eternity gave way to a freedom of expression that emphasized the here-and-now. Aten was worshiped in an open temple that ushered in the sun's rays rather than in the dark, austere sanctuary usually designated for worship. Residential buildings included spacious villas with large gardens and pools to house wealthy officials. In artistic expression, solemnity gave way to an unprecedented liveliness and invention. Artists showed the royal parents playing with their children or dandling them on their laps. Curious depictions of Akhenaten's drooping jaw and misshapen body capture his individuality, marking a departure from the highly stylized representations of previous pharaohs.

Akhenaten's isolated position, both geographically and intellectually, threatened the stability of Egypt's empire. When he died, Akhenaten's successors abandoned Akhetaten and later razed it to the ground. The capital returned to Thebes where the old religious and political order could resume. Subsequent pharaohs so hated Akhenaten's religion that they dismantled the city and used its building materials on other sites.

From this discussion of the varied cities of the Nile Valley with their abundance of archaeological and textual materials, we move eastward about 2500 miles to explore the earliest cities of the Indus valley with their very different structures and materials.

THE INDUS VALLEY CIVILIZATION AND ITS MYSTERIES

The civilizations of ancient Mesopotamia and Egypt never disappeared completely. Hebrew and Greek accounts and surviving artifacts, like the spectacular pyramids, kept them alive in popular imagination. Intermittent discoveries of tombs, and the thefts of their contents, added concrete evidence. Nevertheless, systematic excavating of sites and deciphering of texts did not occur in modern times until the mid-1800s.

The civilization of the Indus valley was lost almost entirely, so it is no surprise that its excavation did not begin until the 1920s and that its script is still not deciphered. The accidental discovery and systematic exploration of this long-lived and far-flung civilization is one of the great stories of mid- and late-twentieth-century archaeology.

The Roots of the Indus Valley Civilization

In 1856, the British colonial rulers of India were supervising construction of a railway between Lahore and Karachi, along the Indus River valley. As they progressed, construction workers discovered hundreds of thousands of old fire-baked bricks in the semi-desert area and used them to lay the road bed. Scattered among the old bricks, workers discovered steatite stone seals marked with artistic designs. These seals and bricks were the first clue that the area had once been home to an ancient and unknown civilization. Some were passed along to officers of the Archaeological Survey of India, and they took note of them, but formal systematic excavations began only in 1920 when John Marshall, Director General of the Archaeological Survey, commissioned his staff to survey a huge mound that rose above the desert floor where the seals had been found.

These excavations soon revealed a 4500-year-old city. They named the site Harappa, and archaeologists often used this name to designate the entire Indus valley civilization. Two years later, R. D. Banerji, an Indian officer of the Survey, recognized and began to excavate a twin site 200 miles to the southwest, later named Mohenjo-Daro, "Hill of the Dead." The two cities had many urban design and architectural features in common. Both were about 3 miles in circumference, large enough to hold populations of 40,000. With these two excavations, an urban civilization that had been lost for thousands of years was uncovered.

Before these excavations, scholars had believed that the civilization of India had begun in the Ganges valley with the arrival of Aryan immigrants from Persia or central

AT A GLANCE : THE INDUS VALLEY

DATE	POLITICAL	RELIGION AND CULTURE	SOCIAL DEVELOPMENT
7000 B.C.E.			■ Traces of settlements; trade with Mesopotamia
3000 B.C.E.			■ Cotton cultivated
2500 B.C.E.	■ Height of Harappan civilization in northern India (2500–2000)		■ Cities of Harappa and Mohenjo-Daro
2000 B.C.E.	■ Collapse of Harappan civilization (2000–1900)	■ Evidence of decline in standards of architecture	
1500 B.C.E.	■ Immigration of Aryans into India (c. 1250)		
1000 B.C.E.	■ Aryan immigrants reach west Ganges valley (c. 1000) and build first cities (c. 750)		■ Iron tools used to clear Ganges valley for agriculture (c. 1000)

Asia *c.* 1250 B.C.E. and the construction of their first cities *c.* 700 B.C.E. The discovery of the Harappan cities pushed the origin of Indian civilization back an additional 1500 years and located it in an entirely different ecological zone.

As archaeologists explored more widely in the Indus valley, they found that civilization there began earlier, lasted longer, and spread farther than anyone had suspected. Some of its roots seem to lie in a settlement called Mehrgarh, in the foothills of the Bolan Pass, that has yielded early settlement artifacts going back to 7000 B.C.E. and, with ever-increasing sophistication, coming forward to 2500–2000 B.C.E. At its height, it had major settlements as far west as the Makran Coast toward Iran, north and east into Punjab and even the upper Ganges River valley, and south and east to Dholavira in Kutch, and on to the banks of the Narmada River.

What was the relationship between this civilization and that of Mesopotamia? At first, many scholars assumed that the Indus valley people learned the art of city-building from the Sumerians and other peoples of Mesopotamia. But later scholars have argued that Harappa was not a derivative of Mesopotamia but had grown up independently. It is conceivable that the civilizations of both Mesopotamia and the Indus had a common ancestor in the settlements of the hills and mountains between them.

Written records, the key that re-opened the civilizations of ancient Mesopotamia and Egypt, are scarce in the Indus valley. The only written materials so far discovered are seal inscriptions that give only limited information. In addition, scholars have not succeeded in their attempts to decipher the script; they differ substantially in their interpretations. As a result, our understanding of Indus civilization is limited. Artifactual remains give a good representation of the physical cities and settlements, but not of their institutions. Moreover, while we can make educated guesses about the function and meaning of the remaining artifacts and physical structures from our own perspective, we do not have the words of the Harappans themselves to explain their own understanding of their civilization.

The Design and Construction of Well-planned Cities

Archaeological evidence to date reveals an urban civilization with its roots beginning as early as 7000 B.C.E. in simple settlements, such as Mehrgarh in the hills. Over the millennia, people moved down into the plains and river valley. At first, they may have moved into the forested river valley only in the colder months, herding their flocks of sheep and cattle, including the humped zebu, back to the hills for the summer. Over time they may have decided to farm the river-watered alluvial lands of the valley. They began to trade by boat along the Indus and even down the Indus into the Arabian Sea and, further, into the Persian Gulf and up the Tigris and Euphrates into Mesopotamia. Goods from the Indus valley have been found in Mesopotamia and vice versa.

Crafts and the Arts. Crafts of the Indus valley included pottery making, dyeing, metal working in bronze, and bead making. Bead materials included jade from the Himalayas, lapis lazuli from Afghanistan, turquoise from Persia, amethyst from Mewar in India, and steatite, which was found locally. All of these items suggest an active interregional trade. Small sculptures in stone, terra cotta, and bronze appear to represent priestly or governmental officials, dancing girls, and, perhaps, mother goddesses. Since there are no accompanying texts to explain exact identities, these can only be guesses. Dice and small sculptures of bullock carts were probably used as toys and games. The first known use of cotton as a fiber for weaving textiles occurred in the Indus valley, introducing one of India's and the world's most enduring and important crops and crafts.

For an interactive version of this map, go to: http://www.prenhall.com/spodek/map3.2

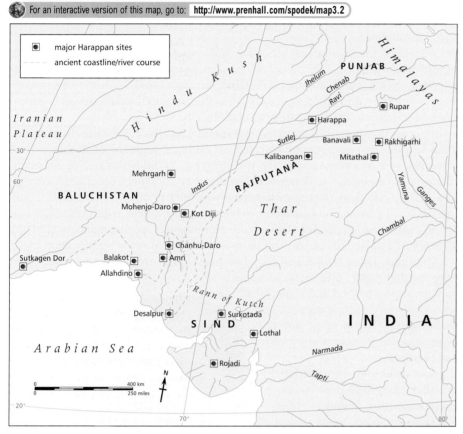

- ◉ major Harappan sites
- - - - ancient coastline/river course

Iranian Plateau
Himalayas
Hindu Kush
PUNJAB
Jhelum
Chenab
Ravi
◉ Rupar
◉ Harappa
Sutlej
Banavali ◉
◉ Rakhigarhi
30°
Kalibangan ◉
Mitathal ◉
Yamuna
Ganges
60°
Mehrgarh ◉
Indus
RAJPUTANA
BALUCHISTAN
Thar Desert
Mohenjo-Daro ◉
◉ Kot Diji
Chambal
◉ Chanhu-Daro
Sutkagen Dor ◉
Balakot ◉
◉ Amri
Allahdino ◉
Rann of Kutch
Desalpur ◉
◉ Surkotada
SIND
INDIA
◉ Lothal
Arabian Sea
Narmada
◉ Rojadi
Tapti
0 400 km
0 250 miles
N
20°
70°
80°

Cities of the Indus. Confined to the north and west by mountains, and to the east by desert, the Indus valley had, by 2500 B.C.E., developed a sophisticated urban culture based on individual walled cities, sharing common patterns of urban design. In terms of geographical extent this civilization was the largest in the world in its time.

Planned Cities. With an area of 150 acres, and about 40,000 inhabitants, Mohenjo-Daro was a thriving Indus city. Excavations reveal a raised citadel area, containing ceremonial and administrative buildings, and a residential quarter centered on boulevards about 45 feet wide, with grid-patterned streets, an underground sewerage and drainage system, and a range of brick-built dwellings.

Carefully Planned Cities. By about 2500 B.C.E., a thriving civilization encompassing 1000 known sites reached its apex and maintained it for about 500 years. Each of the two largest settlements, Harappa and Mohenjo-Daro, had a core area of about 3 miles in circumference, while Mohenjo-Daro also had a suburb—residential or industrial—about a mile away. Each city accommodated about 40,000 people.

Both cities share similar features of design. To the north is a citadel, or raised area; to the south is a lower town. In Mohenjo-Daro, the citadel is built on an architectural platform about 45 feet above the plain, and it measures 1400 by 450 feet. On the summit was a vast, communal bath 8 feet deep and 23 by 29 feet in area. Numerous cubicles—perhaps small, individual baths—flanked it. Adjacent to the large bath was a huge open space, identified as a granary, where food was stored safe from possible flood. Other spaces may have been used for public meetings. Fortified walls mark the southeast corner, and it appears that the entire citadel was walled.

The lower city was laid out in a gridiron, with the main streets about 45 feet wide. Here were the private houses, almost every one with its own well, bathing space, and toilet, consisting of a brick seat over a drainage area. Brick-lined drains flushed by water carried liquid and solid waste to sumps, where it would be collected and carted away, probably to fertilize the nearby fields.

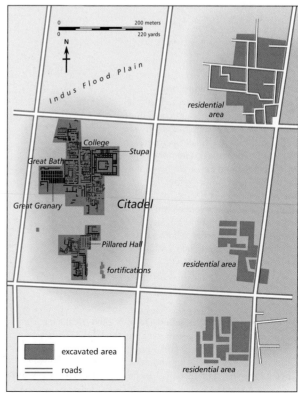

0 200 meters
0 220 yards
N
Indus Flood Plain
residential area
College
Stupa
Great Bath
Citadel
Great Granary
Pillared Hall
residential area
fortifications

- ▨ excavated area
- ══ roads

residential area

The town plan was orderly and regular. Even the prefabricated, fire-baked bricks were uniform in size and shape. A uniform system of weights and measures was also employed throughout.

Excavation of the two largest cities has now reached severe limits. The city of Harappa was vandalized for thousands of years before, as well as during, the railroad construction, and few artifacts remain to be discovered. Mohenjo-Daro sits on a high water table, and any deeper excavation threatens to flood the site. It is impossible to dig down to the foundation level of the city.

Further exploration of Mohenjo-Daro's surface, however, continues to yield fascinating results. A recent survey revealed an outlying segment of Mohenjo-Daro about a mile away from the known city. Was it part of an industrial area or a residential suburb? It is impossible to determine. The discovery, however, identifies Mohenjo-Daro as a larger city than Harappa. Perhaps it was the capital city of the civilization. The regularity of plan and construction suggests a government with great organizational and bureaucratic capacity, but no truly monumental architecture clearly marks the presence of a palace or temple, and there is little sign of social stratification in the plan or buildings. Those burials that have been discovered are regular, with the heads pointing to the north, and with some grave goods, such as pots of food and water, small amounts of jewelry, simple mirrors, and some cosmetics. These were not the extravagant royal burials of Egypt or even of Mesopotamia.

In more recent years additional Indus valley cities have been discovered and excavated, giving a fuller idea of the immense geographical extent of this civilization. The new excavations generally confirm the

Limestone dancing figure from Harappa, c. 2300–1750 B.C.E. This dancing figure displays a grasp of three-dimensional movement and vitality rare in the arts until much later periods. Human sculptures in contemporary Mesopotamia and Egypt are by contrast symbols of pure power, either immutable ideals of divinity or semidivine kingship. Indeed, this Harappan accomplishment is so extraordinary that some scholars have cast doubt on its early date. (*National Museum of India, New Delhi*)

Limestone bust from Mohenjo-Daro, c. 2300–1750 B.C.E. This half-figure with horizontal slits for eyes, flat thick lips, and fringes of beard is thought to have represented a priest or shaman because of the way the robe is hung over its left shoulder. Despite its monumental appearance, the figure is only 7 inches high. (*National Museum of Pakistan, Karachi*)

urban design patterns of the earlier finds, but they add some new elements. The excavations at Dholavira, in Kutch, India, for example, begun in the late 1980s, revealed immense, ornamented gates at the principal entrances to the city and playing fields in the area between upper and lower cities. Dholavira was not located on a river, but in the elevated center of a small region that may have formed an island during the monsoon, when water levels around it were highest. Huge cisterns were cut into the rock of the upper city for collecting rain water in this extremely arid area. Dholavira also demonstrates a stark contrast between the relatively spacious quarters of the upper city and the more modest accommodations of the lower. Among the 20,000 artifacts uncovered, however, the extraordinary extremes of wealth and poverty of Egypt and Mesopotamia do not appear.

Questions of Interpretation. Interpretations of Indus valley artifacts stress the apparent classlessness of the society, its equality, efficiency, and public conveniences. Some interpreters view these qualities negatively, equating them with oppressively rigid governments and drab lives. While some scholars emphasize that the Harappans apparently survived and prospered for centuries, others argue that the cities changed little over long periods of time and lacked the dynamism of the cities in Mesopotamia and Egypt. With no contemporary literature to guide us, interpretation of what is found is in the eyes, and the value system, of the beholder.

We also do not know if this uniform, planned civilization had a single capital city, or several regional capitals, or no centralized political system at all. We see careful planning in the urban forms, but we do not know if the Indus valley civilization developed urban institutions for governance, trade, religion, or worship, much less the quality of any such institutions. While Egypt had a state but, perhaps, few cities, the Indus valley had cities but no clearly delineated state. Indeed, some scholars argue that the Indus valley did not create state structures at all. Was it like Egypt before unification or after unification? Was it like Mesopotamia, with numerous city-states all participating in a single general culture? All three suggestions have been made.

Until the Harappan language is deciphered, its civilization will remain mysterious: How was it organized? Why did it disperse? How did it move eastward? In what ways did it enrich its successor, the Aryan civilization of the Ganges River valley?

Legacies of the Harappan Civilization

Interchange between the resident Harappans and the invading Aryans produced new, hybrid cultural forms that we know primarily from the Aryan records. Ironically, these records are almost entirely literary and artistic. Reversing the Harappan pattern, the early Aryans have left a treasure of literature, but virtually no architectural or design artifacts.

Four legacies of Harappa stand out. First, the Aryan invaders were a nomadic group, who must have adopted at least some of the arts of settlement and civilization from the already settled residents. Second, as newcomers to the ecological zones of India, the Aryans must also have learned methods of farming and animal husbandry from the Harappans. Later, however, as they migrated eastward into the Ganges valley, they confronted

EARLY SCIENCE AND TECHNOLOGY (7000–1000 B.C.E.)	
7000–6000	Pottery made in Middle East
c. 5500	Copper, gold, and silver worked in Mesopotamia and Egypt
c. 4000–3500	In Asia and Africa, potter's wheel and kiln invented; mud bricks used; spindle developed for spinning; basket-making begins
c. 3500–3000	Plow and cart invented; bronze cast and cuneiform writing developed in Sumer
3100	Reed boats in Egypt and Assyria; appearance of hieroglyphs in Egypt
3000	Cotton cultivated in the Indus valley
c. 2500	Wooden boats used in Egypt; ink and papyrus writing material used
2050	First glass in Mesopotamia
1790	Mathematics and medicine practiced in Babylon
1740	War chariots introduced from Persia to Mesopotamia (and later Egypt)
1370	Alphabetic script used in western Syria
1000	Industrial use of iron in Egypt and Mesopotamia

HOW DO WE KNOW?

The Decline of Harappan Civilization

By about 2000 B.C.E. the architecture of the Indus civilization began to decline. New buildings and repairs to existing structures lacked attention to quality and detail. Residents began to leave the cities and towns along the Indus and to relocate northeastward into the Punjab to towns such as Kalibangan, and southeastward to towns such as Lothal in Gujarat. Meanwhile, newcomers—squatters—seem to have moved into the old cities.

Again, a variety of arguments suggest the reasons for the decline in the cities and the geographical redistribution of their populations. Perhaps the river changed course or became erratic; perhaps the soil became too saline; perhaps the forests were cut down and the topsoil eroded.

An older opinion—that the Indus civilization was destroyed by the invasion of Aryan peoples from somewhere northwest of India—is now less widely held. It rested on Harappan archaeological evidence and Aryan literature. Several sets of skeletal remains in Mohenjo-Daro indicate violent deaths, while Aryan religious texts suggest that the invaders burned and destroyed existing settlements. The Rigveda, one of the earliest and most important of these texts, tells of the destructive power of the god Indra:

> With all-outstripping chariot-wheel, O Indra, thou far-famed, hast overthrown the twice ten kings of men
> With sixty thousand nine and ninety followers …
> Thou goest on from fight to fight intrepidly, destroying castle after castle here with strength. (i, 53)
> … in kindled fire he burnt up all their weapons,
> And made him rich with kine and carts and horses. (ii, 15)

The Aryan god of fire, Agni, is still more fearsome:

> Through fear of you the dark people went away, not giving battle, leaving behind their possessions, when, O Vaisvanara, burning brightly for Puru, and destroying the cities, you did shine. (7.5.3)

Newer archaeological evidence, however, suggests that the decline, de-urbanization, and dispersal of the Indus civilization seem to have preceded the Aryan invasion. Further evidence suggests that the Aryans may not have swept into the region in a single all-conquering expedition, but in a series of smaller waves of immigration. The arrival of the Aryans may have only completed the Harappan decay.

- Why does the formation of new cities such as Kalibangan and Lothal suggest the decline of the Indus Valley civilization?
- Why did scholars once believe that Aryan invasions destroyed the Indus Valley civilization? Why do they now question that belief?
- What is the range of alternative explanations that have been offered? Why are scholars uncertain about the accuracy of these explanations?

a new ecology based on rice cultivation and the use of iron. Here Harappan skills were useless. Third, a three-headed figure frequently appearing in Harappan seals resembles later representations of the Aryan god Shiva. Perhaps an earlier Harappan god may have been adopted and adapted by the Aryans.

Finally, the Aryan caste system, which ranked people at birth according to family occupation, color, and ritual purity, and prescribed the people with whom they may enter into social intercourse and marry, may reflect the need of the Aryans to regulate relationships between themselves and the Harappans. To claim and maintain their own supremacy, the Aryans may have elaborated the social structures of an early caste system and relegated the native inhabitants to permanent low status within it.

The Aryan groups grew increasingly skilled and powerful as they moved east. The first known archaeological evidence of their urban structures dates to about 700 B.C.E. and is found in the Ganges valley. We will read more about it when we analyze the first Indian empire in Chapter 8.

THE CITIES OF THE NILE AND THE INDUS WHAT DIFFERENCE DO THEY MAKE?

To what extent do the river valley civilizations of the Indus and the Nile confirm or alter our views of the significance of cities? They do show us that cities come in very different forms and networks. In Mesopotamia they had appeared as warring city-states. Along the Nile they were part of a single state that was first unified by about

3000 B.C.E., and they continued to be unified through most of the next 2500 years. By 2000 B.C.E. they formed the core of an imperial state with foreign conquests. In the Indus valley we do not know if the cities were independent city-states or part of a unified state; it is apparent, however, from their design and cultural products that they were part of a single cultural unit. In all three areas, then, the city created the state and gave concrete form to its value system.

We also learn of the significance of archaeological and textual study in unearthing and recovering all these early civilizations. To greater or lesser degrees, all had been lost to history for thousands of years before being exhumed by scholars in the nineteenth and twentieth centuries. In the task of reconstruction, written records have been critical to understanding the social structures and value systems of these cities. In both Mesopotamia and the Nile valley, excavations and written records enable us to see clearly the presence of cosmo-magical religious elements, alliances between rulers and priests, extensive temple complexes and, in Egypt, burial complexes as well, and, in both civilizations, extensive specialization of labor and social stratification. But before we take these characteristics as the normal ancestry of city life, we pause at the Indus valley excavations, for here we see no record of such intense occupation with the otherworldly or the afterlife. We see no record of such extensive specialization of labor nor of such extreme stratification—although the more recent excavations at Dholavira exhibit significant differences between the richest and poorest residential areas. We also see little evidence of the levels of artistic accomplishments of Mesopotamia and Egypt. And, of course, without texts, we have no clear record of religious, philosophical, legal, or administrative systems in the Indus valley.

The citadel of Mohenjo-Daro, c. 2300 B.C.E. and later. The citadel at Mohenjo-Daro, a massive, mud-filled embankment that rises 43 feet above the lower city, was discovered by archaeologist Daya Ram Sahni while investigating the second-century C.E. Buddhist stupa (burial mound) that can be seen in the distance. The citadel's summit houses the remains of several impressive structures, of which the most prominent is the so-called Great Bath (foreground).

To further explore the global legacy of city and state formation, we now turn to four other regions of indigenous, early city and state formation in places far from those we have studied and far from each other: the Yellow River valley of China, Mesoamerica, South America, and the Niger River valley of West Africa. We are in for some surprises.

Review Questions

- Why is it difficult to determine which Egyptian settlements are cities? Why is Hierakonpolis sometimes called a city, although more often it is designated a very large settlement?
- In what ways did their belief in an afterlife influence the cities that the Egyptians built?
- What can we learn about cities from the autobiographical account by Si-Nuhe of his experience in exile and his return to the capital city of Lisht?
- What kinds of information are available in the written records of Egypt, and of Mesopotamia, that are unavailable for the Indus valley due to the scarcity of written materials and our inability to decipher them?
- In light of the discovery of the likely origins of the Indus valley civilization in the foothills to the west, and of its extensions as far north as Punjab and as far south as the Narmada river, is it appropriate to continue to call it "the Indus valley civilization?" Why or why not? If not, what other name might you give it?
- What is the evidence that scholars use to argue that the Indus valley civilization was more egalitarian, with less class differentiation, than the civilizations of the Nile valley and Mesopotamia?

Suggested Readings

PRINCIPAL SOURCES

Baines, John and Jaromir Malek. *Atlas of Ancient Egypt* (New York: Facts on File Publications, 1980). Another comprehensive and excellent introduction from these publishers, with well-chosen and copious maps, pictures, and charts.

Fagan, Brian. *People of the Earth: An Introduction to World Prehistory* (Upper Saddle River, NJ: Prentice Hall, 10th ed., 2000). The best available textbook introduction to prehistory.

Foster, John L., trans. and ed. *Ancient Egyptian Literature* (Austin, TX: University of Texas Press, 2001). A fine anthology of varied forms of literature, culled from the translator/editors of many previous collections, plus a few new pieces.

Hawass, Z. *Silent Images: Women in Pharaonic Egypt* (New York: Harry N. Abrams, 2000).

Kuhrt, Amélie, *The Ancient Near East, c. 3000–330 B.C.*, 2 vols (New York: Routledge, 1995).

Lesko, Barbara, "Women of Egypt and the Ancient Near East," in *Becoming Visible: Women in European History*, 2nd ed., ed. Renata Bridenthal, Claudia Koonz, and Susan Stuard (Boston, MA: Houghton Mifflin, 1998).

Lesko, Barbara S., ed. *Women's Earliest Records: From Ancient Egypt and Western Asia* (Atlanta, GA: Scholar's Press, 1989).

Manley, Bill. *The Penguin Historical Atlas of Ancient Egypt* (New York: Penguin Books, 1996). Through maps and pictures, an excellent review of Egyptian history from pre-dynastic times through Alexander's conquest. Special sections include coverage of foreign relations and warfare, urbanization, and women. Special emphasis on trade.

Nashat, Guity. " Women in the ancient Middle East," in *Restoring Women to History* (Bloomington, IN: Indiana University Press, 1999).

Past Worlds: The (London) Times Atlas of Archaeology (Maplewood, NJ: Hammond, Inc., 1988). The best available introduction to the archaeological exploration of the world, with attractive and useful maps, pictures, diagrams.

Possehl, Gregory L., ed. *Harappan Civilization: A Recent Perspective* (New Delhi: Oxford University Press and IBH Publishing, 2nd ed., 1993). An comprehensive update of the research.

Spodek, Howard and Doris Meth Srinivasan, eds. *Urban Form and Meaning in South Asia: The*

Shaping of Cities from Prehistoric to Precolonial Times (Washington: National Gallery of Art, 1993). The papers of an international conference by some of the leading archaeologists working in South Asian urbanization including Michael Janson, Jean-Francois Jarrige, Jim Shaffer, and others on the Indus valley civilization and its legacy.

ADDITIONAL SOURCES

Aldred, Cyril. *The Egyptians* (New York: Thames and Hudson, 1986). Useful general introduction, well illustrated.

Allchin, Bridget and Raymond. *The Birth of Indian Civilization: India and Pakistan before 500 B.C.* (Baltimore, MD: Penguin Books, 1968). Now dated, but clear and comprehensive introduction to what we know and how we know it by archaeologists who stress the archaeological record.

Fairservis, Walter. *The Roots of Ancient India* (Chicago, IL: University of Chicago Press, 2nd ed., 1975). An archaeologist's clear and accessible account of his own findings and those of his colleagues up to the date of publication.

Hassan, Fekri A. "The Predynastic of Egypt," *Journal of World Prehistory* II, No. 2 (June 1988), 135–85. Careful and comprehensive account of the research.

Kemp, Barry J. *Ancient Egypt: Anatomy of a Civilization* (London: Routledge, 1989). Stresses what we know about the social structures of ancient Egypt.

Lichtheim, Miriam. *Ancient Egyptian Literature: A Book of Readings* (Berkeley, CA: University of California Press, 3 vols., 1973). Wide-ranging, comprehensive account of 3000 years of literature.

Mumford, Lewis. *The City in History* (New York: Harcourt Brace, and World, 1961). Mumford looks only at cities of the western world, but he is thoughtful, opinionated, and persuasive on what makes a good city.

Noble Wilford, John. "Egypt Carvings Set Earlier Date for Alphabet," *New York Times* (November 14, 1999), A–1, 16. Records the discovery of the earliest alphabetic writing yet discovered.

Possehl, Gregory L., ed. *Ancient Cities of the Indus* (New Delhi: Vikas Publishing, 1979). Scholarly resume of what was known and debated among archaeologists up to the date of publication by an archaeologist practicing primarily in Gujarat.

Pritchard, James B., ed. *Ancient Near Eastern Texts Relating to the Old Testament* (Princeton, NJ: Princeton University Press, 3rd ed. 1969). The most comprehensive and accessible anthology of texts. Presented with full scholarly annotation.

Time-Life Books. *Time Frame 3000–1500: The Age of God-Kings* (Alexandria, VA: Time-Life Books, 1987). Beautifully illustrated, popular presentation of early civilizations including Mesopotamia, Nile valley, and Indus valley.

Wenke, Robert J. "The Evolution of Early Egyptian Civilization: Issues and Evidence," *Journal of World Prehistory* V, No. 1 (September 1991), 279–329. Historiographic study of what we know and how we know.

Wheatley, Paul. *Pivot of the Four Quarters* (Chicago, IL: Aldine Publishing Company, 1971). Very scholarly presentation of the argument that early cities were mostly cosmo-magical cities. Primary focus is China, but total range is global.

Wheeler, Mortimer. *Civilizations of the Indus Valley and Beyond* (London: Thames and Hudson, 1966). Head of the Archaeological Survey of India presents a clear view of its findings in layman's terms.

World History Documents CD-ROM

1.6 Daily Life in Egypt
1.7 A Humble Farmer Pleads His Own Case: The Workings of Ma'at
1.8 Some Commonsense Advice from the Scribe Any to His Son

A POLYCENTRIC WORLD

CITIES AND STATES IN EAST ASIA, THE AMERICAS, AND WEST AFRICA 1700 B.C.E.–1000 C.E.

4

KEY TOPICS
- China: The Xia, Shang, and Zhou Dynasties
- The Western Hemisphere: Mesoamerica and South America
- West Africa: The Niger River Valley

This chapter completes the survey of the seven areas of primary urbanization. It covers the four areas that developed primary urbanization somewhat more recently: the Yellow River valley of China; two regions of the western hemisphere—Mesoamerica and the South American Pacific coastal plain with the adjacent Andes Mountains that tower above it; and the Niger River valley of West Africa. The first cities in these regions date from as early as 1700 B.C.E. in China to as late as 400 C.E. in the Niger valley. They include cities that were not in major river valleys as well as some that were. They all show at least some evidence of state formation, long-distance trade, and religious practices. But they include settlements that did not have written languages and records, and therefore require us to base our understanding entirely on the archaeological record. In at least one of them—west Africa—the settlement pattern is so different from urbanization elsewhere that we are asked to stretch our definition of urbanization and challenge our value system in assessing the significance of it.

CHINA: THE XIA, SHANG, AND ZHOU DYNASTIES

The Earliest Villages

As early as the eighth millennium B.C.E., Neolithic pottery decorations marked the transition from hunting and gathering into the culture of farming and village life. This Yangshao culture, first excavated in 1921, was named for the location where it was discovered in China's western Henan province. Among other fascinating finds, in late 1999 archaeologists uncovered a set of tiny flutes carved some 9000 years ago from the wing bones of a large bird. Three thousand years older than the next known playable instruments, from Sumer, one of them is still playable.

The Yangshao lasted to *c.* 2700 B.C.E. Farmers of this era grew millet, wheat, and rice, and domesticated pigs, dogs, goats, and perhaps horses. They lived mostly in river valleys, and the villages were often surrounded with earthen walls for defense. Ban Po is the best excavated village of the Yangshao culture (see Turning Point, p. 36). From archaeological evidence, it appears that individual nuclear families occupied dwellings, but there was also a larger building found that may have housed clan meetings.

Slightly later and slightly to the northeast, a more sophisticated Neolithic culture, the Longshan, grew up. The people of the Longshan made their pottery on wheels, whereas the Yangshao had coiled or molded their pots by hand. The Longshan people domesticated sheep and cattle, which were not seen in Yangshao sites. Longshan graves were dug under their own homes, while the Yangshao had buried their dead in

Opposite **Warrior ear ornament (above), cleaned and reconstructed (tomb 1), and spider bead (below), cleaned and reconstructed (tomb 3), Moche Royal Tombs, Sipan, Peru, 1st–6th centuries C.E.** The spider that captures its prey in webs and later extracts its vital fluids, and the warrior—along with other human, animal, and ornamental grave goods—suggest a culture dominated by powerful warrior priests.

AT A GLANCE : CHINA

DATE	POLITICAL	RELIGION AND CULTURE	SOCIAL DEVELOPMENT
8000 B.C.E.		■ Neolithic decorated pottery	■ Simple Neolithic society established
5000 B.C.E.	■ Yangshao culture in China (5000–2700)	■ Marks on Yangshao pottery possibly writing	■ Penal code; defensive structures round villages
3500 B.C.E.	■ Longshan late Neolithic culture	■ Delicate Longshan ceramics	■ Farming, with domesticated animals
2000 B.C.E.	■ Xia dynasty (2205–1766) ■ Shang dynasty (1766–1122) ■ City of Zhengzhou (c. 1700) ■ Under Shang, bronze vases found in ceremonial burials	■ The "sage kings" in China known from legend; first known use of writing in this area	■ Agricultural progress ■ Cities (by 1700) under control of Shang kings
1100 B.C.E.	■ Zhou dynasty (1100–256)	■ Poetry extant from Zhou period	■ Under Zhou, iron, money, and written laws in use
500 B.C.E.	■ Warring States period (480–222) ■ Qin Dynasty (221–206)	■ Confucius (d. 479) ■ Great Wall of China begun (214) to keep out Xiongnu	■ Crossbow invented (c. 350)
100 B.C.E.		■ Sima Qian (d. 85)	

Burial pit, unearthed at Liulihe, Hebei province, Western Zhou period. Evidence for the centrality of ritual in ancient Chinese culture can be found in this tomb, which contains the remains of horses and chariots. These important instruments of rule would have been regarded as valuable offerings to the gods and were thus buried along with their owner.

graveyards far from their villages. Sometimes Longshan funeral urns were cemented into foundation walls, suggesting ancestor worship.

Several hundred miles to the east, somewhat further down the Yellow River in Shandong, and one or two centuries later, yet another branch of Longshan culture developed, with yet another distinct type of pottery, often distinctively reddish-brown and gray in color, quite different from the black pottery of the Longshan of Henan. Although the high points of Yangshao and the western and eastern Longshan cultures appeared at successively later times, they overlapped each other to a considerable extent.

The Henan Longshan culture seems to have been a harsh one. Excavations reveal the burials of victims of killing, some decapitated and showing signs of struggle, suggesting warfare between villages. The defensive walls of pounded earth that encircle some of the villages support this hypothesis, as does the presence of bronze knives.

The Beginnings of State Formation

Out of these struggles among villages, larger political units gradually emerged. Ancient Chinese historical texts tell of three early dynasties—the Xia, the Shang, and the Zhou—that ruled over large regions of China. In its time, each ruled over the most powerful single kingdom among the embattled states of northern China. All were based primarily around the Huang He (Yellow River) valley in north China. State formation may have begun under the Xia, c. 2205–1766 B.C.E., although records are too sparse to recreate its cities and institutions. The archaeological record on urbanization under the Shang, c. 1766–1122 B.C.E., is far more revealing and reliable. The Zhou, c. 1100–256 B.C.E., consolidated both city and state, and left extensive archaeological remains and written records.

None of the three dynasties succeeded in annexing all its enemies and building a single unified empire. That process would come later.

The traditional chronological dating suggests that the states succeeded one another, but recent evidence indicates that there may, in fact, have been considerable overlap. For centuries, they may have coexisted in neighboring regions, with first one, then another, having comparatively greater power and prestige.

By the time of the Shang, if not already in the Xia dynasty, people had founded cities in north China as centers of administration and ritual. State formation was well under way, and cities served as capitals and administrative centers. An urban network ruled the entire dynastic state. Capitals were frequently shifted, suggesting that new rulers wanted to make their mark through new construction, or that confrontations with neighboring, enemy states required strategic redeployments for improving offensive or defensive positions. Kings frequently entrusted the regional cities and their administrations to their blood relatives. It appears that rulers performed productive economic functions for their subjects, especially in water control. The ability to organize huge work gangs to construct irrigation channels and dikes for flood control confirmed their power and status. As a result, the lineages on top lived lives of considerable wealth while those on the lower levels had little, as sharp class differences emerged in the early dynastic states. The cemeteries of different classes were geographically segregated into different neighborhoods within the city and its suburbs, and were of different quality.

Like primary cities in other parts of the world, the Chinese cities were also religious centers, with the kings presiding over rituals as well as administration and warfare. Indeed, the warfare was necessary to supply the human and animal sacrifices that were central to the rituals.

Early Evidence of Writing. One of these early rituals has left us evidence of a crucial development in Chinese civilization—the invention of writing. Oracle bones—bones of birds, animals, and especially the shells of turtles—were inscribed with markings and writings for use in predicting the future. After they were marked, these bones were placed in a fire and tapped lightly with a rod until they began to crack. The cracks were then interpreted by specialists in predicting the future. A poem from the later Zhou dynasty noted the use of oracle bones in deciding the location of a new city:

The plain of Chou was very fertile,
Its celery and sowthistle sweet as rice-cakes.
"Here we will make a start; here take counsel,
Here notch our [turtle]."
It says, "Stop," it says, "Halt.
Build houses here." (Chang, *Shang Civilization*, pp. 31–2)

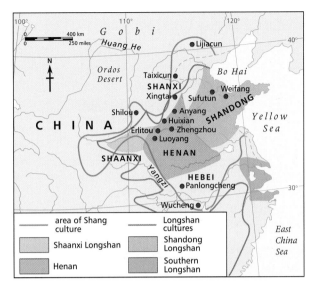

Shang China. Centered where the Huang He (Yellow River) enters its floodplain from the mountains of northeast China, the Longshan farming communities of about 2500 B.C.E benefited from rich alluvial soils and extensive metal ore deposits. By 1800 B.C.E. a powerful, highly organized, urban, metal-working culture, the Shang, had developed.

Inscribed oracle bone, China. Shang kings communicated with their ancestors through both sacrificial rituals and divination. Diviners would pose questions—about health, harvest, or politics—by applying a red-hot poker to animal bones or turtle shells and then analyze the resulting heat-induced cracks. (*East Asian Library, Columbia University*)

EARLY CHINESE CULTURE

5000 (B.C.E.)	Rice cultivation, basketry, weaving, use of wooden tools, primitive writing
3000	Domestication of sheep, cattle, water buffalo
2000	Human grave sacrifices
1900	Metal working, class system, domestication of horse
1200	Chariots in warfare

Some of the oracle bone inscriptions confirm the names and approximate dates of Xia and Shang rulers. Other bones suggest that their purpose was to communicate with the gods. The location of the bones and the content of their inscriptions encouraged archaeologists to search further in the north central Chinese plains, near the point where the Yellow River flows out of the mountains for evidence of China's early dynastic period.

Historical Evidence of the Xia Dynasty. Chinese legend long spoke of three ancient dynasties—the Xia, the Shang, and the Zhou. While many written records exist on the Zhou dynasty, historians were often skeptical of the existence of the earlier dynasties until relatively recently. At Erlitou, east of Luoyang, in western Henan, archaeologists found a culture in precisely the areas described by ancient texts as the

HOW DO WE KNOW?

Ancient China

Three kinds of sources provide most of our direct information about early Chinese cities and dynasties: written texts, oracle bones, and artifacts uncovered archaeologically. (Scholars also sometimes take records, such as poetry, from later eras and infer that they may represent earlier conditions as well, as we shall see in the next pages.)

Texts
We have no literary texts remaining from the Xia and Shang dynasties. Some scholars believe that the Zhou dynasty destroyed those that did exist. Much later texts ascribed to the Chinese teacher Confucius (551–479 B.C.E.) refer to the Xia and Shang dynasties, but give little detail. Later, Sima Qian (Ssu-ma Ch'ien; c. 145–85 B.C.E.), court historian of the Han dynasty, wrote the first of China's official historical annals. Sima, who had access to many texts that have not survived, devoted a chapter to the Shang royal house beginning with its legendary founder Xie, who located his capital to a town called Shang, now believed to have been in eastern Henan. Successive rulers moved this capital eight times. Xie's fourteenth successor, Tang, established the hereditary dynasty of Shang. Sima's sources of information were limited, however, and his chapter mostly outlined the genealogy of the rulers, recounted moralistic tales of their rule, and briefly noted their capital cities.

Oracle Bones
A new source of information came to light in the 1890s and early 1900s. Numerous oracle bones—some apparently hidden away for many years, others recently uncovered—appeared in antique markets in China. Over the decades more than 10,000 were discovered, mostly in the central plains of north China. These bones of birds and animals, and shells of turtles, were inscribed with symbolic notations, placed in a fire, and tapped with a rod until they began to crack. Specialists then "read" the marks to predict the future.

Some of the oracle-bone inscriptions confirmed Sima Qian's accounts of early Shang rulers. The location of the bones and the content of their inscriptions encouraged archaeologists to search further for additional oracle bones and other artifacts in the area around the ancient Shang capital of Anyang.

Archaeology
Archaeology was in fashion in China in the 1920s. Peking Man had been discovered at Zhoukoudian, and in the process a new generation of Chinese archaeologists had received on-the-job training. Meanwhile, the new "doubting antiquity" school of Chinese historiography began to question the dating and to challenge the authenticity of many ancient Chinese historical events. In response, the newly established National Research Institute of History and Philology dispatched the

young archaeologist Dong Zobin to explore the Anyang region. Dong recommended excavating for oracle bones. These excavations, mostly under the direction of Li Ji, uncovered not only bones but also sites from the Shang dynasty. These led to the discovery of artifacts from earlier eras as well. Scholars understood these to be evidence of the existence of the Xia dynasty. Ancient texts, bronzes, oracle bones, and excavations reinforced one another in recounting parts of ancient China's urbanization and state formation. Civil war in China, beginning in 1927, and war with Japan, beginning in 1937 (see Chapter 20), interrupted excavations until 1950, but since then continuous archaeological research has yielded new understandings.

* What historical evidence enabled the Xia dynasty to emerge from the realm of legend to its current status as the accepted first dynasty of ancient China?
* Politics and fashion as well as scholarly motives influence the kind of research that archaeologists can and do undertake. Please discuss this assertion in terms of the excavation of the sites of early Chinese cities and dynasties.
* What kinds of skills do you think a "reader" of oracle bones must have had to be successful? What would have been considered success in this profession?

site of the legendary Xia dynasty. The pottery at Erlitou seemed intermediate in style and quality between the earlier Longshan and the later Shang. Although the link is not certain, many archaeologists took Erlitou to be representative of the Xia dynasty.

The Xia, like the later Shang and Zhou, seems to have been ruled by specific internal clans, each with its own king. As in many cultures, kingship and kinship were linked. As head of both his biological clan and his geographical realm, the king performed rituals, divinations, and sacrifices; waged war; constructed irrigation and flood control works; and administered his government. The king mediated between the world of the spirits and the world of humans. He was thought to be descended from the god of the spirits who controlled human health, wealth, agriculture, and warfare. The king's assertion of his right to perform sacrifice in any particular place was, in effect, his assertion of his right to rule over that place. Rights over ritual implied rights over land and people.

Another critical task of the ruler was taming the waters of the mighty, and hazardous, Yellow River. China's first settlements had avoided the immediate flood plain of the Yellow River, one of the most treacherous in the world. Its bed filled with the silt from the mountains, the Yellow River has jumped its course twenty-six times in recorded history, wreaking untold devastation. As early as the Longshan culture, people built great levees and canals for flood control, drainage, and irrigation. Chinese legend credits the first success in taming the Yellow River to one of the cultural heroes of ancient history, Yu the Great of the twenty-third century B.C.E., legendary founder of the Xia dynasty. The legend reflects the reality of a royal house's gaining power in part through its ability to organize great gangs of laborers to construct a system of water control.

The Xia dynasty went further with human organization. It assembled armies, built cities, carved jade, cast and worked bronze into both weapons and ritual vessels, created the pictograms that would evolve into Chinese script, and may have designed China's first calendar.

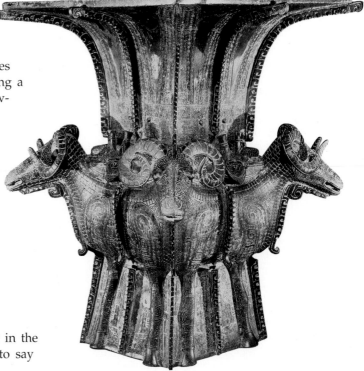

Shang dynasty bronze wine vessel, fourteenth to eleventh century B.C.E. The thousands of Shang bronze vessels that survive today continue to astonish us with their technical mastery and elegance. They testify to the elite's willingness to devote huge quantities of a precious resource to ritual purposes. During times of war, such bronzes were often melted down to produce weapons but once peace resumed, they were recast into ritual objects. (*Historical Museum, Beijing*)

Similarities Among the Three Dynasties. All three of these earliest dynasties, the Xia, Shang, and Zhou, built walled towns. Indeed, in written Chinese the same character, *cheng*, represents both city and city wall. At times these towns were loosely connected to one another, forming a network of rule and trade. At other times, when a single powerful king headed the dynasty, a single capital city predominated. Archaeologists see many similarities among the towns and the political structures of all three dynasties.

In the absence of earlier written records, scholars sometimes use literary evidence from later dynasties as evidence for patterns in the earlier dynasties. For example, in arguing for the supremacy of royal rule during the Shang Dynasty, they find supporting proof from "Pei shan," a poem of the Zhou dynasty:

> Everywhere under Heaven
> Is no land that is not the king's
> To the borders of all those lands
> None but is the king's slave. (trans. Arthur Waley)

There is some evidence that women could wield power in the earliest of Chinese dynasties, but it is otherwise difficult to say much about gender relations in ancient China. By the time of the Shang dynasty, however, all evidence points to China as a very patriarchal society wherein women had many fewer options than men.

City and State under the Shang and Zhou

By the time of the Shang dynasty, the ruler directly controlled a growing network of towns. The king ruled from his capital city. He apportioned regional cities to his designated representatives, who were usually blood relatives. These relatives received

SOURCE

The Cosmo-Magical City

In his classic and convincing Pivot of the Four Quarters, *Paul Wheatley argues that ancient Chinese cities, like most ancient cities, began as ritual centers. He calls these cities "cosmo-magical." Archaeological and textual records support this interpretation for China. Consider, for example, this Zhou poem illustrating the siting of a royal capital. The process begins with reading the oracle shell of a tortoise to determine its location and ends with sacrifices to mark the completion of construction:*

Of old Tan-fu the duke
At coming of day galloped his horses,
Going west along the river bank
Till he came to the foot of Mount Ch'i.
Where with the lady Chiang
He came to look for a home.

The plain of Chou was very fertile,
Its celery and sowthistle sweet as rice-cakes.
"Here we will make a start; here take counsel,
Here notch our tortoise."
It says, "Stop," it says, "Halt.
Build houses here."

So he halted, so he stopped,
And left and right
He drew the boundaries of big plots and little,
He opened up the ground, he counted the acres
From west to east;
Everywhere he took his task in hand.

Then he summoned his Master of Works,
Then he summoned his Master of Lands
And made them build houses
Dead straight was the plumb-line,
The planks were lashed to hold the earth;
They made the Hall of Ancestors, very venerable.

They tilted in the earth with a rattling,
They pounded it with a dull thud,

They beat the walls with a loud clang,
They pared and chiselled them with a faint *p'ing, p'ing*;
The hundred cubits all rose;
The drummers could not hold out.

They raised the outer gate;
The outer gate soared high.
They raised the inner gate;
The inner gate was very strong.
They raised the great earth-mound,
Whence excursions of war might start.

The rituals seem to have conferred worldly benefits. Potential enemies fled. The poem continues:

And in the time that followed they did not abate their sacrifices
Did not let fall their high renown;
The oak forests were laid low,
Roads were opened up.
The K'un tribes scampered away;
Oh, how they panted!

Oracle records recognize more than twenty titles of officials grouped into three categories: ministers, generals, and archivists, "but the most important categories of officials insofar as our available data are concerned are the diviners … and the inquirers. . .. Jao Tsung-yi enumerated the activities of as many as 117 diviners and inquirers in the oracle records. Ch'en Meng-chia counted 120." (Chang, p. 192)

Besides the diviners, a cadre of priests performed religious rituals, including human sacrifices.

Military force was needed to sustain these rituals, by providing the prisoners-of-war to be sacrificed when rituals demanded. Oracle records speak of Shang military campaigns of 3000, 5000, and even 13,000 troops. As many as 30,000 prisoners-of-war were claimed in one large battle, and 300 prisoners were sacrificed in a ritual of ancestor worship. Archaeological finds show that 600 humans were sacrificed at the completion of a single house; 164 for a single tomb.

title to land, shares in the harvests, and rights to build and control the regional capital cities. In exchange, they represented and served the king and his interests in the provinces.

Territorially, the Shang dynasty was always based in northern and central Henan and southwestern Shandong. At its most powerful it extended as far south as Wucheng, south of the Yangzi River; east to the Pacific, incorporating the Shandong Peninsula; north into Hebei and southern Manchuria; and west through Shanxi into the mountains of Shaanxi. At its greatest extent it may have controlled 40,000 square miles. On the fringes, Shang territories were interspersed with those of other rulers, and warfare between them was apparently frequent.

Early Royal Capitals. The capital shifted often, but always remained within the core area of Shang urbanization. One of the earliest capitals was located at Luoyang; later, and for many decades, it was at Zhengzhou; and, finally, *c.* 1384 B.C.E., at Anyang. Luoyang has been difficult to excavate because it lies directly under a modern city. Zhengzhou, however, has been excavated extensively. Founded *c.* 1700 B.C.E., its core covered about 1¼ square miles, enclosed by a wall 4½ miles long and, in places, still surviving to a height of 30 feet.

Inside the walled area lived the royal family, the nobility, and their retainers. Outside this palace/ritual center was a network of residential areas; workshops making bone, pottery, and bronze artifacts; and cemeteries. The class divisions written into this spatial pattern were reinforced by the geography of the suburbs: to the north were the dwellings and graves of the wealthy and powerful, marked by ritual bronze vessels and sacrificial victims; to the south were the dwellings of the commoners and their burial places in trash pits. Occupations tended to be inherited within specific family units (compare the caste system of India discussed in Chapters 8 and 9). Many *zu*, or lineage groups, corresponded to occupational groups.

Anyang: The Last Shang Capital. The final, most powerful, and most elaborate capital of the Shang dynasty was at Anyang. Shang texts report that the nineteenth king, Pan Gieng, moved his capital to Yin and that the dynasty remained there until its fall 273 years later. Archaeologists identify that site as Anyang. This capital was the center of a network of sites stretching about 200 miles from northwest to southeast. The core area around Anyang is difficult to excavate fruitfully. The city burned to the ground,

Headless skeletons of human sacrificial victims, tomb 1001, Anyang, China. The royal tombs discovered at Anyang testify to the wealth and power of the Shang rulers. Numerous servants and prisoners-of-war gave their lives willingly or unwillingly to accompany their masters to the grave. The heads of the decapitated figures shown here were located elsewhere in the tomb.

and farmers have been plowing the area, and robbers pillaging it, for 3000 years. Remains of royal graves and of buildings that appear to be royal palaces hint at the greatness of the ancient city, but they do not yield many secrets. Nonetheless scholars have found yields of bronze treasures in royal graves.

The Shang excelled in crafting bronze. They produced bronze axes, knives, spears, and arrowheads as well as bronze utensils, ritual vessels, and sculptures. They also used horse-drawn chariots, which may have been derived from Indo-Europeans who migrated into China. The ability to use bronze in their weapons gave Chinese kings and warriors a decided advantage over their enemies, but it appears that most bronze was crafted for ritual uses.

The Zhou Dynasty. The Shang dynasty fell to the Zhou around 1122 B.C.E., but it did not disappear, just as the Xia had not disappeared when it had fallen to the Shang. Instead, in defeat, these kingdoms continued to exist, albeit with diminished territories and powers. Until the Qin dynasty unified China in 221 B.C.E., the defeat of a dynasty did not mean that it completely disappeared. Rather, it became one of the many smaller kingdoms competing for power in continuous warfare in north China.

The Zhou survived for more than 600 years, making it one of the longest lasting Chinese dynasties. The Zhou made several important conceptual contributions to Chinese thinking about culture, politics, and military strategy. Moreover, with the advent of substantial written sources, we know much more about the Zhou than the earlier Chinese dynasties.

One of the most important written sources for Zhou political thought is the *Book of Documents*, which describes the Zhou conquest of the Shang. As is often the case, such a book is written from the perspective of the winners. In this case, the Zhou portray their victory as one of heroic soldiers over decadent soldiers led by a clueless king. Nonetheless, they wanted to portray their strong connections and good relations with previous kings so that they will appear legitimate.

They also develop a heretofore unique explanation of why they should be considered the legitimate rulers of the region: the idea of the "Mandate of Heaven." The *Book of History* assumed a close relationship between Heaven and the king, but the king only had the mandate to rule if he acted in the interests of the people. If a king was weak, the theory argued that others had the right to remove him, with the "Mandate of Heaven." This doctrine would shape Chinese thinking on leadership for centuries.

While they were in power, the Zhou made several important contributions to Chinese culture. One of the most important was the *Book of Songs*, which includes a collection of China's earliest poetry, some of which appears to have been from earlier societies and transmitted orally until it was recorded. The poetry focuses on the exploits of kings and aristocrats, but also provides powerful insights into family life and gender relations in early China.

One poem, for example, describes the anxiety of a woman who became too old to marry. It makes clear that men would pursue women in courtship and not the other way around and that the woman would leave her family to join her husband's. Others speak of a deep distrust of women in politics and argue that men alone should be in the public sphere and that women belonged at home. Challenging the notion of the Mandate of Heaven, at least one poem argues that women in politics, not Heaven, sowed disorder in dynasties. Still others deal with the give and take of seduction and love outside of marriage.

The Zhou also transformed warfare, turning away from the chariots that seemed so useful earlier. They both developed the cavalry in which soldiers fought successfully with bows and arrows on horseback, and introduced infantry troops of draft foot soldiers who could effectively fight the cavalry with crossbows.

The Zhou expanded significantly, creating a much larger state than that ruled by the Shang. Recognizing the difficulty of ruling such a large state, the Zhou created a decentralized administration that left much power in local hands. In the end, this contributed to much instability with the Zhou remaining in power at least nominally at the top, while Zhou rulers faced competition from subordinates throughout China. Because of the chaos, by 480 B.C.E. a period subsequent scholars have named "the Warring States period" emerged, which lasted until the Qin dynasty unified the country in 221 B.C.E. (We will continue with this discussion as China enters an imperial age, Chapter 5.)

THE WESTERN HEMISPHERE: MESOAMERICA AND SOUTH AMERICA

The first cities of the Americas share several characteristics with those of east Asia. They began as religious shrine centers, linked by shamans, individuals who had special powers to communicate with the spiritual world on behalf of the community. They developed into city-states with important functions in politics and trade as well as in religion, and some even incorporated whole empires under their sway. Specific individual cities, most notably Teotihuacán, had enormous cultural influence over other settlements that were spread across great distances.

AT A GLANCE : THE EARLY AMERICAS

DATE	POLITICAL	RELIGION AND CULTURE	SOCIAL DEVELOPMENT
6000 B.C.E.		■ Stone tools in Mexico (6700)	
5000 B.C.E.			■ Plants (including maize) cultivated in Mesoamerica
3000 B.C.E.			■ Villages established in Mesoamerica; gourds and beans grown
2500 B.C.E.	■ Maya culture originated (2000)	■ Pottery from Mesoamerica	
1500 B.C.E.	■ Olmecs, Gulf of Mexico (c. 1500 B.C.E.–400 B.C.E.) ■ Zapotecs, S. Mexico (1400 B.C.E–900 C.E.)	■ Olmec center of San Lorenzo; pottery, mirrors, ceramics	
1000 B.C.E.	■ Chavin, N. Peru (c. 900–200 B.C.E) ■ Tiwanaku, Bolivia (c. 800 B.C.E–1200 B.C.E.)		
200 B.C.E.	■ Moche, N. coast of Peru (200 B.C.E.–600 C.E.)	■ First Teotihuacán buildings, Valley of Mexico	
100 B.C.E.	■ Nazca, Peru (1–600 C.E.)		
500 C.E.	■ Maya culture (S. Mexico, Guatemala, Belize) at peak (325–900) ■ Huari, Peru (c. 650–800)	■ Teotihuacán population 100,000 ■ First fully developed towns in the Mississippi valley (c. 700) ■ Teotihuacán culture at peak (500–650)	
1000 C.E	■ Toltecs (c. 900–1170) ■ Chimu, N.W. Peruvian coast (c. 1000–1470)		
1200 C.E	■ Aztecs (c. 1100–1521) ■ Inca, Andean S. America (c. 1200–1535)	■ Aztec pictographs and hieroglyphs ■ Aztec gold, jade, and turquoise jewels, textiles, and sculptures	■ Aztec tribute empire over surrounding lands from capital of Cuzco

There were also great differences between the hemispheres. Geographically, the cities of the western hemisphere were built at water's edge, usually near lakes or small rivers, but not on major river systems. Technologically, the people of the Americas did not use metals in their tools. In fact, they hardly used metal at all except for ornaments, jewelry, and artwork. They used neither wheels nor draft animals in transportation, perhaps because the Americas had no large, domesticable animals to use for pulling carts until horses and cattle were introduced by the Spaniards. Llamas served as pack animals for small loads in the Andes in South America, but otherwise goods were carried by hand, dragged, or shipped by canoe. Construction and transportation were thus far more labor intensive than in most of Afro-Eurasia. Finally, except for the Maya, the native Americans did not create writing systems. Some, like the Zapotecs and Toltecs, used limited hieroglyphic symbols and calendar formats, but these did not develop into full, written languages. In Afro-Eurasia, only in the Niger River area did settlements grow into cities without developing writing systems.

In many respects, the cities of the western hemisphere still had one foot in the stone age. Urban society evolved much later in the Americas. Stone tools ground by hand first appeared in central Mexico about 6700 B.C.E.; the domestication of plants began about 5000 B.C.E.; villages were established about 3000 B.C.E.; pottery appeared about 2300 B.C.E.; and population suddenly increased in about 500 B.C.E. These processes were much slower than in the river-valley civilizations of Eurasia, perhaps because humans arrived in the New World relatively recently.

Origins: Migration and Agriculture

Humans arrived in the western hemisphere from across the Beringia land bridge (connecting Alaska and Siberia) about 15,000 years ago and then spread throughout both North and South America. By 5000 B.C.E., they were cultivating maize, at least in small quantities, as well as gathering wild crops and hunting animals. By around 3000 B.C.E. they also grew beans and gourds.

Archaeologists and botanists have documented the beginnings of domestication of maize in the valley of Tehuacan, 200 miles southeast of Mexico City. Beginning with wild corn cobs about 5000 B.C.E., farmers slowly bred larger and more nutritious varieties, producing an early form of modern corn about 2000 years ago. Later excavations in Peru showed that the cultivation of maize began there by 4000 B.C.E., perhaps introduced from Mesoamerica. In both regions, at about the same time, the other two staples of the American diet, beans and squashes, also appear. Further, in the Andes Mountains, potatoes and rootcrops were also grown. The valley of Mexico and the high Andes of Peru thus became incubators of much of the civilization of the Americas from an early date. Agricultural innovation, urbanization, and the foundation of empires originated in these regions and spread outward.

Mesoamerican Urbanization: The First Stages

By 2000 B.C.E., the agricultural foundations for an urban civilization were in place in Mesoamerica. Farmers throughout present-day Mexico and central America were cultivating maize, gourds, beans, and other food crops. In addition to farming dry fields, their methods included "slash-and-burn agriculture," which kept them moving from place to place in search of new land; "pot irrigation," dipping pots into wells and simply pouring the water onto the fields; canal irrigation; and, in low-lying swamplands, the creation of *chinampas*, raised fields or so-called "hanging gardens." *Chinampas* were created by piling up the mud and the natural vegetation of the swamps into grids of raised land crisscrossed by natural irrigation channels. When the

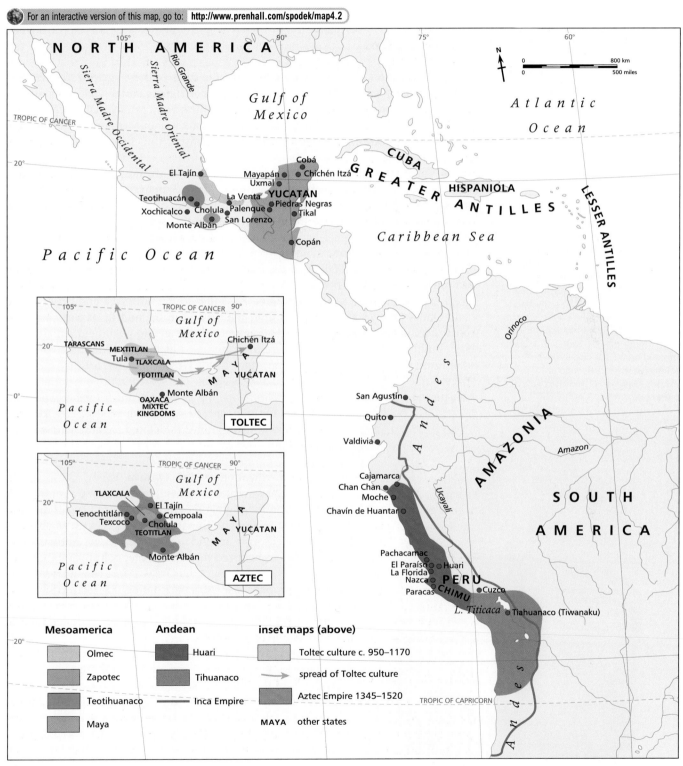

For an interactive version of this map, go to: http://www.prenhall.com/spodek/map4.2

Mesoamerica
- Olmec
- Zapotec
- Teotihuanaco
- Maya

Andean
- Huari
- Tihuanaco
- —— Inca Empire

inset maps (above)
- Toltec culture c. 950–1170
- → spread of Toltec culture
- Aztec Empire 1345–1520
- **MAYA** other states

Classic cultures of the Americas. Sophisticated urban cultures developed in two tropical regions of the Americas: humid southern Mexico and the more temperate valleys of the central Andes. Both regions witnessed a succession of distinctive cultural and political centers. The Maya civilization of the Yucatán emerged, by 250 C.E., as the outstanding power in Mesoamerica, while the Huari empire of the Andes prefigured that of the Inca. In South America, urban civilizations appeared both near sea level along the Pacific coast and in the Andes Mountains, at altitudes from 6,500 to 12,000 feet.

Spanish arrived in 1519, they estimated that the *chinampas* could feed an impressive four persons per acre; more recent archaeological estimates of their productivity suggest eight people.

Olmec Civilization along the Gulf Coast. On the basis of these agricultural systems, localized permanent settlements that centered on religious shrines and were led by local chiefs began to emerge. Trade and shared cultural and ceremonial practices gave a common character to specific geographical regions within Mesoamerica. Along the Gulf coast of Mexico, the earliest of these civilizations, the Olmec, took shape from about 1500 B.C.E.

The Olmec built raised platforms, settlements, and shrines above the low-lying woodlands. The first that we know of was built at San Lorenzo about 1150 B.C.E. Labor brigades constructed *chinampas*, and the population of the settlement may have reached 2500. Olmec artwork—representations of animals and mythological creatures in sculpture and bas relief—suggests a shared religious basis of the society. They also developed rudimentary hieroglyphics, but as of today, no one has been able to decipher them. About 900 B.C.E. the San Lorenzo site was destroyed, its artwork defaced. No one today knows why.

About one hundred years later, some 100 miles to the northeast and closer to the Gulf, Olmec peoples at La Venta built a small island in the middle of a swamp, and constructed on it an earth mound, half again as large as a football field and 100 feet high. Buildings atop the mound were probably used as temples. Monumental stone sculptures, including some of the giant stone heads typical of Olmec art, also mark the space. Some of them probably served also as altars. The stone building materials were transported here from at least 60 miles away, the jade from much further. La Venta flourished for four centuries until about 400 B.C.E. it, too, was destroyed and its monuments defaced. Again, no one today knows why.

Zapotec Civilization in the Oaxaca Valley. Olmec products—pottery, ritual objects, mirrors, and ceramics—appeared in the highlands around modern Oaxaca as early as 1150 B.C.E., along with natural products, such as obsidian and seashells from around the Gulf of Mexico. At first, therefore, scholars believed that the Zapotec culture of the Oaxaca valley was an offshoot of the Olmec. More recent finds in the village of San Jose Mogote, dating to 1400–1150 B.C.E., demonstrate, however, that the Zapotec settlements began as early as the Olmecs. The imported products reflected trading between the two groups.

Zapotec civilization peaked on the slopes of Monte Albán. By 400 B.C.E. ceremonial and public buildings dotted the summits of the hills. The settlement grew over the centuries, reaching its peak in the centuries after 200 C.E., when up to 50,000 people lived there. The settlement was not entirely concentrated into a single city, but extended over 15 square miles, with some 2000 terraces built into the hills, each with a house or two and its own water supply. Temples, pyramids, tombs, and an array of religious images suggest the importance of symbolism among the Zapotecs, too. Monte Albán peaked in population and creativity about 700 C.E. and then declined.

Colossal head from San Lorenzo, Veracruz, Mexico, before 400 B.C.E. Weighing around ten tons, this massive sculpted head is one of nine that were found at San Lorenzo. Made from basalt and carved with stone tools, the heads originally stood in rows on the site and are most probably portraits of Olmec rulers. All display the same full, resolute lips and broad, flat noses. Similar sculptures were also found at La Venta. (*Museo Regional de Veracruz, Jalapa, Mexico*)

The Urban Explosion: Teotihuacán

Meanwhile, in the valley of Mexico, another civilization was coalescing, dominating the lands near it, and finally creating a substantial empire. At its core, about 40 miles to the northeast of present day Mexico City, stood Teotihuacán, one of the great cities of the ancient world. Teotihuacán represented a totally new kind of settlement in the Americas. It marked the beginning of a true urban revolution. At its peak, about 550 C.E., Teotihuacán accommodated about 100,000 inhabitants on some 8 square miles. Teotihuacán civilization had no system of writing so, again, our knowledge is limited to the excavation and interpretation of physical artifacts.

The first buildings of Teotihuacán appeared about 200 B.C.E. One hundred years later, there were still only about 600 inhabitants. By 150 C.E., however, the population had grown to 20,000 and the area to 5 square miles. Then the population multiplied as the city exploded with religious, trade, artisanal, and administrative functions and personnel.

The city sat astride the major communication line between the valley of Mexico and the passes eastward to the Gulf of Mexico. Life in the city was a gift of the low-lying lake system of the valley of Mexico, especially of nearby Lake Texcoco. The lakes provided irrigation waters for the fields of the Teotihuacán valley and salt, fish, and waterfowl. Basalt, limestone, and chert stone for building and clay for pottery were readily available in the valley, but other raw materials were imported, notably obsidian for tools and weapons from Pachuca and Otumba in the surrounding mountains. Marine shells and copal (a tree resin used as incense) were imported from the Gulf region, and feathers of the quetzal bird came from the Maya regions of the southeast. Trading outposts of Teotihuacán appeared 700 miles south in Maya areas, and Teotihuacán ceramics have been found as far south as Tikal (see the discussion of Maya civilization on pp. 103–106). More than 400 workshops in the city produced pottery, obsidian manufactures, ornaments fashioned from seashells, and art and jewelry from jade and onyx.

A huge pyramid, the Pyramid of the Sun, at its base as broad as the great pyramid of Khufu in Egypt, though only half as high, dominated the Teotihuacán cityscape. The pyramid sits above a natural cave that early inhabitants enlarged into a clover-leaf-shaped chamber. The combination of natural cave and pyramid suggests that local people may have believed that this cave was the "navel of the universe." As Mircea Eliade, the historian of religions, has demonstrated, the belief that all human life, or at least the lives of the local people, had emerged upward onto earth from a "navel," a single specific geographical point, was widely held in many civilizations of the ancient world. (The Garden of Eden story is a later variant of this belief.) Two additional massive shrines—the adjacent, smaller Pyramid of the Moon, and a central temple dedicated to the god Quetzalcoatl—enhance the religious dimensions of the city. Throughout its lifetime, and indeed even afterward until the Spanish conquest, Teotihuacán attracted multitudes of pilgrims from as far away as Guatemala.

The city was laid out on a monumental, geometric grid that centered on the 150-foot-wide Avenue of the Dead, the north–south axis of the city. More than seventy-five temples line this road, including the Pyramid of the Sun. The Pyramid of the Moon

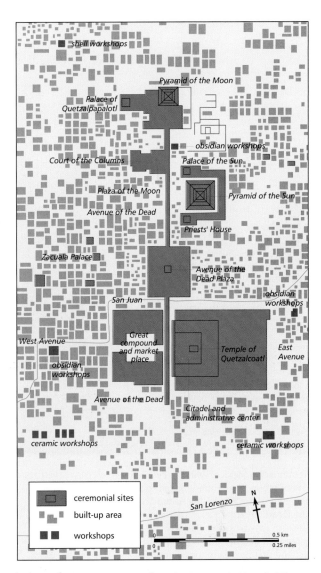

Teotihuacán. Between 400 and 750 C.E., high in the valley of Mexico, Teotihuacán was the dominant power in Mesoamerica. Covering over 7.5 square miles, with a population of 100,000, the city was laid out on a regular grid plan connecting the elements of a massive ceremonial complex. The residents thrived on agriculture, craftwork, and trade in ceramics and locally quarried obsidian.

Teotihuacán, Mexico, with the Pyramid of the Moon (foreground) linked to the Pyramid of the Sun by the Avenue of the Dead. By 200 B.C.E. in the valley of Mexico, the combined effects of intensified trading, growing religious activity, and huge surpluses of food led to the founding of this major city, which for centuries enjoyed religious, political, and economic dominance in the region. Teotihuacán reached an enormous size (8 square miles) and population (100,000) before eventually being deliberately, and mysteriously, burned down in 650 C.E.

demarcated its northern terminal. The regularity of the city plan suggests a powerful government and, indeed, a large administrative headquarters, the Ciudadela, dominates the southeastern terminus of the Avenue. The placement of the central Temple of Quetzalcoatl within the Ciudadela implies a close relationship between religion and administration.

At its peak, 500–650 C.E., Teotihuacán exercised a powerful imperial force over its immediate surrounding area and exerted spiritual, religious, cultural, economic, and military influence for hundreds of miles, especially to the south, into Maya areas. In 650, however, the city was deliberately burned down. Teotihuacán began to decline in significance. By 750 its power was broken, and its population scattered to smaller towns and rural areas. Several reasons have been suggested: the region may have become increasingly arid, incapable of supporting so large a population; increasing density of population, augmented by government programs for moving rural populations into the city, might have led to conflict and revolt from within; neighboring city-states, pressured by the increasing militarization in Teotihuacán, may have attacked the city. These are, however, only educated guesses. In the absence of written records, no one knows for sure.

Cities interact with one another in networks of exchange, so advances or declines in one usually echo in the others. Teotihuacán and Monte Albán both declined simultaneously about 750 C.E., but smaller, nonurban centers kept the political, cultural, and religious legacies of Teotihuacán alive in the region. (Compare this with the experience of western Europe after the decline of Rome, discussed in Chapter 6.) Three subsequent civilizations—the Toltec, the Aztec, and the Maya—absorbed and perpetuated its influence.

Successor States in the Valley of Mexico

When the Toltecs arrived in the valley of Mexico from the north and came to dominate the region from a new capital at Tula, about 900 C.E., they apparently ruled on Teotihuacán foundations and built their chief ceremonial center in honor of Quetzalcoatl. Their rule, however, was shortlived. About 1170 C.E. still newer immigrants destroyed the Toltec temples and government.

After Tula fell, the Aztecs entered the valley. They established settlements on the southeastern shores of Lake Texcoco and built Tenochtitlán as their capital only 40 miles from the earlier site of Teotihuacán. As the Aztecs built their large, militaristic empire, the population of Tenochtitlán grew to 200,000. Militarism and the demand of their gods for human sacrifice led the Aztecs into a constant quest for captives to sacrifice and, therefore, into constant warfare with their neighbors. When the Spanish conquistadores arrived in 1519, the neighboring peoples helped them overthrow the Aztecs and their empire. The Spanish then razed Tenochtitlán to the ground and established their own capital, Mexico City, atop its ruins (see Chapter 12).

The Rise and Fall of the Maya

Teotihuacán's third legacy was to the Maya. The Maya lived where their descendants still dwell today—in the Yucatán peninsula of Mexico, in Guatemala, and in Belize. The Maya built on Olmec and Teotihuacáno foundations as well as on their own practices. Arriving in the Yucatán and central America, they began to construct ceremonial centers by 2000 B.C.E. Between 300 B.C.E. and 300 C.E., they expanded their centers to plazas surrounded by stone pyramids and crowned with temples and palaces. The classic phase, 300–600 C.E., followed with full-fledged cities and monumental architecture, temples, extensive sacrifices, and elaborate burials, and the Olmec and Teotihuacán cultural influences are evident. Maya culture flourished in the southern lowlands, and major construction took place at Palenque, Piedras Negras, Copán, Coba, and elsewhere.

The Great City of Tikal.

Tikal, in today's Guatemala, is one of the largest, most elaborate, and most completely excavated of these cities. In its center, Tikal holds five temple pyramids, up to 200 feet high and built from 300 to 800 C.E. (One appeared so massive, powerful, and exotic that film-maker George Lucas used it as a setting for *Star Wars*.) As the first modern archaeologists hacked away the tropical rainforest and uncovered this temple core, they concluded that Tikal was a spiritual and religious center. Later they uncovered housing and water cisterns that accommodated up to 50,000 people outside the

A blood-letting rite, limestone lintel from Yaxchilán, Mexico (Maya), c. 725 C.E. The king, Lord Shield Jaguar, in his role of shaman, brandishes a flaming torch to illuminate the drama about to unfold. His principal wife, Lady Xoc, kneeling, pulls through her tongue thorn-lined rope that falls into a woven basket holding blood-soaked strips of paper cloth. These will be burned and thereby transmitted to the gods. Few works of art made by the Maya capture so completely the link between their political and religious ideas in an appropriately sacramental style. (Having deciphered the hieroglyphics of the Mayan calendar, scholars know that this event took place on October 28, 709 C.E.) (*British Museum, London*)

temple precincts. This find led them to change their assessment of Tikal. Instead of viewing it as a purely religious shrine, they began to see it as a large city of considerable regional political and economic significance as well. At the height of its powers, Tikal's authority covered almost 1000 square miles containing 360,000 people.

Most Maya states held only 30,000–50,000 subjects. The number of states ruled by kings grew from perhaps a dozen in the first century B.C.E. to as many as sixty at the height of the lowland civilization in the eighth century C.E.

Temple I at Tikal, Guatemala (Mayan), before 800 C.E. At its height the city-state of Tikal covered almost 1000 square miles and was home to 360,000 inhabitants. Its symbols of authority were centralized in its monumental shrines. This unusually steep stepped pyramid—230 feet high—would have been the backdrop for self-inflicted blood-letting and the sacrifice of prisoners-of-war as offerings to the gods.

SOURCE

The Popol Vuh

The Popol Vuh *is the most complete existing collection of creation myths to survive the Spanish conquistadores. Originally written in Maya hieroglyphs, it was transcribed into Latin in the sixteenth century and then translated into Spanish by a Dominican priest in the eighteenth century. The selection cited here is reminiscent of the biblical story of the tree in the garden of Eden whose fruits were forbidden. But the tale in* Popol Vuh *has even more significant differences. The tree, a calabash, is forbidden because the skull of a god, named One Hunahpu, was placed on a fork in it. As a young woman reached out to take the fruit of the tree, the skull spat out saliva on her, making her pregnant and thus preserving the god's lineage among humans.*

And this is when a maiden heard of it, the daughter of a lord. Blood Gatherer is the name of her father, and Blood Woman is the name of the maiden.

And when he heard the account of the fruit of the tree, her father retold it. And she was amazed at the account:

"I'm not acquainted with that tree they talk about. 'Its fruit is truly sweet!' they say." "I hear," she said.

Next she went all alone and arrived where the tree stood. It stood at the Place of Ball Game Sacrifice:

"What? Well! What's the fruit of this tree? Shouldn't this tree bear something sweet? They shouldn't die, they shouldn't be wasted. Should I pick one?" said the maiden.

And then the bone spoke; it was here in the fork of the tree:

"Why do you want a mere bone, a round thing in the branches of a tree?" said the head of One Hunahpu when it spoke to the maiden. "You don't want it," she was told.

"I do want it," said the maiden.

"Very well. Stretch out your right hand here, so I can see it," said the bone.

"Yes," said the maiden. She stretched out her right hand, up there in front of the bone.

And then the bone spat out its saliva, which landed squarely in the hand of the maiden.

And then she looked in her hand, she inspected it right away, but the bone's saliva wasn't in her hand.

"It is just a sign I have given you, my saliva, my spittle. This, my head, has nothing on it—just the bone, nothing of meat. It's just the same with the head of a great lord: it's just the flesh that makes his face look good. And when he dies, people get frightened by his bones. After that, his son is like his saliva, his spittle, in his being, whether it be the son of a lord or the son of a craftsman, an orator. The father does not disappear, but goes on being fulfilled. Neither dimmed nor destroyed is the face of a lord, a warrior, craftsman, orator. Rather, he will leave his daughters and sons. So it is that I have done likewise through you. Now go up there on the face of the earth; you will not die. Keep the word. So be it," said the head of One and Seven Hunahpu—they were of one mind when they did it.

This was the word Hurricane, Newborn Thunderbolt, Raw Thunderbolt had given them. In the same way, by the time the maiden returned to her home, she had been given many instructions. Right away something was generated in her belly, from the saliva alone, and this was the generation of Hunahpu and Xbalanque.

And when the maiden got home and six months had passed, she was found out by her father. Blood Gatherer is the name of her father. (Tedlock, p. 106)

The Maya also created an elaborate calendar that recorded three related chronologies: dates and events in cosmic time periods of thousands of years; historic events in the lives of specific rulers and their states; and the yearly cycle of agricultural activity. Maya rituals were permeated by the sense of living at once in the world of here-and-now and in a spiritual realm connected with other worlds and gods. Their kings were shamans, bridges between the two worlds.

Maya Civilization in Decline. By 900 C.E., the great classical period of the Maya in the southern lowlands ended. No one knows why. The most frequent hypotheses include: excessive population pressure on natural resources, especially agriculture; climatic changes beyond the ability of the Maya to adjust; excessive warfare that wore out the people and destroyed their states. No one knows for sure.

No one knows, either, why at the time of the Maya decline in the lowlands, new Maya cities and states grew up in the northern highlands of the Yucatán peninsula, notably at Uxmal and Chichén Itzá. These cities, in turn, declined by 1200, and the last Maya capital, Mayapán, was constructed between 1263 and 1283. It adapted many of the cultural monuments of Chichén Itzá, but grew only to some 10,000 to 20,000

HOW DO WE KNOW?

Great-Jaguar-Paw: Mayan King of Tikal

By deciphering, translating, and interpreting the stelae at Tikal, Linda Schele and David Freidel recreate an heroic moment of military victory in the life of the king Great-Jaguar-Paw and in the history of his kingdom. Their interpretation is based primarily on the stela illustrated here and on comparison with later stelae representing the same event:

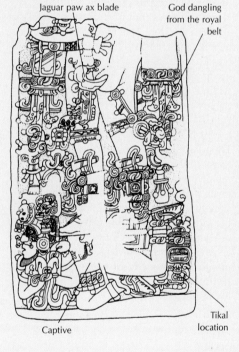

Jaguar paw ax blade

God dangling from the royal belt

Captive

Tikal location

Despite the fact that he was such an important king, we know relatively little about Great-Jaguar-Paw's life outside of the spectacular campaign he waged against Uaxactun. His reign must have been long, but the dates we have on him come only from his last three years. On one of these historical dates, October 21, A.D. *376, we see Great-Jaguar-Paw ending the seventeenth katun [a ritual cycle of twenty years] ... This fragmentary monument shows him only from the waist down, but he is dressed in the same regalia as his royal ancestors, with the god Chac-Xib-Chac dangling from his belt. His ankle cuffs display the sign of day on one leg and night on the other ... He holds an executioner's ax, its flint blade knapped into the image of a jaguar paw. In this guise of warrior and giver of sacrifices, he stands atop a captive he has taken in battle. The unfortunate victim, a bearded noble still wearing part of the regalia that marks his noble station, struggles under the victor's feet, his wrists bound together in front of his chest. He will die to sanctify the katun ending at Tikal.*

Warfare was not new to the Maya. Raiding for captives from one kingdom to another had been going on for centuries, for allusions to decapitation are present in even the earliest architectural decorations celebrating kingship. The hunt for sacrificial gifts to give to the gods and the testing of personal prowess in battle was part of the accepted social order and captive sacrifice was something expected of nobles and kings in the performance of their ritual duties. Just as the gods were sustained by the bloodletting ceremonies of the kings, so they were nourished as

well by the blood of noble captives. Sacrificial victims like these had been buried as offerings in building terminations and dedications from late Preclassic times on, and possibly even earlier ...

The war waged by Great-Jaguar-Paw of Tikal against Uaxactun, however, was not the traditional hand-to-hand combat of proud nobles striving for personal glory and for captives to give to the gods. This was war on an entirely different scale, played by rules never before heard of and for stakes far higher than the reputations or lives of individuals. In this new warfare of death and conquest, the winner would gain the kingdom of the loser. Tikal won the prize on January 16, A.D. *378 ...*

The subjugation of Uaxactun by Great-Jaguar-Paw and Smoking Fog [his commander-in-chief], which precipitated this new kind of war and rituals, survives in the inscriptional record almost entirely in the retrospective histories carved by later rulers at Tikal. The fact that these rulers kept commemorating this event shows both its historical importance and its propaganda value for the descendants of these conquerors.

(Schele and Freidel, pp. 144–8)

- What are all the symbols through which this stela represents the power and strength of Great-Jaguar-Paw?
- What does the war between Tikal and Uaxactun tell us about the increasing power of the state?
- What do you think Schele and Freidel mean by "the propaganda value" of commemorating the victory of Tikal over Uaxactun?

inhabitants. Mayapán seemed militaristic, beleaguered, and possessed of tough sensibilities as evidenced by wholesale human sacrifices. The city was later destroyed in civil wars in the mid-1400s.

By the time the Spanish conquistadores reached Mesoamerica in 1517, only a few small Maya towns remained. The period of Maya power and splendor had ended. The Toltecs, too, had fallen by then. The Aztecs had become the reigning power, and the Spaniards destroyed them.

Urbanization in South America

South America had few established trade links with Mesoamerica, but the two regions share many similarities. Both regions constructed religious shrine centers that seem to have dominated their general cultural foundations by about 1500 B.C.E. Both developed small city-states that defined local cultural variations from 300 to

HOW DO WE KNOW?

The Mysteries of Maya Writing

For centuries the connection between today's Maya—living an often impoverished existence—and the glories of their civilization in the third through the tenth centuries C.E. had been lost. Then, in 1839–41, a New York lawyer, John Lloyd Stephens, and a Scottish artist, Frederick Catherwood, discovered the remnants of the cities of Copán and Palenque in the rainforests of Mesoamerica, and the temples of Uxmal and Chichén Itzà in the Yucatán peninsula. Stephens and Catherwood wrote and painted what they saw and made rubbings of the designs they found on Maya stelae, stone marker tablets. Their research, published in 1841, opened the way for the modern academic study of the Maya at almost exactly the same time as H.C. Rawlinson and others were discovering the great archaeological sites of Mesopotamia and deciphering its language.

Stelae and other inscriptions demonstrated that the Maya had created a written language, but no one could read it. Even the Maya themselves, prevented by the Spanish from keeping their language alive (see Chapter 13), had forgotten the script. Scholars could read parts of the elaborate and sophisticated Maya calendar system, but they could not discern whether the events recorded were historical, mythical, or some combination of the two.

In the 1950s and 1960s, at Harvard University, Tatiana Proskouriakoff began to demonstrate that the Maya stelae recorded the reigns and victories of real kings who had ruled real states. Then the Russian scholar Yuri Knorozov demonstrated, against fierce opposition, that the Maya script included representations of phonetic sounds as well as of full words. By the 1970s a new generation of linguistic scholars began to decode the syntactical structure of the writing. They learned to distinguish the signs for nouns and those for verbs, and their place in the structure of the narrative. They were well on their way to discovering Maya history, and they were surprised by what they found.

The archaeologists Linda Schele and David Freidel finally mastered the hieroglyphs and scripts of the people of the city of Palenque. In contrast to previous beliefs that the Maya were peaceful and somewhat otherworldly in their concerns, as their massive temples seemed to indicate, Schele and Freidel found records of constant warfare among the local shaman kings and their profoundly religious local city-states. The Maya kingdoms fought in order to gain captives who would serve as slaves and human sacrifices to their demanding gods. The temples, it turned out, were the altars on which the sacrifices were performed. Schele and Freidel also discovered the exact lineage of the Palenque kings, and the picture of a tree used to symbolize the king, for the Maya represented their royal families as forests of trees and forests of kings.

- Why was it easier to decipher the cuneiform of Sumer and the hieroglyphs of Egypt than the symbols of Maya writing?
- Why had the Maya forgotten their own written language? Does the reason surprise you? Why or why not?
- On p. 106 you can see an example of Maya writing. As you look at it, what seem to you to be the difficulties in deciphering the Maya written language?

200 B.C.E. Both created proto-empires throughout significant regions about 500–600 C.E.; and generated large, urban empires—the Aztecs in the valley of Mexico, the Inca in the Andes—and developed trading relationships between their coastal regions and their mountainous inland cores. But the contrast between coast and inland mountains is far more striking in South America. The Pacific coast of Ecuador, Peru, and Chile is a desert in most places. The prevailing winds come not from the Pacific, but from the Amazon basin to the east. The Andes Mountains thus have little rainfall from the Pacific Ocean to trap on their western slopes, but they do intercept the precipitation from the Atlantic, making the eastern slopes fertile while leaving the west coast dry. The most spectacular urban civilizations of South America took root in the 10,000-foot-high plains and passes of the Andes rather than in the arid Pacific coast below. The contrast with the river-basin civilizations of Afro-Eurasia could not be more vivid.

Coastal Settlements and Networks

The Pacific coast is not, however, uninhabitable. It yields abundant quantities of fish, seaweed, and salt. Even today these ocean products are traded to the mountain cities in exchange for their food crops. In some areas the cultivation of cotton is also

CIVILIZATIONS FLOURISHING IN CENTRAL AMERICA BEFORE COLUMBUS

Olmec	*c.* 1500–400 B.C.E. Gulf of Mexico. First complex society in region, with centralized authority. Known for carvings of giant stone heads and jade animals.	**Teotihuacán**	*c.* 300 B.C.E.–750 C.E. Valley of Mexico. Major trading and cultural center. At its peak populated by 100,000 inhabitants in an area (8 square miles) larger than Rome. Contains huge Pyramid of the Sun, Mexico's largest pre-Columbian edifice.
Maya	*c.* 2000 B.C.E.–900 C.E. S. Mexico, Guatemala, Belize. Most enduring of the Middle American civilizations, the Mayans had by 325 C.E. become superb astronomers who built stepped pyramids, smelted metal tools, and developed hieroglyphs.	**Toltec**	*c.* 900–1170 C.E. Central Mexico. Toltecs ruled much of the country from Tula (northeast of Mexico City), where symbols of blood and war predominate, and the similar city of Chichén Itzá in Yucatán.
		Aztec	*c.* 1100–1521 C.E. Central Mexico. Sophisticated culture run by priestly aristocracy that built capital of Tenochtitlán. Known for their architecture, textiles, and a complex sacred calendar, the Aztecs were conquered by the Spanish in 1519–21.
Zapotec	*c.* 1400 B.C.E.–900 C.E. S. Mexico. Built ceremonial center of Monte Albán and peaked as a civilization around 200 C.E.		

possible, and coastal Peru rivals the Indus valley as the home of the first production of cotton textiles, about 4500 B.C.E. The quality of the textiles and the colorful designs dyed into the cotton show up most clearly in the burial cloths of semi-mummified bodies in the Paracas peninsula near Pisco, Peru.

In addition, although climatically a desert, the coast does have some small mountain-fed rivers running through it. People who could organize labor brigades to channel the rivers for irrigation also created ceremonial centers along the coast, beginning perhaps by 2000 B.C.E. The oldest of these shrine centers, and the one closest to the Pacific, is El Paraiso, near modern Lima, at the mouth of the Chillon River. Built in a typically U-shaped complex of buildings, El Paraiso appears to have been constructed by people from many separate villages and kin groups. Few lived at El Paraiso, but apparently the shrine served them all, and many used the location as a burial place.

The largest of the shrine centers is Sechin Alto, a 130-foot-high mound, 1000 by 800 feet, on which was built a U-shaped ceremonial complex surrounded by houses and platforms. The oldest building dates to 1300 B.C.E. It continued to expand until 400 B.C.E.

The Moche. In the Moche valley of coastal northern Peru, settlements of up to 2000 separate structures had grown up by 200 B.C.E. From about 200 B.C.E. to 600 C.E., in this and neighboring valleys, the Moche state established itself. The Moche created irrigation systems, spectacular monuments, and important tombs. In the late 1980s, at nearby Sipan, archaeologists discovered three royal tombs that demonstrate the social and political stratification of the society. Each tomb housed a lord, buried in shrouds and adorned with jewellery, some made of gold, and surrounded by servants and perhaps family members, and by animals—llamas, and at least one dog and one snake—that had been buried with him. Paintings and ceramic designs within the tombs show priests engaged in warfare and performing human sacrifices of prisoners-of-war. The Moche built provincial centers in nearby river valleys from which they apparently ruled, traded, and introduced irrigation systems.

The Chimu. By about 600 C.E. the Moche left the region, for reasons that are not entirely clear, and were succeeded by the Chimu kingdom that controlled twelve coastal river valleys. The Chimu built irrigation and water storage facilities, trade networks, and a powerful state that stretched some 1000 miles along the Peruvian coast. Their monumental capital, Chan Chan, built near the earlier Moche, was surrounded by a 35 foot high mud wall, and it covered nearly 4 square miles, with palaces, temples, administrative offices, and housing for the common people. Chan Chan contained ten royal compounds. Apparently each king in turn built his own center, ruled from it during his life, and was buried in it after his death.

In each area they dominated, the Chimu built subsidiary administrative centers that formed a network reaching as far south as modern Lima. The Chimu empire reigned until it was conquered by the Inca in 1470. Ironically, thanks to the Inca transportation and communication network, Chimu artwork influenced western South America even more after the Inca conquest than it had before.

Urbanization in the Andes Mountains

Despite these coastal settlements and networks, most scholars believe that the core areas of South American urbanization were in the Andes, the 20,000-foot-high mountain chain that parallels the Pacific coast for the entire length of South America. From earliest times to today, there has been considerable "vertical trade," linking coastal lowlands with high mountain areas in an exchange of the different products of their different ecologies. With the trade came networks of cultural, religious, and political communication, and some archaeologists have argued that the civilization of the Andes Mountains was developed from a prior foundation along the sea coast far below.

The Chavin. The first known civilization of the Andes, the Chavin, flourished for about a millennium, 1200–200 B.C.E. The civilization is named for its best known and largest ceremonial center at Chavin de Huantar, which flourished in central Peru from about 900 to about 200 B.C.E. Chavin temples include a pantheon of gods preserved in paintings and carvings, including jaguar-like humans with serpents for hair, eagles, caymans, and many mixed figures, part-human, part-animal, reminiscent of similar figures in China. Like El Paraiso and the coastal shrines, Chavin seems to have been built by the joint efforts of many nearby kin and village groups. At its height, it held only 2000 inhabitants, but its culture and its gods inspired common religious forms in the vicinity, and carried them throughout the high Andes.

The Tiwanaku, Huari, and Nazca. Some 600 miles to the south, south of Lake Titicaca, on today's border between Peru and Bolivia, at an elevation of 12,000 feet, lay the largest open, flat plain available for agriculture in the Andes. By 200 C.E., Tiwanaku (Tihuanaco) at the southern end of the lake, near the modern city of La Paz, became the capital of the region. Its rulers irrigated their high plains, *altiplano*, region to support perhaps 20,000 people and to create a ritual center of monumental structures and religious and spiritual practices that suffused the Andes and the coast. When Tiwanaku collapsed, for reasons now lost to history, successor states in the region, notably at Huari and Nazca, kept alive many of their administrative and religious practices.

CIVILIZATIONS OF SOUTH AMERICA

Chavin	c. 1200–200 B.C.E. N. Peru. Farming society, comprising different regional groups, whose main town may have been a pilgrimage site.
Moche	200 B.C.E.–600 C.E. N. coast of Peru. Modeled ceramics of animals in a realistic style. Religious and political life focused on the Huaca de la Luna (artificial platform) and Huaca del Sol (stepped pyramid).
Nazca	?1–600 C.E. Peru. Known principally for its series of enormous figures drawn with lines of pebbles. Best seen from the air, the largest (a hummingbird) is 900 feet long.
Tiwanaku	c. 200 C.E.–1200 C.E. Bolivia. Named for the ancient city, near Lake Titicaca, that was occupied by a series of five different cultures, then abandoned.
Huari	c. 650–800 C.E. Peru. Empire whose style of architecture and artifacts, similar to Tiwanaku's, was dispersed throughout the region.
Chimu	c. 600–1470 C.E. Northwest Peruvian coast. Large urban civilization (capital: Chan Chan) responsible for fine gold work, record-keeping, and aqueducts. Conquered by the Aztecs.
Inca	c. 1476–1534 C.E. Andean South America. Last and largest pre-Columbian civilization (capital: Cuzco) that was destroyed by Spanish conquistadores in the 1530s.

Nazca lines, San Jose pampa, Peru desert, c. 500 C.E. Another of the successor states of Tiwanaku, the Nazca, created great patterns of lines drawn with pebbles on the desert surface. The designs, like this 900-foot-long hummingbird figure, are visible only from the air, and their function and meaning are as elusive as the culture that fashioned them.

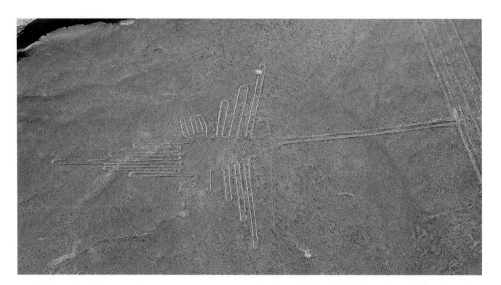

The Inca. These five states—Chimu, Chavin, Tiwanaku, Huari, and Nazca—established foundations on which the Inca built their powerful but shortlived empire, which stretched for 2000 miles from north to south and as far as 200 miles inland, between 1476 and 1534. The Inca adapted many of the gods and religious symbols, artwork, ceramics, and textiles of these earlier states. They built a new capital, Cuzco, at 10,000 feet, and connected it to all the mountain and coastal regions of their empire by an astonishing 25,000-mile system of roads, with tunnels, causeways, suspension bridges, travel lodges, and storage places. The roads were sometimes broad and paved, but often narrow and unpaved, especially because the Inca had no wheeled vehicles. Enforced, *mit'a* labor was exacted from local populations for the construction.

In 1438, Cusi Yupanqui was crowned "Inca," or king-emperor, after he won a victory over a neighboring tribe, and forged his quarreling peoples into a conquering nation. Thereafter, the whole nation was called Inca. Cusi Yupanqui established an hereditary monarchy, and his descendants built a great empire from his early conquests. They employed the *mit'a* system, demanding unpaid labor for public construction for part of each year from all adults in the empire. The Inca did not develop writing, but they did create an abacus-like system of numerical recording through the use of knots tied on strings. These *quipu* held the administrative records of the empire.

In each conquered region, the Inca established administrative centers, from which tax collectors gathered two-thirds of the crops and the manufactured products, like beer and textiles, half of it for the state, half for the gods and their priests. They established state workshops to produce official and consumer goods, and they seem to have encouraged significant standardization of production, for Inca arts and crafts show little variation over time and place. Inca religion apparently encouraged different gods and worship for different people. The sun god was the chief deity, and the emperor was considered his descendant; the nobility worshiped the military god Viracocha; while the common people continued to worship their own indigenous spirits, along with the newer sun god. The organization and the study of empire, however, take us to Part 3.

Agricultural Towns in North America

Agricultural settlements took root in many locations in continental North America in the first few hundred years C.E. Several grew into small towns, reaching their maximum size about 1000–1400 C.E., and some scholars see the signs of early urbanization. Nevertheless, these towns are not included among the seven sites of primary urbanization because few of them reached a population size that might be considered urban; nor do they demonstrate clearly a non-agricultural base to their economies. They may also be derivative of earlier settlements to the south. For example, those in the southwestern United States, like the Hohokam, Mogollon, and Anasazi peoples, show evidence in their artwork and building patterns of influences from Mexico and even South America.

The first fully developed towns in the Mississippi valley appeared about 700 C.E. Their inhabitants built temple mounds and left evidence of elaborate, ritual funerals, suggesting a hierarchical social and political organization. The largest of the temple mound towns, Cahokia, occupied land along the Mississippi, across the river from and a few miles east of present-day Saint Louis. Cahokia held a population of 10,000 in the city and 38,000 in the region in the twelfth and thirteenth centuries. Such a large population probably included many craft specialists. Around the town were sited some 100 mounds, which served as burial tombs or as platforms for homes of the elite. The mounds resemble those of Mexican cities and suggest interchange between the two regions. Evidence indicates that a strong central authority controlled the town. Cahokia, like almost all the towns of North America, was in decline, or even deserted, before the arrival of European invaders, in the early 1500s, for reasons that are not entirely clear. Archaeologists continue active research in the towns of North America, their cultures, and their links to one another and to other regions.

WEST AFRICA: THE NIGER RIVER VALLEY

Until the late 1970s, all the cities in sub-Saharan Africa that were known to archaeologists had developed along patterns introduced from outside the region. Meroe and Kush on the upper Nile had adapted urban patterns from Egypt. Aksum in modern Ethiopia had followed examples of urbanization from both the Nile valley and the trading powers of the Indian Ocean. Port cities along the East African coast, such as Malindi, Kilwa, and Sofala, had been founded by traders from across the Indian Ocean. The walled stone enclosures, called **zimbabwes**, built in the region of modern Zimbabwe and Mozambique to house local royal rulers, had been initiated through contact with Swahili traders from the coast.

In west Africa, the first known cities, such as Timbuktu, Jenne, and Mopti along the Niger River, and Ife and Igbo Ukwu deeper south in the Yoruba lands near the tropical forests, had been built as centers of exchange. They were thought to be responses

zimbabwes Stone-walled enclosures or buildings built during the African Iron Age in the region of modern Zimbabwe and Mozambique. The structures were the courts of local rulers. They have been associated with foreign trade, integrated farming and animal husbandry, and gold production.

AT A GLANCE: THE EARLY AFRICAS

DATE	POLITICAL	RELIGION AND CULTURE	SOCIAL DEVELOPMENT
500 B.C.E.		■ Nok terra cotta sculptures ■ Bantu adopting settled agricultural lives	■ Iron smelting
250 B.C.E.	■ Jenne-jeno founded	■ Copper and semi-precious stone ornaments from Niger	
500 C.E.	■ Ancient Ghana		■ Cities in Niger valley (400) recorded by Arab visitors
1000 C.E.	■ Foundation of Benin (c. 1000)		
1200 C.E.	■ Ghana falls; Kingdom of Mali founded		

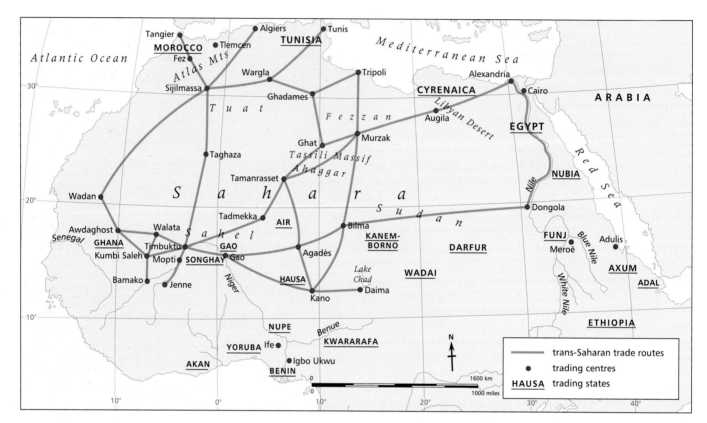

Trade across the Sahara. Ivory, gold, hardwoods, and slaves were the magnets which drew trading caravans south across the arid Saharan wastes, often following routes established before the desert had formed. These routes linked the classical cultures of the Mediterranean and southwest Asia with an array of rich trading states strung along the Sahel/Sudan axis.

to the arrival of Muslim traders from north Africa who crossed the Sahara southward after the seventh century C.E. Archaeologists believed that Africans, like Europeans, had learned of city building from outsiders. But this viewpoint has now been challenged.

West Africa before Urbanization

The most important developments of pre-urban west Africa were iron smelting, apparently initiated by contact with north Africa; the development of new artistic traditions, especially by the Nok peoples; and the spread of agricultural civilization by the Bantu people. Iron smelting entered the archaeological record in west Africa suddenly about 500 B.C.E. In most places the technology jumped from stone to iron directly, with only a few examples of copper-work in between. Most archaeologists interpret this technological jump to indicate that iron working was introduced from outside, probably from the Phoenician colonies along the north African coast, and they find evidence for this idea in the rock art of the Sahara desert. Along the routes crossing the desert, rock engravings and paintings dating from between 1200 B.C.E. and 400 B.C.E. depict two-wheeled chariots that suggest trans-Saharan traffic.

In northern Nigeria, the Nok peoples were producing terra cotta sculptures, especially of human heads, from about 500 B.C.E. Living in settlements along the Niger, near its confluence with the Benue in modern Nigeria, the Nok also built iron-smelting furnaces, dating to 500–450 B.C.E.

Meanwhile, also in the lower Niger, some Bantu peoples were giving up nomadic pastoralism for settled agriculture, although many remained nomadic for a long time. They began great, but gradual, migrations southward and eastward over thousands of miles, introducing their languages, their knowledge of iron production, and their experience with settled agriculture. In one thousand years, 500 B.C.E. to 500 C.E., the Bantu carried their languages, their new, settled way of life, and their metallurgical skills almost to the southern tip of Africa.

Jenne-jeno: A New Urban Pattern?

Neither the Nok nor the Bantu built cities. Other people of the Niger River, however, apparently did. In excavations that began in 1977 and continue today archaeologists Susan and Roderick McIntosh uncovered Jenne-jeno, "Ancient Jenne," the first known indigenous city in sub-Saharan Africa. The Jenne-jeno settlement began about 250 B.C.E. as a small group of round mud huts. Its herding and fishing inhabitants were already using iron implements, and the village grew to urban size by 400 C.E., reaching its peak of settlement by about 900 C.E.

The physical form of the city was different from that of the other six centers we have studied. A central inhabited area of some 80 acres was surrounded by a city wall 10 feet wide and 13 feet high with a perimeter of 1¼ miles. Near this central area were some forty smaller, but still substantial additional settlements. They extended to a radius of 2½ miles. By the year 1000, the settled area may have included 50,000 persons.

Excavations through numerous levels revealed that the people of Jenne-jeno ate fish from the river, rice from their fields, and beef from their herds. They probably drank the cows' milk as well. At least some wore jewelry and ornaments of imported copper and semi-precious stones. Dozens of burial urns, each up to 3 feet high, yielded human skeletons arranged in fetal position. The urns date from 300 to 1400 C.E., and their burial inside and adjacent to the houses suggests a reverence for ancestors. Statuettes in a kneeling position set into walls and under floors further suggest the probability of ancestor worship.

This part of the religious and cultural heritage of Jenne-jeno seems to have endured. Although not built primarily as a shrine center, Jenne-jeno included religious functions as an important part of its activities, as its modern counterpart does today. There are also similarities between the arrangement of the huts of Jenne-jeno 1000 years ago and the grouping of family huts there today. In ancient times as in modern, it appears that the husband–father lived in one large central hut while one of his wives occupied each of the surrounding huts.

Jenne-jeno must have engaged in trade, because even in 250 B.C.E. its inhabitants were using iron and stone that had to be brought from at least 30 miles away. Sandstone for their grinding stones had to have been imported from at least 60 miles away, while copper and salt came from hundreds of miles away. The McIntoshes have also discovered one gold

Two men with an ibex, Tanzoumaitak, Tassili Mountains, Sahara, 7000–6000 B.C.E. Rock painting. Rock art of the Sahara at first represented wild animals such as buffalo, rhinoceros, hippopotamuses, giraffes, and elephants. By 6000 B.C.E. it was representing domesticated animals such as ibex or goats, dogs, horses, and camels, suggesting a transition from hunting to pastoralism and settled agriculture.

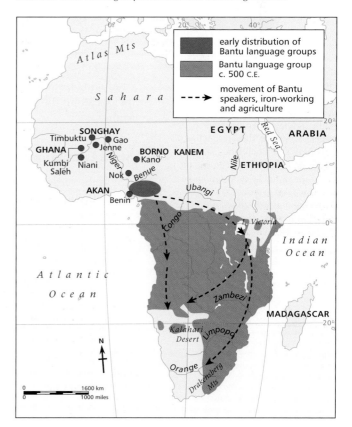

The spread of Bantu. About 1500 B.C.E. an extraordinary cultural migration began to transform sub-Saharan Africa. From their homeland near the Niger delta, groups of Bantu-speaking farmers began to move east and south, spreading cattle domestication, crop cultivation, and iron-working. By about 500 C.E. southern Africa had been reached, the original hunter-gatherers having been marginalized to remote regions such as the Kalahari Desert.

Head from Jemaa, Nigeria, c. 400 B.C.E.
The Nok were a nonliterate farming people that occupied the Jos Plateau in northern Nigeria during the first millennium B.C.E. Their distinctive sculptures—of elephants, snakes, monkeys, people, and even a giant tick—are all boldly modeled and skillfully fired in terra cotta. This powerful lifesize head would probably have formed part of a full-length statue. (*National Museum, Lagos, Nigeria*)

earring, dating to about 750 C.E., in the region. The nearest site of gold mining was 500 miles away. Perhaps the people of Jenne-jeno traded the fish of the Niger and the rice of their fields for these imports. Some Jenne-jenoites may have become professional merchants.

Innovation in architectural concepts may also have come to Jenne from external contacts. By about 900 C.E. some rectangular houses began to appear among the circular ones, perhaps introduced through contact with northern peoples. Outside contacts increased with the introduction of camel transportation across the Sahara about 300 C.E. and with the Muslim Arab conquest of north Africa about 700 C.E. Especially after 1200 C.E., Muslim traders crossing the Sahara linked the savanna and forest lands of the south to the cities of the Mediterranean coast. Most scholars have argued that these external contacts and trade possibilities encouraged the growing importance of new cities like Timbuktu, Jenne, Niani, Gao, Kano, and, further south, Benin. The McIntoshes suggest an opposite perspective: these cities predate the northern connections, and, indeed, their prosperity and control of the trade routes and the gold further to the south encouraged the northerners to dispatch their camel caravans across the Sahara. This debate remains unresolved.

By 1100, the settlements peripheral to Jenne-jeno began to lose population. Some of their inhabitants apparently moved to the central settlement. In another century the rural population also began to decline. By 1400, Jenne-jeno and its satellites were no more. Why? Perhaps warfare and slave-trading upset local stability. It is also possible that land rights and family structures shifted, reducing residents' interest in the region. Finally, it is possible that migration to other places along the Niger River simply allowed Jenne to slowly decline. We just do not know.

State Formation?

Could the settlements of the Middle Niger at Jenne-jeno be an example of early urbanism without a strong centralized government? Without a state? It is possible. The population at Jenne-jeno lived in neighboring clusters that were functionally interdependent rather than in a single urban center with a prominent core marked by large scale, monumental architecture as was found in most of the other centers of primary urbanization. This kind of development might be viewed as "a precocious, indigenous, and highly individual form of urbanism" (R. McIntosh, p. 203). In this case, it is possible that Jenne-jeno rose on the basis of trade and expanded into geographically neighboring, interactive settlements, but without a hierarchical social structure or a strong, central authority. In contrast to primary urbanization in all the other regions of the world we have examined, Jenne-jeno may have experienced relative equality and cooperation among its citizens rather than competition, dominance, and coercion.

On the other hand, a comparative assessment might suggest that Jenne had developed only to about the stage of the Olmec settlements and had not yet created the kind of centralized authority that emerged clearly and powerfully among the later Maya. Had Jenne-jeno persisted longer and grown larger, perhaps centralization and stratification would have developed. Indeed the presence of a central settlement surrounded by smaller adjacent settlements suggests that some hierarchy was already emerging. Did Jenne-jeno represent an alternative kind of urbanization, or was it a settlement that was on its way to full-scale conventional urbanization? These are the kinds of questions of comparison that archaeologists—and historians—love to debate.

THE FIRST CITIES
WHAT DIFFERENCE DO THEY MAKE?

With the creation of cities, humanity entered into many new forms of living. The first of these cities, in the river valleys of Mesopotamia and the Nile almost 5500 years ago, introduced not only new scale and density in human settlement patterns but also new technology in the metallurgy of copper, tin, and bronze; monumental scale in architecture; and specialization and hierarchy in social, political, and economic life. These cities flourished also as nodes in networks for the exchange of goods and ideas. The invention of writing in these cities not only gave new life to cultural creativity, but also provided new means of record keeping for the bureaucrat, businessperson, and scholar. These new cities allowed and demanded complex and hierarchical government to keep them functioning. Although we sometimes see cities today as homes of secularism and heterogeneity, these early cities were also religious in the sense that they often existed to promote dedication to specific gods through their physical and ritual organization. Differences in climate and culture separate Egyptian from Mesopotamian urbanization, but they also shared many similarities. We know somewhat less about Egyptian urbanization because the Nile itself washed away many of its foundations, but more recent archaeology has uncovered Egyptian as well as Sumerian city walls and residential structures, suggesting that they also needed to protect their inhabitants from outsiders.

Sumer and Egypt provide what scholars sometimes refer to as a "master narrative," a conventional, widely accepted view of historical transformation, suggesting that the historical process at other times and places will follow similar patterns. Each of our subsequent case studies has reinforced some dimensions of the "master narrative" while challenging others.

- Indus valley urbanization suggested that a generally consistent civilization could extend over an immense geographical space, over thousands of years. A few of its distinctive, planned cities stood out as capitals, but even after they were evacuated, other cities of the far-flung network kept the civilization alive. Moreover, Indus agricultural practices were adopted and adapted by invaders who transplanted some of them from the Indus valley to the Ganges valley.
- Early Chinese urbanization, represented in the historical record through oracle bones and through the geometrical design of city plans, placed added emphasis on the religious dimension of cities, although the rulers did not neglect to mobilize large and powerful armed forces.
- In the Americas, cities like Teotihuacán and the later cities of the Maya demonstrated again the importance of monumental, religious architecture, although each additional excavation reveals the extent of both long-distance trade and of everyday, mundane activities as well. Urbanization in the Andes mountains indicates that not all early cities needed river beds. Urban rulers could construct fabulous networks for trade, communication, and troop movement at forbidding altitudes. From their capital cities they could launch empires. They could also administer cities, and even empires, without having invented writing.
- In the Niger River valley of west Africa, the single primary urban settlement that has been excavated challenges the "master narrative," suggesting that cities may develop through the interrelationship of adjacent smaller settlements without the need for hierarchy, centralization, government structure, and written language. The data presented thus far may be, however, subject to different interpretations. Perhaps the central mound in Jenne-jeno does, in fact, represent some hierarchical

Bronze kneeling figure, Jenne, Mali, c. 1100–1400. Archaeological activity over the last quarter century has revealed Jenne-jeno, "Old Jenne," as a commercial center on the Niger River from about 250 B.C.E. Its traditions seem to have persisted through the centuries and into "new" Jenne, the city which now stands adjacent to the older excavation. Statuettes such as this one, produced in Jenne, may have been used in worship of and for ancestors. (*Private collection*)

structure. Or perhaps it is a collection of contiguous villages rather than an urban center. The interpretation depends in part on how far the definition of a city and its functions may be—and ought to be—stretched. Continuing excavation and interpretation will help decide the degree to which the "master narrative" concerning early urbanization will hold up, and to what degree new, less rigid ideas of the role of urbanization in human history are yet be formulated.

Review Questions

- Archaeologists working with the earliest cities of Mesopotamia and Egypt asserted that a true city must have writing. In light of the findings in the Americas and in Jenne-jeno, do you agree with those archaeologists that the settlements in these regions are not cities; or do you think that they are cities and that a city's definition should be changed?
- How has the discovery and deciphering of ancient writing helped to form our understanding of urban life in ancient China and Mesoamerica?
- Anthropologist Jared Diamond says that Mesopotamia and Egypt had an advantage in technological and social development over other areas of the world because they were ecologically rich in animal and plant resources. As you compare the early urban developments in China, the Americas, and Jenne-jeno, would you agree or disagree with Diamond? Why?
- In at least six of the early seven urban locations, we find evidence of human sacrifice, or of killing some of the ruler's companions to accompany him (or her) to an afterlife. Why do you think these practices stopped?
- In which of the four urban centers represented in this chapter did the ruler seem to have the most power? What evidence can you cite to support your view?
- Are you convinced by the arguments of the McIntoshes that Jenne-jeno is an example of an unusual kind of city that challenges our understanding of early urbanization? Why or why not?

Suggested Readings

PRINCIPAL SOURCES

Blunden, Caroline and Mark Elvin. *Cultural Atlas of China* (New Haven, CT: Facts on File, 1983). One in the excellent series by this publisher, prepared by an historian and an archaeologist, with text, maps, pictures.

Coe, Michael, Dean Snow, and Elizabeth Benson. *Atlas of Ancient America* (New York: Facts on File, 1986). One in the excellent series by this publisher, prepared by experts, with text, maps, pictures.

Fagan, Brian. *People of the Earth: An Introduction to World Prehistory* (Upper Saddle River, NJ: Prentice Hall, 2000). Outstanding anthropological textbook on prehistory.

McIntosh, Roderick James. *The Peoples of the Middle Niger: the Island of Gold* (Oxford: Blackwell, 1998). Most recent book publication on Jenne-Jeno by one of the two principal archaeologists.

Murray, Jocelyn, ed. *Cultural Atlas of Africa* (New York: Facts on File, 1982). One in the excellent

series by this publisher, prepared by an expert with text, maps, pictures, time lines.

Schele, Linda and David Freidel. *A Forest of Kings: The Untold Story of the Ancient Maya* (New York: William Morrow, 1990). Tells how the Mayan language was deciphered, by those who did it.

Times (London). *Past Worlds* (Maplewood, NJ: Hammond Inc., 1988). Excellent, comprehensive, scholarly introduction to archaeological prehistory, lavishly illustrated with maps and pictures.

ADDITIONAL SOURCES

Alva, Walter and Christopher Donnan. *The Royal Tombs of Sipan* (Los Angeles, CA: Fowler Museum of Cultural History, University of California, Los Angeles, 1993). Lavishly illustrated account of the excavation.

Chang, Kwang-chih. *The Archaeology of Ancient China* (New Haven, CT: Yale University Press,

3rd ed., 1977). THE expert's account, somewhat dated, but still the standard.

Chang, Kwang-chih. *Shang Civilization* (New Haven, CT: Yale University Press, 1980). Comprehensive account by an archaeologist who participated in some of the most significant excavations.

Connah, Graham. *African Civilizations* (Cambridge: Cambridge University Press, 1987). Excellent, comprehensive textbook on prehistoric Africa. Covers the entire continent.

Curtin, Philip, Steven Feierman, Leonard Thompson, and Jan Vansina. *African History from Earliest Times to Independence* (New York: Longman, 2nd ed., 1995). A standard textbook by four distinguished experts.

deBary, William Theodore, *et al.*, comp., *Sources of Chinese Tradition. Vol. 1.* (New York: Columbia University Press, 1998). The best available anthology of classic writings. Good section on oracle bones.

Demarest, Arthur and Geoffrey Conrad, eds. *Ideology and Pre-Columbian Civilizations* (Santa Fe, NM: School of American Research Press, 1992). Scholarly argument on the importance of ideas, both cosmo-magical and political, in the construction of pre-Columbian civilizations.

Eliade, Mircea. *The Sacred and the Profane* (New York: Harper and Row, 1959). The classic argument for the importance of sacred spaces in city development, by a pre-eminent historian of religion.

Keightly, David N., ed. *The Origins of Chinese Civilization* (Berkeley, CA: University of California Press, 1983). An excellent account.

MacNeish, Richard S. "The Origins of New World Civilization," *Scientific American* (November 1964). Reprinted in *Scientific American, Cities: Their Origin, Growth, and Human Impact* (San Francisco, CA: W.H. Freeman and Company, 1973), 63–71. Brief introduction, especially interesting on domestication of crops and animals.

McIntosh, Susan and Roderick McIntosh. "Finding West Africa's Oldest City," *National Geographic* CLXII No. 3 (September 1982), 396–418. Popular introduction based on early archaeological expeditions.

McIntosh, Susan Keech, ed. *Excavations at Jenné-Jeno, Hambarketolo, and Kaniana (Inland Niger Delta, Mali), the 1981 Season* (Berkeley, CA: University of California Press, 1995). Comprehensive, scholarly documentation on the excavations.

Millon, René. "Teotihuacan," *Scientific American* (June 1967). Reprinted in *Scientific American, Cities: Their Origin, Growth, and Human Impact*, 82–91. Basic introduction to the early professional excavations of Mesoamerica's largest prehistoric metropolis.

Moseley, Michael E. *The Maritime Foundations of Andean Civilization* (Menlo Park, CA: Cummings, 1975). Argues that the Andean cities were founded on the basis of the Pacific coastal developments.

Scientific American, ed. *Cities: Their Origin, Growth, and Human Impact* (San Francisco, CA: W.H. Freeman and Company, 1973). Anthology of articles on urbanization culled from *Scientific American* articles. Still useful.

Tedlock, D., trans. *Popol Vuh* (New York: Simon & Schuster, 1985). The definitive edition of the Mayan *Book of the Dawn of Life and the Glories of Gods and Kings*.

Time-Life Books. *Time Frame 3000–1500 BC: The Age of God-Kings* (Alexandria, VA: Time-Life Books, 1987). Popular but authentic, engaging, introduction to many areas of early urbanization: Mesopotamia, the Nile valley, the Indus valley, and the Yellow River valley.

Waley, Arthur, trans. *The Book of Songs* (New York: Grove Press, 1996). Marvelous translation of poetry from the age of Confucius.

World History Documents CD-ROM

2.1 Might Makes Right: the "Shu ching" Sets Forth the Mandate of Heaven
2.2 The Spirit World
2.3 Ch'u Yuan and Sung Yu: Individual Voices in a Chaotic Era
2.4 Confucius: *Analects*
2.5 Mencius: the *Counterattack on Legalism*
2.6 Taoism

From City-State to Empire

Developing military force was the key to transforming a city-state into an empire. City-states already had their offensive and defensive powers: walls, moats, soldiers and troops, and, for those situated at the water's edge, ships and sailors. The literature from Mesopotamia, pre-imperial China, ancient Greece, and Mayan Mesoamerica abounds with evidence of fighting among city-states. From Gilgamesh onward, the rulers of city-states were builders of city walls and commanders of armed forces, famed as much for their military prowess as for their administration. They were engaged in incessant warfare.

Military force turned these city-states into empires. Almost 4000 years earlier, Sargon of Akkad (c. 2330–2280

B.C.E.) had set the example. His victories over the quarreling city-states of Mesopotamia around 2250 B.C.E. created the first empire recorded in history.

Sargon's troops were apparently equipped with the usual weaponry of the day: wooden spears with sharp points made of stone or bone and a range of perhaps 150 feet, simple bows and arrows with a range of somewhat more than 300 feet, leather slings capable of hurling stones with deadly force up to 600 feet, and war chariots—rough wagons with solid wooden wheels, pulled by asses—bearing their spear hurlers and quivers filled with arrows. We do not have visual evidence of Sargon's armies, but we do for the Sumerians whom he defeated. The military standard from Ur depicts not only the foot soldiers, chariots, and weapons of the victors, but also the defeated enemy soldiers, some already dead, some awaiting their fate. Sargon's armies were probably not much different from Ur's in their equipment, but they were greater in numbers, organization, skill, and energy.

Sargon proceeded to conquer the cities of the middle and upper Euphrates and moved on into southern Anatolia. Then he turned eastward to dominate Susa in western Iran, the capital city of the Elamites. Sargon's empire lasted for only about a century, but from his time onward,

Deer hunt relief, Hittite, 9th century B.C.E. **Stone.** (*Museum of Anatolian Civilizations, Ankara, Turkey*)

Macedonian troops in formation, after a painting by G.D. Rowlandson.

Mesopotamia was usually ruled by one empire or another, most frequently an invading force, like his own, but sometimes a revolutionary army arising from within. City-states did not return.

Egypt also established an empire early on, by moving southward, above the first cataract—one of a series of impassable rapids—on the Nile River, into Nubia, a land famed for its gold. As early as 2500 B.C.E., the Egyptians built a city at Buhen, just below the second cataract, in an area not much populated at the time, and held it for centuries as a basis for mining and trade, until it was taken by Nubians. During the twelfth dynasty (1991–1786 B.C.E.), however, Egypt returned to the area. The Egyptians secured passage for ships around the first cataract by constructing a canal and added a parallel land route over the desert sands. At Buhen Egyptian engineers directed the construction of one of the greatest fortresses known to ancient history. Low, outer walls and towering inner walls were each protected by ditches and crenellated on top with loopholes for archers and spear- and stone-throwers. The fortress housed soldiers' barracks surrounded by their own walls, a market, government offices and residences, and, later, a temple dedicated to Horus. Buhen served as the chief outpost of Egyptian military activity, administration, and trade in Nubia. It was once again conquered by Nubians after Egypt itself was defeated by Hyksos invaders, probably from across the deserts of Sinai, about 1600 B.C.E.

At about that time, new instruments of war were being introduced into the fertile crescent by new immigrant groups, probably from the mountains to the northeast. The most significant was a new two-wheeled war chariot, light, fast, easily maneuverable, pulled by horses and commanded by archers in bronze

The Assyrian army and musicians, from the Palace of Ashurbanipal, Nineveh, 7th century B.C.E. Limestone relief. (*Louvre, Paris*)

Although chariots, horses, and asses were employed by early armies, the mainstay of most was the infantry: Greek hoplites, protected by their heavy bronze armor and massed in phalanxes several rows deep; Roman legions, less heavily armed, and grouped into smaller units for greater mobility; and Chinese foot soldiers, also by the thousands. Chinese historical records are abundant in their descriptions of armies and warfare, but archaeologists were nevertheless astonished to uncover in 1974 a ceramic army of 7000 life-sized soldiers and horses (see p. 206) arranged in military formation and armed with bronze weapons, spears, longbows, and crossbows (a Chinese invention). In 1976 a second excavation uncovered the cavalry, 1400 chariots and mounted soldiers in four military units. The next year a much smaller pit was discovered, holding what appeared to be a terra cotta officer corps. These thousands of figures were not mass produced. Each figure was modeled and painted separately, even down to its elaborate hairstyle that symbolized its specific military office. The figures apparently represented the elite of the imperial troops, and were fashioned to accompany the first emperor of China, Qin Shi Huangdi (r. 221–210 B.C.E.), to his own tomb and afterlife.

War took place on sea as well as land. In the eastern Mediterranean, in the fifth century B.C.E., the trireme (see p. 145) was the principal warship of both the Persians and the Greeks as they contested for power. With approximately 170 oarsmen arranged about equally in three tiers along each side, these ships could reach speeds of up to nine knots per hour. When such speeds were not necessary, the ships might hoist square-rigged sails and travel with the wind.

The trireme's hull was of light wooden construction, with the Greek ships usually somewhat lighter than

armor shooting bronze-tipped arrows. This chariot powered the armies of the Middle East for a thousand years. The first to use it successfully were the Mitanni, centered on northern Mesopotamia, about 1500 B.C.E. They were succeeded by the Hittites, based in their capital of Hattushash (Boğazköy) in eastern Anatolia from about 1650 to about 1200 B.C.E. The Hittites, in particular, also developed the use of iron and even steel for use in weapons—defensive armor and offensive spear-, arrow-, and sword-points—and in farm tools that increased agricultural productivity.

the Persians'. This enabled faster speeds, but it also left the ships vulnerable to the bronze-covered rams that they carried as an offensive weapon. At first, spearmen and archers accompanied the rowers. By the end of the fourth century B.C.E., the construction changed, as decks were introduced to accommodate the armed soldiers, and multiple rows of oarsmen replaced the tiers.

Psychological weapons had their place as well. One of the earliest and most common was the use of sound and instruments in urging on one's own troops—and providing communication among them—while frightening and confusing the enemy. There are ancient references to the use of trumpets and other instruments as accompaniments of warfare. The Bible includes instructions in their use as the Hebrews traversed the desert in their exodus from Egypt. As they finally reached their promised land, their leader Joshua's assault on the walled city of Jericho was accompanied by trumpeters blasting on rams' horns that, according to the Book of Judges, caused the city walls to collapse.

The legendary founding of the Persian Empire was recorded long afterwards by the tenth-century C.E. poet Firdowsi in Iran's national epic the *Shah-nameh* ("Book of Kings"). Beloved by its readers, the epic describes the victory by Rustum, one of the legendary founders of the Persian nation, over his arch-enemy Turani. The epic also captures the sounds of musical instruments used in battle.

The written record of warfare is filled with the images of death, destruction, and captivity, from virtually all imperial conquests. One of the closing scenes depicts corpses from the warfare of Mesopotamia, the earliest and most continuous site of imperial battles. The lamentations over the destruction of the third city of Ur, Ur III, is one of the earliest ever recorded, between 2000 and 1500 B.C.E. It reminds us that empire building is deadly business:

O Father Nanna, that city into ruins was made; the people groan.

…

Its walls were breached; the people groan. In its lofty gates, where they were wont to promenade, dead bodies were lying about;

In its boulevards, where the feasts were celebrated, scattered they lay. In all its streets, where they were wont to promenade, dead bodies were lying about; In its places, where the festivities of the land took place, the people lay in heaps.

…

Its dead bodies, like fat placed in the sun, of themselves melted away.

(Pritchard, p. 459)

Battle of Til-Tuba between the Assyrian king Ashurbanipal and the king of Elam, from the palace of Ashurbanipal, 645 B.C.E. Stone relief. (*British Museum, London*)

QUESTIONS

1. How important are warfare and murder in the construction of empire?
2. How closely can you correlate the development of new weapons of warfare with the creation of new empires?
3. What kinds of skills and powers, beyond the military, are necessary in the construction of empires?

3

Empire and Imperialism

2000 B.C.E. –1100 C.E.

WHAT ARE EMPIRES AND WHY ARE THEY IMPORTANT?

The first empires grew up in the areas of the civilizations we studied in Part 2—that is, in Mesopotamia, the Nile valley, and the Yellow River valley. The Akkadian Empire of Sargon, which flourished *c.* 2350 B.C.E., is the first for which we have documentary evidence, and it was followed in the same part of Mesopotamia by the Babylonians and, later, by the Assyrians. In their successions we see a pattern that will become familiar: the building of a large, powerful military force in the hands of a strong ruler, followed by a decline, a challenge by an outsider, the overthrow of the old empire, and the rise of a new one.

Chapter 5 begins with Akkad as the earliest example of empire building. Egypt provides the second example, and then we turn to the Persian Empire. In Persia's struggle against the Greeks in the fifth century B.C.E., we see a fundamental clash between monarchy and democracy and between empire and city-state. A confederation of small, local city-states stopped the conquering force of the world's most powerful empire. Ultimately, however, in the subsequent dissolution of the Greek system into civil war and the succession of Alexander the Great, we see one of the great ironies of history. Those cities that had earlier prided themselves on their independence and their victory over the largest empire of the time lost their independence and became integrated into Alexander's empire.

Chapter 6 will consider in greater depth the empire of Rome, while Chapter 7 examines those of China and, briefly, its daughter civilization in Japan. Chapter 8 explores India and touches on southeast Asia. These three systems controlled vast areas, had an enormous impact on tens of millions of people, and have continued to make their influence felt to our own time. They represent turning points in the history of most of humankind.

Rome, China, and India were so successful that their ideologies of empire—their explanations of why they should rule—prevailed for centuries. Indeed, the Roman Empire endured for almost a thousand years, from about 500 B.C.E. to almost 500 C.E., and if we include the Eastern

Roman soldiers besieging a town, from *The History of the Nations*. Aquatint engraving by A. Nani. Rome's array of military devices—battering rams, equipment for scaling walls, catapults, and horses and chariots waiting at the ready—facilitated its policy of the "new wisdom," namely, to defeat the enemy through patient, deliberate preparation, and the demonstration of overwhelming force. (*Private Collection*)

Empire, based in Constantinople, Rome's duration is some 2000 years. Moreover, Rome inspired an imperial image that was expressed throughout later Europe in the so-called Holy Roman Empire. In the nineteenth and early twentieth centuries, many commentators compared the British Empire with Rome, and in the late twentieth and early twenty-first centuries, many drew a similar comparison with the United States. The Chinese Empire, founded in 221 B.C.E., lasted more or less continuously until 1911 C.E., and some would argue that it persists even today in new, communist garb. The first emperor to rule almost all of the Indian subcontinent, Ashok (Asoka) Maurya (r. 273–232 B.C.E.), is still commemorated today on every rupee currency note printed in India. Throughout these chapters, we also consider the trade routes that kept these three great empires in communication with each other.

DAWN OF THE EMPIRES

EMPIRE-BUILDING IN NORTH AFRICA, WEST ASIA, AND THE MEDITERRANEAN 2000 B.C.E.–300 B.C.E.

KEY TOPICS
- The Meaning of Empire
- The Earliest Empires
- The Persian Empire
- The Greek City-States
- The Empire of Alexander the Great

THE MEANING OF EMPIRE

New York proudly calls itself the Empire State; Chrysler advertises its Chrysler Imperial luxury automobile; until recently, Britain maintained the "imperial gallon" as a measure of volume. Yet today the word "imperialism" has a generally negative connotation. The demise within the past generation of many empires, most recently that of the Soviet Union, has met with general approval around the world. Why does the concept of empire evoke such conflicting attitudes? What is an empire?

Empires grow from the conquest of one people by another—in fact, a definition of empire is the extension of political rule by one people over other, different peoples. Empires have been as natural in human history as the desire of people to exert control over other peoples and their resources, and they have arisen as frequently as rulers have been able to build military organizations capable of attaining those goals.

The word "empire" stirs conflicting images and feelings in most of us. We think of the monumental structures of palaces and the ruling establishments of the emperor and the leadership cadre. In our imaginations we see majestic buildings adorned with the finest artworks. The emperor and the imperial administrators, we imagine, wear the finest clothes, eat the choicest foods, enjoy the most select luxuries, and support and command the most powerful technologies. Often they encourage great creativity in the arts and in learning. Sometimes, however, we see them using their power over others in acts of cruelty, arrogance, irresponsibility, and decadence.

We see, too, vast marketplaces and, perhaps, ports and dockyards processing goods from the far corners of the empire, since one purpose of empire building is to bring natural resources to the mother country. Leading into the capital city, connecting it with the remotest areas of empire, are lines of communication and transportation, sea lanes, and, most important of all, roads. Specific examples stand out. Notable are the grand canals linking the rich agricultural lands of south China to the capital in the north and dating back as early as the Sui dynasty, in the seventh century C.E. Similarly, the phrase "All roads lead to Rome," the capital of an equally powerful empire, may have been an exaggeration, but its central idea was correct. Empires bring exotic goods and diverse peoples together under a common ruler. People of different languages, religions, ethnic origins, and cultural and technological levels are brought under a single, centralized rule.

In order to organize and maintain communication and exchange among all parts of the empire, a system of administration must be established. The administrators and rulers must also regulate the fate of conquered peoples in accordance with the needs of the empire. Some are granted full citizenship, most of the remainder receive fewer rights and privileges, while those at the bottom, especially war captives, might be

Opposite **Apadana, principal audience hall, Persepolis, Iran, 521–486** B.C.E. Persepolis was destroyed by Alexander the Great. Visible here are columns from the Apadana of Darius I.

enslaved. A few—those who proved particularly dangerous or costly to the imperial rulers—might be executed as a warning to potential rebels.

The administration must ensure either that different kinds of monies from various parts of the empire are consolidated into a single system of coinage or that means of exchanging them are readily available. It must communicate across the many languages of the empire, and it may adopt and impose a single administrative language so that the writ of empire is universally understood. It must establish a legal system with at least some degree of uniformity. Indeed, the administration must provide sufficient uniformity in language, currency, weights, measures, and legal systems to enable it to function as a single political structure. Perhaps the most significant administrative task of all is the collection of taxes from its subjects and tribute from the conquered. Such revenues represent the continuing financial profits to the rulers.

Twentieth-century scholars emphasize two forms of imperial rule: **hegemony** and **dominance**. For the imperial power, hegemony is to be preferred, for this is rule that subjects accept willingly if they can be persuaded that it is in their best interests. They may benefit from the stability and peace it imposes; from the technological improvements it introduces; from the more extensive networks it develops and opens to their trade and profit; from the cultural sophistication it exhibits and shares with them; or from the opportunities for new kinds of advancement that membership in the empire may offer. If imperial membership is perceived to have such benefits, the subject peoples may welcome it peacefully, even eagerly. They may accept the ideology of the imperial power and its explanation for the legitimacy and benefit of its foreign rule. In short, hegemony may be defined as foreign rule that governs with the substantial consent of the governed.

Should the imperial ideology not be acceptable, however, rulers will impose their government through dominance, the exercise of sheer power. In these circumstances, military force, and the threat to exercise it, are central to the empire's existence, so the state expends vast sums on recruiting, training, and equipping its armies. The troops mobilize across the vast spaces of empire, using the same roads that carry the imperial commerce.

Resistance to imperial rule is as normal as empires themselves. Rulers of empires usually dominate because they are able to mobilize more power than the peoples they control. Often, intentionally or unintentionally, the secrets of their power spread among the conquered, thereby enriching their lives. The subject populations learn from the technology introduced by their conquerors, whether it is the use of weapons, materials, military formations, agricultural methods, administrative organizations, or techniques of production. Empires that begin by using their superiority to rule, eventually produce change among the peoples they conquer. Subject peoples, who may originally have felt some gratitude toward their imperial benefactors, may later grow resentful, restive, and finally rebellious. Goths, for example, no longer wished to be subordinate to Romans, nor Mongols to Chinese, as we shall see in Chapters 6 and 7. Empires are not static. They rise and they fall. Ironically, the imperial masters are often forced to trade places with those they had subjugated.

The causes of the decline and fall of empires include:

- Failure of leadership—the inability of the empire to produce or select rulers capable of maintaining the imperial structures;
- Overextension of the administration—the inability of the imperial rulers to sustain the costs of a far-flung empire while coping simultaneously with critical domestic problems;
- Collapse of the economy—the overextension of empire to territories so remote or so difficult to subdue and govern that costs outrun benefits;

hegemony The predominance of one unit over the others in a group, for example one state in a confederation. It can also apply to the rule of an empire over its subject peoples, when the foreign government is exercised with their substantial consent.

dominance The imposition of alien government through force, as opposed to hegemony.

- Doubts over the ideology—the end of belief in the justice or benefit of empire, which may occur either when cynical colonizers abandon the colonial enterprise, or when frustrated colonized peoples revolt, or both;
- Military defeat—external enemies and the colonized people combine in revolt.

THE EARLIEST EMPIRES

Mesopotamia and the Fertile Crescent

Mesopotamia's earliest power centers were independent city-states that could not reach political accommodation among themselves. They fought constantly for land, irrigation rights, and prestige, as we can see from the scenes of warfare that fill the bas relief artwork from third-millennium Sumer. From this artwork and from cuneiform records, archaeologists have reconstructed two main antagonists, the cities of Lagash and Umma in Mesopotamia, which, with their allied forces, dominated the warfare of the time. Victory by either one, however, or by any of the city-states over any of the others, was frequently avenged in the next generation.

Sargon of Akkad. Geographically, the city-states of Mesopotamia were also vulnerable to immigrant groups crossing their territory and challenging their powers. About 2350 B.C.E., Sargon (r. *c.* 2334–2279 B.C.E.), leading an immigrant group of Semitic peoples from the Arabian peninsula, entered Sumer. The new arrivals settled in and around northern Sumer and called their land Akkad. Sargon led the Akkadians to victories over the leading cities of Sumer, over the Elamites to the east, over northern Mesopotamia, and over a swath of land connecting Mesopotamia to the Mediterranean. He founded the Akkadian capital at Agade, a city whose exact location is now unknown.

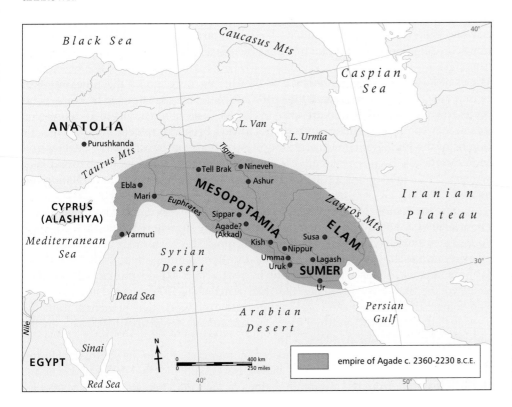

The Empire of Sargon. During the third millennium B.C.E. Sargon established his control over the city-states of southern Mesopotamia, creating the world's first empire. Building a capital at Agade, he founded the Akkadian dynasty, which for a century ruled the fertile crescent, from the Persian Gulf to the Mediterranean Sea.

Bronze head of an Akkadian ruler (Sargon I?), c. **2250** B.C.E. Exuding royal self-confidence, this near-lifesized bronze head probably depicts Sargon I, founder of the Akkadian dynasty. For over half a century, Sargon dominated one city-state after another until he had conquered most of Mesopotamia. After his death, his successors worshiped him as a god.

Historical records are skimpy, but those that do exist correspond to our assessment of the key characteristics of empire. First, the Akkadians conquered widely. Administrative tablets of the Akkad dynasty have been found as far away as Susa, several hundred miles to the east in Persia, suggesting a far-flung governmental administration. Second, after razing the walls of the major cities of Ur, Lagash, and Umma, Sargon displaced the traditional local civilian hierarchies with his own administrators, designated the "sons of Akkad." Third, the Akkadian language was used in administrative documents in Sumer. Fourth, measurements of length, area, dry and liquid quantities, and probably weight were standardized throughout the empire; indeed, people in the region used the Akkadian units of measure for more than a thousand years, far longer than the empire itself survived. Finally, Sargon imposed his own imagery and ideology of empire. Documents were dated from the founding of the Akkadian kingdom, legal oaths were taken in the name of the Akkadian king, and Sargon installed his own daughter as high-priestess of the moon-god Nanna at Ur.

Sargon's empire lasted for about a century and was followed by other outsiders, the Gutians, and then by a revival of internal Sumerian power under Ur-Nammu (r. *c.* 2112–*c.* 2095 B.C.E.). Culturally, Sumer was so advanced that it influenced even its conquerors, the Akkadians, the Gutians, and later arrivals. The Akkadian language, however, did supplant Sumerian by about 2000 B.C.E.

Waves of Invaders: The Babylonians and the Hittites. Throughout this time, waves of immigrants continuously entered the fertile crescent, perhaps attracted by empty land on its fringes, perhaps by the presence in its heartland of already settled peoples on whom they could prey. Historians have not always been able to determine the specific origins of the immigrants, but two groups have stood out most clearly, Semites and Indo-Europeans. Each is designated by the family of languages that it spoke and later wrote; a common language probably indicates a degree of internal ethnic relationship as well.

Among the Semitic groups were the Amorites, who invaded and conquered Sumer about 1900 B.C.E. and founded their own new dynasty slightly to the north at Babylon. At first they employed Sumerian cultural and administrative forms, but over time they created new systems of their own. Their sixth ruler, Hammurabi (r. 1792–1750 B.C.E.), is most famous for his law codes, but he was also a skilled military leader who defeated the Sumerian city-states that had remained independent. He created the Babylonian Empire, imposing an administrative network that stretched from the Persian Gulf to Syria and endured for 250 years, until its defeat about 1500 B.C.E. by the Hittites, a new group of invaders.

While the Semitic Amorites had apparently immigrated from the south, the Hittites arrived as part of a vast movement of Indo-European peoples that originated from the north, apparently from the mountain regions of the Caucasus. This group of peoples spoke "Indo-European" languages, from which developed many of the principal languages of the lands to which they migrated and settled, from Britain in the northwest to Persia and India in the southeast.

In the course of their migrations, the Indo-Europeans also invented the decisive weapon of the age, the two-wheeled war chariot. Drawn by a horse, which bore part of the weight of the chariot, this new war machine had light wheels with a hub and spokes and carried three warriors, at least one of whom could continuously shoot his wooden bow, reinforced with bone and sinew. Unlike the four-wheeled chariot, the new design of the Indo-Europeans had great maneuverability.

The Hittites shared in this invention. When they settled in Anatolia, they also helped usher in another innovation, iron-working technology that they developed in this iron-rich region. They established their capital in Hattushash, modern Boğazköy, Turkey, in the early second millennium B.C.E., extending their power over much of Anatolia and northern Syria. Much of what we know about them comes from some 25,000 cuneiform tablets that were discovered there. About 1590 B.C.E. they invaded and conquered Babylonia. About 1400 to 1200 B.C.E., during the New Kingdom of Egypt, the Hittites ruled as one of the most powerful nations of the Middle East. In c. 1274 B.C.E., in one of the greatest battles of the Middle East, they confronted the Egyptian armies at Qadesh, Syria. The two armies, each with about 20,000 men, and the Hittites with 2500 two-wheeled chariots, fought to a draw. Within a few years these two great powers had concluded treaties of peace and mutual defense, re-affirmed by royal marriages.

The Hittite Empire suddenly collapsed about 1193 B.C.E., perhaps under an onslaught from invaders, the Sea Peoples, who arrived via the Mediterranean. City-state and regional outposts of Hittites survived until about 710 B.C.E., when they were defeated and incorporated by the Assyrians.

The Assyrians. Assyrians, descendants of the Akkadians, were additional major participants in the continuous warfare in Mesopotamia. In the twentieth century B.C.E. they established an independent state and, through the trade of their private businessmen, achieved some prosperity. Then, subjugated by the Mitanni, they regained

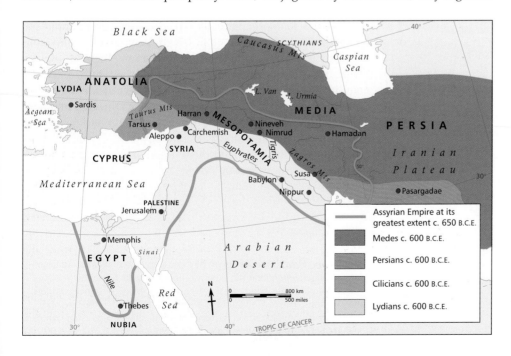

Assyria and its rivals. The shifting political map of southwest Asia was dominated between 850 and 650 B.C.E. by the powerful and martial Assyrians, who even occupied Egypt. Anatolia was fragmented into smaller states. To the north a powerful federation of Median tribes was a growing threat. In 614, in alliance with the Babylonians, they crushed Assyria.

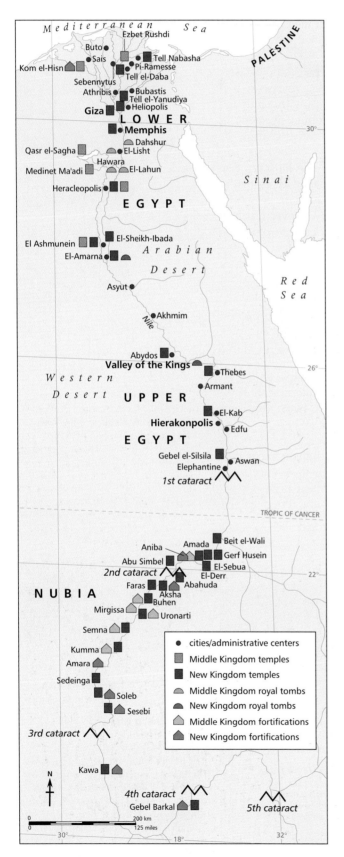

their independence in the thirteenth century only to lose it again to the Arameans *c.* 1000 B.C.E.

Around 900 B.C.E. a Neo-Assyrian (New Assyrian) kingdom began a series of conquests, sweeping westward to the Mediterranean coast, northward to Syria and Palestine, and southeastward into Babylon. Infantry provided their main force, while archers riding in chariots led the attacks, and battering rams and siege towers assaulted fixed positions.

More than most ancient empires, the Assyrians controlled conquered peoples through policies of terror and forced migration. They tortured those they captured to instill fear. They also deported some nations into exile from their homelands, including ten of the tribes of Israel, which were subsequently "lost"—that is, they lost their sense of ethnic and religious identity and presumably ceased their opposition to the Assyrians, just as the conquerors had hoped. In other regions, the Assyrians imported their own people to settle among the defeated peoples and keep them under control.

King Esarhaddon (r. 680–669 B.C.E.) conquered Egypt in 671 B.C.E., making Assyria the greatest power of its day. His successors held the entire province, driving the Nubians from the southern regions and suppressing rebellions. Assyria finally withdrew from Egypt, defeated not primarily by the Egyptians but by internal dynastic struggles and by the combined forces of Babylonians, Arameans, the Medes of Iran, and Scythian invaders, who attacked Assyria's Mesopotamian heartland. The Assyrian capital, Nineveh, fell in 612 B.C.E.

Only the last of the Neo-Assyrian kings, Ashurbanipal (r. 668–627 B.C.E.), is known to have been literate, and he constructed a great library in his capital at Nineveh. Some 20,000 tablets are still preserved from that library, including the earliest complete version of *The Epic of Gilgamesh*.

The city-state organizational structure of Mesopotamia and its geographical openness had left the region very vulnerable. As the city-states fought destructively among themselves, they were repeatedly attacked by, and absorbed into, powerful empires. Some of these empires were based outside the region, others grew up, or transplanted themselves through immigration, within the region. The Mesopotamians had to expend their resources on military technology and organization as their local units of government faced increasing challenges from ever-greater external powers.

Middle and New Kingdom Egypt. By 2040 B.C.E. the unification of Egypt into a centralized, militaristic state was under way. Its hierarchic society focused on the priesthood and the dynastic succession of semi-god rulers, the pharaohs. The consolidation of power was reflected in the size and scale of royal building projects, including fortifications, new cities, temples, and grandiose tombs, and by conquests in Nubia.

Egypt and International Conquest

Egypt's background to empire was very different from Mesopotamia's. From early times Egypt was governed as a unified state. Geography had encouraged Egypt to become a single administrative unit, incorporating the entire Nile valley from the first cataract northward to the Mediterranean Sea. From 3000 B.C.E. to the present, Egypt has usually remained a single political unit, so we think of it as a kingdom with a single government ruling a single civilization rather than as an empire of one people ruling over others.

Egyptian forces did not always stay within their own borders, however. During the Middle Kingdom, *c.* 2000–1650 B.C.E., Egyptians conquered Nubia, the territory stretching southward some 900 miles from just above the first cataract in the Nile, at present-day Aswan in Egypt, to present-day Khartoum, capital of the Sudan. At first, this imperial conquest was only into lower Nubia, and Nubia's success in driving out the Egyptian conquerors was one of the factors that brought Egypt's Middle Kingdom to an end.

During the second intermediate period (1650–1550 B.C.E.), a time of disunity between periods of consolidation, immigrant Semitic groups, referred to in Egyptian texts as the Hyksos, ruled Lower Egypt. It is not clear if the Hyksos first came as traders or as nomadic immigrants, but as the Egyptian kingdom disintegrated they came to rule parts of it. Although later Egyptian rulers despised them, they are recognized as the legitimate sixteenth dynasty. A Semitic people, the Hyksos introduced bronze-making technology and horses and chariots to Egypt.

One of the establishing events of the New Kingdom, as Egypt became consolidated once again (*c.* 1550–*c.* 1070 B.C.E.), was the expulsion of the Hyksos. In pursuing the Hyksos into Palestine, where they apparently had allies, the Egyptians began an active, direct involvement in Middle Eastern affairs that led to their imperial presence in the region for several centuries. Thutmosis I (r. 1504–1492 B.C.E.) not only extended Egypt's control further into Nubia than ever before (see below), but also northeast as far as the Euphrates River, creating Egypt's greatest historical empire. The small states of Syria and Palestine managed to remain self-governing, but Egypt stationed army units and administrative officials in the region and collected taxes. Egypt seemed more interested in access to these taxes, to raw materials, and to trading opportunities than in imperial governance.

Relief from the temple of Beit el-Wali (detail), Lower Nubia, *c.* 2000–1850 B.C.E. The rich variety of produce here presented to Ramses II after his conquest of Lower Nubia—bags of gold, incense, tusks, ebony logs, ostrich eggs, bows, shields, fans, and wild animals—seems to mirror the ethnic diversity on display. Pale-, brown-, and black-skinned peoples coexisted in Egypt and Nubia. (*British Museum, London*)

Royal pyramids and adjacent iron slag heaps at Meroe, Sudan, c. 600 B.C.E. The rulers of Meroe and Egypt shared many artistic traditions, but often gave them a distinctive local interpretation, as can be seen in the forms of their pyramids and palaces.

The Art of Palace and Temple. The colonies of the New Kingdom enriched Egypt, helping to produce a period of great opulence and creativity. Because the pharaoh often traveled throughout the country, the Egyptians built a number of elegant palaces at various points along the Nile, from the delta all the way to the northern edge of Nubia. The state religion and the state administration were closely linked, so temple complexes and the towns that grew up around them were also constructed and reconstructed as important centers of power, faith, and governance. One of the greatest of these temples was constructed by Pharaoh Ramses II (r. c. 1279–1213 B.C.E.) at Abu Simbel, just north of the first cataract, and dedicated to the greatest gods of the New Kingdom and to Ramses II himself. The entire complex, including its grand sculptures, was saved from total destruction in the 1970s by being moved to a new location at the time of the building of the Aswan dam, which completely flooded the entire site. Art was abundant and highly stylized, with fixed proportions for various parts of the body, and fixed, usually stiff, poses.

In addition to Ramses II, at least two other pharaohs call for special note. One of the four female pharaohs, Hatshepsut (c. 1473–c. 1458 B.C.E.) was the widow of one pharaoh and served as regent to her stepson when he succeeded to the throne. For fifteen years, however, until the boy grew up and she died, Hatshepsut declared herself "king," since there was no official sanction for a female ruler. She encouraged artists to represent her as a man, wearing male clothing and with a male king's beard. She built a temple at Deir el-Bahri near Thebes, which was devoted to the worship of the traditional god Amon but which she also hoped would promote her as a deity after her death.

Also departing from Egyptian traditions, in the fifth year of his reign, Amenhotep IV (r. 1352–1336 B.C.E.) changed his name to Akhenaten, "he who serves Aten," the lord of the sun. He challenged the order of ancient Egypt by adopting a new monotheistic religion. Instead of worshiping a pantheon of gods, he worshiped only the sun, and designated himself as mediator between his people and the god. He had the name of

Amon, principal god of the existing religious practice, erased from inscriptions throughout Egypt, and similarly had the words "all gods" removed from certain texts.

To bolster the new order and escape the power of the hostile priesthood, Akhenaten moved his capital 200 miles north from the established center of Thebes to an untouched site in the desert. He named his new city Akhetaten, or "horizon of Aten," present-day Amarna. Here he and his queen Nefertiti and their six daughters practiced their new religion. Akhenaten's religious revolution never caught on. His geographic and intellectual isolation from his people threatened the stability of Egypt's empire. When he died, Akhenaten's successors abandoned Akhetaten and later razed it to the ground. They returned to Thebes where the old religious and political order resumed.

The End of Empire. Egypt's imperial control over remote and diverse peoples met resistance from local powers within the fertile crescent. The Hittites, the Babylonians, and, especially, the Mitanni mounted frequent revolts. (Egyptian pharaoh Ramses II

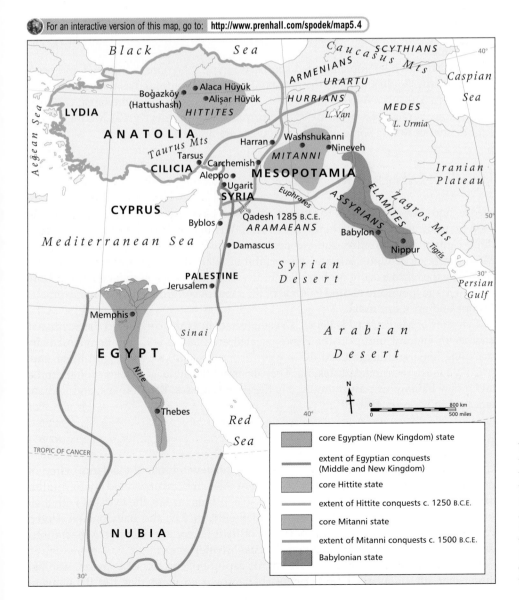

For an interactive version of this map, go to: http://www.prenhall.com/spodek/map5.4

Legend:
- core Egyptian (New Kingdom) state
- extent of Egyptian conquests (Middle and New Kingdom)
- core Hittite state
- extent of Hittite conquests c. 1250 B.C.E.
- core Mitanni state
- extent of Mitanni conquests c. 1500 B.C.E.
- Babylonian state

The empires of southwest Asia. Toward the end of the second millennium B.C.E. three empires fought for control of the fertile crescent. Egyptians, Mitanni of northern Mesopotamia, and Hittites of Anatolia came into direct conflict. Building on strong political control over their core regions, each dispatched powerful armies with the most up-to-date weapons to seize more territory from the others.

reported the great, but indecisive, battle against the Hittites at Qadesh, noted above, as a brilliant victory, neither the first nor last time that a government would falsely claim military honors that it had not won.) Egyptian control ended by about 1200 B.C.E., although its trading interests and political and economic influence in the region continued for centuries.

After suffering defeats in the Levant, Egypt was pushed back within its river domains, but by now these once again included Nubia. Early in the New Kingdom, Egypt had once again conquered the heartland of central Nubia, the core of the sophisticated, independent state and a source of gold, minerals, wood, and recruits for Egypt's army and police. It maintained its imperial power over this southern colony until c. 1050 B.C.E., when the colony broke free. The loss of empire, together with the loss of the gold, supplies, and slaves it had provided, helped to bring an end to the unified New Kingdom of the Egyptians and to usher in the third intermediate period of divided rule (c. 1069–747 B.C.E.).

Three centuries later Nubia marched northward to capture Egypt itself, reversing the relationship between colonizer and colonized. For half a century, 712–657 B.C.E., Nubia ruled over an empire of its own, which included all of Egypt. Thereafter Nubia remained strong, with its capital first at Napata and later at Meroe, while Egypt fell into decline.

In 671 B.C.E., while Nubians ruled southern Egypt, Assyrians conquered and occupied the north. Egypt's fall into the possession of others continued as the Persians conquered it in 525 B.C.E. Two centuries later, in 332 B.C.E., Alexander the Great captured Egypt from Persia, and in 30 B.C.E., Egypt passed to the next great Mediterranean empire, that of Rome. Some of these conquests are noted below.

THE PERSIAN EMPIRE

Medes and Persians began to appear in the region east of Mesopotamia about 1300 B.C.E., bringing with them the use of iron. Written cuneiform records of the mid-ninth century B.C.E. confirm the archaeological evidence of their arrival. At first the Medes were more numerous and powerful, but later the Persians came to predominate. Like the Hittites, both groups were Indo-Europeans—that is, in language and cultural heritage they were related to some of the same major groups who came to inhabit Europe and northern India.

Cyaxares of Media (r. 625–585 B.C.E.) established an army; conquered the Scythians, another immigrant group in the region; sealed an alliance with the Babylonians by marrying his granddaughter to the son of their ruler; and, together with them, captured Nineveh, the capital of Assyria. They destroyed Assyria as a major military force, and a new **balance of power** among the Egyptians, Medes, Babylonians, and Lydians emerged in western Asia.

balance of power In international relations, a policy that aims to secure peace by preventing any one state or alignment of states from becoming too dominant. Alliances are formed in order to build up a force equal or superior to that of the potential enemy.

Persian Expansion

Cyrus II, the Great, of Persia (r. 558–529 B.C.E.), however, broke the balance when he defeated the other three kingdoms of western Asia and incorporated them into his own empire. He conquered, first, the Medes in 550; then, in 546, the Lydians with their king, the fabulously wealthy Croesus; and finally, in 539, the Babylonians. Under Cyrus, the Achaemenids (named in honor of their legendary ancestor Achaemenes) dominated the entire region from Persia to the Mediterranean.

The story of Cyrus' greatest conquest, his capture of the city of Babylon, also has larger-than-life qualities. Cyrus' legend had grown so great that the Babylonians

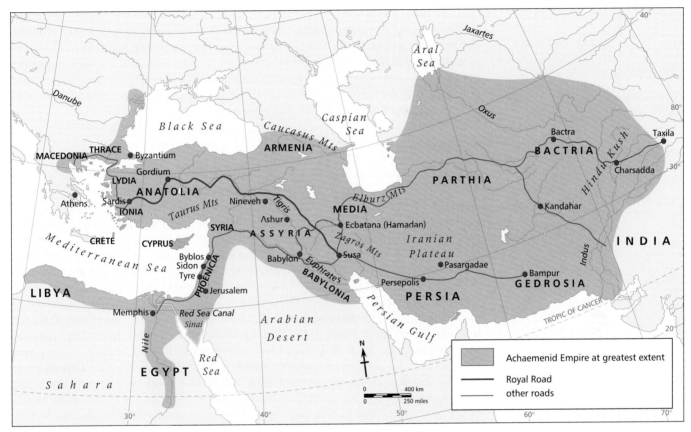

Achaemenid Persia. The Medes and the Persians were united under Cyrus the Great in 550 B.C.E. to form the Achaemenid or Persian Empire. Cyrus and his successors, notably Darius and Xerxes, extended the empire to the Indus in the east and to Egypt and Libya in the west, and twice invaded Greece.

welcomed their new foreign king without even giving battle. Cyrus was also careful to observe the principal ritual of the Babylonian New Year festival, showing honor to the statue of Bel-Marduk, the king of the Babylonian gods. Herodotus' story of Cyrus' death is also of legendary proportions. In conquering the Massagetai nomads, Cyrus killed the son of the woman who ruled them, and the young man committed suicide. The mother swore revenge and ultimately killed Cyrus. This legend is, however, not consistent with the more illustrious story of Cyrus' death in battle. According to this, Cyrus was killed in battle in 529 B.C.E., defending his empire against attacks from the north by a nomadic group of Scythians led by their queen Tomyris.

His eldest son, Cambyses II (r. 529–522 B.C.E.), expanded Cyrus' conquests. Crossing the Sinai Desert, he captured Memphis, the capital of Egypt, and carried its pharaoh back to Susa in captivity, thus completing the conquest of all of the major powers that had influenced the Middle East. Egypt frequently revolted, and large garrisons were required to keep it under control, so the Achaemenids under Darius I (r. 522–486 B.C.E.) completed a canal across the desert, connecting the Nile River and the Red Sea. This early "Suez Canal," first envisioned by the Egyptians as a trade route, became a troop supply line for Persian control over Egypt.

Darius also extended the Persian Empire more deeply into the Indian subcontinent, as far as the Indus River. The Achaemenids now controlled some of the most valuable trade routes in Asia; the **satrapy**, or province, of "India" submitted one-third of the annual cash receipts of the Achaemenids, and Indian troops served in the Achaemenid armies. From this time, Indian- and Persian-based powers would regularly confront one another across the borders of what are today Afghanistan and Pakistan. Meanwhile, in the west, Darius expanded onto the fringes of Europe, capturing Thrace and Macedonia, and bringing the Persian Empire to its greatest extent.

satrapy A province or colony in the Achaemenid or Persian Empire ruled by a satrap or governor. Darius I completed the division of the Empire into provinces, and established 20 satrapies with their annual tributes. The term satrapy can also refer to the period of rule of a satrap.

Attempts to move further were stymied. The Scythians to the north and west fought a kind of guerrilla warfare that the massed forces of the Persians could not overcome. To the south and west, the Greeks defeated Persian armies of invasion. As you will read later in this chapter, a confederation of small, democratic, Greek city-states managed to repulse the mighty Persian Empire. Herodotus' *The Persian Wars*, written in the late fifth century B.C.E. and presenting the story from a Greek perspective, is the first great book of secular history still preserved.

Imperial Policies

The Persian imperial form of rule and administration changed in the three generations from Cyrus II, its chief architect, through his son and successor Cambyses II, to Darius I, its most powerful emperor. The differences among the three emperors became especially clear in their policies for achieving a balance between the power of the central government and the desire of local, conquered peoples for some degree of autonomy. Under Cyrus and Darius, Persia respected local customs and institutions even as the empire expanded. Cambyses was more dictatorial, and met an early end.

Cyrus II. Cyrus (r. 558–529 B.C.E.) respected the dignity of his opponents. When he conquered the Medes, he allowed their king to escape with his life. He administered his newly acquired lands through the existing Median bureaucracy and army, allowing Median officials to keep their positions, though under Persian control. When Cyrus conquered Lydia, he spared Croesus and even enlisted his advice as a consultant. In conquered Ionian cities he retained local rulers who were willing to work under Persian direction. On defeating Babylon, his most powerful rival, Cyrus chose to rule in the name of the Babylonian god Marduk and to worship daily in his temple, thus keeping the support of the priests. He continued to employ local bureaucrats and to protect and secure the trade routes that brought wealth to the empire and secured the loyalty of the merchant classes.

Perhaps most strikingly, Cyrus allowed the peoples that Babylonia had captured and deported to return to their homes. For example, he permitted the Jewish community of exiles in Babylon to return home to Judaea and to rebuild their temple in

Lion killing a bull, bas relief, Persepolis, Iran, 550–330 B.C.E. The great palace complex of Persepolis, encompassing many smaller palaces within it, was designed as the central symbol of Darius' empire. Construction began in 518 B.C.E. and took some seventy years to complete. Scenes such as this bas relief of a lion killing a bull seem to emerge from Achaemenid mythology, which read the signs of the zodiac, Leo following Taurus, as representing the end of the old year and the coming of the new.

Homage rendered to Darius, bas relief, Persepolis, Iran, 550–330 B.C.E. On New Year's Day, ambassadors of each of Persia's twenty and more satrapies presented themselves to the emperor in his audience hall at Persepolis. Darius, bejeweled and arrayed in royal robes of purple and gold, received them.

Jerusalem. He also returned to them the gold and silver that had been taken from the temple. The 40,000 exiles who returned over 1000 miles to Judaea hailed Cyrus as their political savior and kept their renewed state loyal to the Persian Empire.

Cambyses II. Unlike his father, Cambyses II (r. 529–522 B.C.E.) seems to have lost sight of the need for restraint in both the expansion and the administration of his empire. His conquest of Egypt and his use of Egyptians in his own administration of that land followed Cyrus' model, but then he overextended his reach. His attempted campaign against the Phoenician city of Carthage in distant north Africa failed when Phoenician sailors in his own navy refused to fight. An army sent south from Egypt to Nubia, attempting to capture its fabled gold supplies, failed to reach its destination and retreated from the desert in tatters. Cambyses may not have been emotionally stable, and it was rumored that he kicked to death his pregnant wife/sister. When he died, as he was returning to Persia to put down an insurrection, it was further rumored that he had committed suicide. His seven-year rule had been costly to Persia.

Darius I. Darius (r. 522–486 B.C.E.), a general in the Persian army and prince of the Achaemenid dynasty, succeeded to the throne by murdering Bardiya (r. 522), who ruled briefly after Cambyses. Darius ruled for thirty-five years. He was more deliberate, more balanced, and more capable as an administrator than Cambyses, and he became much richer as emperor than either of his predecessors. Like Cyrus, he used local administrators to staff local governments. He sought to create smaller, more efficient units of government by increasing the number of administrative units, or satrapies, even faster than he expanded the empire. Some of the regional administrators, or satraps, were local elites; some were Persian. In each satrapy, loyalty to the empire was assured by the presence of Persian army units, which reported directly back to the king, and by a secretary, who monitored the actions of the satrap and also reported back to Persia.

Darius commissioned the design of the first written Persian script. He established the tradition that royal inscriptions were to be trilingual—in Old Persian, Babylonian, and Elamite. Among these inscriptions were those on the Behistun stone, a proclamation of Darius' ascent to power, that twenty-three centuries later became the key to unlocking cuneiform writing. In the midst of the multitude of languages used across the empire, these were to be the official written languages of administration. The most widely spoken public language was Aramaic, however, and this language of the common people throughout much of the eastern Mediterranean greatly influenced the development of formal Persian.

Legal codes varied among the satrapies to reflect local usage, and the Persian rulers frequently codified and recorded these laws. They rationalized tax codes. They evaluated, measured, and recorded the size and productivity of agricultural fields, and fixed the tax rate at about 20 percent. In each satrapy a Persian collector gathered the various taxes—on industry, mining, ports, water, commerce, and sales. The satraps remitted most of the revenues to Persia, but some were retained locally for administrative and development expenses.

Darius built, maintained, and guarded an imperial system of roads, the most famous of which was a 1700-mile royal road, stretching from his capital at Susa to Sardis across Anatolia (but not quite reaching the Mediterranean). Along these roads he established a series of inns for travelers and a royal courier service with stations at about every 15 miles. He completed the construction of the Nile–Red Sea canal, which the Egyptians themselves had abandoned.

To increase agricultural production, Darius renewed the irrigation systems of Mesopotamia, and encouraged the introduction of new crops from one part of the empire to another. He standardized the empire's gold coinage, and permitted only his own imperial mints to strike the official coinage, the gold daric, in his name. Agriculture and commerce flourished, and not only for the benefit of the wealthy. Craftsmen produced goods for everyday use—leather sandals, cheap cloth, iron implements and utensils, and pottery—in increasing quantities.

Substantial sums of the enormous wealth of the flourishing empire went to the construction of four capital cities. The most sumptuous and lavish of them, and the one most Persian in style, was built by Darius and named "Parsa," Persia. The Greeks later called it "Persepolis," the city of the Persians.

Symbols of Power

Although the records of ancient Persia speak of painting as one of its arts, little has been found. Our greatest knowledge of Persian art comes from imperial architecture and design, most especially at Persepolis. The outstanding architectural monument in this capital was a fortified citadel that held ceremonial and administrative buildings. Immediately below it was a large complex of residential palaces, probably the homes of the court.

Alexander and subsequent conquerors looted and burned the city, and the dominant remains today are forests of 60-foot high columns, which have survived to indicate the grandeur of the city at its height. The largest and highest of all the remaining structures in the palace is the audience hall of Darius. Its façade is covered by creatures—lions, bulls, and griffins—asserting the power of the emperor and intimidating visitors. These visitors—many of them representatives from Persia's subject lands come to pay their respects in a procession before the emperor—are immortalized in bas reliefs on the façades of the building and its stairways. The array of reliefs suggests the imperial power of Persia over its empire, and yet a place of honor seems to have been found for each of the delegates.

In accordance with the political theory that had evolved in imperial Persia, the emperor legally possessed all the property of the realm as well as the power of life and death over his subjects. Darius did not, however, choose to become a god. He was probably a follower of the religion of the teacher Zarathustra, or Zoroaster as the Greeks called him. Zoroastrian scriptures date him to about 600 B.C.E., although modern scholarship places him as much as 1000 years earlier. In a series of hymns, called *Gathas*, Zoroaster described a conflict between Ahuramazda, the god of goodness and light, and Ahriman, who embodied the forces of evil and darkness. Individuals had to choose between them and they would be rewarded or punished for their choice on a final day of judgment. The *Avesta*, a later, fuller book of Zoroastrian scripture, further elaborated on the concept of an afterlife and the resurrection of the dead. Although, like Cyrus, Darius did not impose his own religious beliefs on the peoples he conquered, Zoroastrianism, with its roots in Persia, did spread rapidly under his rule. Darius also tried to soften the imposition of imperial administration and tax collection by maintaining local traditions and by enlisting local elites to serve in his administration. Like Cyrus, Darius managed to balance imperial majesty with local autonomy. At the western end of his empire, however, his neighbors and rivals, the Greeks, fought back against his attempts to rule over them.

THE GREEK CITY-STATES

The Greek city-states had deep historic roots of their own. Long before the Persian Empire, civilizations had risen and fallen on the Greek peninsula, its neighboring islands, and the island of Crete in the eastern Mediterranean Sea. Archaeological excavations show that for some five hundred years in Greece and for a thousand in Crete, local, brilliant, urban civilizations had flourished.

Early City-states of the Aegean

The Minoans. Immigrants began to settle on Crete about 6000 B.C.E. By 3000 B.C.E., they had built villages, and by 2000 B.C.E. at Knossos they erected the first and largest of at least four major palace complexes on the island. The palaces combined three functions:

HOW DO WE KNOW?

Discovering Troy and Mycenae

Until the 1870s, scholars of classical Greece believed that the Greek city-states had begun their slow evolution about the ninth century B.C.E. after hundreds of years of political and military turmoil. Naturally, they knew of Homer's great epic poems of the Trojan War, the Iliad and the Odyssey, in which the king of Mycenae led the Greek city-states in war against Troy around 1400 B.C.E., but they understood these tales of earlier times to be myths without foundation in fact.

Then, in the 1870s, Heinrich Schliemann, a classicist and amateur archaeologist, discovered evidence of the existence of city kingdoms at both Troy and Mycenae dating to about 1600 to 1450 B.C.E. Schliemann popularized archaeology and began to standardize its methods. He sought to buy the site of Knossos located on the island of Crete, but he couldn't afford to pay what the Ottoman Empire wanted for it. When Crete became independent, another archaeologist, Arthur Evans, was able to buy it. Excavating it in 1900, Evans discovered a massive palace complex that confirmed the possible reality of the

mythical king Minos. Thus archaeologists discovered two ancient kingdoms, with trade links, confirming popular folk legends and locating some of the roots of Greek civilization a thousand years further back in time.

- Languages and civilizations have been lost to history. How does the past become lost?
- Nineteenth- and twentieth-century archaeologists recovered some lost languages and civilizations. Besides Troy and Mycenae, what other examples come to mind?

they were elaborately furnished royal residences, centers for religion and ritual, and headquarters for administering the Cretan economy. The craftspeople of Crete produced bronze tools, gems, and extraordinarily fine pottery in the form of eggshell-thin vessels, which they exported throughout the eastern Mediterranean. As an island kingdom located at the crossroads of multiple trade routes, Crete excelled in commerce. Pictographic writing existed from at least 2000 B.C.E., and syllabic writing was introduced *c.* 1700 B.C.E. Known as Linear A, this script has not yet been deciphered.

About 1450 B.C.E., some, now unknown, disaster led to the destruction of three of the major palaces. (For a time scholars believed that eruptions of the volcano Thera might have caused the destruction, but deep-sea excavations show that the eruption was too early, *c.* 1625 B.C.E., and too far distant to have caused such devastation.) Crete seems to have become more deeply enmeshed in the affairs of the Greek mainland at this time. A new script, known as Linear B, was created for transcribing Greek, suggesting that this had now become the language of Crete. In 1370 B.C.E. the palace at

AT A GLANCE: ANCIENT GREECE AND ITS NEIGHBORS

DATE	POLITICAL	RELIGION AND CULTURE	SOCIAL DEVELOPMENT
600 B.C.E.	■ Cyaxares of Media (r. 625–585) ■ Age of Greek tyrants (657–570)	■ Zoroaster (630–553)	■ City-states in Greece
550 B.C.E.	■ Cyrus II (r. 558–529); defeat of Medes, Lydia, Babylon ■ Peisistratus (d. 527) controlled Athens ■ Cambyses II (r. 529–522) conquered Egypt	■ Pasargadae and Susa developed	■ Nile–Red Sea canal
500 B.C.E.	■ Darius I (r. 522–486); Persian Empire extended to Indus River; war against Greek city-states ■ Ionian revolt (499) ■ Battle of Marathon (490) ■ Xerxes I (r. 486–465) ■ War between Athens and Sparta: 1st Peloponnesian War (461–451)	■ Pythagoras (d. *c.* 500) ■ Piraeus established as port of Athens ■ Persepolis built	■ Athens at the height of its power. Acropolis built (*c.* 460); architecture, city-state democracy, political philosophy flourish
450 B.C.E.	■ Pericles (d. 429) and Delian League ■ 2nd Peloponnesian War (431–404) and end of Athenian power	■ Persian script written down ■ "Golden Age" of Athens ■ Aeschylus (d. 456) ■ Herodotus (d. *c.* 420) ■ Sophocles (d. 406) ■ Euripides (d. 406) ■ Thucydides (d. *c.* 401)	■ Persian Empire: regional laws codified; roads built; centralized administration; irrigation systems extended
400 B.C.E.		■ Socrates (d. 399)	
350 B.C.E.	■ Philip II (r. 359–336) and Alexander the Great (r. 336–323) extend Macedonian Empire ■ Athens and Thebes defeated (338), ending Greek independence ■ Alexander conquers Asia Minor (334) and Egypt (332), and reaches Indus (326)	■ Aristophanes (d. *c.* 351) ■ Plato (d. 348) ■ Aristotle (d. 322) ■ Demosthenes (d. 322) ■ Alexandria (Egypt) founded (331) ■ Persepolis burned (331)	■ Spread of Hellenistic culture
300 B.C.E.	■ Ptolemies in Egypt ■ Seleucids in Asia		

Knossos was also destroyed, and Crete came under the sway of Mycenae, the leading city-state of mainland Greece. Finally the glories of Knossos were lost, preserved for thousands of years only in legend.

The Mycenaeans. Homer portrays the Mycenaeans as brave and heroic warriors as well as active sailors and traders. They carried on extensive trade and cultural exchange with Crete, including sharing the use of Linear B script. After 1450, when several of Crete's important towns were destroyed, Mycenae came to dominate the relationship.

Mycenae was home to several small kingdoms, each with its own palace or citadel and accompanying cemetery of beehive-shaped tombs. The greatest of the cities was Mycenae itself, capital of the legendary king Agamemnon. This administrative center of the entire region was surrounded by a colossal wall up to 25 feet thick. Its massive entrance gate was adorned with huge stone lions looking down on all who entered and left. The site is rich in the evidence of warfare: weapons, armor, paintings of warriors, and, at the seashore a few miles distant, ships of war. Some of the kings, at least, were quite wealthy: one was buried with 11 pounds of gold, and the funeral "mask of Agamemnon" was a work of consummate craftsmanship in gold. Scholars have been unable to discover the reason for the fall of Mycenaean civilization; perhaps it was invaded, perhaps it imploded in internal warfare. By the end of the twelfth century B.C.E., all the palaces and towns of Mycenae had been destroyed or abandoned.

Their fall ushered in the Greek "Dark Ages," a period of general upheaval throughout much of the eastern Mediterranean. The Greeks even lost their knowledge of how to write. Apparently, additional waves of nomadic immigrants entered Greece from the north. By about 850 B.C.E. the peoples of Greece began to emerge from an age of darkness and once again to settle, to build towns, to trade overseas, to receive new waves of immigrants that increased their population, and to restore their written culture.

Death mask ("Mask of Agamemnon"), 16th century B.C.E. Gold. When archaeologists in the late nineteenth century discovered this brilliant death mask, in this leading city-state of ancient Greece, they naturally claimed that it represented Mycenae's King Agamemnon himself, leader of the Greek forces in their war against Troy. Later judgments differed, because the date of the mask was too early. (*National Archaeological Museum, Athens*)

The Greek Polis: Image and Reality

By the time the Persian emperor Darius I began to conquer the Greek city-states of western Anatolia (present-day Turkey), the Greeks had developed a very different form of political organization from that of the Persian imperial structure. The Greek city-state, or polis, was an intentionally small, locally organized government based on a single central city with enough surrounding land to support its agricultural needs. Most of the city-states had populations of a few thousand, with only the very largest of them exceeding 40,000 people.

Geography and topography played a large part in limiting the size of the Greek city-state. In and around the Greek peninsula, mountains, rivers, and seas had kept the units of settlement rather small and isolated. (To the north, where farmland was more expansive, as it was in Macedonia, geographically larger states developed within such

SOURCE

Homer and the Value System of Early Greece

Historical folk tales survived from the era of Mycenae through the Dark Ages. From these tales, which had probably circulated orally since the twelfth century B.C.E., the poet Homer (c. eighth century B.C.E.) wove his two great epic poems, the Iliad *and the* Odyssey. *The* Iliad *tells of the Trojan War, which, Homer writes, a coalition of Greek city-states launched against the Trojans in response to the seduction of Helen, the wife of the king of Sparta, by Paris, the son of the king of Troy. Just as the war begins in a personal vendetta, so, too, individual feuds during the war break out among the Greeks themselves, for personal more than for political reasons. The bitter personal quarrel between Agamemnon, brother of the king of Sparta and himself king of Mycenae, and Achilles, the mightiest of the Greek warriors, cripples the effectiveness of the Greek coalition and dominates the storyline of the* Iliad. *The* Odyssey *tells the still more personal post-war story of Odysseus' ten-year struggle to reach his home in Ithaca and of his ultimate reunion with his wife and son in that kingdom.*

Although some literary critics believe that "Homer" was really more than one author, most today believe that just one person wrote, or dictated, the epics. The stories on which Homer bases his poetic accounts were probably well known among the Greeks of his time. Homer's lasting reputation and fame rest on his skill in crafting these stories into coherent narratives told in poetry of great power. Further, by focusing on personal stories within the national epics, Homer created images of human excellence (arete in ancient Greek) at levels of heroism that inspire readers to this day. He writes with equal power of excellence in war and in love.

Bravery in warfare is a cardinal virtue, and, in the Iliad, *Homer portrays Hektor, the mightiest of the Trojans, praying that his son might inherit his own strength in battle, and even surpass it. The child's mother would apparently share this vision of her son as warrior:*

> Zeus, and you other immortals, grant that this boy, who is my son,
> may be as I am, pre-eminent among the Trojans,
> great in strength, as am I, and rule strongly over Ilion;
> and some day let them say of him: "He is better by far than his father,"
> as he comes in from the fighting; and let him kill his enemy
> and bring home the blooded spoils, and delight the heart of his mother.   (*Iliad*, VI: 476–81)

Praising excellence in warfare and combat, Homer portrays Odysseus, Telemachus, and their followers in the Odyssey *as fierce raptors swooping down upon their prey:*

> After them the attackers wheeled, as terrible as falcons
> from eyries in the mountains veering over and diving down
> with talons wide unsheathed on flights of birds,
> who cower down the sky in chutes and bursts along the valley—

> but the pouncing falcons grip their prey, no frantic wing avails,
> and farmers love to watch those beaked hunters.
> So these now fell upon the suitors in that hall,
> turning, turning to strike and strike again,
> while torn men moaned at death, and blood ran smoking over the whole floor. (XXII: 310–19)

Homer sang equally vividly, and far more sweetly and poignantly, of excellence in love. As the Odyssey *moves toward its conclusion, hero and heroine, Odysseus and Penelope, are reunited after a wartime separation of twenty years:*

> Now from his breast into his eyes the ache
> of longing mounted, and he wept at last,
> his dear wife, clear and faithful, in his arms,
> longed for as the sunwarmed earth is longed for by a swimmer
> spent in rough water where his ship went down
> under Poseidon's blows, gale winds and tons of sea.
> Few men can keep alive through a big surf
> to crawl, clotted with brine, on kindly beaches
> in joy, in joy, knowing the abyss behind:

> and so she too rejoiced, her gaze upon her husband,
> her white arms round him pressed as though forever.
> … (XXIII: 234–44)

> So they came
> into that bed so steadfast, loved of old,
> opening glad arms to one another,
> Telemachus by now had hushed the dancing,
> hushed the women. In the darkened hall
> he and the cowherd and the swineherd slept.
> The royal pair mingled in love again
> and afterward lay reveling in stories:
> hers of the siege her beauty stood at home
> from arrogant suitors, crowding on her sight,
> and how they fed their courtship on his cattle,
> oxen and fat sheep, and drank up rivers
> of wine out of the vats.
>   Odysseus told
> of what hard blows he had dealt out to others
> and of what blows he had taken—all that story.
> she could not close her eyes till all was told.
>   (*Odyssey* XXIII: 298–313)

War and love, the bloody heroism of the battlefield and the warm intimacy of family life—Homer addressed both in imagery that has inspired readers, and listeners, to this day.

centralized city capitals.) When a region could no longer support an expanding population, it hived off colonies to new locations. Most of the Greek city-states in Anatolia seem to have originated as colonial settlements of older cities on the Greek mainland, part of an array of Greek city-states that spread throughout the Mediterranean coast, extending as far west as present-day Marseilles in France and Catalonia in Spain. Although separate and usually independent politically, the city-states were united culturally by the use of the Greek language, a myth-history centered on the *Iliad* and *Odyssey* of the poet Homer, and such festivals as the Olympic games, held every four years after 776 B.C.E.

The physical design of a Greek polis told much about its origins, functions, and ideals. Many cities were built on hillsides, at least partly for defense, but also partly because of the mountainous geography of Greece. As the city rose, with each level upward its functions and architecture became more exalted. At the bottom were the houses of the common people, built simply from local materials of stone and mud, with little concern for architectural merit. Private dwellings were relatively plain; the fine art and architecture went into public buildings.

Further up the hill was the **agora**, or civic and market center, with clusters of buildings for trade in goods, ideas, and political maneuvers. These public buildings were more elegant, designed for greater comfort and show. Nearby were gymnasia for exercise and competition. The *agora* and gymnasia demonstrated the value the Greeks placed on public life and physical prowess and discipline. Further off, built into the side of the hill, was an amphitheater where plays were regularly performed, often representing scenes from Greek mythological history and suggesting their significance in understanding the moral issues of the day. In the city of Athens, at the top of the hill, on the Acropolis ("city on high"), surrounded by a wall, were the chief temples of the city, especially the shrine to the goddess Athena who was considered the divine guardian of the city.

agora A central feature of ancient Greek town planning. Its chief function was as a town market, but it also became the main social and political meeting place. Together with the acropolis, it normally housed the most important buildings of the town. Later, the Roman forum fulfilled this function.

Athens and the Development of Democracy

Each polis developed its own form of government. Councils of nobles governed some cities, while others fell under the rule of a single powerful individual. We recount the fate of the city of Athens, in particular, for three reasons: It was a leader among the Greek city-states; it gave birth to the modern concept of political democracy; and it has left us the most historical records. Of all the major cities of Greece—for example, Sparta, Corinth, Thebes, and Syracuse—Athens seems to have moved farthest from rule by kings and oligarchies in the direction of rule by the people, democracy.

In 600 B.C.E., Solon (*c.* 630–*c.* 560 B.C.E.), who had risen to high office as a general and a poet, ended the monopoly over public office held by the Athenian hereditary aristocracy. He opened to all free men participation and voting in the decision-making public assembly, although only those meeting certain income levels could be elected to high public office. The Council of Four Hundred, which Solon also created, represented the interests of the wealthy and noble factions, while the assembly balanced them with the voices of more common men. Perhaps more importantly, Solon canceled all public and private debts, and abolished the practice of enslaving people to pay off their debts.

Solon's reforms crumbled when he left office, and decades of struggle between rich and poor and between men of different hereditary clans ensued until about 550 B.C.E., when Peisistratus seized control of the government as a "tyrant," the Greek term for a one-man autocratic ruler. Peisistratus (d. 527 B.C.E.) fostered economic growth through loans to small farmers; export promotion programs; road construction; and public works, including major building programs for the beautification of Athens and its

Two halves of a red-figure cup by the sculptor Douris, fifth century B.C.E. The figures depict four scenes from the education of a young man: learning to play the lyre and flute, and learning to read and write, all under the watchful eye of a pedagogue.

deme A rural district or village in ancient Greece, or its members or inhabitants. The demes were a constituent part of the polis but had their own corporations with police powers, and their own cults, officials, and property.

Acropolis. On Peisistratus' death, the city-state again fell into disarray and even civil war. In 510 B.C.E., at the invitation of a faction of Athenian noblemen, the king of Sparta, already Athens' greatest rival, invaded Athens, besieged the Acropolis, and deposed the descendants of Peisistratus.

Through all the warfare and strife, the ideals of Solon survived. A new ruler, Cleisthenes (*c.* 570–*c.* 508 B.C.E.), came to power as a tyrant and dramatically reorganized the city and its surrounding countryside. He did away with the aristocratic family centers of power by registering each Athenian as a citizen according to his geographical residence, or **deme**, in the city. Similarly, he reorganized the electoral districts of Attica, the region around Athens, into ten electoral units, creating new political identities and allegiances. The assembly resumed meeting about every ten days, and all male citizens were expected to participate; 6000 were necessary for a quorum. Above the assembly, and setting its agenda, was a Council of Five Hundred, even more open than Solon's Council of Four Hundred had been, since members were selected from each deme, or neighborhood, for one-year terms by lottery, and members were not allowed to serve for more than two terms. In organizing themselves by deme, Athenians based their political identity on geographical residence in the city, not on heredity and kinship, nor on class and wealth.

This new concept of civic identity allowed the city to welcome new residents and the ideas they brought with them, regardless of their place of origin. It allowed people of different ethnic origins, even of enemy ethnic stocks, to enter the city, although they were not eligible for full citizenship, which was restricted to free men born in the deme. The human interaction in the small Greek city-state nurtured the intellect of its citizens. Life in the polis meant constant participation in a kind of ongoing public seminar. As Socrates (c. 470–399 B.C.E.), the leading philosopher of fifth-century Athens, said: "I'm a lover of learning, and trees and open country won't teach me anything, whereas men in the town do."

When Darius I's Persian Empire challenged the Greek city-states, Athens took the lead in forming a coalition against it. The contrast between the combatants was stark: city-state versus empire; local administration versus imperial power; evolving, decentralized democracy versus established, centralized imperial control. Persia was a huge, centrally governed empire; each Greek city-state was individually independent, although many had joined into regional confederations and leagues for mutual assistance and trade. A single emperor who set policies for the entire empire headed Persia; an assembly of all its adult, free, male citizens, for the most part, governed each individual Greek city-state. These assemblies passed laws, judged criminal and civil cases, provided for administration and implementation of legislation, and arranged for military defense as the need arose. The Greek city-states were moving toward democracy; they understood their legal systems to be their own creation and responsibility, neither ordained by the gods nor imposed by a powerful external emperor.

Greek trireme. The Greeks developed triremes (with three banks of oars) as warships and had them specially strengthened so that they could ram other ships. The triremes were slower and less maneuverable than the Persian ships. To compensate, the Greeks put soldiers aboard and, at Salamis, relied mostly on hand-to-hand combat.

War with Persia

Some of the Greek city-states in Anatolia had earlier fallen under Darius' empire. Although they were permitted to retain their own form of local government as long as they paid their taxes to Persia, some of them revolted and called on the Greek cities of the peninsula for help. Athens tried, half-heartedly and unsuccessfully, to assist its overseas relatives with ships and soldiers. According to Herodotus, Darius was furious at this interference. He ordered one of his servants to remind him, every day at dinnertime, "Master, remember the Athenians." In 490, Darius I dispatched a naval expedition directly across the Aegean to punish Athens for its part in the revolt in Anatolia.

War with the Persians tested the Greeks' fundamental mode of political organization. How could the tiny Greek city-states hold off Darius' imperial armies and keep their incipient democracies alive? First, they had the enormous advantage of being close to home, with a good knowledge of local geography and conditions. Second, the largest among them, especially Athens and Sparta, chose to cooperate in defense against a common enemy.

When the Persian fleet of 600 ships landed 48,000 soldiers at Marathon in 490 B.C.E., a force of some 10,000 Greek **hoplite** soldiers, joined by about 1000 soldiers from Plataea and another 1000 slaves, confronted them. The hoplite forces were deployed in solid phalanxes, columns of soldiers arrayed in tight lines, the left arm and shield of one man pressed against the right shoulder of the other, in row on row. If a soldier in the front row fell, one from the next line took his place. (In these hoplite formations, each individual soldier is crucial to the welfare of all. Many analysts have seen in this egalitarian military formation the rationale for Athenian political democracy.)

The discipline of the Athenians defeated their enemy. At the Battle of Marathon in 490 B.C.E., Persia lost 6400 men, Athens 192. The Athenian general sent his fastest runner, Pheidippides, racing back to Athens to tell of the victory at Marathon to strengthen the resolve of the Athenians at home and to hasten their preparations for battle against the surviving Persian forces. Pheidippides delivered the message, and died of exhaustion on the spot. (The marathon race of today is named for his 26-mile run.)

Xerxes I (r. 486–465 B.C.E.), Darius's son, succeeded him and mounted a renewed attack on the Greek mainland by land and sea in 480 B.C.E. Courageous resistance by the Spartan general Leonidas and his troops at Thermopylae cost the lives of all the defenders, but won time for the Athenians to evacuate their city and regroup their forces. Xerxes continued to push onward to Athens, capturing, burning, and plundering the city and its Acropolis, but the Athenian warriors had withdrawn to the nearby port of Piraeus and the Bay of Salamis. At Salamis, a force of some 1000 Persian ships confronted a much smaller fleet of some 300 Greek triremes, named for the three levels in which its approximately 170 rowers were arranged. One of Xerxes' most trusted naval advisers, Artemisia, a widowed queen among the people of Halicarnassus, and a captain of one of the ships, counseled waiting and watching. Xerxes, however, followed the majority and sailed into battle. The Athenians maneuvered the Persians into a bottleneck in the Salamis Channel and destroyed 200 of their ships while losing only 40. Xerxes sailed for home, and Persia never again attacked Greece by sea.

The Persians did, however, continue to fight by land. In 479 B.C.E., in alliance with their subjects in Macedonia and some northern Greeks, they prepared an army of some 100,000 men on the edge of the plains opening southward to Athens and the Peloponnese. Sparta and Athens formed an alliance with some other city-states to field an opposing army of about 40,000. Despite initial confusion in the ranks, the allied Spartan and Athenian forces destroyed the Persian armies and their camp, annihilated

hoplite A heavily armed foot soldier of ancient Greece, whose function was to fight in close formation, usually in ranks of eight men. Each soldier carried a heavy bronze shield, a short iron sword, and a long spear for thrusting.

the elite guard, and killed the leading Persian general. At about the same time, the Greek fleet defeated the surviving Persian fleet at Mycale, on the Ionian coast of Anatolia.

In the face of these losses, and with weaker leadership at home, Persia left Europe, never to return in such force. The small Greek city-states, led by arch-rivals Athens and Sparta, had shown an ability to combine in the face of a common enemy. They had demonstrated the virtues of small-scale, local units of society and the resilience of popular, democratic forms of government. Conversely, the Persians had exhibited one of the great flaws of empire: the tendency to overextend its powers.

Athens: from City-State to Mini-Empire

Ironically, the city-state of Athens, having led the Greeks in their struggle against the Persian Empire, subsequently began to construct an empire of its own. For purposes of the war, Athens had assembled its principal allies into the Delian League, with its council and treasury situated in Delos. At first, membership was voluntary, but soon Athens forbade withdrawal. When Naxos left the league in 470 B.C.E., the Athenians attacked the city, forced it to return, and terminated its independence. Other allies also revolted, usually because they could not meet Athens' demands for tribute and ships. As Athens continued to suppress these revolts, Thucydides reports, "the Athenians as rulers were no longer popular as they used to be."

By 461 B.C.E., many of the Greek city-states turned to Sparta to help them resist Athenian power. For ten years, from 461 to 451, Athens and its allies confronted Sparta and its allies in a series of intermittent battles sometimes called the First Peloponnesian War. During these wars Athens exploited its allies. In 454 B.C.E. the Athenians moved the treasury of the Delian League to Athens and appropriated its funds in order to create in the city a spectacular center of culture and grace. These self-serving actions antagonized its allies and precipitated further war with Sparta. Here we explore Athens, first in its brilliant century of splendor, and later in its wartime suffering and defeats.

Parthenon, Athens, 447–432 B.C.E. The Parthenon on the Athenian Acropolis was a temple dedicated to the goddess Athena, the city's patron-deity. It was built at the instigation of Pericles as a symbol of Athens' growing importance and represents, in architectural terms, the summit of classical Greek achievement.

The Golden Age of Athenian Culture

Under the military and civic leadership of Pericles (c. 495–429 B.C.E.), Athenians took immense pride in their city-state, its democratic philosophy and artistic creativity. During the war years, the Persians had destroyed and burned much of Athens. When victory was secure, the Athenians began the rebuilding of their city.

Athens rose from a plain, and with each level upward its functions and architecture became more exalted. At the bottom were the houses of commoners, built simply from local materials of stone and mud, with little concern for architectural merit. Further up the hill was the *agora*, or civic and market center, with clusters of buildings for trade in goods, ideas, and political decision-making. These public buildings were more elegant, designed for greater comfort and show. In the splendor of the *agora* Athenians demonstrated the value placed on public life and on physical prowess and discipline. Nearby were gymnasia for exercise and competition. An amphitheater where plays were regularly performed was carved out of the hillside. At the top of the hill, on the Acropolis ("city on high"), surrounded by a wall, were the chief temples of the city, especially the shrine of the goddess Athena, the divine guardian of the city. Architects and urban designers Ictinus and Callicrates planned the new Acropolis and built the Parthenon, while the sculptor Phidias carved the friezes on the Parthenon and created a 40-foot-high statue of Athena, the city's patron goddess, to reside within it.

As the architectural projects flourished, Pericles founded a colony in southern Italy and took a fleet into the Black Sea. More important, he encouraged naval battles against Sparta and Corinth, as well as Persia, to promote his radical egalitarian democracy at home. Rowers typically were poorer than hoplites, but benefited from regular salaries and the spoils of war and empire. Eventually, he realized his strategy was flawed, concluding that his imperial ambitions threatened the very Athenian democracy he cherished.

sophist An itinerant professor of higher education in ancient Greece, who gave instruction for a fee. The subjects taught, which included oratory, grammar, ethics, mathematics, and literature, had the practical aim of equipping pupils for successful careers.

Plan of Acropolis. The construction of the Acropolis (Greek for "high city") beginning in c. 460 B.C.E. under the leadership of Pericles, signified the beginning of a Golden Age for Athens. The plan above indicates some of its most celebrated buildings—the Parthenon (1), the Erectheum (2), the Propylaea (3), and the Temple of Athena Nike (4).

Historians. The city's historians began to reflect on its origins, accomplishments, and the challenges it had faced. Indeed, the modern profession of history as a systematic attempt to understand the influence of past experience on the present began in Athens. Two of the most outstanding historians of the fifth century B.C.E. have given us the history of the city and its relationships with its neighbors. Herodotus (d. c. 420 B.C.E.) wrote *The Persian Wars*, and in the narrative recaptured a general, if anecdotal, history of the whole eastern Mediterranean and eastward as far as Persia and India from a Greek perspective. Thucydides (d. c. 401 B.C.E.), far more systematically and carefully, recounted the subsequent *History of the Peloponnesian War*, the war between Athens and Sparta that lasted from 431 B.C.E. until 404 B.C.E.

Philosophers. Philosophers such as Socrates and his student Plato introduced questions, methods of analysis and of teaching, and examinations of the purpose of life, which continue to command attention for their range and depth. Plato's prize student, Aristotle, later wrote that man is a "political animal," a creature of the city-state, and many of the key works in Greek history, drama, and philosophy explored the working of the city-state itself and the relationship of the individual to it.

For the philosopher Socrates (*c.* 470–399 B.C.E.), the Athenian state was father and mother; he derived his sense of self and purpose from the education the state gave him and from his continual debates with fellow citizens both in public and private. Socrates argued for the supremacy of the city-state over the individual. The citizen had obligations to the state for all the benefits he received from it, but had no rights to claim against the power of the state.

Socrates took philosophy personally and seriously. He opposed and satirized the **sophist** philosophers of his day who earned their salaries by training future statesmen how to argue any side of any question without necessarily staking any personal commitment. Through his incessant questions, he taught *his* students to be thoughtful but critical about the truths of others and about their own truths, and, after having reached their own conclusions, to live their own truths fully even if it meant their death, as it did for Socrates himself.

Plato (*c.* 428–348 B.C.E.) was Socrates' leading pupil and the founder of the Academy, which endured for centuries as Athens' leading school of philosophy. His philosophical works dealt with many topics, including love, justice, courage, and the nature of the state. Plato conceived of ideal situations, whether realistic or not. The ideal state, according to Plato, would be administered by a philosopher-king, who by virtue of innate good character and intensive training would know and do what was best for all citizens in the state. Similarly, Plato saw love ascending from the emotional and sexual passion for an individual to the contemplation of universal ideals.

Aristotle (384–322 B.C.E.), Plato's greatest pupil, addressed an astonishing array of subjects—logic, physics, astronomy, metaphysics, religion, rhetoric, literary criticism, and natural science—but he, too, devoted some of his most important writing to ethics and politics. His analysis of the principal forms of constitutional government in his *Politics* remains a useful introduction to the field even today. Aristotle later tutored Alexander the Great of Macedon, although that world-conqueror seems to have thoroughly rejected his teacher's argument for small units of government like the city-state: As Aristotle argued:

> If the citizens of a state are to judge and to distribute offices according to merit, then they must know each other's characters; where they do not possess this knowledge, both the election to offices and the decision of lawsuits will go wrong. When the population is very large they are manifestly settled at haphazard, which clearly ought not to be. (*Politics* VII: 4; p. 326)

Dramatists. Drama developed and flourished in the theaters of Athens. The pursuit of justice, morality, and equity was a core theme. Athenian playwrights invented the

A marble, second-century-C.E. copy of the statue of Athena Parthenos, dedicated in 438 B.C.E. Phidias' 40-foot Athena, the divine guardian of the city, dominated the central chamber of the Parthenon on the Acropolis. This miniature Roman copy of the destroyed statue hardly suggests the glittering magnificence of the enormous gold-and-ivory original, a powerful symbol of the might of the goddess and her city, Athens. (*Acropolis Museum, Athens*)

SOURCE

Socrates on the Rights of the State over the Individual

Condemned to death on trumped-up charges of corrupting the political morals of youth and blaspheming against the gods of Athens, Socrates is offered the opportunity to escape and live out his life in another city-state. He refuses. He notes that the state has acted through formal legal process and has the right to execute him. He, in turn, has the obligation to accept the sentence.

Are you too wise to see that your country is worthier, more to be revered, more sacred, and held in higher honor both by the gods and by all men of understanding, than your father and your mother and all your other ancestors; and that you ought to reverence it, and to submit to it, and to approach it more humbly when it is angry with you than you would approach your father; and either to do whatever it tells you to do or to persuade it to excuse you; and to obey in silence if it orders you to endure flogging or imprisonment, or if it sends you to battle to be wounded or to die? That is just. You must not give way, nor retreat, nor desert your station. In war, and in the court of justice, and everywhere, you must do whatever your state and your country tell you to do, or you must persuade them that their commands are unjust. But it is impious to use violence against your father or your mother; and much more impious to use violence against your country. (Plato, *Crito* XII: 51: b)

dramatic forms of tragedy and comedy, and their most important plays all include themes related to the evolution of their city and its institutions.

The *Oresteia* trilogy by Aeschylus (525–456 B.C.E.) follows three generations of murders within the royal family of Atreus, as one act of revenge provokes the next, until finally, in a trial at Athens, Athena, patron goddess of the city, acquits Orestes, suggesting that divinely ordained vengeance will be replaced by human justice and the cycle of murder will be ended.

Oedipus Rex of Sophocles (c. 496–406 B.C.E.), perhaps the most famous single play of ancient Athens, centers on the family tragedy of Oedipus' murder of his own father, the king of Thebes, and his subsequent marriage to his own mother. (Oedipus, who had been abandoned as an infant and raised by shepherds, did not know that the man he killed was his father and that he had married his mother.) The play opens with the people of Thebes gathered round King Oedipus, before his tragedy is revealed, crying out for his help in arresting a plague that is afflicting the city. Oedipus' own moral corruption has brought the plague on the city, although that is revealed only later. Sophocles' *Antigone* confronts the conflict in loyalty to family versus loyalty to the city-state, as Antigone chooses to bury her brother, Polynices, despite the royal decree to leave his corpse unattended as an enemy of the state.

Euripides (480–406 B.C.E.) saw more clearly Athens' move toward imperialism, and criticized it in *The Trojan Women*. The hilarious, sexually explicit comedy, *Lysistrata*, by Aristophanes (c. 450–385 B.C.E.) portrays the women of Athens and Sparta agreeing to go on strike sexually until their men stop fighting the Peloponnesian Wars. As long as the men make war the women will not make love! The best of the Athenian dramatists addressed directly the political and social issues that confronted their city.

The Limits of City-State Democracy

Socrates' justification of the state demonstrates that even in the most democratic Greek city-state, government could exact respect and service from the citizen, but the citizen had few rights vis-à-vis the state. The citizen had the right, and indeed the obligation, to participate in the activities of the state and to serve the state, but not to have the state serve him.

For women, even the right of participation was absent. Women born of two Athenian parents were regarded as citizens, enjoyed some legal protection, and had responsibilities for performing certain religious rituals of great importance for the state. But, like slaves, they were excluded from attending the meetings of the assembly, holding annual public offices, serving as jurors, initiating legal cases on their own, or owning property in their own names. They had to have a man speak for them before judges and juries. Women's segregation from public life in ancient Greece perpetuated longstanding beliefs that there is a public sphere and a private sphere, and that women should be confined to the latter. Pericles captured this belief in his famous funeral oration, when he delivered this advice to the widows of fallen warriors: "Great will be your glory in not falling short of your natural character; and greatest will be hers who is least talked of among the men, whether for good or for bad."

Since many Greeks believed that true friendship was possible only among equals, many Greek men sought relationships, including sexual relationships, with other men outside their households, even when they held their marriages in high esteem. Greek vases, especially those used in male drinking parties, often carried paintings that glorified the phallus. Given this evidence, some feminist historians have concluded that this culture was misogynistic—hating women—and that the exaltation of masculinity could have been at the root of the constant warfare and militarism of ancient Greek society.

Plato (c. 428–348 B.C.E.) recognized the prejudices against women in his society. When he suggested in his visionary *Republic* that women should be treated equally with men in their access to the highest professional and civic responsibilities, and in the education needed to achieve them, he knew that his ideas were revolutionary for Athens in his time and that they would be greeted with derision. Plato himself believed that men were generally more talented than women, but he argued that both should be offered equal access to political opportunity. On the issue of gender equality, he seemed to remain consistent with his general philosophy: the state should encourage each citizen to reach his or her educational potential, and should direct the most talented into governmental affairs. Plato wrote:

> There is no occupation concerned with the management of social affairs which belongs either to women or to men, as such. Natural gifts are to be found here and there in both creatures alike; and every occupation is open to both, so far as their natures are concerned, though woman is for all purposes the weaker ... Now, for the purpose of producing a woman fit to be a Guardian, we shall not have one education for men and another for women ... If we are to set women to the same tasks as men, we must teach them the same things. They must have the same two branches of training for mind and body and also be taught the art of war, and they must receive the same treatment.

Aristotle confirmed Plato's apprehensions, but not his optimism nor his sense of potential equality. Aristotle wrote of women: "The temperance of a man and of a woman, or the courage and justice of a man and of a woman, are not, as Socrates maintained, the same; the courage of a man is shown in commanding, of a woman in obeying." He quotes with approval the general view that "Silence is a woman's glory."

Psykter (wine cooler) painted by Douris with cavorting satyrs, 500–490 B.C.E. Feminist historian Eva Keuls argues that, contrary to the cradle-of-civilization clichés, Athenian society was excessively warlike and women-hating. She finds much of her evidence on Greek vases of the type used in male drinking parties. (*British Museum, London*)

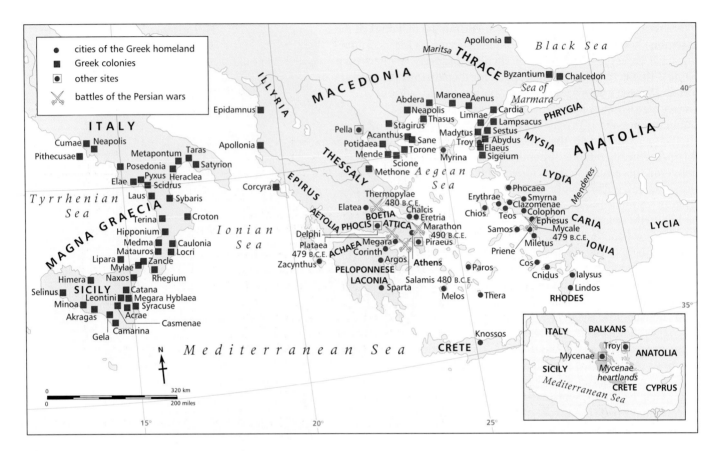

Classical Greece. The hilly terrain and sea-boundaries of Greece discouraged the growth of large settlements, and Greek philosophers also stressed the importance of local community. When population grew too great the citizens encouraged their younger cohort to establish new city-states of their own. The resulting spread of settlements established Greek influence all the way from Sicily to Anatolia.

In practice, Athens followed Aristotelian rather than Platonic views on the role of women in public life.

Even among males, only the sons of native-born Athenian mothers and fathers were eligible for citizenship. Slaves captured in war, and even allies, could not gain citizenship. When Classical Athens reached its maximum population, 250,000, only about one adult Athenian in six qualified for citizenship. These limits on Athenian democracy increased domestic social strains.

Ironically, the city-state of Athens, having led the Greek city-states in the struggle against the Persian Empire, subsequently set out to construct an empire of its own. Following major victories in the Persian wars, Athens assembled its principal allies into the Delian League, with its council and treasury situated in Delos. At first, membership was voluntary, but soon Athens forbade withdrawal. Some cities left the League, usually because they could not pay the tribute Athens demanded. They found it particularly difficult to supply triremes, because they frequently lacked the shipyards of their larger ally. In response, Athens might declare war against them. As a result, "the Athenians as rulers," in the words of Thucydides, "were no longer popular as they used to be."

By 461 B.C.E., many of the Greek city-states turned to Sparta to help them resist Athenian coercion. For ten years, from 461 to 451, Athens and its allies confronted Sparta and its allies in intermittent warfare. During these wars Athens exploited its allies. In 454 B.C.E. Pericles moved the treasury of the Delian League to Athens and appropriated its funds in order to create at Athens a spectacular center of power and authority, particularly by building the Parthenon and expanding the fleet. A democracy at home, Athens was fast becoming an imperial power holding sway over its neighbor.

The Peloponnesian War

Relationships between Athens and its neighbors also deteriorated. Pericles' imperialistic policies encroached on its own allies and on those of Sparta. Fearful that the Athenians would use their navy to destroy Spartan control over its own alliance system, the Peloponnesian League, Sparta became determined to destroy Athens' power. In 432 B.C.E. Sparta attacked Athens, and the Peloponnesian War began in earnest. The struggle was for power, not for higher ideals.

Thucydides, historian of the conflict, portrays Athens setting forth its claims increasingly bluntly in statements of **realpolitik** (power politics). He reports the arrogant Athenian ultimatum ordering the people of the island of Melos to submit to Athenian authority:

> Our opinion of the gods and our knowledge of men lead us to conclude that it is a general and necessary law of nature to rule whatever one can. (V:105; p. 404)

Much weaker than Athens, Melos nevertheless chose to resist. When the Athenians finally conquered the Melians in 415 B.C.E., they killed all the men of military age whom they captured and sold the women and children into slavery. Throughout Greece, admiration for Athens turned to loathing.

By 404 B.C.E. Sparta, supported by Persian funding, defeated Athens and captured the city. The Peloponnesian War between Athens and Sparta and their allies had dragged on for a full generation. Both sides were exhausted. Nevertheless, warfare

realpolitik A German term meaning practical politics, that is, a policy determined by expediency rather than by ethical or ideological considerations.

SOURCE

Pericles' Funeral Oration

As political and military leader of Athens, 460–429 B.C.E., Pericles delivered this eulogy at a mass-funeral of troops who had died in battle in the early years of the Peloponnesian War. As reported by Thucydides, it is one of the great proclamations of the civic, aesthetic, moral, and personal virtues of the Athenian city-state:

Our system of government does not copy the institutions of our neighbors. It is more the case of our being a model to others, than of our imitating anyone else. Our constitution is called a democracy because power is in the hands not of a minority but of the whole people. When it is a question of settling private disputes, everyone is equal before the law; when it is a question of putting one person before another in positions of public responsibility, what counts is not membership of a particular class, but the actual ability which the man possesses. No one, so long as he has it in him to be of service to the state, is kept in political obscurity because of poverty …

We [obey] those whom we put in positions of authority, and we obey the laws themselves, especially those which are for the protection of the oppressed, and those unwritten laws which it is an acknowledged shame to break …

When our work is over, we are in a position to enjoy all kinds of recreation for our spirits … all the good things from all over the world flow in to us, so that to us it seems just as natural to enjoy foreign goods as our own local products …

Our love of what is beautiful does not lead to extravagance; our love of the things of the mind does not make us soft. We regard wealth as something to be properly used, rather than as something to boast about. As for poverty, no one need be ashamed to admit it: the real shame is in not taking practical measures to escape from it. Here each individual is interested not only in his own affairs but in the affairs of the state as well: even those who are mostly occupied with their own business are extremely well informed on general politics—this is a peculiarity of ours: we do not say that a man who takes no interest in politics is a man who minds his own business; we say that he has no business here at all. We Athenians, in our own persons, take our decisions on policy or submit them to proper discussions: for we do not think that there is an incompatibility between words and deeds; the worst thing is to rush into action before the consequences have been properly debated …

I declare that our city is an education to Greece, and I declare that in my opinion each single one of our citizens, in all the manifold aspects of life, is able to show himself the rightful lord and owner of his own person, and do this, moreover, with exceptional grace and exceptional versatility. (Book II:37–41; pp. 145–8)

soon resumed among the Greeks, with Thebes and Corinth now entering the lists as major contenders. Each major city-state sought advantage over the others, and the stronger continued to force the weaker into subordinate alliances as intermittent warfare sputtered on.

THE EMPIRE OF ALEXANDER THE GREAT

To the north of the major Greek city-states lay the rougher, less urbanized Macedonia, a borderland between Greece and the Slavic regions to the north and east. The principal language and culture of Macedonia were Greek, but other languages and cultures were also present. Here in 359 B.C.E., in the Macedonian capital of Pella, Philip II (r. 359–336 B.C.E.) persuaded the Macedonian army to declare him king, in succession to his brother, who had died in warfare.

The Conquests of Philip

The Empire of Alexander. In 338 the Greek city-states were defeated by Philip of Macedon. His son, Alexander, extended the imprint of Greek culture far beyond its Mediterranean homeland. In a series of whirlwind campaigns between 334 and 323 B.C.E., Alexander gained control of Syria and Egypt and then destroyed the might of Persia. He took his armies east to the Indus and north to central Asia, but died age 33 in Babylon.

After consolidating his power in Macedonia, Philip declared two goals. The first of these was to unify and bring peace to Greece; the second was to liberate the Greek city-states in Asia Minor from Persian control. Skillful as a diplomat and careful to introduce economic improvements in the lands he conquered, Philip nevertheless realized that his army was the real key to achieving his goals. He built up its phalanxes, armed the soldiers with spears up to 15 feet long, and augmented the foot soldiers with powerful and swift cavalry. Philip led the troops himself, suffering numerous, serious wounds in battle.

Between 354 and 339 Philip conquered the Balkans from the Danube to the Aegean coast and from the Adriatic to the Black Sea. To pacify and administer the area, he

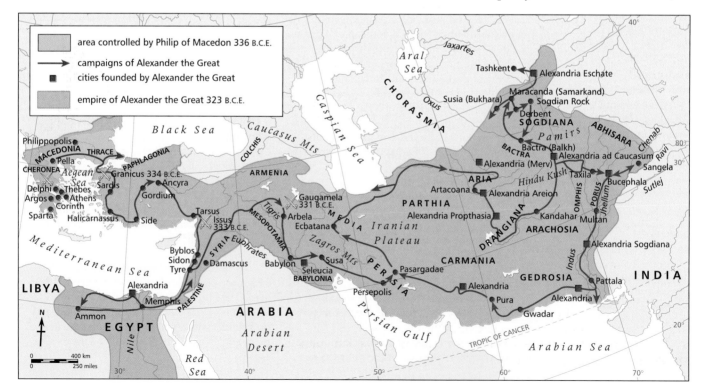

established new towns, which were populated by both Macedonians and local peoples. Similarly, he employed many local people in his administration. Within Greece proper, his accomplishments were more mixed. He won some allies, such as Thessaly; defeated the armies of several city-states; and mediated the end of a war between two coalitions of Greek city-states. He was honored with election as president of the Pythian Games at Delphi in 346, but Athens and Thebes bitterly opposed his overtures for greater power in Greece.

The orator Demosthenes (384–322 B.C.E.) delivered three "Philippics," public addresses calling Athens to battle against the Macedonian king and predicting the end of Athenian democracy if Philip defeated the city-state. In the face of this opposition, Philip met in battle with Athens and its allies, defeating them at Chaeronea in 338 B.C.E. Philip now sought to create a self-governing league of Greek city-states, to accomplish his first goal, and to forge an alliance between Macedonia and the league to fight Persia, his second goal. But he was assassinated in 336. His twenty-year-old son, Alexander, continued his father's mission.

The Reign of Alexander the Great

No stranger to warfare, Alexander had fought by his father's side just two years beforehand as he defeated Athens at the Battle of Chaeronea. Applauded by the army, Alexander succeeded to the throne without opposition and continued his father's career of conquest. Over the next twelve years, his disciplined army traversed some 22,000 miles, conquering lands that stretched from Egypt in the west to the Indus River in the east. Alexander's empire became the largest known up to his time, and in 324 B.C.E. he declared himself a god.

Like his father Philip and like the Persian emperors Cyrus II and Darius I, Alexander (r. 336–323 B.C.E.) followed a policy of benevolent despotism much of the time. But, also like them, he implemented this policy only after his power had been amply demonstrated. Unfortunate Thebes provided an early site for this demonstration. Soon after assuming the throne, Alexander had marched north to the Danube River to suppress revolts in Thrace. Mistakenly informed that Alexander had been killed in battle, Thebes revolted against his local forces. Alexander quickly marched his troops back to Thebes, captured and sacked the rebel city, killed 6000 of its inhabitants, and sold into slavery 20,000 of those who survived.

In 334 Alexander was ready to cross into Asia, where his first major victory came at Granicus. From there he continued southward, forcing the Persians out of the Greek cities that lined the Ionian coast. To make sure that the Persians would not return, Alexander marched eastward through Anatolia with 35,000 Greek troops, routing the 300,000-man army of the Persian emperor Darius III at Issus in 333 B.C.E. and forcing Darius himself into flight.

Alexander continued southward down the coast of the eastern Mediterranean. At Tyre, which held out in siege against him for seven months, he again demonstrated power and brutality, killing 7000 men and selling 30,000, mostly women and children, into slavery. Elsewhere, however, Alexander showed the velvet glove, respecting local religions, ruling through local hierarchies, and maintaining local tax rates. To drive Persia from the Mediterranean basin and to establish his own control, Alexander continued south and then west, conquering Egypt. He was welcomed as Egypt's liberator from Persian rule and treated as a god by the Egyptian priests of the god Amon, whose shrine he visited. At the western end of the Nile delta, Alexander laid the foundation of what would be for several centuries the most attractive and cultured city of the Mediterranean coast, Alexandria.

The "Alexander Mosaic," first century B.C.E. mosaic copy from Pompeii of a painting by Philoxenos, c. 300 B.C.E. This mosaic portrays the Battle of Issus (333 B.C.E.) in terms of a personal duel between Alexander the Great and Darius III, Emperor of Persia. Darius (right) is shown about to turn and flee in his chariot as the youthful Alexander (left), wild-haired and helmetless, charges toward him. (*Museo Archeologico Nazionale, Naples*)

His appetite whetted, again a common experience with empire builders once they begin their careers, Alexander moved onward to conquests previously unplanned. He set out to conquer the Persian Empire and make it his own. He marched northeastward across the fertile crescent and through Mesopotamia. At Gaugamela in 331 B.C.E. he again faced the Persian emperor, Darius III, and again routed him. The historical capital cities of Babylon, Susa, Persepolis, and Pasargadae lay open to Alexander. He destroyed Persepolis, Darius' own capital, almost totally. Then, having captured the heartland of the Persian Empire, he set off to conquer the eastern half as well, finally reaching and capturing the Indus River valley in the east, and Sogdiana, across the Oxus River, in the northeast.

Although Alexander wanted to continue into India as far as the Ganges, his troops mutinied. They would go no farther. As he was returning from his new frontiers, Alexander contracted a fever. Weakened both by the hardships of war and by heavy drinking, he died in Babylon in 323 B.C.E., only thirty-three years old. Several accounts report that he was poisoned; some said the instigator was his own former teacher Aristotle. On his deathbed he reputedly declared, "Let the job go to the strongest." In the battle for succession among his generals, Alexander's wife, Roxane, and their thirteen-year-old son were murdered.

The empire Alexander created did not survive two generations. In the east, local rulers regained power in India and Afghanistan. In the west, the Greeks returned to their internal warfare, finally breaking up once more into individual city-states, kingdoms, and leagues. Macedonia remained a separate kingdom and meddled in Greek affairs.

Two major kingdoms emerged from the wreckage of Alexander's empire: Egypt under the dynasty of Ptolemy, which ruled through a Greek and Macedonian elite until the Roman conquest; and the empire established by Seleucus I Nicator (d. 281 B.C.E.), who was governor of Babylon when the empire split apart, and who added to his own domain Iran, Afghanistan, and Anatolia. But the Seleucid Empire, too, fragmented. Parthians reclaimed Persia in the east, and Anatolia divided into numerous local governments. By 200 B.C.E. the Seleucid Empire was limited primarily to the area around Syria.

HOW DO WE KNOW?

Evaluating Alexander the Great

Alexander remains a controversial figure. He was reputed to have murdered hundreds of thousands to achieve his power, yet his admirers see in him a creative genius who aimed at forging a unified Greco-Persian culture that extended into central Asia. By some he was called Alexander the Great; by others Iskander the Accursed. Subsequent historians and other scholars are unsure whether he was an innocent multiculturalist or an imperial monster. There seems to be no question that he believed in his own divinity, but much about this young man remains unknown.

By the end of his life, however, there were few who sorrowed over Alexander's death. Historian Peter Green, who has written an historiographical sketch of Alexander's reputation through the ages, found that the conqueror's image has changed dramatically over time.

The earliest remaining accounts of Alexander's life date from the first century B.C.E., at least 200 years after his death, while the most reliable and fullest of the earliest biographies still extant, that written by Arrian Flavius Arrianus, dates to the second century C.E. For the most part, all historians work from these same basic records, but their assessments reflect the issues and conditions of their own day.

Arrian, who lived at the height of the Roman empire, and approved of it, praises Alexander for his conquests. Alexander was the prototype of Rome's own Caesars. Closer to our own times, in the late eighteenth and nineteenth centuries, during the democratic era of the American and French revolutions, and of the Greek War for Independence (see Chapter 15), historical opinion turned against Alexander. George Grote's History of Greece (1888) represented both Philip and Alexander as "brutalized adventurers simply out for power, wealth, and territorial expansion, both of them inflamed by the pure lust for conquest" (Green, p. 482).

On the other hand, Johann Gustav Droysen, an ardent advocate of a reunified, powerful Germany (see Chapter 17), saw Alexander as a model. Droysen's scholarly biography, Alexander der Grosse (1833), praised Alexander for introducing Greek culture into large parts of Asia.

As the British Empire expanded in the nineteenth and early twentieth centuries, many British scholars also adopted a favorable view of Alexander. William Tarn's two-volume biography saw his conquests as instrumental in spreading a social philosophy of the Brotherhood of Man, bringing together Greeks and Persians, the conquerors with the conquered. Even in our post-imperial day, Cambridge University scholar N.G.L.

Hammond agrees, citing the essay by the biographer Plutarch (c. 46–126 C.E.):

> He harnessed all resources to one and the same end, mixing as it were in a loving-cup the lives, manners, marriages and customs of men. He ordered them all to regard the inhabited earth as their fatherland and his armed forces as their stronghold and defense.

Nonetheless, Green remains critical, arguing that his own assessment is closest to that at the time of Alexander's death:

> his all-absorbing obsession through a short but crowded life, was war and conquest. It is idle to palliate this central truth, to pretend that he dreamed ... of wading through rivers of blood and violence to achieve the Brotherhood of Man by raping an entire continent. He spent his whole life, with legendary success, in the pursuit of personal glory, Achillean kleos; and until very recent times this was regarded as a wholly laudable aim. The empire he built collapsed the moment he was gone; he came as a conqueror and the work he wrought was destruction. (p. 488)

- What seems to be the basis for Green's interpretation of Alexander's career?
- Would you consider Alexander a hero or a villain?
- In light of America's increasing use of power overseas, how do you think scholarly interpretations of Alexander might change?

The Legacy of Alexander: The Hellenistic Ecumene

What were the legacies of the empire Alexander built? He made the language and culture of Greece dominant among the ruling intellectual and commercial elites from the Mediterranean, east to India, Afghanistan, and the borders of Russia, and south as far as Egypt. A common dialect of Greek, known as Koine, spread as the language of educated people throughout the ancient western world.

Waves of Greek administrators, businessmen, and soldiers followed Alexander's conquests and helped to transmit Greek culture. At the same time, local customs, especially the imperial ceremonial forms of Persia, endured and transformed the simplicity of the earlier Hellenic culture into the more complex, elaborate, and cosmopolitan Hellenistic culture that flourished from the time of Alexander until the death of the last Macedonian queen of Egypt, Cleopatra, in 30 B.C.E. One striking example of the mixture of Hellenistic and local cultures—this time from India—can be seen in some

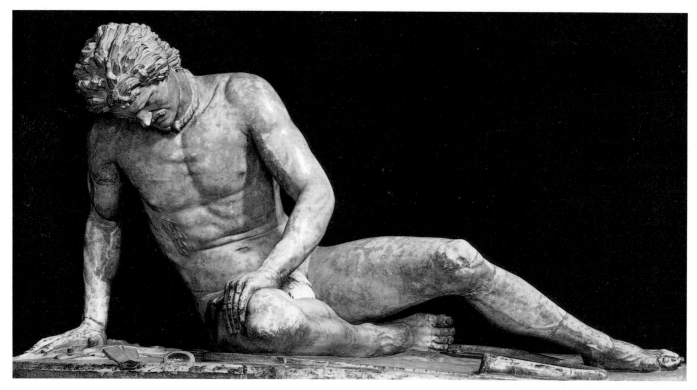

Dying Gaul, Roman copy in marble of a bronze original of c. 230–220 B.C.E. When Attalas I of Pergamum defeated an enemy force of Gauls, a series of statues showing dead or dying invaders was cast. This poignant example illustrates the many artistic developments in sculpture that epitomize Hellenistic Greece: a special emphasis on the portrayal of suffering and pain, dramatically conveyed through facial expression; a widening subject-matter (not merely male and female nudes); a twisting pose for the body; and a design that allows the composition to be viewed from all sides. (*Museo Capitolino, Rome*)

ecumene A Greek word referring to the inhabited world and designating a distinct cultural-historical community.

of the first representations of the Buddha in sculpture from the area of India/Pakistan after it was conquered by Alexander. These sculptures represent the Buddha wearing a toga (see p. 251).

To facilitate travel and commerce, as well as conquest and administration, Alexander built roads, canals, and whole new cities, including at least sixteen Alexandrias across the length and breadth of his conquests, using the gold and silver captured from Persia to finance many of these constructions. The most famous and illustrious Alexandria was the metropolis in Egypt, which became the leading city of its day. Egyptian Alexandria housed palaces, administrative centers, theaters, stadia, the greatest library of Greek knowledge, containing 700,000 manuscripts, and the final resting place of Alexander himself.

At the eastern end of the empire, on the Oxus River in today's Uzbekistan, the Greeks constructed, on Persian foundations, Ai Khanoum, a small, well-defended city centered on a palace. Ai Khanoum was rediscovered and excavated only in the 1960s, and archaeologists believe it may prove to be Alexandria Oxiana, a lost city from the age of Alexander the Great.

Between Alexandria in Egypt and Ai Khanoum in central Asia were dozens of cities and small towns, which served as seeds of Greek culture throughout the empire. The Alexandrian Empire and its successors built a Hellenistic **ecumene**—that is, a unified urban culture, encompassing vast lands and diverse peoples. Some of its cities, which had long, independent Greek heritages, retained strong elements of their pre-Alexandrian culture and even their autonomy. These were the cities of the Greek heartland, such as Athens, Sparta, Thebes, Corinth, and Delphi. Others were cities of empire, built later by Alexander and his successors either from the ground up or on existing but relatively minor urban bases. These cities served as new regional capitals, to administer the new empire, to extend its economy, and to broadcast its culture.

Alexander and his successors also administered their empire through the already existing indigenous urban framework, but added to it the principal institutions and monuments of Hellenistic culture: temples to Greek gods frequently located on a walled acropolis; theaters; an *agora*; civic buildings such as a council chamber and town hall; gymnasia; and stadia. Examples of this style of urban Hellenization in newly conquered lands included Susa, Damascus, Tyre, Kandahar, and Merv. Residents of these varied cities might feel themselves to be both citizens of the locality and participants in a semi-universal ecumene, although the balance of these feelings might vary from city to city and from time to time. A sharp division intensified between the cities with their high culture, now very much Hellenized throughout the empire, and the rural areas, which continued their traditional patterns of life without much change.

The empire encouraged the flow of trade and culture in many directions. Greek ships have been found as far west as the British Isles as well as in the Indian Ocean in the east. European, African, and Asian trade routes intersected at Taxila, Ai Khanoum, Begram, and Merv. The Persians had begun to create an Asian–African–European ecumene; Alexander carried the process further and deeper. Rome, already beginning to rise by the time of Alexander, would later extend a similar imperial mission throughout much of Europe to the west and north, although Rome would not control the east, as we shall see in Chapter 6.

EMPIRE-BUILDING
WHAT DIFFERENCE DOES IT MAKE?

Mesopotamians, Egyptians, Persians, Greeks, and Macedonians launched their imperial ambitions from very different backgrounds. Mesopotamians and Greeks began as city-states, while Egyptians and Persians started as consolidated nations. Out of the fractious chaos of the Greek city-states Macedon built its small state to imperial dimensions under a father and son who ruled as ambitious and skillful kings. Although our coverage was necessarily sketchy, we have seen that each empire erected a central capital; administered a government based in that center that could control the provinces; provided a uniform language, coinage, and legal system across the empire; constructed a road and communication network; articulated an ideology of empire that won the loyalty of many of its citizens and subjects; and created art and architecture to impress on friend and foe alike the power of the empire. Each assembled military forces to apply coercion where necessary.

A time finally came for each empire to rein in its ambitions and limit further expansion. Sometimes it reached the limit of its capacity to conquer and administer profitably; sometimes it was defeated in warfare; often it encountered a combination of both these humbling experiences.

The imperial armies of Alexander the Great refused to proceed to newer, more distant conquests beyond the Indus River. So he turned back toward home. Ironically, Alexander's school tutor had been the philosopher Aristotle, who had written: "To the size of states there is a limit." Aristotle's ideal political unit was the Greek city-state because it promoted the maximum personal participation in democratic government through intense social and political interaction among the citizens.

In choosing to build an empire, Alexander was neither the first nor the last student to disregard his teacher's advice. (Alexander wanted the Greek city-states to be self-governing, but he did not want other areas to have such powers.) Nor was Aristotle the first or last to weigh the relative merits of small, local democratic government units against those of large, centralized bureaucracies. Similar debates still go on in our own day. Debates over the usefulness, limits, and legitimacy of empire were also central to the political thought of ancient Rome, China, and India, the three huge empires that are the focus of Chapters 6, 7, and 8.

Review Questions

- Define "empire" and discuss the chief characteristics generally shared by empires.
- Choose an empire from this chapter. Indicate the degree to which it shares the characteristics noted above.
- Give examples of a culture becoming an empire by conquering an existing empire. Give examples of people creating an empire of their own.
- Apart from the use of sheer military force, what policies do successful empires adopt in order to establish and maintain their power over the peoples they conquer?
- What seem to be the causes of the decline and fall of empires?
- Thucydides wrote, "Our opinion of the gods and our knowledge of men lead us to conclude that it is a general and necessary law of nature to rule whatever one can." Do you agree? Why or why not? Use this chapter's materials to support your view.

Suggested Readings

PRINCIPAL SOURCES

Baines, John and Jaromir Malek. *Atlas of Ancient Egypt* (New York: Facts on File Publications, 1980). Two noted experts continue the excellent books in this series with fine text, maps, pictures, time lines, and breadth of coverage.

Green, Peter. *Alexander of Macedon* (Berkeley, CA: University of California Press, 1991). An excellent, thoughtful, up-to-date biography with good historiographical coverage as well.

Green, Peter. *The Greco-Persian Wars* (Berkeley, CA: University of California Press, 1996). A revision of an older classic on the wars.

Hanson, Victor Davis. *The Wars of the Ancient Greeks* (London: Cassell & Co, 1999). A readable volume that incorporates recent scholarship on Greek warfare.

Kagan, Donald. *The Peloponnesian War* (New York: Viking, 2003). Distills the great scholarship, and increases the readability, of his earlier four-volume work. Based largely on Thucydides, but includes considerable additional scholarship and new perspectives.

Levi, Peter. *Atlas of the Greek World* (New York: Facts on File Publications, 1982). The series continues its excellent, broad coverage with outstanding text, maps, pictures, time lines.

Past Worlds: The (London) Times Atlas of Archaeology (Maplewood, NJ: Hammond, Inc., 1988). Beautifully produced, superbly researched atlas with fine text and excellent pictures as well.

Postgate, J.N. *Early Mesopotamia* (London: Routledge, 1992). Scholarly analysis and clear presentation.

Thucydides. *History of the Peloponnesian War*, trans. Rex Warner (Harmondsworth: Penguin Books, 1972). The definitive primary source, cynically philosophical about political motives, the product of bitter and cynical events.

Wycherley, R.E. *How the Greeks Built Cities* (Garden City, NY: Anchor Books, 1969). Excellent introduction to the urban plans of the Greek cities, with good attention to the significance of the buildings and designs, and to the variety of city-states.

ADDITIONAL SOURCES

Aristotle. *Basic Works*, ed. and trans. Richard McKeon (New York: Random House, 1941). Direct introduction to the work of the philosopher, whose works continued authoritative for at least two thousand years.

Bernal, Martin. *Black Athena: The Afroasiatic Roots of Classical Civilization* (New Brunswick, NJ: Rutgers University Press, 1987). Bernal demonstrates the influence of Egyptian culture on ancient Greece. Because of the title the book became involved in racial debates, but the text does not concentrate on race.

Hamilton, J.R. *Alexander the Great* (London: Hutchison University Library, 1973). A standard biography.

Hammond, Mason. *The City in the Ancient World* (Cambridge, MA: Harvard University Press, 1972). A kind of history of the ancient western world through an analysis of its cities.

Hammond, N.G.L. *The Genius of Alexander the Great* (Chapel Hill, NC: The University of North Carolina Press, 1997). A standard biography.

Herodotus. *The Persian Wars*, trans. George Rawlinson (New York: Modern Library, 1942). Some consider this the first secular book of history. Mixes myth with history in recreating the great clash of civilizations between the Greeks and the Persians.

Homer. *Iliad*, trans. Richmond Lattimore (Chicago, IL: University of Chicago Press, 1951). The story that inspired the ancient Greeks in warfare, and gave us insight into their world.

Homer. *Odyssey*, trans. Robert Fitzgerald (New York: Doubleday & Co., 1961). The great story of the odyssey of Odysseus through one trial after another from the Trojan war back to his home in Greece.

Hornblower, Simon. *The Greek World 479–323 BC* (London: Methuen, 1983). A standard historical survey.

Keuls, Eva C. *The Reign of the Phallus: Sexual Politics in Ancient Athens* (New York: Harper and Row, 1985). Opinionated, belligerent, engaging feminist critique of ancient Athens; evidence based on painting on drinking vessels.

Mumford, Lewis. *The City in History* (New York: Harcourt, Brace and World, 1961). Classic history with a strong argument for small, manageable cities with strong sense of community.

O'Brien, John Maxwell. *Alexander the Great: The Invisible Enemy* (London: Routledge, 1992). Critical biography.

Plato. *The Collected Dialogues of Plato*, ed. Edith Hamilton and Huntington Cairns (New York: Bollingen Foundation [distributed by Pantheon Books], 1961). The complete works of the classic philosopher of ideal types.

Plutarch. *The Lives of the Noble Grecians and Romans*, trans. John Dryden, revised by Arthur Hugh Clough (New York: Modern Library, n.d.). Writing from the height of the Roman Empire, this Greek historian preserves many materials that have otherwise been lost as he assesses the accomplishments of many of the Greek and Roman greats.

Robinson, Eric W., ed. *Ancient Greek Democracy: Readings and Sources* (Malden, MA: Blackwell, 2004). Very useful selection of primary documents on the functioning and limits of ancient Greek democracy.

Saggs, H.W.F. *The Might that Was Assyria* (London: Sidgwick & Jackson, 1984). Fine general survey.

Sophocles. *Oedipus Rex and Oedipus at Colonus*, trans. Robert Fitzgerald in *The Oedipus Cycle* (San Diego: Harcourt Brace Jovanovich, 1969). Two of the most famous plays from ancient Greece.

Tacitus. *The Annals of Imperial Rome*, trans. Michael Grant (Baltimore, MD: Penguin Books, 1959). Primary source by this government official and historian of Rome, often very critical of the growth of empire.

Tarn, W.W. *Alexander the Great*. 2 Vols. (Cambridge: Cambridge University Press, 1948). Laudatory biography.

◉ World History Documents CD-ROM

1.3 The Reign of Sargon

1.5 The Code of Hammurabi

1.10 Assyrian War Tactics

4.1 Homer: The *Iliad*

4.2 Empires and Military Glory: Herodotus Relates the Story of Thermopylae

4.3 Thucydides

4.4 From Confederacy to Empire: Thucydides

4.5 The City-State of Sparta

4.6 The First Philippic: A Great Orator Warns of Macedonian Imperialism

4.7 The Figure of Alexander

4.8a Against Communism

4.8b Virtue and Moderation: The Doctrine of the Mean

ROME AND THE BARBARIANS

THE RISE AND FALL OF EMPIRE
750 B.C.E.–500 C.E.

KEY TOPICS
- From Hill Town to Empire
- The Barbarians and the Fall of the Roman Empire

All roads, by land and sea, led to Rome, the capital of one of the longest lasting and most influential of empires. Situated on the Tiber River, not far from the sea, Rome served as the center of communication and trade for the entire Italian peninsula. To the surrounding sea the Romans gave the name "Mediterranean," the middle of the earth, for it is itself surrounded by the three continents that they knew: southern Europe, northern Africa, and western Asia. Later, as Roman armies conquered and ruled an empire that encompassed all these lands and many territories still more distant, they began to call the Mediterranean *Mare Nostrum* ("Our Sea").

At its greatest extent in the second century C.E., the Roman Empire ruled between 70 and 100 million people of vastly diverse ethnic, racial, religious, and cultural roots. Geographically, it sprawled over 2700 miles east to west and 2500 miles north to south, extending from Scotland to the Persian Gulf. At its most powerful, between 27 B.C.E. and 180 C.E., Rome enforced the **Pax Romana**, the Roman peace, a reign of stability and relative tranquility throughout all these vast regions.

From the first, this empire evoked both praise and condemnation. The Latin poet Virgil (70–19 B.C.E.) led one of the greatest choruses of praise, describing Rome as a gift of the gods, and praising its citizens for successfully carrying out their mandate: "Remember Romans/ To rule the people under law, to establish/ The way of peace." Virgil praised the sheer size of the empire, its roads, its cities, its trade, and its monuments. Most of all, however, he cited the peace and prosperity established through Rome's rule of law, the Pax Romana, enforced by Rome's armies.

The historian Tacitus (*c*. 56–*c*. 120 C.E.) mocked this praise of peace and prosperity: "Robbery, butchery, and rapine they call 'Empire.' They create a desert and call it 'Peace.'" Writing a century after Virgil, and viewing the empire through the eyes of a defeated Celtic chieftain, Tacitus characterized the Pax Romana as a policy of brute military conquest and destruction. This chapter will explore the conditions underlying both of these contradictory points of view.

FROM HILL TOWN TO EMPIRE

The Founding of the Roman Republic

The legendary date for the founding of the city of Rome is 753 B.C.E., and although this is probably not exact, it is approximately correct. According to this legend, beloved by the Romans, Romulus and Remus, twin sons of Mars, the god of War, founded the city at the site where they were rescued from the Tiber River and suckled by a nurturing she-wolf. (See the accompanying Etruscan statue of a she-wolf (p. 164); the suckling

Pax Romana The "Roman Peace," that is, the state of comparative concord prevailing within the boundaries of the Roman Empire from the reign of Augustus (27 B.C.E.–14 C.E.) to that of Marcus Aurelius (161–180 C.E.), enforced by Roman rule and military control.

Opposite **Battle line formed with shields by the Romans against the Dacians, from Trajan's Column, Rome, c. 113 C.E. Plaster cast of marble original.** The Romans adapted the Greek phalanx into a more maneuverable, but tightly configured, array of foot soldiers with shields, spears, and daggers. Victory memorials, like Trajan's column, celebrated the resulting successes in battle. (*Museo della Civiltà, Rome*)

republic A state that is not ruled by a hereditary leader (a monarchy) but by a person or persons appointed under the constitution.

centuries The smallest units of the Roman army, each composed of some 100 foot-soldiers and commanded by a centurion. A legion was made up of 60 centuries. Centuries also formed political divisions of Roman citizens.

Capitoline Wolf, *c.* **500 B.C.E.** According to legend, Rome was founded by Romulus and Remus, twin sons of Mars, at the spot where they were rescued from the Tiber River and suckled by a she-wolf. The group of she-wolf with twins was adopted as the symbol of Rome, although the children in this particular statue were added almost two thousand years later, in the Renaissance. (*Museo Capitolino, Rome*)

children were added two thousand years later, to represent the legend of Romulus and Remus.)

For two and a half centuries, kings of the neighboring Etruria, the land to Rome's north, ruled the city. The Romans learned much from the Etruscans about city building, art, religion, mythology, and even language. As Rome entered the Mediterranean trade networks of the Etruscans, merchants and craft workers immigrated to the city. The Etruscan king Servius Tullius (578–534 B.C.E.) reformed the military, creating the *comitia centuriata*, a deliberative ruling council organized by hundreds (*centuriae*), representing the soldiers of Rome. This assembly of Roman citizens persisted for centuries after Etruscan rule had ended, reinforcing the connection between the armies of Rome and its government.

About 509 B.C.E., the wealthy, powerful, citizens of Rome—all veterans of military service—drove out the Etruscan kings. They declared Rome a **republic**, a government in which power resides in a body of citizens and consists of representatives elected by them. Although they overthrew the monarchy, the new oligarchs—the small, elite group of rulers—retained many other political institutions. Their armies remained the center of power. Because soldiers provided their own arms, only men with some wealth and property could command and rise in the ranks. They in turn were ordered by class, according to the quality and cost of the weapons they provided, and then divided into military units called **centuries**, or groups of one hundred, as they had

been under the Etruscans. The leaders of the centuries continued to meet together in assembly to elect magistrates and decide questions of peace and war.

The magistrates, administrative and judicial officials, administered the Roman Republic. At the lowest level of **quaestor** they had limited financial authority. At the highest level, **consuls** held power that extended over all the lands Rome ruled. As magistrates ended their one-year (renewable) term of office, they automatically entered the Senate of Rome, the highest legislative and consultative body of the government.

At each level, two officials were paired, so that they would have to consult with one another, and neither could seize excessive power. The power of the former kings, for example, was now shared between the two consuls in this new system of checks and balances. (In extraordinary emergencies, one man could be named as dictator for the limited term of six months.)

The Conquest of Italy

The Roman Republic established alliances with other nearby city-states in west-central Italy, and began to challenge the Etruscans. In 396 B.C.E., after a siege of six years, the Romans captured Veii, a principal Etruscan city only 12 miles from Rome. Celtic invaders sacked Rome itself in 390 B.C.E.(see p. 192), but the setback was brief, and Rome's expansion continued.

Its armies, fighting until now in phalanxes, according to the Greek model (see p. 146), were reorganized. Small, flexible units, armed with swords and throwing javelins in place of older spears, lined up with less experienced, younger troops in front, more tested troops behind them, and then, as the final resort, veterans of courage and proved valor. If the front ranks could not hold and fell back into the rear lines, the advancing, over-confident enemy was suddenly confronted by a compact mass of soldiers of the greatest numbers and skill. By 264 B.C.E., Roman armies controlled all of Italy south of the Po valley.

As it expanded, Rome often offered its opponents a choice between alliance and conquest. Subsequently it bestowed various levels of Roman citizenship throughout Italy to induce its residents to support Rome and join its armies.

Rome became a society geared for war. Roman armies, and a new navy created to combat their Mediterranean opponents, continued to expand Roman rule. For the next 140 years its troops were almost constantly on the move. The most bitter and the most decisive of their battles were the three Punic Wars against Carthage.

The Conquest of Carthage and the Western Mediterranean

Carthage, only 130 miles across the narrow waist of the Mediterranean from Italy, had developed as a major trade outpost of Phoenician seafarers. Just as Rome dominated Italy, the Carthaginians controlled the north central coast of Africa and the western Mediterranean. One of their trade networks focused on the mineral wealth of Spain, especially its silver mines. To protect that route, Carthage developed ports and cities in Sicily and Sardinia. It even controlled trade outposts on the Italian mainland in Etruria. Carthage and Rome were set on a collision course.

The three wars that broke out are known as the Punic Wars after the Roman term for Phoenicians, *Punici*. The fighting opened in Sicily in 264 B.C.E. By 241 B.C.E., when the first Punic War ended, Rome was victorious both on land and sea. It took control of Sicily and imposed taxes on the island. Four years later, Rome took advantage of a mutiny among Carthaginian troops in Sardinia to occupy Sardinia and Corsica. In 227 B.C.E., it annexed the islands. For the first time, Rome had provinces outside the Italian peninsula.

quaestor A junior official in ancient Rome. There were originally two, elected annually, but more were appointed as the empire expanded. Most were financial officials.

consul Under the Roman Republic, one of the two magistrates holding supreme civil and military authority. Nominated by the Senate and elected by citizens in the Comitia Centuriata (popular assembly), the consuls held office for one year and each had power of veto over the other.

AT A GLANCE: THE ROMAN EMPIRE

DATE	POLITICAL	RELIGION AND CULTURE	SOCIAL DEVELOPMENT
500 B.C.E.	■ Rome independent of Etruscan rule (509); Republic founded		
450 B.C.E.	■ Rome sacked by Gauls (390)		■ Laws of Twelve Tables promulgated
350 B.C.E.	■ Roman expansion into Italy south of Po (327–304)		
300 B.C.E.	■ 1st Punic War (264–241)		■ Earliest Roman coinage (280–75)
250 B.C.E.	■ 2nd Punic War (218–201) ■ Hannibal invaded Italy ■ Roman conquest of Cisalpine Gaul (202–191)	■ Stoicism – Zeno	
200 B.C.E.	■ Rome annexed Spain (197) ■ Conquest of Macedon (167)	■ Polybius (200–118)	
150 B.C.E.	■ 3rd Punic War (149–146) ■ T. Gracchus tribune (133) ■ G. Gracchus tribune (123 and 122) ■ Gallia Narbonensis a Roman province	■ Carthage destroyed ■ Corinth destroyed	■ Pax Romana led to widespread trade throughout Empire; roads built
100 B.C.E.	■ Sulla conquers Greece ■ Civil war in Rome (83–2) ■ Conquest of Syria (66) ■ 1st Triumvirate (60)		■ Spartacus slave revolt (73–71)
50 B.C.E.	■ Civil war (49) ■ Caesar dictator (47–44) ■ 2nd Triumvirate (43) ■ Annexation of Egypt (30) ■ Augustus Caesar (d. 14 C.E.)	■ Cicero (d. 43) ■ Virgil (d. 19) ■ Augustus deified on his death ■ Forum in Rome ■ Livy (d. 17 C.E.)	

Carthage, however, rebuilt its forces, especially in Spain. When the Spanish city of Saguntum asked for Roman help, the Romans intervened, threatening Carthage's Spanish colonies. The brilliant, twenty-seven-year-old Carthaginian commander Hannibal (247–183 B.C.E.) defeated Rome's troops in 219 B.C.E., and the second Punic War had begun. It continued for almost twenty years.

Hannibal unexpectedly took the offensive by land, marching tens of thousands of troops and thirty-seven elephants 1000 miles along the French coast, over the Alps, into the Po valley, and toward Rome. In two months he overran most of north Italy and destroyed the armies sent against him. But Hannibal could not break the power of Rome. Most of Rome's allies remained loyal and Rome raised new armies. Rome recaptured those cities that had previously gone over to Hannibal, including Capua, Syracuse, and Tarentum. Hannibal did annihilate a Roman army at Cannae in south Italy, but ultimately he was isolated there. Meanwhile, Rome won victories in Spain in 211–206 B.C.E., especially under the general Publius Cornelius Scipio. In 204 B.C.E. Scipio invaded Africa. Hannibal returned to defend his homeland, but Scipio, later named Scipio Africanus for his victory, defeated him at the Battle of Zama (202 B.C.E.). The war was over, and Carthage became a dependency of Rome.

In its treatment of the rebellious city of Capua and its surrounding region of Campania, just to the south of Rome, the Romans exhibited what would become known as their "New Wisdom," a policy of brute force toward their enemies. Roman leaders executed seventy senators, imprisoned three hundred Campanian aristocrats, and put others into the custody of Latin allies. They sold the mass of Campanian citizens into slavery, although they allowed resident aliens, freedmen, and petty tradesmen and artisans to continue to work.

A half-century later, Rome again responded with brute force after Carthage attacked Rome's African ally, King Masinissa of Numidia. Disregarding Carthage's legitimate claims that its land was being encroached upon, Rome sided with its ally and provoked the third Punic War (149–146 B.C.E.). With the aged Cato the Censor calling in the Roman Senate for the complete destruction of Carthage, Rome razed it to the ground, sold its survivors into slavery, and sowed salt into the soil so that it would never again flourish. The Romans annexed all of Carthage into the Roman province of Africa. Rome had become mistress of the Mediterranean.

Rome's brutal use of military power served as a warning to potential foes. Roman generals were not pressed to win quick, brilliant victories, but to defeat the enemy through patient, deliberate preparation, and decisive force. Ideally, the enemy would be so awed by Roman forces that it would never dare oppose them.

Subsequent Expansion

After Rome had eliminated the Carthaginian threat with the end of the second Punic War, in 202–191 B.C.E. it turned to the conquest of the Gauls in northern Italy and annexed their territory. It annexed Spain in 197 B.C.E. but treated that province so harshly that constant revolts simmered until Rome finally crushed them in 133 B.C.E. Rome then turned its power toward Gaul, modern France. In southern Gaul, Rome's

AT A GLANCE: THE ROMAN EMPIRE (continued)

DATE	POLITICAL	RELIGION AND CULTURE	SOCIAL DEVELOPMENT
25 C.E.	■ Christianity reaches Rome ■ Invasion of Britain (43)		
50 C.E.	■ Trajan (98–117)	■ Seneca (d. 65) ■ Destruction of Temple in Jerusalem (70) ■ Pompeii and Herculaneum buried by eruption of Vesuvius (79)	■ Jewish revolt (66–73) ■ Roman women gain new rights
100 C.E.	■ Dacia conquered by Trajan ■ Hadrian (117–38)	■ Tacitus (d. 120) ■ Trajan's column and forum (112–113) ■ Pantheon in Rome ■ Hadrian's Wall	
150 C.E.	■ Marcus Aurelius (161–180)	■ Apuleius (d. c. 170) ■ Galen (d. 199)	
200 C.E.	■ Caracalla (212–217) ■ Decius (249–51)	■ Baths of Caracalla	■ Roman citizenship for all males
250 C.E.	■ Gallienus (253–268)	■ Persecution of Christians	
300 C.E.	■ Constantine (r. 306–337)	■ Edict of Milan (313) ■ Constantinople inaugurated (330)	
350 C.E.		■ St. Augustine (354–430) ■ End of state support for paganism (394)	
400 C.E.	■ Sack of Rome (410)		
450 C.E.	■ End of Roman Empire in West (476)		
550 C.E.			■ Justinian codifies Roman law

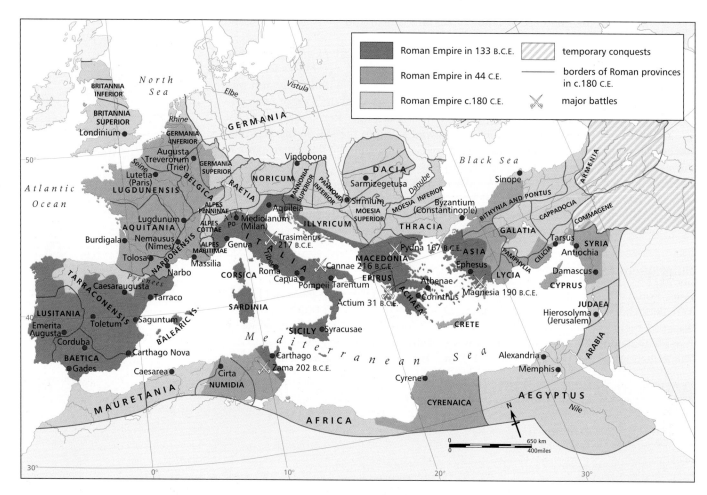

The Roman Empire. Rome built its empire on military expansion, first within Italy by overthrowing its neighbors, then across the Mediterranean by defeating the Carthaginians, then northwest to Gaul and Britain and north to the Danube. Rome offered many benefits to the peoples it conquered, but finally its power rested in its armies.

ally Massilia (Marseilles) asked for help against Gallic tribes, and by 121 B.C.E. Rome had annexed most of the region.

Northern Gaul seemed stably divided among various Gallic peoples until the Helvetii, Celts driven out of Switzerland, began to invade. In response, Julius Caesar (100–44 B.C.E.), the Roman commander in north Italy and southern Gaul, moved with his army into central and northern Gaul. Caesar's *Gallic War* tells of his conquests in 58–52 B.C.E. By the time his campaigns ended in 49 B.C.E., all Gaul belonged to Rome.

The Romans were opportunists, seizing land wherever they saw weakness. Even as they conquered territory in the west, they expanded in the east as well. In the eastern Mediterranean, the Romans encountered Macedonians and Greeks, the proud heirs of Alexander the Great, who still ruled the lands that he had conquered and Hellenized. Rome's first battle on Greek soil came in 200 B.C.E., and it began the complete restructuring of political power in the eastern Mediterranean.

At the death of Alexander the Great in 323 B.C.E. his empire had divided into three regional kingdoms. In 203–202 B.C.E. two of these kingdoms, Macedonia and Syria, where the Seleucid dynasty ruled, combined to threaten the third, Egypt, where the Ptolemaic family ruled. Neighboring Greek city-states encouraged Rome to use these divisions to establish its own balance of power in the region. Rome accepted the invitation. It warned Macedonia not to interfere in Greek affairs. When Philip V of Macedon (r. 211–179 B.C.E.) rejected this warning, the Romans attacked and defeated him. In victory, the Romans declared the Greek city-states of the eastern

SOURCE

Artifactual Records

Rome has bequeathed rich material artifacts. Much of the infrastructure of the empire—its roads, aqueducts, stadia, public baths, forums, temples, triumphal arches—as well as substantial parts of many of the military camps and cities it constructed still stand. Roman coinage and statuary are everywhere.

The cities of Pompeii and Herculaneum, comprising a total population of about 20,000, were buried in dust and cinders in the volcanic eruption of Mount Vesuvius in 79 C.E. Archaeologists uncovered these remains, forgotten for almost two millennia, in the late eighteenth century, providing an unparalleled view of the structure and furnishings of these provincial towns. Preserved like time capsules, they reveal their urban design, buildings, furniture, and household objects.

Pompeii was a walled town, with seven gates, a forum, council chamber, offices of magistrates, temples dedicated to Apollo and Jupiter, market buildings, a stock exchange, law court, theater, auditoriums, an amphitheater for gladiatorial contests and wild beast hunts, three Turkish-style baths, workshops, shops, brothels, and homes. Carbonized food, preserved and sealed in hot volcanic mud, suggests that at least some of the inhabitants ate well. Walls, surviving to their full height, have preserved vivid murals from the residences and businesses. At least some Pompeiians had cultivated aesthetic sensibilities. Some of the art in the seven brothels indicates also a cultivated taste for pornography.

In the countryside, archaeologists have also been able to reconstruct latifundia, *rural estates that were controlled by rich owners who bought up family farms and ran them as plantations. Off-shore searches have uncovered sunken ships in the Italian Mediterranean that shed light on Roman trade missions and their cargoes.*

Archaeological digs have also uncovered the history of the many Gothic, Celtic, and other groups of migrating peoples who lived on the fringes of the empire, later settled within its territories, and finally established their own states on those lands as the empire disintegrated. Their settlements, burial grounds, tools, and artwork yield significant information about their lives, even though they had no writing systems until they learned from the Romans.

With such extensive artifacts complementing the rich documentary record, scholars can reconstruct the rise and fall of the Roman Empire and its relationships with neighboring peoples. Relatively abundant materials provide the sources also to explore new topics such as the extent of slavery, the treatment of women, and patterns of health and disease in ancient Rome.

The young Hercules wrestling with a snake, fresco, House of the Vettii, Pompeii.

The body of a man petrified by ash from the eruption of Mount Vesuvius, Pompeii, 79 C.E.

Mediterranean "free," granting them nominal independence, but, in fact, placing them under Roman control.

Rome had similarly warned Antiochus III, the Great, of Syria (r. 223–187 B.C.E.) to stay out of Europe and Egypt. When Antiochus ignored the warning, Roman forces crushed him, pushed him back to Syria, and forced him to pay a huge indemnity.

In the next generation, Rome decisively defeated Philip V's son Perseus (r.179–168 B.C.E.) in 168 B.C.E., ending the Macedonian monarchy. In the same year, Rome again protected Egypt from the Seleucids, asserting its own control of the eastern Mediterranean.

Here, too, Rome applied the brutal tactics of the "New Wisdom." In 148 B.C.E., when the Greek city-state of Corinth and its allies flouted Roman wishes, and even attacked Roman envoys, Rome razed Corinth to the ground, sold all its surviving inhabitants into slavery, and carried its artistic works to Rome. Recognizing Rome's power, the king of Pergamum, in Asia Minor, bequeathed his lands to Rome at his death in 133 B.C.E. Throughout the Mediterranean, Rome was now the dominant power.

In the east, the general Pompey (106–48 B.C.E.) added Syria and most of Asia Minor to the empire. In 63 B.C.E. he captured Jerusalem, the capital of Judaea, allowing a Jewish king to rule as a client-monarch. Gnaeus Pompeius Magnus (Pompey the Great) favored such indirect rule through local potentates throughout the east, where sophisticated governmental structures had existed for centuries. He also founded some forty cities as centers of Roman political influence.

Institutions of Empire

Empires are ultimately sustained by military force, but successful empires must also win at least some degree of support from among the conquered peoples. Beginning with its early conquests, Rome had often won such support through several of its political, cultural, economic, and ideological policies, most importantly through the granting of citizenship.

Politically, Rome bestowed benefits on conquered peoples, especially the benefits of citizenship. All free men from Rome were citizens automatically; the rest of the men of Italy, however, were not. In 381 B.C.E., the town of Tusculum, some 15 miles from Rome and surrounded by Roman territory, seemed poised to oppose Rome. The Romans won over the Tusculuns by offering incorporation into Rome and full citizenship. In 338 B.C.E. full citizenship was bestowed on four additional Latin cities; others received partial citizenship with no voting rights but with rights of property, contracts, and the right to marry Roman citizens. They were also freed of property taxes. Roman citizenship also protected its beneficiary from arbitrary arrest and violence.

In 91 B.C.E. Marcus Livius Drusus the Younger was elected **tribune**, one of the most powerful offices in ancient Rome. Drusus proposed extending citizenship and the vote to all the Italian allies, but the Roman Senate rejected the proposal. Drusus was later assassinated, leaving the Italians frustrated and furious. So began the "Social War" or "War of the Allies." After two years, however, Rome did offer full citizenship to all Italians who had remained loyal and even to those who agreed to put down their arms. It extended full citizenship north as far as the Po River, and partial citizenship up to the Alps Mountains. So, grudgingly, citizenship was offered as an inducement to loyalty. In newly annexed lands, the aristocrats, the group to whom Rome usually granted these rights and obligations, regarded even partial citizenship as attractive.

tribune In ancient Rome, a plebeian officer elected by the plebeians and charged to protect their lives and properties, with a right of veto against legislative proposals of the Senate.

Patrons and Clients

Asymmetrical power relationships characterized Roman life—private as well as public—under the Republic. The earliest enduring social structure in Rome was the patron–client relationship. Strong men acted as protectors of the weak; the weak, in turn, provided obedience and services for the strong as requested.

In civilian life, patrons, usually patricians, would provide legal protection and representation for their clients, usually **plebeians**, those without longstanding hereditary

plebeian A citizen of ancient Rome who was not a member of the privileged patrician class. From the later Republican period, the term *plebeian* implied low social class.

HOW DO WE KNOW?

Contemporary Historians Evaluate the History of Rome

During the later Republic historians began consciously to write the history of the city. Their accounts were often ambivalent, revealing a mixture of pride in the conquests and achievements of their empire with skepticism and even hostility toward the abandonment of the earlier republican ideals.

The most famous of the early historians was Polybius (c. 200–c. 118 B.C.E.), a Greek taken to Rome as a political captive. Polybius marveled at the overwhelming event of his own time, Rome's conquest of an empire through its victories over Carthage, Macedonia, and Spain:

There can surely be no one so petty or so apathetic in his outlook that he has no desire to discover by what means and under what system of government the Romans succeeded in less than fifty-three years [220–167 B.C.E.] in bringing under their rule almost the whole of the inhabited world, an achievement which is without parallel in human history. (The Histories I:1; p. 443, cited in Finley)

Livy (59 B.C.E.–17 C.E.) praised the glories of Rome's imperial expansion, but he decried the resulting class conflict between Rome's aristocrats and its common people that was currently ripping apart Rome's self-governing, elected, republican form of government.

Tacitus (c. 56–c. 120 C.E.) continued the story to the height of imperial power. He praised the heroism of the Roman conquerors, but he also understood the anguish and bitterness of the conquered peoples. In Agricola, Tacitus attributes to the Celtic chieftain Calgacus one of the most devastating critiques of imperialism ever articulated. In Tacitus' account, Calgacus condemns

the Romans, whose tyranny cannot be escaped by any act of reasonable submission. These brigands of the world have exhausted the land by their rapacity, so they now ransack the sea. When their enemy is rich, they lust after wealth; when the enemy is poor, they lust after power. Neither East nor West has satisfied their hunger. They are unique among humanity insofar as they equally covet the rich and the poor. Robbery, butchery, and rapine they call "Empire." They create a desert and call it "Peace." (I:129, cited in Andrea and Overfield)

As the empire began to decay, mainstream historians added more critical perspectives. Dio Cassius (c. 150–235 C.E.) nostalgically recalled the rule of Augustus as Rome's golden age and lamented the empire's subsequent decline "from a monarchy of gold to one of iron and rust." Like Tacitus, he cited and sympathized with the frustration and rage of those, like Boudicca, the warrior-queen of the Celts, who led her armies in revolt against the Romans in 61 C.E.:

We have been despised and trampled underfoot by men who know nothing else than how to secure gain. (Lewis and Reinhold, II:334)

Other historians illuminated the empire from its fringes rather than from its center, and they, too, were often critical of the effects of empire on its subjects. For Jewish historians, such as Philo of Alexandria (c. 13 B.C.E.–c. 45 C.E.) and Josephus (c. 37–c. 100 C.E.), and for Christian theologians, such as Tertullian (c. 155–c. 225 C.E.) and St. Augustine, bishop of Hippo in north Africa (354–430 C.E.), the Roman Empire was not the central concern, but it was an inescapable presence. These historians, philosophers, and theologians had to take account of Rome's power in their own teaching, writing, and actions. From their marginal positions, they usually counseled realistic accommodation to Rome's power.

In addition to these formal histories, leading men of the empire left important documents that shed light on their times. The great orator and political leader Cicero (106–43 B.C.E.) left dozens of letters, fifty-seven public speeches, and extensive writings on public affairs. Julius Caesar's account of the Gallic War describes his military organization and strategy, the Roman virtues that characterized his troops, and the lands and peoples against which he fought. It is the only account of a Roman war written by a participant that has endured to today. In part, Caesar was writing a propaganda piece, preparing the path for his later assertion of personal power in Rome.

His accounts are filled with great slaughter. For example, in 58 B.C.E., he reported that his armies slaughtered 226,000 Helvetii, with only some 110,000 surviving. In the same year he reports killing almost an entire German army of 120,000 men and, the next year, almost every soldier in a Belgic army of 60,000 men. He captured the region around Namur in northern France and sold all 53,000 inhabitants into slavery. In 56 B.C.E., he massacred two German peoples, killing as many as 460,000 people, including women and children. By the end of nine years of war in Gaul, Caesar reports a total of 1,192,000 enemy killed and another million captured.

- Which Roman authors and historians saw the expansion of the Roman Empire as unfortunate for the people of Rome? Why? Do you agree? Why or why not?
- Name Jews and Christians whose writings shed light on the Roman Empire. What issues did they address that are useful in understanding empires?
- If you could join archaeologists at a Roman site, which site would you like to explore? Why?

ties to the state, and usually without property. In exchange, clients were expected to help pay fines and public charges levied against their patrons and to help provide dowries for their patron's daughters at marriage. To mark the symbolism of the relationship, the client was to present himself periodically at the residence or office of the patron, and the patron was to give him a small gift at that time. The relationship of ex-masters to ex-slaves was of patron to client, and it was frequently characterized by warm feelings, especially if freedom was granted by gift of manumission rather than by the slave's purchase. These relationships often endured through several generations. Similar patron–client relationships between strong and weak later characterized Rome's imperial control over conquered provinces.

The Roman Family. Patron–client relationships also marked the structure of the family. The father of the family, the *paterfamilias*, had the right of life and death over his children as long as he lived. In reality, most fathers were not tyrants, and in exercising the right to choose their children's occupations and spouses, and to control their economic possessions, they would normally try to consider their needs and desires. Nevertheless, fathers had the legal power to act as they wished: they continued to have control over their daughters' economic lives even after their marriages, for these rights did not pass to the husbands. These rights were enshrined in the law of *patria potestas*, the right of the head of the household.

According to Roman custom and practice, woman's role was subordinate to man's. A woman was legally subject to her father as long as he lived. After his death, she was required to obey the advice of her husband or a legally appointed guardian in any kind of legal or business transaction. Actual practice was, however, more liberal. If a woman had reached adulthood, she usually gained her independence at the death of her father, as did her brothers. Also, at least as early as the fifth-century B.C.E. *Law of the Twelve Tables*, women could block the legal powers of their husband by absenting themselves from his home for three nights in a row each year.

The families of the bride and groom arranged their marriages. Motherhood was considered the most significant rite of passage for women. Free-born women were exempted from having a guardian after giving birth to three children, and freed women after four children.

People respected women if they lived chastely and more or less contentedly within these guidelines of family, motherhood, and domesticity. The feminine ideal was the faith-ful and loyal *univira*, the "one-man woman." A woman caught in adultery was banished from her home and might well be executed; men apprehended in adultery were not punished. Women found drinking wine could also be punished; men could not. These principles of behavior were, of course, fully applicable only to the upper classes. The masses of lower-class free women entered the working world outside the home, and slaves had little control over their lives. The prevalence of prostitution and brothels further indicate the limited applicability of the Roman female ideal.

Class and Class Conflict. Despite the structure provided by patron–client relationships, class conflict was a staple of Rome's history. The system of government

paterfamilias The head of a family or household in Roman law—always a male—and the only member to have full legal rights. The *paterfamilias* had absolute power over his family, which extended to life and death.

Mosaic of Neptune and Amphitrite (detail), Herculaneum, before 79 c.e. Art sometimes seems to contradict the legal evidence concerning gender relationships in the Roman Empire. The artist responsible for this mosaic of the sea-god Neptune and his wife Amphitrite has accorded the couple an apparent equality.

under the early Republic had included only 7 to 10 percent of the population: the wealthy, the powerful, and some with hereditary ties to Rome. These were the patricians (from the Latin "pater," father). The overwhelming majority, the plebeians, those without long-standing hereditary ties to the state, and usually without property, could not serve as officers in the military and were thus excluded from government, as were slaves and women.

The two classes, patricians and plebeians, had become increasingly polarized under Etruscan rule. The patricians forbade intermarriage with the plebeians and monopolized for themselves the magistracies, membership of the Senate, and even the religious offices of the state. In response, the plebeians had looked to the Etruscan king as their protector. The fall of the monarchy c. 509 B.C.E. reduced the status of the plebeians still further.

The Struggle of the Orders. The first conflict between patricians and plebeians, the Struggle of the Orders, persisted through more than half a century—494 to 440 B.C.E.—of the early Republic. The plebeians relied on their ultimate strengths: their bodies and their numbers. They were the foot soldiers of Rome, and their periodic boycotts of the patricians, by withdrawing to the Aventine Hill, threatened the city of Rome itself. In 451 B.C.E., in an attempt to resolve the conflict, a commission of ten patricians codified Rome's existing customary practices into the *Law of the Twelve Tables*.

The patricians were pleased with their legal accomplishments and apparent liberality, but the plebeians were horrified when they recognized the force of the laws that were imposed upon them. For example, after a thirty-day grace period, debtors could be arrested and brought to court, held in chains or stocks, and, after sixty days, sold into slavery or killed. The financial punishment for bruising or breaking the bone of a freeman was twice that for similar injuries to a slave. The punishment for pasturing animals on someone else's land or for cutting crops from someone else's field secretly by night was death by hanging. The punishment for theft by a freeman was flogging and arranging some form of repayment; for theft by a slave it was flogging and execution by being thrown from the Tarpeian Rock on the Capitoline Hill in Rome. On the other hand, a patron who defrauded a client was subject to execution, later commuted to exile and confiscation of property (Lewis and Reinhold, I:109–113).

Slowly, under pressure, the patricians yielded power, and the first plebeian consul was elected in 360 B.C.E. A series of laws that relieved debt also helped the plebeians, although indebtedness continued to be a problem throughout Roman history.

Imperial expansion exacerbated class conflicts within Rome. The benefits of the conquests went mostly to the rich, while the yeoman farmers, who supplied the troops, were often bankrupted by the wars. After serving in the army for years, they would return home to find that in their absence their wives and children had not been able to maintain the family farms and might even have sold them to owners of large estates, called *latifundia*, and left for the city, impoverished.

Urban Splendor and Squalor. Class divisions were most glaring in the capital. The city of Rome itself grew seemingly without limit and without adequate planning. As Rome came to control Italy and then the Mediterranean, the city's population multiplied, reaching one million by about the first century C.E.

Some of the newcomers were wealthy and powerful, and they adorned the city by adding new examples of Greek architecture and urban design to the earlier Etruscan forms. They replaced wood, mud, and local volcanic rock with concrete and finer stone. Augustus himself boasted that he had found Rome a city of brick and left it one of marble. A modern urban historian has described the private homes of the wealthy patricians as models of comfort:

Canopus, Hadrian's Villa, Tivoli,
c. **135** C.E. Rome's wealthy and powerful elites commanded private luxuries beyond the imagination of the average Roman. The Villa of the Emperor Hadrian comprised a series of buildings, gardens, and pools—this one representing a well-known Egyptian canal—laid out on the side of a hill in Tivoli. The complex was designed to bring the more sophisticated pleasures of city life to the country.

The houses of the patricians, spacious, airy, sanitary, equipped with bathrooms and water closets, heated in winter by hypocausts, which carried hot air through chambers in the floors, were perhaps the most commodious and comfortable houses built for a temperate climate anywhere until the twentieth century; a triumph of domestic architecture. (Mumford, p. 220)

The poor also came streaming into the city, but from bankrupt family farms. For them, Rome was a nightmare. The contrast was shocking.

Not only were these buildings unheated, unprovided with waste pipes or water closets, unadapted to cooking; not merely did they contain an undue number of airless rooms, indecently overcrowded: though poor in all the facilities that make for decent daily living, they were in addition so badly built and so high that they offered no means of safe exit from the frequent fires that occurred. And if their tenants escaped typhoid, typhus, fire, they might easily meet their death in the collapse of the whole structure. Such accidents were all too frequent …

The main population of the city that boasted its world conquests lived in cramped, noisy, airless, foul-smelling, infected quarters, paying extortionate rents to merciless landlords, undergoing daily indignities and terrors that coarsened and brutalized them, and in turn demanded compensatory outlets. (pp. 220–21)

Attempts at Reform. The most exemplary of the leaders who tried to achieve equity for Rome's poorer citizens were the reforming Gracchi brothers, Tiberius Sempronius Gracchus (163–133 B.C.E.) and Gaius Sempronius Gracchus (153–121 B.C.E.). In 133 B.C.E., while serving as tribune of the people, the office established to protect the interest of the plebeians, Tiberius proposed distributing some public lands among the poor, especially among poor soldiers. Opposed to this liberal proposal and fearing that Gracchus was attempting to gain too much political power for himself, a number of senators, supported by their clients, clubbed Tiberius and 300 of his supporters to death. This was the first political murder over a public policy issue in Rome in nearly 400 years. Despite the murder, the redistribution of public land did take place.

In 123 B.C.E., Gaius Gracchus was elected tribune of the people. He extended his brother's plan for land redistribution by establishing new colonies for the resettlement of some of the poor people of Rome in the regions conquered in the Punic Wars, including Carthage itself. He also introduced subsidized grain sales—later extended into a dole of free bread—to the poor people of Rome. Gaius argued that citizenship should be granted to all Latins and to the local civic officials in all other communities.

He was not equally sensitive to the problems of non-Italians, however, for his legislation exploited the provinces by enabling Roman knights to serve as "publicans" or tax farmers. These tax farmers struck an agreement with the state to turn over a fixed amount of net taxes from their region while retaining the right to collect as much as they were able and to keep the balance for themselves. Tax farming enabled the state to collect taxes without monitoring the process; it enabled the tax farmers to become wealthy; and it exploited the people who were being taxed, leaving them without protection. Gaius auctioned off the collection of taxes in Asia. While this profited the elite and helped to secure their loyalty to him personally, it impoverished the residents of the Roman province of Asia. Many senators became increasingly hostile to Gaius Gracchus, and in 121 B.C.E. he too was assassinated, along with his fellow tribune, Flaccus. Some 3000 of his supporters were executed.

The reforms of the Gracchi brothers seemed blocked, but in fact they laid the foundations for the events that led to the end of the Republic a century later. They challenged the power of the Senate and exposed the problems of the poor and the war veterans, while their enemies employed violence, murder, and thuggery as tools for fashioning and implementing public policy. Julius Caesar and Augustus Caesar, the two men most responsible for finally turning the Republic into a militaristic empire headed by a single person, learned from the experiences of the Gracchi brothers to play on Rome's class divisions by soliciting the support of the lower classes. They created an alliance between the emperor and the urban poor.

"Bread and Circuses." A new method of coping with class conflict developed: "Bread and circuses." Rome bribed the poor, many of them former soldiers from its conquering armies, with a dole of free bread. Up to 200,000 people were served each day. The dole encouraged them to while away their time in public religious festivities, races, the theater, and gladiatorial contests of great cruelty, which pitted man against man and man against beast in spectacles witnessed by tens of thousands. The public arenas of Rome, including Rome's largest race-track and stadia, could accommodate about half of Rome's adult population. On days of gladiatorial contests, as many as 5000 animals, including elephants and water buffalo, were slaughtered. Hundreds of humans, too, were slain in a single day. This combination of spectacle and free food was offered to keep the unemployed urban masses compliant.

Later emperors continued these policies designed to keep the plebeians quiet without actually solving the problems of unemployment and lack of dignity. Until its final collapse, the empire was threatened by unrest and revolt, and one of the reasons for the later popularity of Christianity in Rome was its message of compassion and salvation for the poor and downtrodden (Chapter 10).

Slaves and Slave Revolts

As wealthy Romans assembled vast estates and as Roman armies captured valuable underground mineral resources, they needed labor for farming and mining. Increasingly, they turned to the acquisition of slaves. Through military conquest, piracy, and raids in foreign regions, Rome accumulated slaves numbering perhaps in the millions. Short wars, such as those in Macedonia (197 B.C.E.) and Illyria (177 B.C.E.), yielded thousands; longer conflicts, such as those against the Teutons and Cimbrians (102–101 B.C.E.), hundreds of thousands. In his nine years in Gaul Julius Caesar may have captured nearly half a million. As much as a quarter of Rome's agricultural labor force was slave labor.

"Every slave we own is an enemy we harbor," was a sardonic Roman proverb by the time of Caesar Augustus (Lewis and Reinhold, I:245). That emperor proclaimed in his epitaph that in successful campaigns against pirates, "I turned over to their masters for punishment nearly 30,000 fugitive slaves who had taken up arms against the state" (Lewis and Reinhold, I:569). Three great slave revolts grew into wars. During the Great Slave War in Sicily (134–131 B.C.E.) 70,000 slaves resorted to armed resistance. In 104–100 B.C.E., a second revolt in Sicily broke out when it seemed that Germanic tribes would invade Italy and keep the imperial troops occupied in the north. Finally, Spartacus led a revolt among the gladiators in 73–71 B.C.E. that the Romans crushed. Some 100,000 slaves were killed in the fighting, and 6000 captured slaves were crucified on the roads leading into Rome.

Slaves continued throughout the imperial centuries as a threat within the Roman Empire. As Alaric besieged Rome with an army of Goths in 410 C.E., "Day by day almost all the slaves who were in Rome poured out of the city to join the barbarians, who now numbered about forty thousand" (Zosimus, *New History*, cited in Lewis and Reinhold, II:626).

Military Power

From its beginning, Rome was a military state. According to one legend, its founders, the twin brothers Romulus and Remus, were the sons of Mars, the god of war. An alternative legend, reported in Virgil's *Aeneid*, saw them descended on their mother's side from Aeneas, a pious and devoted warrior-hero from the fallen city of Troy.

Rome's armies were central to its life and they excelled in organization and technology. When necessary they adopted creative innovations. Although at first they copied the Greek hoplite phalanxes (see Chapter 5) in their military deployment, later Roman armies were structured around smaller, more maneuverable units, arrayed together in battle lines from least to most experienced, so that enemies were forced to confront row-on-row of soldiers of increasing skill and valor. Confronting groups of invading Goths, they created new, mobile cavalry units to supplement their more conventional infantry legions of 3000 to 6000 foot soldiers.

Although it had never previously possessed a navy, Rome built one that conquered Carthage, the greatest sea-power of the day. The

Column of Trajan, Rome. Dedicated 113 C.E. The Romans built tall commemorative columns in order to celebrate the power and military might of the empire. The Column of Trajan is covered by a continuous strip of carving that tells the story of the Emperor Trajan's victories over the barbarian tribes along the Danube.

Arch of Trajan, Benevento, 114–117 C.E.
Triumphal arches are another peculiarly Roman means of celebrating the power of the ruler and his empire. This particular arch, dedicated to Trajan, stands at the point where the road to Brindisi, a port on the east coast, branches off the Appian Way, the first major road in the Romans' strategic network.

Romans learned to build sophisticated warships by capturing one from Carthage and copying it. Confronting great walled towns in the east, Rome developed unprecedented machinery to besiege the walls, catapult firepower into them, and batter them down. The Roman preference for massing overwhelming strength and their willingness to let time work on their side through siege warfare, brought many victories with minimal losses of their own.

To be a free man was to serve in the army. Within Italy, captured city-states were required to supply not gold and taxes but men for the armies. At the time of Julius Caesar, the average Italian male served seven years in the army. Under Augustus, soldiering became more professional: men enlisted for between sixteen and twenty-five years and were paid regular wages. Conquered peoples outside Italy also contributed troops to Rome's armies. The Barbarians who invaded the empire were often encouraged to settle in Roman territories and to enlist in Roman armies. An outward spiral of imperial expansion resulted. As Rome expanded, so did its armed forces; it then expanded further in part to capture the wealth needed to pay its larger armies; this expansion, in turn, enlarged its armies once more.

In the field, the soldiers built their support systems: military camps, administrative towns, strings of fortress watch-towers along the borders, roads, and aqueducts. Roman engineering feats astonished the world in their day, and many of them remain to astonish us as well. Many of the walled military camps were kernels from which sprouted later towns and cities, one of Rome's most distinctive contributions. These urban outposts established Rome's military and administrative rule in the midst of remote rural regions. In the reign of Augustus, these nodes were linked by 50,000 miles of first-class roads and 200,000 miles of lesser roads. The roads facilitated commerce and communication, but their original and fundamental purpose was to enable the swift movement of troops throughout the empire.

Generals in Politics

In this militaristic empire, generals gained power. At first Rome's military leaders were constrained by the aristocratic Senate and the general assembly of Rome. Later, the generals began giving the orders. General Gaius Marius campaigned to have himself elected consul in 107 B.C.E. He broke with the normal practice of recruiting only troops who owned property, and accepted soldiers who were indebted to him personally for their maintenance. Elected consul six times between 107 and 100 B.C.E., Marius restructured the armies to increase their efficiency. He arranged large allotments of land for veteran soldiers in north Africa, Gaul, Sicily, Greece, and Macedonia, a move that solved temporarily one of the great problems of Rome: How to accommodate soldiers returning home after long tours of duty. The armies now depended for their welfare on Marius rather than on the state.

The generals began to compete among themselves for power. At the highest level, the struggle between the generals Lucius Sulla and Gaius Marius precipitated civil war in Rome. To fight against Mithridates VI, king of Pontus (r. 120–63 B.C.E.), the Senate called Sulla. Marius, however, arranged to have the command transferred to himself. In response, Sulla rallied soldiers loyal to him and invaded Rome, initiating the first civil war (83–82 B.C.E.). He declared Marius an outlaw and left with his troops for Greece, where he defeated Mithridates. Meanwhile Marius, joined by another general, Lucius Cornelius Cinna, seized Rome and banned Sulla. Sulla returned with his army, invaded Italy and Rome, had himself declared dictator, a position he held for two years, and then abdicated.

Twenty years later, in 60 B.C.E., two great generals, Julius Caesar and Pompey, and Marcus Licinius Crassus, a wealthy businessman who became a military commander, formed a **triumvirate**, an alliance of the three men to rule. The three competed among themselves until Caesar defeated the others. Caesar ruled as dictator from 47 until 44 B.C.E., when rivals assassinated him because they felt he had usurped too much power.

Born in Rome of an aristocratic patrician family about 100 B.C.E., Caesar felt the hand of the military dictator Sulla as a young man when Sulla ordered him to divorce his wife, Cornelia, daughter of Cinna, one of Sulla's greatest rivals. Caesar refused. Biographers are not sure whether this was because of Caesar's love for Cornelia, exceptional personal pride, an assessment that the alliance with Cinna's faction would, in the long run, prove advantageous, or some combination of calculations. In any case, Caesar's refusal was unusual in a world where aristocratic marriages—and divorces—were usually contracted for political purposes. (Caesar, for example, later married his seventeen-year-old daughter to the forty-seven-year-old Pompey.) No one else, even Pompey, refused Sulla's commands. It was also out of character for Caesar himself, a man who had already begun to earn a growing reputation for marital infidelity, including rumors of some homosexual activity (Grant, *Julius Caesar*, pp. 23–4, 33–9).

triumvirate An unofficial coalition between Julius Caesar, Pompey, and Crassus was formed in 60 B.C.E. After Caesar's murder in 44 B.C.E., a triumvirate that included his heir Octavian (later Augustus), Mark Antony, and Marcus Lepidus was appointed to maintain public order.

To escape Sulla's grasp, Caesar fled into exile in the Greek islands where he studied philosophy and oratory until he was pardoned and returned to Rome. He was elected magistrate in 65 B.C.E., with responsibilities for producing public games. Pouring his own money as well as public and borrowed funds into the task, he won widespread acclaim. His prominence increased when he was elected chief priest, *pontifex maximus*, of the Roman state in 63 B.C.E., a position of greater prestige and patronage than of religious significance. Reaching toward the pinnacle of political power, Caesar was elected **praetor** in 60 B.C.E. and consul—the highest elected position in Rome—in 59. A military man, he sometimes used strong-arm methods to intimidate the Senate, on one occasion having his fellow consul attacked and beaten.

In Rome, military prowess counted most, and in 58 B.C.E. Caesar led his armies on a mission to dominate Gaul (modern France) and protect it from invaders. This move also got him out of Rome at the end of his term as consul, thus escaping legal prosecution for his violent acts while serving in that position. Caesar's *Gallic War* tells of the nine years of military campaigns that brought all of Gaul under Rome. Caesar also briefly crossed the Rhine River, to demonstrate that Rome had the capacity to invade the Germanic territories if it wished, and he twice invaded Britain, also briefly. Caesar was Rome's most successful general and one of its best orators as well.

The triumvirate broke down when Crassus was killed during warfare in Turkey, as he sought to extend Rome's empire in the east. Pompey now saw Caesar as his direct rival, and Rome dissolved into civil war. Pompey was defeated in a series of battles and finally killed while seeking refuge in Egypt. Caesar now ruled Rome alone, but only briefly. Jealous of, and frightened by, his extraordinary powers, senators followed Brutus and Cassius in stabbing him to death on the Ides of March, March 15, 44 B.C.E.

In his three years as dictator, Caesar revised the Roman calendar creating the Julian calendar that lasted for 1500 years; re-organized Rome's city government; extended citizenship to the peoples of many conquered provinces; continued the policy of free bread and circuses; and appointed many of his opponents to public office in an attempt at reconciliation. He resolved one of the most intractable problems of Rome's citizens: the debts that had piled up during the years of civil war. He forced creditors to accept payment in land and property valued at pre-war prices, and he canceled all interest due since the wars began. Caesar selected his sister Julia's grandson, Gaius Octavius (63 B.C.E.–14 C.E.), later called Octavian, as his heir. Following Caesar's assassination, this adopted son avenged his death by murdering 300 senators and 2000 knights; triumphed over Lepidus and Mark Antony, the two rivals who had been for sometime his colleagues in a second triumvirate; and became the unchallenged ruler of Rome for almost half a century.

To avert civil war, Octavian used his sister Octavia as a diplomatic and political tool, marrying her to his rival, Antony (83–30 B.C.E.) in 40 B.C.E. In 36 B.C.E., Antony openly married the alluring and seductive queen of Egypt, Cleopatra (r. 51–30 B.C.E.), even though he was already married to Octavia, and established his headquarters in Egypt, the richest state in the east. By sharing local rule with Cleopatra, Antony betrayed Rome's imperial policies. Eventually, Antony discarded and divorced Octavia, humiliating Octavian personally as well as infuriating him politically. The warfare between the two men became especially bitter. Octavian finally defeated Antony and Cleopatra in the decisive naval battle at Actium (31 B.C.E.), formally annexed Egypt, and seized the Egyptian treasury for himself. Octavian now controlled more wealth than the Roman state.

praetor In ancient Rome, the name was originally applied to the consul as leader of an army. In 366 B.C.E. a further praetor was elected with special responsibility for the administration of justice in Rome, with the right of military command. Further praetors were subsequently appointed to administer the increasing number of provinces.

Augustus of Prima Porta, **early 1st century C.E.** With the gratitude of the Senate of Rome that was weary of civil warfare among its generals, Augustus transformed Rome into an imperial monarchy under his control. (*Musei Vaticani, Rome*)

SOURCE

The Legacy and Epitaph of Augustus Caesar

Our primary sources on Augustus' life are limited, and almost all of his own autobiography has been lost. Therefore, the Res Gestae Divi Augusti *("Account of the Accomplishments of Augustus") has become a crucial text. Written for the people of Rome by Augustus himself shortly before he died, and inscribed on several temples throughout the empire, it records the emperor's own statement of how he wanted to be remembered. Its thirty-five paragraphs fall into three sections: the offices and honors bestowed on him; his personal donations for public purposes; and his accomplishments in war and peace:*

1. At the age of nineteen, on my own initiative and at my own expense, I raised an army by means of which I liberated the Republic … the people elected me consul and a triumvir for the settlement of the commonwealth …

3. I waged many wars throughout the whole world by land and by sea … and when victorious I spared all citizens who sought pardon … About 500,000 Roman citizens were under military oath to me.

15. To the Roman plebs I paid 300 sesterces apiece in accordance with the will of my father [Julius Caesar]; and in my fifth consulship [29 B.C.E.] I gave each 400 sesterces in my own name out of the spoil of war, reaching never less than 250,000 persons … In the eighteenth year of my tribunician power and my twelfth consulship [29 B.C.E.] I gave out of the spoils of war 1000 sesterces apiece to my soldiers settled in colonies … received by about 120,000 persons … In my thirteenth consulship [2 B.C.E.] I gave sixty denarii apiece to those of the plebs who at that time were receiving public grain … a little more than 200,000 persons.

19. I built … the senate house and … the temple of Apollo …

22. I gave a gladiatorial show three times in my own name, and five times in the names of my sons or grandsons; at these shows about 10,000 fought … Twenty-six times I provided for the people … hunting spectacles of African wild beasts in the circus or in the Forum or in the amphitheaters …

23. I turned over to their masters for punishment nearly 30,000 slaves who had run away from their owners and taken up arms against the state.

28. I established colonies of soldiers in Africa, Sicily, Macedonia, in both Spanish provinces, in Achaea, Asia, Syria, Narbonese Gaul, and Pisidia. Italy, moreover, has twenty-eight colonies established by me which grew large and prosperous in my lifetime …

31. Royal embassies from India, never previously seen before any Roman general, were often sent to me. (Lewis and Reinhold, I:561–72)

By 30 B.C.E., following fourteen years of civil war, Octavian had become master of a re-unified Roman world. A grateful Senate, weary of seemingly endless civil wars, heaped him with honors, including, in 27 B.C.E., the title "Augustus," meaning "sacred" or "venerable." His achievements were immense, and after his death the Romans designated him a god.

Under one name or another, Augustus ruled Rome for fifty-six years until his death in 14 C.E. He fought wars that stabilized the borders of the empire while ensuring peace and facilitating trade, commerce, and economic growth throughout the Mediterranean. He restructured imperial administration into a form that lasted for almost two centuries. He inaugurated public projects that beautified Rome and kept its workers employed. He pacified the Roman masses and won over the aristocracy. He patronized the arts and literature, which flourished in a "Golden Age." He built new roads and cities throughout the length and breadth of the empire.

Augustus instituted conservative policies concerning religion and family life. The growth of urban life, especially in Rome itself in the first century B.C.E., offered new opportunities to a few upper-class Roman women to gain education and even to participate in public life, although usually behind the scenes. New marriage laws enabled them to live as equals of their husbands and gave them the right to divorce and to act without reference to a legal guardian. They could own and control wealth in their own name. Women did not have access to the professions or to public political office, but several exercised great influence over their husbands, brothers, and sons.

Augustus sought to restore the earlier family order. He made adultery a criminal offense, punishable by exile, confiscation of property, and even execution. Indeed, he exiled his own daughter and only child, Julia, a charming and intelligent woman who offended him with her frequent and publicly known affairs. He encouraged marriage and childbearing and punished celibacy. These laws were widely opposed and disobeyed, but they reveal to us the link in Augustus' mind between a well-ordered family and a well-ordered empire, a link that was repeated in the official policies of many empires throughout history. (Compare China and India in Chapters 7 and 8, Britain in Chapter 16, Japan in Chapter 17, and Germany in Chapter 18.) Moreover, despite the general religious skepticism and indifference of the Roman upper classes, Augustus rebuilt temples and encouraged the worship of ancestral gods as a foundation of state morality.

The End of the Republic

With Augustus, Rome became an imperial monarchy, a territorial, political, and economic empire ruled by a single military commander, the *imperator* (from which the term emperor is derived), and his armies. For years generals had wanted this centralized power. Now, in gratitude, the Senate was willing to turn it over to Augustus. Augustus rejected the title of monarch, preferring to be called princeps, or first citizen. This gesture of humility fooled no one. With Augustus' reign, the imperial form of government begins even though the Senate and the consuls and other magistrates survived. From Augustus on, all real power in the Roman state lay in the hands of the emperor.

As the empire continued to expand through military conquests, Rome's generals demanded, and were granted, increasing powers until, with Augustus, they supplanted republican, civilian government with an administration headed by the military commander-in-chief. Before we analyze the significance of this political transformation, however, let us complete our account of the continuing geographical expansion of the empire.

Augustus annexed modern Switzerland and Noricum (modern Austria and Bavaria) in 16–15 B.C.E., and established Rome's historical frontier in central Europe at the Danube River. After an attempt to conquer central Germany failed in 9 C.E., the Rhine became the normal border in the northeast.

In the 40s C.E. the Romans conquered modern England and Wales, which became the Roman province of Britain. Some 2000 miles to the east, the Emperor Trajan (r. 98–117 C.E.) conquered Dacia (modern Romania), and briefly annexed Armenia and Parthia (Mesopotamia).

Trajan's successor, Hadrian (117–138 C.E.), consolidated Roman gains. He permanently withdrew the Roman forces from Mesopotamia back to the Euphrates and built a wall, west to east, across the narrow neck of the northern part of Britain. Twenty-five years later, his successor, Antoninus Pius (r. 138–161 B.C.E.), built another wall some 50 miles further north. The limits of the Roman Empire had been reached.

The policy of granting citizenship to consolidate empire continued on a limited basis as Rome expanded. In 14 C.E. Augustus Caesar announced that there were 4,937,000 citizens in the empire, about 2 million of them in the provinces. At that time, the total population of the empire was between 70 and 100 million. In 212 C.E., the Emperor Caracalla (r. 212–217) officially proclaimed citizenship for all free males in the empire, although ambiguous legal restrictions limited the effect. Provincials could occupy the highest offices in the empire: senator, consul, and even emperor. The Emperor Trajan was from Spain; Septimius Severus (r. 193–211) was from north Africa; Diocletian (r. 284–305) was from Dalmatia (modern Croatia).

The development of international law, the *jus gentium,* the law of nations, also helped to unite and pacify the empire. After its victory in the first Punic War in 241 B.C.E., Rome interacted more than ever with foreigners and with subjects of Rome who did not have citizenship. To deal with legal cases between Romans and others,

HOW DO WE KNOW?

Roman Law: Theory and Practice

Modern historians have generally praised Rome's incipient international legal system as:

one of the most potent and effective ideas that the Romans ever originated ... It demonstrated that a body of law could be established upon a foundation acceptable to the members of different peoples and races at any and every phase of social, economic, and political evolution; and so it brought the laws of the Romans nearer to universal applicability than any others that have ever been devised. (Grant, pp. 104–5)

Legal theory and practice, however, did not always coincide in ancient Rome (just as they do not always coincide today). The poor did not receive the same protection and benefits as the rich, soldiers abused their authority, and laws were not always applied consistently. The satirist Juvenal (c. 55–c. 127) ridiculed t he inability of Rome's legal system to curb the arbitrary violence of Roman soldiers:

Your teeth are shattered? Face hectically inflamed, with great black welts? You know the doctor wasn't too optimistic about the eye that was left. But it's not a bit of good your running to the courts about it. If you've been beaten up by a soldier, better keep it to yourself. (cited in Boardman et al., p. 575)

In practice, the law was also not always as universal as it claimed, and those challenging the empire might not reap its benefits. Jewish nationalist writers, for example, compared the hypocrisy of Rome's laws to the ambiguous associations of the unclean pig:

Just as a pig lies down and sticks out its trotters as though to say "I am clean" [because they are cloven], so the evil empire robs and oppresses while pretending to execute justice. (cited in Boardman et al., p. 582)

Beginning about the second century C.E., preferential treatment for the wealthy and the powerful entered explicitly into the law, deepening class antagonisms, and weakening the empire.

- On what basis do historians differ when evaluating the quality of the Roman legal system?
- The modern historian Michael Grant writes about Rome's system of international law while the satirist Juvenal lived in ancient Rome and wrote about its local criminal law. How is each author's perspective affected by his time and expertise?
- What do you think is the effect on society of a legal system that gives preferential treatment to one group over another?

a new official, the foreign magistrate, was appointed. The *jus gentium* evolved from his judgments. Over time, this law was codified, first by Hadrian, and later, in the East, by the Emperor Justinian (r. 527–565).

Economic Policies of the Empire

The empire brought extraordinary benefits to the rulers, and sometimes to the ruled. Imperial rule and the opening of imperial markets brought opportunities for economic development and profit in the conquered provinces, although most of these went to the local wealthy elites who possessed the capital and skills to take advantage of them. In general, Roman rulers were solicitous of the upper classes in the provinces, both because of a shared class position and because they believed that the loyalty of these elites was crucial to maintaining Roman hegemony.

The cost of this imperial role, however, could also be heavy and eventually became oppressive. The Romans levied tribute, taxes, and rents, and recruited soldiers from the peoples they conquered. They settled their own soldiers in captured lands, turning those lands into Roman estates and enslaving millions of people to work on them. They exploited their political power for the economic advantage of their own traders and military and administrative elites.

As the size and wealth of the empire grew, many Romans felt that they had conquered the world but lost their souls. They spoke not of victory, but of loss. The historian Livy, writing at the height of the age of Augustus, lamented the end of innocence:

with the gradual relaxation of discipline, morals first gave way, as it were, then sank lower and lower, and finally began the downward plunge which has brought us to the present time, when we can endure neither our vices nor the cure. (cited in Lewis and Reinhold, I:8)

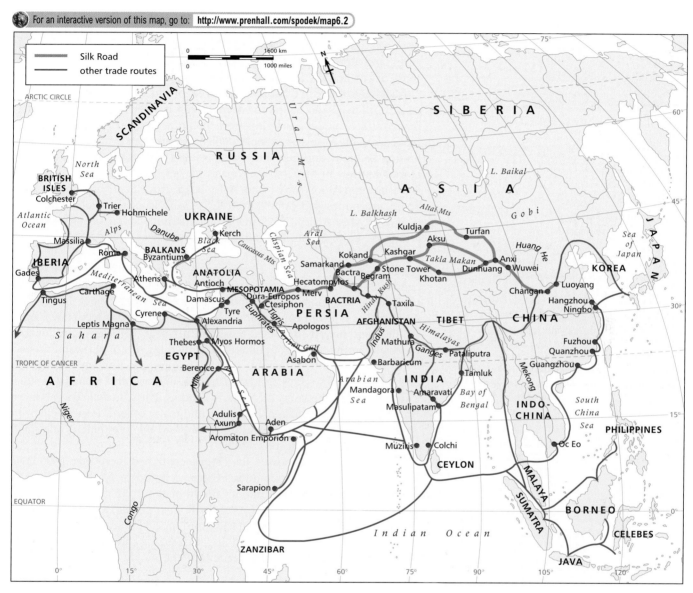

For an interactive version of this map, go to: http://www.prenhall.com/spodek/map6.2

Eurasian trade. The commercial links that bound the ancient world were both extensive and sophisticated. Self-sustaining individual networks—the Saharan caravans, the Arab dhows plying the Indian Ocean, the fleets of Chinese junks coasting east Asia, and most famously the Silk Routes traversing central Asia—linked at key entrepots such as Alexandria and Oc Eo by sea, and Ctesiphon and Kashgar by land, to form a truly intercontinental trading system.

Livy proclaimed the widely held myth of an older, golden age of simplicity and lamented its loss:

> No state was ever greater, none more righteous or richer in good examples, nor ever was where avarice and luxury came into the social order so late, or where humble means and thrift were so highly esteemed and so long held in honor. For true it is that the less men's wealth was, the less was their greed. Of late, riches have brought in avarice, and excessive pleasures the longing to carry wantonness and license to the point of personal ruin and universal destruction. (cited in Lewis and Reinhold, I:8)

This nostalgia had two related, but different versions. One drew on examples from the days of simple, rustic equality before the advent of the Etruscan kings. It condemned the maltreatment of the plebeians and the slaves at the hands of the patricians that had begun under Etruscan rule and intensified under the Republic. The other version wished to re-create the days of the oligarchic, patrician Republic, before the transfer of power from the Senate to the generals.

ROMAN EMPERORS

	Augustus (27 B.C.E.–14 C.E.)
Julio-Claudian dynasty	Tiberius (14–37) Caligula (37–41) Claudius (41–54) Nero (54–68)
Flavian dynasty	Vespasian (69–79) Titus (79–81) Domitian (81–96)
Age of the Antonines	Nerva (96–98) Trajan (98–117) Hadrian (117–138) Antoninus Pius (138–161) Marcus Aurelius (161–180) Commodus (180–193)
Severan dynasty	Septimius Severus (193–211) Caracalla (212–217) Elagabalus (218–222) Severus Alexander (222–235)
The late empire	Philip the Arabian (244–249) Decius (249–251) Gallus (251–253) Valerian (253–260) Gallienus (253–268) Claudius (268–270) Aurelian (270–275) Tacitus (275–276) Florian (276) Probus (276–282) Carus (282–283) Numerianus (283–284) and Carinus (283–285) Diocletian (284–305)

Supplying Rome. Feeding and provisioning the city of Rome, which had a population of about a million by the time of Augustus, called on vast resources throughout the empire. The most important requirement was grain, and Romans imported it from Sicily, Egypt and the north African coast, Spain, and the lands surrounding the Black Sea.

Merchants imported more specialized products from all parts of the empire: olive oil and wine came from within Italy, Spain, and the Mediterranean shores; pottery and glass from the Rhineland; leather from southern France; marble from Asia Minor; woolen textiles from Britain and northern France, Belgium, and the Netherlands; slaves from many lands. For gladiatorial contests in the Colosseum, and for general display in Rome, lions were brought from Africa and Asia, bears from Scotland, horses from Spain, crocodiles and camels from Egypt, and leopards and rhinoceroses from northwest Africa. The transportation of bulk commodities, especially within the empire, was most often by sea.

Building Cities. A few other extremely large cities, such as Alexandria, also needed to import extensively to provide for their hundreds of thousands of inhabitants, but most of the empire was locally self-sufficient. In this pre-industrial age, most people worked on the land, most production was agricultural, and people consumed most produce near the place of production, especially in the newly conquered and settled regions of western Europe.

To incorporate these regions into the empire, the Romans constructed and promoted new cities as administrative, military, and financial centers. These included the cores of modern London, Paris, Lyons, Trier, Nimes, Bruges, Barcelona, Cologne, Budapest, and many other European cities. In an empire that rested on agriculture, Rome laid the foundations of a small but potent ruling urban civilization.

At the height of its power, the empire contained more than 5000 civic bodies. The orator Marcus Tullius Cicero referred to Narbonne, Rome's administrative capital in southern Gaul from about 118 B.C.E., as "a colony of Roman citizens, a watch tower of the Roman people, a bulwark against the wild tribes of Gaul" (cited in Mumford, p. 209). Roman rule especially attracted and benefited the urban upper classes in the conquered regions, and helped to urbanize some leaders of the newly arriving immigrant German settlers.

Luxury Trades. People of wealth and power could command specialty goods. Supplying their demands generated small but significant streams of intercontinental, long-distance, luxury trade. For this commerce to flourish, trade routes had to be protected and kept safe. The Pax Romana secured the Red Sea routes, which allowed the import of frankincense, myrrh, and other spices from the Arabian peninsula and the Horn of Africa and spices and textiles from India, some of them transshipped from China. By the first century C.E., sailors had discovered that by sailing with the summer monsoon winds they could reach India from Egypt in about four months. They could then return with the winter monsoon, completing the round trip within a year.

Rome's repayment in this exchange was mostly precious metals. Hoards of gold coins from Rome have been discovered in south India, with smaller treasuries in China, southeast Asia, and east Africa. The historian Pliny the Elder (23–79) complained that the trade drained Italy's precious metals, but the profits to be made back home were extraordinary: "In no year does India absorb less than 50,000,000 sesterces

The Roman aqueduct at Segovia, Spain, early first or second century c.e. Unlike the Greeks, the Romans are remembered less for their art than for their great engineering feats. The need to improve the water supply to Roman settlements increased along with urban population growth. The popularity of the public bathing houses heightened the demand even more. The Romans developed a massive network of aqueducts to channel water into cities across uneven terrain.

Timgad, North Africa. Timgad, in Algeria, was founded as a military and administrative fortress around 100 C.E. and designed as a perfect square with a grid plan for the streets. The Romans tended to adhere to standard templates of town construction, despite variations in local topography, and Timgad is one of the clearest surviving models of what a provincial headquarters looked like.

of our Empire's wealth, sending back merchandise to be sold with us at a hundred times its original cost" (cited in Lewis and Reinhold, II:120).

Overland routes were also vital. The need for safety and protection was most evident in the silk trade, which prospered when Augustan Rome, Parthian Mesopotamia and Iran, Kushan India, and Han China—the four empires that spanned the silk routes—were at their peaks. Goods from Luoyang and Xian in China crossed the mountains of central Asia, connecting finally at one of the great trading emporia of Begram, Bactra, or Merv. From there, they continued onward into the Mediterranean.

Silk, light and valuable, was the principal export westward, but the caravans also carried lacquerware, bronzes, and other treasures. A storehouse discovered in 1938 in Begram, which stood at the crossroads of China, India, Persia, and the Mediterranean, revealed some of the principal luxury goods of this intercontinental trade: lacquer-work from China; ivory statues and carvings from India; alabaster, bronze, and glass works from the Mediterranean. Astonishingly, many of the carriers of these treasures seem to have been the steppe nomads of central Asia, the Huns and other "barbarians," who at other times attacked and plundered the empires across which they now traded.

Officially, the Roman upper classes scorned trade as beneath their status. Unofficially, they often entered into contracts with freedmen, their own ex-slaves, to front for their commercial enterprises. Trade was lucrative, and the aristocrats did not wish to lose the profits. The preferred methods of earning a livelihood were from land ownership, tax collecting for the state, or military conquest, but even generals, like Julius Caesar, profited from the sale of slaves captured in war.

Roman traders could be very exploitative. Especially when working in Rome's provinces, they often inspired great hatred. When Mithridates VI, king of Pontus in northern Anatolia, invaded the Roman province of Asia in 88 B.C.E. he encouraged Asian debtors to kill their Roman creditors. Eighty thousand Italian and Italian-Greek businessmen were reported murdered (Grant, p. 184).

In the late second century C.E. internal revolts and external attacks by Germanic peoples brought an end to the Pax Romana and introduced major obstacles to this trade. Roads and markets were no longer secure, and only items that could be consumed locally were worth producing. For example, manufacturers cut back sharply the production of glass, metals, and textiles in northern Europe. Provisioning Rome and other cities became more difficult. The population of cities fell and the protection they could offer declined, as did their levels of consumption. They provided less opportunity for making a profit and less incentive to producers. Trade and productivity faltered. As the Pax Romana began to break down politically and militarily, trade declined and became more localized.

Cultural Policies of the Empire

Greco-Roman Culture. To win and secure allies, Rome not only granted citizenship, codified international law, and built a remarkable physical infrastructure of towns and roads for unifying the empire, it also developed a culture that it brought to the people it conquered. Roman cultural achievements had lagged far behind those of

The Colosseum, Rome, c. 72–80 C.E. Built to house spectacular entertainments, such as mock sea-battles and gladiatorial combats, for audiences of up to 50,000 people, the Colosseum combined Greek decorative traditions with Roman engineering ingenuity, epitomized in the advanced use of concrete as a building material.

Greece, but as Rome conquered the Greek city-states, it began to absorb the culture of those it conquered. The Roman aristocratic classes adopted Greek language and literature as well as the architectural, sculptural, and painting traditions of the Greeks. The Romans now borrowed from the Greeks as they had earlier borrowed from the Etruscans.

Rome carried this polyglot culture outward in its conquests in Europe and Asia. Its schools in the provinces spread Greek as well as Latin among the tribal Goths and Gauls. Greek was the language of high culture. Latin, however, became the language of administration. Roman troops constructed amphitheaters, stadia, and baths wherever they went, the Roman invention of concrete making such constructions feasible. In these settings Roman rulers provided theaters and spectacles modeled on those in Rome.

Rome's sense of its own superiority doubtless encouraged its conquest of other peoples, deemed inferior, and was encouraged, in turn, by the success of those conquests. Rome's greatest epic poem, the *Aeneid*, written by Virgil during the reign of Augustus, sings the emperor's praises and celebrates Rome's superiority.

> … Behold the Romans,
> Your very own. These are Iulus' children,
> The race to come. One promise you have heard
> Over and over: here is its fulfillment,
> The son of a god, Augustus Caesar, founder
> Of a new age of gold, in lands where Saturn
> Ruled long ago; he will extend his empire
> Beyond the Indies, beyond the normal measure
> Of years and constellations, where high Atlas
> Turns on his shoulders the star-studded world.

At the same time, Virgil upholds the concept of *noblesse oblige*, the duty of the superior to help the inferior:

> … remember Romans,
> To rule the people under law, to establish
> The way of peace, to battle down the haughty,
> To spare the meek. Our fine arts, these, forever.
> (*Aeneid*, VI:822–31, 893–6; trans. Rolphe Humphries)

In the *Aeneid*, Virgil incorporates many of the forms of the earlier Greek epics, especially of Homer's *Odyssey*, but obviously he adds his own notes of an intensely imperialistic triumphalism.

Stoicism. Romans borrowed philosophical as well as literary ideas from the Greeks. Many thoughtful Romans were attracted to Stoicism, a philosophy founded by the Greek Zeno about 300 B.C.E. Stoicism took its name from the *stoa*, the covered walkway, in Athens where he taught. Zeno began with a cosmic theory of the world as a rational, well-ordered, and coherent system. Therefore humans should accept, without joy or grief, free from passion, everything that takes place in this world. Lucius Annaeus Seneca (*c.* 4 B.C.E.–65 C.E.), a Roman Stoic living three centuries later, elaborated:

> What is the principal thing? A heart … which can go forth to face ill or good dauntless and unembarrassed, paralyzed neither by the tumult of the one nor the glamour of the other. (Seneca, *Natural Questions*, cited in Lewis and Reinhold, II:165–6)

A corollary of Zeno's moral philosophy stated that people should treat one another with decency because we are all brothers and sisters. Marcus Tullius Cicero (106–43

B.C.E.), one of Rome's most important orators, commentators, and statesmen, and much influenced by Stoic beliefs, wrote:

> The private individual ought first, in private relations, to live on fair and equal terms with his fellow citizens, with a spirit neither servile and groveling nor yet domineering. (Cicero, *On Duties*, cited in Lewis and Reinhold, I:273)

How, then, did Stoics address the conditions of slavery in Rome? Although Stoics did not advocate the end of slavery, they did propose more humane treatment. Writing on the treatment of slaves, Seneca proposed a kind of Golden Rule:

> Treat those below you as you would be treated by those above you. (Seneca, *Moral Epistles*, cited in Lewis and Reinhold, II:180)

At this, however, Tacitus accused Seneca, one of Rome's richest citizens, of hypocrisy: "By what wisdom, by what principles of philosophy had he acquired 300,000,000 sesterces within four years of [receiving Emperor Nero's] royal favor? At Rome the childless and their wills are snared in his nets, as it were; Italy and the provinces are drained by his enormous usury" (*Annals* XIII:xlii, cited in Lewis and Reinhold, II:165–6, n. 58).

Stoicism reached the height of its influence in Rome with the selection of Marcus Aurelius Antoninus as emperor (r. 161–180 C.E.). He ruled through two decades of almost continuous warfare, economic upheaval, internal revolts, and plague. Through it all, Marcus Aurelius remained courageous and Stoic. He recorded his thoughts in his *Meditations*, one of the most philosophically reflective works ever written by a man in a position of such power:

> Keep thyself then simple, good, pure, serious, free from affectation, a friend of justice, a worshipper of the gods, and help men. Short is life. The universe is either a confusion, and a mutual involution of things, and a dispersion; or it is unity and order and providence ... If the [latter], I venerate, and I am firm, and I trust in him who governs. (VI:30, 10)

Religion in the Empire. Officially, Rome celebrated a religion centralized on the person of the emperor-god. After the deification of Augustus at his death, the official priesthood offered animal sacrifices to him and later to his successors, adding these to the traditional sacrifices to the major pagan gods, especially Jupiter, Juno, and Minerva. People celebrated the birthdays and death anniversaries of the emperors as holidays.

GREEK AND ROMAN GODS

In the second century B.C.E., Greece was absorbed by the Roman Empire. In the process the Romans adopted and adapted many Greek myths, linking their own gallery of gods to Greek legends and deities.

Greek	Roman	
Aphrodite	Venus	Goddess of love and beauty
Apollo, Phoebus	Apollo, Phoebus	Greek god of sun, god of music, poetry, and prophecy
Ares	Mars	God of war
Artemis	Diana	Virgin huntress, goddess of the moon
Asclepius	Aesculapius	God of medicine
Athena (Pallas)	Minerva	Goddess of wisdom and art
Cronus	Saturn	Father of the supreme god: Zeus or Jupiter
Demeter	Ceres	Goddess of the harvest
Dionysus	Bacchus	God of wine and fertility
Eros	Cupid	God of love
Hades	Pluto, Dis	God of the underworld
Hephaestus	Vulcan	God of fire
Hera	Juno	Queen of heaven, wife of Zeus/Jupiter, goddess of women and marriage
Hermes	Mercury	Messenger of the gods, god of roads, cunning, commerce, wealth, and luck
Hestia	Vesta	Goddess of the hearth
Hymen	Hymen	God of marriage
Irene	Pax	Goddess of peace
Pan	Faunus	God of flocks and shepherds
Persephone	Proserpina	Goddess of corn and the spring, goddess of the dead
Poseidon	Neptune	God of the sea
Zeus	Jupiter, Jove	Supreme ruler of gods and men, king of heaven, and overseer of justice and destiny

Beyond these rituals, however, Roman religious policies allowed a great deal of flexibility. For the most part, as long as people venerated the emperor and did not question the legitimacy of the state, Roman emperors allowed diverse religious practices to flourish. Mithraism, a religion that worshiped the Persian sun god Mithra as mediator between god and man, emphasized discipline and loyalty. It was especially popular within the military, especially among the Germanic and eastern troops who found attractive its message of fighting vigorously against both internal passions and external military opponents.

Two additional religions popular in early imperial Rome centered on female goddesses, and were especially attractive to women. Like Mithraism, both were mystery religions—that is, they had rituals of initiation that defied rational understanding and that were unknown to outsiders. These could include orgies and baptisms. One such faith worshiped Cybele, the venerated earth-mother of Asia Minor. Another worshiped the Egyptian goddess Isis, with her annual promise of rebirth and a variety of dramatic rituals to be observed throughout the year.

Rome did not, however, tolerate sects that challenged the authority of the empire or the emperor. The government cracked down on worship of the god Bacchus, for example, in 186 B.C.E., fearing that lower-class members of this cult might turn against the state. The same antagonism toward potential revolt put Rome on a collision course with the Jews of Judaea, in the eastern Mediterranean.

After conquering the eastern Mediterranean from the Seleucid inheritors of Alexander the Great, the Romans turned their attention to Judaea. For at least a century the region had been fragmented, and often in the throes of open warfare, among contending factions: Seleucids, pagans, and Jews of a wide variety of beliefs and political commitments. In Chapter 10 we shall see how the Jews, from their seventeenth-century B.C.E. roots, developed a religion based on ethical monotheism and a fierce sense of ethnic nationalism. Here, we only note that both of these qualities evoked strong opposition among the Roman rulers. The zealous monotheism of most of the Jews left no room for worship of the Roman emperor as a god, and the ethnic nationalism meant that a spirit of revolt against Roman authority was always simmering. From the time that Rome conquered Judaea and turned it into a subject state, in 63 B.C.E., fighting broke out frequently, not only between Jews and Romans, but also among Jewish political and religious factions that differed on the proper behavior toward the Roman conquerors and toward each other. In response to three major revolts by the Jews—in 66–73 C.E., 115–117 C.E., and 132–135 C.E.—the Romans destroyed Jerusalem and its principal Jewish Temple, established the Roman colony of Aelia Capitolina on its site, destroyed Judaea as a Jewish state, and exiled the Jews from this land, with repercussions that would last for centuries.

One of the religious factions that grew up among the Jews in Judaea was the veneration of the preacher, exorcist, and miracle worker Jesus of Nazareth (c. 4 B.C.E.–c. 30 C.E.). Many of his followers believed him to be divine and later called him Christ, or the Messiah (the anointed one of God). The discussion of his ministry and its emergence from Jewish roots will also wait for Chapter 10 in the unit on religion. Here suffice it to say that the Roman government clashed with the early Christians, followers of Jesus, much as it did with Judaism, on the grounds of its monotheism, resistance to emperor worship, and potential as a force for political revolution. For the first three centuries of its existence, many Romans viewed Christianity as atheistic because it rejected the divinity of the emperor. Some Romans saw the new Christian religion as treasonable because it spoke of a kingdom of heaven that was distinct from the Roman earthly empire. Finally the Roman governor of Judaea, Pontius Pilate, tried and crucified Jesus partly because he was a threat to the religious and political stability of their colony.

Christianity Triumphant. By the time of Marcus Aurelius, however, Christianity was making serious inroads into Roman thought. The Stoic philosophy was not far removed from the Christian concept of an orderly world and concern for social welfare. To these beliefs, Christianity added faith in a god actively intervening in human affairs and, specifically, the doctrines of the birth, life, miracles, and resurrection of Jesus. This combination of beliefs was attractive to increasing numbers of Romans, and despite severe persecution of Christians under several emperors—Nero (r. 54–68), Marcus Aurelius (r. 161–180), Maximinus I (r. 235–238), Decius (r. 249–251), Valerian (r. 253–260), and Diocletian (r. 284–305)—over the course of three centuries Christianity became acceptable in Rome and flourished. At first it attracted the poor, who were moved by Jesus' concern for the downtrodden, but later, more powerful classes also joined, attracted by both the organization and message of Christianity. The new religion promoted greater freedom for women, with a few reaching positions of prominence as deaconesses and abbesses, and it began to incorporate some of the sophistication of Greek philosophy, attracting a new intellectual leadership. By the time of Constantine's legalization of Christianity in 313, estimates suggested that one out of ten inhabitants of the Roman empire was a Christian (Lewis and Reinhold, II: 553).

In 313 the joint emperors, Constantine and Licinius, issued the Edict of Milan, which recognized Christianity as a valid faith, along with polytheism. After 324, when Constantine ruled alone, he favored Christianity as a religion that had brought miraculous benefits to himself personally and to his empire, and he granted it official recognition and legal status. Thereafter Christianity spread freely throughout the conquered lands and peoples of northwestern Europe. The network of roads and towns created to facilitate administration also served to transmit the message of Christianity, and members of the clergy frequently served as a bridge between the religious practices of Christian Rome and those of the "barbarians." After emerging as the official state religion, Christianity succeeded in having government support for polytheistic cults terminated in 394. Even the most widespread of them, Mithraism, with its message of loyalty to the emperor, died out. Christianity emerged triumphant. (For a fuller discussion of early Christianity and its relationship to the Roman Empire, see Chapter 10.)

THE BARBARIANS AND THE FALL OF THE ROMAN EMPIRE

Rome labeled many of its neighbors on its far-flung borders barbarians, including the Celts of central Europe, the various Germanic groups of northern and eastern Europe, and the steppe nomads of central Asia. These peoples spoke unknown foreign languages. They did not have cities, written languages, formal government structures, established geographical boundaries, codified laws, or labor specialization. Some, like the Celts and Germans, lived in villages and carried on settled farming. Nomadic steppe peoples spent their lives riding, herding, and often fighting among themselves in far-off central Asia. Such peoples, the Romans must have thought, could benefit from the civilizing influences of the empire. Perhaps Virgil had this in mind when he was writing the *Aeneid*.

Invaders at the Gates

The Celts had arrived in central Europe as early as 2000 B.C.E. Burials indicate their respect for horse-riding warriors and the slow development among them of iron technology in weapons and tools. The Hallstatt cemetery in Austria reveals a greater use of iron by the eighth century B.C.E. and includes items of Greek manufacture.

A cemetery at La Tène in what is now Switzerland shows continuing Greek and then Roman influences from the fifth century B.C.E. to the first century C.E.

By 400 B.C.E., the Celts were expanding their territory. In 390 B.C.E. they sacked Rome, and by 200 B.C.E. Celtic groups had covered central Europe and were pushing outward toward Spain, the British Isles, the Balkans, and Anatolia. Learning from Greek and Roman examples, they built fortified towns throughout their territories. The largest of these covered more than a half square mile. Celtic women enjoyed more freedom than did the Roman women, and this evoked the scorn of some Roman writers. Tacitus, who seemed to appreciate Calgacus' revolt in 83–84 C.E., was far more critical of the failed Celtic revolt of 61 C.E. in Britain led by the female leader Boudicca at the head of her armies. Ultimately, Rome conquered the Celtic peoples. They were killed, or assimilated, or fled to Ireland, Scotland, and Wales, where, to some degree, they continue today to preserve the Celtic language and culture.

The coming of the Barbarians. Rome's control of northern and western Europe declined in the fourth century C.E. as successive waves of Germanic peoples began to migrate and colonize the outer reaches of the empire. When the Huns began to advance westward from central Asia they pushed before them additional Gothic peoples who increased the pressures on Rome. Other Huns were meanwhile pushing south into India and east into China.

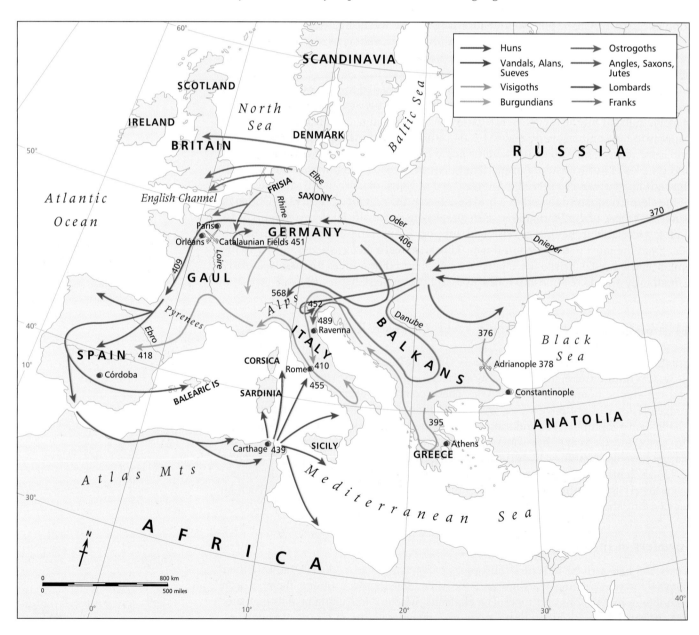

The Goths—an array of Germanic peoples (primarily Visigoths and Ostrogoths), distinguished in part by their use of Germanic languages, in part through their residence in lands that later became Germany—settled at first in northern Europe outside the Celtic and Roman strongholds. Indeed, much of what we know of this early period comes from burials in the bogs of what are now northern Germany and Denmark. By 600 B.C.E. these Germanic peoples had established small villages, and by about 500 B.C.E. they had begun working with iron. With the discovery of richer iron deposits and contact with Greek and Roman technology, the Goths developed more sophisticated tools and weapons.

Romans and Germans had faced each other along the Rhine since Julius Caesar had conquered Gaul, and along the Danube from the time Augustus had secured that border. They had skirmished, traded, and at times penetrated each other's territories. Recent archaeological excavations show that leaders of the Germans adopted for themselves many of the tools, weapons, and luxury goods of the conquering Romans. Roman goods, and some values, spread through imitation as well as by force.

In 370 C.E., steppe nomads began to invade across the thousands of miles from central Asia, bringing pressure to bear on the whole of Europe. In response to this pressure, the Goths began to migrate westward, pushing more vigorously into Roman territories. These massive Germanic invasions upset the rough balance of power that existed between Rome and the Goths, and threatened the stability of the empire. Ultimately, the Goths formed their own states within the imperial territories. A second Germanic emigration occurred about 500 C.E. as a response to floods in the areas of north Germany and Denmark. Among the emigrant Germanic groups, the Saxons sailed across the North Sea and the English Channel to Britain, where they came to form a substantial part of the population.

The Romans called all the steppe peoples who invaded Europe from central Asia in 370 C.E. "Huns." In fact, however, the Huns were only one of the many groups of warrior-nomads who inhabited the flat grasslands from European Russia to Manchuria. They virtually lived on their horses, herding cattle, sheep, and horses as well as hunting. They lived in tents and used wagons to transport their goods as they moved from place to place, especially in their annual shift between summer and winter locations.

Although they lived in tent encampments, the Huns' living arrangements and political structures were by no means random. Many groups had chiefs and even governments, and their leaders lived in the most elaborate of the tents. When the Huns invaded Europe, Romans observed emissaries of various peoples enter the tent of Attila, their leader, to conduct political negotiations.

Funerary bronze couch from the Hallstatt prince's tomb at Eberdingen-Hochdorf, near Stuttgart, Germany, c. 530 B.C.E. This couch demonstrates the remarkable sophistication of some early Celtic art. It was buried in the tomb of a sixth-century B.C.E. Celtic chieftain in Germany, along with other possessions reflecting the wealth and importance of the dead man. (*Württembergisches Landesmuseum, Stuttgart*)

HOW DO WE KNOW?

The "Barbarians"

Chinese Sources

The steppe peoples had no written language, and their nomadic life style has left few archaeological remains. We know about them in part from burials, especially of the Scythians, a group living in southern Russia and in the Altai Mountains of Mongolia. Mostly we know of them from the accounts of the peoples whose lands they invaded: Romans, Greeks, Chinese, and Indians. All these accounts report them as fierce, mobile, swift, and terrifying warriors on horseback, armed with powerful bows, swords, and lances. In more peaceful times, the Huns carried the goods of the overland silk routes through central Asia.

Latin histories did not mention the Huns until Ammianus Marcellinus (330–395 C.E.) described them:

> They are without fixed abode, without hearth, or law, or settled mode of life, and they keep roaming from place to place, like fugitives, accompanied by the wagons in which they live; in wagons their wives weave for them their hideous garments, in wagons they cohabit with their husbands, bear children, and rear them to the age of puberty …
>
> This race of untamed men, without encumbrances, aflame with an inhuman desire for plundering others' property, made their violent way amid the rapine and slaughter of the neighboring peoples as far as the Halani [on the river Don]. (cited in Lewis and Reinhold, II:623)

Five hundred years earlier the Chinese historian Sima Qian had depicted them as coarse warriors:

> During the Ch'ien-yuan reign [140–134 B.C.E.] … the Son of Heaven made inquiries among those of the Hsiung-na [Xiongnu; Huns] who had surrendered and been made prisoners, and they all reported that the Hsiung-na had overcome the king of the Yueh-chih and made a drinking vessel out of his skull. The Yueh-chih had decamped and were hiding somewhere, constantly scheming how to revenge themselves on the Hsiung-na. (Sima Qian, p. 274)

Further elaboration by Sima delineates several groups of steppe nomads who frequently fought among themselves and sometimes invaded China itself. Both his description and that of Ammianus Marcellinus reflect the similar fear with which settled, imperial powers viewed their powerful, nomadic adversaries.

- What examples of barbarism does Ammianus Marcellinus cite from Rome? How do they compare with those cited by Sima Qian from China?
- What advantages did horse-mounted warriors with bows, swords, and lances have against the might of the empires of Rome and China?
- If we had records from the "barbarians" about the "civilized" peoples whose land they were invading, how do you think they would describe them?

At the time Augustus ruled Rome, groups of steppe nomads engaged in battles that would ultimately help to topple the Han dynasty in China. They also launched the attacks on India that would make two of the groups the rulers of north India: the Kushanas, 150–300 C.E., and the Hunas, 500–550 C.E. The Huns arrived in Europe in 370 C.E., defeating and displacing the Alans, Ostrogoths, and Visigoths, and pushing them in the direction of Rome.

The "domino effect" that would ultimately destroy the empire had begun.

The Decline and Dismemberment of the Roman Empire

Rome proved vulnerable to the invaders, especially because of a plague that wiped out up to a quarter of the population of some areas in 165–180 C.E. Historians debate the exact severity and impact of this plague, but it diminished the numbers and undermined the self-confidence of the empire's population. During the reign of Marcus Aurelius (r. 161–180 C.E.), the Marcomanni, a Germanic tribe from Bohemia, began to invade the Danube basin. Some penetrated into Greece, and across the Alps and into Italy. "Barbarian" invasions continued for hundreds of years, ultimately leading to the break-up of the Roman Empire.

For seven years, 168–175, Marcus Aurelius fought against the invaders, but he also recognized that they could be assimilated into the empire for mutual benefit. The Marcomanni wanted to establish settlements, so he offered them land within the borders of the empire that they could farm; they were soldiers, so he also offered them positions in Rome's armies.

Some of the Gothic groups also accepted assimilation into the empire. Others wished simply to plunder and withdraw. Still others wished to seize portions of the empire for themselves and settle.

The Crisis of the Third Century. Invaders repeatedly penetrated the borders represented by the Danube and the Rhine. In 248 the Emperor Decius (r. 249–251) defeated an invasion of Goths in the Balkans but was himself killed by another Gothic group. The Goths continued into the Balkans and beyond into Asia Minor. They took to ships and attacked Black Sea commerce, in the process cutting off large parts of Rome's grain supplies. Meanwhile, further west, Franks and Vandals swept across the Rhine into Gaul, Spain, and as far south as north Africa.

The empire struck back. The Emperor Gallienus (r. 253–268) created a mobile cavalry and moved the imperial military headquarters from Rome to Milan in the north, better to confront invaders into Italy. In a series of battles Roman armies preserved Italy for the empire.

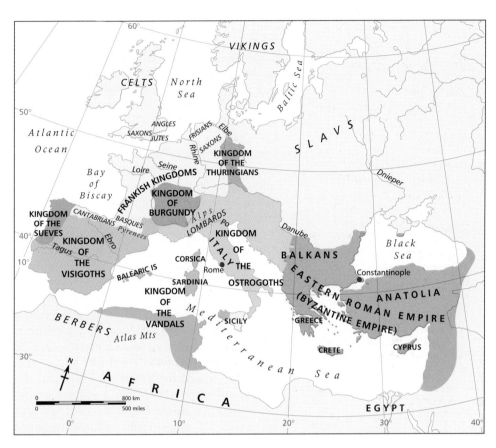

Rome's successors. Following the sack of Rome by the Ostrogoths in 455 C.E., a new map of Europe emerged. The Roman power base had shifted east to Constantinople, forming the Byzantine Empire. The steppe invaders, keen to emulate the Romans, had created new kingdoms in Italy, Africa, and Iberia, while Germanic peoples were struggling to create a new power balance in the north.

Aurelian (r. 270–275), an even more brilliant and energetic general, succeeded Gallienus as emperor after the latter died in a plague. In a series of battles, Aurelian protected Rome's western and northern borders, although he abandoned Dacia and pulled back to the Danube.

In the east, too, Rome defeated revolts. The greatest challenge came as the new, expansive Sassanian dynasty in Persia confronted Rome in Armenia and Syria. In 260 C.E. the Roman Emperor Valerian (r. 253–260) was captured and held prisoner for the rest of his life in humiliating conditions. (Legend told that after his death he was stuffed and preserved in a Persian temple.) Nevertheless, Rome recaptured its eastern areas, partly because the Sassanians treated the inhabitants of these lands so badly that they revolted. In another revolt against Rome, Zenobia, the widow of the leader of semi-independent Palmyra, declared the independence of Syria and Mesopotamia, and annexed Egypt. Her revolt lasted only a few years, and in 273 Aurelian defeated her, took her back to Rome in chains, and put her on public display, fully bedecked in jewels.

The Fragmentation of Authority. Continuing warfare forced the decentralization of Rome's power from the capital to distant provincial battlefields, and from civilian control by the Senate in Rome to generals in the field. Soldiers in Gaul, Britain, and Spain declared their general Postumus (r. 259–268 C.E.) the independent emperor of those regions, but Aurelian defeated their mutiny in 274 C.E. Militarily, the empire staged an extraordinary comeback.

In the belief that an aura of pomp and majesty would be helpful in asserting central control, the Emperor Diocletian (r. 284–305 C.E.) claimed for himself a sanctity and splendor never before seen in Rome. The expense of his battles and the splendor of his court bankrupted the empire and brought misery to its inhabitants. To cope with the attacks on far distant borders, emperors established regional capitals, and in 330 C.E. Constantine established Constantinople as a secondary capital for ruling the entire eastern region. After 395 C.E., one emperor in Rome and another in Constantinople formally divided the empire, west and east.

"Barbarian" tribes continued to breach the imperial borders and defenses. Valentinian I (r. 364–375) was the last emperor capable of driving them back effectively. From this time on, impelled by the invasion of the Huns, the Germans pushed against Roman defenses in increasing numbers. In 378 Valentinian's brother, the eastern Emperor Valens (r. 364–378), lost two-thirds of the eastern armies—and his life—in battle against the Visigoths at Adrianople. Valens' successor, Theodosius I (r. 379–395), who ruled from Constantinople, settled Visigoths within the empire, requiring them to provide soldiers and farmers for the imperial armies and lands. This "federate" status for Goths and other "barbarians" became a common pattern, with Goths, Franks, Alans, and Vandals settling within the imperial borders in increasing numbers. The empire was Roman in name, but was a mixed enterprise in terms of population, armies, and leadership. Increasingly, emperors avoided Rome and preferred to reside in cities such as Milan and Trier.

Alaric, the Visigoth (c. 370–410), invaded Italy in 401 and, in response, the Emperor Honorius (r. 395–423) removed the capital from Milan to Ravenna, a more defensible city on the east coast of Italy. Alaric invaded Italy again in 407, and in 410 he sacked Rome. At the end of 406, combined armies of Goths, Vandals, Suevi, Alans, and Burgundians crossed the Rhine into Gaul and moved into Spain. At first they sacked, looted, and burned, but within a few years they established their own settlements and local kingdoms, displacing or merging with Roman landlords. The Vandal King Geiseric (r. 428–477) crossed into north Africa, seizing Carthage and its agriculturally rich hinterlands. Gaining control of a fleet, he challenged Roman control of the Mediterranean. The Romans could not defeat him.

The Huns were building up their own imperial confederacy in central Europe. Their most powerful leader, Attila (c. 406–453), commanded them from 434 to 453. His territory stretched from the Baltic to the Danube. He invaded Italy in 451, threatening Rome and withdrawing only on the intervention of Pope Leo I. After Attila's death, his armies dissolved and never again regained their power. In 476, the German general Odoacer deposed the last Roman emperor in the west. Odoacer became the first barbarian king of Italy (r. 476–493), and thus the five-centuries-old Roman Empire came to an end.

In the west, the Roman imperial system continued to function for at least two more centuries, but its leadership and its legions were in the hands of Germans and other invading groups. The groups carved the empire up into several distinct regions. There was no central government. Rome was no longer capital of an empire.

Causes of the Decline and Fall

Structural problems had been visible in the Roman Empire even at the height of its power. Internally, the conflict between the elite and the masses continued, under different names, throughout the history of the Republic and the empire. The cost of sustaining the empire by military force overtaxed the imperial economy, impoverishing the middle classes and the remaining agricultural classes. The yeoman-farmer class, the class that had first built up the Roman Republic, was ruined. Although the rich continued to live off their estates in Italy and elsewhere and the senatorial classes continued to do well, popular support for the imperial ideal had disappeared. In earlier times, an ever-expanding frontier had brought new economic resources to support the empire, but expansion had come to an end in the second century. The empire was overextended.

In addition, the quality of the empire depended on the quality of its emperors, but Rome had no viable system of succession. In the century between Marcus Aurelius and Diocletian, more than eighty men assumed command as emperor, and many of these were assassinated. In the third century C.E., as fighting in the border regions decentralized the empire, competing armies fought to have their generals selected as emperor. The results were devastating to the economy, administration, and morale of the empire.

Rome could no longer win its frontier battles against invaders, but neither could it continue to assimilate Goths and others into its armies and settlements as subordinates. The Roman armies and vast territories of the empire had become heavily Germanic, and when whole tribes of Goths began to serve together in single units under Gothic commanders, questions arose concerning the army's loyalty to the empire. Romans and Germans saw each other as "other," alien, and the Romans even forbade intermarriage. As Germanic peoples began to take over leading positions, the empire effectively ceased to be Roman.

The rise of Christianity as the principal religion and philosophy of the empire (see Chapter 10) also suggested that the Roman desire for earthly political power was evaporating. At first, Christianity was accepted by the poor, who used it as a means of expressing their disaffection from the power of the Caesars. Later, however, when Constantine declared Christianity a legitimate state religion in 313, and the official state religion in 324, more mainstream Romans converted. Christianity offered an alternative focus for human energy. The eighteenth-century English historian Edward Gibbon argued in his classic *History of the Decline and Fall of the Roman Empire* that Christianity turned people against this-worldly attractions and power. Later historians

The Byzantine Empire. Despite the erosion of Roman power in western Europe by 457 C.E., the East Roman or Byzantine Empire survived with varying fortunes for another thousand years—albeit Greek-speaking and Orthodox Christian—until 1453. Centered on Constantinople, its heartland straddled the crossroads between Europe and Asia. Only briefly, under Justinian (483–565), did it recover control of the western Mediterranean.

regard this as an overstatement. They point to growing numbers of imperial administrators who converted to Christianity as evidence that the new religion and the Roman empire were compatible. Christianity did preach that eternal salvation was more important than fighting for the empire and it siphoned energy toward more spiritual and humanitarian goals, and toward competition with other religious groups.

More recently, scholars have suggested that climatic change reduced agricultural productivity and hurt the economy. Still others have noted that epidemics killed up to a quarter of the population in some imperial centers between 165 and 180 C.E. and again between 251 and 266 C.E. These diseases sapped the empire of manpower and left it more open to attack. Such biological and ecological arguments complement the more traditional explanations of Rome's fall: overextension; financial and military exhaustion; a failure of leadership; the rise of new, alternative value systems; and the infiltration of Germanic peoples, which fragmented the empire into new, separate, independent states that no longer wished to be subordinated to Rome.

The Empire in the East

On May 11, 330, the Emperor Constantine inaugurated the "New Rome which is Constantinople," to share with Rome, as co-capital, the administration of his huge empire. From its inception three complementary elements characterized the new city: Greek language and culture; Roman law and administration; and Christian faith and organization. While the western half of the empire survived only another century and a half, the eastern empire continued on its own for another thousand years, until 1453. It became an empire in its own right, later called Byzantium after the name of the Greek city around which Constantinople was built.

Resurgence under Justinian. Like the west, the east had to withstand military attack. Germanic tribes crossed the Danube, but found Constantinople impregnable, defended behind huge walls built by the Emperor Theodosius II (r. 408–450). Using German mercenaries, the eastern emperor Justinian I (r. 527–565) recaptured many of the western regions including north Africa, southern Spain, Sicily, Italy, and even Rome itself, but the costs in wealth and manpower crippled his empire. After his death most of these western conquests were lost, while the Persians constantly warred with the remnants of the Roman Empire in the east.

Justinian's legal, administrative, and architectural initiatives produced more lasting results. He had the Roman system of Civil Law codified in four great works, known collectively as the Justinian Code, thus helping to perpetuate an administration of great competence. In time, the Code became the basis for much of modern European law. He adorned Constantinople with numerous new buildings, crowned by the Church of Hagia Sophia, the Church of Holy Wisdom. He had churches, forts, and public works constructed throughout the empire.

Theology was closely intertwined with politics in the eastern empire. Disputes that appeared to concern only theology frequently had political consequences, and here Justinian seemed to over-reach. When many Syrian and Egyptian Christians declared themselves **Monophysites**, believers that Jesus' nature was only divine, not human, Justinian oppressed them in the name of theological conformity and imperial authority. In his religious zeal, he created antagonisms that smoldered for centuries and contributed to the loss of these provinces to the Muslims in the seventh century.

Religious Struggles. Troops burst out of Arabia after 632, inspired with the religious zeal of Islam (Chapter 11). Emperor Heraclius (r. 610–641) had defeated the Persian Empire, but he and his successors could not hold back these new invaders. The Arabs

Monophysites The supporters of a doctrine in the early Christian Church that held that the incarnate Christ possessed a single, wholly divine nature. They opposed the orthodox view that Christ had a double nature, one divine and one human, and emphasized his divinity at the expense of his capacity to experience real human suffering.

captured much of the land of the eastern empire, including Syria and Egypt with their disaffected Monophysites.

By this time, so much had changed in the relationship between Rome and Constantinople that the eastern empire had taken on an identity of its own as the Byzantine Empire. For centuries, the Christian Byzantine empire based in the Balkans and Asia Minor would confront Islam militarily and religiously. The Byzantine Empire organized its armies into **themes**, administrative districts and army units, in which peasants were given farms in payment for their military service. These themes and the impregnable fortifications of Constantinople were the empire's bulwark in confronting Arab armies.

The **iconoclastic** controversy, the bitter battle over the use of images, or icons, in Christian worship, began in 726, in large part as a response, to the Arab invasions. Islam rigorously excluded religious imagery and its armies were hugely successful. Some eastern clergy thought that these two facts might be linked. They became iconoclasts, arguing that Christianity should enforce the biblical commandment against idol worship by also banning icons. They campaigned to break and discard religious images, and the reigning Byzantine emperors supported them. For more than a century, until it was rescinded, this decision split what became known as the Eastern

themes A theme was originally a military unit stationed in one of the provinces of the Byzantine empire, but it later applied to the large military districts that formed buffer zones in the areas most vulnerable to Muslim invasion.

iconoclast An "image-breaker", or a person who rejects the veneration of **icons**, on the grounds that the practice is idolatrous.

Hagia Sophia, Constantinople, 532–7. The Hagia Sophia (Church of the Holy Wisdom), built under the Emperor Justinian, is an imposing visual symbol of the power of the eastern empire. The minarets, or pointed towers at the four corners, were added in the fifteenth century when the Ottomans captured Constantinople and the church was converted into a mosque.

Orthodox hierarchy and positioned its mainstream in opposition to the western Church. It added to the strain in the political-religious relationship between the western Church and the Byzantine Empire.

The great leaders of the Byzantine Empire were known for their combination of military prowess and religious leadership. Basil I (r. 867–886), for example, kept control of the Balkans and crushed the Bulgar invaders; initiated a dynasty which reconquered Crete, Syria, southern Italy, and much of Palestine from the Arabs; and also healed the religious rift with Rome for a time.

Ultimately, however, beginning in the late eleventh century C.E., a combination of religious and political antagonisms contributed to the decline of the Byzantine Empire. Battered from the north by invading Normans and Slavs, the Byzantines turned to the pope in Rome for help against the Islamic Seljuq Turks who had overrun Asia Minor from the east (Chapters 11 and 14). In response, the pope preached the crusades, but in 1204 crusaders—acting against the pope's explicit orders—conquered and sacked Constantinople, poisoning relationships between the eastern and western churches for centuries. The Byzantines recovered the city in 1261, but their empire was irreparably weakened. In 1453 it finally succumbed to the Turks.

A Millennium of Byzantine Strength. How did the Byzantine Empire manage to survive for 1000 years after Rome had fallen? The administrative system of the Byzantines deserved much of the credit, as a modern historian has explained:

> Consisting of a group of highly educated officials trained primarily at the university or, rather "higher school" of Constantinople, the civil service was organized into a hierarchical system of considerable complexity even by today's standards. Taxes were collected regularly, justice was administered, armies were raised and put into the field, and the functions of the state in general were very adequately carried out. It may be said that in its period of greatest power (330–c. 1050) the Byzantine government, despite all its faults (excessive love of pomp and protocol, bureaucratic tendencies, and frequent venality), functioned more effectively, and for a longer period, than virtually any other political organism in history. (Geanakoplos, p. 3)

The ruling classes were never as isolated and alienated from the common people as in the west. The eastern empire was also less geographically overextended. Even when it lost its more distant territories, it could defend its heartland. Its sources of wealth and military manpower were in Thrace and Anatolia, geographically close to its center of political power in Constantinople, which remained an impregnable fortress for almost 1000 years. In these settled lands, the Byzantine Empire had an older and stronger urban tradition than the west, and its cities remained viable centers of commerce long after most cities in the west had all but disappeared. The fiercest of the invading Germanic tribes turned away from these more settled regions and marched westward, toward the more open agricultural lands of the Roman Empire. In all these ways, the east was different from the west and was able to survive as an imperial state for another thousand years.

THE LEGACY OF THE ROMAN EMPIRE
WHAT DIFFERENCE DOES IT MAKE?

The Roman Empire laid foundations that have lasted until today in language, law, urban and regional development, and religious organization. Rome's language, Latin, was the official language of the empire, and it persisted as one of the two languages (with Greek) known by all educated Europeans until the seventeenth century. It survived until the mid-twentieth century as the language of ritual prayer for the Roman Catholic Church. It formed the base of the Romance languages (Italian, Spanish, Catalan, Portuguese, French, and Romanian) and contributed substantially to English.

Roman law, which developed and was codified over several centuries, inspired the transition to modern, codified law in much of Europe. It was the ancestor of the Napoleonic Codes that the French general and emperor institutionalized wherever he ruled in early nineteenth-century Europe (see Chapter 15).

The hundreds of towns that Rome founded and developed as administrative and military centers throughout the empire provided the nuclei around which the urban structure of much of modern Europe and northern Africa developed. The 50,000 miles of well-paved roads that connected the cities of the empire laid the foundation for much of modern Europe's land transportation patterns.

Even after its decline and fall, c. 476, the Roman Empire continued to shape the vision and the administration of hundreds of millions of people. In 330 the Emperor Constantine inaugurated Constantinople as an eastern, sister capital of the Roman Empire, and that city dominated much of the eastern Mediterranean for another thousand years, until 1453.

Meanwhile in western Europe, during that millennium, the Roman Catholic Church adapted the Roman imperial administrative organization for its own uses. This basic organization persists to the present. When the Emperor Constantine gave Christianity legal status throughout the empire, and chose it as his own religion, he opened the gates for its unprecedented growth. What later became known as the Holy Roman Empire, which ruled much of central Europe for some 900 years from 800, also styled itself a successor to Rome, although the comparison was somewhat remote.

Images of the Roman Empire remain powerful even to our own times. The British Empire, which girdled the globe from the eighteenth to the mid-twentieth centuries, proudly described itself as recreating and extending the imperial military power, administration, legal system, and technological superiority that had characterized Rome. Like the early Romans, the British claimed to have stumbled into their imperial possessions rather than to have actively pursued them (see Chapter 16).

They spoke of administering a "Pax Britannica." More recently, many political analysts have referred to the exercise of American political and military power around the globe as the "Pax Americana."

Review Questions

- Why did Rome choose to expand from city-state to empire? What stages marked that expansion?
- What was the policy of the "New Wisdom" in Rome's military strategy? Give examples of its implementation. Do you think it was an appropriate and effective policy? What other strategies did Rome employ to win over its enemies?
- Social hierarchy was fundamental to Roman political and social life at all levels throughout its history. Give examples from domestic life to civic life to imperial life.
- What was the policy of "bread and circuses"? How did it evolve? What do you think were its effects?
- What were the accomplishments in which Roman emperors took the most pride? In our text, the example of Augustus is most fully discussed, but other emperors are also mentioned.

- What changes took place in the Roman Empire and in Christianity that enabled Christianity to become the dominant religion? Please note the stages in this evolution.
- Why might historians say that the Roman Empire was "dismembered," rather than say that it "fell"?
- What factors enabled the eastern, Byzantine Empire to survive for one thousand years after the end of the Roman Empire?

Suggested Readings

PRINCIPAL SOURCES

Boardman, John, Jasper Griffin, and Oswyn Murray, eds. *The Oxford History of the Classical World* (New York: Oxford University Press, 1986). Very useful array of expert articles on Greece and the Roman Empire.

Cornell, Tim and John Matthews. *Atlas of the Roman World* (New York: Facts on File, 1983). The series of atlases in the *Facts on File* series are encyclopedic in their coverage, and extremely accessible as well.

Grant, Michael. *History of Rome* (New York: Scribner's, 1978). Grant is an excellent scholar-writer who leads the reader through the heart of his subject matter. An outstanding introduction to the field. His many other books are also extremely useful. See for example *Julius Caesar* (New York: McGraw-Hill, 1969).

Lewis, Naphtali and Meyer Reinhold, eds. *Roman Civilization: Selected Readings: Vol I: The Republic and the Augustan Age; Vol II: The Empire* (New York: Columbia University Press, 1990). *The* documentary collection. Indispensable.

MacMullen, Ramsay. *Romanization in the Time of Augustus* (New Haven, CT: Yale University Press, 2000). Argues that Roman ways of life were eagerly sought by conquered peoples, especially their leaders, and spread through imitation more than by force. Several of MacMullen's other very readable books illuminate class and religious relationships in imperial and post-imperial Rome. See especially *Roman Social Relations, 50 B.C. to A.D. 284* (New Haven, CT: Yale University Press, 1981).

Time-Life Books. *Time Frame 400 B.C.–200 A.D.: Empires Ascendant* (Alexandria, VA: Time-Life Books, 1988) and *Time Frame A.D. 200–600: Empires Besieged* (Alexandria, VA: Time-Life Books, 1988). These books are more at the advanced high school level than college, but all the books in this series are backed by excellent scholarship, clear and effective prose, and lavish, superb illustrations. These two volumes contain important chapters on Rome.

ADDITIONAL SOURCES

Antoninus, Marcus Aurelius. *Meditations*, trans. by H. G. Long in Whitney J. Oates, ed., *The Stoic and Epicurean Philosophers* (New York: Modern Library, 1940). The classic statement of Stoicism by an emperor of Rome known also for his ruthless military conquests.

Aries, Philippe and Georges Duby, eds. *A History of Private Life: Vol. I: From Pagan Rome to Byzantium* (Cambridge, MA: Harvard University Press, 1987). Life cycle, marriage, family, slavery, the household, architecture, the private attitudes of public officials, work and leisure, wealth, public opinion, pleasure, religion, and community are the subjects of three of the fascinating, lengthy essays in this book.

Bradley, K.R. *Slavery and Society at Rome* (Cambridge: Cambridge University Press, 1994). A comprehensive, accessible, up-to-date review.

Brown, Peter. *The World of Late Antiquity, A.D. 150–750* (New York: Harcourt Brace Jovanovich, 1971) and *The Rise of Western Christendom* (Malden, MA: Blackwell, 1996). Brown's scholarship and clarity of presentation on the world of the late Roman Empire and the rise of Christianity make these excellent introductions.

Carcopino, Jerome. *Daily Life in Ancient Rome* (New Haven, CT: Yale University Press, 1940). Although dated and generalized, Carcopino's introduction to the way in which people actually lived is most useful.

Clark, Gillian. *Women in Late Antiquity: Pagan and Christian Life Styles* (Oxford: Oxford University Press, 1993). Sketchy analysis of gender relations accompanying the introduction of early Christianity.

Fantham, Elaine, *et al. Women in the Classical World* (New York: Oxford University Press, 1994). A collection of essays on gender relations through texts and art work.

Finley, M.I., ed. *The Portable Greek Historians* (New York: Viking Press, 1959).

Frank, Andre Gunder and Barry K. Gillis, eds. *The World System: Five Hundred Years or Five Thousand* (New York: Routledge, 1993). Many new explorations of trade in the ancient world, and new ways of understanding trade as the context of political as well as economic system building, make this a fascinating interpretive study.

Geanakoplos, Deno John. *Byzantium: Church, Society, and Civilization Seen Through Contemporary Eyes* (Chicago, IL: University of Chicago Press, 1984). An excellent analysis of the strengths of the Byzantine empire, stressing its bureaucratic organization.

Gibbon, Edward. *The History of the Decline and Fall of the Roman Empire* (New York: Modern Library, 3 Vols. 1932). Available in several abridgements. This classic, two-century-old, study includes important analyses of the Germanic nations, the Huns, the confrontation with early Islam, and the origins of early modern Europe as well as the fall of Rome. Fascinating for its perspective from the age of the European enlightenment.

Johns, Catherine. *Sex or Symbol? Erotic Images of Greece and Rome* (London: British Museum Press, 1989). An outstanding presentation of selections from the special collections of the British Museum on Greece and Rome introducing an analysis of the function of sexual art in religious rituals, drama, and erotic titillation.

Jones, A.H.M. *Augustus* (New York: W.W. Norton & Co., 1970). The basic introduction to this pivotal emperor and his accomplishments. Jones is another classical master scholar-writer. Among his many other books, note *The Later Roman Empire, 284–602: A Social,*

Economic, and Administrative Survey, 2 Vols. (Oxford: Basil Blackwell, 1990).

Luttwak, Edward N. *The Grand Strategy of the Roman Empire* (Baltimore, MD: Johns Hopkins University Press, 1976). A fascinating analysis of Rome's military strategy, stressing "The New Wisdom" of application of overwhelming strength.

Mumford, Lewis. *The City in History* (New York: Harcourt, Brace, and World, 1961). Mumford's classic, moralistic analysis of historic urbanization sees Rome, both city and empire, as a catastrophe of the exploitation of the poor and vulnerable by the rich and powerful.

Ramage, Nancy and Andrew Ramage. *Roman Art: Romulus to Constantine* (Englewood Cliffs, NJ: Prentice Hall, 1991). Useful, accessible, basic introductory text. Richly illustrated.

Runciman, Steven. *Byzantine Civilization* (Cleveland, OH: World Publishing Co., 1933). Even after seventy years, Runciman is still a fascinating and readable introduction.

Virgil. *Aeneid*, trans. Rolphe Humphries (New York: Charles Scribner's Sons, 1951). Many translations available. Writing in the age of Augustus, Virgil gives the classic, idealized statement of Rome's mission.

Wells, Peter. *The Barbarians Speak: How the Conquered Peoples Shaped Roman Europe* (Princeton, NJ: Princeton University Press, 1999). Reviews and extends studies of the relationships between Romans and "Barbarians" based on recent archaeological findings.

World History Documents CD-ROM

5.1 A Hero Under Fire: Livy Relates the Trials and Tribulations of Scipio Africanus
5.2 "The War with Catiline": Sallust's Insights Into the Roman Republic's Decline
5.3 The Transition from Republic to Principate: Tacitus
5.4 "All Roads Lead to Rome!": Strabo
5.5 Gladiatorial Combat: Seneca
5.6 The Stoic Philosophy
5.7 Sidonius Appolinaris: Rome's Decay, and a Glimpse of the New Order
7.1 Procopius: *History of the Wars*
7.2 Iconoclasm and Orthodoxy: The Second Council of Nicaea (787)
7.3 A Western Attitude Toward the Byzantine Greeks (1147): Odo of Deuil

CHINA

FRACTURE AND UNIFICATION: THE QIN, HAN, SUI, AND TANG DYNASTIES 200 B.C.E.–900 C.E.

KEY TOPICS
- The Qin Dynasty
- The Han Dynasty
- Disintegration and Reunification
- Imperial China

When we last discussed the north China plain in Chapter 4, the Zhou (Chou) dynasty (1100–256 B.C.E.) was in decline. As the dynasty began to weaken, the powerful, independent states of the region fought among themselves so constantly that China's historians have named the years between *c.* 481 and 221 B.C.E. the Warring States period. In 221 B.C.E., after hundreds of years of warfare, the Qin (Ch'in) dynasty defeated the others, unifying north China and creating the first unified Chinese Empire.

This chapter will consider the Chinese Empire during its first 1100 years, from 221 B.C.E. to 907 C.E. During this time China created political and cultural forms that would last for another thousand years, and, as we shall see in Chapter 21, perhaps even to the present.

We will examine the key accomplishments under China's imperial rulers—the conquest, consolidation, and confirmation of the empire—and the expansion of China to include "outer China," the distant, conquered provinces inhabited by people not ethnically Chinese. In addition, we outline relationships with peoples to the south and southwest, who were ultimately incorporated into China, and with Korea and Japan, whose cultures were influenced profoundly by China. We close by comparing and contrasting the Chinese Empire with that of Rome.

THE QIN DYNASTY

The Qin dynasty expanded from a geopolitical base around the confluence of the Yellow and Wei rivers to control the whole of north China and a segment of the south. The Qin conquest ended centuries of fighting among the warring dynasties of north China that began with the decline of the Zhou dynasty and lasted through the period of the Warring States. The Qin defeated other regional states over the course of perhaps a century, until by 221 B.C.E. they could rightfully claim to have established a unified empire, the first in China's history. Although the dynasty itself lasted only a few years after it succeeded in establishing the empire, the new empire itself persisted with few interruptions to the present.

Military Power and Mobilization

Armed force was fundamental in the Qin's conquest. The *Book of Songs*, dating from the early years of the Zhou dynasty, suggests the constant nature of warfare in early China:

Which plant is not yellow?
Which day don't we march?

Opposite **Great Wall of China. Begun 214 B.C.E., rebuilt repeatedly.** "The seven wonders of the world are not comparable to this work," wrote one awestruck seventeenth-century European observer of this most imposing relic of China's past. Faced with brick and stone and averaging 25 feet high and wide, the 1500-mile-long wall is studded with towers that serve as signaling stations, warning of the approach of mobile enemies.

Which man does not go
To bring peace to the four quarters?

Which plant is not brown?
Which man is not sad?
Have pity on us soldiers,
Treated as though we were not men!

… We are neither rhinos nor tigers
Yet are led through the wilds,
Have pity on us soldiers,
Never resting morn or night.

The Qin not only conquered north China but also defeated the Xiongnu (Hsiung-na), border tribes (probably related to the groups that the Romans called the Huns) to the north and west of China proper. They gained authority over northern Korea, and defeated some of the Yue tribes in the south. The first Qin ruler to govern a unified China was Qin Shi Huangdi (r. 221–210 B.C.E.), "the first august emperor of the Qin," not unlike the title "Caesar Augustus of Rome" that Octavian bestowed upon himself.

In addition to their military efforts, the Qin also mobilized tens of thousands of men for enormous public works projects. After conquering the other states of north China they fortified and linked the defensive walls that had been constructed by local rulers into the 1500-mile Great Wall of China in seven years with a work force of one million laborers. This wall was to keep the northern Xiongnu "barbarians" out of China proper and, with its 40-foot high watch-towers constructed every few hundred yards, to serve as a first warning in case of attempted invasion.

The first emperor also conscripted 700,000 laborers to construct his palace, a complex large enough to hold 40,000 people. But perhaps even more impressive was Qin Shi Huangdi's tomb. In 1974 archaeologists digging near his mausoleum

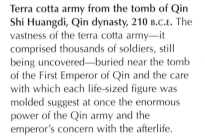

Terra cotta army from the tomb of Qin Shi Huangdi, Qin dynasty, 210 B.C.E. The vastness of the terra cotta army—it comprised thousands of soldiers, still being uncovered—buried near the tomb of the First Emperor of Qin and the care with which each life-sized figure was molded suggest at once the enormous power of the Qin army and the emperor's concern with the afterlife.

discovered a ceramic army of some 7000 life-sized soldiers and horses, arranged in military formation and armed with bronze weapons, spears, longbows, and crossbows (a Chinese invention). In 1976, a second excavation uncovered an additional 1400 chariots and cavalrymen in four military units. The next year archaeologists discovered a much smaller pit, holding what appeared to be a terra cotta officer corps. These thousands of figures were not mass produced. Craftsmen modeled and painted each figure separately, even down to its elaborate hairstyle, which symbolized its specific military office. The figures apparently represented the elite of the imperial troops and were fashioned to accompany the emperor to his own tomb and afterlife.

Economic Power

The Qin undertook some of the enormous public works projects to increase the economic productivity of the empire. During the centuries of their rise to power, the Qin had built canals and river transport systems in both the Wei River system in the north and the Min River system in Sichuan in west-central China. In Sichuan they irrigated the region around Chengdu, turning it into a granary for the nation. The transportation and irrigation systems they built in the northern state of Shanxi transformed it into an area so rich in agricultural productivity and the means of transporting it that they could control all of north China from this base. As ironworking became increasingly important in Chinese military and economic development, the Qin also captured the richest sources of iron ore and two of China's best ironworking facilities, crucial resources for fashioning both tools and weapons.

EARLY ADVANCES IN WEAPONRY	
3000 (B.C.E.)	War chariot invented. In Mesopotamia and southeastern Europe first metal swords and shields made (bronze).
2000	First armor made, from bronze scales, in Mesopotamia.
c. 700	The Phoenicians and Egyptians invent galleys—warships powered by oars.
500	Giant crossbows and catapults used by the Greeks and Carthaginians.
200	Hand-held crossbow now being used in China.
300 (C.E.)	Stirrups used in China.
950	Gunpowder used by Chinese for signaling devices and fireworks.
1250–1300	Bronze and iron cannon probably used by the Chinese; in Europe, first recorded use of cannon is 1326.

Administrative Power

Administratively, Qin Shi Huangdi ruled through a bureaucracy. He did away with the system of personal allegiance by which officials were appointed on the basis of their personal, often family, ties to the court and therefore owed allegiance to the emperor himself rather than to the empire as an institution. Instead, the emperor chose people for office on the basis of ability; their tasks were fixed and governed by systematic, formalized, written rules; and their work was rewarded or punished according to the degree of their efficiency and fidelity. The Qin divided the empire into some forty administrative units called "commanderies." Each commandery was staffed with three leading officials: a civil authority, a military authority, and an inspector representing the emperor. The three officials served as checks and balances on one another: no one individual could assert too much power and threaten the control of the emperor at the center.

The Qin standardized as they centralized. They fixed weights and measures, values of coinage, the size of cart axles and of the roads they traveled. They standardized the legal code. Perhaps most important of all, the Qin standardized the written form of the Chinese language, possibly the most important single act of political and cultural unification in China's history. To this day, despite great variation in the local forms of spoken Chinese, written Chinese is uniform throughout the country, just as the Qin established it.

AT A GLANCE: CHINA

DATE	POLITICAL	RELIGION AND CULTURE	SOCIAL DEVELOPMENT
500 B.C.E.	■ Warring States period (481–221)	■ Confucius (551–479)	
250 B.C.E.	■ Zhou dynasty ends (256) ■ Qin Shi Huangdi initiates Qin dynasty (221–206) ■ Revolts against Qin (207)	■ Han Feizi (d. 233) ■ Daoism ■ Legalism ■ Great Wall	
200 B.C.E.	■ Liu Bang (206–195) first emperor of Han dynasty		
150 B.C.E.	■ Han Wu (141–87)	■ Confucian Academy established (124)	■ Travels of Zhang Qian
100 B.C.E.	■ Reign of usurper Wang Mang (9–23 C.E.)	■ Sima Qian (145–85) ■ Invention of paper	
50 C.E.		■ First mention of Buddhism in China	
200 C.E.	■ Han dynasty ends (220) ■ Age of Disunity (221–331) ■ Three Kingdoms (220–280)		
300 C.E.	■ Jin dynasty (265–316) ■ Northern Wei dynasty (386–534)	■ Buddhism expands ■ Gu Kaizhi (334–406)	
600 C.E.	■ Sui dynasty (581–618) ■ Tang dynasty (618–907)	■ Invention of block printing ■ Grand canal completed (610) ■ Buddhist cave art	■ Boundaries of empire extended to Mongolia, Turkestan, Afghanistan, Pakistan, and Iran ■ Tang briefly held North Korea and Vietnam
650 C.E.	■ Empress Wu (625–705)		■ First pharmacopoeia
700 C.E.	■ Battle of Talas River (751) ■ An Lushan rebellion (755–63)	■ Wang Wei (701–62) ■ Li Bai (701–61) ■ Du Fu (712–70) ■ Porcelain produced	
800 C.E.		■ Repression of Buddhism	
900 C.E.	■ Collapse of Tang, leading to disunity (907–960) ■ Song dynasty (960–1279)		

Competing Ideologies of Empire

In their public proclamations, Chinese emperors stressed the importance of their philosophy to the actual process of building, sustaining, and guiding their empire. In addition, the official historians who compiled China's records were an elite trained in philosophy. As a result, China's history reflects a profound concern with the conflicts over the philosophy and ideology of empire. These philosophies and ideologies themselves emerged in the late Zhou period and the years historians have called the Period of the Warring States (*c.* 481–221 B.C.E.). The chaos of the times induced some individuals either to search for a solution to Chinese political and social problems or to find tranquility apart from society and politics. The three schools of thought—Confucianism, Daoism (Taoism), and Legalism—that emerged in this period deeply influenced the dynasties that sought to rule the Chinese empire after the Qin established their dynasty.

Confucianism. Kong Fuzi (551–479 B.C.E.), known in Latin as Confucius, a philosopher and political adviser from the small state of Lu in modern Shandong, sought to reform

China by redefining Chinese political and ethical thought. Confucius began his career as a scholar. He mastered the six arts of ritual, music, archery, chariot driving, calligraphy, and arithmetic, and then began his career as a teacher. At a time when China was divided into many states, often in conflict, he formulated principles that he thought would bring peace, contentment, dignity, and personal cultural development at least to the elites of his time. Although Confucius was unsuccessful in finding employment as an adviser in any single state, his disciples kept his vision alive, and it has permeated Chinese thought and, often, government policy.

Confucius felt that good government depended on good officials, men of *jen*, or humanity, benevolence, virtue, and culture. Although he was not much concerned with the supernatural, he did believe that a moral order pervaded the universe and that it could be understood. In contrast to the tumult of his own day, Confucius believed that the early days of the Zhou dynasty had been a golden age of peace and order, wisdom and virtue. In those days, political leaders had understood the importance of social hierarchy, ritual, music, and art. The neglect of these elements of humanism and rationalism and the absence of schools that taught them to new leaders, had reduced China to chaos.

Confucius and his disciples canonized five of China's earliest historical texts as especially fine examples of the philosopher's own thought and his concern for history, music, the arts, and rituals:

- the *Book of Documents*, a collection of various statements of early kings and their ministers;
- the *Book of Changes*, the *I Ching*, which details methods of predicting the future through casting sticks;
- the *Book of Songs*, which contains 305 poems, about half of which relate to the everyday lives of ordinary people, half to issues of court politics and rituals;
- the *Spring and Autumn Annals*, which contains brief chronologies from Lu, Confucius' home state;
- *Rites and Rituals* (three texts, grouped together as one), which combines both philosophies and rituals of the court.

In addition to these five, Confucius' disciples recorded his own teachings in *The Analects* (see p. 210). A large body of interpretation and commentary grew up around each of these texts.

Confucius believed in the essential goodness and educability of each individual, and believed that the virtues of the past could be regained. He believed in the centrality of the "gentleman" (*junzi*), the moral leader who had the vision to move the society toward peace and virtue. Such a gentleman would and should be concerned about political leadership and the proper ordering of the state. For Confucius, however, gentlemen were not born but made, fashioned through proper education. Believing that character, not birth, was important, he taught whoever would come to him, but Confucius' own era was too violent for his teachings to find immediate acceptance.

The Qin dynasty did not welcome his teachings either, but the next dynasty, the Han, did. Under the Han, Confucius' ethical and political values came to dominate the culture and thought of China's scholars and intellectuals, and they continued powerful for most of the following 2000 years, also influencing the political thought of Korea, Japan, and southeast Asia.

Moreover, because Confucius expressed his ideas in such general terms, subsequent disciples could adapt them to particular problems. Thus, Confucianism evolved and often transformed into new forms that sometimes maintained its core values and sometimes changed them. For example, Mencius (Mengzi) (*c.* 371–*c.* 289 B.C.E.) had an optimistic view of human nature and believed that education would function to bring

SOURCE

Confucius and The Analects

We have no record that Confucius wrote down his own teachings. The Analects as a collection of thoughtful perceptions attributed to him, was apparently recorded and compiled by disciples of his disciples. Because these aphorisms—497 verses in twenty chapters—are brief, unelaborated, unorganized, and written in ideographic form, their exact meaning is not always clear, but these same qualities promote the reader's engagement with and interpretation of the text. The Analects have been a part of the education of every Chinese school student for centuries, at least until the communist revolution in 1949. The selections here represent typical issues for Confucius: the importance of formal, humanistic education in forming proper character; teaching and learning by example; focus on the world of here-and-now; and respect for others, especially for parents and elders.

A young man is to be filial within his family and respectful outside it. He is to be earnest and faithful, overflowing in his love for living beings and intimate with those who are humane. If after such practice he has strength to spare, he may use it in the study of culture.

Lead them by means of regulations and keep order among them through punishments, and the people will evade them and will lack any sense of shame.

Lead them through moral force (*de*) and keep order among them through rites (*li*), and they will have a sense of shame and will also correct themselves.

In education there should be no class distinctions.

Shall I teach you what knowledge is? When you know something, to know that you know it. When you do not know, to know that you do not know it. That is knowledge.

The noble person is concerned with rightness; the small person is concerned with profit.

I am not one who was born with knowledge; I am one who loves the past and is diligent in seeking it.

The Three Armies can be deprived of their commander, but even a common person cannot be deprived of his will.

The wise have no doubts; the humane have no sorrows; the courageous have no fears.

Before you have learned to serve human beings, how can you serve spirits …

When you do not yet know life, how can you know about death?

Look at nothing contrary to ritual; listen to nothing contrary to ritual; say nothing contrary to ritual; do nothing contrary to ritual.

What you would not want for yourself, do not do to others.

Zigong asked about government. The Master said, "sufficient food, sufficient military force, the confidence of the people." Zigong said, "If one had, unavoidably, to dispense with one of these three, which of them should go first?" The Master said, "Get rid of the military." Zigong said, "If one had, unavoidably, to dispense with one of the remaining two, which should go first?" The Master said, "Dispense with the food. Since ancient times there has always been death, but without confidence a people cannot stand."
(deBary, 1999, pp. 45–60)

Throughout Chinese history, some groups rebelled against Confucius' ethical principles. Peasant rebels, a frequent presence throughout the centuries, condemned Confucius' emphasis on order and harmony. In the late nineteenth and twentieth centuries, as China saw itself fall behind the technological and military achievements of the Western world, Confucian traditions were challenged with renewed vigor (see Chapters 18 and 21). Critics argued that Confucianism was incompatible with equality, scientific education, rebellious youth movements, dignity of physical labor, peasant equity, and equal rights for women. The communist government that has ruled China since 1949 attacked Confucius especially bitterly in 1973 and 1974 during the Cultural Revolution, asserting that in his own day Confucius had served as a representative of the slave-owning aristocracy. As communism has more recently been transformed in contemporary China, the study of Confucianism is returning to China's schools.

out the best in people. He encouraged government leaders to rule in the best interests of the people and society by encouraging harmony according to Confucian principles. Another disciple, Xunzi (Hsün-Tzu) (312–235 B.C.E.), took a more negative view of human nature. Having many years of experience in government, he emphasized different aspects of Confucian thought. Most important, he believed that human nature was inherently bad and that only through education and participation in rituals would people learn to put the needs of society ahead of their private desires. Unlike Mencius, Xunzi believed in an education that would emphasize restraints on human behavior.

Legalism. Rejecting Confucianism, the Qin favored a philosophy of government known as **legalism**, which was characterized by strict laws and strict enforcement, with rewards for those who observed the laws and swift and appropriate punishment for those who broke them. During his reign Qin Shi Huangdi set up inscriptions on stone in various parts of his empire proclaiming his values and policies. For example, after he put down a rebellion in the far northeast, he inscribed on the city walls:

> Then he mobilized armies, and punished the unprincipled, and those who perpetrated rebellion were wiped out.
>
> Armed force exterminates the violent and rebellious, but civil power relieves the guiltless of their labors, and the masses all submit in their hearts.
>
> Achievements and toil are generously assessed, and the rewards even extend to cattle and horses, and his bounty enriches the land.
>
> The August Emperor gave a vigorous display of his authority, and his virtue brought together all the states, and for the first time brought unity and supreme peace.
>
> City walls were demolished [suggesting that peace had been established so that they were no longer necessary for defense], waterways were opened up, and obstacles were flattened.
>
> When the physical features of the land had been determined, there was no conscript labor for the masses, and all under heaven was pacified.
>
> Men take pleasure in their farmland, and women cultivate their tasks, and all matters have their proper arrangement.
>
> His kindness protects all production, and for long they have been coming together in the fields, and everyone is content with his place. (Sima Qian, p. 74)

In another inscription he wrote:

> When the sage of Qin took charge of his state, he first determined punishments and names, and clearly set forth the ancient regulations.
>
> He was the first to standardize the system of laws, examine and demarcate duties and responsibilities, so as to establish unchanging practices. (Sima Qian, p. 82)

He proclaimed a code of sexual conduct:

> If a man commits adultery, to kill him is no crime, so men hang on to the standards of righteousness.
>
> If a wife elopes to remarry, then the son will not have a mother, and so everyone is converted into chastity and purity. (Sima Qian, p. 83)

In his rulings Qin Shi Huangdi followed many of the policies of the political philosopher Han Fei Tzu (d. 233 B.C.E.), a student of the Confucian scholar Xunzi. Han Fei Tzu called himself a Legalist because he believed that strict laws, strictly enforced, were the best assurance of good and stable government. Han Fei Tzu summed up the power of the law:

> To govern the state by law is to praise the right and blame the wrong ... To correct the faults of the high, to rebuke the vices of the low, to suppress disorders, to decide against mistakes, to subdue the arrogant, to straighten the crooked, and to unify the folkways of the masses, nothing could match the law.
>
> The means whereby the intelligent ruler controls his ministers are two handles only. The two handles are chastisement and commendation. (Han Fei Tzu, I:45–7)

Daoism. Daoism (Taoism) was a philosophy of spontaneity in the face of nature and the cosmos. It was a mystical philosophy, not usually directly applicable to government, but often a solace to public men in their private lives, especially after retirement.

legalism A school of Chinese philosophy that came into prominence during the period of the Warring States and had great influence on the policies of the Qin dynasty. Legalists took a pessimistic view of human nature and believed that social harmony could only be attained through strong government control and the imposition of strict laws, enforced absolutely.

Daoism is often seen as an inspiration to artists, and, because it advocates a high regard for nature, it is often seen as an inspiration to natural scientists as well.

The legendary founder of Daoism and the author of its key text, the *Daodejing* ("The Way and its Power"), is Laozi (*c.* 604–*c.* 517 B.C.E.), but the school and the book more likely date to the third or fourth centuries B.C.E. Its teachings are cloaked in paradox and mystery:

> The Way that can be spoken of is not the constant Way;
> The name that can be named is not the constant name.

Rejecting the emphasis on sophisticated learning and education that characterized Confucian thought, Daoists believed that untutored simplicity was powerful:

> Do away with sageliness, discard knowledge,
> And the people will benefit a hundredfold.
> Do away with humaneness, discard righteousness,
> And the people will once more be filial and loving,
> Dispense with cleverness, discard profit,
> And there will be no more bandits and thieves.
> These three, to be regarded as ornaments, are insufficient.
> Therefore let the people have something to cling to:
> Manifest plainness,
> Embrace uncarved wood,
> Diminish selfishness,
> Reduce desires.
>
> What is softest in the world
> Overcomes what is hardest in the world.
> No-thing penetrates where there is no space.
> Thus I know that in doing nothing there is advantage.
> The wordless teaching and the advantage of doing nothing—there are few in the
>   world who understand them.

Those who followed Daoism believed in a natural order or path (Dao). They taught that government should leave people alone:

> The more prohibitions there are in the world,
> The poorer are the people.
> The more sharp weapons people have,
> The more disorder is fomented in the family and the state.
> The more adroit and clever men are,
> The more deceptive things are brought forth.
> The more laws and ordnances are promulgated,
> The more thieves and robbers there are.
> Therefore the sage says:
> I do nothing (*wuwei*),
> And the people are transformed by themselves.
> (deBary, 1999, pp. 79–90)

This Daoist view of simplicity diminishes the need for government: "Let the state be small and the people be few" (deBary, 1999, p. 94). Nor is there need to travel. Beauty, peace, and joy are to be found at home:

> Though neighboring states are within sight of one another,
> And the sound of cocks and dogs is audible from one to the other,
> People will reach old age and yet not visit one another. (deBary, 1999, p. 94)

For an interactive version of this map, go to: http://www.prenhall.com/spodek/map7.1

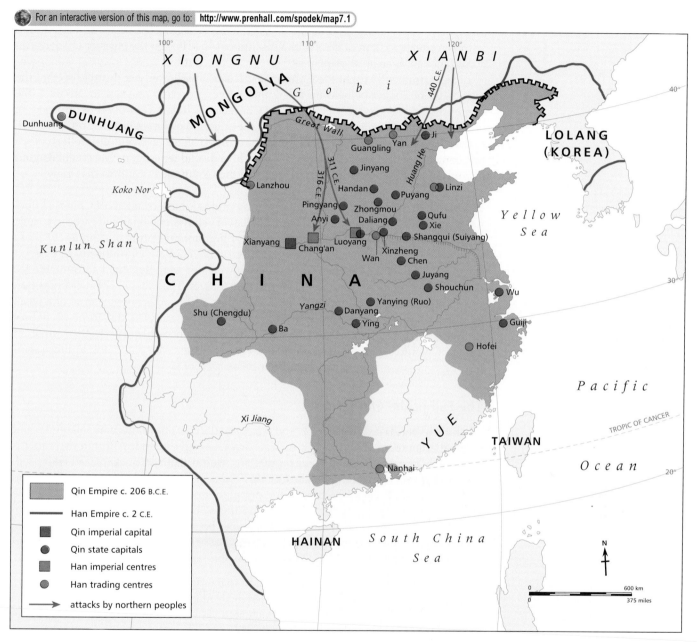

Qin Empire c. 206 B.C.E.

Han Empire c. 2 C.E.

Qin imperial capital

Qin state capitals

Han imperial centres

Han trading centres

attacks by northern peoples

Daoism can be viewed as a rejection of Confucian principles, but over time many Chinese embraced both Confucianism and Daoism, allowing the former to shape their public lives, while gaining solace from the latter in their private lives. Also, because Daoism allowed the individual to find his or her own path, over time it began to embrace a variety of popular beliefs, alchemy, mysticism, and magic, all reinforced through a variety of rituals. Finally, Daoism may have facilitated the acceptance of Mahayana Buddhism in China, since both stressed the idea of transcending the material world.

The Struggle between Legalism and Confucianism. The philosophies of Legalism and Confucianism collided during the Qin dynasty. In direct contrast to the Confucianists' reverence for the past, the prime minister Li Si (Li Ssu) (*c.* 280–208 B.C.E.) argued that

Classical China. In 221 B.C.E. two centuries of internecine rivalry—the "Warring States" period—ended with the rise to centralized power of the Qin dynasty, but internal revolt and external pressures on the borders precipitated further civil war. The Han dynasty emerged as the new rulers in 202 B.C.E. They refortified the northern walls, and extended imperial control far to the south and west, deep into central Asia along the silk route, defining a Chinese territorial extent that has been asserted down to the present day.

the administration of the Qin was far superior to the government of any earlier time. The Qin success was the result of its decision to replace personal, *ad hoc* administration with an orderly system of laws and appointment to office on the basis of efficiency in accordance with Legalist principles.

Li Si recommended that the Confucian classics be collected and burned so that the past could no longer be held up as an alternative to present policies. In 213 B.C.E. the Qin burned the books. Subsequently, as Confucian scholars continued to oppose Qin Shi Huangdi, the emperor had 460 scholars buried alive. Sima Qian, the official, Confucian, historian of the Han government, recorded these acts of anti-intellectualism and brutality, which leave the Legalist Qin with a dismal reputation. The cruel intrigues and struggles for succession that helped end the Qin dynasty confirm that view.

The Mandate of Heaven. One of the enduring philosophical concepts of Chinese imperial politics was the Mandate of Heaven. Heaven—not a personal god but the cosmic forces of the universe—underpinned rulers of high moral stature and undercut those who lacked it. An omnipotent heaven conferred its mandate, or authority to rule, on the moral and revoked it from the immoral. Dynasties were thus held accountable for their actions, and they could not expect to rule forever. Their loss of cosmic connection would be made manifest, not only in the usual political and economic strife of a weak administration, but also through nature itself going awry in the form of floods, droughts, or other natural disasters. Throughout Chinese history, rebels against an emperor would claim evidence of his having lost the "Mandate," while those supporting new rulers would proclaim their possession of it.

The Fall of the Qin Dynasty

Qin Shi Huangdi died in 210 B.C.E. and was buried in the enormous mausoleum he had created, accompanied by the vast ceramic army he had ordered. Within four years his apparently powerful, centralized, productive, well-organized dynasty had collapsed. Despite the apparent strengths, the Qin had oppressed to its breaking point the nation and its peasantry, the 90 percent of the population who paid the taxes, served in the armies, built the public works projects, and the women who supported all these projects through their work at home. The final crisis began when the emperor sent several hundreds of thousands of these peasants to fight the Xiongnu in the far north and northwest on both sides of the Great Wall. As the *Han History* later reported,

> For more than ten years they were exposed to the rigors of military life, and countless numbers died … Although the men toiled at farming, there was not enough grain for rations; and the women could not spin enough yarn for the tents. The common people were ruined. (cited in Elvin, p. 27)

In addition to these systemic problems, the fight over the succession to Qin Shi Huangdi's throne destroyed the dynasty. A contest for power broke out among the late emperor's son, the minister Li Si, and another court official, the eunuch Zhao Gao. In the struggle, the emperor's son murdered many of his father's supporters on advice from his minister. Fear and disloyalty flourished. Each contestant seemed concerned only for his own survival and aggrandizement. Qin Shi Huangdi had instituted bureaucracy in place of personal rule throughout the empire, but personal politics still dominated the imperial court. Finally, Zhao forced the emperor's son to commit suicide, but then he himself was assassinated. While the court was convulsed in these internal struggles, rebels broke into the capital at Xianyang and captured power. Warfare continued until, in 206 B.C.E., the rebel leader Liu Bang emerged victorious and established the Han dynasty.

Han historians proclaimed their belief that the Qin dynasty had lost the Mandate of Heaven. Nevertheless, the Qin had brought China to a new stage of political development: the empire had been founded; an effective bureaucratic administration had been established; and careers had been opened to new men of talent. All these innovations were to last, in changing measures, for 2000 years.

THE HAN DYNASTY

When Liu Bang (r. 206–195 B.C.E.) prevailed in the warfare that ended the Qin dynasty, the empire remained intact. One ruling family fell and another took its place and asserted its own control, but the empire itself continued united under a single emperor. The principal Legalist ministers who had guided the Qin were replaced, but the administrative bureaucracy continued to function.

A Confucian Bureaucracy

Change came in the leadership style of the new dynasty. Liu Bang was himself a commoner and a soldier, perhaps illiterate, with many years of warfare still ahead of him—he died in battle in 195 B.C.E.—but as his ministers he chose educated men with Confucian principles. Slowly, a new social and political hierarchy emerged, with scholars at the top, followed by farmers, artisans, and merchants. Legalism still influenced the administrative systems, and Daoism's emphasis on nature and emotion continued to be attractive, but Confucius' ethical teachings captured the imagination of the court.

The influence of Confucianism appeared in four other areas. First, history became more important than ever. The appointment of Sima Tan and then of his son Sima Qian as court historians established the tradition of imperial record keeping (see p. 217). The Confucian notion of the importance of tradition and continuity prevailed over the Legalist idea of discounting the past.

Second, in 124 B.C.E. the most powerful and longest lived of the Han rulers, Wudi or Emperor Wu (r. 141–87 B.C.E.), the Martial Emperor, established an elite imperial academy to teach specially selected scholar-bureaucrats the wisdom of Confucius and its applicability to problems of governance. The emperor also declared that knowledge of the Confucian classics would be a basis for promotion in the imperial civil service. Although the academy could at first educate only fifty men, it multiplied in size until in the later Han period it could accommodate 30,000 men. In Han times, the landed aristocracy still gained most of the places in the bureaucracy, but the principle of appointment and promotion based not on birth but on success in an examination in the Confucian classics was finally established during the Tang dynasty (618–907 C.E.).

Third, an imperial conference of Confucian legal scholars was convened in the imperial palace in 51 B.C.E. to codify and establish the principles for applying case law. This established and consolidated the Chinese legal system for centuries to come.

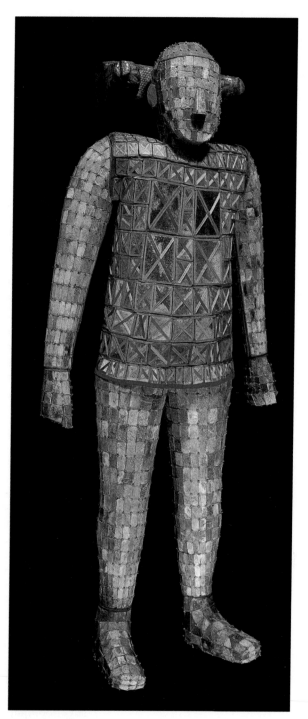

Jade burial suit of Princess Tou Wan, Western Han dynasty, late second century B.C.E. As a very hard stone, jade was believed to be an effective preservative. When the Princess Tou Wan, daughter-in-law of the Emperor Jingdi, died, a burial suit was created for her using 2160 pieces of jade tied together with gold wire.

SOURCE

Treatises about Women in Han Society

During the Han dynasty, several authors decided to address the subject of women's role in society. Unfortunately, we have far more records on aristocratic women than we do on the peasantry. Ban Zhao (45–116 C.E.), sister of the famous court historian Ban Gu, wrote Admonitions for Women, *a text of advice on the virtues appropriate for aristocratic women, which was divided into seven sections on humility, resignation, subservience, self-abasement, obedience, cleanliness, and industry. Ban Zhao explained:*

In ancient times, on the third day after a girl was born, people placed her at the base of the bed, gave her a pot shard to play with, and made a sacrifice to announce her birth. She was put below the bed to show that she was lowly and weak and should concentrate on humbling herself before others. Playing with a shard showed that she should get accustomed to hard work and concentrate on being diligent. Announcing her birth to the ancestors showed that she should focus on continuing the sacrifices. These three customs convey the unchanging path for women and the ritual traditions.

Humility means yielding and acting respectful, putting others first and oneself last, never mentioning one's own good deeds or denying one's own faults, enduring insults and bearing with mistreatment, all with due trepidation.

Industriousness means going to bed late, getting up early, never shirking work morning or night, never refusing to take on domestic work, and completing everything that needs to be done neatly and carefully. Continuing the sacrifices means serving one's husband-master with appropriate demeanor, keeping oneself clean and pure, never joking or laughing, and preparing pure wine and food to offer to the ancestors. (Ebrey, p. 75)

Placing a similar stress on the virtues of self-sacrificing service, Liu Xiang (79–8 B.C.E.) wrote the Biographies of Heroic Women, *which recounted the virtues of 125 women. He especially praised the mother of the philosopher Mencius, the greatest of the Confucian scholars. Liu Xiang quotes Mencius' mother telling her son of her concept of women's obligations:*

A woman's duties are to cook the five grains, heat the wine, look after her parents-in-law, make clothes, and that is all! Therefore she cultivates the skills required in the women's quarters and has no ambition to manage affairs outside of the house. The *Book of Changes* says, "In her central place, she attends to the preparation of the food." The *Book of Songs* says, "It will be theirs neither to do wrong nor to do good, / Only about the spirits and the food will they have to think." This means that a woman's duty is not to control or to take charge. Instead she must follow the "three submissions." When she is young, she must submit to her parents. After her marriage, she must submit to her husband. When she is widowed, she must submit to her son. These are the rules of propriety.

The pervasive Confucian stress on hierarchy and deference permeates these prescriptions for women's conduct. However, throughout Han times—but not after—women could inherit property, divorce, and remarry after divorce or widowhood. And even the most highly placed women sometimes rebelled against Confucian ideals.

Finally, Confucian scholars, both male and female, began to establish principles of conduct for women. Confucius had spoken of the importance of five relationships in human society: ruler–subject; father–son; husband–wife; older brother–younger brother; and friend–friend. The first four were hierarchical relationships of superior–inferior. Little, however, had been written about the role of women. During the Han dynasty several Confucian scholars addressed the issue. They urged women to be self-sacrificing, serving others, especially the males in their lives: father, brother(s), husband, and son(s). The Source box includes examples of such advice by Ban Zhao, sister of one of the Han court historians, and Liu Xiang, who wrote *Biographies of Heroic Women*.

Military Power and Diplomacy

The Han emperors were no less militaristic than the Qin. Confucian principles of moral rectitude held sway among the educated elites, but the government did not dispense with formal legal systems nor did it forsake offensive or defensive warfare. The standing army numbered between 300,000 and 1,000,000, and all able-bodied men between the ages of about twenty and fifty-six were conscripted, serving for one year of training and one year of duty in the capital or in battle on the frontiers. They could be recalled in case of warfare.

Throughout the Han dynasty, China was engaged in incessant battles with the Xiongnu and other tribes around the Great Wall. Indeed, as we shall see shortly, the Han forced open a corridor through Gansu in the direction of Xinjiang (Turkestan). One reason for this expansion was to open markets for silk in the west. Parthian traders carried goods on this trade route as far as Rome. China also wanted to secure a supply of horses from distant Bactria for the military. As the Chinese Empire expanded, emperors sought new ways of regulating foreign affairs with neighboring peoples, including nomadic groups, such as the Xiongnu. They created a "tributary

HOW DO WE KNOW?

The Grand Historians

The Chinese valued recording the past both for itself and for the moral principles it was believed to teach. China therefore prepared and transmitted the most fully and continuously documented history of any ancient empire. Building on this legacy of historical literature, the Han emperor, Wu (r. 141–87 B.C.E.), created a new official position, the Grand Historian of the Han court, with the responsibility of preparing a comprehensive history of the entire Chinese past.

The first to hold the post was Sima Tan (d. 110 B.C.E.). He was succeeded by his son Sima Qian (145–85 B.C.E.), one of the greatest of all historians. Father and son transformed their task from one of writing dynastic chronologies to one of evaluating the quality of governments and rulers. They created the art of Chinese history as a commentary on politics and ethics.

At the very end of his great work, Shi Qi, 130 chapters recounting the history of China from mythological times almost to his own, Sima Qian includes an autobiographical sketch:

Qian was born at Longmen. He ploughed and kept flocks on the sunny slopes of the mountains near the Yellow River. By the age of ten he was reading aloud the ancient writings. At twenty he journeyed south to the Yangtze and Huai rivers, ascended Kuaiji to search for the cave of Yu, espied Jiuyi, went by water down to Yun and Xiang, journeyed north and crossed the

Wen and Si to investigate the traditions in the cities of Qi and Lu, and observed the customs handed down by Master Kong [Confucius], and took part in the archery competition held at Mount Yi in Cou. He suffered distress in Po, Xie, and Pengcheng, and returned home via Liang and Chu. Afterwards Qian served as a palace gentleman, and received orders to be sent on the western expedition to the south of Ba and Shu. Having gone south and captured Qiong, Ze, and Kunming, they returned and made their report on the mission. (Dawson trans., p. xix)

So his training included farming, literature, travel, adventure, anthropological research, archery, court service, and warfare. If historians improve with their own experience of life, since it enables them to understand more fully the lives of the people they study, then Sima Qian was off to a good start.

The highlight of Sima Qian's historical writing is its emphasis on biography, a traditional Chinese literary form that he developed into a vehicle for commenting on the political and ethical policies of the state not only in the past but also in his own time. His judgments could be fierce, and they sometimes got him into trouble. His support for his friend General Li Ling at a time when the general was in great disfavor in court led to Sima Qian's castration. Later, the Han Emperor Wu was so angered by Sima Qian's account of his father, the Emperor Jingdi, that he had this chapter removed. Eventually, however, imperial feelings mellowed, and Sima Qian won his reputation as the

greatest master of the early Chinese historical tradition.

Sima Qian completed his accounts up to c. 100 B.C.E. A later historian, Ban Biao (3–54 C.E.), added tens of chapters of "Supplementary Chronicles," and his son, Ban Gu (32–92 C.E.), wrote the Han Shu ("History of the Han Dynasty") to 22 C.E. Ban Gu established the tradition of compiling a history of each dynasty, a form continued in the Hou-Han shu ("History of the Later Han") and enduring into the twentieth century.

Because the official histories carry their own Confucian, conservative biases and focus almost entirely on issues of the central government and its court, unofficial materials from the provinces are especially useful in giving additional viewpoints. Grave sites and tombs yield documents, inscriptions, and engravings, and these often include relief sculptures of the activities of the deceased during his or her life. The burial goods represent in miniature the deceased's house, tools, carriages, boats, farms, and equipment. They often included terra cotta figures or painted frescoes of entertainers, musicians, servants, and maids, who had enriched the life of the deceased.

- What were the reasons for recording an official court history of each dynasty?
- What were the reasons for the rise, fall, and return to prominence of Sima Qian?
- How would you evaluate the training of Sima Qian as an historian?

system," in which the neighboring tributary group would acknowledge Chinese dominance and offer gifts (tribute) to the emperor. In exchange the emperor would send gifts to the ruler of the tributary group. On the northern and western borders, where Chinese, Mongol, Tibetan, and Barbarian forces fought, each learned the strengths and weaknesses of the other. A Chinese strength was the crossbow. An important Mongol and Tibetan strength was cavalry, mounted on strong, fast horses. To achieve military parity, the Han emperors sought and found a supply of equivalent horses in central Asia. The Gansu corridor served as an access route, and Emperor Wu garrisoned it with 700,000 soldiers. Administrative records written on wooden strips have survived to tell of the lives of these immigrant soldier-colonizers in some detail.

Population and Migration

In both the south and the northern border regions, the Han established military-agricultural colonies to provide military defense and economic development. The Chinese attempted to win the local populations over to Chinese culture. Often they succeeded, but not always. On the borders and in the southeast they met opposition, and rebellions against the Chinese settlers erupted in 86, 83, and 28–25 B.C.E.

During the later Han dynasty the population of northern China declined dramatically, even as the population of the south was expanding, perhaps from immigration from the north as well as from natural growth. The earliest preserved census in the world, taken in China in the year 2 C.E., shows the Chinese heartland clearly in the north; the southern population was sparse, mostly settled along the rivers. The second preserved census, taken 138 years later in 140 C.E., showed a sharp overall decline of 10 million people from about 58 million to about 48 million. The regional distribution had shifted from 76 percent in the north and 24 percent in the south, to 54 and 46 percent, respectively. In absolute terms the population of the south actually went up by more than 50 percent, from 14 million to 22 million, while the entire north declined from 44 million to 26 million.

Xiongnu and Tibetan massacres along the northern and western borders contributed to population losses, as did the floods caused when the Yellow River broke its banks and twice changed course, in c. 4 C.E. and again in 11 C.E. The military and natural turbulence also impoverished China's civilian population. Meanwhile, the imperial government allocated more and more resources to support the army,

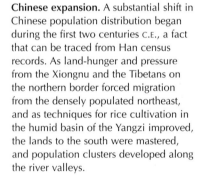

Chinese expansion. A substantial shift in Chinese population distribution began during the first two centuries C.E., a fact that can be traced from Han census records. As land-hunger and pressure from the Xiongnu and the Tibetans on the northern border forced migration from the densely populated northeast, and as techniques for rice cultivation in the humid basin of the Yangzi improved, the lands to the south were mastered, and population clusters developed along the river valleys.

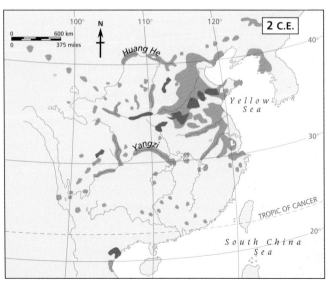

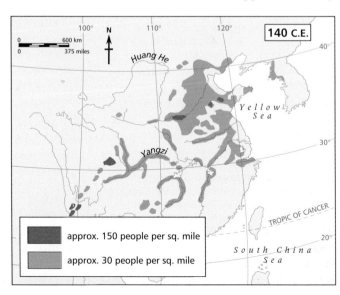

expansionism, and the court in the capital city of Chang'an.

In the south, in general, there was little indigenous population and little hostility or resistance to the increase in Han Chinese. The regional Yue or Viet tribes were more often involved in fighting one another, although in 40 C.E. there was a revolt, and violence broke out on at least seven occasions between 100–184 C.E. Perhaps the increased resistance in the later years was evoked by the vast increase in the flow of population from the north to the south.

Economic Power

Han rulers also encouraged the expansion of China's iron industry. They developed the technique of liquefying iron and pouring it into molds to produce cast iron and later steel. In spite of the demographic decline in the north, the economy of Han China grew with the exploitation of new sources of wealth from along the Yangzi River, Sichuan, and the south. New inventions in mining (including salt mining), paper production, the compass, the breast-strap harness for horses, a redesigned plowshare, hydraulic engineering, and the tapping of natural gas increased wealth and productivity.

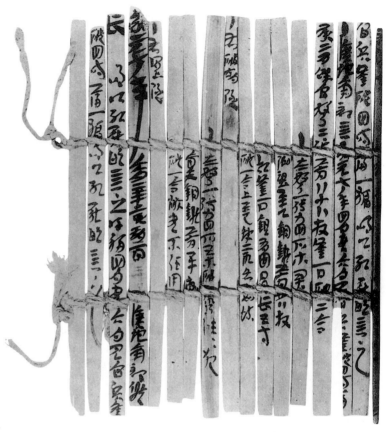

Inventory written on bamboo, 95 C.E. Government bureaucracy expanded with military and economic power under the Han dynasty, producing an enormous number of documents on wooden and bamboo strips. This inventory lists the equipment of two infantry units. (*British Library, London*)

The road through the Gansu corridor to Xinjiang (Turkestan) brought increased knowledge of distant lands and new trade possibilities. In 138 B.C.E. Emperor Wu dispatched Zhang Qian to inner Asia to seek enemies of the Xiongnu who might serve as allies of the Chinese. Zhang returned twelve years later without new alliances but with precious new information on lands as far west as Bactria, in modern northern Afghanistan. New trade possibilities opened not only in horses but also in silk. Parthian traders served as intermediaries between the Chinese and Roman Empires. By 57 B.C.E. Chinese silk had reached Rome. The first silk route had been opened. Geography and cartography flourished, and gazetteers began to be published.

The cost of military expeditions and garrisons, and the expenses of the self-aggrandizing court ate up the gains, however. Having dramatically lowered the land revenues when they first took office, the Han emperors began to raise them again. They also began to nationalize private enterprise by bringing it under state control, not in order to promote efficiency or honesty but to gain the profits for the state. Although commerce and business were theoretically held in low regard by Confucians, businessmen flourished under the Han, and Sima Qian praised their enterprise:

A family with a thousand catties of gold may stand side by side with the lord of a city; the man with a hundred million cash may enjoy the pleasures of a king. Rich men such as these deserve to be called the "untitled nobility," do they not? (Sima Qian, p. 356)

Emperor Wu sought to expropriate some of this wealth to pay for his military ventures and his imperial court. He altered coinage, confiscated the land of the nobility, sold offices and titles, and increased taxes. He established government monopolies in the production of iron, salt, and liquor, and he took over part of the grain trade, arguing that this was a means of stabilizing prices, but actually intending to secure

Stone relief of harnessed cattle found at Mizhi, Shaanxi province.
Technological advancements, such as the development of the animal-drawn plow, went hand in hand with the increase in the area of cultivated land under the Han dynasty.

profits for his government and its border wars. On his death, his successor, the Emperor Zhao, arranged a debate between his chief minister, who advocated continuing the state monopolies on salt and iron, and a number of Confucian scholars, who opposed them. The minister defended and explained the emperor's policy:

He established the salt, iron, and liquor monopolies and the system of equitable marketing in order to raise more funds for expenditures at the borders. … [O]ur critics … would have the men who are defending our passes and patrolling our walls suffer hunger and cold. … Abolition of these measures is not expedient! (deBary, vol. 1: p. 361)

The Confucianists opposed the policy of costly military expansion and the government plan to take over businesses in order to finance it:

Never should material profit appear as a motive of government. Only then can moral instruction succeed and the customs of the people be reformed. But now in the provinces the salt, iron, and liquor monopolies, and the system of equitable marketing have been established to compete with the people for profit, dispelling rustic generosity and teaching the people greed. (deBary, vol. 1: p. 360–1).

The Confucianists also distrusted businessmen as self-seeking and corrupt, and they feared that government-run businesses would increase that corruption. The new emperor came to accept the Confucian argument and relinquished at least some government-run monopolies temporarily.

Fluctuations in Administrative Power

The bureaucracy of the early Han seemed to run well, and the adoption of Confucian principles tempered some of the harshness of the Legalist codes. In addition, the wars that the Qin had pursued to establish China's borders made fighting somewhat less necessary for the Han. For two hundred years even the problems of succession, problems that had ultimately helped destroy the Qin dynasty, were negotiated effectively, if sometimes quite cruelly. Nevertheless, the absence of clear principles of imperial succession continued, and in 9 C.E. the Han temporarily fell from power because there was no clear successor.

An Interregnum. In 1 B.C.E., the eight-year-old Emperor Ping inherited the throne. A regent, Wang Mang, was appointed to run the government during the boy's minority, and when Ping died in 9 C.E., Wang Mang became the *de facto* ruler, declaring himself founder of a new dynasty. His policies, however, alienated virtually everyone. These policies—fighting against the Xiongnu, breaking up large estates, reinstating the prohibition on the sale of land, fixing commodity prices, terminating the status of the Han nobility and reducing them to commoners, cutting bureaucratic salaries, confiscating villagers' gold in exchange for bronze—inflamed rich and poor, nobility and commoners, and urban and rural folk.

To add to his problems, just at the beginning of Wang Mang's regency, the silt-laden, shallow Yellow River again broke its banks and changed course twice in five years, wreaking immense devastation to property, and loss of life. In 23 C.E., a combination of Xiongnu invasions in the north, the rebellion of Han nobles near the capital, and, after 18 C.E., the revolt of the Red Turbans, a mass movement centered in the Shandong peninsula, which had been most devastated by the Yellow River's flooding, brought down Wang Mang and led to the reinstatement of the Han dynasty.

A Weakened Han Dynasty. The later Han dynasty, 23–220 C.E., did not have the same strength as the former Han. To cope with continuing incursions, the later Han made alliances with the barbarians, inviting them to settle within the Great Wall, to provide soldiers for Chinese armies, and even to intermarry with the Chinese, policies that were similar to Rome's actions in its border regions. Although this pattern demonstrated the weakness of the Chinese central government, it also contributed to the **sinicization** of the tribal barbarians, who learned the language, culture, and administrative patterns of the Chinese. Reversing the pattern of tribute of the years of strong government, the later Han gave silk cloth to the border tribes so that they would not invade. Later Han emperors also moved the capital from Chang'an eastward to the less exposed city of Luoyang.

sinicization The adoption and absorption by foreign peoples of Chinese language, customs, and culture.

The movement of population to the south increased the wealth of the empire generally, but the increase went largely to merchants and landlords. Peasants continued to be exploited and oppressed by the exactions of both their landlords and the imperial government. As government taxes increased, peasants sold off their private holdings and went to live and farm under the jurisdictions of local landlords, where they sought to evade government taxes and military conscription.

The landlords themselves faced a dilemma. As members of the governing elite, they were to collect and remit taxes to the central government and to turn over their tenants for conscription, but as landlords and local potentates, it was to their advantage to retain the taxes and the tenants' labor for themselves. Strong central governments were capable of demanding loyalty and collection; the later Han, however, frequently failed. Peasants absconded, the government's tax and labor bases diminished, and provincial notables developed independent power bases. Peasant revolts, which would become endemic in most of China, broke out with increasing frequency.

Gu Kaizhi, two concubines in front of a mirror, *Admonitions ...,* **fourth century C.E.** As the Han Dynasty collapsed, artists lamented the neglect of the Confucian codes of behavior. Here the court painter Gu Kaizhi (334–406) illustrates the text of the poet Zhang Hua (c. 232–300): "Men and women know how to adorn their faces, but there is none who knows how to adorn his character. ..."

Peasant Revolt and the Fall of the Han. The beginning of the end of the Han is usually dated to 184 C.E., when a revolt of hundreds of thousands of peasants broke out. Zhang Jue, a Daoist healer who proclaimed that a new era would begin with the fall of the Han, launched the rebellion, called the Yellow Turban revolt for the headgear worn by the rebels. It broke out simultaneously in sixteen commanderies throughout the south, east, and northeast of China. Although this specific revolt was suppressed, it triggered a continuous string of additional outbreaks.

At least four factions struggled for power within the palace— the emperor, who, after the death of Emperor Ling in 189, was a child; the bureaucrats, advisers, palace guards, and regent to the young emperor; the eunuchs in the court, about 2000 castrated men chosen primarily for their direct loyalty to the emperor and the women of the court; and the women of the court and their families. Since each emperor had several wives and consorts, competition among them was fierce, both for their own recognition and for recognition of their sons at court, especially in the selection of the heir to the emperor. After the death of an emperor, his widows and his mother often remained embroiled in court politics to defend their own positions and those of their family.

In the last decades of Han rule, 189–220 C.E., the court was buffeted from the outside and divided on the inside. For example, on September 25, 189 C.E., generals in the court murdered hundreds of eunuchs to remove their influence. By the year 220, when the last Han emperor, Xian, abdicated, the court had no center and the lands of the empire had already been divided among numerous, competing warlords.

DISINTEGRATION AND REUNIFICATION

The fall of the Han brought the disintegration of China into three separate states, but the ideal of a united Chinese empire was not lost. The empire was restored for fifty years, 265–316 C.E., then divided again for 273 years until 589 C.E., when a new dynasty introduced a unification that would last for more than three centuries. Even during periods of disintegration, elements of an underlying unity endured, for China has deep and pervasive common cultural traditions, just as, during periods of powerful imperial rule, elements of divisive regionalism persisted, for China is a huge and diverse country.

Ecology and Culture

On the fall of the Han dynasty, China divided into three states: the Wei in the north, ruling over some 29 million people; the Wu in the south, ruling over 11 million; and the Shu in the west, ruling over 7 million. From 265 to 316 C.E. a single dynasty, the Jin (Chin), reunited China briefly. Then, for 273 years, 316–589 C.E., China was divided north from south, more or less by the Huai River Basin, halfway between the Yellow River to the north and the Yangzi River to the south.

This division was characterized by a number of geographical features. To the north, the top soil is a fine yellow dust, called loess. Borne by winds from the west, it is 250 feet deep to the north of Chang'an, a region with little irrigation. The agriculture in this region has been dry-field farming not dependent on massive irrigation projects and mostly carried on by owner-operators. Its principal crops are wheat, millet, beans, and turnips. The region is intensely cold in winter. The south, by contrast, has many waterways, which are useful for both irrigation and navigation. The warmer weather, even subtropical in the far south, makes it possible to grow rice and tea, which were introduced from southeast Asia probably toward the end of the Han dynasty. The area is typically organized into landlord-tenant estates.

During the centuries of imperial division, six successive dynasties governed the south, while a series of non-Chinese barbarian dynasties ruled the north. Warfare and ecological disaster in the north steadily reduced the population, while people moved south, shifting the balance of population to a southern majority by this period. It appeared that the Chinese Empire, like that of Rome, had lost control of its original homeland and divided forever.

While China was divided politically, however, its culture and ethical ideologies persisted, keeping alive its traditions of unity. In the south, especially, the arts, painting, calligraphy, and poetry flourished, frequently with the themes of spiritual survival amid political disarray. The Chinese language, too, continued to unite all literate Chinese as their means of communication.

Chinese technology. Classical Chinese cultures were administratively and technologically sophisticated. They mastered diplomacy, bureaucracy, navigation, architecture, chemistry, mechanics, astronomy, printing, and, most dramatically, hydrology. Terraced farming, intensive irrigation systems, and the construction of thousands of miles of navigable canals harnessed the often unpredictable rivers of eastern China, and opened up the inland cities to commerce.

In the north, China was more open to new social and ethnic syntheses. The Chinese absorbed the barbarians into their continuing cultural life, and, through intermarriage, into China's genetic pool as well. When scholars today note the homogeneity of China's population as "95 percent Han," they are referring to cultural rather than ethnic homogeneity and recognizing the openness of China toward accepting and assimilating neighboring peoples who accept the culture of the "Han." The Chinese themselves echo the importance of this common culture, referring to all who have accepted it as "people of the Han." The nomadic peoples living on the northern borders and settling within the Great Wall at the invitation of the later Han emperors had already begun to absorb Chinese culture. When they became powerful enough to conquer north China, they found that they needed to enlist Chinese bureaucrats to administer their gains. In many regions, the administrators appointed by the new rulers were descended from families whom the Han had employed. Thus, below the surface of foreign rule, a powerful stratum of Chinese elites remained in place.

The most powerful and longest ruling of the nomadic conquerors became the most assimilated. These were the Northern Wei dynasty (r. 386–534), also named the Toba Wei after the tribal group that founded it. The longer they ruled, the more assimilated they became. In 493–494 they moved their capital from the far west to one of the former Han capitals, Luoyang, in order to consolidate their control of the northeast. But in Luoyang they wore Chinese dress, adopted Chinese names, and many intermarried. The Toba also made their own contributions to China's administrative practices, instituting a new pattern of urban organization by wards in Luoyang. Subsequent dynasties used this system in laying out the restored capital of Chang'an. Still later, Japanese imperial planners copied it in Nara. Similarly, in their attempts to keep agricultural populations from fleeing from north China, the Toba took over all land ownership for the state and continued to redistribute it in "equal fields" as each generation of cultivators died and new ones inherited the land. According to the "equal fields" system, all families received some land in return for paying a tribute in goods or in labor.

The developing, new aristocracy of mixed Chinese–Toba blood alienated the unassimilated Toba troops who garrisoned the frontiers. They finally revolted and defeated the Northern Wei government in 534, opening the way to the Sui dynasty, a family of mixed Chinese-foreign (barbarian) parentage, that reunited China.

Buddhism Reaches China

While China was beset by this dynastic turmoil, a new religion was spreading through the country. During the Han dynasty, Buddhism had entered China from its birthplace in India. It is first noted in Chinese historical records in the first century C.E.

Siddhartha Gautama, the Buddha, "the enlightened one" (*c.* 563–483 B.C.E.), introduced a religion of compassion in the face of a world of pain. Buddhism is discussed at length in Chapter 9. Here, however, we ask why and how this religion, which later died out in its own native soil in India, was able to take root in far-off China, even in the face of early opposition by Confucian scholars and bureaucrats and an institutionalized Daoist establishment.

Over time, Buddhism's very foreignness may have contributed to its success. The nomadic conquerors who succeeded the Han may have felt comfortable accepting, and even sponsoring a religion which, like themselves, came from outside China.

Second, Buddhism arose in India, to a large degree, as an anti-priestly religion favored by the merchant classes. These merchants sponsored Buddhist monasteries, convents, and cave temples along the silk routes between India and China, some of which remain impressive even today. When Buddhism arrived in China with the silk-route merchants, Chinese merchants were already familiar with it and the new religion appeared cosmopolitan rather than exclusively Indian.

Buddhism persevered in China, securing patronage in several regional courts, capturing the hearts of millions of followers, and ultimately becoming one of the unifying elements in Chinese culture. Eventually it mixed with Confucianism and Daoism, bringing popular new spiritual, intellectual, cultural, and ritual innovations (see Chapter 9).

Reunification under the Sui and Tang Dynasties

Despite almost 400 years of imperial fragmentation, many elements of Chinese unity were potentially at hand: language, ideology, culture, administration at the local level, aristocratic families with deep roots, and sufficient imperial prestige and administrative expertise that even China's conquerors were assimilated to it. To reunite the empire required the restoration of military power, economic productivity, and administrative integration. The Sui dynasty (581–618) provided all three.

The Short-lived Sui Dynasty. The Sui dynasty was founded by the Emperor Wen (Yang Chien) (r. 581–604), a general from one of the northern Chinese states, who usurped power in his own state and then succeeded in conquering and unifying all of inner China. Militarily, Wen raised the status of his militia, settled them on their own lands, and gave them property rights. He thus created an effective, committed, and loyal standing army of peasant-farmers. A powerful crossbow, protective body armor, and constant drills to achieve precision in maneuvers and battle made these troops a formidable fighting force.

Ideologically, the first Sui emperor and his son, Yang (Yang Kuang) (r. 604–615), who succeeded him, employed a combination of Confucian, Daoist, and Buddhist symbolism and practice to win popular loyalty. Administratively, they centralized authority, eliminating a layer of local administrators and transferring their own appointees from one jurisdiction to another every three years to prevent them from establishing their own local power base. They drew up a new centralized legal code that still recognized local customs. Economically, the Sui dynasty completed the Grand Canal from Hangzhou in the south to Luoyang in the center. The canal linked the Yangzi and Yellow River systems, and extensions connected it to the rebuilt capital in Chang'an and, later, to Beijing. The canal provided for the transportation of the agricultural produce of the rapidly developing south to the political-military centers of the north.

The expense of mobilizing and dispatching imperial troops and administrators on their far-flung missions depleted the treasury of the Sui dynasty. The Grand Canal produced many economic benefits, but it cost dearly in manpower. Built in seven years, the canal required the labor of 5.5 million people, and to complete some sections, all commoners between the ages of fifteen and fifty-five were pressed into service. As many as 50,000 police supervised the construction, flogging and chaining those who could not or would not work, and ordering every fifth family to provide one person to supply and prepare food. In addition to these public works, three costly and disastrous military campaigns in Korea and in central Asia wasted lives and treasure and sapped the loyalty of the troops. Finally, the leading general of the Sui seized control of the state and under the imperial name Gaozu established the new Tang dynasty in 618 C.E.

When the Sui fell, after over-extending itself militarily and economically, the Tang dynasty (618–907) continued and even strengthened these attributes of empire. Moreover the Sui and Tang extended China's reign to truly imperial dimensions—that is, beyond China proper to "outer China," Mongolia, Turkestan, and central Asia, as far

Bridge over the outer moat, a connecting link of the Grand Canal at Suzhou. The engineering feats of the Sui dynasty made significant contributions to the closer integration of the empire. By digging the Grand Canal and building roads in the north China plain, rulers ensured effective communication and the opening of new trade routes between diverse regions.

as the frontiers of modern Afghanistan, Pakistan, and Iran. China also held strong cultural sway over Tibet, although without achieving direct political control. These lands were larger than all of "inner China" in area, although they held only perhaps 5 percent of its population. In addition, Tang China held northern Vietnam and, briefly, northern Korea. China's cultural influence at this time was extremely strong in Japan as well (see below).

Arts and Technology under the Tang Dynasty. Tang policies built on those of the Sui, consolidating and improving them where possible. The Tang dynasty relied more than ever on the imperial examination system to provide its administrators, and in 754 the emperor founded a new Imperial Academy, the Han-Lin Yuan (the Forest of Pens).

The arts and technology, often reinforcing one another, flourished under the Tang as never before. The world's first block printing was invented, partly in response to the needs of Buddhists to disseminate their doctrines, for under the Tang the Buddhist religious establishment became increasingly powerful. Buddhist religious art found expression also in further cave sculptures and paintings. New ceramic manufacturing methods led to the production of the first true porcelain, a product of great beauty and durability. For centuries, China alone knew the secret of its manufacture. Millers developed machinery and gears for converting linear and rotary motion, encouraging further development of both water- and windmills. In 659 China produced the world's first pharmacopoeia, which listed the contents and uses of all known medicines.

Finally, Tang era poetry of meditation, nature, politics, fate, suffering, and individual identity transmitted its living legacy even to today's readers in China and beyond.

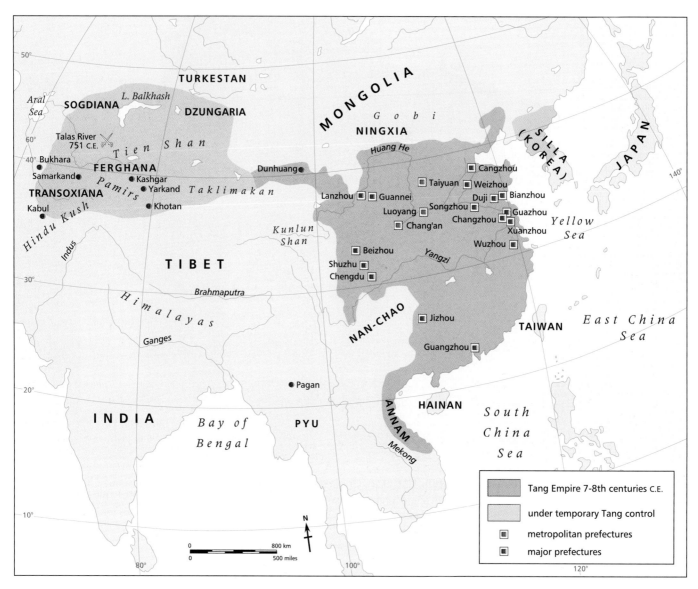

The Tang revival. The Sui Dynasty (581–618 C.E.) and its successor, the politically organized Tang, restored the Chinese imperial impulse four centuries after the decline of the Han, extending control along the silk route as far as the Tien Shan mountain range and the arid Ferghana basin. Trade flourished. China finally reached its western limits when its forces were defeated by the imperial armies of the Muslim Abbasid empire at the Talas River in 751.

Each of the three most famous Tang poets has been seen as linked to a different cultural tradition: Wang Wei (701–762) to Buddhism; Li Bai (Li Bo) (701–761) to Daoism; and Du Fu (Tu Fu) (712–770) to Confucianism, although each was influenced by all three traditions. Du Fu's "Autumn Meditation" expresses the tension between the high-stakes, hustle-bustle of the imperial court under stress and his own desire for a life of peace within nature:

> I've heard them say Chang'an's like a chessboard;
> sad beyond bearing, the happenings of these hundred years!
> Mansions of peers and princes, all with new owners now;
> in civil or martial cap and garb, not the same as before.
> Over mountain passes, due north, gongs and drums resound;
> wagons and horses pressing west speed the feather-decked dispatches.
> Fish and dragons sunk in sleep, autumn rivers cold;
> old homeland, those peaceful times, forever in my thoughts!
>
> (*Du Fu*, Watson translation, p. 134)

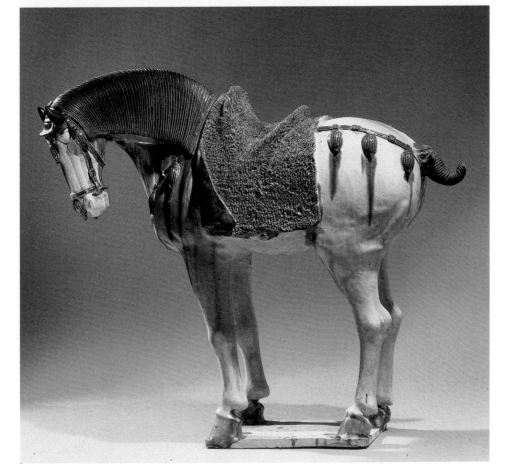

Above **Hill of the Thousand Buddhas, Jinan, Tang dynasty.** The increased power of the Buddhist religious establishment in Tang times is reflected in the growth of cave paintings and sculptures. The merchants and missionaries who brought Buddhism to China along the silk route also brought ideas about the iconography of temples and the depiction of the Buddha.

Pottery figure of a Ferghana horse, excavated from a tomb, Tang dynasty (618–907 C.E.). The Tang dynasty opened the Grand Canal, stimulated growth in trade, and expanded the boundaries of the empire. For much of this they were dependent on the mobility of the army, which in turn was dependent for covering great distances on the famed Ferghana horses, immortalized in literature as "the horses that sweated blood." (*Idemitsu Museum of Arts, Tokyo*)

Ceramic model of a group of musicians seated on a camel, Tang dynasty (618–907 C.E.), excavated from a tomb in the suburb of Xian. The beards, facial features, and costumes of some of the musicians in this group suggest that they are from central Asia. Such models, commonly found in the tombs of the Tang elite, are evidence of a taste for the goods that came along the silk route from the west and the central Asian music that accompanied them.

Caravanserai, Kirghizstan, Tang dynasty, (618–907 C.E.). The silk route led traders through hundreds of miles of inhospitable terrain, such as this barren and mountainous region of Kirghizstan in central Asia. This Tang dynasty-era caravanserai, the oldest complete example in existence, would have protected traders from the elements and from preying bandits.

HOW DO WE KNOW?

Poetry as a Source for History

Du Fu's "Ballad of the Army Carts" repeats the heartbreaking pain of war as the troops describe the seemingly endless fighting and dying:

> Carts rattle and squeak,
> Horses snort and neigh—
> Bows and arrows at their waists, the conscripts march away.
> Fathers, mothers, children, wives run to say goodbye.
> The Xianyang Bridge in clouds of dust is hidden from the eye.
>
> They tug at them and stamp their feet, weep, and obstruct their way.
> The weeping rises to the sky.
> Along a road a passer-by
> Questions the conscripts. They reply:
> They mobilize us constantly. Sent northwards at fifteen
> To guard the River, we were forced once more to volunteer,
> Though we are forty now, to man the western front this year.
> The headman tied our headcloths for us when we first left here.
> We came back white-haired—to be sent again to the frontier.
> Those frontier posts could fill the sea with the blood of those who've died,
> But still the Martial Emperor's aims remain unsatisfied.
> In county after county to the east, Sir, don't you know,
> In village after village only thorns and brambles grow,
> Even if there's a sturdy wife to wield the plough and hoe,

> The borders of the fields have merged, you can't tell east from west.
> It's worse still for the men from Qin, as fighters they're the best—
> And so, like chickens or like dogs, they're driven to and fro.
> Though you are kind enough to ask,
> Dare we complain about our task?
> Take, Sir, this winter. In Guanxi
> The troops have not yet been set free.
> The district officers come to press
> The land tax from us nonetheless.
> But, Sir, how can we possibly pay?
> Having a son's a curse today.
> Far better to have daughters, get them married—
> A son will lie lost in the grass, unburied.
> Why, Sir, on distant Qinhhai shore
> The bleached ungathered bones lie year on year.
> New ghosts complain, and those who died before
> Weep in the wet grey sky and haunt the ear.
> (Seth, pp. 48–9)

Du Fu probably wrote this poem of exhaustion and discontent after two decisive and disastrous military operations. In the first, the Battle of the Talas River, on one of the most distant of China's western frontiers, 2000 miles from Chang'an, Arab armies defeated China in 751. China lost control of its central Asian holdings, and the silk route was opened to the cultural influence of Islam, which displaced Buddhism and Confucianism. Four years later, An Lushan, one of China's frontier generals of Turkish extraction, revolted. Although the Chinese put down the revolt in 763, the cost of the warfare, and the vulnerability it revealed, weakened the Tang dynasty for the entire century and a half leading up to its fall.

The Tang dynasty had extended China's border farther than any other except the Qing (Manchu) that ruled a thousand years later (1644–1912). Tang holdings in central Asia had flanked and protected the silk route and brought new opportunities for wealth. Ultimately, however, these lands cost more than they brought in economically and militarily. The border groups—Turks, Uighurs, Khitans, and other ethnic groups—no longer accepted Chinese domination, but continually probed the Tang border fortifications. Finally, China ceded control of central Asia to them. In China proper, agricultural and commercial wealth continued to grow, but the central, imperial government could no longer control it. Regional rulers grew in authority and power. In 907 the Tang dynasty finally disappeared, as China splintered into ten separate states. Yet the imperial idea and pattern held. In 960 the Song dynasty arose, ruling all of China until 1127, and the south until 1279.

- What elements of the poem might suggest that Du Fu was influenced by Confucianism?
- Who is the poem's main speaker? What are his feelings about the war?
- How does the poem help us understand the feelings of the Chinese after the battle's defeat and subsequent developments?

The three centuries of Sui and Tang rule consolidated the theory and practice of Chinese imperial rule even to the present (although today there is no emperor). Since 581 China has been divided into two administrations only once, in 1127–75, and fragmented into several regions only twice, in 907–959 and 1916–49. Apart from these three periods, totalling 133 years, China has stood united for a continuous period of more than fourteen centuries.

IMPERIAL CHINA

We opened this unit on empires by noting that the word empire signifies rule by one people over another. Let us examine this definition in relation to China. First, within

assimilation The process by which different ethnic groups lose their distinctive cultural identity through contact with the dominant culture of a society, and gradually become absorbed and integrated into it.

the borders of China, empire frequently meant the **assimilation** of others. In the north, many of the tribal groups against which China fought and against which Chinese rulers constructed the Great Wall, nevertheless came to enlist in China's armies, settle its land, assimilate its culture, adopt its language and calligraphy, and intermarry with its peoples.

Both the ethnic Chinese and the "barbarians" regarded this process as mutually beneficial. Both also understood the dangers: the barbarians might lose their culture and even find themselves in civil war with others of their ethnic group who rejected assimilation; the Chinese might be conquered by their new allies. Indeed, both of these results did occur frequently, and the interchanges transformed the cultures of both the barbarians and the Chinese.

The West and Northwest

The most geographically far-reaching of China's expansions beyond the borders of inner China were to the northwest and west. Emperor Wu's expansion into Gansu and beyond did not survive the early Han dynasty; similarly, the expansion of the Sui and Tang even deeper into central Asia did not survive the Battle of the Talas River and the An Lushan revolt. Nevertheless, China's cultural and symbolic influence over these regions persisted, even after its political, military, and direct economic power was gone. (In the seventeenth century, under the Qing dynasty, China returned to dominate these areas, and rules them today; see Chapter 14.)

The South and Southwest

Processes of assimilation also took place in south China, but they have made much less of a mark in the records. China as an ethnic, cultural, and political entity developed first in the north, around the Yellow River, but as Chinese peoples moved south of the Yangzi they met people of other ethnic groups. As the Chinese encroached, some southern peoples retreated still further south to preserve and develop their own separate national identities. The Vietnamese are the clearest example of this pattern. Other groups of southerners remained as distinct, separate tribal groups, usually in remote areas somewhat difficult to access. Occasionally, these peoples revolted against the Chinese invasion and take-over of their land. The Miao gave the clearest example of this response. Most of the rest assimilated, including some Vietnamese and Miao, without making a lasting impression on the historical records.

Vietnam

For a thousand years China held Annam (northern Vietnam) as a colony. The Han dynasty conquered Annam and incorporated the area as a province of China in 111 B.C.E. It remained part of China until 939 C.E., when, not long after the collapse of the Tang, the Vietnamese rebel Ngo Quyen declared himself the king of the independent state of Dai Viet.

CHINA'S IMPERIAL DYNASTIES

Listed below are all the imperial dynasties, starting with the Qin, and the two major pre-imperial ruling houses. Gaps in the date sequences mark those periods when the country was divided between two or more rulers.

Shang	*c.* **1600–1100** B.C.E.
Zhou	*c.* **1100–256**
Qin	**221–206**
Han	**202** B.C.E.–**220** C.E.
Three Kingdoms (Kingdom of Shu Han, Kingdom of Wei, Kingdom of Wu)	**220–65**
Northern and Southern Dynasties	**265–589**
Western Jin	**265–317**
Eastern Jin	**317–419**
Northern Wei	**386–534**
Sui	**581–618**
Tang	**618–907**
Song	**960–1279**
Yuan (Mongol)	**1279–1368**
Ming	**1368–1644**
Manchu (Qing)	**1644–1912**

During and after Chinese colonization, the Vietnamese were locked in a love-hate relationship with Chinese culture and politics. Chinese scholars and officials, many of them fleeing imperial policies in China, brought to Vietnam their own ideographic script, Confucian ethical principles, and the Confucian literary classics. The Vietnamese adopted them all.

Buddhism also arrived in Vietnam by way of China. The rest of southeast Asia absorbed Buddhism in its Theravada form from India; Vietnam adopted Mahayana Buddhism as it had developed in China, after about the fifth century C.E. These cultural innovations appealed primarily to the Vietnamese upper-class aristocracy. At the level of practical technology, the Chinese also introduced a number of valuable agricultural innovations: the construction of a huge network of dams and waterworks that protect against monsoon flooding every year; the use of human excrement as fertilizer; market gardening; and intensive pig farming.

Although they adopted many Chinese customs, the Vietnamese resented foreign hegemony by the colossus to its north. For example, the two Trung sisters led a military revolt in 39 C.E., succeeded in evicting the Chinese, ruled jointly over Vietnam for two years, but committed suicide when their revolt was crushed. They are revered in Vietnam to this day. Leaders of numerous, less dramatic revolts against China are also viewed as national heroes, yet paradoxically, the most profound adoption of Chinese administrative reforms occurred in the fifteenth century, when Vietnam was independent. As a result of Chinese direct rule in the earlier period and Chinese power and proximity during later periods of Vietnamese independence, the country became a Confucian state, with an examination system, an intellectually elitist administration somewhat aloof from the masses, and an intense desire for independence from China.

Korea

Korea came under direct Chinese rule only briefly, but Chinese cultural hegemony profoundly influenced the peninsula. The Han Emperor Wu first conquered northern Korea in 109–108 B.C.E., along with Manchuria. Military garrisons established Chinese control and influence.

Korea, like Vietnam, had borrowed heavily from prehistoric China, including much of Shang technology and, later, iron technology, paper production, printing, lacquerwork, porcelain (although Korean double-fired, greenish, celadon ware had a distinct beauty all its own), wheat and rice agriculture, and the ideographs of written language. In 1446, at the initiative of its king, Koreans created a written system called *han'gul*, based on phonetics, which they proudly describe as the most scientifically formulated of all the world's scripts. Until after World War II, however, Korean elites suppressed the use of the simple *han'gul*, preferring the more prestigious, more elitist, and more difficult Chinese ideographs.

After the collapse of the Han in 220 C.E., Korea broke free of direct control, although it remained a vassal of the Chinese. Some of China's colonies remained in place, but without military capacity. The Sui dynasty sent three expeditions to conquer Korea, but all ended in disaster. The expansive Tang dynasty also tried to retake Korea in the seventh century and succeeded in occupying much of the peninsula in 668–676. Ultimately, however, Korea regained and maintained its independence, although it was often forced to accept tributary status, acknowledging China's regional dominance.

China's power over Korea can be seen far more in terms of cultural hegemony than in political-military rule. Confucianism, law codes, bureaucratic administration, literature, art, and Mahayana Buddhism entered Korean life from China, independent of government pressure. In 935 C.E., after the fall of the Tang, Korea's Silla dynasty also fell. The Koryo dynasty, which took its place, built a new capital at Kaesong, just north

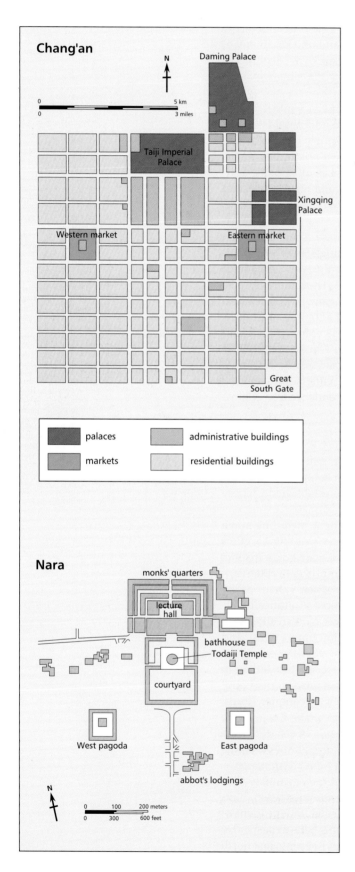

Chang'an

Daming Palace

Taiji Imperial Palace

Xingqing Palace

Western market

Eastern market

Great South Gate

	palaces		administrative buildings
	markets		residential buildings

Nara

monks' quarters

lecture hall

bathhouse
Todaiji Temple

courtyard

West pagoda

East pagoda

abbot's lodgings

of today's South Korean capital at Seoul, and modeled it on Chang'an, the Tang capital in China. Both China and Korea spoke of a "younger brother/older brother" relationship between the two countries.

Japan

China never conquered Japan, but Japan did accept China's cultural hegemony. Indeed, through the seventh and eighth centuries C.E. Japan actively and enthusiastically attempted to model its state, religion, technology, art, and language on those of China. As the Korean peninsula stands between the Chinese mainland and the four major islands of Japan, much of the importation of Chinese forms came to Japan through Korea.

Immigration and Cultural Influences. Although archaeological records show that Japan was populated by the Jomon people of the coastal regions at least as early as 10,000 B.C.E., rice agriculture seems to have begun only about 300 B.C.E., when it was introduced from south China. Bronze tools and weapons arrived about the first century B.C.E. and the technology for making iron tools about 200 years later.

Waves of immigrants from Korea and China arrived in Japan between *c.* 200 B.C.E. and *c.* 500 C.E. By 500 C.E., about one-third of Japan's nobility claimed Korean or Chinese descent, and many artisans and metal workers in Japan had come from Korea. All was not peaceful between Japan and Korea, however, and invasions and raids were launched from both sides. In this period, the Chinese represented the Japanese by an ideograph that signifies "dwarf," presumably suggesting an inferior status.

In 405 C.E., a Korean scribe named Wani traveled to Japan to teach the Chinese script. This became Japan's earliest written language, and Japan's recorded history begins only in the eighth century C.E. Most of our knowledge of these earlier years comes either from archaeological records or from references in the literatures of China and Korea. These archaeological and literary materials tell of the formation of an embryonic Japanese state about the third century C.E., when a clan of people worshiping the sun-goddess established their rule over the Yamato Plain in central Honshu Island. Ultimately, the imperial line of Japan claimed descent from this group. They used Chinese written characters and accepted elements of both Confucianism and Buddhism to

Asian imperial capitals. The Tang capital of Chang'an was grid-planned as a massive rectangle over 5 miles square, focusing on the imperial quarters and housing about a million people within its walls. The newly centralized Japanese Yamato state built Nara in imitation of Chang'an: a grid plan incorporated the Todaiji Temple complexes.

enrich the polytheistic practices of the indigenous religion, Shinto, and its deification of the Japanese emperor.

After China succeeded in re-establishing its own powerful empire under the Sui and Tang dynasties, Japanese rulers dispatched numerous delegations of hundreds of members each to China to learn and adopt Chinese models. The Chinese calendar and many methods of government were introduced. In 604 a new seventeen-point "constitution" was introduced, a guide that was modeled on Chinese practice. The document included reverence for Confucianism and Buddhism, for the sovereign of Japan, and, on a more mundane level, asserted the government's monopoly over the collection of taxes.

Officially, Japanese elites recognized the emperor as the head of Japan, but, in fact, he was little more than a figurehead; real power belonged to those behind the throne. Bloody struggles for control of the court in Japan brought Nakatomi no Kamatari to power in 645. He took the surname Fujiwara, and under this name his family dominated the politics of Japan for centuries to come. (One descendant, Prince Konoe Fumimaro, served as prime minister in 1937–9 and again in 1940–41.) Fujiwara adopted Chinese culture, religion, and government as the way to centralize and unify Japan and to assert his own control. He proclaimed the Taika ("great change") reforms in 646, consolidating provincial administration and constructing an extensive road system. The reforms also abolished private ownership of land and redistributed it at each generational change.

The Nandaimon, or "Great South Gate," of the Todai Buddhist temple, 745–752 C.E. The first Japanese Buddhist temples—modeled on the Buddhist temples of China—are among the oldest surviving timber buildings in the world. So faithful and enduring are they that they have become our best examples of *Chinese* architecture for the period.

In 710 two acts further consolidated centralized rule. First, a new capital, modeled on Chang'an, was built at Nara. Second, the Japanese ruler now claimed to rule through divine mandate, although, unlike the Chinese "Mandate of Heaven", it could never be revoked. (To this day, the same family occupies the imperial throne, although after World War II, its divinity was officially repudiated; see Chapter 19.) At about the same time, again following Chinese models, the Japanese began to record their history for the first time in the *Nihongi*, in Chinese, and their legends in the *Kojiki*, which was written in a mixture of Chinese and Japanese forms.

The emperor served as the chief priest of Japan's Shinto faith, but as Shinto is a religion that worships the gods of nature—streams, trees, rocks—it can be practiced anywhere. Buddhism, by contrast, provides a more centralized form of organization, through monasteries and temples. Many new Buddhist temples were, therefore, constructed in Chinese form at Nara to centralize worship in Japan. From this time onward Buddhism and Shinto have coexisted in Japan, with millions of Japanese declaring themselves devotees of both faiths.

As centuries passed and Japan became more secure in its own political organization and cultural identity, the reliance on Chinese models declined. But in the centuries when its basic cultural and political identity was formed, Japan had followed carefully and devotedly the hegemonic examples of China, without compulsion or force of any sort.

LEGACIES FOR THE FUTURE
WHAT DIFFERENCE DO THEY MAKE?

The Roman and Chinese Empires are among the greatest empires in history in terms of longevity, population, geographical extent, and lasting influence. A comparison between them will help to clarify the characteristics and significance of each and help establish guidelines for thinking about other empires of other times, and our own.

Differences

Not surprisingly, there are important differences between these two huge empires, separated by such great distances.

Geopolitical. China's heartland was far larger and more cohesive, geographically and culturally, than Rome's. Rome had as its heartland only central Italy, and even after conquering Italy, it held just that single peninsula bounded by the Alps Mountains and the Mediterranean Sea. In the time of Augustus in Rome and the Han dynasty in China, the Roman and Chinese empires each held about 60 million people, but in Rome only a few of these millions lived in Italy. In China virtually all inhabited "inner China." Ninety percent of them were in the north China plain.

Ideological. Although Confucian China spoke of a mythological golden age of equality among people living in harmony with each other and with nature, realistically the Confucianists believed that the best possible government was a well-ordered empire. Many philosophers and writers in imperial Rome, on the other hand, believed in an actual, historical republican past (albeit an idealized past) and always looked back to it as a golden age. Roman imperial expansion and stratification were often regarded as violations of the earlier republican ideals.

Longevity and Persistence. Rome's empire rose, fell, and disappeared, although it lived on as a concept. China's empire has lasted for the past 2000 years. Dynasties have come and gone, sometimes the empire has broken into fragments, and sometimes it has been ruled by conquering "barbarians," but finally the empire endured as a single political entity. Today, although there is no emperor, China's geopolitical unity continues.

Policy and Powers of Assimilation. As China moved both north and south, it assimilated a great number of the peoples it invaded and conquered. Non-ethnic Chinese were absorbed culturally and biologically. Many of the 95 percent of today's Chinese population who are called "Han" are descended from ancestors who were not. Confucian and Buddhist ideology held the empire together, supported by the power of the emperor and his armies. Rome's empire was held together by law and backed by military power. Selected non-Romans could gain citizenship under law, but ethnically and culturally the conquered peoples remained "other." Intermarriage with non-citizens was usually forbidden. Romans maintained the cultural distinctions between themselves and those they conquered far more than did the Chinese.

Language Policy. The Chinese language unified the Chinese Empire across space and through time—even today—far more than Latin did the Roman Empire. Chinese was never subordinated to another language and culture, as Latin was to Greek for many years and in many regions. Nor did Chinese compete with regional languages as Latin ultimately did. Indeed, Chinese helped to bring even neighboring countries—Vietnam, Korea, and Japan—together into a single general cultural unit.

Ideology and Cultural Cohesion. China's Confucian bureaucracy provided a core cultural identity throughout the empire and beyond. Even the alternative political-cultural philosophies of China, such as Daoism, Legalism, and later Buddhism, usually (but not always) served to broaden and augment the attraction of Confucianism. Rome's emperor worship did reinforce its cohesion, but its principal philosophies of polytheism, Stoicism, and, later, Christianity did not significantly buttress and augment its imperial rule. The latter two may even have diminished popular loyalty to the empire, except in its later continuation in the east as the Byzantine Empire.

Influence on Neighbors. The Roman Empire influenced the lands it conquered, but had less influence on those outside its boundaries. China exercised lasting hegemonic influence even on neighbors it did not conquer, such as Japan, or conquered only briefly, such as Korea. A considerable part of this legacy was religious and cultural as well as political, economic, and administrative.

Similarities

The many points of similarity between China and Rome reveal some basic truths about the nature of empires.

Relations with Barbarians. Both empires faced nomadic groups from central Asia who threatened and penetrated their boundaries. Indeed, the Huns, who invaded Europe, and the Xiongnu, who invaded China, may have belonged to the same ethnic group. Both empires settled the "barbarians" near their borders and enlisted them in their imperial armies. In both cases, the barbarians came to hold great power. Ultimately, however, they dismembered the Roman Empire, while the Chinese absorbed them.

Religious Policies. Both empires incubated foreign religions, especially in times of imperial disorder. In China, Buddhism was absorbed into Confucianism and Daoism and helped to sustain the national culture in times of political trouble. In Rome, however, Christianity did not save the empire. In fact, by challenging the significance of earthly power it may even have contributed to the empire's weakness.

The Role of the Emperor. Both empires ascribed divine attributes to the emperor, and both frequently had difficulty in establishing rules for imperial succession. The Romans often attempted to choose their best general, while the Chinese selected a man who could control the imperial family and court. Neither empire believed that a single imperial family should rule forever. The Chinese believed that eventually the Mandate of Heaven would pass from one dynasty to another.

Gender Relationships and the Family. The family was extremely important for both empires, and both empires subordinated women to men at all stages of life. Both drew analogies between hierarchies and loyalties in a well-run family and those in a well-run empire. Both empires used marriages as a means of confirming political alliances with foreign powers. Both periodically felt that excessive concern with sexual relationships distracted energy from the demands of sustaining the empire, and both proclaimed strict codes of sexual morality.

The Significance of Imperial Armies. In both empires the army was crucial in creating and sustaining the political structure in the face of domestic and foreign enemies. The Roman Empire was established and ruled by generals, as were the Qin, Han, Sui, and Tang dynasties in China. Both empires were periodically threatened and usurped by rebel generals asserting their own authority. The cost of the armies, especially on distant, unprofitable expeditions, often drained the finances of the government and encouraged its subjects to evade taxes and military service and even to rise in revolt. Both empires established colonies of soldier-colonizers to garrison and develop remote areas while simultaneously providing compensation and retirement benefits for the troops.

Overextension. Both empires suffered their greatest challenges in confronting simultaneously the strains of overexpansion and the subsequent internal revolts that were triggered by the costs. In Rome these dual problems, along with the barbarian invasions, finally precipitated the end of the empire in the west. In China they led to the loss of the Mandate of Heaven and the downfall of dynasties. The external battles against Qin-Jurchen border tribes, for example, combined with the revolt of the Yellow Turbans, brought down the later Han; the loss of the distant Battle of the Talas River, combined with the internal revolt of An Lushan, sapped Tang power.

Public Works Projects. Throughout their empire the Romans built roads, aqueducts, public monumental structures, administrative/military towns, and the great capital cities of Rome and Constantinople. The Chinese built the Great Wall, the Grand Canal, systems of transportation by road and water, public monumental structures, administrative/military towns throughout the empire, and several successive capitals, especially Chang'an and Luoyang.

The Concentration of Wealth. In both empires, the benefits of imperial wealth tended to flow toward the center and to the elites in the capital cities. The capitals grew to unprecedented size. Both Chang'an and Rome housed more than one million people.

Policies for and against Individual Mobility. To maintain power and stability in the face of demands for change, both empires periodically bound their peasantry to the soil and demanded that the sons of soldiers follow their fathers' occupations. Both found these policies difficult to enforce. Both offered some individual mobility through service in their armies. In addition, the Chinese examination system provided for advancement within the imperial bureaucracy.

Revolts. Both empires experienced frequent revolts against the emperor and his policies. In Rome, which housed a much larger slave population, slaves led some of the revolts. In China they were more typically initiated by peasants. Rome attempted to forestall mass revolts in the capital and other large cities through the provision of "bread and circuses." Both empires faced constant challenges from those living on their peripheries.

Peasant Flight. In both empires during times of upheaval, peasants sought to evade taxes and conscription by finding refuge as tenants on large, landed estates. Whenever imperial government was weak, the largest of these estates challenged the power of the central government.

The influence of the early Chinese Empire continues today, not only in China itself, but in east Asia, southeast Asia, and central Asia. Consistent patterns in language, culture, geopolitical organization, and international relations are there to be discovered through the ages. The same is true of Rome throughout the areas it ruled directly in western and southern Europe, the Mediterranean, and North Africa. To a lesser degree, its influence extends to eastern Europe and to the European settler colonies in the Americas, Australia, and New Zealand. The imperial ideals of China and Rome have entranced many who have studied them, and repelled many as well. As we turn to study the empires of ancient India, these models help to guide our thinking.

Review Questions

- Many kinds of standardization accompanied the creation and consolidation of empire in China. What were these forms of standardization, and which do you think were the most important?
- What were the three most prominent philosophies of rule in the Chinese Empire? They seem to have been applied under different circumstances. Under what circumstances do you think each was most appropriate? Why?
- What were the attitudes of Confucianism toward the role of women in society? How did these attitudes compare with those of other Chinese philosophies, and with philosophies from ancient Rome?
- Compare the policies of the Tang dynasty with those of the Han. You might consider the geographical extent of the empire under these dynasties, their administrative mechanisms, philosophies of government, and international relations.
- Why are Vietnam, Korea, and Japan often considered to be daughter civilizations of China?
- How did China regard the barbarians on its borders, in terms of international relations and in terms of assimilation? How did China's policies compare with those of Rome?

Suggested Readings

PRINCIPAL SOURCES

Blunden, Caroline and Mark Elvin. *Cultural Atlas of China* (New York: Facts on File, 1983). Excellent introductory coverage to history and culture, lavishly illustrated with maps, pictures. Excellent as both narrative and reference.

deBary, William Theodore and Irene Bloom, eds., *Sources of Chinese Tradition,* Vol. I: *From Earliest Times to 1600* (New York: Columbia University Press, 2nd ed., 1999). The premier primary source reference to the thought of the elites of ancient China.

Ebrey, Patricia Buckley, ed. *Chinese Civilization: A Sourcebook* (New York: The Free Press, 2nd ed., 1993). This primary sourcebook covers social and economic materials of everyday life of common people.

Elvin, Mark. *The Pattern of the Chinese Past* (Stanford, CA: Stanford University Press, 1973). Most Chinese history has been written dynasty-by-dynasty. Elvin seeks deeper patterns of change in the economy and social life. Introduces new approaches.

Twitchett, Denis and Michael Lowe, eds. *The Cambridge History of China,* Vol. I: *The Ch'in and Han Empires, 221 B.C.–A.D. 220* (Cambridge: Cambridge University Press, 1986). Comprehensive, standard compendium of analysis and narrative.

Twitchett, Denis, ed. *The Cambridge History of China,* Vol. III: *Sui and T'ang China, 589–906,* Part I (Cambridge: Cambridge University Press, 1979). Comprehensive, standard compendium of analysis and narrative.

Waley, Arthur, trans. *The Book of Songs* (New York: Grove Press, 1996). Marvellous collection by master translator.

Watson, Burton, trans. *The Selected Poems of Du Fu* (New York: Columbia University Press, 2002). An excellent selection and translation.

ADDITIONAL SOURCES

Andrea, Alfred and James H. Overfield, eds. *The Human Record:* Vol I (Boston, MA: Houghton Mifflin Co., 3rd ed., 1998). Excellent array of primary sources, arranged and cross-referenced to provide its comprehensive course of study.

Creel, H.G. *Confucius: The Man and the Myth* (Westport, CT: Greenwood Press, reprinted 1972 from 1949 ed.). Little is known about Confucius the man. This classic study tells us what we know and how it has been represented and interpreted.

Fairbank, John K., Edwin O. Reischauer, and Albert M. Craig. *East Asia: Tradition and Transformation* (Boston, MA: Houghton Mifflin, rev. ed., 1989). This is the standard history of the subject, updated from time to time.

Friedman, Edward. "Reconstructing China's National Identity: A Southern Alternative to Mao-Era Anti-Imperialist Nationalism," *Journal of Asian Studies* LIII, No. 1 (February 1994), 67–91. An analysis of continuing differences between China's southern, coastal, commercial regions, and its more bureaucratic and politically oriented interior and north.

Han Fei Tzu. *The Complete Works of Han Fei Tzu,* 2 vols. trans. W.K. Liao (London: Arthur Probsthain, 1959). The basis of the Legalist tradition.

Hughes, Sarah Shaver and Brady Hughes, ed. *Women in World History,* Vol. I (Armonk, NY: M.E. Sharpe, 1995). A reader with materials drawn from all over the world.

Lattimore, Owen. *Inner Asian Frontiers of China* (London: Oxford University Press, 1940). Classic statement of the relationship between China proper and the areas north and west of the Great Wall.

Lockard, Craig A. "Integrating Southeast Asia into the Framework of World History: The Period Before 1500," *The History Teacher* XXIX, No. 1 (November 1995), 7–35. Establishes a point-of-view for understanding southeast Asia as a part of the world. Designed for teaching, but widely useful for its range of subjects and their context.

Murphey, Rhoads. *East Asia: A New History* (Boston, MA: Addison-Wesley, 2nd ed., 2000). Standard textbook history.

Needham, Joseph. *The Shorter Science and Civilization in China,* Vol. I, abridged by Colin A. Ronan (Cambridge: Cambridge University Press, 1978). First volume in Needham's monumental work opening up the scientific accomplishments to an English-reading audience.

Past Worlds: The (London) Times Atlas of Archaeology (Maplewood, NJ: Hammond, 1988). Excellent introduction to the entire subject, including archaeology of ancient China. Lavishly illustrated with maps, pictures, charts.

SarDesai, D.R. *Southeast Asia: Past and Present* (Boulder, CO: Westview Press, 4th ed., 1997).

Schirokauer, Conrad. *A Brief History of Chinese and Japanese Civilizations* (Fort Worth: Harcourt Brace Jovanovich, 2nd ed., 1989).

Schwartz, Benjamin I. *The World of Thought in Ancient China* (Cambridge, MA: Harvard University Press, 1985). Fine analysis of philosophies and policies in ancient Chinese thought and politics.

Seth, Vikram. *Three Chinese Poets: Translations of Poems by Wang Wei, Li Bai, and Du Fu* (New York: HarperCollins, 1993). Translations of classical poetry of classical poets. The insistence on rhyme is sometimes monotonous.

Sima Qian. *Historical Records*, trans. Raymond Dawson (New York: Oxford University Press, 1994). Translation from the works of China's pre-eminent dynastic historian. Clear, readable with introduction to and evaluation of the historian's life and work.

Sima Qian. *Records of the Historian: Chapters from the Shih Chi of Ssu-ma Ch'ien*, trans. Burton Watson (New York: Columbia University Press, 1969). Translation from the works of China's pre-eminent dynastic historian. Places the work in the context of Chinese history and literature.

Sullivan, Michael. *The Arts of China* (Berkeley, CA: University of California Press, 4th ed., rev. 2000). Well illustrated introduction to classical Chinese painting, sculpture, and fine arts.

Sun Tzu [Sunzi]. *The Art of War*, trans. Thomas Cleary (Boston, MA: Shambhala, 1988). Accessible translation of the classic treatise on fighting a war, often through not fighting. A Zen approach. Consulted by Chinese strategists, including Mao.

Waley, Arthur, trans. *Chinese Poems* (New York: Dover, 2000). Marvellous collection by a master translator.

◉ World History Documents CD-ROM

2.7 Sima Qian: The Historian's Historian Writes About the Builder of the Great Wall
2.8 Shi Huang Ti of Qin: A Study in Absolutism
9.1 The Tang Dynasty (618–907): The Art of Government
9.2 Sung (Song) China: Imperial Examination System
9.3 Record of Ancient Matters: Futo No Yasumaro
9.4 Prince Shotoku's Seventeen-Article Constitution
9.5 Pilgrimage to China (840): Ennin
9.6 Thai Civilization: Southeast Asia

INDIAN EMPIRES

CULTURAL COHESION IN A DIVIDED
SUBCONTINENT 1500 B.C.E.–1100 C.E.

KEY TOPICS
- New Arrivals in South Asia
- The Empires of India
- Invasions End the Age of Empires
- India, China, and Rome: Empires and Intermediate Institutions

What do we mean by "India"? In this chapter we include the entire subcontinent of south Asia, which includes not only the present-day country of India, but also its neighbors: Pakistan, Bangladesh, Nepal, and Bhutan. Geographers call the entire region a subcontinent because it is so large and so clearly bounded by powerful natural borders. Along its entire southern perimeter it is a peninsula surrounded by oceanic waters: the Arabian Sea to the west and the Bay of Bengal to the east. To the north, the Himalaya Mountains, the highest in the world, form an almost impenetrable barrier. At the eastern and western ends of the Himalayas, rugged spurs of the great range complete the ring of demarcation, but these mountains are lower and more negotiable. Passes such as the Khyber Pass make entrance accessible through the northwest mountains, as does a route through the desert along the western Makran coast.

The peoples who came to India before 3000 B.C.E., for whom we have no historical record, seem to have arrived from a variety of approaches, probably including some by sea voyages from Africa, southeast Asia, and the islands of the Pacific. Since 3000 B.C.E., all the major immigrations have come from the northwest. In modern times British traders and rulers also came by sea (see Chapters 13 and 16). They had an important impact on the subcontinent, but they did not stay.

The geographical area of the subcontinent is equal to about one-fourth the size of Europe. The entire region has been unified into a single empire only once, under British rule in the nineteenth and early twentieth centuries. Asoka Maurya (r. *c.* 265–238 B.C.E.) was the first person to come close to achieving that goal, but he never captured the far south. Usually, as today, a number of rulers controlled different regions of the subcontinent. It is not surprising, then, that Indian empires did not last more than a few hundred years. Yet unlike Rome, and much more like China, India has maintained a persistent cultural unity over several thousand years. In this chapter we will begin to consider why India dissolved politically into many separate states, and in Chapter 9 we will consider the religious and cultural institutions that nevertheless served to bring a loose unity to the subcontinent. We will consider India as an empire based as much on cultural cohesion as on political and military unity.

NEW ARRIVALS IN SOUTH ASIA

In Chapter 3 we read of the civilization of the Indus valley, which began with the appearance of the first cities in south Asia about 2500 B.C.E. That civilization—the Harappan—began to fade about 1500 B.C.E. for reasons that are not entirely understood. Perhaps simultaneously, perhaps somewhat later, new waves of "Aryan" immigrants arrived.

Opposite **Prince Gautama, Ajanta Cave 1, Maharashtra, India,** *c.* **450–500.** The prince is seated within an ornamental pavilion. Servants are pouring holy water over him.

Indo-Aryan A sub-group of the Indo-Iranian branch of the Indo-European group of languages, also called Indic and spoken in India, Sri Lanka, Bangladesh, and Pakistan. The Indo-Aryan languages descend from Sanskrit, the sacred language of Hinduism.

The Spread of Aryan Settlement

These new arrivals are named not for their race, but for Sanskrit and the other related **Indo-Aryan** languages they spoke. Archaeologists are not certain of the geographical origins of the new arrivals; some claim they came from central Asia, others from the Iranian plateau, while a few suggest Europe. In successive waves of immigration, the nomadic and pastoral Aryans, riding the horses of central Asia and light, spoke-wheeled chariots, mixed with indigenous peoples, migrated slowly eastward, and reached the Ganges valley about the year 1000 B.C.E.

Written Texts

The greatest sources of information for the Aryan immigrations, settlements, and empires are written materials that preserve earlier oral traditions. A special group of bards and chroniclers collected and composed these materials, although they did not attempt to establish a direct chronological, interpretive record of the sort found in Greece or Rome, or in China.

The Vedas. The earliest existing source is one of the four Vedas, the *Rigveda*, 1028 hymns composed in Sanskrit about 1500–1200 B.C.E. at the very time the Aryans were moving into the subcontinent. The Vedas are religious reflections rather than historical accounts, but to the extent that they refer to the life of the Aryan peoples who wrote them, their accounts are probably reliable. They do refer to conquests made by the Aryans in the course of their migrations southward and eastward. Three other Vedas, the *Samaveda*, *Yajurveda*, and *Atharva Veda*, were composed some centuries later. Other religious literature of the Vedic period (1500–500 B.C.E.) include the Brahmanas, which give instructions on rituals and sacrifices, and the Upanishads, which are mystical speculations. These were composed *c.* 700 B.C.E. and afterwards.

The Puranas, or legends and folk tales from earliest times, were finally collected and written down between *c.* 500 B.C.E. and 500 C.E. They contain genealogical lists of rulers from before the first humans were born until historic times, mixing fact and

HOW DO WE KNOW?

Pottery and Philology

Archaeology can tell us comparatively little about the Aryan way of life in the Ganges valley. The valley is a humid, subtropical region, where heavy monsoon rains have not allowed ancient settlements to endure. It is also densely inhabited, making archaeological excavation difficult if not impossible. As a result, we know less about the Aryan settlements along the Ganges than we do about the earlier Indus valley, where the sparsely populated desert sites facilitated relatively easy excavation.

The distribution of pottery—painted grayware dating primarily before 500 B.C.E., and northern black polished ware from after that date—helps us to identify and follow the waves of Aryan

immigration into the Ganges valley. The more recently discovered ocher-colored pottery in the western Ganges valley and the presence of black and red ware further east suggest that by the time the Aryans arrived indigenous peoples had already settled on the land. Since the late 1970s archaeological digs have uncovered small settlement sites dating from 1000–600 B.C.E. throughout the Ganges valley. However, it is difficult to trace in any detail the spread and nature of early Aryan civilization without additional excavations of many other cities and small towns.

Philology helps to establish the dispersion of Indo-Aryan peoples by tracking the spread of their languages. The first known surviving specimens of writing in the Ganges valley are Asoka's rock and

pillar inscriptions in Brahmi script, which date to the third century B.C.E. To track the oral transmission patterns of earlier centuries, anthropologists study texts that recorded them in written form at a much later time, and compare them with the distribution and evolution of today's spoken languages.

- Why is there more archaeological evidence about the Indus valley than the Ganges valley?
- What is the evidence that indigenous peoples preceded the Aryans in the Ganges valley?
- How do the study of pottery and philology complement each other in an analysis of early settlements in the Ganges valley?

fable, human and divine, and making no attempt to distinguish between them. The tales of the Puranas bring the gods of the Aryans into the popular imagination of the multitudes.

The *Mahabharata* and the *Ramayana*. India's two great epics, the *Mahabharata* and the *Ramayana*, recount events that took place between 1000 and 700 B.C.E., although the texts themselves place the action in earlier mythic times. Neither is an historical account, but both provide valuable information on the social structures, the ways of life, and the values of the time in which they were written.

The *Mahabharata* is the longest single poem in the world, some ten times longer than the Bible. Its central story is of a great civil war fought between two branches of the same family. Into its tales, subplots, and asides are woven myth, speculation, folklore, moral teaching, and political reflection that are central to India's living culture. The intermingling of the great themes of life, death, family, warfare, duty, and power give the *Mahabharata* continuing universal appeal. The most famous single segment of the *Mahabharata* is the profound religious meditation and instruction called the *Bhagavad-Gita*, or "Song of God". The *Gita* takes the form of advice given

AT A GLANCE : INDIA

DATE	POLITICAL	RELIGION AND CULTURE	SOCIAL DEVELOPMENT
600 B.C.E.	■ *Janapadas* established		
500 B.C.E.	■ Gandhara and Sind held by Persian Empire (*c.* 518) ■ *Maha-janapadas* established (500–400)	■ Buddha, Siddhartha Gautama (*c.* 563–483) ■ Puranas written (*c.* 500 B.C.E.–500 C.E.) ■ Vedic period ends (1500–500)	
400 B.C.E.	■ Nanda dynasty in Magadha (*c.* 364–324)		
300 B.C.E.	■ Alexander the Great in south Asia (327–325) ■ Chandragupta Maurya (*c.* 321–*c.* 297) founds Mauryan dynasty (324–185) in Magadha ■ Kautilya wrote *Artha–sastra* (*c.* 300)	■ *Mahabharata* and *Ramayana* (*c.* 300 B.C.E.–300 C.E.)	
250 B.C.E.	■ Bindusara Maurya (*c.* 297–*c.* 272) ■ Asoka Maurya (*c.* 265–238)	■ Rock inscriptions of Asoka ■ Asoka enhances spread of Buddhism ■ Asokan lion column (see p. 250)	■ Mauryan empire extended from Afghanistan to Bay of Bengal to Deccan
200 B.C.E.	■ Sunga dynasty (185–173) ■ Mauryan Empire fractures, along with unity of India (185)	■ Jain influence increases	
150 B.C.E.	■ Menander (Milanda) king of Indo–Greek Empire (*c.* 160–135)	■ Sanchi stupa (p. 288)	■ Trade contacts with S.E. Asia
100 B.C.E.	■ First Shaka king in western India (*c.* 94)	■ Sangam poetry from Tamil culture	
50 C.E.	■ Height of Kushana power under Emperor Kanishka (*c.* 78–*c.* 103)	■ Bhagavad-Gita	
100 C.E.		■ Gandhara Buddha (p. 251) ■ Rise of Mahayana Buddhism	■ Trade flourishes between India and the Central Asian trade routes
200 C.E.		■ Beginning of Hindu–Buddhist influence on southeast Asia	

AT A GLANCE : INDIA (continued)

DATE	POLITICAL	RELIGION AND CULTURE	SOCIAL DEVELOPMENT
300 C.E.	■ Gupta Empire (c. 320–540) established by Chandra Gupta (320–c. 330)	■ Sanskrit used for official business ■ Hindu ascendancy over Buddhism	■ Indian trade contacts with Oc Eo, Funan (300–600)
350 C.E.	■ Samudra Gupta (c. 330–c. 380) expands dynasty throughout north and into south		
400 C.E.	■ Chandra Gupta II (c. 380–c. 415) expands empire to maximum ■ Kumara Gupta (c. 415–455)	■ Cultural "golden age" ■ Panini, Sanskrit grammarian (fl. 400) ■ Faxian, Buddhist pilgrim ■ Ajanta caves (c. 5th–8th C.) (pp. 253, 289)	
450 C.E.	■ Skanda Gupta (455–467) repulses Huna invasion from central Asia (c. 460) ■ Budha Gupta (467–497)	■ Kalidasa composes "Meghaduta" and Shakuntala	■ Sanskrit in S.E. Asia; Indian gods; Buddhism
500 C.E.	■ Hunas gain control of north India	■ Classical urban culture declines	
600 C.E.	■ Pallavas rise to power at Kanchipuram under Mahendravarman I (c. 600–c. 611) ■ Harsha-vardhana (606–647) rules north India from Kanauj ■ Chalukyas rule central India under Pulakeshin II at Badami (608–642)	■ Xuanzang, Buddhist pilgrim	
700 C.E.	■ Arabs conquer Sind (712)	■ Ellora temple complex (p. 283) (757–790) ■ Borobudur, Java (p. 258) (778–824) ■ Khajuraho temple complex (p. 282) (1025–1050) ■ Vedantic philosophy flourishes ■ Angkor Wat, Cambodia (p. 259)	
1100 C.E.	■ Cholas defeat Srivijaya Empire, Sumatra		

to a warrior facing battle, but it expands into professional advice on life, death, and rebirth.

The *Ramayana*, which is much shorter, refers to somewhat later times, and there are many versions. The first known written version in Sanskrit was composed by Valmiki about 700 B.C.E. Its core story tells of the mythical god-king Rama's victory over Ravana, the demon king of Sri Lanka, who had kidnapped his wife, Sita. The diverse versions of the *Ramayana* indicate its great popularity and the variety of its uses. Some focus on the battles between north and south, perhaps a reference to the first Aryan invasions of the south about 800 B.C.E. Some southern versions, however, tend to justify Ravana as defending the south against Rama's invasions from the north. The role of Sita is also told in different ways. Men more frequently praise Sita for her adoration of Rama and her willingness to renounce even her life so that his reputation might remain intact. Women, however, are often critical of Rama for inadequately defending Sita in the first place, then for doubting her fidelity to him during her captivity in Sri Lanka, and, finally, for bowing to public skepticism of her loyalty by exiling her from his royal court.

Indian sailors, merchants, and priests carried their culture to southeast Asia, and the *Ramayana* has become a national epic in several of the countries of that region, especially in Thailand and Indonesia, where it is often dramatized by live actors and through puppetry. In India, the story is retold each year on the holiday of Dussehra, which celebrates the victory of good over evil with great color and pageantry. Broadcast on Indian national television in serialized form for about a year each, the *Mahabharata* and the *Ramayana* drew audiences of hundreds of millions for each weekly episode in the mid-1980s. In this way, modern technology keeps alive and vital the ancient literature of India in tens of millions of eagerly receptive homes. The epics live on in the West also. In 1985 the British theatrical producer Peter Brook staged a nine-hour version of the *Mahabharata* in English and French.

Despite these literary sources and their implicit evidence of major political and social change, there are no purely historical written records for these crucial centuries in Indian history. Gradually, however, other records do begin to appear and cast light on the changes that were taking place. Codes of law and statecraft, such as the *Artha-sastra* from around 300 B.C.E., and Asoka's rock inscriptions about a half-century later illuminate politics and imperial ideology. Many more such codes appeared in later times, together with Buddhist and Jain texts that usually include chronologies and some interpretation.

Visitors from outside also give periodic "snapshot" accounts of India. These include the observations by Megasthenes (*c.* 350–*c.* 290 B.C.E.), a Greek ambassador and historian sent to the court of Chandragupta Maurya about 300 B.C.E., and Menander (Milinda; *fl.* 160–135 B.C.E.), a Greek king of northwest India who became a Buddhist. Later, about 400–700 C.E., Faxian (Fa-hsien; *fl.* 399–414 C.E.) and Xuanzang (Hsuan-tsang; 602–664 C.E.), Buddhist pilgrims from China, recorded further observations. The travelers' reflections echo their own positions and interests, but in general depict a prosperous country. The earliest of the four visitors, Megasthenes appears to have been most interested in India's geography and history, one that combines many myths with the actual accomplishments of Alexander and Indian forces. He was also fascinated with India's caste system, which he believed to have included seven castes. Like all the travelers, he was impressed by the Indian

Ahmad Kashmiri, Mughal School, scene from the *Mahabharata*, 1598 C.E. In this illustrated manuscript, a Muslim painter depicts a scene from the great Hindu epic. The god Agni is shown creating fire as a smokescreen to assist his father-in-law, while Arjun quells the flames with magic arrows that release springs of water. (*Oriental & India Office, London*)

Indian School, scene from the *Ramayana*, 1713 C.E. This painting from the *Ramayana* is remarkable for its exquisitely rich gouache illustration. Among the heroes depicted are Rama, his faithful wife Sita, his loyal brother Laxman, and the army of monkey warriors who accompany him in his battle against Ravana, the Lord of Lanka. (*Oriental & India Office, London*)

janapada A large political district in India, beginning about 700 B.C.E.

government's respect for foreigners. Faxian, who came much later, was most interested in visiting places associated with the Buddha's life. He found India a country of rich and prosperous cities, where peace and order prevailed and the wealthy provided for the poor and the disadvantaged.

The Establishment of States

Both archaeological and written sources reveal that, as they settled in India, the Aryans began to build a new urban civilization and to form new states. By 700–600 B.C.E., numerous political groupings, called *janapadas* (populated territories), began to emerge. The leadership of the territories was centered in specific family lineage groups, and as these lineages grew larger and as they cleared more forest land to expand their territorial control, the *janapadas* began to take on the political forms of states with urban capitals and political administrations. Some constituted themselves as republics, others as monarchies. By 500–400 B.C.E., about the time the Persian armies of Darius reached the Indus, sixteen large *maha-janapadas* had emerged in northern India.

By about 300 B.C.E. four of these large states dominated the rest, and one, Magadha, was beginning to emerge as an imperial power over all. As we saw in Chapter 5, Alexander had reached the Indus in 326 B.C.E. and had wanted to continue his sweep all the way across the subcontinent to the ocean that he believed to be at the end of the world. His troops, however, mutinied, refused to proceed further, and forced Alexander to withdraw. Soon thereafter Chandragupta Maurya, the ruler of Magadha, marched his own troops from Magadha into northwest India to fill the power vacuum. With this triumph the Maurya dynasty began to carve out India's first empire.

THE EMPIRES OF INDIA

For the following fifteen centuries, comparatively brief but influential empires alternated with long periods of decentralized and often weak rule. India nevertheless retained a strong sense of cultural unity, based in large part on the intermediate familial, social, economic, and religious institutions that brought cohesion to both ancient and modern India.

In the following pages, therefore, we analyze not only the two major imperial dynasties of ancient India, the Mauryas and the Guptas, but also the more permanent institutions that mediated between the individual and the state. The religious philosophies and social practices of Hinduism that inspire much of the statecraft of these dynasties are discussed briefly here, and are treated much more fully in Chapter 9. Hinduism, as we shall see, is not a specific set of dogmas and rituals, but rather the variety of religious beliefs and practices of the peoples of India—excluding only those who explicitly reject them in favour of a different religion. This separation in the discussion of political and religious practices is somewhat artificial, but it allows us to recognize the importance of each system separately as well as to see them interacting in support of one another.

The Maurya Empire

The Maurya family dynasty succeeded to the throne of Magadha in 324 B.C.E. Its founder, Chandragupta Maurya (r. *c.* 321–*c.* 297 B.C.E.), may have first imagined an India-wide empire from a possible meeting with Alexander the Great, and he conquered much of northern India between 321 and 297 B.C.E. His son, Bindusara (r. *c.* 297–*c.* 272 B.C.E.), expanded still further the empire that his father had created, and Bindusara's son, Asoka (r. *c.* 265–238 B.C.E.), brought the empire of the Mauryas to its greatest extent, ruling from modern Afghanistan in the northwest to the Bay of Bengal in the east and well into the Deccan peninsula in the south. By this time India may have held as many as 100 million people.

Government under the Maurya Dynasty. The Maurya dynasty created an imperial government that ruled over or displaced earlier political structures based only on family lineage. Hereditary family lineage did not cease to be important—after all, the imperial ruling dynasty itself was a lineage—but a new state apparatus stood above it in authority and power. The *Mahabharata* told of a large family of cousins falling into intra-family war over issues of inheritance of power, but by the time of the Mauryas, the state stood above such individual families and lineages.

The new empire expressed its theory of politics in the *Artha-sastra*, or manual of politics and economics, which has been attributed to Kautilya, the minister of Chandragupta Maurya. (The date of composition is not certain, and the text may actually have been written down later, but its ideas were current under the Mauryas. The *Artha-sastra* text had been lost to historians and was rediscovered only in 1909.) The text spoke of *danda niti*, translated into English alternatively and provocatively as the "policy of the scepter" or the "policy of the big stick." It had a cut-throat view of inter-state competition. Even in the earlier age of the *janapadas* (smaller political groupings), Indian political thought had already

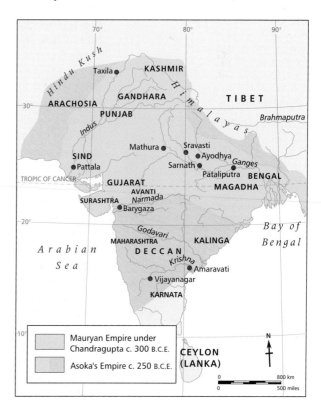

Mauryan India. A contemporary of Alexander the Great, Chandragupta Maurya seized control of the kingdom of Magadha and annexed lands to the west, eventually controlling by 300 B.C.E. the strategic trade routes of the Ganges and Indus basins. His grandson Asoka extended the empire west into Seleucid Persia, and south via the wealthy kingdom of Kalinga to gain control of the Deccan by 250.

expressed itself in terms of the "justice of the fish"—that is, larger states swallowed smaller ones. The *Artha-sastra* postulated that every state must be on constant guard against all its neighbors, for all were potential enemies. It counseled that strong states be hedged in through mutual treaties among their neighbors, providing a balance of power, while weak states should be attacked and conquered. The *Artha-sastra* regarded the immediate circle of neighbors as potential enemies but the next circle beyond them as potential allies, in keeping with the doctrine that the "enemy of my enemy is my friend." Kautilya's advice included suggestions for collecting taxes and encouraging trade. He was also obsessed with using spies. In this competitive world of constant warfare, the state had come into its own.

The state had many internal regulatory functions as well. First among these was the requirement to provide a powerful setting in which people had the opportunity to seek the four major goals of life in accord with Hindu philosophy: *artha* (wealth), *kama* (sensual pleasure), *dharma* (the fulfillment of social and religious duties), and *moksha* (the release from earthly existence and union with the infinite power of the universe, achieved, if at all, at the time of death).

The state helped to enforce rules of behavior between males and females. This relationship charged men with power over women and the responsibility for protecting them, while women were expected to run the household in accordance with the wishes of men and to be available for the pleasure of men. As the *Kama Sutra* explained, "By a girl, by a young woman, or even by an aged one, nothing must be done independently, even in her own house." Women's property rights were always very limited, and in some periods they had none. On the other hand, some professions, notably weaving, were open to women. Hindu views of women's proper role and behavior are discussed briefly on page 257.

The state also regulated the behavior of its subjects in terms of the rules of the caste. In Hindu belief each person has a social, economic, and ritual position, which was inherited at birth directly from his or her parents. Although this status may, in practice, be changed with difficulty, in theory it remains for life and on into future generations. Caste status not only governs private behavior, it also gives people different, unequal status under law. (The origins, rationale, and functions of the caste system as part of Hindu religious belief are discussed in detail on pages 257–8.) It was the task of the state to enforce these caste distinctions, especially their differential rankings, liabilities, and rights in legal proceedings.

The state also regulated religious establishments. The larger Hindu temples and Buddhist monasteries developed considerable economic and political power based on the land and resources that devout followers, especially wealthy landlords, businessmen, and often kings themselves, donated to them. They also influenced a wide range of public and private decisions made by their devotees, and the state attempted to regulate the use of this wealth and power.

guild A sworn association of people who gather for some common purpose, usually economic. In the towns of medieval Europe, guilds of craftsmen or merchants were formed in order to protect and further the members' professional interests and for mutual aid.

The state also enforced rules developed by India's **guilds**, associations of businessmen and producers. Closely associated with the *jati*, or subcastes, these mostly urban groups convened to set work rules, prices, and weights and measures, and to enforce quality control. Independent of the state, the guilds could nevertheless call on the state to enforce the regulations they had agreed upon.

Some students of Indian social structures have asked why the business guilds seem never to have attempted to gain direct control of the government in India as they did in medieval Europe. The answer is not entirely clear, but caste distinctions designated some people for government and military careers, and others for business, separating those who were permitted to take up the bow and the sword in using force to gain government control from those who could wield influence only through wealth. In Europe businessmen both armed themselves and hired troops; in India, it seems, they did

SOURCE

Asoka, India's Buddhist Emperor

Until just over a hundred years ago, little was known about Asoka, the Mauryan emperor who held sway over the bulk of the Indian subcontinent from 265 to 238 B.C.E. In the nineteenth century, however, inscriptions that Asoka had made on pillars and rocks to spread his name and ideals were deciphered, and for the first time in modern history Asoka's identity and teachings were understood.

Asoka had constructed at least seven pillar edicts and had inscribed at least fourteen major and numerous minor rock edicts which have been discovered and excavated across many regions of India. Most are written in Brahmi script and are the oldest existing writing in India. The script, although an early variant of Sanskrit, had been lost for centuries until a British official, James Prinsep, redeciphered it in 1837. He also analyzed the collective significance of the rock and pillar edicts discovered up to his time along with materials on Asoka found in early chronicles in Ceylon (modern-day Sri Lanka).

Asoka's famed conversion to Buddhism, a dramatic turning-point in his life, is described in the Thirteenth Major Rock Edict. The carnage he had created in his military victory at Kalinga and the suffering of his victims had left Asoka with a terrible sense of remorse. As reparation for his actions, he proclaimed his renunciation of violence and acceptance of Dhamma, the teachings of the Buddha that promote compassion, tolerance, and honesty.

A hundred and fifty thousand people were deported, a hundred thousand

Asoka, as depicted in a nineteenth-century engraving.

were killed and many times that number perished. Afterwards, now that Kalinga was annexed, the Beloved of the Gods [Asoka] very earnestly practiced *Dhamma*, desired *Dhamma*, and taught *Dhamma*. (Thapar, *Asoka*, p. 255)

He did not however renounce the conquest and annexation of Kalinga, and while he disavowed violence as a general principle, he seemed to retain it as an option of state policy, especially in dealing with the tribal people of the hills.

the Beloved of the Gods conciliates the forest tribes of his empire, but he warns them that he has power even in his remorse, and he asks them to

repent, lest they be killed. (Thapar, *Asoka*, p. 256)

To spread his message and promote a universal faith, Asoka dispatched missionaries throughout his empire and beyond. He also made his own journeys to practice Dhamma *and help alleviate suffering, especially in rural areas. The Sixth Major Rock Edict proclaims Asoka's dedication to public welfare:*

I consider that I must promote the welfare of the whole world, and hard work and the dispatch of business are the means of doing so. Indeed there is no better work than promoting the welfare of the whole world. And whatever may be my great deeds, I have done them in order to discharge my debt to all beings. (Thapar, *Asoka*, p. 253)

Projects implemented by Asoka to improve the welfare of his people included the founding of hospitals, the planting of medicinal plants and trees, and the building of some 84,000 stupas (Buddhist burial mounds) and monasteries. In his bid to create a more tolerant, compassionate society, Asoka granted religious groups outside of Buddhism the freedom to worship, but at the same time encouraged them to respect the beliefs and practices of other sects. The sacrificial use of animals was banned.

Asoka's active contribution to the spread of Buddhism had a lasting impact. His inscriptions offer us tangible evidence of the great influence Buddhism had not only on his own life but on Indian life and thought as a whole.

neither. They sought to influence the warrior classes, but not by taking up arms against them.

With so many responsibilities for regulating the interests of conflicting groups internally, and recognizing the need to remain constantly vigilant against powerful neighbors, Chandragupta Maurya and his son Bindusara attempted to build a highly centralized administration with a group of well-paid central ministers and bureaucrats, a powerful military, and an efficient system of spies dispersed throughout the empire.

Lion capital of the pillar erected by Asoka at Sarnath, Mauryan, c. 250 B.C.E. The polished sandstone columns erected by the Emperor Asoka at places associated with events in the Buddha's life, or marking pilgrim routes to holy places, are of special interest for their 7-foot-tall capitals. These provide us with the best remaining examples of Mauryan imperial art and are rich in symbolism. For instance, the Buddha was spoken of as a "lion" among spiritual preachers, whose sermon penetrated to all four corners of the world, just as the lion's roar established his authority in the forest.

Asoka, India's Buddhist Emperor. At first Asoka followed similar policies, and he was especially effective at enlarging the empire through military force, but nine years into his administration, he abruptly changed course. In 260 B.C.E. Asoka defeated Kalinga (now Orissa), incorporating this eastern kingdom into his empire. The killing and chaos required to win the victory soured his heart, and he determined to become a different person and a different ruler. He converted to Buddhism, a religion firmly committed to nonviolence, and began to dispatch missionaries throughout his realm as well as to parts of south India beyond his own borders, and to Syria, Greece, Egypt, and, probably, southeast Asia. He sent his own son on a mission to Sri Lanka and the island kingdom permanently converted to Buddhism.

For thirty years after the battle of Kalinga Asoka's reign brought general peace to India and the further expansion of a new, more universalist ethic for a people who were increasingly settling down from nomadism into stable agricultural and urban life. Buddhism, diminishing the importance of the brahmin castes, was especially attractive to merchant castes and guilds, and Asoka's patronage was apparently also good for business.

Successor States Divide the Empire. Following Asoka's death in 238 B.C.E., no emperor was strong enough to maintain centralized power, and the Mauryan Empire went into a half century of decline. One of his military commanders assassinated the last Maurya king in 184 B.C.E. The Mauryan dynasty came to an end, and with it the unity of India. The subcontinent subsequently divided among many regional rulers, including some rulers who invaded and seized control of large territories.

The Mauryas had always depended on the power of their lineage as the core of their rule, but they had not continued to produce emperors of the power and charisma of Chandragupta, Bindusara, and Asoka. The Maurya lineage had not institutionalized its state into a permanent form. India dissolved again into a variety of contesting states.

The Sunga dynasty, 185–173 B.C.E., ruled the core region that remained from Magadha. With Indian governments faltering, Indo-Greeks, the inheritors of Alexander's empire stationed in Afghanistan and Bactria, invaded in 182 B.C.E., capturing the northwest all the way south to the coastal cities of Gujarat. They produced a hybrid culture with the Indians they conquered. King Menander (*fl.* 160–135 B.C.E.), an Indo-Greek, carried on a profound conversation with the Buddhist monk Nagasena, who introduced the king to his religion. Their dialogue is still studied today as the *Questions of King Milinda.* Gandharan art, synthesizing Greek and Indian contributions, flourished in this period, as did the city of Taxila, the great center of trade, culture, and education in the northwest. Finally, large caches of Indo-Greek coinage reflect the importance of trade routes running through the northwest and linking India to the great silk routes of central Asia.

Indo-Greek coins (obverse and reverse), central Asia. The Indian subcontinent was linked to the silk route by trade routes that passsed through Afghanistan and the Kushan Empire and continued westward. These economic connections account for the large quantity of Indo-Greek coinage, like this example showing the Macedonian king Demetrius I (c. 337–283 B.C.E.). (*British Museum, London*)

"The Bimaran reliquary." Gandhara, first century C.E. The central figure of the Buddha is flanked by the Hindu gods Indra and Brahma. This mixed grouping reflects the crossroads nature of the Gandhara region, the border between today's Pakistan and Afghanistan.

New invaders conquered and displaced the old. In Chapter 7 we read of tribal wars in east Asia, on the borders of China, which pushed Mongol groups westward to Rome. The Shakas, who invaded and ruled parts of northwest and western India for about a century, c. 94 B.C.E. to c. 20 C.E., were one of these tribal groups. They, in turn, were displaced by yet another, larger nomadic tribal group from east Asia, known in India as the Kushanas. The geographical extent of Kushana rule is not entirely known, but it seems to have included today's Afghanistan, Pakistan, Kashmir, and India as far south as Gujarat and its ports. The most outstanding Kushana king, Kanishka (r. c. 78–c. 103 C.E.), seems also to have promoted Buddhism and may have adopted it himself. With a single ruler controlling all these lands, trade between the subcontinent and the central Asian silk routes flourished.

The Gupta Empire

In 320 C.E. a new dynasty began its rise to power in the Ganges valley, apparently through a fortunate marriage. The founder came from a dynasty of no historical fame, but he married a princess of the powerful Licchavi lineage. Reflecting a deep sense of history and a desire to gain legitimacy, he deliberately named himself after the founder of the Mauryan Empire and became Chandra Gupta I (r. 320–c. 330). His son, Samudra Gupta (r. c. 330–c. 380), earned a reputation as one of India's greatest military conquerors. The record of his battles, inscribed on an already existing Asoka pillar at Allahabad, touches all regions of India: the far south, the east to Bengal and even Assam, the north to Nepal, and the mountain kingdoms of central India, which had often remained independent because of their inaccessibility.

Samudra's son and successor, Chandra Gupta II (r. c. 380–c. 415), conquered the Shakas and annexed western India, including prosperous Gujarat and its Arabian Sea

Buddha of the "great wonders." Gandhara, third to fourth century C.E. The Hellenistic draping of the Buddha's clothing again represents the crossroads nature of the Gandhara region. The Buddha's right hand is raised in the *abhaya mudra,* or hand position expressing reassurance. His palm is marked with the Wheel of the Buddha's Doctrine of Enlightenment.

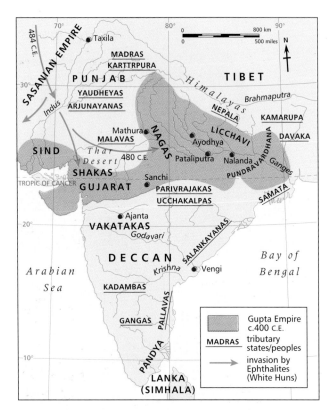

Gupta India. In the fourth century C.E. the indigenous Gupta dynasty gained control of the middle Ganges and rapidly built an empire straddling the subcontinent from Sind to the Ganges delta, augmented by a web of treaty and tributary arrangements with neighboring powers. This classical age of Indian civilization was destroyed by invasions of central Asian peoples in the fifth century.

ports, for the first time in five centuries. By marrying his daughter to the head of the Vakataka lineage, he cemented an alliance with his kingdom in central India. Other Gupta alliances were established through marriages with other powerful lineages in the Deccan. The fourth Gupta emperor, Kumara Gupta (r. *c.* 415–455), presided over a great empire now at peace.

Gupta rule was often indirect. Following many of their distant military victories, the Gupta emperors abdicated the tasks of administration and withdrew, demanding only tribute payments. Nor did their alliances with other kingdoms and lineages call for direct rule. In the Ganges valley heartland of the empire, the Gupta emperor himself appointed governors at provincial levels, and sometimes even at the district level. At the most local level of the village and the city, however, the Guptas allowed considerable independence to local administrators. The area they administered directly was much smaller than the Mauryan Empire, and the two centuries of Gupta rule and influence are considered India's "golden age" more for their cultural brilliance than for their political power.

A Golden Age of Learning. The Guptas presided over a resurgence of Sanskrit literature and Hindu philosophy. The great playwright Kalidasa (fifth century C.E.) composed two epic poems, a lyrical poem "Meghaduta," and the great drama *Shakuntala*, the first Sanskrit drama translated into a Western language in modern times. Much of the important literature that had been transmitted orally was now transcribed into writing, including the Purana stories of legend and myth. Further emendations were made to the great epics, the *Mahabharata* and *Ramayana*.

Plaque of musician with lyre, central India, fifth century C.E. During the Gupta period terra cotta plaques, such as this cross-legged lyre-player, were used to adorn the exterior of temples. It comes from one of the few surviving examples of free-standing brick temples decorated in this way at Bhitargaon in the Gupta heartland. (*British Museum, London*)

The Gupta Empire began to use Sanskrit for its official correspondence. The great grammarian Panini (*fl. c.* 400 B.C.E.) had fixed the essentials of Sanskrit grammar in his *Astadhyayi* (perhaps the most systematic grammar ever produced in any language), but the Mauryas and most other earlier rulers had used Prakrit, a variant of Sanskrit that was closer to the common language of the people. Now Sanskrit law codes, such as the *Laws of Manu*, and manuals of statecraft, such as Kautilya's *Artha-sastra*, were studied, revised, and further codified. Many locally powerful officials patronized scholars, humanists, and artists. Important academic centers for Buddhist learning flourished at Taxila in the northwest and Nalanda in the Ganges valley. Chinese Buddhist scholars visited and described these academies, although their descriptions of Hindu academies have not been preserved to the present.

The Resurgence of Hinduism. This was especially an age of the resurgence of Hindu religious authority, and major systems of Hindu philosophy were articulated. The most influential, Vedanta (the culmination, or end, of the Vedas), expanded upon the teachings of the Upanishads. Vedanta philosophy posed a powerful, attractive alternative vision to Buddhism, and Hinduism began to regain ascendancy over Buddhism in India.

Wall-painting illustrating the *Vishvantara Jataka*, Cave 17, Ajanta. Gupta period, fifth century C.E. The rock-cut sanctuaries of Ajanta in northwest Deccan were abandoned for centuries until they were rediscovered in 1817 by British soldiers hunting tigers. The twenty-nine cave temples contain some of the earliest surviving Indian painting and mark the last true flowering of Buddhist art in the subcontinent prior to the ascendancy of Hinduism. This erotic fresco, taken from a folk tale, portrays Prince Vishvantara informing his queen that he has been banished from his father's kingdom.

The caste system was elaborated and enforced in more detail. Rulers, high-level administrators, and wealthy landlords gave patronage to brahmins in the form of land grants and court positions. Brahmin priests also asserted their role in ritual performance. Buddhism, which had flourished through the patronage of earlier empires, and the support of business classes, ceded the performance of many of its own rituals to brahmin priests, and began to decline.

Despite its military and cultural achievements, the Gupta dynasty's power began to wane in the late fifth century C.E. The subcontinent was once again politically divided and subject to one wave of invader-rulers after another. These internal divisions and conquests by outsiders continued until the modern independence of India and Pakistan in 1947, and of Bangladesh in 1971.

INVASIONS END THE AGE OF EMPIRES

In the fifth century, new conquerors came through the passes of the northwest, over-throwing the Gupta Empire and establishing their own headquarters in Bamiyan, Afghanistan. These invaders were the Hunas, a branch of the Xiongnu, the nomadic Mongol tribes that roamed the regions north of the Great Wall of China and sometimes invaded. In previous expansions, they had driven other groups west, even into the Roman Empire, as we saw in Chapter 6. Domino fashion, these groups pushed one another westward. The Shakas had invaded India as a result of this sequence in about 94 B.C.E. The Kushanas followed about a century later. Now the Hunas themselves arrived in force. These same ethnic peoples were called Huns in the Roman Empire, which they invaded under Attila in 454 C.E.

The Hunas and their Legacy

Skanda Gupta (r. 455–467) repulsed the first Huna invasions, which occurred about 460 C.E. But the continuing Huna presence across India's northwest border seems to have disrupted international trade and reduced Gupta wealth. Skanda's successor apparently could not hold the empire together, and regional strongmen began to assert their independence. With central control thus weakened, Huna armies invaded again in about 500 C.E., and for the next half-century they fought in, and controlled much of, northern and central India.

From their capital in Bamiyan, Afghanistan, the Hunas ruled parts of India as their own imperial provinces. As in Rome, they earned a reputation for great cruelty, reported not only by Indians but also by Chinese and Greek travelers who visited the region. Huna rule proved brief, however. In 528 C.E. Indian regional princes drove them northwest as far as Kashmir. About a generation later Turkic and Persian armies defeated the main Huna concentrations in Bactria, removing them as a force in India.

Although it was short-lived, the Hunas' impact on India was considerable. Their invasion further weakened the Gupta Empire, enabling regional powers to dismember it and to declare their own independence. Except for a brief reign by Harshavardhana or Harsa (r. 606–647), king of the north Indian region of Kanauj, no further unification of all of India was ever seriously attempted from inside the subcontinent until the twentieth century. (The Moghul and British Empires, discussed in Chapters 14 and 16, were created by invasions from outside, although the Moghuls later settled within the subcontinent.)

The urban culture of north India dimmed. The Buddhist monasteries, which the Hunas attacked with especial force, never recovered. On the other hand, by opening up their invasion routes the Hunas indirectly enriched India's population pool.

Gurjaras and Rajputs entered western India more or less along with the Hunas and settled permanently. The modern Indian states of Gujarat and Rajasthan are named for them and their descendants.

The legacies of the Hunas in India—the destruction and dismemberment of the Gupta Empire, the reduction in inter-regional trade, the decline of culture, and the introduction of new nomadic groups into already settled imperial lands—quite closely mirror those of their Hun brothers in the Roman Empire. Even the timings were similar, products of the same emigration from central Asia. Of the great empires of the ancient world, only China was capable of defeating or assimilating these invaders without losing its own coherence and identity.

Regional Diversity and Power

The history of the Indian subcontinent tends to be written from the perspective of the Ganges valley as the center of political power and influence. (The settlements of the central Indus valley discussed in Chapter 3 did not endure, and the region is now a desert.) The Aryans established their centers in the Ganges region; the Mauryas continued the pattern; so did the Guptas; the later Moghuls established their capitals there; the British ultimately followed Moghul patterns by also placing their capital at Delhi; and today's government of independent India has followed suit. But other regions of India have always been important, too. Even at times when India has been unified, regional powers have regularly challenged the supremacy of the Ganges heartland. In periods such as the millennium from 500 C.E. to 1500 C.E., when India had no central empire, the outlying regions asserted their status as independent states.

The major regions of India speak different languages from one another, although imperial rulers have usually introduced a unifying link language for inter-regional communication: Prakrit under Asoka; Sanskrit under the Guptas; Persian under the Moghuls; and English under the British. Today, India uses two

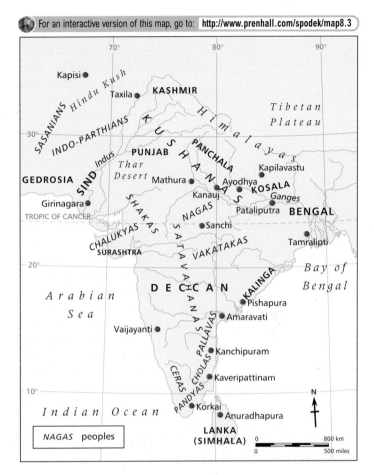

For an interactive version of this map, go to: **http://www.prenhall.com/spodek/map8.3**

Classical South Asia. As kingdoms rose and fell, India had no centralized empire for almost a thousand years. Local powers grew up, often based on different languages and ethnicities. More powerful groups occupied the richest lands, while the weaker were forced into the hills. The roots of today's separate states of India lie in some of these early ethnic kingdoms.

Earthenware sculpture, Nilgiri Hills, south India, early centuries c.e. The Tamil culture of southern India generated not only a separate language and an expressive literary tradition, but also distinctive artifacts. A buffalo cult among the Todas, the largest of the Nilgiri Hills tribal groups, led to the creation of this characterful figurine, made to decorate the lid of an urn containing ashes. (*British Museum, London*)

official languages, Hindi and English. Pakistan uses Urdu and English, and Bangladesh, Bengali.

The peoples of different regions have immigrated into the subcontinent from different places and at different times, some preceding the Aryans, others following them. In regions dominated by Aryans, many of these non-Aryans (people who spoke other languages) found a place within the social system of the Aryans. The highly stratified Aryan society—marked by caste and *jati*—could make room for the absorption of various groups by creating new categories for them within the hierarchy. When not consolidated into larger empires, these diverse groups have created their own political-cultural administrations. The peoples of Gujarat in the west and of Bengal and Orissa in the east have all seen themselves as distinct ethnic groups, even when they were ruled from the north, and as independent when that rule was broken. Regional dynasties came and went.

The indigenous tribal peoples whose immigration predates any historical records, referred to today as *"adivasis"*—that is, "original inhabitants," or **tribals**—generally inhabit less accessible areas, frequently in hilly tracts not easy to farm. They have attempted to protect their independence from outside exploitation by maintaining their inaccessibility.

The most distinct and separate region was the far south. Here, several lineage and ethnic groups fought to maintain their independence: the Pandyas in the extreme southeast; the Pallavas just north of them along the coast; and then the Cholas and the

tribals The aboriginal peoples of the Indian sub-continent, who are outside the **caste** system and live quite separately from the rest of society, generally in remote places.

SOURCE

Tamil Culture in Southeast India

The dominant language of the southeast was Tamil, and it developed an especially expressive literature. The poetry of the southern Tamilian academies, called sangam *poetry and written 100 B.C.E.– 250 C.E., set in counterpoint the private, bittersweet play of love against a public atmosphere of warfare and strife. This poetry was lost until scholars rediscovered it in the later decades of the nineteenth century. It has been brought to the attention of the English-speaking world especially by the efforts of the late A.K. Ramanujan.*

A King's Double Nature

His armies love massacre,
he loves war,

yet gifts
flow from him ceaselessly.

Come, dear singers,
let's go and see him in Naravu

where, on trees
no axe can fell,
fruits ripen, unharmed
by swarms of bees,
egg-shaped, ready
for the weary traveller
in the fields of steady, unfailing harvests;
where warriors with bows
that never tire of arrows
shiver
but stand austere
in the sea winds
mixed with the lit cloud
and the spray of seafoam.

There he is,
in the town of Naravu,
tender among tender women.

Harvest of War

Great king,

you shield your men from ruin,
so your victories, your greatness
are bywords.

Loose chariot wheels
lie about the battleground
with the long white tusks
of bull-elephants.

Flocks of male eagles
eat carrion
with their mates.

Headless bodies
dance about
before they fall
to the ground.

Blood glows,
like the sky before nightfall,
in the red center
of the battlefield.

Demons dance there.
And your kingdom
is an unfailing harvest
of victorious wars.

(trans. by A.K. Ramanujan, pp. 131, 115)

Coins and Excavations

About 50 C.E., a Greek merchant wrote of the Roman trade with Malabar, the southwest coast of India, in his great compendium of trade in the Indian Ocean, The Periplus of the Erythrean Sea:

They send large ships to the market-towns on account of the great quantity and bulk of pepper and [cinnamon]. There are imported here, in the first place, a great quantity of coin; topaz, thin clothing, not much; figured linens, antimony, coral, crude glass, copper, tin, lead, wine, not much, but as much as at Barygaza [the flourishing port of Gujarat, further north] ... There is exported pepper, which is produced in quantity in only one region near these markets ... Besides this there are exported great quantities of fine

pearls, ivory, silk cloth, spikenard from the Ganges, [cinnamon] from the places in the interior, transparent stones of all kinds, diamonds and sapphires, and tortoise shell. (cited in Kulke and Rothermund, p. 106)

Numerous hoards of Roman gold coins throughout south India provide archaeological evidence of trade between Rome and India. In 1945, the British archaeologist Sir Mortimer Wheeler discovered the remnants of a Roman trading post at Arikamedu, a fishing village adjacent to Chennai (formerly Madras), and he excavated the brick foundations of large halls and terraces, cisterns, fortifications, and ceramics that had been produced in Italy between 30 B.C.E. and 35 C.E. This outpost suggests that the traders actually

carrying the goods across the Arabian Sea were foreign rather than Indian: Arabs, Jews, and Romans. The Roman historian Pliny complained that Rome was sending around 50 million sesterces a year to India to buy its luxuries, although he also noted that they sold in Rome for one hundred times that amount.

- What seems to have been the main item exported from Europe to pay for Indian goods?
- Why was this pattern of exports disturbing to the Roman Pliny?
- Is it surprising to you that India's import-export trade with Rome was apparently not carried by Indians, but by Arabs, Jews, and Romans? Why or why not?

Chalukyas. Along the southwest coast, the Perumal and Cera lineages dominated. The place of their origin and the time of their immigration are not clearly known, but their languages form a linguistic family called Dravidian, not related to the Sanskritic family of languages of the north.

Sea Trade and Cultural Influence: From Rome to Southeast Asia

Imperial governments based inland in the Ganges valley and even further to the northwest tended to draw their economic power from their control over those rich lands and from trade through the mountain passes connecting to the silk routes. Many of the regional, coastal powers, on the other hand, traded by sea. This gave them wide-ranging external connections, from the Roman Empire in the west to southeast Asia in the east.

Under the Roman emperor Caesar Augustus (r. 27 B.C.E.–14 C.E.), Rome annexed Egypt, thereby opening up a trade route to the east by way of the Red Sea. Rome controlled enormous wealth, which generated a powerful economic demand for goods from Asia. Roman traders learned from the Arabs to sail with the southwest monsoon winds from the Red Sea to the west coast of India; about six months later they could sail back with the northeast monsoon.

Southeast Asia: "Greater India"

Some of the luxuries shipped to Rome were first brought to India from southeast Asia. Indian sailors traveled to all the coastal countries of modern southeast Asia: Myanmar (formerly Burma), Thailand, Cambodia, Vietnam, Malaysia, and Indonesia. To anchor this trade, they established settlements in port cities such as Oc Eo in Funan, in the southernmost part of modern Vietnam. Brahmin priests and Buddhist monks settled along with the traders, serving the Indian expatriates and attracting local converts at the same time.

Long before any of these trade ventures, in the third century B.C.E. King Asoka had dispatched missionaries to Sri Lanka and to Myanmar to begin the process of converting these lands to Buddhism. Local mythology and Chinese historical records tell (quite different) stories of the arrival of a brahmin priest named Kaundinya. As a result of his activities, Funan adopted Sanskrit as the language of the court and encouraged Hinduism.

Funan remained an independent state, not an Indian province. Indeed, in the third century C.E. Funan extended its own rule to southern Vietnam, Cambodia, central Thailand, northern Malaya, and southern Myanmar from its capital at Vyadhapura, near present-day Phnom Penh. Wherever Funan expanded, it encouraged the adoption of Indian culture.

Ironically, Funan later infused Indian culture even among those who conquered it. When Champa expanded southward into Funan lands, the kings of Champa began to adopt the cultural, linguistic, and architectural styles of the Pallavas of south India that were then current in Funan. Bhadravarman, a Champa king, built the first Champa temple to the Hindu god Shiva.

Two additional areas under Funan hegemony later established independent states with strong Hindu and Buddhist cultural elements: Java, which was ruled by the Sailendra lineage, and the kingdom of Srivijaya in Sumatra. In Java, the Sailendras built an extraordinary Buddhist temple at Borobudur in 778–824. When the Sailendras

Borobudur, Java, late eighth century.
This monument, the supreme example of Buddhist art in southeast Asia and Indonesia, is a fantastic microcosm, reproducing the universe as it was known and imagined in the Mahayana school of Buddhist theology. The relief sculptures, of which there are some 10 miles, represent the doctrine of karma, the cycle of birth and rebirth, of striving, and release from the Wheel of Life.

attacked the Khmer peoples of present-day Cambodia, the Khmers unified their defenses under King Jayavarman II (r. 790–850). He established a new capital and introduced Hindu temples and philosophies into the whole region around it at Angkor, which later became the location of one of Hinduism's greatest temples constructed by Jayavarman VII (r. 1181–1219).

The diffusion of Indian religious and cultural forms continued for centuries throughout southeast Asia. It proceeded almost entirely peacefully, spread by priests and traders. A few exceptions, however, stand out. The Pallava king Nandivarman III (r. c. 844–866) supported a military camp on the Isthmus of Siam to protect a group of south Indian merchants who were living and working there. The Chola king Rajendra I (r. 1014–47) dispatched a fleet to Sumatra and Malaya and defeated the Srivijaya Empire. It appears that his goal was to keep the trade routes open and to support India's shippers on the competitive sea lanes; he claimed no territory. In 1068–9, the Cholas apparently intervened in a dispute among rival claimants to rule in Malaya, conquered a large part of the region, but then turned it over to their local client.

Angkor Wat, Angkor, Cambodia, early twelfth century C.E. Dedicated to the Hindu god Vishnu, this huge, jungle-bound temple complex once served as the centerpiece of the Khmer Empire, originally founded in 880. Decorated with extensive relief sculpture, the temples of Angkor Wat were intended to emulate mountains in dressed stone.

INDIA, CHINA, AND ROME: EMPIRES AND INTERMEDIATE INSTITUTIONS

Chapter 7 ended with a comparison of the long-lived and far-flung Roman and Chinese empires. The following section extends that comparison to include the Indian empires. The comparison alerts us to the need to analyze empires not only from the top-down perspective of the central administration but also from the bottom-up—from their foundations in local regions and institutions.

Sources

Comparing India, China, and Rome is not straightforward. To begin with, India lacks the detailed political, military, economic, administrative, and personal records that would facilitate comparison in any detail. Rome and China compiled official histories, and a wide variety of personal accounts have also survived to the present. For India, on the other hand, we must often rely on the observations of foreign visitors for our best accounts. Even the life, writings, and policies of Asoka, now regarded as ancient India's greatest emperor, were lost from historical consciousness for centuries until his rock and pillar edicts were deciphered in the nineteenth century.

Administration

Second, both Rome and China built institutionalized bureaucracies and systems of administration, lasting for centuries in Rome and millennia in China. By contrast, India's states and empires generally seemed to be extensions of family lineages. Even the most powerful of ancient India's empires, the Mauryan and Gupta, were family holdings. Despite the administrative rigor suggested by Kautilya's *Artha-sastra*, even Chandragupta Maurya's dynasty began to weaken after the death of his grandson Asoka. In India, power remained more personal than institutional.

International Relations

The *Artha-sastra* characterized inter-state relations by the law of the fish, the large swallow the small: "When one king is weaker than the other, he should make peace with him. When he is stronger than the other, he should make war with him." Despite Asoka's renunciation of the excessive use of force, the constant rise and fall of kingdoms and small empires throughout India suggest that Kautilya's view generally prevailed. We do not have records of internal revolts against states and empires in India. Instead, dissidents would abscond to a neighboring state where they felt they could live more freely and where they might join the official military to fight against their former ruler.

Invasion of the Hunas

Indian empires did not expand beyond the borders of the subcontinent. Indian trade missions in southeast Asia exported cultural and religious innovations along with their material cargo, but they made little attempt to establish political rule there. On the other hand, outsiders frequently invaded the subcontinent.

Remarkably, the one political experience that the empires of India, Rome, and China shared was invasion and at least partial conquest by the Hunas (Huns, Xiongnu) and by the peoples they displaced. Indeed, the last three chapters point to the great importance of the Hunas/Huns in world history, especially from the third through the sixth centuries C.E. Historical records include not only the builders and sustainers of sedentary empire, but also their nomadic challengers. (We will explore this issue further in considering the Mongols in Chapters 12 and 14.)

Local Institutions and the State

In Rome and China, government touched much of the population directly, through taxes, military conscription, imperial service, and aggressive bureaucracies. The state was fundamental to all areas of life. In India, on the other hand, the state seemed to preside over a set of social institutions that had previously existed, were more deeply rooted, and were more persistent through time. These institutions included family lineages, aware and proud of their histories; caste groups, each presiding over its own occupational, ritual, and ethnic niche; guild associations, overseeing the conditions of economic production and distribution; local councils, providing government at the village and town level; and religious sects, which gave their members a sense of belonging, identity, and purpose. The state was important in overseeing the activities of all of these groups, but it existed only in the context of their existence. States and empires came and went, but these varied, pervasive institutions carried on in their own rhythms. In India political authority was intimately connected, and sometimes subordinated, to familial, cultural, and religious power. In the next chapters on religion in world history, and especially in Chapter 9 on Hinduism and Buddhism, we will explore these connections.

INDIAN EMPIRES
WHAT DIFFERENCE DO THEY MAKE?

Ancient Indian empires shed light both on the later history of India and on the structure of empires generally. Modern India is a direct descendant of its ancient empires and shares their diversity, their many languages and ethnic groups incorporated into the whole, their "unity in diversity." The ancient texts—philosophical, political, and epic—continue to provide a common cultural imagery to the majority of Indians today, and their influence extends to large parts of southeast Asia. Questions concerning the ethics of rule, answered quite differently by such practitioners of politics as Emperor Asoka and such political advisers as Kautilya, author of the *Artha-sastra*, continue to be debated. Most of all, the power of the subdivisions of empire—regions, castes, guilds, village organizations—retain their importance in modern India and in its south Asian neighbors as well.

The tensions between center and periphery, between centralized bureaucracy and regional interest groups, that mark all empires to some degree were—and are—especially prominent in India. While China and Rome draw most attention for their ability to build the central institutions of empire and impose them on their subjects, India teaches more lessons in imperial structures that integrate and balance already existing local forms of organization. This is more a matter of degree than of complete difference in philosophy of government: Asoka was willing to use brute force to conquer and subdue enemies of his empire even after his adoption of Buddhism; Rome and China were willing to accommodate local interests if they did not threaten imperial control. Nevertheless, more than Rome or China, India gives us an example of empire built up by integrating its constituent parts rather than by defeating them or completely assimilating them.

Because these patterns continue to re-appear in empires throughout history and around the globe, these early explorations of Rome, China, and India give us some of the tools we need to analyze the successes—and the failures—of imperial structures down to our own times.

Review Questions

- India is almost always described as "diverse." Why? What are the bases of its diversity?
- Modern historians sometimes complain that too much attention is paid to Aryans and not enough to other groups in early India. What are some of these other groups, and why do you think they may not receive adequate attention?
- Asoka has gained a reputation as perhaps the greatest of all Indian emperors. What do you think is the basis of that judgment?
- What were the most important consequences of the successful invasion of India by the Hunas?
- Discuss the overseas influences of India on the broader world from the time of the Emperor Asoka until about 1000 C.E.
- Compare the power of the Maurya and Gupta Empires in India with the Roman Empire and the Chinese Empire under the Qin and Han Dynasties.

Suggested Readings

PRINCIPAL SOURCES

Basham, A.L. *The Wonder That Was India* (New York: Grove Press, 1954). Graceful, comprehensive, standard introduction to early Indian history. Dated on Indus valley, but still valid on imperial India.

Embree, Ainslee, ed. and rev. *Sources of Indian Tradition*, Vol. I: *From the Beginning to 1800* (New York: Columbia University Press, 2nd ed., 1988). The principal source for materials on ancient India, especially on high culture, philosophy, and politics.

Kulke, Hersmann and Dietmar Rothermund. *A History of India* (Totowa, NJ: Barnes and Noble Books, 1986). Brief, accessible, excellent introductory history. Kulke brings his considerable expertise on ancient India to the section on empires.

Thapar, Romila. *Ancient Indian Social History* (New Delhi: Orient Longman, 1978). Principal introduction to the institutions of ancient India.

Thapar, Romila. *Asoka and the Decline of the Mauryas* (Delhi: Oxford University Press, 1963). Principal introduction to the empire of the Mauryas.

Thapar, Romila. *A History of India*, Vol. I (Baltimore, MD: Penguin Books, 1966). Principal general introduction to ancient Indian history.

Thapar, Romila. *Early India: From the Origins to A.D. 1300* (Berkeley, CA: University of California Press, 2003).

Thapar, Romila. *Interpreting Early India* (New York: Oxford University Press, 1992). Philosophy of studying ancient India, opposing the use of history to advance political programs.

ADDITIONAL SOURCES

Allchin, F.R., *et al. The Archaeology of Early Historic South Asia: The Emergence of Cities and States* (Cambridge: Cambridge University Press, 1995). Somewhat dated, but very accessible, wide ranging introduction for a non-specialist.

Craven, Roy C. *A Concise History of Indian Art* (New York: Oxford University Press, n.d.).

Green, Peter. *Alexander of Macedon, 356–323 B.C.* (Berkeley, CA: University of California Press, 1991). For Alexander at the threshold of India.

Hughes, Sarah Shaver and Brady Hughes, eds. *Women in World History*, Vol. I: *Readings from Prehistory to 1500* (Armonk, NY: M.E. Sharpe, 1995). Good readings on India.

Lockhard, Craig A. "Integrating Southeast Asia into the Framework of World History: The Period Before 1500," *The History Teacher* XXIX, No. 1 (November 1995), 7–35. Designed for preparing syllabi, with good conceptual scheme for understanding southeast Asia.

Hammond Atlas of World History (Maplewood, NJ: Hammond, 5th ed., 1999). Indispensable world history atlas.

Past Worlds: The (London) Times Atlas of Archaeology (Maplewood, NJ: Hammond, 1988). Fascinating introduction to history through archaeological finds. Lavishly illustrated with maps, pictures, charts.

Ramanujan, A.K., ed. and trans. *Poems of Love and War: From the Eight Anthologies and the Ten Long Poems of Classical Tamil* (New York: Columbia University Press, 1985). An outstanding modern poet and scholar translating classical Tamil poetry.

Richman, Paula, ed. *Many Ramayanas: The Diversity of a Narrative Tradition in South Asia*

(Berkeley, CA: University of California Press, 1991). The Ramayana has many interpretations and uses. Richman provides an astonishing, scholarly array of them.

Rowland, Benjamin. *The Art and Architecture of India: Buddhist/Hindu/Jain* (New York: Penguin Books, 1977). Still a useful introduction.

SarDesai, D.R. *Southeast Asia: Past and Present* (Boulder, CO: Westview Press, 1994). A standard introduction to an understudied field.

Schwartzberg, Joseph E., ed. *A Historical Atlas of South Asia* (Chicago, IL: University of Chicago Press, 1978). A scholarly, encyclopedic coverage of history through geography. Superb research tool.

Spodek, Howard and Doris Srinivasan, eds. *Urban Form and Meaning in South Asia: The Shaping of Cities from Prehistoric to Precolonial Times* (Washington D.C.: National Gallery of Art, 1993). Papers from an outstanding international scholarly seminar.

Thapar, Romila. *Cultural Pasts: Essays in Early Indian History* (New Delhi: Oxford University Press, 2000). Principal introduction to the institutions of ancient India.

Tharu, Susie and K. Lalita, eds. *Women Writing in India 600 B.C. to the Present*, Vol. I (New York: The Feminist Press, 1991). Beginning of the movement to include women's materials in the history of ancient India. Wide-ranging subjects.

⊙ World History Documents CD-ROM

3.7 "King Milinda": The Greek World's Incursion Into India

3.8 Fa-Hsien: A Chinese Perspective on Gupta India

Politics and Religion

Religions, the subject of our next unit, have at least two faces: the personal and the public. As a personal experience, religion is a search for meaning and purpose in the life of each individual. When whole societies seek meaning and purpose, however, the path can lead to the union of religion and politics. This union has existed through most of human history. The separation of religion and politics—the separation of Church and state—that we find in the United States and other modern nations, marks a turning point in world history. From earliest times, priests of religion and political rulers usually made common cause. Often high priest and ruling king would be united in a single person. We have seen examples in Gilgamesh of Mesopotamia, the pharaohs of ancient Egypt, and, at least in name, the emperors of Rome following Augustus Caesar. The authority and power of the ruler and of the priest reinforced one another.

Even in the ancient world, however, there were occasions when religious leaders would challenge and confront political rulers, accusing them of transgressing the will of god. Most notably, the Hebrew prophets confronted their kings with these accusations, as we will see in Chapter 10.

Religion reinforced the powers of legislation as well as those of administration. About 1750 B.C.E., when Hammurabi composed one of the earliest known legal codes, he did so in the name of the gods of Babylonia. The stele on which the code was inscribed is topped by a relief showing the god of justice, the sun-god Shamash, commissioning Hammurabi to write down his law code. The inscription itself opens with the words

> … lofty Anum, king of the Anunnaki,
> (and) Enlil, lord of heaven and earth …
> named me
> to promote the welfare of the people,
> me, Hammurabi, the devout, god-fearing prince,
> to cause justice to prevail in the land,
> to destroy the wicked and the evil,
> that the strong might not oppress the weak.
> (Pritchard, p. 164)

Hammurabi's Code, Susa, c. 1700 B.C.E. Diorite stele. (*Louvre, Paris*)

The stele itself was carried from Babylon to Susa apparently as a spoil of war about 1200 B.C.E., and in the winter of 1901–2 French archaeologists moved it to Paris.

Many subsequent legal codes were also said to be the word of god, delivered in person or through a supernatural presence. In the Jewish tradition, for example, Moses ascended Mount Sinai to receive directly from God the Ten Commandments engraved in stone, and, orally, the remainder of the earliest Jewish code of laws. As the biblical Book of Exodus describes the process, Moses became the ethical, legislative, executive, judicial, and inspirational leader of the Jewish people, largely through his constant contact with God. Moses' brother Aaron served as high priest, performing the ritual celebrations of the nation.

Michelangelo's famous sculpture of Moses descending Mount Sinai with the engraved tablets of the Ten Commandments in his hands captures this sense of merged religious and political authority. The commandments themselves are a mixture of religious rules—"Thou shalt have no other gods before me"—with civil laws—"Do not murder. Do not steal." But several of the commandments seem to lie somewhere between these two spaces, such as "Observe the Sabbath Day. Honor Thy Father and Thy Mother. Do not covet."

Christianity was transformed from an often-persecuted religion, mostly of the downtrodden, to the dominant religion of the Roman Empire by the conversion of the Emperor Constantine. Jesus' sermons, addressed primarily to the humble, meek, and poor, condemned the power of the wealthy and preached aloofness from political power. St. Paul, as he went on his missionary voyages to spread the new faith, often ran afoul of Roman authorities. Several emperors launched campaigns against the early Christians. But after Constantine accepted Christianity, in 313 C.E., formally converting on his deathbed, the Roman government began withdrawing its

Michelangelo Buonarroti, Moses, Tomb of Pope Julius II, Rome, 1513. Marble. (*San Pietro in Vincoli, Rome*)

support from pagan religious groups and transferring funds instead to Christian churches. With this imperial backing, Christianity soon triumphed over all the other religions contesting for recognition and followers to begin its reign as the dominant religion of Europe and, subsequently, the largest religious group in the world.

Islam merged political and religious authority even more fully. Muhammad was both the prophet of the message of God and the political commander of the *umma*, the international community of Muslim believers. Indeed, it was only after he assumed political leadership of the city-state of Medina, that Muhammad's teachings were recognized as authoritative. Until that time in his life, unsympathetic observers, seeing him enter a cave on a mountainside and return with tales of receiving truths—ultimately written down in the Quran—thought of Muhammad as somewhat deranged. Only after his successful political leadership was joined to his religious vision in Medina, and then after his return to Mecca as conqueror of that city, was he widely received as the final Prophet of God. From Muhammad's time onward, Islam saw religious law and political authority united in one institution headed by one person, the caliph. Not until the twentieth century did this union of religion and politics come under serious attack.

Hinduism, with its many deities, portrayed gods intervening in political and military activity on a regular basis. The most famous and best-loved Hindu religious text, the *Bhagavad-Gita*, tells of a civil war between two branches of the same family. The Lord Krishna serves as the chariot driver and military and spiritual guide to Arjuna, leader of the Pandava branch. As Arjuna despairs of a war in which either he dies or he kills members of his own family, Lord Krishna teaches him lessons to guide him to a deeper understanding of life and death.

On a more mundane level, earthly Hindu kings were in charge not only of the secular administration of their

Krishna instructs Arjuna, India, 10th century C.E.

realm, but also of the administration of temple estates, which could be quite large and quite wealthy, and of ensuring that the rules of social order, including the rules of caste hierarchy, were enforced. In effect, that meant that while brahmins might be the leading caste group in theory, it was only the supporting force of the king-rulers that secured their position in practice. In exchange for this royal support, brahmins were expected to endorse the kings' authority.

The Buddha, son of a king, left his father's palace to seek truths about life and suffering. His discoveries through meditation led him on a path that diverged from both the warrior-ideal of his family and the Hinduism of his youth. He became instead a great and compassionate teacher of many monk-disciples. His message became the basis of a major religion, only three centuries after his death, however, when it was adopted by King Asoka, ruler of India. When Asoka found that rule meant warfare, killing, and suffering, he found solace in the Buddha's message of nonviolent compassion toward all creatures. He tried to live this message himself, to the extent that it was consistent with the demands of government, and he spread it throughout his kingdom. According to tradition, he dispatched missionaries to give instruction in Buddhist ethics throughout east Asia, and sent his own son to spread the message to Sri Lanka. Within India, he erected numerous pillars and rock edicts inscribed with references to the influence of the Buddha's teaching on his own administration. Many later kings—and merchant-princes as well—followed Asoka's example in adopting Buddhism. They may have been attracted not only by its message of compassion, but also by its emphasis on equality among castes; this equality reduced the prestige of the brahmins and raised their own.

The next section will discuss the evolution of world religions in terms of their doctrines, organization, cultural contributions, and their impact on individuals. It will also point out the importance of the relationship between government and religion in the evolution of both.

Marble head of Constantine, Palazzo dei Conservatori, Rome, 313 C.E.

QUESTIONS

1. To what degree is the importance of religions related to their spiritual and ethical messages?
2. To what degree is the importance of religions related to their cultural contributions to the arts and the humanities?
3. To what degree is the importance of religions related to their alliances with political and economic institutions?

PART 4

The Rise of World Religions 2500 B.C.E. –1500 C.E.

NOT BY BREAD ALONE: RELIGION IN WORLD HISTORY

Religion is the sense of human relationship with the sacred, with forces in and beyond nature. Throughout history people have felt the need to establish such relationships with powers that they believed capable of protecting and supporting them and capable of providing a deeper sense of significance to life and the possibility of some form of existence after death. Some people have thought of these forces as abstract and remote; others have regarded them as having personalities, as gods. Some people, of course, do not believe in such powers at all, or they are skeptical.

Mircea Eliade (1907–86), perhaps the leading historian of religion in the mid- and late twentieth century, wrote:

> In the most archaic phases of culture, *to live as a human being* was in itself *a religious act*, since eating, sexual activity, and labor all had a sacramental value. Experience of the sacred is inherent in man's mode of being in the world.
>
> When we think of the sacred we must not limit it to divine figures. The sacred does not necessarily imply belief in God or gods or spirits … it is the experience of a reality and the source of an awareness of existing in the world … The sacred cannot be recognized "from outside." It is by means of internal experience that each individual will be able to recognize it in the religious acts of a Christian or a "primitive" man. (Eliade, *Ordeal by Labyrinth*, p. 154)

From the earliest human records we have encountered such religious needs. More than 100,000 years ago Neanderthals buried their dead in anticipation of their journey to an afterlife. Archaeologists have found Neanderthal burials with flint tools, food, and cooked meat at Teshik-Tash in Siberia; the burial of a man with a crippled right arm at the Shanidar cave in the Zagros Mountains of Iraq; and graves covered with red ocher powder, including some group burials, in France and central Europe. With the evolution to modern humans, far more elaborate burials appear. Perhaps the most extraordinary yet uncovered are at Sungir about 100 miles east of Moscow, in Russia. Dating back 32,000 years, the five skeletons uncovered there include one—apparently an adolescent boy—buried with about 5000 beads, 250 canine teeth of foxes, and carved ivory statues and pendants, and another—apparently an adolescent girl—with 5274 beads in addition to other objects.

Burial rituals—the formal recognition of our common mortality—suggest that the earliest humans thought about the significance of their lives. They hoped that life might

Stonehenge, Salisbury Plain, England, Neolithic period. Stonehenge was once believed to be a temple of Druids or Romans, but even its third phase, about 2000 B.C.E., preceded these groups in England.

continue in some form, even after death, and they must also have dedicated a part of their energies to transmitting values that would continue after they died and to creating institutions to perpetuate those values.

In Part 2 we saw that many early cities and states were dedicated to particular gods or goddesses, sometimes even carrying their names. Gilgamesh, builder of the city of Uruk in Mesopotamia, was two-thirds a god and sought eternal life. In Babylon, Hammurabi transmitted his legal code in the name of the god Shamash. Egyptian hymns proclaimed the divinity of the pharaohs. Chinese of the Shang dynasty used oracle bones to augur the will of transcendent powers. Athens was named for the goddess Athena.

The empires we discussed in Part 3 sought the validation provided by religious leaders and, in exchange, gave financial and political backing to religious institutions. The emperors of Rome and China served also as high-priests for their people. When the Roman emperor Constantine believed that he had been miraculously assisted by Jesus, he transferred his allegiance from paganism to the embattled Christian church. Hinduism and its caste system provided India with a sense of unity and continuity. In several states of south and southeast Asia, Buddhist priests were called upon to validate the authority of rulers. Confucianism, which was discussed in

Chapter 7 as one of the pillars of the Chinese imperial system, presents a profound theory of ethical human relationships. Unlike the religions just mentioned, however, Confucianism has very little otherworldly focus.

This part focuses in greater depth on the role of religion in human history. Chronologically, the part spans the entire period, from earliest humans to about 1500 C.E. Its key focus, however, is from c. 300 C.E. to c. 1200 C.E. In this period Hinduism became more fully defined and systematized throughout India; Buddhism rose to great importance in China, Japan, and southeast Asia; Judaism, exiled from its original home in Israel, spread with the exiles throughout much of west Asia, the Mediterranean basin, and northern Europe; Christianity grew into the great cultural system of Europe; and Islam radiated outward from the pivotal center of Afro-Eurasia to the far corners of the eastern hemisphere. These five religions often confronted one another, sometimes leading to syncretism, the borrowing and adaptation of ideas and practices; sometimes to competition; and sometimes to direct conflict.

HINDUISM AND BUDDHISM

THE SACRED SUBCONTINENT: THE SPREAD OF RELIGION IN INDIA AND BEYOND
1500 B.C.E.–1200 C.E.

KEY TOPICS
- Examining Religious Beliefs
- Hinduism
- Buddhism
- Comparing Hinduism and Buddhism

This chapter begins with a definition of religion and a description of early religious practices. It proceeds to a brief history of early Hinduism, the most ancient of existing major religions, and analyzes its evolution as the principal cultural system of the Indian subcontinent. Buddhism emerged out of Hinduism in India and spread throughout central, eastern, and southeastern Asia, defining much of the cultural and religious life of this vast region. Its history concludes this chapter.

EXAMINING RELIGIOUS BELIEFS

Organized religious groups usually build on the religious experiences proclaimed by their founders and early teachers. All five of the religions we study in this part grew from such experiences, and many of these experiences were called miraculous—that is, they are contrary to everyday experience, and they can be neither proved nor disproved. For example, most Hindus believe that gods have regularly intervened in human life, as Krishna is said to have done at the Battle of Kurukshetra. They also believe in the reincarnation of all living creatures, including gods. Buddhists believe in the revelation of the Four Noble Truths and the Eightfold Path to Siddhartha Gautama (the Buddha) under the bodhi (bo) tree at Bodh Gaya in northern India; most also believe that Siddhartha was a reborn soul of an earlier Buddha and would himself be born again. Most Jews have believed in special divine intervention in the lives of Abraham and his descendants, a special divine covenant with the Jewish people, and a revelation of divine law at Mount Sinai. Most Christians have believed in the miracle of Jesus' incarnation as the Son of God and his resurrection after death. Most Muslims believe that God revealed his teachings to Muhammad through the angel Gabriel.

Historians, however, cannot study miracles. Historical study seeks proof of events, and such proof is not usually available for miracles. Almost by definition, a belief in miracles is a matter of faith, not of proof. Moreover, history is the study of the regular processes of change over time, and miracles, again by definition, are one-time-only events, which stand outside and defy the normal processes of change.

What can be studied are the manifestations and effects of religious beliefs on people's behavior. Sincere believers in religious miracles restructure their lives accordingly, creating and joining religious organizations to spread the word about these miracles and about their own experiences with them. These new organizations formulate rules of membership, and they infuse their beliefs into everyday life by establishing sacred time, sacred space, sacred liturgy, and sacred literature and culture. Historically,

Opposite **Shiva with the corpse of the goddess Sati, southern India, 17th century. Bronze.** Lord Shiva, one of the most revered of all the gods of Hinduism, is usually portrayed in awe-inspiring forms because he is the god of destruction, but that destruction sets the stage for later rebirth and reconsruction. (*Trivandrum, Government Museum*)

when religious identity combined with political power, group boundaries became even more important, marking in-group from out-group, separating "us" from "them," sometimes even leading to violent conflict. Historians do study these manifestations and effects of religious beliefs:

- **The sanctification of time** Each religion creates its own sacred calendar, linking the present with the past by commemorating each year the key dates in the history of the religion and in the life of its community. It marks dates for the performance of special rituals, celebrations, fasts, and community assemblies. In addition to the community calendar, members of religious organizations create their own individual and family calendars to mark the rites of passage—the great life cycle events of birth, puberty, marriage, maturity, and death—so that each event has its own ritual observance. Religions especially formulate rules of marriage in an attempt to channel the raw, powerful, mysterious, and often indiscriminate forces of youthful sexuality to conform to the norms of the group.
- **The sanctification of space** Each religion creates its own sacred geography by establishing shrines where miraculous acts are said to have occurred; where saints had been born, flourished, or met their deaths; and where relics from the lives of holy people are preserved and venerated. The most sacred of these sites become centers of pilgrimage. As we have seen in earlier chapters, whole cities, and especially their sacred quarters, were dedicated to gods and goddesses, and thought to be under their special protection.
- **The sanctification of language and literature** Each religion shapes its own use of language, literature, and artistic imagery. The Hebrew Bible, the Greek New Testament, the Arabic Quran, the Sanskrit Veda and epics, and the Pali Buddhist Tripitaka have provided linguistic and literary canons across the millennia. In translation these texts have given character to new languages. For example, translations of the Bible by St. Jerome (c. 347–419), William Tyndale (c. 1494–1536), and Martin Luther (1483–1546) have enriched Latin, English, and German, respectively. The retelling in Hindi by Tulsidas (c. 1543–1623) of the Sanskrit Ramayana helped to establish the importance of that modern language in north India. This religious literature usually provides the core of religious liturgy and thus becomes part of the daily expression of faith of the common people. Part 4 quotes religious scriptures extensively because of their centrality to the world's languages, literatures, and imagery.
- **The sanctification of artistic and cultural creativity** Religious sensibilities often inspire specific creative efforts, and religious groups often encourage the creation of art and music to express and enhance their message.
- **The sanctification of family and ancestors** Many religions not only celebrate events of the life cycle, but they also link living generations to those that have gone before. Through prayers and periodic ritual performances such as visits to graves and shrines, current generations are informed that even ancestors who are no longer living still deserve, and require, respect and reverence. Ancestor remembrance and worship situate current life into a deeper historical context and may promote a more conservative outlook on life.
- **The creation of religious organization** As religion moves from individual experience to group membership, organization develops. At one extreme this may be a hierarchical structure with a single leader at the apex and an array of administrative and spiritual orders down to the most local level, the form of the Roman Catholic Church. At another extreme there may be no formal overall organization, and no formal set of rules and regulations, but instead a loose association of local communities related to one another through common beliefs and social structures, the form of Hinduism.

HINDUISM

Hinduism began before recorded time. The other major religions of the world claim the inspiration of a specific person or event—Abraham's covenant; the Buddha's enlightenment; Jesus' birth; Muhammad's revelation—but Hinduism emerged through the weaving together of many diverse, ancient religious traditions of India, some of which precede written records. Hinduism evolved from the experience of the peoples of India.

The Origins of Hinduism

Because Hinduism preserves a rich body of religious literature written in Sanskrit, the language of the Aryan invaders of 1700–1200 B.C.E., scholars believed until recently that Hinduism was a product of that invasion. Even the excavations at Mohenjo-Daro and Harappa, which uncovered a pre-Aryan civilization (see Chapter 3), did not at first alter these beliefs. But as excavation and analysis have continued, many scholars have come to believe that the Indus valley civilization may have contributed many of Hinduism's principal gods and ceremonies. Excavated statues seem to represent the

AT A GLANCE: HINDUISM AND BUDDHISM

DATE	POLITICAL/SOCIAL EVENTS	LITERARY/PHILOSOPHICAL EVENTS
1500 B.C.E.	■ Caste system	■ *Rigveda* (1500–1200)
900 B.C.E.		■ Brahmanas (900–500)
800 B.C.E.		■ Upanishads (800–500)
500 B.C.E.	■ Siddhartha Gautama (Buddha) (c. 563–483) ■ Mahavir (b. 540), Jain teacher	■ Buddha delivers sermon on the Four Noble Truths and the Noble Eightfold Path
300 B.C.E.		■ *Mahabharata* (c. 300 B.C.E.–300 C.E.) ■ *Ramayana* (c. 300 B.C.E.–300 C.E.)
200 B.C.E	■ Buddhism more widespread than Hinduism in India (until 200 C.E.); spreading in Sri Lanka ■ Mahayana Buddhism growing in popularity	
10 C.E	■ 4th general council of Buddhism codified Theravada doctrines ■ Buddhist missionaries in China (65 C.E.)	■ Nagarjuna (c. 50–150 C.E.), philosopher of Mahayana Buddhism
300 C.E	■ Spread of Hinduism to southeast Asia	
400 C.E.	■ Hindu pantheon established ■ Buddhism declining in India	■ Puranas written (400–1000) ■ Faxian's pilgrimage to India ■ Sanskrit; Hindu gods, temples, and priests in southeast Asia; Buddhism in southeast Asia
500 C.E.	■ Bhakti begun in south India ■ Buddhist monks to Japan	
600 C.E.	■ Buddhist monks to southeast Asia ■ Buddhism flourishes under Tang dynasty (618–907)	■ Xuanzang's pilgrimage to India
700 C.E.	■ Hindu temples and shrines begin to appear in India ■ Buddhism begins to decline in China ■ Buddhism becoming established in Japan	■ Hindu philosopher Shankaracharya (788–820) ■ Saicho (767–822), Japanese Buddhist priest ■ Kukai (774–835), Japanese Buddhist priest
800 C.E.	■ Hindu priests in southeast Asia ■ Emperor Wuzong attacks Buddhism in China	■ Earliest printed book (*The Diamond Sutra*) (868)
1000 C.E.	■ Muslim invasion of India (1000–1200) ■ Buddhist institutions close in India	■ Hindu philosopher Ramanuja (c. 1017–1137)

god Shiva (see p. 270), the sacred bull Nandi on which he rides, a man practicing yogic meditation, a sacred tree, and a mother goddess. Archaeologists increasingly argue that the invading Aryans absorbed religious beliefs and practices, along with secular culture, from the Indus valley and from other groups already living in India when they arrived.

Contemporary anthropological accounts support this idea that Hinduism is an amalgam of beliefs and practices. These accounts emphasize Hinduism's remarkable ability to absorb and assimilate tribal peoples and their gods. Today, about 100 million people, about 10 percent of India's population, are officially regarded as "tribals." These peoples were living in India before the arrival of the Aryans, and they have largely attempted to escape Aryan domination by retreating into remote hilly and forested regions, where they could preserve their own social systems. Hindus have, however, pursued them and their lands, building temples in and around tribal areas. These temples recognize tribal gods and incorporate them with the mainstream deities in an attempt to persuade the tribals to accept Hindu religious patterns. Indeed, one of Hinduism's most important gods, Krishna, the blue/black god, was apparently a tribal god who gained national recognition.

As India's peoples have been diverse, so its evolving religious system is diverse. The concept of "Hinduism" as a unified religion comes from outsiders. Greeks and Persians first encountering India spoke of India's belief systems and practices collectively as "Hinduism," that is, the ways of the peoples on the far side of the Indus River. When Muslims began to arrive in India, beginning in the eighth century C.E., they adopted the same terminology.

Hindu south Asia. Hinduism is the oldest of the world's leading religions, although its geographic range is confined to the peoples of south Asia. Here its impact has been profound, exemplified by the sacred geography of the subcontinent; rivers, mountains, and regions associated with divine mythology are important, and networks of pilgrimage centers and temples provide cultural unity.

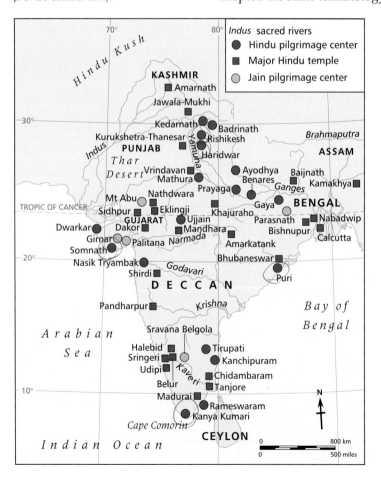

Sacred Geography and Pilgrimage

Hinduism is closely associated with a specific territory, India. Almost all Hindus live in India or are of Indian descent. Within India itself a sacred geography has developed. Places visited by gods and by saints, as well as places of great natural sanctity, have become shrines and pilgrim destinations. Pilgrims traveling these routes have created a geography of religious/national integration, and modern transportation, in the form of trains, buses, and airplanes, has increased the pilgrim traffic throughout India. Some of the most important shrines are at the far corners of India, such as Somnath on the far west coast, Haridwar and Rishikesh in the far north on the upper Ganges, Puri on the east coast, and Kanya Kumari (Cape Comorin) at the extreme southern tip. Travel to all of these shrines would thus provide the pilgrim with a "Bharat Darshan," a view of the entire geography of India. Such pilgrimage routes have helped to unify both Hinduism and India.

Each locality in city and village is also knit together by religious shrines, ranging from the simple prayer niche, containing pictures and statues of the gods of the kind found in even the most humble home; through neighborhood shrines, nestled perhaps into the trunk of an especially sacred tree; to local and regional temples.

CHRONOLOGY OF THE WORLD'S RELIGIOUS CULTURES

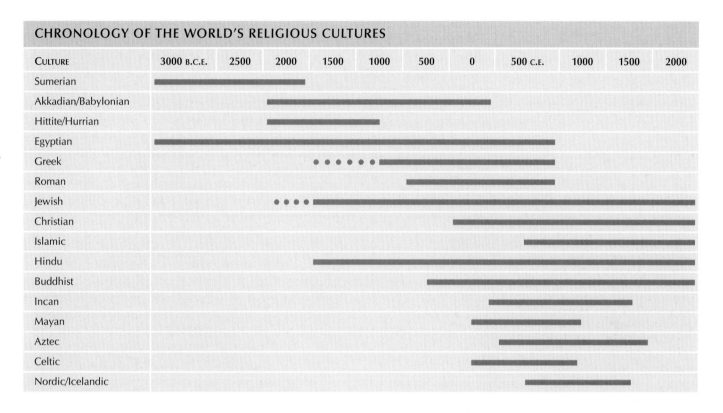

CULTURE	3000 B.C.E.	2500	2000	1500	1000	500	0	500 C.E.	1000	1500	2000
Sumerian											
Akkadian/Babylonian											
Hittite/Hurrian											
Egyptian											
Greek											
Roman											
Jewish											
Christian											
Islamic											
Hindu											
Buddhist											
Incan											
Mayan											
Aztec											
Celtic											
Nordic/Icelandic											

The Central Beliefs of Hinduism

Hinduism has none of the fixed dogmas of most other-worldly religions, and great flexibility and variety of beliefs exist under the general term "Hindu." Nevertheless, sacred texts do provide a set of beliefs and orientations toward life that are very widely shared. Over time, the introduction of new texts to the Hindu legacy marked the evolution of Hinduism as a living, changing system of beliefs and practices.

The *Rigveda*. Between *c.* 1500 and 1200 B.C.E. brahmin priests of the nomadic pastoralist Aryan peoples entering India composed the *Rigveda*, a collection of 1028 verses of Sanskrit poetry, the oldest and most venerated of the four books called, collectively, Vedas. These verses invoke many early gods, including Agni, the god of various kinds of fire; Indra, a phallic god of rain and fertility; Surya, god of the sun; and Varuna, the sovereign of the world who assures that the cosmic law is maintained. They include references to music, dance, and acting as modes of worship. Vedic worship also takes the form of animal sacrifice offered on sacred altars. The *Rigveda* speculates on the creation of the world and on the significance of life in this world, but it does not pretend to offer conclusive answers:

> Who really knows? Who shall here proclaim it? whence things came to be, whence this creation. … This creation, whence it came to be, whether it was made or not—he who is its overseer in the highest heaven, he surely knows. Or if he does not know …? (X:129, Embree, p. 21)

Caste. The *Rigveda* also introduces the mythic origin and rationale of the caste system, one of the most distinctive features of Hindu life. Caste began, the *Rigveda* suggests, in a primeval sacrifice of a mythical creature, Purusha. He was carved into four sections, each symbolizing one of the principal divisions of the caste system:

When they divided Purusha, in how many different portions did they arrange him? What became of his mouth, what of his two arms? What were his two thighs and his two feet called? His mouth became the *brahman* [priest]; his two arms were made into the *rajanya* [or *kshatriya*, warrior]; his two thighs the *vaishyas* [business people and farmer/landlords]; from his two feet the *shudra* [person of the lower working class] was born. (X:90 Embree, pp. 18–19)

Apparently, the Aryan invaders were even then thinking of a social system that separated people by occupation and sanctioned that separation through religion. The caste system that developed in India was probably the most rigidly unequal and hierarchical of any in the world. Caste status was hereditary, passing from parent to child at birth. Each caste was subject to different local legal rules, with upper castes being rewarded more generously and punished less severely than lower. Only upper castes were permitted to receive formal education, and the separate castes were not to intermarry nor to even dine with one another. Their vital fluids were distinct and different, and the blood and semen of one group were not to mingle with those of another. The food fit for one group was not necessarily appropriate for others: brahmin priests were to be vegetarians, but *kshatriya* warriors were to eat meat.

Commentators throughout the centuries have searched for additional roots of the caste system, more grounded in social, economic, and political rationales. Many have seen India's caste system as a means of ordering relationships among the multitude of

Gouache illustration from Bhanudatta's *Rasamanjari*, 1685. Krishna, the eighth *avatar* (incarnation) of Vishnu, is always depicted with blue/black skin and is renowned for his prowess as a warrior and a lover. In this scene from one of his amorous adventures, a woman hinders a forester from felling the tree under which she has arranged to meet Krishna for a romantic tryst.

Prayer room and shrine, India. Nearly every Hindu home in India has a shrine with pictures or small statues of various deities, and many have a special prayer room set aside for their worship. For *puja*, or worship, which is observed every day, ritual purity is emphasized; the time for offerings to the gods is after the morning bath or evening wash.

MAJOR RELIGIONS OF THE WORLD, 2002

Religion	Number of followers	Percentage of world population
Christians	2,019,052,000	32.9
Roman Catholics	1,067,053,000	17.4
Protestants	345,855,000	5.6
Orthodox	216,314,000	3.5
Anglicans	80,644,000	1.3
Independents	391,856,000	6.4
Unaffiliated Christians	111,689,000	1.8
Muslims	1,207,148,000	19.7
Hindus	819,689,000	13.4
Nonreligious	771,345,000	12.6
Chinese folk religionists	387,167,000	6.3
Buddhists	361,985,000	5.9
Ethnic religionists	230,026,000	3.8
Atheists	150,252,000	2.5
New-religionists	102,801,000	1.7
Sikhs	23,538,000	0.4
Jews	14,484,000	0.2
Baha'is	7,254,000	0.1
Confucianists	6,313,000	0.1
Jains	4,281,000	0.1
Shintoists	2,732,000	0.0
Zoroastrians	2,601,000	0.0

(Encyclopedia Britannica Book of the Year 2002)

immigrant groups in India's multi-ethnic population, consolidating some at the top and relegating others to the bottom. Others have seen caste as the result of a frozen economic system, with parents doing all they could to make sure that their children maintained at least the family's current occupational status. They sacrificed the possibility of upward mobility in exchange for the security that they would not fall lower on the social scale.

Many suggested that the system was imposed on the rest of the population by an extremely powerful coalition of brahmin priests and *kshatriya* warrior-rulers. Such a dominant coalition is common in world history, and the Indian situation was simply more entrenched than most.

MAJOR HINDU GODS AND GODDESSES

A shrine with images of one or more of the thousands of gods in the pantheon can be found in every devout Hindu home. The most widely worshiped gods are probably Shiva with his consort Parvati, and Vishnu with his consorts Lakshmi and Saraswati. But most Hindus offer at least some form of devotion to more than one god.

Brahma	The creator god, whose four heads and arms represent the four vedas (scriptures), castes, and yugas (ages of the world).
Ganesh	The elephant-headed god, bringer of good luck.
Kali	Shiva's fierce consort—the goddess of death—is shown as a fearsome, blood-drinking, four-armed black woman.
Krishna	The eighth avatar (incarnation) of Vishnu, depicted with blue or black skin. He is honored for his skills as a lover and a warrior; with his consort **Radha**.
Rama	The personification of virtue, reason and chivalry; with his consort **Sita**, revered for her loyalty.
Shiva	God of destruction, whose dancing in a circle of fire symbolizes the eternal cycle of creation and destruction.
Sitala	Mothers traditionally pray to this goddess to protect their children from disease.
Vishnu	The preserver, a kindly god, who protects those who worship him, banishes bad luck, and restores good health; with his consorts **Lakshmi**, the goddess of wealth, and **Saraswati**, the goddess of wisdom and the arts.

Historians employ the insights of anthropologists as they attempt to understand the historical origins and basis of the caste system. Anthropological observation shows that the four generalized castes of the Veda are not the actual groupings that function in practice today. Instead, India has tens of thousands of localized castes, called *jatis*—indeed, there are thousands of different brahmin groups alone. In practice, caste is lived in accordance with the accepted practices of these local groupings, in the 750,000 villages, towns, and cities of India. From customary law to dining patterns to marriage arrangements, caste relationships are determined locally, and there is no national over-arching religious system to formulate and enforce rules. Residents of any given village, for example, may represent some twenty to thirty castes, including all the various craftspeople and artisans. There may be more than one caste claiming brahmin status, or *kshatriya*, or *vaishya*, or *shudra*. Anthropologists therefore differentiate between the mythological four *varna* groups of the Vedic caste system and the thousands of *jati* groups through which caste is actually lived in India. Both historians and anthropologists are convinced that the same multitude of castes that they find "on the ground" today existed also in the past. Eventually, "outcastes," or "untouchables" emerged, people who were outside the caste system because of the "polluting" work they performed, which might include dealing with dead animals or handling those who died.

Throughout Indian history there have been revolts against the hierarchy of the caste system. In the twentieth century and into the present century the government of India has acted assertively to eliminate the historic discrimination of the caste system, as we shall see in Chapter 20. Nevertheless, through the millennia, caste has usually been more important than government in determining the conditions of life of most people. Personal identity and group loyalty were formed far more by caste locally than by government, which tended to be remote.

The Brahmanas and Upanishads. A second collection of Sanskrit religious literature, dating from *c.* 900–500 B.C.E., sets out rules for brahmins, including procedures for sacrifice and worship. These scriptures, the Brahmanas, include discussions of the origins of various rituals and myths of the immortal gods.

The Upanishads, composed 800–500 B.C.E., are devoted primarily to mystical speculation and proclaim the oneness of the individual and the universe. The universal spirit, Brahman, and the soul of each individual, *atman*, are ultimately the same substance, just as individual sparks are the same substance as a large fire. In time, each *atman* will be united with the universal Brahman. To reach this unity, each soul will experience reincarnation (*samsara*) in a series of bodies, until it is purged of its attachments to the physical world and achieves pure spirituality. Then, at the death of this final body, the *atman* is released to its union with the Brahman.

The Upanishads introduce several concepts fundamental to almost all strands of Hinduism. *Dharma* is the set of religious and ethical duties to which each living creature in the universe is subject. These duties are not the same, however, for each creature; they differ according to ritual status. *Karma* is the set of activities of each creature and the effects that these activities have on its *atman*. Each action has an effect on the *atman*; activities in accord with one's *dharma* purify the *atman*; activities in opposition to one's *dharma* pollute it. "Good *karma*," the good effects brought about by actions in accord with *dharma*, will finally enable the *atman* to escape *samsara*, or reincarnation, and reach *moksha*, release from the travails of life on earth and ultimate union with the Brahman. Thus Hinduism sees reward and punishment in the universe as a natural consequence. Good, *dharmic* actions carry their own reward for the *atman*; activities opposed to *dharma* carry their own negative consequences. Activities in this life earn good or bad *karma*.

The Upanishads also introduce the concept of the life cycle, with its different duties at each stage. The first stage, *brahmacharya*, is the youthful time of studies and celibacy; the second, *gruhasta*, the householder stage, is for raising a family; the third, *vanaprastha*, literally forest-wandering, is for reflection outside the demands of everyday life; and the last, *sannyasin*, is for total immersion in meditation in preparation for death and, ideally, for *moksha*.

These early scriptures established a set of principles that constitute the core of Hindu belief: caste, *dharma*, *karma*, life stages, *samsara*, and, ultimately, *moksha*, the union of *atman* and Brahman. They represent a rational system of order in the universe and in individual life. They teach the importance of dharmic activities in this world in order to reach *moksha* in the deeper reality beyond. They are transmitted from *guru*, or teacher, to *shishya*, or student. The codification of many of these specific behavioral norms for each caste in *The Law of Manu* attempted to institutionalize the position of the priests and to elaborate on core Hindu beliefs. Written in the first or second century B.C.E., the treatise almost certainly reflected earlier practices, spelling out the appropriate relationships between social classes and between men and women.

Although it reveres the brahmin priest (not to be confused with the Brahman spirit of the universe), Hinduism is ultimately accessible to each individual, even to those of low caste. Despite the hierarchy of the caste system, Hinduism allows enormous spiritual scope to each individual. It has no core dogma that each must affirm. Each individual Hindu may claim his or her own unique sense of spirituality. This universal accessibility of Hinduism is most clear in three later forms of literature that have become a kind of folk treasury (in contrast to the Vedas, Brahmanas, and Upanishads, which are the province of the brahmin priests).

The Great Epics. In the last chapter we discussed India's two great epic poems, the *Ramayana* and the *Mahabharata*. The latter's central story revolves around the civil war between two branches of the family of the Bharatas (from whom India derives its current Hindi name, Bharat). The *Mahabharata* presents moral conflicts, the dilemma of taking sides, and the necessity of acting decisively. At its center stands the *Bhagavad-Gita* ("Song of God"), a philosophical discourse on the duties and the meaning of life and death.

The *Bhagavad-Gita* opens on the field of Kurukshetra before the final battle between the two branches of the Bharata family. Arjun, leader of one branch, despairs of his choices: if he fights, he kills his cousins; if he does not fight, he dies. He turns to his chariot driver, the Lord Krishna, for advice. Krishna's reply incorporates many fundamental principles of Hindu thought.

SACRED WRITINGS OF HINDUISM

Veda	The most sacred of the Hindu scriptures, meaning "divine knowledge." They consist of collections of writings compiled by the Aryans: *Rigveda* (hymns and praises), *Yajurveda* (prayers and sacrificial formulas), *Samaveda* (tunes and chants), and *Atharva-Veda* (Veda of the Atharvans, the priests who officiate at sacrifices).
Upanishads	Philosophical treatises, centering on the doctrine of Brahma.
Brahamanas	Instructions on ritual and sacrifice.
Ramayana	An epic poem, telling how Rama (an incarnation of the god Vishnu) and his devotee Hanuman, the monkey god, recover Rama's wife, Sita, who has been abducted by the demon king Ravana.
Mahabharata	("Great Poem of the Bharatas") It includes the *Bhagavad-Gita* ("Song of God") and consists of eighteen books and 90,000 stanzas. The central narrative of civil war, and the innumerable sidebars, emphasize the struggle to do one's duty faithfully.

Actor in the *Ramayana* festival, 1996.
Dressed in the classical Yogya style, the actor portrays the enemy of Lord Rama, Ravana, in this tale of the battle of good versus evil.

First, Krishna speaks of the duty of Arjun, a *kshatriya* by caste, to fight: "For a *kshatriya* there does not exist another greater good than war enjoined by *dharma*" (II:31). Each person has a unique *dharma*, largely determined by caste. In this philosophy, changing one's vocational duty is no virtue:

> Better is one's own *dharma* that one may be able to fulfill but imperfectly, than the *dharma* of others that is more easily accomplished. Better is death in the fulfillment of one's own *dharma*. To adopt the *dharma* of others is perilous. (III:35)

The *Bhagavad-Gita* summarizes many of the key doctrines of Hinduism. Lord Krishna promises to help people who do their duty, and points the way toward spiritual fulfillment. The text demonstrates considerable assimilation within Hinduism, for the Lord Krishna is dark-skinned, usually represented as blue-black in color. He appears to be originally a non-Vedic, non-Aryan tribal god, perhaps from the south. His centrality in this most revered Sanskrit text suggests the continuing accommodation

SOURCE

The Bhagavad-Gita *from the* Mahabharata

Lord Krishna counsels Arjun to do his duty in leading the fighting of a civil war, even though the warrior has no desire to shed the blood of his relatives. Krishna continues with additional advice—on the importance of proper action for its own sake regardless of praise or condemnation, on reincarnation, and on Lord Krishna's grace upon those who seek him—much of which has been accepted by many Hindus then and now as key principles of life.

Krishna counsels Arjun to action. He notes three kinds of yoga, or discipline, which bring people to spiritual liberation: the yoga of knowledge; the yoga of devotion; and the yoga of action. (The yoga of physical discipline and meditation, known widely today in the West, is yet another form.) In this case, Krishna tells Arjun, the yoga of action is required:

Do your allotted work, for action is superior to nonaction. Even the normal functioning of your body cannot be accomplished through actionlessness. (III:8)

The key, however, is performing the action because it is right, without concern for its results or rewards.

Action alone is your concern, never at all its fruits. Let not the fruits of action be your motive, nor let yourself be attached to inaction … Seek refuge in the right mental attitude. Wretched are those who are motivated by the fruits of action. (II:49)

Non-attachment is the ideal:

He who feels no attachment toward anything; who, having encountered the various good or evil things, neither rejoices nor loathes—his wisdom is steadfast. (II:59)

He who behaves alike to foe and friend; who likewise is even-poised in honor or dishonor; who is even-tempered in cold and heat, happiness and sorrow; who is free from attachment; who regards praise and censure with equanimity; who is silent, content with anything whatever; who has no fixed abode, who is steadfast in mind, who is full of devotion—that man is dear to me. (XII:18–19)

In reply to Arjun's specific anxiety about killing his cousins, Krishna reminds him of the doctrine of reincarnation:

As a man discards worn-out clothes to put on new and different ones, so the disembodied self discards its worn-out bodies to take on other new ones.

Death is certain for anyone born, and birth is certain for the dead; since the cycle is inevitable, you have no cause to grieve! (II:22, 27)

Krishna also assures Arjun of his abiding concern for him, and of the god's power to help him: "If I am in your thought, by my grace you will transcend all dangers" (XVIII:58). Arjun does fight, and wins, and in the end all the warriors who die are reborn.

between the Aryans and the indigenous peoples of India. The *Gita* provided the basis for the continuing emphasis in Hinduism on *bhakti*, mystical devotion to god. "No one devoted to me is lost … Keep me in your mind and devotion, sacrifice to me, bow to me, discipline your self toward me, and you will reach me," (IX:31,34) is one of many statements in the *Gita* that called for this devotion. Bhakti was a revolt within Hinduism against formality in religion, against hierarchy, and against the power of the brahmin priesthood. Bhakti continues today in the hymns and poetry of the common people and in the multitudes of devotional prayer meetings in every corner of India.

The two epics generally also reflect greater prestige for women than did earlier Sanskrit texts. In the *Ramayana*, Sita appears as a traditionally subordinate wife to Rama, but her commitment to honor and duty surpasses even his; she defends Rama's honor even when he fails to defend hers. She is more heroic than he, although her heroism is defined by her role as dutiful wife. Rama is implicitly criticized for his inability to defend her both from Ravana and from the gossip of his own subjects. In some versions, the criticism is made explicit. In the *Mahabharata* Draupadi is the wife of five noble brothers, and she protects, defends, and inspires them in their struggles, going far beyond the subservient role that women play in the majority of Aryan literature. In the epics, the female force, *shakti*, has gained recognition.

The Puranas. The most popular of the gods of Hinduism, Vishnu and Shiva, appear in the Puranas, a collection of ancient stories. Here, too, appear female goddesses, often as consorts of the principal gods, such as the goddesses Lakshmi and Saraswati with the lord Vishnu; and the goddesses Parvati, Durga, and Kali with the lord Shiva. These goddesses also help to balance the rather suppressed position of females evident in the earlier Aryan literature.

Temples and Shrines

By the seventh century C.E. fundamental changes had taken place in the form of Hindu worship. Personal prayer, often addressed to representations of the gods in statues and pictures, displaced sacrifice. Hindus built temples of great beauty. The caves at Ellora in western India were fashioned into temples in the eighth century, reflecting the early importance of caves in Hindu worship. Within the cave-temples, sculpture and painting demonstrate the artistic development in religious worship.

Bronze sculpture of Vishnu, early Chola period, first half of tenth century. Vishnu is beloved as the tender, merciful deity—the Preserver—and as the second member of the Hindu trinity he complements Brahma the Creator and Shiva the Destroyer. He is said to come to earth periodically as an *avatar*, an incarnation in various forms, to help humankind in times of crisis. (*Metropolitan Museum of Art, New York*)

Kandariya Mahadeo Temple at Khajuraho, Chandela, c. 1025–1050 C.E. The twenty surviving temples at Khajuraho, though maimed by time, are still among the greatest examples of medieval Hindu architecture and sculpture in north India. Beneath the soaring towers, multilayered bands of sculptures writhe in a pulsating tableau of human and divine activity. The depictions of athletic lovemaking, which so scandalized nineteenth-century European travelers, can be linked to tantric sects of Hinduism, then prevalent in the Chandela region.

Kailasanatha Temple at Ellora, Rashtrakuta, c. 757–790 C.E. Carved into an escarpment of volcanic stone, the thirty-three shrines of Ellora have for centuries been a pilgrimage center for Hindus, Buddhists, and Jains. The monolithic stone shaft in the foreground, 60 feet high, would have originally supported a trident symbol of Shiva, to whom this temple is dedicated.

The bas reliefs and artwork in the temples at Kanchi and Mahabalipuram in the south, also built in the eighth century, continue to dazzle viewers today. Magnificent temples flourished everywhere in India, but especially in the south of the subcontinent. Sexual passion and the union of male and female entered into forms of worship, symbolically representing passion for, and union with, god, as the temple sculptures at Khajuraho in north India about 1000 C.E. illustrate.

Religion and Rule

Wealthy landowners and rulers, who sought validation of their power and rule through the prestige of brahmin priests, often patronized temples. As in many religions, rulers supported priests, while priests affirmed the authority of the rulers. This was especially true in the south. At least as early as the eighth century, new rulers who seized lands occupied by indigenous tribal peoples often imported brahmin priests to overawe the tribals with their learning, piety, and rituals, and to persuade the tribals of the proper authority of the king. To pacify the tribals, their gods might be incorporated into the array of gods worshiped in the temple by the priests, just as the tribal peoples would begin to worship the major gods of Hinduism. Anthropologists describe this process as an interplay between the "great" national tradition and the "little" local tradition. As new lands were opened, and tribals were persuaded to accept the new ruling coalition, the temples grew larger and more wealthy.

In exchange for their support, kings rewarded priests with land grants, court subsidies, and temple bequests. Brahmin priests and Tamil rulers in south India prospered together as temples took on important economic functions in banking and money-lending for the villages in their region. Hindu colleges, rest-houses for pilgrims, centers of administration, and even cities grew up around some of these temples.

Hinduism in Southeast Asia

Hinduism did not generally attract, nor seek, converts outside of India, but southeast Asia was an exception. Here, the initiative for conversion grew out of politics, as it had in southern India. The powers of the Hindu temple and the brahmin priesthood were imported to validate royal authority in southeast Asia from as early as the third century C.E. to as late as the fourteenth century.

Trade contacts between India and southeast Asia date back to at least 150 B.C.E. Indian sailors carried cargoes to and from Myanmar, the Straits of Malacca, the

Asian trade. Ports along the Indus and Ganges served Arab maritime traders for many centuries, and provided links to the kingdoms of southeast Asia and the South China Sea. To the north, roads following river valleys and passes through the towering Himalayas and the Hindu Kush provided contact with China and the silk route respectively.

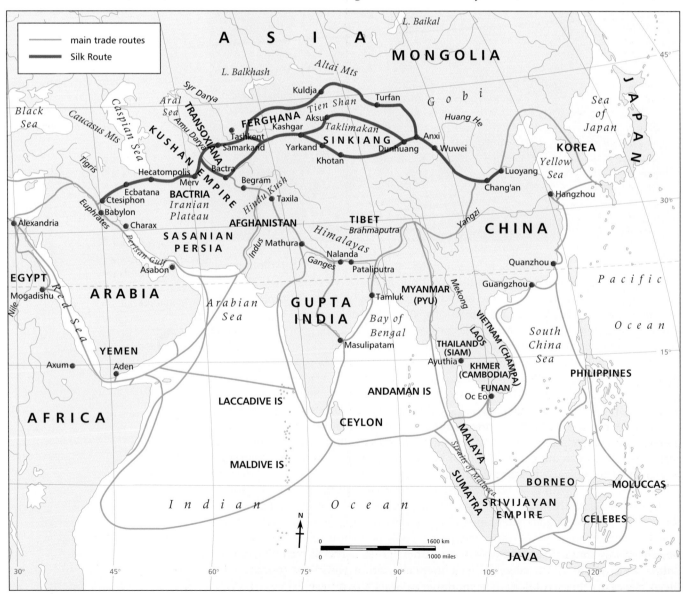

HOW DO WE KNOW?

Hinduism in Southeast Asia

Evidence for the influence of Hinduism in southeast Asia comes from a variety of sources. Even today, the historical stamp of Hinduism endures in southeast Asia in the names of cities, including Ayuthia in Thailand, derived from Ayodhya in northern India; in the influence of Sanskrit on several southeast Asian languages; in the popularity of the Ramayana and other Hindu literature in the folklore and theater of the region. Moreover, Hindu temples still stand, most spectacularly the Angkor Wat temple complex in Cambodia.

Evidence of Hindu influence in southeast Asia appears also in early reports of Chinese visitors, archaeological remains, and epigraphy (inscriptions on metal and rock). These records are, nevertheless, sparse. Brahmin priests appear in the southeast-Asian records only after 800 C.E. It is, therefore, difficult to answer the question: "What brought Indian power and prestige into southeast Asia from about the third century to about the fourteenth century?"

Three theories explaining the appearance of Indian influence in southeast Asia have been suggested. One theory argued that Indians initiated contact and attempted to introduce their religion and culture into southeast Asia. This theory, which stressed the use of military might, is no longer accepted. As noted in Chapter 8, there is very little record of Indian military action in the area, and none suggesting a desire for conquest. A second theory—that Indian traders brought their culture with them—has wider acceptance, but it also encounters serious opposition. Trade connections between India and southeast Asia were numerous, long-standing, and intense. Some cultural and religious influence must have accompanied them, but these contacts were by sea, while much of the Hindu influence was found inland.

A third theory argued that local rulers invited brahmin priests to come from India to southeast Asia to build temples, to promote agricultural development on land specially granted to them, to invoke the Hindu gods to validate their authority, and to convince the local population of this divine validation. In the words of one historian, these priests were to serve as "development planners." They brought with them from India principles of government, religious law, administration, art, and architecture. In promoting these religious/political practices through the priests, southeast-Asian rulers were emulating the policies of the Pallava and Chola kings of southern India. But Hinduism did not survive in southeast Asia. It was superseded by Buddhism and, later, by Islam.

Local kings and southeast-Asian rulers also invited Buddhist monks as well as Hindu priests to southeast Asia to help establish and consolidate their power, and they found the Buddhist monks to be as useful as the Hindu brahmins, for they served similar political and administrative functions, but in the name of Buddhism. For example, the ruler of the Srivijaya Empire in the East Indies welcomed 1000 Buddhist monks to his kingdom in the late seventh century C.E. Jayavarman VII, the Buddhist ruler of the Khmer kingdom at the end of the twelfth century, added Buddhist images in the great temple of Angkor Wat, which had been built earlier in the century to honor the Hindu god Vishnu.

By about the fourteenth century, Hinduism had died out in southeast Asia, while Buddhism continued to thrive. In fact, Buddhism became an enormously successful proselytizing religion throughout Asia. In India, on the other hand, Buddhism withered away, while Hinduism flourished.

- Of the theories explaining the spread of Hinduism in southeast Asia, why does the theory of the priest as "development planner" seem the most convincing?
- What is the evidence for the co-existence of Hinduism and Buddhism, for a time, in southeast Asia?
- What was the functional relationship between priests and rulers in southeast Asia?

Kingdom of Funan in modern Cambodia and Vietnam, and Java in modern Indonesia. By the third century C.E., Funan had accepted many elements of Indian culture, religion, and political practice. Chinese envoys reported a prosperous state with walled cities, palaces, and houses. Sanskrit was in use, as was some Indian technology for irrigation and farming. By the fifth century it appears that Sanskrit had spread, Indian calendars marked the dates, and Indian gods, including Shiva and Vishnu, were worshiped, as were representations of the Buddha (see below). Hindu temples began to appear with brahmin priests to staff them.

BUDDHISM

Buddhism was born in India, within the culture of Hinduism, and then charted its own path. Like Hinduism, it questioned the reality of this earthly world and speculated on the existence of other worlds. Unlike Hinduism, however, Buddhism had a founder, a set of originating scriptures, and an order of monks. In opposition to Hinduism, it renounced hereditary caste organization and the supremacy of the brahmin priests. Buddhism spread to southeast Asia, gaining acceptance as the principal religion of Myanmar (Burma), Thailand, Cambodia, Laos, and Vietnam until today. It won multitudes of adherents throughout the rest of Asia as well, in Sri Lanka, Tibet, China, Korea, and Japan. Yet in India itself, Buddhism lost out in competition with Hinduism and its priesthood, virtually vanishing from the subcontinent by about the twelfth century C.E.

The Origins of Buddhism

All we know of the Buddha's life and teaching comes from much later accounts, embellished by his followers. While there is much doubt about almost every aspect of the Buddha's life and teachings, the accounts that exist tell the following story.

The Life of the Buddha. Siddhartha Gautama was born *c.* 563 B.C.E. in the foothills of the Himalayan mountains of what is now Nepal. His father, a warrior chief of the *kshatriya* caste, received a prophecy that Siddhartha would become either a great emperor or a great religious teacher. Hoping that his son would follow the former vocation, the chief sheltered him as best he could so that he would experience neither pain nor disillusionment.

When he was twenty-nine years old, Siddhartha started to grow curious about what lay beyond the confines of his father's palace. Leaving his wife, Yasadhara, and their son, Rahula, he instructed his charioteer to take him to the city, where he came across a frail, elderly man. Never having encountered old age, Siddhartha was confused. His companion explained that aging was an inevitable and painful part of human experience. As Siddhartha took further excursions outside the palace, he soon came to see that pain was an integral part of life, experienced in illness, aging, death, and birth. The search for a remedy for this pervasive sorrow became his quest.

On his fourth and final trip he met a wandering holy man who had shunned the trappings of wealth and material gain. Siddhartha decided to do likewise. Bidding farewell to his family for the last time, he set out on horseback in search of an antidote to sorrow and a means of teaching it to others.

For six years Siddhartha wandered as an ascetic. Nearing starvation, however, he gave up the path of asceticism. Determined to achieve enlightenment, he began to meditate, sitting under a tree at Bodh Gaya near modern Patna, in India. Mara, the spirit of this world, who tempted him to give up his meditation with both threats of punishment and promises of rewards, tested his concentration and fortitude. Touching the ground with his hand in a gesture, or *mudra*, repeated often in sculptures of the Buddha, Siddhartha revealed these temptations to be illusions. On the forty-ninth day of meditation he reached enlightenment, becoming the Buddha, He Who Has Awakened. He had found an antidote to pain and suffering. He proceeded to the Deer Park at Sarnath, near Banaras, where he delivered his first sermon, beginning by setting forth the Four Noble Truths of suffering. Its source, he taught, was personal desire and passion:

> This is the [first] Noble Truth of Sorrow. Birth is sorrow, age is sorrow, disease is sorrow, death is sorrow, contact with the unpleasant is sorrow, separation from the pleasant is sorrow, every wish unfulfilled is sorrow—in short all the five components of individuality are sorrow. This is the [second] Noble Truth of the Arising of Sorrow. [It arises from] thirst, which leads to rebirth, which brings delight and passion, and seeks pleasure now here, now there—the thirst for sensual pleasure, the thirst for continued life, the thirst for power. (Basham, p. 269)

Teaching Buddha, from Sarnath, India, Gupta dynasty, fifth century C.E. Siddhartha Gautama sought to understand the causes of and remedy for human suffering. After many trials, he finally found his answer on the forty-ninth day of intense meditation. As the Buddha, the Enlightened One, he began to teach his new message. The *mudra*, the hand gesture, here represents the Buddha teaching. (*Archaeological Musem, Sarnath*)

SOURCE

The Address to Sigala: Buddhism in Everyday Life

Much of the Buddha's moral and ethical instruction is directed to the monks of the Sangha. In the Address to Sigala, however, he speaks to laypeople about their relationships and responsibilities toward one another. The address includes practical advice to husbands and wives, friends, employers, and employees. The lengthy address is translated and summarized here by A.L. Basham.

Husbands should respect their wives, and comply as far as possible with their requests. They should not commit adultery. They should give their wives full charge of the home, and supply them with fine clothes and jewelry as far as their means permit. Wives should be thorough in their duties, gentle and kind to the whole household, chaste, and careful in housekeeping, and should carry out their work with skill and enthusiasm.

A man should be generous to his friends, speak kindly of them, act in their interest in every way possible, treat them as his equals, and keep his word to them. They in turn should watch over his interests and property, take care of him when he is "off his guard" [i.e., intoxicated, infatuated, or otherwise liable to commit rash and careless actions], stand by him and help him in time of trouble, and respect other members of his family.

Employers should treat their servants and workpeople decently. They should not be given tasks beyond their strength. They should receive adequate food and wages, be cared for in time of sickness and infirmity, and be given regular holidays and bonuses in times of prosperity. They should rise early and go to bed late in the service of their master, be content with their just wages, work thoroughly, and maintain their master's reputation. (Digha Nikaya, iii:161; cited in Basham, p. 286)

Its antidote followed from this analysis:

> This is the [third] Noble Truth of the Stopping of Sorrow. It is the complete stopping of that thirst, so that no passion remains, leaving it, being emancipated from it, being released from it, giving no place to it. And this is the [fourth] Noble Truth of the Way which Leads to the Stopping of Sorrow. It is the Noble Eightfold Path—Right Views, Right Resolve, Right Speech, Right Conduct, Right Livelihood, Right Effort, Right Recollection and Right Meditation. (Basham, p. 269)

A new consciousness could be achieved by a combination of disciplining the mind and observing ethical precepts in human relationships. In the face of continuing rebirths into the pain of life, the Buddha taught that right living could bring release from the cycle of mortality and pain, and entry into *nirvana*, a kind of blissful nothingness. On the metaphysical plane, the Buddha taught that everything in the universe is transient; there is no "being." There exists neither an immortal soul nor a god, neither *atman* nor Brahman. The Buddha's teachings about the illusion of life and about rebirth and release were consistent with Hindu concepts of *maya*, *samsara*, and *moksha*, but the Buddha's denial of god put him on the fringes of Hindu thought. His rejection of caste as an organizing hierarchy and of the Hindu priests as connoisseurs of religious truth, won him powerful allies—and powerful opponents.

Although much of the Hindu priesthood opposed the Buddha's teachings, the kings of Magadha and Koshala, whose territories included most of the lower Gangetic plain, befriended and supported him and the small band of followers gathered around him. The Buddha taught peacefully and calmly until about 483 B.C.E., when, at the age of eighty, he died, surrounded by a cadre of dedicated monks and believers, the original Buddhist Sangha (order of monks). The three-fold motto of all devout Buddhists became, "I seek refuge in the Buddha; I seek refuge in the Doctrine; I seek refuge in the Sangha."

The Sangha. The Sangha was open to all men regardless of caste and thus drew the antagonism of brahmins, although some did join. For a time, women were permitted to form their own convents, but only under special restrictions. Today Buddhist nuns exist only in Tibet.

The monks wore saffron robes and shaved their heads. They practiced celibacy and renounced alcohol, but did not have to take a vow of obedience to the order. The monks were intellectually and spiritually free. Decisions were made through group discussion, perpetuating the pattern of the early republics of the north Indian hills. Monks studied, disciplined their spirits, meditated, and did the physical work of their monasteries. At first, they wandered, begging for their living, except during the rainy months of the monsoon. But as monasteries became richer, through donations of money and land, the monks tended to settle down. They also tended to give up begging, which diminished their contact with the common people to some degree.

The Emergence of Mahayana Buddhism

A series of general councils began to codify the principles, doctrines, and texts of the emerging community. The first council, convened shortly after the Buddha's death, began the continuing process of collecting his teachings. The second, about a century later, began to dispute the essential meaning of Buddhism. The third, convened at Pataliputra, Asoka's capital, revealed more of the differences that would soon lead to a split over the question of whether the Buddha was a human or a god.

By this time an array of Buddhist *caityas*, or shrines, was growing. In addition to monasteries, great stupas, or monuments filled with Buddhist relics, were built at Barhut, Sanchi, and Amaravati. Between 200 B.C.E. and 200 C.E. there were more

Great Stupa, Sanchi, third century B.C.E.–first century C.E. With its four gloriously carved gates and majestic central hemisphere, the Great Stupa of Sanchi is the most remarkable surviving example of the 84,000 such Buddhist shrines reputedly erected by the emperor Asoka during the Mauryan Empire. This "world mountain," oriented to the four corners of the universe, contained a holy relic, the object of pilgrims' devotion, and is topped by a three-tiered umbrella representing the Three Jewels of Buddhism: the Buddha, the Law, and the community of monks.

SACRED WRITINGS OF BUDDHISM

Tripitaka	"The Three Baskets": **Vinaya**, on the proper conduct of Buddhist monks and nuns; **Sutta**, discourses attributed to the Buddha; and **Abhidhamma**, supplementary doctrines. Written in Pali.
The Mahayanas	(Mahayana is Sanskrit for "Greater Vehicle.") The body of writings associated with the school of Buddhism dominant in Tibet, Mongolia, China, Korea, and Japan. Includes the famous allegory, the Lotus Sutra, the Buddhist Parable of the Prodigal Son.
Milindapanha	Dialogue between the Greek king Milinda and the Buddhist monk Nagasena on the philosophy of Buddhism.
Buddha's Four Noble Truths	Suffering is always present in life; desire is the cause of suffering; freedom from suffering can be achieved in nirvana (perfect peace and bliss); the Eightfold Path leads to nirvana.

Seated Buddhas, Cave 2, Ajanta, Maharashtra, India, fifth century C.E. While the original Theravada Buddhism saw the Buddha as a human being of great enlightenment, later forms of Buddhism, especially Mahayana Buddhism, taught that there had been many Buddhas who had lived at different times and continued to live on in various heavens, and that others would follow.

Buddhist than Hindu shrines in India. Theological discussion flourished, with a heavy emphasis on *metta*, or benevolence; nonviolence; *dharma*, or proper behavior (although not related to caste, since Buddhism rejected hereditary caste); and tolerance for all religions.

The fourth general council, convened in the first century C.E. in Kashmir, codified the key doctrines of Buddhism as they had developed from earliest times. These were the principles of the Theravada ("Doctrine of the Elders") branch of Buddhism, which we have been examining and which is today the prevailing form in Sri Lanka and southeast Asia, except for Vietnam.

By now, however, a newer school of Mahayana Buddhism had been growing for perhaps two centuries and had become a serious challenge to Theravada. Mahayana means "the Greater Vehicle," and its advocates claimed that their practices could carry more Buddhists to nirvana because they had bodhisattvas to help. A bodhisattva was a "being of wisdom" on the verge of achieving nirvana but so concerned about the welfare of fellow humans that he postponed his entrance into nirvana to remain on earth, or to be reborn, in order to help others.

In addition, Mahayana Buddhism taught that religious merit, achieved through performing good deeds, could be transferred from one person to another. It embellished the concept of nirvana with the vision of a Mahayana heaven, presided over by Amitabha Buddha, a Buddha who had lived on earth and had now become a kind of father in heaven. Subsequently, Mahayanists developed the concept of numerous heavens with numerous forms of the Buddha presiding over them. They also developed the concept of the Maitreya Buddha, a suffering servant who will come to redeem humanity.

Some theologians note the similarity of the concept of this Maitreya Buddha to the Christian Messiah, and some suggest that the Buddhists may have borrowed it. They also suggest that Christians may have borrowed the narratives of the virgin birth of the Buddha and of his temptation in his search for enlightenment, and applied them to Jesus. There are significant similarities in the stories of these two men/gods and their biographies. Further, Mahayanists spoke of three aspects of the Buddha: Amitabha, the Buddha in heaven; Gautama, the historical Buddha on earth; and the most revered of all the bodhisattvas, the freely moving Avalokiteshvara. Theologians ask: To what degree do these three Buddhist forms correspond to the Father, Son, and Holy Spirit of Christianity as it was developing at the same time? How much borrowing took place between India and the Mediterranean coast, and in which direction?

Within India, Mahayana Buddhism began to challenge Hinduism more boldly than Theravada had. Wishing to compete for upper-caste and upper-class audiences, Mahayanists began to record their theology in Sanskrit, the language of the elite, rather than the more colloquial Pali language, which Theravada had preferred. Mahayana theologians, most notably Nagarjuna (*fl. c.* 50–150 C.E.), elaborated Buddhist philosophy and debated directly with brahmin priests. Buddhist monasteries established major educational programs, especially at Nalanda in Bihar, where the Buddha had spent much of his life, and at Taxila, on the international trade routes in the northern Punjab.

The Decline of Buddhism in India

From its beginnings in India, Buddhism's strongest appeal had been to *kshatriya* rulers and *vaishya* businessmen, who felt that brahmin priests did not respect them. The Buddha himself came from a *kshatriya* family, and his early friendship with the *kshatriya* kings of Magadha and Koshala had ensured their support for his movement. Later kings and merchants also donated huge sums of money to support Buddhist monks, temples, and monasteries. Many people of the lower castes, who felt the weight and the arrogance of all the other castes pressing down on them, also joined the newly forming religion. They were especially attracted by the use of the vernacular Pali and Magadhi languages in place of Sanskrit, and the absence of the financial demands of the brahmins.

Buddhism began to lose strength in India around the time of the decline of the Gupta Empire (*c.* 320–550 C.E.). Regional rulers began to choose Hinduism over Buddhism, and alliances with priests rather than with monks. At the popular level, lower castes—who had found the anti-caste philosophy of Buddhism attractive—apparently also began to shift their allegiances back toward more orthodox Hinduism as an anchor in a time of political change. Also, without imperial assistance, merchants' incomes may have decreased within India, reducing their contributions to Buddhist temples. By the fifth century C.E., the Chinese Buddhist pilgrim Faxian noted weaknesses in Indian Buddhism.

Mahayana Buddhism, with its many god-like Buddhas and bodhisattvas inhabiting a multitude of heavens, seemed so close to Hinduism that many Buddhists must have seen little purpose in maintaining a distinction. Finally, Buddhists throughout their history in India had relied upon Hindu brahmin priests to officiate at their life cycle ceremonies of birth, marriage, and death, so Hindu priests could argue that they always had a significant claim on Buddhist allegiance.

Readers who are accustomed to the monotheistic pattern of religions claiming the undivided loyalty of their followers will recognize here a very different pattern. Many religions, especially polytheistic religions, expect that individuals will incorporate diverse elements of different religions into their personal philosophy and ritual. We

For an interactive version of this map, go to: http://www.prenhall.com/spodek/map9.3

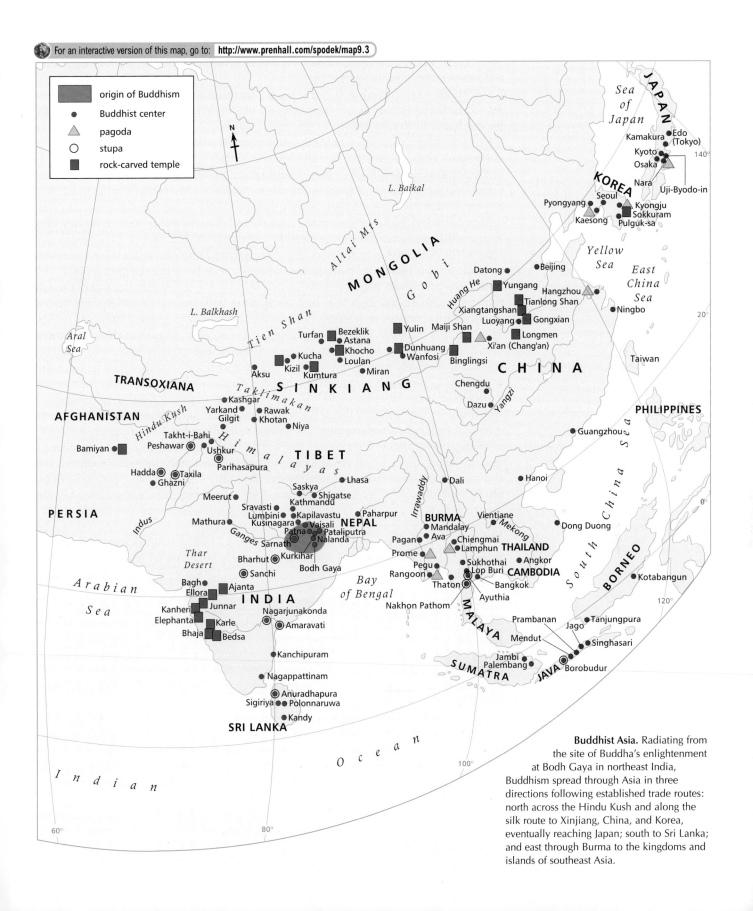

origin of Buddhism
● Buddhist center
▲ pagoda
○ stupa
■ rock-carved temple

Buddhist Asia. Radiating from the site of Buddha's enlightenment at Bodh Gaya in northeast India, Buddhism spread through Asia in three directions following established trade routes: north across the Hindu Kush and along the silk route to Xinjiang, China, and Korea, eventually reaching Japan; south to Sri Lanka; and east through Burma to the kingdoms and islands of southeast Asia.

will see more examples of this personal syncretism and loyalty to multiple religions as we examine Buddhism's relationship with Confucianism in China and with both Confucianism and Shinto in Japan.

As Hinduism evolved, it became more attractive to Buddhists. Theologians like Shankaracharya (788–820) and Ramanuja (c. 1017–1137) advanced philosophies based on the Vedic literature known to the common people and built many temples and schools to spread their thought. At the same time, Hinduism, following its tradition of syncretism, incorporated the Buddha himself within its own polytheistic universe as an incarnation of Vishnu. A devotee could revere the Buddha within the overarching framework of Hinduism. Finally, neither Buddhism nor Hinduism gave much scope to women within their official institutions of temples, schools, and monasteries. For Hinduism, however, the home was much more central than the public institution, and here women did have a central role in worship and ritual. Buddhism was much more centered on its monasteries and monks. The comparative lack of a role for women, and the comparative uninterest in domestic life generally, may have impeded its spread.

Buddhism in India began to wane when Muslim traders gained control of the silk routes through central Asia. The final blow came with the arrival of Muslims during the first two centuries of their major invasions into India, between 1000 and 1200 C.E. Muslims saw Buddhism as a competitive, proselytizing religion, unlike Hinduism, and did not wish to coexist with it. Because Buddhism was, by this time, relatively weak and relatively centralized within its monasteries and schools, Muslims were able to destroy the remnants of the religion by attacking these institutions. Buddhist monks were killed or forced to flee from India to centers in southeast Asia, Nepal, and Tibet. Hinduism survived the challenge because it was much more broadly based as the religion of home and community and far more deeply rooted in Indian culture.

In the 1950s, almost a thousand years after Buddhism's demise in India, about 5 million "outcastes" revived Buddhism in India in protest at the inequalities of the caste system and declared their allegiance to the old/new religion. These "neo-Buddhists" are virtually the only Buddhists to be found in India today (see Chapter 20).

Jainism

Jainism is another religion of India, with many similarities to early Buddhism. At about the time of the Buddha, the teacher Mahavir (c. 540 B.C.E.), the twenty-fourth in

Jainist nuns on their way to worship. Although most Jains are laypersons, important monasteries house priests and nuns. These nuns wear mouth-cloths to prevent injury to insects that might otherwise be inhaled.

a long lineage of Jain religious leaders, guided the religion into its modern form. The religion takes its name from Mahavir's designation *jina*, or conqueror. Like Theravada Buddhists, Jains reject the caste system and the supremacy of brahmin priests, postulating instead that there is no god, but that humans do have souls that they can purify by careful attention to their actions, and especially by practicing nonviolence. If they follow the eternal law of ethical treatment of others and devotion to the rather austere rituals of the faith, Jains believe they will reach nirvana, which is an end to the cycle of rebirths rather than a rewarding afterlife.

Jainism's emphasis on nonviolence is so powerful that Jains typically do not become farmers lest they kill living creatures in the soil. In a country overwhelmingly agricultural, Jains are usually urban and often businessmen. Jainism did not spread outside India, and its 4 million adherents today live almost entirely in India. Because Jains, like earlier Buddhists, employ brahmin priests to officiate at their life cycle events, and because Jains intermarry freely with several Hindu *vaishya* (business) subcastes, some consider them a branch of Hinduism, although they do not usually regard themselves as Hindus. One of the regions of Jain strength in India is western Gujarat, the region where Mahatma Gandhi grew up (see Chapter 20). The Mahatma attributed his adherence to nonviolence in large part to the influence of Jainism.

Buddhism in China

Because of its decentralization and vast geographical diffusion, Buddhism has taken on different forms from place to place, time to time, and state to state. It arrived in new locations in foreign form, but over time each regional culture put its own stamp on Buddhism. We must, therefore, examine the faith and practice of Buddhism in each region separately, by studying the works of the monks, missionaries, poets, architects, and sculptors who spread the faith.

Arrival in China: The Silk Route. The long, thin line of communication over which pilgrims and missionaries carried the message of the Buddha from India to China and beyond was the silk route, the same route that carried luxury products between China and India and then on to the West. The first Buddhist missionaries are mentioned in Chinese records about 65 C.E. They established their first monastery at Luoyang. Over the centuries, many more were built within China and along the silk route.

Chinese pilgrims traveled the silk route in the opposite direction to visit and study in the land of the Buddha, and some, most notably Faxian, who visited in 399–414, left important records of their observations. Thousands came to study at Taxila and Nalanda.

Several of the pilgrims who traveled these routes, especially Faxian, in the early years of the fifth century C.E., and Xuanzang, in the early years

Guanyin, Buddhist deity, Northern Song dynasty, China, *c.* 1200 C.E. Guanyin, a bodhisattva, or enlightened being, who remains in this world to relieve human suffering, was a very popular subject in Chinese art: this painted-wood example is particularly sensuous and refined. Buddhist deities are considered to have the spiritual qualities of both genders and by this date the feminine qualities were accentuated. (*Nelson-Atkins Museum of Art, Kansas City, Missouri*)

of the seventh, brought back both Buddhist texts and important first-hand information from India and the lands along the silk routes. Turning north from India through Kashgar, and then east to Khotan, Turfan, Dunhuang, and on to Chang'an in the heart of China, Buddhist pilgrims improved these trade routes with rest-houses, temples, and monasteries, some of them built into caves.

Relations with Daoism and Confucianism. Although Buddhism first appeared in China in the first century C.E., at the height of the Han dynasty, it took firmer root after the dynasty eventually fell. Confucianism, China's dominant philosophy, was intimately tied to the fate of the imperial government, and only after this central political structure collapsed could Mahayana Buddhism find a place. The mystical character of Mahayana Buddhism especially attracted Daoists. To some degree, the two beliefs competed, but some of the competition eventually led to each validating the other. For example, some Daoists claimed that the Buddha was actually Laozi as he appeared in his travels in India. Many Buddhists, in turn, accorded to Laozi and Confucius the status of bodhisattva. In this way, competition sometimes turned into mutual recognition.

As a foreign religion, Buddhism also had special appeal for some of the rulers of northern China in the third through the sixth centuries, since they, too, were outsiders. The Toba rulers of the Northern Wei dynasty (386–534) occasionally persecuted Buddhists as a threat to the state, but mostly they felt some kinship to this religion of outsiders. They patronized Buddhist shrines and monks, but they also regulated them.

In the south, with its abundance of émigrés from the northern court, Confucianism was crippled by the severance of its connection with the government. In contrast, newly arriving Buddhists won followers by proposing an organized, aesthetic philosophy for coping with the hazards of life in semi-exile. In southern China Buddhist arts of poetry, painting, and calligraphy flourished, and monasteries in the south offered refuge to the men who might have been part of the governing Confucian aristocracy in other times. In the southern state of Liang, the Emperor Wu (r. 502–549) declared Buddhism the official state religion, built temples, sponsored Buddhist assemblies, and wrote Buddhist commentaries.

Doctrinally, Buddhism had important differences from Confucianism, but the two world perspectives seem to have reached mutual accommodation. For example, Confucianism encouraged family cohesion and the veneration of ancestors, while Buddhist monks followed lives of celibacy; but Buddhist laypeople also valued family, and the monks themselves venerated the Buddha and bodhisattvas as their spiritual ancestors. Nevertheless, tension between the two belief systems and organizations never completely dissipated. Confucians thought in terms of government order and control, while Buddhists tended toward decentralized congregational worship within a loose doctrinal framework. In many areas of China, as Buddhist monasteries became wealthy from the donations of local magnates and landlords, Confucian governments moved to regulate their power.

Buddhism's network of pilgrims and monks crisscrossed China, helping to integrate the nation. Through almost four centuries of division in China, from the fall of the Han (220 C.E.) to the rise of the Sui (581), Buddhism continued to grow in both north and south. Indeed, the founder of the Sui dynasty, a Buddhist himself, also patronized Confucianism and Daoism, seeing all these belief systems as vital to earning legitimacy for his government. The Tang extended this veneration.

Buddhism under the Tang Dynasty. For most of the Tang dynasty (618–907), the intellectual, spiritual, and artistic life of Buddhism flourished. Eight major sects developed, each with a different interpretation of the original message of the Buddha, the

SOURCE

The Transience of Life: A Woman's Perspective from the Tang Dynasty

This anonymous poem of the Tang dynasty, discovered in the Dunhuang cave and translated by Patricia Ebrey and Lily Hwa, illuminates the Buddhist sense of the transience of life as experienced by a woman of high status.

A Woman's Hundred Years

At ten, like a flowering branch in the rain,
She is slender, delicate, and full of grace.
Her parents are themselves as young as the
rising moon
And do not allow her past the red curtain
without a reason.

At twenty, receiving the hairpin, she is a
spring bud.
Her parents arrange her betrothal; the
matter's well done.
A fragrant carriage comes at evening to
carry her to her lord.
Like Xioshi and his wife, at dawn they
depart with the clouds.

At thirty, perfect as a pearl, full of the beauty
of youth,
At her window, by the gauze curtain, she
makes up in front of the mirror.
With her singing companions, in the
waterlily season,
She rows a boat and plucks the blue flowers.

At forty, she is mistress of a prosperous
house and makes plans.
Three sons and five daughters give her some
trouble.
With her lute not far away, she toils always
at her loom.
Her only fear that the sun will set too soon.

At fifty, afraid of her husband's dislike,
She strains to please him with every charm.
Trying to remember the many tricks she had
learned since the age of sixteen.

No longer is she afraid of mothers- and
sisters-in-law.

At sixty, face wrinkled and hair like silk
thread,
She walks unsteadily and speaks little.
Distressed that her sons can find no brides,
Grieved that her daughters have departed
for their husbands' homes.

At seventy, frail and thin, but not knowing
what to do about it,
She is no longer able to learn the Buddhist
Law even if she tries.
In the morning a light breeze
Makes her joints crack like clanging gongs.

At eighty, eyes blinded and ears half-deaf,
When she goes out she cannot tell north
from east.
Dreaming always of departed loves,
Who persuade her to chase the dying breeze.

At ninety, the glow fades like spent
lightning.
Human affairs are no longer her concern.
Lying on a pillow, solitary on her high bed,
She resembles the dying leaves that fall in
autumn.

At a hundred, like a cliff crumbling in the
wind,
For her body it is the moment to become
dust.
Children and grandchildren will perform
sacrifices to her spirit.
And clear moonlight will forever illumine
her patch of earth.   (Ebrey, p. 104)

importance of rules and regulations, rituals, meditation, scholarship, disciplinary exercises, and devotion. Among the larger and more significant schools was the Pure Land Sect. Its devotees believed that anyone could reach the Pure Land of paradise after death through faith in the Buddha Amitabha, the presiding authority in that realm. Members of the sect demonstrated their faith by continuously repeating the name Amitabha. Devotees also meditated on the Bodhisattva Guanyin, the bodhisattva of mercy (see picture, p. 293).

Another sect, Chan Buddhism, taught the importance of meditation. Some followers believed in lengthy disciplines of meditation, which would gradually lead to enlightenment; others in spontaneous flashes of insight, which would lead to the same goal. Both Pure Land and Chan were adopted in Japan as well, where the meditative exercises of Chan became known as Zen.

Buddhists are credited with inventing woodblock printing as a means of reproducing their sacred texts. The earliest woodblock print known is an illustrated copy of the *Diamond Sutra* from 868 C.E., discovered in the Dunhuang Caves. Most of the Buddhist

Diamond Sutra, 868 C.E. This superb frontispiece, showing the Buddha preaching to an elderly disciple, comes from the *Diamond Sutra*, a Sanskrit tale transmitted along the silk route and translated into Chinese in the fifth century. Produced by woodblock to a high standard of technical and artistic achievement, the 17-foot-long sutra is the world's earliest dated printed book. (*British Library, London*)

art and architecture of Tang China was destroyed in later persecution, confiscation, and warfare. Its leading representations are now seen in Japan, which at just about this time adopted much of Chinese Buddhism as its own and then modified it (see pp. 297–301).

The only woman ever to rule China in her own name, the "Emperor" Wu (625–705), was a great patron of Buddhism. First ruling indirectly through the Emperor Gaozong (d. 683), whose concubine she was, and then, after his death, through two of their sons, in 690 she proclaimed herself the emperor of a new dynasty, which she named the Zhou (not to be confused with the earlier Zhou dynasty discussed in Chapter 3). She patronized Buddhism as a means of legitimizing her rule, declaring herself a reincarnation of Maitreya, the Buddha of future salvation. The empress built temples in every province of China. Before she was deposed in 705, she had overseen the warfare that expanded the Tang to its greatest geographical extent, including Xinjiang and Tibet.

Dying Buddha, Cave 428, Dunhuang, China, early sixth century C.E. The monastery at Dunhuang was one of the most important of those along the Silk Route, and the paintings in its 460 caves are spectacular. Here, bodhisattvas attend the Buddha at his death, appearing rather ascetic, abstract, and enchanted. Compare the scene from Japan on p. 297.

Buddhism's Decline in China. Political and military defeats started Buddhism on its decline during the late Tang period in China. In far-off central Asia, Muslim forces defeated Chinese forces in the decisive Battle of the Talas River in 751. Four years later, the revolt of General An Lushan in northeast China occupied the imperial armies for eight years. China's power in central Asia was broken, and with it the power of Buddhism in these regions. Islam would become the world religion of most of central Asia (see Chapter 11). In these vast regions, Buddhism remained powerful, and was supported by state power, only in Tibet. It was carried there from eastern India about the eighth century in a newly emerging form called *vajrayana* Buddhism, "the vehicle of the thunderbolt," or tantric Buddhism, for its *tantras*, or scriptures advocating magic rituals. Tantric Buddhism venerated not only buddhas, bodhisattvas, and other divinities, but also their wives or feminine counterparts, new additions to the growing array of sacred personalities. Tantric rituals were secret, esoteric, sometimes sexual, and only for the initiated.

Almost a century later, the Tang emperor Wuzong (r. 840–846) attacked Buddhism and its monasteries. Wuzong was a Daoist, personally opposed to Buddhism. He feared the power of the Buddhist establishment, and the wealth and influence of its various monasteries, especially when the Tang had been weakened by external defeats and internal revolts. Wuzong confiscated the lands and wealth of the Buddhist monasteries. He forced monks and nuns to leave the monasteries, claiming that he personally had defrocked 260,500 monks and nuns. He destroyed sacred texts, statues, and shrines, leaving only 49 monasteries and 800 monks in all of China. Later rulers alternated between reversing and re-imposing Wuzong's policies. Although Buddhism has remained a presence in China, even to today, it has never recovered its numbers, vitality, or influence.

Buddhism in Japan

Long before Buddhism arrived in Japan, the people of Japan followed "The Way of the *Kami*," later called Shinto. *Kamis* were the powers and spirits inherent in nature. Found everywhere, they could be called upon to help in time of human need. Shrines to the *kami* were built throughout the land, always including a mirror in tribute to the sun-goddess, a sword, and a jewel.

Accounts of the *kami* appear in the earliest Japanese records, the *Kojiki* (712 C.E.) and *Nihon shoki* (720 C.E.). These semi-mythological records give a basic history of early Japan, but these documents—and all accounts of Buddhist saints—must be read with some caution, because they blend myth with factual record. According to the *Kojiki* and *Nihon shoki*, the highest of the *kami* were Amaterasu, the sun-goddess, and her obstreperous brother Susa-no-o. Amaterasu's grandson, Niniqi, descended to earth and set out to conquer Japan. He established himself as Japan's first emperor in 660 B.C.E., and all subsequent emperors trace their lineage directly back to this mythological founder.

With the later arrival of Buddhism, the *kami* continued to have a distinguished and venerated position, often as minor Buddhas or bodhisattvas. Conversely, the Buddhas and bodhisattvas were accepted as especially powerful and exalted *kami*, capable of helping those in adversity. The royal family in Japan knew that the Emperor Asoka in India had adopted Buddhism and they emulated his decision.

Buddhism's Arrival in Japan. Buddhism first came to Japan from China in 552 C.E. via the Paekche kingdom of southwest Korea. The *Nihon shoki* tells of the Paekche king sending Buddhist texts and statues and asking help in a war against another Korean kingdom, the Silla.

From the beginning, Buddhism had political as well as religious implications. Clans close to the Japanese emperor were divided in their reception of the foreign religion. Those who accepted it regarded Buddhism as a force for

Dying Buddha, Japanese scroll, seventeenth to eighteenth century C.E. Here the dying Buddha is attended by human disciples, bodhisattvas, grieving animals, and representatives of other worlds. From across the river, another disciple leads the Buddha's mother and her retinue down from heaven to attend his last teaching.

Horyuji Temple, Nara, Japan, 670 C.E. Through the seventh and eighth centuries the Japanese court enthusiastically welcomed Chinese political and artistic forms (see Chapter 7). This is Japan's earliest surviving example of Buddhist architecture, which was adopted along with Chinese writing, painting, and sculpture. It became a central shrine for all of Japan.

performing miracles, especially healing the sick, and many Buddhist monks were especially skilled in medicine. A minority, however, thought the new religion ought to be banned.

Buddhism found acceptance at a political level in Japan a half century later under Prince Shotoku Taishi (573–621). The prince effectively ruled the country as the regent to the ruler of the Yamato Plain, the western region of Japan. An enthusiastic Buddhist, Shotoku built many temples, including the Horyuji in the capital city of Nara. A scholar of Buddhist theology, he invited Buddhist clergy from Korea, and he dispatched four Japanese missions to Sui China to learn more about Buddhism, both as a religious system and as a model for centralizing his political rule. At this time China was the premier state of eastern Asia, and Buddhism was seen as one of the principal constituents of its power. In 604, Prince Shotoku introduced a kind of constitution to centralize and strengthen the Japanese government. Among its seventeen articles, the first promoted Confucian principles of social organization and the second declared that the Japanese people should, "Sincerely reverence the three treasures ... the Buddha, the Law, and the Monastic orders" (Embree, p. 50).

Buddhism's Role in Unifying Japan. A century later, in 710, the ruling clans of Japan moved their capital to Nara, then called Heijo. Continuing to regard China as the model state of their day, the Japanese rulers copied much of the Chinese structures of authority and administration. They used Chinese ideographs as their written language and adopted Chinese patterns of bureaucracy, taxation, architecture, and land reforms. They modeled their new capital on the city plan of Chang'an, building a smaller version of that Chinese capital at Nara.

Within Nara, Japan's rulers built numerous Buddhist temples, including several of national significance. They encouraged the creation of a system of monasteries and convents throughout the provinces, with the Todaiji monastery, built by the Emperor Shomu (r. 715–749), at the apex. Inside that great temple is one of the world's great repositories of art, holding several thousand treasures from the eighth century, including painting, sculptures, calligraphy, textiles, ceramics, jade, metal and lacquer work, masks for drama, and musical instruments.

Buddhism became a pillar in the structure of Japanese national unity and administration. Buddhism did not replace Shinto, the indigenous worship of spirits, especially spirits of nature. Rather, it complemented the indigenous system. The emperor performed the official rituals of both Shinto and Buddhist worship.

Buddhism introduced a measure of centralization. Shinto, a looser system of belief and worship, had spread throughout all of Japan with no need of a central shrine for its worship of nature. By contrast, the Horyuji Temple near Nara became a central shrine for all of Japan. In 741 the emperor ordered that a Buddhist temple and pagoda be established in each province. Buddhism and Shinto coexisted in Japan in a pattern that continues today.

As in China, the power and wealth of Buddhist monasteries and temples in Japan, and especially in Nara, alarmed some members of the court. To reduce the power of the Buddhist clergy and to increase the power of his own lineage, Emperor Kammu (r. 781–806) moved the capital again, from Nara to Heian (modern Kyoto) in 794. This move initiated the Heian period in Japanese history and coincided with the decline of the Tang Empire in China. The Japanese government dispatched its last official mission to China in 838. With Japan on the ascendant and China in decline, Japan's Buddhism developed along its own paths, helped by substantial imperial patronage. The emperor himself patronized two young Japanese monks who founded the Tendai and Shingon schools of Buddhism, the two most powerful and enduring Buddhist movements in Japan.

Japanese Buddhism Develops New Forms. The Buddhist priesthood itself became increasingly Japanese, no longer reliant on priests from the Chinese mainland. It also entered more profoundly into politics. The priest Saicho (767–822) studied Tiantai (Tendai in Japanese) Buddhism in China and introduced it into Japan. Based on the Lotus Sutra, Tendai taught that each person could achieve enlightenment through sincere religious devotion. On Mount Hiei, northeast of Kyoto, Saicho built the Enryakuji monastery, which grew rapidly and steadily into one of the most important temple communities in Japan.

Saicho had intended his monastery to remain aloof from politics, and he therefore built it far from the national capital in Nara. Ironically, however, when the capital was moved to Kyoto, the monastery again found itself geographically close to the national political center. Saicho encouraged the monks to add teaching, administration, and social work in the service of the nation to their religious duties, merging Confucian and Buddhist value systems. His monastery grew to house tens of thousands of monks in some 3000 buildings. By the eleventh century, an era of deep and violent political fissures in Japanese political life, many Shinto and Buddhist temples supported standing armies to protect themselves and their extensive land holdings and branch temples. Troops from the Mount Hiei monastery began to enter the capital, demanding additional lands and thus completely reversing Saicho's original wishes. The Buddhist clergy thereafter became increasingly intertwined with Japanese politics.

Kukai (774–835), another Japanese Buddhist priest who had studied in China, also returned home to preach a new form of Buddhism. He became abbot of the monastery

Hoodo (Phoenix Hall), Byodoin Temple, Uji, Japan, eleventh century. The Phoenix Hall of the Byodoin Temple, with its jauntily uplifted roof-corners, indicates how over time the Buddhist style took on a distinctively Japanese flavor and shed its Chinese influence (contrast with picture, p. 286).

mantra A formula of utterances of words and sounds that are believed to possess spiritual power, a practice of both Hinduism and Buddhism.

mandala A symbolic circular diagram of complex geometric design used as an instrument of meditation or in the performance of sacred rites in Hinduism and Buddhism.

syllabary A writing system in which each symbol represents the syllable of a word (cf. ideogram).

ideogram (alternative: ideograph) A character or figure in a writing system in which the idea of a thing is represented rather than its name.

of the great Toji temple at Kyoto, where he introduced Shingon ("True Word") Buddhism. Shingon emphasizes the repetition of mystic incantations or **mantras**; meditation on colorful, sometimes stunning, geometrically ordered religious paintings, called **mandalas**, of Buddhas and bodhisattvas in their heavens; complicated rituals; music; and ecstatic dancing. Because the transmission of these forms was closely guarded among believers, Shingon was also called Esoteric Buddhism. Creating more accessible forms as well, Kukai introduced rituals, such as the austere and beautiful tea ceremony, in which a formal ritual surrounding the serving and drinking of tea invites deep meditation. Kukai is also credited with inventing the *kana* **syllabary**, a Japanese script in phonetic letters rather than **ideograms**. These innovations, in addition to mysterious, secret rituals, use of herbal medicines, and the elegant pageantry of Shingon, gave Kukai's monastery great popularity and power.

Another Chinese form of Buddhism that deeply influenced Japan was dedicated to Amida, or, in Sanskrit, Amitabha, the Buddha of the Infinite Light. In the tenth century, two priests, Kuya (903–972) and Genshin (942–1017), popularized this sect, which taught the importance of chanting the mantra *nembutsu*, "Praise to Amida Buddha." Amidism grew in subsequent generations through the organizational abilities of a series of monks, including Ryonin (1072–1132), who taught the counting of rosary beads to accompany the repetition of the *nembutsu*, a practice that spread to most sects of Japanese Buddhism. By the late twelfth century, Amidism established its independence from other Buddhist sects and at last reached a mass audience for whom its message of uncomplicated, universal access to salvation had great appeal.

Chan Buddhism, Zen in Japanese, appeared in Japan during the seventh century, but began to flourish only after the twelfth century. Much of Zen's popularity resulted from the teachings of Eisai, a Buddhist monk who believed that in addition to meditation, Zen should defend the state. Its emphasis on martial arts made Zen Buddhism particularly attractive to the increasingly powerful warrior class. Since then it has deeply influenced Japanese culture and remains important in Japan today.

Lasting Buddhist Elements in Japanese Society. Three other elements gave Buddhism a prominence and significance in Japanese life that has continued till today. First, Japanese Buddhism cultivated an especially pure aesthetic dimension, which we have seen here in the representations of the Buddha and bodhisattvas and of the architecture and art of the Japanese Buddhist temples. This appreciation of artistic creativity is apparent throughout Japan in formal gardens, in painting and calligraphy, and in the art of presentation of everything from self, to gifts, to tea, to food. Second, Buddhism's emphasis on the transience of all life has inspired much of the greatest Japanese literature, from the *Tale of Genji*, written by Lady Murasaki (*c.* 978–*c.* 1015) at the Japanese court a thousand years ago, to the novels of Mishima Yukio (1925–70), who committed *seppuku*, ritual suicide, immediately after completing his last novel. Third, Buddhism has coexisted and even merged to some degree with indigenous Shinto worship and belief.

By the twelfth century Japan had entered its Buddhist Age. Despite occasional attacks on Buddhism as a foreign religion and as an excessively wealthy and powerful organization, Buddhism has remained one of the two national religions of Japan. Most Japanese continue to mingle Buddhism and Shinto in their aesthetic and spiritual lives as well as in their ritual practices.

COMPARING HINDUISM AND BUDDHISM

Hinduism and Buddhism have undergone enormous transformations through their thousands of years of history. Geographically, Hinduism spread across the Indian subcontinent from its roots in the encounter between Aryan invaders and the indigenous peoples of the Indus valley and north India. It extended briefly even to southeast Asia (where a single Hindu outpost still remains on the Indonesian island of Bali). Buddhism spread from the Buddha's home region in the Himalayan foothills throughout India, where it subsequently died out, and most of east and southeast Asia, where it flourishes. Buddhism's array of monasteries and temples, and its veneration of the homeland of the Buddha himself, mark its sacred geography.

Both religions established their own sacred calendars and their control over life cycle events. In this, Hindu priests took a commanding position since even Buddhists (and Jains) employed them to officiate. Within India this continuing role of the brahmin priests ultimately helped Hinduism to absorb Buddhism. Outside India, where no other major religion was already in place, Buddhist priests performed their own rituals and came to predominate.

Both groups developed sacred languages. Buddhists felt that Sanskrit was narrowly limited to Hindu priests and so used Pali, a language closer to the vernacular. Over time, as the common people expressed their own religious feelings in their own languages, the leaders of both religions responded by also using the vernacular. Both religions inspired extensive literatures, including philosophy, mystical poetry, drama, and folk tales. Both generated their own artistic traditions in painting, sculpture, and temple architecture.

Organizationally, Buddhism, especially in its early Theravada form, was seen as a religion of its monks. Many common people found comfort and meaning in their philosophy and supported them, but ultimately they turned to brahmin priests for their ritual needs. Within Hinduism the caste system structured all classes and occupations into a single framework of relationships, with brahmins, *kshatriyas*, and sometimes *vaishyas*, predominating. Buddhism's later Mahayana form, with its multitudes of gods, bodhisattvas, and heavens, reached out to more people ritually as well as emotionally.

The evolution of Hinduism and Buddhism demonstrates the flexibility of great world religions. A small sect may define itself narrowly, proclaiming a core set of principles and practices and adhering to them rigidly. For its small membership, these restrictions may be the very attraction of the sect. But for a religion to grow in numbers, it must be open organizationally, doctrinally, and ritually to the varied spiritual, psychic, and social needs of diverse peoples. Like the empires we studied in Part 3, a world religion must be able to accommodate, satisfy, and absorb people of various languages, regions, classes, and previous spiritual beliefs and practices. World religions expand their theologies and practices to incorporate ever more members, until they reach the limits of their flexibility.

Finally, religions and governments have been historically interdependent. Buddhism flourished thanks to the early support of the Buddha's royal allies and later through the backing of the Emperor Asoka. It spread to southeast Asia and to Japan as kings offered their support in exchange for Buddhist legitimation. In China, Buddhism found its opening after Confucian dynasties fell and people searched for new belief systems and new leaders. Hinduism flourished as kings in India struck their own agreements with brahmin priests. Conversely, when governments turned against particular religious groups, they could devastate them. And when sizable religious groups shifted their support away from a ruler, they undermined his authority. We shall find more examples of this mutual antagonism in the next chapters.

HINDUISM AND BUDDHISM
WHAT DIFFERENCE DO THEY MAKE?

Hinduism keeps alive a major religion of active polytheism. Although many Hindus would argue that behind all of the gods a single reality pervades the world, others would argue, more literally, that there are indeed many very different gods with influence over the world and its creatures. These advocates of polytheism find a consistency between the diversity of life forms and life experiences and the multitude of gods of existence.

Hinduism has given a general cultural unity and depth to much of south Asia, in its arts and literature, its complex and sophisticated philosophical systems, and its hierarchical social, economic, and political order, which is based on caste forms. Today, the government and people of India cope with these legacies in a world that generally proclaims publicly the equality of all people. As a result, many political and religious questions regarding the relationships between the historic claims of hierarchy and the contemporary demands for equality confront India, and there are conflicting arguments about the most appropriate direction for future development, as we shall see in Chapter 20.

Buddhism also continues as the basis of the culture and religion of hundreds of millions of people, most of them in east and southeast Asia. The religion takes many different forms, from the relative austerity of the Theravada Buddhism of Sri Lanka, to the more elaborated and otherworldly Mahayana forms of southeast Asia, and the more mystical and isolated forms of Tibetan Buddhism. In many lands Buddhism is practiced freely, often in conjunction with other religions, as in Japan. In China, however, especially in Tibet, Buddhism struggles for survival against a hostile government, as we shall also see in Chapter 20. To understand religions in history, we must see them in the context of the political, social, and economic systems in which they are embedded.

We turn in the next chapters to three religions—Judaism, Christianity, and Islam— that have been militantly monotheistic. Although Judaism has remained relatively limited in its numbers, Christianity and Islam have been aggressive in their desire to win converts and are now the largest of the world's religions, with about 2 billion and 1.2 billion followers, respectively. Their relationships with the governments alongside which they exist have been checkered. Their impact on spiritual, cultural, social, and aesthetic life has been immense.

Review Questions

- What is the difference between studying a religion and studying about a religion? How does this compare to the differences between the studies of theologians and of historians?
- In what ways is Hinduism especially related to the land of India?
- Beginning with the emergence of Buddhism out of early brahminic beliefs and practices, what were the key turning points in the evolution of Buddhism?
- Describe the key elements in the competition between Hinduism and Buddhism, including such issues as principal beliefs, role of the clergy, role of the home, social hierarchy, and support of the government.
- What are the geographical distributions of Hindus and Buddhists? How and why have they changed over time?
- What have been the relationships between Buddhism and Confucianism in China? In Japan?

Suggested Readings

PRINCIPAL SOURCES

Basham, A.L. *The Wonder That Was India* (New York: Grove Press, 1954). Graceful, comprehensive, standard introduction to early Indian history. Dated on Indus valley, but still valid on imperial India.

Bhagavad Gita, trans. Barbara Stoler Miller (New York: Bantam Books, 1986). A fine, readable, clear translation of one of the greatest classics of Hinduism.

deBary, William Theodore and Irene Bloom, eds., *Sources of Chinese Tradition*, Vol. I: *From Earliest Times to 1600* (New York: Columbia University Press, 2nd ed., 1999). The best available repository of primary sources from the literature.

Ebrey, Patricia Buckley, ed. *Chinese Civilization: A Sourcebook* (New York: The Free Press, 2nd ed., 1993). An excellent sourcebook, drawn much more from the lives of common people.

Embree, Ainslee, ed. and rev. *Sources of Indian Tradition*, Vol. I: *From the Beginning to 1800* (New York: Columbia University Press, 2nd ed., 1988). The best available repository of primary sources from the literature.

Tsunoda, Ryusaku, William Theodore deBary, and Donald Keene, comps. *Sources of Japanese Tradition* (New York: Columbia University Press, 1958). The best available repository of primary sources from the literature.

ADDITIONAL SOURCES

Allchin, F.R., *et al. The Archaeology of Early Historic South Asia: The Emergence of Cities and States* (Cambridge: Cambridge University Press, 1995). Accessible, wide-ranging introduction, for non-specialists.

Andrea, Alfred and James Overfield, eds. *The Human Record*, Vol. I (Boston, MA: Houghton Mifflin Company, 3rd ed., 1998). Excellent collection of primary sources on world history.

Appadurai, Arjun. *Worship and Conflict under Colonial Rule* (Cambridge: Cambridge University Press, 1981). Demonstrates the interweaving of the major temples with the politics, economics, and social structures of their region.

Berger, Peter L. *The Sacred Canopy* (New York: Anchor Books, 1967). A classic introduction to the importance of religion and religious organizations in society.

Blunden, Caroline and Mark Elvin. *Cultural Atlas of China* (New York: Facts on File, 1983). Superb introduction to China, with fine interpretive essays, maps, pictures. Especially strong on geography and its implications.

Bodde, Derk. *Essays on Chinese Civilization*, ed. Charles Le Blanc and Dorothy Borei (Princeton, NJ: Princeton University Press, 1981). A classic set of essays on the significance of Chinese civilization.

Britannica Book of the Year 2002 (Chicago, IL: Encyclopedia Britannica, Inc., 2001) Updates a great deal of basic information, especially quantitative information on societies around the world.

Conze, Edward. *Buddhist Scriptures* (New York: Penguin Books, 1959). Basic source readings.

Craven, Roy C. *A Concise History of Indian Art* (New York: Oxford University Press, n.d.). Excellent introduction to Indian art, especially of the classical period.

The Dhammapada, trans. by Juan Mascaro (New York: Penguin Books, 1973). Fine translation and introduction to this Buddhist literary and religious classic.

Dimmitt, Cornelia and J.A.B. van Buitenen, ed. and trans. *Classical Hindu Mythology* (Philadelphia, PA: Temple University Press, 1978). An exposition of Indian mythology and texts by masters of the field.

Eberhard, Wolfram. *China's Minorities: Yesterday and Today* (Belmont, CA: Wadsworth Publishing, 1982). Fills in the picture for non-Han Chinese, a subject often overlooked.

Eliade, Mircea. *Ordeal by Labyrinth* (Chicago, IL: University of Chicago Press, 1982). Elegant exposition of the role of religion in society.

Eliade, Mircea. *The Sacred and the Profane* (New York: Harper Torchbooks, 1959). Thought provoking introduction to the way in which religion moves people and encourages them to create institutions.

Eliade, Mircea. *Yoga: Immortality and Freedom* (Princeton, NJ: Princeton University Press, 1969). The philosophy of yoga presented clearly and profoundly.

Elvin, Mark. *The Pattern of the Chinese Past* (Stanford, CA: Stanford University Press, 1973). Elvin explores especially the economy of China, its highs and lows.

Hall, Kenneth R. *Maritime Trade and State Development in Early Southeast Asia* (Honolulu: University of Hawaii, 1985). Especially good on the relationships between India and southeast Asia in trade and in political evolution.

Hall, Kenneth R. and John K. Whitmore, eds. *Explorations in Early Southeast Asian History: The Origins of Southeast Asian Statecraft* (Ann Arbor, MI: Center for South and Southeast Asian Studies, University of Michigan, 1976). Set of outstanding seminar papers.

Hammond Atlas of World History (Maplewood, NJ: Hammond, 5th ed., 1999). Indispensable world history atlas.

Hughes, Sarah Shaver and Brady Hughes, eds. *Women in World History*, Vol. I: *Readings from Prehistory to 1500* (Armonk, NY: M.E. Sharpe, 1995). Includes short, but interesting sections on husbands and wives, Sita and Rama, and Buddhist nuns.

Kulke, Hermann and Dietmar Rothermund. *A History of India* (Totowa, NJ: Barnes and Noble Books, 1986). Brief, accessible, excellent introductory history.

Lewis-Williams, David. *The Mind in the Cave: Consciousness in the Origins of Art* (London: Thames and Hudson, 2002). Exploration of meaning in earliest art includes religious speculations.

Lockard, Craig A. "Integrating Southeast Asia into the Framework of World History: The Period Before 1500," *The History Teacher* XXIX, No. 1 (November 1995), 7–35. Concern with pedagogy leads also to good conceptual scheme for understanding southeast Asia.

Martin, Rafe. *The Hungry Tigress: Buddhist Legends and Jataka Tales* (Berkeley, CA: Parallax Press, 1990). Classic legends and tales as means of transmitting the essential moral lessons of Buddhism.

Murphey, Rhoads. *A Brief History of Asia* (New York: HarperCollins, 1992). Useful especially for its cross-regional explorations.

Needham, Joseph. *The Shorter Science and Civilization in China*, Vol. I, abridged by Colin A. Ronan (Cambridge: Cambridge University Press, 1978). The classic study of Chinese science, demonstrating its methods, findings, and significance.

Nelson, Lynn and Patrick Peebles, eds. *Classics of Eastern Thought* (San Diego, CA: Harcourt Brace Jovanovich, 1991). Fine collection of basic texts.

Past Worlds: The (London) Times Atlas of Archaeology (Maplewood, NJ: Hammond, 1988). Fascinating introduction to history through archaeological finds. Lavishly illustrated with maps, pictures, charts.

Ramanujan, A.K., ed. and trans. *Poems of Love and War: From the Eight Anthologies and the Ten Long Poems of Classical Tamil* (New York: Columbia University Press, 1985). An outstanding modern poet and scholar translating classical Tamil poetry.

Ramanujan, A.K., trans. *Speaking of Síva* (Harmondsworth, England: Penguin Books, 1973). Further translations specifically on the Lord Shiva in the imagination of India.

Richman, Paula, ed. *Many Ramayanas: The Diversity of a Narrative Tradition in South Asia* (Berkeley, CA: University of California Press, 1991). The Ramayana has many interpretations and uses. Richman provides an astonishing, scholarly array of them.

Rowland, Benjamin. *The Art and Architecture of India: Buddhist/Hindu/Jain* (New York: Penguin Books, 1977). Indian religion can be understood only with reference to its art and architecture. A fine introduction.

SarDesai, D.R. *Southeast Asia: Past and Present* (Boulder, CO: Westview Press, 3rd ed., 1994). Good on the context of the spread of Buddhism.

Schwartzberg, Joseph E., ed. *A Historical Atlas of South Asia* (Chicago, IL: University of Chicago Press, 1978). A scholarly, encyclopedic coverage of history through geography. Superb research tool.

Smart, Ninian. *The World's Religions* (Cambridge: Cambridge University Press , 1989). Fine, comprehensive introduction to the major religions.

Stein, Burton. *Peasant State and Society in Medieval South India* (New Delhi: Oxford University Press, 1980). Provides context for understanding religion and religious institutions in the life of the society.

Thapar, Romila. *Ancient Indian Social History* (New Delhi: Orient Longman, 1978). Thapar's works are the most accessible, clear, comprehensive introduction to ancient India, its politics, institutions, leaders, economy, social groups, and religions.

——. *Asoka and the Decline of the Mauryas* (New Delhi: Oxford University Press, 1963).

——. *A History of India*, Vol. I (Baltimore, MD: Penguin Books, 1966).

——. *Early India: From the Origins to AD 300* (Berkeley, CA: University of California Press, 2003).

——. *Interpreting Early India* (New York: Oxford University Press, 1992).

Tharu, Susie and K. Lalita, eds. *Women Writing in India 600 B.C. to the Present*, Vol. I (New York: The Feminist Press, 1991). Includes writings from various regions of India, and puts them into context.

Twitchett, Denis and Michael Lowe, eds. *The Cambridge History of China*, Vol. I: *The Ch'in and Han Empires, 221 B.C.–A.D. 220* (Cambridge: Cambridge University Press, 1986). Comprehensive, scholarly, helps understand early Buddhism in China.

Twitchett, Denis, ed. *The Cambridge History of China*, Vol. III: *Sui and T'ang China, 589–906*, Part I (Cambridge: Cambridge University Press, 1979). Comprehensive, scholarly, follows Buddhism through its flourishing in China.

Zimmer, Heinrich. *Philosophies of India* (New York: Meridian Books, 1956). Classic introduction to the texts and concepts.

◉ World History Documents CD-ROM

3.1 *Rig Veda*

3.2 *Bhagavad Gita*: Hinduism

3.3 The Foundation of the Kingdom of Righteousness

3.4 Dhammapada: Buddhism

3.5 Mahavira: The "Great Hero" of the Jain Religion

3.6 Asoka: How a Life Was Turned Around

JUDAISM AND CHRISTIANITY

PEOPLES OF THE BIBLE: GOD'S EVOLUTION IN WEST ASIA AND EUROPE 1700 B.C.E.–1100 C.E.

KEY TOPICS
- Judaism
- Christianity
- Christianity in the Wake of Empire

Into a world that believed in many gods who often fought with one another and inter-fered capriciously in human life, the Hebrews introduced and perpetuated the concept of a single god whose rule was both orderly and just. In contrast with the many gods of polytheism, each with his or her own temperament and judgment, the new monotheism provided a more definitive statement of right and wrong. At the same time it demanded much greater conformity in both faith and action, calling for adher-ence to a strict code of ethics within a community governed by laws proclaimed by a single god. The Hebrews' belief in one god was not simply a reduction in the number of gods from many to one. Their god represented a new religious category of a god above nature and free of compulsion and fate. Their belief in only one god, however, also confronted them with a fundamental theological dilemma, a dilemma for all monotheistic religions: If there is only one god, and if the god is both all-powerful and caring, then why does human life on earth often appear so difficult and unjust?

The Hebrews' early home was in the Middle East, and other peoples in that region sometimes expressed similar ideas. In Egypt, for example, Akhenaten also proclaimed a belief in one god. His declaration of faith, however, came several centuries after that of the Hebrews. More importantly, his new faith did not survive his death and had no lasting effects on his country. Later pharaohs rejected Akhenaten's beliefs and his style of worship. In Mesopotamia, Hammurabi of Babylon issued a law code in the name of his god Shamash, by the year 1750 B.C.E., some 500 years before Hebrew sacred texts record a similar gift of a legal system from their god YHWH, through their leader Moses. Over time, however, the code of Hammurabi was forgotten in Mesopotamia while the Hebrew people kept their legal codes alive as they evolved into the Jewish people.

In their early years the "Hebrews" were known as the people whose legendary founder, Abraham, came from "eber," meaning "the other side" of the Euphrates River. Later they took on the name of Jews, in honor of one of their tribes, Judah, and of the new territory that they claimed in Judaea, in the modern land of Israel and Palestine.

Today there are only about 14 million Jews worldwide, but their role in history has been disproportionate to their numbers. Many of their core beliefs were incorporated into Christianity and Islam, the two great monotheistic faiths that have come to include half the world's population today. Meanwhile Judaism itself adapted to chang-ing conditions over time and space, maintaining its own core beliefs, traditions, and identity as an independent religious community. We begin this chapter with a study of Judaism and then proceed to Christianity, which emerged from it, and challenged it. In the next chapter we explore Islam and the interactions among all three of these closely related, but often bitterly antagonistic, monotheistic religions.

Opposite **The four evangelists, from the *Gospel Book of Charlemagne*, early ninth century.** With the exception of the cross, the best-known symbols in early Christianity were associated with the four gospels. Based on a text in the Book of Revelation (4:7), Matthew was represented by a man, Mark by a lion, Luke by a winged ox, and John by an eagle. (*Cathedral Treasury, Aachen, Germany*)

AT A GLANCE : JUDAISM AND CHRISTIANITY

DATE	POLITICAL/SOCIAL EVENTS	LITERARY/PHILOSOPHICAL EVENTS
1700 B.C.E.	■ Abraham travels from Mesopotamia to Israel (c. 1750)	
1600 B.C.E.	■ Hebrew slavery in Egypt	
1200 B.C.E.	■ Moses (?1300–?1200) ■ Exodus from Egypt; legal codes formulated; return to Palestine; tribal government under Judges	
1000 B.C.E.	■ Period of Kings begins with Saul, David, and Solomon ■ First temple in Jerusalem	
900 B.C.E	■ Jewish kingdom divides into Israel and Judaea	
800 B.C.E.	■ Prophets exhort Jewish nation (800–500) ■ Assyrians conquer Israel and exile Jews (721)	■ Numbers (850–650) ■ Genesis (mid 5th–8th century) ■ Prophets Isaiah, Amos, Micah
700 B.C.E.		■ Josiah begins to write down Torah (640) ■ Deuteronomy (mid 7th century) ■ Leviticus (mid 7th century) ■ Jeremiah
600 B.C.E.	■ Babylonians conquer Judaea, exile the people, and destroy the first temple (586) ■ Jews permitted to return to Judaea and rebuild the temple (538)	■ Book of Job (600)
300 B.C.E.		■ Books of TaNaKh (the Torah) edited and canonized
100 B.C.E.	■ Birth and death of Jesus (c. 4 B.C.E.–c. 30 C.E.)	
10 C.E.	■ Rome captures Jerusalem (63) ■ Christianity emerges from Judaism ■ St. Paul, Saul of Tarsus, organizes early Christianity (d. c. 67) ■ Rome destroys second temple (70)	■ Gospels (70–100) ■ Acts (70–80) ■ Epistles of Paul (50–120)
100 C.E.	■ Rome exiles Jews from Judaea; Jewish diaspora throughout Mediterranean basin and west Asia (135) ■ Rabbinical tradition developed (1st to 4th century)	
200 C.E.	■ Christians persecuted under Severus, Decius, and Diocletian	■ Babylonian and Jerusalem Talmuds edited and published (200–500)
300 C.E.	■ Christianity legalized (313) and then declared the official religion of the Roman Empire (392) ■ Council of Nicaea (325) ■ Georgia and Armenia convert to Christianity (c. 330)	■ Augustine's *The City of God* and *Confessions*
400 C.E.	■ Council of Chalcedon (451)	
500 C.E.	■ Monasticism in Europe ■ Clovis converted to Christianity ■ St. Benedict founds monastery of Monte Cassino	
600 C.E.	■ England converted to Christianity	■ Venerable Bede, Ecclesiastical *History of the English People*
700 C.E.	■ Iconoclastic controversy	
800 C.E.	■ Coronation of Charlemagne (800) ■ St. Cyril and St. Methodius convert Russia, translate the Bible, and create the Cyrillic alphabet	■ Einhard, *Life of Charlemagne*
900 C.E.	■ Missionaries proliferate among the Vikings	

AT A GLANCE : JUDAISM AND CHRISTIANITY (continued)

DATE	POLITICAL/SOCIAL EVENTS	LITERARY/PHILOSOPHICAL EVENTS
1000 C.E.	■ Christians capture Toledo from Muslim control and begin *reconquista* (1085) ■ Split of Western and Eastern Christianity (1054) ■ 1st Crusade (1095–9)	
1100 C.E.	■ 2nd Crusade (1147–9) ■ 3rd Crusade (1189–92)	
1200 C.E.	■ 4th Crusade (1202–04) ■ Children's Crusade (1212) ■ Crusaders capture Constantinople (1204–61) ■ 5th–8th Crusades (1218–91)	
1300 C.E.	■ Monastic orders	
1400 C.E.	■ Christians capture Granada, Spain, complete the *reconquista* (1492), expel Jews and Muslims	

JUDAISM

The story of Judaism, as recorded in Hebrew scriptures, begins some 3800 years ago with one man's vision of a single, unique God of all creation. They tell us that God and Abraham sealed a covenant stating that Abraham's descendants would forever revere and worship that God, and God, in return, would forever watch over and protect them. From then until now Judaism has remained a relatively small, family-based religion, with branches throughout the world, but focused in part in Israel, the land that Jews believe God promised to Abraham.

The Sacred Scriptures

Our knowledge of early Jewish history comes from the scriptures known collectively as the **TaNaKh**: Torah (the Five Books of Moses), Nevi'im (the Books of the Prophets), and Ketuvim (additional historical, poetic, and philosophic writings). Christians have incorporated the entire TaNaKh into their Bible, referring to these scriptures collectively as the "Old Testament." Because the New Testament is written in Greek and the Old Testament in Hebrew, the TaNaKh is often referred to as the Hebrew Bible.

TaNaKh A Hebrew term for the books of the Bible that are written in Hebrew. The word is composed of the initial letters of the words Torah (first five books of the Bible, traditionally attributed to Moses), Nevi'im (the books of the Prophets) and the Ketuvim (additional historical, poetic, and philosophic writings). These are the three sections of the Hebrew Bible.

The narratives of the five books of the Torah abound with miracles, as God intervenes continuously in the history of the Jews. The Torah begins with God's creating the world and contracting his covenant with Abraham. Over the next several generations, the Torah continues, famine struck Israel (then called Canaan), the land God promised to Abraham. Abraham's grandson and his family traveled to the Nile valley of Egypt in search of food. At first invited by the pharaoh to remain as permanent residents, they were later enslaved. About 1200 B.C.E., after 400 years of slavery, the Jews won their freedom and escaped from Egypt under the leadership of Moses through the miraculous intervention of God. During their journey back to Israel through the wilderness of the Sinai Desert, the contentious group of ex-slaves was forged into a small but militant nation. The Torah records a dramatic miracle at Mount Sinai in which God revealed a set of religious and civil laws for them to follow.

For centuries, Jews and Christians believed that these earliest books of the Bible, which describe the creation of the world and the earliest history of the Jewish people, were the literal word of God. During the past two centuries, scholarship has given us a new sense of the historical place of these books. Today historians ask: When and

The Kingdom of Israel. The first unified Jewish state in Palestine emerged around 980 B.C.E. under King David. He united the tribes of Israel during a period of decline among their more powerful neighbors—Egypt and the Hittites. After the death of his son Solomon (926 B.C.E.), tribal rivalries divided the empire into the kingdoms of Judah and Israel, but the sense of cultural unity survived.

where were the books of the Hebrew Bible composed and how valid are they as historical documents?

Modern scholarly analysis of the TaNaKh texts became a prominent academic enterprise in Germany during the early nineteenth century. The founders of "biblical criticism" noted certain inconsistencies in the biblical texts. For example, the first chapter of Genesis reports that God created man and woman simultaneously, "male and female he created them," while the second chapter reports that God first created man and then removed one of his ribs and created woman from it. The critics noted also that different names are used for God in the Hebrew text—most notably YHWH and Elohim—and they suggested that the different names represent the stylistic preferences of different authors. They noted similarities between the stories and laws of the Bible and those in the literature of other peoples of the region, and they suggested that some of the external stories had found their way into the biblical accounts. Through rigorous analysis, the biblical scholars argued persuasively that Josiah (r. 640–609 B.C.E.), the king of the Jewish state of Judaea, first made the decision to begin to edit and write down the definitive edition of oral texts that had been passed from generation to generation.

The story of Josiah's reign is told in the biblical book of 2 Kings, chapters 20–21. Struggling to survive in the face of the powerful Assyrian Empire, Josiah was anxious to promote allegiance to the state and its religion. He centralized Jewish worship in the national temple in Jerusalem and collected and transcribed the most important texts of his people. Josiah regarded adherence to the laws laid down in these scriptures as fundamental to the maintenance of the Jewish religion, the Jewish people, and his own Jewish kingdom. From existing literary fragments, folk wisdom, and oral history he had the book of Deuteronomy, the fifth book of the TaNaKh, written down. Soon, additional literary materials from at least three other major interpretive traditions were also woven together to create the books of Genesis, Exodus, Leviticus, and Numbers. Together with Deuteronomy, these books formed the Torah or "Five Books of Moses."

With the ravages of time, older copies of the Torah, written in Hebrew on parchment scrolls, began to perish and new ones were copied. The oldest existing Hebrew manuscripts of the entire Torah date only to the ninth to the eleventh centuries C.E., but fragments dating to as early as the second century B.C.E. have been discovered. Stored in caves near the Dead Sea in Israel, these Dead Sea Scrolls have been rediscovered only since 1947. Another very early edition of the Torah is a Greek translation from the Hebrew, the Septuagint. It was prepared for the Greek-speaking Jews of Egypt in the third and second centuries B.C.E. It still exists and is consistent with the Hebrew texts of our own time. In short, the written text of the Torah appears to have been preserved with great fidelity for at least 2600 years. The oral texts on which the written scriptures were based date back much further.

The Torah remains one of the greatest examples of myth-history. Although its stories should not necessarily be read as literal, historical records, their version of events gave birth to the Jewish people's concept of itself and helped to define its character and principal beliefs. The stories of the Torah tell us what the Jewish people, and especially its literate leadership, have thought important about their own origins and mission. They also define images of God that have profoundly influenced the imagination and action of Jews, Christians, and Muslims for millennia.

Essential Beliefs of Judaism in Early Scriptures

The Torah fixes many of the essential beliefs and principles of Judaism:

- A single caring God, demanding obedience, who administers rewards and punishments fairly and in accordance with his fixed laws:

  Hear, O Israel, the Lord is our God, the Lord alone. You shall love the Lord your God with all your heart, and with all your soul, and with all your might. (Deuteronomy 6:4–5)

  Know therefore that the Lord your God is God, the faithful God who maintains covenant loyalty with those who love him and keep his commandments, to a thousand generations, and who repays in their own person those who reject him. (Deuteronomy 7:9–10)

- A God of history, whose power affects the destiny of individuals and nations:

  I am the Lord your God who brought you out of Egypt, out of the land of slavery. (Exodus 20:2–3)

- A community rooted in a divinely chosen family and ethnic group:

  Now the Lord said to Abram, "Go from your country and your kindred and your father's house to the land that I will show you. I will make of you a great nation, and I will bless you, and make your name great, so that you will be a blessing." (Genesis 12:1–2)

- A specific, "promised," geographical homeland:

  When Abraham reached Canaan, God said to him: "Raise your eyes now, and look from the place where you are, northward and southward and eastward and westward; for all the land that you see I will give to you and to your offspring forever." (Genesis 13:14–15)

- A legal system to guide proper behavior: religious, familial, sexual, commercial, civic, ethical, and ritual. The introduction to this code was the Ten Commandments, revered as the heart of the revelation to Moses at Mount Sinai.

Dead Sea Scrolls, Isaiah scroll 1Q Is. 9 verses 58.6–63.4. The five hundred or so documents that make up the Dead Sea Scrolls—which date between about 250 B.C.E. and 70 C.E.—appear at one time to have formed the library of a Jewish community. As well as providing evidence of the accuracy of Hebrew biblical texts, they give information about the life of the community itself. *(Israel Museum, Jerusalem)*

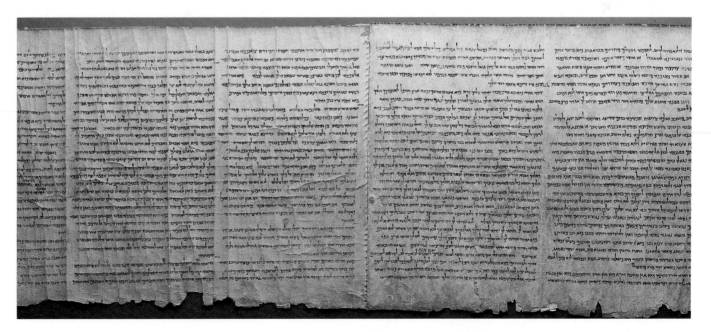

SOURCE

The Ten Commandments

The Torah contains legal codes governing many aspects of life, including family rules concerning marriage, divorce, and inheritance; civil laws regulating business practices and responsibilities; criminal law mandating rules of evidence and of punishment; rules commanding ethical and charitable behavior especially toward the weak and helpless, strangers, orphans, and widows; and extensive rules concerning ritual practices of prayer, sacrifice, food, and priestly behavior. At the center of the codes are the Ten Commandments, given, according to the Torah account, directly by God to Moses atop Mount Sinai amidst terrifying thunder, lightning, clouds, and trumpet blasts. These commandments dictate behavior toward God, parents, and fellow humans. They also proclaim the importance of observing a Sabbath day once a week.

I am the Lord your God who brought you out of Egypt, out of the house of slavery.

You shall have no other gods before me.

You shall not make for yourself an idol, whether in the form of anything that is in heaven above, or that is on the earth beneath, or that is in the water under the earth.

You shall not bow down to them or worship them; for I the Lord your God am a jealous god, punishing children for the iniquity of parents, to the third and fourth generation of those who reject me, but showing steadfast love to the thousandth generation of those who love me and keep my commandments.

You shall not make wrongful use of the name of the Lord your God, for the Lord will not acquit anyone who misuses his name.

Remember the Sabbath day, and keep it holy. Six days you shall labor and do all your work. But the seventh day is a Sabbath to the Lord your God; you shall not do any work—you, your son or your daughter, your male or female slave, your livestock, or the alien resident in your towns. For in six days the Lord made heaven and earth, the sea, and all that is in them, but rested the seventh day; therefore the Lord blessed the Sabbath day and consecrated it.

Honor your father and your mother, so that your days may be long in the land that the Lord your God is giving you.

You shall not murder.

You shall not commit adultery.

You shall not steal.

You shall not bear false witness against your neighbor.

You shall not covet your neighbor's house; you shall not covet your neighbor's wife, or male or female slave, or ox, or donkey, or anything that belongs to your neighbor.
(Exodus 20:2–17; see also Deuteronomy 5)

- A sacred calendar: Jewish religious leaders reconstituted earlier polytheistic celebrations of nature into a calendar of national religious celebration. A spring festival of renewal was incorporated into Passover, the commemoration of the exodus from Egypt; an early summer festival of first harvest was subsumed into Shavuot, a rejoicing in the revelation of the Ten Commandments at Sinai; and an early fall harvest festival became part of Sukkot (Succoth), a remembrance of the years of wandering in the desert. All these festivals were to be celebrated, if possible, by pilgrimage to the central, national temple in Jerusalem. Celebrations of nature, history, and national identity were fused together.

To ground the mystical beliefs and forge the Jewish people into a "kingdom of priests and a sacred nation," rules issued in the name of God forbade intermarriage with outsiders; prohibited eating animals which do not have cloven hooves and chew their cud, and fish that do not have scales and fins (Deuteronomy 14 and Leviticus 11); and centralized worship in the hands of a priestly aristocracy. Animal sacrifices were to be offered, but only by the hereditary priests and only in a single national temple in Jerusalem.

The Later Books of Jewish Scripture

The later volumes of the TaNaKh, the books of Nevi'im and Ketuvim, carry an account of the history of the Jewish people from about 1200 B.C.E. to about the fifth century B.C.E. God continues as a constant presence in these narratives, but he intervenes less openly and less frequently. These later records can generally be cross-checked against

Moses, mosaic in San Vitale, Ravenna, Italy, sixth century C.E. After he had led the Israelite slaves out of Egypt by the miracle of parting the Red Sea), Moses ascended Mount Sinai. There he received from God the Torah, or sacred teachings, beginning with the two tablets of the Ten Commandments. He led his quarrelsome people across the Sinai desert but died at the border of the promised land.

the archaeology of the region and the history of neighboring peoples, and they seem generally consistent.

The Book of Joshua begins the story about the year 1200 B.C.E., as the Jews returned to Canaan, or Israel, the land promised to them, and made it their home. This biblical account tells of continuous, violent, political and religious warfare between the invading Jews and the resident Canaanite peoples. Modern scholarship suggests, however, that re-entry into the land of Israel was a gradual process, with fewer, more localized battles and considerably more cultural borrowing among all the groups in the region.

Rule by Judges and by Kings. Arriving in Canaan, the Jews first organized themselves in a loose tribal confederacy led by a series of "Judges," *ad hoc* leaders who took

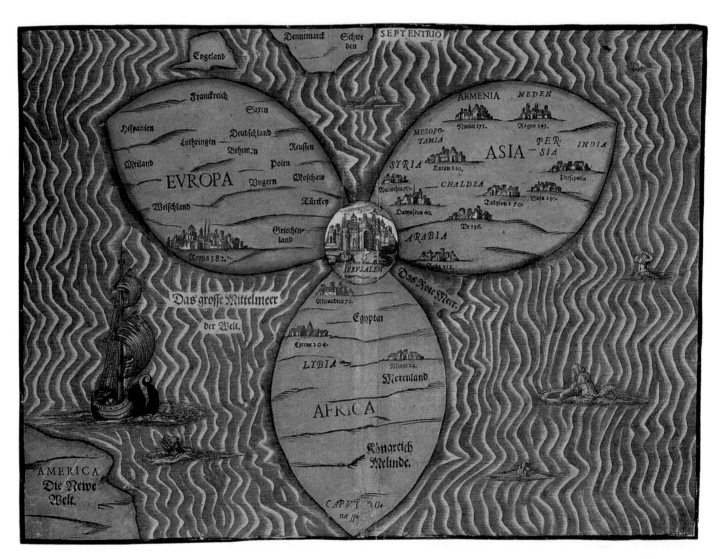

Map of the world by Heinrich Bunting, 1585. Many peoples believed that their capital city was the cosmo-magical axis of the universe. This map, shaped like a clover leaf, places Jerusalem at the center, uniting Africa, Asia, and Europe.

command at critical periods, especially at times of war. Later, despite warnings that a monarchy would lead to increased warfare, profligate leaders, extortionate taxes, and the impressment of young men and women into royal service, the Jews anointed a king. For three generations (c. 1020–950 B.C.E.), strong kings, Saul, David, and Solomon, are said to have ruled and expanded the geographic base of the people. They established a national center in Jerusalem, where they united political and religious power by building both palace and temple, exalting both king and priest. The earlier warnings against royal excesses, however, proved correct. Unable to sustain Solomon's legendary extravagances in expenditure and in his relationships with 700 wives, many of them foreign princesses, and 300 concubines, the kingdom split in two, the kingdom of Judah and the kingdom of Israel.

The Teachings of the Prophets: Morality and Hope. Continuing despotism by their kings and greed on the part of their wealthier citizens ripped apart the social fabric of the two splinter kingdoms. A group of prophets emerged, demanding reform. In powerful and sublime language, these men called for a reinstitution of justice, compassion, and ethics. Speaking in the name of God and of the people, they cried out against the hypocritical misuse of religious and political power.

The prophet Isaiah, in the eighth century B.C.E., led the charge:

> When you stretch out your hands, I will hide my eyes from you; even though you
> make many prayers, I will not listen; your hands are full of blood.
> Wash yourselves; make yourselves clean; remove the evil of your doings from before
> my eyes; cease to do evil,
> Learn to do good; seek justice, rescue the oppressed, defend the orphan, plead for the
> widow. (Isaiah 1:15–17)

A century later, Jeremiah continued in the same spirit of moral outrage, rebuking the
rulers and people of Judah, the southern kingdom:

> You keep saying, "This place is the temple of the Lord, the temple of the Lord, the
> temple of the Lord!" This catchword of yours is a lie; put no trust in it. Mend your
> ways and your doings, deal fairly with one another, do not oppress the alien, the
> orphan, and the widow, shed no innocent blood in this place, do not run after other
> gods to your own ruin. (Jeremiah 7:4–6)

So even at the time that Israel and Judah developed into powerful kingdoms, the
prophets remembered that the beginnings of the Jewish people were in slavery and
that a significant part of its mission was to identify with and help the downtrodden.
When destruction came, the prophets interpreted it as punishment not *of* their God, as
earlier peoples had often done, but *by* their God. Destruction of a corrupt nation indicated not the weakness of its God, but his ethical consistency.

Finally, the prophets not only harangued, blamed, and condemned, they also held
up visions of a future to inspire their listeners. They saw God transforming human
history. He offered rewards as well as punishments. He offered hope. Micah's
prophecy in the eighth century B.C.E. is one of the most exalted, and perhaps utopian:

> He shall judge between many peoples, and shall arbitrate between strong nations far
> away; they shall beat their swords into plowshares, and their spears into pruning
> hooks; nation shall not lift up sword against nation, neither shall they learn war any
> more; but they shall all sit under their own vines and under their own fig trees, and
> no one shall make them afraid; for the mouth of the Lord of hosts has spoken.
> (Micah 4:1–4)

Micah closed with a vision of great Jewish religious commitment, balanced by equally
great appreciation for the diversity of others:

> For all the peoples walk each in the name of its god, but we will walk in the name of
> the Lord our God forever and ever. (Micah 4:5)

The Evolution of the Image of God

The Torah portrays God as an evolving moral force in dialogue with humans. In God's
early interactions with humans, his nature is still malleable. Disgusted at human disobedience, he destroys almost all humankind through a flood, but he then pledges
never to be so destructive again, creating a rainbow as a kind of treaty of peace with
humanity (Genesis 6–8). Still fearful of the collective power of humanity, God confounds their inter-communication by dividing them into separate language groups at
the Tower of Babel (Genesis 11). While deciding the fate of the sinful cities of Sodom
and Gomorrah, God listens to Abraham's plea for the defense: "Far be it from thee to
do this—to kill good and bad together; for then the good would suffer with the bad.
Far be it from thee. Shall not the judge of all the earth do what is just?" (Genesis 18–19).
God apparently bans child sacrifice when he stops Abraham from killing his son Isaac.
(The Muslim Quran reports this to be Abraham's son Ishmael.)

When asked by Moses to identify himself by name, God replies enigmatically and powerfully, "I am who I am" (Exodus 3:14). The Hebrew designation for God's name is YHWH, "Being." English-speaking readers have usually rendered it either Jehovah or Yahweh.

In Jewish theology, God is almighty but still directly accessible to every human being through prayer and even through dialogue. Indeed, humans and God come to understand each other by arguing with one another in a process that the contemporary rabbi Arthur Waskow has called "Godwrestling." If Jews are to be God's people and to follow his will, he, in turn, is expected to be a compassionate and attentive ruler.

This view challenged the polytheistic beliefs in self-willed gods, but it left Judaism with no strong answer to the eternal problem of evil in the universe: If there is a single God, and if he is good, why do the wicked often prosper and the righteous often suffer? One biblical response is found in the Book of Job (*c.* 600 B.C.E.). To the questions of the innocent, suffering Job, God finally responds with overwhelming power:

Who is this whose ignorant words cloud my design in darkness?
Brace yourself and stand up like a man; I will ask the questions, and you shall answer.
Where were you when I laid the earth's foundations? Tell me, if you know and
     understand.
Who settled its dimensions? Surely you should know …
Is it for a man who disputes with the Almighty to be stubborn?
Should he that argues with God answer back? (Job 38:2–5; 40:2)

But while God lectures Job for his brashness in questioning his authority and power, he understands Job's anguish at the apparent injustice in the world and ultimately rewards Job with health, a restored family, and abundance for his honesty in raising his questions.

Crossing the Red Sea, c. 245 C.E. Fresco, synagogue at Dura Europos, Syria. The Old Testament tells of God's miraculous intervention in helping Moses and the people of Israel escape enslavement in Egypt. Hotly pursued by pharaoh's soldiers to the banks of the Red Sea, Moses saw the waves draw back in front of him to allow the Jews to pass. When the Egyptians tried to follow, the sea engulfed them and they were drowned. (*National Archaeological Museum, Damascus, Syria*)

Patriarchy and Gender Relations

The Torah grants women fewer civil and religious rights (and obligations) than men. By conventional interpretation, women were expected to be responsible for nursing and child care, tasks that know no time constraints, and they were therefore freed of all ritual obligations that had to be performed at specific times, for instance prayers at specific times of day.

The regulation of sexuality is a fundamental issue in biblical Jewish law, as it is in most religions. Women are regarded as ritually unclean each month at times of menstruation and in childbirth. Men may be ritually unclean as a result of wet dreams or sexual diseases (Leviticus 15), but these occurred with less regularity. Marriage is regarded as the norm, with a strong emphasis on bearing children. Homosexual behavior is strongly rejected. (Today, however, many branches of Judaism have revised gender rules and discarded prohibitions on homosexuality.)

Jewish scriptures credit a few women with heroic roles. Sarah, Abraham's wife, forced him to choose her son as his proper successor, and she gained God's approval (Genesis 16). Deborah led Israel in peace and war during the period of conquering the land of Israel (Judges 4–5). Ruth, a convert, taught the importance of openness to the outside world; she became an ancestor of King David and, therefore, in Christian belief, of Jesus (Book of Ruth). Esther was married to the Persian king and used her position to block the attempts of a court minister to kill the Jews of the Persian Empire (Book of Esther). Although none of these stories can be authenticated externally nor dated exactly, they speak to the significance of individual, exceptional women at turning points in Jewish history, and in the collective mind of the Jewish people.

JEWISH FESTIVALS AND FAST DAYS		
Hebrew date	Gregorian date	Name of festival
1–2 Tishri	Sept–Oct	Rosh Hashana (New Year)
10 Tishri	Sept–Oct	Yom Kippur (Day of Atonement)
15–21 Tishri	Sept–Oct	Sukkot (Feast of the Tabernacles)
22 Tishri	Sept–Oct	Shemini Atzeret (8th Day of the Solemn Assembly)
23 Tishri	Sept–Oct	Simchat Torah (Rejoicing of the Law)
25 Kislev–2–3 Tevet	Nov–Dec	Hannukah (Feast of Dedication)
14–15 Adar	Feb–Mar	Purim (Feast of Lots)
14–20 Nisan	Mar–Apr	Pesach (Passover)
5 Iyar	Apr–May	Israel Independence Day
6–7 Sivan	May–Jun	Shavuot (Feast of Weeks)
9 Av	Jul–Aug	Tisha be–Av (Fast of 9th Av)

Defeat, Exile, and Redefinition

Jews represent both an ethnic community and a universal religion. This dual identity became especially clear when foreign conquerors exiled part of the Jewish population from Israel as part of a plan to encourage their assimilation and to open the land to foreign immigration. This dispersion of Jews to various lands ruled by other peoples is known as the **diaspora**.

First, Sennacherib of Assyria dispersed the Jews of the northern kingdom of Israel in 721 B.C.E. These exiles drifted into assimilation and were subsequently referred to as the "Lost Ten Tribes of Israel." In 586 B.C.E., Babylonian conquerors destroyed the temple in Jerusalem and exiled thousands of Jews from the southern kingdom of Judah to Babylon, but these Jews remained loyal to their unique identity as a separate community, remembering their homeland:

diaspora A dispersion of peoples. Most commonly used to refer to the dispersion of Jews among the gentiles, which began with the Babylonian captivity of the sixth century B.C.E.

> By the rivers of Babylon—there we sat down and wept when we remembered Zion …
> Our captors asked us for songs: "Sing us one of the songs of Zion!"
> How could we sing the Lord's song in a foreign land?
> If I forget you, O Jerusalem, let my right hand wither!
> Let my tongue cling to the roof of my mouth if I do not remember you, if I do not set
>   Jerusalem above my highest joy. (Psalm 137)

The second (Herod's) temple (model), 20 B.C.E. The temple at Jerusalem was originally built in the tenth century B.C.E. by King Solomon as a symbol of national unity and as a religious pilgrimage center. Razed by the Babylonians in 586 B.C.E., it was rebuilt sixty years later. It was finally destroyed by the Romans in 70 C.E. as part of the campaign to crush Jewish rebellion.

When the emperor Cyrus permitted the Jews to return to Judaea some sixty years later, many Jews left Babylonia, returned to Judaea, rebuilt their temple, and reconstructed national life. But many did not. Those who stayed behind did not assimilate into the Babylonian culture, however. Instead, they reconstituted their religion, replacing the sacrificial services of the temple with meditation and prayers offered privately or in synagogues. They replaced the hereditary priesthood with teachers and rabbis, positions earned through study and piety. In academies at Sura and Pumbeditha, towns adjacent to Babylon, rabbis continued the study of the Torah. They interpreted and edited Jewish law, and they elaborated Jewish stories and myths, which often conveyed moral principles. The multi-volumed record of their proceedings, the Babylonian Talmud, was completed about 500 C.E. So distinguished was the Jewish scholarship of Babylonia, that this Talmud was considered superior in coverage and scholarship to the Jerusalem Talmud, which was produced about the same time in academies in Israel.

Jews lived in substantial numbers both in Israel and in the diaspora. Many had chosen to remain in Babylonia even after they were permitted to return to Judaea. Many others traveled by free choice throughout the trade and cultural networks that were established by the Persians in the sixth century B.C.E., enhanced by Alexander the Great in the fourth century B.C.E., and eventually extended by the Roman Empire.

A census of the Roman Empire undertaken by the Emperor Claudius in 48 C.E. showed 5,984,072 Jews. This figure suggests a total global Jewish population of about 8 million. At the time, the population of the Roman Empire was perhaps 60 million, while that of the Afro-Eurasian world was about 170 million. Most Jews outside Israel continued to look to Jerusalem as a spiritual center, and they sent funds to support the temple.

Judaea itself passed from one conqueror to another, from the Persians to Alexander the Great and his successors, and then to the Roman Empire in 63 B.C.E. As noted in Chapter 6, struggles simmered continuously under Roman rule, not only between Jews and Romans, but also among Jewish political and religious factions. Three major revolts broke out and Roman authorities responded with overwhelming force in suppressing them. In 70 C.E. they destroyed the Jewish temple in Jerusalem, exiled all Jews

from the city, and turned it into their regional capital. In 135 C.E. they dismantled the political structure of the Jewish state and exiled almost all Jews from Judaea.

Unlike earlier exiles, this Roman dispersion fundamentally and permanently altered Jewish existence, removing all but a few Jews from the region of Israel until the twentieth century. This final exile established the principal contours of Jewish diaspora existence from then on: life as a minority group; dispersed among various peoples around the world; with distinct religious and social practices; united in reverence for sacred texts and their teachings, as interpreted by rabbi-scholars; usually dependent on the widely varying policies of the peoples among whom they lived; and sometimes forced to choose between religious conversion, emigration, or death. Jews preserved their cohesion through their acceptance of the authority of the TaNaKh and the importance of studying it, and their persistence in seeing themselves as a special kind of family even in dispersion.

Menorah procession, Arch of Titus, Rome, c. 81 C.E. The Romans put down the Jewish revolt of 70 C.E. by recapturing Jerusalem, destroying the temple, and looting its sacred objects. This relief from Emperor Titus' triumphal arch shows Roman soldiers with the temple *menorah*, a seven-branched candelabrum, which today serves as an official emblem of the state of Israel.

Minority–Majority Relations in the Diaspora

In general, Jews remained socially and religiously distinct wherever they traveled. This identification was imposed partially from the outside by others, partially by internal discipline and loyalty to the group, its traditions, and its laws. Jewish history becomes a case study also of tolerance and intolerance of minorities by majority peoples around the world.

In some civilizations, Jewish life in the diaspora survived and even flourished. For example, Rabbi Benjamin of Tudela, Spain, visited Muslim Baghdad in 1160–70 C.E. and reported: "In Baghdad there are about 40,000 Jews, and they dwell in security, prosperity, and honor under the great Caliph, and amongst them are great sages, the heads of Academies engaged in the study of the law. In this city there are ten Academies ... and twenty-eight Jewish synagogues" (Andrea & Overfield, Vol. I, pp. 248–9).

There were contrary examples, however. The Book of Esther, written about (and probably during) the Persian diaspora, 638–333 B.C.E., captures the vulnerability of minority existence. A royal minister sees his chance to advance his career and profit and argues to the king:

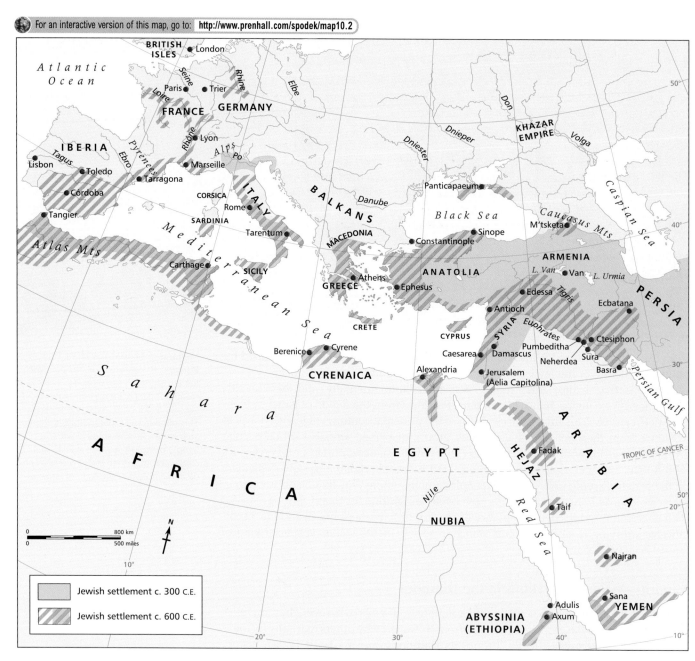

For an interactive version of this map, go to: http://www.prenhall.com/spodek/map10.2

Jewish settlement c. 300 C.E.

Jewish settlement c. 600 C.E.

The Jewish diaspora. Following the Jewish Revolt in 66 C.E., the Roman destruction of the temple in Jerusalem in 70, and the defeat of the Bar-Cochba revolt in 135, the Roman government expelled the Jews from Judaea. These migrations spread Judaism north into Mesopotamia and Anatolia, followed trade routes throughout the Mediterranean and the Red Sea, and eventually resulted in Jewish communities being established as far afield as northwest Europe and Ethiopia.

There is a certain people, dispersed among the many peoples in all the provinces of your kingdom, who keep themselves apart. Their laws are different from those of every other people; they do not keep your majesty's laws. It does not befit your majesty to tolerate them. If it please your majesty, let an order be made in writing for their destruction; and I will pay ten thousand talents of silver to your majesty's officials, to be deposited in the royal treasury. (Esther 3:8–9)

The king agrees: "The money and the people are yours; deal with them as you wish" (Esther 3:11). On this occasion, according to Jewish traditions, the actions of Esther saved these Jews from destruction. But the biblical account captures a pattern of official xenophobia and greed, repeated frequently in Jewish history—and in the history of many minorities.

CHRISTIANITY

Christianity Emerges from Judaism

At the height of Roman rule over Judaea, a splinter group within the Jewish people was forming around the person and teachings of Jesus of Nazareth. External histories indicate that the times were turbulent and difficult. As a colony of the Roman Empire, Judaea was taxed heavily and suppressed economically and politically. The Romans also demanded emperor worship from a people who were devoted to monotheism. Religious and political antagonisms were closely intertwined in an explosive mixture. The Jewish prophets of the Old Testament had promised a final end to such anguish, and many of Jesus's followers believed that he was the "servant" that had been promised to lead them into a brighter future.

In the face of Roman colonialism, the Jews were divided into at least four conflicting groups. The largest of these groups, the Pharisees, identified with the masses of the population in resenting the Roman occupation, but, seeing no realistic alternative to it, found some comfort in keeping alive and reinterpreting Jewish religious traditions. The more elite Sadducees, the temple priesthood and their allies, had become servants of the Roman state and preached accommodation to it. A much smaller, militant group of Zealots sought, quixotically, to drive out the Romans through violence. A fourth, still smaller group, the Essenes, lived a prayerful existence by the shores of the Dead Sea, stayed aloof from politics, and preached the imminent end of the world as they knew it.

Into this volatile and complex society, Jesus was born to Joseph, a carpenter, and Mary, his betrothed, about the year 4 B.C.E., in the town of Bethlehem, about 10 miles southwest of Jerusalem. (The year of Jesus' birth is not recorded. The Christian calendar places it at the beginning of the year 1, but it must have taken place no later than 4 B.C.E., for Herod, king at the time of Jesus' birth, died that year.) Biblical accounts report little about his early life, except that his parents took him to Jerusalem to celebrate the Passover holiday when he was twelve years old, and he entered there into probing discussions of religion with teachers sitting in the temple, astonishing onlookers and his parents. Jesus next emerges, at about the age of thirty, as a powerful preacher, attracting multitudes to his sermons that are filled with allegories and parables concerning ethical life, moral teachings, and predictions of the future.

In his calls for rapid and radical religious reform, Jesus found himself in opposition to the more conservative Pharisees, whom he frequently referred to as hypocrites. Like the Essenes, he spoke often of an imminent day of divine judgment of the whole world. He promised eternal life and happiness to the poor and downtrodden people of colonial Judaea if only they would keep their faith in God. Similar predictions had also been common among the Jewish prophets centuries before, and Jesus' emphasis on the coming of the kingdom of God resonated strongly with the earlier voices as well as with the Essenes. Jesus' message, however, stressed a future not on earth during people's lifetimes, but in heaven after their deaths. In this he differed from most Jewish beliefs of his time. In addition to his preaching, according to biblical accounts Jesus also performed exorcisms and miracles, fed multitudes of people, cured the blind and lame among his followers, and even brought the dead back to life. He pursued his unorthodox search for truth in the Galilee, the beautiful and lush northern region of Judaea, only recently converted to Judaism. There he continued his preaching, angering both the Jewish religious establishment, which viewed him as a heretic, and the Roman imperial government, which feared the revolutionary potential of his rabble rousing.

Jesus' followers, however—mostly common people—revered him as one specially chosen and anointed by God (*Messiah* in Hebrew, *Christos* in Greek). They proclaimed

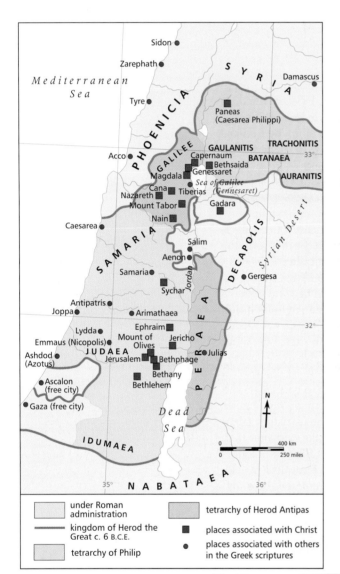

Silver crucifix from Birka, Sweden, *c.* 900 C.E. The cross—signifying Christ's crucifixion—was adopted by Christians as a symbol of their faith as early as the second century. Making "the sign of the cross" was believed powerful in warding off evil, and, in later centuries, crusaders were said to "take the cross" when they set off on crusade (a word itself derived from the Latin for cross, *crux*). (*Historiska Museet, Stockholm*)

Palestine at the time of Jesus. Christianity first emerged as a sect within Judaism when Roman control of Palestine was increasing. Shortly before Jesus' birth, Rome had granted Herod the Great the Kingdom of Judaea as a client ruler. Upon his death in 4 B.C.E. the kingdom was divided among his sons, and Judaea itself came under direct Roman military rule.

Jesus to be the source of eternal life and accepted him as a miracle-worker and the son of God. They believed, according to the biblical accounts, that his birth had been a miracle, that he had been conceived by the Holy Spirit of God and born to Mary, who was a virgin.

Jesus said that he had come "not to abolish the Jewish law but to fulfill it," and his followers accepted much of the moral code of Jewish teachings, but they rejected most parts of its legal and separatist covenant. Beginning in a few towns at the eastern end of the Mediterranean Sea, Jesus' followers built an entirely new organizational structure for sustaining and spreading their new faith in this man whom they called Christ, God's anointed representative.

As Jesus' fame spread, the fears of the Jewish religious authorities and the Roman colonial administrators increased. To prevent any potential rebellion, the Roman government seized him when he once again returned to Jerusalem to preach and to celebrate the Passover, and executed him by crucifixion when he was thirty-three years old.

But death did not stop Jesus' message. His followers believed that he arose from the grave in a miraculous resurrection and triumph over death, and ascended to heaven to join God the Father. Their belief contained equal measures of admiration for his message of compassion and salvation and for his ability to perform miracles. Jesus' disciples took his message of compassion, salvation, and eternal life to Rome. The proud upper classes of Rome scoffed at first, but more and more of the simple people believed. Despite early persecution, Christianity increased in influence, until, in the fourth century, it became the official religion of the empire.

Spread through the networks of the empire, the Christian Church ultimately became the most important organizing force in post-Roman Europe. The message of Christianity and the organization of the Church expanded throughout the world. Today almost 2 billion people, one-third of the world's population, distributed among numerous different churches and denominations, declare themselves followers of Jesus, the simple preacher from Judaea.

HOW DO WE KNOW?

The Search for the Historical Jesus

The only records of Jesus's life are the four gospels, "the good news accounts," the first four books of the New Testament, which is the second section of the Christian Bible. Named for their authors—Matthew, Mark, Luke, and John—the gospels are neither unbiased nor contemporary. Mark, probably the oldest of the four, dates to 70 C.E., forty years after Jesus' death. As with the early literature of Hinduism, Buddhism, and Judaism, the gospels represent written recordings of oral traditions. They bring together traditions surrounding Jesus's life as they were transmitted among his followers. Although individual names are associated with them, the actual authors of the gospels are unknown. Mark, for example, was the most common name in the Roman Empire at the time. Moreover, it appears that they were written for different audiences and therefore tell their stories somewhat differently. Mark, for example, addressed his beliefs in a future life to Christians who were being persecuted in Rome.

Fifty-two additional texts, called by scholars the Gnostic gospels, were discovered near the town of Nag Hammadi in upper Egypt in 1945, and have been subject to intense study ever since. Scholars believe that these texts were transcribed at about the same time as the four gospels of the Christian Bible, but that they contain accounts of Jesus'

teachings that were inconsistent with them and that they were therefore banned by Church leaders and hidden away.

According to the most important of the Gnostic gospels, The Secret Gospel of Thomas, Jesus taught that each individual could find the light of God within him or herself, without the necessity of belief in Jesus. "The kingdom is inside of you, and it is outside of you. When you come to know yourselves, then you will become known, and you will realize that it is you who are the sons of the living father." The search for meaning is most important: "Jesus said, 'Let him who seeks continue seeking until he finds. When he finds, he will become troubled. When he becomes troubled he will be astonished, and he will rule over the all.'"

The Gnostic gospels also give a greater place to women in the search for religious truth, and they suggest that Jesus had some measure of physical relationship with Mary Magdalene, a prostitute whom he brought back to respectable society. These somewhat mystical gospels, with their message of a greater sexuality for Jesus, were suppressed as heresies in the wake of theological struggles within the Church in the late second century.

The four biblical gospels themselves also present additional problems for historical analysis. They begin with the story of the birth of Jesus told as a miracle. According to the gospels, Jesus was the son of God, born miraculously through Mary, a virgin betrothed to Joseph, a carpenter from Nazareth in the region of the Galilee. Believers certainly

accept such an account, but it is not subject to historical verification. Moreover, despite the gospels' accounts of Jesus' multitudes of followers, and his political and religious influence, neither Roman nor Jewish records of the time take note of his life or his teachings. Tacitus, although scornful of the early Christians, does take note of Jesus' death.

Modern scholars who have attempted to reconstruct the life of Jesus have reached very different conclusions about his essential character, depicting Jesus as political revolutionary, magician, Galilean charismatic, Galilean rabbi, proto-Pharisee, Essene, prophet of the end of days, exorcist, miracle worker, and marginal Jew. All the research, however, no matter how scholarly and how inventive, remains inconclusive. The four biblical gospels, despite their richness as religious teachings, have serious shortcomings as religious texts, and the historical validity of the Gnostic gospels is clouded by their official suppression.

- What are the shortcomings of the gospels as historical texts for understanding the life of Jesus? What are their strengths?
- Historians attempting to characterize the life of Jesus, have reached very different conclusions. What kinds of sources do you think they used?
- If the Gnostic gospels had not been suppressed by powerful theologians, do you think the Church might have developed differently? If so, how? If not, why not?

Jesus' Life, Teachings, and Disciples

Whatever the reality of the miracles associated with Jesus, clearly a new religion, Christianity, emerged from earlier Jewish roots, and in this process, a number of adaptations and innovations took place.

Adapting Rituals to New Purposes. As we have seen, newly forming religions often adapt rituals and philosophies from already existing religions, as, for example, Buddhism adapted the concept of *dharma* from Hinduism. This borrowing and adaptation can be attractive to members of the existing religion who wish to join the new one, for it assures them that their spiritual customs will be maintained. At the same time, a new interpretation gives the ritual a new meaning for the new faith. Jesus' form of prayer and much of his preaching were fully in accord with Jewish tradition. When he accepted baptism from the desert preacher John the Baptist, however, Jesus prepared the way for adapting an existing practice and giving it new meaning for his followers. A minor practice within Judaism, baptism would later become in Christianity a central **sacrament** of purification enjoined on all members.

Another example of adaptation is Jesus' "last supper," a Passover ritual meal. Jesus ate unleavened, flat bread as a symbol of slavery in Egypt, and he drank the wine that accompanies all Jewish festivals as a symbol of joy. Then he offered the bread and wine also to his disciples with the words, "This is my body ... this is my blood." Thus he transformed the foods of the Passover meal into the **Eucharist**, or Holy Communion, another central sacrament, a mystery through which Christians believe the invisible Christ grants communion to them.

Overturning the Old Order. In his teachings, Jesus also addressed political and social issues, staking out his own often ambiguous positions in relationship to the different and competing philosophies of the day. When Jesus, following John the Baptist, taught, "Repent; for the kingdom of heaven has come near" (Matthew 4:17), he was not explicit in describing that kingdom or its date of arrival. But in metaphor and parable he preached that life as we know it on earth would soon change dramatically, or even come to an end.

sacrament In Christian theology, a rite or ritual that is an outward sign of a spiritual grace conveyed on the believer by Christ through the ministry of the Church.

Eucharist From the Greek *eucharistia*, thanksgiving. The central **sacrament** and act of worship of the Christian Church, culminating in Holy Communion.

SOURCE

The Beatitudes from the Sermon on the Mount

Jesus' teaching—powerful in direct address, in parable, and in allegory—established his identification with the poor and oppressed, his disdain for the Roman authorities, and his scorn for the Jewish religious leadership of his time. He sounded much like a latterday Jewish prophet calling his people to reform. The Beatitudes, a list of promises of God's rewards for the simple, righteous people, the first of Jesus' great sermons recorded in the New Testament, was delivered from the top of a hill in Galilee.

Blessed are the poor in spirit, for theirs is the kingdom of heaven.
Blessed are those who mourn, for they will be comforted.
Blessed are the meek, for they will inherit the earth.
Blessed are those who hunger and thirst for righteousness, for they will be filled.
Blessed are the merciful, for they will receive mercy.
Blessed are the poor in heart, for they will see God.
Blessed are the peacemakers, for they will be called children of God.
Blessed are those who are persecuted for righteousness' sake, for theirs is the kingdom of heaven. (Matthew 5:3–10)

Jesus' words must have been especially welcome to the poor, as he spoke repeatedly of the "Kingdom of Heaven" in which the tables would be turned:

> It will be hard for a rich person to enter the kingdom of heaven. Again I tell you, it is easier for a camel to go through the eye of a needle than for someone who is rich to enter the kingdom of God. (Matthew 19:23–4)

Jesus declared that the most important commandment was to "Love the Lord your God with all your heart, and with all your soul, and with all your mind," and the second was "Love your neighbor as yourself," both directly cited from the TaNaKh (Deuteronomy 6:7 and Leviticus 19:18). Indeed, he projected these principles into new dimensions, declaring "Love your enemies and pray for your persecutors" (Matthew 5:44). But he also warned that the coming apocalypse would be violent:

> Do not think that I have come to bring peace to earth; I have not come to bring peace, but a sword. (Matthew 10:34)

Jesus and the Jewish Establishment. The gospels depict Jesus' attitude toward Jewish law as ambivalent but often condescending, and his relationship toward the Jewish religious leadership as confrontational. He scoffed at Jewish dietary laws: "It is not what goes into the mouth that defiles a person, but it is what comes out of the mouth that defiles" (Matthew 15:11). He constantly tested the limits of Sabbath restrictions, declaring that: "The Sabbath is made for man, not man for the Sabbath" (Mark 2:27). He restricted divorce, announcing that: "If a man divorces his wife for any cause other than unchastity he involves her in adultery; and anyone who marries a divorced woman commits adultery" (Matthew 5:32). Many of his teachings may have reflected his desire to return to earlier beliefs in faith and spirituality and his belief that the future lay in heaven, not on earth.

Miracles and Resurrection. The gospels describe Jesus' ministry as filled with miracles—healing the sick, restoring sight to the blind, feeding multitudes of followers from just a few loaves and fishes, walking on water, calming storms, and even raising the dead. Reports of these miracles, perhaps even more than his ethical teachings, brought followers flocking to him. The gospel narrative of Jesus' suffering on the cross, presenting him at the final moment of his life as both human and divine in one personage, and finally his miraculous resurrection from the grave, his appearances to his disciples, and his ascent to heaven, complete the miracle and the majesty of his life and embody his promise of eternal life for those who believe in his power.

The stories of Jesus's life and death, message and miracles, form the basis for Christianity, at first a new sect located within Judaism. Although different followers attributed more or less divinity and greater or lesser miracles to him, apparently all accepted Jesus as a new, reforming teacher. Many saw him as the long-awaited "Messiah," a messenger and savior specially anointed by God. His apostles, especially Paul of Tarsus (d. 67), now refocused Jesus's message and built the Christian sect into a new, powerful religion. The apostles' preaching, organizational work, and letters to fledgling Christian communities fill most of the rest of the New Testament.

The Growth of the Early Church

At first, the followers of Jesus functioned as a sect within Judaism, continuing to meet in synagogues and to identify themselves as Jews. Peter, described in the gospels as Jesus' chosen organizational leader, first took the Christian message outside the Jewish community (Acts 10). Declaring circumcision unnecessary for membership, he

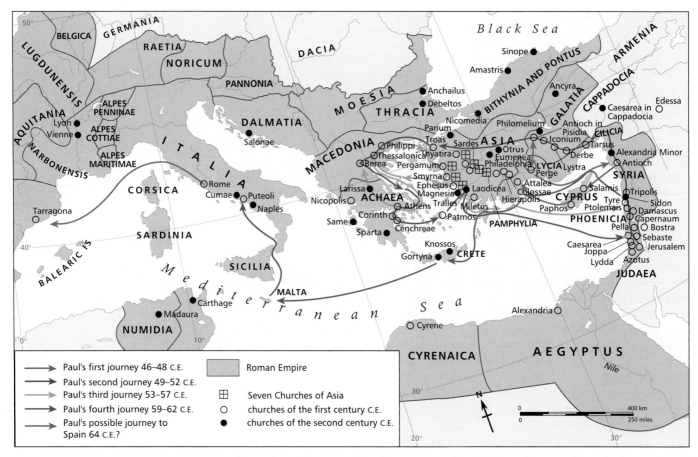

Paul's missionary journeys. Following Jesus' trial and crucifixion, about 29 C.E., his disciples, notably the Roman convert Paul, set out to convert non-Jews or gentiles. Paul's journeys took him throughout the Greco-Roman east Mediterranean, and beyond. These journeys and the epistles Paul wrote began to weave struggling Christian groups into a new religious organization, the Christian Church. Paul died in Rome, apparently a martyr to the Emperor Nero.

welcomed gentiles, people who were not Jewish, into the new Church. James, Jesus' brother and leader of the Christian community of Jerusalem, abrogated most of the Jewish dietary laws for the new community (Acts 15). These apostles believed that the rigorous ritual laws of Judaism inhibited the spread of its ethical message. Instead, they chose to emphasize the miraculous powers of Jesus and his followers. They spoke little of their master's views on the coming apocalypse but stressed his statements on the importance of love and redemption.

Paul Organizes the Early Church. Tensions continued to simmer between mainstream Jewish leaders and the early Christians. One of the fiercest opponents of the new sect was Saul from the Anatolian town of Tarsus. Saul was traveling to confront the Christian community in Damascus when he experienced an overpowering mystical vision of Jesus that literally knocked him to the ground. Reversing his previous position, Saul now affirmed his belief in the authenticity of Jesus as the divine Son of God. In speaking within the Jewish community, he had preferred his Hebrew name, Saul. Now, as he took his new message to gentiles, he preferred his Roman name, Paul. Jewish by ethnicity and early religious choice, Roman by citizenship, and Greek by culture, Paul was ideally placed to refine and explicate Jesus' message. He became the second founder of Christianity and dedicated himself to establishing Christianity as an independent, organized religion.

To link the flourishing, but separate, Christian communities, Paul undertook three missionary voyages in the eastern Mediterranean, and he kept in continuous communication through a series of letters, Paul's "Epistles" of the New Testament. He advised the leadership emerging within each local church organization: the presbyters, or elders; the deacons above them; and, at the head, the bishop. He promised eternal life to those who believed in Jesus' power. He declared Jewish ritual laws an obstacle to spiritual progress (Galatians 5:2–6). Neither membership in a chosen family nor observance of laws or rituals was necessary in the new religion. Paul proclaimed a new equality in Christianity:

> There is no longer Jew or Greek, there is no longer slave or free, there is no longer male or female; for all of you are one in Christ Jesus. (Galatians 3:28)

Paul formulated a new concept of "original sin" and redemption from it. Jews had accepted the story told in Genesis of Adam and Eve's disobedience in the Garden of Eden as a mythical explanation of some of life's harsh realities: the pain of childbirth, the struggle to earn a living, the dangers of wild beasts, and, most of all, human mortality. Paul now proclaimed that Adam and Eve's "original sin" could be forgiven. Humanity could, in a sense, return to paradise and eternal life. Jesus' death on the cross atoned for original sin. According to Paul, those who believed in Jesus and accepted membership in the new Christian community would be forgiven by God and "saved." Although they would still be mortal, at the end of their earthly lives they would inherit a life in heaven, and, much later, would even be reborn on earth (Romans 5–6).

The Christian Calendar. Like other religions, Christianity established a sacred calendar. People had long celebrated the winter solstice; in the fourth century Christians fixed the observance of Jesus' birth, **Christmas**, at that time of year, although no one knew the actual date of his birth. Good Friday, at about the time of Passover, mourned Jesus' crucifixion and death; three days later his resurrection was celebrated in the joyous festival of **Easter**. Corresponding to the Jewish holiday of **Pentecost**, the anniversary of receiving the Ten Commandments fifty days after the Passover, Christianity introduced its own holiday of Pentecost. It commemorates the date when, according to Acts 2, the "Holy Spirit," the third element of the Trinity along with God the Father and Jesus the son, filled Jesus' disciples and they "began to talk in other tongues, as the Spirit gave them power of utterance," enabling them to preach to the various peoples of the world. (Modern-day Christian Pentecostals "speak in tongues," praying and uttering praises ecstatically, healing through prayer and laying on of hands, and speaking of experiencing spiritual miracles.)

Over time, special saints' days were designated to mark the lives and deaths of people who helped to spread the new religion. The new Christian calendar, which has become the most widely used in the world, fixed its first year at the approximate date of Jesus' birth. The Jewish Sabbath, a weekly day of rest and reflection, was transferred from Saturday to Sunday.

Gender Relations. Jesus attracted many women as followers, and women led in the organization of several of the early churches. Paul welcomed them warmly and treated them respectfully at first, but women gradually lost their influence as Jesus' disciples institutionalized the Church. Although they taught spiritual equality, early Christians allowed gender and social inequalities to remain. Paul had proclaimed that in Jesus "There is no longer male or female," but he seemed to distrust

Christmas The Christian feast celebrating the birth of Jesus Christ.

Easter The principal feast of the Christian calendar celebrating the resurrection of Christ.

Pentecost This festival commemorates the descent of the Holy Spirit on the Apostles of Christ and the beginning of their preaching mission on the fiftieth day after the resurrection of Christ at Easter.

MAJOR CHRISTIAN FESTIVALS

January 6	Epiphany
February–March	Shrove Tuesday, or Mardi Gras (day before Ash Wednesday)
February–March	Ash Wednesday (first day of Lent)
February–April	Lent
February 2	Candlemas Day
March–April	Easter
March 25	Feast of Annunciation
April–June	Ascension (40 days after Easter)
May–June	Pentecost/Whit Sunday (50 days after Easter)
May–June	Trinity Sunday (Sunday after Pentecost)
November–December	Advent
December 24	Christmas Eve
December 25	Christmas Day

sexual energies. Like Jesus he was unmarried. He recommended celibacy and, for those unable to meet that standard, monogamous marriage as a means of sexual restraint:

> It is well for a man not to touch a woman. But because of cases of sexual immorality, each man should have his own wife and each woman her own husband. The husband should give to his wife her conjugal rights, and likewise the wife to her husband. (1 Corinthians 7:1–3)

In addition, Paul moved to subordinate women, first at home:

> I want you to understand that Christ is the head of every man, and the husband is the head of the wife … he is the image and reflection of God; but woman is the reflection of man. Indeed, man was not made from woman, but woman from man. Neither was man created for the sake of woman, but woman for the sake of man. (1 Corinthians 11:3–9)

Then in church:

> Women should be silent in the churches. For they are not permitted to speak, but should be subordinate, as the law also says. If there is anything they desire to know, let them ask their husbands at home. (1 Corinthians 14:34–35)

Paul had also declared that spiritually "There is no longer slave or free," but in practice he accepted slavery, saying, "Slaves, obey your earthly masters with fear and trembling." He did urge masters to be kind to slaves and to "stop threatening them for you know that both of you have the same Master in heaven, and with him there is no partiality" (Ephesians 6:5–9).

From Persecution to Triumph

Having established the central doctrines of the new religion and stabilized its core communities, both Peter and Paul moved to expand its geographical scope. They saw Rome as the capital of empire and the center of the international communication network of the time, and they traveled there to preach and teach. Tradition holds that both were martyred there in the persecutions of the Emperor Nero, about 67 C.E., and that both are entombed and enshrined there.

In this capital of empire, Christianity appeared as one of several mystery religions, all of which were based on beliefs in supernatural beings. They included the religion of Mithra, a Persian sun-god; Demeter, a Greek goddess; YHWH the god of the Jews; and an eclectic mixture of beliefs called Gnosticism. Romans seemed to be in search of a more inspiring, otherworldly faith than paganism provided, but at the time of the deaths of Peter and Paul, Christianity was still a relatively weak force.

The first Christians, Jews by nationality, were scorned as provincial foreigners. Some Roman authorities thought that Christian beliefs in resurrection and an afterlife undermined pride in citizenship and willingness to serve in the army. About the year 100, the historian Tacitus wrote of:

> a class of persons hated for their vices whom the crowd called Christians. Christus, after whom they were named, had undergone the death penalty in the reign of Tiberius, by sentence of the procurator Pontius Pilate, and the pernicious superstition was checked for a moment only to break out once more, not only in Judaea, the home of the disease, but in the Capital itself, where everything horrible or shameful in the world gathers and becomes fashionable. (Tacitus, *Annales* XV:44)

Paradoxically, because they refused to worship the emperor or to take oaths in his name, official Rome viewed Christians as atheists. Their emphasis on otherworldly salvation and their strong internal organization were seen as threats to the state's authority. Roman leaders also mocked the sacrament of the Eucharist, in which Christians consumed consecrated wafers and wine as the body and blood of Christ, as a sign of cannibalism. Official treatment of Christianity was erratic but often marked by severe persecution. Nero (r. 54–68) scapegoated the Christians, blaming them for the great fire in 64, apparently executing both Peter and Paul among his victims, and sending hundreds of Christians to die in public gladiatorial contests and by burning. Edicts of persecution were issued by Emperors Antoninus Pius (r. 138–161), Marcus Aurelius (r. 161–180), Septimius Severus (r. 193–211), Decius (c. 201–251), and Diocletian (r. 284–305). In 257 the Emperor Valerian (r. 253–260) was prepared to launch a major persecution of Christians, but he was captured in battle by Persians. In these early years of persecution, thousands of Christians suffered martyrdom.

Despite the scorn and the persecution, Christianity continued to grow. Its key doctrines and texts were written, edited, and approved by leaders in the network of Christian churches. After years of debates, Christian leaders and scholars agreed on the contents of the New Testament by about the year 200, and by 250 the city of Rome alone held about 50,000 Christians among its million inhabitants. Most were of the lower classes, attracted by Jesus' message to the poor, but middle- and upper-class Romans had also joined. In particular, Christianity proved attractive to the wives of Roman leaders, who often contributed to their husbands' conversions. By the reign of Constantine, estimates reported that one out of ten inhabitants of the Roman Empire was Christian.

The Conversion of Constantine. In 313, Constantine (r. 306–337) had a vision in which a cross and the words *in hoc signo vinces*, "in this sign you will be victorious," appeared to him the night before he won the critical battle that made him sole emperor in the western empire. He immediately declared Christianity legal. He funded Christian leaders and their construction of churches, while he withdrew official support from the pagan churches, making Christianity the *de facto* official religion of the Roman Empire. On a personal level, Constantine encouraged his mother Helena to embrace Christianity, which she did enthusiastically. Helena had churches built in Asia Minor and the Holy Land, and traveled to Jerusalem seeking the cross on which Jesus died. After her death, she was canonized as a saint in the Catholic Church.

As emperor, Constantine took a leading part in Church affairs. He sponsored the Council of Nicaea in 325, the largest assembly of bishops of local Christian churches up to that time. He convened the council primarily to establish the central theological doctrines of Christianity, but it also established a Church organization for the Roman Empire, a network of urban bishoprics grouped into provinces, with each province headed by the chief bishop of its largest city. In 337, on his deathbed, Constantine accepted baptism.

In 392, Emperor Theodosius (r. 379–395) declared Christianity to be the official religion of the Roman Empire. He outlawed the worship of the traditional Roman gods and severely restricted Judaism, initiating centuries of bitter Christian persecution of both traditions.

How Had Christianity Succeeded? How had Christianity, once scorned and persecuted, achieved such power? Christian believers attributed the success to divine assistance. Historians seek more earthly explanations. Let us consider one of the major historians to tackle the topic, Edward Gibbon (1737–94).

In 1776, Gibbon began the publication of his six-volume masterpiece, *The History of the Decline and Fall of the Roman Empire*. A child of the Enlightenment philosophy of his time, which rejected supernatural explanations (see Chapter 15), Gibbon rather

HOW DO WE KNOW?

Explanations for the Spread of Christianity

Many historians of our own time accept the thrust of Gibbon's explanations, but tend to emphasize more the importance of community within the Church.

"*From the outset, the major goal of the Jesus movement was to call into existence a new kind of inclusive community that might arch over all the ordinary human distinctions of race and religion,*" *writes Howard Clark Kee (1991, p. 2). Kee analyzes five different kinds of community that were active in the Roman world during the first two centuries of the Christian era and suggests that Christianity developed an appeal to each of them: The community of the wise, seeking special knowledge of the future; the community of the law-abiding, seeking appropriate rules of guidance in the present; the community where God dwells among his people, seeking assurance that it was specially selected and cared for; the community of mystical participation, influenced by the mystery religions of the time; and the ethnically and culturally inclusive community, outsiders seeking a place of belonging. Different aspects of the Christian message, developed by different Church leaders, spoke to each of these communities and succeeded in drawing them in (Kee, 1995).*

Historical sociologist Michael Mann cites the psychological and practical rewards of the growing Christian "ecumene," the worldwide community of the Church, with its comprehensive philosophy for living and organizing. Although much of Christianity's message targeted the poor, Mann notes that the religion also drew a large following of urban artisans, whom the aristocratic Roman Empire devalued. Excluded from political power, these working-class people were in search of a comprehensive and welcoming community. They wanted to recreate an earlier, simpler, more participatory era, and they became Christians. As imperial power became increasingly centralized, remote, insensitive, and, later, unstable, "In many ways Christianity represented how Rome liked to idealize its republican past" (Mann, p. 325).*

- *Jesus and St. Paul promised life after death to Christians. Do Kee and Mann cite this as a reason for Christianity's success in winning new adherents? If so, what terms do they use to indicate this promise? If not, why do you think they omit it?*
- *Gibbon suggests that a large part of the appeal of early Christianity was the miracles that Christ and his disciples were said to have performed. Kee and Mann don't emphasize miracles. Why?*
- *Both Kee and Mann suggest that different groups were attracted to Christianity for different reasons. Give examples. Based on people's motivations for joining religious groups, with which of their reasons would you agree? Disagree?*

Neoplatonic A philosophical system founded by Plotinus (205–270 C.E.) and influenced by Plato's theory of ideas. It emphasizes the transcendent, impersonal, and indefinable "One" as the ground of all existence and the source of an eternal world of goodness, beauty, and order, of which material existence is but a feeble copy.

sarcastically presented five reasons for Christianity's victories. But beneath his sarcasm Gibbon revealed the profound strengths of the new religion:

- Its "inflexible and intolerant" zeal, derived from its Jewish roots.
- Its promise of resurrection and a future life for believers, soon augmented by the threat of eternal damnation for nonbelievers.
- Its assertion of miraculous accomplishments.
- The austere morals of the first Christians. The Christian search for spiritual perfection, a monogamous sexual code, the rejection of worldly honor, and a general emphasis on equality attracted many converts. In the extreme case, martyrdom won admiration, sympathy, and followers. Later commentators noted that the simplicity and self-sacrifice of the early Christians reminded some Romans of the ideals of the early Republic.
- The Church gradually generated a state within a state through the decentralized leadership of its local bishops and presbyters, the structure Paul had begun to knit together. As imperial structures weakened, Christianity provided an alternative community. This Christian community distributed philanthropy to needy people, Christian and non-Christian alike. It also publicized its message effectively—in Greek, the language of the eastern part of the empire.
- Many later commentators noted that the Christian community included a local church in which to share the joys and sorrows of everyday life, celebrate life-cycle events, and commemorate major events in the history of the group. At the same time it provided membership in a universal Church that extended to the entire known world, and suggested participation in a life that transcended earthly concerns altogether.

Doctrine: Definition and Dispute

As it grew after receiving official recognition, institutional Christianity refined its theology. The most influential theologian of the period, St. Augustine (354–430), bishop of Hippo in north Africa, wrote *The City of God* (413–426) to explain Christianity's relationship to competing religions and philosophies, and to the Roman government with which it was increasingly intertwined.

Despite Christianity's designation as the official religion of the empire, Augustine declared its message to be spiritual rather than political. Christianity, he argued, should be concerned with the mystical, heavenly City of Jerusalem rather than with earthly politics. Although Augustine encouraged the Roman emperors to suppress certain religious groups, some elements of his theology supported the separation of Church and state.

Augustine built philosophical bridges to Platonic philosophy, the dominant system of the Hellenistic world of his time and place. Christianity envisioned Jesus, God's son, walking the earth and suffering for his people. He was, literally, very down-to-earth. God, the Father, had more transcendent characteristics, but they were less emphasized in Christian theology at the time. Plato (*c.* 428–348 B.C.E.) and later **Neoplatonic** philosophers, however, provided the model of a more exalted, more remote god, a god that was more accepted among the leading thinkers of Augustine's time. According to Augustine, Plato's god was:

> the maker of all created things, the light by which things are known, and the good in reference to which things are to be done; … we have in him the first principle of nature, the truth of doctrines, and the happiness of life. (p. 253)

In addition, Plato's god existed in the soul of every person, perhaps a borrowing from Hinduism (see Chapter 9).

Augustine married these Platonic and Neoplatonic views to the transcendent characteristics of God in Christian theology. This provided Christianity with a new intellectual respectability, which attracted new audiences in the vast Hellenistic world. He also encouraged contemplation and meditation within Christianity, an important element in the monastic life that was beginning to emerge among Christians (as it had among Buddhists). Augustine himself organized a community of monks in Tegaste (now Souk-Ahras), the city of his birth.

In his earlier *Confessions* (*c.* 400), Augustine had written of his personal life of relatively mild sin before his conversion to Christianity. Now he warned Christians that Adam and Eve's willfulness had led to original sin; sin had unlocked the forces of lust, turning the flesh against the spirit; and lust had called forth a death sentence on all humans in place of the immortality originally intended for them:

> As soon as our first parents had transgressed the commandment, divine grace forsook them, and they were confounded at their own wickedness … They experienced a new motion of their flesh which had become disobedient to them, in strict retribution of their own disobedience to God … Then began the flesh to lust against the Spirit

El Greco, *St. Augustine*, c. 1580. Oil on canvas. El Greco's painting captures the formal power of Augustine's position within the early Church as Bishop and theologian. Augustine emphasized spiritual rather than worldly issues, encouraged contemplation and meditation, and incorporated Platonic and Neoplatonic concepts of a transcendent god into Christianity. (*Museo de Santa Cruz, Toledo*)

... And thus, from the bad use of free will, there originated the whole train of evil ... on to the destruction of the second death, which has no end, those only being excepted who are freed by the grace of God. (pp. 422–3)

For Augustine as for Paul, and thus for early Christianity, sexuality was perilous and woman suspect. In early Christian theology, profane flesh and divine spirit confronted each other uneasily.

Augustine also believed that Christians should subordinate their will and reason to the teachings and authority of the Church. Although it is usually associated with the development of Protestant religions much later, the idea of predestination—that is, that individuals could do nothing through their own actions to obtain salvation and entrance to heaven—dominated Augustine's theology. Some Christian theologians, such as Pelagius (c. 354–after 418), rejected Augustine's argument about original sin and taught that human beings could chose between good and evil to determine their own fate. They feared that the growing acceptance of Augustine's beliefs would devalue both public service for the poor and private initiative by less disciplined Christians. Ultimately, Augustine's views prevailed, and popes at the time labeled those of Pelagius heresy.

Battles over Dogma. Some theological disputes led to violence, especially as the Church attempted to suppress doctrinal disagreement. The most divisive dispute concerned the nature of the divinity of Jesus. The theologian Arius (c. 250–336) taught that Christ's humanity limited his divinity, and that God the Father, wholly transcendent, was more sacred than the son who had walked the earth. The Council of Nicaea, which was convened in 325 to resolve this dispute, issued an official statement of creed affirming Jesus' complete divinity and his indivisibility from God. The Arian controversy continued, however, especially on the fringes of empire, where Arian missionaries converted many of the Gothic tribes to their own beliefs. Wars between the new Arian converts and the Roman Church ensued, until finally Arianism was defeated in armed battle. Of these struggles, the historian Ammianus Marcellinus (c. 330–395) wrote: "No wild beasts are such enemies to mankind as are most of the Christians in the deadly hatred they feel for one another."

In the eastern Mediterranean, too, bitter and violent conflicts broke out among rival Christian theological factions, again over the precise balance between Jesus' divinity and his humanity. Persecution of dissidents by the Orthodox Church in Carthage, Syria, and Egypt was so severe that the arrival in the seventh century of Muslim rule, which treated all the Christian sects equally, was often welcomed as a respite from the struggles.

By the sixth century Christians far surpassed Jews in numbers, geographical spread, power, and influence. Christian missionaries continued their attempts to convert Jews, often by coercion. In 576, for example, a Gallic bishop gave the Jews of his city the choice between baptism and expulsion, a pattern that was repeated periodically, although Jews had not yet immigrated into western Europe in large numbers.

CHRISTIANITY IN THE WAKE OF EMPIRE

Christianity spread to western and northern Europe along the communication and transportation networks of the Roman Empire. Born in Judaea under Roman occupation, Christianity now spread throughout the empire, spoke its languages of Greek and Latin, preached the gospel along its trade routes, and constructed church communities in its cities. Thanks to official recognition and patronage, the Church grew steadily. As the Roman imperial government weakened, it enlisted the now official Church as a kind of department of state. While the empire weakened and dissolved, Christianity emerged and flourished.

The Conversion of the Barbarians

During the first millennium C.E. bishops in the western Church came "from the ranks of the senatorial governing class ... they stood for continuity of the old Roman values ... The eventual conversion of the barbarian leaders was due to their influence" (Matthew, p. 21). "None of the major Germanic peoples who entered the Roman provinces in the fourth and fifth centuries remained pagan for more than a generation after they crossed the frontier" (Mann, p. 335). About 496 Clovis, chief of the Merovingian Franks, rejected Arianism and converted to Roman Christianity, the first barbarian to accept the religion of the empire. He established his capital in Paris and had thousands of his tribesmen converted, for, in general, followers accepted the religion of their leader. Clovis' acceptance of Christianity brought him the support of the Roman ecclesiastical hierarchy, including the pope, and insured the triumph of this version of Christianity in Gaul.

Decentralized Power and Monastic Life

In western Europe, Christianity developed a multitude of local institutions. Churches, monasteries, and convents were established, and leadership was decentralized. In regions that lacked organized government and administration, local Church leaders and institutions provided whatever existed of order, administration, and a sense of larger community. For several centuries, "Christendom was dominated by thousands of dedicated unmarried men and women" (McManners, p. 89), the clergy of the Church. Missionary activity continued enthusiastically, but now turned northward toward the Vikings and the Slavs, as other geographical doors had been forcibly shut.

Pope Gregory I (r. 590–604) saw the usefulness of the monasteries and monks in converting and disciplining the barbarians, and he began to encourage the monastic movement. By the year 600 there were about 200 monasteries in Gaul alone, and the first missionaries dispatched by Rome arrived in England c. 597. By 700 much of England had been converted. In the ninth, tenth, and eleventh centuries, missionary activity was directed toward the "Northmen," the Vikings from Scandinavia, who raided and traded for goods and slaves from North America and Greenland, through the North Sea and the Baltic, down the Volga River, across the Caspian Sea, and on as far as Baghdad. The Vikings came into the Christian fold with only a tenuous link to Rome and a strong admixture of pagan ritual.

Although the pope in Rome had nominal authority over Christian affairs in the west, the Church's power was, in fact, fragmented and decentralized between 500 and 1000. Christianity spread in urban areas through its bishops in their large churches. In rural and remote areas, monks, acting as missionaries, carried the message.

Monasteries, which were small, isolated communities, each under the local control of a single abbot, modeled the spirituality and simplicity of the earliest Christian communities. Because sexual activity was ruled out, monasticism became as accessible to women in convents as to men in monasteries, and was equally valued by both. Many monasteries contained both men and women, each living in celibacy.

The most famous of the early monastics, St. Benedict (c. 480–547), founded a monastery at Monte Cassino, about 100 miles southeast of Rome. The writings of Pope Gregory I give us the most detailed information on the life, regulations, and discipline of that exemplary institution, although each monastery had its own variations in administration and practice.

Monastery of St. Catherine, Mount Sinai, 557 C.E. According to the Torah, Moses received the tablets of the law from God on Mount Sinai. It was for this reason that the Byzantine emperor Justinian I (r. 527–565) chose to found the monastery of St. Catherine here. The remote beauty of the place also made it ideal for spiritual meditation.

Through a variety of educational institutions, the churches, monasteries, convents, and bishops kept Rome's culture alive in northern and western Europe. In much of rural western Europe, local authorities valued the monks not just as the only literate people in the region but also as the most capable persons in administering land and agriculture. These authorities also sought an alliance with the prestige and power of the Church. They granted land and administrative powers to nearby monasteries, transforming them into important local economic forces. (Compare the administrative roles of Hindu priests and Buddhist monks in south and southeast Asia; Chapter 9.) Monks became courtiers and bishops as well as missionaries as they expanded the geographic, social, and economic dimensions of the Church. Until the Fourth Lateran Council (1216) under Pope Innocent III (r. 1198–1216), monasteries could form and dissolve at local initiatives, so we have no record of their exact numbers in the early centuries.

A history of the very decentralized Church of this time would have to be written from the bottom up. The Church in the west was decentralized partly because the Roman Empire was decentralized, having lost its administrative power. There was no longer an emperor in Rome. The Church and what was left of the government in western Europe groped toward a new mutual relationship.

The Church Divides into East and West

In the far more literate and sophisticated Byzantine Empire, political leaders did not relinquish their power to Church authorities. Indeed, the emperor at Constantinople served as administrative head of the Church, a pattern that had been set by Constantine when he presided over the Council of Nicaea, outside Constantinople.

Today, Eastern Orthodoxy and Roman Catholicism share the same fundamental faith and scripture and they maintain official communication with each other, but they developed many historic differences over Church organization, authority, and language. Doctrinally, at the Council of Chalcedon (451) both Eastern Orthodoxy and the Roman Church accepted the belief that Jesus was simultaneously an historical person and one with God. Organizationally, however, the Eastern Church remained far more urban. The west had so few roads and so little trade that it was held together organizationally by its military and ecclesiastical strongholds. The Council of Chalcedon recognized four centers of Church organization, or sees, in the east—Antioch, Jerusalem, Alexandria, and Constantinople—with Constantinople predominating and having the same leadership role in the east as Rome had in the west. Rome, once one of the patriarchates, and the only one in the west, was now deemed an entirely separate administrative center, still under its own emperor and with its own bishop.

The Split between Rome and Constantinople. Rome and Byzantium have remained divided over the authority of the bishop of Rome to the present. From the sixth century, he has claimed to be pope, *pappa*, father of the (Roman) Catholic Church and the direct organizational successor of the apostle Peter. Eastern Orthodox Christianity, however, has never recognized the pope's claim to pre-eminent authority, accepting as their principal authority the patriarch or bishop of Constantinople. Also, unlike the Roman practice, all but the highest clergy in Eastern Orthodoxy are permitted to marry, so here again the two clergies have not accepted each other's authority. The language of Rome is Latin, while the East uses Greek and the various Slavic languages of eastern Europe.

When Leo IX became pope in 1048, he aimed to expand his influence over all of Europe and sponsored the writing of a treatise that emphasized the pope's power. He sent one of his more zealous reformers to Constantinople to argue against the patriarch of Constantinople's claims to be independent of Rome's control. After failed negotiations, the reformer excommunicated the patriarch; in response, the patriarch excommunicated the reformer. Through this mutual rejection, called the Great Schism of 1054, the two Churches divided definitively

Icon of Mary, Jesus, and SS. Theodore and George, St. Catherine's Monastery, Israel, sixth to seventh century C.E. The dispute over the use of icons in worship divided the Eastern Orthodox Church for over a century, 726–843, between iconoclasts who wanted them banned and iconodules who continued to venerate them.

Icon of the "Triumph of Orthodoxy," Constantinople, late fourteenth/early fifteenth century C.E. In 843 the Empress Theodora restored the use of icons, an event still celebrated in the Eastern Church on the first Sunday in Lent.

into the Latin (later Roman Catholic) Church, which is predominant in western Europe, and the Greek Orthodox Church, which prevailed in the east. Friction between the two groups has waxed and waned over time, with the most direct confrontation coming in 1204, when crusaders dispatched by Rome to fight against Muslims in Jerusalem turned northward and sacked Constantinople instead.

New Areas Adopt Orthodox Christianity. As in the west, monastic life flourished in the Byzantine Empire, with exemplary institutions at remote, starkly beautiful sites such as Mount Sinai and Mount Athos. The greatest missionary activity of the Orthodox monks came later than in the west. Hemmed in by the Roman Church to the west and by the growing power of Islam to the east after about 650, Byzantium turned its missionary efforts northward, toward Russia. The brothers St. Cyril (*c.* 827–869) and St. Methodius (*c.* 825–884) translated the Bible into Slavonic, creating the Cyrillic alphabet in which to transcribe and publish it. When Russia embraced Orthodox Christianity in the tenth century it also adopted this alphabet. In the late fifteenth century, after the fall of Constantinople to the Turks (1453), Moscow began to refer to itself as the "Third Rome," the spiritual and political heir to the Caesars and the Byzantine Empire.

In other regions of east-central Europe, Rome and Byzantium competed in spreading their religious and cultural messages and organizations. Rome won in Poland, Bohemia, Lithuania, and Ukraine; the Orthodox Church in Bulgaria, Romania, and Serbia. Other national Churches also grew up beyond Rome's jurisdiction, including the Coptic in Egypt, the Armenian, and the Ethiopian. They also asserted their independence from Constantinople, creating a pattern of distinct national Churches that the Protestant Reformation would later adopt (see Chapter 13).

Christianity in Western Europe

The abrupt, dramatic rise of Islam throughout the Middle East and into the Mediterranean, which we will examine in the next chapter, had an immediate and profound influence on Christianity. By the year 700, Muslim armies had conquered the eastern Mediterranean and the north coast of Africa, key regions of both Christianity and the former Roman Empire. The Muslim Umayyad dynasty pushed on into Spain and crossed the Pyrenees. Stopped in southern France by the Frankish ruler Charles Martel (*c.* 688–741) at the Battle of Tours in 732, the Umayyad forces withdrew to Spain. Muslim troops captured segments of the southern Italian peninsula, Sicily, and other Mediterranean islands. These Muslim conquests cut Christianity off geographically from the lands of its birth and early vigor. As a result, Christianity became primarily a religion of Europe, where many of its members were recently converted "barbarian" warrior nobles.

For an interactive version of this map, go to: http://www.prenhall.com/spodek/map10.5

Legend:

- Coptic (Monophysite) church
- core Catholic church
- Celtic church
- spread of Catholic church 800–1200
- Orthodox church
- Islamic

- → Coptic (Monophysite) missions
- → Celtic missions 600–1200
- → Catholic missions 800–1200
- → Orthodox missions 800–1200
- → Nestorian missions
- ◎ major churches founded by 800
- ⊞ major churches founded 800–1000
- ⊕ major churches founded 1000–1200

The spread of Christianity. The disciples and early missionaries established Christian communities in southwest Asia, Greece, Italy, north Africa, and India. On the other hand, Roman persecution, the decline of western Rome, and the rise of Islam hindered its dissemination. The Orthodox Church of Constantinople converted eastern Europe, penetrating Russia; Rome became reestablished as a powerful center; and Celtic missionaries traveled throughout northwest Europe.

Christ triumphing over evil, Frankish terra cotta plaque, *c.* 500–750 C.E. It was not unusual for western Europeans to represent Christ in contemporary local costume. Here, dressed as a member of the German warrior nobility, he treads the serpent, an emblem of the devil, underfoot. (*Musée des Antiquités, St-Germain-en-Laye, France*)

Bronze and gilt statuette of Charlemagne, *c.* 860–870 C.E. Charlemagne's ceaseless warfare spread Christianity and Frankish rule across western Europe, while repelling barbarian intruders and enemies of Rome. In 800 C.E. Pope Leo III showed his gratitude by crowning him Holy Roman Emperor. (*Louvre, Paris*)

The Pope Allies with the Franks. In Rome, the pope felt surrounded by the hostile powers of Constantinople and Islam to the east and south, and several Gothic kings to the north and west. Seeking alliances with strong men, he turned to a Frank, Charles (Carolus) Martel, who gave his name to the Carolingian family. As we have seen, Martel had repulsed the Muslims at Tours in 732. In 754 his son, Pepin III (r. 751–768), answered the call of Pope Stephen II (r. 752–757) for help in fighting the Lombards who were invading Italy and threatening the papal possessions. Pepin secured a swath of lands from Rome to Ravenna and turned them over to papal rule. In exchange, the pope anointed Pepin and his two sons, confirming the succession of the Carolingian family as the royal house ruling the Franks.

SOURCE

Charlemagne and Harun-al-Rashid

Charlemagne spent his lifetime fighting in the name of the pope and on behalf of Christianity. In 777 he invaded Muslim Spain and by 801 had captured Barcelona. (His campaigns in Spain gave rise to the epic poem The Song of Roland *about the defeat of his rearguard in the pass of Roncesvalles. This became the most celebrated poem of medieval French chivalry.)*

Yet Charlemagne carried on a valued diplomatic friendship with the most powerful Muslim ruler of his day, Harun-al-Rashid, Caliph of Baghdad (r. 786–809). Charlemagne's adviser, friend, and biographer Einhard (c. 770–840) describes the friendship:

With Harun-al-Rachid [*sic*], King of the Persians, who held almost the whole of the East in fee, always excepting India, Charlemagne was on such friendly terms that Harun valued his goodwill more than the approval of all the other kings and princes in the entire world, and considered that he alone was worthy of being honoured and propitiated with gifts. When Charlemagne's messengers, whom he had sent with offerings to the most Holy Sepulchre of our Lord and Saviour and to the place of His resurrection, came to Harun and told him of their master's intention, he not only granted all that was asked but even went so far as to agree that this sacred scene of our redemption should be placed under Charlemagne's own jurisdiction. When the time came for these messengers to turn homewards, Harun sent some of his own men to accompany them and dispatched to Charlemagne costly gifts, which included robes, spices and other marvels of the lands of the Orient. A few years earlier Harun had sent Charlemagne the only elephant he possessed, simply because the Frankish King asked for it. (Einhard, p. 70)

Einhard does not note what gifts Charlemagne might have sent to Baghdad in return, nor does he comment on the political benefits of this interfaith diplomacy between the two great empires—empires that flanked, and confronted, the Byzantine Empire lying between them.

Charlemagne Revives the Idea of Empire. Pepin's son Charles ruled between 768 and 814, achieving the greatest recognition of his power when Pope Leo III (r. 795–816) crowned him Roman Emperor on Christmas Day, 800. In spite of this seeming unity of interests, Charles, who became known as Charles the Great or Charlemagne, rejected the title throughout most of his life and was often at odds with the various popes as he sought to expand an empire of his own. To achieve his goal, Charlemagne spent all his adult lifetime in warfare, continuing the military expeditions of his father and grandfather. He reconquered the northeastern corner of Spain from its Muslim rulers, defeated the Lombard rulers of Italy and relieved their pressure on the pope, seized Bavaria and Bohemia, killed and looted the entire nobility of the Avars in Pannonia (modern Austria and Hungary), and subdued the German Saxon populations along the Elbe River after thirty-three years of warfare. Himself a German Frank, Charlemagne offered the German Saxons a choice of conversion to Christianity or death.

With Charlemagne's victories, the borders of his kingdom came to match the borders of the dominance of the Church of Rome, except for the British Isles, which he did not enter. The political capital of western Europe passed from Rome to Charlemagne's own palace in Aachen (Aix-la-Chapelle) in modern Germany. Although Charlemagne was barely literate, he established within this palace a center of learning that attracted Church scholars from throughout Europe, initiating what historians call the Carolingian Renaissance.

THE CAROLINGIAN DYNASTY

751	Pepin III "the Short" becomes King of the Franks
755	Franks drive Lombards out of central Italy; creation of Papal States
768–814	Charlemagne rules as King of the Franks
774	Charlemagne defeats Lombards in northern Italy
800	Pope Leo III crowns Charlemagne
814–840	Louis the Pious succeeds Charlemagne as "emperor"
843	Treaty of Verdun partitions the Carolingian Empire
870	Treaty of Mersen further divides Carolingian Empire
875–950	New invasions of Vikings, Muslims, and Magyars
962	Ottonian dynasty succeeds Carolingian in Germany
987	Capetian dynasty succeeds Carolingian in France

Laon Cathedral, west front, c. 1190–95.
Gothic architecture was the dominant style in Europe after the twelfth century and was based on northern European models. Gothic churches were built to communicate, announcing the glories of heaven with their confident mastery of space and light and, at the same time, heralding the wealth and power of the Church.

Charles persuaded the noted scholar Alcuin of York (c. 730–804), England, to come to Aachen as head of the palace school and as his own personal adviser. The goals of the school were Christian and basic: reading and writing of biblical texts in Latin, chanting of prayers, knowledge of grammar and arithmetic. This training would prepare missionaries for their work among the peoples of northern Europe. Scribes at the school prepared copies of prayers and biblical texts for the liturgical and scholarly needs of churches and scholars. In the process they created a new form of Latin script that forms the basis of the lower-case (small) letters we use today. Charlemagne also fostered the arts by bringing to his capital sculpture from Italy and by patronizing local artisans and craftspeople. Alcuin himself had the ear of the emperor, criticizing him for using force in converting the Saxons and convincing him not to repeat the practice by invading England.

Charlemagne's coronation challenged the authority of the eastern emperor in Constantinople, but during the next years Charlemagne managed, through negotiation and warfare, to gain Constantinople's recognition of his title. There were once again two emperors, east and west.

The Attempt at Empire Fails. The Carolingian family remained powerful until about the end of the ninth century. But then they could no longer fight off the new invasions of the western Christian world by Magyars (Hungarians), Norsemen, and Arabs. Regional administrators, emboldened by the Carolingian emperor's weakness, began to act independently of his authority. Only after yet another century would militarily powerful leaders begin once again to cobble together loosely structured kingdoms in northwestern Europe. Meanwhile, political leadership in Europe was generally decentralized in rural manor estates controlled by local lords.

Religious leadership in the cathedrals, churches, monasteries, and convents filled the gap, providing a greater sense of overall community and order. In this era, 600–1100 C.E., the Church gave Europe its fundamental character and order. The Magyar and Norse invaders, like the Germans before them, converted to Christianity. By the end of the eleventh century, the Roman Church, as well as the political authorities of western Europe, were preparing to confront Islam.

EARLY CHRISTIANITY
WHAT DIFFERENCE DOES IT MAKE?

Christianity completed its first millennium during the High Middle Ages in Europe. It had originated in the eastern Mediterranean and spread throughout Europe. It had begun with the teachings of one man preached by a handful of disciples and institutionalized through the zeal of a single missionary, and had flowered into two separate, far-flung Church hierarchies and several localized structures. It had begun with a membership of downtrodden Jews, added middling-level gentiles, attracted some of the elites of Rome, and finally converted multitudes of Europe's invading barbarians. It had expanded its own organizational establishment via the network of transportation, communication, and trade put in place by the Roman Empire. And when that empire dissolved and contracted, the Church maintained and consolidated its position within the remains of those old Roman administrative and market centers. As European society became more rural, Christian monasteries and convents were founded in the countryside and often took on administrative and developmental roles alongside their spiritual missions. In short, the Church, like the empire, was much transformed. By the year 1000 it had become the most important organizational and cultural force in western Europe.

The transformations of both the Christian religious world and the European political world continued after 1000 with extraordinary developments in crusading vigor, trade and commerce, urbanization, intellectual and artistic creativity, and religious reform. We will explore these transformations in Chapter 12. First, however, we turn to equally startling and revolutionary developments that had created another world religion, originating in the Arabian peninsula only a few hundred miles from the birth place of both Judaism and Christianity. By the year 1000 it had spread across north Africa, northward into Spain, throughout the Middle East, and on through Iran and Afghanistan into India. Our study of Islam in Chapter 11 will complete our introduction to the origins and early life of the three major monotheistic religions.

Review Questions

- In what ways did the Judaism of the prophets differ from the Judaism of the Torah? In what ways were they similar?
- Early Judaism was very closely associated with the land of Israel. How did exile force the Jewish people to restructure their religion in order to survive?
- What were the reasons for Christians and Muslims to treat their Jewish minorities respectfully? What were the reasons for treating them spitefully?
- What elements from Judaism were incorporated into Christianity? What elements were rejected?
- How did St. Paul take the original teachings and organization created by Jesus and build them into a Christian Church?
- Christianity began in Judaea and became the dominant religion in Europe. What were the key steps in making and consolidating that geographical move?

Suggested Readings

PRINCIPAL SOURCES

The New English Bible with the Apocrypha. Oxford Study Edition (New York: Oxford University Press, 1970). Clear, readable, authentic text produced by interfaith team of scholars.

Brown, Peter. *The Rise of Western Christendom* (Malden, MA: Blackwell Publishers, 1996). Brown brings to bear expertise on the Roman empire at the time of Christ to provide context to early Christianity.

Crossan, John Dominic. *The Historical Jesus. The Life of a Mediterranean Jewish Peasant* (San Francisco, CA: HarperCollins, 1991). One of the clearest interpretations of Jesus in his time.

Kee, Howard Clark, *et al. Christianity: A Social and Cultural History* (New York: Macmillan Publishers, 1991). Excellent, scholarly analysis and narrative of early Christianity.

Pagels, Elaine. *The Gnostic Gospels* (New York: Random House, 1979). Clear, concise explanation of the significance to our understanding of early Christianity of the Gnostic manuscripts discovered at Nag Hammadi in 1945.

Smart, Ninian. *The World's Religions* (Cambridge: Cambridge University Press, 1989). Useful general survey, clearly written.

Smeltzer, Robert M. *Jewish People, Jewish Thought* (New York: Macmillan Publishing Co., Inc., 1980). Excellent general history.

ADDITIONAL SOURCES

Andrea, Alfred and James Overfield, eds. *The Human Record*, Vol. I (Boston, MA: Houghton Mifflin Company, 3rd ed., 1998). Superbly chosen selections.

Armstrong, Karen. *A History of God* (New York: Knopf, 1993). Concise history of the evolution of the three major monotheistic religions.

Augustine. *The City of God*, trans. Marcus Dods (New York: Modern Library, 1950). A central work of Christian theology from the late Roman Empire.

Baron, Salo Wittmayer. *A Social and Religious History of the Jews*, Vol. 1 (New York: Columbia University Press, 1952). First in a multivolume series by one of the leading Jewish historians of his time.

Holy Bible. New Revised Standard Version (Grand Rapids, MI: Zondervan Publishing House, 1989). Another excellent, standard translation.

de Lange, Nicholas. *Atlas of the Jewish World* (New York: Facts on File, 1984). Excellent text, helpful maps. Beautiful illustrations.

Einhard and Notker the Stammerer. *Two Lives of Charlemagne*, trans. Lewis Thorpe (Harmondsworth, England: Penguin Books, 1969). The standard primary source on Charlemagne.

Eliade, Mircea. *Ordeal by Labyrinth* (Chicago, IL: University of Chicago Press, 1982). The leading religious historian of the early twentieth century explains principles of his view of religious history.

——. *The Sacred and the Profane* (New York: Harper Torchbooks, 1959). Explains his view of religion in history.

Gibbon, Edward. *The History of the Decline and Fall of the Roman Empire*, 3 vols., abridged by D.M. Low (New York: Washington Square Books, 1962). The classic from the age of the Enlightenment. Follows and projects the story through the fall of Constantinople to the Turks.

Grant, Michael. *History of Rome* (New York: Charles Scribner's Sons, 1978). Readable, basic text.

——. *Jesus: An Historian's Review of the Gospels* (New York: Touchstone, 1995). Does the best he can to reconstruct Jesus' life and teachings based on the gospels.

Halpern, Baruch. *The First Historians: The Hebrew Bible and History* (San Francisco, CA: Harper and Row, 1988). Attempts to demonstrate the extent to which Hebrew stories from the Bible can be authenticated.

Honour, Hugh and John Fleming. *The Visual Arts: A History* (Englewood Cliffs, NJ: Prentice-Hall, 4th ed., 1995). Excellent textbook approach to the history of art.

Hopfe, Lewis M. *Religions of the World* (New York: Macmillan Publishing Company, 5th ed., 1991). Useful textbook survey.

Kaufmann, Yehezkel. *The Religion of Israel* (Chicago, IL: University of Chicago Press, 1960). Fascinating analysis of biblical Judaism, stressing the inability of the early Jews even to comprehend the significance of images in worship.

Kee, Howard Clark. *Who Are The People of God: Early Christian Models of Community* (New Haven, CT: Yale University Press, 1995). Kee stresses the importance of the community of believers in the success of the early Christian Church.

Mann, Michael. *A History of Power from the Beginning to A.D. 1760* (Cambridge: Cambridge University Press, 1986). Mann searches for the success of early Christianity in its sociological composition and appeal.

Matthew, Donald. *Atlas of Medieval Europe* (New York: Facts on File, 1983). Excellent text. Useful maps. Beautiful illustrations.

McManners, John, ed. *The Oxford Illustrated History of Christianity* (New York: Oxford University Press, 1990). Outstanding set of basic introductory articles by major scholars, highly illustrated.

Meier, John P. *A Marginal Jew: Rethinking the Historical Jesus* 2 vols. (New York: Doubleday, 1991, 1994). Meier emphasizes Jesus' abilities as a magician and exorcist in attracting followers.

Momigliano, Arnaldo. *On Pagans, Jews, and Christians* (Hanover, NH: University Press of New England for Wesleyan University Press, 1987). Compares the attractions of each of these perspectives, and their confrontations with one another in the early years of Christianity.

Pagels, Elaine. *Beyond Belief: The Secret Gospel of Thomas* (New York: Random House, 2003). Pagels' analysis of the most significant of the Gnostic gospels, and its meaning for her.

Palmer, R.R. and Joel Colton. *A History of the Modern World*, 8th ed. (New York: Knopf, 1984). Eurocentric and mostly centered on the period since 1500, nevertheless an excellent, readable text, strongest on the French Revolution.

Pritchard, James B., ed. *Ancient Near Eastern Texts Relating to the Old Testament* (Princeton, NJ: Princeton University Press, 3rd ed., 1969). Basic compendium of the most important documents. Indispensable for the subject.

Rosenberg, David and Harold Bloom. *The Book of J* (New York: Grove Weidenfeld, 1990). Analyses the four major editorial strands in the composition of the Torah, stressing the one that refers to god by his Hebrew name of JHWH.

Rubenstein, Richard L. *When Jesus Became God* (New York: Harcourt Brace, 1999). An account of the armed battle and victory of the Roman Church over the theologian Arius who declared that Christ's human nature diminished his divine nature.

Smart, Ninian and Richard D. Hecht, eds. *Sacred Texts of the World: A Universal Anthology* (New York: Crossroad Publishing, 1982). Useful selection of religious texts.

◉ World History Documents CD-ROM

ISLAM

SUBMISSION TO ALLAH: MUSLIM CIVILIZATION BRIDGES THE WORLD 570 C.E.–1500 C.E.

KEY TOPICS
- The Origins of Islam
- Successors to the Prophet
- Spiritual, Religious, and Cultural Flowering
- Relations with Non-Muslims

Islam, in Arabic, means "submission." Islam teaches submission to the word of God, called "Allah" in Arabic. Muslims, "those who submit," know God's word primarily through the Quran, the Arabic book that records the teachings of God as they were transmitted to the Prophet Muhammad (570–632). Stories of Muhammad's life, words, and deeds (*hadith*), carefully collected, sifted, and transmitted over many generations, provide Muslims with models of the righteous life and how to live it. According to Islam's holy book, the Quran, Muhammad was the most recent prophet of God's message of ethical monotheism. Devout Muslims declare this belief in prayers, which are recited five times each day: "There is no God but God, and Muhammad is his Prophet."

For Islam the teachings of the Quran and of Muhammad's life are fulfilled only with the creation of a community of believers, the *umma*, and its proper regulation through political structures. Through its early centuries, Islam established administrative and legal systems in the areas to which it spread: Arabia, western Asia, northern Africa, and Spain. As Islam spread later to eastern Europe, central Asia, south Asia, and sub-Saharan Africa, it arrived sometimes with government backing, sometimes without. After the twelfth century, Islam expanded into China and southeast Asia as a religious and cultural system without government support.

Islam is considered here as a world religion, but because it often unified government and religion into a single system, it may also be compared with the materials in Part 3 on the expansion of world empires. In this chapter, we shall trace the growth and spread of Islam as a religious, governmental, and cultural system. We shall also examine its encounters with other religions and empires.

umma The community of believers in Islam, which transcends ethnic and political boundaries.

THE ORIGINS OF ISLAM

Islam emerged in the Arabian peninsula, an area largely inhabited by nomadic Bedouin tribes. The Bedouins organized themselves as clans. Inhabiting the desert, they lacked the sources of water so crucial for the emergence of cities and civilizations in the ancient world, although a few cities, such as Mecca, grew up alongside major oases. Mecca flourished as a trading center in the seventh century, but the region, in general, lacked the governmental institutions and the powerful emperors that supported the emergence of major religions elsewhere. Religiously, the region was polytheistic, worshiping many gods. Mecca held an especially prominent role in this worship. It held the Ka'aba, a rectangular building that housed a cubical black stone structure, and the sacred tokens of all the clans of Mecca and of many of the surrounding tribes as well. Serving as a center of pilgrimage and trade, Mecca brought enormous economic benefits to the traders of the Quraysh tribes who controlled the city and its shrine.

Opposite **Niche (*Mihrab*) with Islamic calligraphy.** Islamic design features a meandering pattern made up of repetitive motifs and a suggestion of infinite extension. (*Metropolitan Museum, New York*)

AT A GLANCE: ISLAM

DATE	POLITICAL/SOCIAL EVENTS	LITERARY/PHILOSOPHICAL EVENTS
500 C.E.	■ Muhammad (570–632)	
600 C.E.	■ Hijra (622) ■ Muslim conquest of Mecca ■ Orthodox or Rightly Guided Caliphs (632–661) ■ Muslim conquest of Iraq, Syria, Palestine, Egypt, western Iran (632–642), Cyprus (649), and Persian Empire (650s) ■ Umayyad caliphate (661–750); capital in Damascus ■ Muslim conquest of Carthage (698) and central Asia (650–712) ■ Husayn killed at Karbala (680); Sunni–Shi'ite split	■ Revelation of the Quran to Muhammad (610) ■ Persian becomes second language of Islam
700 C.E.	■ Muslim conquest of Tunis (700), Spain (711–716), Sind and lower Indus valley ■ Muslim defeat at Battle of Tours (732) ■ Muslims defeat Chinese at battle of Talas River (751) ■ Abbasid caliphate (750–1258) ■ Baghdad founded (762)	■ Biography of Muhammad by Ibn Ishaq (d. 767) ■ Formulation of major systems of Islamic law
800 C.E.	■ Divisions in Muslim Empire (833–945) ■ Fez founded (808)	■ al–Tabari, *History of Prophets and Kings* ■ al–Khwarazmi develops algebra ■ Abbasid caliphate establishes "House of Wisdom" translation bureau in Baghdad ■ Sufi tariqat
900 C.E.	■ Persians seize Baghdad (945) ■ Cairo founded (969)	■ Ferdowsi, *Shah Nama* ■ al–Razi, *Encyclopedia of Medicine* ■ Turkish becomes third language of Islam ■ Mutazilites challenge Islamic orthodoxy
1000 C.E.	■ Seljuk Turks dominate Abbasid caliphate (1038) ■ Almoravid dynasty in north Africa and Spain (1061–1145) ■ Battle of Manzikert (1071) ■ 1st Crusade (1095–9)	■ Ibn Sina (Avicenna), philosopher, produces "Canon of Medicine" ■ al–Biruni writes on mathematics and astronomy (d. 1046)
1100 C.E.	■ Almohad dynasty rules north Africa and Spain (1145–1269) ■ 2nd Crusade (1147–9) ■ Salah al–Din (Saladin) recaptures Jerusalem (1187) ■ 3rd Crusade (1189–92)	■ al–Ghazzali (d. 1111), Muslim philosopher and theologian ■ Ibn Rushd (Avarroes; 1126–98) ■ Maimonides (1135–1204), Jewish physician, philosopher, and theologian
1200 C.E.	■ 4th Crusade (1202–04) ■ Sultanate of Delhi (1211–1526) ■ Children's Crusade (1212) ■ 5th–8th Crusades (1218–91) ■ Crusaders driven from west Asia (1291) ■ Fall of Baghdad to Mongols (1258); end of Abbasid Caliphate	■ Jalal al–Din Rumi, *Mathnawi* ■ al–Juvaini, *History of the World Conquerors* ■ Rashid al–Din, *World History*
1300 C.E.	■ Mansa Musa's pilgrimage to Mecca (1324) ■ Conversion of Malayans and Indonesians to Islam	■ Ibn Battuta (1304–c. 1368), traveler ■ Ibn Khaldun, *Universal History*
1400 C.E.	■ Ottoman Turks conquer Constantinople (1453) ■ Christians capture Granada, complete *reconquista* (1492)	

The Prophet: His Life and Teaching

Born in 570 to parents eminent in the Quraysh tribe, Muhammad was orphaned at an early age, and he was raised by his grandfather and later his uncle. He became a merchant, employed by a wealthy widow named Khadija. When he was twenty-five years old, he married her and they had four children together.

Muhammad was a deeply meditative person, retreating regularly to a nearby hill to pray and reflect. In 610, when he was forty years old, his reflections were interrupted, according to Islamic teachings, by the voice of the angel Gabriel, who instructed him: "Recite: In the name of the Lord who created Man of a blood-clot." Over the next two decades, according to Islamic theology, God continued to reveal his messages to Muhammad through Gabriel. Muhammad transmitted these revelations to professionals whose task it was to commit them to memory. The verses were also transcribed on palm leaves, stone, and other material. Soon after Muhammad's death, during the rule of Umar I, the second leader of the Islamic community (r. 634–644), scribes and editors compiled the entire collection of written and oral recitations into the Quran, which in Arabic means recitations. Umar's successor, Uthman (r. 644–656), issued an officially authorized edition of the Quran.

Approximately the length of the Christian New Testament, the Quran is considered by Muslims to be the absolute, uncorrupted, word of God. Composed in poetic form, the Quran helped to define the literary standards of the Arabic language. Muslims chant and study its text in Arabic, considering each syllable sacred. Even today many Muslims reject translations of the Quran into other languages as inadequate.

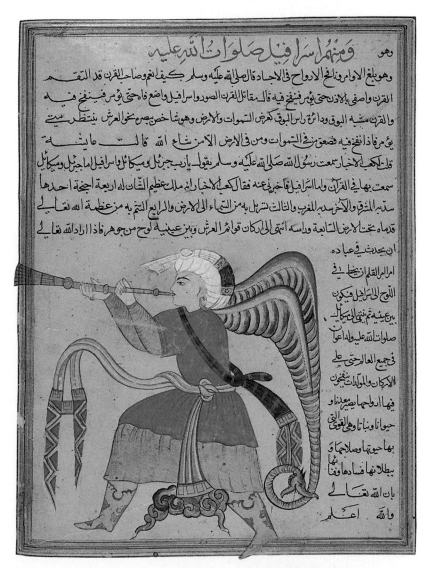

Trumpet call of the archangel Gabriel. Muhammad's religious career as a prophet seems to have been inspired by his early supernatural experiences. Once, he encountered a mighty being, the archangel Gabriel, on the horizon, who commanded him to recite … This was the first *surah* (section from the Quran) revealed to humanity, and is symbolized here by Gabriel's blowing on a trumpet. (*British Library, London*)

In the next century, new technologies led to broader dispersion of the Quran. During the middle eighth century, as Arab armies defeated Chinese forces in central Asia, the Muslim victors learned from their prisoners-of-war the technology of papermaking. By the end of the eighth century Baghdad had a paper mill; Egypt by 900; Morocco and Spain by 1100. Turks brought the art of papermaking to north India in the twelfth century. One use of paper was, of course, in the administration of the government bureaucracy. Another, perhaps even more important, was in the copying and diffusion of the Quran.

The Five Pillars of Islam

The Quran reveals the "five pillars" of Islam, the five ritual expressions that define orthodox Muslim religious belief and practice:

- Declaring the creed, "There is no god but God, and Muhammad is his Prophet."
- Praying five times daily while facing Mecca (2:144), and, if possible, praying also in public assembly at midday each Friday.

- Giving alms to the poor in the community, especially to widows and orphans (2:212 ff.), later recommended at 2½ percent of income.
- Fasting each day during the month of Ramadan, the ninth month of the lunar year, although eating is permitted at night, with a major feast marking the month's end (2:179–84).
- Making the *hajj*, a pilgrimage to Mecca, at least once in a lifetime, if possible (2:185 ff.).

Jihad, or sacred struggle, is sometimes called a "sixth pillar" of Islam. It was less stringently required and has been interpreted in different ways. Some scholars interpret *jihad* as a call to physical warfare to preserve and extend the **dar al-Islam**, the "abode of Islam," the lands under Muslim rule, or, later, the lands in which Islam could be practiced freely, even if not under Muslim political rule. Even in this interpretation, however, *jihad* should be practiced only in self-defense, for "God loves not the aggressors" (2:187). Other scholars understand *jihad* as a personal call to the individual, internal, spiritual struggle to live Islam as fully as possible. The Quran gives a capsule description of this proper life:

> true piety is this: to believe in God, and the Last Day, the angels, the Book, and the Prophets, to give of one's substance, however cherished, to kinsmen, and orphans, the needy, the traveller, beggars, and to ransom the slave, to perform the prayer, to pay the alms. And they who fulfil their covenant, and endure with fortitude misfortune, hardship and peril, these are they who are true in their faith, these are the truly godfearing. (2:172–3)

Finally, the Quran promises repeatedly that those who observe Islam faithfully will find their reward in paradise, described as "gardens underneath which rivers flow … a shelter of plenteous shade" (4:60). On the other hand, those who reject the opportunity to fulfill the teachings of Islam will burn in a fiery Hell forever. Humans must choose between doing good and evil, but the Quran asserts that ultimately free will is limited: "God has power over everything" (4:87).

The Quran emphasized many of the same principles as those of Judaism and Christianity, including the importance of worshiping a single God—Allah in Arabic—and the obligation of the rich to help the poor. As in Christianity, the Quran taught that there would be a final Judgment Day. Many of the Quran's practices, too, were consistent with the existing rituals of Christians, Jews, and Zoroastrians living in Arabia at the time, and this made acceptance of the new religion easier. For example, regular prayer times and recitals of creed were also central to Judaism and Christianity, as was institutionalized charity. Animal sacrifice was a part of pagan and Zoroastrian religions, and had once been central to Judaism as it was now of Islam. Ritual slaughter of animals for food mirrored Jewish practice, as did male circumcision. Ritual washing before public prayers was also practiced by Zoroastrians.

Responses to Muhammad

In Mecca, Muhammad created the nucleus of the *umma*, or community of Muslims, as people converted to his message. Some were successful business people, some slaves, some tribeless people, some were family members. His wife Khadija became his first disciple, his cousin, Ali, seems to have been the second.

Most Meccans, however, found Muhammad's moral teachings too demanding, and, when he told them of the physical state—resembling an epileptic fit—in which he received some of the revelations from the angel Gabriel, many questioned his stability. On more practical grounds, they feared that his teachings threatened their own beliefs,

dar al-Islam The literal meaning of the Arabic words is "the abode of peace." The term refers to the land of Islam, or the territories in which Islam and its religious laws (shari'a) may be freely practiced.

Opposite **"Celebration of the End of Ramadan,"** from *The Maqamat (The Meetings)*, c. **1325–50 C.E.** At the end of Ramadan, the month of fasting, Muslims don new clothes, throng the congregational mosques, and share their mingled senses of joy, relief, and achievement. Here a cavalcade, brandishing flags bearing religious inscriptions, unites in celebration. (*Bibliothèque Nationale, Paris*)

HOW DO WE KNOW?

Sources on Early Islam

Much of the historical writing on Islam is based on orthodox Islamic sources or, conversely, on the writings of their opponents. Such sources are not unbiased. In addition, several key documents were written down long after the events they describe, allowing possible alterations in the text. The Quran itself, for example, was compiled some fifty years after Muhammad received his first revelation. Muhammad ibn Ishaq (c. 704–767) wrote the first Arabic biography of the Prophet more than a century after his death.

Moreover, Islam suffered three civil wars in its first 120 years and considerable internal fighting thereafter, and many of the "official" histories were prepared in support of one position or another. Finally, as Islam confronted other

religious civilizations, the accounts of its history were frequently tendentious, again supporting one side or another.

In their search for unbiased information, recent historians have made use of sources that were not recorded as historical narratives but that provide data from which history can be written:

The new generation of historians thus uncovered an impressive variety of sources: commercial documents, tax registers, official land grants, administrative seals, census records, coins, gravestones, magical incantations written on bowls, memoirs of pilgrims, archeological and architectural data, biographical dictionaries, inscriptional evidence, and, more recently, oral history. (Eaton in Adas, p. 4)

From these records has emerged a deeper understanding of the culture of Muhammad's homeland in Arabia and of the adjacent Byzantine and Sasanid

Persian Empires. These records suggest that Islam did not develop within a national vacuum. It incorporated religious, cultural, and social structures that were already present among its neighbors. As it grew and expanded, it incorporated aspects of Arab, Greek, Roman, and Persian civilizations.

- *What are some issues in the early history of Islam that have led to the creation of primary source documents with conflicting interpretations?*
- *What use are tax registers, official land grant documents, and census records in interpreting the early history of Islam?*
- *If you were to study the degree to which Islam adopted practices from either the Greco-Roman or Persian civilizations, what primary sources would you seek?*

especially the idol worship in their homes and in the Ka'aba. Some Meccans were already monotheists, especially the Jews and Christians who lived in the city, but most of them also rejected his message for they did not believe that their own religions needed the purification that Muhammad proposed. Despite this intense opposition, including apparent threats on Muhammad's life, his family and his branch of the Quraysh tribe stood by him, including some who did not accept his message but trusted his integrity.

After Khadija and some others of his early supporters died, however, Muhammad's position in Mecca became more precarious. Some members of the Muslim community began to leave Mecca in search of a home more accepting of the new teachings.

The Hijra and the Islamic Calendar. Largely rejected by his own tribe and the inhabitants of Mecca, Muhammad, too, sought a place that would be more receptive. He welcomed an invitation from the elders of the city of Medina to come with his followers to their oasis city some 200 miles to the north to adjudicate bitter disputes that had arisen among local tribes and to take over the reins of government. Muhammad may also have been attracted because Medina had a large Jewish population. As monotheists, they shared the most central principle of his faith, and he may have thought that he could ultimately convert them.

Known as the **hijra**, Muhammad's flight under pressure to Medina became a central moment in Islamic history. As Christians begin the year 1 of their calendar with an event in the life of Jesus—his birth—so Muslims begin theirs with the *hijra* and Muhammad's assertion of governmental leadership in Medina, a year that corresponds to the year 622 on the Christian calendar.

Though he failed to convert many Jews, Muhammad found many other inhabitants of Medina who did accept his religious message. This allowed him to consolidate the *umma* as the unified religious community of Muslims. He believed that for Islam to

hijra The "migration" or flight of Muhammad from Mecca, where his life was in danger, to Medina (then called Yathrib), where he was welcomed as a potential leader in 622 C.E. The Islamic era (A.H.: After Hijra) is calculated from this date.

survive, he needed to create an Islamic government, a *dar al-Islam* ("an abode of Islam"), that included institutions that would protect the faith. In Medina he promulgated codes of business ethics as well as family laws of marriage, divorce, and inheritance, all based on the teachings of the Quran.

Muhammad Extends his Authority. After establishing his authority in Medina, Muhammad sought to gain converts in Mecca and ended up in skirmishes with the Quraysh tribes that opposed him. In 624 he and his followers successfully raided a large Meccan caravan train in the Battle of Badr, reducing Mecca's prosperity by cutting important trade routes and winning local fame for themselves. In 625 the Meccans fought back, defeating Muhammad and his forces at Uhud. In 627 the two sides fought to a draw at the Battle of the Ditch, but Muhammad's reputation grew as he stood up to the proud and powerful Meccans. In 630, following a dispute between the tribes of the two cities, Mecca surrendered to Medina. Muslims gained control of the Ka'aba, destroyed the Meccan idols, and turned the building with its sacred black rock into an Islamic shrine. By the time he died in 632, Muhammad was well on his way to creating from the warring tribes an Arabia-wide federation dedicated to the faith and the political structure of Islam.

Connections to Other Monotheistic Faiths. According to the Quran, Muhammad was only a messenger of God, not the originator of a new doctrine. Indeed, he was not even the founder of Islam: Several prophets came before him, including Adam, Noah, Abraham, Ishmael, Moses, and Jesus:

> We believe in God, and in that which has been sent down on us and sent down on Abraham, Ishmael, Isaac and Jacob, and the tribes, and that which was given to Moses and Jesus and the Prophets, of their Lord; we make no division between any of them, and to Him we surrender. (Quran, 2:130–32)

Muslims claim the Hebrew Abraham, whom Jews see as the father of Jewish monotheism, as the first Muslim: "Abraham in truth was not a Jew, neither a Christian; but he was a Muslim and one of pure faith" (Quran, 3:60). For this reason, Muslims often refer to Jews, Christians, and Muslims collectively as "children of Abraham."

The teachings of each of the earlier prophets, Muslims believe, were corrupted over time by their followers. Muslims challenged the Christian belief in Jesus as the son of God and maintain that the Christian doctrine of Jesus' divinity conflicts with the fundamental concept of pure monotheism. The Quran deplored this heresy, declaring, "It is not for God to take a son unto Him" (19:36). The Jews' error was in refusing to accept the Quran as a revised and updated version of the truth already given to them:

> When they were told, "Believe in that God has sent down," They said, "We believe in what was sent down on us"; and they disbelieve in what is beyond that. (2:85)

Muhammad and his followers came to believe that the revelations he received were final, uncorrupted, and true. Muhammad did not formulate this message; he only transmitted it as received. For Muslims, in the chain of prophets, Muhammad is the last and final link.

Christian Arabs remained largely aloof from Muhammad's alliances, while some Jews actively opposed his political goals and rejected his claims to religious prophecy. Disappointed in his wish to unite the members of the two monotheistic religions of the region under his leadership, and especially infuriated that some Jewish families had joined his Meccan enemies in war, he had the Jewish men of the Banu Qurayza clan executed, and the women and children enslaved. Elsewhere in Arabia, however, Jews and Christians, though subject to a special tax, were free to practice their religion.

HOW DO WE KNOW?

Gender Relations in Islam

Although many readers might consider the relationships between men and women a private matter, in fact in each religion—and empire—that we have studied some official doctrines attempted to regulate gender relationships. In general, they placed women under the authority of men and granted men more legal rights than they accorded to women. Although they often gave women greater importance than men in the private realm of house and hearth, they vested more public power and responsibility with men. Islam also follows this general pattern. The Quran states:

> Men have authority over women because God has made the one superior to the other, and because they spend their wealth to maintain them. Good women are obedient. They guard their unseen parts because God has guarded them. As for those from whom you fear disobedience, admonish them and send them to beds apart and beat them. Then if they obey you, take no further action against them. God is high, supreme. (4:34)

According to the Quran, women are to satisfy men's sexual desires and to bear children:

> Women are your fields: go, then, into your fields whence you please. (2:223)

Although, as in Judaism and Hinduism, sexual intercourse is forbidden during a woman's menstrual period:

> Keep aloof from women during their menstrual periods and do not touch them until they are clean again. (2:222)

It might appear that men are the initiators of sexual relations, but women are considered sexually seductive, and the Quran therefore urges the Prophet to:

> Enjoin believing women to turn their eyes away from temptation and to preserve their chastity; to cover their adornments (except such as are normally displayed); to draw their veils over their bosoms and not to reveal their finery except to their husbands, close relatives, and the very old and very young. (24:31)

As witnesses in legal matters, the testimony of two women equals that of a single man (2:282). Similarly in matters of inheritance, "A male shall inherit twice as much as a female" (4:11).

Despite these regulations that apparently limit the status of women, some modern scholars assert that Islam actually introduced "a positive social revolution" (Tucker, p. 42) in gender relations. Compared to what came before, Islam introduced new rights for women and gave them greater security in marriage. Islamic law, shari'a, safeguarded the rights of both partners in marriage through contractual responsibilities: it insisted on the consent of the bride; it specified that dowry, or bridal gift, go to the bride herself and not to her family; and it spelled out the husband's obligations to support his wives and children, even wives that he might divorce. Although men were allowed to take up to four wives, the Quran added, "But if you fear that you cannot maintain equality among them, marry one only or any slave-girls you may own. This will make it easier for you to avoid injustice" (4:3); so, in practice, only one wife was normally permitted.

These scholars note also that in the life of Muhammad, three women played exemplary roles: his first wife, Khadija, who supported him economically and emotionally when the revelations he received brought him scorn from others; Aisha, the most beloved of the wives he took after Khadija's death; and Fatima, the daughter of the Prophet and wife of the fourth caliph, Ali. Nevertheless, these women drew their importance from their service to prominent men, and were criticized when they asserted more independent roles.

Other scholars, on the other hand, have argued that Islam made the plight of women worse than it had been. These scholars argue that in pre-Islamic Arabia, women could initiate marriage, they could have more than one husband, they could divorce their husbands, they could remain in their parents' home area and have their husbands come to live with

them, and they could keep custody of their children in case of divorce. In pre-Islamic Arabia, some, like Allat, al-Uzza, and Manat were worshiped with great honor, suggesting there was considerable respect for females.

Of those scholars who feel that the position of women declined under Islam, some put the blame on Islam itself, but others suggest that the teachings of Islam were actually comparatively liberal. These scholars argue that it was contact with the Byzantine and Sasanid Empires that reduced women's status. They argue that tribal, nomadic Arabia had treated women with relative equality, but the neighboring empires, with their settled, urban civilizations, veiled women and kept them mostly at home under male domination. The Arabs adopted these practices. In effect, this group of scholars is also saying that the more liberal Quranic rules regarding women were reinterpreted after contact with societies outside Arabia. Whatever the rules of the Quran, in practice gender relations varied widely in different parts of the world of Islam.

Ibn Battuta (1304–c. 1368), a famous Berber (North African) traveler whose adventures took him to much of the known world, learned his concepts of gender relations in the Arab heartland of Islam. As he traveled, he was often astonished, and sometimes shocked, by the status of women in other Islamic countries. In the Turkish and Mongol regions between the Black and Caspian Seas, wives of local, ruling khans (sultans) owned property. When the senior wife appeared at the khan's residence, Ibn Battuta observes, the khan (sultan)

> advances to the entrance to the pavilion to meet her, salutes her, takes her by the hand, and only after she has mounted to the couch and taken her seat does the sultan himself sit down. All this is done in full view of those present, and without any use of veils. (Dunn, p. 168)

In the Maldive Islands, in the Indian Ocean, Ibn Battuta was even more scandalized:

Divorce proceedings. A scribe records the accusations of a husband and wife as they petition for a divorce in front of a *qadi*, or judge. A woman had limited rights to divorce her husband, but a man could divorce his wife without stipulating a reason, though in practice matters were rarely this simple. A *qadi* would bring to bear the combined wisdom of scriptural knowledge, local custom, and his own judgment in making an adjudication. (*Bibliothèque Nationale, Paris*)

HOW DO WE KNOW? (continued)

Their womenfolk do not cover their hands, not even their queen does so, and they comb their hair and gather it at one side. Most of them wear only an apron from their waists to the ground, the rest of their bodies being uncovered. When I held the qadiship [judge] there, I tried to put an end to this practice and ordered them to wear clothes, but I met with no success. No woman was admitted to my presence in a lawsuit unless her body was covered, but apart from that I was unable to effect anything. (McNeill, p. 276)

In Mali, west Africa, female slaves and servants went publicly into the ruler's court completely naked. When Ibn

Battuta found a scholar's wife chatting with another man, he complained to the scholar. But the scholar quickly put Ibn Battuta in his place:

> *The association of women with men is agreeable to us and a part of good conduct, to which no suspicion attaches. They are not like the women of your country. (Dunn, p. 300)*

Ibn Battuta left immediately and never returned to the man's home.

- In terms of gender relationships, to what degree is Islam concerned with

regulating biological, sexual relations? Family relationships? Social and legal relationships outside the family? How do regulations in Islam compare with those from other religions?

- What is the evidence that Islam in its early years was more egalitarian toward women than were either the other groups in Arabia or the Byzantine and Sasanid Empires outside Arabia? What is the evidence that it was less egalitarian?

- Ibn Battuta was surprised that the treatment of women varied quite widely in the various lands of Islam. Are you surprised? Why or why not?

SUCCESSORS TO THE PROPHET

When the Prophet died leaving no male heir, the Muslim community feared that the *umma* and its political organization would break up. To preserve them, the Muslim leadership elected Abu Bakr (r. 632–634), one of Muhammad's closest associates and the father of his wife Aisha, as **caliph**—that is, successor to the Prophet and head of the Muslim community. The next three caliphs were similarly elected from among Muhammad's relatives and companions, but amidst much more dissension.

Abu Bakr mobilized to prevent Muslims from deserting their new religion and the authority of its government, attacking those who tried. Arabia was convulsed in tribal warfare. The contending tribes fought for power and looted one another, as they had traditionally. Their battles spilled over the borders of the Arabian peninsula, as did their search for allies. The Byzantine and Sasanid Empires saw the Arab troops encroaching on their territories and fought back, but at the Battle of Ajnadayn (634), in southern Palestine, the Arab clans combined to form a unified army and defeated the Byzantine army. With their victory at Ajnadayn, the Arab warriors were no longer simple raiders in search of plunder. They were now at war for the control of settled empires.

Conquest followed conquest—Damascus in 636, Jerusalem in 638—but the northward march stopped as Byzantine troops held fast at the borders of the Anatolian peninsula. The Byzantine Empire defended its Anatolian borders for another four

caliph The spiritual head and temporal ruler of the Muslim community.

The expansion of Islam. The Muslim faith spread with astonishing speed from its center at Mecca, exploiting the weakness of the Byzantine and Sasanid Empires. Within a century of the death of the Prophet Muhammad in 632 C.E., Arab armies had reached the Atlantic coast in the west, and the borders of India and China in the east.

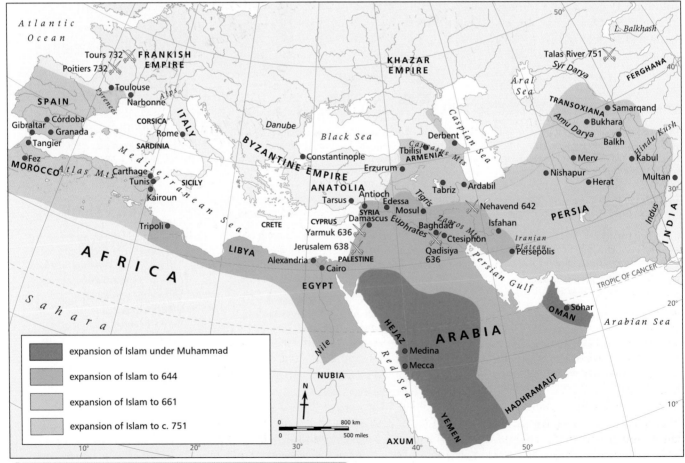

expansion of Islam under Muhammad

expansion of Islam to 644

expansion of Islam to 661

expansion of Islam to c. 751

For an interactive version of this map, go to: **http://www.prenhall.com/spodek/map11.1**

centuries, and its Balkan territories for eight. But the Sasanid Empire collapsed almost immediately. In 637 Arab armies defeated the Persians in battle, seized their capital, Ctesiphon, and forced the last emperor to flee. Meeting little opposition, Arab armies swept across Iraq, Iran, Afghanistan, and central Asia. Other Arab armies now turned toward northern Africa, taking Egypt in 641–643 and Tripoli in 643.

The second caliph, Umar I (r. 634–644), established the early principles of political administration, as a "rightly guided" caliph, in the conquered territories. The troops were not to interfere with the way of life of the conquered populations. The early caliphs did not encourage conversion to Islam, lest the political and social status of conqueror and conquered become confused. Also, since Muslims were exempted from land taxes and poll taxes, the conversion of conquered peoples would cause considerable loss of tax revenue to Umar's government.

To prevent the armies and the administrators from interfering with the economy and the social traditions of the newly conquered territories, Umar ordered the occupiers to live somewhat apart from the conquered populations. Muslim armies built new garrison cities, such as Basra, Kufa, Fustat, and Merv, and added new neighborhoods to existing cities for their troops and administrators. They largely left local systems of taxation and administration in place, and incumbent personnel often kept their jobs, but the new government confiscated lands that had been owned by the state and its officials and claimed them for itself.

These new arrangements proved unstable. In the new garrison cities, conqueror and conquered lived side by side, and they could not effectively be segregated socially and culturally. In addition, the troops soon argued that their pay was not adequate. Their incomes lagged, even as the new conquests enriched the top-level administrators. What had become of Islam's call for a more egalitarian society? In essence, the imperial aims of the ruling class and the religious goals of Islam were pulling in opposite directions.

Civil War: Religious Conflict and the Sunni-Shi'a Division

The jockeying for power among various political, economic, tribal, and religious interest groups precipitated a series of civil wars. A contingent of Arab troops from Egypt assassinated the third caliph, Uthman (r. 644–656), complaining that under his administration their local governors were cruel, their pay was inadequate, and class divisions were destroying Arab unity.

Uthman's successor, Ali (r. 656–661), was elected despite considerable opposition. Supporting his election most strongly was the *shiat Ali*, "the party of Ali," usually referred to simply as the Shi'a or Shi'ites. This group felt that the caliph should be chosen from the family of the Prophet. They had opposed the election of the first three caliphs. Ali, as the cousin and also the son-in-law of Muhammad, having married his daughter Fatima, was the first caliph to fit their requirement. In opposition, members of Uthman's family, the Ummayad clan, preferred one of their own. They argued for acceptance of the first three caliphs as legitimate since they were chosen by the *umma* and reflected the *sunna*, or example, of the Prophet. They and their followers called themselves Sunnis. Finally, a third group, who had long opposed the Umayyad for their own reasons, feared that Ali might reach an accommodation with their rivals, and assassinated him.

After Ali's assassination, the Umayyad leader, Mu'awiya (r. 661–680), declared himself caliph. Moving the capital out of Arabia to Damascus in Syria, Mu'awiya distanced himself from the original Muslim elite of the Arabian peninsula. He opened Islam to more cosmopolitan influences and a more professional style of imperial administration.

Read:

The exterior of the Dome of the Rock, Jerusalem, first constructed in 692 C.E. The first Umayyad caliph, Abd al-Malik (r. 685–705) built this shrine as the first major monument in Islamic history. It celebrates the triumphal conquests of the Umayyad dynasty as it emerged from Arabia and defeated both the Byzantine and Persian Empires to carve out a new empire of its own.

imam In Islam, a title for a person whose leadership or example is to be followed.

mahdi According to Islamic tradition, a messianic leader will appear to restore justice, truth, and religion for a brief period before the Day of Judgment.

Tension remained high among the various religious and tribal factions, however, and civil war broke out again on Mu'awiya's death in 680. His son, Yazid I (r. 680–683), claimed the caliphate, but Husayn, son of the assassinated Ali, took the field against him. When Husayn was killed in battle at Karbala, Iraq, in the year 680, he joined his father as the second martyr of the Shi'a branch of Islam.

The Shi'as stressed the importance of religious purity and they wanted the caliph to represent Islam's religious principles rather than its imperial aspirations. They felt that Ali, in addition to his heritage as a member of the family of the Prophet, represented that purer orientation, and they would recognize only descendants of Ali as **imams**, religious leaders who were also rightful caliphs. From 680 onward, Shi'as went into battle for the appointment of their imams to fill the position of caliph.

One after another, all of the first eleven Shi'a imams are believed to have died as martyrs, either in battle or through assassination. After the death of the eleventh imam in 874, and the disappearance of his son, the hereditary line ended. From that time onward, "twelver" Shi'as have looked forward to the reappearance of the "hidden" twelfth imam, referred to as the **mahdi**, or the "rightly guided one," a messiah, to usher in a new age of Islam, truth, and justice. Meanwhile, they have usually been willing to accept the authority of the current government, while stressing matters of the spiritual rather than the temporal world.

The great majority of Muslims, however, regarded the caliph as primarily a political official, administering the empire of Islam. They accepted the rule of the Umayyads, based on *sunni* teachings and the importance of the *umma* in making political decisions.

The division between Sunni and Shi'a, which began over the proper succession to the caliphate, has continued to the present, long after the caliphate has ceased to exist, as the principal sectarian division within Islam. Some 83 percent of the world's Muslims today are Sunnis, 16 percent Shi'as. The split is largely geographical with Shi'as forming 95 percent of the population of Iran and about 60 percent of Iraq. Ismailis, a branch of Shi'as, are found mostly in Pakistan and India. Elsewhere Sunnis are the overwhelming majority.

The Sunni-Shi'a division is the most significant in Islam, but it is not the only one. At the death of the sixth imam in 765, there was another conflict over acceptance of the seventh. The majority chose the imam's younger son, but a minority followed the elder son Ismail. The Ismailis proselytized actively and led frequent rebellions against the caliphate. Later the Ismailis also divided. One branch lives on today, revering the Aga Khan as its leader.

The Umayyad Caliphs Build an Empire

After the succession struggle on Mu'awiya's death, the Umayyads consolidated their rule and embarked on wars of imperial conquest. To symbolize their imperial power, the Umayyad caliphs constructed elegant, monumental mosques in Jerusalem in 691 (the Dome of the Rock); in Medina, 706–710; Damascus, 706–714; and, again, Jerusalem (the al-Aqsa Mosque), 709–715. They began also to create an imperial bureaucracy which owed its allegiance to the state rather than to the current ruler personally.

Life in the cities eroded the solidarity of tribal society. A new social structure was developing that was dividing the Arab upper and lower classes while mixing together the Arab and non-Arab elites. The Umayyad caliphs looked to Islam as the glue that could hold the splintered society together. They sought actively to convert the conquered peoples and assimilate them into a single Muslim *umma*. By the middle of the eighth century, conversions to Islam were increasing among the urban populations, as was the use of Arabic as the language of administration, literature, and everyday speech.

The Umayyads quickly expanded their empire through a series of enormously successful imperial conquests. Arab armies conquered the entire northern coast of Africa by 711. In north Africa, after initial resistance, most of the conquered Berber tribes converted to Islam. At one extreme, conversion was accompanied by intermarriage, and some of the Arab conquerors and Berber peoples intermingled to the point where it was no longer possible to distinguish among them ethnically. In other cases, whole tribes converted. They became part of the Islamic world but remained in their tribal groupings. Often they conducted their own internal administration as if they were a small state. Other Muslim armies marched eastward, capturing large parts of central Asia, and raiding repeatedly in the Indus valley region of Sind.

Between 711 and 756, Arab and Berber forces crossed the Straits of Gibraltar and completed the conquest of Spain. Muslim raiders also moved into France, but Charles Martel and Frankish armies pushed them back south of the Pyrenees in 732 after the Battle of Tours.

Muslim governments continued to rule at least parts of Spain for seven and a half centuries, until 1492. During those years the relationships between Muslims, Christians, and Jews were sometimes severe. Sometimes, however, they were very fruitful.

Clay figurine of a female slave from Khirbat al-Mafjar, Syria, c. eighth century. Female slaves had their place in the world of the Umayyad dynasty and beyond. Often the objects of passionate love, many were accomplished singers and highly educated.

The Umayyads copied the imperial structures of the Byzantine and Persian Empires: wars of imperial conquest, bureaucracy in administration, monumentality in architecture, and regal opulence at court. They used Arabic as their language of administration and encouraged conversion to Islam.

However, Umar's successors were not so committed to the program of equality under Islam as earlier caliphs had been. Their implementation was inconsistent, and various interest groups were frustrated by the vagaries of their changing fortunes. Many Sunni religious leaders, although pleased with the new emphasis on Islam, were offended by the imperial pomp of the Umayyads and their use of religion for blatantly political purposes. Many Shi'as continued to nourish the hope that one of their imams would displace the Umayyads and take his rightful place as caliph. In Kufa, Iraq, Shi'as revolted in 740, but the revolt was suppressed, and its leaders were executed.

The Ummayads had raised conflicting expectations. Non-Arab Muslims, whose taxes were not lowered or were lowered only temporarily, railed against the government for not delivering on its promises. Arabs were unhappy that their own taxes were being raised to compensate for the reductions offered to others.

The Umayyad armies, which were overextended and exhausted, began to lose major battles. The Turks drove them from Transoxiania in central Asia; the Khazars stopped them in Armenia in 730; Charles Martel halted the Umayyad advance in France in 732; the Greeks destroyed a major Muslim army in Anatolia in 740; in north Africa Berber rebels, although defeated in 742, destroyed an Umayyad army of 27,000 in the process. Umayyad forces did win the critical Battle of the Talas River in 751, halting the advance of Chinese forces westward and opening central Asia and its silk routes to Islamic religious and cultural missions, but they did not push forward. Military advances stopped. Pulled in many conflicting directions, without the strength to reply, the caliphate was drawn into a third civil war.

Portrait of Mahmud of Ghazni, from Rashid al-Din's *World History*, 1306–7. Mahmud (998–1030), a Sunni Muslim prince, is shown putting on the traditional diplomatic gift of a robe of honor, bestowed by the Abbasid caliph. Regional rulers sometimes declared their independence from central control, but Mahmud of Ghazni was careful to include the caliph's name on his coinage, thereby presenting himself as a loyal subject. (*Edinburgh University Library*)

The Third Civil War and the Abbasid Caliphs

The Abbasid clan in northern Iran—descended from an uncle of Muhammad named Abbas and also claiming support from descendants from the line of Ali—revolted against the Umayyads. Supported by Arab settlers in Iran who were protesting against high taxes, by Shi'as who were seeking their own rule, and also by a faction from Yemen, the Abbasid clan overthrew the Umayyad caliphate. In 750, Abu al-Abbas al-Saffah initiated the new Abbasid caliphate, which ruled in reality for a century and a half but held power in name until 1258. Signaling new policy directions, the Abbasid caliph built a new capital at Baghdad, 500 miles east of Damascus, along the banks of the Tigris River, in the heart of the historic fertile crescent.

The Abbasid caliphs continued the tasks of the Umayyads in trying to bring order and unity to an empire of heterogeneous peoples, and they followed many of the principles set forth by Umar II. They used Arabic as a unifying language of official communication and administration, and continued to urge non-Muslims to convert. They recruited widely among all the peoples of the empire to fill administrative and military positions, and as the bureaucracy expanded, Nestorian Christians, Jews, Shi'as, and numerous ethnic groups became prominent in the Abbasid administration.

For a century the Abbasids succeeded—to a surprising degree—in solving the problems of administering large empires. They kept their administration cosmopolitan and centralized, yet at the same time in touch with local communities. They rotated their officers so that none could become entrenched and semi-independent in a distant posting. They regularized taxes. They employed spies as well as troops of soldiers and armed police. They also attempted to maintain good relations with local notables, such as village headmen, large landowners, qadis (judges), officials of local mosques, religious teachers, moneylenders, accountants, merchants, and family patriarchs, who were the critical sources of information and power in the villages and towns.

The Weakening of the Caliphate

Inevitably, however, the Abbasid caliphate, too, encountered difficulties. The process of choosing a successor to the caliph remained unresolved. At the death of Caliph Harun-al-Rashid (r. 786–809), his two sons fought for the throne, provoking a fourth civil war. Recruiting troops proved an even bigger problem. Throughout the empire, local strongmen were invited to ally their troops to the caliph's armies, but these military contingents naturally owed their allegiance not to Baghdad but to the local potentate.

The caliphs expanded sharply the use of slave troops in their armies. Slave troops, mostly from central Asia, were often poorly disciplined, and sometimes various contingents turned on one another. At the same time the civilian bureaucracy became more corrupt and more distant from the general population, and tax collection was increasingly turned over to exploitive, semi-independent tax farmers. Corruption and reliance on slaves isolated the caliphs from their own civilian populations. The rulers became increasingly remote from the people they ruled—the more imperial the caliphate, the more distant it became from the original Islamic ideals of equality and simplicity.

The Emergence of Quasi-independent States. As a consequence, revolts struck the caliphate. In 868 a Turkish commander established a virtually independent dynasty that included Egypt and Syria, until the caliph regained them in 905. The slaves in the salt mines of southern Iraq waged a successful revolt for fifteen years, 868–883. In 867, frontier troops in central Iran revolted and won control of southern and western Iran.

Ismaili and Shi'a religious leaders organized revolts throughout the empire. Denying the legitimacy of Abbasid claims to rule and highlighting the exploitation of the village and tribal masses by the distant and corrupt administration in Baghdad, they won many victories in the name of their own views of Islam. Inspired by the Ismailis, peasant and Bedouin raiders attacked Mecca, briefly carrying away the sacred Ka'aba stone, the most venerated shrine in the holy city.

The Fatimid clan, claiming to be the rightful successors of the Prophet, conquered Egypt and much of northern Africa. They broke openly with Baghdad, declaring themselves the legitimate caliphs. In Iraq, other rebels took control first of the regions around Baghdad and then, in 945, of Baghdad itself. The caliph was permitted to continue to rule in name, but in effect the empire as a unified, centralized administration was finished. The unity of the Abbasid state dissolved, although the nominal authority of the caliph was still accepted everywhere.

Seljuk Turks and their Sultanate. Meanwhile, in the seventh and eighth centuries, the consolidation of the Tang dynasty in China had revived the pressure on the pastoral, nomadic peoples of inner Asia, pushing them westward, just as the Han had done centuries before (see Chapter 7). This time the pastoral nomads encountered peoples who had been converted to Islam. As a result of contacts with Muslim scholars and mystics, many of the nomadic peoples converted as well.

One of these groups, the Turkish-speaking Qarluq peoples, gained control of Bukhara (992) and Samarqand (999) in modern Uzbekistan. They propagated Islam and began to sponsor the development of the Turkish language and a Turkish-Islamic civilization.

Another Turkish-speaking group, led by the Seljuk (or Saljuq) family, entered central Asia, conquered Afghanistan and Iran, and seized Baghdad in 1055. In Baghdad, the Seljuk Turks kept the Abbasid caliph on his throne and ruled in his name.

Byzantium and Islam. The Byzantine Empire remained the bastion of Christian political power in Asia Minor for a thousand years after the fall of Rome. A powerful new force for Islam, the Seljuk Turks, appeared out of central Asia in the eleventh century. After invading Persia and Syria, they defeated a Byzantine army at Manzikert in 1071 and began to infiltrate the Byzantine heartland.

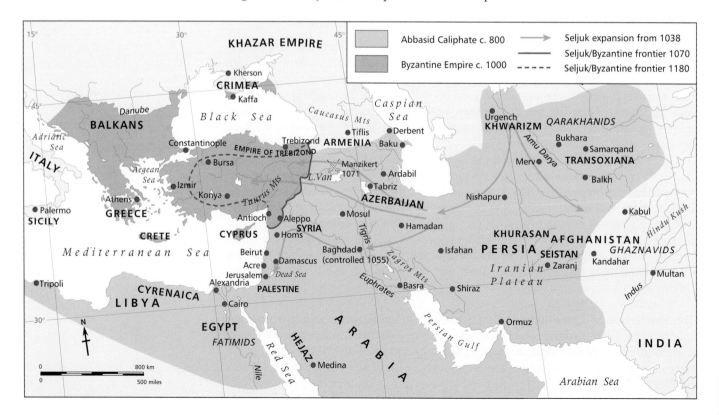

For an interactive version of this map, go to: http://www.prenhall.com/spodek/map11.3

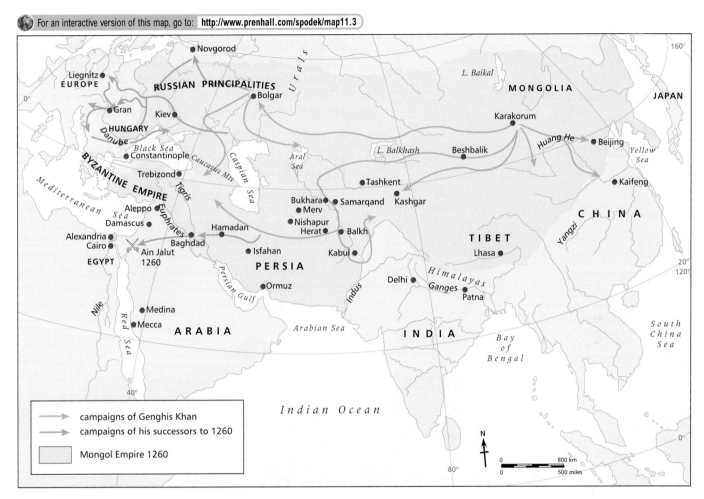

campaigns of Genghis Khan

campaigns of his successors to 1260

Mongol Empire 1260

They titled themselves sultans, claiming authority over the secular side of government, while leaving the administration of religious affairs to the caliph.

The Mongols and the Destruction of the Caliphate. In the twelfth century, a new threat destabilized empires from China to Europe, including the areas under Muslim rule. In Karakorum, Mongolia, Temujin (*c.* 1162–1227), later called Chinngis (Genghis) Khan ("Universal Ruler"), forged a confederation of Mongol and Turkish peoples, who rode outward, east and west, creating the largest land-based empire in history. The story of the Mongol expansion is told in Chapter 12.

Muslims whose lands the Mongols conquered felt devastated. An eyewitness observer, Ibn al-Athir, records his response to the early waves of invasions in 1220–21:

> For some years I continued averse from mentioning this event, deeming it so horrible that I shrank from recording it. To whom, indeed can it be easy to write the announcement of the death-blow of Islam and the Muslims, or who is he on whom the remembrance thereof can weigh lightly? O would that my mother had not born me, or that I had died and become a forgotten thing ere this befell … These [Mongols] spared none, slaying women and men and children, ripping open pregnant women and killing unborn babes. (McNeill and Waldman, pp. 249–51)

In 1258, Chinngis' grandson Hülegü (*c.* 1217–65) conquered Baghdad and executed the caliph, ending the Abbasid empire. The Mongols might have continued further on

The Mongol world. The irruption across Eurasia of the Mongols, an aggressive steppe nomad people, remains one of the most successful military undertakings of all time. Within thirty years the campaigns of Genghis Khan took the Mongol cavalry east to the Chinese heartland and west to Kievan Russia, the Caucasus, and Persia. His immediate successors consolidated China, entered Europe, and went on to establish a network of trans-Asian empires.

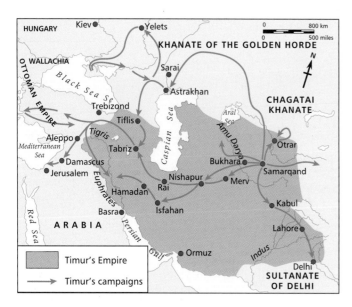

The Empire of Timur. The final stage of Mongol power was inspired by Timur's ambitions. Originating in Samarqand, his armies struck southeast to India, north to the Khanate of the Golden Horde, and west against the Ottoman and Egyptian Mameluke empires. Despite brilliant, brutal, early successes, the empire was unable to sustain its internal dynamics, and its collapse saw the exit of Mongol power from the world stage.

their conquests in west Asia, but the death of Hülegü's brother in China diverted their attention. Meanwhile, the sultan in Cairo defeated the Mongol troops at the Battle of Ain Jalut (1260), near Nazareth, ending their threat of further advance. Mongol rule in west Asia continued, however, until 1336. Significantly, even after it lost its political power to the Mongols, Islam continued to expand and gain converts.

SPIRITUAL, RELIGIOUS, AND CULTURAL FLOWERING

When the caliphate fell, the universal Muslim community, the *umma*, seemed to fall with it. Its central political focus was destroyed. Earlier historians have therefore characterized 1258 as a downward turning point, ushering in a protracted decline. More recent writers, however, emphasize the continuing growth of Islam outside the Arab world. The descendants of the Mongols themselves converted to Islam

Delivering a lecture. A traditional saying—"Kings are the rulers of the people, but scholars are the rulers of kings"—indicates the esteem in which learning is traditionally held by Muslims. Moreover, the transmission of knowledge was deemed a major act of piety. A well-stocked library serves as the backdrop for a lecture, in which a teacher would first dictate a text, then discourse upon it. (*Bibliothèque Nationale, Paris*)

within a century of their arrival in Islamic lands. Muslim scholars, mystics, and merchants carried Islam throughout the entire region of the Indian Ocean by sea, and along the length of the silk routes by land.

When Timur the Lame (Tamerlane or Tamburlane; 1336–1405) led his Turkish invaders along many of the routes and in many of the same kinds of campaigns as Genghis Khan had done, sacking or capturing Delhi (1398), Aleppo (1400), Damascus (1401), Ankara (1402), and Bukhara (1402), he had the support of Islamic scholars, *ulama* and mystics, **Sufis**. Timur's descendants patronized Islamic scholarship, and within a century Samarqand and Bukhara had become major capitals of Islamic culture. They also patronized Turkish as a literary language, encouraging its development as the third language of Islam along with Arabic and Persian.

Today, approximately 17 percent of the world's Muslim population lives in southeast Asia, an area never subject to the rule of the caliphate; 30 percent lives in south Asia, where conversion took place almost entirely after its fall; 12 percent lives in sub-Saharan Africa, again virtually untouched by the caliphate. In short, some 60 percent of today's Muslims are descended from peoples who had no connection to the Abbasid caliphate in Baghdad. In the following pages we consider the factors that enabled Islam to flourish and spread as a religion and a civilization even after its historic political center collapsed.

Islam Reaches New Peoples

The end of the caliphate did not mean the end of the spread of Islam. Quite the contrary. Regional rulers, finding themselves more independent, pursued policies of political and military expansion while proclaiming the religion and culture of Islam as their own.

India. A Muslim government run by slave soldiers who had earned their freedom had established itself in Ghazni, Afghanistan, as early as 962. From that base, Muslims launched raids into India and established their rule over the Punjab. In 1211, the Muslim general who conquered Delhi declared himself an independent sultan, initiating a series of five dynasties, which are known collectively as the Sultanate of Delhi (1211–1526). By 1236 they controlled north India; by 1335, almost the entire subcontinent.

When Delhi's power dimmed, numerous Muslim rulers controlled other regions of India. These regional governments, in particular, stayed close to their subjects, encouraged the development of regional languages, and provided new opportunities to Sufis, Muslim mystics and teachers, to introduce and practice Islam in new areas. In 1526, temporarily, and in 1556, more permanently, a mixture of Mongol and Turkish Muslim invaders conquered India, heralding the start of a new era, the Mughal Empire.

Most, but not all, of the Muslim rulers recognized the importance of a respectful religious accommodation with the overwhelming Hindu majority. The first Muslim invaders in Sind in the eighth century extended a protected status to Hindus usually granted only to monotheists. They argued that behind the many forms of god in Hinduism there was just one reality They also recognized that warfare against so

ulama The theologians and legal experts of Islam.

Sufi In Islam, a member of one of the orders practicing mystical forms of worship that first arose in the eighth and ninth centuries C.E.

The rise of the Delhi Sultanate. The Muslim Afghan Ghaznavid Empire was the first of a number of Afghan and Turkic powers who, exploiting divisions among local Hindu rulers, established their hegemony in northern India. Based at Delhi, six successive Muslim dynasties commanded varying territorial extents, but only briefly in the mid-fourteenth century did they completely control the Deccan.

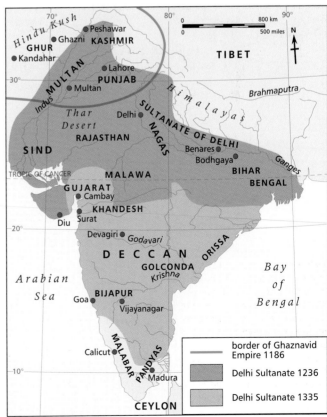

large a majority of Hindus was impossible. They allowed Hindus the right to practice their own religion as long as they accepted Islamic rule. Usually they protected Hindu temples, although in some instances they defaced shrines as a means of asserting their own supremacy. For example, they destroyed the famous Shaivite temple at Somnath, western India, in 1024. The Turkish forces occupying Bengal and Bihar also destroyed the last remaining libraries and monasteries of Buddhism in that region, delivering the final death blow to a religion that had already seen most of its following in India disappear.

The Muslim conquest of India opened the subcontinent to Persians, Afghans, Turks, and Mongols seeking jobs with the new governments (see Chapter 14). This immigration brought a variety of Islamic practices to India, where no single orthodoxy prevailed. Diverse Muslims coexisted with diverse Hindus, venerating some saints and sharing some devotions in common. India's population became 20–25 percent Muslim. Many were descendants of Muslim immigrants near the top of the social hierarchy;

Islam in south and southeast Asia. The disruption of centralized political power in the Muslim world did not stop the expansion of Islam in Africa and southern Asia. Arab maritime traders carried their faith to the shores of India and onward throughout maritime southeast Asia. The Indian heartland was conquered by successive waves of Muslim invaders, who, by 1400, secured the key Indo-Gangetic plain.

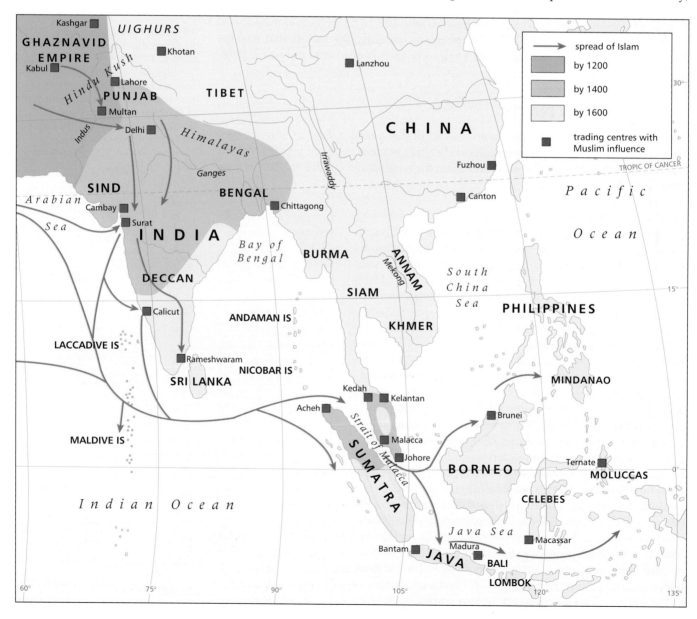

others were converts, escaping untouchability at the bottom of the caste system. The majority of India's population, however, remained Hindu.

Southeast Asia. The beginning of mass conversions of southeast Asians to Islam came in the fourteenth and fifteenth centuries, and today, Malaysia and Indonesia are overwhelmingly Muslim. Ocean traders and Sufis from India seem to have accomplished most of the missionary work. The traders offered increased economic opportunities to local people who would adopt Islam, while the Sufis and the regional kings of southeast Asia exchanged support for one another in a familiar pattern of interdependence between religious and political leaders. We will consider this further in Chapter 12.

Sub-Saharan Africa. As in southeast Asia, Islam was first carried to sub-Saharan Africa by traders and Sufis. They came from three directions: from Mediterranean north Africa across the Sahara to west Africa; from Egypt up the Nile to east Africa; and from India and Arabia across the Indian Ocean to the coast of east Africa.

The Arab conquest of north Africa in the seventh and early eighth centuries set the scene for increasing contacts between Arab and Black Africans. As traders, and sometimes as warriors, the Arabs began to cross the Sahara. When they arrived, they found flourishing kingdoms in place, their power derived from control of the desert trade routes and the taxes they imposed on this trade. Founded (according to legend) about 300 c.e., Ghana was the largest of these sub-Saharan kingdoms. (This Ghana is located approximately in the area of modern Mali, and is not to be confused with modern Ghana to the southeast.) By the ninth century Ghana was both a partner and a rival of the northern Berbers for control of Saharan trade. Along these routes, gold, slaves, hides, and ivory were transported northward in exchange for copper, silver, metal goods, horses, dried fruit, cloth, and salt transported southward.

By the eleventh century, a network of Islamic traders extended from the Atlantic Ocean in the west to modern-day Nigeria in the east, from the Sahara in the north to the fringes of the forested areas in the south. The traders included people of the Mandingo, Jakhande, and Dyula ethnic groups. Traders from the north invited their southern counterparts to adopt their religion, and Sufis came to establish new communities of faith and good works. Although the common people were not much affected until the nineteenth century, leading traders and rulers began to convert to Islam.

Trade connections were not the only source of converts. A wave of conversions also followed the domination of Ghana in the eleventh century by the Almoravid dynasty of Morocco. The Almoravids and their Berber allies waged a holy war to convert the Ghanaians, although many of the new converts continued to participate in indigenous religious practices even while officially accepting Islam. The Almoravids fought among themselves, as well as against the Ghanaians, and their cattle degraded the ecology of the region. Groups that had been ruled by, or allied with, the kingdom of Ghana began to assert their autonomy, until about 1235 the Keita kings of Mali, with greater access to the Niger River, surpassed Ghana in importance. Mali's founding king, Sundiata, is commemorated in the national epic of his nation, the *Sundiata*, as a great hunter and warrior possessed of magical powers. Although he himself observed African religious practices along with Islam, he encouraged his people to accept Islam.

About a century later, a more orthodox Muslim came to rule Mali. Mansa Musa (r. 1307–1332) made the *hajj* (pilgrimage) to Mecca in 1324, disbursing legendary amounts of gold along the way. He and subsequent rulers of Mali sought prestige through public affiliation with, and support for, Islamic institutions. They made improvements in Timbuktu, the most important trading city on the Niger River, at its northern bend

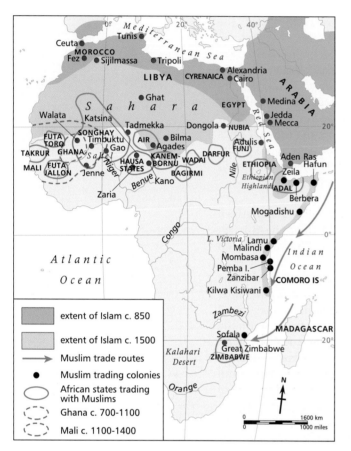

Islam in Africa. Islam entered sub-Saharan Africa as a result of trade. Trans-Saharan caravans from Egypt, Libya, and Morocco gradually introduced the faith overland among the trading kingdoms of west Africa, while the Arab traders of the Indian Ocean carried the message south by sea along the east coast of the continent.

near the Sahara, transforming the city into a major center of Arabic and Islamic studies. In the late fifteenth century, however, Sonni Ali (1464–1492), king of the Songhay people, slightly to the east, destroyed the empire of Mali and diminished its connection to the Islamic world of north Africa. Mali's rulers and people resumed the kind of halfway position between Islam and traditional African religions that Sundiata had held. Islam continued to be important in the private life but not the governance of the country. Mosques, for example, were treated as sanctuaries, so long as they were not used for political meetings. Ironically, at the death of Sonni Ali, one of his former generals, al-Hajj (the informal title often given to a person who has completed the *hajj* pilgrimage) Muhammad Askia (1493–1528) helped to restore connections with major Islamic centers in north Africa. Timbuktu resumed its growth. By the mid-sixteenth century, when it was under the rule of Songhay, Timbuktu held between 150 and 180 Quranic elementary schools that, in turn, laid the foundations for more advanced education. Timbuktu's scholarship matched that of Morocco, and leading scholars of Morocco came to learn from Timbuktu's leading scholar, Ahmad Baba (1556–1627). In 1591, however, the power of the city and its trading networks were undercut by the conquest of the region by Moroccan forces. Although the Moroccans were also Muslims, they acted as conquerors rather than as members of the same community, and the status of Muslims actually declined.

From Ghana, Mali, and Songhay, Islam was spreading eastward across Africa. For example, in the beginning of the twelfth century, the king of Kanem converted to Islam, made a pilgrimage to Mecca, and constructed a religious school in Cairo for students from Kanem. His subjects followed him in converting to Islam. When his Saifawa ruling dynasty was forced militarily to leave Kanem in the mid-fourteenth century, they reestablished their Muslim state in nearby Bornu. Islamic influences from Kanem and Bornu, in turn, reinforced the religious message that the *ulama* accompanying traders from Mali brought to the neighboring Hausa people in Kano in modern northern Nigeria. In these lands, too, Islamic practices and local religious practices often blended, with the people choosing whichever seemed most efficacious in their personal lives. Kings often responded similarly, following the practices that seemed most associated with their military victories, and abandoning those that seemed to accompany defeats. Still farther east, the upper Nile valley had been mostly Christianized by the time Muslim traders, gold miners, and slave traders arrived. As Muslim governments in Egypt began to push southward, however, they defeated the Nubian Christian kingdom and Islam began to take root, with the first Islamic states in Nubia dating to around 1500. The state of Sinnar, ruled by the Funj dynasty, became the most important of these states, in part because its subjects were expected to accept the Islamic religion of its rulers, and it gave special privileges to Islamic holy men and scholars.

Islam arrived on Africa's east coast by the eighth century. As Islam crossed from Arabia and the Yemen into east Africa, it met fierce resistance in Ethiopia, which had become staunchly Christian. Nevertheless, about 1630, a Portuguese missionary estimated that Muslims made up one-third of Ethiopia's population. A mosque at Shanga, off the east coast of Kenya, dates to about the beginning of the ninth century.

At about the same time, al-Masudi, an Arab historian and sailor, reported Muslim settlers on the east coast of Africa. Much larger growth appeared in the thirteenth century, and by the fourteenth century more than thirty communities, with mosques, lined the east African coast. Kilwa in southeastern Tanzania was the most important settlement and port, and modern archaeologists have been busy excavating its medieval remains along with those of other coastal towns. Philologists also study the interaction between the Arabic language of the overseas traders with the Swahili language of the African coast as trading necessities brought the two languages—and the two peoples—together.

Law Provides an Institutional Foundation

One of the central features of Islamic society that survived the fall of the caliphate was the law. The legal systems of Islam, *shari'a*, lived on and flourished. For Muslims, as for other populations, law expresses in formal terms the standards of proper conduct. Law supports the fundamental Islamic duty of *hisba*, "to promote what is right and to prevent what is wrong" (Musallam in Robinson, p. 175). Muslims encounter their legal system in the regulation of public life; in family matters of marriage, divorce, parental responsibilities, and inheritance; and in the *shari'a*'s advice on daily activities such as eating, dressing, and housekeeping.

As the early caliphs and the Abbasids began to confront legal questions, they appointed *qadis* (judges) to resolve them. The *qadis* searched the classical texts of the Quran, the **hadith** (quotations from Muhammad), and biographies of the Prophet for their core teachings, and then relied on a combination of local custom and their own deliberation and judgment (*ijtihad*) in rendering final decisions.

Seeking to overcome wide differences in local practices, four great legal scholars of the eighth and ninth centuries formulated the major systems of Islamic law that endure today: the system of Abu Hanifah (699–767) is in use mostly in the Arab Middle East and south Asia; of Malik ibn Anas (*c.* 715–795) in north, central, and west Africa; of Muhammad al-Shafii (767–820) in east Africa, southern Arabia, and southeast Asia; and of Ahmad ibn Hanbal (780–855) in Saudi Arabia. Although most localities have followed one or another of these systems since about the tenth century, the existence of multiple systems has allowed flexibility in interpretation. Under certain circumstances, local legal experts have the option of drawing on any of the four texts. Because Shi'ites maintain different traditions of authority, encompassing the teachings of Ali and the early imams, they have also developed different schools of law. The most widespread is that of Jafar al-Sadiq (d. 765).

The personnel of the legal system are the *ulama* (singular *alim*), the religiously trained scholars of Islam who interpret and implement the law. The *ulama* constitute a class that includes *qadis* and their assistants, Quran reciters, prayer leaders, and preachers. The *ulama* are sometimes trained in formal theological schools or, more frequently, are simply apprenticed to senior *ulama*. Islam has no formal hierarchical, bureaucratic institution of *ulama*—indeed, it has no official Church. Informal networks of respected *ulama* have provided cohesion, stability, and flexibility within Islam, regardless of the changing forms of government.

Ideally, *ulama* and ruler worked together to decide and implement religious policy, but when Caliph al-Mamun (r. 813–833) proclaimed that he had the right to give authoritative interpretations of the Quran, the *ulama* mobilized the population of Baghdad against him. He responded with an inquisition to root out these opponents. The only major leader who stood up to him was Ahmad ibn Hanbal, the greatest *hadith* scholar of his generation, who argued that only the scholars had the authority to interpret Quranic text. The people supported him, and to escape the continuing popular

hadith Traditional records of the deeds and utterances of the prophet Muhammad, and the basis, after the Quran, for Islamic theology and law.

protest, Caliph al-Mutasim (r. 833–842) moved his capital from densely populated Baghdad to Samarra, 60 miles away.

In 848–849 the Caliph al-Mutawakkil (d. 861) withdrew the claim of caliphal authority in religious matters. The *ulama* had won, but the battle had so embittered relations between caliph and *ulama* that their spheres of influence were forever separated: the caliph had authority over matters of state; the *ulama* over matters of religion. The caliphs came to represent the imperial aspirations of the state, while the *ulama* represented the everyday needs and wishes of the people. Over time, such departures from popular accountability cost them the caliphate. But the *ulama* endured, in touch with the people, and serving as their guides.

Sufis Provide Religious Mysticism

Law brings order to life. It makes concrete the responsibilities of one individual to another and to society in general. In Islam it also fixes the formal obligations due to God. The *ulama* conveyed and interpreted this message, carrying it to people in vastly different societies. Sufis also spread Islam to many parts of the world, but were much less interested than the *ulama* in strict religious doctrine and emphasized devotion to Allah instead.

The Role of Mysticism. As the Umayyad empire weakened, many people inhabiting it began to reject the materialism of its leaders and turned to a pious asceticism. For these spiritual seekers, Sufis revealed Islam's inner, mystical path to God. Early Sufis found and transmitted the inner disciplines of mind and body, the purifications of the heart

Whirling Dervishes. Sufism represents the mystical, contemplative strand of Islam—a strand that is captured vividly by the "Whirling Dervishes," a religious order closely linked to the teachings of the thirteenth-century Persian poet Jalal al-Din Rumi. Their slow, revolving dance helps to create higher states of consciousness, while being a ceremonial ritual in its own right.

SOURCE

Al-Ghazzali, "the Renewer of Islam."

The more solemn ulama *and the more emotional Sufis were often suspicious of one another. Deeply disturbed by the tension between the two perspectives, the revered scholar Abu Hamid Muhammad al-Ghazzali (1058–1111) finally formulated a synthesis of the intellectual and the mystical sides of Islam that has proved satisfying to Muslims ever since.*

Born and educated in Iran, al-Ghazzali was appointed at the age of thirty-three to teach philosophy at the leading madrasa, *or theological institute, in Baghdad. During four years there, Ghazzali began to doubt the role of rationality in life and searched for more holistic ways of experiencing the world. Torn between holding his prestigious tenure at the* madrasa *or giving it up to pursue new roads toward truth, Ghazzali was on the verge of breakdown:*

For nearly six months ... I was continuously tossed about between the attractions of worldly desires and the impulses towards eternal life. In that month the matter ceased to be one of choice and became one of compulsion. God caused my tongue to dry up so that I was prevented from lecturing. One particular day I would make an effort to lecture in order to gratify the hearts of my following, but my tongue would not utter a single word nor could I accomplish anything at all. This impediment in my speech produced grief in my heart, and at the same time my power to digest and assimilate food and drink was impaired; I could hardly swallow or digest a single mouthful of food. (al-Ghazzali, p. 57)

In 1095 Ghazzali resigned his post. He traveled to Damascus, Jerusalem, and Mecca, and then returned to his home town, where he lived the monastic life of a Sufi mystic, for ten years:

I learnt with certainty that it is above all the mystics who walk on the road of God; their life is the best life, their method the soundest method, their character the purest character. (p. 60)

During his time of contemplation, Ghazzali wrote a great number of philosophical and theological works, including the influential Revival of the Religious Sciences, *exploring the relationship between religion and reason. He asserted the importance of mystical experience and a direct, personal understanding of God, while at the same time defending the doctrine and authority of the Islamic faith.*

In 1106 Ghazzali was persuaded to return to teaching, now proclaiming the complementarity of Sufism and rationality:

Just as intellect is one of the stages of human development in which there is an "eye" which sees the various types of intelligible objects, which are beyond the ken of the senses, so prophecy also is the description of a state in which there is an eye endowed with light such that in that light the unseen and other supra-intellectual objects become visible. (p. 65)

By the end of his life, Ghazzali's reconciliation of Sufism and rationality within Islam had earned him the title "Renewer of Islam."

that enabled their followers to feel that they experienced God directly as the ultimate reality. They usually disdained worldly pleasures. One of the earliest of the Sufis, Hasan al-Basri (643–728), concluded: "This world has neither worth nor weight with God, so slight it is" (Esposito, p. 102). Though most Sufis were men, some, like Rabi'a al-Adawiyya (d. 801), were women. Rabi'a, like the Hindu Mirabai, rejected marriage to devote herself to God: "Love of God hath so absorbed me that neither love nor hate of any other thing remain in my heart" (Embree, p. 448).

As we have seen throughout this part, every theistic religion has an aspect of devotional love of god, expressed through spontaneous prayer, private meditation, fasting and asceticism, and, often, of physical disciplines, music, dance, and poetry. In Islam these aspects were adopted by the Sufis, who also absorbed influences from the mystics of other religions, especially monasticism from Christianity and Buddhism, and ecstasy in prayer from Hinduism.

Through their lives of exemplary devotion to God and people, the Sufis enhanced the message of Islam. They attracted people through the simplicity of their piety, their personal love of God, and their dedication to the needs of others. Some developed reputations for magical powers. The mosques where they lived and prayed, and the mausolea in which they were buried, were revered as sacred shrines. A sixteenth-century folk ballad of eastern Bengal tells of one such Sufi saint:

> At that time there came a Mahomedan *pir* [Sufi] to that village. He built a mosque in its outskirts, and for the whole day sat under a fig tree ... His fame soon spread far and wide. Everybody talked of the occult powers that he possessed. If a sick man called on him he would cure him at once by dust or some trifle touched by him. He read and spoke the innermost thoughts of a man before he opened his mouth ... Hundreds of men and women came every day to pay him their respects. Whatever they wanted they miraculously got from this saint. Presents of rice, fruits, and other delicious food, goats, chickens, and fowls came in large quantities to his doors. Of these offerings the *pir* did not touch a bit but freely distributed all among the poor. (Eaton in Adas, pp. 21–2)

tariqa In Islam a generic term meaning "path," referring to the doctrines and methods of mysticism and esoterism. The word also refers to schools or brotherhoods of mystics, which were often situated at a mosque or the tomb of a Muslim saint.

Individual mystics appeared in Islam from its earliest days, drawing their inspiration directly from the Quran. Centuries later, they began to form **tariqas**, or mystical brotherhoods, often located at the mosque or mausoleum of an especially revered saint. Some *tariqas* emphasized ecstatic practices; others were more sober and meditative. The *tariqa mawlawiya* was founded by Jalal-al-Din Rumi (1207–73) in Konya, Turkey. Rumi is most famous for his expression of ecstatic worship through the dance of the "whirling dervishes." Rumi's Persian language text, the *Mathnawi*, expressed in rich and evocative lyrics his love of God: "The result of religion is nothing but rapture" (Rumi, *Mathnawi* 1:312, Vitray-Meyerovitch, p. 83).

Intellectual Achievements

As the *ulama* provided order to the social structures of Islam, and the Sufis spread its spiritual powers, other intellectuals further enriched its cultural depth.

History. The historian and theologian al-Tabari (c. 839–923) introduced formal historical writings with his *History of Prophets and Kings*. The segment on prophecy recorded the contributions from Abraham through Muhammad; the record of kings covered rulers from biblical times to his own and included eyewitness reports of relatively recent events.

With the conquest of Iran in the mid-seventh century, Persian became the second language of Islam. (The arrival of the Turks in 923 introduced Turkish as the third.) The Persian poet Ferdowsi (940–1020) wrote an epic poem on the mythical origins of the Persian peoples, in which one of his central themes is the tragedy that befalls "a good man whose king is a fool."

The Mongols also supported historical writing, including al-Juvaini's (1226–83) *History of the World Conquerors*, which told of Chinggis Khan's conquests, especially in Iran. Rashid al-Din (1247–1318) wrote *World History*, which many regard as the first attempt at a history of humanity, as it integrates Chinese, Indian, European, Muslim, and Mongol history into a single cosmopolitan perspective.

Although others, notably Rashid al-Din, had attempted to write comprehensive, narrative histories before him, Ibn Khaldun (1332–1406) of Tunis is often viewed as the first to apply social science theory to the study of history. His *Universal History* stressed a cyclical theory of history, in which vigorous nomadic peoples regularly conquered urban peoples who were settled, cultured, and contented, took over their cities, settled into lives of luxury, and then themselves fell prey to the next round of invasion from more robust nomads. The theory seemed to fit the comings and goings of nomadic invaders from Arabia, Mongolia, and central Asia that characterized his times. Among Ibn Khaldun's other interpretive themes that still seem insightful today are: "The differences between Easterners and Westerners are cultural [not innate]"(p. 51); "The differences between peoples arise principally from the differences in their occupations" (p. 80); and, perhaps, "Scholars are of all men those least fitted for politics and its ways" (p. 64).

Philosophy. Theology and philosophy had been regarded as inferior to revelation in early Islam, but as Muslims came into contact with the philosophies of the Hellenistic and Indian worlds, they were drawn to concepts of Platonism and Neoplatonism in particular. The caliphate established in Baghdad a "house of wisdom," a translation bureau under Hunayn ibn Ishaq (803–873). In the next 200 years some eighty Greek authors were translated, including Aristotle, Plato, Galen, and Euclid. So, too, were writings from Syriac, Sanskrit, and Persian.

Mihrab in the Great Mosque, Cordoba, Spain, c. 961–976. Under the Umayyads, Cordoba grew to be by far the most prosperous city in western Europe, second only to Baghdad in the Islamic world. At its height, the city is said to have contained some 300 public baths and 3000 mosques within its walls. Shown here is the most important surviving example. Great attention was lavished on the decoration of the Great Mosque, and the *mihrab*, a small domed chamber indicating the direction of Mecca, is considered unique for its horseshoe-shaped doorway, a stylistic innovation of the Muslims in Spain.

A group of Islamic philosophers, called *Mutazilites*, "those who keep themselves apart," began to challenge orthodox Islamic belief, arguing that the attributes of God in the Quran were not literal but metaphorical, that human actions and life were not pre-determined, and that the Quran had not existed eternally. Al-Farabi (*c.* 870–950) argued that philosophical knowledge gained through study and thought was of higher value than revelation from God. Similar notions of the supremacy of philosophy were expressed by al-Kindi (d. 870), Ibn Sina (Avicenna; d. 1037), and Ibn Rushd (Averroes; 1126–98). Such philosophical speculation was marginal to mainstream Islamic thought and actually found more resonance among Christian and Jewish philosophers of the time.

Christian thinkers in Europe were indebted to the Muslims for keeping alive the Hellenistic traditions, for with the fall of the Roman Empire in the west the intellectual traditions and resources of Christianity had been neglected and forgotten. Now, thanks to Arabic translations and Islamic thought, Christian and Jewish philosophers grappled both with the original texts from Greece and India, and with the newer concepts introduced by Muslim thinkers.

Mathematics, Astronomy, and Medicine. The intersection of intellectual traditions also enriched mathematics, astronomy, and medicine. Indian scholars brought their texts on astronomy to Baghdad as early as 770. The caliph had them translated into Arabic, which was becoming the common language of scholarship throughout the empire. Arabs adopted and transmitted Hindi numerals and the decimal system, including the zero, throughout the empire and into Europe, where they were (mis)named "Arabic" numerals. A few decades later, al-Khwarazmi (d. *c.* 846) used Indian texts in conjunction with scholarship from Greece and Iran to develop algebra (from the Arabic *al-jabr*, "restoration"). (The word *algorithm* comes from al-Khwarazmi's name.) Al-Biruni (d. 1046) wrote extensively on number theory and computation, and later scholars developed the trigonometry we study today.

Al-Biruni also wrote *al-Qanun al-Mas'udi*, a compendium of Islamic astronomy, which incorporated findings from throughout the empire. Arabic mathematical and astronomical theories apparently informed Copernicus as he proposed a **heliocentric** universe in the sixteenth century (see Chapter 13).

heliocentric A system in which the sun is assumed to be at the center of the solar system—or of the universe—while Earth and the planets move around it.

Medical wisdom and herbal remedies were transmitted from one end of the empire to the other. Al-Razi (Rhazes; *c.* 865–*c.* 935) compiled an encyclopedia of medicine giving the views of Greek, Syrian, Indian, Iranian, and Arab writers on each disease, and including his own clinical observations and opinions. Ibn Sina, noted above for his contributions to philosophy, produced the even more encyclopedic *Qanun fi'l-tibb* ("Canon of Medicine"), which included volumes on the pharmacology of herbs, the functioning of organs, fevers, and surgery. The *Qanun* was translated into Latin and dominated medical thinking for 300 years.

The Extension of Technology

By 751, at the end of the Umayyad dynasty, Islam served as a network of communication that linked all the major civilizations of Eurasia. For example, as we noted above, Muslims learned papermaking from the Chinese and transmitted the technology throughout their domain. European Christians learned the art from Muslims in Spain.

Exchanges of information on agriculture and crops also enriched the world of Islam. Between the eighth and tenth centuries, Arabs brought from India hard wheat, rice, varieties of sorghum, sugarcane, bananas, sour oranges, lemons, limes, mangoes, watermelon, coconut palm, spinach, artichokes, eggplants, and the key industrial crop, cotton. All these crops were introduced throughout the empire, wherever climatic conditions were favorable. This may well have been the largest agricultural exchange in world history up to that time. Because most of these crops from India were warm-weather crops, many of them facilitated summer cropping in areas that had previously lain fallow in that season. To replicate the monsoon climate of India, Muslim officials improved existing forms of irrigation (underground water canals and water-lifting mechanisms) and invented new ones (certain kinds of cisterns). Agricultural productivity diversified and increased, encouraging population increase in general and urban growth in particular.

City Design and Architecture

Muslim governments built great cities and adorned their public spaces lavishly and often exquisitely. The largest of the cities were the political capitals. Baghdad was built along the west bank of the Tigris River in 762 to serve as the capital of the Abbasid dynasty, and it served that purpose for almost 500 years. In the ninth century, with between 300,000 and 500,000 people in 25 square miles, Baghdad became the largest city in the world outside China.

As the caliphate declined, and Baghdad with it, regional capitals grew in importance: Bukhara, Nishapur, and Isfahan in the east, and Cairo, Fez, and Cordoba in the west. The Fatimid rulers of Egypt began their administration in Fustat and expanded

The Great Mosque and minaret of al-Mutawakkil, Samarra, Iraq, 848–52. Though now only a shadow of its former glory, this 1150-year-old mosque remains the largest of its kind in the world. The three essential elements of simple mosque architecture emerge clearly through the ruins: a central courtyard or atrium, a (formerly) covered sanctuary inside the perimeter walls, and a minaret, or tower, from which the *muezzin* (crier) summons the community to worship.

that already existing city into al-Qahira (Cairo) in 969. In Morocco, King Idris II (r. 791–828) built Fez in 808 as the capital of the Idrisid dynasty, which had been founded by his father. A later dynasty, the Almoravids built their capital Marrakesh in 1070. In Andalusia, southern Spain, the Umayyads developed Cordoba into one of the most cosmopolitan cities of the Islamic world. It achieved its greatest splendor in the mid-tenth century, but was sacked by Berbers in 1013 and never fully recovered. The architecture of these cities proclaimed the splendor of Islam and the power of the Muslim ruler.

Although the daily prayers in Islam may be performed privately, Friday noon prayers require collective assembly, so all cities and most neighborhoods within cities also constructed mosques for public services. Wealthy rulers proclaimed their power and piety by building monumental central mosques, as they did early on in Jerusalem, Medina, and Damascus. The Abbasids constructed an enormous central mosque in Baghdad, and during the years that Samarra served as their capital (848–852) a huge mosque was constructed there, too. Great mosques were also built at Qayrawan in Tunisia, Fez in Morocco, and Cordoba in Spain.

Bronzesmith, Isfahan bazaar, Iran. In Islam, religion and business are integrally linked, in that the land adjoining mosques is often leased to market traders whose rents support the buildings and their activities. Here a bronzesmith works outside his shop in the bazaar at Isfahan, which has been thriving since the third century C.E.

As the Seljuk Turks conquered and then joined the world of Islam, they built an especially monumental mosque at Isfahan in the late eleventh century, and then rebuilt it fifty years later after Ismaili Shi'as burned it down. Ottoman architects, most notably Hoja Sinan (1490–1578), constructed magnificent mosques, such as the Selimiye at Edirne and the Sulaymaniye in Istanbul, and other public buildings that incorporated Byzantine and Islamic forms. When Islam crossed the Sahara desert, a new architectural form developed: the Sahelian mosque. When Mansa Musa returned from his trip to Mecca in 1325, he brought with him an Arab architect to supervise the construction of mosques and madrasas (theological schools) especially in Timbuktu.

Because Islam teaches that all the dead should be honored, and some believe that the saintly among them could confer blessings, mausolea have a special significance and sanctity. The followers of Timur (Tamerlane), for example, built for him an enormous tomb at Samarqand in 1405. Some burial shrines reveal extraordinary personal love and devotion. In 1632–49 the Emperor Shah Jahan built perhaps the best known of all Islamic buildings, the Taj Mahal in Agra, India, as a mausoleum for his wife Mumtaz Mahal, who died giving birth to their fifteenth child. At a more humble level, simple tombs of local holy men are found throughout the Islamic world, attracting followers, especially women, who pour out their hearts in prayer, trusting that the sanctity of the saint will carry it to God.

The public architecture of mosques, mausolea, and, to a lesser extent, the royal and governmental

The Taj Mahal, Agra, India, 1632–48.
Perhaps the best known of all Islamic buildings, the Taj Mahal was built by India's Emperor Shah Jahan as a mausoleum for his beloved wife Mumtaz Mahal, who died giving birth to their fifteenth child.

buildings that frequently adjoin them, anchored the formal religious and political institutions of the Islamic city. The bazaar, or market area, was home to business activities. Business in Islam was an honored profession. Muhammad himself had been a caravan operator, and his first wife, Khadija, had been a businesswoman. Even today mosques often control the land immediately adjacent to them and lease it out to businesses so that the rents can support the mosques.

Islamic cities were, in effect, nodes on international trade routes linking the Islamic world from China to Morocco and Spain. These trade routes enabled the movement not only of goods but also of people and ideas from one end of Eurasia to the other (see Chapter 12). The *hajj* (pilgrimage) to Mecca was also instrumental in creating a communication network among the regions and peoples of Islam.

The *Rihla* or travelogues of Ibn Battuta demonstrate the opportunities for travel open to a person of culture. In thirty years of traveling from his home in Tangier, he traversed approximately 73,000 miles of territories that today belong to some fifty different countries. Thanks to his mastery of Arabic and his knowledge of *shari'a*, he found a welcome reception, and frequently temporary employment and gifts of wives and wealth in the lands he traversed. Muhammad Tughluq, sultan of Delhi, appointed him a *qadi* and, later, his envoy to China.

Ibn Battuta's tales of adventure reflect the unity of the Islamic world. Despite its diversity, this world was held together by reverence for the Quran, the *shari'a*, the Arabic language (supplemented by Persian and Turkish), the political officials who ruled in its cities, and the scholars and merchants who traveled through them.

RELATIONS WITH NON-MUSLIMS

Early Islamic governments spread their worldly power by the sword. As a result, popular belief in the West has held that the religion of Islam spread in the same way. Although conversion by force was practiced occasionally (just as it was by Christianity), by and large forced conversion to Islam was unusual. For example, the early "rightly guided" caliphs and the early Umayyads did not seek to convert the people they conquered. They preferred to rule as Arab Muslim conquerors over non-Arab, non-Muslim subjects. Only when the later Umayyads feared that they could not continue minority rule over so large a majority, did they decide actively to seek conversion of, and alliance with, the conquered peoples.

Dhimmi Status

Non-Muslims were offered three choices. The first was to convert to Islam. The second was to accept "protected," *dhimmi*, status as worshipers of one God who accepted Muslim rule. All the monotheistic "peoples of the book" were eligible for this status, including Christians, Jews, and Zoroastrians. Later, Islamic governments in India also extended *dhimmi* status to Hindus. The *dhimmi* were often required to pay a special poll tax, but they could follow their own religion and their own personal law regarding marriage, divorce, and inheritance, and they were to be protected by the Muslim government. The third option was to fight against the Muslim state, an option that few chose.

The status of the *dhimmi* was spelled out in "The Pact of Umar," a document ascribed to Umar I (r. 634–644). This document prescribed second-class status for the *dhimmi*. They were not to build new houses of worship nor to reconstruct old ones. They were not to convert anyone to their religion. They were not to wear the same clothing as Muslims, but to wear distinguishing garments. The sounds of their prayers, their calls to prayer, and their funeral processions were to be muted. Their houses were not to be higher than the houses of Muslims. The poll tax, however, was not mentioned in this document. Perhaps designed to encourage non-Muslims to gain first-class citizenship by converting, these rules were nevertheless not crippling to life, and, indeed, they were often unenforced. Travelers throughout the Muslim world noted that Jews and Christians often held some of the highest positions in public and private life, and were self-governing in their religious life.

A principal goal of conquest, however, remained the creation of a *dar al-Islam*, "an abode of Islam," a land with a government under which Islam could be practiced freely. This did not mean that the people of the land were forced to become Muslims, only that the Muslims among them must have the freedom to practice their religion and sustain their culture.

Later, when many Muslims lived under non-Muslim governments, the *ulama* declared that any government that permitted freedom of religion to Muslims could be a *dar al-Islam*. The alternative was a *dar al-Harb*, an "abode of war," which had to be opposed because it restricted the practice of Islam.

The Crusades

At opposite ends of the Mediterranean, Muslims and Christians fought each other in war. The crusades (1095–1291) were as much political and economic as religious in their motivation. After Arab armies captured Jerusalem in 638, they built new, glorious mosques to indicate their own dominance, but they allowed Christians to continue their religious practices without hindrance and permitted Jews to return to Jerusalem officially for the first time since their exile by the Romans in 135 C.E.

Only centuries later, after Muslim Turkish armies won the Battle of Manzikert in 1071 and opened Anatolia to conquest, did the Byzantine emperor Alexius I call on Pope Urban II to help fight the Muslims and to recapture Jerusalem and the "Holy Land." The pope seized this opportunity to unite western Europe and its various rulers under his own banner in the name of religion. For those who would undertake the crusades, he promised indulgences that would reduce the time that they would serve in purgatory—before entering heaven—after their death. On a more earthly level, the pope promised that their property and assets would be protected in their absence. Many pious Christians responded to his call: rich and poor, men and women, old people and children. Christian rulers, knights, and merchants joined in, driven not only by religious inspiration but also by their own political and military ambitions, and by the promise of trade opportunities that would accompany the establishment of a Latin kingdom in the Middle East. In the course of the first four crusades—the major crusades—more than 100,000 people participated.

At first, the European Christian crusaders were successful—and brutal. In 1099 they captured Jerusalem, killing its Muslim residents, men, women, and children. They turned the Dome of the Rock into a church and the adjacent al-Aqsa mosque into an official residence. The savagery of the crusaders—reported in both Christian and Muslim sources—ushered in centuries of confrontation far more bitter than ever before. At the time, Muslim leadership in the region was divided, however, and did not respond. Then Salah al-Din (Saladin) (c. 1137–93), who had established a new dynasty in Egypt, recaptured Jerusalem in 1187. Records show that he treated the crusaders reasonably and humanely. But more crusades followed. When Richard I of England, called the Lion-Heart (r. 1189–99), captured Acre on the Mediterranean coast in the Third Crusade (1189–92), he also massacred its men, women, and children. By 1291, however, Muslim forces had reconquered Acre and all other crusader outposts. Although four minor crusades followed, none succeeded in capturing and holding any outposts in the Holy Land.

The crusader soldiers themselves were largely mercenaries with worldly motives who attacked many in their path for their own profit. As early as 1096, *en route* overland to Jerusalem on the First Crusade, crusaders paused to slaughter Jews. In 1204, during the Fourth Crusade, Roman Catholic armies, acting against the direct orders of the pope, attacked the city of Zara in Croatia and Constantinople, the capital of the Byzantine Empire, their presumed ally. Instead of uniting Christianity and defeating the Muslims, the crusaders had divided Christianity and were defeated by the Muslims.

THE CRUSADES

First Crusade (1095–9)	Proclaimed by Pope Urban II, the crusade was motivated by the occupation of Anatolia and Jerusalem by the Seljuk Turks. The crusaders recaptured Jerusalem and established several Latin kingdoms on the Syrian coast.
Second Crusade (1147–9)	Led by Louis VII of France and the Holy Roman Emperor, Conrad III, this was a disaster from the crusaders' point of view.
Third Crusade (1189–92)	Mounted to recapture Jerusalem, which had been taken by Saladin in 1187. Personal rivalry between the leaders, Philip II Augustus of France and Richard I of England, undermined the crusaders' unity.
Fourth Crusade (1202–04)	This crusade against Egypt was diverted, at the instigation of the Venetians, to sack and divide Constantinople, which led to half a century of western rule over Byzantium.
Children's Crusade (1212)	Thousands of children crossed Europe on their way to Palestine. Untold numbers were sold into slavery in Marseilles, France, or died of disease and malnutrition.
Fifth Crusade (1218–21)	King Andrew of Hungary, Cardinal Pelagius, King John of Jerusalem, and King Hugh of Cyprus captured, then lost, Damietta, Egypt.
Sixth Crusade (1228–9)	The Holy Roman Emperor, Frederick II (r. 1212–50), led the crusade that, through negotiation with the sultan of Egypt, recovered Jerusalem. The city was finally lost in 1244.
Seventh Crusade (1249–54) and Eighth (1270–91)	Both led by Louis IX of France (r. 1226–70), who was inspired by religious motives, but both were personal disasters. Louis was later canonized.

Illustration of the Second Crusade (1147–9). Lance-bearing Christian forces face a Muslim army in this scene from the Second Crusade. The fleur-de-lys emblem, here sported on his shield by the French king, Louis VII, was adopted at almost the same time by his opponent, the ruler of Aleppo. (*British Library, London*)

A Golden Age in Spain

At the other end of the Mediterranean, in Spain, Islam flourished and coexisted with the Christian and Jewish communities of the peninsula. Through a century of immigration, conquest, administration, and intermarriage, beginning in 711, Umayyad and Berber invaders brought Islam to a central position in Spain. They also revitalized trade by breaking the monopoly of Byzantine control over the western Mediterranean. They introduced new crops and new irrigation techniques from west Asia. Abd al-Rahman III (r. 912–961) asserted his separation from the Abbasids by declaring himself a caliph rather than just a sultan. A series of rulers expanded the ornate mosque at Cordoba, making it one of the architectural showcases of Islam.

Eastern scholars of law and philosophy immigrated to the flourishing court. Poets developed new styles, based in Arabic but also influenced by local Spanish and Latin styles. Greek philosophical and medical treatises were translated into Latin as well as Arabic, thus opening intellectual communication with the educated classes in Christendom. Although some Christians revolted against Islamic and Arabic inroads, and were killed in battle (850–859), many more adopted Arabic lifestyles.

By 1030, the caliphate in Spain had disintegrated. Various armed struggles broke out between the provinces and the capital, between townsmen and rural Berber immigrants, and between converts and Arabs. The conflicts did not, however, impede the spread of Islam. As in the eastern Mediterranean, provincial administrations replaced the central caliphate and brought the culture of their courts closer to the general population. Sufis spread their ascetic and devotional teachings.

The vacuum in the central government did, however, provide an opening to various Christian forces to begin the *reconquista*, the Christian reconquest of Spain. In 1085 Alfonso VI (r. 1065–1109), king of Leon, then king of Leon and Castile, captured Toledo. By the mid-thirteenth century all of Spain with the exception of Granada was in Christian hands.

During the years of the *reconquista*, culture continued to flourish. Until the mid-thirteenth century, Christian rulers in Spain patronized the rich, hybrid culture. They translated the Bible, the Talmud, and the Quran into Castilian. Arabic texts on astrology and astronomy, and the philosophical works of Muslim thinkers, including al-Kindi, al-Farabi, and Ibn Sina (Avicenna), were translated into Castilian and Latin, as was the philosophy of the Jewish thinker Moses Maimonides and his codification of Jewish religious law. Spain was the entry-way into western Europe for classical writings and their reworking through the prism of Islamic civilization.

With the fall of Seville to the Christian *reconquista* in 1248, Granada remained as the only Islamic kingdom in Spain. Nestled on a spur of the Sierra Nevada mountains in the south, the city flourished thanks to an influx of talented Muslims fleeing the advancing Christian armies, and the enterprise and vigor of its rulers. Two of the kings of the Nasrid dynasty, Yusuf I (1333–54) and Muhammad V (1354–9, 1362–91), built a complex of buildings called in Arabic "Qalat al-hamra," or the Alhambra. This red citadel served as their home, a city within a city. Their legacy is today the best-preserved palace of medieval Spain.

By the fourteenth century, Christianity had become triumphal and intolerant. Jews and Muslims were forced to accept baptism and convert to Christianity, although many of them continued to practice their original religions in secret. In 1478, at the request of the Spanish rulers, the Roman Catholic Church established the Spanish Inquisition to hunt down those suspected of being insincere converts, whether Jewish (called Marranos) or Muslims (called Moriscos). The first Grand Inquisitor, Tomás de Torquemada, began his work in 1483, and brought people to trial not only for apostasy and heresy, but also for sorcery, sodomy, polygamy, blasphemy, and usury. Under Torquemada's direction, about 2000 people were burned at the stake, making his name a watchword for the fanatical misuse of religious authority.

The Court of Lions, Alhambra Palace, Granada, 14th century. The elegance of this courtyard, with its central fountain and a dozen stone lions whose mouths are waterspouts, testifies to the power and aesthetic taste of the last Islamic kingdom left in Spain as the Christian reconquista was completed in 1492.

HOW DO WE KNOW?

Conversion and Assimilation

Only in the last two decades has serious research been done on conversion to Islam, asking exactly how the process worked. For example, Nehemia Levtzion edited a set of studies on Conversion to Islam in 1979 examining the motives of converts. Levtzion argued that "assimilation" was a better term than "conversion" for describing the process of becoming a Muslim. People in conquered areas, especially, were not so much overwhelmed by political conquest as they were impressed with the richness of the culture that Islam brought to them. They found that their lives were enriched by the rituals, philosophy, art, and sense of belonging to a world system that came with joining the umma, the Islamic community.

Richard Bulliet's Conversion to Islam in the Medieval Period: An Essay in Quantitative History demonstrates that conversion took place at different rates of speed in each of the six societies he examines: Arabia, Egypt, Iraq, Syria, Iran, and Spain. He notes the problems of finding data to understand the process,

since "medieval Islam produced no missionaries, bishops, baptismal rites, or other indicators of conversion that could be conveniently recorded by the Muslim chronicler" (p. 4). For data, Bulliet examines the speed of adoption of Muslim names in each of the six societies. He concludes that rapid acceptance of Islam went hand in hand with a breakdown in central political rule. As centralized Islamic rule broke down, paradoxically, Sufis carried the word of Islam more freely and with more backing from local governments.

We also know of the very large-scale assimilation to Islam by the Mongol successors of Genghis Khan and of the followers of Timur the Lame (Tamerlane). These ruling groups were assimilated by Islam because the new civilization they encountered offered them cultural, political, social, economic, and spiritual rewards that were not available in the religions and cultures of their birth.

Finally, the great assimilation that took place outside the heartlands of Islamic conquest, in sub-Saharan Africa and southeast Asia, was carried by traders and

later supported by Sufis and ulama. In both these huge areas, the trade networks by land and sea were so densely worked by Muslims that indigenous traders began to assimilate Islam into their lives, either from religious conviction or from the promise of trade advantage. They stayed to join in one of the world's richest and most widespread civilizations, the umma of Islam.

- Nehemia Levtzion prefers the term "assimilation" rather than "conversion" to describe the process by which people adopted Islam. What does he mean by each term? Do you agree with his argument? Why or why not?
- Besides political rulers, what other groups successfully encouraged large numbers of people to accept Islam? In what geographical regions of the world were they most effective?
- What was the problem faced by Richard Bulliet in determining thow many people accepted Islam? How did he attempt to solve this problem? Do you think his solution appropriate? Why or why not?

Granada fell in 1492 to the Catholic rulers Ferdinand and Isabella. Muslim rule in Spain was broken. In 1492 Ferdinand and Isabella expelled the Jewish population from Spain. After an unsuccessful revolt of 1499–1500, Muslims, too, had to choose between exile and conversion to Christianity. In 1566 use of the Arabic language was banned in Spain. The golden age of religious tolerance and cultural exchange was over.

JUDAISM, CHRISTIANITY, AND ISLAM WHAT DIFFERENCE DO THEY MAKE?

Judaism, Christianity, and Islam shared many common ancestors. They all were monotheistic religions and believed in divinely given written scriptures. Each of them had common rituals and practices. These included encouraging regular prayer, providing charity for the poor, and valuing pilgrimages to sacred holy places. Each also promised that behavior will receive its proper rewards and punishments in the future, on earth and in an afterlife. Finally, all balanced and integrated strands of mysticism, legalism, and pious devotion. Given these commonalities, the three religions of Judaism, Christianity, and Islam would appear to be naturally suited to coexistence and even to mutual reinforcement. And indeed at times, notably in Spain for many years, the three faiths did coexist and gladly learned from one another. But such warm, reciprocally beneficial coexistence has been the exception rather than the rule.

Perhaps two factors can explain the friction that has often characterized the relationships among these religions. First, all three have been proselytizing religions—although Judaism abandoned this practice early in the Christian era—and their very closeness has made them bitterly competitive. Each has had some feeling that it has come the closest to the essential truths of God and the world, and that the others have somehow failed to recognize this. Both Christianity and Islam, for example, accuse Judaism of stubbornly refusing to accept later revelations that modify and update its original truths. Both Judaism and Islam accuse Christianity of a kind of idolatry in claiming that God begat a son who was actually a form of God and who walked the earth in human form. Both Judaism and Christianity argue that God did not give a special, final revelation to Muhammad. In each case these religions have looked at one another and said that, despite elements of deep commonality, there exist also fundamental antagonisms. Indeed within each of these religions, at various times, internal divisions have turned one group against another amid cries of heresy and calls to armed opposition. Truth was to be maintained, asserted, and defended through the force of arms. (Religions with less insistence on doctrinal correctness, such as Hinduism and Buddhism, have had fewer, and less violent, religious wars.)

Second, as each religion developed, it sought the support of government. It often sought to *be* the government. Truth was to be reinforced by power. Basic competition over spiritual and philosophical truths spilled over into competition also for tax monies, office, land, and public acceptance of specific ritual and architectural symbols, and suppression of opposition. When they could, these religions marched through the world armed. Until recently, in the lands where these three religions predominated, the state and religion were usually intimately bound up with one another, and in many places the leader of the state expected that his subjects would accept his religion as their own, or at least give it preferential treatment.

Historically, Christianity came to dominate the European lands formerly held by the Roman Empire and, as we shall see, traveled with its European faithful to the New World. Islam dominated north Africa and the Asian lands formerly held by the Persian and Alexandrine Empires, and it traveled with armies, saints, and traders to India and southeast Asia. Judaism, which lost out to its younger successors both in numbers and in gaining the support of governments, remained everywhere a minority religion, dependent on the tolerance of others. This identification of different religions with particular geographical parts of the world was typical also of Hinduism, identified with India and, to a much lesser extent, with southeast Asia; and of Buddhism, identified with the Indian subcontinent, east and southeast Asia, and the routes connecting them.

Nevertheless, amid the carving up of the world into zones of religious dominance backed by supportive governments and frequent warfare among religious groups, there were also times of mutually beneficial coexistence, sharing of cultures, and recognition of the commonalities of these religions and of the common humanity of their faithful. In many regions, like the Middle East, and in cities along the various trade routes all over the world, members of different religions lived side-by-side, often developing mutual understanding, respect, and trust. And always the voice of the mystic, like that of Jalal al-Din Rumi, called out for recognition of the oneness of God and the unity of God's universe:

What is to be done, O Moslems? for I do not recognize myself.
I am neither Christian, nor Jew, nor Gabr [Zoroastrian], nor Moslem.
I am not of the East, nor of the West, nor of the land, nor of the sea;
I am not of Nature's mint, nor of the circling heavens.
I am not of earth, nor of water, nor of air, nor of fire;

I am not of the empyrian, nor of the dust, nor of existence, nor of entity.
I am not of India, nor of China, nor of Bulgaria, nor of Saqsin;
I am not of the kingdom of Iraqain, nor of the country of Khorasan.
I am not of this world, nor of the next, nor of Paradise, nor of Hell;
I am not of Adam, nor of Eve, nor of Eden and [the angel] Rizwan.
My place is the Placeless, my trace is the Traceless;
'Tis neither body nor soul, for I belong to the soul of the Beloved.
I have put duality away, I have seen that the two worlds are one;
One I seek, One I know, One I see, One I call. (McNeill and Waldman, p. 242)

Review Questions

- What is the *umma* in Islamic philosophy and practice? Why did Muhammad and later Muslim leaders think that it was important? What did they do to construct and preserve the *umma*?
- To what degree did the philosophy and practices of Islam appear to be new in Arabia? To what extent did they fit into existing philosophies and practices?
- Why have scholars disagreed as to whether early Islam improved the lives of women or made them more difficult?
- What is the basis for the division in Islam between Shi'a and Sunni groups?
- The political capital of Islam was moved from Medina to Mecca to Damascus to Baghdad. When did each of these moves occur, and for what reason?
- As between Sufis and the *ulama*, which group do you think did more to promote Islam in the world? Why do you hold this opinion? How did they do it?
- What were the ways in which Muslims preserved, enhanced, and transmitted knowledge and technology throughout their own domains and beyond?
- Give some historical examples of tensions and warfare between Muslims and Christians. Other examples of peaceful, mutually beneficial coexistence? Some historical examples of tensions and warfare between Muslims and Hindus? Other examples of peaceful, mutually beneficial coexistence?

Suggested Readings

PRINCIPAL SOURCES

Esposito, John. *Islam: The Straight Path* (New York: Oxford University Press, 1991). Clear, basic, exposition of the development and significance of Islam by a lifelong, non-Muslim scholar.

Esposito, John, ed. *The Oxford History of Islam* (New York. Oxford University Press, 1999). Brings together an array of clear, well-illustrated essays by outstanding scholars on the origin and evolution of Islam, including materials on law, society, science, medicine, technology, philosophy, and Islam and Christianity.

Hodgson, Marshall G.S. *The Venture of Islam*, 3 vols. (Chicago, IL: University of Chicago Press, 1974). Hodgson's classic reinterpretation of Islam, seeing it not only in alliance with political power, but also as an attractive global culture.

Keddie, Nikki R. and Beth Baron, eds. *Women in Middle Eastern History* (New Haven, CT: Yale University Press, 1991). Presents a wide variety of feminist perspectives on women in Islamic cultures.

Lapidus, Ira M. *A History of Islamic Societies* (Cambridge: Cambridge University Press, 1988). A comprehensive, even encyclopedic account by a single scholar.

Lewis, Bernard, ed. and trans. *Islam from the Prophet Muhammad to the Capture of Constantinople*, 2 vols. (New York: Oxford University Press, 1987). Outstanding anthology of primary sources, grouped as politics, war, religion, and society.

McNeill, William H. and Marilyn Robinson Waldman, eds. *The Islamic World* (Chicago, IL: University of Chicago Press, 1983). Outstanding anthology of primary sources.

Watson, Andrew. *Agricultural Innovation in the Early Islamic World* (Cambridge: Cambridge University Press, 1983). An account of the major crops of India transplanted westward to the very ends of the Islamic world. A kind of precursor to the later Columbian exchange.

ADDITIONAL SOURCES

Adas, Michael. *Islamic and European Expansion* (Philadelphia, PA: Temple University Press, 1993). Contains excellent interpretive historiographic articles on Islam in world history.

Ahmed, Leila. *Women and Gender in Islam* (New Haven, CT: Yale University Press, 1992). Demonstrates the variety of practices chronologically around the world.

Bulliet, Richard W. *Conversion to Islam in the Medieval Period: An Essay in Quantitative History* (Cambridge, MA: Harvard University Press, 1979). An innovative assessment of the rate of conversion through a study of name change.

E.J. Costello, trans. (from Gabrieli Francesco, trans. from Arabic), *Arab Historians of the Crusades* (Berkeley, CA: University of California Press, 1969). Through the eyes of Arab historians, the Crusades appear less religious, more brutal and cruel, and much more concerned with money, than in most western accounts.

Dunn, Ross E. *The Adventures of Ibn Battuta* (Berkeley, CA: University of California Press, 1986). An interpretive study of the great Muslim traveler as an introduction to the culture and lands of his travels.

Eaton, Richard M. "Islamic History as Global History," in Adas, *op. cit.*, 1–36. Brings new social-science sources to bear in interpreting the rise and significance of Islam.

Eaton, Richard M. *The Rise of Islam and the Bengal Frontier, 1204–1760* (Berkeley, CA: University of California Press, 1993). Innovative assessment of how the region of modern Bangladesh became Islamic.

Eaton, Richard M. *Essays on Islam and Indian History* (New York: Oxford University Press, 2000). Important revisionist views of Muslim-Hindu interaction, usually emphasizing the achievement of accommodation.

Embree, Ainslee T., ed. *Sources of Indian Tradition, Volume I: From the Beginning to 1800* (New York: Columbia University Press, 2nd ed., 1988). The outstanding anthology of primary sources.

Ferdowsi. *The Legend of Seyavash* (London: Penguin Books, 1992). Classic tales of the early rulers of Persia.

al-Ghazzali. *The Faith and Practice of al-Ghazali*, trans. W. Montgomery Watt (London: Allen and Unwin, 1953). Tells of the tribulations of the master as he painfully sought a synthesis between legalism and mysticism in Islam.

Grabar, Oleg. *The Alhambra* (Cambridge, MA: Harvard University Press, 1978). A beautiful, scholarly account of the architectural marvel.

Hodgson, Marshall G.S. *Rethinking World History: Essays on Europe, Islam, and World History*, ed. Edmund Burke III (Cambridge: Cambridge University Press, 1993). A re-assessment of Hodgson's classic scholarship on Islam to demonstrate its relevance to world history.

Ibn Khaldun. *An Arab Philosophy of History*, ed. Charles Issawi (London: John Murray, 1950). An abridgement of this fourteenth-century classic of contemporary social science.

Johns, Jeremy. "Christianity and Islam," in John McManners, ed. *The Oxford Illustrated History of Christianity* (Oxford: Oxford University Press, 1990), 163–95. A basic sketch of the interaction of these religions, positive and negative.

The Koran trans. N.J. Dawood (London: Penguin Books, 1990). Probably the most readable translation.

The Koran Interpreted trans. A.J. Arberry (New York: Macmillan Publishing Co., 1955). The most acceptable translation to Muslim scholars.

Levtzion, Nehemia, ed. *Conversion to Islam* (New York: Holmes and Meier, 1979). Argues that conversion to Islam was at least as much a cultural process of assimilation as a sudden change in belief.

Levtzion, Nehemia. "Islam in Africa to 1800s: Merchants, Chiefs, and Saints," in Esposito (1999), 475–507. Very useful overview of many of the states and regions of sub-Saharan Africa.

Lewis, Bernard. *Islam and the West* (New York: Oxford University Press, 1993). Basic, but controversial interpretive account of cultural and political interaction, by a master.

Morony, Michael. *Iraq after the Muslim Conquest* (Princeton, NJ: Princeton University Press, 1984). Account of the conquests of Genghis Khan, his successors, and their legacies.

Nashat, Guity. "Women in the Middle East, 8000 B.C.–A.D. 1800," in *Expanding the Boundaries of Women's History: Essays on Women in the Third World*, eds. Cheryl Johnson-Odim and Margaret Strobel. (Bloomington, IN: Published for the Journal of Women's History, 1992). An introductory bibliographic survey of existing literature.

Niane, D.T. *Sundiata: an Epic of Old Mali* (Harlow, Essex, England: Longman, 1965). The classic epic of the founder-ruler of Mali.

Riley-Smith, Jonathan, ed. *The Oxford Illustrated History of the Crusades* (New York: Oxford University Press, 2001). A dozen articles by experts mostly from Western, Christian perspectives.

Robinson, Francis, ed. *The Cambridge Illustrated History of the Islamic World* (Cambridge: Cambridge University Press, 1996). Beautifully produced, one volume scholarly introduction to the Islamic world, lavishly illustrated.

Trimingham, John S. *Sufi Orders in Islam* (Oxford: Oxford University Press, 1971). An account of several different Sufi tariqas, their leadership, history, and commitments.

Tucker, Judith. "Gender and Islamic History," in Adas, op. cit., pp. 37–74. A succinct, provocative historiographical assessment of various interpretations of the status of Muslim women through the ages and around the world.

Vitray-Meyerovitch, Eva de. *Rumi and Sufism* (Sausalito, CA: Post-Apollo Press, 1987). Basic introduction to Rumi, his poetry, and his place in the Sufi movement.

⊚ World History Documents CD-ROM

8.1 Muhammad: Koran

8.2 Al-Tabari: An Early Biography of Islam's Prophet

8.3 Orations: The Words of the Prophet Through His Speeches

8.4 Islam in the Prophet's Absence: Continuation Under the Caliphate

8.5 Harun al-Rashid and the Zenith of the Caliphate

8.6 Al-Farabi: The Perfect State

8.7 Islamic Science and Mathematics

8.8 The Caliphate in Decline: Al-Matawwakil's Murder

8.9 Shiism and Caliph Ali: Controversy Over the Prophetic Succession

12.1 Sunni versus Shi'ite: "We Exhort You to Embrace the True Faith!"

12.2 Süleyman "The Lawgiver" and the Advantages of Islam: Oigier de Busbecq

12.3 Women in Ottoman Society: Oigier de Busbecq

12.4 The Ottomans: Empire-builders at the Crossroads of Three Continents

12.5 The Safavid Shi'ite Empire of Persia

12.6 Shah Abbas the Great: The Resurgence of the Persian Empire

12.7 Moghul Apogee: Akbar the Enlightened

Religion to Trade

Moving from the theme of religion in Part 4 to the theme of trade in Part 5 may seem a big jump. Are not matters of the spirit quite separate from matters of commerce? In Christianity, did not both the Gospel of Matthew (6:24) and of Luke (16:13) quote Jesus as saying, "No servant can be the slave of two masters … You cannot serve God and Money"? Did not Matthew quote Jesus as saying, "It is easier for a camel to pass thorough the eye of a needle than for a rich man to enter the kingdom of God" (Matthew 19: 23-24). Christian clergy were sworn to lives of poverty.

As the Church became wealthy at various times in its history, reformers lamented its departure from the ascetic standards of its early years. Martin Luther proclaimed his reformation of the Church in the mid-fifteenth century in part as a protest against the Church's sale of "indulgences," documents granting forgiveness of sin in exchange for donations to the Church. Luther argued that money could not take the place of honest penance.

Lucas Cranach the Elder, The Pope's Selling of Indulgences, 1521. Woodcut.

A bishop blessing the annual market, St. Denis, near Paris, 14th century. Miniature. (*Bibliothèque Nationale, Paris*)

Church might bless their economic interests. See for example the illustration (*left*) depicting a bishop blessing the annual market at St. Denis, near Paris.

Other religions generally began with a more accommodating view of the relationship of religion and trade. The Book of Genesis portrays Judaism's founder, Abraham, as a semi-nomadic owner of flocks of sheep and goats, and a man who bargained actively in purchasing a burial site for his wife. In more systemic terms, the rabbis interpreted the Biblical injunction against taking interest as applying to loans among friends and family members; they devised methods of allowing modest interest to be taken on commercial loans. Islam, which views Abraham also as the first Muslim, worked out similar practical methods of discriminating between personal loans and business loans. Islam's great Prophet, Muhammad, was himself a businessman married to a businesswoman. Many mosques are constructed with business properties adjacent to them, the rent of which goes to support the mosque. See the illustration below.

Large and popular religions must, however, have some flexibility in their belief systems, and we find in Christianity many examples of the accommodation of spiritual and financial interests. The Church became wealthy because many people tithed, they gave ten percent of their earnings to the Church. In exchange, the

H. Griffiths, *Mosque of Bajazet with the Seraskier's Gate*, Istanbul, c. 1850. Engraving. (*Stapleton Collection, England*)

Hinduism designates the pursuit of "artha," wealth and power, as an important life goal, and sets aside the longest stage of the life cycle to the practicalities of administering a household. One whole caste category, the vaishyas, is composed of business people. In parts of India, especially Gujarat, at New Year's time, businessmen invite brahmin priests to bless their account books for the coming year in an elaborate ceremony called chopada puja, or the worship of the account books. The illustration on this page indicates that as Hindu businessmen have traveled overseas in modern times, they have continued this custom of integrating business practice with religious ritual.

His Holiness Pramukh Swami Maharaj sanctifying books of account during the Chopada Puja ceremony at the Shri Swaminarayan Mandir, Neasden, London.

QUESTIONS

1. To what degree have religious and business leaders accommodated one another – or failed to find such accommodation?
2. What have been the terms of the accommodation?
3. How have the members of each group benefited or lost out from the accommodation or the failure of accommodation?

PART 5

The Movement of Goods and Peoples 1000–1776

CHANNELS OF COMMUNICATION: THE EXCHANGE OF COMMODITIES, DISEASES, AND CULTURE

We have frequently noted the importance of trade in regional and world economies. Trade linked the oldest centers of urban civilization—Mesopotamia, the Indus valley, and the Nile valley—as we noted in Part 2. In Part 3 we saw that empires sought to protect the principal transportation routes and that emperors sought to capture their profits. In Part 4 we noted that world religions spread along the same routes as trade and that religions were often carried by merchants. Both Buddhism and Islam spread to eastern Asia via the overland silk routes, and to Southeast Asia via the shipping lanes of the Indian Ocean. The exchange of ideas and cultures went hand-in-hand with the exchange of commodities.

In this Part trade is our central focus. In Chapter 12 we explore the role of traders and their relationships with political rulers from about 1100 to about 1500. We study the geography of the principal trade routes. They were not yet fully unified, and certainly not yet global, but they were linked together and capable of delivering goods from one end of Afro-Eurasia to the other. The transportation networks of those days required considerable coordination by merchants from various parts of the world, and considerable off-loading and re-loading of merchandise to move it from one region to the next—but they could deliver the goods.

Epidemics sometimes accompanied trade missions. The most devastating of them, the "Black Plague" of the mid-fourteenth century, wiped out more than one-third of the population in many places from China to western Europe, dramatically restructuring relationships of wealth and power in its wake. Security was critically important along the trade routes, as were the Mongol descendants of Chinggis Khan in providing that security along the silk routes of Central Asia. We read personal accounts of great traders and travelers like Marco Polo and Ibn Battuta. We close with an examination of the expansion of trade in Europe, the growing importance of traders, the resurrection of cities and trade routes and the cultural renaissance that these movements inspired.

Chapter 13 explores some of the oceans and seas of the world. For thousands of years, the Indian Ocean, the Red Sea, the Persian Gulf, the Arabian Sea, the Bay of Bengal the Mediterranean Sea, and the South China Sea, had been principal highways of seaborne trade. But the Atlantic and Pacific Oceans had not. Some evidence suggests that an occasional, rare voyage might have crossed these vast bodies of water, but establishing regular contact awaited Columbus' four voyages across the Atlantic 1492–1504, and Magellan's circumnavigation of the earth, 1519–22. The chapter charts the background of the voyages that provided the first continuous linkage of the three continents of North and South America, and Australia,

Marco Polo, from *Romance of Alexander*, c. 1340. The great world traveler is shown setting sail for China from Venice in 1271. Europe was eager for news of the Mongol Empire—potential allies against the ancient Muslim enemy—and a steady stream of intrepid merchants and missionaries brought back amazing reports of the Khan's court. The exotic reminiscences of Marco Polo are, however, by far the most famous. (*Bodleian Library, Oxford*)

to the core area of Afro-Eurasia and examines the astonishing results of these voyages.

Chapter 14 describes trade becoming global and the rulers of nation-states encouraging their merchants to participate in it. The Spanish and Portuguese came first, followed by the Dutch, French, and English. The search for wealth inspired the creation of new economic institutions and the reform of cultural and religious thought. In 1776 the Scottish philosopher and economist Adam Smith published *The Wealth of Nations*, signaling the arrival of a new philosophy of economic organization called capitalism, an economic system in which the means of production are privately owned and goods and services are exchanged according to levels of supply and demand in markets. Smith applauded the work of private businesspeople who pursued their own profit, and proclaimed them the chief engine of progressive change in world history. He opposed both governmental and religious control of trade—the existing system—and proposed instead free trade, mostly unregulated markets, and independent merchant-capitalists.

Smith's word was not final, and the market-based, supply-and-demand philosophy of capitalism is still debated today—reviled by some, extolled by others—significant to virtually all considerations of economic systems and to many questions of politics, culture, and religion as well. The final section of chapter 14 indicates how the economic and political leadership of a variety of countries, from Russia in the west to Japan in the east, responded to the new wealth and power of western Europe.

ESTABLISHING WORLD TRADE ROUTES

THE GEOGRAPHY AND PHILOSOPHIES OF EARLY ECONOMIC SYSTEMS
TRADE AND TRADERS: GOALS AND FUNCTIONS
1000–1500

KEY TOPICS

- World Trade: An Historical Analysis
- Trade Networks
- Trade in the Americas before 1500
- Trade in Sub-Saharan Africa
- Muslim and Jewish Traders
- Asia's Complex Trade Patterns
- The Mongols

Today, long-distance, international trade forms a substantial part of the world's commerce and includes even the most basic products of everyday food and clothing. In earlier times, however, long-distance trade represented only a small fraction of overall trade, mostly supplying luxury goods—silks, gold, spices, and the like—for the wealthy upper classes. Because these goods were extremely valuable relative to their weight, merchants could carry them over hundreds or even thousands of miles and still sell them for handsome profits. Some commercial goods, like raw wool and cotton, were also traded over medium distances, a few hundred miles. The transportation costs were justified because these raw materials became more valuable after importation and manufacture into finished products.

Before 1500, by far the largest share of trade was local—food crops traded for local hand manufactures or raw materials. These goods were necessities, but they had little value in relationship to their weight: the cost of transportation was a substantial part of their final price. They were, therefore, traded over only short distances. Often, they were bartered in exchange for other local goods rather than sold for money in more distant markets. This local exchange of goods is a fundamental part of local and regional history, but the study of world history focuses on long-distance trade and its importance in knitting together distant regions of the world.

Trade provides an index of economic vitality. It stimulates economic growth; people produce goods and provide services only if markets exist for them. Anyone who has ever looked for a job has experienced this economic truth. If jobs exist, people can find work; if jobs do not exist, they remain unemployed and economically unproductive. Similarly, both production and consumption are limited by the availability of markets. If markets are easily accessible, products can be bought and sold easily; if not, then trade, production, and consumption stagnate.

WORLD TRADE: AN HISTORICAL ANALYSIS

Historians studying world trade seek to understand its purposes, conditions, and regulations. We ask about social as well as economic values. For example: What benefits have different systems of trade achieved? Which systems have benefited which

Opposite **Boucicault Master, Trade in the Gulf of Cambay (detail), India, 1410. Vellum.** As the main port of northeastern India, Cambay excited the wonder of painters and artists in far-off Europe. This illustration from the *Livre des Merveilles* (*The Book of Wonders*) (1410) represents Cambay's ships and traders in European guise, not surprisingly because the artist had never been to the city. (*Bibliothèque Nationale, Paris*)

members of society? Which systems have harmed which members of society? What have been the trade-offs in benefits and losses under each system? These questions, of course, are not only historical. The present-day debates over the "globalization" of trade—the opening of more and more countries of the world, and more and more products, to import and export trade—demonstrate their enduring significance. The street demonstrations in Seattle in 1999, and subsequently in other cities around the globe, against the World Trade Organization, which attempts to expand, facilitate, and regulate international trade, reveal the intense passions underlying these debates today.

To what degree do governments regulate or control economic markets? To what degree should they? In a completely **free market economy**, conditions of trade would not be regulated at all. Prices would vary only in terms of the relationship between the **supply** of goods and the economic **demand** for them, and business-people would be free to seek their fortune as they choose. Societies, however, do regulate trade to some degree in order to serve the greater good of the society. For example, governments may wish to ensure that everyone has enough food for survival. They may therefore decide that agricultural production should be expanded and industrial production limited. In time of scarcity—in wartime, for example—governments may ration food and essential commodities to ensure that everyone has access to at least minimum quantities. By taxing some items at high rates and

free market economy An economic system in which the means of production are largely privately owned and there is little or no government control over the markets.

supply and demand In economics, the relationship between the amount of a commodity that producers are able and willing to sell (supply), and the quantity that consumers can afford and wish to buy (demand).

AT A GLANCE: MEDIEVAL WORLD TRADE

DATE	POLITICAL/SOCIAL EVENTS	TRADE DEVELOPMENTS	EXPLORATION
1050 C.E.	■ Almoravids destroy Kingdom of Ghana (1067)		
1100 C.E.		■ Age of Great Zimbabwe in southern Africa	
1150 C.E.		■ Paper-making spreads from Muslim world to Europe	
1200 C.E.	■ Foundation of first Muslim empire in India ■ Chinggis Khan establishes Mongol Empire (1206–1405) ■ Collapse of Mayan civilization in Central America; rise of Incas in Peru ■ Rise of Mali, west Africa		
1250 C.E.	■ Osman I founds Ottoman dynasty in Turkey (1290–1326) ■ Emergence of Empire of Benin ■ Mongols fail to conquer Japan (1281)		■ Marco Polo arrives in China (1275)
1300 C.E.	■ Height of Mali (Mandingo) Empire under Sultan Mansa Musa		■ Ibn Battuta's travels in East Asia and Africa (c. 1330–60)
1350 C.E.	■ Ming dynasty in China (1368)		
1400 C.E.	■ Ottoman Turks establish foothold in Europe at Gallipoli	■ China reconstructs and extends Grand Canal	
1450 C.E.		■ Decline of Kilwa and Great Zimbabwe in southeast Africa (c. 1450)	
1500 C.E.	■ Zenith of Songay Empire of the middle Niger region (1492–1529) ■ Hernán Cortés and Spanish conquistadors defeat Aztecs and seize Mexico (1519–21) ■ Francisco Pizarro and Spanish conquistadors defeat Incas and seize Peru		

others at low rates, governments promote or limit various kinds of production and trade. Business may be more regulated or less regulated, but it is never completely unregulated.

In the earliest societies, such as Egypt, Mesopotamia, and China, government officials, often in alliance with priests, had more power than did private merchants, and trade was highly regulated. Nevertheless, considerable evidence suggests that market economies based on private profit did exist from earliest times. This trade for private profit was embedded in deeper political, social, religious, and moral structures of society. Long-distance private trade flourished most profitably in major port cities around the world. The merchants who carried on this port-city trade were often foreigners, with some independence from local political and social structures. They tended to occupy marginal positions in the host society, but central positions in the international trade networks.

TRADE NETWORKS

These long-distance merchants encouraged and brokered trade between the society in which they were living and far-flung networks of international merchants. They formed "trade diasporas," networks of interconnected commercial communities living and working in major trade cities throughout Africa, Europe, and Asia. As historians of trade have pointed out, trade diasporas appear in the archaeological record as early as 3500 B.C.E.

World trade routes. Between 1100 and 1500 a relay system of trade by land and sea connected almost all populous regions of Eurasia, as well as north and east Africa. Long-distance traders carried goods along their own segments of these routes, and then turned them over to traders in the next sector. The western hemisphere was still separate, and had two major trade networks of its own.

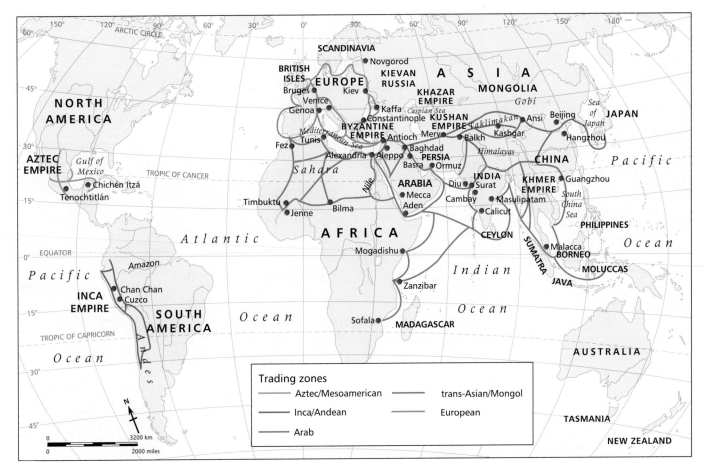

Some of them have endured for millennia. During the height of the Roman Empire, for example, traders from Rome sailed the waters of the Mediterranean Sea and the Indian Ocean. On rare occasions they continued all the way to China. Usually, these traders were not ethnically Roman. Most frequently they were descendants of the major trading communities of the eastern Mediterranean: Jews, Greek-speaking Egyptians, and Arabs. Roman trade left a heritage of these diaspora traders—in the form of small religious communities of Jews, Christians, and Muslim Arabs—living along the southwest coast of India long after the sack of Rome in 410.

Typically, the visiting merchants who carried the trade were marginal to their host societies rather than embedded within them. They were not unregulated by the hosts, nor were they totally subordinated. They were expected to take a reasonable profit in exchange for the benefits they brought to the port city.

TRADE IN THE AMERICAS BEFORE 1500

In the western hemisphere, two major trade networks had developed. The northern network served primarily the area that is Mexico today, although in those years it was ruled by several different groups. The southern network ran north–south both along the Pacific Coast and inland along the spine of the Andes Mountains. East–west routes rose to altitudes of 15,000 feet, linking the coastal settlements with those of the mountains. There was little traffic between North and South America and virtually none between the eastern and western hemispheres, except for rare voyages, such as that of Leif Eriksson, the Viking explorer who reached Newfoundland about the year 1000 (see Chapter 13).

Trade in the Inca Empire

In the Andes Mountains of South America, a significant and long-lasting hub of civilization grew up after 600 C.E. By the time the Incas consolidated their empire in the early fifteenth century, the mountain peoples generated extensive trade, connecting

Photograph of a quipu. In the Inca empire, which extended from Ecuador to central Chile, trading was facilitated by an extensive road network. This *quipu*, a device of knotted string used to record dates and accounts, would have been a handy aid to the traveling South American businessman in the early 1400s.

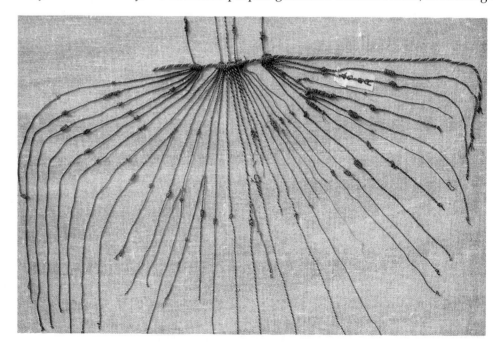

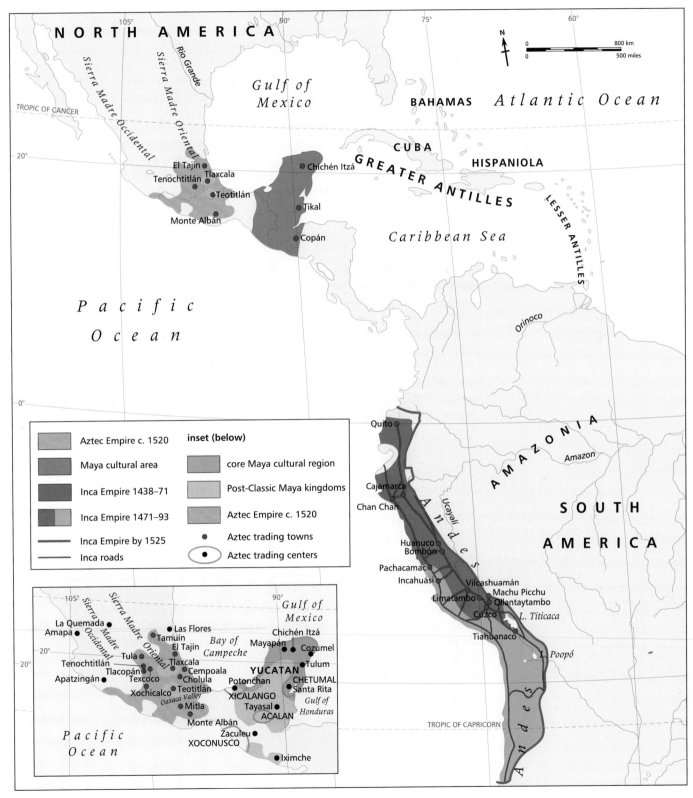

Pre-Columbian America. Pre-Columbian America had two great regions of trade and political power. In the north, the Aztec kingdom, centered on Tenochtitlán, dominated. The adjacent Maya of Central America were in decline. In South America, about 1500, the Inca dominated the Andes mountain regions, linking them together through an extensive system of roads.

Map labels

NORTH AMERICA

Sierra Madre Occidental
Sierra Madre Oriental
Río Grande

Gulf of Mexico

BAHAMAS   Atlantic Ocean

TROPIC OF CANCER

CUBA
GREATER ANTILLES
HISPANIOLA
LESSER ANTILLES

El Tajín
Tlaxcala
Tenochtitlán
Teotitlán
Monte Albán

Chichén Itzá
Tikal
Copán

Caribbean Sea

Pacific Ocean

Orinoco

AMAZONIA
Amazon

SOUTH AMERICA

Quito
Cajamarca
Chan Chan
Huanuco
Bombón
Pachacamac
Incahuási
Limatambo
Vilcashuamán
Machu Picchu
Ollantaytambo
Cuzco
L. Titicaca
Tiahuanaco
L. Poopó
Andes

TROPIC OF CAPRICORN

Legend

- Aztec Empire c. 1520
- Maya cultural area
- Inca Empire 1438–71
- Inca Empire 1471–93
- Inca Empire by 1525
- Inca roads
- Aztec trading towns
- Aztec trading centers

inset (below)
- core Maya cultural region
- Post-Classic Maya kingdoms
- Aztec Empire c. 1520

Inset labels

Sierra Madre Occidental
Sierra Madre Oriental

La Quemada
Amapa
Tamuín
Las Flores
El Tajín
Tula
Tenochtitlán
Tlacopán
Texcoco
Apatzingán
Xochicalco
Teotitlán
Oaxaca Valley
Mitla
Monte Albán
Zaculeu
XOCONUSCO
Iximche

Tlaxcala
Cempoala
Cholula

Gulf of Mexico
Bay of Campeche

Chichén Itzá
Mayapán
Cozumel
Tulum
YUCATAN
Potonchan
CHETUMAL
Santa Rita
XICALANGO
Tayasal
ACALAN
Gulf of Honduras

Pacific Ocean

Scale: 800 km / 500 miles

settlements over hundreds of miles north to south and linking together some 32 million people.

Trade was important up and down the mountainsides. With peaks rising up to 20,000 feet, these mountain slopes hosted several different ecological zones, encouraging product differentiation and trade. The valleys below provided sweet potatoes, maize, manioc, squash, beans, chili peppers, peanuts, and cotton. The hills above produced white potatoes, a cereal grain called quinoa, coca, medicines, feathers, and animal skins. The highland people specialized in manufacture and crafts, including gold working.

The state and its semi-divine rulers controlled this trade between the ecological zones. Under Inca rulers, from the early 1400s until the Spanish conquest in 1535, many of the best of the 15,000 miles of roads through the Andes were open only to government officials.

Trade in Central America and Mexico

In the Yucatán peninsula of Central and North America, the Mayan peoples had flourished from 200 B.C.E. to 900 C.E. Mayan traders flourished relatively independently, amassing a disproportionate share of wealth. Archaeologists suggest that the increasing wealth of the traders created social tensions and that ultimately the traders were brought under the control of the hierarchical state, creating a new set of unequal relations dominated by kings rather than merchants.

By the time the Spanish arrived in the 1520s, the Maya had weakened in the Yucatán, and the Aztecs dominated the valley of Mexico. The Spanish conquistadors wrote vivid accounts of the great marketplace of the Aztec capital, Tenochtitlán. As the Spanish leader Hernán Cortés summarizes in one of his letters:

> This city has many squares where trading is done and markets are held continuously. There is also one square twice as big as that of Salamanca, with arcades all around … There are streets of herbalists where all the medicinal herbs and roots found in the land are sold. There are shops like apothecaries', where they sell ready-made medicines as well as liquid ointments and plasters. There are shops like barbers', where they have their hair washed and shaved, and shops where they sell food and drink. (*The Second Letter*, pp. 103–104)

The market met every fifth day, with perhaps 40,000 to 50,000 merchants swarming in, rowing their canoes across the lake to the island on which Tenochtitlán was built. In many ways, the market was like the great fairs that were held in medieval Europe, drawing merchants from distant corners of the kingdom and beyond.

But how independent were these Tenochtitlán merchants? The Spanish described the city's market as being under tight government control. In addition to officers who kept the peace, collected taxes, and checked the accuracy of weights and measures, a court of twelve judges sat to decide cases immediately.

A guild of traders, called *pochteca*, carried on long-distance trade, which expanded steadily through the fifteenth century. They led trade expeditions for hundreds of miles, exchanging city-crafted obsidian knives, fur blankets, clothes, herbs, and dyes for such raw materials as jade, seashells, jaguar skins, feathers from forest birds, and, in the greatest volume, cotton from the Gulf coast. They were to marry only within the guild, and, though they were commoners, they could send their sons to temple schools and they had their own courts.

Because the American Indians had not invented the wheel, goods were carried by pack animals—and by humans. Boats were used on streams and rivers. Along the South American coast, near the equator, the Incas sailed boats constructed of balsa wood, while the Mayans paddled canoes through the river systems of the Yucatán.

The traders often gathered both goods and military intelligence for the ruling Aztec families. Royal troops protected them and sometimes used attacks on traveling *pochteca* as a justification for punishing the attackers and confiscating their lands. The *pochteca* lived in their own wards in the towns, had their own magistrates, and supervised the markets on their own. Their main god, Yiacatecutli, seemed akin to the Toltec god Quetzalcoatl, and this, too, suggests that they were to some degree foreigners living in a trade diaspora, with a high degree of independence from the state and temple.

The two major civilizational hubs functioned independently of one another and both were, of course, virtually completely cut off from Afro-Eurasia. When Europeans arrived in the sixteenth century brandishing new weapons, commanding new military organizations, and transmitting new diseases, the American residents were unprepared for the challenges.

TRADE IN SUB-SAHARAN AFRICA

Africa south of the Sahara was also well-integrated into webs of trade relationships. In West Africa, traders dispatched caravans of goods on camel back across the Sahara, linking the forest cultivators and miners in the south with the merchants and rulers of the Mediterranean coast. In East Africa traders along the coast procured gold and ivory from the interior of the continent and sold them to the seafaring merchants of the Indian Ocean.

West Africa

The domestication of the camel in the second to fifth century C.E. opened the possibility of regular trans-Saharan trade. Oases provided the necessary rest and watering points for caravans, as well as producing dates, a major commodity of trade. The

Mosque at Jenne, Mali, first built fourteenth century C.E. The spectacular mud-brick mosques found in the major towns of the African savanna states, such as Jenne and Timbuktu, point to the acceptance of Islam by the merchant and ruling classes in the thirteenth and fourteenth centuries. The mud, which washes away in the rain, needs continual renewal—hence the built-in "scaffolding" of the structure.

For an interactive version of this map, go to: http://www.prenhall.com/spodek/map12.3

African kingdoms. Many states appeared in 1000–1500 in northern and western Africa, their power based on control over long-distance trade—gold, ivory, and slaves moving north; metalware, textiles, and salt carried south. Ghana, Mali, and Songhay are discussed in the text. These states, protected from marauders by the Sahara, could usually maintain their independence.

earliest written records of this trans-Saharan trade begin with the arrival of Muslim traders in the eighth century.

For the most part, African political units were local, but three large empires in succession arose around the northern bend in the Niger, near Timbuktu, where the sahel, the arid fringe of the desert, meets the vast Sahara itself. These three empires—Ghana (about 700 to about 1100), Mali (about 1100 to about 1400), and Songhay (about 1300 to about 1600)—kept the trade routes open and secure. In contrast with most governments in other parts of the world that amassed wealth and power by controlling land and agriculture, these empires drew their power from control over trade, traders, and trade routes.

Gold, slaves, cloth, ivory, ebony, pepper, and kola nuts (stimulants) moved north across the Sahara; salt, dates, horses, brass, copper, glassware, beads, leather, textiles, clothing, and foodstuffs moved south. Gold was the central attraction. In the fourteenth century, the gold mines of West Africa provided about two-thirds of the gold used to finance trade in the eastern hemisphere. In 1324, when the Muslim emperor of Mali, Mansa Musa (r. 1307–32), passed through Cairo on his way to Mecca, he dispensed so much gold in gifts to court officials and in purchases in the bazaar that local prices in Cairo were inflated for years to come. A European map of 1375 showing a seated Mansa Musa as ruler of Mali is noted as follows: "So abundant is the gold found in his country that he is the richest and most noble king in all the land."

There were many natural break-points for the north–south trade: From the Mediterranean coast to the northern fringe of the desert, trade was borne by pack horse; across the desert, via oases, by camel; across the arid sahel and the grassy savanna lands south of the Sahara again by pack animal; and finally, through the tropical forest, impenetrable to larger animals and afflicted with the lethal tsetse fly, it was borne by human porters. For the most part, locally dominant trade groups carried the trade from one market center to the next in short relays. A few trading communities, however, notably the Soninke and, especially, their Mande-speaking Dyula branch, established trade diasporas that negotiated with the rulers.

East Africa

In the fourth century, the kingdom of Axum in Christian Ethiopia dominated the trade of the Red Sea and to some extent the Arabian Sea. With the rise of Islam, however, Arab traders gained control of the flow of merchandise and Arab armies began restricting Ethiopian power. After the ninth century, and south of the Horn of Africa, Arab merchants provided the main trading link between East Africa and the Indian Ocean. The first major port to spring up had been Manda, followed in the thirteenth century by Kilwa. The ruling Arab dynasty along the coast also seized control of the port of Sofala further to the south. Through local African merchants they exchanged goods with the peoples of the interior, especially at the trading post of

sahel "Shore"—the northern and southern edges of the Sahara Desert. A semi-arid region of Africa, extending from Senegal eastward to the Sudan.

Great Zimbabwe. The biggest and most celebrated of several stone enclosures in east Africa dating from the tenth to fifteenth centuries, Great Zimbabwe provided raw materials for trade at the coastal settlements, especially gold, copper, tin, and iron, and was also a trading post for luxury goods—Islamic pottery and cowrie shells were dug up at the site.

Great Zimbabwe. Here they found abundant supplies of valuable metals such as gold and copper (often cast into ingots) and animal products: ivory, horns, skins, and tortoise shells. Slaves were also an important commodity. Great Zimbabwe was the largest and most remarkable of all the developing towns. Architecturally, it featured a 100-acre stone enclosure and another 100 smaller enclosures in the surrounding region.

From these inland sources, goods were transported to the coastal ports and shipped onward to Arabia and India in exchange for spices, pottery, glass beads, and cloth. In the port cities of Africa's east coast, the Swahili language of the nearby African peoples received from these Indian Ocean traders a strong admixture of Arabic vocabulary, enriching Swahili and ensuring its place as the dominant language of the coastal trade.

MUSLIM AND JEWISH TRADERS

Muslim Arab traders played critical roles in the development of African trade networks, from north to south across the Sahara and overseas from the East African coast to various ports along the shores of the Indian Ocean. Their religion and ethnicity formed the basis of community and trust necessary for conducting business in a world that had no international courts or legal systems. A much smaller group, Jews, too, were able to carry on international trade across the entire eastern hemisphere from China to western Europe and Africa. For Jews, like Arabs, religion and ethnicity were the underlying basis of their trade diaspora. Within their overseas communities they quickly learned whom they could trust and this enabled them to establish highly efficient trade networks. Other groups of global traders also formed commercial networks on the basis of shared religion and ethnicity, although they were generally less extensive geographically, for example Christian Armenians, Jain and Hindu Gujaratis from western India, and Fukienese from the southeast coast of China. Small overseas Muslim trade communities also often attracted local traders to assimilate to Islam, as happened especially in Indonesia and southeast Asia. The other trading communities generally stayed within their own social and religious networks, enjoying trade relations with local groups, but not encouraging their conversion.

Jewish Traders

During the period of Tang-Abbasid control over the silk route—the eighth and early ninth centuries—Jews had once again emerged as a preeminent trading community throughout the diaspora linking Europe and China. The emigration of Jews to many far distant points of settlement facilitated their trade connections. Their religious diaspora supported their trade diaspora. Charlemagne's ninth-century European empire employed them to carry trade in southern Europe. Baghdad, astride many of the key trade routes in western Asia, held the most prominent Jewish community in the world at the time, but there were also small Jewish communities in Calicut and Cochin in south India and in Kaifeng, China. When the Portuguese explorer Vasco da Gama reached Calicut in 1498, a local Jewish merchant was able to serve as interpreter. Cairo, Egypt, one of the world's great trade centers, also sheltered a very significant Jewish community.

Statuette of Semitic trader, Chinese, 10th century. Traders from the Roman Empire traveling the silk routes were likely to be Jews from the Fertile Crescent, Greek-speaking Egyptians, and other Levantines. They and their descendants eventually settled along the trans-Asian routes, which most likely explains the Chinese derivation of this glazed porcelain Semitic peddler, made during Tang dynasty times. (*The Seattle Art Museum*)

Muslim Traders

With the rise of Islam (see Chapter 11), and especially after the Abbasid caliphs shifted their capital to Baghdad in 762, Muslim traders dominated the routes through the Indian Ocean. Ethnically, most were Arabs and Persians. In the thirteenth century, as the Muslim sultanate of Delhi came to rule most of India, many of the Hindu ocean-going traders, especially those in the western Indian region of Gujarat, converted to Islam. Along with their trade goods, they carried their culture and religion. Distant merchants who encountered them in order to trade, slowly also absorbed elements of Islam. In regions as distant as Malaysia and Indonesia local merchants began to assimilate to the religion of these oceanic traders. When the ruler of Malacca converted to Islam, about 1400, the trading circuit of Muslim merchants was complete.

Islam encouraged trade. The *hajj* (pilgrimage), advocated for every Muslim at least once during his or her lifetime, demanded international travel; trade connections flourished with the *hajj*. A Muslim trade colony had operated in Sri Lanka from about 700 C.E. Arab traders sailed with the monsoon winds first to India, then on to Southeast Asia, and some even on to the southeast coast of China. Catching the proper seasonal winds in each direction and using their **lateen (triangular)** sails to maximum effect, sailors could complete a round trip from Mesopotamia to China in less than two years. Carried not by military power but by traders, Islam came to be the dominant religion in Indonesia (the most populous Muslim country in the world today), and to attract tens of millions of Chinese adherents. The entire length of the Indian Ocean

lateen A triangular sail affixed to a long yard or crossbar at an angle of about 45 degrees to the mast, with the other free corner secured near the stern. The sail was capable of taking the wind on either side.

Anon., *King Edward I Returns from Gascony*, 1470. **Miniature.** This is an example of a ship with lateen sails. Europeans adapted these sails from Arab models because they enabled ships to tack against the wind as well as run with it. (*British Library, London*)

HOW DO WE KNOW?

The Records in the Cairo Genizah

Information on Mediterranean cultures and their trade connections into the Indian Ocean, from the tenth through the thirteenth centuries, has come to historians from the Cairo Genizah (Hebrew for a repository of old papers), studied by Solomon Goitein from the 1950s through the 1980s. Jewish law requires that the written name of "God" not be destroyed but stored for later burial; the Genizah was the storage point in Cairo for such documents for several centuries. Because paper was scarce and often re-used, the manuscripts in the Genizah include massive bundles of notes and manuscripts on secular as well as sacred aspects of life: on trade and commerce, on social organization in general, and on the Jewish community in particular. Marriage contracts "state in detail and with great variety the conditions regulating the future relations of the newly married, and thus constitute a precious source for our knowledge of family life" (I:10). Wills and inventories of estates are "veritable mines of information" (I:10). Letters of correspondence, both personal and business, "form the largest and most important group [of manuscripts]. They are our main source not only for our knowledge of commerce and industry, but also for various other subjects, such as travel and seafaring" (I:11). "There are hundreds of letters addressed to various authorities containing reports, petitions, requests for help, demands for redress of injustice, applications for appointments, and a great variety of other matters" (I:12). Religious responsa are frequent, questions and answers between commoners and sages concerning religious philosophy, doctrine, and practice. Most women were illiterate, but they dictated many letters to scribes: "We hear the female voice guiding the male pen" (I:12). For the most part the writing is in Arabic, but transcribed in Hebrew letters. These centuries-old manuscripts have proven to be a gold mine for historians studying the life of Cairo, its citizens, and their external connections throughout the Mediterranean Sea and the Indian Ocean.

- Given the nature of the Genizah repository, what kinds of records do you think would be most fully represented? Least well represented?
- How might records of family life and records dictated by women help to fill out the records of business transactions?
- How important was Cairo as a trade center at this time?

littoral, from East Africa through India and on to Indonesia, housed a Muslim, largely Arab, trading diaspora.

ASIA'S COMPLEX TRADE PATTERNS

As the largest continent, with the largest population and the oldest civilizations, it is not surprising that Asia developed complex trade networks thousands of years ago. As early as 1250, a set of interlinked trade networks connected the main population and production centers of Asia, Africa, and Europe. The earlier map (p. 377) illustrates their vast and comprehensive geographic coverage. From east to west, Japan and China were linked by land routes to Central Asia and by sea lanes to the Indian Ocean. Both land and sea routes continued westward to Arabia, western Asia, and on to the Mediterranean and Europe. Well-developed sea traffic linked also to the East African coast, where land routes extended into the African continent. North–south routes ran through China, Central and West Asia, and Europe, and from the Mediterranean across the Sahara by camel. At this time there was not yet any central transportation headquarters or company that could carry goods all the way from East Asia to western Europe, for example, but arrangements could be made for even this long voyage to be completed stage by stage.

The Polynesians of the South Pacific

The Polynesians are Austronesian-speaking peoples who migrated from south China and Southeast Asia perhaps 6000 years ago to Taiwan, the Philippines, and eastern Indonesia (see Chapter 1). Those who settled in the islands adjacent to these areas became known as Melanesians. Those who continued on eastward became known as

Polynesians. These Polynesians continued to sail eastward in single and double canoes, 100 to 150 feet long, made of wooden components fitted together and held in place by ropes and cords of fiber. These ships, with their single, square, woven-mat sails, could carry not only men and women but also food supplies and even live animals. In these simple, elegant craft, the Polynesians began vast ocean voyages that would take them as far northeastward as Hawaii (400 C.E.), as far southeastward as Easter Island (400 C.E.), and as far southwestward as New Zealand (750 C.E.). They became the greatest seafaring peoples of pre-modern times. Students of Polynesian history marvel both at the enormous stone statues erected on some of the Polynesian islands, most spectacularly on Easter Island, and at the accomplishments of their sea voyages. Polynesians apparently visited every island within the huge triangle of Hawaii, Easter Island, and New Zealand. Nevertheless, despite traveling through thousands of years and thousands of miles, the Polynesians preserved several remarkably similar elements of culture throughout their domains. Anthropologists note the similarities across the islands of Polynesia of tools, names of plants, terms of kinship, and artistic styles.

Were Polynesians capable of sailing across the Pacific and establishing contact with the Americas? Apparently so. The Hawaiian Islands are closer to the Americas than to Asia, and Easter Island is only 2200 miles off the coast of South America. Indeed, many scholars argue that this contact was accomplished, citing the sweet potatoes and manioc of Polynesia as their evidence. But, whatever the capabilities of the Polynesians and their canoes, and whatever the source of these food supplies, the Polynesians did not establish permanent connections to the Americas. Apparently they were not interested in sailing for the sake of exploration, but only to find places in which to settle, raise families, and obtain necessary food supplies. Although they were among the greatest sailors in human history, they apparently did not sail just for the excitement of the voyage, but rather for more specific and immediate needs.

Malay Sailors in the South China Sea and the Indian Ocean

Extraordinary as the Polynesian sailors were, apparently they adopted their sails from the Malay sailors of the South China Seas probably late in the first millennium B.C.E. These sailors left four major legacies to world seafaring, one primarily in their own neighborhood, the other three of much wider significance. The first was the most important: cargo ships—*jongs*, or junks as they are usually called in English. These ships with multilayered hulls, two to four masts, two rudders, and a normal capacity of 400 to 500 tons, seem to have inspired the junks used by Chinese merchant sailors to the north. Second, their balance-lug square sails seem to have inspired a series of adaptations and inventions, from the sails used by the Polynesians, to the sails used by Arab sailors, later modified to triangular sails, called lateen sails. (Other authorities believe that the balance-lug sail developed on the Nile River, also in the first millennium B.C.E., and they argue that this Egyptian invention was the background source for the Arab lateen

Johannes Baptista van Doetechum, *A Chinese Junk*, from *Jan Huyghen van Linschoten: His Discourse of Voyages into the East and West Indies*, 1579–92. Engraving. Apparently first an invention of the Malay sailors of the South China Sea, and adapted by the Chinese, these ships could carry more than a thousand tons of cargo and hundreds of sailors. (*Private Collection*)

sails.) These lateen sails were subsequently copied by European sailors in the Mediterranean and used for their voyages in the Atlantic. The balance-lug sail could be turned to face into the wind or to tack against it, allowing sailors to set their course with much greater maneuverability. As the sail was turned, from an angle it appeared to be triangular, and sailors learned that a triangular sail would work equally well. Thus the lateen sail was born and ultimately carried to the sailing paths of the world.

Third, the Malay sailors learned the patterns of the seasonal monsoon winds of the Indian Ocean and learned to sail with them. The rain-laden monsoon winds are attracted from the Indian Ocean inward toward Central Asia during the summer months, when the continental interior is much hotter than the oceans around it, and blow outward from the continent toward the ocean in the cooler months, when the ocean is warmer than the interior. The Greeks, too, learned how to use the monsoon winds of the Indian Ocean effectively in the first few centuries B.C.E. Whether from the Malays or the Greeks, the knowledge of the wind patterns soon reached all the sailors of the Indian Ocean, including the Europeans when they arrived in 1498.

Finally, using their ship technology and knowledge of the winds, Malay sailors made regular voyages of 3000 miles across the Indian Ocean—probably via the Maldive, Seychelles, and Comoro islands—to the large island of Madagascar, 250 miles off the coast of East Africa, where they established themselves as the majority population, as they remain to this day. The Malay sailors brought to Madagascar bananas, coconuts, taro, and their language, which also continues as the dominant language of the island.

Along with their settlements, the Malay sailors established sea routes from East Africa to China. They carried frankincense and myrrh from East Africa, Arabia, southwest Iran, and the Makran Coast of India to present day Vietnam and China. From Timor, 1800 miles to the southeast of Vietnam, they brought aromatic woods, especially sandalwood. From the "Spice Islands," the Moluccas, 1000 miles east of Java, they brought cloves, nutmeg, and mace. For more than a thousand years they were the master sailors of the South China Sea.

Sailors and Merchants of the Indian Ocean

The great crossroads of the world's shipping lanes in the period 1100–1500 was the Indian Ocean. Its waters encompass three distinct geographical sectors, each with its own cultural orientation. The western sector sweeps from the East African coast across Arabia and continues on to the west coast of India. From the time of Alexander the Great and the Roman Empire, Greek sailors participated in this trade. By the first century B.C.E. Greek sailors had learned to use the monsoon winds to navigate these waters swiftly and effectively. From the fourth to the eighth centuries, following the decline and fall of the Roman Empire, two new groups dominated this western region of the Indian Ocean: sailors from Axum (modern Ethiopia and Eritrea), and its Red Sea port of Adulis, and sailors from Sassanian Persia, an empire that was in the ascendant in western Asia at the time.

From the eighth to the sixteenth century, Arab Muslim traders and sailors became masters of the western Indian Ocean sea lanes. This was the area made famous by the legendary exploits of Sinbad the Sailor. As Islam inspired the people of Arabia to undertake expeditions of conquest by land beginning in the seventh century (see Chapter 11), Arab sailors also began to assume prominence in the Indian Ocean trade. Among the Arabs living at the southern end of the Arabian peninsula, some had experience with sea trade, but those to the north, the majority, did not. As Arab armies moved still further north, however, they came into contact with, conquered, and learned from previous masters of the Indian Ocean, the Sassanians of Iran. Mastering

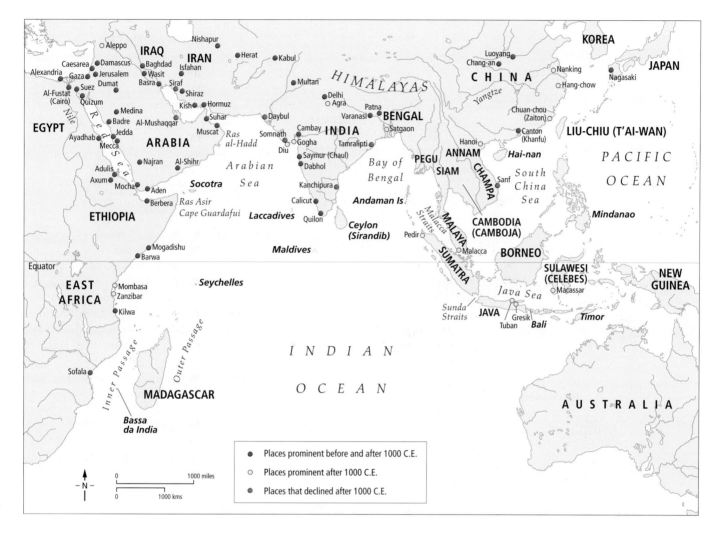

Trading ports and cities, Indian Ocean, 618–1500 C.E. The Indian Ocean was the pivot of long-distance seaborne trade from the Mediterranean to the South China Sea. Each of its port cities housed a rich diversity of merchants of many ethnicities and cultures.

these new skills, and inspired by their own expansionism, Arab sailors displaced the Sassanians. In 762 C.E. the new Abbasid dynasty built a new capital in Baghdad, in the heartland of Mesopotamia. In this land that had participated in sea trade for millennia, the Arabs' concern for oceanic trade increased further.

As they increasingly participated in sea trade, Arab sailors became true masters of the Indian Ocean trade. Lacking wood in Arabia, they depended on others to build their ships, or obtained teak from southern India to build their own. For reasons that remain unclear, they did not use metal nails in ship construction, but "stitched" the wooden planks together with coir—the fiber of coconut husks—or other fibers. Like the Malay and the Greek sailors before them, they learned to sail with the monsoon winds. The Arab Muslim Ahmad Ibn Majid included extensive recommendations on travel dates appropriate to the monsoon winds in his comprehensive fifteenth-century guide to navigation throughout the Indian Ocean. For example:

Travelling from Bengal and connected regions [begins] in the 40th day of the year [1st January] and its end is the 70th day [31st January]: it is no good travelling later than that if bound for Hormuz or Yemen or the Hijaz. Travelling to Ceylon and the Maldives is possible until the 70th and 80th days although it is a gamble in some years by the 80th and the same from Malacca, Pegu, and Siam. But from Java, Sumatra, Malacca, and Tanasari to Bengal, sailing takes place from the 90th to the 140th days.

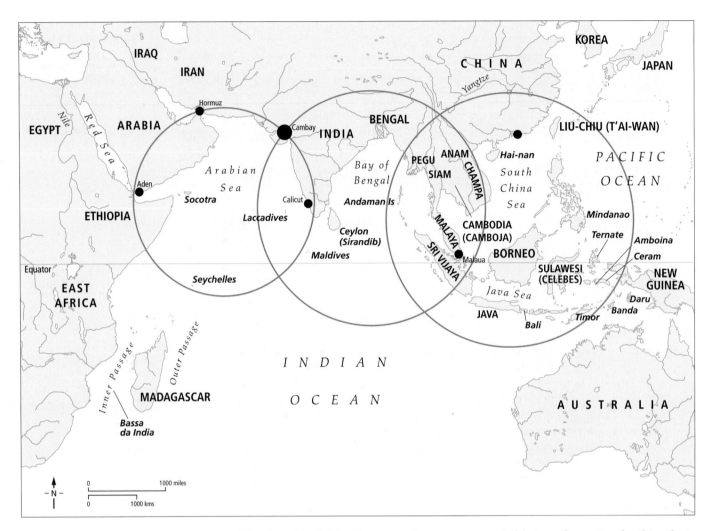

The pattern of emporia trade in the Indian Ocean, c. 1000–1500. Trade goods did not travel on a single ship the whole length of this region. Rather, they would be loaded at a port in one of the three regions, off-loaded and reloaded in the next for shipment to the third region.

The rise of Arab Muslim sea traders was a remarkable transformation for this ethnic and religious group. The Arabs had been quite accustomed to trade—Muhammad himself was a camel driver and leader of caravans—but trade by sea was different. They took to this new way of life eagerly and came to dominate the sea lanes from the Mediterranean coast in the west all the way east to Guangzhou (Canton) and Hangzhou in China, frequently displacing previous communities of sailors.

In the eastern waters of the Indian Ocean, for example—from India and the Bay of Bengal to Indo-China and the Malacca Straits—Indian sailors and merchants, largely Hindu, had predominated. East of the Malacca Straits, these sailors entered into the South China Sea, attracted by China's wealth and luxury products. Despite the geographical distance of their homes from this region, they came to surpass in import-ance the more local Chinese and East Asian merchants.

Until the tenth century, much of the cultural influence in this region came from India, as evidenced in the many astonishingly large and beautiful temple complexes of this region—for example, Borobudur and Prambanan in Java, Angkor Wat in Cambo-dia, Pagan in Burma, and the Cham Shaivite temple of central Vietnam. These Bud-dhist and Hindu temples marked centers of cultural as well as political and economic dominance. From the seventh to the tenth century, south Sumatra was home to the Buddhist Srivijayan maritime empire, the largest and most powerful of the Indian-influenced Southeast Asian kingdoms.

Boucicault Master, Trade in the Gulf of Cambay, India, 1410. Vellum. Merchants and travelers carried exciting tales of their adventures, but when European painters sought to represent these wonders they could only fill in their imagination with scenes from their own experience. Hence this illustration looks more like a European town than an Indian city port. (*Bibliothèque Nationale, Paris*)

By the end of the thirteenth century, however, Muslim traders, mostly from India, began their trade and proselytization through the entire Southeast Asian archipelago of islands—today's Indonesia, Borneo, Celebes, the Moluccas, and the Philippines. By the fourteenth century, most of the ocean-going merchants appear to have been Muslims, either Arabs or Indian converts from Hinduism, and their descendants. On the basis of their economic strength as traders they attracted local peoples and encouraged them to assimilate to Islam. When the ruler of Malacca converted, about 1400, Muslim supremacy in Indian Ocean trade reached its zenith. From west to east, Muslim merchants dominated the major ports. In Indonesia and the Malaysian

SOURCE

The Arabian Nights

Arab Muslim traders of the Indian Ocean fill the pages of some of the best loved tales of world literature. The Thousand Nights and One Night, *also called the* Arabian Nights, *fables originally written in Persian during the years of the Abbasid Empire (750–1258), include the tales of the seven voyages of Sinbad (Sindbad) the Sailor, who won a fortune through a series of hazardous (if unbelievable) adventures at sea. The adventures, supposedly told night after night by Scheherazade to the emperor, Haroun al-Rashid (r. 786–809), as a ploy to postpone her scheduled execution, are fanciful, but Sinbad's descriptions of his departures on each of his voyages are based on the reality of Indian Ocean shipping. This translation from the beginning of the third voyage is by Richard F. Burton who brought the complete tales to the English-speaking world in the late nineteenth century.*

I returned from my second voyage overjoyed at my safety and with great increase of wealth, Allah having requited me all that I had wasted and lost, and I abode awhile in Baghdad-city savouring the utmost ease and prosperity and comfort and happiness, till the carnal man was once more seized with longing for travel and diversion and adventure, and yearned after traffic and lucre and emolument, for that the human heart is naturally prone to evil. So making up my mind I laid in great plenty of goods suitable for a sea voyage and repairing to Bassorah [Basra], went down to the shore and found there a fine ship ready to sail, with a full crew and a numerous company of merchants, men of worth and substance; Faith, piety and consideration. I embarked with them and we set sail on the blessing of Allah Almighty and on His aidance and His favour to bring our voyage to a safe and prosperous issue and already we congratulated one another on our good fortune and bon voyage. We fared on from sea to sea and from island to island and city to city, in all delight and contentment, buying and selling wherever we touched, and taking our solace and our pleasure, till one day … [and here begin the fabulous adventures of the third voyage]. (*The Thousand Nights and One Night*, Vol. 4, pp. 2031–2)

Arab trader, illustration from the *Maqamat* of al-Hariri, 12th century. Regional shipping routes linked into the oceanic, intercontinental routes. This ship, with Arab passengers and Indian, and perhaps African, crew, sailed the Persian Gulf connecting Mesopotamia and the Indian Ocean.

peninsula Islam displaced the Hindu and Buddhist cultures that had already taken root, and today both Malaya and Indonesia are primarily Muslim countries.

Arabs did not sail further, into the Atlantic or Pacific Oceans, simply because they had no need. They sailed at will throughout the most valued seas of the world that they knew. They had no problem of access. While Europeans were beginning to attempt to find new routes to India and China in the fifteenth century, the Arabs were already there.

China

By 1500 China was the most economically advanced region in the world, a magnet for world trade. China is so huge, however, that its internal trade far outweighed its external trade. It is so rich and varied in its productivity that others came to China to obtain its products far more regularly than the Chinese traveled abroad in search of the products of others. China's policies towards trade have, nevertheless, altered through the centuries we are considering here, partly as a result of changes in imperial leadership, partly in response to external pressures. Even though it created a highly integrated system of internal markets and reached extraordinary levels of agricultural and industrial productivity under the Song Dynasty, China was defeated by Mongol invaders and had to abandon a large part of its territories, relocate to the south, and reconstruct its economy. The Ming Dynasty overthrew the Mongols and undertook a series of spectacular ocean voyages. Then, in another change of policy, later Ming emperors forbade the Chinese to trade overseas. Nevertheless, overseas merchants continued to pour in, eager to do business with the Central Kingdom.

International Trade. As early as the fourth century C.E. the Chinese also participated in the trade of the South China Sea and the Indian Ocean, although probably only as far west as Sri Lanka. Their oceanic trade activity increased with the rise of the Tang dynasty (618–907 C.E.). During much of this period, the Abbasid Empire (750–1258) was at its height, and helped to protect the sea lanes of the Indian Ocean. But with the decline of both empires in the ninth century, the Chinese largely withdrew from this oceanic trade and concentrated instead on inland issues, in accord with their geographical position centered on the Yellow River valley and the north. After 1127, however, they returned to oceanic enterprise, when the Song dynasty was driven from north China by the invasions of the Tatars and other northern peoples. As they moved south, establishing a new capital at Hangzhou, about 100 miles from the modern-day port-metropolis of Shanghai, they turned their attention back to the sea. With various northern groups in control of the old overland silk routes, sea-borne trade was an obvious transportation and communication alternative. For this purpose, the Chinese mastered the craft of building large ships and merchants created new patterns of commercial exchange, including sophisticated credit systems. In addition to a merchant marine, China constructed a powerful navy.

Ink and watercolor print showing silk manufacture, Chinese, early 17th century. During the Song dynasty (960–1279), long-distance trade across Central Asia dwindled. Maritime trade, with its very much safer and cheaper routes, now offered a viable alternative, and silk, along with porcelain and tea, continued to attract the merchants of the world. Unwinding filaments from silkworm cocoons in order to make yarn was considered women's work, as this Ming dynasty print suggests. (*Victoria & Albert Museum, London*)

In 1368, a new dynasty, the Ming, came to power. Especially in the early years of the dynasty, Ming emperors adopted policies of expansionism by land and self-assertion by sea. The Ming Emperor Yung-lo (r. 1402–24) dispatched a series of seven spectacular ocean voyages under the Muslim eunuch, Admiral Zheng He. The first voyage set out in 1405 with sixty-two large junks, 100 smaller ships, and 30,000 crew. The largest ships were 450 feet long, displaced 1600 tons, held a crew of about 500, and were the largest ships built anywhere up to that time. They carried silks, porcelains, and pepper. The first expedition sailed as far as Calicut, near the southwest tip of India. In six further missions between 1407 and 1433, Zheng He sailed to ports all along the Indian Ocean shores, at least twice reaching the East African ports of Mogadishu, Brava, Malindi, and Kilwa. Interested in exotic treasures that could not be found in China, Emperor Yung-lo seemed most pleased with a giraffe sent to him by the sultan of Malindi on the fourth voyage, in 1416–19. These colossal expeditions demonstrated both the skill of Admiral Zheng He and the vision of Emperor Yung-lo. On the basis of these accomplishments, many historians believe that the Chinese would have been able to cross either the Atlantic or the Pacific Ocean—had they wished. But they did not push their expeditions any further and, in 1433, the Ming emperor terminated the great, state-sponsored Indian Ocean voyages.

Why did the emperor terminate these voyages? Why did China not dispatch its own missions to Europe, and even to the western hemisphere? It appeared to have the

SOURCE

Chinese Ships in South Indian Harbors: An Account by Ibn Battuta

The fourteenth-century traveler Ibn Battuta (1304–68) did not usually comment on ships and sailors. He was far more interested in his encounters with people on land. In the south Indian port of Calicut, however, he was so impressed with the capacity and design of the Chinese ships in the harbor that he gave a remarkable description. He notes that while the Chinese allowed only Chinese ships to dock in their ports, the pilots and crew were not necessarily Chinese:

We traveled to the city of Calicut, which is one of the chief ports in Malabar [the southwest coast of India], and one of the largest harbors in the world. It is visited by men from China, Sumatra, Ceylon, the Maldives, Yemen, and Fars [Persia], and in it gather merchants from all quarters ... there were at the time thirteen Chinese vessels, and we disembarked. Every one of us was lodged in a house and we stayed there three months as the guests of the infidel [Zamorin ruler of Calicut], awaiting the season of the voyage to China. On the Sea of China traveling is done in Chinese ships only, so we shall describe their arrangements.

The Chinese vessels are of three kinds; large ships called *chunks* [junks], middle-sized ones called *zaws* [dhows], and small ones called *kakams*. The large ships have anything from twelve down to three sails, which are made of bamboo rods plaited like mats. They are never lowered, but turned according to the direction of the wind; at anchor they are left floating in the wind. A ship carries a complement of a thousand men, six hundred of whom are sailors and four hundred men-at-arms, including archers, men with shields and arbalests, who throw naphtha. Each large vessel is accompanied by three smaller ones, the "half," the "third," and the "quarter." These vessels are built only in the towns of Zaytun and Canton. The vessel has four decks and contains rooms, cabins, and saloons for merchants; a cabin has chambers and a lavatory, and can be locked by its occupant, who takes along with him slave girls and wives. Often a man will live in his cabin unknown to any of the others on board until they meet on reaching some town. The sailors have their children living on board ship, and they cultivate green stuffs, vegetables and ginger in wooden tanks. The owner's factor [representative] on board ship is like a great *amir* [nobleman]. When he goes on shore he is preceded by archers and Abyssinians with javelins, swords, drums, trumpets, and bugles. On reaching the house where he stays they stand their lances on both sides of the door, and continue thus during his stay. Some of the Chinese own large numbers of ships on which their factors are sent to foreign countries. There is no people in the world wealthier than the Chinese. (Ibn Battuta, pp. 234–6)

technological capability to do so. Why did Chinese emperors choose only to receive European shipping—rather than to dispatch their own ships—beginning with the Portuguese in 1514?

Many answers appear plausible. The Ming turned their energies inward, toward consolidation and internal development. At first they pushed the Mongols further north from the Great Wall, but an invasion of Mongolia failed in 1449. Thereafter, the Ming limited their military goals, rebuilt the Great Wall, and restricted their forces to more defensible borders.

In 1411 the Ming reconstructed and extended the Grand Canal from Hangzhou in the south to Beijing in the north. The canal was the cheapest, most efficient means of shipping the grain and produce required by the northern capital. The man-made inland waterway also reduced the importance of coastal shipping, enabling the Ming emperors to turn their backs on the seas and ocean. The faction of eunuchs, dedicated court servants like Zheng He, who urged the government to continue its sponsorship of foreign trade, lost out in palace competition to other factions that promoted internal development. International private shipping was also curtailed.

The Ming government limited contacts with foreigners and prohibited private overseas trade by Chinese merchants. In 1371, coastal residents were forbidden to travel overseas. Recognizing the smuggling that resulted, the government issued further prohibitions in 1390, 1394, 1397, 1433, 1449, and 1452. The repetition of this legislation reveals that smuggling did continue, but, for the most part, private Chinese sailors were cut off from foreign trade. The government defined the expeditions of Zheng He as political missions that sought tribute to China from outlying countries. Although products were exchanged on these voyages, officially trade was not their goal. So, while both private and government trade flourished in the interior of China, and while thousands of Chinese emigrated to carry on private businesses throughout Southeast Asia, China's official overseas trade virtually stopped. Zheng He's expeditions stand out as spectacular exceptions to generally restrictive policies.

These decisions to limit China's international trade, both official and private, proved enormously costly. Chinese society became introverted and, although economic growth continued, innovation stagnated. Under the Song dynasty (960–1279) Chinese technology had been the most innovative in the world. Creativity continued under the Mongols, but by about the beginning of the Ming dynasty, China became more conservative. Military technology improved but then it, too, stagnated. China had invented gunpowder before 1000 C.E., but used it only sporadically. Ming cannon in the early fifteenth century were at least equal to those anywhere in the world, but metal was in short supply, limiting further development. The Ming fought few battles against fortress cities, where cannon were most useful, so they also saw little need to invest further in developing this heavy weaponry. No enemies appeared against whom they needed such weapons. In fighting against invasions from the north, the crossbow was of more importance to the infantrymen, who made up China's armies of a million and more soldiers. At first, when China was itself very advanced, these decisions to limit further military innovation seemed not so consequential. Later, however, they would render the country vulnerable to newly rising powers.

Internal Trade. When Marco Polo arrived in China in 1275, the splendor and wealth of the country overwhelmed him. He described its ruler, Kublai Khan, as "the mightiest man, whether in respect of subjects or of territory or of treasure, who is in the world today or who ever has been, from Adam our first parent down to the present moment." Polo correctly informed the West that China in the late 1200s was the richest, most technologically progressive, and largest politically unified country in the world.

The foundations of China's wealth had been in place for centuries. We have already read in Chapter 7 of China's generally growing population, territory, power, and wealth through its successive dynasties from Qin to Tang. Under the Song dynasty (Northern Song, 960–1126; Southern Song, 1127–1279), China underwent an economic revolution. A revolution in agriculture underpinned the advance: better soil preparation and conservation; improved seeds that often allowed more than one crop per season; better water control and irrigation; and more local specialization of crops. The new techniques were implemented most intensively in the lower Yangzi valley, as the Song moved south from China's historic northern base around the Yellow River. Indeed, they maintained regional capitals, two of which served as national capitals: Kaifeng in the north and Hangzhou in the south, near the mouth of the Yangzi. Thanks to the invention of woodblock printing in the ninth century under the Tang dynasty, ideas could spread in China more rapidly than anywhere else. One of the first uses of print had been to conserve and spread religious concepts; the oldest printed book extant in the world is a copy of the Buddhist *Diamond Sutra* from 868. Now the new method of printing was put into the service of disseminating the new farming methods.

Agricultural improvements—plus China's traditional excellence in textile production and remarkable innovations in the most advanced coal and iron industry in the world—inspired a trade revolution. Common people became involved in the mass production of goods for sale. Domestically this included the production of military goods for the Song army of over one million men; internationally it emphasized traditional silks and porcelain ceramics now supplemented with the export of iron and steel products. Trade became monetized, with copper as the principal currency. Chinese currency was so popular in Japan at this time that it became the most important medium of trade. Chinese ships sailed as far as East Africa, returning with exotic goods, such as gold, ivory, tortoise-shell, rhinoceros horns (regarded as aphrodisiacs), leopard skins, ambergris, and some slaves. Large numbers of Song coins were excavated in Zanzibar in 1888. Ships returning from Southeast Asia also brought luxuries: aromatic herbs and spices, rhinoceros horns, pearls, and camphor. From Arabian lands came frankincense.

In 1024, in Sichuan province, China, paper money was printed for the first time in the world. (Sometimes the government printed an excess of paper money, giving rise to inflation.) Merchants invented new credit mechanisms to facilitate trade. Government control of trade, quite marked under the Tang, was sharply reduced in favor of greater market freedom and trade made up an increasing share of government revenue. Customs offices in the nine official ports, especially the largest, Canton and Zaitun (Quanzhou), collected import taxes of 10 to 15 percent of the value of goods. In 1128, maritime trade brought in 20 percent of China's total cash revenues. Merchants were valued for the taxes the state could collect from them. Those who paid the most were rewarded with official rank.

The great luxury products of China—silk, porcelain, and tea—continued to attract thousands of foreign merchants as they had since Tang times. Many were Muslim Arabs. A few Lombards, Germans, and French were also present. They were treated as welcome guests, and special quarters in the port cities were set aside for them. In issues that involved no Chinese but only these foreigners, they could apply their own laws. Shops with foreign goods and foreign schools catered to their interests. Nevertheless, these merchants followed Chinese commercial rules, and many became quite Sinicized in their manners. When they ended their sojourn in China, they were feted with large farewell feasts.

The international merchants were at the peak of a highly integrated national system of trade and commerce, a system that was built on domestic and international water transport. To integrate the system of waterways, portage of goods was arranged at points of dangerous rapids and cataracts. To ensure smooth passage, double locks were installed on the man-made Grand Canal, which extended from Hangzhou in the

River traffic at Qing Ming festival, Kaifeng, by Zhang Zeduan, Song dynasty scroll. The multitude of Chinese junks on the Yellow River suggest the well-developed channels of trade in northern China. (*National Palace Museum, Taiwan*)

SOURCE

River Trade in China

Just as the vast and profitable trade in silk depended ultimately on the hard work of millions of spinners and weavers and their families, so river trade in China depended, at least partially, on the investments of common people. The three sources below support that assertion. The first is from Marco Polo attesting to the abundance of river trade in China. The second is from Pao Hui, writing in the thirteenth century about the financing of overseas river trade. The third is a Song dynasty scroll illustrating the multitude of Chinese junks sailing on the Yellow River at Kaifeng.

First, Marco Polo writing of the Yangzi River:

I assure that this river runs for such a distance and through so many regions and there are so many cities on its banks that truth to tell, in the amount of shipping it carries and the total volume and value of its traffic, it exceeds all the rivers of the Christians put together and their seas into the bargain. I give you my word that I have seen in this city [I-ching] fully five thousand ships at once, all afloat on this river. Then you may reflect, since this city, which is not very big has so many ships, how many there must be in the others. (cited in Elvin, pp. 144–5)

Then compare Pao Hui on the financing of river trade in Southern Song China:

All the people along the coast are on intimate terms with the merchants who engage in overseas trade, either because they are fellow countrymen or personal acquaintances. Leakage [of copper currency] through entrusting occurs when the former give the latter money to take with them on their ships for the purchase and return conveyance of foreign goods. They invest from ten to a hundred strings of cash, and regularly make profits of several hundred per cent. (Shiba Yoshinobu, p. 33)

Finally, examine Zhang Zeduan's twelfth-century scroll painting, Going on the River at the Qingming Festival. *At this time, the city of Kaifeng, situated on the Yellow River and at the crossroads of some of China's most important canals, was the hub of water-borne traffic for all of northern China. Inland Kaifeng and Hangzhou, on the coast, were China's most important regional capitals. They formed the apex of a regional system of urbanization that unified the whole country.*

Market towns sprang up throughout China, enabling virtually every rural family to sell its products for cash and to buy city goods. In turn, the small market towns were linked to larger cities, which provided more specialized products and access to government administrators. Here, families could buy and sell, arrange a marriage, determine the latest government rulings, hear about new farming possibilities, learn the dates and the results of academic examinations. These towns were so widespread that nearly every farm family lived within reach of one.

At the base were the rural families, struggling to survive by producing commodities demanded by the traders. Hand manufacture, especially of cotton and silk cloth, often supplemented farm production in rural areas. Invention made the process more productive. In particular a reeling machine, invented around the eleventh century, drew several silk filaments at once from silkworm cocoons immersed in boiling water. It then drew the filaments through eyelets and hooks and finally banded them into silk thread.

The rural producers were integrated into the market system either through direct, personal access or through brokers who supplied raw materials and bought the finished product. Women were the chief producers in this supplemental rural industry. They also carried the finished product to market. Conditions of production and of marketing could be savage. Xu Xianzhong's "Prose Poem on Cotton Cloth" presents the harshness of both aspects. It is not clear whether the women in the marketplace are selling their cloth, or themselves, or both:

Why do you ignore their toil? Why are you touched
Only by the loveliness that is born from toil?
…
Shall I tell you how their work exhausts them?
By hand and treadle they turn the rollers of wood and iron,
Feeling their fibre in between their fingers;
The cotton comes out fluffy and the seeds fall away.
The string of the cotton bow is stretched so taut
It twangs with a sob from its pillar.
They draw out slivers, spin them on their wheels
To the accompaniment of a medley of creakings.
Working through the darkness by candlelight,
Forgetful of bed. When energy ebbs, they sing.
The quilts are cold. Unheard, the waterclock flows over.
…
When a woman leaves for market
She does not look at her hungry husband.
Afraid her cloth's not good enough,
She adorns her face with cream and powder,
Touches men's shoulders to arouse their lust,
And sells herself with pleasant words.
Money she thinks of as a beast its prey;
Merchants she coaxes as she would her father.
Nor is her burden lifted till one buys.
(Elvin, pp. 273–4)

south to administrative centers, including Beijing, in the north; this system helped to link the agricultural wealth of the south with the administrative cities of the north. Tugboats with human-powered paddle-wheels serviced the main ports. Chinese oceangoing ships, equipped with axial rudders, watertight bulkheads, and magnetic compasses, gained a reputation as the best in the world.

THE MONGOLS

The Song dynasty (960–1279) developed the waterways of China, but the great Central Asian overland silk routes had declined after the ninth century along with the Abbasid and Tang dynasties that had protected and encouraged them. Under the Mongol Empire (1206–1405), the largest land empire ever known, traffic on the silk routes revived.

The two million Mongols who inhabited the plateau region of Central Asia were divided into several warring tribes, each led by a *khan*. The land was poor and the climate harsh. The Mongols shepherded their cattle, sheep, and goats in a circular pattern of migration called transhumance: in the brief summers they moved their herds northward to pasture; in winter they turned back south. They spent most of their waking hours on horseback and mastered the art of warfare from the stirrups, with bow and arrow as well as sword by their side.

The "Pax Mongolica"

Cultural historians credit the Mongols with little permanent contribution because they were absorbed into other, more settled and sophisticated cultures. But they did establish, for about a century, the "Pax Mongolica," the Mongolian Peace, over a vast region, in which intercontinental trade could flourish across the reopened silk route. Reports from two world travelers, Ibn Battuta (1304–68) of Morocco and Marco Polo (1254–1324) of Venice, give vivid insights into that exotic trade route.

During his thirty years and 73,000 miles of travel, Ibn Battuta commented extensively on conditions of travel and trade. For example, in Central Asia Ibn Battuta encountered a military expedition of Oz Beg Khan (d. 1341), the ruler of the khanate of the Golden Horde:

> We saw a vast city on the move with its inhabitants, with mosques and bazaars in it, the smoke of the kitchens rising in the air (for they cook while on the march), and horse-drawn wagons transporting the people. (Dunn, p. 167)

yurts A portable dwelling used by the nomadic people of Central Asia, consisting of a tentlike structure of skin, felt, or hand-woven textiles arranged over wooden poles, simply furnished with brightly colored rugs.

The tents of this camp/city were Mongol yurts. Made of wooden poles covered with leather pelt, and with rugs on the floor, the yurts could be disassembled quickly for travel.

Later, Ibn Battuta was granted his request to travel with one of Oz Beg Khan's wives along the trade route as she returned to her father's home in Constantinople to give birth to her child. Ibn Battuta reported that the princess traveled with 5000 horsemen under military command, 500 of her own troops and servants, 200 female slave girls, 20 Greek and Indian pages, 400 wagons, 2000 horses, and about 500 oxen and camels. They crossed from Islamic Mongol territory to Christian Byzantium.

Marco Polo was a merchant in a family of merchants, and his account of his travels to and in China was thus particularly attuned to patterns of trade. His numerous descriptions of urban markets support the idea of an urban-centered trade diaspora. For example, consider Marco Polo's description of Tabriz in northwest Persia:

HOW DO WE KNOW?

The Mongol Empire

Because it was the largest contiguous land empire in history, understanding the entire Mongol Empire requires language competence in Mongolian, Chinese, Persian, Arabic, Turkish, Japanese, Russian, Armenian, Georgian, and Latin. No scholar can be expected to master all of these languages, but serious scholars are expected to know at least one or two of them and to use others in translation. Surprisingly, Mongolian may not be the most important. Before Chinggis Khan, the language was not written and there are no archives of the Mongol Empire, at least none that have survived. The only major historical text in Mongolian is The Secret History of the Mongols, and, although some scholars think it inauthentic, it is our principal source for the biography of Chinggis Khan. Another text from the days of Chinggis Khan, the Altan Debter, or Golden Book, is lost, but Persian and Chinese historians mention it, and their references show the book to be consistent with, although not the same as, The Secret History.

Chinese and Persian texts are the next most important, discussing Mongol rule over the two empires flanking, and captured by, the Mongol Empire. In China, the major text is the official dynastic history of the Yuan, or Mongol, dynasty. In Persia, several authors are important, most notably Rashid al-Din. Until his time, the Mongol conquest posed a problem for Muslim historians: The conquest of the Abbasid Empire was not supposed to happen. Muslims were to conquer others, as they had done with great consistency; they were not supposed to be conquered themselves. During Rashid al-Din's time, however, the Mongols converted to Islam. Rashid al-Din must have understood this well, since he himself had converted from Judaism. Rashid al-Din wrote the history of the Mongol Empire which, he said, marked a new era in world history. Later, he wrote Jami' al-tawarikh, a Collection of Histories, recording the history of all the peoples touched by the Mongols from the Chinese in the east to the Franks in the west. It was the first example of the form of a world history. For the last twenty years of his life, until he was assassinated as the result of a court intrigue in 1318, Rashid al-Din served as principal adviser to the Il-Khan ruler of Persia.

Distant Europe held relatively little importance for the Mongols, but a number of European sources discuss their conquests. These included men such as Giovanni de Piano Carpini, who was sent by Pope Innocent IV to visit the Khans, and William of Rubruck, who visited the Mongols at the behest of the king of France, Louis IX. The most comprehensive account is by Matthew Paris, who chronicled European reactions to the Mongol advances from his post at St. Albans, England, but the most popular came from travelers, of whom the most famous was Marco Polo.

- Mongolian may not be the most important language in the study of the Mongolian empire, yet the most important biography of Chinggis Khan is in Mongolian. How do you explain this paradox?
- Why are Chinese and Persian important languages for studying the Mongol Empire?
- Would you consider Rashid-al-Din's Collection of Histories a history of the world? Why or why not?

The people of Tabriz live by trade and industry; for cloth of gold and silk is woven here in great quantity and of great value. The city is so favourably situated that it is a market for merchandise from India and Baghdad, from Mosul and Hormuz, and from many other places; and many Latin merchants come here to buy the merchandise imported from foreign lands. It is also a market for precious stones, which are found here in great abundance. It is a city where good profits are made by traveling merchants. The inhabitants are a mixed lot and good for very little. There are Armenians and Nestorians, Jacobites and Georgians and Persians; and there are also worshippers of Mahomet, who are the natives of the city and are called Tabrizis. (Marco Polo, p. 57)

Central Asian routes challenged travelers and their animals. Despite the Pax Mongolica, merchants still had to be prepared to defend themselves from attack. As Marco Polo recounts:

Among the people of these kingdoms there are many who are brutal and bloodthirsty. They are forever slaughtering one another; and, were it not for fear of the government … they would do great mischief to traveling merchants. The government imposes severe penalties upon them and has ordered that along all dangerous routes the inhabitants at the request of the merchants shall supply good and efficient escorts from district to district for their safe conduct on payment of two or three groats for each loaded beast according to the length of the journey. Yet, for all that the government can do, these brigands are not to be deterred from frequent depredations. Unless the merchants are well armed and equipped with bows, they slay and harry them unsparingly. (Polo, p. 61)

For those merchants and statesmen who did reach Beijing, the Khan maintained a massive service industry to provide hospitality. Polo noted, in particular, an army of prostitutes:

I assure you that there are fully 20,000 of them, all serving the needs of men for money. They have a captain general, and there are chiefs of hundreds and of thousands responsible to the captain. This is because, whenever ambassadors come to the Great Khan on his business and are maintained at his expense, which is done on a lavish scale, the captain is called upon to provide one of these women every night for the ambassador and one for each of his attendants. They are changed each night and receive no payment; for this is the tax they pay to the Great Khan. (Polo, p. 129)

Almost everything we know about Marco Polo's life is based on the colorful account he left us of his travels through Asia. Little is known of his childhood years in Venice or his education. Marco's father and uncle, both Venetian merchants, traveled from their home in 1260 on a trade mission as far as the northern end of the Caspian Sea. Then war broke out, and their route back home was blocked. But the route eastward was open, so the brothers traveled on to Beijing, where Chinggis Khan's grandson, Kublai Khan (1215–94), ruled.

The Great Khan invited the men to return with more information on Christianity and a delegation from the pope. The information and delegation never materialized, but in 1271 the two brothers, along with the seventeen-year-old Marco, set out for China again. They arrived in 1275 and remained there for seventeen years. How exactly they occupied themselves during this time is unclear from Marco's account, but it was not uncommon for foreigners to find employment in the Mongol state. Kublai Khan, it appears, was so enchanted by Marco's tales of foreign lands that he sent him on repeated reconnaissance trips throughout the empire. The Polos eventually set off for home in about 1292, reaching Venice in 1295 and reuniting with relatives and friends who had believed them long-since dead.

Soon after his homecoming, Marco was captured in battle by Genoese sailors and imprisoned. He dictated the tales of his travels to his fellow prisoner Rustichello, a writer of romances. Europe now had its most complete and consistent account up to that date of the silk route and of the fabulous Chinese empire of Kublai Khan. Marco's *Travels* was soon translated into several European languages, introducing to Christian Europe a new understanding of the world.

For seven centuries scholars have hotly debated the authenticity of Marco Polo's account. No original copy of *The Travels* exists, and scholars have been faced with some 140 manuscript versions that were copied in various languages and dialects from scribe to scribe before the invention of printing. Frances Wood, head of the China Department at the British Library, has asked, *Did Marco Polo Go to China?* (1996). Wood emphasizes the arguments against. Polo did not mention any of the phenomena that should have caught his attention during his reported time in China: Chinese writing, tea, chopsticks, foot binding, the Great Wall. Despite his claims to frequent meetings with Kublai Khan, Marco Polo is not mentioned in any Chinese records of the time. Wood concludes that Polo's work is actually based on materials gathered from others and that he himself never traveled beyond the Black Sea. As a travel narrative, Wood asserts, the book was a fabrication, but as an account of what was known of China at the time, it was a very rich and very influential source of information. Many commentators are therefore equally adamant that Polo did complete all the travels that he claimed, and the debate over the extent of Marco Polo's own travels continues.

Chinggis Khan

Chinggis (Genghis) Khan Temujin, later called Chinggis (Genghis) Khan, was born about 1162 into one of the more powerful and more militant Mongol tribes. His father, chief of his tribe, was poisoned by a rival tribe. About three generations before Temujin's birth, one of his ancestors, Kabul Khan, had briefly united the Mongols, and Chinggis made it his own mission to unify them once again. He conquered the surrounding tribes, one by one, and united them at Karakorum, his capital. Although skilled at negotiation, Chinggis was also infamous for his brutality. Historian Rashid al-Din (1247–1318), writing almost a century after his conquests, reports Chinggis Khan's declaration of purpose, emphasizing women as the spoils of warfare:

> Man's greatest good fortune is to chase and defeat his enemy, seize all his possessions, leave his married women weeping and wailing, ride his gelding, and use the bodies of his women as a nightshirt and support, gazing upon and kissing their rosy breasts, sucking their lips which are as sweet as the berries of their breasts. (cited in Ratchnevsky, p. 153)

Chinggis defeated the Tartars and killed all surviving males taller than a cart axle. He defeated the rival Mongol clans and boiled alive all their chiefs. In 1206, an assembly of all the chiefs of the steppe regions proclaimed him Chinggis Khan—"Universal Ruler." He organized them for further battle under a pyramid of officers leading units of 100, 1000, and 10,000 mounted warriors, commanded, as they grew older, by his four sons. Promotion within the fighting machine was by merit. Internal feuding among the Mongols ended and a new legal code, based on written and recorded case law, called for high moral standards from all Mongols.

Chinggis turned east toward China. On the way he captured the Tangut kingdom of Xixia, and from Chinese engineers he mastered the weapons of siege warfare: the mangonel and trebuchet, which could catapult great rocks; giant crossbows mounted on stands; and gunpowder, which could be launched from longbows in bamboo-tube rockets. In 1211 Chinggis pierced the Great Wall of China, and in 1215 he conquered the capital, Zhongdu (modern Beijing), killing thousands.

Chinggis departed from China to conquer other kingdoms. His officials and successors continued moving south, however, until they

Chinggis Khan, from Rashid al-Din's world history, 13th century. Chinggis Khan's conquests had as much impact on West Asia as they did on China. This Persian illustration of Chinggis pursuing his enemies comes from a history, which some consider to be the first world history, written by Rashid al-Din (1247–1318), a Persian administrator employed by Mongol Il-Khans in Iran. (*Bibliothèque Nationale, Paris*)

captured all of China, establishing the Mongol dynasty, 1276–1368. They conquered Korea, large parts of Southeast Asia as far as Java, and attempted, but failed, to take Japan as well. The planned assault on Japan in 1281 was stopped by *kamikaze*, divine winds, which prevented the Mongol fleet from sailing.

Chinggis himself turned west, conquering the Kara-Khitai Empire, which included the major cities of Tashkent and Samarkand. He turned southward toward India, reaching the Indus River and stationing troops in the Punjab, but he was unable to penetrate further. Turning northwest, he proceeded to conquer Khwarizm. In the great cities of Bukhara, Nishapur, Merv, Herat, Balkh, and Gurgan, millions were reported killed, an exaggeration, but still an indication of great slaughter. Chinggis went on to capture Tabriz and Tbilisi.

After Chinggis's death in 1227, his four sons continued the expansion relentlessly. In the northwest they defeated the Bulgars along the Volga and the Cumans of the southern steppes and then entered Russia. They took Moscow, destroyed Kiev, overran Moravia and Silesia, and set their sights on the conquest of Hungary. To the terrified peoples in their path, it looked as if nothing could stop the Mongols' relentless expansion. But in 1241, internal quarrels did what opposing armies could not: they brought the Mongol advance in Europe to a halt. During the dispute over succession that followed the death of Chinggis's son Ogedei (1185–1241), the Mongols withdrew east of Kiev. They never resumed their westward movement, and central and western Europe remained untouched.

The Mongol successor states. After the death of Chinggis Khan's grandson Mongke in 1259, the Mongol world devolved into four successor states. Kublai Khan's emerged as the most powerful, but only after a long struggle with Song China. In Central Asia, the Chagatai dominated the eastern steppe; the Golden Horde became established in southwest Russia; and the Il-Khan in Persia ruled from Kabul to Anatolia.

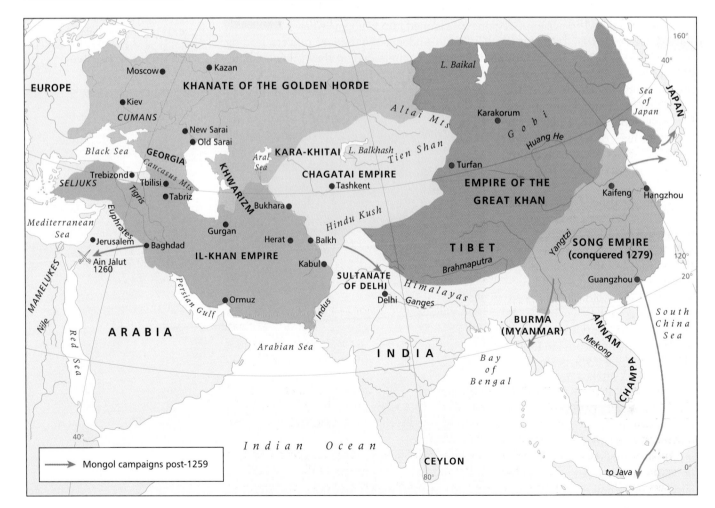

In the southwest, under Chinggis's grandson Hulegu (*c.* 1217–65), the Mongols captured and destroyed Baghdad in 1258, ending the five-century-old Abbasid dynasty by killing the caliph. But in the next year, Mongke, Chinggis's grandson and the fourth and last successor to his title as "Great Khan," died while campaigning in China, and many of the Mongol forces withdrew to attend a general conclave in Karakorum to choose his successor. In 1260, Mongol forces were defeated by a Mamluk army at the battle of Ain Jalut, in modern Jordan, and never again pushed further to the southwest.

The End of the Mongol Empire

Mongol rule was extensive but brief. At their apogee, 1279–1350, the Mongols had ruled all of China, almost all of Russia, Iran, Iraq, and Central Asia. The huge empire was administered and ruled through four separate geographical *khanates*, or sub-empires, each under the authority of a branch of Chinggis Khan's family. Over time central authority declined and the four khanates separated, each becoming an independent empire.

The Mongols could not govern their empire from horseback, and they were soon absorbed by the peoples they had conquered. They intermarried freely with the Turks who had joined them as allies in conquest. In Russia, Mongols and Turks merged with Slavs and Finns in a new Turkish-speaking ethnic group, the Tartars. In Persia and China they assimilated into local culture, converting to various religions, including Christianity, Buddhism, and Confucianism. In most of the areas inhabited by Muslims, the Mongols and their Turkish allies typically converted to Islam.

As the four segments of Chinggis's empire went their own separate ways, slowly they were driven from their conquests. By 1335 the male line of Chinggis and his grandson Hulegu died out in the Il-Khan Empire in Persia. The Ming dynasty defeated and evicted the Mongol (or Yuan) rulers in 1368. The Chagatai khanate was destroyed by Timur the Lame (Tamerlane) after 1369. The Russians pushed out the Golden Horde (named not, as one might think, for their numbers, but for their tents, *Ordu* in Turkish) more slowly. The last Mongol state in the Crimea was conquered only in the eighteenth century.

Plague and the Trade Routes

In addition to commerce and religion, disease also followed the trade routes. An unexpected side effect of the Pax Mongolica was the spread of a plague—called the Black Death—that devastated Eurasia's population in the 1300s. Until recently this mortal disease was believed to be the bubonic plague, but research within the last decade suggests that it may have been a different, unknown, disease. Whatever the disease was, it apparently followed the Mongols from Central Asia into China in 1331 and decimated its population. China's population, estimated at 123 million in 1200, dropped to 65 million in the census of 1393. Part of the decrease was caused by warfare between Chinese and Mongols, but a large part must also have been caused by the plague.

Along the silk routes, after the mid-fourteenth century, the presence and the role of the Mongols declined, probably also as a result of plague deaths. The plague reached the Crimea in 1346. There, plague-infested rats boarded ships, disembarking with the disease at all the ports of Europe and the Near East.

Within the next five years, in Europe, where the plague was new and people had no natural immunity, one-third of the population died. The ravages of the plague fore-shadowed further, even worse epidemics that would sweep across the continents of

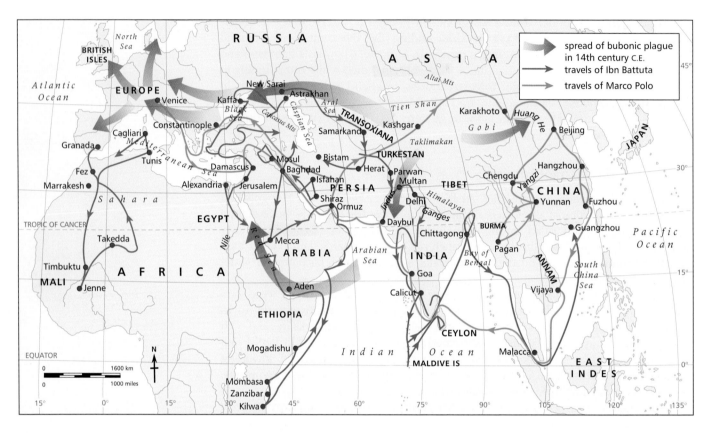

The routes of the plague. The central and east Asian stability imposed by Mongol rule—the "Mongol Peace"—brought mixed benefits. Trade flourished, and travelers such as Ibn Battuta and Marco Polo were able to write remarkable accounts of the lands they visited. At the same time, however, vectors for other travelers, such as the rats that carried bubonic plague, also opened up. The Black Death, originating in Central Asia, was one of a succession of plagues that followed the trade routes by land and sea, decimating parts of Europe and China.

the New World, as groups of people who had not previously been exposed to one another's diseases began to meet for the first time (see Chapter 14).

From Mongol to Ming: Dynastic Transition

During the ninety years of Mongol rule, 1279–1368, China's population plummeted from a high of 100 million to just over 50 million. Despite the splendor of Kublai Khan in his capital at Beijing, the Chinese economy did not serve everyone equally well. Marco Polo told of especially bitter poverty and class division in south China where the Han Chinese of the Southern Song dynasty experienced Mongol rule as cruel and exploitative:

> In the province of Manzi almost all the poor and needy sell some of their sons and daughters to the rich and noble, so that they may support themselves on the price paid for them and the children may be better fed in their new homes. (Polo, p. 227)

Revolution simmered until 1368, when the Ming dynasty overthrew the Mongols and ruled for almost three centuries, until 1644.

Under the Ming dynasty, the population increased sharply. By 1450 it had reached 100 million again, and by 1580 the population was at least 130 million. Plagues and rebellions again caused the population to fall back to 100 million by 1650, but from that trough it rose consistently into present times.

The population settled new territories as it grew. The origins of the Chinese Empire had been in the Yellow River valley in the north (see Chapter 4). At the time of the Han dynasty, more than 80 percent of the population of China lived north of the Yangzi valley. Under the late Tang dynasty, the population was divided about equally between north and south. Warfare with the Mongols in the north drove more migrants south, and at the height of the Mongol dynasty up to 90 percent of the population lived in the south. Economically, the south produced rice, cotton, and tea, three of China's most valuable products, not available in the northern climate. Closer to the sea lanes of Southeast Asia and the Indian Ocean, the south also developed China's principal ports for international commerce. The Song built a powerful navy and Chinese merchants carried on regular trade with Southeast Asia, India, and the Persian Gulf. After the Mongols were defeated, however, migration began to reverse. By about 1500, 75 percent lived in the south, and movement back to the north was continuing.

LEGACIES TO THE PRESENT
WHAT DIFFERENCE DO THEY MAKE?

The years shortly before and after 1500 marked a turning point in world trade patterns. Before 1500 trading routes criss-crossed Africa, Europe, and Asia. These routes connected with one another, but they were not unified into a single system of trade. Long-distance trade goods would travel in stages from one set of routes to the next, carried first by one set of traders and then transferred to another, as goods were transported to their final destination. The most important long-distance traders were the Muslim Arab sailors and merchants of the Indian Ocean routes and beyond to the ports of China. Chinese traders dominated the East Asian waterways and occasionally, and spectacularly, sailed into and across the Indian Ocean. At this time, few European traders journeyed into Asia. In the thirteenth century, Mongol rulers provided protection along the old silk routes, reopening these land passages through Central Asia.

The western hemisphere had two sets of regional routes—mostly unconnected with each other—one centering on Mesoamerica, the other on the Andes Mountains of South America. Except for rare voyages, the American routes and the Afro-Eurasian routes remained separated from each other by the vast expanses of the Atlantic and Pacific Oceans.

As European traders grew more powerful after 1500, they attempted to subordinate pre-existing regional systems to their own centralized control from European headquarters. Within a single generation they seized control of the Americas. Asian powers, however, were much less vulnerable and they tended to pay little attention to the newly arriving Europeans. China and Japan mostly kept them out. European control increased as northwestern Europe industrialized after 1750 (see Chapter 16). Then the European traders, and their governments, supported by new productivity at home, as well as new ships and new guns, began to declare supremacy in global trade. They challenged the legacies of Arab and Chinese supremacy in the east, and Native American isolation in the west, and began to introduce new regimes of trade and domination into world history.

Review Questions

- What is a "trade diaspora"? What was the importance of trade diasporas to the spread of world trade before 1500? What advantages did Jews and Muslims have for exercising world trade in the period 1000–1500?
- What were the principle inter-regional trading networks in 1300?
- What is a lateen sail? Where did it originate? What is its significance?
- How would you compare the relative importance of inland and overseas trade for China in the fifteenth century?
- How did the Mongol Empire facilitate world trade?

• Trace the rise of Arab seafaring to show how it came to be predominant in the Indian Ocean and South China Sea.

Suggested Readings

PRINCIPAL SOURCES

Abu-Lughod, Janet L. *Before European Hegemony: The World System A.D. 1250–1350* (New York: Oxford University Press, 1989). A résumé of the principal trade routes around 1250. Unfortunately omits African routes.

Adas, Michael, ed. *Islamic and European Expansion* (Philadelphia: Temple University Press, 1993). Key collection of historiographical essays on major topics in world history, 1200–1900. Articles by Eaton and Tucker on Islam, and McNeill on "gunpowder empires" are especially helpful for this unit.

Chaudhuri, K.N. *Trade and Civilization in the Indian Ocean: An Economic History from the Rise of Islam to 1750* (Cambridge: Cambridge University Press, 1985). A survey of goods, traders, ships, regulations, and competition among those who sailed and claimed to control the Indian Ocean.

Cortés, Hernán. *Letters from Mexico*, trans. from the Spanish and ed. by Anthony Pagden (New Haven: Yale University Press, 1986). Newest edition of Cortés' letters.

Curtin, Philip. *Cross-Cultural Trade in World History* (Cambridge: Cambridge University Press, 1984). Classical statement of the significance and ubiquity of trade diasporas.

Dunn, Ross. *The Adventures of Ibn Battuta* (Berkeley: University of California Press, 1986). Dunn uses Ibn Battuta and his travels as the center-point of an analysis of Islamic life throughout the Islamic ecumene in the fourteenth century.

Elvin, Mark. *The Pattern of the Chinese Past* (Stanford: Stanford University Press, 1973). Primarily economic history, focused heavily on the central questions of why China did so well economically until about 1700, and then why it did so badly after that time.

ADDITIONAL SOURCES

The Book of the Thousand Nights and a Night: A Plain and Literal Translation of the Arabian Nights Entertainment, 6 vols. in 3, trans. by Richard F. Burton (New York: Heritage Press, 1946).

Bentley, Jerry H. *Old World Encounters* (New York: Oxford University Press, 1993). Survey of the range of cross-cultural, long-distance encounters—especially through trade, religion, and culture—throughout Afro-Eurasia from earliest times to about 1500. Engaging.

Chaudhuri, K. N. *Asia Before Europe* (Cambridge: Cambridge University Press, 1990). Survey of the economic and political systems of Asia before the impact of colonialism and the industrial revolution. Comprehensive, comparative, and thoughtful.

Columbia College. Columbia University. *Introduction to Contemporary Civilization in the West*, Vol. I (New York: Columbia University Press, 2nd ed., 1954). Very well-chosen, long source readings from leading thinkers of the time and place. Vol. I covers *c.* 1000 to 1800.

Crosby, Alfred W. *Ecological Imperialism: The Biological Expansion of Europe, 900–1900* (Cambridge: Cambridge University Press, 1986). The biological—mostly destructive—impact of European settlement around the world, a tragedy for native peoples from the Americas to Oceania.

Frank, Andre Gunder and Barry K. Gills, eds. *The World System: Five Hundred Years or Five Thousand?* (London: Routledge, 1993). In this somewhat tendentious, but well argued, account, globalization is nothing new.

Ghosh, Amitav. *In an Antique Land* (New York: Knopf, 1993). A novel, travelogue, historical fiction of Indian Ocean exchanges in the twelfth century and today. Captivating. Much of the tale is based on the research in Goitein's study, below.

Goitein, Shelomo Dov. *A Mediterranean Society: The Jewish Communities of the Arab World as Portrayed in the Documents of the Cairo Genizah*, 6 vols. (Berkeley: University of California Press, 1967–83). Extraordinary research resulting from the examination of a discovered treasury of about ten thousand documents from about 1000–1300. Despite the title, gives insight into a variety of communities of the time.

Hanbury-Tenison, Robin. *The Oxford Book of Exploration* (New York: Oxford University Press, 1994). An excellent collection of primary sources on exploration.

Hourani, George Fadlo. *Arab Seafaring in the Indian Ocean in Ancient and Early Medieval Times* (Princeton: Princeton University Press, 1951, reprinted 1995). The standard introduction. Examines the trade routes and the ships prior to and after the coming of Islam.

Ibn Battuta. *Travels in Asia and Africa 1325–1354*, trans. and selected from the Arabic by H.A.R. Gibb (New Delhi: Saeed International, edition 1990). Selections from the writings of one of the greatest travelers in history.

Ibn Majid, Ahmad. *Arab Navigation in the Indian Ocean Before the Coming of the Portuguese*, trans., introduced, and annotated by G.R. Tibbetts (London: Royal Asiatic Society of Great Britain and Ireland, 1971). Translation of Ibn Majid's classic fifteenth-century guide for navigators, along with very extensive discussion by Tibbetts placing the author and work in context and discussing contemporary theories of navigation.

Komaroff, Linda and Stefano Carboni, eds. *The Legacy of Genghis Khan: Courtly Art and Culture in Western Asia, 1256–1353* (New York: Metropolitan Museum of Art and New Haven: Yale University Press, 2002). Lavishly illustrated catalogue of blockbuster art exhibit, with numerous interpretive essays as well.

Levathes, Louise. *When China Ruled the Seas: The Treasure Fleet of the Dragon Throne, 1405–33* (New York: Oxford University Press, 1996). Scholarly study of the expeditions of Zheng He.

Ma, Laurence J.C. *Commercial Development and Urban Change in Sung China (960–1279)* (Ann Arbor: Department of Geography, University of Michigan, 1971). Careful, scholarly, detailed research monograph.

Menzies, Gavin. *1421: The Year China Discovered America* (New York: William Morrow, 2003). Menzies brings together many scraps of evidence in concocting the argument that Zheng He actually did sail to America. The evidence does not hold.

Polanyi, Karl, Conrad M. Arensberg, and Harry W. Pearson, eds. *Trade and Market in the Early Empires* (Chicago: The Free Press, 1957). Fundamental argument by historical anthropologists that early trade was mostly regulated by rulers and priests.

Polo, Marco. *The Travels*, trans. from the French by Ronald Latham (London: Penguin Books, 1958). One of the most fascinating and influential travelogues ever written.

Ratchnevsky, Paul. *Genghis Khan: His Life and Legacy*, trans. and ed. by Thomas Nivison Haining (Oxford: Blackwell, 1991). The current standard biography of the personally elusive Chinggis Khan.

Raychaudhuri, Tapan and Irfan Habib, eds. *The Cambridge Economic History of India*. Vol. 1: *c. 122–c. 1750* (Cambridge: Cambridge University Press, 1982). Collection of articles of fundamental significance.

Risso, Patricia. *Merchants and Faith. Muslim Commerce and Culture in the Indian Ocean*. (Boulder: Westview Press, 1995). Among the questions explored: "What difference did it make to be a Muslim?"

Schele, Linda and David Freidel. *A Forest of Kings: The Untold Story of the Ancient Maya* (New York: William Morrow and Co., 1990). The story of the deciphering of the Mayan ideographs and the histories of warfare that they reveal, by two of the leading researchers.

Shaffer, Lynda Norene. *Maritime Southeast Asia to 1500* (Armonk, NY: M.E. Sharpe, 1996). Useful survey on the voyages, trade goods, markets, towns, and government of the region—from earliest times.

Shiba Yoshinobu. *Commerce and Society in Sung China*, trans. by Mark Elvin (Ann Arbor: Michigan Abstracts of Chinese and Japanese Works on Chinese History, 1970). Scholarly source materials with annotations from the economic transformation of the Song dynasty.

Skinner, G. William. "Marketing and Social Structure in Rural China," *Journal of Asian Studies* XXIV, No. 1 (November 1964), 3–43. Classic account of the interlocking structure of urban development in China from local market towns through national capitals of trade.

Toussaint, Auguste. *History of the Indian Ocean*. Trans. from the French by June Guicharnaud (Chicago: University of Chicago Press, 1966). Broad historical sweep of exploration, trade, cultural exchange, fighting, and rule in and of the Indian Ocean from earliest times to the 1960s. Very useful survey.

Wood, Frances. *Did Marco Polo Go to China?* (Boulder, CO: Westview Press, 1996). One of the more recent, and lucid, statements of the controversy.

◉ World History Documents CD-ROM

ILLꟼ DE MAGELLAM

MER DV SV

EUROPEAN VISIONS

ECONOMIC GROWTH, RELIGION AND RENAISSANCE, GLOBAL CONNECTIONS 1100–1776

KEY TOPICS
- The Atlantic
- The Decline of Trade in the Mediterranean
- Trade and Social Change in Europe
- The Renaissance
- A New World
- Oceania

Until 1492 no continuous links connected the eastern and western hemispheres although there had certainly been some voyages between them. The expeditions of Leif Eriksson and other Vikings from Scandinavia around the year 1000 are well known, documented, and authenticated in the artifacts they left behind in their temporary settlements on the northeast coast of North America. Some of the foods of Polynesia—sweet potatoes and manioc—that apparently came from South America present evidence of other contacts, even more fleeting, across the Pacific. Permanent contact between the two major continental landmasses of the world was established, however, only with Christopher Columbus' conquest of the Atlantic Ocean in 1492. The consequences for the people of both hemispheres were enormous.

We have seen that three groups had the capacity to cross the oceans prior to Columbus' expedition. Polynesians and South Americans apparently made contact in some fashion, but neither felt the need to continue their brief encounter. Arab traders of the Indian Ocean probably had the shipping capacity to make the voyage to the Americas, but they also had no need. The Indian Ocean with its neighboring Mediterranean Sea and South China Sea provided all the trading opportunities they required. The Chinese, who were capable of dispatching fleets as far as East Africa, had the capacity, but the imperial decision to terminate these voyages ended their explorations. The Europeans, except for the Vikings, also did not venture out so long as the ports of the Middle East provided access to the great markets of Asia. Only when that access was reduced and profits were curtailed, and when their own economies and technologies grew stronger, did their imaginations expand. Even then, the western Europeans who set off exploring were not looking for new lands, but only for new routes to well-known markets. Columbus did not realize that he had discovered two new continents. In this chapter we discuss the great voyages of exploration of Columbus, Vespucci, Magellan, Tasman, and Cook, who opened new oceanic perspectives to an incredulous world.

THE ATLANTIC

From the eighth until the twelfth century, the European north Atlantic was primarily the province of marauding sailors and raiders from the north. These Vikings were the ancestors of today's Norwegians, Swedes, and Danes. They were also colonizers, fishermen, and traders. One group from Norway began to settle Iceland around 870 and Greenland about 982. Under Leif Eriksson they reached Newfoundland in North America about 1000 and established a settlement there as well, but it did not endure. Danes and Norwegians plundered along the entire Atlantic coast of Europe, with

Opposite **French caravel, 1555. Watercolor on paper.** The sturdy caravel, adapted by Europeans from the Arab ships of the Indian Ocean, became the ship of choice for oceanic exploration. Columbus and Vasco da Gama both sailed in caravels. By arming his caravel with cannon, Gama transformed it into a weapon of war.

The Arrival of King Sweyn and Danish Troops in England, 11th century. Vellum. Sweyn Forkbeard (c. 987–1014), a formidable Viking warrior from Denmark, created a Danish North Sea empire, gaining control over Norway (1000) and conquering England (1013). He is shown here disembarking from his warship.

especially early and devastating attacks on Lindisfarne off the northern coast of England (793), Dorestad in Frisia (834), and Nantes in France (842), where they murdered the bishop and all his clergy. In 859 they sailed through the Strait of Gibraltar and attacked ports along the Mediterranean. Arabs from North Africa and Spain were launching similar attacks in the Mediterranean at about the same time.

These Vikings were also traders and colonizers who often fostered urban development and trade in the places they conquered. They founded the town of Dublin, in Ireland, in 841, and they conquered much of northern England, establishing the kingdom of York in the 870s. Vikings also conquered the French territory of Normandy in the late eighth century, from where in 1066 their leader, William of Normandy (William the Conqueror), conquered England. The Normans, as these "Northmen" came to be known, also founded a kingdom in southern Italy and Sicily and established a principality in Antioch.

The Swedes turned eastward across the Baltic Sea and founded trading cities along the river systems of Russia, establishing their capital first at Novgorod in the early ninth century and in Kiev in 882. They proceeded all the way south to the Black Sea, where they traded with the Byzantine Empire. The Swedish settlements became catalysts for the formation of the political and economic organization of the Slavic people in whose midst they were established. Kiev became the capital of the first Russian state; its people were called the "Rus." Historians continue to debate whether that term refers to the Vikings, the Slavs, or the hybrid group that emerged as the Slavic majority assimilated the Viking minority. By about 1000 the fierce Vikings became more peaceful, and their raids ceased as their home regions of Scandinavia developed into organized states and accepted Christianity. They lost interest in further exploration westward across the ocean.

Voyages across the north Atlantic, except those of the Vikings, are not recorded historically and are unlikely to have occurred. In the south Atlantic even less travel took place. There is no known crossing of the south Atlantic. Africans carried on only limited coastal shipping and Europeans were frightened of the unknown hazards of the west African coast, especially south of Cape Bojador. In addition, they recognized that the prevailing winds on the African coast blew from north to south and they feared that while they might be able to proceed to the south they might not be able to return north.

THE DECLINE OF TRADE IN THE MEDITERRANEAN

As Arab armies swept across the Middle East and North Africa, they hesitated before taking to sea battles in the Mediterranean Sea. Nevertheless, in 643 they captured

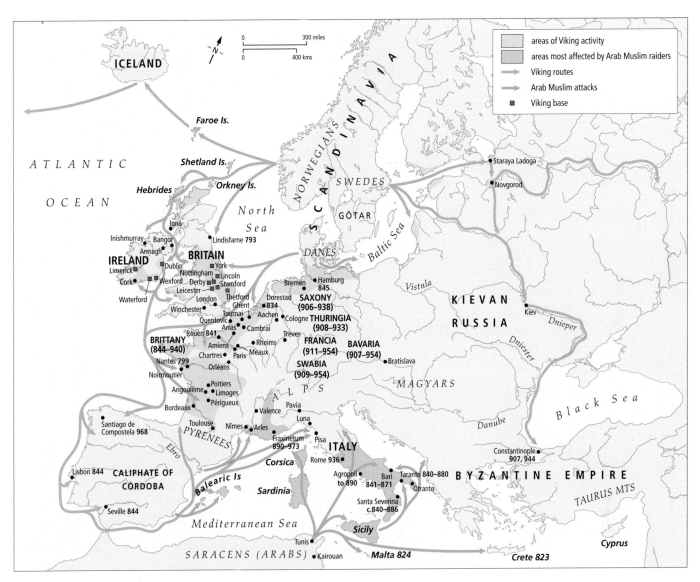

ICELAND

Faroe Is.

Shetland Is.

Hebrides   *Orkney Is.*

A T L A N T I C

O C E A N

North Sea

N O R W E G I A N S

S C A N D I N A V I A

SWEDES

GÖTAR

Baltic Sea

• Staraya Ladoga

• Novgorod

Iona •

• Lindisfarne 793

DANES

Inishmurray •   • Bangor

• Armagh

IRELAND   **BRITAIN**

Limerick •   • York
• Dublin
Cork •   Nottingham • Lincoln
    • Wexford   Derby • Stamford
    Leicester •
Waterford •   Thetford
    London   Bremen •   • Hamburg
Winchester •   Dorestad   845
    Ghent • 834   **SAXONY**
    Tournai   Aachen   **(906–938)**
    Quentovic   Cologne • **THURINGIA**
    Arras • Cambrai   **(908–933)**
Rouen 841 •   Treves •
BRITTANY   Amiens •   • Rheims   **FRANCIA**   **BAVARIA**
(844–940)   Chartres • Paris   Meaux •   **(911–954)**   **(907–954)**
Nantes 799 •   Orléans •   **SWABIA**   • Bratislava
Noirmoutier •   **(909–954)**
    • Poitiers
Angoulême •   • Limoges   **A L P S**
Bordeaux •   • Périgueux   Pavia
    Valence •   • Luna   **M A G Y A R S**
Santiago de   Toulouse •   Nîmes • Arles •   *Danube*
Compostela 968   **P Y R E N E E S**   Fraxinetum   Pisa •
    890–973   **ITALY**
    Corsica   Rome 936 •
Lisbon 844 •   **CALIPHATE OF**   Agropoli   • Bari
    CÓRDOBA   to 890   841–871   Taranto 840–880
    Balearic Is   *Sardinia*   • Otranto
Seville 844 •   Santa Severina
    c.840–886
    Mediterranean Sea   *Sicily*
    Tunis •
    S A R A C E N S   (A R A B S)   • Kairouan   **Malta 824**

• Kiev   **K I E V A N**

R U S S I A

Vistula

Dnieper

Dniester

Black Sea

Constantinople •
907, 944

B Y Z A N T I N E   E M P I R E

TAURUS MTS

Cyprus

Crete 823

Ebro

Legend:
- areas of Viking activity
- areas most affected by Arab Muslim raiders
- → Viking routes
- → Arab Muslim attacks
- ■ Viking base

0   300 miles
0   400 kms

Alexandria, the most important port in the eastern Mediterranean, and in 655 they engaged and defeated a fleet of the Byzantine Empire at Dhat al-Sawari, off the south-western coast of modern Turkey. They established their dominion by land along the eastern and southern coasts of the Mediterranean and had enough sea power in the eastern Mediterranean to hold their own against the Byzantine Empire, and even to expand. By about 950 they held parts of southern Italy as well as major islands in the Mediterranean: Cyprus, Crete, and Sicily. The southern and southeastern Mediterranean had become a "Muslim lake." The Byzantine Empire continued, however, to control the northeastern shores of the Mediterranean, and various Frankish and Germanic Christian powers held the north-central coast. The Mediterranean Sea, and its coastline, were divided into three major cultural and political spheres of control: Muslim to the south and southeast, Byzantine to the northeast, and Roman Catholic to the northwest. The Mediterranean is so large and so diverse that such divisions seem natural enough. (Look carefully at the accompanying map of the Mediterranean Sea on page 429 to see the many islands and peninsulas and the many smaller seas that mark its inlets.)

Scandinavian and Arab Muslim, and East Slav invasions, 9th–10th centuries. Europe was subjected to repeated invasions that temporarily weakened the continent but then increased its power. The Vikings settled and developed Scandinavia, and their interaction with the Slavs gave shape to Russia. The Muslims brought with them an understanding of the culture of ancient Greece and Rome that Europeans had forgotten. (Adapted from *The Times Atlas of World History*, 5th edition. London. Times Books.)

Three developments followed these divisions. First, the Mediterranean once again became a war zone. Battles between the Christians of southern Europe and the Muslims of the Middle East and North Africa persisted from the eighth century until 1571, when the naval Battle of Lepanto, in Greek waters, fixed generally accepted zones of control between them. Second, trade continued but oscillated with the fate of Europe's internal economy and with warfare in the Mediterranean. Finally, in the southeastern Mediterranean, where land separated the Mediterranean Sea from the Indian Ocean—where today the Suez Canal provides that link—the European merchants felt blocked. The valuable and profitable merchandise coming from the Indian Ocean basin—the spices of India and Indonesia; the silk and porcelain of China; and the gold and ivory and slaves of East Africa—were controlled by Middle Eastern Muslim traders. The eastern Mediterranean trade blockage is often seen as a religious confrontation. On several occasions, for example, popes forbade Catholics to trade with Muslims. But

AT A GLANCE : MEDIEVAL WORLD TRADE

DATE	POLITICAL/SOCIAL EVENTS	TRADE DEVELOPMENTS	EXPLORATION
1050 C.E.	■ Normans under William I invade England (1066) ■ Seljuk Turks take Baghdad ■ Franks invade Anatolia and Syria and found Crusader states	■ Venice dominates Adriatic; trading ports set up throughout eastern Mediterranean (1000–1100)	
1100 C.E.		■ Wool trade flourishing between England and Flanders	
1150 C.E.	■ Salah al-Din, sultan of Turkish Syria and Egypt, retakes Jerusalem (1187) ■ St. Francis of Assisi (1181–1226) ■ St. Dominic (1170–1221) ■ St. Clare of Assisi (1194–1253)	■ Market fairs in the Champagne region, France	
1200 C.E.		■ Rise of craft guilds in towns of western Europe ■ Foundation of Hanseatic League (1241)	
1250 C.E.		■ Increasing Venetian links with Central Asia and China (1255–95) ■ Revolt of craftspeople in Flanders	
1300 C.E.	■ Hundred Years War between England and France (1337–1453) ■ Bubonic plague in Europe (1346–50)	■ West Africa provides two-thirds of the gold of the eastern hemisphere	
1350 C.E.	■ Ghettoization of Jews in western Europe ■ Ashigawa Shoguns dominate Japan (1338–1573)	■ Revolts of urban workers in Italy and Flanders	
1400 C.E.	■ Ottoman Turks establish foothold in Europe at Gallipoli	■ Great Chinese naval expeditions reach east coast of Africa and India under Zheng He	■ Portugal's Prince Henry the Navigator sponsors expeditions to West Africa
1450 C.E.	■ Printing of Gutenberg's Bible (1455) ■ War of the Roses in England (1453–85) ■ Turks capture Constantinople (1453) ■ Jews driven from Spain (1492) ■ Treaty of Tordesillas (1494)	■ Medici family in Florence: Giovanni, Cosimo, Lorenzo	■ Bartholomeu Dias sails round Cape of Good Hope (1488) ■ Columbus reaches the Americas (1492) ■ Vasco da Gama reaches the Malabar coast, India (1498)
1500 C.E.	■ Machiavelli, *The Prince* (1513) ■ Muslims in Spain forced to convert or leave	■ Portugal sets up trading port of Goa, in India (1502); Portuguese ships armed with cannon	■ Ferdinand Magellan's voyage round globe (1519–22)

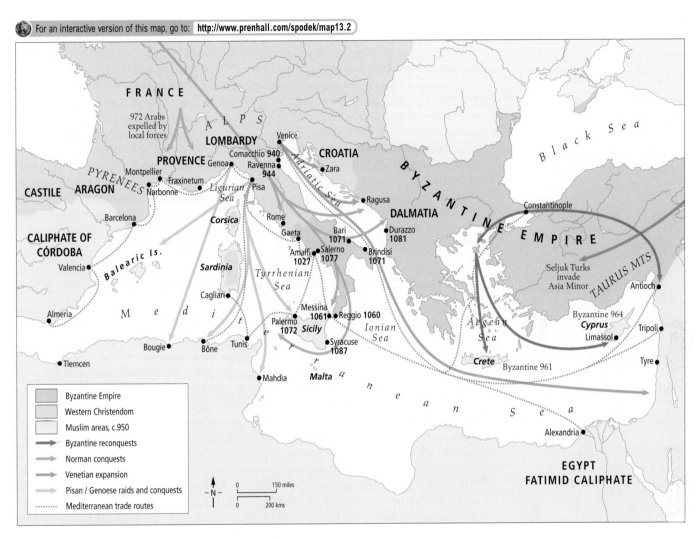

For an interactive version of this map, go to: http://www.prenhall.com/spodek/map13.2

European resurgence in the Mediterranean, c. 1000. After centuries of attacks from Vikings and Muslims, the Europeans of the Mediterranean began to fight back effectively, but the Mediterranean continued as a zone of intermittent warfare between Christians and Muslims until the Battle of Lepanto, 1571. (Adapted from *The Times Atlas of World History*, 5th edition. London. Times Books.)

these prohibitions were generally disregarded. More critical was the competition for profits among the many different groups of traders. The Muslim traders themselves were not a unified group. Most were Arabs, but many of the Egyptian traders were Mamluks, and later Seljuk and Ottoman Turks invaded the area as well. Among the European trading communities, many felt that the city-state of Venice, with its skilled merchants and sailors, controlled the eastern Mediterranean trade in spices, cotton, and silk textiles for its own advantage. Religious and ethnic differences may have exaggerated the tensions among the traders, but the main contest was the competition for profits.

In search of higher profits and easier access to trade commodities, some merchants and some princes began seeking alternative routes to the Indian Ocean. This search took on special intensity in western Europe, which was geographically farther from the Middle East and closer to the Atlantic. Beginning in 1277, a maritime route between Italy and Spain in the Mediterranean and England and Flanders in northwestern Europe brought regular trade to the north Atlantic seacoast of Europe. Also, European trade generally was picking up in the early fifteenth century, as the continent recovered from the devastation of the plague. One search now began to explore the southern Atlantic Ocean for routes around the coast of Africa to India; another sought routes directly across the north Atlantic.

TRADE AND SOCIAL CHANGE IN EUROPE

The popularity of Marco Polo's accounts of his travels reflects the increasing interest of western Europeans in international trade. The Vikings and others were opening a new world of trade in the eastern fringes of Europe by the mid-1200s, and at about this time western Europeans were beginning to emerge from localized, agrarian, manorial economies and from the localized political systems of administration and order that had marked the Middle Ages. This was a period in which agricultural productivity increased and additional lands were brought under the plow as forests were cut down. New wealth enriched the towns and stimulated trade within Europe, while the crusades brought new opportunities for renewed commerce across the Mediterranean to ports of the Middle East and the merchandise that arrived there from Asia. This rebirth of long-distance trade in Europe aggravated the frustrations of the traders of western Europe with the problems of doing business in the Middle East and the eastern Mediterranean generally.

Guilds and City-states Confront Rural Aristocrats

As business increased, local traders and manufacturers formed trade organizations called **guilds**. These guilds regulated prices, wages, the quality and quantity of production and trade, and the recruitment, training, and certification of apprentices, journeymen, and masters. The guilds also represented their members in town governments and thus helped to keep industrial and commercial interests at the forefront of the civic agenda. The guilds were the principal organization through which the merchants successfully confronted the landed aristocrats and won legal rights and privileges for their businesses and their cities. Guild members were mostly males, but widowed heads of households and workshops were also included among the voting members.

Most guilds were organized locally, within their hometowns, but international traders organized international guilds corresponding to their commercial interests. The most famous and powerful of them, the Hanseatic League, though lacking the social and religious dimensions of a true guild, was founded in the mid-thirteenth century to represent the interests of leading shippers of the cities of Germany and the Baltic Sea. Headquartered in the city of Lübeck, the League established its own commercial trading posts as far west as London and Bruges (modern Belgium), and as far east as Novgorod in Russia. Throughout the region, it lobbied for legal systems that favored its members. Ships belonging to the League carried grain, timber, furs, tar, honey, and flax westward from Russia and Poland, and woolen goods eastward from England. From Sweden they carried copper and iron ore. In the fourteenth century about 100 towns were affiliated with the League. As states such as the Netherlands (United Provinces), England, and Sweden grew powerful, they asserted their control of the Baltic and the League began to die a natural death after dominating the commerce of its region for almost two centuries.

Economic and Social Conflict within the City

In two regions of western Europe, north Italy and Flanders, the manufacture of textiles came to dominate the urban economies. In Florence, between 200 and 300 workshops provided a livelihood for one-fourth of the city's population, producing a total of 100,000 pieces of woolen cloth each year. Other cities of northern Italy, though smaller, had similar workshops. The economies of Flanders and the neighboring regions of northern France and what is now Belgium were increasingly dominated by the production of textiles.

guild A sworn association of people who gather for some common purpose. In the towns of medieval Europe, guilds of craftsmen or merchants were formed in order to protect and further the members' professional interests and for mutual aid.

Opposite **Italian School, The Oar Makers, 18th-century painting of a medieval guild sign.** By the thirteenth century, as the advantages of corporate organizations over individual enterprise loomed larger, specific craftsmen's guilds began to appear—in this case, that of the oar makers. Guilds issued regulations that covered everything from protecting the welfare of deceased members' families to ensuring quality of production. (*Museo Correr, Venice*)

HOW DO WE KNOW?

Fernand Braudel Begins the Historical Study of Oceans

Fernand Braudel (1902–1985) was studying for his doctorate in Paris in the 1920s, specializing in the Mediterranean foreign policy of Phillip II of Spain, when he decided to change course:

> I was already beginning to move outside the traditional bounds of diplomatic history when I began to ask myself finally whether the Mediterranean did not possess ... a history and a destiny of its own, a powerful vitality, and whether this vitality did not in fact deserve something better than the role of a picturesque background ... (The Mediterranean, p. 1)

Braudel left his studies of diplomatic history and joined the group of young Parisian scholars—the "Annales" School—that was transforming the study of history from narrowly political questions to encompass much broader issues of geography, ecology, social structures, and "mentalités," or attitudes. As his work progressed, he became one of the school's most prominent leaders.

Braudel's first great historical work was The Mediterranean and the Mediterranean World in the Age of Phillip II, in two volumes, first published in 1949. Here Braudel worked out in practice his concept of three time frames always operating simultaneously: most deeply rooted, the longue durée, extending back even to geologic times and establishing the fundamental conditions of material life, states of mind, natural environment, and geography; the middle time frame of social, economic, and political organization; and the short term, the time of an individual life, the time frame of most conventional historical study of events. Implementing this concept of diverse time frames, Braudel began with the physical and human geography of the Mediterranean basin, went on to its political systems, and ended with the specific policies of Philip II and other rulers of his time. He examined general population figures, the everyday food that people ate, the houses they lived in, the clothes they wore, the fashions they affected, the technology they used, their money and media of exchange, and the cities they built and used. His work revolutionized the way many historians understood their discipline.

Two generations later, K.N. Chaudhuri encountered Braudel and his work. Chaudhuri explains the impact of that meeting on his own historical research and writing:

> The idea that the study of a civilization might be named after a sea originated with Fernand Braudel. Arab geographers were aware a thousand years ago of the relationship between different oceans and the Bilad al-Islam [the lands of Islam]. In our own times, Braudel remains one of a select group of French historians and geographers who have perceived with rare clarity the connection between the sea and the people who lived around its shores. For him the interaction between space, the passage of solar time, and the identity of civilizations constitutes one of the most important latent forces of history ... a whole generation of historians have learnt their craft from this great teacher. (Trade and Civilization, p. 1)

Chaudhuri then began writing Trade and Civilisation in the Indian Ocean, which he named in tribute to Braudel's pioneering work on the Mediterranean. Other scholars have followed this lead, and its comprehensive perspective has influenced many more.

- What was Braudel's motivation for leaving his studies of diplomatic history to study the Mediterranean Sea?
- What was new about his work?
- In light of Chaudhuri's comments, what questions that Braudel was asking about the Mediterranean might be useful to ask about other great bodies of water?

Left **Aerial view of present-day Delft, west Netherlands.** Here, gabled medieval townhouses are seen surrounding the bustling market square in Delft. Since the late 1500s the town has been famous for its pottery and porcelain known as delftware. Dutch products began to compete in European markets with porcelain imports from China.

Right **Painting of Hertogenbosch, Netherlands, 1530.** Compare today's photograph of a medieval square on market day *(left)* with this view of a cloth market in another Dutch town painted in 1530. The layout and construction of the stalls are virtually identical.

The new organization of textile production created a complex class structure with some possibility of upward mobility. Capitalist traders organized the manufacture. They estimated the market demand for production and supplied workers with the raw materials and equipment necessary to meet it. Below them, guild masters and the aspiring journeymen and apprentices within the guilds held the best positions among the manual workers: shearing the sheep; fulling the cloth (that is, shrinking and thickening it by moistening, heating, and pressing it); and dyeing the wool. Weavers, carders, and combers were lower on the pay and social scales, and of these, only the weavers were likely to organize a guild. Below all these, an army of poor people washed, warped, and spun the wool. Female and child laborers, employed at even lower pay and in worse conditions than the men, enabled working families to survive. Latent class antagonisms between employer and employee occasionally broke out in open conflict.

Revolts broke out in the Flemish cities of Douai, Tournai, Ypres, and Bruges at the end of the thirteenth century. The leaders were usually craftsmen, and they usually demanded that guild members be allowed to participate in government. The proletariat, the workers outside the guild organizations, could hope only that increased wages, shorter hours, and better conditions of work might trickle down to their level as well.

In the fourteenth century, class antagonisms increased. Increasingly impoverished workers, suffering also from plagues, wars, and bad harvests, confronted increasingly wealthy traders and industrialists. Workers were forbidden to strike and, in some towns, forbidden even to assemble. Nevertheless, a limited class consciousness was growing, especially in Florence, the greatest industrial center of western Europe. In 1345 ten wool-carders were hanged for organizing workers.

New Directions in Philosophy and Learning

On the basis of merchant wealth in the cities, a Renaissance—a rebirth in thought, literature, art, manners, and sensibilities—arose throughout central and western Europe. Most historians see the Renaissance emerging in the fourteenth century with the rise of trade and the increasingly favorable emphasis placed upon the profit motive in western Europe. Historians of the Church, however, detect the roots of this transformation as early as the mid-eleventh century—a period usually referred to as the High Middle Ages—when a shift occurred in religious as well as secular values.

Philosophers in the eleventh century began to suggest that pure faith was not enough to attain salvation. They spoke of additional values that opened the way to a new understanding and experience of the world. St. Anselm (1033–1109) stressed the need for an intellectual basis for faith. Peter Abelard (1079–1142) emphasized the need for a rational approach to the interpretation of texts. St. Bernard of Clairvaux (1090–1153) sought to combine love and spirituality with faith. Meanwhile, the new wealth and power of their Church offended some Roman Catholics, and they challenged the Church to live up to its early ideals of compassion for the poor and simplicity in everyday living. New orders of priests and nuns began to form as a way of returning to these early ideals: Franciscans followed the teachings of St. Francis of Assisi (1181–1226), Dominicans followed St. Dominic (1170–1221), and the "Poor Clares", an order of nuns, followed St. Clare of Assisi (1194–1253).

The same era witnessed an intellectual opening to the Arab world, especially through links in Spain. Christian scholars began the systematic translation of Arabic texts into Latin, reestablishing the link with the ancient Roman and Greek texts that the Arabs had preserved and developed, and that the European world had lost. The works of Avicenna (Ibn Sina) (980–1037), Averroes (Ibn Rushd) (1126–98), and the Jewish philosopher Maimonides (1135–1204) helped restore the emphasis upon logic and philosophy that Aristotle had taught.

Universities were founded to preserve, enhance, and transmit knowledge. Most emphasized practical disciplines: medical studies at Salerno and legal studies at Bologna; theological studies at Paris. All were founded before 1200. Later, students and professors from Paris crossed the English Channel and founded the University

Simone Martini, *St. Francis,* **c. 1320. Fresco. Church of S. Francesco, Assisi.** St. Francis of Assisi (c. 1182–1226) gave away all his possesssions to the poor. When his father disowned him, he stripped naked and, cloaked in a robe given by the Bishop of Assisi, went from place to place begging for food, offering service, and preaching. The religious order that he founded became the largest in Europe.

French School, *Avicenna*, 18th century. Oil on canvas. Ibn Sina, called Avicenna by Christian Europeans, was one of the foremost Islamic students of Aristotle's work. He influenced Church scholars, who re-learned Greek scholarship through him. (*Bibliothèque de la Faculté de Médecine, Paris*)

of Oxford about 1200, with Cambridge following shortly afterward. By 1300 there were about a dozen universities in western Europe; by 1500, nearly one hundred.

Curricula usually centered on theology, but they included grammar, dialectic, rhetoric, arithmetic, music, geometry, and astronomy. The theology curriculum, in particular, required the approval of the Church. This could be problematic, as illustrated by the case of St. Thomas Aquinas (1225–74). St. Thomas was the greatest Christian theologian of his age and paved the way for the new ideas of the Renaissance. Contentiously, he also welcomed the rationality of Aristotle. While many Church leaders rejected Aristotelian logic as contradicting the teachings of the Church, Aquinas saw no conflict. Instead, he declared that logic and reason, as taught by Aristotle, and faith, as taught by the Church, were complementary. In places where they did

Theological lecture at the Sorbonne, Paris, 15th century. Ms illumination. Sponsored by the Church, universities were founded primarily for the study of theology, but some included specializations in medecine and law. All the students were male and most were quite serious-minded. (*Bibliothèque de Troyes*)

HOW DO WE KNOW?

Islamic Influences on the European Renaissance

Arab thinkers, their translations of classical Greek works, and their comments on them, helped inspire the European Renaissance. Ibn Rushd's (Averroes') Arabic translations of and commentaries on Aristotle revealed that philosopher's works to western Europeans who had lost contact with the originals. In addition to his philosophy, Ibn Sina's (Avicenna's) Qanun (Canon) of medicine remained central to European medical thought for centuries. Al-Khuwarizmi's work in mathematics remained influential for centuries, and lives on in our lexicon today in the word algorithm, based on his name. From the tenth to the twelfth century Arabs, Christians, and Jews lived in such proximity, and even harmony, in parts of Spain—the home of these three scholars—that linguistic borrowing back and forth became common. Poetic and prose forms were also borrowed, especially from Arabic literature to Latin and the Romance languages. European scholars, such as Gerard of Cremona, sought out the best in Arabic thought in order to translate it. We have also seen that Europeans adapted Arab technology, such as the caravel, which gave them access to the oceans of the world.

Despite this rich harvest of culture and technology from the Arab world, we have the harsh, even hysterical judgment of Petrarch (1304-1374), one of the greatest Italian poets of the Renaissance, often called "the father of humanism":

I implore you to keep these Arabs from giving me advice about my personal condition. Let them stay in exile. I hate the whole lot … You know what kind of physicians the Arabs are. I know what kind of poets they are. Nobody has such winning ways; nobody, also, is more tender and more lacking in vigor, and, to use the right words, meaner and more perverted. The minds of men are inclined to act differently; but, as you used to say, every man radiates his own peculiar mental disposition. To sum up: I will not be persuaded that any good can come from Arabia. (Cassirer, et al., p. 142.)

What has happened between the early welcome given to Arabic learning and its bitter, summary rejection by Petrarch? Several interpretations are possible: First, Arabic influence was always greatest in Spain, where Muslims ruled much of the country for centuries, in some regions for almost eight centuries. Other European countries were less influenced. Even in Spain, as Christians began to reconquer the country, they began to focus on Muslims as political and religious enemies rather than as cultural colleagues. A similar change over time occurred throughout the Christian world as the launching of the crusades, after 1095, crystallized a new political antagonism between the two religious communities. The passing of time also brought new cultural currents to Europe, the development of new vernaculars especially in the Romance languages, such as Spanish, Italian, and French, broadening and deepening the base of culture, and making it more nationalistic. The Western Europeans also developed their own intellectual competences and institutions, reducing their reliance on others. The European Renaissance took Western Europeans in new directions.

Scholars sometimes designate three different periods as "renaissances" in Western Europe. The first was the Carolingian Renaissance, initiated by Charlemagne, about 800; the second was the Renaissance of the High Middle Ages, about the middle of the eleventh to the middle of the thirteenth centuries, significantly influenced by Muslim scholarship and learning; the third was the best known, and most influential, the Renaissance of the mid-fourteenth to the mid-sixteenth centuries. Each of the later renaissances built on the earlier ones, but also discarded some of their qualities. In Petrarch's dismissal of Arabic poetry and of Arabs generally we see a dramatic transformation in the attitudes of Christian thinkers, as their own religious and philosophical traditions become less open, and more hostile, to the influences of other cultures.

- The fourteenth century Renaissance took place primarily in Italy and in northwestern Europe. Why do you think it did not take place in Spain, where so much earlier cultural development took place?
- Petrarch turned against Arabic learning, but not against the early Greek philosophers. Would such a division have been possible in twelfth-century Spain? Why or why not?
- Arabic learning could be seen as more successful because it continued to hew to traditional paths, whereas Western Christian scholarship could be seen as a failure for turning in new directions. Would you accept such a characterization?

appear to conflict, however, he conceded that divine truths must take precedence: "Some divine truths are attainable by human reason, while others altogether surpass the power of human reason." Clerics should attempt to reach truth through reason, but when that proved too difficult, divine truths as revealed through the Church were the most reliable guide in showing the true path in life.

Aquinas was ahead of his time. For more than fifty years, the Franciscan order banned the reading of his works. Universities at Paris and Oxford condemned many of his doctrines. But within a century, Aquinas' synthesis of logic and faith, of Aristotle and the Church, became the standard orthodoxy of Roman Catholicism. Although Aquinas gave divine revelation precedence over human reason, on the eve of the

Renaissance he opened the door of the Church to the importance of reason in all human endeavors.

No matter how rigorous the rules and regulations of the universities, the assembly of dozens of inquisitive and exuberant young male students led to challenges to authority and quests for individualism. The "Golliard Poets" took their name from the biblical Goliath, a kind of early anti-Christ. These poets reveled in the pleasures of youth and ridiculed the conventions of sobriety, solemnity, and sanctity. They wrote parodies that were usually irreverent and sometimes obscene, for example, a *Drunkard's Mass*, a *Glutton's Mass*, and an *Office of Ribalds*. They mocked the most sacred beliefs of their time, declaring "I believe in dice … and love the tavern more than Jesus." They declared their blessings for one another: "Fraud be with you."

Today most scholars agree that these many changes in religious and philosophical attitudes opened the way to the European Renaissance, a philosophical and artistic movement that reached its greatest creativity in the two centuries stretching from the mid-1300s through the mid-1500s.

Disasters of the Fourteenth Century: Famine, Plague, and War

Paradoxically, the Renaissance was ushered in not only by an increase in scholarship and cultural borrowing, but also by extraordinary disasters that afflicted Europe in the fourteenth century. The area was plunged into famine, civil upheavals, and, worst of all, a plague that halted its general economic prosperity and its population growth for a century. These catastrophes led to a reshuffling of classes and a reevaluation of values, which provided receptive soil for a renaissance.

For some four hundred years, beginning about 900, Europe's rural population had been increasing in size and density as farmers chopped down forests and brought new land under the plow. However, scarcity of resources then resulted, and by the mid-thirteenth century parts of central Italy, for example, began to suffer depopulation. In addition, in the fourteenth century the climate turned wetter and colder, the winters more severe, reducing harvests. Consequently, the resistance to disease was reduced among populations everywhere.

The plague had begun in Asia and China's population had dropped from about 123 million in 1200 to about 65 million in 1393. When the plague reached Europe by way

Sheep in pen being milked, Luttrell Psalter, 14th century. Woolen-cloth merchants had congregated in Flanders from an early stage, and by the twelfth century the industry there needed English wool to function to capacity. Prior to medieval times overland traders could transport only small and valuable objects over long distances; by the fourteenth century the emergence of sea routes meant that bulk goods, such as wool and grain, could be traded internationally. (*British Museum, London*)

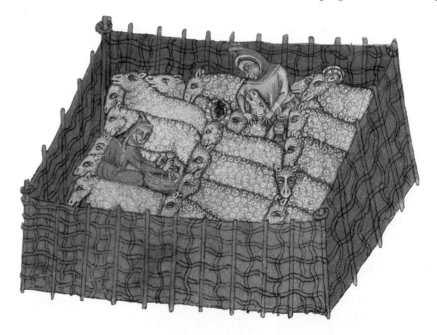

SOURCE

Giovanni Boccaccio Describes the Plague

Giovanni Boccaccio (1313–75) captured the horror of the plague in the introduction to his otherwise droll and humanistic classic of the era, The Decameron:

In the year of Our Lord 1348 the deadly plague broke out in the great city of Florence … At the onset of the disease both men and women were afflicted by a sort of swelling in the groin or under the armpits which sometimes attained the size of a common apple or egg. Some of these swellings were larger and some smaller, and all were commonly called boils. From these two starting points the boils began in a little while to spread and appear generally all over the body. Afterwards, the manifestation of the disease changed into black or livid spots on the arms, thighs, and the whole person … Neither the advice of physicians nor the virtue of any medicine seemed to help … almost everyone died within three days of the appearance of the signs—some sooner, some later …

The calamity had instilled such horror into the hearts of men and women that brother abandoned brother, uncles, sisters, and wives left their dear ones to perish and, what is more serious and almost incredible, parents avoided visiting or nursing their very children, as though these were not their own flesh. (xxiii–xxiv)

The Triumph of Death, French, 1503. This sixteenth-century work recalls the enormous loss of life caused by the Black Death of 1348. Brought back from East Asia by Genoese merchants, the bubonic plague is estimated to have killed between 20 and 50 percent of Europe's inhabitants. Contemporary medicine was impotent in the face of the disease, whose onset meant almost certain death. (*Bibliothèque Nationale, Paris*)

of trading ships in 1348, it killed off a third of Europe's population, reducing it from 70 million in 1300 to only 45 million in 1400.

Social Unrest Follows the Plague

Peasants who survived the plague benefited from the labor shortages that followed, gaining higher wages and access to more land, freedom from labor services, and geographical mobility. They began to form a new class of property-owning farmers. Together with urban industrial workers and guild members, they rioted more frequently and boldly against kings and nobles who attempted to raise taxes to fund their wars.

In urban areas, too, the new scarcity of workers encouraged those who survived to demand higher wages, better working conditions, and more civic rights. In industrialized Florence, the *Ciompi* (the lowest class of workers, named for the neighborhood of Florence in which they lived), revolted, supported by lower level artisans. In 1378 they presented their demands to the officials of Florence. They wanted open access to the guilds, the right to unionize, a reduction of worker fines and punishments, and the right "to participate in the government of the City." They gained some of their goals, but the powerful business leaders of the city ultimately triumphed. By 1382 the major guilds were back in control, and soon a more dictatorial government under the Medici family was installed. Similar revolts occurred in Flanders, but on a smaller scale, and with no more success. The dissolution of the norms of everyday life, and the certainties of the class structure, inspired a reassessment of fundamental values and institutions that may have helped carry Renaissance values of individualism and a humanistic perspective to the common people as well as the elites.

THE RENAISSANCE

The central motivating philosophy of the Renaissance was **humanism**, the belief that the proper study of man is man. Renaissance humanism held strongly to a belief in God, but assigned Him a less overwhelming, less intimidating role in human life and action. Asserting the importance of the individual, it challenged the monopoly of the Church over the interpretation of cultural life. In his *Oration on the Dignity of Man*, Giovanni Pico della Mirandola (1463–94) places in the mouth of God Himself the most succinct statement of this humanistic perspective of the Renaissance:

I have given you, Adam, neither a predetermined place nor a particular aspect nor any special prerogatives in order that you may take and possess these through your own decision and choice. The limitations on the nature of other creatures are contained within my prescribed laws. You shall determine your own nature without constraint from any barrier, by means of the freedom to whose power I have entrusted you … I have made you neither heavenly nor earthly, neither mortal nor immortal so that, like a free and sovereign artificer, you might mold and fashion yourself into that form you yourself shall have chosen.

According to this typical Renaissance perspective, God gives mankind the power to shape its own destiny.

New Artistic Styles

Renaissance art continued to emphasize religious themes, but it also began to reveal the influence of humanistic and commercial values. Masaccio's painting of *Trinity with the Virgin* (1427) demonstrates the evolution of geometric perspective in painting, suggesting not only a new artistic technique but also a new relationship of individuals to space.

Renaissance in Italy, 1300–1570. From 1300–1570 in Italy, artists and intellectuals worked to fuse the Christian tradition (originating in antiquity but developed during the Middle Ages) with the Greco-Roman tradition in a movement fundamental for the later evolution of the modern civilization of the West: the Renaissance. This map shows the principal places that are associated with the names of important figures.

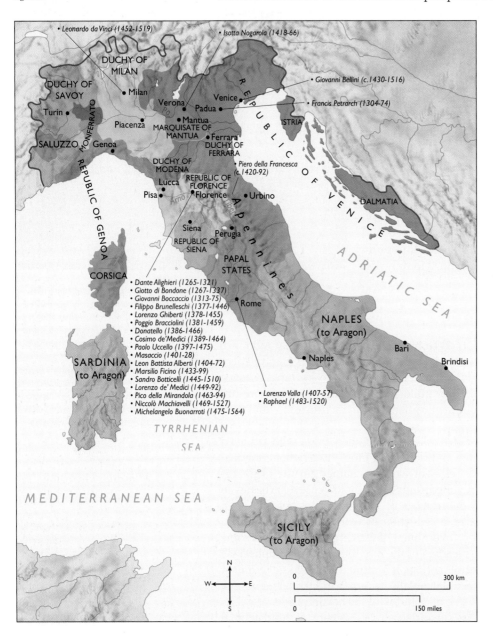

- Leonardo da Vinci (1452-1519)
- Isotta Nogarola (1418-66)
- Giovanni Bellini (c.1430-1516)
- Francis Petrarch (1304-74)
- Piero della Francesca (c.1420-92)

DUCHY OF MILAN
DUCHY OF SAVOY
Milan
Verona
Venice
Padua
Turin
MONFERRATO
Piacenza
Mantua
MARQUISATE OF MANTUA
ISTRIA
Ferrara
DUCHY OF FERRARA
SALUZZO
Genoa
DUCHY OF MODENA
REPUBLIC OF GENOA
Lucca
REPUBLIC OF FLORENCE
Pisa
Arno
Florence
Urbino
DALMATIA
REPUBLIC OF VENICE
Siena
Perugia
REPUBLIC OF SIENA
Apennines
ADRIATIC SEA
CORSICA
PAPAL STATES

- Dante Alighieri (1265-1321)
- Giotto di Bondone (1267-1337)
- Giovanni Boccaccio (1313-75)
- Filippo Brunelleschi (1377-1446)
- Lorenzo Ghiberti (1378-1455)
- Poggio Bracciolini (1381-1459)
- Donatello (1386-1466)
- Cosimo de'Medici (1389-1464)
- Paolo Uccello (1397-1475)
- Masaccio (1401-28)
- Leon Battista Alberti (1404-72)
- Marsilio Ficino (1433-99)
- Sandro Botticelli (1445-1510)
- Lorenzo de' Medici (1449-92)
- Pico della Mirandola (1463-94)
- Niccolò Machiavelli (1469-1527)
- Michelangelo Buonarroti (1475-1564)

Rome
NAPLES (to Aragon)
Bari
Naples
Brindisi

SARDINIA (to Aragon)

- Lorenzo Valla (1407-57)
- Raphael (1483-1520)

TYRRHENIAN SEA

MEDITERRANEAN SEA

SICILY (to Aragon)

N
W   E
S

0   300 km
0   150 miles

By the fifteenth century, artistic and commercial sensibilities had joined together. *The Arnolfini Wedding Portrait*, painted in 1434 in Flanders by Jan van Eyck, depicts in a realistic setting and clothing the marriage of a businessman, probably an Italian stationed in Flanders, and his perhaps already pregnant wife. Renaissance artists frequently merged their concerns for secular business affairs with their concerns for a spiritual life.

The richest fruits of Renaissance creativity matured in Florence, where the illustrious Medici family provided lavish patronage. The family's fortune had been built by

humanism A term applied to the intellectual movement initiated in Western Europe in the fourteenth century by such men as Petrarch and Boccaccio and deriving from the rediscovery and study of Classical, particularly Latin, literary texts.

Left **Masaccio,** *Trinity with the Virgin, St. John, and Donors***, 1427.** During the Renaissance, people began to rethink their relationship to God and the world around them; at the same time, artists were developing a new means of depicting reality. According to some art history scholars, Masaccio's monumental fresco is the first painting created in correct geometric perspective (the single vanishing point lies at the foot of the cross). (*S. Maria Novella, Florence*)

Below **Jan van Eyck,** *The Arnolfini Wedding Portrait***, 1434.** Giovanni Arnolfini, an Italian merchant living in Flanders, commissioned this pictorial record of his marriage. On the far wall, van Eyck has written in Latin "Jan van Eyck was here," much as a notary would sign a document. (*National Gallery, London*)

Right **Michelangelo Buonarroti, Sistine Chapel Ceiling (post restoration), 1508–12. Fresco.** Renaissance humanism praised the ability of human beings to be creative and original, yet it continued to be anchored in classical, religious imagery. Pope Sixtus IV commissioned Michelangelo to use his imagination in painting the Sistine Chapel ceiling in the Vatican, Rome, with biblical scenes. (*Vatican Museums and Galleries, Vatican City*)

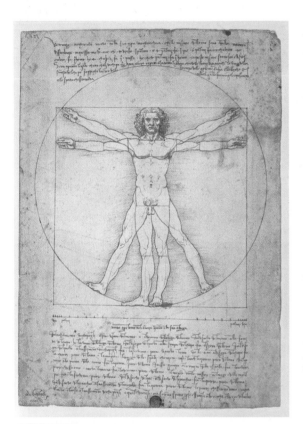

Leonardo da Vinci, *Vitruvian Man,* **c. 1492. Pen and ink on paper.** Renaissance artists studied the proportions of the human body carefully and represented it accurately. Leonardo's drawing suggests the geometric perfection of the body, relating it both to the circle and the square, and thus to a perfect and harmonious cosmos (*Galleria dell'Accademia, Venice*)

the merchant-banker Giovanni de' Medici (1360–1429), and was enhanced by his son Cosimo (1389–1464) and grandson Lorenzo (1449–92). In this supportive environment creative artists developed and expressed their genius. They included Michelangelo (1475–1564), the sculptor of such masterpieces as *David, Moses,* and the *Pietà,* and the painter of the Sistine Chapel ceiling in Rome; Leonardo da Vinci (1452–1519), scientific inventor and painter of the *Mona Lisa;* and Niccolò Machiavelli (1469–1527), author of *The Prince,* a harsh, and hard-nosed philosophy of government. At the same time, the general population of the city of Florence enjoyed high standards of literacy and expressiveness.

Developments in Technology

Creativity flourished in the practical arts as well as the fine arts, and it contributed substantially to the rise of merchant power. In 1317 merchants in Venice established regular commercial voyages through the Strait of Gibraltar and northward along the Atlantic coast to France and Flanders. Many innovations resulted from amalgamating local techniques with those encountered in the course of trade, especially with Arab civilization. Improvements in sailing technology included a new design in the ships themselves. In the thirteenth century the caravel of the Mediterranean, with its triangular, or lateen (Latin) sails, used mostly by Arab sailors, was blended with the straight sternpost and stern rudder of northern Europe. The caravel could also be rerigged with a square sail for greater speed in a tail wind. The astrolabe, again an Arab invention, helped sailors determine their longitude at sea. The rediscovery in the early fifteenth century of Ptolemy's *Geography*, written in the second century C.E., and preserved in the Arab world, helped to spark interest in proper mapping. (An error in longitude in Ptolemy's map led Columbus to underestimate the size of the globe by about one-third and to think that he could reach East Asia by sailing across the Atlantic.)

Cannon, especially when mounted on ships, gave European merchants firepower not available to others. Although the Chinese had invented gunpowder centuries before, the Europeans put it to practical use in warfare in the fourteenth century to become the masters of gunmaking. By the early 1400s they were firing cannonballs. The Ottoman Turks employed western European Christians to build and operate the cannons they used in 1453 to besiege and conquer Constantinople. The Turkish rulers of Persia also employed European gunners and gun manufacturers, and copied their works. By the late 1400s European warring powers were competing energetically in an "arms race" to develop the most powerful and effective cannons and guns. Leonardo and others worked on the mathematics of the projectiles. When Portuguese ships began to sail into the waters of the Indian Ocean after 1498, claiming the right to regulate commerce, their guns and cannons sank all opposition. Some historians have designated this era the Age of Gunpowder Empires.

The Chinese had also invented the principle of movable type and the printing press, but, again, European technology surpassed them in implementation. Movable type was better suited to Europe's alphabetic languages than to Chinese ideographs. By 1455, in Mainz, Germany, Johannes Gutenberg (*c.* 1390–1486) had printed the first major book set in movable type, the Bible. By the end of the century at least 10 million individual books in some 30,000 different editions had been produced and distributed.

In fourteenth-century Italy, two centuries after the decimal system had been absorbed from India via the Arab world, businesspeople began to develop double-entry bookkeeping. This facilitated the accurate accounting of transactions and the efficient tracking of business profits and losses. In 1494 Luca Pacioli (*c.* 1445–*c.* 1514), a Franciscan friar and mathematician, first published the method in systematic form.

The cannon. From the 1450s, innovations in weapons changed the nature of warfare. The most dramatic changes affected the cannon, as shown here in *Four Books of Knighthood*, 1528.

The Church Revises its Economic Policies

In establishing its independent power, the urban business community confronted not only landed aristocrats on the one hand and organizations of urban workers on the other, but it also faced an often hostile clergy. From its earliest times, the Church had taken a dim view of the quest for private profit and wealth. St. Augustine perpetuated the disdain. In the High Middle Ages theologians seriously debated whether it was possible for a merchant to attain salvation.

The Church forbade Christians to take and give interest on loans. For this reason, Jews carried out much of the business of moneylending. In fact, Jews were so much a part of the merchant classes in early medieval northern Europe that a traditional administrative phrase referred to "Jews and other merchants." Church laws forbidding Jews to own land also pushed them into urban life and commerce. By the end of the thirteenth century, Christian rulers forced Jews to live in ghettos, specific areas of the cities to which they were confined each night. In European society, Jews were stigmatized four times over: alien by religion, foreign by ancestry, moneylenders by occupation, and segregated by residence. Nevertheless, Jews were tolerated as an economically vital trade diaspora until local people mastered the intricacies of business. After that, Jews

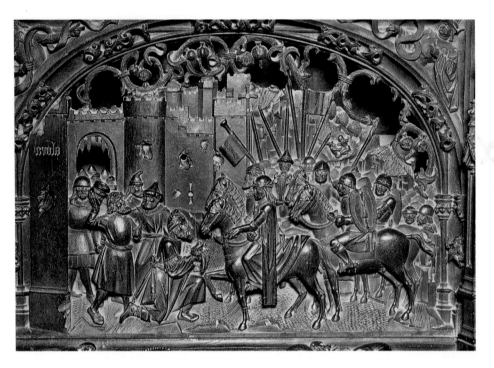

Rodrigo Aleman, *The Conquest of Granada on January 2, 1492*, Toledo Cathedral, late 15th century. The conquest of Granada by the Catholic King Ferdinand II and Queen Isabella I of Spain marked the final victory of the *reconquista*, the Christian recovery of all of Spain from Muslim rule. Here the Moorish king Boabdil is handing over the keys to the town.

were often persecuted, sometimes murdered, and repeatedly exiled—from England in 1290, from France in 1394, from Spain in 1492, and from many German cities.

As commerce increased, the Church began to revise its opposition to business and businessmen. St. Thomas Aquinas addressed the issue directly in his *Summa Theologica*. Aquinas justified commerce: "Buying and selling seem to be established for the common advantage of both parties." He wrote of a "just" price, determined by negotiation between buyer and seller. Neither Church nor government needed to regulate prices: "The just price of things is not fixed with mathematical precision, but depends on a kind of estimate, so that a slight addition or subtraction would not seem to destroy the equality of justice." Profit was allowed if its uses were deemed appropriate: "Nothing prevents gain from being directed to some necessary or even virtuous end, and thus trading becomes lawful." Traders were allowed compensation for their labor: "A man may take to trade ... and seek gain, not as an end, but as payment for his labor." Aquinas elaborated similar interpretations to allow interest on commercial loans.

Most of the dynamism of western European trade through the fifteenth century emanated from the relatively secular city-states of Flanders and Italy, but in the Iberian peninsula, Portugal and Spain created a powerful new merger of the desire to spread missionary Catholicism with the desire for economic profit. The Portuguese crown dispatched sailing missions along the African coast that ultimately reached the Cape of Good Hope, turned north into the Indian Ocean and onward to India, and were poised to continue on to China. The newly unified government of Spain commissioned Christopher Columbus to sail westward in search of a new route to the Indies. Instead he discovered a "New World."

A NEW WORLD

Portugal was particularly well situated geographically to explore the Atlantic coast of Africa as the opening step in finding an alternative route to India. At first, however, the main goal was to achieve supremacy over the Muslims who controlled the southern shores of the Mediterranean. King John I (*c.* 1385–1435) launched a crusade to capture at least part of North Africa from Muslim control. In 1415 he succeeded in taking Ceuta, a local trading center on the African side of the Strait of Gibraltar. John thought he would achieve both spiritual and economic gain, but once the trans-Saharan caravans saw that Ceuta had fallen to Christians, they turned their trade to other coastal cities.

John's third son, Prince Henry (1394–1460), later called the Navigator, expanded on his father's goals. He, too, wished to defeat Muslim power, but he thought the best

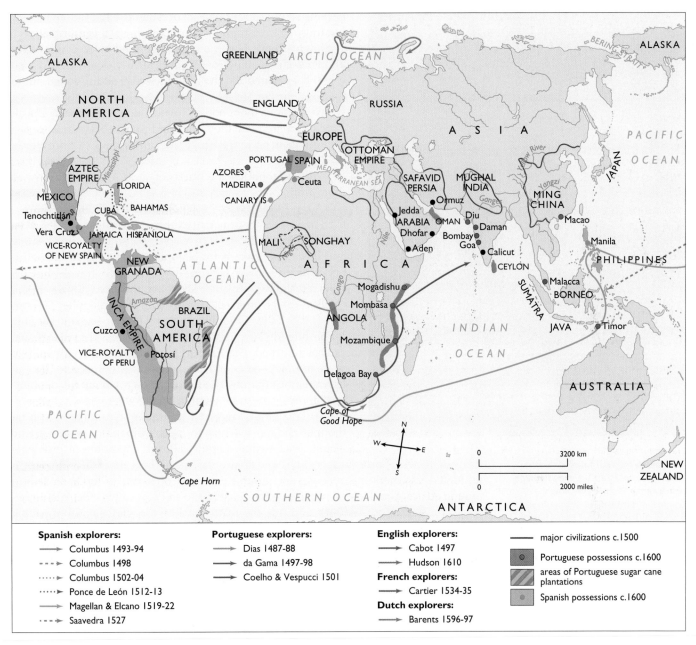

Spanish explorers:
→ Columbus 1493-94
--→ Columbus 1498
····→ Columbus 1502-04
·····→ Ponce de León 1512-13
→ Magellan & Elcano 1519-22
--→ Saavedra 1527

Portuguese explorers:
→ Dias 1487-88
→ da Gama 1497-98
→ Coelho & Vespucci 1501

English explorers:
→ Cabot 1497
→ Hudson 1610

French explorers:
→ Cartier 1534-35

Dutch explorers:
→ Barents 1596-97

— major civilizations c.1500
Portuguese possessions c.1600
areas of Portuguese sugar cane plantations
Spanish possessions c.1600

policy was to outflank the Muslims by sailing down the coast of Africa and striking them from the south. Legends of a Christian king, Prester John, sometimes said to rule in Mesopotamia, sometimes in Africa, led Henry, first, to believe that he would find an ally. Second, Henry was curious about the possibility of oceanic exploration. Finally, he believed that it might be possible to reach India by sailing around Africa, although no-one in Europe had any idea of the size and shape of that continent. At the southwestern tip of Portugal he established a center for the study of navigation and the building of ships. He gathered a staff of experts, who tested existing navigational tools, such as the magnetic compass, astrolabe, and compass, and created new geographical and mathematical tables. They constructed caravels modeled on Arab ships, with lateen sails, which could sail with the wind or tack against it, so they would be able to return, no matter what the direction of the prevailing wind. Caravels with lateen sails

European exploration, 1450–1600.
Spanish and Portuguese explorers and traders had established settlements in South America and the Caribbean by 1600, and commercial depots on the coasts of Africa, India, the Pacific islands, China, and Japan—at a time when English, Dutch, and French explorations of North America had just begun.

Portuguese School, *Vasco da Gama,* **c. 1524.** Gama's 1497–9 expedition on behalf of the Portuguese Crown completed the sea link from Europe around Africa to India. On his next voyage, 1502–3, he established the policy of using military force to create Portuguese power in the Indian Ocean.

became standard for voyages of Atlantic exploration, including those of Christopher Columbus almost a century later.

Slowly, Prince Henry's men attempted a series of explorations, each reaching just a little further down the African coast. They feared the shoals of the coast, and so sailed out to the west, farther out into the ocean, and allowed the northern winds to blow them south, further down the coast. On an expedition in 1444 they captured some 200 Africans and brought them back to Portugal for sale as slaves. Prince Henry died in 1460, but the project continued. As the Portuguese expeditions rounded the hump of west Africa, they proved their profitability as they reached what they called the grain coast, the ivory coast, the gold coast, and the slave coast—each named for its principal exports to Portugal. In 1488, Bartolomeu Dias (*c.* 1450–1500) reached the southern tip of Africa and turned northward for 300 miles. He would have continued onward—toward India—with his two caravels, but his crew refused to go further. The route, however, now lay open.

Dias' career intersected with that of Christopher Columbus (1451–1506). Columbus was in Lisbon seeking support for his intended exploration westward across the Atlantic just as Dias returned. Dias' report made clear that an alternative route to India had been found: there was no need to risk the transatlantic attempt. The Portuguese crown rejected Columbus' appeal, and so he went to Spain, where he was successful. In 1492 he discovered a transatlantic passage, which he thought had carried him to Japan (Cipangu), or at least its vicinity. Meanwhile, disputes at court and domestic problems delayed further Portuguese sailing, and it was not until 1498 that Vasco da Gama (*c.* 1460–1524) made his epic voyage around the coast of Africa to India. In sailing around Africa, Gama chose not to hug the coast but to sail far out into the Atlantic, as far as the Cape Verde Islands, and ride the winds back to the southern tip of Africa. Once he began the voyage northward, there was another touch of irony. The sea captain who guided him from East Africa to India was, according to legend, Ahmad Ibn Majid, the most famous navigator of his day. Thus, Ibn Majid, quite unknowingly, conveyed to India the first of the European Christians, who would soon displace the Arab Muslim merchants and sailors of the Indian Ocean.

Gama made a triumphal return to Lisbon, although he brought back only two of his four ships and only 55 of his 170 men survived. On his return visit in 1502, Gama initiated the policies of destroying ships, persons, and property, and of seizing goods that marked the early centuries of Portuguese conduct in Asia. His ships were armed with cannon, and he was prepared to use them. For example, he confronted a large dhow carrying pilgrims to Mecca. He burned the ship, apparently killing all the people on board, and seized from it 12,000 ducats and goods worth another 10,000. When Gama returned to Lisbon this time, he left behind a permanent armed naval force of five ships to begin to claim control of the waters of the Indian Ocean. In India and the Indian Ocean, Portuguese navies subsequently destroyed the Muslim fleet in 1509, conquered Hormuz at the entrance to the Persian Gulf, established Goa as the capital of Portuguese activities in Asia, captured Malacca in 1511, and opened oceanic trade with the lands of east and Southeast Asia. Wherever they went, they actively sought converts to Christianity, often by force. By establishing its new trade routes to the east, Portugal achieved its economic goals. In 1503 the price of pepper in Lisbon was one-fifth the price in Venice, and thus trade in the eastern Mediterranean between Venice and Alexandria was undermined.

By 1488, when Columbus' plea to the Portuguese court for support was aborted by Dias' voyage, Columbus had already been trying for three years to gain backing for his venture. He was known in Portugal, for he had sailed on various Portuguese ships as far north as the Arctic Circle, south almost to the equator, east to the Aegean, and west to the Azores. Finally, in Spain he received from the newly merged thrones of Ferdinand of Castile and Isabella of Aragon the backing he needed. In his voyage, Columbus depended on two geographical estimates and he got both wrong. He underestimated the total circumference of the earth and he overestimated the total east–west span of the Eurasian continent. The globe was bigger than he thought, and so was the oceanic distance that he had to traverse. And nowhere in his figures was there the space for two continents of which he and the people of Europe knew nothing, despite Leif Eriksson's voyages. When Columbus arrived in the New World, he thought he had reached islands off the eastern coast of Asia. Although he found only a little gold, he believed—and promised his patrons—that an abundance of it yet awaited him. He promised also a virtually limitless supply of cotton, spices and aromatics, timber, and slaves. He characterized the people of the lands he had come upon as ready for conversion to Christianity. He reported all these observations in a letter addressed to Ferdinand and Isabella.

Six months later Columbus embarked on a much larger expedition with seventeen ships, 1200 men, including six priests to carry on the work of conversion, and enough supplies to establish a permanent settlement. The expedition, however, yielded no serious commercial gains and it took Columbus two years to gain support for a third expedition, in 1498, with only six ships. For the first time, he landed on the continental landmass, in what is today Venezuela. Even at the end of his life, after yet another, fourth voyage that brought him to Central America, Columbus recognized neither the enormity of his mistake nor the enormity of his discovery. He never realized that he had not found China, Japan, India, or islands off the coast of Asia. Nor did he realize that he had discovered a "New World."

Amerigo Vespucci (1454–1512) of Florence was the first person clearly to recognize Columbus' error and his success. In 1499, sailing with a Spanish fleet after Columbus' third expedition, Vespucci traveled some 1200 miles along the coast of South America. He recognized clearly that this was a continental landmass, but he did not yet realize which one. In a second voyage, 1501–2, this one under the flag of Portugal, he traveled some 2400 miles down the coast of South America. He reported carefully on all that he saw: humans and their customs and tools, animals, plants, and hints of great treasures. Unlike Columbus, however, Vespucci was cautious: "The natives told us of gold and other metals and many miracle-working drugs, but I am one of those followers of Saint Thomas, who are slow to believe. Time will reveal everything" (Boorstin, p. 250). On his return to Spain, Vespucci was asked by Queen Isabella to establish a school for pilots and a clearing house for information brought back from the New World. In 1507 the clergyman and mapmaker Martin Waldseemüller published a new map of the world as known at the time, and on it he named the new western areas "America." In 1538, Gerardus Mercator published his large and influential map of the world designating two new continents as North America and South America. Vespucci himself died in 1512 of malaria, contracted on his voyages.

Only the eastern coast of the Americas was known to Europeans when Vasco Nuñez de Balboa (1474–1517) followed the guidance of one of his Native American allies, crossed the Isthmus of Panama, climbed a peak, and, in 1513, became the first European to see the Pacific Ocean. Four years later, Balboa was falsely accused of treason toward the king of Spain and was beheaded. With the recognition that the Americas

SOURCE

The Journal of Columbus' First Voyage to the Americas

Columbus kept a day-by-day journal of his first voyage. Columbus' original has been lost, but fortunately the priest Bartolomé de Las Casas (1474–1566) prepared an abstract that he used in writing his own Historia de las Indias. *Columbus' leading biographer in English, Samuel Eliot Morison, calls the abstract, "The most important document in the entire history of American discovery." This account of what Columbus saw and how he related to it is written sometimes in the first person of Columbus, sometimes in the third person, as the voice of Las Casas. Note especially the overwhelming importance given to religion:*

Prologue: Your Highnesses, as Catholic Christians and Princes devoted to the Holy Christian Faith and the propagators thereof, and enemies of the sect of Mahomet and of all idolatries and heresies, resolved to send me, Christopher Columbus, to the said regions of India, to see the said princes and peoples and lands and the disposition of them and of all, and the manner which may be undertaken their conversion to our Holy Faith, and ordained that I should not go by (the usual way) to the Orient, but by the route of the Occident, by which no one to this day knows for sure that anyone has gone …

12 October 1492: At two hours after midnight appeared the land, at a distance of two leagues … Presently they saw naked people, and the Admiral went ashore in his barge, and [others] followed. The Admiral broke out the royal standard, and the captains [displayed] two banners of the Green Cross, which the Admiral flew on all the vessels as a signal, with an F and a Y, one at one arm of the cross and the other on the other, and over each letter his or her crown … and said that they should bear faith and witness how he before them all was taking, as in fact he took, possession of the said island for the King and Queen …

15 October: It was my wish to bypass no island without taking possession, although having taken one you can claim all …

22 October: All this night and today I was here, waiting to see if the king here or other people would bring gold or anything substantial, and many of this people came, like the others of the other islands, as naked and as painted, some of them white, others red, others black, and [painted] in many ways … any little thing I gave them, and also our coming, they considered a great wonder, and believed that we had come from the sky …

1 November: It is certain that this is the mainland and that I am before Zayto [Zaytun] and Quisay [Hangzhou], [two great port cities of China] 100 leagues more or less distant the one from the other …

6 November: If they had access to devout religious persons knowing the language, they would all turn Christian, and so I hope in Our Lord that Your Highnesses will do something about it with much care … And after your days (for we are all mortal) … you will be well received before the eternal Creator …

12 November: Yesterday came aboard the ship a dugout with six young men, and five came on board; these I ordered to be detained and I am bringing them. Afterwards I sent to a house which is on the western bank of the river, and they brought seven women, small and large, and three boys. I did this because the [Indian] men would behave better in Spain with women of their country than without them …

27 November: Your Highnesses ought not to consent that any foreigner does business or sets foot here, except Christian Catholics, since this was the end and the beginning of the enterprise …

22 December: The Indians were so free, and the Spaniards so covetous and overreaching, that it was not enough that for a lace-tip or a little piece of glass and crockery or other things of no value, the Indians should give them what they asked; even without giving anything they [the Spaniards] wanted to get and take all, which the Admiral had always forbidden …

23 December: In that hour … more than 1000 persons had come to the ship, and that all brought something that they owned, and that before they come within half a crossbow shot of the ship, they stand up in their canoes with what they brought in their hands, saying "Take! Take!" (Morrison, pp. 41–179)

were continental in size, and that another ocean lay between them and Asia, Charles V of Spain commissioned Ferdinand Magellan (c. 1480–1521) to sail west, find a passage around the southern tip of South America, and proceed across the Pacific—no matter how big it was—and reach the Spice Islands of East Asia. Magellan set out in 1519 with five ships and about 250 sailors from several different European countries. The voyage became the first circumnavigation of the globe, yielding the first accurate picture of the full magnitude of the planet and completing the picture of most of its main contours. It took just twelve days less than three years. Only eighteen men completed the trip. Magellan himself was killed in a skirmish with Mactan tribal warriors in the Philippine island of Cebu.

OCEANIA

One inhabited continent remained unmapped. Europeans had touched on the northern and western coasts of Australia, but without gaining a clear idea of the continent's size, shape, or character. In 1642, the Dutch East India Company commissioned Abel Tasman (c. 1603–59), a Dutch navigator, to explore the continent. On two voyages, Tasman circumnavigated Australia without actually exploring it. In the process, he also discovered the island later named Tasmania. In 1768, the British government commissioned James Cook (1728–79) to carry out astronomical observations in Tahiti as well as to explore the south Pacific in search of a Great Southern Continent which had been rumored to exist, but whose existence was not proved. He sailed on the *Endeavour*, a sturdy 368 ton, 98 feet long ship, of the sort used to carry coal. He took along with him the young scientist Joseph Banks (1743–1820), who made vast contributions to botany and zoology on the basis of his findings on this voyage. Indeed because of Banks' discoveries, one of the most important harbors in southeast Australia was named Botany Bay. Cook charted the coasts of New Zealand and explored the eastern coast of Australia, but he found no other continent. His voyage of two years and eleven months became the second circumnavigation of the earth. On a second, even more adventuresome voyage, 1772–5, Cook saw the mist, fogs, and icebergs of the Antarctic Ocean, but never landed on or even saw the continent, although he reached within 75 miles of its coast. With these major oceanic adventures, and others, the main contours of the world's oceans and landmasses became known, and, at least geographically speaking, all humanity had come to live in a single, interconnected world.

LEGACIES TO THE FUTURE
WHAT DIFFERENCE DO THEY MAKE?

Voyages of exploration, trade, conquest, and settlement evoke a sense of wonder at the courage, daring, and skill of the captains and sailors who embarked on them, and the governments and businesspeople who organized and financed them. Each participant was called by a different set of values: the desire to chart the unknown; the pressure to find a new home; the quest for profit; the urge to proselytize; the lust for conquest; the competition for superiority. Often, many of these motives were mixed together. Their legacy has left us with admiration for the conquest for the skill of individual European captains to sail into the unknown with such limited ships and equipment. The legacy of these people is the achievement of a geographically known and integrated globe. It is not, however, a single, simple legacy, but a variegated set of mixed legacies that includes competition, greed, self-righteousness, and violence in the achievement of global integration. Few participants prepared for oceanic voyages with the greater good of the entire world at heart. Most, instead, sought benefits for themselves, their region or nation, or their religious group. They looked out on a huge and diverse world from relatively narrow and often self-interested perspectives.

By 1500 European traders had established a permanent connection between the eastern and western hemispheres for the first time, following Columbus' voyages across the Atlantic and Magellan's circumnavigation of the world. Inspired by the early explorations of Prince Henry the Navigator around the west coast of Africa, Portuguese sailors rounded the Cape of Good Hope and opened new routes into the Indian Ocean. These explorations followed centuries of western European economic expansion, national consolidation, and intellectual renaissance. Explorers were motivated by their mixed desire for knowledge, profit, national aggrandizement, and Christian proselytizing.

Review Questions

- Of the groups—Polynesians, Malays, Indians, Chinese, Arabs, and Europeans—discussed in this chapter and in Chapter 12, why do you think that the Europeans were the first to circumnavigate the globe?
- How did the Portuguese displace the Arabs as the predominant maritime power in the Indian Ocean?
- Why do you think that Columbus could not, or did not, recognize that he had not reached East Asia? (There is no single correct answer to this question.)
- What were the demographic, economic, and social effects of the plague in the fourteenth century?
- What was the European Renaissance? To what did degree did it develop from contacts with non-European peoples?

Suggested Readings

PRINCIPAL SOURCES

Adas, Michael, ed. *Islamic and European Expansion* (Philadelphia: Temple University Press, 1993). Key collection of historiographical essays on major topics in world history, 1200–1900. Articles by Eaton and Tucker on Islam, and McNeill on "gunpowder empires" are especially helpful for this section.

Boorstin, Daniel J. *The Discoverers* (New York: Random House, 1983). Extremely well-written, engaging history of four kinds of invention and discovery. One is maritime, mostly European explorers and cartographers 1400–1800.

Chaudhuri, K.N. *Trade and Civilization in the Indian Ocean: An Economic History from the Rise of Islam to 1750* (Cambridge: Cambridge University Press, 1985). A survey of goods, traders, ships, regulations, and competition among those who sailed and claimed to control the Indian Ocean.

Crosby, Alfred W. *Ecological Imperialism: The Biological Expansion of Europe, 900–1900* (Cambridge: Cambridge University Press, 1986). The biological—mostly destructive—impact of European settlement around the world: a tragedy for native peoples from the Americas to Oceania.

Curtin, Philip. *Cross-Cultural Trade in World History* (Cambridge: Cambridge University Press, 1984). Classical statement of the significance and ubiquity of trade diasporas.

SECONDARY SOURCES

Aquinas, St. Thomas. *Summa contra Gentiles* and *Governance of Rulers* (excerpts) in *Introduction to Contemporary Civilization in the West*, cited below. Aquinas defined the field of thirteenth-century Roman Catholic theology—and beyond.

Bloch, Marc. *Feudal Society*, 2 vols. (Chicago: University of Chicago Press, 1961). Classic, if dated, comprehensive view of the workings of feudalism in western Europe.

Boccaccio, Giovanni. *The Decameron*, trans. by Frances Winwar (New York: Modern Library, 1955). Delightful tales, set against the background of the plague raging through western Europe in the 1340s.

Braudel, Fernand. *Capitalism and Material Life, 1400–1800*, trans. from the French by Miriam Kochan (New York: Harper and Row, 1973). Comprehensive survey of the beginnings of the modern capitalist system in Europe.

——. *The Mediterranean and the Mediterranean World in the Age of Phillip II*, 2 vols, trans. Sian Reynolds (New York: Harper and Row, 1973). Comprehensive survey of the beginnings of the modern capitalist system in Europe.

Cassirer, Ernst, Paul Oskar Kristeller, and John Herman Randall, jr. eds. *The Renaissance Philosophy of Man* (Chicago, IL: University of Chicago Press, 1948).

Chaudhuri, K. N. *Asia Before Europe* (Cambridge: Cambridge University Press, 1990). Survey of the economic and political systems of Asia before the impact of colonialism and the industrial revolution. Comprehensive, comparative, and thoughtful.

Cohn, Samuel K., Jr. *The Black Death Transformed: Disease and Culture in Early Renaissance Europe* (London: Arnold, 2002). Studies and summarizes the research on the nature of the plague and its longer term effects.

Columbia College. Columbia University. *Introduction to Contemporary Civilization in the West*, Vol. 1 (New York: Columbia University Press, 2nd ed., 1954). Very well-chosen, long source readings from leading thinkers of the time and place. Vol. I covers about 1000–1800.

Fernandez-Armesto, Felipe. *Columbus* (New York: Oxford University Press, 1991). Careful, sensitive biography of the man and his times.

Frank, Andre Gunder and Barry K. Gills, eds. *The World System: Five Hundred Years or Five Thousand?* (London: Routledge, 1993). In this somewhat tendentious, but well argued, account, globalization is nothing new.

Gabrieli, F. "The Transmission of Learning and Literary Influences to Western Europe,' in Holt, P.M., Ann K.S. Lambton, and Bernard Lewis, eds. *The Cambridge History of Islam, Vol. 2B: Islamic Society and Civilization* (Cambridge, MA: Cambridge University Press, 1970, pp. 851–89). Comprehensive summary of the influence of Islamic learning on Europe, especially good on contrasting different time periods.

The Hammond Atlas of World History ed. Richard Overy (Maplewood, NJ: Hammond, 1999). Excellent, standard historical atlas.

Havighurst, Alfred F., ed. *The Pirenne Thesis: Analysis, Criticism, and Revision* (Lexington, MA: D.C. Heath, rev. ed. 1969). Well-selected pieces from Pirenne, his critics, and supporters. Well introduced, supported, and summarized, although mostly European in orientation.

Hohenberg, Paul M. and Lynn Hollen Lees. *The Making of Urban Europe, 1000–1950.* (Cambridge: Harvard University Press, 1985). Brief, but comprehensive text on the significance of cities to the history of Europe. Special attention to the social development of cities and their residents.

Kee, Howard Clark, *et al. Christianity: A Social and Cultural History* (New York: Macmillan, 1991). An accessible and insightful introduction to a huge subject.

Lindberg, Carter. "The Late Middle Ages and the Reformations of the Sixteenth Century," in Kee, *et al. Christianity*, pp. 257–423. Excellent survey.

Levenson, Jay A. *Circa 1492: Art in the Age of Exploration* (Washington: National Gallery of Art, 1991). Catalogue of an astounding art exhibit, covering the arts in all the major regions in the world at the time of Columbus' voyages.

Morison, Samuel Eliot, trans. and ed. *Journals and Other Documents on the Life and Voyages of Christopher Columbus* (New York: The Heritage Press, 1963). The crucial documents.

Nicholas, David. *The Evolution of the Medieval World* (New York: Longman, 1992). Useful survey.

Pirenne, Henri. *Medieval Cities: Their Origins and the Revival of Trade*, trans. from the French by Frank D. Halsey (Princeton: Princeton University Press, 1925). Classic statement of the importance of free merchants to the rise of commercial cities and the development of the modern world. Dated, and more limited than claimed, but pathbreaking and enormously influential.

——. *Mohammed and Charlemagne*, trans. from the 10th French edition by Bernard Miall (New York: W.W. Norton, 1939). Key revisionist text citing the Islamic victories in the Mediterranean as the end of Roman Europe and the beginning of rebirth in the north under Charlemagne.

Polanyi, Karl, Conrad M. Arensberg, and Harry W. Pearson, eds. *Trade and Market in the Early Empires* (Chicago: The Free Press, 1957). Fundamental argument by historical anthropologists that early trade was mostly regulated by rulers and priests.

Reynolds, Susan. *Fiefs and Vassals* (Oxford: Clarendon Press, 1994). Scholarly, influential examination of "feudalism," arguing that the word is misused to cover too wide a variety of regional and temporal patterns.

Subrahmanyam, Sanjay. *The Career and Legend of Vasco da Gama* (Cambridge: Cambridge University Press, 1997). The most thorough available account of the man, his contributions, and the historical puzzles surrounding them, presented in overwhelming scholarly detail.

Tuchman, Barbara. *A Distant Mirror: The Calamitous Fourteenth Century* (New York: Knopf, 1978). Engaging history of a century filled with war and plague.

Wills, John E., Jr. "Maritime Asia, 1500–1800: the Interactive Emergence of European Domination," *American Historical Review* XCVIII, No. 1 (February 1993), 83–05. Survey of European entrance into and domination of Indian Ocean and Chinese sea lanes.

⊙ World History Documents CD-ROM

THE UNIFICATION OF WORLD TRADE

NEW PHILOSOPHIES FOR NEW TRADE PATTERNS, 1500–1776

KEY TOPICS
- The Expansion of Europe and the Birth of Capitalism
- The Empires of Spain and Portugal
- Trade and Religion in Western Europe: The Protestant Reformation and the Catholic Reformation
- The Nation-State
- Russia's Empire under Peter the Great
- Diverse Cultures, Diverse Trade Systems
- The Influence of World Trade: What Difference Does It Make?

THE EXPANSION OF EUROPE AND THE BIRTH OF CAPITALISM

By 1500, ocean voyages of exploration and trade had brought the eastern and western hemispheres together, initiating a new phase of world history. During the next three centuries most of the regions of the world began to enter into a single system of trade and exchange. The organization of this emerging system generally followed the economic principles of capitalism, being dedicated to the pursuit of private economic profit through the private ownership of wealth and the means of producing wealth.

Capitalism claimed to allow individuals to exchange their products and labor in free, unregulated markets. It had little place for the restrictive rules of Church and government. Free-market exchange would determine the prices of goods and labor by reaching a balance between supply and demand. These market prices would then influence what would be produced and what would be consumed. The lure of the market would encourage people to invest their capital, or accumulated wealth, in economic activities that might earn profits (or suffer losses). Despite these free-market claims and their desire to be free of regulation, capitalists frequently persuaded governments to support and assist them in their money-making projects. In exchange, capitalists lent their financial support to government.

Major west European governments had been following principles of mercantilism, the belief that government should regulate trade—especially by restricting the outflow of gold and silver—for the greater strength of the state. Slowly these governments were persuaded that allowing businessmen more freedom of trade would in fact benefit the state even more by generating more taxable wealth. Capitalists and the governments worked together to achieve the goals of both: protection and encouragement for the businessmen, taxes for the state.

Western European businessmen led in sponsoring new international trade initiatives that emphasized private profit and national aggrandizement. As a result, the trading centers of northwestern Europe grew ever larger. By 1700, London had a population of 550,000, Paris, 530,000, Lisbon, 188,000, and Amsterdam, 172,000. Each of

capitalism An economic system characterized by private or corporate ownership of the means of production and by private control over decisions on prices, production, and distribution of goods in a free, competitive market of supply and demand.

mercantilism An economic policy pursued by many European nations between the sixteenth and eighteenth centuries. It aimed to strengthen an individual nation's economic power at the expense of its rivals by stockpiling reserves of bullion, which involved government regulation of trade.

Opposite **Imam Quli**
boats being repulse
at Hormuz. Miniatu
century.

these cities was both a national capital and a major trading center. Economic and political interests reinforced one another.

In western Europe, overseas trade was restructuring public life, but it was not equally important in other parts of the world. In several very large empires, government by itself continued to be a formidable force and more important than private business. The largest city in Europe, for example, was not an Atlantic Ocean port but Constantinople (modern-day Istanbul), the capital of the Ottoman Empire. It, too, was an important commercial city, serving the eastern Mediterranean and the Middle East, but it owed its size—700,000 residents—and importance more to its political role than to its trade. In India, China, Japan, and Southeast Asia, too, government authorities generally dominated business interests. There were exceptions, but government control was the pattern.

Each major region of the world also had a very different experience in confronting the new international world system of trade being fashioned by the Europeans. The Americas, for example, succumbed almost immediately. The Chinese, on the other hand, remained somewhat independent of the system until the mid-nineteenth century, and in some ways China actually dominated the system. Even though the Chinese and Indians were not the shippers carrying the goods overseas, it was their products and their economies that evoked a very large proportion of international trade. Chinese products—especially tea, silk, and porcelain—were the objects of a great deal of the trade. The Europeans sailed in order to get them—as well as the spices and textiles of India and Indonesia, and the gold and, later, some 10 million enslaved people of Africa. Almost half the silver of the New World mines went to China to pay for exports to Europe. Asians and Africans may not have sailed as widely and aggressively as Europeans did after 1500, but it was the goods of Asia and Africa that motivated the European voyages. Later, as in the Americas, Europeans would seek ever greater control over the terms of trade. Finally they would impose colonial rule, in part to create new terms of trade more favorable to themselves. In many respects, these societies let others dominate ocean trade because of geographical factors as well as the belief that they produced everything they needed at home.

THE EMPIRES OF SPAIN AND PORTUGAL

The Ottoman conquest of Constantinople in 1453 gave it control of the eastern Mediterranean trade and encouraged the Atlantic countries to seek new routes to Asia, inspiring Columbus' and Vasco da Gama's voyages of exploration. The first European nations to dominate the new overseas trade and colonization were the Spanish and the Portuguese. Both faced directly on the Atlantic Ocean. Portugal's rulers saw the Atlantic as their front door to the world. Spain's rulers, just consolidating their country in 1492, saw it as a new route to riches, power, and proselytization.

Spain's New World Conquests

The four voyages of Christopher Columbus between 1492 and 1504 revealed to the Spanish crown some of the opportunities for agricultural development, religious conversion, and exploitation of resources in gold and silver to be found in the Americas. Spanish settlers began to colonize the islands of the Caribbean and the north coast of South America. In response to tales of great riches, Spanish conquistadors marched inland to conquer what they could. In 1519, Hernán Cortés began his expedition from Veracruz with 600 Spaniards, a few guns, and sixteen horses. Because the Aztecs under Moctezuma II engaged in frequent wars and collected extensive tribute from various

SOURCE

Adam Smith on Capitalism

By the late eighteenth century, as European economies were expanding, they became the subject of discussion and debate among businesspeople, political leaders, and philosophers. Adam Smith (1723–90) had already established his reputation as a moral philosopher before he turned to writing what became his most famous work. In 1776 Smith published The Wealth of Nations, a book of a thousand pages, the first systematic explanation of a newly emerging philosophy of economics, later called capitalism.

In contrast to the mercantilist views of his day, Smith argued that national wealth was not to be measured by treasuries of precious metals, but rather by quantities of productivity and of trade. He opened his great work with an illustration from a pin factory where a division of labor into specialized tasks of production increased output dramatically. Smith further argued that when workers specialize in what they do best, and then exchange their products in the market, productivity increases. The competitive free market guides production: Goods that consumers want to buy attract higher prices, and producers supply them in order to earn good profits; unwanted goods earn no profits, and producers stop producing them. This law of supply and demand in the market, argues Smith, leads to the production of the amounts and kinds of goods that suit the wishes of consumers and the capacity of producers. According to Smith's Law of Accumulation, profits are reinvested in further production.

Smith reached a new and surprising conclusion: Wealth comes not from the command of a ruler, nor the regulations of the clergy, nor the altruism of members of the community, but as a result of people pursuing their own economic self-interest and exchanging the fruits of their labor in the market.

It is not from the benevolence of the butcher, the brewer, or the baker that we expect our dinner, but from their regard to their self-interest. We address ourselves, not to their humanity, but to their self-love, and never talk to them of our necessities, but of their advantages. (Smith, p. 14)

Although Smith did not use the term, today we call the system he analyzed capitalism— that is, most wealth, or capital, rests in private, non-governmental hands, and economic decisions on price, supply, and demand are made through the free market rather than by government decision. Critics of this capitalist market system, in which buyer and seller negotiate freely over prices, equated capitalism's self-interest with greed, but Smith explained how competition transformed self-interest into community benefit: If a greedy producer charges too much for his goods, someone else will undercut him and lower prices will result; if he pays his employees too little, they will abandon him and seek work elsewhere. Out of the conflicting self-interests of individual members of the society, paradoxically, social harmony will emerge. Smith, who was a professor of moral philosophy at the University of Edinburgh, disagreed with those who said that rulers or priests must regulate the economy to achieve equity. Like an "invisible hand," the impersonal market would do the job.

Believing that the free, unregulated market would correct most economic imbalances, Smith opposed government intervention. He argued for a hands-off government policy of laissez-faire toward the market—that is, let people do as they choose. But he did recognize that some necessities for economic growth were beyond the powers of any single, small producer. "The erection and maintenance of the public works which facilitate the commerce of any country, such as good roads, bridges, navigable canals, harbors, et cetera, must require very

different degrees of expense" (Vol. 5, p. 1), and therefore Smith urged government to promote these public works. He believed that education was fundamental to economic productivity. Private education was more effective than public education, but government-supported public education was better than none.

Smith recognized, of course, that the market did not always succeed in balancing supply and demand. Huge businesses that formed virtual monopolies could control whole industries and manipulate market forces. Their size gave them unfair leverage and Smith wanted them broken up. The Wealth of Nations attacked the British East India Company, the joint stock company that monopolized virtually all of Britain's trade in Asia and had even become the acting government of Bengal in India. Smith argued that its monopoly should be broken. His plea, however, did not bring about a change.

Capitalism was the prevailing economic philosophy in Britain in the years of its economic supremacy in the nineteenth century, and the new system spread to many other countries as well. As we shall see in the following chapters, many critics blamed capitalism for the inhumanity and cruelty of the slave trade, the seizure of colonies overseas, and the vulnerability of workers at home. Smith understood these problems, but argued that they were corruptions of the market system rather than natural products of it. He condemned slavery as a form of kidnapping and theft of human beings, rather than a free-market exchange. Similarly he deplored the European destruction of the Native American states and populations as a violation of human ethics:

The savage injustice of the Europeans rendered an event which ought to have been beneficial to all ruinous and destructive to several of those unfortunate countries. (Smith, p. 416)

---

laissez-faire An economic policy of non-interference by government in the working of the market and the economic affairs of individuals.

monopoly The exclusive control over the production or supply of a particular commodity or service for which there is no substitute.

Emperor Atahualpa arrested by Francisco Pizarro in 1532. When Pizarro landed on the northern coast of Peru on May 13, 1532 he brought with him a force of 200 men with horses, guns, and swords. The Inca Emperor Atahualpa, backed up by thousands of troops, felt he had little to fear from the Spanish and, as this contemporary Peruvian drawing shows, he accepted Pizarro's seemingly friendly invitation to meet accompanied only by his bodyguards. It was a trap, and Pizarro arrested and later executed him.

Inca-Spanish wooden drinking vessel, Peru, c. 1650. This painted Inca ritual drinking vessel made of wood, known as a *kero*, represents people of three different cultures: to the left, an Inca dignitary; in the center, a Spaniard playing a trumpet; and on the right, one of the earliest depictions of a black African in South America, a man playing a drum.

tribes living in the region, Cortés was joined by thousands of Native Americans from the various states through which he passed, who wished to overthrow the powerful Aztec empire at Tenochtitlán, modern-day Mexico City. Cortés' small force entered the city without a struggle on November 8, 1519, possibly helped by a woman, Malinche or Marina, who became his mistress and translator. The peace didn't last, however, and after the Spaniards massacred several Aztec leaders during a festival, the population revolted. They killed Moctezuma believing that he had collaborated with Cortés, and they forced the conquistadors to leave the city on June 30, 1520. Cortés suffered heavy losses, perhaps as many as two-thirds of his men and several horses, but the Spaniards reached Tlaxcala, where their new Native American allies nursed them back to health and helped them plan to retake Tenochtitlán. The Spaniards conquered the capital city again on August 13, 1521 after a bitter four-month siege, and the empire fell to them. In the next twenty years they captured the Yucatán and most of Central America, although revolts continued in the region. Cortés became ruler of the Kingdom of New Spain, reorganized in 1535 as the Vice-Royalty of New Spain.

In South America, the Inca Empire of the west coast and Andes Mountains became accessible to Spanish conquistadors after Vasco Nuñez de Balboa found a portage across the Isthmus of Panama in 1513. Now the Spanish could transport their ships from the Atlantic coast overland across the Isthmus and sail south along the Pacific Coast to Peru. Rumors of great stores of gold encouraged these voyages. Like the Aztecs, the Inca were divided. In 1525, after the death of Huayna Capec, possibly from smallpox, a civil war broke out between two of his sons—Huáscar and Atahualpa—over who should rule the empire. Fighting was fierce and ended only in 1532, when Atahuallpa captured Huáscar and executed him In the same year, Francisco Pizarro, leading a force of some two hundred men, captured Atahualpa. Although given a room full of gold as ransom for the emperor's life, Pizarro nevertheless feared a revolt and killed him. In 1533 he captured the Inca capital, Cuzco. The Spanish conquistadors fought among themselves for years until Spain established the Vice-Royalty of Peru in the mid-sixteenth century as the South American counterpart to the Vice-Royalty of New Spain in the north. Revolts against the Spaniards continued until they captured and beheaded the last Inca emperor, Tupac Amarú, in 1572.

How had a few hundred Spanish soldiers and their Indian allies succeeded in overthrowing the two largest empires in the Americas? The conquered Native Americans:

- were divided and fought among themselves. The Native Americans were not a single united people, but many different, competitive, and even warring peoples. In conquering the

AT A GLANCE : THE INTERCONNECTING WORLD

DATE	EUROPE	THE AMERICAS	ASIA AND AFRICA
1500	■ Communero revolt in Spain (1520–21) ■ Luther excommunicated (1521)	■ Four voyages of Christopher Columbus (1492–1504) ■ Cortés conquers Tenochtitlán (1521)	■ Portuguese establish trading posts in East Africa (1505) ■ Portugal captures Goa, India (1510) ■ Portuguese missionaries arrive in China (1514)
1525	■ Henry VIII becomes head of new Anglican church (1534) ■ First stock exchange in Antwerp (1538) ■ Calvin establishes Presbyterian theocracy in Geneva (1541)	■ Pizarro captures Inca emperor Atahualpa (1532) ■ Potosí silver mine discovered (1545)	■ Mughals invade India (1526) ■ St. Francis Xavier arrives in Japan (1549)
1550	■ Council of Trent (1545–63) ■ End of Hundred Years War (1558) ■ Tobacco first introduced into Europe (1559); potato (c. 1565)	■ Portuguese begin sugar cultivation in Brazil (c. 1560)	■ Akbar consolidates Mughal Empire (1556–1605) ■ Spanish capture Manila, Philippines (1571) ■ Portuguese establish colony in Angola (1571)
1575	■ Spanish Armada defeated by England (1588) ■ Henry IV of France issues Edict of Nantes (1598)		■ Matteo Ricci arrives in China (1582) ■ Japan invades Korea (1592)
1600	■ Dutch, English, and French East India companies founded ■ Holland wins independence from Spain; Bank of Amsterdam established (1609)		■ Tokugawa shoguns begin consolidation of Japan (1603) ■ Christianity outlawed in Japan (1606) ■ Dutch found Batavia (Jakarta), Indonesia (1619)
1625	■ Portugal declares independence from Spain (1640) ■ Russia captures Siberia (1649)		■ Manchus conquer China and form Qing dynasty (1644)
1650	■ English Navigation Act (1651) ■ Louis XIV of France, the "Sun King" (1643–1715)		■ Dutch capture Cape of Good Hope (1652)
1675	■ War of the League of Augsburg (1688–97) ■ Bank of England created (1694)		■ Qing dynasty establishes "Canton system" (1683)
1700	■ Peter the Great founds St. Petersburg (1704) ■ War of the Spanish Succession (1702–13) ■ Act of Union creates Great Britain (1707)		■ Edo, Japan, has 1 million people
1725	■ War of Austrian Succession (1740–8)		
1750	■ Seven Years War (1756–63) ■ Adam Smith, *The Wealth of Nations* (1776)	■ War of American Independence (1775–81)	■ After English victory at Plassey, English gain Bengal (1757)

dominant groups—Moctezuma's Aztecs in Mexico and Atahualpa's Inca in Peru—the Spanish found many allies among the enemies of these groups. In addition, the Inca were weakened by their own civil war.

- lacked the Spaniards' military technology and organization. The Spanish introduced firearms, steel armor and weapons, and horses—animals that had never previously been seen in the Americas. The Spaniards also fought differently from the indigenous populations, shooting from a distance rather than engaging in the hand-to-hand warfare practiced by the Aztecs.

World exploration. The limitations on sea routes through the Middle East drove the trading nations of western Europe to seek alternate maritime passages to Asia. European navigators and cartographers rapidly built a map of the globe which included, by sailing west, the "New World" of the Americas and, by sailing south, a passage around Africa, linking with the Arab trading routes of the Indian Ocean. The voyages of the Ming Chinese admiral Zheng He were undertaken to demonstrate China's strength even more than for trade.

- were demoralized when their commanders-in-chief, Moctezuma II in Mexico and Atahualpa in Peru, were captured. The Indian empires were highly centralized so that the capture and murder of their leaders left them disorganized. Less centralized and more remote groups, like the Araucanians of central Chile, held out far longer, winning a revered place in Latin American history and poetry.
- succumbed to European diseases, such as smallpox. The Native Americans had no immunity to these diseases that were new to the Americas. The diseases proved far more deadly than the warfare.

Legend had it that the Indians also viewed the Spanish as gods returning to their homelands and therefore deserving of obedience rather than resistance, but recent scholarship has dispelled this myth as a fiction later created by the Spanish.

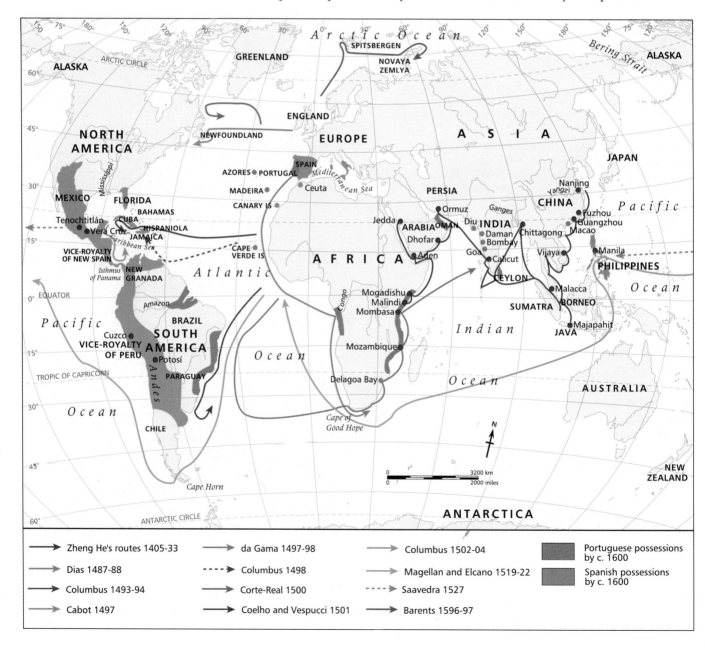

Zheng He's routes 1405-33		da Gama 1497-98		Columbus 1502-04		Portuguese possessions by c. 1600
Dias 1487-88		Columbus 1498		Magellan and Elcano 1519-22		Spanish possessions by c. 1600
Columbus 1493-94		Corte-Real 1500		Saavedra 1527		
Cabot 1497		Coelho and Vespucci 1501		Barents 1596-97		

Making the Conquests Pay. After the conquests, the Spanish began to reorganize the economies of the Americas. They established the *encomienda* system, assigning the taxes and the labor of local Indian populations to Spanish colonists who were also to convert them to Christianity, if possible. The Indians were enslaved under conditions of great cruelty. The *encomienda* system was first established on the island of Hispaniola, where in twenty years the Indian population fell from several million to 29,000. Humane voices, especially of priests such as Bartolomé de Las Casas, opposed the *encomienda* system, but it continued until so many Indians died that it could function no longer. In most of Mexico and Peru the system had ended by the late 1500s, but it operated for another century in Venezuela; for another two centuries, until 1791, in Chile; and until the early 1800s in Paraguay.

The systems that replaced it were not much more humane. The *repartimiento* system in central Mexico and the similar *mita* system in Peru forced Indians into low-paid or unpaid labor for a portion of each year on Spanish-owned farms, in mines and workshops, and on public works projects. These systems, too, were forms of unofficial slavery. Not all labor was coerced, however. Spanish-owned plantations or *haciendas*, agricultural estates producing commercial crops and livestock, employed both free and indentured labor. The *haciendas* often produced commercially the newly imported products of the eastern hemisphere—wheat, cattle, pigs, sheep, chickens, horses, and mules—in addition to the indigenous local crops of maize, potatoes, and manioc (cassava).

Perhaps the worst conditions existed in silver mines, which also used paid labor at very low wages. The immense Potosí mine in Upper Peru (today's Bolivia) employed 40,000 Indian miners in the seventeenth century. Tunnels were dug that destroyed the landscape, and working conditions were inhuman. Children were forced to crawl through cracks and were often made to work without breaks.

As sugar plantations were introduced into the Caribbean islands and into Portuguese-held Brazil, Indian laborers were unable or unwilling to perform the gang labor of the cane fields, so slaves were imported by the millions from Africa. African slaves also worked the tobacco, cacao, and indigo plantations.

From the Spanish perspective, the most valuable products of the Americas throughout the sixteenth century were gold and silver. The mine at Potosí, discovered in 1545, was the largest silver mine in the world. Smaller mines were opened in Mexico in 1545 and 1558. In 1556 a new method of separating silver from ore by using mercury, available from Almadén in Spain, was discovered. Between 1550 and 1800 Mexico and South America produced more than 80 percent of the world's silver and more than 70 percent of its gold. The precious metals were exported each year from Latin America eastward to Europe and westward to

encomienda A concession from the Spanish crown to a colonist, giving him permission to exact tribute from a specified number of Indians living in a certain area.

repartimiento A system by which the Spanish crown allowed colonists to employ Indians for forced labor.

mita A system of forced labor in Peru, begun under Inca rule, by which Indian communities were required to contribute a set number of laborers for public works for a given period.

hacienda A large rural estate in Spanish America, originating with Spanish colonialization in the sixteenth century.

Plan of Potosí and the Cerro Rico (Rich Hill), Upper Peru. This seventeenth-century painting shows Potosí and the hills in which the lucrative silver mines were located. The mines at Potosí employed some 40,000 poorly paid Indian laborers and tens of thousands of horses—shown in this painting ascending and descending the hills—to transport the material and drive the machinery.

the Philippines, where the Spanish had captured Manila in 1571 and established it as their chief trade center for East Asia. They were ultimately used to pay for European purchases of silks, tea, textiles, and spices from India and China. Between one-third and one-half of all American silver produced between 1527 and 1821 found its way to China. The Mexican peso became a legal currency in China. Asian traders demanded payment in gold and especially silver because Europe itself produced very little of interest to them.

Merchant Profits. The gold and silver mines of the Americas brought enslavement and poverty to the Native Americans, and they benefited the Spaniards less than the merchants of Antwerp, Genoa, Amsterdam, London, and Paris. The Spanish did not have the commercial infrastructure to employ their newly captured resources in profitable investments, and they lacked the ships to carry the trade generated by the new finds of gold and silver. The experienced merchants of the trade cities of Europe organized the necessary commercial services. They exchanged the raw metals for cash and bills of exchange, provided loans to tide over the period from the arrival of one shipment of silver to the next, arranged the purchase of goods needed by the Spanish, and supplied the necessary shipping. In the sixteenth century, the most important of these commercial centers was Antwerp (Belgium), with its skilled and wealthy merchants from Antwerp and from England, France, Portugal, Italy, Spain, and Germany.

Warfare and Bankruptcy. Many regions of Europe at this time were "owned" by particular families, who had the responsibility to protect them and the rights to tax them and bequeath them to others. These families often intermarried—and whole countries changed rulers. Charles V (r. 1515–56) inherited Spain and the Spanish colonies in Africa, the Americas, Naples, and Sicily from his mother's parents, Ferdinand of Aragon and Isabella of Castile. From his father's family, the House of Burgundy, he inherited the Netherlands and the German lands owned by the Habsburg family. Charles was the most powerful ruler in Europe.

Charles V had been raised in Flanders by his father's family of the House of Burgundy. He spoke no Spanish, and his pride and foreignness alienated the Spanish. He appointed foreign courtiers from Flanders to offices in Spain, and he used Spanish wealth to fund his political programs in central European territories. Spaniards revolted. The nobles wanted to stop the drain of money to central Europe and the assignment of offices to foreigners. They wanted Charles to return to Spain. As civil order broke down, artisans and business classes in Castile revolted against the great landholders in the Communero revolt of 1520–21. The revolutionaries held conflicting goals, and as they fought one another to exhaustion Charles easily retained his hold on government.

But when Charles entered into wars against the Ottoman Turkish Empire in eastern Europe and on the Mediterranean, and into the Christian religious wars of Catholic versus Protestant in northern and central Europe (see next section on the Protestant Reformation and the Catholic Reformation), he bankrupted even the silver-rich treasury of Spain. After Charles's abdication in 1556, his son Philip II (r. 1556–98) continued the politics of warfare and suffered much the same fate. Even his military victories were financial defeats.

Portugal's Empire

Isabella and Ferdinand united their thrones, creating modern Spain in 1492, but the western third of the Iberian peninsula, Portugal, remained a separate state. For sixty years, from 1580 to 1640, it was incorporated into Spain, but otherwise it has

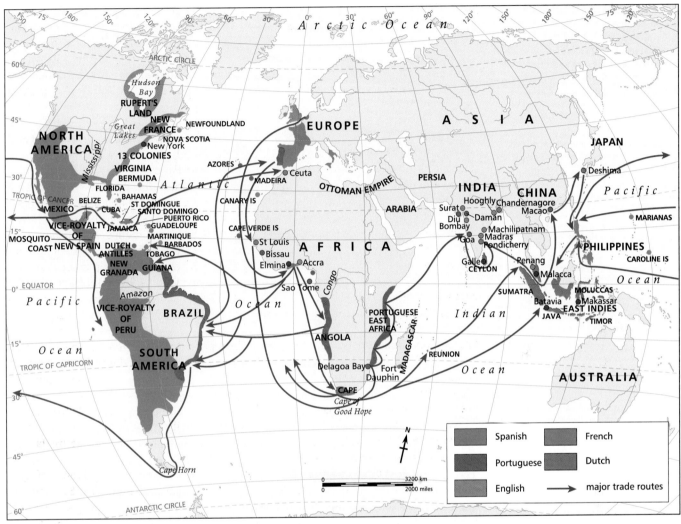

The first European trading empires about 1750. European seaborne intercontinental trade was dominated by Spain and Portugal in the sixteenth century. The Spanish rapidly colonized Central America, the Andes mountain regions, and the Philippines. The Portuguese concentrated on the coasts of Brazil, east and west Africa, and the Arabian Sea ports of India. A century later the Dutch, English, and French followed, establishing settler colonies in North America and South Africa and fortified trading posts along the coasts elsewhere.

remained separate until today. In terms of worldwide exploration and trade, Portugal, under the leadership of Prince Henry the Navigator (1394–1460), who sponsored many voyages along the coast of Africa, had entered the field earlier and more vigorously than Spain.

Portugal in Africa. Portugal sought souls for Christianity, gold for its national treasury, grain and fish for its domestic food supply, and slaves for its new sugar plantations. Portuguese entrepreneurs, having seen sugar plantations in the eastern Mediterranean, planted their own on Madeira and other islands in the Atlantic Ocean off the coast of Africa. (Spanish landlords and businessmen did the same in the Canary Islands.) These new plantations needed laborers. Portugal went to Africa to obtain them.

In 1415 Portugal captured Ceuta on the Moroccan coast of North Africa, one of the major points of the trans-Saharan trade in gold and slaves. Then, to get closer to the sources of supply, Portuguese ships, supported by the crown, sailed down the coast of West Africa, rounding Cape Bojador in 1434 and continuing on to the Gold Coast in 1472. Bartholomeu Dias reached the Cape of Good Hope and continued northward, sailing his slim, long caravels, a few hundred miles up the east coast of Africa in 1488. As the Portuguese explored they also built fortresses—such as El Mina in modern Ghana—as assembly and shipping points for their purchases of slaves and gold. For

The fortress of São Jorge da Mina (later called El Mina), African Gold Coast, 1482. Built at the order of King John II of Portugal in 1482, this fortress—like many others—provided a fortified trading post designed both to protect Portuguese trade from rival Europeans and to serve as a supply base. At the beginning of the sixteenth century trade was in gold and kola nuts with imports of American crops such as maize and cassava, and trans-shipment of slaves. It was not until the late seventeenth century that the export of slaves became the main trade on the Gold Coast.

the most part, the Portuguese remained in their coastal enclaves of fortresses, trading posts, and Christian missionary outposts.

At some points, however, the Portuguese did venture inland to explore, trade, evangelize, and attempt to conquer. From El Mina, on the Gold Coast, for example, they went inland to trade directly with Mane and Soninke merchants. In the Kongo, they converted King Nzinga Mbembe (1507–43) and many of his people to Christianity, although the Portuguese slave trade in the Kongo ultimately alienated people from their king. He wrote to the king of Portugal, on humanitarian grounds, that the slave trade was destroying the Kongo as its people turned predatory towards one another. He wanted the trade stopped. His plea was ignored. The Portuguese, and the Kongolese themselves, desired the profits of the trade.

In Angola, on the west coast, the Portuguese went directly inland to bring slaves to the coast, and claimed the region as their colony in 1484. By 1500, Lisbon was receiving some 1500 pounds of gold and 10,000 slaves each year from west Africa. On the east coast of Africa, they sacked the Swahili trading city of Kilwa to gain control of the Indian Ocean trade and claimed Mozambique for its rich gold supplies. Although the Portuguese mostly stayed in coastal enclaves like Sofala, and established an outpost on Mozambique Island, they also traveled inland along the Zambezi River.

Portugal in Brazil. In 1500, a Portuguese expedition headed for India was blown off course in the Atlantic and landed briefly in Brazil. The Portuguese claimed the land but did little to develop it until pressed by competition from other European powers. By the mid-sixteenth century they had established some coastal towns, including a colonial capital at Salvador, introduced Jesuit missionaries, and planted the first of the plantations that would make Brazil the first of the huge plantation colonies in the Americas. By 1700 Brazil had 150,000 slaves—half its total population—working its sugar plantations.

By this time, other nations had developed sugar plantations in the Caribbean, contesting Brazil's leadership and undercutting prices and profits. In 1695, however, gold and diamonds were discovered in the interior mountains of Brazil (in the state later named Minas Gerais, General Mines), and by the mid-eighteenth century Brazil was mining some 3000 tons of gold each year, mostly through slave labor. Unfortunately, as often happens with windfall profits from the discovery of raw materials, Portugal and Brazil spent the profits on goods from other countries, especially Britain, without developing new economic enterprises of their own. When the gold began to run out in the mid-eighteenth century, Brazil and Portugal found themselves in debt to Britain, but hooked on British imports, without further means of paying.

Portugal in the Indian Ocean. Throughout the sixteenth century, even taking into account the emerging sugar profits from Brazil, Portugal's main overseas interests lay in Asia. In 1498 Vasco da Gama had extended Portugal's voyages of exploration eastward. Departing from the east coast of Africa, with the assistance of a local pilot who knew the route, he sailed into one of the world's liveliest arenas of trade, the Indian Ocean and the west coast of India (see Chapter 13). Almost immediately the Portuguese introduced armed violence into trade relations that had been peaceful. In 1500 an armed Portuguese expedition under Pedro Alvarez Cabral (c. 1468–1520) was under instructions from the government to establish a fort and trading post at Cochin, India, to promote relations with other "Christian kingdoms" in India, and to impede Muslim shipping to the Red Sea. Cabral had numerous armed engagements with ships in the Indian Ocean and in ports on India's southwest coast. In fighting at Calicut, fifty-four of Cabral's men were killed and substantial goods were lost. In response, Cabral bombarded Cochin, killing between 400 and 500 people and destroying considerable goods and property.

When da Gama returned on his second voyage in 1502 he came with twenty-one armed ships to assert Portuguese power in the Indian Ocean. Seven years later, at the Battle of Diu, Portuguese cannon devastated a combined Egyptian–Gujarati–Calicut fleet. Under Governor Afonso de Albuquerque (1509–15) Portugal captured Goa in 1510, Malacca in 1511, and Hormuz in 1515. At the height of their Indian Ocean power, Portugal held some fifty ports, with Goa serving as their Indian Ocean capital. The Portuguese imposed a system of passes in the Indian Ocean. To the extent that they could enforce it, the Portuguese forced ocean traders to pay them a tax of passage—previously unheard of—and demanded that many of them put into port at Portuguese centers, especially Goa. The Portuguese were making money as much from their own kind of piracy as from trade. Their reputation for violence spread.

By the end of the century, however, it became clear that the Portuguese could not maintain their coercive system. Many of their own merchants operated as private traders despite the official state monopoly; Portuguese officers were often corrupt; their military was not well disciplined; and they lacked the manpower to actually enforce the controls that they asserted over Indian Ocean traders. Most of all, beginning in the seventeenth century, the much larger ocean-going nations of the Netherlands, England, and France entered the Indian Ocean waters in substantial force, and tiny Portugal was no match for them. Portugal remained in the East, but only as a minor power.

Evaluating the Spanish and the Portuguese Empires

Critics who claim that Europe's wealth was built on the exploitation of people overseas certainly have some justification, but the experiences of Spain and Portugal demonstrate that exploitation alone was not enough. To build and sustain wealth, countries must be able to use wealth effectively. They must conceive and implement policies of economic growth. They require banks and instruments of exchange to store and transmit money. They need commercial intelligence to create and evaluate strategies for investing capital sensibly and profitably. They must develop efficient means of transporting goods and people. They must not allow their commercial aims to be excessively deflected by warfare. Both Spain and Portugal lacked these facilities. Both societies, too, were hierarchical societies, where prestige belonged to those in the nobility, the aristocracy. It was common in both Spain and Portugal for people to use whatever mercantile wealth they accumulated to buy into the nobility and buy land, then cease to engage in trade and commerce. Thus, both countries built enormous global empires in the sixteenth century based on their ocean explorations (see Chapter 13), but by the end of the sixteenth century both these empires were on the wane, first challenged and then surpassed by the Netherlands, France, and England, countries that established successful commercial communities.

Culturally, Spain and Portugal were far more successful. The influence of their languages and cultures remains dominant in Latin America until today, and they continue to have an effect on areas as far as the Philippines (for Spain) and Angola, Mozambique, Goa, and tiny Macao (for Portugal). But as economic and political powers, Spain and Portugal, despite their early, extraordinary successes, were soon eclipsed by the commercially astute nations of northwest Europe.

TRADE AND RELIGION IN WESTERN EUROPE: THE PROTESTANT REFORMATION AND THE CATHOLIC REFORMATION

Charles V and his son Philip II fought against Protestant countries in wars explicitly devoted to matters of religion. These wars siphoned off vast treasures that Spain brought from the Americas and diverted her from economic and commercial growth. To understand the choice that Spain made, we must analyze the warfare between Catholics and Protestants that divided Europe in the sixteenth and seventeenth centuries. We will also consider scholarly arguments over the extent to which religious philosophies have a direct impact on national economic development.

The Reformation

Catholicism had won the hearts, spirits, and tithes of the overwhelming majority of the population of western and central Europe. By 1500 the Church had become so wealthy and powerful that several reformers charged the Church with straying from Jesus' early simplicity and his message of compassion for the poor.

Martin Luther (1483–1546), a pious German monk who lived in a monastery in Wittenberg and taught in the university there, shared these criticisms of the Church's wealth and further asserted that it claimed too much power over individual conscience. Luther doubted the importance of sacraments and authority. He kept his doubts private, however, until in 1517 a friar came to Wittenberg selling **indulgences**, which offered exemption from punishment for sins in exchange for donations to the Church. Outraged, Luther posted on the door of the castle church **ninety-five theses**, or statements of his belief, asserting the importance of faith and grace alone. Priests, he wrote, were not needed to mediate between humans and God. Pressed to recant, Luther refused, declaring "it is neither right nor safe to act against conscience."

indulgences In the Roman Catholic church, the remission from the punishments of an absolved sin, obtainable through good works or special prayers and granted by the Church through the merits of Christ and the saints. The sale of indulgences in the late medieval church led to widespread abuse.

ninety-five theses Luther's exposition of his beliefs and his differences with the Catholic Church, posted publicly as a challenge to Church authority.

For an interactive version of this map, go to: http://www.prenhall.com/spodek/map14.3

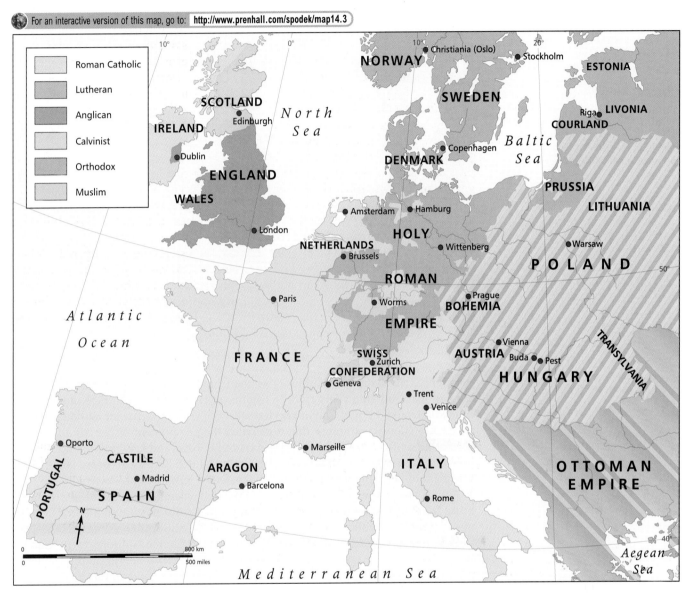

Legend:
- Roman Catholic
- Lutheran
- Anglican
- Calvinist
- Orthodox
- Muslim

The Reformation in Europe. The tide of religious reform was felt throughout Europe and changed its political map. The early commitment of most of northern Europe to Calvinism, Lutheranism, or Anglicanism was counterbalanced by the recovery to Catholicism of France and Poland. Counter-Reformation zeal, combined with political confrontation and dynastic rivalry, culminated in the Thirty Years' War (1618–48), fought across Europe's heartland at enormous cost.

When Pope Leo X excommunicated Luther, several local rulers in Germany protected him. They used the occasion to assert their independence of Charles V, who was not only king of Spain but also Holy Roman Emperor, with powers over Germany. From this time, Luther often aligned himself with local rulers. When a revolt of peasants against their landlords swept Germany in 1524, Luther urged the local princes to suppress the revolt by force, and thousands were killed. The kings of Denmark and Sweden and many of the princes of Germany adopted this branch of Protestantism, which is called Lutheranism in America, making this region of northern Europe the heartland of the new denomination. Printing presses using movable type, introduced into Europe by Johannes Gutenberg about 1450, helped to spread the new message as well as new German translations of the Bible, making the sacred text available to ordinary readers who could not read Latin, the language of earlier Christianity, and freeing them from dependence on priestly readings and interpretations.

In Geneva, Switzerland, John Calvin (1509–64) preached another doctrine of reform. Like Luther, Calvin spoke of justification by faith and the supremacy of individual

John Calvin weighing the Bible against Popish Pomp. Calvin had studied the writings of the first generation of reformers such as Martin Luther and accepted without question the idea of justification by faith alone and the biblical foundation of religious authority. This contemporary woodcut shows him weighing what he saw as the extraneous ceremonial trappings and overweening bishops of the Catholic Church against the simple truth of the Bible.

conscience. He denied the authority of the Church. Calvin went beyond Luther in arguing that God grants His grace to whomever He chooses, regardless of individual behavior. Unlike Luther, Calvin rejected alliances with government, although he did create a religious community that dominated the government of the city of Geneva. Calvinism spread widely in western and central Europe, and in New England, without the patronage of any political authority. (In the United States Calvinism is the dominant faith of Presbyterianism, named for its elected leaders or presbyters.)

A third major strand of reform arose in England, where King Henry VIII (r. 1509–47) broke from the Church not for reasons of doctrine, but to claim authority for England over the entire Catholic establishment within the country—churches, monasteries, and clergy—and to gain for himself a divorce, which the Church had forbidden, from the first of his six wives. Henry had no doctrinal quarrel with Rome. He simply wanted to head the English Church himself, and in 1534 Parliament named him "Protector and Only Supreme Head of the Church and Clergy of England," a title that was passed in slightly modified form to later English sovereigns. In England, Henry's new church was called Anglican. (Its followers in the United States are called Episcopalians.)

Each of the three reform movements rejected the authority of the pope, stressed the freedom of individual conscience in matters of faith, and permitted their clergy to marry. Collectively, these various protests against the power and doctrine of the Catholic Church were called Protestantism or the Protestant Reformation.

The Catholic Reformation (the Counter-Reformation)

Its religious monopoly challenged, the Catholic Church countered with the Council of Trent to intensify its own efforts at internal reform. The Council met irregularly for eighteen years, 1545–63, reaffirming the basic doctrines of Catholicism. It reasserted the necessity of the celibacy of the clergy and encouraged greater religious devotion among them. It created new religious orders to purify the Church and transmit its teachings. In 1534 Ignatius Loyola (1491–1556) founded the Society of Jesus, which was especially dedicated to education, secular as well as religious, and to carrying the message of the Church around the world. From 1540 Francis Xavier (1506–52) introduced the Jesuit vision to India, Indonesia, and Japan, baptizing thousands of new Christians. In Paris in 1625, Vincent de Paul (1581–1660) began his work among the wretched of the slums, a humanitarian mission that continues around the world today.

The Catholic Church was fighting for an international, universal vision of the world under its own leadership, while the various Protestant movements encouraged separate national states. In response, several of the new national states encouraged the Protestant movement.

HOW DO WE KNOW?

Weber and Tawney on Religion and Capitalism

The social scientist Max Weber (1864–1920), writing The Protestant Ethic and the Spirit of Capitalism in the early twentieth century, argued that Protestantism's emphasis on individual achievement and divine grace tended to promote economic enterprise and capitalism. Weber claimed that Protestant ministers urged their followers to demonstrate their virtue through devotion to thrift, discipline, industriousness, and business.

> Striving for wealth is objectionable only when it has the aim of a carefree and merry existence. But as exercise of duty in a calling it is not only morally permitted but actually commanded . . . Worldly Protestant asceticism acted effectively against the spontaneous enjoyment of wealth; it limited consumption, especially that of luxuries. On the other hand, it eliminated traditional inhibitions against the acquisition of property; it burst the bonds of the profit motive by not only legalizing it, but even viewing it as directly willed by God . . . He desired rational and utilitarian use of wealth for the purposes of the individual and the community. (Columbia University, pp. 84, 89)

According to Weber, Protestantism encouraged entrepreneurs to dedicate themselves to making money and laborers to finding satisfaction in hard work.

> The bourgeois entrepreneur could, and felt that he ought to, follow his economic self-interest in the certainty of being in God's good grace, and of being visibly blessed by Him. This remained true as long as he observed the formal rules of the game, kept his morals spotless, and did not make objectionable use of his wealth. In addition, the power of religious asceticism made available to him sober, conscientious, eminently capable workers who regarded their labor as their divinely ordained purpose in life. Even more, it gave him the comforting assurance that the unequal distribution of the goods of this world was the direct consequence of God's Providence which followed out His unknown aims by these distinctions as well as by this selective show of grace. (Columbia University, p. 93)

Weber extended these arguments to assert that ultimately Protestant religious leaders had made the pursuit of profit through hard work into the essence of religion.

Subsequent authors, however, notably the British social historian R.H. Tawney, rejected Weber's arguments. Capitalist thought and practice had preceded Protestantism, and some Catholic areas, such as northern Italy and parts of France, were strongly capitalistic, while some Protestant areas, notably in north Germany, were not. "There was plenty of the 'capitalist spirit' in fifteenth-century Venice and Florence, or in south Germany and Flanders, for the simple reason that these areas were the greatest commercial and financial centers of the age, though all were, at least nominally, Catholic" (Tawney, p. 262, n. 32). It was difficult to show any historically consistent correlation between religious doctrines and economic policy.

Tawney's most significant quarrel with Weber, however, was over Weber's argument that religion had ceded the central place in life to the pursuit of economic gain, at least temporarily. Weber was not pleased with this transformation, but he claimed to observe it. Tawney, on the contrary, argued that moral issues concerning the welfare of the entire society always underpin economic ones. They never become secondary.

> A reasonable estimate of economic organization must allow for the fact that, unless industry is to be paralyzed by recurrent revolts on the part of outraged human nature, it must satisfy criteria which are not purely economic . . . natural appetites may be purified or restrained, as, in fact, in some considerable measure they already have been, by being submitted to the control of some larger body of interests. (Tawney, p. 233)

Debates over the relationship between religious doctrine and business practice continue unabated and unresolved until today in relation to religion in general and to all major religions in particular. These debates continue also outside the Western world. Today when East Asian economies are flourishing, Confucian traditions are praised for encouraging development. A century ago, the same traditions, interpreted differently, had been blamed for a lack of development.

- Can you cite examples of religious sentiments influencing economic actions?
- Can you cite examples of economic actions having no relation to religious, moral, or social concerns?
- Do you side with Weber's argument that to a large degree the pursuit of economic growth has taken precedence over religious, moral, and social concerns? Or would you agree with Tawney that, in the long run, economic issues must always be subordinated to larger issues?

The Dutch Republic, France, and England

Spanish Defeats. Inspired by Protestant doctrines and chafing under Spanish rule, the Netherlands, including today's Holland and Belgium, rose in revolt against control by the Habsburg family. Although geographically small, they were among the wealthiest of Philip's possessions. They were offended by the excessive quantity and deficient quality of the Spanish administrators sent to govern them. They also feared that Philip would extend to the Netherlands and all non-Catholics the Spanish Inquisition, a royal court originally established to combat Islam and Judaism in Spain. Many of the peoples of the Netherlands had left Catholicism for new Protestant movements, and many Protestants from other countries had come seeking asylum. In the Netherlands, Protestants and Catholics had reached an accommodation and neither community wished to see that harmony destroyed by the Inquisition. Philip's government refused to pay attention, and the Netherlands erupted in fury. A civil war ensued in which thousands were killed, property was destroyed, and churches were desecrated. By 1576, however, the Netherlands had suffered enough, and representatives of all the Netherlands united across religious lines to expel the Spanish.

In the same year, Queen Elizabeth I of England (r. 1558–1603), the daughter of Henry VIII, officially and publicly aligned her country with the rebels in the Netherlands and began to pursue a policy of alliance with Protestant forces throughout Europe. In reply, Philip II prepared to invade England. In 1588 the Spanish Armada set sail for England with 130 ships, 30,000 men, and 2400 pieces of artillery. In an astonishing reversal, the Armada was destroyed by the English and by a fierce storm, which was quickly named "the Protestant wind."

Spain entered a century-long decline. The northern Netherlands won its independence in 1609, although Spain did not fully and formally acknowledge it until 1648, after years of intermittent warfare. In 1640 Portugal, which had been united with Spain since 1580, declared its independence once again, and constituent units of Spain, especially Catalonia in the northeast, fought costly, if unsuccessful, wars for independence. Philip III (r. 1598–1621) and Philip IV (r. 1621–65) were incompetent rulers; Charles II (r. 1665–1700) was mentally incapable of ruling. And finally, about mid-century, the stream of silver from the Americas dried up, dwindling from 135 million pesos in the decade 1591–1600 to 19 million in 1651–60. Spain had squandered a fabulous windfall of silver and gold. England, France, and the Netherlands emerged as the rising powers of Europe; their self-confidence and their economies flourished; and their merchant classes organized to travel the world.

The Dutch Republic: Seaborne Merchant Enterprise. In the early seventeenth century, the Dutch had the most efficient economic system in Europe. The Dutch Republic bordered the North Sea, reclaimed land from its waters, and lived from its largesse. Fishing was the Republic's great national industry. One out of every four Dutch persons was reliant on the herring industry—catching, salting, smoking, pickling, selling—and others depended on cod fishing and whaling. With their windmills and their dikes, the Dutch reclaimed land from the sea—364,565 acres between 1540 and 1715—and also from inland lakes—another 84,638 acres. With such an investment of capital and energy the Dutch worked their land carefully and efficiently. They developed new methods of crop rotation, planting turnips in the fall to provide winter food for humans and sheep. At other times of year they raised peas, beans, and clover to restore nitrogen to the soil. With these cropping patterns, the Dutch no longer had to leave one-third of their land fallow each year. They farmed it all, increasing productivity by 50 percent. In addition, the Dutch built one of the largest textile industries in Europe, based on wool from their own sheep and on huge quantities imported from England.

On the seas and in the rivers, the Dutch were sailing 10,000 ships as early as 1600, and for the next century they dominated the shipping of northern Europe. From the Baltic they brought timber and grain to Amsterdam and western Europe. In exchange, from the ports of Portugal, Spain, and France they carried salt, oil, wool, wine, and, most of all, the silver and gold of the New World. Often they warehoused in Amsterdam the trade goods en route to other ports, earning additional profits on the storage. They used substantial amounts of the timber themselves to build the most seaworthy, yet economical, ships of the day.

The Dutch also developed commercial institutions to underpin their dominance in trade. The **bourse**, or stock exchange, was opened in Amsterdam in the mid-sixteenth century as the Dutch were gaining control of the Baltic trade, and it was reopened in 1592 as they captured a dominant role in supplying grain to Mediterranean countries. In 1598 they initiated a Chamber of Insurance; in 1609 the Bank of Amsterdam was established. This bank accepted coins from all over the world, assessed their gold and silver content, and exchanged them for gold florin coins that were fixed in weight and value and became the standard everywhere. The Dutch government guaranteed the safety of deposits in the national bank, thereby attracting capital from through-out Europe. Depositors were able to draw checks on their accounts. For two centuries, until the French Revolution in 1789, Amsterdam was the financial center of Europe.

In 1602 Dutch businessmen founded the Dutch East India Company, a joint stock company dedicated to trade in Asia. The Company captured several Portuguese ports, but concentrated on the most lucrative of all the East Asian centers, Java and the Moluccas, the Spice Islands of today's Indonesia. In 1619 the Dutch East India

bourse stock exchange

Andries van Eertvel, *The Return to Amsterdam of the Fleet of the Dutch East India Company*, 1599. The Dutch East India Company was founded in 1602 to create a monopoly over Dutch trade and to seize control of the Portuguese trade routes in the Indian Ocean. The company owned a fleet of ships armed with cannon which carried pepper, indigo, raw silk, saltpeter, and textiles from India to western Europe. In the later 1600s, large-scale exports of textiles were also carried from India to Africa in payment for slaves going to the Caribbean. (*Johnny Van Haeften Gallery, London*)

SOURCE

National Joint Stock Companies: Instruments of Trade and Colonization

National joint stock companies were one of the key commercial innovations of Dutch, French, and English financiers in the seventeenth century, giving them an enormous advantage in overseas trade. Forerunners of the modern business corporation, the companies sold stock publicly, sometimes for a single expedition, more commonly for all the expeditions and activities of the company. Financiers invested in expectation of the great profits that might come from successful shipping ventures. Their potential losses and liabilities were limited to the value of their investment; the rest of their personal property was protected. Individual states gave legal charters to these companies in expectation of the benefits of trade for the country. These national companies were chartered for expeditions throughout the world. Those headed toward the Americas were designated "West India Companies," those toward Asia were "East India Companies." The companies of each state usually saw themselves in competition with each other, sometimes leading to armed struggle. And their missions included colonization, and sometimes proselytization, as well as trade.

The government "Edict Providing for the Establishment of a Company of the West Indies," establishing the French West India Company in 1664, is representative of the aspirations of the state and of the merchants looking to the Americas for both settlement and trade:

> We have recognized that colonial trade and navigation are the only and true means of raising commerce to the brilliant position it holds in foreign lands; to achieve this and to stimulate our subjects to form powerful companies we have promised them such great advantages that there is reason to hope that all those who take interests in the glory of the State, and who wish to profit by honorable and legitimate means will willingly participate . . . but as it is not sufficient for these companies to take possession of the lands which we grant them, and have them cleared and cultivated by the people they send there at great expense, if they do not equip themselves to carry on . . . commerce . . . it is also absolutely necessary, in order to carry on this trade, to provide numerous ships to carry each day the goods which are to be sold in the said countries, and bring back to France those which they export. (Columbia College, *Contemporary Civilization*, I: 815–20)

Investment in the Company was open to foreigners as well as to native-born French. The Company was "obliged to introduce into the lands granted above, the number of clergy necessary for preaching the Holy Gospel, and instructing these peoples in the faith of the Catholic, Apostolic and Roman religion; and also to build churches." It also had many of the attributes of a sovereign state:

> The said Company may build forts in all places it shall judge necessary for the defense of the said country . . . may arm and equip for war such number of vessels as it shall deem fitting for the defense of the said countries and the security of the said commerce . . . may negotiate peace and alliances in our name, with the Kings and Princes of the countries where it wishes to establish its settlements and trade . . . and, in case of insult, declare war on them, attack them, and defend itself by force of arms. (ibid).

In the Indian Ocean, trade in spices was a large part of the Companies' business. Between them the English and Dutch East India Companies carried 13.5 million pounds of pepper to Europe in the peak year of 1670, the British share mostly from India, the Dutch share from Indonesia. Other goods included indigo, raw silk, saltpeter, and, increasingly, Indian textiles. There were also large-scale exports of textiles carried by Europeans from India to Africa in payment for slaves going to the Caribbean.

The Companies' ships were armed, and their representatives established fortresses and trading centers on the coasts of Asia and of the Americas, and the Companies became, in effect, miniature governments. Malachy Postlethwayt's Universal Dictionary of 1751 wrote that the Dutch East India Company

> makes peace and war at pleasure, and by its own authority; administers justice to all . . . settles colonies, builds fortifications, levies troops, maintains numerous armies and garrisons, fits out fleets, and coins money. (cited in Tracy, *The Political Economy of Merchant Empires*, p. 196)

In India, in the seventeenth century, the English, French, and Dutch East India Companies set up trading posts within towns. Until the end of the century, the Mughal emperors and local governments generally welcomed the foreign traders as means of stimulating the Indian economy through trade and enriching the government through taxes. Following its victories at Plassey in 1757 and Buxar in 1765, however, the British East India Company became the de facto government of the province of Bengal in India—with the rights of collecting taxes and the responsibility for providing order and administration. The Company's holdings continued to expand until it was effectively the ruler of almost all of India. The British government regulated the East India Company from its founding in 1600, and finally disbanded it and took over direct rule of India after the Indian revolt of 1857.

Company founded Jakarta, which served as its regional headquarters until 1950 when Indonesia won its independence. In 1623 they seized Amboina in the Moluccas, killing a group of Englishmen they found there, and forcing the English back to India. The profits from these possessions reinforced Dutch economic precedence in Europe.

In 1600 a group of Dutch traders reached Japan. In 1641, all other foreigners were expelled, but, because they did not engage in missionary activity, the Dutch were permitted a small settlement on Deshima Island, off Nagasaki, and for two centuries they were the only European traders allowed in Japan. In 1652, the Dutch captured from the Portuguese the Cape of Good Hope at the southernmost tip of Africa and established there the first settlement of Afrikaners, South Africans of Dutch descent.

In the Americas, the Dutch West India Company raided the shipping of the Spanish and the Portuguese, and then founded their own rich sugar plantations in Caracas, Curaçao, and Guiana. For a few decades they held Bahia in Brazil, but the Portuguese drove them out in 1654. In North America they established New Amsterdam on Manhattan Island. The English, however, conquered and annexed it and in 1664 renamed it New York.

Despite their commercial skill and success, the Dutch could not ultimately retain their supremacy. The English Navigation Act of 1651 permitted imports to England and its dependencies only in English ships or in those of the exporting country, and this effectively restricted Dutch shipping. Three indecisive, draining wars followed, from 1652 to 1674. Additional years of warfare on land against France further exhausted Dutch resources. In 1700 the Dutch Republic had a population of 2 million people; at this time the population of the British Isles was 9 million, and that of France 19 million. An aggressive, skilled small country simply could not continue to compete with two aggressive, skilled large countries.

Indian cotton cloth, late seventeenth century. This detailed portrayal of Dutch traders suggests that they have come from far across the seas to trade in a rich array of goods. The Indian gentleman on the far right may find the Dutch doffing of caps and handshakes a strange form of greeting, quite different from the form used in India of joining one's hands in the "namaste" salutation.

France and Britain

France and Britain surpassed the Dutch and competed for dominance in world trade. For two centuries each pursued its own strategy of economic development—France primarily by land and Britain primarily by sea. Leadership finally went to the mistress of the waves. (The names of Britain and England are often used interchangeably. Formally, however, before the 1707 Act of Union, England and Wales were one country, Scotland another. By the Act of 1707 they were united into the single state of Great Britain.)

France: Consolidating the Nation. In the second half of the sixteenth century, France endured four decades of civil warfare because the crown was unable to control the various factions, religious groups, and regions of the country. Struggles between

Huguenot Any protestants in France in the sixteenth and seventeenth centuries. Their legal status changed according to the wishes of the monarch on the throne at the time.

Catholics and Protestants, called **Huguenots** in France, helped to fuel the warfare. So, too, did the desire of the nobles to have more independence from the king. In 1589 Henry of Navarre, a Huguenot, came to the throne as Henry IV (r. 1589–1610). Recognizing the importance of Catholicism to the majority of the French people, he joined the Catholic Church with the apocryphal comment, "Paris is worth a Mass." In 1598, however, hoping to heal the schism between the religious communities, he issued the Edict of Nantes, which gave Protestants the same civil rights as Catholics. He was not entirely successful, however, and, indeed, was assassinated by a Catholic militant. His successor, Louis XIII (r. 1610–43), following the advice of his chief minister, the Cardinal Richelieu, encouraged nobles to invest in trade by land and sea, built up France's armies, and cultivated allies among France's neighbors. Internally he captured several Huguenot strongholds in France, and concluded a truce with these French Protestants. Externally he joined with Protestant rulers in Sweden, the United Netherlands, and parts of Germany to defeat the Catholic Hapsburg Empire and increase the stature of France.

Louis XIV, in an extraordinarily long and forceful reign (1643–1715), made France the most powerful country in Europe. Under the Sun King, as Louis was known, France set the standard throughout Europe for administration, war, diplomacy, language, thought, literature, music, architecture, fashion, cooking, and etiquette. Although they had been slower than other European countries to enter transoceanic trade, the French now began to assert a global presence, trading in India, Madagascar, the American Great Lakes, and the Mississippi River; establishing colonies in the West Indies; and staking a claim to Canada. By 1690 Louis XIV had raised an army of 400,000 men, equal to the combined armies of England, the Habsburg Empire, Prussia, Russia, and the Dutch Republic. At this time, the French navy was also larger than the English, with 120 ships of the line (warships) compared to the English navy's 100. Also, as we have seen, in 1700, France had a population of 19 million, more than double that of the British Isles.

Louis XIV boasted "L'état, c'est moi" ("I am the state") by which he meant that the powers of the state rested in him alone. His leading religious adviser, Bishop Jacques-Bénigne Bossuet (1627–1704), linked the king's power to divine right, asserting that "Royalty has its origin in the divinity itself." Louis XIV continued to assert the right of the king to appoint the Catholic clergy in France, and in 1685 he revoked the Edict of Nantes in the belief that a single, dominant religion was more important than the toleration of minorities within his kingdom. This act cost France the services of many of its Protestant artisans, who fled to the Netherlands and Britain.

Economically, Louis XIV's chief economic adviser, Jean-Baptiste Colbert (1625–96), pursued a policy of mercantilism—fostering the economic welfare of one's own state against all others—by strengthening state control over the national economy even more aggressively than had Richelieu. To facilitate trade, he abolished local taxes on trade throughout central France (a region as large as England), although his government was not powerful enough to do away with these internal tariffs throughout the entire country. Colbert established a Commercial Code to unify business practice throughout the country. To improve communication and transportation, he built roads and canals, including a link between the Bay of Biscay and the Mediterranean. He set quality standards for hand manufacturers to improve their marketability and gave financial incentives to the French manufacturers of such luxury goods as silks, tapestries, glass, and woolens. Meanwhile, the needs of the army created huge national markets for uniforms, equipment, and provisions. All these policies benefited private business as well as the state, but the mercantilist insistence that the export of gold and silver weakened the national economy and that state monopolies should dominate certain economic fields, including much of foreign trade, was opposed by many business people who sought greater freedom of trade.

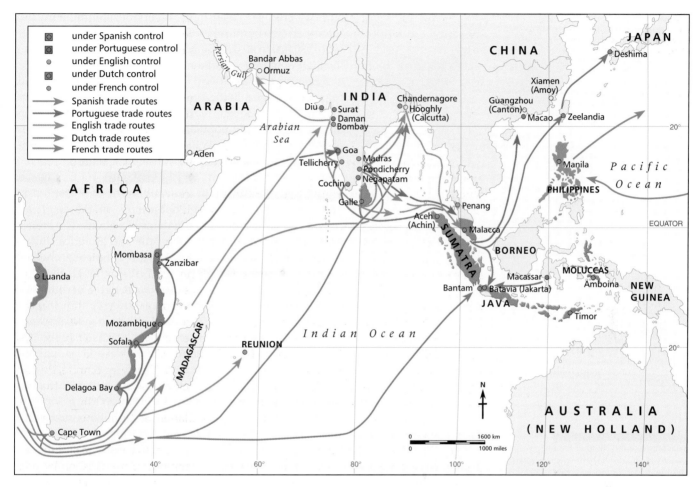

The growth of French military and economic strength disturbed the **balance of power** among the leading states of Europe and precipitated a series of wars. The War of the League of Augsburg, 1688–97, and the War of the Spanish Succession, 1702–13, reduced France's power when she was forced to cede to Britain the North American colonies of Newfoundland and Nova Scotia and all French claims to the Hudson Bay territory. Britain began to pull ahead in overseas possessions.

Britain: Establishing Commercial Supremacy. In the same wars, Britain won from Spain the *asiento*, the right to carry all the slave cargoes from Africa to Spanish America, plus one shipload of more conventional goods each year to Panama. These officially recognized trading rights also provided cover for British ships to engage illegally in the business of piracy and smuggling that flourished in the Caribbean, where buccaneers preyed on Spanish commerce.

In the eighteenth century the most valued properties in the Americas were the sugar-producing islands of the Caribbean. In the Atlantic the most valuable trade was in human cargo—the slaves who worked the sugar plantations. In Asia, control of sea lanes and of the outposts established by the various East India companies was the prize.

Competition for dominance in all three regions continued between the French and the British through four more wars in the eighteenth century: the War of Austrian Succession, 1740–48; the Seven Years' War, 1756–63; the War of American Independence (the American Revolution), 1775–81. These wars demonstrated the importance of sea power, and here the British triumphed. Around 1790, the French population

Indian Ocean trade in the seventeenth century. Prior to the sixteenth century, Arabs and other local traders had dominated Indian Ocean commerce. When the Portuguese arrived in 1498, however, European nations entered directly into these trade routes in armed ships. Controlled from headquarters in Europe, they established coastal trade enclaves throughout the region. They began to battle each other for supremacy, projecting European competition into these distant waters and shores.

balance of power In international relations, a policy that aims to secure peace by preventing any one state or alignment of states from becoming too dominant. Alliances are formed to build up a force equal or superior to that of the potential enemy.

asiento A contract between the Spanish crown and a private individual or sovereign power, giving the latter exclusive rights to import a stipulated number of slaves into the Spanish American colonies in exchange for a fee.

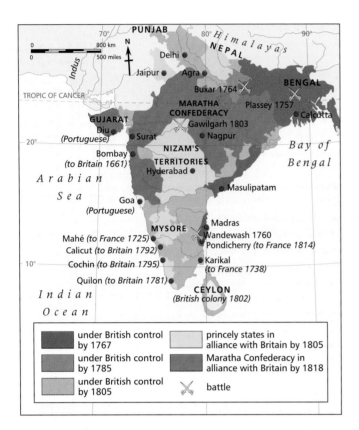

British power in India to 1818. The weakening of the Mughal Empire created a situation which was exploited by the English and French East India companies. They created strategic alliances with local independent princes and competed for power on land and sea. With Clive's victory at Plassey (1757) the English gained Bengal, a power base which allowed them to expand steadily, but their control over India was not secure until their final defeat of the Maratha confederation in 1818.

outnumbered the British 28 million to 16 million, and French armies outnumbered the British by an even greater ratio, 180,000 to 40,000. But the British navy had 195 ships of the line compared with France's 81.

Suffering defeats at sea, the French retreated from their colonial positions. In the Peace Settlement at Paris in 1763 at the end of the Seven Years' War they turned over their immense, but thinly populated, holdings in North America east of the Mississippi to the British and those west of the Mississippi to Spain. They kept their rich, sugar-producing islands in the Caribbean: Saint-Domingue (Haiti), Guadeloupe, and Martinique. In India, although they lost out in other locations, they kept Pondicherry on the southeast coast and a few additional commercial locations. The French navy was deployed against the British in America during the American Revolution, but it was completely crushed during the Napoleonic Wars. The British, though they lost the thirteen colonies of the United States in 1783, triumphed everywhere else because of the great strength of their navy. They held Canada. They held their islands in the Caribbean. They increased their holdings in India, and they dominated the sea lanes both across the Atlantic Ocean and through the Indian Ocean.

Institutionally, Britain surpassed all other European countries, even the Netherlands, in supporting sophisticated economic enterprise. Recognizing the importance of a stable currency, England had fixed the value of the pound sterling in 1560–61 at 4 ounces of silver, and maintained that valuation for two and a half centuries, until after World War I. Britain surpassed Amsterdam as the center of Europe's international trade. The Bank of England, created in 1694, could transact its business with a currency of fixed value. Moreover, Britain never defaulted on her debts and so earned the trust of the international financial community. In times of war as well as of peace, Britain could borrow whatever sums she needed. Politically, England developed a new system of constitutional monarchy after 1688 that gave strong support to private commercial interests, as we shall see in more detail in Chapter 15. The French later ridiculed Britain as "a nation of shopkeepers," but geographically, militarily, institutionally, politically, and agriculturally, the British were building the capacity to become the most effective businessmen in the world. They were building a nation-state and a capitalist economy.

THE NATION-STATE

The term nation-state is generally used to describe the combination of a political state with the emotional sensibility of a collective social identity. The state is a geographic territory with its own independent government, and it must have enough size and force that it is not swallowed up by another. The nation is based on some combination of shared language, religion, history, ethnicity, future aspiration, and a sense of distinctiveness from, competition with, or antagonism toward, some other nation-state or states. Nation-states may emerge from the break-up of larger empires—which may contain several nations within themselves—or from the aggrandizement of small units into larger ones through conquest or merger. Both these processes had been continuing in western Europe for centuries. Small units, like the region around Paris under Hugh Capet, were expanding into states, while large units, like Charlemagne's empire, were dissolving.

The nation-states had developed relatively efficient central governments that were capable of collecting taxes, keeping the peace, and raising and deploying armies and navies effectively in waging war. Their authority was generally recognized and accepted—even welcomed—by most of the people within their borders. That authority was different in different nation-states: England, France, and Portugal were monarchies; the Netherlands was ruled by a coalition of businessmen; Spain was a part of the larger Habsburg Empire.

Nation-states took an interest in the economic welfare of their people, although here too different states adopted different policies at different times, some capitalist, some mercantilist but with independent merchants, some state controlled. They engaged in external, overseas trade and commerce and, in this period of time, colonization. The development of overseas trade and colonization that we have studied in this chapter and in Chapter 13 was a large part of their transformation from small, locally governed units into nation-states. They also defined themselves by their relationship to one another—generally competitive, often hostile, sometimes belligerent.

By the mid-1700s the nation-states of western Europe had become the object of both fear and emulation. They were feared because of their economic and military powers. They could, and did, fight wars, conquer territories, create colonies, and dominate trade networks. Many societies and governments feared victimization by them. Consider, for example, the fate of the Aztecs, Inca, and other Native Americans. These fears led some states to keep these new nation-states at arm's length as long as they could. China and Japan remained essentially closed for centuries. It led still other governments to emulate them, to develop the strength to resist them even while becoming more like them. This was the response of Russia under Peter the Great.

The period we are now studying is critical to the formation of nation-states because in their competition over trade routes and colonies around the world, these nation-states defined themselves in relation to one another and in relation to the other civilizations with which they were engaging. This self-definition in terms of the "Other" is certainly not the only element in the definition of the nation-state, but it is important. Moreover, as the trade and colonization of European nation-states encountered other groupings of people around the world, both the Europeans and the peoples they encountered began to redefine themselves politically and culturally. The European nation-state evoked many different responses. In the rest of this chapter we shall consider some of the most important in this early era of European trade and colonial expansion.

RUSSIA'S EMPIRE UNDER PETER THE GREAT

At the end of the seventeenth century Russia had little direct contact with the market economies of northwestern Europe. The country was geographically remote by land, and by sea its principal ocean port was Archangel at the extreme north, on the White Sea, ice-bound for most of the year. The foreign trade that did exist was carried by foreign ships traveling Russia's great rivers, especially the Volga. Russia belonged to the Greek Orthodox branch of Christianity, so communication with the Church of Rome and its western European networks was also limited. Mongol rule had further isolated Russia culturally from western Europe, tying it more closely to Central Asia.

Russia began to take its modern form only after Ivan III (r. 1462–1505) overthrew Mongol domination in 1480. Muscovy, the territory around Moscow, became the core of an expanding independent state. At first, Russia expanded southeastward, defeating the khanate of Astrakhan in 1556 and capturing the Volga River basin south to the Caspian Sea with its access to the silk trade of Persia. It also expanded eastward all the way to the Pacific (1649), capturing Siberia and its rich population of fur-bearing animals.

Because of its isolation and foreign rule, Russia had only a tiny urban trading class and very few big city markets. As late as 1811, only 4 percent of its population was urban. The overwhelming majority of its people lived in serfdom, which bound people not directly to specific owners, but to specific land and its landlords, with little possibility for economic, social, or geographic mobility. After 1675 landlords gained the right to sell serfs off the land, even to urban owners. Occasional serf uprisings, like that led by Stepan Razin (Stenka Razin; d. 1671) in 1667, were brutally suppressed, and the gulf between free persons and serfs increased.

When Peter I, the Great (r. 1682–96 as co-emperor with his half-brother; 1696–1725 as sole emperor), became sole emperor, he saw Sweden as his principal external enemy. Sweden already held Finland and the entire eastern shore of the Baltic, bottling up Russia without any Baltic port. Worse, in a crushing blow, 8000 Swedish troops defeated 40,000 Russians at the Battle of Narva in 1700. Humiliated, Peter set out to construct in Russia a powerful state based on a powerful army and navy. In 1697, traveling under an assumed name in order to evade royal protocol, Peter had embarked on a "Grand Embassy of Western Europe," especially England and the Netherlands, but also Baltic ports and the Holy Roman Empire. He searched for allies for the wars he expected against the Turks as Russia pushed toward the Black Sea; he gathered information on the economic, cultural, and military-industrial practices of the western European powers; and for several months he even worked as a ship's carpenter in Amsterdam.

Impressed by the strength of the western European countries, Peter invited to Russia military experts from the West to train and lead his troops. He bought western European artillery and copied it. He established naval forces and reorganized the army along Western lines, in uniformed regiments, armed with muskets. He promoted mining, metallurgy, and textile manufacture, largely as means of supplying his troops. By 1703–4 Peter had started to build a new capital, an all-weather port and "window on the West," in St. Petersburg on land that he conquered from Sweden. Commercially, geographically, and architecturally, he

serf An agricultural worker or peasant bound to the land and legally dependent on the lord. Serfs had their own homes, plots, and livestock but they owed the lord labor, dues, and services. These services could be commuted to rent, but serfs remained chattels of the lord unless they were emancipated, or escaped. Serfdom declined in western Europe in the late medieval period, but persisted in parts of eastern Europe until the nineteenth century.

Left Russia in 1682 and Peter the Great's acquisitions thereafter.

Right Peter the Great in armor. Alarmed by the growing power of his western European neighbors, and by Russia's relative weakness, Peter the Great undertook to modernize his country, especially its military, economic, and cultural life. He built his program, however, on the backs of Russia's serfs.

ARCTIC OCEAN

White Sea — Archangel

SWEDEN

St. Petersburg

INGRIA AND LIVONIA, 1720

Moscow

Baltic Sea

Smolensk

Warsaw

POLAND

Kiev

Astrakhan

Azov

Volga

Caspian Sea

CAUCASUS

Black Sea

Constantinople

OTTOMAN EMPIRE

Russia in 1682

Acquisitions of Peter the Great, 1682–1725

designed St. Petersburg as a Western city. Thirty thousand died in the construction of the city from disease, drowning, or lack of food.

In 1709, when Sweden again invaded Russia, Peter was prepared. He retreated until the Swedes fell from the exhaustion of pursuing him through the severe Russian winter. Then, holding his ground at Poltava in south Russia, he defeated the remaining Swedish troops. The Swedish army was finished as an imperial force, and Russia began to seize additional Baltic possessions.

Peter's goals for Westernization were not exclusively military. He wanted Russia to be counted among the powers of Europe, and this would require cultural and economic ties as well. Peter required Western-style education for all male nobles. He established schools for their children, and sent many to study in western Europe. He demanded that aristocrats acquire the morals and tastes of Europe's elites. He made them abandon their Russian dress in favor of the clothing of western Europe, and forced the men to shave or trim their beards in the Western style, He introduced "cipher schools" for teaching basic reading and arithmetic, established a printing press, established and edited Russia's first newspaper, and funded the Academy of Sciences, which opened in 1724, a year before his death. Collectively, all these revolutionary reforms drove a wedge between the nobility and the mass of Russians.

Economically, Peter pushed for the creation of new enterprises. He built a fleet on the Baltic and encouraged exports. He organized new companies headed by groups of Russians and foreigners, and supplied them with working capital and serf laborers. He accepted the mercantilist concept of an economically strong state and saw no role for a free market in achieving it. To finance these state-organized initiatives, Peter introduced heavy taxes, which fell especially severely on the peasantry.

No democrat, Peter demanded loyalty and obedience to himself. He created a new system of administration with himself as head. He brought the Eastern Orthodox Church under state control and subordinated its clergy to his own leadership. He streamlined local and central government. He created a new "state service," including both civil and military officials, and made appointments to it completely without regard to family status, birth, or seniority. Foreigners could serve within this service, serfs could be elevated, and nobles could be demoted. All depended on performance. In 1722 he introduced a new Table of Ranks, which automatically gave noble status to officials who reached the eighth position out of fourteen. The newly elevated nobility were the chief administrators of his new policies of Westernization. These moves were revolutionary and did not survive long after Peter's death.

Peter strengthened the economic and political position of the ruling classes, the landowners, and the rising bourgeoisie while exploiting the peasantry ruthlessly. He allotted to the nobility some 175,000 serfs and 100,000 acres of land in the first half of his reign alone. Conscription, programs of forced labor, a poll tax, and indirect taxes on everything from bee-keeping to salt provoked two major uprisings in the Russian interior between 1705 and 1708. The czar suppressed them brutally. An iron-willed autocrat, Peter brought his nation into Europe and made it an important military and economic power, but millions of Russians paid a terrible price.

Peter achieved many of his goals, establishing a strong central administration, a powerful military, some commercial enterprise, international trade connections, and diplomatic contact with the nations of western Europe. He did not, however, free Russia's merchants to carry on the kinds of independent economic activity characteristic of western European commerce. And he kept the largest enterprises, like weapons

Bartolomeo Carlo Rastrelli, *The Founding of St. Petersburg*, Russia, 1723. This bronze relief commemorates the founding of St. Petersburg in 1704. Peter the Great intended his capital to be an all-weather port and a "window on the West." As part of his drive for Westernization he decreed that the aristocracy must abandon their Russian dress in favor of European clothes. The garb of the men depicted here indicates clearly that the edict was already in place. (*Hermitage, St. Petersburg*)

enlightened despotism A benevolent form of absolutism, a system of government in which the ruler has absolute rights over his or her subjects. It implies that the ruler acts for the good of the people, not in self-interest.

manufacture and shipping, in the hands of the state. Considered an **enlightened despot**—a ruler who advanced new concepts of intellectual inquiry and legal rights, at least for the nobility, but held on to power for himself—Peter died in 1725. Since he had killed his own son rather than permit him to sidetrack reforms, Peter was succeeded for two years by his wife and then by other family members.

In 1762 Catherine II, the Great, assumed the throne and ruled for thirty-four years. At least as despotic as Peter, Catherine won especially important victories over Poles and Turks, expanding the borders of Russia to the Black Sea. After brutally suppressing a revolt by hundreds of thousands of serfs led by Yemelyan Pugachev (1726–75), she further reduced the power of Russia's serfs.

DIVERSE CULTURES, DIVERSE TRADE SYSTEMS

Ottomans and Mughals

Two powerful empires, the Ottoman and the Mughal, were rising in Asia at about the same time as Spain and Portugal were advancing in Europe and overseas. Indeed, there was some connection. In 1600 all four empires were approaching the height of their powers. By 1700 all were in severe decline because of overextension, draining warfare, weak state systems, and lack of attention to technological improvements, especially in the military. All four also allowed control of their economic affairs to fall into the hands of foreigners. By the end of our period, all were subordinated to greater or lesser degree under the power of the newly risen French and British.

The Ottomans did not control their own trade and its profits. At first, because of political alliances with France, only French ships were allowed to trade with the Ottomans. After 1580, trade opened more widely and the English and Dutch entered the trade, along with Jews, Armenians, Venetians, and Genoese. The situation came to resemble Spain's, in which the empire's new riches went into the hands of foreign merchants. A shift in the balance of trade also weakened the central government. To pay for increasing amounts of imported manufactured goods the Ottomans exported more agricultural raw materials, increasing the wealth of landed estate holders and enabling them to break free of central control.

In India, between 1556 and 1605, the Mughal emperor Akbar established one of the great empires of the world. Akbar's administrative reforms brought change in trade and economies as well. City markets encouraged the production of luxury goods for the court and everyday goods for the common people and even village India joined the city-based cash economy. The markets contained a wide array of craftsmen, shopkeepers, and sophisticated specialists. Moneylenders and moneychangers were active throughout the urban system, enabling the smooth transfer of funds across the empire. Their *hundis* (bills of exchange) were accepted throughout the empire, and these financial instruments facilitated the work of government officials in collecting and transmitting in cash the taxes and rents on land. Indian cities boasted very wealthy financiers and important guild organizations. The guilds, much like those in contemporary Europe, regulated and supervised the major trades. Contrary to popular beliefs sometimes mistakenly held about India as an otherworldly culture, business flourished and prospered. After all, among the multitude of India's castes, were baniyas or vaishyas who were charged specifically with carrying on business.

Indian traders were highly mobile and therefore had some independence from the political fortunes of the rulers of the time. If a particular ruler could not defend his territory against foreign invasion or maintain internal law and order, or if he tried to extort excessive taxes, the merchant communities could leave for other cities more amenable to their pursuits. Conversely, rulers who wanted to improve their commercial prospects lured these footloose merchants with offers of free land and low taxes. Thus, even in the event of political decline or catastrophe, India's business might continue.

Indian businessmen continued to carry on coastal and ocean-going trade, but the imperial government could not support these ventures very effectively. They had no navy. In 1686, for example, the English blocked Indian trade between Bengal and Southeast Asia and even seized ships belonging to the officers and family members of the Mughal rulers. The Emperor Aurangzeb replied by land, forcing the English out of their settlement at Hoogly. But the English relocated, built a new town, Calcutta, and continued their mari-time commerce and armed competition. Furthermore, despite sophisticated economic institutions developed within family-held firms, Indian merchants did not developimpersonal business firms like the European joint stock companies. When the European joint stock companies arrived on the subcontinent, they opened a new scale of overseas operations. Finally, Indian merchants did not normally arm themselves or contract for armed forces, as did many European merchants, especially the joint stock companies. Although they might flee particular rulers, business elites did not directly challenge the power of the ruler or seek to supplant it with their own forces.

Ming and Qing Dynasties in China

The Ming dynasty in China, as we saw in Chapters 12 and 13, had largely closed China to foreign trade in favor of developing the internal economy and of defending the northern borders against Mongol and Manchu attack. They repaired the Great Wall and extended it by an additional 600 miles. Having limited the size and power of their navy, the Ming were harassed by Japanese and Chinese pirates on their coasts. The Ming responded meekly by avoiding the sea and reviving the system of inland transportation by canals. The pirate attacks increased and became minor invasions of the mainland, even up the Yangzi River. Following national unification at the end of the sixteenth century, the new Japanese government brought their pirates under control, but in 1592 Japan invaded Korea, intending ultimately to invade China. Warfare continued for years, mostly within the Korean peninsula, but also within north China, until Japan finally withdrew in 1598.

The Western presence was limited at this stage. The few Portuguese who arrived in China after 1514 were mostly Jesuit missionaries whose influence was felt far more in the culture of the court than in the commerce of the marketplace. Matteo Ricci (1552–1610), one of the most prominent of the Jesuit missionaries to China, shared with government officials in Beijing his knowledge of mathematics, cartography, astronomy, mechanics, and clocks, while hemastered the Chinese language and many of the Confucian classics. The Jesuits concentrated their efforts on winning the elites of China, and by 1700 some 300,000 Chinese had converted to Christianity.

Despite the shutdown of most international trade, China's economy expanded, at least until about 1600. China, after all, contained one-fifth of the

"Idris giving instruction to mankind on the art of weaving," Mughal period, c. 1590. In the Islamic tradition, the mythical Idris gives instruction and protection to pious and skilled weavers. Here weavers wash, dry, spin, skein, and weave their wool, while courtiers present rolls of cloth for inspection. Most production was localized, as suggested here, although a few examples of large, well organized workshops, with wage labor and centralized management, mostly under the control of Mughal courts, also existed. When pressured, weavers organized in boycotts and strikes to resist the exactions of rulers and merchants, and to defend the honor of their religion.

world's population and generated an immense internal economy. The canal system encouraged north–south trade. Using kaolin clay, Chinese artisans created porcelain more beautiful and stronger than ever. Weaving and dyeing of silk expanded near Suzhou; cotton textiles flourished at Nanjing; Hebei specialized in iron manufacture.

In the late Ming period, private sea-going trade with Southeast Asia began to flourish again, often carried by families who had sent emigrants to the region and thus had local contacts. Within China, however, local authorities on the south China coast regulated and limited this trade. Fascinating research by a modern scholar on the success of overseas Chinese merchants suggests that had the Chinese government supported its own traders at home, instead of restricting them, they too might have been effective in building overseas merchant empires. The Chinese merchants

could, in terms of entrepreneurship and daring, do everything that the various Europeans could do. But they were helpless to produce the necessary institutional change in China to match European or even Japanese power. They were never the instruments of any effort by Ming or Qing authorities to build merchant empires; nor could they hope to get mandarin or ideological support for any innovative efforts of their own. (Gungwu, cited in Tracy, *The Rise of Merchant Empires*, p. 401)

When Europeans came to trade, the Chinese government restricted them to coastal enclaves. First, the Ming dynasty limited the Portuguese to Macao in 1557 (where they remained until 1999 under agreement with the current Chinese government). Nevertheless, as noted above, between one-third and one-half of all the silver of the New World ultimately went to China to pay for purchases of silk, porcelain, tea, and other products. Despite this new wealth, by the time the Dutch and British arrived in the 1600s the quality of the Ming administration had weakened.

The Qing dynasty, Manchus from north of the Great Wall, captured the government of China in 1644 and secured the southeast coast in 1683. They established the "Canton system," restricting European traders to the area around Canton (Guangzhou), and entrusting their supervision and control to a monopoly of Chinese firms called the Cohong. Because of these restrictions, and because of the vast size of China, European merchants had little effect on China.

Although most historians have emphasized the role of Europe in enlarging the world economy through its overseas voyages, some are beginning to see it was the vast internal markets of China and the wealth of its luxury goods—along with the spices of India and the Spice Islands—that attracted the Europeans. According to this perspective, the dominant economic

Portuguese ships and sailors, lacquer screen, Chinese, seventeenth century. The faces of the sailors and the ship itself are not depicted as hostile, although at the beginning of the previous century the Portuguese had been expelled for aggressive actions and by mid century were restricted to coastal enclaves.

force in the world economy between 1500 and 1776 was not the vigor of European exploration and trade but the richness of Asian markets that attracted them in the first place. The "pull" of the Chinese market attracted the "push" of the European merchants.

HOW DO WE KNOW?

How Europe Surpassed China Economically and Militarily

During the period covered in this chapter, the relative balance of power between Europe and Asia was shifting. The most remarkable shift was the slow but steady economic progress of western European nations compared to China, still the most powerful and wealthy nation of the time. We have examined the sheer prowess of European shipping, shipboard armaments, and the consolidation of their commercial classes and their nation states. Why did China not keep pace?

Mark Elvin, an economic historian, tackled this question in a classic study, The Pattern of the Chinese Past (1973), a sketch of Chinese economic and social history from earliest times. In a series of chapters Elvin praises the creativity of the Tang and Song dynasties, crediting the period from the eighth to the twelfth centuries with "revolutions" in farming, water transport, money and credit, market structure and urbanization, science and technology. But "the dynamic quality of the medieval Chinese economy disappeared . . . some time around the middle of the fourteenth century" (p. 203). Elvin gives three reasons for this disappearance: The Chinese frontier began to fill up with people and resources; commerce with the outside world decreased sharply; and philosophy became introspective, less concerned with engaging practical problems. The result was "quantitative growth, qualitative standstill," or what Elvin calls a "high-equilibrium trap." That is, economic growth continued and new natural resources were tapped, but most of the gains were eaten up by the population growth. For example, Elvin writes, in the sixteenth through the nineteenth centuries, New World crops were introduced, agricultural techniques were improved, market networks were extended, the legal status of the peasantry was improved, and entrepreneurship and invention flourished. But the population doubled from about 200 million people in 1580 to about 400 million in 1850. "Agricultural productivity per acre had nearly reached the limits of what was possible without industrial-scientific inputs" (p. 312), and these inputs were simply unavailable. Technological innovation occurred, but resources for implementing them were scarce. Wood, clothing fibers, land, draught animals, and metals were in short supply. In this "high-level equilibrium trap," the Chinese economy worked well enough in its traditional forms that there were few incentives for making changes. More important, the changes that would have been necessary to increase production substantially would have required more capital and human resources than were available. China was stuck.

Had the West faced such a trap, and, if so, how had the West avoided it? Kenneth Pomeranz, another economic historian, gives his answers in The Great Divergence: China, Europe, and the Making of the Modern World Economy (2000). Yes, he says, "Europe, too, could have wound up on an 'east Asian,' labor-intensive path" (p. 13) in which there were few incentives and even fewer resources available to create innovations to improve productivity. Its escape was "the result of important and sharp discontinuities, based on both fossil fuels [coal] and access to New World resources" (p. 13). The fossil fuels became important only later, during the industrial revolution, but the New World resources became important almost immediately after their discovery by Europeans. The New World "relieved the strain on Europe's supply of what was truly scarce: land and energy . . . crucial factors leading out of a world of Malthusian constraints" (p. 23). The New World provided a place for some of Europe's "excess" population. It also provided richly productive land, an abundance of gold and silver, the lucrative slave trade, and millions of slaves who created a new market for European products.

Was the lucky discovery of the New World the major differentiation between the European economic experience and the Chinese? Pomeranz also credits "war, armed long distance trade and colonization" (p. 166). The joint stock company organized for overseas trade and colonization was a significant breakthrough for the "unified management of trading voyages and cargoes too big for a single investor" (p. 171). The backing of the state for these ventures—without excessive, crippling interference—was probably another (p. 173). The use of "force to create monopolies or near-monopolies (mostly in spices)" was a third (p. 182). The competition among the European powers for trading and colonizing supremacy was a fourth element in driving their economic success (p. 194).

Between Elvin and Pomeranz we get a comprehensive, comparative survey of the factors at work in China and in Europe—ecological, demographic, and institutional—that led to China's stagnation and western Europe's dynamism in economic creativity in the era of the Ming and early Qing dynasties in China, the era of overseas exploration, trade, and early colonization in western Europe.

- When did the economic productivity and wealth of Western Europe surpass that of China?
- To what degree did the stagnation in China's economy result from a lack of planning and hard work?
- To what degree did the success of Western Europe's economy result from planning and hard work?

Tokugawa Japan

As in China, the early European influences on Japan were both economic and religious. Roman Catholicism appeared with the Jesuit priest Francis Xavier (1506–52), who arrived in 1549. Like Matteo Ricci in China, Xavier adapted to local cultural practices in dress, food, residence, and, of course, language. For their religious ideas, their culture, and trade, Europeans were at first warmly welcomed. Japan's **shogun**, or chief military administrator, Oda Nobunaga (1534–82), encouraged the Jesuits in their missionary work, and even after Nobunaga's assassination, Christianity found a foothold in Japan. As in China, converts numbered in the hundreds of thousands, and they were mostly from among the Japanese elites. (Among the European contributions to Japanese everyday life were tobacco, bread, playing cards, and deep-fat frying, which inspired the Japanese specialty of tempura.)

The Japanese government became apprehensive about so large a group of elite converts. There had been early signs of the change in policy. In 1597, after a Spanish ship captain boasted of the power of his king, and after Spain had colonized Manila making that power more blatant, the shogun Toyotomi Hideyoshi crucified six Franciscan missionaries and eighteen Japanese converts. In 1606 Christianity was outlawed, and in 1614 the shogun, Tokugawa Ieyasu, began to expel all Christian missionaries. Three thousand Japanese Christians were murdered. In 1623 the British left Japan; in 1624 the Spanish were expelled; in 1630 Japanese were forbidden to travel overseas. In 1637–8, in reaction to a revolt that was more a rural economic protest than a religious uprising, 37,000 Christians were killed. The Portuguese were expelled. Only a small contingent of Dutch traders was permitted to remain, confined to Deshima Island off Nagasaki. A limited number of Chinese ships continued to visit Japan each year and some diplomatic contact with Korea continued, but Japan chose to live largely in isolation.

As in China, the suppression of contact with outsiders did not cripple Japan. Its process of political consolidation continued under the three shoguns of the Tokugawa family, from the 1600 battle of Sekigahara until 1651. The country was unified and peaceful. Privately held guns were virtually banned. Agriculture prospered as the area of land under cultivation doubled, and the production of cash crops, such as indigo, tobacco (from the New World), sugar cane, and mulberry leaves as food for silk worms, increased. The population almost doubled, from 18 million in 1600 to 30 million by the mid-1700s, at which point it stabilized temporarily.

The new government was in the hands of the *samurai* warrior classes, who made up about 7 percent of the population. They benefited most from the improved conditions, and there were sometimes violent protests against increasing disparities in income, but standards of living and of education generally improved. City merchants, *chonin*, emerged as a newly wealthy and powerful class, dealing in the new cash commodities of farm and hand manufacture. They supplied banking, shipping, loans, and other commercial services, and founded family businesses, some of which endure even today. The Tokugawa capital Edo (Tokyo) grew to a million people by 1700, among the largest cities in the world at the time. In a reversal of the European pattern of the time, Japan was doing well despite cutting off almost all international trade.

Southeast Asia

Southeast Asia was one of the great prizes of international commerce throughout our period, and foreign merchants from China, Japan, India, Arabia, and Europe were active in its markets. Yet the merchants of the region did not themselves become major factors in the international side of the trade. Foreign traders began their activities on

shogun The military dictator of Japan, a hereditary title held by three families between 1192 and 1867. Although they were legally subservient to the emperor, their military power gave them effective control of the country.

samurai A member of the warrior class of feudal Japan, who became vassals of the daimyo. Characterized by their military skills and stoical pride, they valued personal loyalty, bravery, and honor more than life. During the peaceful years of the Tokugawa shogunate (1603–1867) they became scholars, bureaucrats, and merchants. The class was officially abolished in 1871.

chonin City merchants and their collective class. During the Tokugawa shogunate this class grew in wealth, power, and sophistication.

the coast and then moved inland, taking control of local markets. They also fought among themselves. The Dutch East India Company, for example, expelled from the Indonesian archipelago not only the local merchants but also European competitors by 1640. By this time, the spice trade was beginning to level off and the Dutch were in the process of restructuring the economies of Southeast Asia, especially Indonesia, to produce such commercial crops as sugar, coffee, and tobacco. In the Philippines, the Spanish asserted similar power.

Local rulers entered into commercial agreements with the foreign traders that enriched themselves, but not their merchant communities. Commercial profits were repatriated from Southeast Asia back to Europe, creating ever more serious imbalances of power and wealth. Capitalist enterprise in the hands of merchants, backed by the state and by military power, was radiating outward from Europe; Southeast Asia had become a participant in this new system, and a victim of it.

THE INFLUENCE OF WORLD TRADE
WHAT DIFFERENCE DOES IT MAKE?

As we close this exploration of world trade in 1776, we have witnessed enormous changes from 1100, when we began, and even from 1500, when European explorers began their oceanic voyages. During these centuries, an entirely new set of trade networks opened, crisscrossing the Atlantic Ocean. Major elements in these new trade relationships included the export from the western hemisphere of enormous quantities of gold and silver to Europe and to Asia, across the Pacific, and the taking of millions of people in slavery from Africa to the plantations of the Americas.

The earlier center of ocean trade, the Indian Ocean, continued to be important, but now European traders—Portuguese, followed by Dutch, British, and French—gained control of the intercontinental segments of that trade. The variety of traders in coastal port cities around the world increased, with some exceptions, as in Japan, and the trade outposts of the Europeans were fortified militarily. Within Europe, the power of nation-states and of private traders increased, in large part because of the profits of international trade and because of the perceived need to support it with ocean-going fleets and navies. The new philosophy of capitalism explained and justified the rising power of private business at home and abroad. New religious denominations also arose, with philosophies that rationalized the new economic acquisitiveness. Competition increased in the technology of shipping, the sophistication of commercial strategies, the manufacture of armaments, and the training and disciplining of armed forces at home and overseas. Leadership passed from the Spanish and Portuguese to the Dutch, French, and British.

Throughout this era, the most powerful and wealthy of the world's empires were in Asia, but by the end of it, Europeans, hungry for profit, and often eager to spread the gospel of Christianity, were fashioning overseas empires of unprecedented extent.

Review Questions

- Define capitalism and discuss its strengths and weaknesses as an economic system as described by Adam Smith.
- What were the chief causes of the decline of the Portuguese empire and of the Spanish empire?
- What were the chief causes of the rise of the British, French, and Dutch empires?

- What is a nation-state? Why did European rulers seek to consolidate their countries as nation-states in the period 1500–1750?
- What were the goals of Peter the Great of Russia? In what ways did contact with the outside world encourage him to pursue these goals? To what extent did he accomplish them?

Suggested Readings

PRINCIPAL SOURCES

Braudel, Fernand. *Capitalism and Material Life 1400–1800*, trans. by Miriam Kochan (New York: Harper and Row, 1973). Highly influential overview of the beginning of capitalism as the guiding economic force in modern Europe.

Chaudhuri, K.N. *Trade and Civilization in the Indian Ocean* (Cambridge: Cambridge University Press, 1985). Comprehensive survey of the ecology, politics, traders, and the trade of the Indian Ocean.

Elvin, Mark. *The Pattern of the Chinese Past* (Stanford: Stanford University Press, 1973). An interpretive economic history from pre-Han to Qing China. Thoughtful analyses of successes and failures.

Kennedy, Paul. *The Rise and Fall of the Great Powers* (New York: Vintage Books, 1987). Examines histories of great power rivalries, including the western European rivalries in the age of exploration and trade. Seeks balance between military power and economic health.

McNeill, William H. "The Age of Gunpowder Empires, 1450–1800," in Michael Adas, ed., *Islamic and European Expansion* (Philadelphia: Temple University Press, 1993), 103–9. Brief survey of the effects of gunpowder on warfare and on the nations that use it in warfare.

Mintz, Sidney W. *Sweetness and Power: The Place of Sugar in Modern History* (New York: Penguin Books, 1985). Anthropological focus on the Caribbean sugar plantation, but places it also in the context of world trade patterns, advertising, and changing food choices.

Thornton, John. *Africa and Africans in the Making of the Atlantic World, 1400–1680* (Cambridge: Cambridge University Press, 1992). Sees Africans as active participants in the slave trade and other trading activities, not simply as passive recipients in the affairs of others.

Tracy, James D., ed. *The Political Economy of Merchant Empires* (Cambridge: Cambridge University Press, 1991). An excellent account of the merchant empires that emerged in the Early Modern period.

——, ed. *The Rise of Merchant Empires* (Cambridge: Cambridge University Press, 1990). Tracy brings together the papers of an exciting academic conference on the merchant empires of the age of exploration and early colonization. Specialized, but very important

coverage. "The Rise" discusses primarily the merchant activity; "Political Economy," primarily the imperial effects.

ADDITIONAL SOURCES

Bayly, C.A. *Indian Society and the Making of the British Empire* (Cambridge: Cambridge University Press, 1988). Sees the effects of British colonization in the early years through the eyes and activities of Indians.

Braudel, Fernand. *Civilization and Capitalism 15th–18th Century.* Vol. 2: *The Wheels of Commerce*, trans. by Sian Reynolds (New York: Harper and Row, 1986). Remarkable synthesis of the transformation of early modern Europe through its economy, social life, and culture. Volume 1 is published as *Capitalism and Material Life, 1400–1800*, see above.

——. *Civilization and Capitalism 15th–18th Century.* Vol. 3: *The Perspective of the World*, trans. by Sian Reynolds (New York: Harper and Row, 1986). Third volume in the series, looks more at the importance of international relations.

——. *The Mediterranean and the Mediterranean World in the Age of Philip II*, 2 vols, trans. by Sian Reynolds (New York: Harper Torchbooks, Vol. 1: 1972; Vol. 2: 1973). This study of the Mediterranean demonstrated Braudel's style of history, including geological influences, long-time institutional influences, and short-run political and personal influences. Highly influential for its style of history as well as its subject matter.

Columbia University. *Introduction to Contemporary Civilization in the West*, 2 vols. (New York: Columbia University Press, 2nd ed., 1954). A superb reader of some of the most influential thinkers, presented in long, rich excerpts.

Curtin, Philip, Steven Feierman, Leonard Thompson, and Jan Vansina. *African History from Earliest Times to Independence* (New York: Longman, 2nd ed. 1995). Excellent, textbook survey emphasizing anthropology as well as history.

Das Gupta, Ashin and M.N. Pearson, eds. *India and the Indian Ocean 1500–1800* (Calcutta: Oxford University Press, 1987). Articles on the vital trade and politics of the major actors in the Indian Ocean.

Duara, Prasenjit. *Rescuing History from the Nation* (Chicago: University of Chicago Press, 1995). A critical challenge to the ideas that the nation state is a creation of the modern West and that it has a fixed meaning.

Ebrey, Patricia Buckley. *Cambridge Illustrated History of China* (Cambridge: Cambridge University Press, 1996). Excellent basic survey. Pictures help tell the story. Some emphasis on women in Chinese history.

Gungwu, Wang, "Merchants without Empire: the Hokkien Sojourning Communities," in Tracy, *The Rise of Merchant Empires*, 400–21. Traces the overseas activities of merchants of the south China coast, whose opportunities in China were blocked by government.

Kamen, Henry. *Empire: How Spain Became a World Power, 1492–176,* (New York: Harper Collins, 2003). Analyzes the empire globally, accounting for the many non-Spanish groups that participated in constructing and administering it.

Lapidus, Ira. *A History of Islamic Societies* (Cambridge: Cambridge University Press, 2nd ed., 2002). A 1000+ page, comprehensive, well-written history.

Palmer, R.R. and Joel Colton. *A History of the Modern World* (New York: Knopf, 9th ed., 2002). Once THE major text; now considered too Eurocentric, and very Francophile, but still excellent.

Pearson, M.N., "Merchants and States," in Tracy, ed., *The Political Economy of Merchant Empires*, 41–116. Discusses the role of the state in encouraging business, mostly in Europe, but considers Asia as well.

Pomeranz, Kenneth. *The Great Divergence: Europe, China, and the Making of the Modern World Economy* (Princeton: Princeton University Press, 2000). How did Europe surpass China? An economic historian explores various explanations. He suggests: The exploitation of New World resources; coal in Britain; armed merchant exploration and trade.

Reid, Anthony. *Southeast Asia in the Age of Commerce 1450–1680*. Vol 1: *The Land Below the Winds*; Vol 2: *Expansion and Crisis* (New Haven: Yale University Press, Vol. 1: 1988; Vol.

2: 1993). Excellent collection of conference papers on foreign merchant impacts on Southeast Asia.

Rothermund, Dietmar. *Asian Trade and European Expansion in the Age of Mercantilism* (Delhi: Manohar, 1981). Survey of economic history.

Schama, Simon. *The Embarrassment of Riches* (New York: Knopf, 1987). Study of early modern Netherlands, especially its artistic production.

Smith, Adam. *An Inquiry into the Nature and Causes of the Wealth of Nations* (New York: Modern Library, 1937). The classic philosophical rationale for capitalism.

Spence, Jonathan D. *The Memory Palace of Matteo Ricci* (New York: Penguin Books, 1985). An account of the work and the significance of Matteo Ricci in China, filled with cultural information, as on the function of memory.

Steensgaard, Niels. *The Asian Trade Revolution of the Seventeenth Century* (Chicago: University of Chicago Press, 1973). Argues that most Asian traders were small scale and not well organized.

Tawney, R.H. *Religion and the Rise of Capitalism* (New York: Harcourt, Brace, & Co., 1926). Argues, against Max Weber, that Catholicism also showed substantial economic entrepreneurship and that religious and moral principles will always be included in economic considerations.

Thomas, Hugh. *Rivers of Gold: The Rise of the Spanish Empire, from Columbus to Magellan* (New York: Random House, 2004). The first thirty years of conquest seen largely through the eyes of the men who carried it out.

Weber, Max. *The Protestant Ethic and the Spirit of Capitalism*, trans. by Talcott Parsons (London, 1930). Argues that religious beliefs do have considerable impact on economic performance. Also, in the modern world, religious enthusiasm had been supplanted by economic aspirations.

Wolf, Eric. *Europe and the People without History* (Berkeley: University of California Press, 1982). Historical anthropologist demonstrates that non-European societies are not unchanging. Their recent history has been heavily influenced by the capitalist West.

◉ World History Documents CD-ROM

14.2 Vasco da Gama: Journey to India
16.1 Matteo Ricci: Journals
16.2 Dynastic Change in China Tears a Family Apart
16.3 Ceremonial for Visitors: Court Tribute
16.4 Taisuke Mitamura: The Palace Eunuchs of Imperial China
16.5 Letter to King George: China and Great Britain
16.6 Japan Encounters the West
16.7 The Laws for the Military House (Buke Shohatto), 1615

MIGRATION

DEMOGRAPHIC CHANGES IN A NEW GLOBAL ECUMENE, 1300–1750

KEY TOPICS
- The "New Europes"
- Slavery: Enforced Migration, 1500–1750
- Asian Migrations, 1300–1750
- Global Population Growth and Movement
- Cities and Demographics
- Migration and Demography: What Difference Do They Make?

In the past, historians have chosen most frequently to write about great individuals, major institutions, and the politics and wards of particular peoples. In the twentieth century, however, and especially in its second half, historians began to examine demographics—that is, human populations viewed collectively and usually represented in quantitative terms. They asked such questions as: When and why do populations grow and decline? What are the impacts on population of disease, war, famine, and more efficient farming methods? What is the distribution of population by age, gender, class, and household size? They utilize life expectancy and other "vital statistics" such as birth rates, death rates, and marriage rates. They may analyze the average age at marriage, and rates of childbirth, legitimacy, and illegitimacy.

Through large-scale analyses of such data demographers seek to understand and interpret patterns of change and, although the statistics may sometimes seem dry, they tell stories of fundamental structures and changes in human society. Today, most governments gather this sort of information as a matter of course. To find information on earlier periods that lack such systematic official data collection, historians search for other sources. Church registers of birth and death, travelers' estimates of sudden population expansion and of catastrophes, ships' records of passengers and cargo, for example, have all proved valuable sources. In this chapter we shall examine demographic data specifically concerned with migration, the movement of large groups of people across geographical space, from one region to another, and between countryside and city. We touched on some of these issues from the beginning with the migration of *Homo sapiens* around the globe

New topics in the study of the past are often inspired by new experiences in the present. In our own time, demographic shifts are dramatically altering our world, both in the population explosion that has doubled the earth's population in the last thirty years and in the migrations of hundreds of millions of people both from one region to another and from rural areas to cities. The United States, in particular, stresses its importance as a nation of immigrants, a pattern that has continued from before its beginnings as a nation down to our own times. In addition, the USA continues to experience massive population shifts, especially from north to south and from east to west, and also from countryside to city and from city to suburb. These demographic transformations evoke comparisons with earlier historical eras, especially the period 1500–1750, when the population of whole continents was restructured as new peoples immigrated and native populations perished. At the same time, great capital cities, some of them newly founded, also experienced enormous population growth.

There is another reason for choosing to study aggregate populations instead of individual lives. Such studies are often the closest we can come to understanding the lives of average people. They may not have left written records—most were not literate

Opposite **Albrecht Dürer, *Portrait of a Black Man*, 1508. Charcoal on paper.** Europeans saw black Africans mostly in slavery. This *Portrait of a Black Man* by the great German painter Albrecht Dürer is exceptional, portraying the subject as intelligent, clear-eyed, thoughtful, and independent of spirit. (*Graphische Sammlung Albertina, Vienna*).

(they could not read or write)—so we are not able to know their individual biographies, but through demographic studies of aggregate groups we may be able to gain a better understanding of the societies in which they lived and died.

Finally, new kinds of research often require new kinds of tools; sometimes the research is motivated by the availability of these new tools. Population history requires quantitative information and the statistical tools to work with it. Within the last generation demographers have made great strides in methodology, some of it as a result of new computers and data-processing capabilities. Their quantitative researches provide additional, new replies to the question "How Do We Know?"

Our explorations will take us to four major issues: First, the formation of "New Europes" around the globe as settlers from Europe set out in all directions—often with catastrophic consequences for native populations in each of these areas. Second, the trade in slaves that brought some 10 million people from Africa to the Americas—against a background of the longstanding historic trade in slaves in many parts of the globe. Third, very long-distance migrations of Mongols and Turks, groups of people emerging from Central Asia and invading and conquering lands from China in the east, to Russia and the Balkans in the west, to India in the south. Finally, we will analyze migrations from rural areas to cities in several different parts of the world and compare and contrast peoples' reasons for moving.

THE "NEW EUROPES"

From 1500 to 1750 internal developments within Europe began to increase the area's influence in the world and expedited the emigration of millions of Europeans to establish "New Europes" around the globe. Many of these developments were discussed in Chapter 14. These included:

- increasing powers of the traders in the diaspora cities of trade around the globe;
- increasing power of European nation-states and their support for overseas trade;
- shifting of trade to the Atlantic (rather than the Indian) Ocean;
- increasing pace of technological invention in Europe, especially in guns and ships;
- increasing discipline and order within European armies;
- importation of immense quantities of gold and silver from the New World, much of which was sent to China and India to pay for imports to Europe;
- exploitation of the labor of millions of slaves taken from Africa to work the plantations of the New World;
- spreading the message of aggressive Christianity.

Some historians see the crusades as a precursor of the massive movements of population after 1500. These religious campaigns to seize and settle the "Holy Land" lasted from 1096 until just after the last crusader kingdom was destroyed in 1291. The crusaders established commercial settlements along with their fortresses, and their new settlements also housed at least some missionaries. The crusades thus prefigured the European expansion after 1500 in including goals of conquest, settlement, economic gain, and missionary activity.

As we have seen in Chapter 14, in the sixteenth century both Spain and Portugal built enormous global empires. The voyages of Columbus revealed gold and silver reserves in the Americas, and many Europeans who followed him were prepared to kill Native Americans and to take over their lands. Cortés conquered the Aztec nation of Mexico in 1519 and Pizarro the Incas in 1533. The death and destruction that followed were monumental, but warfare was not the greatest killer: disease was even more deadly.

The Columbian Exchanges of Plants, Animals, and Disease

The peoples of the eastern and western hemispheres had had no sustained contact for thousands of years. Columbus' voyages therefore ushered in a new era of interaction. This "Columbian Exchange" brought in its wake both catastrophe and new opportunities. The catastrophe befell the Amerindians, who had no resistance to the diseases carried by the Europeans. The new opportunities came with the intercontinental exchange of new plants and animals.

The Devastation of the Amerindian Population.
Historian Alfred Crosby, a pioneer in the study of the exchange of microbes, cites the lowest currently accepted estimate of the Amerindian population in 1492 as 33 million, the highest as perhaps 50 million. By comparison, Europe at the time had a population of 80 million. The death of millions of Amerindians followed almost immediately after Europeans began to arrive. At their lowest point after the coming of Europeans, the populations of the western hemisphere dropped to 4.5 million. The biggest killers in this demographic catastrophe were not guns, but diseases: smallpox, measles, whooping cough, chicken pox, bubonic plague, malaria, diphtheria, amoebic dysentery, and influenza. The populations of the New World, separated by thousands of years and thousands of miles from those of the Old, had little resistance to its diseases. Up to 90 percent of the population died.

Benefits of the Columbian Exchanges.
Ironically, but more happily, links between the hemispheres also brought an exchange of food sources, which later facilitated the multiplication of human lives. From South America, the cassava spread to Africa and Asia and the white potato to northern Europe. Sweet potatoes traveled to China, as did maize (corn), of which China is today the second largest producer after the United States. Today, the former Soviet Union produces ten times more potatoes by weight than does South America; Africa produces almost twice as much cassava as does South America.

The migration of flora and fauna went from east to west as well. Wheat was the leading Old World crop to come to the New World, but perhaps an even greater contribution came in domesticated animals: cattle, sheep, pigs, and goats. Domesticated horses, too, were imported from the Old World to the New. In the long run, these exchanges of food sources did much to increase the population of the world more than ten times, from about 500 million in 1492 to about 6 billion today. But not everyone participated in this growth. There were demographic winners and losers. Peoples of the European continent in 1492 were the biggest winners; Asians generally did well; Amerindians were among the biggest losers.

North America

By the early 1600s, Spanish supremacy in the New World was being challenged by the Dutch Republic, England, and France. All three had developed expertise in the construction of high quality ships, and all three fostered business groups skilled in

Aztec smallpox victims, sixteenth century. The Spanish conquest of the Americas owed more to the diseases they brought with them than to their armed forces. The Native Americans had never encountered these diseases, especially smallpox, and had no immunity. They died in horrific numbers—up to 90 percent in many regions. (*Peabody Museum of Archaeology and Ethnology, Harvard University*)

European settlement in eastern North America. Along the Atlantic coast of North America, Britain established an array of colonies. Thirteen of them revolted in 1776 to form the United States, but the northern areas remained loyal. The British restricted settlement across the Appalachian Mountains so that land was held by Indian nations and, still further west, claimed by the French. Florida was held by the British, 1763–83, but otherwise was a Spanish possession until invaded and conquered by the US in 1818.

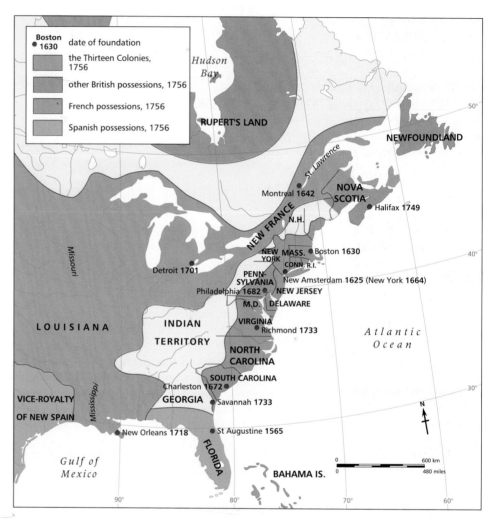

trade and motivated by profit, with strong ties to political leadership. At first, all three concentrated on the Caribbean and its potential for profits from plantations. They seized and settled outposts: England most notably in the Bahamas and Jamaica, France in Saint-Domingue (modern Haiti), and the Dutch along the Brazilian coast and in Curaçao. Later they turned to the North American mainland.

North America had its own attractions for farmers, artisans, laborers, and agricultural workers who came to settle. Some of the earliest settlers were pushed out of Europe by the "price revolution" created by the availability of New World silver. The influx of the precious metal into Europe, and into the European trade networks in Asia, inflated prices; wages did not keep pace. Pressured by this decline in their economic condition, people living at the margins of European society sought the opportunity of new frontiers in North America.

Later, through the seventeenth and early eighteenth centuries, the European invaders into the New World came in different waves and appropriated different regions for their purposes. In Virginia they came at first looking for gold, beaver furs, deer skin, and a northwest passage to Asia. They failed in all these goals, and at first they failed even to survive. Of the first 900 colonists arriving in 1607–9, only sixty were alive at the end of the two years, most dying from famine and disease. Some 9000 came between 1610 and 1622; at the later date, only 2000 were alive. After 1618 the crown-appointed administrators of the colony offered 50 acres to any settler who would come, and by this date Virginia's tobacco crop became the staple product of its economy. Settlers continued to come, but the life was difficult, attractive mostly to people of the lower social classes. Many signed on as **indentured laborers**, contracting to work for a fixed period of years, usually about seven, in exchange for ocean passage and fixed labor with a specific employer in the New World. About three-fourths of these laborers were male, and most aged between fifteen and twenty-four. Since their masters cared little for them, they were bought and sold, and sometimes worked to death, not much different from slaves. With life so cheap, at the whim of both man and nature, the further massacre of Native Americans, who were seen as alien, savage, non-Christian, and an obstacle to European invasion and expansion, became a way of life for the land-hungry settlers.

Maryland also grew tobacco, but its goals included more than mere economic profit. In 1632 the English Crown had given the land to George Calvert, Lord Baltimore, and he established here a religious refuge for Catholics, who were at that time an oppressed minority in England. Catholics formed a minority of the population of the colony, but they were legally protected. Their relationships with the Native Americans, however, were also murderous.

In New England, the first collective settlement of Europeans was the Pilgrim colony founded in 1620. Dissenters from the official doctrines of the Church of England, the Pilgrims also sought a religious haven in the New World. Their community was bound together by the Mayflower Compact, an agreement they drafted on board ship to the New World, establishing a governing body "for the general good of the colony; unto which, we promise all due submission and obedience." Of the 102 Pilgrims who landed at Plymouth, fewer than half survived the first year, but, with the help of Native Americans who befriended the settlers, the colony took root.

indentured labor Labor performed under signed indenture, or contract, which binds the laborer to work for a specific employer, for a specified time, usually years, often in a distant place, in exchange for transportation and maintenance.

EUROPEAN MIGRATION TO NORTH AMERICA	
1565	Spanish settle in Florida
1604	Nova Scotia settled by French
1607	First permanent English settlement at Jamestown, Virginia
1608	"New France" in Canada settled by French
1611	Dutch settle on Manhattan Island
1619	Europeans bring first black Africans, as slaves, to Virginia
1620	Mayflower sails from Plymouth, England, with Pilgrim Fathers to found first colony in New England, at Plymouth, Massachusetts
1622	Maine settled by English
1624	New York settled by Dutch
1630	Massachusetts settled by Massachusetts Bay Co.
1634	English Catholics found Maryland
1635–8	Connecticut settled by English
1638	Rhode Island settled by groups from Massachusetts
1638	Delaware settled by Swedes
1663	Carolina settled by English
1670	Rupert's Land claimed by Hudson Bay Co.
1681	Pennsylvania settled by English Quakers
1682	French claim Mississippi area
1713	British sovereignty over Newfoundland recognized

Puritans arrive in New England. Religious freedom and economic opportunity were the two great attractions for European immigrants to the New World. Many of the immigrants from England were dissenters from the established official Church. Their independence was a background factor that later helped to inspire the American Revolution in 1776. Some of the dissenters, however, like the Puritans, were themselves intolerant toward others who settled in their communities, forcing them to conform or to leave.

In 1630 another group of settlers, the Puritans, arrived in New England. The Pilgrims wished to separate from the Church of England; the Puritans wished only to purify it. They were richer and better educated than the Pilgrims. Many had some college education. English King Charles I (whom many suspected of secret Catholicism and who conflicted with Protestant hardliners at home), eager to get them out of England, gave them a charter to establish the Company of the Massachusetts Bay. By the end of the year, 1000 had settled; within a decade, 20,000. Many more chose to settle in the sugar plantations of the Caribbean islands.

The Puritans had left England for their own religious freedom, but in New England, they denied it to others. People like Roger Williams, a minister who wanted the separation of Church and state, were forced to flee. The Puritans were narrow in their outlook, but fiercely devoted to community, discipline, work, education, and spreading their view of religion. They scorned Indians, fought them, and confiscated their land with little compunction.

The Dutch had settled the area around New Amsterdam until the English seized it in 1664 and, after a brief loss, recaptured it in 1673. The English renamed it New York, and the area developed its own polyglot, pragmatic, tolerant business ethic instituted by the Dutch.

Perhaps the most inspiring settlement was the Quaker colony of Pennsylvania, founded by William Penn, a British aristocrat who had joined the Society of Friends, as Quakers are called formally, inspired by a lecture on the Society's basic principles of freedom of conscience, non-violence, and pacifism. Pennsylvania and its first capital, Philadelphia (whose name means "brotherly love"), became known throughout western Europe for their religious toleration, and people of many countries and faiths immigrated here: "English, Highland Scots, French, Germans, Irish, Welsh, Swedes, Finns, and Swiss … Mennonites, Lutherans, Dutch Reformed, Baptists, Anglicans, Presbyterians, Catholics, Jews," and a few hermits and mystics). Indeed, even Native Americans immigrated to flee the violence against them that was endemic elsewhere. Unfortunately, the non-Quaker immigrant-invaders did not share Penn's early commitment to tolerant, peaceful inter-racial relationships with the Native Americans, regulated by legal contracts and personal contacts. After Penn's death, they too pushed Indians off the land, although with less violence than elsewhere.

While the English were establishing numerous, diverse, thriving colonies along the Atlantic Coast, from Newfoundland to South Carolina, and inland on Hudson's Bay, the French were settling, lightly, the inland waterways of the St. Lawrence River, the Great Lakes, and the Mississippi River, as well as Gulf Coast Louisiana. During the global warfare between Britain and France, the Seven Years War of 1756–63, British military forces conquered the North American mainland from the Atlantic to the Mississippi. Their victory ensured that North America would be English-speaking. French cultural influences and migration, however, continued to be felt in the region of Quebec, and it continues as a French-speaking province until today. By 1750, about four million people of European origin inhabited North America.

The Antipodes: Australia and New Zealand, 1600–1900

The English also conquered and sent migrants to the Pacific Islands. Crossing the Atlantic became relatively quick and easy, but reaching Australia and New Zealand, on the opposite side of the globe, was quite a different matter. Even their neighbors had established only minimal contacts with them. There had been some landings by Asians in the sixteenth century. They came to the north coast of Australia in search of a species of sea slug that looked like a withered penis when smoked and dried. The slugs became Indonesia's largest export to the Chinese, who valued them as aphrodisiacs.

Spanish copies of Portuguese charts suggest that Portuguese sailors had landed on and mapped the northern and eastern coasts of Australia, and that the Spanish may also have known about them, but no continuing contact resulted. In the early 1600s, a few Dutch sailors reached parts of the coast, several wrecking their ships in the process. Between 1642 and 1644, under commission from the Dutch East India Company, the Dutch commander Abel Tasman (c. 1605–59) began the systematic exploration of New Zealand, the sea—later named for him—that separates Australia from New Zealand, the island that was later named Tasmania, and the north coast of Australia. He reported "naked beach-roving wretches, destitute even of rice . . . miserably poor, and in many places of a very bad disposition" (cited in Hughes, p. 48). With such unpromising descriptions reaching England, and the general decline of Spanish, Dutch, and Portuguese power, Australia remained virtually untouched by Europeans for a century and a half, and the pattern of immigration from Europe lags behind the pattern going to the western hemisphere by a similar amount of time.

In 1768, the English Captain James Cook (1728–79) set out on a three-year voyage, which took him to Tahiti to record astronomical observations; to Australia to determine the nature of the "Southern Continent" reported by Tasman; to map New Zealand; and, thanks to the zeal of a young amateur botanist, Joseph Banks (1743–1820), to report on the natural resources of all these distant lands. The success of Cook's three-year voyage was made possible by discoveries of proper food supplements to prevent scurvy among the sailors and of new instrumentation to chart longitude and thus

SOURCE

Captain Cook Encounters the Aboriginals of Australia

Abel Tasman's description of the fierce Maori of New Zealand discouraged Europeans from further explorations of those islands. A similarly dismal, and racist, report on Australia was written by the only European to have visited it, William Dampier, who had come to the north coast from New Holland (Indonesia) in 1688:

The inhabitants of this country are the miserablest people in the World . . . They have great Heads, round Foreheads, and great Brows. Their Eye-lids are always half closed, to keep the Flies out of their Eyes . . . therefore they cannot see far.

They are long-visaged, and of a very unpleasing aspect; having no one graceful feature in their faces.

They have no houses, but lye in the open Air, without any covering; the Earth being their Bed, and the Heaven their Canopy . . .

I did not perceive that they did worship anything. (cited in Hughes, p. 48)

Captain Cook's view was the absolute contrary:

They may appear to some to be the most wretched people upon Earth, but in reality they are far happier than we Europeans; being wholly unacquainted not only with the superfluous, but the necessary Conveniencies so much sought after in Europe, they are happy in not knowing the use of them. They live in Tranquility which is not disturb'd by the Inequality of Condition: The Earth and sea of their own accord furnishes them with all things necessary for life, they covet not Magnificent Houses, Houshold-stuff, etc., they live in a warm and fine Climate and enjoy a very wholesome Air, so that they have very little need of Clothing and this they seem to be fully sencible of, for many to whome we gave Cloth etc. to, left it carlessly upon the Sea beach and in the woods as a thing they had no manner of use for. In short they seem'd to set no Value upon any thing we gave them, nor would they ever part with any thing of their own for any one article we could offer them; this in my opinion argues that they think themselves provided with all the necessarys of Life and that they have no superfluities. (Cook, Vol. I, p. 399)

Cook took with him on the voyage a young botanist, Joseph Banks. Bank's descriptions of the Aboriginals presented them as timid, without property, and few in number. Although Banks was not proposing colonization, those who wished it could find encouragement in his comments. Banks and his associate Daniel Solander brought back from the three-year trip some 30,000 specimens representing 3000 species, of which 1600 had never before been seen by European scientists. Not all of these were from Australia, but in honor of the work of Banks and Solander, Cook named his principal harbor in Australia "Botany Bay."

Australia was distant from Europe, but based on Cook's discoveries, it seemed to hold rich promise for future encounters.

establish location at sea. Cook's descriptions of the people he encountered in Australia differed sharply from those of Tasman. He found them peaceful—unlike the Maori of New Zealand. This sealed the fate of Australia.

On the basis of Cook's report, the British government decided that Australia could serve as the "dumping ground" it had been seeking for the prisoners who were overcrowding the jails at home. (Until the Revolutionary War, the American colonies had served this purpose.) British settlement in Australia thus began in the form of penal colonies. From 1788, when the first shipload of convicts arrived, until the 1850s, "transportation" to Australia was the only alternative to hanging for British prisoners. Under the "assignment system," convicts were assigned for the duration of their sentences to particular masters, about 90 percent of them private individuals, about 10 percent government officials superintending public works projects. Conditions among the prisoners were extremely harsh, and sexual relationships in particular reflected both the demography and the harshness. Men outnumbered women among the prisoners by a ratio of 6 to 1; in the cities, 4 to 1; in the countryside, 20 to 1. Both prostitution and rape were common among the women; homosexuality flourished among the men. Beginning in 1835, new prison acts in Britain began to provide for prisons at home and the use of Australia as a prison colony quickly declined. By 1868, the last convict ship unloaded its cargo—Irish prisoners deposited in Western Australia.

The early British colonization of Australia began at Botany Bay, adjacent to Sydney, and then at other points along the southeast coast, the best watered and most fertile part of Australia. Because mountains flanked close against the coast and fresh water was scarce, progress inland was problematic, and settlement by Europeans was slow, based on commercial agriculture in wool, dairy cattle, and sugar cultivation.

In the 1850s and again in the 1890s, however, gold was discovered and newcomers rushed in. The advent of faster shipping stimulated wheat exports, and refrigeration increased the frozen meat trade after 1880. Even so, the population in 1861 was only 1,200,000; by 1901 it had climbed to 3,800,000.

The coming of Europeans, even in small numbers, destroyed the fragile ecology of aboriginal civilization, which survived only in the center and far north of the

A government jail gang, Sydney, New South Wales, eighteenth century. After they lost their colonies in the American Revolution and their prison colonies among them, the British were searching for a new dumping ground for their convicts. Australia met their needs. The first shipload of convicts arrived in 1788. (*Private Collection*)

A model war canoe, Gisbourne, New Zealand, eighteenth century. Until the end of the eighteenth century, a Maori war canoe was the most prized and decorated clan possession.

continent. As in other "New Europes," European diseases killed off the overwhelming majority of the Aboriginals. In addition, their hunting grounds were displaced by the sheep and cattle, the fences and the pasturage of the British settlers. Finally, the savagery and the explicit policies of the British, both official and unofficial, overwhelmed them. A large proprietor of sheep and cattle

> narrated as a good thing, that he had been one of party who had pursued the blacks, in consequence of cattle having been rushed by them, and he was sure they shot upwards of a hundred . . . [H]e maintained that there was nothing wrong in it, that it was preposterous to suppose they had souls. (Hughes, p. 277)

At first, the Australian Aborigines, who lived nomadically by hunting and gathering, retreated in the face of white advances, but later they began to resist, to defend their ancestral territories as best they could with bows and arrows and spears against British weaponry. They resisted in some places for up to ten years, stealing British guns and learning to use them, attacking sheep, cattle, horses, and homes. British response to the resistance was intensified by the belief that the Aborigines could neither be attracted nor compelled into productive work for the British. In 1788, when Europeans first arrived to settle Australia, there had been perhaps 300,000 Aborigines. By 2000, the 19 million inhabitants of Australia were 92 percent European, 7 percent Asian, 1 percent aboriginal. Today, most of Australia's 50,000 full-blooded Aborigines, and many of its 150,000 part-Aborigines, live on reservations in arid inland regions.

The devastation caused by the arrival of British settlers was repeated in New Zealand. The Maori, an East Polynesian people, had arrived and settled in New Zealand about 750 C.E. They had lived there for almost a thousand years, probably in isolation, until Tasman reached New Zealand's west coast in 1642. The Maori killed four members of his party and prevented his landing. More than a century later, James Cook explored New Zealand for four months and found the Maori brave, warlike, and cannabalistic. Joseph Banks, who was on the voyage, wrote: "I suppose they live intirely [sic] on fish, dogs, and enemies".

The people may have been fierce, but the seals and whales in the coastal waters, and the flax and timber on the land, attracted hunters and traders from Australia, America, and Britain. The first missionaries came in 1814 to convert the Maori. Warfare against and among the Maori was made more deadly by weapons introduced by Europeans. Diseases accompanying the European arrival, especially tuberculosis, venereal diseases, and measles, cut the Maori population from about 200,000 when Cook arrived to perhaps 100,000 in 1840 and to 42,000 by the end of the century. In 1840, British settlers signed a treaty with a group of Maori chiefs that gave sovereignty to the British Crown. Although they declared equal rights under law for Maoris and Europeans, in practice they enforced racial inequality. The British confiscated Maori lands on North Island and precipitated wars that drove the Maori from some of New Zealand's richest lands.

Captain Hobson signing the Treaty of Waitanga with Maori chiefs, 1840. The treaty was intended to secure the annexation of New Zealand to the British government, while guaranteeing the constitutional rights of the Maoris. But language difficulties and cultural differences caused misinterpretation of the fine print and the settlers' sense of racial superiority over the "natives" eventually precipitated wars and the forfeiture of Maori lands.

South Africa, 1652–1902

The Dutch East India Company sent the first European settlers to South Africa in 1652 to set up a base at Cape Town to facilitate shipping between Europe and Asia. The Company soon invited Dutch, French, and German settlers to move inland and to establish ranches in Cape Colony. By 1700, the Europeans held most of the good farmland in the region; by 1795, they had spread 300 miles north and 500 miles east of Cape Town. The colony then had a total population of 60,000, of which one-third were whites. Most of the African peoples were of two main ethnic groups—the Khoikhoi herdsmen and the San hunters—with some from other African groups, and some peoples of mixed ancestry.

In 1795, Britain took control of the Cape Colony from its Dutch settlers to prevent it from falling to France, which had conquered the Netherlands during the Wars of the French Revolution. In 1814, the Dutch formally gave the Cape to the British, and the first British colonists arrived in 1820. The continuing struggle for land and power among the British, Dutch, and Africans is discussed in Chapter 16.

SLAVERY: ENFORCED MIGRATION, 1500–1750

Most of the migrations of Europeans were of free peoples, who moved by choice. But throughout the seventeenth and eighteenth centuries, Africa contributed more immigrants to the New World than did Europe. These Africans came as slaves, taken as captives and transported against their will.

Trading in African slaves was not new. The Romans had included Africans among their slaves and, as we have seen in Chapter 12, since about the seventh century C.E. Arab camel caravans had carried gold and slaves northward across the Sahara to the Mediterranean in exchange for European cotton and woolen textiles, copper, and brass. On its east coast, Africa had been long integrated into the Indian Ocean trade by Muslim and Arab traders. They exported from Africa gold, slaves, ivory, and amber and imported cotton and silk cloth.

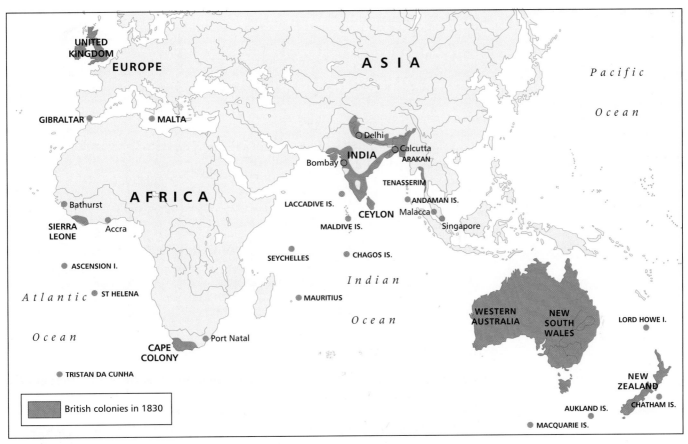

British colonies in 1830

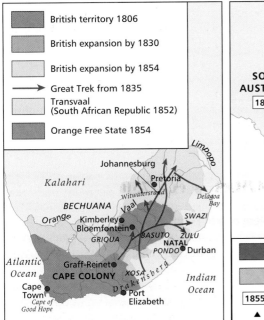

British territory 1806

British expansion by 1830

British expansion by 1854

→ Great Trek from 1835

Transvaal (South African Republic 1852)

Orange Free State 1854

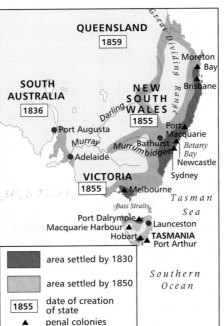

area settled by 1830

area settled by 1850

1855 date of creation of state

▲ penal colonies

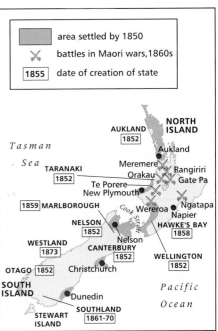

area settled by 1850

⚔ battles in Maori wars, 1860s

1855 date of creation of state

British settlement in Australia, New Zealand, and South Africa. British expansion in the scramble for empire, driven by land hunger and mineral wealth, was unparalleled. In addition to the riches of India, British colonists ousted the Dutch from Cape Colony, grasped the habitable littoral of southeast Australia (initially colonizing it with prisoners and other social outcasts), and laid claim to the world's most southerly inhabitable territory, New Zealand, as a promised land for its burgeoning early nineteenth-century population.

For an interactive version of this map, go to: http://www.prenhall.com/spodek/map15.3

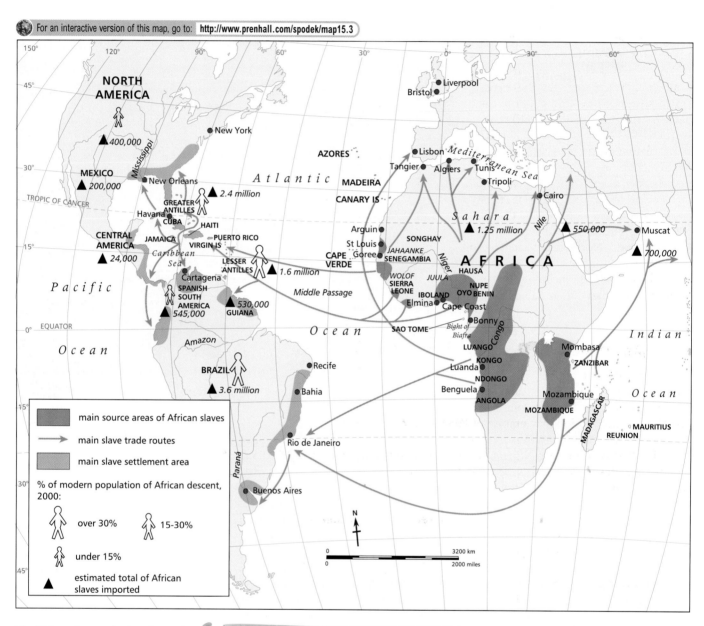

The African slave trade. A trade in sub-Saharan African slaves dated from the Roman Empire, and had been lucratively developed by Arab merchants from the eighth century. But the impact of western European entrepreneurs, seeking cheap labor for the Americas, was unparalleled. The millions of Africans who survived the Middle Passage by boat from Africa to the Americas between about 1550 and the late nineteenth century formed a new African diaspora in the New World.

Portuguese and, later, other European ships reoriented the trade routes of Africa to the Atlantic coast. Caravans continued to cross the desert, but far more trade now came to the new coastal town fortresses constructed at such places as St. Louis, Cape Coast, Elmina, Bonny, Luanda, Benguela, and on São Tomé Island. Here, Africans brought gold and slaves to trade to the European shippers. The number of slaves sold rose from under a thousand a year in 1451–75, when Portugal began to trade in slaves from the West African coast, to about 7500 a year in the first half of the seventeenth century, to about 50,000 a year throughout the eighteenth and first half of the nineteenth centuries. In all, the transatlantic slave trade carried some 10 million people from Africa to the western hemisphere to work as slaves, generally on sugar, tobacco, and cotton plantations.

The slaves took on economic importance in direct proportion to the expansion of the sugar plantation economy of the Caribbean after 1650. In the 1700s, the plantations reached their maximum productivity and profitability. Between 1713 and 1792 Britain alone imported £162 million of goods from the Caribbean, almost all of it sugar. This was half again as much as all British imports from Asia during the same period. France held the richest single sugar colony in the Caribbean, Saint-Domingue, (modern Haiti).

The slaves often fared poorly on the sugar plantations of the Caribbean and Brazil, where owners often believed it was cheaper to work them to death and buy replacements from among those coming from Africa rather than to feed, clothe, and house them adequately to sustain life. In North America, which concentrated on producing other crops and where planters encouraged their reproduction, they often fared much better.

Reinterpreting the Slave Trade

From the fifteenth to the nineteenth centuries, many individual states were taking form on the African continent. The largest, like the Songhay empire of West Africa, was about the size of France or Spain. Medium-sized states, the size of Portugal or of England, were more numerous, including the Oyo Empire in Nigeria, Nupe, Igala, and Benin in the lower Niger Valley, the Hausa states of northern Nigeria, and Kongo, in central Africa. Slavery and the slave trade were important to the rise and decline of these states. First, in a region where land was not privately owned, slaves represented the main form of wealth. A rich state held many slaves. Second, the slaves were a source of labor, a means for their owners to increase wealth. Third, the trade in slaves was a means of still further increasing wealth, either for the state itself or for private traders. Long before Europeans arrived on the Atlantic coast, slavery was big business in these African states.

This prevalence of slavery in Africa helps to explain a turn-about in the interpretation of the slave trade. In this interpretation Africans are seen as active participants who helped build up this important trade. When European traders offered new opportunities, African businessmen, who were already active in the internal slave trade, joined in, continuing to control the trade up to the water's edge. Europeans lacked the military strength, the immunity to disease, and the knowledge of the terrain to enter the interior of the continent. They stayed in coastal enclaves, while Africans captured the slaves and brought them to be purchased. Occasionally, African rulers attempted to limit the trade, but both African and European traders seemed beyond their control. The lure of profit increased as the demand for slaves multiplied in the next two centuries.

Some of the trading communities of Africa—ethnic groups that traditionally facilitated and controlled trade—probably profited, including the Jahaanke of the Gambia–River Niger region; the Juula of northern Ghana, Côte d'Ivoire, and Upper Niger River; the Wolof of Senegal; and the Awka and Aro of Iboland in Nigeria. A new community of African–Portuguese traders was also born as Portuguese and Africans along the coast bonded and had children.

A slave market, from *Al Magamat (The Meetings)*, fourteenth century. Muslims owned and traded slaves from the earliest days of the Islamic religion. Their trade in slaves included Africa, southeastern Europe, Arabia, and the lands surrounding the Indian Ocean. Islamic law governing the treatment of slaves made the practice relatively humane; slaves were used more frequently for domestic service than for gang labor. (*Bibliothèque Nationale, Paris*)

HOW DO WE KNOW?

How Many Slaves?

Philip Curtin's The Atlantic Slave Trade: A Census, *published in 1969, remains the landmark study on the demographics of the slave trade. Curtin examined the existing estimate of 15 million as the number of slaves carried from Africa to the New World and concluded that it had been accepted with little basis in research. Curtin undertook a fundamental investigation of the numbers, limiting himself to data already published rather than undertaking original archival searches of his own. The accounts included import records of specific African and American ports, shipping records, and projections based on historical slave populations in the Americas. From these records, Curtin produced the first systemic analysis of the quantity of slaves from Africa landed in the Americas.*

First he analyzed the structure of the plantation economy that produced the sugar, and stressed six key points:

- it relied on slave labor;
- it was organized as an early large-scale capitalist enterprise with gangs of laborers;
- its owners held "feudal," legal rights over the workers;
- it supplied a crop for export to distant European markets but often did not grow its own food; it was completely reliant on international trade for profits and for necessities;
- "political control over the system lay on another continent and in another kind of society";
- in its organization, the sugar plantation was a forerunner of factory labor.

Curtin begins his analysis with the importation of slaves into Europe, including Sicily, Portugal, Spain, and Italy, as well as to the sugar-producing islands off the coasts of these countries. Evaluating and revising the statistics of previous demographers for the period 1450–1500, Curtin estimates that 50,000 Africans were imported as slaves into Europe and 25,000 into the Atlantic islands of Madeira, Cape Verde, and the Canaries. Another 100,000 were transported off the African coast to São Tomé.

Based primarily on the records of asientos, shipping licenses issued by Spanish authorities to foreign firms between 1521 and 1773, and government records, especially from Britain, Curtin estimates that up to 1865 the entire import of Africans to Spanish America was 1,552,000, with 702,000 of these going to Cuba. For the entire period from 1640 to 1807 (when the British outlawed the slave trade), Curtin estimates that 1,665,000 people were imported as slaves to the British West Indies. To the French West Indies Curtin estimates that 1,600,200 were imported between 1664 and 1838, and that in Portuguese America, these numbers were more than double. To Brazil alone, with its massive sugar plantations in Bahia, Curtin accepts the estimates of two earlier demographers, who suggested a figure of about 3,646,800. To the Dutch West Indies, 500,000 people were imported as slaves; to the Danish West Indies, now the American Virgin Islands, 28,000. Imports to the United States and pre-1776 North America totaled about 399,000.

Thus, Curtin's 1969 estimate for the total importation of slaves to the Americas was 9,566,000. Overall, "more Africans than Europeans arrived in the Americas between, say, 1492 and 1770" (p. 87). Curtin noted that, although his estimates could well be off by as much as 50 percent, they were, nevertheless, "correct enough to point out contradictions in present hypotheses and to raise new questions for comparative demography and social history" (p. 93).

Curtin also explored the effects on reproduction of the slave trade. Only about one-third of the slaves sold overseas were women, so that in Africa population losses to the next generation were proportionately limited, but in the Americas, with fewer females, the slaves did not reproduce their own numbers. Even these rates of reproduction were, however, different in different areas.

North America, for example, imported relatively few slaves because those that were imported had relatively high birth rates. They reproduced more abundantly than slaves elsewhere.

The USA and Canada imported only 4.2 percent of all the slaves imported into the Americas, about 400,000 out of 9,566,000.

> Contrary to the parochial view of history that most North Americans pick up in school, the United States was only a marginal recipient of slaves from Africa. The real center of the trade was tropical America, with almost 90 percent going to the Atlantic fringe from Brazil through the Guianas to the Caribbean coast and islands. (p. 74)

Birth rates among the North American slaves were proportionately higher than elsewhere. No one knows quite why:

> Rather than sustaining the regular excess of deaths over births typical of tropical America, the North American colonies developed a pattern of natural growth among the slaves ... By the end of the eighteenth century, North American s lave populations were growing at nearly the same rate as that of the settler populations from Europe ... Historians have neglected [this] almost completely, even though it has an obvious and important bearing on such recent historical problems as the comparative history of slavery in the New World. Nor have demographic historians yet produced a complete or satisfactory explanation of this phenomenon. (p. 73)

Two different hypotheses have attempted to explain the higher rates of reproduction in North America. The first, and perhaps most obvious, was that slaves in North America may have been better treated than elsewhere. Second, slaves in North America apparently breast fed their children for only one year, in contrast to the two years more typical in the Caribbean. Breast-feeding has a contraceptive effect that would have reduced birth rates more in the Caribbean than in the USA.

Additional demographic inquiries have followed Curtin's Census. For example,

HOW DO WE KNOW? (continued)

Curtin pointed out that the location of the most active slave trading varied over time, according to the law of supply and demand. Where slaves were plentiful, often because of warfare and the seizing of captives who could be sold into slavery, prices fell; then more European slavers arrived to take advantage of the low prices, increasing demand, raising prices, and encouraging European slavers to look elsewhere. The marketplace shifted as prices oscillated. The result seems to be that no area was constantly a supplier, but that each area had time t o recover some of its population losses. On the other hand, no area remained

immune to the economic attractions of the market. The sale and purchase of slaves infected the entire coastline. Later historians have sought to locate more precisely the geographical source of slaves exported from Africa. Paul Lovejoy, for example, found that of the 5.5 million exported in the hundred years between 1701 and 1800, the three largest sources were west central Africa, with 2 million, the Bight of Biafra, with 814,000, and the Senegambia, with 201,000 (Lovejoy, p. 50)

Curtin's work initiated continuing statistical research for greater precision, but we now have a clear, empirical basis

for understanding the general dimensions of three centuries of Atlantic trade in human beings.

- Philip Curtin's studies of the slave trade say very little about moral issues. What is the importance of information about the systems and statistics of plantation slavery separate from the consideration of moral issues?
- Please give examples of ways in which the slave trade was subject to the economic laws of supply and demand.
- What regions of the Americas imported the most slaves?

The effects of the slave trade on the total economy of Africa remain much disputed. Some scholars, following the pioneering work of Walter Rodney in his *How Europe Underdeveloped Africa* (1972), continue to cite dire economic consequences. Some more recent writers, however, suggest that the slave trade, despite its enormous absolute size, was small relative to the total size of Africa's population and internal economy and therefore had little effect. This debate over size and significance continues.

No one, however, can estimate the lost opportunities for African development represented by the export of so many millions of its strongest and most resilient men and women. Crosby points out ironically that Africa received new crops such as maize, manioc, and cassava as part of the Atlantic exchange. These became staple foods and may actually have increased the population more than the export of slaves depleted it. And, of course, slavery established a new population of African–Americans throughout the western hemisphere.

ASIAN MIGRATIONS, 1300–1750

Just as Europeans were transforming the Americas and other parts of the world through their migrations, Asians were moving into other parts of the world they conquered. In Chapters 12 and 13, we analyzed the geographical patterns and economic institutions of trade and traders, and found that they developed differently in Europe and in Asia. The differences became especially sharp as the Europeans set out on their voyages of transoceanic exploration and trade across the Atlantic. Now we shall see that patterns of migration also differed sharply between Europe and Asia—and yet there were striking similarities.

We focus especially on the vast, successive waves of immigrant conquerors that swept out of Central Asia between 1300 and 1750 and created three new empires and several new ruling dynasties within the already existing empire of China. Turkic-speaking invaders founded the Ottoman Empire that sprawled across western Asia, southeastern Europe, and North Africa; the Safavid Empire in Persia; and the Mughal Empire in South Asia; while in China the Mongol descendants of Chinggis Khan and, later, the Manchus introduced new dynasties to the existing empire.

The conquests of the western Europeans and the Central Asians show remarkable similarities. The time frame for these invasions and conquests is roughly parallel. (The Ottoman conquests, blocking access to the eastern Mediterranean and the Middle East, provided the inspiration for the Europeans to launch their overseas explorations.) The distances they traveled, across thousands of miles, were equally vast. Both were ultimately motivated by a desire to conquer and subdue that frequently led to ruthless cruelty. Both imposed new cultures on the peoples they conquered—but the degree of this imposition was starkly different.

The contrasts are altogether quite remarkable. The Asians traveled over land. Although they could be very violent, they did not so utterly destroy the peoples they conquered, perhaps because unlike the Amerindians, the people Asians conquered had immunity to each other's diseases because of their long contact with each other. Since the Asian conquerors were mostly immigrants on horseback with little experience of sedentary societies, they were limited in the degree to which they could influence their subjects. Over time they tended to adopt the more sophisticated and efficient ruling ideologies and institutions of the peoples they conquered. They did not displace existing societies with new ones largely of their own design. In large measure they were assimilated by the peoples they defeated. And by the early eighteenth century, as western Europe was increasing in power and wealth, most of the Asian empires were in decline.

The Ottoman Empire 1300–1700

The Ottoman Empire was named for Osman, a Turkish leader whose military victory in 1301 established its foundation in northwest Anatolia. As the Ottomans expanded from this local base they confronted the Byzantine Empire to the west and the Seljuq Turks—another Turkic-speaking group—to the east. Through the thirteenth and fourteenth centuries they expanded their holdings, capturing much of Anatolia and crossing into Europe to take Gallipoli in 1354. The Ottoman Empire rose to prominence at

Eurasian empires, 1300–1700. Eurasia on the eve of European expansion was dominated by a complex of huge, interlocking, land-based empires, linked by overland trade routes, and by the Arab trading ecumene of the Indian Ocean. The four empires highlighted here were land-based, inward-looking, and ill-prepared for the challenge of European imperialism that would arrive by sea and, over the next four hundred years, effectively undermine them.

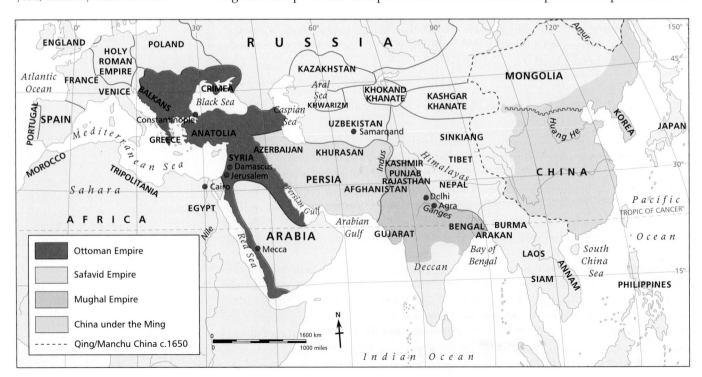

the same time as Spain and Portugal did in western Europe (see Chapter 14) and was at its height in 1600. By 1700, however, it had begun to decline.

Three groups led and sustained the Turkish invasions: **gazis**, Turkish warriors inspired by Islam to conquer territories and bring them under **Dar al-Islam**, a government hospitable to Islam; **Sufis**, members of religious orders, often practicing mystical and ecstatic rituals, who accompanied the troops and introduced Islam within the conquered regions; and **janissaries**, slaves captured or bought from among the conquered populations, usually from among the Christians of the Balkans, to be converted to Islam and serve in the elite Turkish armies and, occasionally, in the administration. In 1527 the slave infantry numbered about 28,000. In conquering Anatolia, Turks displaced the local agricultural communities and became the majority population.

After establishing a foothold in Europe, the Ottomans invited Turkish warriors into the Balkans and occupied northern Greece, Macedonia, and Bulgaria. At the Battle of Kosovo in 1389 they secured Serbia and took control of the western Balkans. Demographically, however, the invaders were not so numerous in this region nor did they force widespread conversion. A census of 1520–30 showed that about one-fifth of the Balkan population was Muslim, about four-fifths was Christian, and there was a small Jewish minority, many of whom moved to the empire after they were expelled from Spain in 1492.

Under Mehmed II, "The Conqueror" (r. 1451–81), the Ottomans moved on to conquer Constantinople in 1453 and then the remainder of Anatolia, the Crimea on the north of the Black Sea, and substantial areas of Venice's empire in Greece and the Aegean. They began the process of rebuilding Constantinople into a great capital city, and by 1600 it had become the largest city in Europe with 700,000 inhabitants. The capital attracted a great influx of immigrant scholars to its **madrasas**, religious schools, and its bureaucratic jobs, which required Islamic learning and knowledge of the law.

Selim I (r. 1512–20) decisively defeated the Shi'a Safavid Empire in Persia at the Battle of Chaldiran in 1514. He turned next against the Mameluke Empire of Egypt, conquering its key cities of Aleppo and Damascus, and its capital, Cairo. These victories also gave the Ottomans control of the holy cities of Jerusalem, Mecca, and Medina, and of both coasts of the Red Sea.

Suleiman (Süleyman) I, "the Magnificent" (r. 1520–66), returned to battle in Europe, adding Hungary to his empire and pushing to the gates of Vienna. As they entered central Europe, the Ottomans confronted the Habsburg Empire. Alliances here crossed religious lines, with Catholic France sometimes joining with the Muslim Ottomans in alliance against the Catholic Habsburgs. In a series of battles, which collectively formed a kind of world war, the Ottomans were defeated at sea in 1571 at Lepanto, off the coast of Greece, by a coalition of the papacy, Venice, and the Habsburgs. Finally, in 1580, a peace treaty confirmed the informal boundaries that endure in the Mediterranean until today between

gazi A warrior or war leader in Islam, sometimes used as a military title among the Turks.

Dar al-Islam Lands under the jurisdiction of Muslim rulers and law; by extension, lands in which Muslims are free to practice their religion.

Sufi In Islam, a member of one of the orders practicing mystical forms of worship that first arose in the 8th and 9th centuries C.E.

janissary A member of the elite corps of Ottoman footsoldiers.

madrasa A traditional Islamic school of higher education, principally of theology and law, literally a "place of study." The madrasa usually comprised a central courtyard surrounded by rooms in which the students resided and a prayer room or mosque, where instruction took place.

Siege of Beograd (Belgrade) by Mehmed II, sixteenth-century Persian manuscript. After the setback of defeat by Central Asian conqueror Tamerlane in 1402, the Ottoman Empire rebuilt, consolidated, and extended its power. A major watershed was passed when Sultan Mehmed II conquered Constantinople (Istanbul) in 1453, making it the third and last Ottoman capital city. This Turkish empire endured for 600 years (1300–1922) and at its height spanned three continents. (*Topkapi Palace, Istanbul*)

predominantly Christian Europe to the north and west, and predominantly Muslim North Africa and West Asia to the south and east.

Battles on land continued until 1606, when the peace treaty of Zsitva Torok confirmed Ottoman rule over Romania, Hungary, and Transylvania, but recognized the Habsburgs as their equals. Financially and militarily drained by two centuries of warfare with the Habsburgs in the Balkans and southeastern Europe, the Ottomans halted their expansion into these areas in 1606. In 1683, a last attempt to seize Vienna failed. North of the Black Sea, where Russia, Poland, and the Ottomans fought, the empire had greater success, taking control of substantial parts of the Ukraine in 1676. These victories, however, marked the maximum extent of Ottoman dominance in the region. Russia had built up its military power under Peter I, the Great (r. 1682–1725), and consolidated it under Catherine II, the Great (r. 1762–96), and now, in the mid-1700s, pushed the Ottomans back. Attempting to regain lost territory, throughout the late 1700s the Ottomans once again brought in western European experts to retrain their military, as they had in capturing Constantinople, but this effort was too little, too late. The Ottoman Empire had fallen too far behind the western Europeans and the Russians both economically and militarily, and they could no longer catch up.

Through both immigration and natural increase, the population of the Ottoman Empire seems to have more than doubled, from 12–13 million in 1520–30 in the early years of the rule of Suleiman I (at a time when Spain may have had 5 million inhabitants; England 2.5 million; Portugal 1 million) to 17–18 million in 1580, to possibly 30–35 million by 1600. This doubling, or even tripling, of the empire's population was consistent with the general population increase of the Mediterranean basin, which rose from 30–35 million in 1500 to 60–70 million in 1600.

India: The Mughal Empire, 1526–1707

The Mughals, a mixture of Mongol and Turkish peoples from Central Asia, rose to power a little later than the Ottomans, beginning their invasion of India in 1526. Under four generations of commanding emperors—Akbar (r. 1556–1605), Jehangir (r. 1605–27), Shah Jahan (r. 1627–58), and Aurangzeb (r. 1658–1707)—they dominated most of the subcontinent, ruling it from splendid capitals that they built in the north, and from mobile tent-cities that they occupied while fighting throughout the subcontinent. Although they continued to rule in name until 1858, the Mughals began to decline as a result of Aurangzeb's extended military campaigns, which wasted the financial and human resources of his empire and also antagonized the Hindu majority population over whom the Mughals, who were Muslims, ruled.

In 1526 Babur (Zahir-ud-Din Mohammad, 1483–1530), a descendant of Timur on his father's side and of Chinggis Khan on his mother's side, invaded India and conquered Delhi and Agra, establishing himself as sultan. His son, Humayun, was defeated in battles with Afghans and driven out of India, but he fought his way back through Afghanistan and into north India before his death. The task of continuing the conquest and consolidating its administration fell to Humayun's son, Akbar (1542–1605), perhaps India's greatest ruler.

Akbar, Emperor of India. Born in 1542, Akbar was reared in exile with his father, the Mughal ruler Humayun, in the rugged terrain of Afghanistan. His childhood was dominated by physical pursuits, and he grew up without learning to read and write, although he loved to have others read to him. Akbar's father Humayun succeeded in returning to India and re-establishing his authority in Delhi when he fell down a staircase and died. Akbar acceded to the throne at age fourteen.

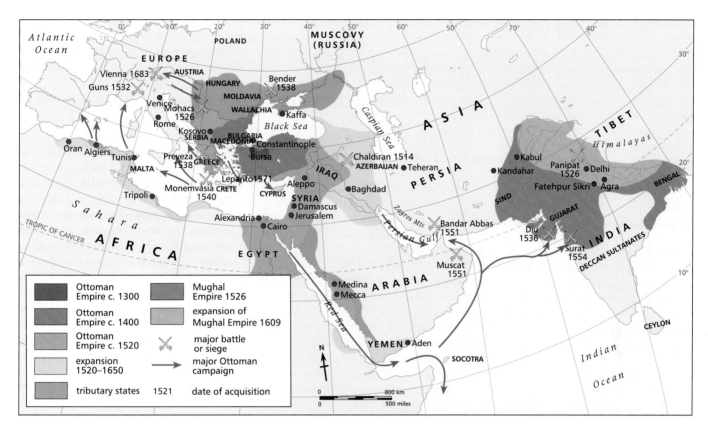

Ottoman and Mughal Empires, 1300–1700. As the Mongols ceased their advance, some of the peoples who had traveled with them began to assert their power. The Ottoman Turks began to establish their new empire, which conquered Constantinople in 1453 and thrust into southeastern Europe as well as the Mediterranean coast. Babur, a Mughal, began the conquest of India in 1526 and his grandson Akbar proceeded to construct one of the largest, most powerful, and most cultured empires of his day.

Four years later, he began to govern on his own as absolute monarch. Raised on stories of his ancestors, Timur the Lame and Chinggis Khan, and of his grandfather, Babur, Akbar now set about creating an empire of his own. He showed no mercy to those who would not submit to his rule. In 1568 protracted fighting in the Mewar district culminated in a siege of the historic fortress of Chitor and ultimately the massacre of its entire population of 30,000 inhabitants. In 1572–3 Akbar conquered Gujarat, gaining control of its extensive commercial networks and its rich resources of cotton and indigo. Then came Bengal to the east, with its rice, silk, and saltpeter. Kashmir to the north, Orissa to the south, and Sind to the west followed. Each new conquest brought greater riches.

A great conqueror, Akbar spent years on the move with his troops, but he also built new capitals for himself, first at Agra (where his grandson later built the Taj Mahal), later at Fatehpur Sikri nearby. With his chief revenue officer, Todar Mal, he established an administrative bureaucracy modeled on a military hierarchy. He surveyed each region of India down to the village level, evaluated its fertility, and thus established the land revenue each was to pay. His administrators collected the payment in cash. These reforms brought village India into a cash economy, while city markets encouraged the production of luxury goods for the court and everyday goods for the common people. Mughal officials, aware that their wealth would revert to the emperor at death, lived a life of lavish consumption.

Akbar understood immediately that as a foreigner and a Muslim in an overwhelmingly Hindu country, he would have to temper conquest with conciliation. He allowed the fiercely independent Hindu Rajputs, who controlled the hilly territory of Rajasthan, to keep their ancestral lands, and he offered them roles in his government and armies. In return they paid tribute to him, supplied him with troops, and gave him their daughters in marriage alliances, since Muslims could practice polygamy. He appointed Hindus to a third of the posts in his centralized administration, although two-thirds went to Muslims who immigrated in large numbers from Iran, Afghanistan, and Central Asia to the expanding Mughal court. In 1562 Akbar discontinued the practice of enslaving prisoners of war and forcing them to convert to Islam. In 1563 he abolished a tax on Hindu pilgrims traveling to sacred shrines. The next year, most importantly, he revoked the **jizya**, the head tax levied on non-Muslims. Between 20 and 25 percent of India's population became Muslim, most through conversion, the rest the result of immigration from outside.

Akbar encouraged and participated personally in religious discussions among Muslims, Hindus, Parsis (Indians who followed Zoroaster, their name means "Persians," where Zoroaster had his greatest influence), and Christians. (Jesuits visiting the court mistook his enquiries into Catholic doctrine as a willingness to convert.) Sufis spread their message in Hindi, a modern derivative of Sanskrit, the sacred language of Hindus. At the same time they inspired the creation of the Urdu (camp) language, the language of common exchange between the invaders and the resident population. Urdu used the syntactical structure of Hindi, the alphabet of Arabic and Persian, and a vocabulary of words drawn from Sanskrit, Persian,

Abul-Fazl presenting his book of the Akbarnama to Akbar, c. 1600. Surrounded by his courtiers, the emperor Akbar receives from his principal administrator, Abul-Fazl, the Akbarnama, an array of Mughal miniature paintings which illustrate the military, diplomatic, economic, and administrative life of Akbar's empire and government. Note the diversity in appearance and dress of the courtiers. Abul-Fazl himself was an Indian Muslim educated in Persian fashion, while Akbar was a soldier of Turkish and Mongol descent. At its best, such diversity was a mark of strength in the Mughal court. (*Chester Beatty Library, Dublin*)

and Arabic. Akbar, in particular, encouraged these kinds of cultural **syncretism** and the mixing of groups. These new practices and mixing groups encouraged still more individuals to migrate to India.

In 1582 he declared a new personal religion, the Din-i-Ilahi, or Divine Faith, an amalgam of Islamic, Hindu, and Parsi perspectives. He also incorporated some concepts of Divine Rights, declaring himself the vice-regent of God and appointing himself ultimate arbiter on disputes concerning Islamic law. Elaborate ceremonials at court emphasized the emperor's supremacy, and he was careful to encourage reverence among the common people as well. Orthodox Muslims, however, saw Akbar's pronouncements as heresies and went into opposition. Several were jailed.

In 1600, at the height of Akbar's rule, the population of India reached 140–150 million, with about 110 million contained within the Mughal Empire, about the same population as China and twice that of the Ottoman Empire at its largest. The population increase that occurred all over Afro-Eurasia at this time affected India as well, and the population of the subcontinent in 1800 probably reached about 200 million.

During a reign that spanned half a century, Akbar presided over a glittering court, in which the fine arts, literature, and architecture flourished. He transformed himself from conquering despot of a foreign religious minority to respected emperor of all Hindustan. In a half century of rule, 1556–1605, Akbar had established one of the great empires of the world.

Akbar's great-grandson, and third successor, Aurangzeb (Alamgir, 1658–1707), continued the Mughal conquest almost to the southern tip of the country. But Aurangzeb forsook Akbar's tolerance. He imposed a poll tax on Hindus and desecrated their shrines and statues, antagonizing them and fomenting resentment. Aurangzeb's military adventures in the south overextended his armies and overtaxed the peasantry to the point of revolt. Hindu Marathas in western India and **Sikhs** in the north, as well as the Afghan Nadir Shah, who invaded from Iran in 1739, rose against the Mughal Empire. By the middle of the eighteenth century, the empire lay weak and open to new invaders from western Europe—the British and the French.

Safavid Persia, 1400–1700

In the thirteenth century the Mongols and Turks first devastated and then repopulated Persia. At first the invaders systematically exterminated the populations of the cities they confronted; others, hearing of the massacres, fled. The invading Mongols and Turks then settled on the land, reducing to serfdom those who remained behind, and

jizya A tax levied on non-Muslims who were considered monotheistic people-of-the-book and therefore to be protected: Jews, Christians, and, later, Zoroastrians and Hindus.

syncretism The mixture of different religious traditions. The term is also used to refer to hybridity in other areas, such as art and culture.

Sikhs Members of a religious community founded in the Punjab region of North India by Guru Nanak in the sixteenth century. Sikhism combines *bhakti*, devotional Hinduism with Islamic Sufism. In the face of the militant opposition of its neighbors, Sikhs also became a militant armed group.

MIGRATION 1200–1930	
1211	Chinggis (Genghis) Khan conquers China
1301	Osman establishes the foundation of the Turkish Empire in northwest Anatolia
1370–1405	Timur the Lame's victories over Iran, northern India, Anatolia, and northern Syria
c. 1450	Portugal begins to trade in slaves from the West African coast
1453	Ottoman Empire conquers Constantinople beginning big thrust into Europe
1500–1888	About 9.6 million slaves are transported to the Americas
1521–35	Hernán Cortés captures most of Mesoamerica and the Yucatán for Spain
1533	Francisco Pizarro defeats Incas; establishes Spanish colony in South America
1565–1605	Akbar establishes Mughal Empire, gaining dominion over two-thirds of India
1607	English found colony in Virginia in North America
1600	Ottoman Empire population (c. 30–35 million) has more than doubled in sixty years
1619	First African slaves brought to British North America
1620	*Mayflower* sets sail for New World
c. 1640	Russia gains control over most of North Asia
1652	Dutch settlers set up a base at Cape Town, South Africa
1680–1800	Chinese imperial expansion to most of Central Asia
1788	British settlement of Australia
1840	Britain annexes New Zealand
1820–1930	50 million Europeans migrate to North and South America, Australia, and New Zealand

The Defeat of Pir Padishah by Shah Rukh in 1403, Persian, 1420–30. Shah Rukh, son of Timur the Lame, was a direct ancestor of the Safavid Persians. During his reign, he had to deal with several rebellions, including one by the Sarbadars, a brigand community in Khurasan. Leading the decisive charge, Shah Rukh's army commander beheads one of the rebel cavalrymen. (*Victoria & Albert Museum. London*)

taxing them into poverty. By the end of the century, however, the invaders began to assimilate Persian ways, rebuilding the cities, redeveloping the irrigation works, supporting agriculture and trade, including the silk routes to China, and adopting both the religion of Islam and the culture of Persia, with its monarchical traditions.

In 1370 the successor to the Chaghatay branch of the Mongols, Timur the Lame (Tamerlane, as Europeans called him; *c.* 1336–1405) came to power, ruling Iran, and much of northern India, Anatolia, and northern Syria from his capital in Samarqand until his death in 1405. With this further set of invasions, Turkish peoples came to constitute about one-fourth of Iran's population, which is the ratio today. The Mongol/Turkish invaders were pastoral peoples, and under their rule substantial agricultural land once again reverted to pasturage and villagers turned to nomadic existences, farming in valley bottoms and herding sheep in nearby mountain highlands.

Culturally, some of the Turks, as well as other ethnic groups in Iran, later came to accept the militantly religious teachings of Shaykh Safi al-Din (1252–1334). His followers, called Safavids, claimed political as well as religious authority. In 1501, a disciple of the teachings of Safi, Shah Isma'il (1487–1524) declared himself the hidden imam, the long-awaited political/religious messiah of Shi'ite Muslims. He occupied Tabriz and proclaimed himself the Shah of Iran.

The Safavids found it difficult to bring together the diverse peoples and interests of Iran. The greatest achievement was by Shah Abbas (1588–1629), who built up the military capacity of the country. He did this, in part, by importing European weapons, equipment, technicians, and advisers. He acquired and built muskets and artillery that were capable of matching the Ottomans. Like other Safavid rulers, he brought slaves from Georgia, Armenia, and Turkish lands to form the core of his armies. Abbas also built a great, new capital city at Isfahan. He encouraged trade and commerce there by inviting Armenian merchants as well as many artisans, including ceramicists who could produce "Chinese" porcelains. He invited some Chinese potters to teach Iranians their trade, and some of them remained and settled in Isfahan. Abbas, however, murdered competing religious leaders and groups, including other Shi'a groups as well as Sunnis and Sufis. His successors in the middle of the century gave official sanction to efforts to convert both Jews and Zoroastrians to Islam by force. But they did not succeed in bringing all the powers of his decentralized realm into a centralized monarchy.

By the end of the seventeenth century, the Safavid army was unraveling, its central administration was failing, regional powers were reasserting themselves, and Iran was in anarchy. Despite the occasional brilliant military conqueror, such as Nadir Shah (1688–1747), another Turkish/Mongol immigrant who took the throne in 1736, Iran was already moving toward partition, first internally, and later at the hands of Europeans and Russians.

China: The Ming and Manchu Dynasties, 1368–1750

In 1211 Chinggis Khan invaded and conquered China, destroying the Song dynasty in the process. His descendants established the Yuan dynasty, which ruled for a century (1271–1368) until the Ming dynasty drove them out and established its own long and successful rule (1368–1644).

By 1600 China's economy was flourishing and the country contained one-fifth of the world's population, about 150 million people. Ming border policy was to pacify and to accommodate the Mongol peoples of the north. The emperors stationed large numbers of troops there and rebuilt the Great Wall. Ming anxieties were well founded. In 1644 China was once again conquered by invaders from the north, as the Jurchen, or Manchus, of Manchuria established a new dynasty, the Qing (1644–1911). The Manchu invasions undercut China's power and sophistication, and contributed—along with natural disasters, virulent epidemics, and the failure of irrigation systems—to a catastrophic fall in China's population. The Mandate of Heaven had surely passed from the Ming.

The Qing expanded the borders of China, more than doubling the geographical size of the country. They conquered and controlled Tibet, Xinjiang, Outer Mongolia, and the Tarim Basin, the heartland of the old silk routes. One of their most important European contacts was with Russia, and disputes between the two empires were negotiated in the Treaty of Nerchinsk (1689), the first Chinese–European treaty negotiated on terms of equality. The treaty facilitated trade between China and Russia and delimited their border along the Amur River, although the border between Mongolia and Siberia was not fixed.

The country's population began to grow again in the eighteenth century. This was made possible by the introduction of new crops into China from the New World. Sweet potatoes, for example, were widespread in coastal China by the mid-eighteenth century, while maize and the Irish potato became common in the north and in the southwest at the same time. Peanuts had spread rapidly in south and southwestern China in the late Ming, and were also becoming an important crop in north China by the end of Qianlong's reign (r. 1736–95). All these crops helped to improve the health of China's rural workers and, because the crops grew well, even in poor and hilly land, they enabled the population to increase rapidly.

Attacks on the borders by land and sea. Through the fifteenth and sixteenth centuries, the Ming dynasty was bedeviled by raids and attacks from the Mongols and other barbarian peoples on China's northern frontiers. The Great Wall underwent major reconstruction in this period. Meanwhile coastal residents were forced to take to their boats to battle the pirates who attacked their settlements. (*Historiographical Institute, University of Tokyo*).

GLOBAL POPULATION GROWTH AND MOVEMENT

Population size is both the result and the cause of larger changes in society. The numbers are important.

Demographers estimate that Europe's population more than tripled between 1000 and 1700, with the greatest growth coming after the Black Death of 1348–51. The plague killed off perhaps a third of Europe's population, but it soon increased again to its former levels and then continued to multiply. The "New World" across the Atlantic provided a new home to some of the increased millions.

Meanwhile, the population of Africa was reduced, in large part by the loss of some 10 million slaves. The native populations of the Americas were devastated, with up to 90 percent of the Native American populations lost, in some areas, although numbers were slowly augmented by European migrants. The population of Asia more than held its own with about two-thirds of the world's population. Between 1000 and 1800 the proportion actually grew from 63 percent to 69 percent of the total. Although there were massive population movements of Mongols and Turks, these migrations do not register in these charts since almost all of the movement was from one location to another within Asia.

Europeans increased fastest of all. They multiplied not only within Europe but, in the words of Alfred Crosby, a leading scholar on the demographic effects of European expansion, they also "leapfrogged around the globe [to found] Neo-Europes, lands thousands of kilometers from Europe and from each other" (Crosby, p. 2). In 1800 North America held almost 5 million whites, South America about 500,000, Australia 10,000, and New Zealand a few thousand.

Then came the deluge. "Between 1820 and 1930, well over fifty million Europeans migrated to the Neo-European lands overseas … approximately one-fifth of the entire population of Europe at the beginning of that period" (Crosby, p. 5). The number of peoples of European ancestry who settled outside Europe grew from 5.7 million in 1810 to 200 million in 1910. These nineteenth-century figures take us into the times of the industrial revolution and its massive transformations, which are covered in the next part, but the demographic diffusion across the world had already begun by 1800.

The expansion of Europe was not unique in world history, yet it was probably the most numerically sizeable and geographically widespread mass migration ever seen; a migration across vast expanses of water; creating permanent links among continents of the world that had been almost entirely separate; and bringing European dominion over three continents besides its own.

CITIES AND DEMOGRAPHICS

Studies of population movement analyze not only migration across global regions, but also the movement from rural to urban areas, and from one urban area to another. Because cities serve as centers for rule, administration, economic production, trade, and cosmopolitan philosophy and art, migration into (or out of) the cities also tells us something of the transformation of society. Here, we combine demographic data with our information on the nature of the city or cities under study to assess these transformations. The movement from nomadic to urban society is one of the most striking examples.

As we know from Part 2, we expect urban occupations, diversity of population, and rates of innovation to be very different from those of the countryside. What then was happening in terms of rural–urban movement in the various regions of the world—and in the capital cities of the empires—we have been studying? Although an examination of capital cities is not decisive, it is suggestive. We expect that capitals of strong states will attract large and vibrant populations. Here we will look at four capital cities that were especially important in attracting migrants in the various empires we have examined.

Delhi/Shahjahanabad

Each Mughal emperor built his own capital. The sultans immediately preceding them had ruled from Delhi. Akbar ruled primarily from Agra, about 100 miles south of Delhi, but in 1569 he built a new capital, about 20 miles from Agra, at Fatehpur Sikri to honor a Sufi saint who had prayed there for a male heir for the emperor. By the end of the century, however, a shortage of water at the beautiful, architecturally eclectic capital forced Akbar to abandon the city and return to Agra. His son, Jahangir, preferred to rule from Lahore and he built up that Punjabi city as his capital. Akbar's grandson, Shah Jahan, rebuilt Delhi as his own capital and gave it his own name.

Built in a semicircular shape, with a radius of 10–12 miles, Shahjahanabad (City of Shah Jahan) apparently had a population reaching 2 million by the mid-seventeenth century. As a newly rebuilt city, almost all its residents were immigrants. The merchant and artisan population, in particular, was composed of foreign merchants such as Armenians, Persians, Central Asians, and Kashmiris.

Stephen Blake in his study *Shahjahanabad* describes the Delhi of Shah Jahan as recapturing the spirit of imperial authority vested in it over centuries, most recently by the Delhi sultanate. It served also as a religious center, a place of pilgrimage revered throughout India for its tombs and graves of saints and holy men. The inner city was encircled by a massive stone wall, 3.8 miles long, 27 feet high, 12 feet thick. At the convergence of the main streets stood the palace-fort, the home of the emperor, the administrative center of the Mughal Empire. The city had its splendors. The poet Amir Khusrau inscribed on the walls of the private audience hall of the emperor, above the peacock throne: "If there is a paradise on earth, it is here, it is here, it is here." Opposite it, a thousand yards west, set on a small hill, rose the *masjid-i-jami*, the Friday mosque, or chief public mosque of the city. In keeping with Islamic architectural principles, gardens with streams of water running through them to delight the eye and the ear were included in the landscaping.

The larger city housed an assembly of military camps, each under the leadership of one of the emperor's leading generals. M. Gentile, a visiting Frenchman in the mid-eighteenth century wrote: "There are many mansions of the nobles, which one can compare to small towns and in which reside the women, equipment, and bazaars (or public markets) of the nobles" (Blake, p. 179). The twentieth-century historian Percival Spear referred to Shahjahanabad's "nomadic court and its tents of stone" (Toynbee, p. 237), the architecture reminding the viewer that the

Shah Jahan leaving the Great Mosque at Delhi by elephant, seventeenth century. Akbar's grandson Shah Jahan restored and rebuilt Delhi in the 1600s to serve as the capital of the Mughal Empire. In 1739 the Persian emperor Nadir Shah conquered the city and looted its treasures, including the famous Peacock Throne. Today, with neighboring New Delhi, it is India's capital and third largest city.

Mughals "had started as nomads in the central Asian steppes, and until their last days they never forgot their origin" (p. 238). Each nobleman also built his own mosque. But the main function of the city was as the center of administrative and military power. Visitors to India observed that in reality the largest city in India was the military camp commanded by the emperor in the field. When he went to war, as Aurangzeb did for years at a time, hundreds of thousands of soldiers and camp followers accompanied him; Shahjahanabad itself was deserted.

Isfahan

In Iran, Shah Abbas (1537–1628) made Isfahan his capital in 1598. One of the largest and most beautiful cities of its time, it contained perhaps a half-million people in its 25-mile circumference. Its two most monumental features were a 2½ mile long elegant promenade, the Chahar Bagh, lined by gardens and court residences encouraged by Shah Abbas and, in the center of the city, the *maidan*, a large public square a third of a mile long by a tenth of a mile wide. The *maidan* was lined on one side by two tiers of shops, on the other sides by the royal palace, the royal mosque, and the smaller Lutfullah mosque. The *maidan* served as marketplace, meeting place, and even as a sportsfield where polo was played.

Shah Abbas fostered artisanal production and trade, and Isfahan welcomed merchants and craftsmen from around the world. In the extended bazaar, which stretched for 1½ miles from the *maidan* to the main mosque, were located shops, factories, and

---

SOURCE

Ibn Khaldun on Urban Life in the Fourteenth Century

The great social philosopher Ibn Khaldun of Tunis (1332–1406) described the transition from nomadic to sedentary and urban forms, and the "softening" of the invaders that occurred in the process of urbanization. Ibn Khaldun's analysis presents a very early philosophy of the flowering and decline of civilization, an analysis that other historians would later repeat. This analysis also presents Arab peoples as nomadic and rough, at first, but urbane and sophisticated after two or three generations of urban life.

It is rare that the age of the state should exceed three generations, a generation being the average age of an individual, that is forty years or the time necessary for full growth and development.

We said that the age of the state rarely exceeds three generations because the first generation still retains its nomadic roughness and savagery, and such nomadic characteristics as a hard life, courage, predatoriness, and the desire to share glory. All this means that the strength of the solidarity uniting the people is still firm, which makes that people feared and powerful and able to dominate others.

The second generation, however, have already passed from the nomadic to the sedentary way of life, owing to the power they wield and the luxury they enjoy. They have abandoned their rough life for an easy and luxurious one …

As for the third generation, they have completely forgotten the nomadic and rough stage, as though it had never existed. They have also lost their love of power and their social solidarity through having been accustomed to being ruled. Luxury corrupts them, because of the pleasant and easy way of living in which they have been brought up. As a result, they become a liability on the state, like women and children who need to be protected …

… the rulers of a state, once they have become sedentary, always imitate in their ways of living those of the state to which they have succeeded and whose condition they have seen and generally adopted.

This is what happened to the Arabs, when they conquered and ruled over the Persian and Byzantine empires … Up until then they had known nothing of civilization. (Ibn Khaldun, pp. 117–19)

Ibn Khaldun's depiction of nomadic conquerors being ultimately absorbed and assimilated into the civilizations they conquer presents a process that is frequently repeated in world history. We have seen it in the barbarian conquests of Rome and China in Chapters 6 and 7. His portrait of the decadence and decay of civilizations does not, however, fit all cases. In India, for example, Aurangzeb provoked fatal rebellions when he tried to rule too strictly over too many people, from too remote a location. Aurangzeb's fatal flaw was not decadence but excessive zeal.

warehouses, as well as smaller mosques, *madrasas* (Islamic schools), baths, and *caravanserais* (travelers' hostels). Up to 25,000 people worked in the textile industry alone. Chinese ceramicists were imported to train workers in Chinese porcelain manufacture, and carpets and metalwork were also anchors of Isfahan's craft production.

Despite their differences in religion, Shah Abbas and the European powers shared a common political and military opposition to the Ottoman Empire, which lay between them. In the early 1600s Shah Abbas allowed both the English and the Dutch to open trade offices in Isfahan. He also practiced religious tolerance, perhaps for reasons of practical statecraft. Augustinian, Carmelite, and Capuchin missions were established. Christian Armenians, forced by Shah Abbas to immigrate from their earlier home in Julfa to expand Isfahan's commerce, built their own suburb, called New Julfa, appropriate to their status as prosperous merchants. A Jewish quarter also grew up in the northwestern part of the city, but later in Shah Abbas' reign Jews were persecuted and forced to convert to Islam or to leave.

Shah Abbas maintained absolute command and imported soldiers who were totally loyal to him. He also kept his forces supplied with up-to-date weapons, for he understood that Iran's status and survival depended upon them, surrounded as it was by the hostile Ottoman Empire on the west, continuing threats from nomads to the north, and a powerful, if friendly, Mughal Empire on the east. In a report of 1605 to Pope Paul V, the friar Paul Simon described the Shah as ruthless, dictatorial, and militarily prepared with forces recruited from far and near:

> His militia is divided into three kinds of troops: one of Georgians, who will be about 25,000 and are mounted; the second force ... is made up of slaves of various races, many of them Christian renegades: their number will be as many again ... The third body consists of soldiers whom the great governors of Persia are obliged to maintain and pay the whole year; they will be about 50,000. (Andrea and Overfield, pp. 91–2)

Constantinople (Istanbul)

Constantinople had been the capital of the much-reduced Byzantine Empire when Sultan Mehmed II captured it and made it his own capital in 1453. He renamed the city Istanbul and began to recast it as the administrative center of the Ottoman Empire, which he was rapidly enlarging. In 1478 Istanbul had about 80,000 inhabitants; between 1520 and 1535, there were 400,000; and some Western observers estimated a population of 700,000 by 1600. Istanbul had become a city of Turks—58 percent of the population in the sixteenth and seventeenth centuries—but there were also Greeks, Jews, Armenians, and Tziganes.

The vast **conurbation** was composed of three major segments plus numerous suburbs. Central Istanbul housed the government center, with trees, gardens, fountains, promenades, and 400 mosques; sprawling, uneven bazaars where luxuries as well as day-to-day necessities could be purchased; and the Serai, near the tip of the peninsula, where the government officials lived in their palaces and gardens. Across the small waterway, called the Golden Horn, were the ports and major commercial establishments of Galata. Here the Western ships came; here were the Jewish businessmen; the shops and warehouses; cabarets; the French ambassador; Latin and Greek merchants dressing in the Turkish style and living in grand houses. On Galata, too, were the two major arsenals—that of Kasim Pasha and the Topkhana—marking the Ottoman commitment to military power. On the Asian side of the Straits of the Bosphorus was the third part of Istanbul, Üsküdar, a more Turkish city, and the terminus of the great land routes through Asia.

conurbation An enormous, complex city, made up of many parts, each of which is a small town or city by itself—a megalopolis.

Historian Fernand Braudel sees in Istanbul the prototype of the great modern European capitals that would arise a century later. Economically these cities produced little, but they processed goods passing through, and were the "hothouses of civilization", where new ideas and patterns arose and created an order. Braudel remarks that cities that were only political capitals would not fare well in the next century; those that were economically productive would. Beginning in the late sixteenth century, the economy of Istanbul was undercut by changes in the world economy. As trade shifted to the Atlantic and to European powers that carried their own commerce around the African continent instead of through the Middle East, the Ottoman Empire and its capital were left as a backwater. Trade deserted them.

London

By comparison with the Asian and east European capitals, London had a very different pattern of immigration and employment. While Delhi, Isfahan, and Istanbul declined during the late seventeenth and early eighteenth centuries in response to negative political and economic factors, London grew, primarily because of economic factors.

E.A. Wrigley, one of the founding members of the Cambridge Group for the History of Population and Social Structure, has examined the changing demography of London between 1650 and 1750 to analyze the city's relationship with English society and economy. Wrigley begins with London's extraordinary population growth, from 200,000 in 1600, to 400,000 in 1650 and 575,000 by 1700, when it became the largest city in western Europe, to 675,000 in 1750 and 900,000 in 1800. London dominated the development of all of England. In 1650 London held 7 percent of England's total population; in 1750, 11 percent.

Before the twentieth century, as a rule, large cities everywhere in the world were so unsanitary that death rates exceeded birth rates, so London's extraordinary population growth reflects not only births within the city, but also extraordinary immigration to compensate for high death rates. Wrigley estimates that by the end of the 1600s, 8000 people a year were migrating into London. Since the entire population of England at this time was only 5 million, London was siphoning half of England's population growth into itself.

With so high a proportion of England's population living in London, or at least visiting the city for a substantial part of their lives, Wrigley suggests that the capital must have had significant influence on the country as a whole. He suggests that the high levels of population growth in London in the seventeenth century may have been a significant factor in giving birth to the industrialization of the eighteenth.

Wrigley suggests several relevant causal relationships. The first group concerns economics: London's growth promoted the creation of a national market, including transportation and communication facilities; it evoked increasing agricultural productivity to feed the urban population; it developed new sources of raw materials, especially coal, to provide for them; it led to the development of new commercial instruments; and it had the effect of increasing productivity and purchasing power. Demographically, London's high death and immigration rates kept England's rate of population growth relatively low. Sociologically, London's growth disseminated new ways of thinking about economics and its importance. Londoners placed increasing value on production and consumption for the common person, encouraging higher levels of entrepreneurship throughout the country.

Wrigley does not here discuss the political variables, but without them London's growth could have simply led to parasitism, with the urban ruling elites commandeering the production of the countryside for their own good. Such parasitism was common in imperial capitals elsewhere, as we have seen above in the Asian capital cities. In London, however, a government increasingly dominated by commercial classes reinforced the values of production and increased consumption for the common person.

MIGRATION AND DEMOGRAPHY
WHAT DIFFERENCE DO THEY MAKE?

Numbers count. Demography helps us to discover patterns in history and to formulate questions about issues that need further study. In this chapter, we have employed the methods and insights of demography to examine four great migrations in world history between 1500 and 1750. We have explored the formation of "New Europes" around the globe, the numbers and motivations of the new immigrants, and the (often catastrophic) fate of the original inhabitants. Second, we have analyzed the size, geography, and economic consequences of the slave trade both in Africa, where people were seized, sold, and exported, and in the plantation economies that absorbed most of them. Third, we have compared the migrations and conquests of Turkic-speaking and Mongol peoples from Central Asia—establishing new empires in India, Persia, and the Middle East, and a new dynasty in China—with the trans-Atlantic migrations. Finally we have discussed the move from rural areas to cities—the spread of urbanization—and contrasted the motives for this move in more traditional political capitals of empire with those in younger, more trade-oriented capitals.

These migrations have attracted the continuing interest of demographic historians like Fernand Braudel, Philip Curtin, and E.A. Wrigley. Their research and the research of their colleagues have helped us to assess the connections between these great migrations of the past and events in our own world. They have also helped alert us to related demographic processes continuing in our own world at present: rapid population growth and its consequences for global ecology; global migrations for economic opportunity—both of highly skilled technical workers seeking high-paying jobs and of unskilled day laborers seeking subsistence work; the migration of jobs from richer, higher wage areas of the world to poorer, lower wage areas of the world—labor remaining stationary but jobs moving from one location to another; migration from rural areas to cities, and from cities to suburbs; migration of refugees fleeing warfare and oppressive governments; the global diffusion of diseases, such as AIDS, West Nile disease, and SARS that seem to originate in one location and spread rapidly around the world.

These migration issues also alert us to related policy issues that persist to our own times. One example is the debate over national and regional language policies in areas where the ethnic composition of the population is changing: In the southwestern United States, for example, the growing proportion of Spanish-speaking people forces constant reconsideration of the importance of bilingualism. Another issue is the encouraging of migration as a policy to change the ethnic composition of a region. The Chinese government, for example, steadily encourages people of Han Chinese ancestry to immigrate into Tibet and Xinjiang in order to make these two provinces more Chinese and less Tibetan and Uighur. Even worse, some governments have undertaken programs of mass murder—genocide—to rid their territories of unwanted peoples. The government of Serbia implemented "ethnic cleansing" in 1999 against Albanian Muslims as part of the battle for control of Kosovo province (with constant, conscious references on both sides to the conquest of Kosovo by the Ottoman Turks in 1389); the Ottoman Turkish government murdered more than 1.5 million Armenians in 1915. In the most extreme case, the government of Germany enforced against Jews in the 1930s and 1940s. These and other issues of demography continue to arise around the globe and alter human history. We will return to them repeatedly in our study.

Review Questions

- What were the "New Europes?" What characteristics did they share in common?
- What were the main reasons for the rise of slavery in the Atlantic Ocean basin between 1400 and 1750?
- What were the similarities and the differences between the great migrations from the eastern hemisphere across the Atlantic to the western hemisphere, 1500–1750, and the migrations from Central Asia to Turkey, Iran, and India at about the same time and slightly earlier?
- The populations of which continents were growing fastest and which slowest in the period 1000–1800? How do you explain the differences between their comparative growth (or decline) in these years?
- What were the principal reasons for the growth of most very large cities before the industrial revolution of about 1800?

Suggested Readings

PRINCIPAL SOURCES

Braudel, Fernand. *Capitalism and Material Life 1400–1800*, trans. by Miriam Kochan (New York: Harper & Row, 1973). Introduction to a whole new way of thinking about the rise of capitalism in Europe, emphasizing both institutions and natural ecology.

——. *The Mediterranean and the Mediterranean World in the Age of Philip II*, 2 vols., trans. by Sian Reynolds (New York: Harper and Row, 1973). Braudel looks at long-run ecological issues, medium-run institutional configurations, and short-run political decisions in this landmark study.

Crosby, Alfred W. *Ecological Imperialism: The Biological Expansion of Europe, 900–1900* (Cambridge: Cambridge University Press, 1986). Extremely well-written and well-argued discussion of the biological consequences of the encounters of distant civilizations with one another.

Curtin, Philip D. *The Atlantic Slave Trade: A Census* (Madison: University of Wisconsin Press, 1969). The pioneering work in quantifying the Atlantic slave trade.

——. *The Rise and Fall of the Plantation Complex: Essays in Atlantic History* (Cambridge: Cambridge University Press, 1990). Comprehensive account of the plantation organization, economy, and significance.

Hughes, Robert. *The Fatal Shore. The Epic of Australia's Founding* (New York: Knopf, 1986). Engagingly written, exciting, thoughtful presentation of Australian history from the first arrival of Europeans to about 1870 when the system of penal transportation ended.

Mintz, Sidney W. *Sweetness and Power: The Place of Sugar in Modern History* (New York: Penguin Books, 1985). Fascinating anthropological study that begins with the Caribbean sugar plantation, extends to the uses of sugar by the wealthy, the sugared cup of tea of the British industrial worker, the Chinese tea crop, and the advertising industry that brought much of this together.

Northrup, David, ed. *The Atlantic Slave Trade* (Lexington, MA: D.C. Heath, 1994; 2nd ed., 2001). Excellent selection of articles on causes, effects, demography, and economics of the slave trade and of abolition.

——. *Indentured Labor in the Age of Imperialism, 1834–1922* (Cambridge: Cambridge University Press, 1995). Comprehensive survey of the system of indentured labor that followed the abolition of the slave trade and slavery, and its demographics.

ADDITIONAL SOURCES

Andrea, Alfred J. and James H. Overfield, eds., *The Human Record: Sources of Global History*, Vol. 2 (Boston: Houghton Mifflin Co., 3rd ed., 1998). The excerpts are extremely well chosen for global and topical coverage.

Blake, Stephen P. *Shahjahanabad* (Cambridge: Cambridge University Press, 1990). Scholarly study of the capital city of Shah Jahan, demonstrating the influence of military camp architecture and design.

Cook, James. *The Journals of Captain James Cook on His Voyages of Discovery*, ed. by J.C. Beaglehole, 2 vols. (Cambridge: Cambridge University Press (for the Hakluyt Society), 1955 and 1961).

Frykenberg, R.E., ed., *Delhi through the Ages: Essays in Urban History, Culture and Society* (Delhi: Oxford University Press, 1986). Wide-ranging collection of scholarly articles from an important conference, covering Delhi from earliest times to almost the present.

Gates, Henry Louis, Jr. *Wonders of The African World* (New York: Knopf, 1999). Introduction to Africa for a general audience by a leading Harvard scholar.

Henige, David, "Measuring the Immeasurable: The Atlantic Slave Trade, West African Population and the Pyrrhonian Critic," *Journal of African History* XXVII.2 (1986), 303–13. Surveys the attempts to evaluate the effects of the slave trade and emigration on African life.

Ibn Khaldun. *An Arab Philosophy of History*, trans. by Charles Issawi (London: John Murray, 1950). In the 14th century, Ibn Khaldun of Tunis, an early social scientist, proposed a reading of history consistent with the experiences of both the nomadic and the sedentary people of North Africa and the Middle East.

Inalcik, Halil. *The Ottoman Empire: The Classical Age, 1300–1600*, trans. by Norman Itzkowitz and Colin Imber (New York: Praeger Publishers, 1973). A standard, accessible history by an eminent scholar.

Keegan, John. *A History of Warfare* (New York: Knopf, 1993). An eminent British scholar analyzes why, how, and with what weapons people have fought throughout history and across geography.

Klein, Herbert S., "Economic Aspects of the Eighteenth-century Atlantic Slave Trade," in James D. Tracy, ed. *The Rise of Merchant Empires* (Cambridge: Cambridge University Press, 1990), 287–310. Important new analyses of the slave trade, including birth rates and survival rates of slaves.

Lapidus, Ira M. *A History of Islamic Societies* (Berkeley: University of California Press, 1988). An excellent, comprehensive, global presentation.

Lovejoy, Paul E., "The Volume of the Atlantic Slave Trade: A Synthesis," *Journal of African History* XXIII (1982), 473–500. Another contribution to the demographic study.

New York Times 2003 Almanac (New York: Penguin, 2002). Standard reference work. Annual.

Robinson, Francis. *Atlas of the Islamic World since 1500* (New York: Facts on File, Inc., 1982). Excellent reference work by an outstanding British scholar. Well written, beautifully illustrated.

Rodney, Walter. *How Europe Underdeveloped Africa* (Washington: Howard University Press, 1972). Classic statement of the exploitation of Africa by the European slave trade and imperialism.

Segal, Ronald. *Islam's Black Slaves: The Other Black Diaspora* (New York: Farrar, Straus, and Giroux, 2001). A general survey of the history of the Arab slave trade in Africa and the Indian Ocean region.

Spence, Jonathan D. *The Search for Modern China* (New York: W.W. Norton and Co., 1990). A standard history, engagingly written, thorough, good on narrative and analysis.

The [London] Times Atlas of World History ed. Geoffrey Parker (London: Times Books, 5th ed., 1999).

Thornton, John. *Africa and Africans in the Making of the Atlantic World, 1400–1640* (Cambridge: Cambridge University Press, 1992). Sees Africans as active in creating their own world, including as businessmen conducting the slave trade.

Toynbee, Arnold. *Cities of Destiny* (New York: Weathervane Books, 1967). Colorful introduction to some of the most famous and influential cities. Illustrations and maps are lavish in this coffee-table book.

Willigan, J. Dennis and Katherine A. Lynch. *Sources and Methods of Historical Demography* (New York: Academic Press, 1982). Useful introduction to significance and methods.

Wolf, Eric. *Europe and the People without History* (Berkeley: University of California Press, 1982). An historical anthropologist writes revisionist history bringing third world people into history as important agents in creating the world as it is, in a generally Marxist framework

Wrigley, E.A. *Population and History* (New York: McGraw-Hill Book Company, 1969). Explains the uses of demographic study in history.

——. "A Simple Model of London's Importance in Changing English Society and Economy 1650–1750," *Past and Present* XXXVII (1967), 44–70. Demographic analysis suggests the importance of London in preparing the way for the industrialization of England.

World History Documents CD-ROM

15.1 Bartolomé de las Casas: The "Black Legend" of Spain
15.2 Nzinga Mbemba (Afonso I): *Our Kingdom Is Being Lost*
15.3 Olaudah Equiano: *The Life of Olaudah Equiano*, or Gustavus Vassa: *The African*
15.4 Commerce, Slavery, and Religion in North Africa
15.5 Thomas Nelson: Slavery and the Slave Trade of Brazil

An Album of Comparisons

This picture album enables us to revisit three important places across periods of time. This before-and-after perspective yields some startling comparisons leading to a deeper understanding of the last century and a half.

Both the first two pictures are from Philadelphia, their perspective separated by three city blocks and 125 years. The first presents Philadelphia's Independence Hall, the site of the Second Continental Congress that adopted the Declaration of Independence on July 4, 1776, and of the Convention that adopted the Constitution of 1787. The second centers on Strawbridge and Clothier, a department store. Although no industry appears in the photograph, the electric trolley cars, the store itself, and the new "downtown" speak volumes about the transformation of the city. The photograph itself represents a medium invented only in the 1830s. From 1780 to 1907 the city had grown from about 25,000 to about 1,250,000 people.

Independence Hall, Philadelphia, c. 1780. Painting.

Strawbridge and Clothier Department Store, Philadelphia, c. 1907.

The illustrations from India suggest the continuous build up of British imperial power and wealth. In 1775 the British annexed Benaras to their holdings in eastern India, providing the background for this imagined, fawning reception of Warren Hastings, the British Governor General, by the Rajah of Benares. But it hardly compares with the actual triumphal splendor and majesty staged for George V and Queen Mary when they visited India. Their 1911 state visit marked a high point of imperial splendor.

The final pairing of pictures creates a great irony. François Biard has painted a disturbing image of the traffic in people, as they are inspected, purchased, branded, and whipped. To the rear right of the market, located on the African coast, rows of shackled slaves await their turn on the block. While a white man brands one female slave, a black man whips another. Despite its touches of voyeurism and pornography, Biard's painting unequivocally condemns slavery. During the nineteenth century slavery was abolished throughout the European-controlled world. But in Africa, European colonialism sanctioned new kinds of plantation—for example, for the production of

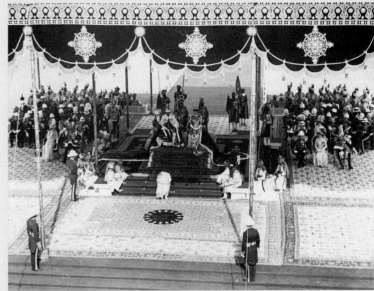

Left Anon. Cheyle Singh, Rajah of Benares, flatters
Warren Hastings, 1784. Engraving.

Above King George V and Queen Mary of England in Delhi during a
State Visit (*Darbar*) to India, 1911.

François Biard, *Slave Market on the Kambia River, Africa*, n.d. Painting.

Norman H. Hardy, 'Beating rubber and beating
time–to the tune of an old love song.' Illustration from
the *Illustrated London News*, October 2, 1905.

rubber in the Congo—so the
equivalent of slavery was simply
moved back to the African continent
itself. The photograph from the
Illustrated London News represents the
processing of the raw natural rubber
as an energetic activity for a lively
group, but the presence of the
overseer suggests that the truth was
much harsher, as we shall read in this
part of the book.

QUESTIONS

1. These six pictures are either illustrations or photographs, photography being
   invented around 1840. Which medium seems more powerful to you?
2. Within each pairing, do you think the sequence of representations suggests
   "progress," a process much heralded in the nineteenth century, or only
   difference? Why? From whose perspective?

6

Social Change
1640–1914

WESTERN REVOLUTIONS
AND THEIR INFLUENCE

Unprecedented activity in global exploration, commerce, and migration began in the thirteenth century (see Parts 5 and 6). By the seventeenth century traditional political, economic, and social philosophies and organizations seemed to be increasingly obsolete. New accommodations first took form in Europe and the Americas. Later, through political colonialism, economic imperialism, and Christian missionary activity, they spread to the rest of the world. The new forms percolated into everyday life and consciousness everywhere, but each society adapted in its own way. The results were diverse and quite often unexpected.

Many of these new forms emerged from new ways of thinking about the world. First, individuals began to think about how to understand the universe through a study of the natural sciences, culminating in Sir Isaac Newton's theory of universal gravitation. Social philosophers subsequently began to apply Newton's methods to understanding the social, political, and economic worlds. Others began to apply them in ways that resulted in major political upheavals.

Explosive events, "revolutions," punctuated the years 1640–1914. One cluster of revolutions—in England, North America, France, Haiti, and Latin America—promoted new political philosophies and introduced new political structures. Many historians refer to them collectively as constituting the "Age of Democratic Revolution."

Francisco de Goya, *Execution of the Defenders of Madrid, 3rd May, 1808*, 1814. Goya, a Spaniard, saw the French revolution and the Napoleonic wars that followed through the prism of their violence. The bitter warfare at the French invasion of Spain, and the Spanish resistance, inspired this agonized painting. (*Prado, Madrid*)

Beginning about the same time, a series of innovations in economic organization and the uses of machinery dramatically increased the quantity and quality of economic productivity. Most historians name this transformation the "Industrial Revolution." These revolutions in politics and economics were accompanied by equally dramatic social changes, which affected the individual, the family, the neighborhood, and the community. Many of these transformations originated in western Europe, but ultimately people all over the world were affected and formulated their own varied responses, adaptations, and rejections. For purposes of analysis, this part will consider these three transformations sequentially: political change in this chapter, industrial change in Chapter 17, and social change in Chapter 18.

POLITICAL REVOLUTIONS IN EUROPE AND THE AMERICAS

THE BIRTH OF HUMAN RIGHTS IN THE AGE OF ENLIGHTENMENT, 1649–1830

KEY TOPICS
- Political Revolution
- Human Rights in the Age of Enlightenment
- England's Glorious Revolution, 1688
- The *Philosophes* and the Enlightenment in the Eighteenth Century
- Revolution in North America, 1776
- The French Revolution and Napoleon, 1789–1812
- Haiti: Slave Revolution and the Overthrow of Colonialism, 1791–1804
- The Abolition of Slavery and the Slave Trade
- The End of Colonialism in Latin America: Independence and Disillusionment, 1810–30
- Political Revolutions: What Difference Do They Make?

POLITICAL REVOLUTION

A revolution is a fundamental and often rapid change in the way a system operates—whether political, economic, intellectual, or social. A political revolution, for example, not only removes some people from office and replaces them with others, it also changes the fundamental basis on which the new leaders come to power, the authority they claim, and their mission in office. Leaders of revolutions usually state their goals in terms of high, non-negotiable principles. As revolutionary struggles unfold and as different groups rise and fall, however, they may lurch from one political position to another relatively swiftly and often violently.

In a major revolution several groups may participate and cooperate in the struggle to replace an existing government. Each group may have its own goals, and these goals may be in conflict. As their joint movement appears to be nearing success and it becomes likely that a new government will replace the old, the differences among the various participating groups will emerge. Each group will seek fiercely to incorporate its own programs and personnel into the new government and even to dominate it. This struggle to control the new government may be even more brutal, violent, chaotic, and unpredictable than the battle to overthrow the old. The stakes are high. Major revolutions can have significant, lasting consequences, not only for participants in that place and time but also for people of later generations and far-flung locations.

The first three political revolutions we will consider all share these characteristics of major revolutions. The "Glorious Revolution" of 1688 in England, the revolt of the American colonies against British rule in 1776, and the French Revolution of 1789

Opposite **Francisco de Goya, *The Sleep of Reason Produces Monsters*, 1797. Engraving.** Goya (1746–1828) creates a terrifying scene challenging a key tenet of the Enlightenment: that human reason will produce progress. The title, *The Sleep of Reason Produces Monsters*, is seen within the etching itself and suggests that when the mind's defenses are down, as in sleep, we are prey to internal monsters.

removed one set of rulers and replaced them with another; changed the basis of authority of the state and its relationship to its citizens; and proposed new missions for the state. By "state" we mean the entire mechanism of government, its officers, its institutions, and its organization. All of these revolutions were fought in the name of principle. The English revolution was considered "bloodless," although it was the culmination of a lengthy period of national violence and civil warfare. The American and French revolutions precipitated lengthy wars.

All three of these revolutions have been characterized as "democratic" because they increased the participation of more (but not all) of the people in government. All of them at some time tried to balance two additional, competing goals: they sought to protect the rights of propertied people while increasing the power of the state (although not of the king). These goals were not, and to this day are not, fully

AT A GLANCE: THE AGE OF REVOLUTIONS

DATE	EUROPE	NORTH AMERICA	LATIN AMERICA
1640	■ Galileo dies; Newton is born (1642) ■ Civil wars in England (1642–6; 1647–9) ■ Execution of King Charles I of England (1649) ■ Restoration of English monarchy (1660) ■ Royal Society of London founded (1662)		■ Portugal takes Brazil from the Dutch (1654)
1670	■ The "Glorious Revolution" in England (1688) ■ The English Bill of Rights (1689) ■ John Locke's *Second Treatise on Government* (1689) ■ *Philosophes*: Diderot (1713–84); Voltaire (1694–1778); Rousseau (1712–78); Montesquieu (1689–1755)		
1760	■ Tennis Court Oath (June 20, 1789) ■ French Revolution (1789–99) ■ "March of the Women" (1789) ■ "Great Fear" (1789) ■ "Second French Revolution" (1791–9)	■ British levy taxes on Americans in the Stamp Act (1765) ■ American Declaration of Independence (1776); War (1775–83) ■ Constitution (1789)	■ Revolts against European rule in Peru, Colombia, and Brazil (1780–98) ■ Tupac Amaru revolt, Peru (1780)
1790	■ "Reign of Terror" (1793–5) ■ Napoleon seizes power (1799); Emperor (1804) ■ Napoleon issues Civil Code (1804) ■ Napoleon invades Russia; finally defeated (1812)	■ Bill of Rights ratified (1791) ■ Louisiana Purchase from France (1803)	■ Toussaint L'Ouverture leads slave revolt against French in Saint-Domingue (Haiti) (1791) ■ Haiti proclaims independence (1804) ■ Joseph Bonaparte, King of Spain (1808) ■ Bolívar and San Martin lead revolts against Spain (1808–28) ■ Paraguay declares independence (1810–11)
1820	■ Congress of Vienna (1814–15) ■ Reform Act extends voting franchise in Britain (1832) ■ Britain abolishes slavery in its empire (1833)	■ President Andrew Jackson evicts Cherokee Indian Nation: "Trail of Tears" (1838) ■ Warfare with Mexico ends in victory for America (1848) ■ United States abolishes slavery (1863, 1865)	■ Mexico wins independence (1821) ■ Prince Pedro declares Brazil independent (1822)

compatible. Individual rights to private property and the rights of the state often conflict. So we must be careful in our understanding of the "democracy" that emerged from these revolutions.

Collectively, for Europeans and Americans, the revolutions that occurred in the years between 1688 and 1789:

- situated the authority of government on earth rather than in heaven and thus increased the influence of the secular over the otherworldly;
- rejected the theory that governments were based on a **divine right of kings** in favor of the theory that governments derive their just powers from the consent of the governed;
- encouraged the creation of an effective bureaucracy to administer the affairs of government;
- emphasized the principle of individual merit, of "a career open to talent," rather than promoting people on the basis of personal and hereditary connections;
- helped to solidify the nation-state as the principal unit of government;
- extended effective power over the state to classes of people hitherto excluded, especially to men of the professions and business;
- encouraged the growth of business and industry for private profit;
- inspired the revolutionary leaders to export their new ideologies and methods to new geographical areas, sometimes by force; and
- precipitated wars of heretofore unknown degrees of military mobilization, geographical extent, and human destructiveness.

"Liberty," "equality," "fraternity," "natural rights," "the pursuit of happiness," "property," and "no taxation without representation" were the battle cries of these various revolutions. As frequently happens, the results were often unintended, unanticipated, and ironic. The political forms that actually resulted did increase human freedom for many people in many countries, but they often coexisted with slavery, patriarchy, colonialism, and warfare.

To understand these ironies more fully, we examine two further revolutions that were inspired in part by these first three. In 1791, the slaves of Haiti, a French colony, revolted and abolished slavery. The French reluctance, and later refusal, to sanction the revolution against slavery—despite their own revolution for human rights—demonstrated the serious shortcomings in that revolution. Then, in the first three decades of the nineteenth century, all the colonies of Spain and Portugal in Latin America fought for and won their independence. But the triumphant generals of the revolution fought among themselves as their dreams of vast, unified, powerful nations dissolved into the reality of smaller, weaker states. And the triumphant **creole** elite—the descendants of the European settlers in these colonies—suppressed indigenous peoples, people of mixed Spanish-Amerindian ancestry (**mestizos**), and African-Americans, thereby spreading disillusionment throughout the continent.

divine right of kings A political doctrine influential in the sixteenth and seventeenth centuries. It held that the monarch derived his authority from God and was therefore not accountable to earthly authority. James I of England (1603–25) was a foremost exponent.

creole In the sixteenth to eighteenth centuries, a white person born in Spanish America of Spanish parents.

mestizo A person of mixed race. In Central and South America it usually denotes a person of combined Indian and European descent.

HUMAN RIGHTS IN THE AGE OF ENLIGHTENMENT

Philosophical Rationales

The philosophy justifying England's Glorious Revolution of 1688 developed over many years. Thomas Hobbes (1588–1679), one of England's leading political philosophers, seemed to justify the enormous, existing power of the king over the citizens. In his most influential work, *Leviathan*, of 1651, he declared: "Nothing the sovereign representative can do to a subject, on what pretence soever, can properly be called injustice, or injury." But Hobbes was simultaneously providing a rationale for limiting the king's power. He declared that the king could claim his authority not by virtue of special, personal rights, nor by virtue of representing God on earth, but because "Every subject is author of every act the sovereign doth." In other words, the king has authority to the extent that he represents the will of the people.

Hobbes and the "State of Nature." Hobbes, like others of his time, was trying to understand the English monarchy in terms of its origins. He postulated the myth of a prehistoric, individualistic, unruly, "state of nature," which people had rejected in order to create a society that would protect them individually and collectively. Uncontrolled by law and a king, Hobbes wrote, "the life of man [is] solitary, poor, nasty, brutish, and short … During the time men live without a common power to keep them all in awe, they are in that condition which is called war; and such a war, as is of every man against every man." To escape such lawlessness, men had exchanged their individual liberties for social and political order. Their (mythical) **social contract**, not divine appointment, had created monarchy in order to serve the people.

social contract A mythical, unwritten agreement among early people in a "state of nature" to establish some form of government. This "contract" generally defines the rights and obligations of the individuals and of the government.

Locke and the Enlightenment. The philosophical accomplishments of the Glorious Revolution are even more closely associated with the writings of John Locke (1632–1704), who had fled England in 1683 for the Netherlands, returning only after the revolution was complete. While he was in the Netherlands, Locke wrote his most important essay on political philosophy, *Second Treatise on Government*, although it was not published until 1689, after the Glorious Revolution had been implemented and Locke felt it safe to return to England. Since Locke's philosophy parallels not only the English revolution but also many subsequent ones, his arguments deserve attention.

Like Hobbes, Locke argued that government is a secular compact entered into voluntarily and freely by individuals. If there are to be kings, they too must live under the constitution. Locke, like Hobbes, based his argument on a mythical, prehistoric, "state of nature," which people forsook in order to provide for their common defense and needs. He, however, stressed the importance of common consent in the earlier mythical contract. The legitimacy of the contract continues only as long as the consent continues. If they no longer consent to the contract, the people have the right to terminate it. Going beyond Hobbes, Locke explicitly proclaimed the right of revolution in his *Second Treatise on Government*:

> There remains still in the people a supreme power to remove or alter the legislative, when they find the legislative act contrary to the trust reposed in them. For all power given with trust for the attaining of an end, being limited by that end, whenever that end is manifestly neglected, or opposed, the trust must necessarily be forfeited, and the power devolves into the hands of those that gave it, who may place it anew where they shall think best for their safety and security. (p. 92)

Locke postulated the "equal right that every man hath to his natural freedom, without being subjected to the will or authority of any other man". "Absolute monarchy, which by some men is counted the only government in the world, is indeed inconsistent with civil society". Majority rule is Locke's basis of government: "the act of the majority passes for the act of the whole, and of course determines as having by the law of nature and reason, the power of the whole".

A Theory of Government by Property Owners. Locke was not, however, proposing radical democracy; he was not advocating one person, one vote. For Locke, government was for property owners. "Government," Locke proclaimed, "has no other end but the preservation of property". "The great and chief end therefore, of men's uniting into commonwealths, and putting themselves under government, is the preservation of their property". Indeed, after the initial, mythical social contract had established the government's authority, succeeding generations had signalled their continuing acceptance of that contract by allowing their property to be protected by the government. "The supreme power cannot take from any man any part of his property without his own consent. For the preservation of property being the end of government, and that for which men enter into society, it necessarily supposes and requires, that the people should have property".

Taxes, therefore, cannot be levied unilaterally or arbitrarily. "If anyone shall claim a power to lay and levy taxes on the people, by his own authority, and without such consent of the people, he thereby invades the fundamental law of property, and subverts the end of government".

Hobbes had already indicated the growing importance of property and industry to seventeenth-century England. Without peace and stability, he wrote:

> there is no place for industry; because the fruit thereof is uncertain; and consequently no culture of the earth; no navigation, nor use of the commodities that may be imported by sea; no commodious building; no instruments of moving, and removing, such things as require much force; no knowledge of the face of the earth; no account of time; no arts; no letters; no society. (p. 895)

Hobbes wanted a society of economic productivity achieved through industry, commerce, and invention. Locke saw private ownership of property and private profit as the means to achieving that end. He saw the property-owning classes of England, the men who made the Glorious Revolution, as the nation's proper leaders and administrators, and he asserted the importance of the enclosure acts by which England was dividing up the common lands of each village, turning them into private property, and

An Eyewitness Representation of the Execution of Charles I, by Weesop, 1649. Charles' belief in the divine right of kings and the authority of the Church of England led eventually to a civil war with Parliament—which he and his supporters lost. At his subsequent trial, the king was sentenced to death as a tyrant, murderer, and enemy of the nation and beheaded at Whitehall, London, on January 30, 1649. (*Private Collection*)

selling them. These enclosure acts were creating a new, wealthier landlord class, which turned its energies to increasing agricultural productivity. At the same time the acts forced rural people, who had owned no land of their own but who had been grazing their animals on common land, to give up their independence. Most found work with more prosperous landlords and some moved to the cities in search of new jobs.

Locke is today usually criticized for overlooking the situation of the non-propertied classes. In his mythical state of nature land had been abundant—available for the taking—and anyone could become a property owner. But in both Locke's time and our own, access to unclaimed, unowned property is not so easy. Indeed, when Locke notes that "the turfs my servant has cut ... become my property", he credits the labor of the landless servant to his landed master. In practice, Locke's theory justified the government of England by Parliament under constitutional law, which limited the power of the king and transferred it to the hands of the propertied classes—the system that was evolving in his time. Locke's is the voice of the improving landlords and the rising commercial classes who made the Glorious Revolution.

Intellectual Revolutions in Science and Philosophy

During the time between the two English political revolutions (1649 and 1688) of the seventeenth century, the Royal Society of London was founded in 1662. The study of science was beginning to be institutionalized, both as knowledge for its own sake and as technological application to practical problems. Ultimately, the new methods in science led to new ways of thinking about the world more generally. Thus, in some ways, our brief survey of the advancement of science might fit more appropriately in Chapter 13 on advances in global commerce or in Chapter 17 on the industrial revolution. But changes in scientific thinking proceeded step-by-step with changes in politics, so we examine them here in the midst of the revolution in political thought.

In his 1985 book *Revolution in Science*, Harvard University historian of science I. Bernard Cohen writes that the study of the history of science is a surprisingly new field. Although some of the scientists we shall consider here—Copernicus, Pascal, Galileo, Descartes, Newton, Harvey, Leeuwenhoek, and Linnaeus—spoke of their findings as revolutionary, the first academic historian to write of a scientific revolution seems to have been a Ph.D. candidate at Columbia University, Martha (Bronfenbrenner) Ornstein. In her 1913 dissertation she summarized the importance of the array of scientific discoveries and inventions that included the telescope, which "utterly revolutionized the science of astronomy," "revolutionary changes in optics," "Linnaeus's revolutionary work" in plant and animal classification, "the revolution in the universities" toward systematic, empirical research, and the role of scientific societies as carriers of culture. There had been, she wrote, "a revolution in the established habits of thought and inquiry, compared to which most revolutions registered in history seem insignificant".

In 1948, in a series of lectures, one of the most distinguished of professional historians, Herbert Butterfield, wrote that the scientific revolution of the seventeenth century "overturned the authority in science not only of the Middle Ages but of the ancient world ... [It] outshines everything since the rise of Christianity and reduces the Renaissance and Reformation to the rank of mere episodes, mere internal displacements, within the system of medieval Christendom". Butterfield refrained from calling this transformation a one-time revolution, since he saw it as a kind of "continuing historical, or history making force acting right up to the present time". Beginning in the 1950s, especially in *The Copernican Revolution* (1957) and *The Structure of Scientific Revolutions* (1962, 3rd ed., 1996), Thomas Kuhn turned his attention to the process of scientific investigation as a method of thought and research that constantly challenges conventional thinking and stands ready to overthrow it. Kuhn argued that most scientific research is based on small, incremental advances in human knowledge. Kuhn called this "normal science." "Revolutionary science" occurs when scientists break completely with existing explanations of their field, finding them inadequate, and create new theories that are better able to account for all the data available. Galileo and Newton created such great revolutions.

What then was this revolution in seventeenth-century science? First, the seventeenth century marked the move from the individual scientist working alone to the creation of a community of scientists, in touch with one another, sharing knowledge and ideas, and building a collective structure of thought and method. It would still be possible for a scientific genius like Leonardo da Vinci (1452–1519) to die with his work unrecognized, and even unknown, but this would be less likely. Leonardo, most famous for his paintings of *The Last Supper* and the *Mona Lisa*, also carried out research in human anatomy through the dissection of cadavers; he wrote of the circulation of the blood through the body and of the path of the earth around the sun; he drew sketches for inventions such as submarines and airplanes. But he did not circulate these scientific and technological ideas. At the time of his death they remained confined to his own notebooks and were not discovered until the twentieth century. The creation of scientific academies in the seventeenth century made it much less likely that such genius would remain hidden.

Second, science added four new qualities to its methods: mathematical formulations, quantifying and expressing relationships in nature in mathematical forms; **empiricism**, accepting the evidence of direct observation over theoretical and philosophical explanations; technological innovations in equipment, such as the telescope and microscope; and freedom of inquiry, encouraging scientists to follow their findings and their imagination regardless of received opinion and official doctrines. All of these qualities are found in the great revolution in astronomy and physics from Copernicus through Kepler and Galileo, and on to Newton. Indeed, many historians would call this *the* scientific revolution of the sixteenth and seventeenth centuries.

Nicholas Copernicus (1473–1543), an outstanding Polish astronomer, was commissioned by Pope Paul III to devise a new calendar that would correct the errors of the Julian calendar. The Julian calendar was based on a 365¼-day year, while the actual time it takes the earth to circle the sun is eleven minutes and fourteen seconds less. So the calendar year was continuously losing time, just a few minutes each year, but by the sixteenth century this amounted to about ten days. Holidays, like Christmas and Easter, began to slip backward into different seasons. The pope commissioned Copernicus to analyze the astronomy underlying the calendar.

In the sixteenth century, people accepted the model of the second-century C.E. Greek astronomer Ptolemy showing the earth at the center of the universe. The sun, the moon, the planets, and the stars went around it. As a mathematician, Copernicus began tracking the movements of all these bodies. He was able to fashion a

Map of the heavens according to Nicholas Copernicus, c. 1543. Copernicus placed the sun in the middle of his solar system with the earth circling around it. He also demonstrated the tilt and rotation of the earth's axis as it traveled in its yearly orbit. In these findings he differed from Ptolemy, the second century C.E. Greek astronomer, but he did continue to see the solar system as bounded, with an array of fixed stars and constellations marking its outer limits.

empiricism The theory that all knowledge originates in experience; the practice of relying on direct observation of events and experience for determining reality.

mathematical system that showed the earth at the center of the universe, as accepted belief had it, but he also found a much simpler, though still complicated, formula that showed the sun, not the earth, at the center of the solar system. His new formulation also showed the earth turning on its axis every twenty-four hours rather than having the entire cosmos revolve around the earth. As a rule, scientists faced with more than one workable explanation choose the simpler, and with his new, simpler model of a solar system Copernicus could explain the calendrical difficulties that had been his principal assignment. But this new explanation would land him in serious trouble with the Church, and he knew it.

The concept of the earth at the center of the universe as taught by Ptolemy had been adopted as the official doctrine of the Catholic Church because it was consistent with biblical passages (Joshua 10:13; Ecclesiastes 1:4-5) that spoke of the sun's circle around the earth. The consequences of challenging that belief frightened Copernicus, as he wrote to the pope in his letter of transmission introducing his findings:

> I may well presume, most Holy Father, that certain people, as soon as they hear that in this book about the Revolutions of the Spheres of the Universe I ascribe movement to the earthly globe, will cry out that . . . I should at once be hissed off the stage . . . Thinking therefore within myself that to ascribe movement to the Earth must indeed seem an absurd performance on my part to those who know that many centuries have consented to the establishment of the contrary judgment, namely that the Earth is placed immovably as the central point in the middle of the Universe, I hesitated long whether, on the one hand, I should give to the light these my Commentaries written to prove the Earth's motion . . . These misgivings and actual protests have been overcome by my friends . . . [one of whom] often urged and even importuned me to publish this work which I had kept in store not for nine years only, but to a fourth period of nine years . . . They urged that I should not, on account of my fears, refuse any longer to contribute the fruits of my labors to the common advantage of those interested in mathematics . . . Yielding then to their persuasion I at last permitted my friends to publish that work which they have so long demanded. (Kuhn, 1957, pp. 137–38)

In the end, Copernicus stuck to the principles of his mathematical commitments and his conscience. He presented the truth as he understood it, but he published his complete findings only on his deathbed. They created much less stir than might have been expected, since they were published as a mathematical study, comprehensible only to the most learned astronomers and mathematicians of his day. They became more the object of technical study than of theological debate.

The greatest astronomer of the next generation, Tycho Brahe (1546–1601), re-examined the mathematics of Copernicus and propounded a new schema that showed the sun and moon circling the earth in the middle of the solar system, and all the other planets circling the sun. It was a more complicated model, but one consistent with the data. The breakthrough that enshrined the sun-centered universe was made by Johannes Kepler (1571–1630). Kepler worked with Brahe toward the end of Brahe's life. For ten years he worked through the rich data he inherited, and finally reached a new understanding. The sun was at the center of the solar system and the planets, including earth, moved around it, but their orbits were not circles but ellipses, and they moved not at a fixed speed, but at a varying speed depending on their position on the ellipse. With these new insights, Kepler designed a model of the solar system that was simple, comprehensive, and mathematically consistent with the data available. He published his results in 1609 in *On the Motion of Mars.*

The theological argument was now clearly drawn. Kuhn writes, "Copernicanism required a transformation in man's view of his relation to God and of the bases of his morality". The earth was no longer the center of God's creation. There was no longer a fixed, heavenly location for God's throne. The perfection of the universe—with the earth at the center of a series of fixed, concentric, crystalline circles in which the planets traveled—was contaminated. Protestant leaders, believing in the literal word of the Bible and led by Luther himself, had attacked the heliocentric universe of Copernicus as early as 1539. The Catholic Church, at first allowing much more latitude to individual belief in this matter, was slower to condemn, but in 1610 the Church officially designated the Copernican model a heresy, and in 1616, *De Revolutionibus* and all other writings that affirmed the earth's motion were put on the *Index,* a list of writings that were forbidden to be taught or even read.

For many years the split between the mathematical astronomers and the Church continued rather quietly, with the mathematicians generally winning out among educated audiences. Then, in 1609, Galileo Galilei (1564–1642), the Italian astronomer, turned the newly invented telescope skyward and changed forever what we know about the heavens, how we know it, and its significance in the eyes of the non-specialist, general public. Galileo added new empirical evidence and new technology to the toolkit of astronomy, opening new avenues of knowledge and popularizing them. The telescope had been created in the Netherlands; Galileo was the first to turn it toward the skies, and he made one discovery after another: The Milky Way is not just a dull glow in the sky but a gigantic collection of stars; the moon's surface is irregular, covered with craters and hills; the moon's radiant light is a reflection from the sun; the sun has imperfections, dark spots which appear and disappear across its surface; the earth is not the only planet with moons—Galileo observed at least four satellites circling Jupiter.

Galileo wrote, "We shall prove the earth to be a wandering body [in orbit around the sun] … This we shall support by an infinitude of arguments drawn from nature" (Galileo, p. 45). Over and over Galileo stressed the validity of his own empirical observations. "With the aid of the telescope this has been scrutinized so directly and with such ocular certainty that all the disputes which have vexed the philosophers through so many ages have been resolved, and we are at last freed from wordy debates about it". "One may learn with all the certainty of sense evidence"; "All these facts were discovered and observed by me not many days ago with the aid of a spyglass which I devised, after first being illuminated by divine grace"; "our own eyes show us". Galileo's appeal to sense evidence, to direct observation, to empirically based information, and to its complete accessibility to anyone who looks through a telescope, found enormous resonance. He wrote for a general audience, not for university scholars; he wrote in Italian, not in Latin. The publication of Galileo's discoveries increased public interest in astronomy, and that public interest gradually turned into general acceptance.

The Catholic Church, deeply enmeshed in its cold war with Protestantism, finally turned against him. In 1633 Galileo was tried by the Inquisition and found guilty of having taught his doctrines against the orders of the Church. Under threat of torture, the sixty-nine-year-old scientist recanted his beliefs and was sentenced to house arrest in his villa near Florence for the rest of his life. (In 1992, 359 years later, Pope John Paul II officially and publicly spoke of the ruling of the Inquisition as a "sad misunderstanding which now belongs to the past," and suggested that there is no incompatibility between "the spirit of science and its rules of research on the one hand, and the Christian faith on the other" [*Philadelphia Inquirer*, November 1, 1992].)

In the same year as Galileo's death Isaac Newton was born in England, on Christmas Day, 1642. He studied at Cambridge University and became a professor of mathematics there at age twenty-six. In the course of his research, he discovered the calculus, a discovery he shared, separately, with the German mathematician Gottfried Wilhelm Leibnitz (1646–1716). A mathematical system especially useful in calculating motion along curved lines, the calculus was immediately valuable in predicting the

Newton experiments with light.
Newton's first published papers were in optics. Here he worked as an experimental scientist rather than as a theoretical mathematician. By passing the rays of the sun through a prism he demonstrated that white light was an amalgam of colored rays. Using this information he built a reflecting telescope, using a mirror to focus light and thus to avoid the chromatic aberration that appeared in a refracting telescope.

celestial course of planets and the earthly trajectory of artillery shells. Another area of Newton's early research was in optics, focusing on the spectrum of light as it passed through a prism. Then he turned his attention to the new issues raised by Copernicus, Kepler, and Galileo: Why do heavy bodies always fall toward earth even as the earth is moving through space? What moves the earth? What moves the planets and what keeps them in their orbits? Before Copernicus, Ptolemy's view of the fixed spheres of the universe answered those questions. But without those fixed spheres, how should we understand the movements of the heavens?

In finding the universal law of gravity, Newton showed that the laws of planetary motion that Kepler formulated, and the laws of earthly movement that Galileo discovered in his later career, along with additional principles of inertia of motion discovered by the French mathematician and philosopher René Descartes (1596–1650), were all consistent. The universal principle of gravitation, coupled with the principle of inertia—that a body once set in motion tends to continue moving at the same speed in the same direction—gives a form for understanding the means by which the universe holds together. Moreover, these forces of inertia and gravity are universal, operating in the same way on earth as in the wider universe. Asserting the principle of the universal law of gravity was the imaginative leap of Newton's new discovery; working out the mathematics was the toil of genius, and he produced it in 1687 in his *Mathematical Principles of Natural Philosophy*. He worked out the formula for the pull of gravity: all matter moves as if every particle attracts every other particle with a force proportional to the product of the two masses, and inversely proportional to the square of the distance between them. This force is universal gravitation.

Like all later scientists, Newton did not try to explain *why* this force worked, only *how* it worked. This new law had enormous philosophical implications, for it explained the "glue" in the Copernican system of the universe. It also had very practical consequences in the understanding and prediction of the tides. The great advances in mathematics underpinned not only theoretical research, but also practical invention in the form of time-keeping, mapping, and processes that required accuracy such as the aiming of artillery and the construction of steam engines. In light of his revolutionary contributions, Newton was named President of the Royal Society in 1703.

The discoveries in astronomy, physics, and mathematics were the leading sectors in the scientific revolution of the seventeenth century, but they were not alone. In England, William Harvey published *On the Movement of the Heart and Blood*, based on years of laboratory research and vivisection of animals, demonstrating the circulation of blood through the body. In the Netherlands, Anthony van Leeuwenhoek (1632–1723) improved the newly invented microscope, the other great advance in optics along with the telescope, to see and then create drawings of blood corpuscles, spermatozoa, and bacteria. His observations enabled him to argue that reproduction even among tiny creatures was through sexual mating, not spontaneous generation. Leeuwenhoek was a businessman in the cloth trade, not specially educated in the sciences, and his election as a Fellow of the Royal Society of London in 1680 demonstrated that amateurs were entering avidly into this new research.

Leeuwenhoek's researches expanded the knowledge of the number and variety of tiny, microscopic creatures. Carolus Linnaeus (1707–78) developed a system of classification for these and all other known creatures in nature, *Systema Naturae* (1735), including an analysis of sexual reproduction in plants. The further evolution of eighteenth-century science was well underway.

The new science both reduced and expanded human powers and self-understanding. Some, frightened, agreed with Blaise Pascal, a devout Christian French mathematician: "I am terrified by the eternal silence of these infinite spaces." But more took heart along with Alexander Pope, that a brave, new world was dawning:

Nature and nature's law lay hid in night;
God said, "Let Newton be," and all was light.

The new world of science swept away much superstition, at least for the time, and suggested that rationality and science could create a new world in which people would trust their senses to gather empirical information and to act upon it, a world in which the laws of nature could be discovered and calculated, a world in which science would inspire technological invention in the practical arts of making human life more productive and more comfortable. Throughout the eighteenth century, this vision of natural law and the power of human reason spilled over from science and technology to philosophy and political theory. Just as scientists began to undermine traditional ideas about the nature of the universe, philosophers began to challenge traditional ideas about the relationship between monarchy and populations.

ENGLAND'S GLORIOUS REVOLUTION, 1688

At about the time Hobbes was writing, England was in continuing revolt against its sovereigns. Religion was a burning issue, and it seemed that no sovereign could satisfy all the conflicting wishes of dissenters—Roman Catholics, Presbyterians, Puritans, and Quakers—and the official Anglican Church. Frustrations simmered but had no focus until both James I (r. 1603–25) and his son Charles I (r. 1625–49) ran out of money to administer their governments, especially the naval and military departments, and therefore convened Parliament to request additional funds. Many members of Parliament—landowners, increasingly wealthy city merchants, lawyers, Puritans and other religious dissenters, as well as Anglican clergy—were not inclined to give the kings the money they requested. They challenged royal authority, proposed increased power for an elected legislature, promotion by merit in government jobs, and, most of all, religious tolerance in private and public life. When Charles I nevertheless attempted to levy taxes without its sanction, the Parliament he had convened in 1640 came to open warfare with him and ultimately, under the leadership of Oliver Cromwell (Lord Protector of England, 1653–8), executed him. Cromwell, an ardent Calvinist and military genius, ruled in a rather arbitrary fashion until he died in 1658. He conquered rebels in both Ireland and Scotland and joined them with England to form the British Commonwealth. In spite of his conquests, neither Cromwell nor Parliament had been able to achieve a new form of effective government and the monarchy was restored in 1660. However, the Civil War established the notion that the monarchy could be abolished and in many ways provided the theoretical framework that led to the subsequent revolution of 1688.

SOURCE

Universal Suffrage vs. Property Rights

E.P. Thompson, the twentieth-century British historian, emphasized the contributions of common people to history. In his ground-breaking The Making of the English Working Class *(pp. 22–3), Thompson cites statements made in 1647 at an army council meeting that attempted to find a constitutional solution to the struggle between the king and Parliament and to determine the role of the common people in electing Parliament.*

Oliver Cromwell's son-in-law, General Ireton, proposed extending the franchise, but only to men of property, fearing that private property might otherwise be abolished: "No person hath a right to an interest or share in the disposing of the affairs of the kingdom ... that hath not a permanent fixed interest in this kingdom ... If you admit any man that hath a breath and being, Why may not those men vote against all property?"

The common soldiers replied more democratically and more bitterly. One asserted: "There are many thousands of us soldiers that have ventured our lives; we have had little property in the kingdom as to our estates, yet we have had a birthright. But it seems now, except a man hath a fixed estate in this kingdom, he hath no right ... I wonder we were so much deceived." If we are asked to fight on behalf of the government, we should have a voice in its election.

The Bill of Rights, 1689

Charles II (r. 1660–85) and his brother James II (r. 1685–90) continued to claim more powers than Parliament wished to sanction. James II, a Catholic, favored Catholics in many of his official appointments. When a son was born to James, leading nobles feared that James and his successors might reinstitute Catholicism as England's official religion a century and a half after Henry VIII had disestablished it in favor of the Church of England. They invited James II's daughter, Mary, and her husband William of Orange, ruler of the United Provinces of the Netherlands, both resolute Protestants, to return to England and assume the monarchy. In 1688 William and Mary arrived in England and confirmed their new rule by defeating the troops still loyal to James II at the Battle of the Boyne in Ireland in 1690.

Although the new king and queen had been invited primarily to resolve religious conflicts, their ascension to the throne also brought resolution to the power conflict between monarch and Parliament. The Bill of Rights that was enacted by Parliament in 1689 stating clearly principles that had been evolving for decades in the relationship between the monarchy and the people of England. It stipulated, among other clauses, that no taxes could be raised, nor armies recruited without prior parliamentary approval; no subject could be arrested and detained without legal process; and no law could be suspended by the king unilaterally. The Glorious Revolution thus not only displaced one monarch in favor of another but also limited the powers of the monarch under constitutional law. After all, this new monarch had been selected by noblemen and confirmed by Parliament. In addition, as William continued his wars against France, he had to defer to Parliament for funds. The Anglican Church remained the established Church of England, but the Toleration Act of 1689 granted Puritan Dissenters—but not Roman Catholics—the right of free public worship. Cromwell had already permitted Jews to return to England, almost 400 years after their expulsion in 1290. Parliament did not yet revoke the Test Act, which reserved military and civil offices for Anglicans only. Nevertheless, these settlements brought some resolution to the issues of religion in politics that had beset England for so long, although rebellion against the religious provisions continued in Scotland and especially Ireland.

The Reality of Government by Male Property Owners. For its time the Glorious Revolution may have been democratic because it placed the king under constitutional rule. But until 1820 fewer than 500 influential men in all of Britain, it has been estimated, could control the election of the majority of the Parliament. The 1832 Reform Act expanded the actual electorate in the British Isles from less than half million to about 800,000. Not until 1867 and 1884 did Reform Acts extend the vote to the middle and lower classes as well as to Catholics, Dissenters, and Jews. By that time the Industrial Revolution had created an entirely new class of occupations and workers who could successfully demand representation, as we shall see in the next chapter. Women got the vote in Britain only in the twentieth century.

THE *PHILOSOPHES* AND THE ENLIGHTENMENT IN THE EIGHTEENTH CENTURY

In the century between the Glorious Revolution in England and the American and French revolutions, a movement in philosophic thought emerged called the Enlightenment. Its intellectual center was in France, although key participants lived in America, Scotland, England, Prussia, Russia, and elsewhere. The French leaders of the Enlightenment were called **philosophes**, and their philosophy helped inspire the American and the French revolutions.

Following on the scientific revolution of the seventeenth century the *philosophes* believed in a world of rationality, in which collected human knowledge and systematic thought could serve as powerful tools for finding order in the universe and for solving key problems in political and economic life. Their concerns for clarity of thought, combined with the desire to solve practical problems in public life, gave them considerable influence over the restructuring of new political institutions in their age of revolution. The authors of the American Declaration of Independence and of the French Declaration of the Rights of Man and the Citizen drew much of their inspiration from the *philosophes*. The *philosophes* believed in order, but also in freedom of thought and expression. For them, public discussion and debate were the means toward finding better ideas and solutions. Indeed, the *philosophes* were in constant dialogue and debate with one another.

Travel influenced the *philosophes'* thought, opening them to a wider range of ideas. Charles de Secondat, the Baron de Montesquieu (1689–1755), traveled widely himself and presented satiric criticism of French institutions, including the monarchy and the Catholic Church, in the form of *Persian Letters*, supposedly dispatched by two visitors to France writing their observations to readers at home. Twenty-seven years later, in 1748, Montesquieu wrote his most influential work, *The Spirit of Laws*, in which he recognized that different countries need different kinds of governments, and advocated a separation of powers based on his (mis)understanding of the British system. The authors of the United States constitution later acknowledged their debt to Montesquieu's thought.

In terms of spiritual and religious beliefs, most *philosophes* were deists. They allowed that the world may have required an original creator, like Aristotle's prime mover, but once the processes of life had begun, he had withdrawn. Their metaphor was that of a watchmaker who built the mechanism, started it moving, and departed. Humanity's fate thereafter was in its own hands.

In contrast to such Catholic doctrines as original sin and the authority of the Church over human reason, the *philosophes* argued that human progress was possible through the steady and unrestricted expansion of knowledge or "enlightenment." Jean-Antoine-Nicolas de Caritat, Marquis de Condorcet (1743–94), author of the *Sketch of the Progress*

philosophes A group of eighteenth-century French writers and philosophers who emphasized the supremacy of human reason and advocated freedom of expression and social, economic, and political reform. They included Voltaire, Montesquieu, Rousseau, and Diderot, editor of the *Encyclopédie* (1751–72), which embodied many of their ideas.

of the Human Mind (published in 1795), proclaimed "the perfectibility of humanity is indefinite". The most famous academic product of the *philosophes* and the Enlightenment was the *Encyclopedia, or Rational Dictionary of the Arts, Sciences, and Crafts*, compiled by Denis Diderot (1713–84) and containing articles by leading scholars and *philosophes*. The *Encyclopedia* reaffirmed this faith in human progress based on education:

> The aim of an Encyclopedia is to collect all the knowledge that now lies scattered over the face of the earth, to make known its general structure to the men among whom we live, and to transmit it to those who will come after us, in order that the labors of past ages may be useful to the ages that will follow, that our grandsons, as they become better educated, may become at the same time more virtuous and more happy, and that we may not die without having deserved well of the human race. (Columbia University, *Contemporary Civilization*, pp. 988–9)

Diderot called for further social and political revolution. "We are beginning to shake off the yoke of authority and tradition in order to hold fast to the laws of reason". Challenging authority meant being open to multiple perspectives rather than holding a single truth, and Diderot built this concept into the structure of his volumes.

> By giving cross-references to articles where solid principles serve as foundation for the diametrically opposed truths we shall be able to throw down the whole edifice of mud and scatter the idle heap of dust. ... If these cross-references, which now confirm and now refute, are carried out artistically according to a plan carefully conceived in advance, they will give to the Encyclopedia the ... ability to change men's common way of thinking. (p. 996)

The *Encyclopedia* ultimately filled seventeen volumes of text and eleven of illustrations.

Another *philosophe*, François-Marie Arouet, better known as Voltaire (1694–1778), spoke out with courage and wit. His *Elements of the Philosophy of Newton* (1738) explicated new scientific evidence of the rational order and the human ability to comprehend the universe; *Philosophical Letters on the English* (1734) argued for freedom of religion, inquiry, and the press; *Essai sur les moeurs* (1756), translated as *Universal History*, gave a humanistic context to historical development and placed responsibility

Jean Huber, *The Philosophers at Supper,* **1750.** Voltaire (1), Condorcet (5), and Diderot (6) are among the figures depicted in this engraving, a visual checklist of important Enlightenment thinkers. Seeing the Western world as emerging from centuries of darkness and ignorance, these Frenchmen promoted reason, science, and a respect for humanity—ideas that would underpin the intellectual case for the French Revolution of 1789. (*Bibliothèque Nationale, Paris*)

in human hands. Voltaire cried *"Ecrasez l'infame!"*—"crush the infamy" of superstition, intolerance, and the power of the clergy.

The *philosophes* were not, however, committed to popular democracy. Voltaire preferred benevolent and **enlightened despotism** to badly administered self-rule. In the best of all possible worlds, there would be an enlightened ruler like Frederick II, the Great, of Prussia (r. 1740–86), at whose court Voltaire lived for several years, or Catherine II, the Great, Empress of Russia (r. 1762–96), of whom he was a close friend, or Joseph II, Emperor of Austria (r. 1765–90). All three ruled countries in which the administration was efficient, taxes were reasonable, agricultural and handicraft production was encouraged, freedom of expression and religion was allowed, the military was strengthened, and powerful empires resulted. The enlightened despot acted in disciplined ways, subject in his or her mind to the law of nature. But the population at large had no say or vote in the administration. In other words, for these rulers, and for Voltaire, good government did not necessarily require self government.

Colonial governments often claimed the mantle of the Enlightenment to justify their rule, arguing that they were utilizing knowledge and reason, to soften the use of brute force, as the foundation of their administration. In 1784 Warren Hastings, Governor General of the British holdings in India explained:

> Every accumulation of knowledge and especially such as is obtained by social communication with people over whom we exercise dominion founded on the right of conquest, is useful to the state … it attracts and conciliates distant affections; it lessens the weight of the chain by which the natives are held in subjection; and it imprints on the hearts of our countrymen the sense of obligation and benevolence. (Metcalf and Metcalf, p. 61)

Implementing this Enlightenment philosophy, Hastings founded the Asiatic Society of Bengal, dedicated primarily to the translation and analysis of ancient Indian texts.

Skepticism regarding democratic government was carried further in the works of Jean-Jacques Rousseau (1712–78), perhaps the most enigmatic and ambiguous of all of the eighteenth-century French thinkers. Rousseau questioned the primacy of intellect and human ingenuity. Like Hobbes and Locke, he wrote of the "state of nature," but, unlike them, he seemed, in some ways, to wish to return to it. His *Social Contract* (1762) lamented, "Man is born free; and everywhere he is in chains." In his *Discourse on the Origin of Inequality* (1755) he wrote:

> There is hardly any inequality in the state of nature; all the inequality which now prevails owes its strength and growth to the development of our faculties and the advance of the human mind, and becomes at last permanent and legitimate by the establishment of property and laws. (Columbia University, *Contemporary Civilization*, p. 1147)

Rousseau proposed a democracy far more radical than that of the other *philosophes*, yet he also seemed to justify a repressive tyranny of the majority. Like Locke and Hobbes, Rousseau mythologized an original social contract transforming a state of nature into a community, and he attributed great power to that community: "Each of us puts his person and all his power in common under the supreme direction of the general will". "Whoever refuses to obey the general will shall be compelled to do so by the whole body. This means nothing less than that he will be forced to be free" (p. 1153). Political philosophers have argued for more than two centuries over the paradox of Rousseau's "general will." How is the citizen "forced to be free"? Is this a proclamation of freedom, justification for suppressing minorities, or a proposal for creating a totalitarian state?

Adam Smith, whose economic ideas we have already examined, is sometimes grouped with the *philosophes*, with whom he carried on extensive discussions and correspondence. Like Locke, Smith believed it was normal for people to want to

enlightened despotism A system of government in which the ruler has absolute rights over his or her subjects, but uses this power for their benefit.

"better their condition" materially. He saw that this attempt was not always successful, but suggested:

> it is well that nature imposes upon us in this manner. It is this deception which rouses and keeps in continual motion the industry of mankind. It is this which first prompted them to cultivate the ground, to build houses, to found cities and commonwealths, and to invent and improve all the sciences and arts, which ennoble and embellish human life. (*Moral Sentiments*, IV.1.10)

Much less optimistically, Smith recognized that private enrichment would engender jealousy and envy. Private property, therefore, needed to be protected and this, he agreed with Locke, was the task of government:

> Civil government, so far as it is instituted for the security of property, is in reality instituted for the defense of the rich against the poor, or of those who have some property against those who have none at all. (*The Wealth of Nations*, p. 674)

At the time of the American and French revolutions these arguments for enlightenment, rationality, experimental science, secularism, private profit and ownership, "fellow feeling," and limitations on the power of government all clamored for changes in politics, economics, and social life. But what would be the substance and direction of those changes? How would they be implemented and by whom?

REVOLUTION IN NORTH AMERICA, 1776

As British settlers began to colonize North America, Australia, and South Africa in the seventeenth and eighteenth centuries, they assumed that they shared in the rights of all Britons. By the 1760s, however, North American settlers were beginning to resent the control over their political and economic life exerted by rulers in Britain. British control over American trade, restrictions on the development of American shipping, and the resulting limitations on the development of certain kinds of manufacture, were as galling as the issue of taxation. The 1763 British victory over the French in the Seven Years War in North America, concluding a global cluster of wars between the two powers for commercial and naval supremacy, ended the threat of attacks by French or Indians, and freed the American colonists from further need of British troops. However, the British decided to maintain a large army in North America and to tax the colonies directly to pay for it. The 1765 Stamp Act levied taxes on a long list of commercial and legal documents. The colonists protested vigorously until Parliament repealed the Act because of serious rioting and a boycot of British goods.

Additional grievances against further imperious decrees of King George III built up until finally the Americans declared themselves an independent country in 1776 and fought to end British rule over them. The American Declaration of Independence set out a list of these

John Trumbull, *Signing of the Declaration of Independence, July 4, 1776*, 1786–97. What began as a protest against colonial trade restrictions and the limiting of political liberty grew into a revolutionary struggle and the birth of a nation. The Declaration of Independence enshrined the principles underlying the new United States and later influenced freedom-fighters all over the world. (*Capitol Collection, Washington*)

"injuries and usurpations." It reflected the American resolve to secure the same legal rights as Britons had won at home almost a century earlier. It charged the king with "taking away our Charters, abolishing our most valuable Laws, and altering fundamentally the Forms of our Governments." It declared the social contract that bound the colonies to Britain had been broken. It declared, ultimately, the right of revolution.

The American Revolution went further in establishing political democracy than had the Glorious Revolution in Britain. It abolished the monarchy entirely, replacing it with an elected government. Having declared that "all men are created equal," with unalienable rights not only to life and liberty, but also to the vague but seductive "pursuit of happiness," the revolutionaries now set out to consolidate their commitments in a new legal structure. Their leaders, men like George Washington, Benjamin Franklin, Thomas Jefferson, and James Madison, were soldiers, entrepreneurs, and statesmen of considerable erudition, common sense, restraint, and balance.

The Constitution and the Bill of Rights, 1789

After the Americans won their war for independence, 1775–81, and in 1783 achieved a peace treaty with Britain, political leaders of the thirteen colonies met in Philadelphia to establish a framework for their new nation. They drafted a new Constitution in 1789, and a Bill of Rights, which was ratified in 1791. The American Bill of Rights, the first ten amendments to the Constitution, guaranteed to Americans not only the basic rights enjoyed by the British at the time, but more: freedom of religion (and the separation of Church and state), press, assembly, and petition; the right to bear arms; protection against unreasonable searches and against cruel and unusual punishment; and the right to a speedy and proper trial by a jury of peers. The Americans established a federal system of government. The states individually set the rules for voting and many, but not all, removed the property requirements. By 1800 Vermont had instituted universal manhood suffrage, and South Carolina, Pennsylvania, New Hampshire, and Delaware extended the vote to virtually every adult white male taxpayer.

Historians of the early United States situate the more radical American approach to political liberty in at least four factors: religious, geographic, social, and philosophical. First, a disproportionate share of the settlers coming to America from Britain and Europe were religious dissenters seeking spiritual independence outside the established churches of their countries. Their widespread, popular beliefs in the importance of individual liberties carried over from religion into politics.

Second, the availability of apparently open land presented abundant individual opportunity to the new Americans (as they dispossessed Native Americans). Later, the historian Frederick Jackson Turner would extend this "frontier thesis," arguing that the relative freedom and openness of American life was based psychologically as well as materially on the presence of seemingly endless open frontier land. Third, the absence of landed and aristocratic privilege, and the strength of artisan classes in the urban population increased the demand for more democracy. Finally, eighteenth-century political thought had

The Boston Tea Party, 1773. On December 16, 1773, American colonists cheer as some radicals dressed up as Indians throw tea from British ships into Boston harbor. (*Yale University Art Gallery, New Haven, Connecticut*)

generally grown more radical, especially among the *philosophes* in France. By the time the Americans wrote their Bill of Rights, the French Revolution was well underway.

The First Anti-imperial Revolution

The American Revolution, in addition to securing British rights for Americans, was also, and perhaps more importantly, the first modern anti-colonial revolution. The trade and taxation policies imposed by Britain had pushed businessmen and artisans into opposition to British rule. Other nations, notably France, eager to embarrass Britain and to detach its most promising colonies, provided financial and military support, which helped the Americans to win their independence. One of the goals of the Revolution was to open the North American continent west of the Appalachian Mountains to settlement. The British prohibition on this westward movement had stood in stark contrast to Spanish and Portuguese settlement policy in Latin America. As the newly independent Americans migrated westward, annexing land as they went, they began to develop imperial interests that were expressed in the mystique of "Manifest Destiny." This popular belief in America's natural growth across the continent was consolidated with the huge Louisiana Purchase from France in 1803. Texans were encouraged to assert their independence from Mexico in 1836 and were then absorbed into the American Union in 1845. Warfare with Mexico in 1846–8 ended in victory for the United States and the annexation of the southwest. Other annexations of land in North America took place more peacefully, with negotiations with Britain for the Oregon country in 1844–6 and with Russia for the purchase of Alaska in 1867.

Over the centuries America served as an inspiration to anti-colonial forces. Jawaharlal Nehru, leading India's twentieth-century struggle for independence from Britain, cited the American Revolution as a model for his own country: "This political change in America was important and destined to bear great results. The American colonies which became free then have grown today [1932] into the most powerful, the richest, and industrially the most advanced country in the world".

The American Revolution, however, did not bring democracy to everyone. The greatest shortcoming was the American perpetuation of slavery. The system was finally ended only by the American Civil War, 1861–5, the bloodiest in the history of the nation. Even afterward, racial discrimination characterized American law until the 1960s and continues to mark American practice up to the present. The status of the Native American population actually worsened after the revolution, as settlers of European extraction headed west, first by wagon train and later by railroad. They slaughtered American Indians, pushed them out of the way, confined them to remote, semi-barren reservations, destroyed the buffalo herds on which their nomadic existence depended, and discouraged the preservation of their separate cultures and languages. For the indigenous Indians the effects of the revolution were exactly opposite to those of the settler-invaders: expansion became contraction, democracy became tyranny, prosperity became poverty, and liberty became confinement.

The hypocrisy of democratic statements, on the one hand, and atrocities against Indians, on the other, peaked in the presidency of Andrew Jackson (1829–37). Jackson fought against economic and political privilege and to extend opportunity to the common man, yet he ordered the United States Army to evict the Cherokee Nation from their lands in Georgia and to drive them to the "Great American Desert" in the west in direct defiance of the Supreme Court of the United States. About one-fourth of the 15,000 Indians forced onto this "Trail of Tears" died *en route*.

How did America reconcile its ideals of equality and liberty with the enslavement of blacks and the confinement of Indians at home? It did so by considering non-whites and non-Europeans as "other"—that is, as not quite equal biologically. Race was often

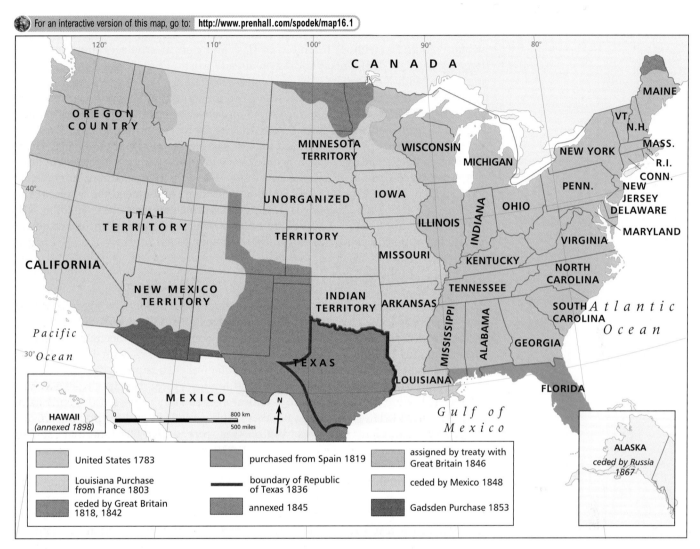

For an interactive version of this map, go to: http://www.prenhall.com/spodek/map16.1

Legend:

- United States 1783
- Louisiana Purchase from France 1803
- ceded by Great Britain 1818, 1842
- purchased from Spain 1819
- boundary of Republic of Texas 1836
- annexed 1845
- assigned by treaty with Great Britain 1846
- ceded by Mexico 1848
- Gadsden Purchase 1853

HAWAII *(annexed 1898)*

ALASKA *ceded by Russia 1867*

used as a definition, usually made by a quick, if approximate and sometimes inaccurate, visual measure, and often as a legal standard. The fixing of legal identity by race, which had been heretofore a flexible category, became especially common in the southern United States in dealing with slaves, ex-slaves, and free blacks. For many years, racial definition was used as a legal standard in excluding Asians from immigrating as well. If non-whites were considered not quite equal biologically, the unalienable right to liberty could be abridged. Once the revolutionary principle of equality was accepted in America and elsewhere, the battle was drawn between those who wished to narrow its application to an "in-group" while excluding "others" and those who wished to apply it to all peoples. That battle continues today, in law and in practice, in the United States and around the globe.

THE FRENCH REVOLUTION AND NAPOLEON, 1789–1812

The American Revolution, with its combined messages of colonial revolt, constitutional government, individual freedom, and equality under law, inspired many peoples at the time and over the centuries. But in comparison with European countries

The growth of the United States. The westward expansion of the United States was effected by territorial cession, acquisition, and conquest. Following independence in 1783, the Louisiana Purchase from France (1803) and the annexations of West and East Florida from Spain, doubled the nation's size. Another doubling occurred with the annexation of Texas (1845), the acquisition of Oregon (1846), and military victory over Mexico (1848), which brought the southwest. Alaska was purchased from Russia (1867). Hawaii was annexed in 1898. In all cases, European immigrants and their descendants displaced Native Americans, and in less than a century the United States had become one of the world's largest nations.

and their experiences, America and its revolution were unique. At the end of the eighteenth century, America was a country of four million people on the fringes of a continental wilderness, without traditions of class and clerical privilege, and founded in large measure by dissidents. Building on already existing British freedoms and fighting a war (with the support of several international allies) against a distant colonial government, the leaders of the revolution were an educated, comfortable elite. The French Revolution, on the other hand, was an internal revolt against entrenched feudal, clerical, and monarchical privilege within the most populous (24 million people) and most powerful European state of its time. It unleashed powerful, combative internal factions, none of which could control the direction or the velocity of revolutionary events inside or outside of France. The French Revolution immediately affected all of Europe, most of the western hemisphere, and indeed the whole world. Some would argue that the battles over its central principles continue even today. The twentieth-century Chinese leader Zhou Enlai, when asked to assess the effects of the French Revolution, legendarily replied: "It's too soon to tell."

The Origins of Revolution

The French Revolution, like the English Civil Wars of the 1640s, was triggered by the king's need for funds. Much like Charles I, King Louis XVI (r. 1774–92) decided to solicit these funds by convening leaders of the French people through the Estates-General in 1789.

From this point on, political, social, and ideological change proceeded very rapidly as political institutions, social classes, and philosophical beliefs challenged one another in a continuous unfolding of critical events. France was divided, hierarchically, into three Estates: the clergy, numbering about 100,000 and controlling perhaps 10 percent of the land of France; the nobility, perhaps 300,000 men, who owned approximately 25 percent of the land; and everyone else. The Third Estate included a rising and prosperous group of urban merchants and professionals (estimated at 8 percent of the total population), as well as working-class artisans, and the four-fifths of France who were farmers. The wealth that the king wished to tap was concentrated in the first two estates and the **bourgeoisie**, or leading urban professional and commercial classes, of the third.

The Revolt of the Third Estate

The Estates-General had not been convened since 1614, and the procedures for its meeting were disputed, revealing grievances not only against the king but also among the representatives. The nobles wished to seize the moment to make the Estates-General into the constitutional government of France, with the king subordinate to them. They wanted guarantees of personal liberty, freedom of the press and speech, and freedom from arbitrary arrest. They also wanted minimal taxation, but they might have conceded this point in exchange for greater political power. Under their proposed constitution, the Estates-General would meet in three separate chambers: one for the nobility; one for the clergy, in which the nobility also had a powerful voice; and a third for everyone else.

The Third Estate, which had long regarded the nobility as parasitic and resented their multitude of special privileges, viewed the new proposals with suspicion. The members of the Third Estate drew their inspiration for a more democratic, representative, inclusive, and accountable government from the writings of the *philosophes*, and the experience of the revolutions in England and, especially, in America. Their local spokesman and leading pamphleteer was actually a clergyman, the Abbé Emmanuel-

bourgeoisie A French word that originally applied to the inhabitants of walled towns, who occupied a socio-economic position between the rural peasantry and the feudal aristocracy; with the development of industry, it became identified more with employers, as well as with other members of the "middle class," professionals, artisans, and shopkeepers.

Joseph Sieyès (1748–1836), who wrote *What Is the Third Estate?* (1789). The tract opened with a catechism of three political questions and answers: "(1) What is the Third Estate? Everything. (2) What has it been in the political order up to the present? Nothing. (3) What does it demand? To Become Something." The leaders of the Third Estate asked for an end to the privileges that had enriched and empowered the clergy and the nobility while reducing the opportunities available to everyone else and impoverishing the French crown. Many saw the king as an ally in the struggle against the nobility. They proposed that the entire Estates-General meet in a single body, since the king had granted them as many representatives as both of the other two estates combined.

The Oath of the Tennis Court by Jacques-Louis David, 1790. In this dramatic composition, David captures the moment when the Third Estate asserted their sovereignty as the elected representatives of France. The merchants, professionals, and artisans who attended the hastily convened meeting swore to remain in session until they had drawn up a new constitution—one that would end the vested interests of the nobility and clergy. (*Musée Carnavalet, Paris*)

When the Parlement of Paris ruled that the three estates should meet separately, as the nobility had wished, the Third Estate was enraged. For six weeks its members boycotted the Estates-General when it was convened in May 1789. On June 13 a few priests joined them, and four days later the Third Estate, with its allies, declared itself the "National Assembly." The king locked them out of their meeting hall. On June 20 they met on a nearby indoor tennis court and swore the "Oath of the Tennis Court," claiming legal power, and declaring that they would not disband until a new constitution was drafted. Louis XVI, frightened by these events, and unwilling or unable to assert his own leadership, called up some 18,000 troops to defend himself from possible attack at his palace in Versailles where all these events were taking place.

The Revolt of the Poor

Meanwhile, in Paris, 12 miles away, and throughout France, mobs of people were rising against organized authority. The harvest had been poor, and the price of bread in 1789 was near record heights. Some farmers refused to pay their taxes and their manorial dues, and many city people were hungry. Beggars and brigands began to roam the countryside and move toward Paris.

In the capital, mobs stormed the Bastille, which was a combination of jail and armory. Meeting violent resistance, they murdered the governor of the Bastille, the mayor of Paris, and a number of soldiers. Hearing of events in Paris, peasants organized against remaining feudalism. Though there was little violence against people, peasants seized and destroyed documents that demanded feudal dues and taxes. In an attempt to contain these revolutionary disorders, the king, in Versailles, recognized the National Assembly, the new group formed by the Third Estate and its allies, as representatives of the people and authorized it to draft a new constitution.

The National Assembly abolished what was left of feudalism and serfdom, the tithe for the church, and the special privileges of the nobility. It issued the "Declaration of the Rights of Man and the Citizen" with seventeen articles, including:

- Men are born and remain free and equal in rights; social distinctions may be based only upon general usefulness.
- The aim of every political association is the preservation of the natural and inalienable rights of man; these rights are liberty, property, security, and resistance to oppression.
- The source of all sovereignty resides essentially in the nation …
- Law is the expression of the general will … All citizens, being equal before it, are equally admissible to all public offices, positions, and employments, according to their capacity, and without other distinction than that of virtues and talents …
- For the maintenance of the public force and for the expenses of administration a common tax is indispensable; it must be assessed equally on all citizens in proportion to their means …
- Society has the right to require of every public agent an accounting of his administration.

The Declaration further affirmed freedom of thought, religion, petition, and due process under law. It represented a triumph for the doctrines of the *philosophes*.

Meanwhile, hungry mobs in Paris continued toward insurrection. In October, led by a demonstration of housewives, market women, and revolutionary militants protesting the high price of bread, 20,000 Parisians marched to the royal palace in Versailles. This "March of the Women" broke into the palace, overwhelmed the National Guard, and forced the royal family to return to Paris where they could be kept under surveillance. In the meantime, in the countryside peasants felt an (unfounded) "Great Fear" that landlords were attempting to block reform by hiring thugs to burn the harvest. In response, peasants attacked the estates of the nobility and the clergy, and their managers.

Over the next two years, the National Assembly drew up a constitution, which called for a constitutional monarchy; did away with the titles and perquisites of nobility and clergy; introduced uniform government across the country; disestablished the Roman Catholic clergy and confiscated the property of the Church; and convened a new Legislative Assembly, for which about one-half of adult, male Frenchmen were entitled to vote, essentially by a property qualification. Protestants, Jews, and agnostics were admitted to full citizenship and could vote and run for office if they met the property qualifications. Citizenship would be based not on religious affiliation but on residence in the country and allegiance to its government. Except for the radical—and polarizing—anticlerical position, the actions of the French Revolution thus far seemed quite similar to those of England and America. They were consistent with the optimistic and activist worldview of the *philosophes*. The new constitution was finally promulgated in September 1791 following a wave of strikes and an official ban on labor organizations.

International War, the "Second" Revolution, and the Terror, 1791–99

In June 1791 Louis XVI and his queen Marie-Antoinette attempted to flee France but were apprehended and,

Contemporary colored engraving showing women marching to Versailles on 5 October 1789. Angered by reports of a luxurious banquet staged by the king, a large crowd of Parisians, mostly women, stormed Versailles and laid siege to the royal palace. Louis XVI and his family, though later executed, were at this point saved by the intervention of the French general, the Marquis de Lafayette.

thereafter, held as virtual prisoners in the royal palace. Shocked and frightened, thousands of aristocrats emigrated to neighboring countries that were more respectful of monarchy and aristocracy. News of the abolition of feudal privilege and of the Civil Constitution of the Clergy filled the nobility and clergy across Europe with dread. Leopold II, the Habsburg emperor (r. 1790–92) and brother of Marie-Antoinette, entered into discussions with other rulers to consider war against the new French government. The French National Assembly, meeting under the new constitution, began to mobilize both in response to this threat and in anticipation of extending the revolution. In April 1792 it declared war on the Austrian monarchy, and for the next twenty-three years, France would be at war with several of the major countries of Europe.

Events careered onward at a revolutionary pace. The war went poorly and mobs stormed the royal palace attempting to kill the king and beginning the "Second French Revolution." Louis sought protection in the National Assembly and was imprisoned; all his official powers were terminated. The Assembly disbanded and called for a new National Convention—to be elected by universal male suffrage—to draw up a new constitution. Amid mob violence, the new Convention met in September 1792. Its leaders were **Jacobins**, members of a nationwide network of political clubs named (ironically) for a former convent in Paris where they had first met. They divided into the more moderate **Girondins**, named for a region of France and in general representing the provinces, and the **Montagnards**, representatives mostly from Paris, who drew their name from the benches they occupied on the uppermost left side of the assembly hall. By 361 to 359 votes, the Convention voted to execute the king in January 1793. The "Second Revolution" was well underway.

Outside the Assembly, the Paris Commune, the government of Paris, represented the workers, merchants, and artisans of the city, who were generally more radical than the Convention. They were called the **sansculottes**, "without breeches," because the men wore long trousers rather than the knee breeches of the middle and aristocratic classes. In June 1793, the Commune invaded the National Convention and forced the arrest of thirty-one Girondins on charges of treason, leaving the more radical Montagnards in control.

To govern in the midst of the combined international and civil warfare, the Convention created a Committee of Public Safety, which launched a Reign of Terror against "counter-revolutionaries." It executed about 40,000 people between mid-1793 and mid-1794. At Nantes, in the Vendée region of western France, the center of the royalist counter-revolution, the Committee intentionally drowned 2000 people. To wage war abroad it instituted a *levée en masse,* or national military draft, which raised an unprecedented army of 800,000 men, and mobilized the economic resources of France to support it.

The Committee intensified the campaign against feudal privilege, rejecting the payment of compensation to the manor lords, who lost their special rights over their tenants. It promoted instruction in practical farming and craft production, spoke of introducing universal elementary education, and abolished slavery throughout France's colonies. It introduced a new calendar, counting Year 1 from the founding of the French Republic in 1793, giving new names to the twelve months, and dividing each

SOURCE

Olympe de Gouges, "The Rights of Women"

Writing under the pen name Olympe de Gouges, Marie Gouze (1748–93) directly appropriated the language of the Revolution's Declaration of the Rights of Man and the Citizen *(1789). Her* Declaration of the Rights of Woman and the Citizen *exposed its lack of concern for the rights of women:*

> Article I. Woman is born free and remains equal in rights to man. Social distinctions can be founded only on general utility …
> Article XVII. The right of property is inviolable and sacred to both sexes, jointly or separately. (Bell and Offen, pp. 105–6)

Gouges addressed this document to the French queen, Marie-Antoinette, urging her to adopt this feminist program as her own and thus win over France to the royalist cause. In 1793 the radical Jacobins in the Assembly, condemning Gouges for both royalism and feminism, had her guillotined.

Jacobins A French revolutionary party founded in 1789. It later became the most radical party of the Revolution, responsible for implementing the Reign of Terror and the execution of the king (1793).

Girondins A French revolutionary group formed largely from the middle classes, many of them originally from the Gironde region.

Montagnards Members of a radical French revolutionary party, closely associated with the Jacobins and supported by the artisans, shopkeepers, and sansculottes. They opposed the more moderate Girondins.

sansculottes (French: "without knee-breeches") In the French Revolution, members of the militant, generally poorer classes of Paris, so-called because they wore trousers rather than the knee-breeches of affluent society.

Le ROI ESCLAVE ou les SUJETS ROIS   FEMALE PATRIOTISM

The women of Les Halles taking Louis XVI from Versailles, 1789. Engraving. The illustration on page 542 shows the women setting out for Versailles, angry, determined, struggling. Here they return in triumph with their quarry. Contemporary cartoons and engravings told the story of the Revolution as it unfolded. (*Bibliothèque Nationale, Paris*)

month into three weeks of ten days each. The most important leader of the Committee, Maximilien Robespierre (1758–94), introduced in 1794 the Worship of the Supreme Being, a kind of civic religious ritual that alienated the Catholic majority in France.

By July 1794, however, French armies were winning wars against the other European powers, and the domestic economy seemed to be recovering. The members of the Convention, partly out of fear for their own lives, managed to end both the mob-inspired violence and the official Terror. The Convention outlawed and guillotined Robespierre. It relaxed price controls and, when working-class mobs threatened the Convention, called in the troops and suppressed the revolt. In 1795 it instituted yet another constitution, this time calling for a three-stage election of a representative government. Almost all adult males could vote for electors who, in turn, chose a

HOW DO WE KNOW?

The Historiography of the French Revolution

The study of the French Revolution remains the pre-eminent subject of French historiography, producing a seemingly endless variety of interpretations. Three approaches, however, have predominated. The first emphasizes the importance of ideas, stressing the philosophes *as the precursors of revolution. This interpretation tends to focus on the first three months of the revolution and the significance of the "Declaration of the Rights of Man and the Citizen." R.R. Palmer's* The Age of the Democratic Revolution *(1959), for example, favors this reading. A second interpretation stresses the significance of class interests in the revolution, and tends to highlight the next chronological stage, as urban workers and rural peasantry escalated their protests and demonstrations. Georges Lefebvre's* The Coming of the French Revolution *(1939) represents this*

position. A more recent interpretation (influenced by literary theory) speaks of the revolution as "discourse," an interplay of ideas and interest groups that constantly shifts, or "skids," as events unfold. As the direction of the revolution changed irrevocably with each new event—for example, the execution of Louis XVI—ideas were reassessed and classes reshuffled themselves into new alignments. François Furet's Interpreting the French Revolution *(1978) is the leading statement of this point of view. Our narrative incorporates elements of all three interpretive perspectives.*

There is a broader issue, too. Historians sometimes envision events as part of a long sweep of related trends. Sometimes they see them as contingencies, occurring because of circumstances that are unique and unpredictable. The French Revolution presents both aspects. On the one hand, it was an outgrowth of larger trends, the ideals of the philosophes *and the legacies*

of the British and American revolutions. On the other hand, specific events unfolded day-by-day in quite unpredictable ways; had they turned out differently—for example, had the one vote majority to guillotine the king been reversed—the outcome of the revolution might have been quite different. To understand the French Revolution, both these perspectives—the grand sweep and the contingency—are necessary.

- *In your own understanding of historical change, which do you think counts for more, the ideas or interests? Why?*
- *In the French Revolution, what is the evidence for the importance of ideas? For the importance of interests?*
- *In your own understanding of historical change, which do you think counts for more, the grand sweep or contingency? Give an example from one of the revolutions other than the French Revolution that illustrates your point of view.*

national legislative assembly composed of men who did have to meet property qualifications and who, in turn, chose an executive of five Directors. When the 1795 elections were threatened by insurrection, the Convention called upon General Napoleon Bonaparte (1769–1821) to protect the process.

The Directory, as the executive body was called, governed from 1795 to 1799. With the execution of the monarch, the manorial system and the privileges of the nobility and clergy had come to an end, and the Directory ratified the new peasant and commercial landowners in the possession of their new property. However, the Directory itself was unpopular and unstable, and the greater freedom benefited its opponents while at the same time enabling the Catholic Church to make a strong comeback. The elections of Directors in 1797, 1798, and 1799 were disputed, and on each occasion army officers were called in to dismiss the Directors, until, in 1799, Bonaparte, acting with the Abbé Sieyès, staged a *coup d'état* and had himself appointed First Consul. In 1802 his position was upgraded to consul for life and, in 1804, to emperor. Losing the right of free elections, France itself became a (benevolent) despotism. The process that historians usually call the French Revolution was over.

Napoleon in Power, 1799–1812

As head of government, Napoleon consolidated and even expanded many of the innovations of the revolution. To maintain the equality of classes and to systematize the administration of justice, he codified the laws of France. The Code Napoléon or Civil Code, which was issued in 1804, pressed for equality before the law and the principle of a "career open to talents," that is, all people should have access to professional advancement according to their ability, rather than by birth or social status. Uniform codes of criminal, commercial, and penal law were also introduced. The administration was organized into a smoothly functioning service throughout France.

Fearing a counter-revolution led by the Church, Napoleon reached a **concordat** with the pope. The French government continued to hold the former church lands, but agreed in exchange to pay the salaries of the clergy (including Protestants and others) and to allow the pope to regain authority over the appointment and discipline of Roman Catholic clergy. Protestants, dissenters, Jews, and others were reaffirmed in full citizenship, with all the rights and obligations that such status entailed, as long as they swore their allegiance to the state. In many conquered cities, including Rome and Frankfurt, French armies pulled down the ghetto walls that for centuries had segregated Jews. The government hired a large bureaucracy to administer the state. It selected personnel mostly on the revolutionary principle of a "career open to talent," hiring the best-qualified personnel rather than those with personal or hereditary connections.

This openness of opportunity suited Napoleon very well. He had come from Corsica, of a modest

Concordat A public agreement, subject to international law, between the pope as head of the Roman Catholic Church and a temporal ruler regulating the status, rights, and liberties of the Church within the country concerned.

Napoleon Crossing the Alps by Jacques-Louis David, c. 1800. Having chronicled the revolution with his brush, David became Napoleon's official painter. The heroic style of the portrait projects the Emperor's enormous confidence as he heads for military glory in the Italian campaigns of 1796–7. The truth of the journey was rather different: Napoleon crossed the Alps on a docile but footsure mule, not a fiery stallion. (*Palace of Versailles, near Paris*)

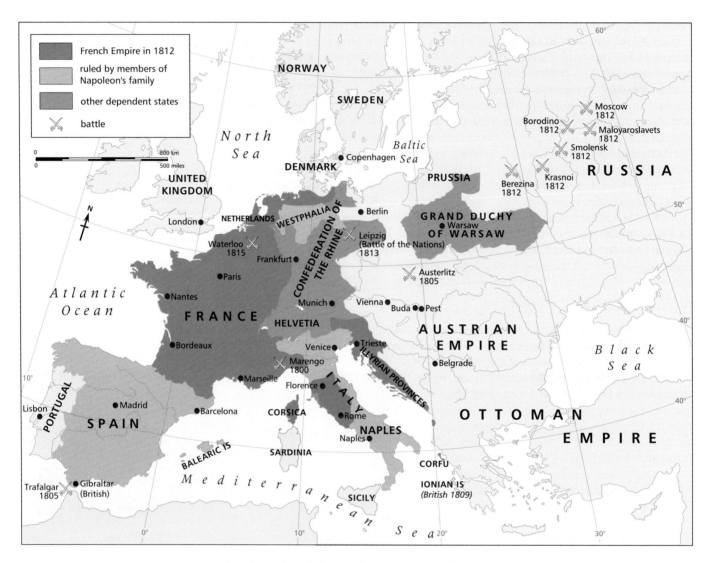

The empire of Napoleon. Napoleon, fired by revolutionary zeal, fought brilliantly to bring much of Europe under his dominion, often installing relatives as rulers. Napoleonic institutions were introduced to Italy, the Low Countries, Germany, and then Poland by force of arms. By 1812 Napoleon seemed invincible, but Britain's strength at sea and Napoleon's disastrous losses on land in his invasion of Russia (1812) led to his downfall.

family, and made his mark as a military officer. He had no respect for unearned authority. Nor was he formally religious. He earned his power through his military, administrative, and leadership skills. In a striking exception to the good principle of advancement by merit, however, Napoleon appointed his brothers as kings of Spain, Holland, and Westphalia, his brother-in-law as king of Naples, and his stepson as viceroy of the kingdom of Italy. He himself continued to lead the forces of France in military victories over the powers of Europe.

The Napoleonic Wars and the Spread of Revolution, 1799–1812

As a son of the revolution, Napoleon sought to spread its principles by force of arms. By 1810 he had conquered or entered into alliances with all the major powers and regions of Europe except Portugal, the Ottoman-held Balkans, and Britain. In each conquered state, Napoleon introduced the principal legal and administrative reforms of the revolution: an end to feudal privilege, equality of rights, religious toleration, codified law, free trade, and efficient and systematic administration, including statistical accounting, registration of documents, and the use of the metric system. In many areas of Europe, Napoleon was welcomed for the reforms he brought.

There were, however, flaws in Napoleon's policies, and they finally brought his rule to an end. First, Napoleon attempted to conquer Britain, and ultimately the naval power of that island nation and the land forces of its allies, especially those of Russia, proved too strong. Napoleon could not break the British hold on continental shipping and he was defeated at sea by Lord Nelson at the Battle of Trafalgar in 1805. When the Russian emperor supported Britain, Napoleon invaded Russia in 1812 and mired his army irretrievably in the vastness of that country during the bitterness of its winter. During that campaign, 400,000 of Napoleon's troops died from battle, starvation, and exposure; another 100,000 were captured.

Finally, the nations Napoleon conquered began to experience the stirrings of nationalism and the desire to rule themselves. Haiti, which had achieved virtual independence in the 1790s, resisted Napoleon's attempt to re-impose French rule and re-institute slavery in the island. Some 50,000 French troops perished in Haiti, most by diseases such as yellow fever, but many at the hands of revolutionary slaves. European peoples, too, did not want their countries to be colonies of France. By 1813 Napoleon had been defeated by his disastrous losses in Russia and by a coalition of European armies; the French were driven back to their borders. In 1814 Napoleon abdicated and Louis XVIII (r. 1814–15; 1815–24) assumed the throne of France. Napoleon escaped from exile on the Mediterranean island of Elba only to be defeated and exiled again in 1815, this time to St. Helena in the South Atlantic. The Napoleonic era was over. The Congress of Vienna, an assembly of representatives of all the powers of Europe, led by the most influential states, concluded diplomatic agreements that established a **balance of power** among them and redrew the post-war map of Europe. Political conservatism enveloped France and Europe for a generation.

HAITI: SLAVE REVOLUTION AND THE OVERTHROW OF COLONIALISM, 1791–1804

The formal philosophy and rhetoric of enlightenment and revolution proclaimed the natural desire of all humans to be free, and in the slave plantations of the Caribbean local slave revolts were common, feared, and ruthlessly suppressed. In the western sector of the island of Hispaniola in the colony of Saint-Domingue (modern Haiti), French planters had established one of the most brutal of the slave plantation systems. By 1791, 500,000 black slaves formed the overwhelming majority of the population, with 40,000 whites, many of them owners of plantations and slaves, and 30,000 free people of color, both **mulatto** and black. For decades, the slaves had escaped psychologically and culturally through the practice of **vodoun** (voodoo), a religion that blended the Catholicism of their masters with religious practices brought from Africa. Physically, they had escaped through **maroonage,** flight from the plantations to the surrounding hills. Sometimes the

balance of power In international relations, a policy that aims to secure peace by preventing any one state or alignment of states from becoming too dominant. Alliances are formed in order to build up a force equal or superior to that of the potential enemy.

mulatto In the Americas, a person of mixed race, usually with parents of European and African origin.

vodoun The popular religious cult of Haiti, as well as other areas of the Caribbean. It combines ritual elements from Roman Catholicism with theological and magical elements of West African origin.

maroonage The condition of some escaped slaves in the West Indian islands in the early eighteenth century. Following their successful escape, they sometimes established communities in inaccessible mountainous regions or forests.

The revolution in Haiti. One of the most dramatic revolutions occurred on the Caribbean island of Hispaniola. A slave revolt in 1791 in the French region, Saint-Domingue, spread rapidly, briefly penetrating and uniting with the Spanish sector, Santo Domingo. Despite interventions by French and British forces, and the incarceration and exile of its leader, Toussaint L'Ouverture, in 1802, Haiti gained its independence from France in 1804, the first successful slave revolt in history.

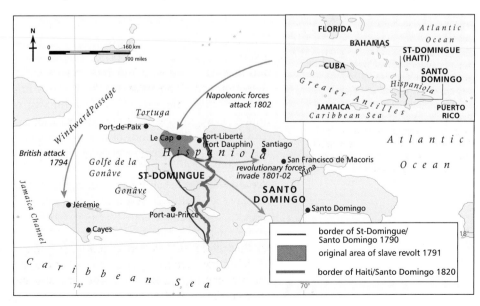

French lithograph of Pierre Dominique Toussaint L'Ouverture, early nineteenth century. The colony of Saint-Domingue (present-day Haiti) in the West Indies had made a fortune for the French through sugar plantations worked by African slaves. In the 1790s, under the leadership of Toussaint L'Ouverture, it became the site of a slave revolution that eventually led to independence. The former slave acquired his surname because of the ferocity with which he made an opening ("ouverture") in the enemy ranks.

escaped slaves, maroons, established their own colonies. In the 1750s one of the maroons, François Makandal, built among the maroon colonies a network of resistance to slavery. Inspired to independence by vodoun beliefs and using poison to attack individual plantation owners, Makandal apparently planned to poison the water supply of Le Cap, the main town of northern Saint-Domingue, but he was captured and burned at the stake in 1758.

The Slave Revolt

In 1791, slave revolts broke out across Saint-Domingue. The inspiration seems to have been the natural desire for freedom, perhaps abetted by news of the American and French revolutions. One of the earliest rallying cries, delivered by the poet Boukman Dutty in Haitian–French patois, *"Coute la liberté li pale nan coeur nous tous"*—"Listen to the voice of liberty which speaks in the hearts of all of us," implied no knowledge of the European and American revolutions.

The revolt spread. From guerrilla warfare by maroon bands, it grew to general armed struggle and civil warfare. In the western part of Saint-Domingue, white planters welcomed the support of British troops who came as allies to suppress the slave revolt and also to drive out the French. The mulattoes—those of mixed race parentage—were free people, and some of them owned slaves. They now sought their own rights of representation and were divided over the issue of slavery. In the eastern part of Saint-Domingue, a new leader, Toussaint L'Ouverture (*c.* 1743–1803), a freed black, established an alliance with the Spanish rulers against both the slave system in Saint-Domingue (but not in the Spanish part of the island) and the French. Toussaint incorporated the rhetoric of the French Revolution into his own. In 1794, under Robespierre, the French National Assembly abolished slavery in all French colonies. In response, Toussaint linked himself to France as he continued his war against slaveowners, who were now aligned with the British and who resisted the new French decree. By May 1800 Toussaint had become the effective ruler of Saint-Domingue.

The Anti-Imperial Revolt

When Napoleon came to power in 1799 he reversed French policy on slavery. He dispatched 20,000 French troops to recapture the island and to reinstitute slavery as he had done in Guadeloupe in 1802. Napoleon's representative deceived Toussaint into suspending his revolution. Toussaint was imprisoned in 1802 and exiled to France, where he died the next year. Nevertheless, unified black and mulatto armies, now under many different cooperating leaders, continued the struggle against France, drove out its forces, and, once again, abolished slavery. As many as 50,000 French troops died of yellow fever, and thousands more became military casualties. On January 1, 1804, Saint-Domingue at last proclaimed its independence and its new name of Haiti, the Carib name for mountain. This completed the only known successful slave revolution in history.

econometrics The use of statistical techniques and mathematical models to analyze economic relationships. Econometrics may be applied by a government or private business to test the validity of an economic theory or to forecast future trends.

THE ABOLITION OF SLAVERY AND THE SLAVE TRADE

Initially, the British tried to assist in putting down the slave rebellion in Haiti. When they failed, their subsequent decision to limit the spread of slavery by abolishing the

HOW DO WE KNOW?

Abolition: Historians Debate the Causes

Why were the slave trade, and then slavery itself, abolished in the Atlantic countries? To what extent was the spread of democratic revolution responsible? Analyses differ. Historians who emphasize the significance of the Haitian Revolution, as C.L.R. James and David Nicholls do, stress the fear that the uprising of the slaves engendered among slave owners. In the lands of the Caribbean, including northeastern Brazil, black slaves working the high-mortality plantations formed up to 90 percent of the population. Local rebellions already occurred frequently, and large-scale revolution now appeared as a real possibility. The abolition of the slave trade provided some limit on the size of the slave population, although total abolition—a much more expensive act for the slave owners—would come only later.

A second school of thought, shared by historians such as David Brion Davis and Orlando Patterson, stresses the importance of compassion as a motive. Davis emphasizes the increasing influence of humanitarian sentiment in European Christian thought from the seventeenth century:

> The philosophy of benevolence was a product of the seventeenth century, when certain British Protestants, shaken by theological controversy and the implications of modern science, looked increasingly to human nature and conduct as a basis for faith. In their impatience with theological dogma, their distaste for the doctrine of original sin, their appreciation for human feeling and sentiment, and their confidence in man's capacity for moral improvement, these Latitudinarians, as they were called, anticipated the main concerns of the Enlightenment, and laid an indispensable foundation for social reform. (pp. 348–49)

The emphasis on compassion increased in reaction against the growing scale and unprecedented cruelty of slavery in the New World. Among Christian groups opposing slavery, Quakers and Methodists stood out. The birth and growth of both these denominations— Quakerism under the leadership of George Fox (1624–91) and Methodism under John Wesley (1703–91)—were contemporary with the development of mass slavery in the Americas. Other branches of Christianity had long since made peace with the institution of slavery, contenting themselves with promising a gentler existence in life after death. Quakers and Methodists, however, had to confront the reality of slavery for the first time in one of its cruelest, New World, forms. In Britain, William Wilberforce (1759–1833), a philanthropist and member of the Clapham Sect—a group of well-to-do Evangelicals—played a major part in the antislavery movement. As a Member of Parliament, he led the campaign to abolish the slave trade and to emancipate existing slaves.

The philosophes argued a third, similar but more intellectual position against slavery. They argued that slavery violated the law of nature; it was inconsistent with the nature of humankind. Montesquieu (1689–1755), in his assessments of the nature of laws and government, argued that "the call for slavery was the call of the wealthy and the decadent, not for the general welfare of mankind".

Finally, an economic critique began to develop in the eighteenth century. Slavery was not profitable to the society, certainly not to the slave, and not to the development of a more productive economy in the long run. In The Wealth of Nations Adam Smith argued that slavery, like all examples of monopoly and special privilege, inhibited economic growth. Lacking the opportunity to acquire wealth and property for himself, the slave would find it in his interest to work as little as possible. Slave owners advocated their system not so much for its economic benefits but for the power it gave them over others, despite economic losses. The leading exponents of this rationale for abolition in recent times have been Marxists, led by Eric Williams in his classic Capitalism and Slavery (1944). Many economic historians disagreed with this analysis, most notably Robert Fogel and Stanley Engerman, who published Time on the Cross in 1974, an elaborate two-volume statistical study linking economics with statistics (econometrics) to show the profitability of slavery. Historian Seymour Drescher arguing bluntly (1977) that abolition was "econocide," economic disaster, for Britain. Drescher sided with the humanitarian assessment: abolition was implemented despite its economic costs.

What to do without slaves? The successor system to slavery was not free labor. Indentured labor, supplied in large part by vast contract immigration from India and China, filled the labor needs of the post-slavery Caribbean as well as those of new plantation economies in the Indian Ocean in Fiji, Mauritius, and Réunion, and in south and east Africa. Although not quite slaves, indentured servants traded many of their basic economic and political rights for a number of years in exchange for their livelihood.

Finally, with the export of slave labor from Africa banned, European entre-preneurs began in the later 1800s to explore the possibilities of shifting the production of primary products to Africa itself and to employ on-site personnel to perform the necessary work. Although this system sounded like free labor, in fact the wages were so low and conditions so abysmal, that many observers saw these economic initiatives as a newer form of slavery transplanted back to Africa.

- What evidence have we seen in this chapter that the Haitian revolution played an important part in the abolition of slavery?
- What evidence do you have from this chapter, and from other studies, that would support the importance of humanitarianism in the abolition of slavery? What evidence do you have for the importance of economics?
- What is the difference between slavery and indentured labor?

slave trade in 1807 reflected, in part, their fear of further revolts. In 1833 Britain abolished slavery throughout its Empire, although "freed" slaves were required to work for their former masters for a period of time to compensate them for their loss of "property." The United States, a slave-holding country, feared that the Haitian slave revolt might spread northward and prohibited all trade with Haiti in 1806. In 1808, following Britain's lead, America outlawed participation in the international slave trade, although it abolished internal slavery only with the Civil War (1861–5). It recognized Haiti as an independent country also during that war, in 1862. Slavery was not the only issue at stake in the United States' Civil War, but each of the other issues was linked to it. Would the United States follow the model of the Northern states and become an urban, free-labor, industrial nation, or follow the Southern pattern with its rural, slave-holding plantation economy? As the North grew more populous and wealthier, the South began to feel itself an internal colony within the United States and grew increasingly resentful and rebellious. An even more central question was states' rights: Did individual states have the right to secede from the Union? The question arose primarily because the slave-holding Southern states preferred secession rather than face the possibility of abolition. When Abraham Lincoln was elected President in 1860, they feared the worst and began to secede. Lincoln, a man who would have preferred peace, recognized that to preserve the Union he would have to go to war. The American Civil War saw more than one-half million dead, the bloodiest war in the history of the country. In the midst of the war, in 1863, Lincoln issued the Emancipation Proclamation, declaring free all slaves in areas that had seceded and were fighting against the Union. In 1865, after the Union victory and Lincoln's assassination, the Thirteenth Amendment to the Constitution officially abolished slavery throughout the country. No compensation was paid. As a class, the Southern slave owners were ruined. Their way of life was finished. Elsewhere, however, the Atlantic slave trade continued at about three-quarters of its highest volume. That trade did not end effectively until slavery was abolished in 1876 in Puerto Rico, in 1886 in Cuba, and in 1888 in Brazil.

THE END OF COLONIALISM IN LATIN AMERICA: INDEPENDENCE AND DISILLUSIONMENT, 1810–30

Independence Movements

In the period 1810 to 1826 virtually all the countries of Latin America expelled their European colonial rulers and established their independence. Latin Americans drew inspiration from the intellectual and political legacies of the American, French, and Haitian revolutions, although few wanted to move so far toward democratic rights as the Europeans had done, and many were frightened by the events in Haiti.

The revolts of the early nineteenth century were led, for the most part, by creole elites, American-born direct descendants of Spanish settlers. These leaders wanted more economic and political rights for themselves, especially after Napoleon occupied Spain and installed his relatives on the Spanish throne. A series of earlier revolts, however, had been led by Amerindians and mestizos. In 1780, in Cuzco, Peru, Tupac Amaru, a mestizo with Inca ancestors, led 70,000 rebels against Spanish rule. Creoles did not join in this revolt and Tupac Amaru was captured and executed in 1783. The entire revolt was brutally crushed. The Comunero Revolt in Colombia in 1781 drove the viceroy from Bogotá but ended with only some concessions by the Spanish and internal fighting among the rebels. Mulattoes led a revolt in Bahia, Brazil, in 1798. At the time of all these revolts, Spain and Portugal were still independent, powerful countries and, with the aid of creoles and **mazombos** (American-born direct descendants of Portuguese settlers), they suppressed the revolts. In general, the creoles and *mazombos*

mazombo A direct descendant of Portuguese settlers in the Americas.

saw their fate linked more to the Spanish and Portuguese rulers than to the Amerindians or to those of mixed parentage. The Napoleonic wars in Spain, however, gave the colonies the opportunity to declare their independence, with the creoles leading the way. The revolts were bloody and successful.

In virtually every revolt, leadership was provided by a creole elite, most of whom feared the potential power of the Amerindian, mestizo, mulatto, and African majority. Such men as Father Miguel Hidalgo (1753–1811) in Mexico, Simón Bolívar (1783–1830; in northern South America, and José de San Martín (1778–1850) in southern South America, were all creoles, as were their leading generals, administrators, and supporters. They were familiar with European traditions and events, and many of them had studied in Europe. Indeed, many of the revolutions seemed to be fought for the benefit of the creoles, who actually formed less than 5 percent of the total population. Believing their own livelihood depended on low-paid and slave labor, these elites were determined to preserve the old system without Spanish and Portuguese domi-

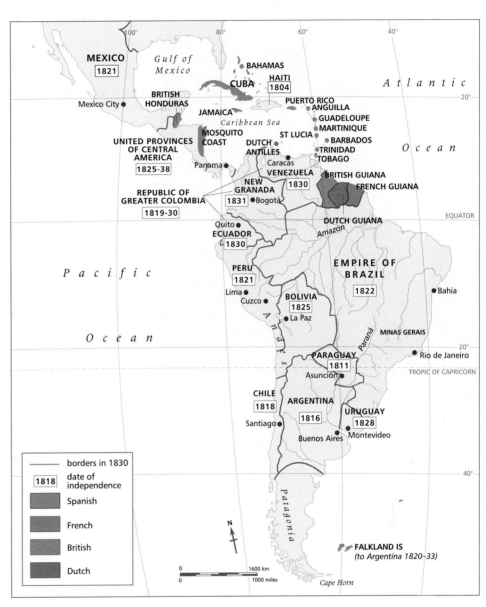

Liberation movements in Latin America. The collapse of Iberian rule in Latin America was virtually complete by 1826. Sustained campaigns by Simón Bolívar and Antonio José de Sucre demolished Spanish control of Venezuela, Colombia, and Peru while, from the south, José de San Martin led the Argentine and Chilean Army of the Andes north to Lima. Liberation brought many internal power struggles and divisions, leaving the present-day South American map with an array of some twenty republics.

nance. Other Latin Americans, mestizos and Amerindians, gained little. On the Caribbean islands of Cuba and Puerto Rico there were no rebellions. Here the elites, frightened lest the slave revolt of Haiti be repeated on their own islands, remained loyal to Spain.

After Independence

The continent—except for Portuguese Brazil—was wrested from Spain by the sword. The greatest of the revolutionary leaders—Simón Bolívar of Venezuela in the north, José de San Martín of Argentina in the south, Antonio José de Sucré of Ecuador, and Bernardo O'Higgins of Chile—combined military excellence with intellectual, administrative, and diplomatic accomplishments.

Simón Bolívar and the Challenge of Unification. As soldier, diplomat, general, administrator, visionary, newspaper publisher, law giver, national president, dictator, lover,

Antonio Salas (attrib.), *Simón Bolívar,* **1825.** Bolívar was the most important military leader of the Latin American revolution. Despite a life of extraordinary adventure and accomplishment, he failed to bring about the unification of South America that he so passionately desired.

and disillusioned revolutionary, Simón Bolívar dominated public life in Latin America for most of two decades, from 1810 until his death in 1830. Son of a Venezuelen creole aristocrat, Bolívar studied in Europe from age sixteen to nineteen, primarily in Spain. On return to Caracas, his chosen bride died in their first year together, and Bolívar vowed to devote his life to politics. He returned to Europe for travel and continued study of the *philosophes.* Returning to Venezuela in 1807, he joined in the movements for independence that swept the region, especially after Napoleon's troops invaded Spain, undercutting Spanish authority and power in the Americas.

In many of his early efforts he failed. Assigned to diplomatic duty in England, he was unable to gain recognition and material support for the Venezuelan revolution. In 1811, when Venezuela lost its independence within a year of declaring it, he was serving as an army officer. In 1813 he captured Caracas and reasserted Venezuelan independence, but he was defeated and exiled in 1814. In defeat, however, he wrote visionary documents. His *Manifesto of Cartagena,* 1812, was a rallying cry for revolutionary forces to continue the struggle against Spain. His *Letter from Jamaica* of September 1815, written in exile, underlined not only Latin America's political suppression, but also its economic servitude.

Bolívar renewed his military expeditions and began to earn fabulous success, especially after he got monetary and military support from Haiti and Britain in return for freeing South American slaves. In 1819 his forces defeated the Spanish and established the Republic of Colombia with himself as president and military dictator. Within two more years they liberated Venezuela and Ecuador, filling out the borders of the federation. In Quito, Ecuador, he met Manuela Saenz, who left her husband to join Bolívar and remain by his side to the last day of his life, despite his numerous affairs and the public scandal of their own relationship.

As Bolívar made conquests from the north, various movements began their struggles for independence from the region of Rio Plate, now Argentina. One of the leaders who has emerged as one of the great military strategists of history was José San Martín. He put together a massive Army of the Andes and promised freedom to slaves who joined his forces. He later claimed they were his best soldiers. Bringing together former slaves and soldiers, he crossed the high Andes mountains with mules and llamas, successfully defeating the Spaniards in Chile and mounting attacks on Peru. He refused to rule over Chile in favor of Bernardo O'Higgins, the creole leader there, but he couldn't effectively take Peru. Ultimately, he met with Bolívar in Guayaquil, Ecuador, in 1822. No one really knows what they discussed, but after the meeting, San Martín retired to France, leaving the conquest of South America to Bolívar.

By 1825, through brilliant military action Bolívar captured Peru and Upper Peru, later named Bolivia in his honor, and became president of both.

Just as his dreams of a single united region seemed to reach fruition, however, they dissolved in warfare among his generals, who now fought for the independence of each of the constituent units. Bolívar tried to hold the federation together through dictatorial rulings, but his high-handedness further alienated his former supporters and he narrowly escaped an assassination attempt in 1828 as Manuela Saenz covered his exit. Bolívar withdrew from political leadership in 1830. A few months later he died in the agony of tuberculosis, indebted and disillusioned.

"Gran Colombia" dissolved into Colombia, Venezuela, and Ecuador. Further south, the Spanish viceroyalty of La Plata dissolved into Argentina, Paraguay, Uruguay, and Bolivia. For a decade, 1829–39, under General Andrés Santa Cruz, a mestizo, Peru and Bolivia were united, but then broke apart, to the relief of some of their neighbors. Chile, isolated by the Andes to its east, and open to the outside world via the Pacific Ocean to its west, also became a separate, independent nation. In total, eighteen nations emerged from Spanish America.

Warfare among many of the new states and the violent repression of the Indian and African-American populations (one-fourth of Brazil's population in 1850 were slaves) gave prominence and power both to national armies and to private military forces throughout Latin America. The military strongmen, or *caudillos*, came to control local areas and even national governments. Personal rule, only minimally controlled by official codes of law and formal election procedures, prevailed in many countries up to the late twentieth century. (See Pablo Neruda's epic history of Latin America in verse, p. 555.)

Mexico. Father Miguel Hidalgo led the first wave of Mexico's revolt until he was executed in 1811. Father José María Morelos (1765–1815) then took command of the revolutionary movement. Morelos sought to displace the Spanish and creole elites, to abolish slavery, and, unlike Hidalgo, to revoke the special privileges and landholdings of the Church. The early Mexican independence movement differed from that in South America because of its attack on creole elites, itself inspired by the incipient "liberation theology" of the priests Hidalgo and Morelos. Close to their parishioners, they understood that peasant poverty was a product of Spanish and creole rule. The Spanish captured and executed Morelos in 1815. By the time Mexico won its independence in 1821, its revolution was controlled by its most conservative creole elite. For two years Mexico was ruled as a monarchy, but in 1823 it was proclaimed a republic. Military leaders, businessmen, and foreign powers all struggled for control, and Mexico remained unstable for decades. Its size was also reduced by half. Central American regions, after years of rebellions, broke away from Mexico and formed a union; it dissolved in internal regional antagonisms in 1838. Texas, with waves of immigrants entering from the United States, and encouraged by the United States government, declared its independence from Mexico in 1836. Nine years later the United States annexed Texas, precipitating the Mexican–American war. In the peace settlement, America gained the territories of its current southwestern States.

Brazil. Brazil, the largest country in Latin America in terms of both geography and population, had a different method of achieving independence, and this helps to explain why it did not break apart after independence. When Napoleon invaded Portugal in 1807, the Portuguese royal family, assisted by Britain, fled to Rio de Janeiro and ruled the Portuguese Empire from the Brazilian capital for thirteen years. King Dom João (John) VI (r. 1816–26) raised Brazil's legal status to equal that of Portugal and expanded Rio as a center of trade, administration, education, and cultural institutions.

In 1821 João returned with his court to Lisbon, but left his son and heir, Prince Pedro, in Rio. When the Parliament, or Cortes, in Lisbon attempted to cut Brazil and Rio back to size, the American-born Brazilian elite, the *mazombos*, counseled defiance. In 1822 Pedro declared Brazil independent, and Portugal did little to stop

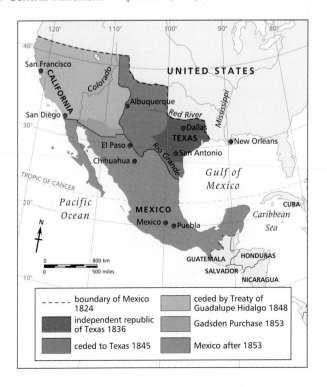

Mexico, 1824–53. In 1821 the Viceroyalty of New Spain, with its capital in Mexico City, won its independence from Spain. By 1823, the Central American countries seceded, leaving Mexico with its current southern border. Then, piece by piece, the northern areas were lost to the United States: Texas through secession from Mexico (1836) and annexation by the US (1845); some territories through warfare (1846–48); and some through purchase (1853).

Jean-Baptiste Debret, *Early Evening Refreshment in the Praca do Palaccio, Rio de Janeiro*, 1835. Lithograph. The port and capital city of Rio has long been famous for its fun-loving life and for a modicum of racial integration. But Brazil did not abolish slavery until 1888. All three of these elements are suggested in this 1835 lithograph. (*Bibliothèque Nationale, Paris*)

the move. Pedro was soon crowned "Constitutional Emperor and Perpetual Defender of Brazil," but the effective rulers of Brazil were its *mazombo* elites. Brazil was thus spared the warfare and disintegration characteristic of Spanish Latin America, but it was ruled by similar American-born descendants of Iberian families. While the former Spanish colonies became republics, Brazil became a monarchy under a member of the Portuguese royal family.

Paraguay: The New Historiography. Tiny landlocked Paraguay, with a population of 150,000, declared its independence in 1810–11 from the viceroyalty of La Plata as well as from Spain and defeated an Argentine army that had been sent to subdue it. Its dictator, José Gaspar Rodríguez de Francia, who governed until his death in 1840, has been characterized negatively by historians of several nations, including his own, but more recent revisionist studies by historians such as Richard Alan White portray Francia as a revolutionary who led his country to a period of exemplary economic and cultural independence. They suggest that Francia's negative evaluations resulted from his harsh treatment of creole elites and from his autocratic policies, but that his concern for economic development helped the Amerindians of Paraguay by keeping them isolated from exploitative world markets.

Paraguay based its revolution on self-government and land redistribution. For a half century, rulers redistributed lands of the government, the Church, and private large-scale landowners to the masses of mestizo and Indian cultivators. Paraguay became self-sufficient in food production. The government established a simple but effective education system that virtually eliminated illiteracy. The state established iron works, textile mills, and livestock industries. It did not accept foreign investment or entanglement. Paraguay's achievements in political independence, economic growth, self-reliance, and raising the standards of its native and mestizo populations, engendered envy in its neighbors and apprehension among foreign financiers.

From 1865 to 1870 Argentina, Brazil, and Uruguay, backed by loans from Britain, fought against Paraguay to destroy its populist policies. After the invaders won, they killed off the majority of Paraguay's adult male population, dismantled its political institutions, and opened its economy to foreign investment and control. Paraguay's unique experiment was over.

Religious and Economic Issues

Many of the new nations of Latin America wished to increase their own power by breaking the authority and wealth of the Catholic Church. Many confiscated church lands, refused the official collection of tithes to fund the Church, demanded a voice in the selection of clergy, and limited church control over educational facilities. To some degree, these crusades against church power reflected also Indian advocacy for a greater appreciation of indigenous cultures, both outside of Christianity and in syncretic movements to join Christian practices to existing indigenous beliefs and rituals. Mexico, which had a large Indian and mestizo population, was most eager to limit church power, and its continuing struggles were the bloodiest. Over time, in each country, individual accommodations were made between Church and state, and to this day they continue to renegotiate their positions.

Economically, until at least 1870, Latin America remained overwhelmingly agrarian, with the hacienda, a kind of feudal estate, continuing as the principal institution for organizing production and labor. The vast majority of the hacienda owners were creole, while the workers were overwhelmingly Indian and mestizo. Many Indians

SOURCE

An Epic Verse History of Latin America

In many parts of the world, historical traditions are kept alive not only in formal historical writing, but also in the arts, music, and poetry. Some of Latin America's most distinguished authors work in this tradition. The Chilean writer Pablo Neruda (1904–73), a recipient of the Nobel Prize for Literature in 1971, advanced a critical and disillusioned vision of Latin America in its first century of independence. In Canto General (1950), Neruda's epic poem of Latin American history, he paints the Spanish settlement of the land as a harsh and tawdry process.

> The land passed between the entailed estates,
> doubloon to doubloon, dispossessed,
> paste of apparitions and convents
> until the entire blue geography was
> divided into haciendas and encomiendas.
> The mestizo's ulcer, the overseer's
> and slaver's whip
> moved through the lifeless space.
> The Creole was an impoverished specter
> who picked up the crumbs,
> until he saved enough
> to acquire a little title
> painted with gilt letters.
> And in the dark carnival
> he masqueraded as a count
> a proud man among beggars,
> with his little silver cane ...

The conquistadors of the sixteenth century had been expelled by the libertadors of the early nineteenth century, but the infrastructure of shopkeepers, clergy, administrators, and hangers-on that had become established in Latin America remained in place as the real inheritors of the revolution. Neruda scowled:

> Soon, undershirt by undershirt,
> they expelled the conquistador
> and established the conquest
> of the grocery store.
> Then they acquired pride
> bought on the black market.
> They were adjudged
> haciendas, whips, slaves,
> catechisms, commissaries,
> alms boxes, tenements, brothels,
> and all this they called
> holy western culture.

Neruda singles out the petty businessmen as the new, but unworthy, elite of Latin America. In more enterprising regions bigger businessmen and investors occupied the leadership positions. These men of practical affairs combined with craftsmen on the one hand, and with government policy makers on the other, to introduce limited industrial development in the twentieth century (see Chapter 23).

remained in villages, where their participation in any larger, external, national economy was marginal. Since ancestry counted so profoundly for each group, the ethnic and racial composition of the population, whether native-born or foreign-born, whether Indian, African, *mestizo*, or Caucasian, in large measure determined the fate and the culture of each colony.

As production for foreign markets increased, new forms of foreign domination, **neo-colonialism**, arose. The principal new power was Britain, and its method was economic investment and control. By 1824, there were 100 British commercial firms functioning in Latin America staffed by 3000 British citizens. Shipping to and from Latin America was carried primarily by British ships. Britain's economic domination of Latin American economies increased with the growing productivity and profitability of its industrial revolution at home.

In the mid-nineteenth century, Latin America was home to a mixed amalgam of philosophies and practices. From the United States and France, it inherited a legacy of revolution in the name of representative democracy and individual freedom. It inherited from Spain and Portugal a loyalty to more conservative, religious, hierarchical traditions. From Africa it inherited rich traditions of religion, food, music, and dance. From its own history of settlement it received a diverse mix of peoples from three continents, often in uneasy relationship to one another. From the international economy Latin America inherited a subordinate position, dependent on outside supply, demand, and control.

neo-colonialism The control exercised by a state or group of states of the developed world over the economies and societies of the developing world.

POLITICAL REVOLUTIONS
WHAT DIFFERENCE DO THEY MAKE?

Charles Dickens opened *A Tale of Two Cities*, his novel set against the background of the French Revolution, with the famous passage: "It was the best of times. It was the worst of times … it was the season of Light, it was the season of Darkness, it was the spring of hope, it was the winter of despair." Having examined the unfolding of this period of political revolution we can better understand Dickens' paradoxical characterization. We began with the successes of the English revolutions in establishing constitutional government. That revolution slowly expanded to include ever larger segments of the population, and to include freedom of religion among its guarantees. But that same government refused to grant the rights of Britons to its American subjects, provoking the American War for Independence. It did abolish the slave trade and slavery, but only in the early nineteenth century, and by that time, as we shall see in Chapter 17, Britain had captured extensive, non-settler colonies overseas.

The *philosophes* spoke of human perfectibility and advocated human reason. They provided rationales that inspired the American, French, and Latin American revolutions, yet many of them preferred benevolent despotism as more efficient. One of the greatest of the *philosophes*, Rousseau, has been interpreted variously as espousing a variety of government alternatives, from radical democracy to totalitarian dictatorship. And later experience would test the limits of the power of rationality in the governance of human affairs.

The War for Independence in North America freed Britain's thirteen colonies and created the United States. It introduced a limited democracy that nonetheless sanctioned attacks on Indians and permitted slavery. The most profound of all the revolutions of its time, the French Revolution, ended in class antagonism, with the monarchy restored, after much of Europe had been convulsed in more extensive warfare than it had ever seen before. Yet in the course of Napoleon's conquests, he abolished feudal privileges throughout Europe and introduced new codes of law and bureaucracies recruited on the basis of merit. Ironically, Napoleon's imperialism also provoked new nationalism among the peoples he conquered. In Haiti, in response to the slave revolt, Napoleon reversed France's stated opposition to slavery, and lost tens of thousands of soldiers to battle and disease. Haiti's successful slave revolt became a successful war for independence. Wars for independence in Latin America freed that continent from direct, political control from overseas, but power was seized by creole and *mazombo* elites who lorded it over the Native American multitudes. In addition, the new nations soon fell into economic dependence on their former colonizers.

Of all these revolutions, the French Revolution's legacies are the most ambiguous. Many scholars have looked to the radical Terror as a precursor to twentieth-century totalitarianism. Other scholars, however, have examined the revolution in terms of what it accomplished rather than what it failed to do. The French Revolution ended religious discrimination, and France went much further than England in allowing worshipers of all faiths, including Jews, to become full citizens. Though Napoleon reversed the decision, the National Convention abolished slavery, making it clear that distinctions of color and race should not matter in civic life. Still others have recognized that while class antagonisms remained, the revolution established legal equality for most males, including freed slaves and Jews, who inhabited the country. Finally, the French Revolution in many ways legitimized the notion of revolution to achieve political and social change. It inspired the Russian Revolution of 1917 and the Chinese student movement, which held a revolutionary parade at Tiananmen Square, Beijing, in support of French revolutionary ideals on the bicentenary of the storming of the Bastille on July 14, 1789. In short, the ideas of the French Revolution remain a powerful inspirational force today.

Review Questions

- What is the difference between a political revolution and a simple change of political administration?
- What were the characteristics of the "Democratic Revolutions?"
- At the celebration of the 200th anniversary of the French Revolution in 1989, the Prime Minister of England remarked that the earlier British revolution had accomplished all that the French Revolution had accomplished—without the violence. Do you agree with her assessment?
- What are the differences between a revolution against a foreign colonial government, as in the revolution of the thirteen American colonies against Britain, and a revolution against an indigenous government, as in France?
- What was the importance of the Haitian Revolution?
- Why did many of the leaders of the revolutions in Latin America feel disillusioned despite their accomplishments?

Suggested Readings

PRINCIPAL SOURCES

Burns, E. Bradford and Julie Charlip. *Latin America* (Englewood Cliffs, NJ: Prentice Hall, 7th ed, 2001).

Furet, François. *Interpreting the French Revolution,* trans. by Elborg Foster (Cambridge: Cambridge University Press, 1978). A masterful summary by one of the leading experts.

Galilei, Galileo. *Discoveries and Opinions of Galileo,* trans. by Stillman Drake (New York: Anchor Books, 1957). Gallileo's own observations and statements, fresh and clear, with helpful commentary.

Hobsbawm, Eric. *The Age of Revolution 1789–1848* (New York: New American Library, 1962). A personal, magisterial, interpretive summary, from a somewhat Marxist perspective. Excellent introduction to the period and issues.

James, C.L.R., *The Black Jacobins* (New York: Random House, 1963). A stirring account of the activities and significance of the Haitian revolution.

Knight, Franklin W. "The Haitian Revolution," *American Historical Review* 105:1 (February 2000), 103–115. A review of the most recent scholarship on the revolution.

Kuhn, Thomas S. *The Copernican Revolution* (Cambridge, MA: Harvard University Press, 1957). A case study of the methods of science in working through received interpretations and developing new ones through the experiences of Copernicus.

——. *The Structure of Scientific Revolutions* (Chicago: University of Chicago Press, 3rd edn, 1996). A generalized assessment of the methods through which scientists revise and sometimes discard older theories and develop new ones.

Lefebvre, Georges. *The Coming of the French Revolution*, trans. by R.R. Palmer (Princeton: Princeton University Press, 1947). A classic Marxist interpretation of the revolution.

Nash, Gary B., *et al. The American People: Creating a Nation and a Society* (New York: Harper and Row, 5th ed. 2003). Leading textbook account.

Palmer, R.R. *The Age of Democratic Revolution* (Princeton: Princeton University Press, 1969). A lucid, standard, comprehensive interpretive account of the revolutions covered in this chapter.

Thompson, E.P. *The Making of the English Working Class* (New York: Vintage Books, 1966). Cultural as well as economic factors that inspired working people to see themselves as a class and to struggle for rights.

White, Richard Alan. *Paraguay's Autonomous Revolution, 1810–1840* (Albuquerque: University of New Mexico Press, 1978). A controversial study presenting Paraguay as attempting to create a more democratic government that is suppressed by its neighbors.

Williams, Eric. *Capitalism and Slavery* (Chapel Hill: University of North Carolina Press, 1944). Williams portrays capitalism as promoting slavery when it is in the economic interests of slave owners, and as working for abolition when these interests change.

ADDITIONAL SOURCES

Abernethy, David B. *The Dynamics of Global Dominance: European Overseas Empires, 1415–1980* (New Haven: Yale University Press, 2000). Traces and analyzes the expansion and contraction of empire, and evaluates its legacy. The writing is thoughtful, lucid, and engaging.

Andrea, Alfred and James Overfield, eds. *The Human Record*, 2 vols. (Boston: Houghton Mifflin Co., 4th ed. 2001). Excellent selection of documents and visuals.

Boorstin, Daniel. *The Discoverers* (New York: Random House, 1983). Lucid, engaging account of the work of specific scientists and explorers and their impact on events.

Cohen I., Bernard. *Revolution in Science* (Cambridge, MA: Harvard University Press, 1985). Analyzes 450 years of major scientific revolutions and their interaction with the larger society. Magisterial yet lucid.

Columbia College, Columbia University. *Contemporary Civilization in the West*, Vol. 2 (New York: Columbia University Press, 3rd ed. 1960). Outstanding sourcebook with lengthy excerpts from highly influential thinkers and actors.

Curtin, Philip. *The Rise and Fall of the Plantation Complex* (New York: Cambridge University Press, 1989). Excellent analysis of the plantation itself and its significance to world trade and politics.

Davis, David Brion. *The Problem of Slavery in the Age of Revolution, 1770–1823* (Ithaca: Cornell University Press, 1975). Analyzes the tensions between the idea of freedom and the practice of slavery.

——. "Looking at Slavery from Broader Perspectives," *American Historical Review* 105:2 (April, 2000), 452–66. Global, comprehensive review of the literature at present.

Drescher, Seymour. *Econocide* (Pittsburgh: University of Pittsburgh Press, 1977). Argues that the abolition of slavery was an economically costly decision, taken, primarily, for moral reasons.

——. *The Problem of Slavery in Western Culture* (New York: Oxford University Press, 1966). Explores the tensions between slavery and the ideals of individual freedom and democracy.

Fick, Carolyn E. *The Making of Haiti* (Knoxville: University of Tennessee Press, 1990). A recent, comprehensive, cogent account.

Fogel, Robert William and Stanley L. Engerman. *Time on the Cross*, 2 vols. (Boston: Little, Brown, 1974). A controversial, influential, assessment of the economics of slavery.

Genovese, Eugene. *From Rebellion to Revolution* (Baton Rouge: Louisiana University Press, 1979). A study of slave revolts and their significance to abolition.

Halévy, Élie. *England in 1815* (New York: Barnes and Noble, 1961). A classic account of a society successfully avoiding revolution.

Hammond Atlas of World History ed. Geoffrey Parker (Maplewood, NJ: Hammond, 5th ed. 1999).

Hanke, Lewis and Jane M. Rausch, eds. *People and Issues in Latin American History* (New York: Markus Weiner, 2nd ed. 2000). A useful reader.

Hobbes, Thomas. *Selections*, ed. Frederick J.E. Woodbridge (New York: Charles Scribner's Sons, 1958). Primary sources.

Hobsbawm, Eric. *The Age of Empire 1875–1914* (New York: Vintage Books, 1987). Excellent, comprehensive account.

Hughes, Robert. *Goya* (New York: Knopf, 2003). Thoughtful, thorough, provocative, well-illustrated interpretation of the man and his art in their time.

Kolchin, Peter. *American Slavery 1619–1877* (New York: Hill and Wang, 1993). Comprehensive treatment, even after 1865, with comparisons to slavery in other societies.

Locke, John. *Second Treatise on Government* (Arlington Heights, IL: Crofts Classics, 1982). Primary source.

McClellan III, James F. and Harold Dorn. *Science and Technology in World History* (Baltimore: Johns Hopkins University Press, 1999). Outstanding coverage of science and technology from various parts of the world.

Márquez, Gabriel García. *The General in His Labyrinth.* trans. by Edith Grossman (New York: Knopf, 1990). Fictionalized account of the end of the life of General Simón Bolívar.

Metcalf, Barbara D. and Thomas R. Metcalf. *A Concise History of India* (Cambridge: Cambridge University Press, 2002). Especially strong on issues of identity and the importance of Muslims and of women.

Nehru, Jawaharlal. *Glimpses of World History* (New Delhi: Jawaharlal Nehru Memorial Fund and Oxford University Press, ed. 1982). Nehru wrote this socialistic account of world history from jail as a series of letters to his daughter.

Neruda, Pablo. *Canto General,* trans. by Jack Schmitt (Berkeley: University of California Press, 1991). A personal, critical assessment of Latin American history in verse by a master poet.

Nicholls, David, "Haiti: Race, Slavery and Independence (1804–1825)," in Archer, ed., *Slavery,* pp. 225–38. On the relationship of slavery to race in Haiti.

Patterson, Orlando. *Freedom in the Making of Western Culture* (New York: Basic Books, 1991). Slavery and racism conflict with the promise of freedom and democracy.

Rousseau, Jean-Jacques. *The Social Contract,* trans. by Maurice Cranston (New York: Viking Penguin, 1968). Primary source.

Smith, Adam. *The Theory of Moral Sentiments* (Charlottesville, VA: Lincoln-Rembrandt Publishers, 6th ed., 1986). Primary source.

——. *The Wealth of Nations,* Books I–III (New York: Viking Penguin Classics, 1986). Primary source.

Thompson, Vincent Bakpetu. *The Making of the African Diaspora in the Americas 1441–1900* (New York: Longman, 1987). A view that transcends the experience of individual countries to see the comprehensive picture.

Tocqueville, Alexis de. *The Old Regime and the French Revolution,* trans. by Gilbert Stuart (Garden City, New York: Doubleday Anchor Books, 1955). Classic analysis that locates precipitating factors in the revolution, and indicates that many endured long afterwards.

Turner, Frederick Jackson. *The Frontier in American History* (New York; Henry Holt, 1920). Classic interpretation of the significance to America of huge, frontier spaces in the West.

Wilentz, Sean. *Chants Democratic: New York and the Rise of the American Working Class, 1788–1850* (New York: Oxford University Press, 1984). Important contribution to working-class history.

⊚ World History Documents CD-ROM

THE INDUSTRIAL REVOLUTION

A GLOBAL PROCESS, 1700–1914

KEY TOPICS

- The Industrial Revolution: What Was Its Significance?
- Britain, 1700–1860
- The Second Stage of Industrialization, 1860–1914
- Social Changes: The Conditions of Working People
- Political Reaction in Britain and Europe, 1800–1914
- New Patterns of Urban Life
- The Industrial Revolution: What Difference Does It Make?

THE INDUSTRIAL REVOLUTION: WHAT WAS ITS SIGNIFICANCE?

One of the key indices of human progress has always been the improvement in the quality and quantity of the tools that we use and the ways in which we organize production. Perhaps the most advanced civilization of pre-modern times was China of the Song dynasty (960–1279). It earned its reputation not only for its neo-Confucian high culture—its painting, poetry, and classical education—but also for its agricultural progress with new crops and more efficient harvesting. It also produced armaments—including gunpowder and siege machines—government-issued paper money, commercial ships, and extensive river and canal networks, all on a massive scale. Finally, China was technically innovative, inventing the compass, making technical improvements in the production of silk, ceramics, and lacquer, and vastly expanding printing and book production. China's advances in iron production were so extensive that deforestation became a problem in parts of the north because wood was used to smelt the ores until coal took its place. The iron was used in tools, weapons, and bridge building. Other parts of the world were, by comparison, backward in trade, commerce, and industry.

The modern industrial revolution beginning in the eighteenth century marked the transformation by which western Europe, and especially Britain, caught up with and surpassed China, and the rest of the world, in economic power and productivity. In Part 5, we surveyed some of the changes that enabled regions of western Europe to emerge from their singular concentration on agriculture as the basis of their economy; to increase their concern with commerce, trade, and exploration; to develop new technologies; and to make a general commitment to financial success and the pursuit of profit. Slowly these new economic interests led to the creation of new tools: better ships, new and improved commercial instruments and organizations, such as the joint stock company, and even the adoption and adaptation of some of China's earlier inventions, including the compass, the use of gunpowder, and movable type for printing. Business people in western Europe actively sought out new economic possibilities. They pursued them with a vigor and flexibility that were sometimes admirable, as the search for new technologies, and sometimes morally reprehensible, as in the use of millions of slaves in the creation of vast sugar plantations in the Caribbean basin, and in the extraction of gold and silver from New World sources, through coerced labor, for the benefit of European businessmen. All these economic initiatives paved the way for the industrial revolution that began in the eighteenth century.

Opposite **International Exhibition, World's Fair, South Kensington, London, 1862.** At its core, the industrial revolution substituted inanimate power for human and animal energy. Before the industrial revolution, Western Europe had lagged economically behind China and India. New machinery dramatically altered that balance.

This modern industrial revolution began with the search for profit from the manufacture of cotton textiles. The search began as European explorers and traders working in India realized that the staple cloth of India—cotton—was far more comfortable and far easier to keep clean than wool, the staple cloth of England and continental Europe. Explorers and traders began to import cotton cloth from India. Cotton cloth also became extremely important in producing clothes for the many slaves who toiled in hot climates of the Americas. As the level of imports increased, enterprising businessmen sought ways to produce the cloth in Europe. They could not grow cotton in Europe—the climate was too cold—but perhaps the cloth could be manufactured in Europe at least as economically as in India from raw cotton imported from overseas, first from India and later from the United States. Britons, after the early 1600s the most active of all Europeans in the India trade, began experimenting with new ways of manufacturing cotton cloth from the imported raw material. Their activity triggered a cascade of changes that we call collectively the "industrial revolution."

The industrial revolution began with simple new machinery and minor changes in the organization of the workplace, but these initial changes were only the first steps.

AT A GLANCE : INDUSTRIALIZATION IN THE WEST

DATE	BRITAIN	REST OF EUROPE	NORTH AMERICA
1760	■ James Watt improves Newcomen's steam engine (1763) ■ James Hargreaves introduces spinning jenny (1764)		
1780	■ Combination Act forbids workers to unionize (1799); repealed 1824		■ Eli Whitney invents cotton gin (1793)
1800	■ Luddite riots (1810–20) ■ Peterloo Massacre, Manchester (1819)		
1820	■ George Stephenson's locomotive *Rocket* (1829) ■ Factory Act forbids employment of children (1833) ■ Chartist movement calls for universal male suffrage (1838)	■ Invention of photography in France by Louis Jacques Mandé Daguerre (1839) ■ Worker revolts in Paris, Prague, Vienna, and Russia (1830)	■ First transatlantic steamship lines in operation (1838) ■ Revolver invented by Samuel Colt (1836)
1840	■ Sir Edwin Chadwick issues report on the Poor Laws (1842) ■ Friedrich Engels, *The Condition of the Working Class in England* (1845) ■ Repeal of the Corn Laws (1846) ■ Bessemer steel converter (1856) ■ Samuel Smiles, *Self Help* (1859)	■ Year of Revolutions—in France, Austria, and Prussia (1848) ■ Marx and Engels, *Communist Manifesto* (1848) ■ Siemens-Martin open-hearth steel production, Germany (1864)	■ Invention of the sewing machine (1846)
1860	■ Under Prime Minister Gladstone, Liberal government begins to provide universal state-supported education (1870) ■ Liberals under Gladstone and Tories under Disraeli compete for workers' votes ■ Trade Union Act guarantees right to strike (1871)	■ Growth of chemical industries (after 1870) ■ Massacre of the Paris Commune (1871) ■ Bismarck unifies Germany (1871) ■ Germany's SPD is first working-class political party (1875)	■ American Civil War (1861–65) ■ Richard Gatling invents the machine gun (1861) ■ Thomas Edison invents early form of telegraph (1864) ■ Invention of the typewriter (1867) ■ Canada becomes unified Dominion (1867) ■ Edison establishes private industrial development lab (1876)
1880	■ London Dock strike (1889)	■ Labor unions legalized in France (1884) ■ May 1 recognized in France as annual "Labor Day" (1890)	■ American Federation of Labor founded (1886) ■ Kodak camera (1888) ■ Homestead Steel strike (1892)

Ultimately the industrial revolution multiplied the profits of the business classes and increased their power in government and public life. It broadened and deepened in its scope until it affected humanity globally, transforming the locations of our workplaces and homes, the size and composition of our families and the quality and quantity of the time we spend with them, the educational systems we create, the wars we fight, and the relationships among nations. As a global process the industrial revolution restructured the procurement of raw materials in the fields and mines of the world, the location of manufacture, and the range of international marketplaces in which new products might be sold. As the masters of the new industrial productivity adopted this global view of their own economic activities, their ventures became imperial in scope. They marshaled the powers of their governments to support their global economic capacities. Reciprocally, the governments relied on the power of industrialists and business-people to increase their own international strength politically, diplomatically, and militarily. The balance of wealth and power in the world shifted, for the first time, toward Europe, and especially toward Britain, the first home of the industrial revolution.

BRITAIN, 1700–1860

The industrial revolution began in Britain around 1700, and although it is called a "revolution," it took over 150 years to be fully realized in 1860. During this period, the British cotton textile industry grew into the world's most productive; its railway network became the nation's principal means of inland transportation and communication; and a new fleet of steam-powered ships enabled Britain to project its new productivity and power around the globe. Economic historians agree, however, that the industrial changes were possible because agriculture in Britain—the basis of its pre-industrial economy—was already undergoing a process of continuing improvement. The transformation was so fundamental that it is called an agricultural revolution.

A Revolution in Agriculture

Britain (along with the Dutch Republic, as the Netherlands was known until 1648) had the most productive and efficient commercial agriculture in Europe. Inventors created new farm equipment and farmers were quick to adopt it. Jethro Tull (1674–1741), as an outstanding example, invented the seed drill that replaced the old method of scattering seeds by hand on the surface of the soil with a new method of planting systematically in regular rows at fixed depths, a horse drawn hoe, and an iron plow that could be set at an angle that would pull up grasses and roots and leave them out to dry. New crops, like turnips and potatoes, were introduced, and farmers and large landlords initiated huge irrigation and drainage projects, increasing the productivity of land already under cultivation and opening up new land.

New laws regarding land ownership changed fundamentally the relationships between tenants and landlords. In Britain and the Netherlands peasants began to pay commercial rents to landowners in a business relationship, rather than paying fixed customary rents based on changing market values and performing labor services for them as in the past. Moreover, lands that had been held in common by the village community and had been used for grazing sheep and cattle by shepherds and livestock owners who had no lands of their own were now parceled out for private ownership through a series of enclosure acts.

Enclosures had begun in England in a limited way in the late 1400s. In the eighteenth century the process resumed and the pace increased. In the period 1714–1801, about one-fourth of the land in Britain was converted from community property to

enclosure acts Laws passed in England in the late 1700s to 1800s that converted public lands held in common into parcels of land to be sold to private owners.

Isaac Claesz Swanenburgh, *Spinning and Weaving Wool,*
c. **1600. Oil on wood.** This image shows the steps involved in
spinning wool for the textile industry in the Dutch Republic.
(*Stedelijk Museum, Leiden*)

private property through enclosures. The results were favorable to
landowners, and urban businessmen began to buy land as agricultural investment property. Agricultural productivity shot up;
landowners prospered. But hundreds of thousands of farmers with
small plots and cottagers who had subsisted through the use of the
common lands for grazing their animals were now turned into
tenant farmers and wage laborers. The results were revolutionary
and profoundly disturbing to the society. Peasant riots broke out as
early as the middle of the sixteenth century. In one of the uprisings,
3500 people were killed.

The process continued throughout the period of the early
industrial revolution as many of the dispossessed farmers turned to
rural or domestic industry to supplement their meager incomes.
Merchants would drop off raw cotton to workers' homes where

Seed drill, 1701. Jethro Tull (1674–1741) is a key figure of the eighteenth–century
agricultural revolution, which saw new technology harnessed to farming
techniques. Tull's machine drill employed a rotary mechanism that sowed seeds in
rows, permitting cultivation between the rows and thus reducing the need for
weeding.

women would spin it into yarn, which men would then weave into cloth, which merchants would later pick up. Later, rural workers left the land altogether and headed for new industrial jobs in Britain's growing cities. The capitalist market system transformed British agriculture and emptied the countryside, providing capital and workers for the industrial revolution. The economist Joseph Schumpeter (1883–1950) called capitalism a process of "creative destruction." In the agricultural revolution and in the industrial revolution that followed it, we see evidence of both: the often painful destruction of older ways of life and the creation of uncharted new ways.

A Revolution in Textile Manufacture

Until the mid-eighteenth century, the staple British textile had been woolens, woven from the wool of locally reared sheep. Then India's light, colorful, durable cotton textiles began to displace woolens in the market. Britain responded by manipulating tariffs and import regulations to restrict Indian cotton textiles, while British inventors began to produce new machinery that enabled Britain to surpass Indian production in both quantity and quality. The raw cotton would still have to be imported from subtropical India (and later from the southern United States and Egypt), but the manufacturing processes that turned it into cloth could be done in Britain, increasing British jobs and profits, and cutting back on cloth purchases in India, thus undercutting jobs and profits there.

When rural workers produced textiles in their home in the eighteenth century, most spinning was accomplished using a spinning wheel, first invented in India. The spinning wheel allowed women to produce fairly uniform yarn. Men wove the yarn on looms that required two men sitting next to each other passing the shuttle of the loom from left to right and back again. In 1733, John Kay (1704–64) invented the "flying shuttle," which allowed a single weaver to send the shuttle forth and back across the loom automatically, without the need of a second operator to push it. The spinners could not keep up with the increased demand of the weavers until, in 1764, James Hargreaves (d. 1778) introduced the spinning jenny, a machine that allowed the operator to spin several threads at once. The earliest jennies could run eight spindles at once; by 1770, sixteen; by the end of the century, 120. Machines to card and comb the cotton to prepare it for spinning were also developed.

Thus far, the machinery was new, but the power source was still human labor, and production was still concentrated in rural homes and small workshops. In 1769, Richard Arkwright (1732–92) patented the "water frame," a machine that could spin several strands simultaneously. Powered by water, it could run continuously. In 1779, Samuel Crompton (1753–1827) developed a "spinning mule," a hybrid that joined the principles of the spinning jenny and the water frame to produce a better quality and higher quantity of cotton thread. Unfortunately, he was too poor to patent it, but he sold designs for it to others. Now British cloth could rival that of India. Fasci-

James Hargreaves' spinning jenny. Named for his daughter, Hargreaves' invention was a spinning machine that prepared natural fibers for weaving. It thus made possible the expanded production of cotton cloth. The industrial revolution was built on relatively simple innovations like this jenny and the even earlier "flying shuttle" of John Kay, 1733.

nated by Arkwright's water frame, Edmund Cartwright (1743–1822) believed he could make a fortune by applying the principles of the technology to weaving. After some experiments, he patented the power loom in 1785, but struggled to benefit from it financially.

Meanwhile, in the coalfields of Britain, mine owners were seeking more efficient means of pumping water out of mine shafts, enabling deeper digging. By 1712, Thomas Newcomen (1663–1729) had mastered the use of steam power to drive these pumps. In 1763, James Watt (1736–1819), a technician at the University of Glasgow, was experimenting with improvements to Newcomen's steam engine, when Matthew Boulton (1728–1809), a small manufacturer, provided him with the capital necessary to develop larger and more costly steam engines. By 1785 the firm of Boulton and Watt was manufacturing new steam engines for use in Britain and for export. In the 1780s, Arkwright used a new Boulton and Watt steam engine instead of water power. From this point, equipment grew more sophisticated and more expensive. Spinning and weaving moved from the producer's home or small workshop adjacent to a stream of

The industrial revolution. In the early nineteenth century the industrial revolution spread throughout the trading nations of western Europe (and enmeshed their colonies, which provided both raw materials and markets). The earlier use of water power gave way to steam engines; coal became the power source. Canal transportation was superseded by railways, driven by steam.

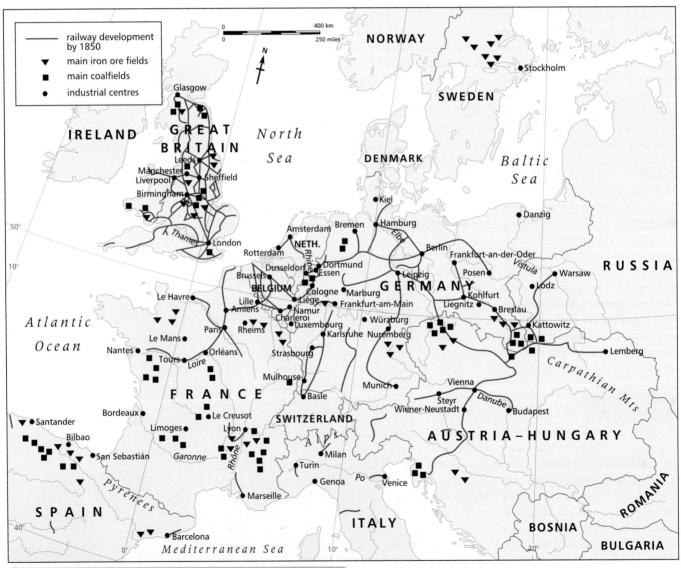

For an interactive version of this map, go to: http://www.prenhall.com/spodek/map17.1

water to new steam-powered cotton textile mills, which increased continuously in size and productivity. Power looms, like Cartwright's, invented to cope with increased spinning capacity, became commercially profitable by about 1800. Increasingly, in the 1800s, power looms became one of the most important technologies of the industrial revolution.

The new productivity of the machines transformed Britain's economy. It took hand spinners in India 50,000 hours to produce 100 pounds of cotton yarn. Crompton's mule could do the same task in 2000 hours; Arkwright's steam-powered frame, available by 1795, took 300 hours; and automatic mules, available by 1825, took 135 hours. Moreover, the quality of the finished product steadily increased in strength, durability, and texture. The number of mule spindles rose from 50,000 in 1788 to 4.6 million in 1811. Cotton textiles became the most important product of British industries by 1820, making up almost half of Britain's exports.

Prior to this mechanization most families had spun and woven their own clothing by hand so the availability of machine-made yarn and cloth affected millions of spinners and weavers throughout Great Britain. As late as 1815 owners of new weaving mills continued the putting-out system, providing home-based weavers with cotton thread and paying them for the finished, woven product. When cutbacks in production were necessary, the home workers could be cut, while the large factories continued to run. The burden of recession could be shifted to the shoulders of the home producer, leaving the factory owners and laborers relatively unscathed. In 1791, home-based workers in the north of England burned down one of the new power-loom factories in Manchester. Machine-wrecking riots followed for several decades, culminating in the Luddite riots of 1810–20. Named for their mythical leader, Ned Ludd, the rioters wanted the new machines banned. Soldiers were called in to suppress the riots.

The textile revolution also generated spin-off effects around the world. India's industrial position was reversed as the country became a supplier of raw cotton to Britain and an importer of machine-manufactured cotton textiles from Britain. Britain's new mills required unprecedented quantities of good-quality cotton. Raw cotton resembled cotton balls, but it was oily and full of seeds. It was impossible to process the cotton into yarn without first cleaning it or removing the seeds from the raw cotton. In the United States, the invention of the cotton gin by Eli Whitney (1765–1825) in 1793 meant that a worker could clean 50 pounds of cotton in the time it had taken to clean one. This solved part of the supply problem. The plantation economy of the United States revived and expanded, providing the necessary raw cotton, but, unfortunately, giving slavery a new lease on life. American cotton production rose from 3000 bales in 1790 to 178,000 bales in 1810; 732,000 bales in 1830; and 4,500,000 bales in 1860. Industrialization in Britain was reshaping the world economy.

Capital Goods: Iron, Steam Engines, Railways, and Steamships

The textile industry began with a consumer product that everyone used and that already employed a substantial handicraft labor force; it mechanized and reorganized the production process in factories. Other industrial innovations created new products. Many were in the capital goods sector of the economy—that is, they produced tools to expand production rather than goods for private consumption. Britain's iron industry, which had been established since the mid-1500s, at first used wood to heat iron ore and extract molten iron, but by about 1750 new mining processes provided coal, a more efficient fuel, more abundantly and cheaply. About 1775, the iron industry relocated to the coal and iron fields of the English Midlands. A process of stirring the molten iron ore at high temperatures was introduced by Henry Cort

MAJOR DISCOVERIES AND INVENTIONS—1640–1830

Year	Discovery / Invention
1640	Theory of numbers: Pierre de Fermat
1642	Calculating machine: Blaise Pascal
1650	Air pump: Otto von Guericke
1656	Pendulum clock: Otto von Guericke
1665–75	Calculus: Isaac Newton and Gottfried Leibnitz (independently)
1698	Steam pump: Thomas Savory
c. 1701	Seed drill: Jethro Tull
1712	Steam engine: Thomas Newcomen
1714	Mercury thermometer: Gabriel Fahrenheit
1733	Flying shuttle: John Kay
1752	Lightning conductor: Benjamin Franklin
1764	Spinning jenny: James Hargreaves
1765	Condensing steam engine: James Watt
1768	Hydrometer: Antoine Baumé
1783	Hot air balloon: Joseph and Étienne Montgolfier
1783	Parachute: Louis Lenormand
1785	Power loom: Edmund Cartwright
1789	Combustion: Antoine Lavoisier
1793	Cotton gin: Eli Whitney
1800	Electric battery: Alessandro Volta
1807	Steamboat: Robert Fulton
1815	Miner's safety lamp: Humphry Davy
1818	Bicycle: Karl von Sauerbrun
1823	Digital calculating machine: Charles Babbage
1824	Portland cement: Joseph Aspdin
1825	Electromagnet: William Sturgeon
1826	Heliography (pre-photography): Joseph Niépce
1828	Blast furnace: James Neilson
1829	Steam locomotive: George Stephenson

(1740–1800) in the 1780s. This "puddling" encouraged the use of larger ovens and integrated the processes of melting, hammering, and rolling the iron into high-quality bars. Productivity increased dramatically. As the price of production dropped and the quality increased, iron was introduced into building construction. The greatest demand for the metal came, however, with new inventions. The steam engine, railroad track and locomotives, steamships, and new urban systems of gas supply and solid and liquid waste disposal all depended on iron for their construction. Britain produced 25,000 tons of pig iron (an extremely high quality of iron, named for the round ingots or pigs it was cast in) in 1720, 125,000 tons in 1796, and 250,000 tons in 1804. Its world market share was 19 percent in 1800 and 52 percent in 1840—that is, Britain produced as much manufactured iron as the rest of the world.

With the new steam engine and the increased availability and quality of iron, the railroad industry was born. The first reliable locomotive, George Stephenson's *Rocket*, was produced in 1829. It serviced the Manchester–Liverpool route, reaching a speed of 16 miles per hour. By the 1840s, a railroad boom swept Britain, Europe, and crossed the Atlantic to the United States, where it facilitated the westward expansion of that rapidly expanding country. By the 1850s most of the 23,500 miles of today's railway network in Britain were already in place, and entrepreneurs found new foreign markets for their locomotives and tracks in India and Latin America.

The new locomotives quickly superseded the canal systems of Britain and the United States, which had been built mostly since the 1750s as the favored means of transporting raw materials and bulk goods between industrial cities. Until the coming of the steam-powered train, canals had been considered the transportation means of the future. (The speed with which the newer technology displaced the older is one reason

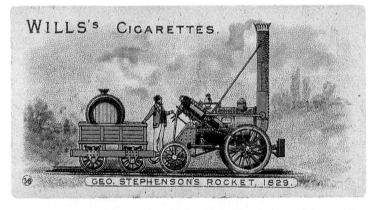

George Stephenson's locomotive *Rocket*, 1829, from a chromolithographic cigarette card of 1901. On October 14, 1829, the *Rocket* won a competition for an engine to haul freight and passengers on the Manchester–Liverpool Railway. The success of Stephenson's invention stimulated a boom in locomotive construction and track laying around the world.

HOW DO WE KNOW?

Why Did the Industrial Revolution Begin in Britain?

Historians have long debated the origins of the industrial revolution. The term itself was used at least as early as 1845, in the opening of Friedrich Engels' The Condition of the Working Class in England:

The history of the English working classes begins in the second half of the eighteenth century with the invention of the steam engine and of machines for spinning and weaving cotton. It is well known that these inventions gave the impetus to the genesis of an industrial revolution. This revolution had a social as well as an economic aspect since it changed the entire structure of middle-class society. (p. 9)

Arnold Toynbee (uncle of a twentieth-century historian with the same name) was apparently the first professional historian to use the term. In a set of lectures delivered in 1880–81, Toynbee identified 1760 as the beginning of the process. He chose this date in recognition of the inventions we have been discussing here. In 1934, John Nef, economic historian at the University of Chicago, argued that the iron industry had already been in place by the mid-sixteenth century and that date was a more appropriate choice. More recent historians, such as Fernand Braudel, have also seen the roots of industrialization stretching back for centuries. They have stressed the underlying economic, political, social, intellectual, and scientific transformations that we have discussed in the last few chapters. All these processes coalesced in the British economy in the late eighteenth century to create the industrial revolution:

- increasing productivity in agriculture;
- new merchant classes in power, and the evolution of a capitalist philosophy of economics that justified their power;
- a powerful state that supported economic development, despite the capitalist doctrine of laissez-faire that called for the state to stay out of business;
- the rise of science, with its new, empirical view of the world, and of technology, with its determination to find practical solutions to practical problems;
- a social structure that allowed and even encouraged people of different classes to work together, especially artisans, who worked with their hands, and financiers, who provided capital;
- more intense patterns of global trading for buying raw materials and for selling manufactured products;
- an expanding population that increased both the labor supply and the demand for more production;
- slave labor in plantation economies, which brought more than a century of exceptional capital accumulation;
- the discovery of massive deposits of gold and silver in the New World, which also increased capital accumulation; and
- "proto-industrialization"—that is, early forms of industrial organization that introduced new skills to both management and labor, paving the way to large-scale factory production.

This question of the origins of the industrial revolution is not purely academic. The debate carries serious implications for planning industrial development in today's world. As many newly independent nations with little industry seek to industrialize, they ask: Does industrialization mean simply the acquisition of machinery and the adaptation of advanced technology? Or must a nation also experience a much wider range of agricultural, economic, philosophical, scientific, political, and social changes? How, and under what terms, can it raise the capital necessary to begin? What are the tasks confronting a government wishing to promote industrialization? We shall examine these twentieth-century questions in Chapters 20 through 24. Those countries that have achieved high levels of industrialization—mostly the countries of Europe and their daughter civilizations overseas; Japan; and now some of the countries of East Asia (see Chapter 22)—have experienced a wide range of fundamental changes, akin to many of those that Britain experienced.

- Among the characteristics that made the industrial revolution possible, do some seem to you more important than others? Which ones? Why?
- Which processes that we usually include in the "industrial revolution" are changes in machinery and equipment? Which are changes in the social structure of the society?
- Which of these processes seem to be continuing to the present and continuing to influence contemporary economics?

historians resist predicting the future. Events do not necessarily proceed in a straight-line process of development, and new, unanticipated developments frequently displace older patterns quite unexpectedly.)

Steamships, using much the same technology as steam locomotives, were introduced at about the same time. The first transatlantic steamship lines began operation in 1838. World steamship tonnage multiplied more than 100 times, from 32,000 tons in 1831 to 3,300,000 tons in 1876. With its new textile mills, iron factories, and steam-driven transportation networks, Britain soon became the "workshop of the world."

Interior of Crystal Palace, designed by Joseph Paxton for the Great Exhibition of 1851 in London. This glass-and-iron exhibition hall, a landmark of early modern architecture, was a celebration of the powerful Victorian economy and an expression of British technological accomplishment and imperial might.

SOURCE

Conflicting Images of Early Industrial Life: The English Romantic Poets

In the century 1750–1850, Britain was transformed by industrialization. Factories, cities, and the working classes all multiplied. One response to the turmoil created by these changes was Romanticism, a new international movement in literature and the arts, which opposed the rationalism of the Enlightenment and glorified emotion. Romantic poets in Britain, such as William Wordsworth (1770–1850) and Samuel Taylor Coleridge (1772–1834), turned away from the belief in modern progress through science and rational knowledge toward nature, history, and their own inner feelings. They saw a great vision of a new aesthetic beauty emerging. Wordsworth's view of London's natural glories represents this Romantic perspective.

Upon Westminster Bridge, September 3, 1802

Earth has not anything to show more fair:
Dull would he be of soul who could pass by
A sight so touching in its majesty;
This City now doth, like a garment, wear
The beauty of the morning; silent, bare,
Ships, towers, domes, theatres, and
    temples lie
Open unto the fields, and to the sky;
All bright and glittering in the smokeless
    air.
Never did sun more beautifully steep
In his first splendour, valley, rock, or hill;
Ne'er saw I, never felt, a calm so deep!
The river glideth at his own sweet will:
Dear God! the very houses seem asleep;
And all that mighty heart is lying still!
                        William Wordsworth

Others, such as the poet William Blake (1757–1827), who were closer to the lives of working-class people, saw the great suffering caused by industrialization. Devoutly religious and nationalistic, Blake nevertheless condemned the people, the government, and the Church of England for tolerating "a land of poverty" in the very midst of "a rich and fruitful land." While Wordsworth looks over London from the vantage point of a bridge, Blake walks its streets and looks into the faces of its inhabitants.

London

I wander thro' each charter'd* street,
Near where the charter'd Thames does
    flow,
And mark in every face I meet
Marks of weakness, marks of woe.

In every cry of every Man,
In every Infant's cry of fear,
In every voice, in every ban,
The mind-forg'd manacles I hear.

How the Chimney-sweeper's cry
Every blackning Church appalls;
And the hapless Soldier's sigh
Runs in blood down Palace walls.

But most thro' midnight streets I hear
How the youthful Harlot's curse
Blasts the new-born Infant's tear**,
And blights with plagues the Marriage
    hearse.
                            William Blake

*charter'd = licensed by the government, controlled, owned
**the infant is blind at birth, from venereal disease transmitted by the parent

No matter how upsetting Blake's view of London may be, the even more lacerated heart of the industrial revolution was actually in the Midlands and north of England, around the cities of Manchester, Birmingham, and Liverpool.

THE SECOND STAGE OF INDUSTRIALIZATION, 1860–1914

New Products and New Nations

Between 1860 and the outbreak of World War I in 1914, a "second industrial revolution" further transformed world productivity, the ways in which humans lived their lives, and the power balances among the major nations and regions of the world. The principal technological advances came in steel, chemicals, and electricity, and these were supported by organizational breakthroughs in shipping, banking, and insurance.

Steel and Chemical Industries. New technologies—the Bessemer steel converter (1856) in Britain followed by the Siemens–Martin open-hearth method of production (1864) in Germany—soon allowed iron ore to be converted to steel cheaply and abundantly. Iron is produced in blast furnaces and can be of high quality, but the final product contains some impurities. Steel production involves removing the impurities first then adding carbon to the iron ore to create a much stronger and more versatile product, which can be shaped into bars, plates, and other structural components, like girders. Germany, united as a country in 1871 under Otto von Bismarck, forged ahead. By 1900 it was producing more steel than Britain, 6.3 million tons to 5.0 million tons; in 1913, on the eve of World War I, Germany's lead had grown to 17.6 million tons against 7.7 million tons. Germany also led in the invention of a number of additional new technologies, especially the internal combustion engine, the diesel engine, and the automobile.

Chemical industries grew, especially after 1870, as synthetic substances, notably derivatives from coal, began to augment and replace the earlier reliance on natural substances from vegetables, such as alkalis and dyes. Now, synthetic, aniline dyes were made from coal tar. Both fertilizers and explosives could be made from synthetic nitrogen and phosphates. Artificial fertilizers added to a revolution in agricultural productivity, while explosives helped in the construction of engineering feats, such as the new tunnels through the Alps in Europe, the Suez Canal in North Africa, and the Panama Canal in Central America. Soda, made from the coal by-product of ammonia, was used in manufacturing both soap and glass. New drugs and insecticides enhanced the quality of life, while perfumes, and cosmetics were produced and made their way to the marketplace, as many middle-class and some working-class women, like department store clerks, sought luxury goods to add a touch of romance to their lives. Plastics, produced from coal tar acids, became available in the late nineteenth century.

Electricity. Electrical inventions sparked one another throughout Europe and across the Atlantic to the United States, as well. In 1831 Michael Faraday (1791–1867) in Britain first demonstrated the principle of electromagnetic induction by moving a metal conductor through a magnetic field to generate electricity, a process repeated regularly today in high-school classrooms. By 1850, several companies were producing simple electric generators. In the 1860s, Ernst Werner von Siemens (1816–92) in Germany developed a practical dynamo. In the United

A canal connects two oceans. The construction of the Panama Canal in 1905, linking the Atlantic and Pacific oceans, ranks as one of the greatest engineering feats of all time. The task involved removing about 175 million cubic yards of earth as well as sanitizing the entire area, which was infested by mosquitoes that spread yellow fever and malaria.

States in the 1880s, Nikola Tesla (1856–1943) invented methods to transmit power effectively over long distances, patenting the alternating current generator in 1892.

The best-known inventor of the age was the American Thomas Alva Edison (1847–1931), who acquired more than one thousand patents for his innovations, 225 of which were patented between 1879 and 1882, for incandescent light bulbs, fuses, sockets, switches, circuit breakers, and meters. Others included an early form of telegraph in 1864; the stock ticker in 1870; the phonograph based on a metal cylinder in 1877; and the wax cylinder recorder in 1888, forerunner of the vinyl record player; and the kinetoscope in 1889, a forerunner of the moving picture. More important than any single invention, however, was Edison's establishment in 1876 of (probably the first) private industrial development laboratory in Menlo Park, New Jersey, a rural area halfway between New York and Philadelphia. Until this time, invention had been largely an individual achievement, based on the skills and luck of the individual inventor. Edison's new research facility institutionalized the process of invention, and encouraged research and development and the commercialization of products like the phonograph.

Factory Production

Production, too, began to be concentrated into immense, impersonal corporations. The second industrial revolution corresponded to the era of big business. In Germany, the rising power in Europe, two large cartels, collaborative business associations, were formed for the production of electronic equipment: Siemens–Schuckert and Allgemeine Elektrizitäts Gesellschaft (AEG). Two others, specializing in chemical production, later merged into I.G. Farben (1925). For steel production, each major producing country had its own giants: Krupp in Germany, Schneider–Creusot in France, Vickers-Armstrong in Britain, and, largest of all, the United States Steel Corporation. These huge corporations integrated the entire process of production from raw material to finished product. They owned their own coal mines and iron works, produced steel, and manufactured such final products as ships, railway equipment, and armaments.

Industrial concentration displaced the artisan in favor of mass-production and mass-consumption. In these mass-market innovations, the United States was frequently the leader, producing the sewing machine (invented by Elias Howe in 1846); the typewriter (1867); clocks and watches, the everyday timekeepers of the new office and factory routines; the telephone, phonograph, and cinema; the bicycle, invented in its modern form in Britain by John Kemp Starley and William Sutton in 1885; and small arms, like the revolver, invented by Samuel Colt in 1836, and the rifle, invented by Oliver Winchester, and improved to a repeating rifle by Christopher Spencer in 1860.

Warfare and Industrialization

Warfare and industrialization went hand-in-hand. In the United States, for example, the Civil War (1861–5) not only restored a political union but also marked the victory of the industrializing, urban, free-labor North over the rural, plantation economy, slave-holding South. It marked a transformation that soon placed the United States among the leaders of world industrialization. Wars of white immigrants against Native American Indians, which soon turned to slaughters and forcible relocations to reservations, accompanied the new cross-continental railroads. Wars against Mexico completed the borders of the contiguous United States, and wars against Spain brought the United States its first overseas colonies.

The machine gun, invented by Richard Gatling in 1862, was improved several times. In 1883 it took on the name of the Maxim gun, for the American Hiram Maxim

cartel An association of independent producers or businessmen whose aim is to control the supply of a particular commodity or group of commodities in order to regulate or push up prices.

who created a gun that had a range of almost 1½ miles and could shoot eleven rounds per second. The Maxim won its greatest fame in Africa, where Europeans found it indispensable in their colonization efforts. In Germany, the Krupp family of steel manufacturers concentrated on producing the heavy armaments that enabled Prussia to defeat France in 1870, to forge a united Germany (see Chapter 18), and to prove a formidable combatant in both World Wars (see Chapter 19).

The Effects of the Second Industrial Revolution Worldwide

Profits from all these businesses, civilian and military, spilled over into finance capital, the purposeful reinvestment of capital into new business to reap new profits. Financiers sought new opportunities in far-flung regions of the world. The industrial development of the Americas offered huge opportunities, and Britain became the largest investor. From the 1840s, for example, the railway networks of both North and South America were in large part financed by British investors. The availability of such investment capital made the task of industrial and urban development easier in the Americas, because the necessary sums could be borrowed and repaid later.

These borrowings, and the industrialization and urbanization that came from them, encouraged the immigration that helped increase the population of North America from 39 million in 1850 to 106 million in 1900, and that of South America from 20 million to 38 million in the same period. The United States absorbed these

Machine shop, West Lynn works, USA, c. 1898. The United States led the way in mass production of household goods. In the nineteenth century, people immigrated to the big cities from rural America and from overseas to work in factories—often for low pay, with long hours and in hot, noisy conditions. The factory system expanded hugely after 1913 when Henry Ford introduced assembly-line technologies to motor-car production.

MAJOR DISCOVERIES AND INVENTIONS—1830–1914	
1831	Dynamo: Michael Faraday
1834	Reaping machine: Cyrus McCormick
1834	Photography: Louis M. Daguerre; William Henry Fox Talbot
1836	Revolver: Samuel Colt
1837	Telegraph: Samuel Morse
1839	Vulcanized rubber: Charles Goodyear
1852	Gyroscope: Léon Foucault
1853	Passenger elevator: Elisha Otis
1856	Celluloid: Alexander Parkes Bessemer converter: Henry Bessemer Bunsen burner: Robert Bunsen
1858	Refrigerator: Ferdinand Carré Washing machine: Hamilton Smith
1859	Internal combustion engine: Etienne Lenoir
1862	Rapid-fire gun: Richard Gatling
1866	Dynamite: Alfred Nobel
1876	Telephone: Alexander Graham Bell
1877	Phonograph: Thomas Edison
1879	Incandescent lamp: Thomas Edison
1885	Motorcycle: Edward Butler Electric transformer: William Stanley Vacuum flask: James Dewar
1887	Motorcar engine: Gottlieb Daimler/Karl Benz
1888	Pneumatic tire: John Boyd Dunlop Kodak camera: George Eastman
1895	Wireless: Nikola Tesla X-rays: Wilhelm Roentgen
1896	Radioactivity: Antoine Becquerel
1897	Diesel engine: Rudolf Diesel
1898	Submarine: John P. Holland Radium and polonium: Pierre and Marie Curie
1902	Radio-telephone: Reginald Fessenden
1903	Airplane: Wilbur and Orville Wright
1905	Theory of relativity: Albert Einstein
1911	Combine harvester: Benjamin Holt
1914	Tank: Ernest Swinton

investments without losing political control of its own internal development and became the most industrialized of all countries. South America, however, became an early example of neo-colonialism, in which foreign economic control leads to indirect foreign political control as well.

Canada enjoyed internal self-government within the British Empire from 1840 and became a unified Dominion, including Ontario, Quebec, Nova Scotia, and New Brunswick, in 1867. It attracted increasing immigration and investment, especially after the United States' frontier was filled in with its own immigrants. Nova Scotia and New Brunswick had joined the original provinces of Quebec and Ontario on condition that a railroad be built to link them with Quebec. More dramatically, the Canadian Pacific Railway was completed in 1885, spanning Canada from east to west. Between 1900 and 1916, 73 million acres of land were planted with wheat and other commercial agriculture. $400 million per year was invested in this sector and in the mining of coal, gold, lead, zinc, nickel, and copper.

In Russia and the Ottoman Empire, the largest investments came from France. For the six decades leading up to World War I, Russia's industrial output grew at the rate of 5 percent per year. It produced more steel than France, Italy, or Japan, and by 1914 it had 46,000 miles of railroad track and was the world's fourth largest industrial power. It could not, however, keep up with the industrial advances of the United States and Germany. Similarly, Russia's railway mileage seems less adequate when the immense expanse of the country, by far the largest in the world, is considered. The proportion of Russian industrial production remained at about 8 percent of the world total from 1880 to 1914, and most of its heavy industry was owned by foreigners.

For reasons that will be explained in Chapter 18, total foreign investment in the Ottoman Empire was much less, about $1.2 billion in 1914, and the empire's industrial base became progressively less competitive than those of western European nations. Increasingly, the Ottoman Empire was seen as the "sick man of Europe".

Overall global investments were immense, with Britain far in the lead. By 1914 Britain had invested some $20 billion, France about $8.7 billion, and Germany about $6 billion. The global age of finance capital was in full swing.

SOCIAL CHANGES: THE CONDITIONS OF WORKING PEOPLE

So far we have concentrated on the immense new productivity of industrialization, and on the abundance and the wonders of new products. But how did the workers fare? What were the conditions of life for those who worked the machines that produced this new wealth? Reports from the early years in Britain, the birthplace of the industrial revolution, relate with horrifying regularity the wretched conditions of the working class. Popular literature, official government reports, political tracts, and the cries of labor organizers repeat the same theme: In the midst of increasing national wealth, workers suffered wracking poverty and degradation. On the other hand, by the end of our period (1914), the condition of working-class people in western Europe and the United States, at least, was becoming comfortable. What had changed? How? What was the significance of the change? These questions remain important today as increasingly sophisticated machines continue to produce more abundant and more sophisticated products and more anxiety in the life of workers.

Demographic Causes and Effects of the Industrial Revolution

Many demographic studies suggest that levels of population and industrialization increased together. The population of Europe almost doubled between 1750 and 1850, from 140 million to 265 million, and then jumped another 50 percent to 400 million by 1900. At the same time, emigration carried an additional 50 million people outward from Europe, especially to the Americas, Australia, and South Africa. Much of this increase occurred before the introduction of machinery. Also, the increase seems to have been worldwide: China's population multiplied four times between 1650 and 1850. Historians now believe the main cause was the availability of new foods, such as maize, provided by the "Columbian exchange".

Demographers note two waves of change that followed the industrial revolution. First, death rates fell as people ate better and kept cleaner, and as public health measures increased the safety of the water supply, improved the sanitation of cities, combated epidemics, and taught new standards of personal hygiene. Second, parents began to realize that improved health increased the likelihood that their children would live to adulthood, and that it was not necessary to produce numerous children to ensure that two or three or four would survive. Urban birth rates went down as parents began to practice family planning. The old "iron law of wages" had argued that as income increased people would simply use the surplus to have more children; this did not continue. After years of rapid growth, by about 1900, the populations of industrial areas began to stabilize.

Winners and Losers in the Industrial Revolution

New entrepreneurs, men creating successful new industrial enterprises, often profited handsomely in this era. Their literary representative was Samuel Smiles (1812–1904), whose *Self-Help*, published in 1859, advocated self-reliance as the key to "a harvest of wealth and prosperity." Smiles described the careers of many of these self-made new men—the "industrial heroes of the civilized world"—for example, Josiah Wedgwood, a potter, son and grandson of potters, who created a new form of pottery that still bears his name. Wedgwood transformed the British pottery industry, earning great profits for himself and providing employment in his factories for 20,000 workers. As industries of all sorts expanded, each nation had its own examples of "captains of industry"—for example, four generations of the Friedrich Krupp family, manufacturers of steel and weapons in Germany; Andrew Carnegie, also in steel manufacture, in the USA; and J. Pierpont Morgan in investment banking also in the USA. In Britain, the economic and political power of the inherited nobility declined. Their wealth, based on land ownership, diminished as that of the new industrial class grew.

Handicraft workers were displaced by the new mechanization. In 1820 there were 240,000 handloom weavers in Britain; in 1840, 123,000; in 1856, 23,000. Some of these workers found jobs running the new power looms, but many could not make the transition and fell into poverty.

While attending his father's cotton mill in Manchester, Friedrich Engels (1820–95) compiled devastating accounts of *The Condition of the Working Class in England* (1845). His description of the St. Giles slum in London demonstrates the moral outrage that led him to join with Karl Marx in calling for revolution:

> Heaps of garbage and ashes lie in all directions, and the foul liquids emptied before the doors gather in stinking pools. Here live the poorest of the poor, the worst paid workers with thieves and the victims of prostitution indiscriminately huddled together … [T]hey who have some kind of shelter are fortunate in comparison with the utterly homeless. In London fifty thousand human beings get up every morning, not knowing where they are to lay their heads at night. (pp. 34–38)

Government reports, although more restrained in tone, sustained these horrific views. They called for, and got, remedial legislation. Official committees studied conditions

Putters or trolley boys, from *Mines and Miners* by L. Simonin, early nineteenth century. Until the reforms of the 1870s, owners of factories and mines were able to force children as young as five and six to work up to sixteen hours a day—often in hazardous conditions. Orphans and pauper children were especially vulnerable since capitalists merely had to keep them fed and sheltered in return for their services. The resulting disease, industrial injury, and illiteracy tended to make poor families even poorer.

in the factories and neighborhoods of Britain's growing industrial cities and in its mines. In 1831, a committee chaired by the Member of Parliament Michael Thomas Sadler (1780–1835) investigated the conditions of child labor in cotton and linen factories. It found children beginning work at the age of six, usually for twelve- and thirteen-hour days. They were often given food so wretched that, despite their hunger, they left it for pigs to eat. Workplaces were cramped and dirty all year long, and were especially damaging to health during the long nights of winter, when gas, candles, and oil lamps added their soot and smoke to the air of the factory. Still worse conditions were revealed by the Committee on the Conditions in Mines that was appointed in 1842 and chaired by Anthony Ashley Cooper, 7th earl of Shaftesbury. Children worked for fourteen hours underground each day. Legally, they could work from the age of nine, but parents needing extra income frequently brought even younger children.

Sir Edwin Chadwick (1800–90), an investigator for the Royal Commission on the Poor Laws, issued his *Inquiry into the Condition of the Poor* in 1842 after taking abundant testimony from workers in factories and mines, homes and workplaces.

Chadwick noted that the British government had already begun legislating the conditions of child labor and of tenement construction. He now urged further legislation to provide for sewage, drainage, sanitation, and a clean water supply. His report suggested that not only the poor workers but also their employers, the community, and the government would benefit. Chadwick's report helped inspire broad public support for the Public Health Act of 1848 and the creation of a Board of Health.

Gender Relationships and the Industrial Revolution

By creating factories, the industrial revolution drove a wedge between the home and the workplace that dramatically affected both. Wives who had been accustomed to working alongside, or at least in proximity to, their husbands on the farm or in the shop or workshop now found that the major source of employment was away from home. The industrial revolution forced redefinitions of identities. What should the woman's role and place be now? How should motherhood and work be balanced? In a world that expected most females to be under the protection of males, how were single women to define, and fend for, themselves? In what voice should the feminist movement address these complex issues?

As the industrial revolution began in semi-rural locations, its labor force was drawn primarily from young, (as yet) unmarried women, frequently daughters of local farmers. Some of the early factory owners built boarding houses for the women and treated them protectively, as young wards. Francis Cabot Lowell (1775–1817) built mills at Waltham, Massachusetts, on this principle. He promised the women hard work, with pay adequate to help their families and to save toward marriage. After his death, his partners extended his example by establishing a new town, Lowell, with the largest cotton mill built to that date. By the 1840s, about half the mills in New England followed this model. Factory work had its demands of order, discipline, and the clock, and the dormitory-boarding houses were somewhat crowded, but labor historian Alice Kessler-Harris quotes approvingly the very warm assessment of the Lowell experience from one of its workers in the 1830s: It was "the first field that had ever been open to her outside of her own restricted home … the first money they earned! When they felt the jingle of silver in their pocket, there for the first time, their heads became erect and they walked as if on air."

As new machinery became heavier, as factory work became more prevalent, and as economic depression pressed down on both American and British economies, the workforce shifted. Men, often farmers and immigrants, moved into the factories, displacing the women. The men demanded higher pay, which factory owners had previously hoped to avoid by hiring women. The culture of the industrializing world of that time, primarily in Britain, called for men to support their families. A young, unmarried woman might earn just enough for herself and that would be adequate. A man required a "family wage." The rising productivity of constantly improving machinery made this "family wage" possible, and it became the baseline standard for industry, although workers had to struggle for it for decades. Women were thus displaced from factory work and brought back to the home.

By the second half of the nineteenth century, "domesticity" became the desired norm for middle- and even working-class women and their families. Most middle-class women spent a great deal of time caring for their families and homes, and the new urban domesticity increased their level of security and comfort. Life expectancy, a basic index of well-being, rose rapidly for women in Britain, even slightly more than for men. It increased from forty-four years in 1890, to fifty-two in 1910, to sixty in 1920. Living standards began to rise and generally continued to rise into the twentieth century. New systems of ventilation, heating, lighting, indoor plumbing, and running hot and cold water contributed to domestic comfort and made life easier for those who could afford these services, although they often did not reach working-class neighborhoods.

Urban conditions made children less of an economic benefit, as they had been on family farms, and more of an economic burden. Family planning increased. Child-bearing became less frequent, freer from infection thanks to antisepsis, less painful with the use of anesthesia, and safer with the professionalization of the practice of medicine. The presence of children in the home also decreased as free, compulsory education, beginning as early as the 1830s and 1840s, began to take them to school for several hours each day.

With more time freed from traditional domestic responsibilities, some women began to enter into the array of white-collar jobs that were opening. The most respectable jobs provided satisfying work that also fit the culturally approved role of women as care givers and nurturers: teaching in the new school systems and nursing in the new hospitals. Other women worked as sales

Anon., "The New Machine for Winding up the Ladies," English cartoon, c. 1840. Upper-class English women wore corsets, devices made of whalebone that constricted the waist painfully, making it appear as tiny as possible and, by contrast, accentuating the hips, buttocks, and breasts. The corsets were often so tight that they interfered with women's ability to breathe properly and encouraged "swooning." The cartoonist mocks these practices.

personnel in the new department stores (where they also shopped) and as secretaries and clerks in the new offices, although this was primarily a male occupation in the nineteenth century. A very few went into professions.

While domestic concerns and new technological wonders engaged the middle classes, and were desired by the working classes, for a great number of people they were out of reach. The 15–20 percent of adult females who had to work as principal breadwinners for themselves and their families confronted more basic problems of earning a living. The value placed on domesticity as the proper role for females, and the concomitant view that men should earn a "family wage" but that women needed only supplementary income, made the plight of the working woman doubly difficult. These women, often immigrants, desperately poor, and without male support, were no longer seen, as the first industrial women workers had been, as proud and independent, but as unfortunate objects of sympathy and pity.

They found jobs where they could. Domestic service was most common, employing two to three times as many women as industry, even in industrialized countries. On the margins of society, other women earned a living through prostitution. In the second half of the nineteenth century, censuses in the largest cities, London and Paris, routinely reported tens of thousands of prostitutes walking the streets, serving in brothels, or, occasionally, employed in more comfortable settings by more prosperous clients. These women were often condemned by more conventional society, but they often found this job the only one that paid enough to enable them to support their families. Most of them worked only until about the age of twenty-five, by which time they usually found other work or were married, a rosy picture painted by the middle classes, but often contradicted by working-class experience.

The socialist wing of the feminist movement understood that class differences often inhibited solidarity among women. Karl Marx spoke of the difference between the bourgeois and the proletarian family. He wrote of the conflict between the roles of mother and of worker. With Engels, Marx condemned the "double oppression" of women by both capitalism and the family, but he praised capitalism for freeing women from being regarded as property. He encouraged women in their struggle for citizens' rights and economic independence. In *The Origin of the Family, Private Property and the State* (1884), Engels argued that the form of the family was not fixed. It had evolved substantially in the past, and he proposed further, revolutionary change:

> The peculiar character of the supremacy of the husband over the wife in the modern family, the necessity of creating real social equality between them and the way to do it, will only be seen in the clear light of day when both possess legally complete equality of rights. Then it will be plain that the first condition for the liberation of the wife is to bring the whole female sex back into public industry, and that this in turn demands that the characteristic of the monogamous family as the economic unit of society be abolished. (Engels, 137–8)

In Germany, the Social Democratic Party (SPD) created a separate organizational structure for women that enlisted 174,751 women members by 1914, the largest movement of women in Europe. The number reflects, however, not only women seeking independent expression, but also women who sought to ally themselves with their husbands as members of the party. Working women's organizations were undercut by the opposition of male unionized workers who feared that the women would take away their jobs or, at least, increase the labor pool and thus drive down wages.

POLITICAL REACTION IN BRITAIN AND EUROPE, 1800–1914

Political, Economic, and Social Reform in Britain

Britain had a growing urban, industrial population that demanded political, economic, and social change. The government, recognizing that industrialization was transforming Britain away from its aristocratic and agrarian traditions and fearful of the consequences, responded initially by trying to repress the movement for reform. The Peterloo Massacre at St. Peter's Fields in Manchester in 1819 demonstrated the government's position. A huge but peaceful demonstration by 80,000 people called for universal male suffrage, the annual election of the House of Commons in Parliament, and the abolition of the Corn Laws. The Corn Laws had raised the tariff on grain to levels that effectively banned importation, thus keeping the price of basic foodstuffs high, favoring landowners and farmers at the expense of the growing urban, industrial population. Soldiers fired on the demonstrators, killing eleven and wounding some 400. The government applauded the soldiers and passed further legislation to restrict free expression.

The mood of Parliament had changed by 1832, becoming more fearful but also more accommodating, partly because of revolutions on the European continent, and partly because of riots in Britain. Fearing the possibility of revolution, the Whig party in Parliament forced through the Reform Bill of 1832. Its most significant provision was to shift 143 seats in Parliament from rural constituencies, which were losing population and were often dominated by single families, to expanding urban constituencies. The number of voters increased by about 60 percent but still totaled only about 800,000 in all of Britain. A far greater proportion of the new voters, however, were professionals: doctors, lawyers, businessmen, and journalists. The benefits of the 1832 reforms went to the middle classes, but soon the two main parties, conservative Tories and more liberal Whigs, jockeying for power, began to craft new programs to protect and enfranchise urban working people. Some commentators at the time and afterward viewed these political moves as sincere attempts to broaden the base of British political participation. Others saw them as cynical attempts to add voters from the new middle class while leaving industrial workers unrepresented. Whatever the motivation, they were effective in forestalling revolution during extremely tense times, and over several decades they did increase the (male) electorate significantly.

In addition to political reform, Parliament addressed the demands of economic and social legislation. The Factory Act of 1833 not only forbade the employment of children under the age of nine in textile mills, it also, for the first time, provided for paid inspectors to enforce the legislation.

Parliament abolished slavery in the British Empire in 1833 and passed a new Poor Law in 1834, which provided assistance just adequate to sustain life. The law required that recipients live in government workhouses and participate in government-created work projects, but this provision was not usually enforced. In 1835 it enacted a Municipal Corporations Act, which reformed elections and administrations in large cities, enabling them to cope more successfully with the problems of growth and industrialization. In 1842 the employment of women and of children under the age of ten was forbidden in coal mines. The Ten Hour Act of 1847 extended this ruling to

The Chartists. As this contemporary cartoon implies, the sheer weight of support received by the Chartists was a powerful argument in favor of voting rights being extended to all men (though not yet women). Parliament rejected increasingly large charters, or petitions, on three occasions and it was not until 1918 that universal male suffrage was adopted in Great Britain.

cover factories and limited the hours of work for women. In practice, men's hours were also soon reduced.

On some fundamental issues Parliament moved slowly, and sometimes it refused to move at all. The Chartist movement, a national working-class movement dissatisfied with both the 1832 Reform Bill and the new Poor Law, presented a Charter or petition with more than a million signatures to Parliament in 1838 calling for universal male suffrage, an end to property qualifications for members of parliament, and equal electoral districts. The Chartists hoped to achieve reform by gaining access to politics rather than by destroying machines, as their Luddite forbears had done. Despite, or perhaps because of, a wave of violence instigated by some of the few "physical force" Chartists, the House of Commons rejected the petition. When it was resubmitted in 1842, with more than 3.3 million signatures, the Charter was rejected again, overwhelmingly, by 287 votes to 49. Parliament feared that universal suffrage would bring an end to the sanctity of property and the capitalist economic system.

In 1846, however, under a Tory government led by Robert Peel, Parliament did repeal the Corn Laws, signaling the victory of the urban constituencies and the triumph of free trade. Britain gave up its policy of self-sufficiency in food and entered fully into the international trade system to purchase its food and sell its manufactured goods. A second Reform Bill in 1867, passed by the Tory government of Benjamin Disraeli, doubled the electorate to about 2 million, about one-third of all adult males. The Bill enfranchised many urban working men, although it continued to exclude most of those agricultural and industrial workers who lived in the countryside.

The two major political parties, Liberals and Tories, now competed directly for the favor of the industrial workers. In 1870, the Liberal government of William Gladstone began to provide universal, state-supported education and, in the next year, it formally legalized labor unions. The Tories, under Disraeli's second administration, 1876–80, extended the acts regulating public sanitation and conditions of labor in factories and mines. They also regulated the conditions of housing for the poor. In 1884, under Gladstone, a third Reform Bill doubled the electorate again. Not until 1918 did Britain adopt universal male suffrage for men 21 years of age and over and extend the vote to

The Great Procession, June 18, 1910. Not only women campaigned for their right to vote: in this procession of the WSPU (Women's Social and Political Union) a hunger strikers' banner is hoisted aloft by male supporters. Emmeline Pankhurst, frustrated that politicians would not pass legislation to allow women to vote, organized the WSPU and began a militant campaign to secure women's suffrage in Britain. She used assaults on public property to call attention to her cause, and spent time in prison where she and other jailed suffragettes went on hunger strike.

women over the age of 30 who were either ratepayers or married to ratepayers.

While women finally gained the right to vote in both Britain and the United States after World War I, it was not without a long and often violent struggle. The Chartists had peacefully demanded that women obtain the right to vote in the 1840s without success. Women's suffrage committees were formed, but legislators in Parliament rejected most of their demands. Their failure to win suffrage through peaceful means led Emmeline Pankhurst and her daughter Christabel to form suffragette organizations, which became increasingly violent. Though many abhorred the violence, many more grew sympathetic to giving women the right to vote. The participation of suffragettes in the national effort in World War I softened opposition, and in 1918 British women aged thirty or over received the complete franchise. In 1928 the Representation of the People Act gave British women voting rights equal to those of men.

In the United States, women turned to conventions and voluntary associations to promote suffrage. One of the most important conventions was held in Seneca Falls, New York, on July 19–20, 1848. The declaration that came out of this convention called not only for the right to vote but also for increased educational and employment opportunities for women. Other conventions followed. Women first gained the right to vote in local and school board elections in some western states and finally gained national voting rights with the ratification of the Nineteenth Amendment to the U.S. Constitution in August, 1920.

Emmeline Pankhurst with her daughter Christabel, 1908. These were the mother and daughter founders of the Women's Social and Political Union (1903), the most renowned of Britain's suffrage movements. Their campaigns were militant and disruptive. They set fire to public buildings, smashed windows, sabotaged mailboxes, slashed paintings in London's National Gallery, and pelted government officials with eggs. Emmeline was jailed repeatedly, and force-fed when she went on hunger-strikes.

Labor Organization

Like women, who organized to obtain political rights, the working class organized to improve labor conditions. Social historian E.P. Thompson identifies the London Corresponding Society, founded in 1792, as perhaps "the first definitely working-class political organization formed in Britain." Unions were forbidden to unionize under the Combination Act of 1799, but in 1824 this law was repealed. Small trade unions took root, usually finding their greatest success among the better-off "aristocracy of labor"—the machinists, carpenters, printers, and spinners. Sometimes they would go on strike; politically they organized for suffrage campaigns; and some helped organize cooperative enterprises. Only under the Trade Union Act of 1871 was the right to strike recognized officially. Unskilled workers began increasingly to join unions, with miners and transport workers usually in the lead. They drew encouragement from the Fabian Society, a group of intellectuals centered in the Bloomsbury area of London that sought to make government and society more receptive to working-class interests without violence. They supported the London Dock strike of 1889, which demonstrated working-class strength by closing that great port. They formed the core constituency of the new Labour Party. The Party won only two seats in the 1900 elections, but in 1906 it captured twenty-nine seats and began its permanent role in parliamentary politics in Britain. By 1914, 4 million Britons held membership in trade unions.

Karl Marx and Theories of Worker Revolution. In Britain, workers created their own organizations, which then gained the support of political party leaders. Elsewhere, political leaders and theorists attempted to provide leadership in organizing much smaller groups of workers. Foremost among the theoreticians was Karl Marx (1818–83). A well-educated and trained German journalist of Jewish ancestry, Marx

WOMEN'S EMANCIPATION 1790–1928

c. 1790	Olympe de Gouges writes the polemical *Declaration of the Rights of Woman and the Citizen*
1792	Mary Wollstonecraft writes *A Vindication of the Rights of Woman*, regarded as the first manifesto of the women's movement in Britain
1794	Condorcet writes of the desirability of establishing equality of civil and political rights for men and women in *Progrès de l'esprit*
1829	*Sati* (ritual suicide by Hindu widows) is banned in India
1848	Elizabeth Cady Stanton and Lucretia Mott organize the first women's rights convention at Seneca Falls, New York
1850	Beginnings in Britain of national agitation for women's suffrage
1857–72	Married Women's Property Acts allow British women to keep their own possessions on marriage
1866	Mott founds American Equal Rights Association
1868	First public meeting of women's suffrage movement held in Manchester, England
1869	In Britain women ratepayers may vote in municipal elections; Cady Stanton is first president of US National Woman Suffrage Association
1890	Footbinding beginning to die out in China
1903	Emmeline Pankhurst founds Women's Social and Political Union
1906	Pankhurst and her daughters launch militant campaign in Britain
1913	Suffragettes protest in Washington, D.C.; International Women's Peace Conference held in the Netherlands
1914–18	Women assume responsibilities outside the home during World War I
1918	British women householders over 30 years granted the vote
1919	Constance de Markiewicz is the first woman elected to Parliament in Britain
1920	19th amendment to the Constitution gives US women the vote
1928	British women over 21 years granted the vote

called for a worker-led revolution. He organized revolutionary socialists through active campaigning, wrote polemical tracts calling for revolution, such as *The Communist Manifesto* (with Friedrich Engels) and produced three volumes of scholarly analysis and critique of the capitalist system called *Das Kapital*.

Marx began his studies in Berlin at a time when western and central Europe were alive with revolutionary sentiments—both of workers seeking new rights and of nationalists seeking greater political representation. In 1848, many of these revolutionary pressures came to a head—and were crushed. In France, a revolt against the monarchy of Louis Philippe (r. 1830–48) and the proclamation of a provisional republic was followed by the establishment of government-sponsored workshops to provide employment for the poor. A new, far more conservative government was elected, however, and it closed the workshops in Paris. The poor people of the city barricaded city streets, and the army was called out. More than 10,000 people were killed or injured in the ensuing street riots.

In Austria, protesting students and workers briefly took control of Prague and Vienna and then were suppressed in both cities by regular forces of the Austrian army at the cost of thousands of casualties. In Prussia, in the same year, worker demands for more democracy and more worker rights joined with demands for a new constitution that would lead toward the merger of Prussia with the many small German-speaking states of the former Holy Roman Empire into a new country of Germany. At first it appeared that the Prussian king Frederick William IV (r. 1840–61) would grant these demands, and a Constituent Assembly was convened in Frankfurt to write a new German constitution. In the end, however, the king reasserted his divine right to rule and rejected the constitution. Under these circumstances, the smaller states refused to join in a unified government. Conservative forces remained in control of central Europe, and Marx moved to London, where he spent the rest of his life, much of it in active scholarship in the British Museum.

Marx believed that wealth is produced not so much by capitalists, who control the finances, but by the proletariat—the laborers—who do the actual physical work of production. Because employers do not generally accept this point of view, workers do not receive proper compensation for their contributions. Violent revolution is the only recourse "to raise the proletariat to the position of ruling class, to establish democracy." In a stirring call to this revolution, Marx and Engels declared the Communist Party as its leader:

proletariat In Marxist theory, those who live solely by the sale of their labor.

> Let the ruling classes tremble at a Communist revolution. The proletarians have nothing to lose but their chains. They have a world to win. Workingmen of all countries, unite! (*The Communist Manifesto* p. 44)

Until the revolution would take place, Marx and Engels called for many shorter term legislative goals, including: "a heavy progressive or graduated income tax ... free education for all children in public schools ... and ... abolition of child factory labor in its present form." Many other labor groups shared these goals, and they were subsequently adopted in virtually all industrialized countries.

After the revolution would occur, Marx and Engels called for the establishment of a powerful, worker-led government to assume control of the economy, and they looked forward to a still later time when the state would be unnecessary and would "wither away". They identified the state as "the organized power of one class for oppressing another," so when workers ruled the state there would be no need for further oppression and the state would vanish. Marx and Engels gave no further description of this utopia, but it would be based on their most central and most radical tenet:

> The theory of the Communists may be summed up in the single sentence: Abolition of private property. (p. 23)

Marx's theory included a view of history that saw class struggle as perpetual: "The history of all hitherto existing society is the history of class struggles." The current form of the struggle was bourgeoisie vs. proletariat. The bourgeoisie themselves had created the proletariat by organizing the new factories that employed and exploited them. Marx condemned the sexual ethics of the bourgeoisie. Despite their official reverence for the family, Marx accused them of sexual abuse of their workers, economic perpetuation of prostitution, and wife-swapping among themselves: "Our bourgeois, not content with having the wives and daughters of their proletarians at their disposal, not to speak of common prostitutes, take the greatest pleasure in seducing each other's wives." Marx heaped scorn on religion, charging the bourgeoisie with using it as an "opiate" to divert the proletariat from its fundamental economic concerns. Marx was a materialist, arguing that economics is the basis of life; ideas and intellectual life are based on economic status: "Man's consciousness changes with every change in the conditions of his material existence, in his social relations and in his social life ... The ruling ideas of each age have ever been the ideas of its ruling class."

The proletarian revolution predicted as inevitable by Marx and Engels did not take place in the nineteenth century. (In Chapter 20 we will consider the extent to which the 1917 Russian Revolution was proletarian and Marxist and in Chapter 22 we will ask the same question about the Chinese revolution of 1949.) As we have seen, in Britain three factors worked toward a relatively peaceful resolution of class tensions. First, workers' unions began to win their demands for higher pay, shorter hours, and better working conditions. Second, political institutions expanded to assimilate the new worker organizations and accommodate many of their demands. Third, legislation favorable to workers was passed, the franchise was extended, and the Labour party took its place in Parliament.

In retrospect, some of Marx and Engels' most enduring criticisms have been cultural rather than economic. They identified five critical areas of social-cultural tension during the height of the industrial revolution:

- the problem of coping with rapid change, as *The Communist Manifesto* observed: "all that is solid melts into air";
- the alienation of factory workers from their work, as they became insignificant cogs in great systems of production;
- the alienation of workers from nature, as farmers left the countryside to find jobs in urban industries;
- the dominance of the husband over the wife in the modern family and the earlier conditions of equality ended; and
- the economic competition that drove workers as well as owners to subordinate their own humanitarian and personal goals to the unceasing economic demands of the capitalist system.

Germany, 1870–1914. Although Marx was frustrated by the revival of conservative forces in continental Europe around 1848, a new wave of labor unrest and strikes swept across the region in the late 1860s and early 1870s, signaling the growing strength of labor. In Germany chief minister Otto von Bismarck (1815–98) pursued diverse and sometimes conflicting strategies to keep working people allied to his government. He extended universal male suffrage to the North German Confederation in 1867 and then to all of Germany when he unified the country in 1871 (see Chapter 18). But he limited the power of the legislature and diluted the power of the vote because government ministers were responsible to the king, not to Parliament. When Germany's opposition Social Democratic Party became Europe's first political party based on the working classes, in 1875, Bismarck sharply restricted its organizational activities. On the other hand, declaring "I too am a socialist," he passed legislation providing workers' disability and accident insurance and, in the 1880s, the first compulsory social security system in Europe. This legislation, however, covered only male industrial workers, not women or children. Thanks to government policies, worker militancy, and its learning from Britain's painful experiences, Germany did not repeat the worst conditions of child and female labor, and of the excessive hours and brutal conditions of industrial work.

The United States, 1870–1914. In the United States, labor began to organize especially with the industrialization that began after the Civil War (1861–5). A number of craft unions joined together to form the National Labor Union in 1866. It claimed 300,000 members by the early 1870s, but it did not survive the depression of 1873. The Noble Order of the Knights of Labor, founded as a secret society in 1869, grew into a mass union, open to all workers, with 700,000 members in 1886. The leadership of the Knights of Labor could not control its members, however, and various wildcat strikes broke out, some of them violent, alienating much of the rest of the membership. America's most successful labor organization was the American Federation of Labor, a union of skilled craft workers, founded in 1886 by Samuel Gompers (1850–1924). Its membership grew to 1 million by 1900 and 2 million by 1914. Women were not allowed to join, but in 1900 the International Ladies Garment Workers Union (ILGWU), which organized male and female workers who made women's clothing, was formed—with men dominating its leadership.

A series of strikes in America throughout the 1890s led to violence, sometimes in response to falling wages, often in response to poor working conditions or paternalism, the excessive control managers and owners held over workers' lives. Hired detectives, local police, and even soldiers attacked strikers and were attacked in return. Near Pittsburgh, steel workers lost the Homestead Steel strike in 1892 as the governor of Pennsylvania sent in 8000 troops. The American Railway Union under Eugene Debs lost a strike at the Pullman Palace Car Company in Chicago when the Governor of Illinois obtained a court injunction to force the workers back to their jobs. Violence ensued, leaving scores of workers dead. In resolving a 1908 strike of hat makers, the United States Supreme Court ruled that trade unions were subject to the Sherman Anti-Trust Act, leaving their members personally liable for business losses suffered during strikes. Until this ruling was reversed in the 1930s, militant unionism was virtually dead, although the small Industrial Workers of the World (IWW), representing a radical perspective on labor organization, did form in 1905 and was responsible for several major strikes, especially in western states.

The United States did develop powerful labor organizations, mostly in the twentieth century, but it never produced a significant political party based primarily on labor. Labor organization in the United States was fragmented into craft-specific unions. In this nation of immigrants, workers also held multiple identities; their ethnic identities frequently inhibited them from building union solidarity with those of other ethnic groups. Many immigrants came to America to earn money and return home; these workers did not usually have a commitment to active unionization. Pay scales and working conditions in the United States were significantly better than in Europe, further muting worker grievances. Finally, the capitalist ideology of the country discouraged class divisions, and the government restricted labor organization.

France, 1870–1914. As we have seen, worker revolts broke out repeatedly in France, many of them inspired by the French revolutionary tradition and others by the low wages and poor working conditions that characterized French industry. Skilled

Massacre of the Paris radicals. The slaughter meted out to the Paris Commune of 1871 is graphically depicted by the Post-Impressionist painter Edouard Manet. Left-wing urban leaders tried to set up their own state-within-a-state, but the communards were put down brutally by the national government. At least 20,000 were summarily executed and over 40,000 were taken prisoner. (*Museum Folkwang, Essen*)

artisans, displaced by new industries, often organized these revolts. Even before the industrial revolution took root, worker and artisanal revolts played a leading role in the French Revolution—and were crushed along with it. They boiled over again in 1848 and were crushed again as the army killed as many as 10,000 workers in street riots in Paris. Later in the century, the revolts were increasingly dominated by industrial workers. In 1871, much of the potential leadership of a workers' movement was once again wiped out. The French national government killed at least 20,000 people and exiled another 10,000 in the Paris Commune, an uprising of urban leaders in Paris.

A decade later, however, some of the exiles from the Paris Commune returned and organization began again, this time with greater success. In 1884 *syndicats*, labor unions, were legalized. Two competing federations were formed, one calling primarily for mutual help, the other for political action. Together, they numbered 140,000 members in 1890, a figure that more than tripled to 580,000 by the end of the century. By 1909, an umbrella group, the Confédération Génerale de Travail, numbered nearly a million. In 1890, May 1 was recognized as an annual "Labor Day." French politics, however, was dominated by the wealthier business leaders. Industrial workers organized, but they commanded less influence than farmers, shopkeepers, and small businessmen.

Labor in the Non-industrialized World. Wherever they reached, the new industrial products displaced old handicraft industries and workers. The craftsmen could not compete with the speed, consistent quality, and low price of the machine-made products. Many of them were ruined. The Indian cotton textile industry provided the most striking example. In 1834–5, the highest ranking British official in India lamented, "The bones of the cotton weavers are bleaching the plains of India." Lord Bentinck's remark was especially true in Bengal, in eastern India, a region that had participated heavily in the export trade, but to some degree it was true throughout India. And as a general observation on the fate of handicraft workers, the comment correctly captured the problem globally. Some of the displaced workers could find jobs in other crafts, not yet overtaken by the new industries. Some could continue their old crafts by cutting back farther and farther on their meager profits and incomes in order to try to compete with the machines. A few could produce fine handicrafts for the specialized luxury market. Many were pushed into agricultural work, especially as their countries could no longer compete as exporters of (hand) manufactured goods and were transformed into exporters of raw materials and importers of finished manufactures. In the industrializing world artisans were also displaced, but the rapidly expanding industries could absorb many of them. The craftspeople mourned the devaluation of their handicraft skills, and the cold, standardized rhythms of the machines wore down their spirits, but they had jobs and, as industrialization increased productivity, their incomes rose.

In some of the poorest countries—most notably India and China—indentured labor overseas became an alternative to unemployment for a wide range of peoples. Between 1831 and 1921, about 2 million people made their way from India and China and, to a lesser extent from Africa, the Pacific Islands, and Japan as indentured laborers to work primarily in the sugar plantations of the Caribbean, Mauritius and Réunion in the Indian Ocean, Hawaii, Fiji, and Peru. Four factors encouraged this mass migration. First, the end of slavery forced a search for alternative labor sources. Slavery did not end all at once, with the British ban on the slave trade in 1807, nor with Britain's outlawing slavery in its colonies in 1833. It continued in the USA until 1863, in Cuba until 1886, and in Brazil until 1888, and, illegally, even until today in many locations. After the formal end of slavery, many slaves continued to labor in conditions of semi-slavery. Nevertheless, the system was finished and a new source of labor was needed to supplement the quasi-slave population that continued. Second, the production of sugar increased globally, and dramatically, throughout the nineteenth century,

SOURCE

Tariffs, Wealth, and Poverty: Reflections on America and India by Pandita Ramabai

Pandita Ramabai (1858–1922) traveled in the United States for three years, 1886–9, and on her return home published a travelogue in Marathi. Translated literally as The Peoples of the United States, *it has recently been published in English as* Pandita Ramabai's American Encounter. *In India, Ramabai was a pioneering reformer for women's education. American women impressed her for their public accomplishments individually and in the groups that they often organized. Indeed, the whole country impressed her favorably. One of the areas in which America compared most favorably with India was in its control of its own tariff policy. American industry did so well, Ramabai argues, because it closed its markets to imports that might be competitive. She criticizes the Indian people for not similarly excluding foreign competitive goods, but she does not give any indication of recognizing that America was free to set its own exclusionary tariffs; India, under British colonial rule, had no such freedom. Her audience, however, would surely have understood that. Or was Ramabai urging her fellow Indians simply to boycott foreign goods voluntarily—to just say no— even without formal tariffs? Some Indian nationalists of her time were beginning to argue for that position, and by the early twentieth century, this would be the official position of the Indian National Congress, as we shall see in Chapter 22.*

The goods which come into this country from foreign countries are charged a heavy customs duty . . . The people here take great precautions to prevent the domination of foreign countries in trade and in other matters, and to prevent their becoming slaves of others . . . This is worth remembering by the people of our country who look to England for everything, who rely entirely on England, and who use English goods to the detriment of native industries and trade. The American said that drinking the tea and wearing the clothes imported from England harms the industries of his country; therefore he would never drink such tea or wear English clothes, but would content himself with whatever good or bad clothes were available in his own country. And he also acted accordingly. That is why this country has reached such prosperity today. And what have we achieved? We have given our gold and bought pots of pewter in return; we have shut down our handlooms and started wearing cheap English clothes. Like the Indians of North America, we have succumbed to the lure of shiny, colored glass beads; and we have sold our precious gem-studded land to foreigners in return for glass beads and glass bottles filled with wine. Now we are screaming because the wine has started to claim our lives, and the fragments of broken glass have made gaping wounds in our feet. This is why our country is in such a wretched state! This clearly shows that the United States and India are on opposite sides of the globe! (Ramabai, p. 227)

from 300,000 tons in 1790 to 10 million tons in 1914. Laborers were required even beyond the number of slaves previously employed in its cultivation and harvest.

Third, imperial reach connected far-flung regions of the world, making possible this international flow of labor. Indian indentured laborers traveling to the West Indies, or Mauritius, or Fiji remained within a single imperial system, with relatively similar laws, a single language of rule, and established systems of transportation and communication. One and a third million of them made the move. Similarly, indentured laborers from France's West African colonies migrating to the French Caribbean or to Réunion moved within a single system. The 387,000 Chinese who emigrated under terms of indenture—the majority of them to Cuba and Peru—were less tied into a single empire, but they were part of the global economic system that the Europeans had developed. This was also true for the 65,000 Japanese who migrated to Hawaii. The fourth element in the indentured traffic was the technological capacity to move so many people around the globe, forth and back, because the indentures of the servants were for limited time periods, usually five to seven years, after which they might go "back home." Sometimes they were encouraged to return, sometimes not.

The indentured laborers were not displaced persons in the industrial system as the craftsmen were. Most were farm laborers to begin with, but it was the industrial system that created the mechanisms of the indenture system. And many observers compared the conditions of gang labor on sugar plantations to the rigors and routinization of the factory work floor. The overwhelming majority of the servants were male, and the absence of females was probably relieved by the knowledge that after five or seven years the servants might return home to establish family life.

Many observers thought that the women who did sign on as indentured laborers were mostly prostitutes. Some were, but most, like the men, recognized that even the low pay of the overseas indentured laborer was at least double that of the Indian or Chinese agricultural worker. They moved to try to improve their situation. Although indentured servitude had some of the attributes of temporary slavery, it had a limited time frame, and thus the prospect of freedom at the end of years of indenture. For many it was a trap. For some it was an escape.

NEW PATTERNS OF URBAN LIFE

The core habitat of industrialization was the city. During the eighteenth century, cities began a period of growth that has continued without break until today. In the largest cities, by the late 1800s this process began to include middle-class suburbanization, which was made possible by the new railroad transportation systems for goods and passengers. In the early twentieth century, automobiles, buses, and trucks enlarged the system to ever-greater dimensions.

Much of the urban growth in the nineteenth century was a direct result of industrialization. The steam engine, which could be constructed anywhere, made the location of industries more flexible. Factories sprang up near port facilities, at inland transportation hubs, in the heart of raw materials resource centers, such as the Midlands of England, or Silesia in central Europe, and near large concentrations of consumers, like the great cities of Paris and London. New industrial metropolises dotted the map.

Immigrants streamed into the new cities for jobs. Farmers became factory workers and the balance between urban and rural populations tilted continuously cityward. Within cities, the children of artisans became factory workers. Both farmers and artisans found the new industrial city shocking. They were exchanging the styles of life of

SOURCE

Diverse Perspectives

Like the proverbial elephant that appeared different to each person who approached it from a different perspective, the industrial city signified something different to each observer. Wordsworth and Blake (p. 570) had certainly seen early nineteenth-century London very differently. From the middle of the century, two additional poets from two additional cities provide still different points of view. Charles Baudelaire presents the hard-working people of Paris—indeed the city itself— as just struggling to get by at the break of a new day.

The crow of a rooster, far off, cuts
   through the hazy air.
A sea of fog bathes the buildings.
Men in agony in the workhouses
Heave their dying breath in
   undignified gasps.
The debauched return home,
   broken by their work.
The shivering dawn robed in pink
   and green
Advances slowly along the
   deserted Seine,
And somber, aging, Paris, rubbing
   its eyes,
Picks up its tools, and sets to work

While Baudelaire anguished with his city's lonely despair, in the United States, Walt Whitman sang rapturously of the dynamism of his own Manhattan, New York:

The down-town streets, the jobbers' houses of
   business, the houses of business of the
ship-merchants and money-brokers, the river-
   streets,
Immigrants arriving, fifteen or twenty thousand in
   a week,
The carts hauling goods, the manly race of drivers
   of horses, the brown-faced sailors,
The summer air, the bright sun shining, and the
   sailing clouds aloft,
The winter snows, the sleigh-bells, the broken ice in
   the river, passing along up or down
with the flood-tide or ebb-tide,
The mechanics of the city, the masters, well-form'd,
   beautiful faced, looking you straight in the eyes,
Trottoirs throng'd, vehicles, Broadway, the women,
   the shops and shows,
A million people—manners free and superb—open
   voices—hospitality—the most
courageous and friendly young men,
City of hurried and sparkling waters! City of spires
   and masts!
City nested in bays! My city!

Back Queen Street, Deansgate, Manchester. As this *Illustrated London News* drawing of housing conditions of the Manchester cotton operatives in 1862 shows, accommodation in this city could be spartan. Manchester in particular, with its high mortality rate, desperately needed the attentions of voluntary agencies that were attempting to better the living conditions of those who had been drawn to work in the new industries. Despite the fact that many workers emigrated to the United States or to British colonies overseas, the population continued to grow at a great rate, with adverse consequences for public health and housing.

farm and workshop for regimes of routinization, standardization, and regulation. The skills that they had previously mastered were of little use here. At the same time, opportunities beckoned: cultural, educational, recreational, social, and, most important, economic. In the early years of the industrial revolution, conditions of labor and of public health were abysmal; later, as productivity increased, workers organized, employers and governments paid heed, and conditions started to improve. "City lights" began to appear more attractive. The nineteenth century began the age of global urbanization.

Philosophical and sociological speculations on the nature of the city also flourished and were equally diverse. In Germany, Max Weber (1864–1920) analyzed the modern industrial city as a new creation. He contrasted, negatively, its freewheeling life and amorphous institutions against the close-knit guilds and political and religious associations of earlier self-governing European cities, especially medieval cities (see Chapter 13). Weber concluded that the sprawling industrial city—open to any immigrant who wished to come and embedded within a nation-state that controlled its life and politics—was quite different from the self-contained city of earlier times. Europe, at least, was living in a new era.

Many observers agreed that the openness of the industrial city and the lack of institutional ties among its citizens were leading to a breakdown of the social fabric and a breakdown of the individual personality. The division of labor was turning the individual into a specialist concerned only with narrow interests; the sense of personal or community wholeness was lost. And the sheer multitude of people and experiences in the city was also forcing the individual to retreat even further into a small, private niche. The urban dweller was evolving into a person swift of intellect to achieve his own needs, but lacking concern for and integration with the larger community. Georg Simmel (1858–1918), a social psychologist in Germany, wrote in 1903 of the destabilizing effects of these new cities:

The individual has become a mere cog in an enormous organization of things and powers which tears from his hands all progress, spirituality, and value in order to transform them from their subjective form into the form of a purely objective life … the metropolis is the genuine arena of this culture which outgrows all personal life.

Here … is offered such an overwhelming fullness of crystallized and impersonalized spirit that the personality, so to speak, cannot maintain itself under its impact. (Sennett, pp. 58–9)

Some observers claimed to see the negative effects of urban individualism as part of an historical process that would ultimately lead to disaster. Oswald Spengler (1880–1936), a German philosopher of history, declared that the enormous "world-cities" of his day were inevitably destroying the spirit of the folk peoples that had built them. In his famous book *The Decline of the West* he argued that this destructive cycle of urban growth and decay had occurred before:

This, then, is the conclusion of the city's history; growing from primitive barter-center to culture-city and at last to world-city, it sacrifices first the blood and soul of its creators to the needs of its majestic evolution, and then the last flower of that growth to the spirit of Civilization—and so, doomed, moves on to final self-destruction. (Sennett, p. 85)

These attacks on urban life perpetuated the centuries-old cultural struggle between the cosmopolitan city of businessmen and the (perhaps imagined) homogeneous country-side of the common folk. The struggle was most extreme in rapidly industrializing Germany. German cities like Berlin had not experienced the same rise and liberation of the merchant classes as had those in Britain, the Netherlands, and France. A generation after Spengler, Germany would turn inward, filled with praise for the traditional values of "the Volk, the People"—meaning the native-born, rural people—and scorn the more diverse, cosmopolitan urbanites (see Chapter 19).

Within this array of sociological, psychological, mythological, and pathological evaluations of the industrial city, many scholars believed that quantitative statistical studies would enable both residents of the industrial city and their observers to understand most clearly the processes through which they were living and to make plans for future directions. Just as accurate measurement and assessment had helped bring in the industrial era, so they helped in its evaluation. Two men—Adna Ferrin Weber, an academic researcher, and Charles Booth, a businessman who wanted to understand the problems of urban poverty in order to combat them—launched quite different, exemplary, quantitative studies of the city that inspired public action as well as further research. Weber's study was global, looking at cities around the world, wherever statistics were available, and found clear correlations between the rate of industrialization, the growth of cities, the strength of immigration, and the increase in standard of living. Booth dispatched researchers throughout London to quantify the conditions of life among the poor. His findings inspired new social movements and legislation.

In the United States, with millions of immigrants streaming into its cities in

Gustave Caillebotte, *Paris, a Rainy Day*, 1876–77. An Impressionist's-eye-view of life in an urban setting. Although a number of studies suggest that the burgeoning urban development of the turn of the century ground down the lives of the poor, for the bourgeoisie, with leisure time on their hands, cities provided a backdrop for pleasure. (*Musée Marmottan, Paris*)

HOW DO WE KNOW?

Quantifying the Conditions of Industrial Urbanization

"The most remarkable social phenomenon of the present century is the concentration of population in cities." These words open Adna Ferrin Weber's The Growth of Cities in the Nineteenth Century, published in 1899, the first comprehensive quantitative study of the subject. A century later it remains an invaluable introduction to the central issues. In the rivalry between city and countryside, Weber generally paid tribute to the role of the city:

> In the last half-century [1848–98], all the agencies of modern civilization have worked together to abolish this rural isolation; the cities have torn down their fortifications, which separated them from the open country; while the railways, the newspaper press, freedom of migration and settlement, etc., cause the spread of the ideas originating in the cities and lift the people of the rural districts out of their state of mental stagnation. Industry is also carried on outside of the cities, so that the medieval distinction between town and country has lost its meaning in the advanced countries. (pp. 7–8)

Apart from their cultural contributions, cities and industry were needed to absorb the surplus growth of rural population. In most of Europe, except France, he writes, "the rural populations, by reason of their continuous increase, produce a surplus which must migrate either to the cities or foreign lands" (p. 67). Without cities and industrial jobs, what would happen to this surplus population? This rhetorical question implied by Weber continues to our own day.

Weber began with a statistical summary and an analysis of levels of urbanization in his own time, and traced it back through the nineteenth century. As part of his research, Weber attempted global coverage and he gathered his data from official government publications as well as unofficial population estimates from around the world. In general, he found industrialization the main reason for city growth. England and Wales, 62 percent urban, were by far the most industrialized and the most urbanized regions on earth. The next closest were Australia, at 42 percent, and various parts of Germany, at about 30 percent. In general, the largest cities were growing fastest. London, the world's largest city in 1890, held 4.2 million people; New York, the second largest, 2.7 million. The least industrialized countries were the least urbanized—below 10 percent—but most of these countries did not maintain statistical records.

In contrast to the gloom of poverty and oppression pictured by Marx and Engels a half century earlier, Weber radiated optimism about the direction of urban life, including increasing levels of longevity and personal comfort. Describing conditions that only the wealthiest could enjoy, he wrote:

> Consider the conveniences at the disposal of the fin de siècle [end of the century] housewife: a house with a good part of the old-fashioned portable furniture built into it, e.g., china cabinets, refrigerators, wardrobes, sideboards, cheval glasses [full-length, swivel mirrors], bath tubs, etc.; electric lights, telephones and electric buttons in every room, automatic burglar alarms, etc. … [Weber then quotes another urban advocate:] Thus has vanished the necessity for drawing water, hewing wood, keeping a cow, churning, laundering clothes, cleaning house, beating carpets, and very much of the rest of the onerous duties of housekeeping, as our mothers knew it. (pp. 218–20)

A judicious scholar, Weber did not omit the many negative aspects of city life at the end of the nineteenth century. Although death rates in the city had been declining steadily, urban death rates in 1899 remained higher than rural ones in most countries. In one of the worst examples, during the decade 1880–90, when the expected length of life at birth for all of England and Wales was forty-seven years, in Manchester, one of the greatest centers of the early industrial revolution, it was twenty-nine. Industrialization exacted its costs. Nevertheless, Weber reviewed the public health measures such as water and sewage systems and the provision of clinics that had already been effective in other places, strongly advocated more of them, and remained optimistic about the urban future—if urbanites could cooperate for the common good.

Weber's pioneering statistical work gives us one flavor of industrial urbanization at the end of the nineteenth-century. Charles Booth (1840–1916) gives quite another. Booth led a team of researchers in London, which produced the seventeen volumes of Life and Labour of the People in London. Between 1886 and 1903, Booth and his colleagues systematically visited thousands of homes throughout London, interviewing workers to discover how the working people of the metropolis labored and lived. They concentrated their efforts in East London, the most industrialized, and most distressed, area of the city. The researchers asked questions about such critical issues as occupations, levels of income and consumption, housing size and quality, quantity and quality of amenities. They began with these statistical questions and then proceeded to qualitative discussion of the neighborhoods and their character. They concluded by asking what was being done, and what could be done, to improve conditions, especially through religious institutions.

- For Weber and for Booth, what was the relationship between formal, quantitative study of the city, and action to deal with its problems?
- How might the global research of Weber be integrated with the local, community research of Booth? How might the research of one influence the research of the other?
- Based on other readings from this chapter, what, if anything, is surprising about the research findings of Weber and Booth?

Guaranty Building in Buffalo, New York, designed by Louis Henry Sullivan, 1894–96. Sullivan's designs for steel-frame construction of large buildings—made possible because steel was now readily available and the elevator had been invented—were the forerunners of today's skyscrapers. A glance at the skyline of any large American or European city will confirm that Sullivan greatly influenced twentieth-century architecture, particularly in the United States. Sullivan's working principle that form follows function applied to the tall buildings (up to ten stories in the late nineteenth century) that he designed. It was important to maximize the limited space in city centers, and the idea of carrying buildings upward instead of outward met the need.

search of industrial jobs, urban diversity was accepted, even valued, and certainly studied. The "Chicago School of urban ecology" took form about the time of World War I as scholars at the University of Chicago studied their own city, the world's fastest growing industrial metropolis of the day. To some degree, they philosophized and speculated as did the Germans, but, building on studies like those of Weber and Booth, they also launched empirical research into conditions in the city. They studied neighborhoods within the city as well as the metropolis as a whole.

The Chicago School argued that urbanites did not live their lives downtown, as so many previous scholars had implied, but in local neighborhoods, each of which had its own characteristics. Within these neighborhoods, people's lives were not so disconnected, isolated, or alienated as they might appear superficially. At the end of the day, most people went back to their own homes in their own neighborhoods, places where they had a strong sense of self and community. The variety of social and economic lifestyles multiplied with the size of the city and the diversity of its functions. Neighborhoods reflected this diversity.

A comprehensive perspective on the city would have to take account of neighborhoods as well as business districts. These commercial areas themselves were quickly increasing in size, complexity, and facilities. By the 1870s, department stores, coffeehouses, pubs, and restaurants had added urbanity to the central business district, attracting retail shoppers, window shoppers, and people with some leisure time. Theaters, concert houses, museums, the press and publishing houses, libraries, clubs, and a multitude of new voluntary associations provided culture and entertainment. They also created a "public sphere"—a setting in which citizens form and circulate their most influential civic ideas, goals, and aspirations. Here was the modern analogue of the ancient Greek *agora*.

A new transportation system made possible this specialization of commercial, cultural, industrial, and residential neighborhoods within the city. London opened its first underground railway system in 1863, the first major subway system in the world, and others followed. From the 1870s, commuter railways began to service new suburbs, and electric trolleys came into service after 1885. The availability of steel at commercial prices made possible the construction of skyscrapers, and the invention of elevators made them accessible. The first skyscrapers rose in the 1880s, beginning with ten-story buildings in Chicago.

Urban Planning: The Middle Ground of Optimists and Pessimists

Both optimists like Weber and pessimists (or realists) like Booth agreed that the industrial city had serious problems, and both agreed that serious planning was necessary to cope with them. Town planning as a profession was born. One of the central problems of the industrializing city of the early nineteenth century was crowding. Poor ventilation, inadequate sanitation, unclean water, alienation from nature, and poor health—especially tuberculosis—resulted as densities in urban cores reached, and even surpassed, 100,000 people per square mile. By the last decades of the century the electric trolley cars and commuter railways offered the means to suburbanize, and the city expanded in area as never before. At first the densities in the center did not appear to diminish, for the stream of new immigrants to the city matched and even exceeded those who were suburbanizing.

By the late 1800s, town planners began seeking comprehensive solutions to the new problem: How to provide space for population increase, allow for geographical expansion, yet continue to provide green space, while fostering participation in both the local community and the metropolis as a whole? The British reformer Ebenezer Howard (1850–1928) provided one of the first proposals in his book *Tomorrow: A Peaceful Path to Real Reform* (1898), later revised and reissued as *Garden Cities of Tomorrow* (1902). Howard's schematic plan for a "Group of Slumless Smokeless Cities" illustrates his provocative concept of a region of about 250,000 people on 66,000 acres. This would be far too miniature to cope with the problems of a London or a New York. Its intense control over the planning process also demanded political decisions that might not be possible within a participatory democracy. Nevertheless, the **garden city** concept of a core city ringed by separate suburbs, each set in a green belt, linked to one another by rapid transit, provided provocative, creative, somewhat utopian thinking for the new urban problems dawning with the new century.

garden city A planned town combining work, residential, agricultural, and recreational facilities, and surrounded by a rural belt.

THE INDUSTRIAL REVOLUTION
WHAT DIFFERENCE DOES IT MAKE?

By the beginning of the twentieth century, the industrial revolution had brought unprecedented wealth and power to those who had mastered its technologies—especially the rulers and elites of the nations of Western Europe and the United States. Applying inanimate power, where previously there had been only humans and animals, had brought new productivity. Agriculture changed first, through enclosures and changing agricultural practices, becoming both more intensive and more extensive, so that fewer farmers could feed more people, freeing—and forcing—many of their fellow workers to leave their farms for urban, industrial jobs. In the cities, steam power and later electrical power enabled factories and the new goods they produced to multiply. Families were restructured in the new urban, industrial settings, with changing relationships between husbands and wives, and more formal schooling for children. Women raised their voices, demanding an equality that they had felt on the family farm and were in danger of losing on the factory floor and in the urban household, with its smaller family groups, greater longevity, and proportionately fewer years that parents spent in raising children. Railway track and steamship lines girdled the earth, and the oceans were connected by canals. Electricity lit up the night, provided the bright lights of the city, powered telephones and telegraphs, and supplied energy to factories and homes in remote areas. With a feeling of self-satisfied triumphalism, the masters of this industrializing world conquered much of the land surface of the world and made it their colonial possession, thus bringing remote areas into the web of the industrial world, whether they wished to be there or not.

In the industrialized countries, the earlier years of poverty, insecurity, filth, and high death rates for industrial workers seemed to be passing as increasing productivity provided more material benefits, unions provided representation, and governments began to legislate in their favor—although the battles for workers' welfare were far from over. Antagonism between captains of industry and their workers continued. New kinds of social relationships formed among industrial workers as they arrived in new urban neighborhoods, with opportunities and constraints quite different from those they had known in their rural homes. They were living in a world transformed and now they were transforming themselves by building new kinds of communities along with their neighbors, friends, and co-workers.

Millions of migrants were on the move, from village to city, from country to country, and from continent to continent. Most traveled as free immigrants, but almost ten million people from poorer countries traveled as indentured laborers to supply the still-flourishing plantations of the world in the aftermath of the abolition of slavery.

The condition of many of the "free" migrants, too, was often precarious. All of these groups formed new kinds of communities in their new homes. The study of sociology was born and flourished.

The industrial revolution restructured the world profoundly, as thoroughly as the agricultural revolution had done some five thousand years earlier. Today we speak of living in a post-industrial world. Our sources of energy, our means of transportation and communication, our international and intercontinental connectivity, our cities, our political institutions, our levels of technical and professional education, our family and gender relationships are in many respects different from those at the height of the industrial revolution, yet they are all built on the transformations of that era. Those of us who live in countries that went through the industrial revolution as it unfolded still live with its infrastructure. Those of us who live in countries that did not directly experience the full weight of that revolution—in large parts of Africa and Asia, in particular—are now trying to understand what parts of that revolution we must recreate in order to cope with the modern world, and what parts we may "leapfrog," finding a new way of achieving some of the benefits of that revolution without going directly through it; establishing networks of cell phone communication, for example, and using that technology, without ever establishing a network of land lines, with all of their infrastructure and expense. While one group is emerging from the industrial revolution, another may be attempting to bypass it.

Review Questions

In answering the first five questions, you may wish to specify different perspectives for different countries and time periods.

- What would you identify as the key social changes introduced by the industrial revolution?
- To what degree do you see rural people benefiting or losing out as a result of the industrial revolution?
- How are industrialization, urbanization, and immigration related to one another?
- In which ways do you see women benefiting from the industrial revolution? In which ways to you see them losing out?
- What were the new political problems raised by the industrial revolution?
- To what degree do you think we can consider the world today as still living in a period of industrial revolution? To what degree do you think that period is past?

Suggested Readings

PRINCIPAL SOURCES

Adas, Michael, ed. *Islamic and European Expansion* (Philadelphia: Temple University Press, 1993). Excellent anthology of historiographical articles that introduce modern world history. Several articles on the period of the industrial revolution and its effects on men and women.

Headrick, Daniel R. *The Tools of Empire* (New York: Oxford University Press, 1981). The industrial revolution gave to Europeans the tools to create empire: weapons, steamships, quinine.

Marx, Karl and Frederick Engels. *The Communist Manifesto* (New York: International Publishers, 1948). The great critique of the evils of industrial capitalism and a revolutionary agenda to overthrow it.

Stearns, Peter N. *The Industrial Revolution in World History* (Boulder, CO: Westview Press, 1993). Excellent introduction to the background, development, and significance of the industrial revolution in global scope and historical time depth.

Thompson, E.P. *The Making of the English Working Class* (New York: Vintage, 1966). Thompson taught us to see the working class not only in Marxist terms but also in cultural terms, to understand their lives as more than just revolutionary fighters.

ADDITIONAL SOURCES

Andrea, Alfred and James Overfield, eds. *The Human Record*, Vol. 2 (Boston: Houghton Mifflin, 3rd ed., 1998). Excellent anthology for world history.

Bairoch, Paul. *Cities and Economic Development*, trans. by Christopher Braider (Chicago: University of Chicago Press, 1988). Heavily quantitative assessment of cities' role in economic development.

Bell, Susan Groag and Karen M. Offen, eds. *Women, the Family, and Freedom: The Debate in Documents, Vol. 1, 1750–1880* (Stanford: Stanford University Press, 1985). Excellent selection of documents on the feminist movement, with insightful commentary.

Braudel, Fernand. *Civilization and Capitalism 15th–18th Century: The Perspective of the World*, trans. by Sian Reynolds (New York: Harper and Row, 1984). Excellent, sweeping background to the industrial revolution.

Davis, Lance E. and Robert A. Huttenback. *Mammon and the Pursuit of Empire* (New York: Cambridge University Press, 1989). Stresses the importance of economic interests, private and public, in the creation of empire.

Engels, Friedrich. *The Condition of the Working Class in England*, trans. by W.O. Henderson and W.H. Chaloner (Stanford: Stanford University Press, 1968). THE explication of the horrors of early industrialization in England, written by a young businessman who became a communist because of what he saw with his own eyes.

——. *The Origins of the Family, Private Property, and the State*, ed. by Eleanor Burke Leacock (New York: International Publishers, 1973). Condemns the contemporary (1884) status of women and urges fundamental restructuring.

Hobsbawm, Eric. *The Age of Capital 1848–1875* (New York: Vintage Books, 1975). This series by Hobsbawm provides an excellent overview of the period of the industrial revolution. Global, but strongest on Europe. Critical of capitalism.

——. *The Age of Empire 1875–1914* (New York: Vintage, 1987).

Kennedy, Paul. *The Rise and Fall of the Great Powers* (New York: Random House, 1987). Great empires since 1500 have been built and preserved by careful attention to the balance between guns and butter, military expenditure and a thriving civilian economy.

Lenin, V.I. *Imperialism, the Highest Stage of Capitalism* (Peking: Foreign Languages Press, 1965). The classic view that industrial nations seek empires as marketplaces for buying raw materials and selling finished products because home markets alone are insufficient.

Perrot, Michelle. *Workers on Strike; France, 1871–1890*, trans. by Chris Turner with Erica Carter and Claire Laudet (Leamington Spa: Berg, 1987). Useful study of labor organization in industrial France.

Ramabai Sarasvati, Pandita. *Pandita Ramabai's American Encounter: The Peoples of the United States (1889)* trans. and ed. by Meera Kosambi (Bloomington: University of Indiana Press, 2003). A rare travelogue by an Indian woman, concerned with economic, social, and political development in America with special attention to women's progress.

Revel, Jacques and Lynn Hunt, eds. *Histories: French Constructions of the Past*, trans. by Arthur Goldhammer *et al.* (New York: New York Press, 1995). How French historians understand the significance of their nation's history. New interpretations for new times.

Sennett, Richard, ed. *Classic Essays on the Culture of Cities* (Englewood Cliffs: Prentice Hall, 1969). An excellent selection of classical sociological essays.

Wallerstein, Immanuel. *The Modern World-system 1: Capitalist Agriculture and the Origins of the European World-economy in the Sixteenth Century* (San Diego: Academic Press, 1974). The fullest exposition of the theory of core-periphery exploitative development, with Europe and the US as the core and Asia, Africa, and Latin America as the periphery.

Weber, Adina Ferrin. *The Growth of Cities in the Nineteenth Century: A Study in Statistics* (Ithaca: Cornell University Press, 1963). A dissertation that became a key to the quantitative understanding of urban growth worldwide.

World History Documents CD-ROM

19.1 Benjamin Disraeli: *Sybil* (1845)
19.2 Women Miners in the English Coal Pits
19.3 Sadler Report: Child Labor
19.4 Andrew Ure: *A Defense of the Factory System* (1835)
19.5 The Chartist Demands (1838)
19.6 Luddism: An Assault on Technology
19.7 Robert Owen: *Utopian Socialism* (1816)
19.8 Karl Marx and Friedrich Engels

NATIONALISM, IMPERIALISM, AND RESISTANCE

COMPETITION AMONG INDUSTRIAL POWERS 1650–1914

KEY TOPICS

- Nationalism
- The Quest for Empire
- Africa, 1652–1912
- Gender Relationships in Colonization
- Anti-Colonial Revolts, 1857–1914
- Japan: from Isolation to Equality, 1867–1914
- Nationalism and Imperialism: What Difference Do They Make?

NATIONALISM

The political and industrial revolutions of the seventeenth, eighteenth, and nineteenth centuries gave birth to modern nationalism, a commitment to building up the nation as a central part of the identity of the citizen and as a powerful force in world affairs. Like the ideals of democracy and the productivity of the industrial revolution, the belief in nationalism has continued to shape the world to this day.

The French Revolution, the Napoleonic Wars, and Nationalism

The ideology and actions of the French Revolution gave a new definition to the concept of the nation and introduced new political and cultural loyalties. In 1789, the members of the National Assembly, declaring themselves "the representatives of the people of France," proclaimed in the *Declaration of the Rights of Man and the Citizen*: "The source of all sovereignty is located essentially in the nation; no body, no individual can exercise authority which does not emanate from it expressly." This Declaration proclaimed that the people of France were forging a social contract, swearing allegiance not to a ruler, religion, or language/ethnic group but to all the people of the nation—a common political group. The Declaration seemed to take for granted the primordial elements of French nationality—a common language, history, geography, and vision for the future. It ratified a new national identity for France. The French state took to itself new, unprecedented powers. It had the authority to tax in the name of the nation, the very authority that Louis XVI had sought for himself when he had convened the Estates General. Asserting the authority to draft virtually the entire adult male population of the country for the army in the new *levée en masse*, France conscripted an army numbering hundreds of thousands. Backed by this army, France swept across Europe between 1791 and 1815, not only to conquer others but also to promote its idea of nationalism. French armies imposed their imperial governments on the nations they conquered, and, after the promulgation of the Napoleonic Code in 1804, they imposed their legal system as well. The new message seemed

Opposite **Kobaysgu Kiyochika, The Sino-Japanese War in Korea, 1894. Engraving.** Japanese forces are shown firing down on their Korean enemy as a journalist makes notes in the foreground. (*Victoria & Albert Museum, London*)

clear: A people organized under a national banner of its own making could act with unprecedented power to tax, to fight, to legislate, to conquer, and to rule.

French nationalism and French military power evoked the nationalism of other countries in response, especially in Britain and Russia. Russia's nationalism expressed itself in the power to resist, to stage a strategic retreat until Napoleon's French army was mired, frozen, and starved in the depths of Russia's winter, and then to fight back. The British, by contrast, mobilized their navy and army immediately to confront the French and ultimately to prevail. The wealth generated by the early stages of its industrial revolution enabled Britain to finance these armed struggles.

These wars demonstrated that nations could mobilize powerful forces militarily, economically, and politically. Disorganized nations, on the other hand, lay open to conquest. At least in part as a response to the power that France demonstrated in its Napoleonic Wars, new nations asserted their independence in many regions of the

AT A GLANCE: THE WORLD BEYOND THE INDUSTRIALIZED WEST

DATE	OTTOMAN EMPIRE	INDIA, S-E ASIA & CHINA	AFRICA
1800		■ Sir Stamford Raffles establishes Singapore for the British (1819) ■ Shaka seizes leadership of the Zulu kingdom near the Cape Colony (1816)	■ British forces drive Napoleon from Egypt (1801); Muhammad Ali assumes rule (1807)
1820	■ Greece wins independence; Serbia, Wallachia, and Moldavia gain autonomy (1829) ■ French gain control of Algeria from empire (1830) ■ Muhammad Ali renders Egypt effectively independent (1832)	■ Java War, Dutch vs. Indonesians (1825–30) ■ Dutch introduce cultivation system in Indonesia (1830) ■ First Opium War (1839–42): China cedes Hong Kong to the British	■ Great Trek north by the Boers (Afrikaners) (1834–41) ■ French invade Algeria (1830); warfare with al-Qadir (1841)
1840	■ Crimean War (1853–4) ■ Westernization encouraged in the Hatt-i Humayun edict (1856)	■ Taiping Rebellion begins (1850); suppressed 1864 ■ "First War for National Independence" in India (1857) ■ Russians seize Amur River region (1858) ■ Second Opium War (1856–60): Beijing occupied by French and British	■ David Livingstone lands along Angola coast for first African expedition (1841)
1860	■ Young Turks go into exile (1876) ■ Russian attack through the Balkans reaches Istanbul (1877)	■ Russians seize Maritime Provinces (1860) and Ili valley in Turkestan (1871–81)	■ Suez Canal opens (1869) ■ Diamonds and gold discovered in the Cape Colony region ■ Egyptian khedive forced to add European representatives to his cabinet (1878)
1880		■ France seizes all of Indochina (1883–93) ■ Germany annexes Eastern New Guinea and the Marshall and Solomon Islands (1880s) ■ Japan defeats China in warfare (1894–5) ■ Boxer Rebellion (1898–1900) ■ Ethiopia defeats Italian forces at Adowa (1896)	■ Bismarck's Berlin Convention apportions Africa among competing powers (1884) ■ General Kitchener retakes Sudan in Battle of Omdurman (1898) ■ Rhodesia (now Zimbabwe and Zambia) named after Cecil John Rhodes (1898) ■ Boer War (1899–1902)
1900	■ Italy takes Libya from weakened empire (1911)	■ India's first steel mill at Jamshedpur, Bihar (1911) ■ Subcontinent has 35,000 miles of railroad track (1914)	■ Maji-Maji revolt against German rule in Tanganyika (1905–07) ■ Belgian Parliament takes over control of the Congo (1908) ■ British form Union of South Africa (1910) ■ Natives Land Act closes 87 percent of South African land to African ownership (1913)

world in the early nineteenth century. In the Balkans, Greece achieved its independence from the Ottoman Empire in 1829, and other break-away regions soon followed. The regions of South America claimed their independence of Spain and Portugal. Canada asserted its unity and its autonomy from Britain. Italy and Germany successfully created unified countries out of disparate petty states. And the United States survived a civil war to re-assert its unity as a powerful, expanding nation.

The Periphery of Western Europe

Nationalists—people who asserted their wish and responsibility to create, strengthen, and consolidate their nations—were most active on the periphery of western Europe. In southeastern Europe, revolts in the Balkans broke out from 1815 onward in the name of individual nationalities. The first successful revolt was that of the Greek peoples against the Ottoman Empire. Greece won its independence in 1829 with the backing of military forces dispatched by Britain, France, and Russia. At the same time, other Ottoman territories also gained autonomy: Serbia, Wallachia and Moldavia in present-day Romania, and Egypt. The western European powers supported these aggressive nationalisms in the Balkans and northeast Africa because they diminished the power of the Ottoman Empire while increasing their own leverage within the regions.

Nationalism always has two faces. As a positive force, it promises to empower the masses of a nation with freedom and evoke their collective participation in building new futures. As a negative force, it threatens to compel the masses to serve the state and to turn one nation against another in destructive warfare. The Balkans have seen both these faces. Some nationalist movements won independence and the possibility of greater freedom and creativity. On the other hand, a century of simmering nationalism throughout the region climaxed in 1914 when a Serbian nationalist assassinated the Crown Prince of Austria-Hungary in Sarajevo after the Emperor Franz Joseph annexed Bosnia—a territory Serbia desired for itself—in 1908. The major powers of Europe soon took sides, and World War I began (see Chapter 19). And, as we shall see in Chapter 24, nationalism in the Balkans continues today as a potent and often violent force.

In Chapter 16 we noted the revolutions in Latin America. Continent-wide revolts broke down into individual national movements, undermining the unifying visions of Simón Bolívar and José de San Martín. Nationalism did not represent everyone within Latin America. Although nationalists spoke in the name of "the people," they mostly represented specific groups: lawyers, journalists, teachers, and military officials. Nationalism in South America was a "top-down" movement of elites.

In Canada, the Report to the British government by the Earl of Durham in 1839 led to the unification of mostly English-speaking Upper Canada, today's Ontario, with mostly French-speaking Lower Canada, today's Quebec. Lord Durham urged the institution of responsible government over domestic affairs and the rapid development of railways and canals to consolidate the nation. The British Government quickly accepted and implemented the Durham Report. In 1867, Britain established the Dominion of Canada, increasing the scope of parliamentary democracy and adding the eastern maritime provinces to the core of Quebec and Ontario. Tensions between the British and French regions of Canada diminished, but they have not disappeared. Nevertheless, Canadian nationalism has continued to prevail over regionalism.

The United States, a land of immigrants from its inception, had established itself as a nation based on an oath binding all of its diverse citizens to the common good. Americans declared in their Constitution:

We, the People of the United States, in Order to form a more perfect Union, establish Justice, insure domestic Tranquility, provide for the common defence, promote the general Welfare, and secure the blessings of Liberty to ourselves and our Posterity, do ordain and establish this Constitution for the United States of America.

With this Constitution the United States declared that the nation was not necessarily an array of people who shared a common history, geography, language, race, ethnicity, religion, and language. A nation could be formed on the basis of a new vision of the present and future and adherence to a common law.

Foreign observers, like Alexis de Tocqueville (1805–59), commented on the newness of America and its lack of history. A substantial proportion of America's institutions, and of its population, was drawn from the British Isles, but immigrants came from all over the world. Some were excluded from full citizenship, including African-American slaves, Native American Indians, and women. But the pattern for future inclusion was also being set. Many, but not all, new immigrants could join this nation, and, after slaves were freed, so could they, although racism remained a powerful force. Native Americans remained torn between allegiances to Indian nations and the American nation. Despite these divisions, the American Constitution illustrated the degree to which a nation was constituted by the will of its people, and especially of its leaders, rather than by primordial historical legacies.

In 1861, the American nation was faced with a struggle for survival when the eleven Confederate States of America seceded from the Union. The Confederacy claimed greater rights for constituent states, especially the right to sanction slavery, and it favored agrarian rather than industrial economic policies. Some 500,000 men were killed in the Civil War that followed. Immediately following the war, the victorious central government instituted generous policies favoring reconciliation (often at the expense of the recently freed ex-slaves), although later these policies became more punitive. After the war, with unity secure, and Northern business leaders asserting great powers, the industrial and economic expansion of the United States set a pace exceeding that of any other nation.

Italy and Germany

In the heart of Europe, nationalism grew in hard soil. The great powers of Austria, Prussia, Russia, France, and Britain suppressed new national uprisings by peoples within their empires. At their meeting to draft the peace settlements at the Congress of Vienna in 1814–15 after the Napoleonic Wars, they set limits on national movements in central Europe. Led by Prince Clemens von Metternich (1773–1859), foreign minister of Austria, conservative leaders of the major European powers were successful in quelling powerful nationalistic uprisings in Poland, Prussia, Italy, and Hungary between 1846 and 1849. (Belgium did gain national independence, from the Dutch, in 1830.) In western Europe, Irish nationalism became increasingly important as the Irish wanted to abrogate the Act of Union of 1801 that made Ireland a part of Great Britain and to preserve the Gaelic language. Under the leadership of Daniel O'Connell, Young Ireland organized hundreds of thousands of people until the British arrested him on conspiracy charges. Only in the 1850s did nationalism win major victories in lands under these empires. Then Italy and Germany began successfully to unite their several divided regions to form new nations. In each country, cultural nationalism preceded political mobilization.

Before 1870, neither Italy nor Germany existed as the unified nations we know today. Each was divided up into many petty states under the control of different rulers. In Italy, the largest single state was the kingdom of Sardinia-Piedmont, but other states

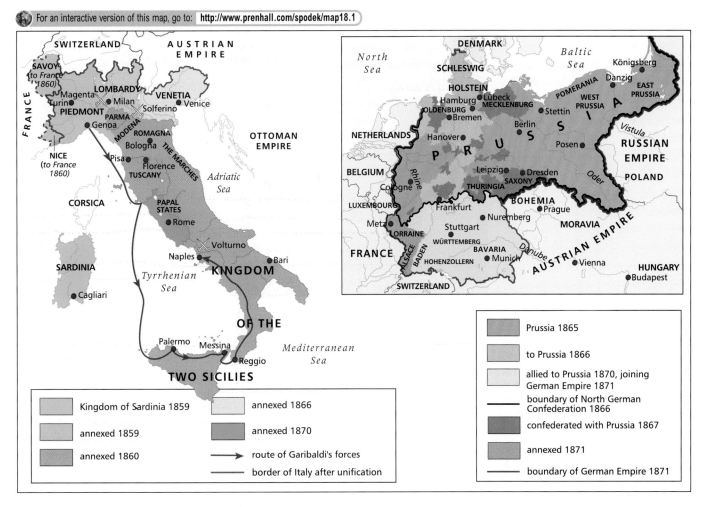

For an interactive version of this map, go to: **http://www.prenhall.com/spodek/map18.1**

The unification of Italy and Germany.
The middle years of the nineteenth century saw popular forces drawing together the disparate territories of central Europe into modern nation states. In Germany the political, military, and economic strength of Prussia had been growing for over two centuries, and Bismarck's wars with Denmark (1864), Austria (1866), and France (1870) eventually secured the union. In Italy the expansion of Piedmont–Sardinia into Lombardy, Venetia, and Rome, and Garibaldi's march through the south, united the nation.

were controlled by other rulers. The area around Venice was controlled by Austria, and the region around Rome by the pope. Most of the small states of Germany had been included within Charlemagne's empire, founded in 800 C.E., and then within its successor institution, the Holy Roman Empire. Each of these states had its own ruler and even its own system of government. The largest, Austria, was in itself a significant state. The smallest had only a few thousand inhabitants. In addition, to the east lay Prussia, a powerful state that was beginning to think of itself as the leader of the German-speaking peoples.

As nation-states formed in western Europe and demonstrated the economic, political, military, and cultural power that came from unity, regional leaders in Italy and Germany also sought unification for themselves. A common language and clearly demarcated geographical borders were considered vital elements in national unity, and were helpful to Italy in consolidating its peninsular nation. Germany, however, lacked clear natural geographic boundaries and faced the question as to which German-speaking states would be included within the new country and which would be excluded.

Giuseppe Mazzini (1805–72) provided a prophetic vision for Italy. In 1831 he founded Young Italy, a secret association urging Italian unification and independence from foreign control by the French, Austrians, and Spanish. Mazzini's *On the Duties of Man* expressed his nationalistic, democratic, and humanistic views:

Anon., **Giuseppe Garibaldi meets Victor Emmanuel II, King of Sardinia, c. 1860.** Several different leaders contributed to the creation of the modern nation of Italy. Garibaldi led armed "red shirts" and freed southern Italy to join the Italian nation. The core of the new Italy was the Kingdom of Sardinia-Piedmont under King Victor Emmanuel II.

O my brothers, love your Country! Our country is our Home, the House that God has given us, placing therein a numerous family that loves us, and whom we love; a family with whom we sympathize more readily, and whom we understand more quickly, than we do others; and which, from its being centred round a given spot, and from the homogeneous nature of its elements, is adapted to a special branch of activity. (Columbia University, p. 570)

When Mazzini's cultural view was joined to the political organization of **Camillo Cavour** (1810–61), prime minister of Sardinia-Piedmont in 1852 under **King Victor Emmanuel II**, the nationalist movement was poised for political victory. Cavour formed a brief alliance with Napoleon III of France against Austria. This enabled the king to annex Lombardy. The adjacent regions of Parma, Modena, and Tuscany joined by plebiscite, in which the population could either agree or disagree to accept a decree issued by their rulers. In 1860, the popular mercenary Giuseppe Garibaldi (1807–82) led 1150 followers, wearing red shirts, into the south Italian Kingdom of the Two Sicilies, which collapsed and subsequently also joined Piedmont after a plebiscite. Venetia, the region around Venice, was added after a war in which Italy allied with Prussia against Austria. Finally, Rome was annexed in 1870 after French troops were withdrawn to fight against Prussia. Through the various contributions of Mazzini, Cavour, Garibaldi, Victor Emmanuel II, Napoleon III, war, and popular votes, Italy had become a unified nation.

At about the same time, prime minister Otto von Bismarck of Prussia (1815–98) was unifying the multitude of small German states

French cartoon portraying Prince Otto Eduard Leopold von Bismarck, Prime Minister of Prussia, 1870. Political figures have traditionally been treated irreverently by cartoonists, but this caricature is savage. The French were outraged by Bismarck's ambitions to get the Prussian prince Leopold on to the Spanish throne—a key factor in the war between the two countries.

HOW DO WE KNOW?

What is Nationalism?

For most people in today's world, nationality is an important part of personal identity, and historians find nationalism to be a central concern of the past two centuries. Some stress the significance of particular forms of nationalism, others argue that national identity is, and can be, constantly shaped and reshaped. In this sense historians of national identity are similar to historians of gender identity: They not only wish to understand where we have been, they also want to use these explorations of the past as a means to search for alternative futures.

One of the first historians and philosophers of nationalism, the Frenchman Joseph-Ernest Renan (1823–92), captured the twofold nature of nationalism in his 1882 lecture "What is a Nation?" It looks both backward and forward in creating a unified vision. Nationalism requires a fundamental shared history in the lives of the citizens, but the past alone is not enough for constructing a nation. That task requires also a vision of what the nation might become and a political commitment to constructing such a future. More dramatically, in considering the nation as a "spiritual principle," Renan asserted his belief that in his time nationalism was displacing religion as a central concern:

A nation is a spiritual principle, the outcome of the profound complications of history; it is a spiritual family not a group determined by the shape of the earth. We have now seen what things are not [by themselves] adequate for the creation of such a spiritual principle, namely, race, language, material interest, religious affinities, geography, and military necessity. What [else] then is required? …

A nation is therefore a large-scale solidarity, constituted by the feeling of the sacrifices that one has made in the past and of those that one is prepared to make in the future. It presupposes a past; it is summarized, however, in the present by a tangible fact, namely, consent, the clearly expressed desire to continue a common life.

More recently, anthropologist Benedict Anderson has referred to the nation as an "imagined political community," stressing the importance of human imagination, creativity, and persuasion—all expressed through the public media—as the means by which the idea of the nation is created, refined, and disseminated. "It is imagined because the members of even the smallest nation will never know most of their fellow-members, meet them, or even hear of them, yet in the minds of each lives the image of their communion" (Anderson, p. 15). For Anderson, as for Renan, the nation is not so much an entity existing in nature as it is an institution created by leaders who are successful in gaining acceptance for their idea of the nation.

In addition to Renan's "spiritual principle," modern nationalism comprises two additional elements. First, at least since the French Revolution, the modern nation exists in a world of other nations, frequently competitive with one another. To some degree, each nation defines itself in its relationship with others. Second, at least since the French Revolution and the industrial revolution, the nation has been the vehicle for the spread of trade networks and capitalism throughout the world. The significance of the nation in achieving economic goals has given great power to national identity.

- How well does Renan's concept of the nation as a "spiritual family" fit the nationalism expressed in the American Constitution? and the nationalism of the various Italian and German spokesmen?
- How might a nation express its desire to continue a common life? How might it reject that desire?
- How does Renan's concept of a "spiritual family" compare with Anderson's idea of an "imagined community?" Are they actually referring to the same relationship but with different words, or are their concepts different?

into a single German nation under William I (King of Prussia 1861–88, Emperor of Germany 1871–88). The cultural basis of German unity was solidly established. The brothers Jakob and Wilhelm Grimm, founders of the modern science of linguistics, analyzed the various dialects of German and collected fairy tales from all parts of the region, publishing them in 1812 as a unifying folklore for the nation. A series of philosophers and historians, including J.G. von Herder (1744–1803), J.G. Fichte (1762–1814), Georg Wilhelm Friedrich Hegel (1770–1831), Leopold von Ranke (1795–1886), and Heinrich von Treitschke (1834–96), urged Germany to fulfill its natural destiny, just as Mazzini had done in Italy.

From 1828 a customs union, *zollverein*, that created a free trade area throughout many of the German states, had already established an economic foundation for unification. Increasing industrialization provided the financial and military underpinnings for it. Now Bismarck instituted a policy of "Blood and Iron." Two wars were the key. In 1866, Bismarck defeated Austria and formed the North German Confederation, leaving Austria out. In 1871, he defeated France, annexing Alsace and Lorraine. In light of these victories the southern states of Germany—Bavaria, Baden, and Württemberg—also joined the newly formed nation.

The Rise of Zionism in Europe

One of the last of the nationalist movements to arise in nineteenth-century Europe was Zionism, the movement to recreate a Jewish homeland. Jews had been dispersed into Europe even during the time of the Roman Empire. By the beginning of the twentieth century, their principal European locations were in Poland, Russia, and Ukraine. Through the centuries Jews had prayed for a return to Zion, their ancestral homeland in modern Israel. In the second half of the nineteenth century, under the influence of various European nationalist movements, some philosophers proposed going beyond prayer. They looked forward to the establishment of a political state.

The move from prayer to political organization took concrete form at the very end of the nineteenth century. Suffering from pogroms in the Russian Empire and discrimination in much of the Austro-Hungarian Empire, Jews felt increasingly persecuted. On assignment in Paris to report on the trial of Alfred Dreyfus, a Jewish officer in the French army unjustly accused of treason, the Viennese Jewish journalist Theodor Herzl (1860–1904) encountered fierce anti-Semitism. Shocked to find such ethnic and religious hatred in the capital of the liberal world, where Jews had gained citizenship during the French Revolution, Herzl concluded that Jews could be free, independent, and safe only in a country of their own. In 1897, he founded the Zionist movement. Because Palestine, the goal of most of the early Zionists, was already the home of 600,000 Arabs, Jewish nationalism simultaneously, if unintentionally, took the form of a colonizing movement originating in Europe. Not all Jews embraced Zionism, although as discrimination and persecution increased in the twentieth century, the Zionist dream became an increasingly desirable alternative to remaining in Europe. The consequences of this nationalistic/colonizing effort are traced in Chapter 24.

THE QUEST FOR EMPIRE

The triumph of nationalism, the rise of the modern nation state, was accompanied by fierce and violent competition for power among the new states, especially during, and as a result of, the wars of the French Revolution and the Napoleonic Wars (Chapter 16). Similarly, the emergence of a global capitalist marketplace (Chapter 14) was also based on sharp competition—much of it between joint stock companies backed by their home governments. The industrial revolution (Chapter 17) also led to sharp competition, first between industrialized and non-industrialized countries—such as Britain and India—and later among the new industrialists and their newly industrializing nations. The very first triumph of British cotton textile manufacture over the traditional handicraft spinning industry of India illustrated this competition between industrialized and non-industrialized nations. The British government made sure that the field of competition between its new industrialists and the Indians was inclined in favor of its own nationals. The very first triumph of British cotton textile manufacture over the traditional handicraft spinning industry of India illustrated this unequal competition between industrialized and non-industrialized nations. The British government assisted its industrialists by protecting their infant industries with high tariffs that made the import of Indian textiles very costly. It also allowed the British East India Company to take over large parts of India as a colony and to fix low tariffs there, thus aiding and encouraging the import of British textiles to India. In these colonized regions the British also gained the power to collect taxes. These taxes enriched the British; a portion of the taxes were sent back to Britain thus draining India of a part of its wealth. Similar policies were common between colonizing and colonized countries throughout the world. As a result of their industrial ingenuity and their

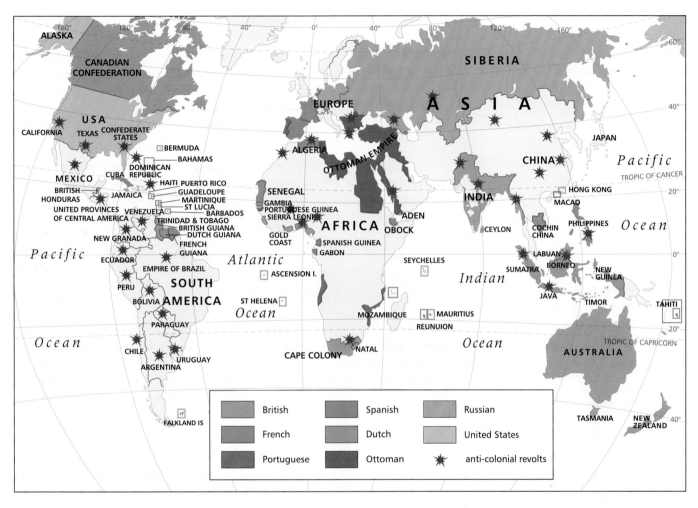

European imperialism 1815–70. By the middle of the nineteenth century, revolutions had brought independence to most of the Americas. With Africa largely impenetrable, European imperialists now focused on Asia. Russia had spread across Siberia to the Pacific, and the United States extended from the Atlantic to the Pacific, while Britain controlled India, South Africa, Australia, and New Zealand. In 1867 Canada achieved "dominion" status, virtual political independence.

political machinations, Europeans increased their share of manufacturing output from 23 percent of the global share in 1750 to 63 percent in 1900. India's, by contrast, plummeted in those same years from 24.5 percent to 1.7; China's from 32.8 percent to 6.2.

As newly industrializing nations began to compete with the British for markets for their finished products and for sources of raw materials another competition opened. At first, Britain stood pre-eminent among the newly industrializing nations, but by the mid-nineteenth century rivals had begun to appear. By the late 1800s, several of them were engaged in this industrial and commercial competition. Mostly the competition was economic, but the wealth of the nation depended in part on the success of the new industrialists, so governments regularly intervened to aid them. It seemed natural that national pride also entered into people's thinking.

Three countries provided the fiercest competition. The United States emerged from its Civil War in 1865 with a powerful industrial base and a rapidly growing immigrant population. In a quest for new land and resources to develop, Americans moved westward by railway across a continent that was abundant in both, removing Indians who blocked their way. By 1900, the US had an industrial base of production that surpassed Britain's. Germany unified its constituent states into a single country under King William I and his chief minister Otto von Bismarck in 1871, and also surpassed Britain in the early years of the twentieth century. In addition, Germany's population at 67 million was almost 50 percent greater than Britain's and was growing faster. France produced only half the industrial output of Britain or Germany, but nevertheless ranked third among European powers.

The greatest competition took place overseas, beyond the borders of Europe, in the quest for imperial power. Empires were not new, of course, but the use of advanced technology and new strategies of financial and economic dominance gave them more power than ever before. By 1914, peoples of Europe and of European ancestry had settled and were ruling, directly or indirectly, 85 percent of the earth's land surface: Canada, the United States, most of Latin America, Siberia, Australia, New Zealand, and substantial parts of South Africa by invasion, settlement, and conquest; most of India, Southeast Asia, and Africa by direct rule over indigenous populations; China by indirect rule. The map below indicates the holdings of each major imperial power in the eastern hemisphere. The British held the most overseas land, and the most people, with their dominant concentration in India, East Africa almost from north to south, large segments of West Africa, and the British settler colonies of Australia and New Zealand. British holdings were so widespread that it was said that "the sun never sets

European empires in 1914. By the beginning of World War I, European imperialism had reached its zenith, with four-fifths of the globe under the direct political control of Europeans or people of European ancestry. Only Antarctica remained unclaimed. Although this power was sustained by technological, naval, and military superiority, insurrections were widespread and increasingly well organized. Imperial trade established a global economic system and spread European cultural values.

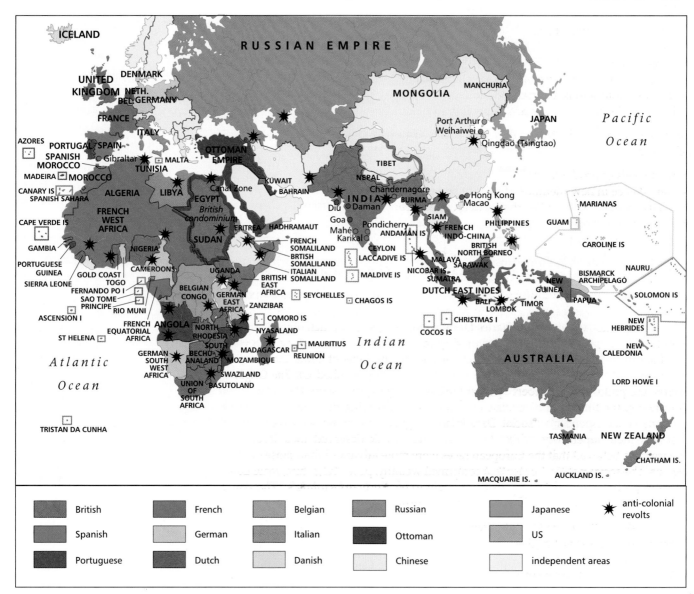

on the British Empire." The French dominated West Africa, beginning with regions directly across the Mediterranean from France itself, and important parts of Southeast Asia.

Many regions of the world were nominally independent, but in fact their economies were controlled by others. Much of Latin America, although politically independent, was dominated internally by elites of European ancestry and externally by European financial investors and their governments, especially by the British. Some states, like Russia and the Ottoman Empire, were dominated in large part by capital from north-western Europe but also, in turn, held their own colonial areas. Northwest Europe and the United States had become the *core* regions in this emerging world system, dominating world economic and political power, while most of the rest of the world, excepting Japan, was incorporated and subordinated into their *periphery*, where economic and political power was subordinated to the core.

The leading states of western Europe had achieved their power through their "dual revolutions," political and industrial. Politically and socially they had achieved, or seemed to be in the process of achieving:

- consolidated nation-states;
- parliamentary democracies;
- bureaucratic administrations;
- freedom of the press, assembly, and religion;
- freedom from wrongful arrest and torture;
- increased levels of literacy and general, public education.

Economically and industrially, they had achieved or seemed to be in the process of achieving:

- high levels of productivity;
- competence in new methods of science and technology;
- relatively high levels of health and of medical care;
- an integrated world economy;
- powerful weaponry;
- high levels of trade and international exchange;
- high levels of economic entrepreneurship and legal protection of property.

Western Europeans, especially Britons, began to define themselves as people who had mastered these qualities, in contrast to the peoples whom they were colonizing and dominating, who lacked them. Charles Darwin (1809–82) shook much of the Christian world when he published *On the Origin of Species* in 1859. In this work he suggested that life developed through chance mechanisms over millions of years that allowed some species to survive over others. Soon after Darwin published *On The Origin of Species*, the philosopher Herbert Spencer (1820–1903) (mis)represented the concept of "survival of the fittest" as a doctrine explaining and justifying the rule by the strong over the weak. Spencer's "social Darwinism" argued that those who were strong deserved their superiority, while those who were weak deserved their inferiority. Spencer also believed that the European races were more advanced than those of other regions. The social-political order that confirmed wealthy, powerful, white, male Europeans in positions of dominance was as it ought to be. Rudyard Kipling's "The White Man's Burden" expressed these beliefs in poetic form.

> Take up the White Man's burden—
> Send forth the best ye breed—
> Go bind your sons to exile
> To serve your captives' need;

To wait in heavy harness,
On fluttered folk and wild—
Your new-caught, sullen peoples,
Half-devil and half-child.

Kipling argued in racial terms that because Europeans were more advanced than others they had an obligation to bring their civilization to those they conquered, although he saw this civilizing mission as a thankless task. Kipling's poem, perhaps naively, perhaps self-righteously, perhaps sarcastically, cites only the moral burdens of colonization without any references to its economic and political profits for the colonizer.

The Ottoman Empire: The "Sick Man of Europe," 1829–76

As the industrializing and colonizing powers of the world built their empires, they cast predatory gazes on the weaknesses of many of the formerly powerful empires around them. The closest geographically, the Ottoman Empire, had been in continuous decline since it lost control of Hungary in 1699. In 1829, the British, French, and Russians gave their support to Greece as it won its independence from the Ottomans, and aided three Balkan states—Serbia, Wallachia, and Moldavia—in gaining recognition as autonomous provinces with limited self-government, although still formally under the Ottoman Empire. In the aftermath of these imperial defeats, Muhammad (Mehemet) Ali seized his opportunity to make Egypt effectively independent of the Ottomans in 1832; the Saud family had already won similar autonomy for parts of Arabia in the early nineteenth century; and the French began their occupation of Algeria in 1830. The Ottoman Empire was unable to hold on to its territories. It had become the "sick man of Europe."

Traditionally the Ottomans had organized people by the millet system, which differentiated subjects by religious communities. Each millet had a religious leader responsible for enforcing its religion's laws and customs and for collecting taxes on behalf of the imperial government. Asserting that sometimes the influence of religion in the empire's organization created religious antagonisms, the Western, industrializing powers, used religious affiliations as an entering wedge in their move to further weaken and dismember the Ottoman Empire. Under these circumstances, different religious groups within the empire looked outward to their co-religionists in other countries for protection, if necessary. The Greek Orthodox community, in particular, looked toward Russia; the Roman Catholics looked to France, and Protestants to Britain. Religious missions from these countries received special privileges within the Ottoman Empire, and often served as bases for trade and intelligence-gathering as well. Foreigners trading within the empire were permitted the right to trial by judges of their own nation. The Ottoman theory and practice of government were quite different from those of western Europe, where the unified nation-state was becoming the norm. In addition, the Ottomans had not kept up with the industrial development of the rest of Europe. In the 1840s Sultan Abdul Mejid enacted the *Tanzimat* (Restructuring) reforms to bring the Ottoman legal code and its social and educational standards into closer conformity with those of western European states, but with very limited success because of internal opposition. The reforms created a new Western-oriented elite that threatened traditional government and its administrative and military officials.

The Crimean War of 1854–6 further revealed the weakness of the Ottoman system. On the north shore of the Black Sea, the major powers of Europe confronted one another in a conflict that tested their abilities both to fight wars and to negotiate diplomatic settlements. The war began as Russia, seeking a warm-water port, probed

Ottoman strength by attacking it in the Crimean peninsula. France and Britain came to the aid of the Ottomans, pushing back the Russian assault and restoring Crimea to the Ottomans. Austria seized this opportunity to occupy Wallachia and Moldavia, and the final peace treaty ending the war recognized both Romania and Serbia as self-governing principalities, free of Ottoman control, and under the protection of other European powers.

In an attempt to remedy its weaknesses, the Ottoman government issued the Hatt-i Humayun edict in 1856. This once again ushered in numerous changes to conform to western European standards, including equality under a common law for all citizens, tax reform, security of property, the end of torture, more honest administration, and greater freedom of the press. The Young Turks, a group of modernizing intellectuals, were delighted, and nationalistic Armenians, Bulgars, Macedonians, and Cretans hoped for greater autonomy. A change of sultan in 1876, however, brought a reverse of all these policies and aspirations. The Young Turks went into exile, and Bulgarian and Armenian nationalists were massacred.

A weak Ottoman Empire left a power vacuum in southeast Europe, which invited continuing foreign intervention and competition. A new Russian attack through the Balkans reached Istanbul itself in 1877. Britain threatened to go to war with Russia, but Bismarck convened an international conference in Berlin in 1878 to resolve the conflict through diplomacy. War was averted for the moment, but tensions ran high. The mixture of Ottoman weakness, aggressive expansionism on the part of other European countries, assertive nationalism in the Balkans, and increasing militarization with increasingly powerful weapons threatened a later, larger war. It arrived in 1914.

Florence Nightingale, Turkey, c. 1854. During the Crimean War "the Lady of the Lamp" established and supervised efficient nursing departments at Scutari and Balaklava. Her unflagging efforts ensured that the mortality rate among the injured was greatly reduced. The effect of her reforms would transform nursing from the realm of menial drudgery into a skilled medical profession with high standards of education.

Southeast Asia and Indonesia, 1795–1880

In Southeast Asia, the colonial competition that had marked the period from 1500 to 1750 continued. The British established a settlement at Penang, Malaya; took Malacca from the Dutch in 1795; and, under Sir Stamford Raffles, established Singapore in 1819 as their major port in the region. In a series of wars, the British took control of Burma and turned it into a major exporter of rice, timber, teak, and oil, and developed the port of Rangoon to handle the trade. Tin was discovered in Malaya, and its rubber plantations became the world's largest producers.

France began its conquest of Indochina in 1859, completing the takeover by 1893, ostensibly to protect French Catholic missionaries. In dislodging Vietnam from China's tributary sphere, the French interrupted a centuries-old relationship. Vietnam's leading products for export were rice and rubber. Germany, entering late into the colonial competition, annexed eastern New Guinea and the Marshall and Solomon Islands in the 1880s.

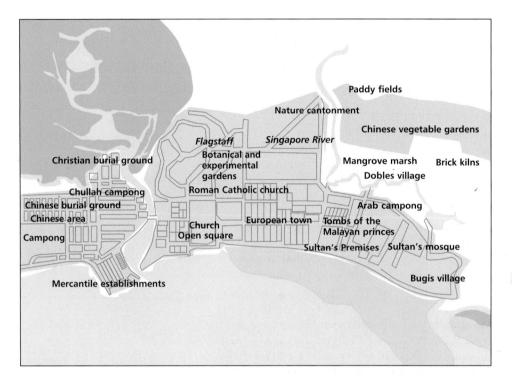

Paddy fields

Nature cantonment

Chinese vegetable gardens

Flagstaff   Singapore River

Christian burial ground

Botanical and experimental gardens

Mangrove marsh   Brick kilns

Dobles village

Chullah campong

Roman Catholic church

Chinese burial ground

Chinese area

Arab campong

Campong

Church   European town   Tombs of the Malayan princes

Open square

Sultan's Premises   Sultan's mosque

Mercantile establishments

Bugis village

A map of the town and environs of Singapore, from an actual survey by G.D. Coleman, 1839. Singapore was not an indigenous town that gradually grew up around a bustling port; it was purposely founded in 1819 on the site of a fishing village by Sir Stamford Raffles, who saw its potential as a trading center. The British actively encouraged immigration to the new port, and divided the thriving city into separate areas for the different ethnic groups that lived and worked there. The divisions can be seen clearly on the map.

Sharing in the expansionist spirit of the times, the Netherlands decided to annex the entire Indonesian archipelago, building on its administrative center at Batavia (Jakarta) in Java and the trading posts it already occupied. The Dutch wished to dissuade other European powers from intruding and to add the profits from rubber, oil, tin, and tobacco from the other islands to those from sugar, coffee, tea, and tobacco from Java. The Dutch ruled through especially high levels of violence and cruelty. The Java War, 1825–30, had many background provocations and finally erupted when the Dutch built a highway through property housing the tomb of a Muslim saint. In five years of brutal combat between the Dutch and Javanese, 15,000 government soldiers were killed, including 8000 Dutch. Some 200,000 Javanese died in the war and in the famine and disease that followed.

In 1830 the Dutch introduced a new, particularly exploitative economic policy called "the cultivation system," *Kulturstelsel*. The Indonesian peasants were forced to devote one-fifth of their land to the production of cash crops, especially coffee, sugar, and indigo, to be turned over to the Dutch for export to the Netherlands as a kind of taxation. From 1840 to 1880 the estimated profits repatriated, or sent back, to the imperial country equaled one-fourth of the total budget of the Netherlands.

India, 1858–1914

The English East India Company had come to India in the seventeenth century to buy spices and hand-made cotton textiles in exchange for bullion, wool, and metals. The Mughal government of India granted the Company permission to trade, and through the seventeenth century it established trading posts, called factories, first at Surat on India's west coast, and then at Madras (1639), Bombay (1661), and Calcutta (1690). During the eighteenth century, the Mughal imperial government began to weaken. Imperial policies of overexpansion in the south drained the empire of funds and manpower, and alienated rural landlords whose taxes were raised to pay the costs. In addition, Emperor Aurangzeb (r. 1659–1707) imposed additional taxes on non-Muslims, which his predecessors had not done, provoking rebellions in several regions of his Hindu-majority country. As the empire weakened, various regional contestants for power sought alliances with the British traders in their by-now well-fortified trading outposts.

The British were not the only European power active in India. The French, too, controlled fortified trading posts and had entered into alliances with regional Indian powers. The French Governor, Joseph Francis Dupleix, had drilled Indian troops under his command to fight in regular formations, armed with muskets that they were trained to shoot accurately and effectively. On the British side, Robert Clive, in the service of the East India Company, similarly trained his soldiers. The British and the French in India seemed poised to reach a truce between themselves, but the general warfare that engulfed the British and French elsewhere (1744–48) pulled them into conflict. Each side won significant victories, but the French East India Company saw the cost to its trade as too great and it sharply cut back its troops and its trading enterprises. When warfare resumed, as a result of the Seven Years' War (1755–63), a global struggle between Britain and France, the British in India easily defeated the French. This victory left the British as the principal European power in India, and their services were much in demand by several emerging regional powers. In exchange for their financial and military support, the British were offered a share in the taxes and the governmental authority of these break-away regions. Beginning in Bengal with the battles of Plassey (1757) and Buxar (1765), the British began to gain control of large areas of India. The British East India Company was the instrument of rule, since it was the actual British representation in India. The British Parliament established a Board of Control in London to oversee the activities of the Company, but in large measure a joint stock trading company had become master of large, and increasing, regions of Indian territory.

The Company's principal motive was the acquisition of profits, and, now as rulers, they adopted two policies to maximize them. First, they increased tax collection, both by raising rates and by increasing the efficiency of collection. Second, they manipulated tariffs, lowering them in India so that British manufactures would have easy access to Indian markets, and lobbying to raise them in Britain in order to block the import of Indian textiles. The beginning of Britain's industrial revolution and of the Company's establishment of control over large regions of India occurred at more or less the same time, in the middle of the eighteenth century. Colonial control thus immediately protected and facilitated the development of British industry, while effectively blocking Indian competition.

British machine-made cotton textiles flooded India's markets. India was transformed into the model colony, importing manufactured goods from Britain's industries and exporting raw materials to its factories and distribution centers: raw cotton, which the British manufactured into cloth; jute for making sacks; leather; and enormous quantities of tea, as India displaced China as the leading provider of tea to Europe. Throughout the second half of the nineteenth century and the first years of the twentieth, two-thirds of India's imports from Britain were machine-manufactured textiles. Iron and steel goods came second. India became a lucrative destination for overseas investment, and about one-fifth of all overseas British investment in the late nineteenth century was in India.

India's own taxes, however, paid for the building and maintenance of the Indian railway system, one of the most extensive in the world with some 35,000 miles of track by 1914. Demonstrating the power of colonial rule, the British manufactured all of the components of the system—engines, cars, tracks—in Britain. Thus, even though the financing was drawn from India, the profits of the manufacture, the expertise in engineering, and the industrial plant that built the railway industry went to Britain rather than to India. The railway system in India made possible a wide range of diverse activities: the widespread deployment of colonial troops, increased commerce that benefited both Indians and British businessmen, the relief of famine through the shipping of food from areas of surplus harvests to areas of shortfall, the geographical spread of political dissidence, and pilgrimage visits to religious shrines throughout the country.

Under British colonial rule, India began its own industrial revolution with cotton textiles, primarily in Bombay. This textile industry was started by local Gujaratis, inhabitants of the western Indian region of Gujarat, who had long family histories of

SOURCE

"The Attack of King Industry"

Communities in India that were already active in business provided many of the new industrialists. Indian financiers became industrialists by importing the new industrial machinery ready-made from Europe. In Ahmedabad, the capital of Gujarat, local businessmen, led by an administrator with close ties to British entrepreneurs, followed Mumbai (Bombay) in establishing a local cotton textile industry in 1861. A few years earlier Dalpatram Kavi, a local poet and intellectual leader, had called on his fellow countrymen to recognize the importance of industry to their future. His Gujarati poem, "Hunnarkhan-ni Chadayi" ("The Attack of King Industry"), presents a far-reaching agenda for reform centering on industrial change and proposes social restructuring as well. It suggests that the British had brought much of value to India and that Indians were prepared to absorb and implement some of this legacy, but without the British imperial presence and its costs.

Fellow countrymen, let us remove all the miseries of our country,
Do work, for the new kingdom has come. Its king is industry.

Our wealth has gone into the hands of foreigners. The great blunder is yours
For you did not unite yourselves—fellow countrymen.

Consider the time, see for yourselves. All our people have become poor,
Many men of business have fallen—fellow countrymen.

Put away idleness. Fill the treasuries with knowledge.
Now awake and work new wonders—fellow countrymen.

With kith and kin keep harmony. Do not enter into debt.
Limit the dinners for your caste—fellow countrymen.

Introduce industry from countries abroad and master the modern machinery.
Please attend to this plea from the Poet Dalpat—fellow countrymen.

(trans. by Chimanbhai Trivedi and Howard Spodek)

involvement in business. The need to found new industries found expression even in local poetry, as "The Attack of King Industry" makes clear. (In Calcutta, where jute textiles were produced, industry was largely pioneered by British investors.) Mining began in the coal fields of Bengal, Bihar, Orissa, and Assam, and in 1911 the Tata family of Bombay—a Parsi family, descendants of immigrants from Persia who had come to India in the eighth century—built India's first steel mill at Jamshedpur, Bihar. At the start of World War I, factory employment in all of India had reached about 1 million (out of a total population of about 300 million). While employment in large, mechanized factories was increasing, many hand craftsmen were being displaced, so the actual percentage of people earning their living by manufacturing of all sorts stayed approximately the same, at about 10 percent of the workforce (and has continued about the same till today).

In 1857 Indians revolted against rule by the British East India Company. The British called this a "Mutiny" of army troops, but later scholars have shown it to be a more geographically widespread and more general opposition to British rule. Some nationalist historians have called it "India's First War for National Independence," but the revolt lacked unified leadership and direction, The British crushed the revolt, and from then onward they ruled India directly, imposing their influence throughout the administrative and educational systems of the country. Concepts based on European political revolutions were introduced directly and indirectly through the formal secondary and post-secondary education system, the law courts, the press, and even through very limited elections. English was designated the official language of government. As a result, imperialism confronted its internal contradiction: How could an imperial power preach and teach the values of self-rule and democracy while maintaining its own foreign rule?

When more organized movements for independence began in India in the late nineteenth century, their leaders first had to evaluate the effects of British rule and to find a balance between acceptance and rejection of its political, economic, social, and cultural models. By the early twentieth century, most politically conscious Indians had come to believe that whatever benefits British rule might have conferred, the time had come for the British to go home. It was time for India to control its own economy and to choose its own political, social, and cultural directions.

China, 1800–1914

We began Chapter 17, on the industrial revolution, with a flashback to the Song dynasty (960–1279) when China—with its sailing expertise and equipment, iron manufacturing, gunpowder, waterwheels, and canal systems—was the most technologically advanced country in the world. We also know from our survey of Zheng He's fifteenth-century seafaring expeditions under the Ming dynasty that China's astonishing maritime capabilities continued to be the most outstanding in the world. On the other hand, we also know that China fell to Chinggis Khan's onslaughts in the thirteenth century and was ruled by these foreigners until the Ming dynasty recaptured power for the Han Chinese (1368–1644). But the Ming also fell to "barbarians," Manchu invaders from north of the Great Wall, who established the Qing dynasty (1644–1911). The Ming invited Manchu warriors to help suppress a band of rebels that had seized Beijing, but after the task was complete, the Manchu refused to leave. They pushed onward to capture all of China for themselves.

The Manchus were enthusiastic colonizers. Even before they invaded and ruled China, they had established a state in their homeland of Manchuria, made Korea a vassal state, and controlled Inner Mongolia as a dependency. After establishing their rule in China, the Qing expanded westward. In the eighteenth century they annexed new lands equal to the size of China itself in Outer Mongolia, Dzungaria, the Tarim Basin, Eastern Turkestan, Tsinghai, and Tibet. They also conquered Taiwan and subordinated the peoples of Southeast Asia into tributary relationships. Revolts broke out against Manchu rule, but until 1800 they occurred mostly at the periphery of the empire and posed no serious threat to the dynasty.

Some scholars believe that the very size and power of China created a sense of invulnerability among its leaders that sometimes led the country to ignore threats from the outside until it was too late. (Of course, the court was often divided within itself, also weakening the government.) As an example, a letter from the Chinese emperor Qianlong (1736–95) to the king of Britain in 1793, is frequently cited. Britain's King George III had dispatched a mission under Lord George Macartney to open trade and diplomatic negotiations with China. For the Chinese emperor, nearing the end of his long reign, the concept of permanent representation by a European power at the Chinese court was inconceivable. The emperor replied to the British monarch in a letter that was, perhaps unintentionally, condescending. It expressed the emperor's continuing belief in China's central position in the world, and his lack of appreciation and understanding of the changes that were taking place in the West in the early stages of the industrial revolution:

> As to the request made in your memorial, O King, to send one of your nationals to stay at the Celestial Court to take care of your country's trade with China, this is not in harmony with the state system of our dynasty and will definitely not be permitted.
>
> The various articles presented by you, O King, this time are accepted by my special order to the office in charge of such functions in consideration of the offerings having come from a long distance with sincere good wishes . . . [but] there is nothing we lack, as your principal envoy and others have themselves observed. We have never set much store on strange or ingenious objects, nor do we need any more of your country's manufactures. (Teng and Fairbank, p. 19)

Although some scholars at the court warned against this policy of isolation and complacency, their opinions were disregarded.

By the early 1800s, however, China faced a range of internal problems that demanded attention. A continuously rising population put pressure on resources and government administrative capacity. The 100 million people of 1650 tripled to 300 million by 1800 and reached 420 million by 1850. More land was needed. Allowing the settlement of Manchuria seemed a suitable reply to the problem, but the Manchus would not permit Chinese settlement in their homeland. Nor did the Manchus increase the size of their bureaucracy to service the rising population, preferring to delegate administrative responsibilities to local authorities, a response that was inadequate.

One strength of the Chinese economy was the sale of tea, silk, and porcelains to the West in exchange for silver and gold. The Europeans trading with China, however, wished to staunch this flow of bullion. Finally, the Europeans trading with China, especially the British, discovered that China would accept opium in place of precious metals. Taking advantage of its multinational commercial connections, the British encouraged the growth of opium in their Indian colony and carried it from the ports of Bombay, Calcutta, and Madras to Canton in China. The centuries of paying for Chinese exports with silver and gold came to an end. By the 1820s China was purchasing so much opium that it began to export silver!

The Opium Wars, 1839–42 and 1856–60. Seeking to staunch the drain of silver and to stop the importation of opium, the Chinese attempted to ban and resist its import in 1839. It was too late. By now the British proclaimed the ideology of "free trade." When the incorruptible Imperial Commissioner Lin Zexu tried to confiscate and destroy the opium, British shipboard cannon destroyed Chinese ships and port installations in the harbor at Guangzhou (Canton). This Opium War of 1839–42 was no contest because the Chinese emperors' lack of interest in Western science and technology meant that China lacked both modern cannons and steamships. China ceded to Britain the island

extraterritoriality Legal immunities enjoyed by the citizens of a sovereign state or international organization within a host country.

The steamer *Nemesis* destroying eleven Chinese junks at Cherpez Canton, China, by E. Duncan, 1843. The two separate wars fought between Britain and China in the 1840s and 1850s began when the Chinese government tried to prevent British merchants from illegally importing opium. The British responded militarily precipitating The Opium Wars (1839–42). (*National Maritime Museum, Canada*)

of Hong Kong as a colony and opened five treaty ports in which foreigners could live and conduct business under their own laws rather than under the laws of China—a condition known as **extraterritoriality**. France and the United States soon gained similar concessions. Foreign settlements were established in the new treaty ports and became the centers of new industry, education, and publishing. The focus of international trade began to relocate from Guangzhou to Shanghai, at the mouth of the Yangzi River, a more central location along the Chinese coast.

The decline of the Qing dynasty. During the course of the nineteenth century, the authority of the Qing (Manchu) dynasty in China was undermined. Beset by the aggressive actions of European colonial powers, the Qing granted extensive trade and territorial concessions. Internally, a series of increasingly violent rebellions, both within the Chinese heartland and in the western (often Muslim) regions, brought the dynasty to the verge of collapse by the turn of the century.

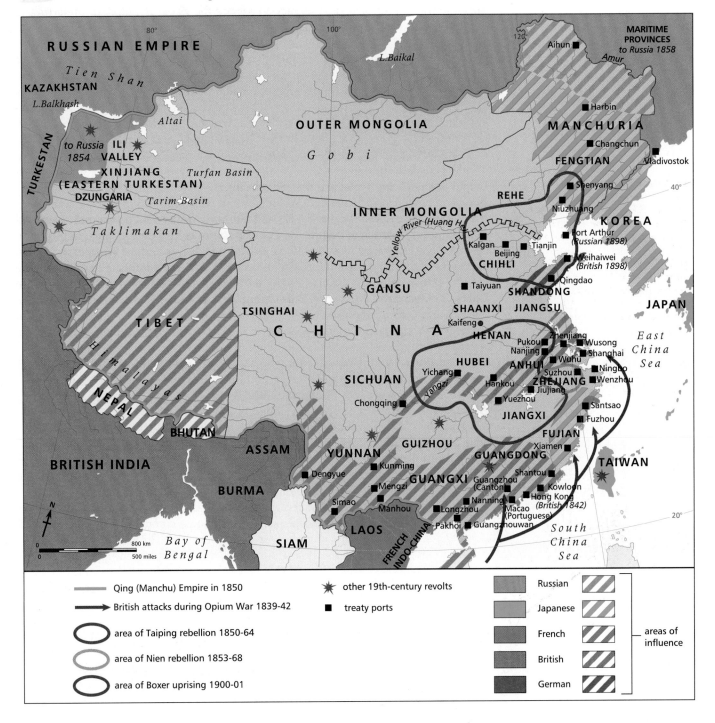

	Qing (Manchu) Empire in 1850
➤	British attacks during Opium War 1839–42
⬭	area of Taiping rebellion 1850–64
⬭	area of Nien rebellion 1853–68
⬭	area of Boxer uprising 1900–01
✳	other 19th-century revolts
■	treaty ports

		areas of influence
Russian		
Japanese		
French		
British		
German		

Marble boat in the gardens of the Summer Palace, Beijing. In the last years of the nineteenth century Chinese reformers clamored for industrial, military, and administrative reform. They were incensed when the dowager empress of China built not a navy but a marble boat for entertainment in her Summer Palace.

comprador (Portuguese: "buyer") A Chinese merchant hired by Western traders to assist with their dealings in China.

Still China did not establish the formal diplomatic recognition and exchange that European powers had demanded. A second set of wars followed in 1856–60, and these led to the occupation of Beijing by 17,000 French and British soldiers and the sacking of the imperial Summer Palace. More treaty ports were opened, including inland centers along the Yangzi River, now patrolled by British gunboats. Europeans gained control over the administration of China's foreign trade and tariffs. The opium trade continued to expand. Christian missionaries were given freedom to travel throughout China. Some Chinese worked with the foreigners as **compradors**, or intermediaries in business and administration.

As the Manchu government weakened in the last decades of the nineteenth century, revolts broke out, foreign powers continued to seize parts of the country and its tributaries, and there were more calls for internal reform. (The Chinese situation showed similarities with events in the Ottoman Empire at about the same time.) The greatest of the internal revolts, the Taiping Rebellion, began in 1850 and was led by Hong Xiuquan, a frustrated scholar who claimed visions of himself as the younger brother of Jesus Christ. The main demands of the Taiping leaders, however, were quite concrete: an end to the corrupt and inefficient Manchu imperial rule, an end to extortionate landlord demands, and the alleviation of poverty. Beginning in the southwest, the Taiping came to dominate the Yangzi valley and established their capital in Nanjing in 1853. The imperial government was unable to respond effectively, but regional military leaders, equipped with more modern weapons, finally defeated the revolt with the help of the "Ever Victorious Army," a mercenary force composed of American and European soldiers, winning more power for themselves. Throughout the struggle, American officers recognized Chinese authority over military operations, while most British and French generals did not. By the time the Taiping Rebellion was suppressed in 1864, some 20 million people had been killed. At about the same time, additional rebellions broke out among tribal peoples near Guangzhou, among the Miao tribals in Guizhou, and among Muslims in Yunnan and Gansu. The largest of all the rebel groups, the Nien, controlled much of the territory between Nanjing and Kaifeng. Collectively, these rebellions cost another 10 million lives.

With the central government fully occupied with these internal revolts, foreign imperialists began to establish their territorial claims as well. Russians seized border areas in the Amur River region (1858), the Maritime Provinces (1860), and, for ten years, the Ili valley in Turkestan (1871–81). France defeated Chinese forces in a local war and seized all of Indochina (1883–4). Most humiliating of all, Japan, having embraced Western technology and imperialist ambitions, defeated China in warfare in 1894–5. China ceded Taiwan to Japan, granted it the right to operate factories in the treaty ports, and paid a huge indemnity. Korea also passed to Japanese control, although formal colonial rule did not follow until 1910. The historic relationship of China as teacher and Japan as disciple, which dated back at least to 600 C.E., had been abruptly reversed. The new industrial age had introduced new values and new power relationships.

The Boxer Rebellion, 1898–1900. In the last years of the nineteenth century, China was in turmoil. In Beijing, a group of nationalists, called "Boxers" by the Europeans, because of their belief that martial arts rendered them invincible in struggle, were enraged by foreign arrogance in China. They burned Christian missions, killed missionaries, and laid siege to the foreign legations for two months. The imperial powers of Europe and the United States put down this revolt and exacted yet another exorbitant indemnity. The Europeans and Americans did not, however, wish to take over the government of China directly. They wanted to have a Chinese government responsible for China. They wanted to preserve China as a quasi-colony, and they therefore supported the Manchus in the formalities of power, even as they steadily hollowed out the content of that power.

A group of Chinese modernizers began to organize new industries, beginning with textiles, later developing Western weapons and steamships, but the government, now in the hands of the aging dowager Empress Cixi, who controlled the heir apparent until she died in 1908, blocked their reforms. Frustrated nationalists called for revolution. Their leading organizer was Sun Yat-sen, a Cantonese educated in Honolulu, where he became a Christian, and in Hong Kong, where he became a doctor. Sun called for a twofold anticolonial revolution: first against the Manchus and then against the European, American, and Japanese powers. Only after the first revolution was successful in overthrowing Manchu rule in 1911 did Sun begin to push against the Western powers and Japan. The story of that struggle is told in Chapter 22.

AFRICA, 1652–1912

When European traders arrived in India and China they found huge countries governed by powerful empires. Africa was quite different. Africa was an entire continent, second only to Asia in size, with many states and with even more areas under the control of local families, clans, and ethnicities. Each area had its own history, and the experience of each different European group varied in each different region.

In sub-Saharan Africa, for the most part the early European experience was limited to the

Boxers on the march. The mostly poor peasants who formed the Boxer Rebellion of 1898–1900 blamed hard times on foreign interference and Christian missionaries. Renowned for the ferocity of their attacks, the rebels terrified Western residents as they marched into Tianjin (pictured). A 20,000-strong force, comprising soldiers from different colonial powers, finally crushed the revolt in Beijing.

PS 494

shoreline of the west coast. The Europeans came in search of a shipping route to Asia, and this required only coastal contact in Africa. They found that they could buy the slaves they wanted in port towns that they established also along the coast. Africans would capture, collect, and bring the slaves to them for sale. The Europeans for the most part accepted this commercial arrangement as economically efficient. It saved them from conflict with local African rulers, who resisted the entrance of Europeans into their territories and opposed them by force. It also did not endanger their health with diseases against which the Europeans had no immunity. Even from their coastal enclaves the Europeans were able to make a considerable mark on Africa, purchasing and transporting more than 10 million slaves to the New World over a period of four centuries.

South Africa, 1652–1910

The first substantial European colony in sub-Saharan Africa was established at the Cape of Good Hope on the southern tip of the continent, not for the purchase of slaves, but for fostering ocean shipping. The Dutch established a colony at the Cape of Good Hope in South Africa in 1652 as a way station en route to and from India and the Spice Islands. The settlement grew steadily, and immigrants from other European countries—especially Britain—also joined it.

European expansion at the Cape had disruptive effects on local populations. As the Dutch and the British set out to the rural areas to farm, they displaced the Khoikhoi people who had been resident in the area. The Khoikhoi chiefdoms dissolved in the face of warfare, displacement, and catastrophic smallpox epidemics that decimated their numbers. Some of the Khoikhoi, along with other African peoples, were taken as slaves to fill the labor needs of the Europeans. In 1708 the population of the Cape was about 1700 free citizens and 1700 slaves. By about 1800 it totaled about 75,000, of whom about one-third were free and two-thirds were slaves, mostly African but some of mixed race.

As a result of their victories in the Napoleonic Wars, military and legal control of the Cape Colony passed to the British. British laws and social practices were instituted, including freedom of the press and of assembly, the development of representative government, the abolition of the slave trade, and, in 1834, with the abolition of slavery throughout the British Empire, the emancipation of slaves. Nevertheless, Europeans controlled the best land of the region, leaving their former slaves to be wage workers rather than land-owners and farmers. Property restrictions on voting effectively kept Africans out of power, and the Masters and Servants Act limited the freedom of movement of black workers.

Some 8000 people of Dutch descent, unhappy with the increasingly British customs of the colony, especially the abolition of slavery went in search of new land for farming. They departed on a great march, or trek, northward in the years between 1834 and 1841. These people, usually called Boers (meaning farmers in Dutch), or Afrikaners (for the African dialect of Dutch they spoke), ultimately founded two new republics, the Orange Free State and the Transvaal. Meanwhile, the Cape Colony expanded eastward, annexing Natal in 1843, partly to keep out the Boers. As they migrated, the Boers fought, conquered, displaced, and restricted to reservations the African peoples they encountered. Seeking labor to work the land, they often captured and virtually enslaved Africans living around them.

The expansion of the European Cape Colony further destabilized a region already passing through a *mfecane*, or time of troubles. In 1816, Shaka (c. 1787–1828) seized the leadership of his small Zulu kingdom just to the north and east of the Cape Colony. He organized a standing army of 40,000 soldiers, rigorously trained and disciplined them,

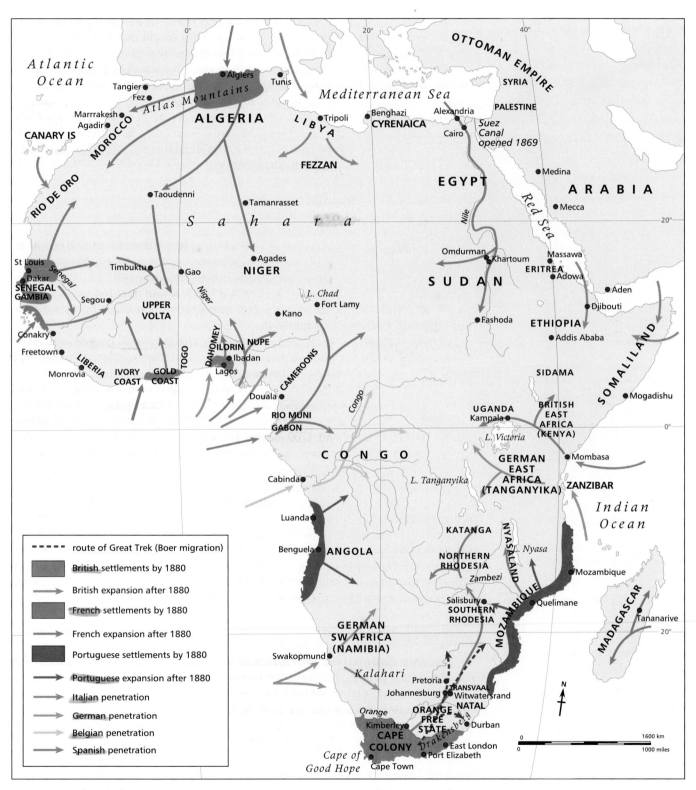

European expansion in Africa. Steamboats, machine-guns, and quinine (to combat malaria) all gave Europeans new access to the interior of Africa in the later nineteenth century, and they intensified their nationalistic competition. The British pursued the dream of linking their possessions from Cape Town to Cairo, while France seized much of North and Central Africa. Bismarck's Berlin Conference of 1884 tried to apportion the spoils among all the competing powers.

THE RHODES COLOSSUS
STRIDING FROM CAPE TOWN TO CAIRO.

The Rhodes Colossus. Cecil John Rhodes became one of the main champions of British rule in southern Africa, promoting colonization "from Cape Town to Cairo." The statesman and financier divided his time between diamond mining and annexing territories to British imperial rule. Rhodesia (now Zimbabwe and Zambia) was named for him in 1894.

housed them in stockades separate from the rest of the population, and armed them with newly designed short, stabbing spears, which gave them enormous power over their enemies in hand-to-hand combat. He instituted new battle formations, similar to those used by the ancient Greeks, with a massed center and flanks that could encircle the enemy and cut off its rear. By 1828, when Shaka was assassinated by two half-brothers, his kingdom had expanded, forcing the Soshagane, Nguni, Ndebele, Sotho, Ngwane, and Mfengu peoples to flee their lands. Some moved into the Cape Colony, but the vast majority turned north and east, traveling hundreds of miles into what is today Mozambique, Zimbabwe, Zambia, and even Tanzania, and displacing other peoples in turn. All of these movements combined—the Boer trek, Shaka's Zulu expansion, and the migration of peoples fleeing before both of these advances—created the *mfecane* in southern and eastern Africa. Cape Colony itself, however, remained relatively tranquil, continuing to serve as a port in transoceanic trade.

When the Suez Canal restructured the shipping routes between Asia and Europe in 1869, ending the need for the long voyage around Africa, South Africa might have become a quiet colonial backwater. But in the 1870s diamonds were discovered at Kimberley, and in the 1880s the world's largest known deposit of gold was found at Witwatersrand. Competition for this new wealth intensified the general hostility between the Boers and the British into full-scale warfare. The British army of 450,000 men finally defeated the Boer army of 88,000 in the three-year-long South African War (which the British called the Boer War), 1899–1902. In 1910, the British consolidated their own two colonies (Cape and Natal) with the two Boer republics into the Union of South Africa, which became a self-governing country. After 1913 whites in South Africa had the same sorts of political institutions and rights as in the British Dominions of Australia and Canada. Because of the European domination of the life of the colony, South Africa was considered a white settler colony despite its black majority.

Egypt, 1798–1882

The European invasion of Egypt in 1798 turned out to be very brief and yet very influential. Napoleon's forces invaded Egypt in 1798 and held it until British forces drove them out in 1801. During the fighting, the Ottoman sultan called in a troop of Albanian cavalry to lead the Ottoman resistance. The commander of the troops, Muhammad (Mehemet) Ali (1769–1849), remained after both French and British troops left and took over the effective rule of Egypt in 1807, although he served nominally as a viceroy of the Ottoman Empire. He introduced some new industries and then decided to concentrate on the cultivation of cotton as a cash crop for Europe's booming textile industry. To enable year-round cultivation, he built extensive new irrigation works. He also encouraged the development of Egypt's own textile mills. For the most part, he kept this economic modernization in the hands of the state rather than of private entrepreneurs. He streamlined the administration and built a system of secular state schools to train administrators and officers, especially by training students in Western scholarship. He introduced a government printing press, which in turn encouraged translations of European books into Arabic.

A professional soldier, Muhammad Ali modernized the army and marched his newly equipped forces up the Nile, captured the Sudan, and built the city of Khartoum to serve as its capital in 1830. He also gained control of the holy cities of Mecca and Medina in Arabia to counter the power of the militantly Islamic Wahabi movement there. Threatened by trends toward Westernization and Europeanization in the Middle East, the Wahabis taught that the Quran and the traditions of Muhammad (the Hadith) contained all of the fundamental beliefs of Islam. Further, they believed that governments should be based on strict interpretations of Islamic law. (This conflict between fundamentalist Muslims and Western-oriented leadership remains a central tension in the Middle Eastern world today.) Fundamentally secular in outlook, Muhammad Ali attempted to reach accommodation with the moderate Islamic forces in Egypt rather than attempting either to attack them or to bring them around to his own perspectives. He occupied Syria and Palestine and threatened Istanbul itself until Britain and France blocked his path, offering him, instead, recognition as the hereditary ruler of Egypt. Muhammad Ali's son, Ishmail, succeeded him and commissioned a French firm to build the Suez Canal, which was opened in 1869. His grandson expanded Egyptian territorial holdings both along the coast of the Red Sea and inland toward the headwaters of the Nile.

Muhammad Ali's modernization program brought mixed results. Egypt entered the international economy based in Europe, but soon was spending more on imports, military modernization, and beautification projects in Cairo than it was earning in exports. In addition, it made commitments to cash cropping of cotton as the principal export item and thus left the country vulnerable to the instability of international price fluctuations on this single crop. As Egyptian debts rose, European creditors pressured their governments to force the khedive (the title given to Muhammad Ali and his successors) to appoint European experts as Commissioners of the Debt in 1876. In 1878 the khedive was forced to add a French and a British representative to his cabinet. Even so, in 1881 the European powers had the Ottoman sultan dismiss the khedive, Muhammad Ali's grandson. When an Egyptian military revolt then seized power, Britain sent in its forces, primarily to protect the Suez Canal, and stayed on as the power behind the throne until the 1950s. For Egypt, entanglement with Europe proved a two-edged sword.

Algeria, 1830–71

The rule of the Ottoman Empire weakened not only in Egypt, but all across North Africa. By the late seventeenth and early eighteenth century, the regions of both Tunis and Algiers were only nominally under Ottoman rule. Both regions profited from piracy and were finally invaded by seafaring nations that sought to suppress the pirates, Tunis by the Americans (from which expedition comes the phrase "to the shores of Tripoli" in the American marine corps hymn) and Algeria by the French. The French attack on Algeria in 1830 began as a campaign against piracy, but relations between the ruler of Algiers and the French government spun out of control, and ultimately the French demanded and got his surrender and control over his possessions. Political control over Algiers was fragmented, however, and the French found themselves at war with other regional leaders, especially Abd al-Qadir, son of the head of one of the most important Muslim brotherhoods, or religious/political organizations, in the Middle East. Resistance swelled under al-Qadir, and he began to build a small state with its own administration and a modernized army of 10,000 men trained by

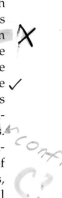

European advisers. At first, the French avoided confrontation with al-Qadir, who stayed south of their holdings, but in 1841 bitter warfare broke out. Before the French won, they had committed 110,000 troops (a third of their army) to the war and had attacked neighboring Morocco to block reinforcements to their enemy. Revolts continued to simmer, with the last and largest repressed in 1871, with 3000 French soldiers reported killed. Since the French resorted to a policy of destroying the crops of al-Qadir's army, Algerian casualties were almost certainly much greater. French armies took over rural areas, opening them for French military occupation and settlement.

During the years of fighting and thereafter, tens of thousands of Europeans came to settle in Algiers, some in connection with the military, some in search of economic opportunity. About half were French, but all began to adopt French language and culture and to think of themselves as French people living in Algeria. By the 1850s there were 130,000 of them and by 1900 more than a half-million, about 13 percent of the population. Christians (and Jews after 1870) were deemed to be citizens of France, Muslims were legally subjects. After a change of government in France in 1870, Algeria was formally annexed to France and French citizens—but not subjects—in Algeria received the right to vote for members of the French National Assembly in Paris. Through official land transfers and sales, the best land came into French hands and was developed into commercial agriculture, while Algerian farmers were generally left with small, under-capitalized holdings. This unequal pattern of representation and development continued until the end of the very bitter and costly Algerian war for independence in 1962. Following the war, almost all of the one million descendants of the French settlers fled to France.

Islamic Religious Revival

In the western and eastern *sahel*, the dry, semi-desert area immediately south of the Sahara, stretching almost from the Atlantic Ocean to the Red Sea, political and religious movements of Islamic revival flourished. Although in some places Islamic forces engaged European Christian forces in armed conflict, these Islamic movements were not directly related to European activities in Africa. Most of them were directed at keeping Muslims loyal to the faith and at bringing polytheistic Africans under Muslim rule rather than at opposing Christians. Some historians do believe, however, that the movements drew some of their inspiration from the knowledge among the Muslims that the balance of power was shifting from an increasingly weak Muslim Middle East and Africa to an increasingly powerful Christian Europe.

In West Africa three movements stand out for special attention. They began in states founded in the eighteenth century by the Fulani peoples. In Hausaland, modern northern Nigeria, Uthman dan Fodio (1754–1817), a prominent *sufi* teacher, began to condemn the rulers of Hausaland for corruption, sacrilege, persecution of true Muslims, and polytheistic practices. After years of this opposition, of gathering supporters from nearby groups, and of receiving inconsistent responses from the Hausaland rulers, Uthman urged his followers to arm themselves for coming conflict. The outbreak of hostilities began when a new sultan attacked a group of Uthman's followers in 1804. In response, Uthman called on his son and brother to lead the military campaigns that ultimately brought all of Hausaland under his control from his new capital at Sokoto. The new empire continued until the 1890s. Under its Islamic umbrella, the Sokoto empire tended to favor Fulani people over Hausa, even though not all of the Fulani were Muslims. For the most part, however, it encouraged both Fulani and Hausa to unite in a single Islamic empire.

Other jihads, or African holy wars, were smaller in geographical and military scale. They were usually concerned with purifying the Islamic faith and practices of rulers and subjects. These included jihads in western Africa in the small states of Futa Toro, Futa Jallon, and the somewhat larger Massina. In Massina, al-Hajj Umar (c. 1794–1864), having returned from a pilgrimage to Mecca, and having visited Sokoto, gathered followers and armed them. He captured the kingdom of Massina and made it the center of his empire. Umar attempted to gain support from the French on the coast of West Africa, but they were uneasy with his proposal. When he attacked French river traders, perhaps seeking to capture their guns, the French-controlled armed forces repulsed his attack.

Another leader who built an empire in the name of Islam, Samori Toure (c. 1830–1900), organized Mandinka and Diola ethnic groups under his military leadership. Although at one point he declared

Aloysius O'Kelly, *African Musician*, c. 1880. **Oil on canvas.** As European artists painted African scenes they often portrayed people of striking beauty and strength against exotic backgrounds. The musician may have been a *griot*, a bard whose songs and chants preserved the history of his people. (*Taylor Gallery, London*)

himself *almami*, or leader of the faithful, his devotion to Islam was sometimes compromised by battles against fellow Muslims and his murder of Muslim scholars in his capture of the town of Kong.

Toure's empire, just south of the bend of the Niger River, as well as the empire founded by al-Hajj Umar, were situated in the path of French imperial conquest eastward from the Atlantic. In 1893–4, both were defeated and brought under French control. Although Toure's record is marred by his raiding for slaves (in order to barter them for guns), by his scorched earth policy of retreat before the French, and by his destruction of Kong, the town to which he moved his capital as he retreated, he is nevertheless viewed by most historians as a guerrilla leader who could hold off the French for two years in his original empire and for two more in his second empire. In 1898 the French captured him and exiled him to Gabon, where he died in 1900.

In East Africa, near Khartoum, the city founded by Muhammad Ali, a man named Muhammad Ahmed declared that he was the Mahdi, a messiah figure who would bring a new age that would restore the true religion. In 1881, he began to build a state in the Sudan. The Mahdi began his movement in opposition to the Egyptian government, but in 1882 the British re-entered Egypt, seized Cairo and claimed the Nile valley as effective rulers of the region. The British and the Mahdi were on a collision course. At first the Mahdi was victorious. In 1885, he defeated an Egyptian force commanded by British General Charles Gordon at Khartoum. Later that year the Mahdi died, leaving his state to a successor who, though Muslim, was far less militant than the founder. For some time Britain did not respond to this new state and its successes. A decade later, however, it sent another force under General Horatio Herbert Kitchener to retake the Sudan for Egypt and to revenge Gordon's defeat and death. At Omdurman, Kitchener's army destroyed the Mahdists, killing 11,000 men and wounding 16,000 in a single battle on September 2, 1898, while losing just forty of its own soldiers. They then proceeded to reclaim Khartoum. The British forces had machine guns while the Mahdists believed they were impervious to bullets. The total imbalance of military force and strategy between the British and the Muslim forces could not have been more clear, and neither could the willingness of the African Muslims to fight and die for their cause.

A Western Orientation in West Africa. Europeans and Africans, working together, created two new responses to the abolition of the slave trade and slavery: They established two colonies as refuges for freed slaves, and they began to found businesses, mostly based on tropical agricultural products, to replace slave trading in the export economy. European port towns along the coast were always more Afro-European than European, since the Europeans stayed only briefly while their mixed-race descendants remained along with a much larger number of slaves. Saint Louis, for example, in modern Senegal, was home in 1810 to about ten Europeans, 500 Afro-Europeans, 500 free Africans who had absorbed European culture, and about 2200 slaves.

The most significant of the west coast settlements was Sierra Leone. Its capital, Freetown, was founded in 1787 and, as the name suggests, it was to serve as a haven for freed slaves. At first these were mostly black Americans who had been freed by the British in their struggle against the American revolutionaries and rebels from Jamaican slavery. After the abolition of the slave trade in 1807, increasing numbers were slaves recaptured at sea by the British navy. In 1808 the British reorganized Sierra Leone as a formal British colony and promoted Christianity and Western culture among its residents. The numbers of recaptured slaves continued to add to the size of the colony, and an important institution for training African clergy, Fourah Bay College, opened in 1827. One of its first graduates, Samuel Crowther, became the first African bishop of the Anglican Church. The overwhelming majority of the population, however, were Africans who joined the colony on their own. Some of the former slaves, especially the Yoruba, used Sierra Leone as a staging point from which to return inland to the societies from which they had been taken.

Following the example of Sierra Leone, the American Colonization Society received a charter from the United States government in 1816 to found a site on the west African coast for the repatriation of freed American slaves. In 1822, the first settlers arrived at the site that later became Monrovia, named for American President James Monroe. In 1847, at a time when Monrovia held about 5000 settlers, it formally declared its independence from the United States government. Nine years later it joined with its surrounding settlements to form the country of Liberia as an independent state, although it was still heavily reliant on American assistance. Americans supported Liberia for diverse reasons: Some saw it as a haven for former slaves; others saw it as a dumping ground in which America could rid itself of ex-slaves. As in Sierra Leone, the population of freed slaves always formed a small minority of the total population. Even today, descendants of repatriated slaves, known as Americo-Liberians, form only 2.5 percent of the total population of about 3.2 million.

As the overseas slave trade ended in the north Atlantic, Europeans and Africans sought new export communities. British schemes to develop cotton plantations on the Niger River failed disastrously as the European personnel fell sick and succumbed to tropical illnesses against which they had no resistance. French schemes for plantations in the Ivory Coast and Gabon similarly failed. Foreigners did establish some economic enterprises inland—and often the same person served as the representative of government and the representative of European business interests. Most of the basic agricultural and animal commodities, however, were produced and transported by Africans. Ivory—much in demand in the West for piano keys and billiard balls—continued as a staple throughout much of the continent. New market crops included palm nuts and kernels, peanuts, timber, dyes, wax, honey, and redwood. As steamships started to ply Africa's rivers, bulkier crops were added: cotton, coffee, sugarcane, and sugar products. Rubber came in the 1870s. In the area around the Congo River, cassava, citrus fruits, tobacco, and maize were introduced. Despite the abolition of the slave trade in the British Empire and the areas it controlled, the slave trade flourished throughout most of the nineteenth century in the south Atlantic and throughout Africa. The increase in commercial cropping, ivory harvesting, and copper and metal mining and production required labor, and slavery provided much of it. Often "freed" slaves were forced into labor on the new plantations and in the expanding caravan trade, especially in East Africa. Arab caravan leaders impressed slaves into the ivory trade in great numbers and with high mortality rates.

The transport networks within Africa were for the most part traditional ones run by groups such as the Hausa, Yoruba, and Asante in West Africa, and by the Yao, the Kamba, and especially the Nyamwezi in East Africa, with their caravans of up to several thousands of people carrying ivory from far inland to the coast. In the east, Arab traders sometimes also conducted caravans from the coast to the Lake District, especially Lake Tanganyika. The Arab traders were backed financially and militarily by the Arab planters of Zanzibar with their rich harvests of cloves. The profit to be made in Zanzibar from cloves and from coordinating caravan transportation in East Africa was so great that the Arab ruler of the Oman empire, Sayyid Said, moved his capital from Muscat in Oman to Zanzibar in 1840. Said was "pulled" to Zanzibar by its promise of profits; he was also "pushed" from Oman by increasing British naval control of the Arabian coast and sea.

River transport by ship developed along with relatively short stretches of railroads to connect the river systems or to stretch short distances from the ports to nearby inland production centers. As steamboat transportation penetrated more deeply into the continent, many of the indigenous transport groups were displaced from their jobs, and some European commercial and administrative systems were positioned inland. Some great industries were owned and run by Europeans: rubber in the Congo, coffee plantations in East Africa, and diamonds and copper in the Congo and South Africa.

During most of the nineteenth century, the Afro-Europeans did well in business, education, and local public affairs in a relatively open environment. Commercial profit became more important than political power. Beginning with the 1880s, however, Europeans in larger numbers came directly from Europe, taking over direct political and economic power and imposing increasingly racist polices. Joseph Conrad's great novel, *Heart of Darkness*, captures the mood and setting of that transformation.

European Explorers and the Scramble for Africa

To extend their commercial ventures, their political power, and their missionary activities, Europeans wanted more knowledge of Africa. Exploration of the interior attracted many adventurers: In the late eighteenth and early nineteenth centuries West Africa and the Niger River were the main attractions for men such as Mungo Park, René Caillié, Hugh Clapperton, the Lander brothers Richard and John, and Heinrich Barth. By the middle of the nineteenth century the mystery and potential of central and East Africa attracted some of the most daring explorers. David Livingstone (1813–73), a Scottish missionary and able scientist, began his career in Africa intent upon establishing a missionary station and providing medical assistance. He began in South Africa in 1841, establishing stations, providing assistance, and exploring. In 1852 he returned home briefly. In 1853 he returned to Africa, landing at Luanda along the Angola Coast. For three years he continued to explore, crossing and re-crossing the continent. Livingstone was distinguished for learning African languages, treating Africans with respect, and constantly campaigning against the slave trade that was endemic in the African interior. In his popular writings on his explorations, he included pleas to the British government to extend its power in Africa to combat this trade. Two subsequent, grueling adventures of exploration in equatorial Africa lasted a total of thirteen years. Livingstone died in the course of his explorations in what is

HOW DO WE KNOW?

Why did Europeans Colonize the World?

The industrial revolution in western Europe and the United States ushered in an era of imperialism that brought most of the world's land under European political control. Why did the industrializing nations assert their powers in this way? To some extent, the answer seems obvious: They relished the power, wealth, and prestige that apparently came with imperial possessions. They also claimed to welcome the opportunity to serve others. Further, the industrial system that they were building took on a life of its own, requiring ever-increasing sources of raw materials and more markets in which to sell. But why was trade alone not enough? Why did the industrialists feel it was necessary to take political control as well? Were there additional motives behind imperialism? And did the results of imperialism match the aspirations of the imperial rulers?

We cannot answer all these questions fully, but a review article by Patrick Wolfe in The American Historical Review, "History and Imperialism: A Century of Theory, from Marx to Postcolonialism," helps us to review and sort out some of the most prominent explanations.

Karl Marx deplored the exploitation of colonialism, but, as a European, he valued some of its contributions. Britain, he emphasized, brought to India a new economic dynamism, with railroads, industrial infrastructure, and communication networks. Ultimately this transformation would lead to capitalism and then socialism. Marx wrote in 1853: "Whatever may have been the crimes of England, she was the unconscious tool of history in bringing about that revolution" (Marx and Engels, First Indian War, p. 21).

J.A. Hobson, a British economist writing in 1902, and V.I. Lenin, the leader of the communist revolution in Russia (see Chapter 19), writing in 1916, agreed that the desire to control raw materials and markets drove imperialism.

Hobson pointed out that the profits of the imperial system went mostly to the rich. He believed that if imperialism were ended overseas, a concentration on investment and industry at home would provide greater opportunities to the working classes in Europe. M.N. Roy, a founder of the Communist Party of India, disagreed with Hobson, arguing that the profits of imperialism did provide economic gains to European workers and that they would therefore support the system. The revolt against the imperial, and capitalist, system would have to begin among the workers in the colonies who were more exploited.

Several analysts have tried to grasp the imperial system as a whole, understanding the impact of colonizer and colonized upon one another. Some, like Marx, above, saw the system introducing valuable modernization into the colonies. Most, like Immanuel Wallerstein and the American economists Paul Baran and Paul Sweezy, argued that the imperial power would always seek to keep the colonies in a position of dependency and underdevelopment. The imperial rulers might introduce some technological innovations, such as railways that were necessary for their trade, but they had no interest in enabling the colonies to become economic and technological rivals. Indeed, one reason for imposing imperial domination was to prevent the colony from taking control of its own economic policies.

Ronald Robinson and John Gallagher, British historians writing in the 1960s, and French philosopher Louis Althusser, writing in the 1970s and 1980s, stressed the need to evaluate imperialism on a case-by-case basis. British imperialism in Egypt, for example, was quite sophisticated and benign compared with the raw cruelty of Belgian imperialism in the Congo. Even within individual colonies, imperialists treated different regions and groups differently, for example incorporating educated urban groups into the administration while treating plantation workers almost like

slave labor. Imperial rule also varied considerably depending on the administration in power in the imperial country and also on the local imperial representatives on the scene. All three scholars eschewed generalizations and emphasized the complexity of the imperial enterprise.

Finally, some of the most recent scholarly analyses of imperialism—often referred to as postcolonial analyses—have stressed the cultural impact of imperialism on both colonized and colonizer. Imperial rulers usually drew a sense of pride from their conquest and exalted their own culture for possessing colonies. Colonized peoples, on the other hand, often suffered a sense of inferiority. They had to re-examine their historic cultural traditions and identities in light of the fact that they had been conquered by foreigners. The postcolonial literature that analyzes this cultural confrontation has expanded rapidly, with contributions by literary critics such as Edward Said, Homi Bhabha, and Gayatri Chakravorty Spivak. Indeed, as industrialization has brought peoples of the world into ever closer contact, and political philosophies have collided with one another, questions of personal and group identity have increased everywhere. We will explore these questions of identity in Chapters 23 and 24.

- Among the scholars who argue that economics is the main force behind imperialism, there are differences of opinion. What are these differences? Which point of view seems most persuasive to you?
- Some scholars have argued that political gain has been the main force behind imperialism. What evidence do you see to support this viewpoint?
- Many contemporary scholars argue that the colonizing countries have been influenced by colonialism culturally just as much as the colonized have been. What examples of this influence can you cite?

today Zambia in 1873. In accordance with his wishes, his heart was buried in Africa, under a tree near the place where he died. His body was returned to England and buried in Westminster Abbey.

In 1871, when premature rumors of Livingstone's death reached Europe, the *New York Herald* dispatched Henry Morton Stanley (1841–1904) to try to find him in the course of his third expedition. Not only did Stanley locate Livingstone, he also carried out expeditions of his own—traveling with an armed retinue that resembled a military expedition or a slave caravan—through the Lake District of East Africa and along the Congo River. On Stanley's return through Europe, King Leopold II of Belgium (r. 1865–1909) engaged him to establish trading stations along the Congo River. Unlike Livingstone, Stanley treated the Africans who worked for him harshly and sought personal profit. He accepted the king's proposal. The colonization of central Africa was beginning.

Stanley, representing the king and his International Association for the Exploration and Civilization of Africa, negotiated treaties with hundreds of local chiefs. The treaties gave him, personally, the power to establish a Confederation of Free Negro Republics, an estate of some 900,000 square miles, which functioned as a kind of slave plantation within Africa for the personal economic benefit of King Leopold. The brutality of his treatment of Africans was perhaps the worst in the annals of European colonialism in Africa.

As European powers explored and colonized central Africa, they came into direct competition with each other. Fearing the consequences of this competition, Germany's Bismarck employed diplomacy to defuse European conflict, as he had done a few years earlier in the Balkans. He convened a conference in Berlin in 1884–5 to determine the allocation of Congo lands and to establish ground rules for fixing borders among European colonies in Africa. The Berlin Conference assigned the administration of the Congo, an area one-third the size of the continental United States, to Leopold II personally as a kind of company government. The Congo became, in effect, his private estate, eighty times larger than Belgium itself. Its economic purpose was, first, the harvesting of natural rubber from vines in the jungles and, later, the exploitation of the area's rich mineral reserves, especially copper. Laborers were forced to work as slaves at the point of a gun. Workers could be killed or have their hands cut off for failing to make quotas. Company agents killed and maimed workers who offered resistance. During the years of the king's rule, ten million Congolese died as a result of his policies. In 1908, recognizing both the cruelty and the economic losses of the Congo administration, the Belgian parliament took over control of the colony from the king, but the Congo remained one of the most harshly administered of all the African colonies.

The Berlin Conference also divided up the lands of Africa on paper, generally apportioning inland areas to the European nations already settled on the adjacent coast. These nations were then charged with establishing actual inland settlements in those regions, and they quickly did so, dispatching settlers in a "scramble for Africa." Portugal added to its domains in Angola and Mozambique. Italy captured a piece of Somaliland at the horn of Africa and Eritrea on the Red Sea. It also attempted to conquer proud Ethiopia, but King Menelik II (r. 1889–1913) had purchased sufficient guns and trained his forces well enough to defeat Italy at the Battle of Adowa in 1896. Italy did succeed, however, in taking Libya from the weakened Ottoman Empire in 1911. Germany established colonies in German East Africa (Tanganyika), the Cameroons, Togo, and German Southwest Africa (Namibia). The Germans, like the British and French before them, established treaties with African chiefs who often did not understand the significance of the documents they ratified but nevertheless found their power over their people strengthened. The chiefs frequently became, in effect, the agents of Europeans for recruiting labor and collecting taxes. In exchange, the Europeans protected the chiefs from resistance and rebellion.

On the occasions when Africans resisted these one-sided agreements, Europeans responded with force. Between 1884 and 1898, the French put down the rebellion of the Mande peoples under the Muslim Samori Toure. The British finally quelled a series of Asante revolts in the Gold Coast in 1900. The Germans crushed perhaps the greatest of the unsuccessful rebellions, the Maji-Maji revolt of 1905–7 in Tanganyika. Led by Kinjikitile Ngwele, who claimed to have magic water (*maji*), which would make his followers invulnerable to wounds, the rebels had refused to perform forced labor on the cotton plantations. The uprising ended with 70,000 rebels dead, including those who succumbed to disease and malnutrition. Other less spectacular revolts were similarly suppressed with violence.

As British forces began to connect the north–south route through East Africa, French forces were proceeding from their huge holdings in West Africa to link up with their small toehold in the east at French Somaliland. In 1898 General Kitchener confronted French Captain Jean-Baptiste Marchand at Fashoda. War threatened, as provocative correspondence and news accounts were issued on both sides. In the end, the heavily outnumbered French backed down, and France retreated to its substantial holdings in Algeria, and to Morocco, which it later divided with Spain in 1912.

Labor Issues: Coercion and Unionization. Throughout Africa, Europeans confronted the problem of finding labor for their new farms and enterprises. By confiscating African land and redistributing it among themselves, Europeans took farms away from Africans and produced a new wage-labor force. The 1913 Natives Land Act of South Africa closed 87 percent of South African land to African ownership; the remaining 13 percent was the most marginal land. The newly displaced labor force was especially vital for the new coffee plantations in the highlands of East Africa. In the farming areas of Kenya, Northern Rhodesia, Nyasaland, and Angola a system of tenancy without wages developed, a kind of share-cropping system. Within their colonies in Angola and Mozambique, the Portuguese used intimidation to coerce labor, but the Africans often fled or otherwise subverted the plans of their colonizers. The British colonies, which used the carrot of (low) wages, seemed more successful in eliciting production. Along the coast, indentured laborers from India, China, and Southeast Asia were imported by the thousands to work in the sugar plantations.

The greatest problem was finding labor for the South African diamond and gold mines (and later for the great copper mines in the Congo as well). Taxation was introduced that had to be paid in cash, forcing all Africans to find some way of raising the money. Jobs in the mines were one alternative. Because the Europeans feared the revolutionary potential of a stable African labor force in the mines, they usually recruited workers on contracts for only one or two years at a time. They split up families, housing the male workers in barracks-like accommodations near the mines while exiling their families to distant reservations, where the women and children carried on limited farming and craft production. The mine owners did not pay the workers enough to support their families so the farming and handicrafts of the women in effect subsidized the workers' salaries.

Trade unions in the mines organized only the white skilled workers and kept Africans out of these jobs. In 1906, when the mines employed 18,000 whites, 94,000 Africans, and 51,000 Chinese indentured laborers, the white skilled workers went on strike to protest their being squeezed out by the Chinese and Blacks. Owners broke this strike through the use of Afrikaner strike breakers, but ultimately the Chinese miners were repatriated and the skilled jobs were reserved for whites. Race thus trumped both the free markets of capitalism and the solidarity of labor unions.

GENDER RELATIONSHIPS IN COLONIZATION

The Europeans who traveled overseas to trade beginning in the sixteenth century were almost invariably males, and they frequently entered into sexual liaisons with local women. As the men stayed longer, these relationships became increasingly important for business and administration as well as for social and sexual pleasure. One example was the **signares**, concubines or mistresses, of French traders in the Senegambia, present-day Senegal and Gambia. As the Senegal Company forbade its traders to marry locally, the men found concubines among the local Wolof and Lebou peoples. These women helped the men to negotiate local languages, customs, and health conditions.

In India, the **nabobs**, the successful traders who often became wealthy, frequently took local women in much the same way. Not forbidden to marry, they fathered Anglo-Indian children who came to form a small but important community of their own, especially in the large port cities of Bombay, Madras, and Calcutta.

As Europeans began to establish colonies, and as women began to travel to these colonies, usually with husbands, or in search of husbands, European women discouraged relationships between the colonizing men and the colonized women. More rigid boundaries were established. In both India and Africa observers saw increasing distance and racism enter into sexual and gender relationships between colonizer and colonized. The new guidelines for inter-racial behavior restricted not only sexual but also social relationships. As these relationships between men and women became less free, so, too, did the informality among the men.

Earlier historians had attributed this increasing distance to the restrictive attitudes of the European women, who wished to prevent their husbands' mixing with the local women. More recent, feminist scholarship has attributed the responsibility for the increased distance to both husband and wife. Both exhibited racism. Whatever may have been the differences of opinion between European men and women concerning the relationships between European men and the colonized women, both usually wished to restrict local men from intimate contact with European women. As colonial settlements increased in size and stability, each family tended to view itself, somewhat pompously, as a representative of the rulers, a colonial outpost in miniature.

Did the colonizing women form a solidarity with their colonized sisters? Most contemporary historians think not. The colonizers tended to fasten on flaws in the gender relations among the colonized peoples, and then set out to introduce reforms. In India the British outlawed *sati*, the practice of widows burning themselves to death on their deceased husbands' funeral pyres; they introduced a minimum age of marriage; they urged widow remarriage despite upper-caste Hindu resistance. In Africa they sought to end polygamy. In each case, the colonial government emphasized the superiority of its own practices, and the good fortune of the colonized to have the Europeans there to save them from themselves. The European colonizers pointed to their

signares African concubines of French traders in the Senegambia.

nabob A British employee of the East India Company who made a huge fortune in India, often through corruption, in the eighteenth century.

Christmas in India, a sketch by E.K. Johnson, *The Graphic*, 1881. Just as, for the most part, European men did not socialize or form a solidarity with the men whose country they had colonized, so, too, the women kept themselves apart and their lives centered on their families and their European friends. The wife would oversee the running of the household as she was accustomed to doing at home. Here the *ayah* looks after the youngest child in much the same way that Nanny would have back in England.

Sati ceremony, Allahabad, India, 1946. A widow on a funeral pyre, prepared to commit *sati* (suttee), ritual suicide, in order to accompany her husband in his death. *Sati* had been practiced for centuries by a very small number of upper caste Hindu women. The British outlawed *sati* in 1829, with the support of some Indians and against the opposition of others. Although illegal and very rare, the practice occasionally continues.

interventions in gender relations to justify and praise their own colonial rule. The colonizing women did the same.

The colonial presence did, however, introduce new patterns of gender relations into the colonies, based on the European models. At least some of the colonized peoples chose to move toward a more European style of gender relations. They wanted more education for women, more freedom of choice in marriage, more companionate marriages, and an end to *sati* in India, to polygamy in parts of Africa, and to footbinding in China. Sometimes people adopted new customs because they seemed better, sometimes because the new behavior won favor for the colonized peoples with the colonizing masters.

Later, as nationalism took root, people began to reject at least some of the foreign practices because of their colonial associations. Some women who had begun by welcoming the aspirations of Western feminist freedoms, such as equal educational opportunity, the right to work outside the home, setting limits on family size, owning property, and equal rights under law, later began to feel that these "freedoms" contradicted traditional family values in their own society, and came to reject them. They also analyzed the relationships between European men and women more closely, and often found them fraught with tension and anxiety. They caricatured at least some of the colonial intrusions into their family and gender relationships as "white men saving brown women from brown men."

ANTI-COLONIAL REVOLTS, 1857–1914

To be conquered by European colonial powers generally evoked anxiety and resentment. Not everyone, of course, shared these emotions. Some of the conquered people found new opportunities in working with or for the conquering powers. Personally, they might find jobs, education, business opportunities, and new professions. For their countries, they might find the imperial powers imposing peace among otherwise warring factions and a rule of law that might displace the arbitrary rule of local officials. New medical and technological systems might raise the standard of living.

For the most part, however, the conquered peoples usually were resentful. Or they became resentful. They might see some benefits to early colonial rule, but after a time they were usually irritated by the "glass ceilings" that kept local people out of higher level jobs in the administration, even when they were qualified. Even if new colonial businesses offered new opportunities, the bulk of the profits was sent back to the colonizing country. The new educational, legal, and administrative systems undermined local traditions, culture, and religion. The use of a foreign language in public life—the norm in colonial situations—also inhibited the development of indigenous cultures. At least as significant as any of these more tangible frustrations were the racism and disrespect that colonized peoples experienced from most of the colonizers, and that they deeply resented. Sooner or later, most colonized people wanted their independence. In region after region they rose in revolt against colonial rule.

Many of these, however, looked backward, to restoring the institutions that had preceded colonialism. This was a common early reaction to colonialism. The 1857–8 revolt in India took this position; as did the Mahdist revolt on the upper Nile (1881–98); so, too, did Shamil, "ruler of the righteous and destroyer of the unbeliever," inspired by an Islamic mystical brotherhood against Russia in the Caucasus (between 1834 and 1859); Emilio Aguinaldo against the United States in the Philippines (1898–1902); and peasant warfare against the Dutch in Bali and Lombok, Indonesia (1881–94), and in Sumatra (1881–1908).

Later, armed revolts and nonviolent political movements against colonial rule became more forward-looking. Their leaders sought not a simple return to the past but a newly restructured nation, usually incorporating significant elements of the past with new goals based in part on innovations introduced by colonial powers. In India, the Indian National Congress, founded in 1885, proposed a pattern of parliamentary democracy for India, often (but not always) with an admixture of Hindu reformism. In 1907, in Egypt, Saad Zaghlul (1857–1927) founded the Hizb al-Umma or People's Party, a reformist party which, in turn, became the core of the nationalist Wafd party after 1919. By 1911, the authors of the Chinese revolution looked forward to modernizing their country. The Young Turk party, formed in 1878 in patriotic anger against the Ottoman defeats in the Balkans, grew into a revolutionary party by 1908. The Young Turks, like the Chinese nationalists, saw as their first task the removal of the ruling government, the Ottomans, before going on to further reforms. Indonesia's first nationalist association, the Budi Utomo, was formed in 1908; South Africa's National Congress in 1912; and Viet Nam's Viet Nam Quang Phuc Hoi in 1913.

Each of these organizations had a conception of the future nation it was constructing, modeled in part on European military, economic, political, and administrative forms, but also incorporating its own cultural, religious, and social dimensions. Perhaps the most interesting of all these responses was that of Japan. By the mid-1850s, Japan had witnessed the partial colonization and humbling of China before the Western powers. When American warships entered Japanese waters in 1853, the Japanese feared that a similar fate awaited them. They took dramatic action to insure that they would not fall victim to colonial rule.

JAPAN: FROM ISOLATION TO EQUALITY, 1867–1914

In terms of nationalism, Japan was unified by race, with accepted legends of its national history and with a single dynasty of emperors that related back to the founding of the nation in the seventh century B.C.E., a single national language, an integrated national political structure, and an island-based geography. Japan's insular nature was intensified in the early 1600s when the government closed the country to foreign, especially European, contact. Rather than accept the European model of competitive nation-states, Japan at this point chose relative isolation. Faced with a challenge from Western nations in 1853, however, Japan recognized the need to transform itself militarily, economically, diplomatically, politically, and culturally. The history of Japan after 1853 charts its move from isolation to full, prominent participation in the world of nation-states.

The End of the Shogunate

By 1639, Japan had shut down commerce and contact with the European world, except for a Dutch outpost, virtually quarantined on Deshima Island in Nagasaki harbor, which was allowed to receive one ship each year. The Japanese also permitted the Chinese to trade at Nagasaki, but only under severe restrictions. Some trade could also pass through the Ryukyu Islands to China, under the guise of "tribute," and Korea could trade through the islands of Tsushima. Otherwise, Japan was isolated. In the late 1700s and early 1800s, European ships would occasionally attempt to establish contact, but the Japanese turned them away.

In 1853, however, the United States dispatched Commodore Matthew Perry (1794–1858) with a small squadron, including three steam frigates, to force Japan to open to trade as China had been opened in the Opium War a decade before. Japan lacked the means to resist the Americans and the European powers that soon followed, and over the next few years the country opened more ports, at first on the periphery, but then at Nagasaki, Kobe, and Yokahama. Japan opened Edo (Tokyo) and Osaka to foreign residents, and then granted the foreigners extraterritorial legal rights. Foreigners were permitted to stipulate Japan's tariff policies. In 1863 and 1864, in the face of firing on their ships, British, French, Dutch, and American naval forces demolished Japanese coastal forts and supplies and forced Japan to pay an indemnity. Like China, Japan seemed headed toward control by foreigners.

Unlike China, however, young, vigorous leaders seized control of the government of Japan, forcing a dramatic restructuring of the nation's politics, administration, class structure, economy, technology, and culture. These leaders, for the most part young samurai warriors in the **han** (feudal estates) of Choshu and Satsuma at the southern extreme of Japan, decided that Japan's current government was not capable of coping with the European threat. Great diversity of opinion flourished among the approximately 250 different *han* in Japan, but the most powerful regional leaders felt that the **shogun** or military governor, who ruled Japan in the name of the emperor, should be removed and the emperor himself should be restored as the direct ruler of Japan. The young samurai, members of Japan's hereditary military elite, should formulate the policies of the new administration.

The samurai were able to employ some of the technological information introduced by the Dutch from their station in Nagasaki harbor. Indeed, in 1811 the shogunate had established an office for translating Dutch material, and it was expanded into a school for European languages and science in 1857. Some of the *han*, including Satsuma, Choshu, and Mito, did the same. By 1840, some Japanese were already casting Western guns and artillery. Sakuma Zozan (1811–64), one of the advocates of adopting Western military methods, coined the motto of the movement: "Eastern Ethics; Western Science." Japan could adopt Western technology, he counseled, especially military technology, while still maintaining its own culture.

Sakuma believed that opening the country was both necessary and beneficial. Not everyone agreed, however, and in 1860 a group of samurai from the conservative

han In Japan, a territory or feudal estate controlled by a **daimyo** under the Tokugawa shogunate (1603–1868). They were abolished in 1871.

shogun The military leader who ruled Japan in the name of the emperor.

han of Mito argued a contrary position: "Revere the Emperor; Expel the Barbarian." The lines of conflict were sharpening. Political violence increased as exponents of the opposing positions attacked each other. Mito loyalists assassinated Sakuma and another reform leader in 1864 and then committed ritual suicide. Attacks on foreigners taking up residence and conducting business in Japan also increased.

In 1865, a group of young samurai in Choshu attacked and defeated their **daimyo**, the ruler of their *han*, establishing control of the government of Choshu. Next year, the armed forces of Choshu confronted and defeated those of the shogun, while the other *daimyo* sat out the contest. In 1868, the forces of Choshu and Satsuma, joining with those of several other more remote *han*, seized control of the emperor's palace in Kyoto and declared the shogunate ended, the lands of the shogun confiscated, and the emperor restored to imperial power. Most of the fighting was over by November, although naval battles continued into early 1869. The **Meiji restoration** ended the power of the shogunate forever and brought the *daimyo* and their young samurai to power in the name of the Emperor Meiji (r. 1867–1912). The emperor assumed the throne at the age of fourteen and reigned over a national transformation of astonishing scope and speed.

Policies of the Meiji Government

On April 8, 1868, the revolutionary leaders issued a Charter Oath in the name of the Emperor Meiji. The fifth and last article proved the most important: "Knowledge shall be sought throughout the world so as to strengthen the foundations of imperial rule." The new goal was "a rich country and a strong military." The new leaders had already begun to search the world for new political, economic, and military models that might be adapted to Japan's needs.

After treaty agreements had been signed in 1858, the shogun had already dispatched embassies to the United States in 1860 and to Europe in 1862, beginning official exchanges of information. Now a two-year overseas goodwill mission, headed by Prince Iwakura Tonomi (1825–83), set out in 1871 to deepen relationships with the heads of state of the treaty powers, to discuss future treaty revisions, and to enable Japanese leaders to experience the West at first hand. Fifty-four students accompanied the mission. A ministry of education was established in 1871, and its first budget (1873) included funds for sending 250 students abroad to study. Many of these students became leaders in the new Japan. Foreign instructors were also brought to Japan. The late shogun's government had employed some foreigners in industrial enterprises, but the Meiji rulers imported far more. They set out to develop Hokkaido, the northern island, and brought in American experts,

daimyo The feudal lords of Japan, who by the sixteenth century controlled almost the entire country.

Meiji restoration The reforms effected in Japan in the name of the emperor Mutsuhito (r. 1867–1912), who was known as the Meiji emperor. During his reign constitutional changes restored the emperor to full power, displacing the militarily powerful shogun, and Japan adopted many Western innovations as it became a modern industrial state.

THE MEIJI RESTORATION AND INDUSTRIALIZATION IN JAPAN

1853	Commander Perry sails into Edo Bay, ending 250 years' isolation
1854	Treaty of Kanagawa gives US trading rights with Japan
1860s	Series of "unequal treaties" gives US, Britain, France, Russia, and Netherlands commercial and territorial privileges
1868	Tokugawa shogun forced to abdicate. Executive power vested with emperor in Meiji restoration
1871	Administration is overhauled; Western-style changes introduced
1872	National education system introduced, providing teaching for 90 per cent of children by 1900 First railway opened
1873	Old order changed by removal of privileges of samurai class
1876	Koreans, under threat, agree to open three of their ports to the Japanese and exchange diplomats
1877	Satsuma rebellion represented last great (unsuccessful) challenge of conservative forces
1879	Representative system of local government introduced
1884	Western-style peerage (upper house) is created
1885	Cabinet government introduced
1889	Adoption of constitution based on Bismarck's Germany
1889	Number of cotton mills has risen from 3 (1877) to 83
1894–5	War with China ends in Japanese victory
1895	Japan annexes Taiwan and Pescadores Islands
1902	Britain and Japan sign military pact
1904–5	War with Russia ends in Japanese victory
1910	Japan annexes Korea
1914	Japan joins World War I on side of Allies

who introduced large-scale farming practices. By 1879 the ministry of industry employed 130 foreigners. Doctors were brought from Germany to teach medicine, and from America to teach natural and social sciences. After a few years, however, the cost of importing foreign experts outweighed the benefits, and fewer were employed. Missionaries, who came at their own expense, were an important exception.

Restructuring Government. The emperor was brought from his home in Kyoto to Edo, the former capital of the shogun, which was renamed Tokyo ("Eastern Capital") in 1868. In 1869, the *daimyo* of four of the most important *han*—Choshu, Satsuma, Tosa, and Hizen—turned over their estates to the emperor, setting the pattern for other *daimyo*. At first the *daimyo* were appointed governors, but two years later their domains were abolished and reorganized among the other prefectures of Japan. The *daimyo* retained certain rights of tax collection, which kept them financially well off, and stipends were paid to the samurai to avoid outright revolt. Nevertheless, a decade of samurai revolts in Choshu, Kyushu, Hizen, and, by far the largest, in Satsuma did challenge the new government. In Satsuma 40,000 troops, under the reluctant leadership of Saigo Takamori, confronted the government and were crushed. Japan's national government held firm.

The core of the central government's new army, 10,000 men drawn from Satsuma, Choshu, and Tosa, was established in 1871. In 1878, the army was reorganized and money was invested in modern equipment, much of it manufactured in Japan. An army staff college began to train an officer corps following a German model, while the navy adapted a British model, often purchasing its ships from Britain. Service in the armed forces introduced Japanese conscripts to new ways of life, some travel, reading and writing, Western-style uniforms and shoes, nationalism, and reverence for the emperor. Japan was becoming the most powerful nation in East Asia.

SOURCE

Fukuzawa Yukichi: Cultural Interpreter

Born into the lower levels of the feudal aristocracy in Kyushu, Fukuzawa Yukichi (1834–1901) had a thirst for knowledge that took him to Osaka, Nagasaki (for Dutch learning), to the United States in 1860 with the very first Japanese official mission (and again in 1867), and to Europe in 1862. Fukuzawa rejected government office, the usual alternative, in favor of private life as a journalist and teacher. He earned a reputation as the foremost interpreter of the West to Japan and his books describing the West as he understood it sold in the hundreds of thousands to a nation hungry for such observation and interpretation. He founded a school in Tokyo that later became Keio University, the training ground of many of Japan's business

leaders. The following excerpts are from Fukuzawa's Autobiography, *published in 1899. He states his goal of interpreting the West fairly, even though he knows that he will face opposition.*

The final purpose of all my work was to create in Japan a civilized nation, as well equipped in both the arts of war and peace as those of the Western world. I acted as if I had become the sole functioning agent for the introduction of Western culture. It was natural then that I would be disliked by the older type of Japanese, and suspected of working for the benefit of foreigners. ... I regard the human being as the most sacred and responsible of all orders, unable in reason to do anything base. ... In short, my creed is that a man should find his faith in independence and self-respect. (p. 214)

He investigates the style of Western institutions:

For instance, when I saw a hospital, I wanted to know how it was run—who paid the running expenses; when I visited a bank, I wished to learn how the money was deposited and paid out. By similar first-hand queries, I learned something of the postal system and the military conscription then in force in France but not in England. A perplexing institution was representative government. ... For some time it was beyond my comprehension to understand what they [political parties] were "fighting" for, and what was meant, anyway, by "fighting" in peace time. "This man and that man are 'enemies' in the House," they would tell me. But these "enemies" were to be seen at the same table, eating and drinking with each other. (p. 134)

Restructuring the Economy. Recognizing an economic principle that underlay the industrial revolution in Britain, Japan first built up its agriculture. It needed the profits, and it needed the food and manpower that an effective agriculture would make available for urban industry. New seeds, fertilizer, and methods were introduced throughout the islands, and Hokkaido was opened to farming. Agricultural colleges spread the new techniques and information. In the 1880s, agricultural production went up by about 30 percent, and from 1890 to 1915 by 100 percent. This production included not only food crops but also tea, cotton, and silk, mostly for the export market. The profits from increased agricultural production did not go to the peasants but to the landlord, who invested them in commerce or industry. Poorer peasants were squeezed off the land by high rents, and all peasants were heavily taxed to fund the large expenses of industrialization and militarization.

In large-scale industrialization, the government was the entrepreneur. It built the first railway line, between Tokyo and Yokohama, in 1872. In two decades about 2000 miles of track followed. Within the cities, trolleys and *rikishas* (rickshaws) supplemented the train lines. Telegraph lines linked all the major cities by 1880. The government financed coal mines, iron mines, a machine-tool factory, cement works, glass and tile factories, wool and cotton textile mills, shipyards, mines, and weapons manufacture. In 1873 it established the Imperial College of Engineering. But the industry that contributed the most, silk, which accounted for more than 40 percent of all of Japan's exports, was developed largely by private entrepreneurs.

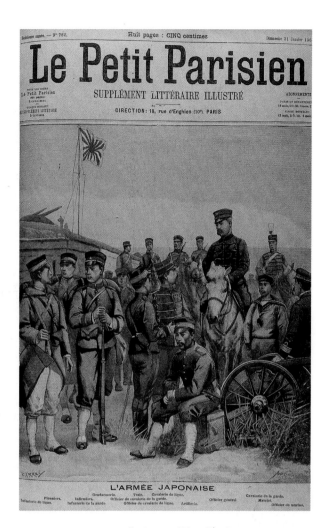

L'ARMÉE JAPONAISE

East wears West. The Japanese troops pictured on the front of this French magazine are a perfect example of the detail to which the government of Japan was willing to go in their efforts to fit into the modern world of early twentieth-century politics and fashions.

Urbanization. Under the Tokugawa shogunate, 1603–1867, each *daimyo* had his own capital. As a result, Japan had a rich array of administrative towns and cities spread throughout the country. During the Meiji restoration, they provided the network for the diffusion of new cultural patterns. Some cities stood out: Kyoto, the home of the emperor, was the center of traditional culture; Osaka was the most important business center; and Edo (Tokyo) was, by the mid-1800s, the largest and most flourishing of the major cities, with a population of a half million to a million people.

Tokugawa urban culture had mixed strains. At the center of business life were merchants dedicated to making money. Yet they liked entertainment and found it outside their homes. Homes were for wives, children, and household duties. The amusement quarters of the city were for restaurants, theater, artistic culture, the female companionship of *geisha* personal entertainers, and prostitutes.

Social networks based on neighborhoods, shrines, guilds, and civic needs, such as firefighting, provided a sense of community, and cities grew relatively slowly in the first generation of the restoration. By 1895 only 12 percent of Japan's population of 42 million lived in cities. Industrialization in large factories had barely begun. In 1897 only 400,000 workers in all of Japan were working in factories employing more than five workers. By the turn of the century, however, the institutional and economic changes of the restoration were taking effect, and urban populations multiplied, so that by the mid-1930s 45 percent of the 69 million people of Japan were living in cities. The industrial labor force reached 1.7 million in 1920 (and 6 million by 1936).

The culture of the cities changed dramatically. Japanese cities, crowded and subject to fire and earthquake, changed not only with cultural and technological innovations,

Advertisement throwaway from the Mitsui dry-goods store (later Mitsuoki Department Store), Tokyo, c. 1895. Retail outlets were obvious signs of the drive to embrace industrialized Western culture, as this "before" and "after" picture aptly demonstrates. The traditional first floor (bottom), with its legions of clerks haggling over material, has been augmented by the new-fangled second floor (top), where a more serene atmosphere and slick glass display cases proclaim a new style of consumerism.

but also with the necessity to rebuild from time to time. Edward Seidensticker's remarkable study of Tokyo between 1867 and 1923, *Low City, High City*, describes a double transformation. The old heart of Tokyo, the low city, developed bigger businesses, more raucous entertainment, and newer fashions, but it remained rooted in the plebeian culture of the Tokugawa period of Edo. The high city, built literally on somewhat higher ground, was developed later, with modern buildings, more refinement of a Western sort, and a more modernist culture.

Cultural and Educational Change. Western cultural styles, superficial and profound, proliferated in Meiji Japan. The Gregorian calendar and the seven-day week, with Sunday as a holiday, were adopted in 1882, and the metric system in 1886. Samurai men began to prefer Western haircuts to the traditional shaved head and topknot. The military dressed in Western-style uniforms, and in 1872 Western dress became mandatory at all official ceremonies. Meat eating was encouraged, despite Buddhist ethics, and *sukiyaki*, a meat and vegetable dish especially cooked at the table, was developed as part of Japanese cuisine.

Japanese readers turned avidly to Western texts. Philosophers of the Enlightenment drew attention to individual rights, and Utilitarians, such as John Stuart Mill, were read and appreciated. The more combative social Darwinism of Herbert Spencer proved attractive as a justification for Japan's sense of its growing power and coming imperialism, and Samuel Smiles' emphasis on *Self Help* also found a receptive readership.

Tokugawa Japan had valued formal education. Samurai had attended Confucian-based schools run by the *han*; commoners had studied in schools located in Buddhist temples. At the time of the Meiji restoration, an estimated 45 percent of adult males and 15 percent of adult females could read and write, about the same proportions as

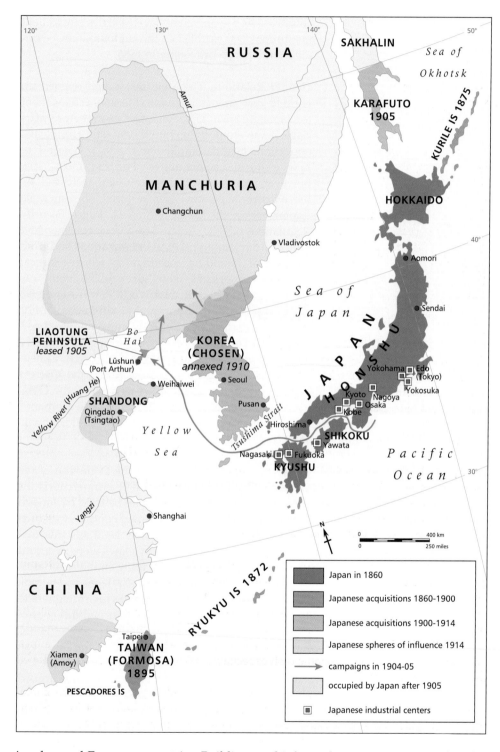

120°   130°   140°   50°

RUSSIA   SAKHALIN   Sea of Okhotsk

KARAFUTO 1905   KURILE IS 1875

MANCHURIA

• Changchun   HOKKAIDO

• Vladivostok   40°

• Aomori

Sea of Japan   • Sendai

LIAOTUNG PENINSULA *leased 1905*   Bo Hai   KOREA (CHOSEN) *annexed 1910*   J A P A N   H O N S H U

Lüshun (Port Arthur) •   Yokohama ▢ ▢ Edo (Tokyo)
          Yokosuka
Weihaiwei •   Seoul •   Kyoto ▢ Nagoya
          Osaka ▢ ▢
SHANDONG   Pusan •   Kobe ▢
Yellow River (Huang He)   Hiroshima ▢ •
Qingdao (Tsingtao) •   Tsushima Strait   SHIKOKU
          ▢ Yawata
Yellow Sea   Nagasaki ▢ ▢ Fukuoka   *Pacific Ocean*
          KYUSHU   30°

Yangzi

• Shanghai

          N
          0   400 km
          0   250 miles

C H I N A

          RYUKYU IS 1872

Taipei •
Xiamen (Amoy) •   TAIWAN (FORMOSA) 1895

PESCADORES IS

Legend:
- ▢ Japan in 1860
- ▢ Japanese acquisitions 1860-1900
- ▢ Japanese acquisitions 1900-1914
- ▢ Japanese spheres of influence 1914
- → campaigns in 1904-05
- ▢ occupied by Japan after 1905
- ▢ Japanese industrial centers

The expansion and modernization of Japan. Responding to the threats of foreign gunboats, Japanese samurai leaders overthrew the long-established Tokugawa shogunate and restored imperial power under the Emperor Meiji in 1868. Within fifty years, industrial development, growing international trade, and territorial expansion made Japan a world power. Initially asserting its control of neighboring islands, and then taking advantage of Manchu decline, its victories over China (1894–95) and Russia (1904–05) established Japanese control over Taiwan, Korea, and Karafuto (southern Sakhalin), and its dominant influence over Manchuria and even parts of mainland China.

in advanced European countries. Building on this base, the government introduced a highly centralized system of education and then mandated compulsory attendance. By 1905, over 90 percent of both boys and girls of primary school age were attending school. The schools were recognized for high quality, for providing public education superior to private schools, and for helping move Japan from the feudal, hierarchical society of Tokugawa Japan to a more egalitarian system than that of most European

Meiji classroom scene c. 1900. The Meiji rulers saw education as critical to Japan's modernization. The Charter Oath declared that, "Knowledge shall be sought throughout the world." Even before the Meiji, educational standards had been high; under the Meiji they approached 100 percent literacy.

countries. At the university level, a series of excellent institutions was established throughout Japan, beginning with Tokyo University in 1886.

Gender Relations. The Meiji restoration opened up entirely new arenas of public life and achievement for Japanese men, and, for a few years before marriage, some women also found new opportunities in education, factory employment, and a handful of new cultural opportunities. For the most part, however, women's public options were restricted. As the emperor's position was restored, so was male dominance in the home reinforced. Police Security Regulations of 1890, Article 5, prohibited women and minors from joining political organizations and from holding or attending meetings in which political speeches or lectures were given. (The vote was granted to women only after World War II.) The 1898 Civil Code reinforced patriarchy within the family, granting the male head of the family unquestioned authority. Women had few legal rights. At marriage, control over a woman's property passed to her husband. Fathers held exclusive right to custody over children. Concubinage was abolished in 1880, but society sanctioned prostitution and the discreet keeping of mistresses. As high school education was extended to women, the Girls' High School Law of 1899 declared its goal to create "good wives and wise mothers." Within the home, women held great authority and respect, but they were allowed virtually no place in the public life of Japan.

War, Colonialism, and Equality in the Family of Nations. From the beginning of the Meiji restoration, Japan sought to end the demeaning provisions of extraterritoriality, which required that foreigners charged with legal crimes in Japan be tried by foreign courts rather than by Japanese courts. Japan also sought to regain control of its own tariffs. These goals provided the rationales for introducing new legal systems that were more consistent with those of Western countries. If Japan's laws were in accord with those of Europe, there would be no justification for continuing extraterritoriality. The British relinquished extraterritoriality in 1899 when the new legal codes took effect. Other nations followed suit, and Japan reciprocated by allowing foreigners to establish residences outside the treaty ports. Additional treaties returned full control over tariffs to Japan in 1911.

War and colonization also seemed important to full membership in the European community of nations. Yamagata Aritomo (1838–1922), the chief proponent of the law of universal conscription in 1873 and the chief architect of Japan's new army, argued this position, and turned his attention to the conquest of Korea. Japan had forced the establishment of a legation in Korea in 1876. As political leaders in that country divided over policy issues, some sought support from more conservative China, others from more progressive Japan. When fighting between the groups broke out in 1894, both China and Japan sent in troops, and war began between the two powers. On land, Japanese armies seized all of Korea and pushed on into Manchuria. At sea, they defeated the Chinese fleet, captured Port Arthur, the naval base in southern Manchuria, and the port of Weihaiwei on the Shandong peninsula. Peace negotiations gave Japan Taiwan and the Pescadores Islands, and Japan supplanted China as the dominant nation of East Asia. Korea was formally recognized as independent, but Japan held sway there nonetheless. Japan was also to receive control over the Liaotung Peninsula, but an international diplomatic consortium led by Russia forced it to withdraw, despite Japan's resentment.

In the first years of the twentieth century, two further engagements with the West ratified Japan's arrival among the powers of the world. First, in 1902, Britain and Japan signed an alliance, the first military pact on equal terms between a European and a non-Western country. It brought together the most powerful navies of Europe and of East Asia. The treaty blocked Russian aspirations and further secured Japan's semicolonial control over China. Second, in response to continuing Russian penetration of Manchuria and increasingly hostile diplomacy, Japan attacked the Russian fleet in Port Arthur in 1904 and declared war. Fighting far from the center of their country, the Russian army was defeated. A Russian fleet dispatched from the Baltic was intercepted and annihilated by the Japanese in 1905 as it crossed the Straits of Tsushima.

An Asian power had defeated a European power for the first time since the victories of the Ottomans in eastern Europe in the seventeenth century. (In Russia, the defeat precipitated a revolution against the government in 1905.) In the peace conference convened by American President Theodore Roosevelt, Japan was given a protectorate over Korea, predominant rights over southern Manchuria (including the Liaotung Peninsula), and control of southern Sakhalin Island. In 1910, with no European power protesting, Japan formally annexed Korea. Japan had reached the international status it had desired—less than a half-century after embarking on its quest. The values of nationalism, technological innovation, and imperialism had become as supreme in Japan as they were in Europe.

NATIONALISM AND IMPERIALISM
WHAT DIFFERENCE DO THEY MAKE?

Nationalism often inspired existing nations with pride in their past and aspirations for their future. It gave them a sense of their potential strength and power. It often united people together in mutual endeavors and encouraged a greater sense of equality and common purpose among them. This was part of the message of the English, American, and French revolutions. For regional groups that were not political nations, like Italy and Germany, the spirit of nationalism often inspired action toward unifying the regions into nations. For groups that felt themselves denied their national identity by a larger power that had colonized them—like the Greeks, Romanians, and Bulgarians under the Ottoman Empire, and much of the world under European colonialism—nationalism offered the promise of autonomy and control over their own affairs. At its best, nationalism encouraged nations to learn from one another, as each had something unique to contribute.

Nationalism has also inspired competition among nations that has sometimes evoked greatness, but has also frequently led to warfare, conquest, and colonialism. It has led to disputes among groups claiming national identity and national geographic borders that are difficult, if not impossible, to resolve. It has accompanied, and

RUSSO-JAPANESE WAR 1904–5: KEY EVENTS	
The war arose from conflicting ambitions in Manchuria and Korea, in particular the Russian occupation of Port Arthur (1896) and Amur province (1900).	
May 1904	Battle of Yalu River: the Russians are defeated by the Japanese in the vicinity of Antung (now Dandong), Manchuria. The river forms the border with Korea, and the Japanese army forces a crossing against light opposition. Quickly overcoming the Russians, who retreat north, the Japanese move to besiege Port Arthur (Lushun).
May 1904–January 1905	Siege of Port Arthur: the Japanese fleet blockades the harbor, keeping the Russian fleet bottled up, while the army launches a series of minor attacks. Japanese eventually overcome garrison, which surrenders, after heavy losses. Japanese lose some 58,000 men.
February–May 1905	Battle of Mukden (Shenyang): Japanese defeat Russians outside the capital city of Manchuria, in the last major engagement of the war, in which 41,000 Japanese were killed and wounded and the Russian dead and wounded totaled more than 32,000. The czar is finally persuaded to accept US mediation. Russia's Baltic Fleet is annihilated in the Tsushima Straits.
August 1905	Peace agreement: Russia surrendered its lease on Port Arthur, ceded South Sakhalin to Japan, evacuated Manchuria, and recognized Japanese interests in Korea. For the first time in more than two centuries an Asian power had defeated a European power. US president Theodore Roosevelt mediated the agreement and was awarded the Nobel Prize for peace (1906).

sometimes encouraged, racism and arrogance. It has created and perpetuated economic systems of great inequality in which the terms of trade are set by the powerful for their own benefit, often causing great suffering to the weak. All these aspects of nationalism—positive and negative—continued into the twentieth century—in ways that we shall explore in the next Part—and remain powerful today.

The political and industrial revolutions of the eighteenth and nineteenth centuries bound nations and peoples together more tightly than ever before. Historically great nations like China and Japan, which had lived mostly within their own regions, were pulled into greater participation in the global economy, politics, and culture. New political and industrial relations raised questions about the goals and the proper functions of the international economy: Is it to create profits or to provide for overall human welfare? Can it do both? How? Can the benefits of international competition be encouraged and its powers of destruction limited?

In this chapter we have seen European nations, and later Japan and the United States, backed by the power of their industrial revolutions, assert their control over much of the globe. Imperialists usually claimed that they were benefiting the peoples they ruled and cited statistics on new transport lines, new health clinics, new schools, and new political institutions. The conquered peoples usually pointed to evidence to the contrary: economies devastated, politics suppressed, and cultural traditions undermined. These legacies continued into the twentieth century, and they continue today as former colonizers and former colonies adjust their economies, cultures, and foreign relations to one another. Consciously and unconsciously the world proceeds against a background in which some nations conquered and lorded it over others. The sensitivities of those relationships are still quite raw as we see today when powerful nations attempt to exert their will politically, economically, and culturally, over weaker ones—and as the weaker choose to accept these conditions, to modify them, or to resist.

Review Questions

- How do you define nationalism? Would a strong nation and a weak nation use the same definition?
- Give examples of nations that formed by bringing together groups and regions, and give other examples of nations that formed by breaking apart from larger powers.
- In what ways were the colonization of India and China similar to each other? In what ways were they different?
- What benefits did colonialism bring to late-nineteenth-century colonies? Please cite specific examples. What benefits did it bring to colonizers? Please consider economic, political, and cultural aspects of colonialism. What were its negative effects on both colonizer and colonized?
- What do you believe to be the most important results of the coming of large numbers of European women to the colonies?
- What were the principal steps in Japan's actions to stave off colonial control?

Suggested Readings

PRINCIPAL SOURCES

Abernethy, David. *The Dynamics of Global Dominance: European Overseas Empires, 1415–1980* (New Haven: Yale University Press, 2000). Presents European expansion through a series of phases, notes its extraordinary power in reshaping the world, but sees it as ultimately self-liquidating. Comprehensive.

Bayly, C.A. *The Birth of the Modern World 1780–1914* (Malden, MA:Blackwell, 2004). A masterpiece of synthesis, combining political, economic, social, and cultural history in a global, interactive framework, by a master historian.

Cooper, Frederick and Ann Laura Stoler, eds. *Tensions of Empire* (Berkeley: University of California Press, 1997). Excellent anthology of recent writings on the social conditions in colonial life, including several essays on feminist perspectives.

Curtin, Philip, *et al. African History from Earliest Times to Independence*, 2nd ed. (New York: Longman, 1995). Masterly study especially good on the combination of history and anthropology. Four authors bring specialization across regions, disciplines, and styles of understanding. The narrative sometimes wanders among them.

Davis, Mike. *Late Victorian Holocausts: El Nino Famines and the Making of the Third World* (New York: Verso, 2001). Brings together many classic arguments about imperial exploitation of colonies, and emphasizes the cruelty of this exploitation at the time when major famines were also devastating colonial economies.

de Bary, William Theodore and Richard Lufrano, eds. *Sources of Chinese Tradition*, Vol. 2, 2nd ed. (New York: Columbia University Press, 2000). Outstanding source book, especially on cultural issues, from the Qing dynasty, to the present. Vol. 1 carries the earlier history.

Hay, Stephen, ed. *Sources of Indian Tradition*, Vol. 2, 2nd ed. (New York: Columbia University Press, 1988). Superb anthology of primary sources, especially strong on the religious and cultural bases of modern India, and their influence on its politics, about 1500 to the present. Vol. 1 carries earlier periods.

Hobsbawm, Eric. *The Age of Capital 1848–1875* (New York: Vintage Books, 1975). This series of Hobsbawm's books provide a well-written narrative sweep of world history through this period, from a leftist perspective. Often uses examples from popular culture, especially music.

——. *The Age of Empire 1875–1914* (New York: Vintage, 1987).

——. *The Age of Revolution 1789–1848* (New York: New American Library, 1962).

Hochschild, Adam. *King Leopold's Ghost* (New York: Houghton Mifflin, 1998). Narrates the horrifying story of the king's rule of the Congo, and the shipping agent who discovered and exposed it.

July, Robert J. *A History of the African People*, 4th ed. (Prospect Heights, IL: Waveland Press, 1992). Clearly written survey, especially good on political history.

Morris-Suzuki, Tessa. *The Technological Transformation of Japan* (Cambridge: Cambridge University Press, 1994). Follows the technical and managerial decisions that brought Japan to parity and even superiority in economic and technological modernization.

Said, Edward W. *Culture and Imperialism* (New York: Vintage Books, 1993). Said's various books emphasize the ways in which imperial powers used their own interpretations of culture to assert their supremacy over the countries they dominated and, often, to get the colonized people to believe it.

Tsunoda, Ryusaku, William Theodore de Bary, and Donald Keene, comps. *Sources of Japanese Tradition* (New York: Columbia University Press, 1958). Outstanding collection of primary sources, especially on the cultural leaders and philosophies of Japan, from earliest to modern times.

ADDITIONAL SOURCES

Adas, Michael, ed. *Islamic and European Expansion* (Philadelphia: Temple University Press, 1993). Still the best collection of introductory historiographic essays on the period 1000 to 1914 in world history.

Anderson, Benedict. *Imagined Communities* (London: Verso, 1983). Stresses the importance of the vision of nationalists in creating new nations, and the critical role of commercial publishing (print capitalism) in popularizing these visions.

Andrea, Alfred and James Overfield, eds., *The Human Record*, Vol. 2 (Boston: Houghton Mifflin, 3rd ed., 1998). Superb collection of primary documents on modern history.

Bayly, C.A. *Origins of Nationality in South Asia* (New York: Oxford University Press, 1998). Seeks to discover how Indians developed the concept of a modern nation from their own cultural materials as well as from new conceptions brought from the West.

Braudel, Fernand. *The Identity of France*, trans. by Sian Reynolds (New York; Harper and Row, 1988). Fascinating discussion of the process by which the various, disparate regions of France were unified into a single nation.

Briggs, Asa. *A Social History of England* (New York: Viking Press, 1983). Standard, well-written, well-illustrated history, stressing social conditions and change more than politics or economics.

Burns, E. Bradford. *Latin America: A Concise Interpretive History* (Englewood Cliffs: Prentice Hall, 6th ed., 1993). Excellent survey from a slightly leftist and critical perspective.

Burton, Antoinette. *Burdens of History* (Chapel Hill: University of North Carolina Press, 1994). Sees European women adopting positions sympathetic to imperialism as a means of showing that they deserved the same rights as men because they shared the same political perspectives.

Cheng, Pei-kai and Michael Lestz with Jonathan Spence, eds. *The Search for Modern China: A Documentary Collection* (New York: W.W. Norton, 1999). Excellent selection, very well annotated. Designed to accompany Spence's textbook of the same name, but also stands alone.

Chatterjee, Partha. *The Nation and Its Fragments* (Princeton: Princeton University Press, 1993). Analyzes some of the movements by which India began to come together as a nation. Thematically notes the importance of religion. Geographically stresses the Bengal region.

Collcutt, Martin, Marius Jansen, and Isao Kumakura. *Cultural Atlas of Japan* (New York: Facts on File, 1988). Superb introduction with fine text, maps, and illustrations that all work well together.

Columbia College, Columbia University. *Introduction to Contemporary Civilization in the West*, Vol. 2 (New York: Columbia University Press, 3rd ed. 1960). Outstanding sourcebook with lengthy excerpts from highly influential thinkers and actors.

Conrad, Joseph. *Heart of Darkness* (Mineola: New York: Dover Publications, 1990). A classic, brief novel on the cruelty and corruption of the "ruler" of a European outpost in the Congo interior.

Dalpat-Kavya Navnit (Selections from Dalpat the Poet), in Gujarati, ed. Deshavram Kashiram Shastri (Ahmedabad: Gujarat Vidyasabha, 1949). Dalpat's poetry expressed his beliefs that Indians in the mid-nineteenth century had much to learn from the British, including the methods of industrialization.

Davis, Lance E. and Robert A. Huttenback. *Mammon and the Pursuit of Empire* (New York: Cambridge University Press, 1989). Argues that imperialism did not pay, at least not financially, at least not after the beginning phases. A careful economic analysis.

Eley, Geoff and Ronald Grigor Suny, eds. *Becoming National* (New York: Oxford University Press, 1996). Excellent analysis of several major Western theories on the meaning of nationalism.

Engels, Friedrich. *The Origins of the Family, Private Property and the State*, ed. by Eleanor Burke Leacock (New York: International Publishers, 1973). Engels saw the exploitation of women as the first kind of economic exploitation that ultimately led to its fullest expression in the capitalist system.

Fujimura-Fanselow, Kumiko and Atsuko Kameda, eds. *Japanese Women* (New York: Feminist Press, 1995). Twenty-seven essays on many aspects of women in public and private life, their changing status, including men's views of the change.

Gluck, Carol. *Japan's Modern Myths: Ideology in the Late Meiji Period* (Princeton: Princeton University Press, 1985). Analyzes not only the formal ideologies, but also how they were received and perceived by the Japanese public.

Haldane, Charlotte. *The Last Great Empress of China* (Indianapolis: Bobbs-Merrill, 1965). A portrait of the powerful woman who effectively ruled China at the end of the nineteenth century and opposed reform.

Hanke, Lewis and Jane M. Rausch, eds. *People and Issues in Latin American History* (New York: Markus Wiener Publishing, 1990). Standard historical survey often presented through biography.

Headrick, Daniel R. *The Tools of Empire* (New York: Oxford University Press, 1981). Steamships, guns, and quinine were among the prerequisites of the European conquest of Africa.

Hertzberg, Arthur, ed. *The Zionist Idea* (Philadelpia: Jewish Publication Society, 1997). Still the best primary source introduction to early Zionist thought and its evolution, with a 100-page introduction.

Hirschmeier, Johannes. *The Origins of Entrepreneurship in Meiji Japan* (Cambridge, MA: Harvard University Press, 1964). Sees the economic transformation of Japan as the key to its development and demonstrates how it developed under government guidance.

Hutchinson, John and Anthony D. Smith, eds. *Nationalism* (New York: Oxford University Press, 1994). Survey of source materials on the meaning and significance of nationalism by nationalist leaders from around the world.

Kennedy, Paul. *The Rise and Fall of the Great Powers* (New York: Random House, 1987). Kennedy's discussion of what makes empires powerful, and what weakens them is engaging and provocative.

Lenin, V.I. *Imperialism, the Highest Stage of Capitalism* (Peking: Foreign Languages Press, 1965). Perhaps the strongest argument ever for the importance of the capitalist competition for markets, both for raw materials and for finished goods, as the basis for imperialism.

Magraw, Roger. *France 1815–1914: The Bourgeois Century* (Oxford: Oxford University Press, 1983). Useful survey stressing the importance of the middle classes.

Marx, Karl. *The First Indian War of Independence 1857–1859* (Moscow: Foreign Languages Press, n.d., c. 1960). As a journalist covering this war, Marx took a pro-European, imperialist position, that British rule in India was a benefit that would bring the colony into the modern world. Surprising?

Moore, Barrington, Jr. *The Social Origins of Dictatorship and Democracy* (Boston: Beacon Press, 1966). A classic of comparative history analyzing especially the role of the peasantry in revolutions from England to China.

Murphey, Rhoads. *A History of Asia* (New York: Addison Wesley Longman, 3rd ed., 1999). Useful survey.

Oliver, Roland. *The African Experience* (New York: Harper Collins, 1991). Sensitive, thoughtful brief survey of African history by a master of the field.

Renan, Ernest, "What is a Nation?" in Eley and Suny, pp. 42–55. A classic essay.

Restoring Women to History (Bloomington, IN: Organization of American Historians, 1988). Set of historiographic essays covering what we know of women's history around the world. Dated. Still useful.

SarDesai, D.R. *Southeast Asia Past and Present* (Boulder, CO: Westview Press, 3rd ed., 1994). Useful survey text.

Schirokauer, Conrad. *A Brief History of Chinese and Japanese Civilizations* (Fort Worth: Harcourt Brace Jovanovich, 2nd ed., 1989). Useful survey text.

Seagrave, Sterling, with Peggy Seagrave. *Dragon Lady: The Life and Legend of the Last Empress of China* (New York: Knopf, 1992). Biography of the woman who ran China's politics for her young son, and actively opposed modernization.

Spivak, Gayatri Chakravorty, "Subaltern Studies: Deconstructing Historiography," in Ranajit Guha and Gayatri Chakravorty Spivak, eds., *Selected Subaltern Studies* (New York: Oxford University Press, 1988), pp. 3–32. The subaltern scholars set out to reveal the importance of the little guy who had been left out; Spivak notes that the scholars left out women.

Strobel, Margaret, "Gender, Sex, and Empire," in Adas, pp. 345–75. Excellent introduction to issues of gender relations in imperial settings.

Teng, Ssu-yu and John K. Fairbank. *China's Response to the West: A Documentary Survey, 1839–1923* (New York: Atheneum, 1963). A superb, standard source book.

Wallerstein, Immanuel. *The Modern World-system 1: Capitalist Agriculture and the Origins of the European World-economy in the Sixteenth Century* (San Diego: Academic Press, 1974). Wallerstein's perspective on the core countries' dominance over the periphery is classic, but Eurocentric, problematic, and densely argued.

Wilentz, Sean. *Chants Democratic: New York City and the Rise of the American Working Class, 1788–1850* (New York: Oxford University Press, 1984). What was special about the American working class? Why did it not form a working-class political party? Wilentz' answers are cogent and lucid.

Wolf, Eric R. *Europe and the People without History* (Berkeley: University of California Press, 1982). Historical anthropologist Wolf looks at the systems of domination in modern history from the viewpoint of the colonized and the worker.

Wolfe, Patrick, "Imperialism and History: A Century of Theory, from Marx to Postcolonialism," *American Historical Review* CII, No. 2 (April 1997), 388–420. Enormously useful survey.

Yukichi, Fukuzawa. *The Autobiography of Yukichi Fukuzawa*, trans. by Eiichi Kiyooka (New York: Columbia University Press, 1966). Yukichi's nineteenth-century views of the West are insightful.

World History Documents CD-ROM

The Olympics and International Politics

Sports such as organized, competitive athletics reflect the world around them. When, where, by whom, in front of what audiences, and for what stakes sports are to be "played" are questions decided through political, economic, and cultural negotiations. In the most famous of all competitions, the modern Olympics, these external forces appear clearly and repeatedly. The ups-and-downs of the Olympics reflect the ups-and-downs of the world outside the arena.

For example, the reopening of the Olympic Games in Athens in 1896 was due to the enthusiastic promotions of a Frenchman, Baron Pierre de Coubertin. As a founding member of the International Olympic Committee, Coubertin struggled for many years to revive the Olympic Games of ancient Greece since their last staging some fifteen hundred years ago. Although Coubertin stressed his love of athletics, he succeeded in part because of the rampant nationalism of his age. Nations were eager to compete against one another, and sports provided a welcome, non-violent forum. The competition among athletes also became a competition among nations. In 1896, thirteen nations of Western Europe and the United States participated; by 2004, some two hundred nations from all over the world took part.

The decision to hold this first revived Olympic Games in Greece was in part to reconnect with the home of

Above The Olympic Games, Athens, 1896.

Right Women racing in the 100 meters, Olympic Games, Amsterdam, 1928.

the original Olympics, but it was designed also to deliver a political message to the Ottoman Empire, Greece's former colonial ruler and hostile neighbor: that Greece had revived as an independent nation, and that other regions of the Balkans were also seeking their independence.

Women competed in track-and-field events for the first time in the 1928 Amsterdam Olympics. This breakthrough in gender relations mirrored more wide-ranging victories for feminism in society at large, most especially the right to vote, which was accorded to women in several European countries and the United States in the decade just after World War I.

Germany staged the 1936 Berlin Olympics as a showcase for Hitler and his National Socialist (Nazi) Party. Leni Riefenstahl's documentary film, *Triumph of the Will*, produced for the government, captured the intensely nationalistic spirit that was proclaimed in parades and demonstrations for the occasion. Many nations hesitated to participate since they were quite aware of the dictatorship and racism of Hitler's government; nevertheless, forty-nine did. In the end they

witnessed the African-American athlete Jesse Owens deliver a great slap in the face to Hitler's racial theories of Aryan supremacy by winning the gold medal in both the 100 and 200 meter races, the long jump, and as part of the 400 meter relay race. Altogether, American track-and-field teams, including several African-American athletes, won twelve gold medals.

There were no Olympic Games in 1940 and 1944 because of World War II.

The right to host the Olympics has been a mark of national accomplishment. All of the first thirteen summer Games were hosted by cities in Western Europe and the United States. The fourteenth Games, held in Melbourne, Australia, in 1956, were the first departure from that pattern. From that time onward hosting of the Games became far more international. By according Japan the right to host the sixteenth Games in 1964, the International Olympic Committee recognized Japan's re-entry into the community of nations after World War II, and Japan went all-out in demonstrating its return to economic and political health. The new Olympic stadium designed by architect Kenzo Tange, along with the new *shinkansen*, or "bullet train" line (the fastest in the world), made clear Japan's renewed status as a world leader. In subsequent years, additional nations outside Western Europe, the United States, and Canada sought and

Above left Jesse Owens signals his acceptance of the gold medal in the long jump, and his defiance, with an American salute at Hitler's Berlin Olympics, 1936.

Above right The Tokyo Stadium (now the Yoyogi National Stadium) built by Kenzo Tange for the Tokyo Olympics, 1964.

Right A member of the International Olympic Committee talks with a masked PLO terrorist, Munich Olympics, 1972.

received the right to host the Olympics as a badge of their significance in international affairs: Mexico in 1968, Moscow in 1980, Korea in 1988. Beijing is scheduled to host the Games in 2008.

The dark as well as the bright side of international politics has spilled over into the Olympic Games. During the 1972 Munich Games, eight Palestinian terrorists brought the warfare of the Middle East to the Olympics. They invaded the Olympic Village, where athletes live during the Games, murdered two Israeli athletes, and seized nine more as hostages. Negotiations between Olympics officials and the terrorists failed. All

the Israeli hostages, one West German policeman, and five of the Palestinians were killed.

In 1979, the USSR invaded Afghanistan in support of a pro-Soviet faction in the ongoing civil war there. President Jimmy Carter responded symbolically by refusing to allow America to compete in the 1980 Olympics in Moscow. In retaliation, the USSR refused to participate in the 1984 Olympics in Los Angeles. Despite the high aspirations of Baron Coubertin in 1896, Olympic competition could not be sealed off from international political competition; on the contrary, they have always been tightly intertwined.

QUESTIONS

1. Can you imagine an Olympic Games in which athletes compete as individuals rather than as part of national teams? How would this be different?
2. Do you agree that sports as public competition mirror world events? Give examples.
3. In 1936 most eligible nations attended Hitler's Munich Olympics. In 1976, the United States boycotted the Moscow Olympics because of Russia's invasion of Afghanistan. Do you think either of these decisions was appropriate? Why?

PART 7

Exploding Technologies 1914–91

CONTESTED VISIONS OF A NEW INTERNATIONAL ORDER

The twentieth century began with great promise. The political and industrial revolutions of the previous two centuries encouraged western Europeans to believe that they were mastering the secrets of securing a long, productive, comfortable, and meaningful life for the individual and the community. They believed that they were transmitting these benefits around the globe through their colonial policies, and that their colonial possessions would continue long into the foreseeable future. Polish poet Wislawa Szymborska captured the optimism:

> Our twentieth century was going to improve on others . . .
> A couple of problems weren't going to come up anymore:
> Hunger, for example, and war, and so forth.

World War I, global economic depression, World War II, the Cold War, and revolts throughout the colonial world shattered many of these European illusions. "Anyone who planned to enjoy the world is now faced with a hopeless task," Szymborska wrote. (For the complete poem, "How Should We Live," see p. 681.)

What had gone wrong? Technology can produce catastrophe as well as creativity. Optimists at the beginning of the century overemphasized its positive potentials. They underestimated the problems of deciding its purposes, uses, and controls in a world of competition among nations, religions, ethnic groups, and ideologies.

The first half of the century saw technology put to use more in warfare than in peace (Chapters 19 and 20), but the second half brought a resurgence of optimism (Chapter 21): the United Nations emerged as a potential venue for conflict resolution and international bargaining, and the Cold War was contained as an armed truce and then came to an end virtually without bloodshed (although many

Atomic weapons test in the Marshall Islands, 1950.

proxy wars had been fought in its name). Technology—especially information and communication technology and biotechnology—was once again promising beneficial revolutions globally and in everyday life.

The world had heard such promises before, and once again the voices of caution were loud and clear: prosperity and opportunity were not trickling down to billions of impoverished people, neither in rich nor in poor countries; identity conflicts remained powerful and unresolved, and ethnic and religious violence broke out repeatedly around the globe; issues of gender identity, growing increasingly sensitive throughout the twentieth century, continued to expose tensions in family and public life; and technologies of destruction continued to multiply side by side with technologies of productivity.

METHODS OF MASS PRODUCTION AND DESTRUCTION

TECHNOLOGICAL SYSTEMS, 1914–37

"Technology" includes not only inventions but also the systems that produce and sustain them. Thomas Hughes, a historian of science and technology, explains this comprehensive definition:

> In popular accounts of technology, inventions of the late nineteenth century, such as the incandescent light, the radio, the airplane, and the gasoline-driven automobile, occupy center stage, but these inventions were embedded within technological systems. Such systems involve far more than the so-called hardware, devices, machines and processes, and the transportation, communication, and information networks that interconnect them. Such systems consist also of people and organizations. An electric light-and-power system, for instance, may involve generators, motors, transmission lines, utility companies, manufacturing enterprises, and banks. Even a regulatory body may be co-opted into the system. (Hughes, p. 3)

The technological enterprise grew into the most pervasive characteristic of the twentieth century and continues to grow. It has dramatically altered:

- the number, longevity, and health of the people who inhabit the globe;
- the size and organization of families;
- the location, design, and equipment of homes, neighborhoods, and workplaces;
- the nature and organization of work and the training necessary to do it;
- the quantities and varieties of food people eat as well as the regions of the globe from which they come;
- clothing;
- travel for business and pleasure;
- recreation;
- the strategies and destructive potentials of wars;
- the complexity and structure of economic, social, and governmental organizations; and
- the ecology—that is, the interaction of the life systems—of the earth.

Opposite **The Great Depression, 1929.** This photograph captures one of the many bread lines that wove their way through New York City during the Great Depression, this one being at Sixth Avenue and 42nd Street.

New farm technology. The American Burger tractor, invented in 1889, was the first to install an internal-combustion engine. With the introduction of automated farm machinery huge tracts of land around the world were brought under cultivation and food productivity soared. Here, in 1917, a woman from Vassar College in Poughkeepsie, New York, plows a field as part of the war effort.

SCIENTIFIC AND TECHNOLOGICAL CREATIVITY

The twentieth century continued to build on the inventions of the nineteenth and demonstrated an array of scientific and technological creativity never before known. As more people began to prosper, as business grew, and as new manufacturing processes spurred the development of new industries, demand led to an increasingly rapid pace of production. The ability to transmit electricity over long distances through the use of alternating current made widespread commercial grids possible. In 1886, a hydroelectric generating system was established at Niagara Falls, and by 1900, the basis of the modern electrical supply industry was in place. The first widespread application of the new energy was in lighting, with the creation of the incandescent lightbulb. Cities were eager to construct or buy into electrical grids to light up the night. In addition to street lighting and domestic lighting, workshops and factories could now operate round the clock. "Labor-saving" electrical appliances entered the home as well. The electric washing machine was patented in 1901, the vacuum cleaner in 1907. Both dramatically simplified women's domestic work. Electricity made possible the widespread use of the telegraph, telephone, and radio transmission. The phonograph had been invented by Thomas Alva Edison in 1877; by 1902, it had become a household product, with recordings of popular opera stars like Enrico Caruso and current vogues like ragtime music becoming increasingly widely available. Motion pictures had been created technologically in the 1890s, and by the early 1900s, they had become a popular entertainment. In 1909, newsreels appeared. Until 1927, the movies were silent, relying mostly on visual effects like slapstick comedy, as in the early films of Charlie Chaplin, perhaps the first great star of film. Not only was electricity functional for industry and the home, it also brought a world of fantasy to life. It encouraged people to dream.

Home life was enriched not only by the new electronic marvels, but new sources of heat made homes more comfortable and safer. Gas was beginning to displace open-fire heating, and kerosene heaters, utilizing the new by-products of the petroleum industry, were also popular. Oil lamps were used where electric lighting was not yet available, and both gas and electric cooking ranges were introduced.

In the mid-nineteenth century, the invention of the internal combustion engine, at first powered by coal gas, provided the motive force for a new industry that revolutionized transportation. The first automobiles to use these engines were produced in Germany in 1885 by Gottlieb Daimler and Karl Benz, working independently of one another. In 1908, Henry Ford produced 10,607 model T cars. In 1913, he created and shifted to assembly-line production, turning out a car every 93 minutes and making the automobile practical and cheap enough to be available for a mass market. In that year his factory produced 300,000 cars. Trucks were marketed at first in the hundreds and, by 1918, in the hundreds of thousands. Commercial bus operations began in Birmingham, England, in 1904 and in New York, Paris, and London in the next year. As automobiles, trucks, and buses multiplied, pressure mounted for road construction, and vast industries developed around the new vehicles: rubber for tires, glass for windows, steel for bodies and engines, and electrical systems for lights, starters, and, later, luxury equipment. Like the electrical industry, automobiles provided both workhorses for industry and fantasies for private consumption, opening up new vistas of personal mobility and, for courting couples, new possibilities of privacy.

Airplanes were still in their infancy. In 1903, the Wright brothers proved that heavier-than-air flight was possible, and by 1914, airplanes could fly at 60 to 70 miles per hour. Ships were certainly not new, and even steamships had existed for decades, but their design was improved. In 1907, the *Lusitania* crossed the Atlantic in five days.

Communication as well as transportation took on new speed and reach. Telegraphy had been invented by Samuel B. Morse in 1844; underwater cables connected Europe and Asia in 1866, and virtually instantaneous radio telegraphy was in place across the Atlantic in 1901 and across the Pacific in 1902. In 1904, telegraphic communication of photographs became possible. The telephone was invented in 1876. By 1907, there were 6 million phone users in the United States alone.

Chemical industries were especially creative. Industrial chemists developed new filaments that made incandescent lighting commercially viable. They created purer and stronger steel. Organic chemists working with coal and coal tar developed a wide array of new synthetic products, beginning with dyes, like indigo. The German chemist Adolf von Baeyer first determined the chemical structure of the dye in 1883, and in 1897 his company made synthetic indigo available commercially. Similar processes of chemical analysis and synthesis were applied to a wide range of consumer products. Most notably, in 1912, Fritz Haber and his colleagues in Germany invented a process for making ammonia (NH_3) directly from nitrogen and hydrogen found in the air, paving the way to the production of artificial fertilizers as well as explosives.

In medicine, antiseptic surgery had already been demonstrated in 1867. The twentieth century saw the development of the new science of bacteriology and its early success in 1909 in finding a drug with some effectiveness in curing syphilis in humans. In 1895, W.K. Roentgen discovered X-rays, and in 1898, Marie and Pierre Curie discovered radium and coined the term radioactivity, providing medicine with important new diagnostic and curative tools. In 1903, the first electrocardiograph was built.

The most significant improvements in health, however, resulted from improvements in basic cleanliness and sanitation. Public health services, and the provision of a clean water supply and adequate facilities for the sanitary disposal of waste, sharply reduced gastro-intestinal diseases and the death rates due to cholera and typhoid. Fine-sand filtration was replaced or joined by coarse-sand filters and, often, aluminum sulphate. By 1896, chlorine gas was used in the United States to purify water; in France ozone was preferred. By 1910, average life expectancy at birth in the United States reached 50 years.

Marie Curie and Pierre Curie.
Nineteenth- and early twentieth-century women increasingly carved out places for themselves at the forefront of intellectual, scientific, and political life. The Polish-born French scientist Marie Curie, seen here in a scene from 1895 relaxing with her husband-collaborator Pierre, pioneered the study of radiation.

Industrial power rose steadily and could be measured quantitatively. Between 1900 and 1913 alone, the production of steel by the world's six largest producing countries—the United States, Britain, Germany, France, Austria-Hungary, and Russia—rose from 26.4 million tons to 69.1 million tons. The energy consumption of these same six nations increased during the same 13 years from the equivalent of 638 million metric tons of coal to 1,089 million metric tons (Kennedy, pp. 200–1).

As science and technology produced one new marvel after another, the creation of large-scale facilities for research and development was both an effect and a cause. Germany and German-speaking regions of the Austrian Empire and Switzerland led the way in creating educational institutions appropriate to the needs of science and technology. In the early 1800s, they created polytechnic institutions at the high school level. Some were later upgraded as technical universities. By 1870, they began to link teaching and experimental research. Based on these models, German chemical firms created the in-house research and development laboratory in the 1870s. Bayer, Hoechst, and Badische Anilin und Soda Fabrik (BASF), the developers of synthetic indigo and other dyes, were the first. The electrical industries followed shortly afterwards. In America, Edison established his research laboratory at Menlo Park, New Jersey, in 1876. Many others followed: Standard Oil (1880), General Electric (1901), DuPont (1902), Parke-Davis (1902), Corning Glass (1908), Bell Labs (1911), Eastman Kodak (1913), and General Motors (1919).

Whereas discoveries and inventions in chemistry and biology had immediate commercial effects, in physics the major discoveries in the early years of the twentieth century were in theory and could be accomplished by individual thinkers, who were in touch with the society of scientists but worked mostly alone. The most revolutionary of the theoretical physicists was Albert Einstein (1879–1955), whose theory of special relativity was published in 1905, when he was twenty-six years old. Practical applications implicit in this theory came—explosively, in the form of the atomic bomb—decades later, but the philosophical significance (for those who could understand it) was immediate and revolutionary.

Einstein changed the way we look at the world. In an earlier paper, also published in 1905, he had helped to found the field of quantum physics by resolving the long-standing debate over the essential nature of light: was light essentially a wave-like flow, or did it take the form of small packets—quanta—of material? Einstein argued that light had both qualities. This explained, for example, the photoelectric effect, the escape of electrons from some solids when they are struck by ultraviolet light. Later in the same year, Einstein's special theory of relativity started from the postulate that the speed of light is constant and unchanging. If that is so, he argued, neither time nor motion is fixed. Both appear relative to the observer. For example, light from two stars may appear to arrive at the same time on earth, but the light has actually left each star at different times relative to earth because each star is a different distance from earth. In yet a third paper published later in the same year, Einstein set forth the principle that mass and energy are interchangeable, a relationship he expressed in the equation $E = mc^2$, energy equals matter times the speed of light squared. (The search for the atomic bomb was later undertaken on the basis of this formula, for the bomb represented the transformation of matter into enormous quantities of energy.) Throughout his life, Einstein sought a unified field theory that would explain the relationship among all the important force fields in nature. He never found this theory, but in 1916, he did publish his general theory of relativity which explored the nature of gravity and gave a new explanation for it. Physical masses do not attract other masses, rather they actually bend space toward themselves, so that objects roll toward them. Einstein thus overturned the basis of Newtonian physics, the intellectual structure on which physics had rested for two centuries, a structure with fixed space, time, matter, and light waves that appealed to "common sense." Instead, only the speed of light remained fixed. Space, time, motion, matter, energy—all were relative to one another. None was stable and predictable in itself. The time for a process to unfold and the weight and size of a material object depended on the speed and position of the observer. This indeterminacy in physics unsettled centuries of scientific thought and helped usher in a period of great indeterminacy in the affairs of the world in general.

GENDER RELATIONS

Changes in technology precipitated profound changes in gender relationships. The invention of new household appliances facilitated women's domestic work, though some historians have also argued that by making such work easier, they created a culture in which women did more of it. For example, instead of one annual "spring cleaning," women began to use their vacuum cleaners to clean the house more frequently. The invention of the telephone and the typewriter in the late nineteenth century led to the creation of the "female" occupations of telephone operator and secretary. Other women became department store clerks, selling to their customers the newest fashions produced with sewing machines. For many women, the invention of the bicycle was even more important than the car because it provided them with increased mobility, which also allowed them more flexibility in seeking work. Some women began to see themselves as professionals. Women's colleges were founded at the end of the nineteenth century, opening up still more possible careers, especially in health care, to them.

Out of the sight of parents, adolescents began exploring their sexuality. Before film censorship exploded in the 1920s, Hollywood films began to explore risqué themes and to feature the best of American technology as props. Many individuals believed that films sold a culture of sex that needed to be combated, hence the censorship of the Hays Code that emerged in the 1920s. Technology made birth control easier. Family size declined from 6.16 children in England and Wales in the 1860s to 2.82 children in 1910–14. But not everyone was pleased with the changes. Many people continued to believe that a woman's traditional role was to raise children. Margaret Sanger in the United States, Marie Stopes in Britain, and Theodore van de Velde in the Netherlands published manuals emphasizing the enjoyment of sex by both men and women in marriage and, at the same time, advocating family planning. Sanger was arrested for sending her magazines through the mail, then for opening the first "family planning" clinic in New York in 1916. Police booked her as a "public nuisance." Only in 1936 did courts in the United States decide that information on birth control was not pornographic and gave doctors the right to discuss it with their patients.

Scholars began to debate the nature of sexuality and the differences between men and women. The father of modern psychiatry, Sigmund Freud (1856–1939), believed that innate drives, especially sex, governed the behaviour of individuals. Another psychoanalyst, Karen Horney (1885–1952), who had initially studied with one of Freud's followers, began to question Freud's theories later in her life, coming to the conclusion that social and cultural factors were far more important than innate drives.

Anthropology added its insights as Margaret Mead brought back observations from New Guinea in the 1920s of aggressive women and passive men, reversing the conventional stereotypes of the West. Mead argued that sex traits were cultural and malleable, not biological and fixed. The debate continues today.

URBANIZATION AND MIGRATION

The world's growing population moved steadily into cities as the mechanization of agriculture drove people out of farming. Jobs in manufacture, bureaucracy, and service industries drew them to the cities. At the beginning of the century, urbanization was still linked to industrial growth, although many newcomers also found the cities exciting and full of attractions. Movie theaters screened sound entertainment. Department stores offered fashionable displays to entice buyers. City streets themselves provided spectacle, where men and women could see and be seen.

THE DOWNSIDE OF PROGRESS

In the early years of the twentieth century, technology and science offered seemingly endless improvements in health, wealth, invention, and the ability of humans to manufacture power and resolve problems. Progress continued in the ascendant as it had since the days of the *philosophes*. But many thoughtful people asked if this progress was only a veneer that covered more persistent problems. Even worse, perhaps the problems were multiplying even faster than "progress" was solving them.

Militarized Competition among the Great Powers

Not all scientific and industrial progress was directed toward peaceful uses. The chemical, metallurgical, and electrical marvels of the early twentieth century were devoted to military as well as to civilian goals, and the peaceful competition in invention and production was matched by military competition. The competition between Britain and Germany was especially sharp. From 1880 to 1913, Britain's share of world manufacturing output dropped from 22.9 percent to 13.6 percent, while Germany's rose from 8.5 percent to 14.8 percent. The greatest gains were actually made by the United States, which more than doubled its share, from 14.7 percent to 32 percent, but America was far away and was perceived by itself and by Europeans as relatively uninvolved. The British–German competition compelled attention. This was evident in the size of their armed forces. In 1914, on the eve of World War I, Germany's lead over Britain in terms of army and navy personnel stood at 891,000 against 532,000. In fact, both Russia, with 1,352,000, and France, with 910,000, had more men under arms. (The United States had only 164,000 in its armed forces.) In naval tonnage, however, Britain held the lead with 2,714,000 warship tons to Germany's 1,305,000 tons. The United States—bordered by two oceans—was third at 985,000 tons.

Most observers did not expect the competition to lead to war because the great powers were careful to build up systems of alliances that were expected to preserve the peace. The **balance of power** between the Triple Alliance of Germany, Austria-Hungary, and Italy and the Triple Entente of France, Russia, and Britain was expected to keep each side aware of the potential costs of war and the benefits of peace. People understood that a miscalculation could embroil all these nations and empires in catastrophic war, and the images of rationality and progress led them to discount such fears.

balance of power In international relations, a policy that aims to secure peace by preventing any one state or alignment of states from becoming too dominant.

In a very different kind of enterprise, the founder of modern psychiatry, Sigmund Freud, was developing at just this time his own concept of a balance of forces within each human being. Freud saw the primal force of the **libido** or **id** driving toward unrestrained aggression; the force of the super ego, representing the caution of parents and society, advocating almost saintly restraint; and the ego, the force for rational action, mediating between them. Freud argued that the balance was not always maintained, and when it failed individual breakdown resulted. An analogy to the military balance of forces among the European powers—and its potential for breakdown—was clear, at least to those who looked.

libido, id In Freudian psychology, the aggressive force in humans largely representing the drive for sex and power.

OUTSIDE EUROPE

Since the industrial revolution began, inventions in Europe had challenged, displaced, and even destroyed hand manufacture in the vast areas of the world that did not experience this revolution. As the pace of scientific invention and technological application increased, this displacement of traditional ways of production intensified, causing immense turmoil. In several cases, foreign colonial rule compounded the economic and technological disparities. Four examples—from India, China, Latin America, and the Ottoman Empire—reveal the process. Before the industrial revolution, India had the largest textile industry in the world, and China manufactured fine silks, porcelain, and iron. When the Spaniards first entered Mexico City, they were awed by its advanced urban structures. The Ottoman Empire preserved and exchanged with Europeans much of the knowledge of the ancient world during the late medieval and early modern periods. Yet for complex geopolitical and cultural reasons, these societies did not easily embrace the European industrial revolution, and soon the Europeans surpassed them in Science and Technology.

India

In the nineteenth century the hand spinners and weavers of India had been superseded and impoverished by the mechanized spindles and looms of Britain (see Chapter 18). Now, in the late nineteenth and early twentieth century, continuing invention in Europe destroyed still more of India's industries. In 1897, the Bayer Company of Germany succeeded in synthesizing indigo as a laboratory-produced dye. At that time, Indian farmers were producing about 9,000 tons of indigo per year. By 1913, India produced only 1,000 tons and was importing indigo from Germany. Later developments—in plastics, for example—would similarly displace hand-manufactured goods and the jobs that went with them. Technological progress in one region caused economic dislocation and suffering in other regions, a process that continues to this day.

In 1911, Britain asserted its supremacy over India through the majestic symbolism of the 1911 *darbar*—royal convocation—in Delhi, presided over by the King Emperor George V, who traveled to India to make the first-ever appearance of a British monarch in the colony, and attended by the princes and the elites of India in subordinate positions. The British proclaimed their power and enumerated their contributions to Indian progress, but in their pride and hubris the British willfully overlooked the disruptions that their rule was causing and the rising resentment against them on the part of the masses and of the elites who represented them.

The *darbar* was held in Delhi because Calcutta, the city that had served as the capital of British India for a century and a half, was seething with discontent against British rule. Indians were protesting not only Britain's economic and technological policies

The importance of prestige. European nations saw their empires—in Asia and elsewhere—as sources of both prestige and economic benefit. The benefit of prestige is well illustrated by A.E. Harris's illustration of the British King George V as he receives a group of maharajahs and other dignitaries, who are clothed in their finest garments for the honor, in 1910. (*Roy Miles Gallery, London*)

but also their political policies of control and their religious policies of "divide and rule," which were designed to turn Hindus and Muslims against each other. The combined outcry against all of these policies forced the government to transfer the capital itself. Indian leaders increasingly called for self-rule. Bal Gangadhar Tilak (1856–1920) summed up their growing demand: "Freedom is my birthright and I shall have it." Their struggle was yet in its early stages. It would take another decade, and new leadership, to consolidate the anti-colonial political alliance between leaders and masses.

China

We have already seen the struggles that occurred in China in the last years of the nineteenth century over the proper policies for confronting Western domination. For the most part, the traditionalists gathered around the dowager empress Cixi defeated the reformers at the imperial court. China chose the "self-strengthening" of its industrial capacities and a restructuring of the official civil service examinations to put greater emphasis on science and technology, but the attempted reforms were too little and too late. In 1911, out of a population of 400 million, China had only one million industrial workers. Most industry was on a small scale, much of it in textiles. Faith in the viability of the Confucian traditions and in the government that was to implement them was dying out. After seventy years of military defeat, colonial subordination, peasant revolt, and intellectual contentiousness, China was ripe for revolution. The Mandate of Heaven was passing from the Manchu dynasty.

Revolution began in China in October 1911 with a bomb explosion in the Wuhan area that triggered a series of army mutinies and civilian revolts. Within a month, the Manchu government promulgated a civil constitution and convened a provisional national assembly. Yuan Shihkai (1859–1916), the most powerful military official in China, was elected premier. In January 1912, the boy emperor Puyi (r. 1908–12) abdicated, ending 2,000 years of China's imperial tradition, and Yuan received full powers to organize a provisional republican government. But he exceeded his mandate. In January 1916, Yuan took the title of emperor, provoking widespread revolt. Under severe military attack and critically ill, Yuan died in June. With no effective governing center, China entered a decade of rule by warlords, regional strongmen who had their own independent militias.

Some of the warlords controlled whole provinces, others only a few towns or segments of railway line; some had formal military training, others were simply local strongmen; some sought to play a role in forming a powerful national government, others to continue China's division. Many were rapacious. In many parts of China, old, painful proverbs took on new reality: "In an age of chaos, don't miss the chance to loot during the fire" and "In the official's house, wine and meat are allowed to rot, but on the roads are the bones of those who starved to death".

The leading revolutionaries looked to Sun Yat-sen (1866–1925) as their mentor. Although raised in a peasant household, Sun received his secondary education in a missionary school in Hawaii and his medical training in Hong Kong. He spent most of his adult life in China's port cities or abroad.

In 1895, Sun attempted a coup in Guangzhou. It failed and he was exiled. He was in the United States organizing for revolution when the 1911 uprising began. He returned to help found the Guomindang (GMD), the leading revolutionary party. He was elected first president of the United Provinces of China, but then a jealous and fearful Yuan exiled him in 1913. He returned to Guangzhou in the early 1920s and led his movement from that port city, but he never regained power.

Sun's "Three People's Principles" included a heavy admixture of Western thought. The first, nationalism, called for revolution against foreign political control, beginning with the ousting of the Manchus from China, and against foreign economic control, which had rendered China:

> the colony of every nation with which it has concluded treaties; each of them is China's master. China is not just the colony of one country, but the colony of many countries. We are not just the slaves of one country, but the slaves of many countries … Today we are the poorest and weakest nation in the world, and occupy the lowest position in international affairs … other men are the carving knife and serving dish; we are the fish and the meat … we must espouse nationalism and bring this national spirit to the salvation of the country.

His second principle, democracy, emphasized a predominantly Western political model: "Since we have had only ideas about popular rights, and no democratic system has evolved, we have to go to Europe and America for a republican form of government" (Andrea and Overfield, p. 350). He did, however, claim the separation of powers as an ancient Chinese tradition.

The third principle, under the heading "People's Livelihood," revealed Sun's ambivalence toward Western technology and organization. He proclaimed the need for new technology:

> First we must build means of communication, railroads and waterways, on a large scale. Second we must open up mines. Third we must hasten to develop manufacturing. Although China has a multitude of workers, she has no machinery and so cannot compete with other countries. Goods used throughout China have to be manufactured and imported from other countries, with the result that our rights and interests are simply leaking away.

Founder of the GMD. Sun Yat-sen (Yixian), photographed here in Western dress according to his custom, is considered the "father of the nation" even though he spent much of his life abroad and never achieved his own political ambitions. He was a revolutionary and helped to found the Guomindang. Although unable to stay in power himself, he influenced China's most important figures of the next generation: Chiang Kai-shek and Mao Zedong.

But Western-style industrialization was not his chosen model:

> With the invention of modern machines, the phenomenon of uneven distribution of wealth in the West has become all the more marked ... On my tour of Europe and America, I saw with my own eyes the instability of their economic structure and the deep concern of their leaders in groping for a solution. (Andrea and Overfield, p. 351)

Fearing "the expansion of private capital and the emergence of a great wealthy class with the consequent inequalities" in China, Sun called for a different path: state ownership and "state power to build up these enterprises." But he thought Marxism irrelevant for China: "In China, where industry is not yet developed, Marx's class war and dictatorship of the proletariat are impracticable". China's economic problem was not unequal distribution but lack of production.

Chinese of all political parties revered Sun, but they could not implement his plans. Sun, however, inspired the two leaders—Chiang Kai-shek and Mao Zedong—who contested for dominance in China for a quarter century following his death in 1925. We shall read about their struggles in Chapter 22.

Latin America

Through the late nineteenth and early twentieth centuries, Latin America began to industrialize, largely with investments from overseas. At first, Britain was the principal investor, but after World War I the United States assumed that role. For the most part, economic and technological innovations were initiated by foreigners in search of profits. Most of the investments were concentrated in primary production—that is, farming and mining—rather than in industrial manufacturing. At the time of World War I (1914–18), for example, the United States was buying about one-third of Brazil's exports, mostly coffee, rubber, and cocoa. (Half of Brazil's exports consisted of coffee.) Members of the creole elites, who saw that they too could share in the new earnings and win some acceptability among Europeans, joined in the new commerce. But for the most part the initiatives came from outside.

Most of the creole elites were content to treat their nations as private estates. Control and patronage mattered—money and profits were means to an end, not ends in themselves. In an essay, *Ariel*, written in 1898, the Uruguayan philosopher José Enrique Rodó (1872–1917) analyzed Latin America's move in the direction of an industrial democracy on the United States model and rejected it. He saw that path as barbaric and inconsistent with the more leisurely, elitist, cultured world of the creole rulers of Latin America. In the absence of democratic systems, most governments in Latin America were still in the hands of *caudillos*, strongmen who governed on their own authority.

Not everyone was content with a system of control by *haciendado* and *caudillo* elites. Businessmen who were participating in the new commerce and industry began to think of new goals: more education, more industrialization, more independence from foreign investors, and more consistent government, with a larger, formal voice in politics for themselves. Toward the end of the nineteenth century, a huge influx of immigrants from Europe, especially Italy, brought with it ideas of industrial development and union representation, and by the early twentieth century, important labor unions were in place in the larger nations of Latin America. Another group advocating reform and national pride was the army, especially its junior officers. Often drawn from middle-class urban families and aware of modern technology through their knowledge of weaponry, army officers were more used to the importance of education, industrialization, business, and stable government.

In some countries these groups worked together and achieved their goals, but even the most progressive states, like Argentina and Uruguay, failed to undertake what might have been the most influential reform of all. They did not restructure the land-holding patterns that left wealthy landlords in charge of impoverished peasants. The reformers were urban people, and they were frequently related to the landlords; they had little practical sympathy for the agricultural laborers and no intention of sharing power or profits with them.

The Mexican Revolution, 1910–20 In 1910, in Mexico, urban and rural leaders rose up against the dictatorship of Porfirio Díaz (1830–1915), who had been ruling the country since 1876. At the age of eighty, Díaz seemed poised to retire from the presidency. Under his leadership Mexico had seen the development of mining, oil drilling, and railways, in addition to increasing exports of raw agricultural products, especially henequen fibers used in making rope. The middle-class urban creole elite had prospered, but the salaries of the urban workers had declined, and rural peasants had fared even worse. Ninety-five percent of the rural peasantry owned no land, while fewer than 200 Mexican families owned 25 percent of all of the land of Mexico, and foreign investors owned another 20–25 percent. One single hacienda spread over 13 million acres and another over 11 million acres. Huge tracts of land lay fallow and unused while peasants went hungry. Finally, on a political level, no system of orderly succession had been worked out for Mexico. The reins of power rested in the hands of Díaz and his allies alone.

Democratic voting existed for a limited electorate, but when Díaz changed his mind and ran again for president, he imprisoned his principal challenger, Francisco Madero (1873–1913). Díaz won, but rebellions against his continuing rule broke out across Mexico, and he soon resigned and went into exile in Paris. Regional leaders then asserted their influence as Mexico erupted into civil war. The warfare was both personal and factional. It concerned differences in policy among the factions and the appropriate division of power between the central government and the states.

Many of the leaders who contested for power were mestizos, people of mixed race and culture (see Chapter 15), who demanded a dramatic break with the past control by the creole elite. The two most radical, Francisco "Pancho" Villa (1878–1923) from the northern border region and Emiliano Zapata (1879–1919) from the state of Morelos, just south of Mexico City, advocated significant land reform, and implemented it in the areas they captured during the civil war. They attracted mixed groups of followers, including farm workers, agricultural colonists, former soldiers, unemployed laborers, cowboys, and delinquents. In November 1911, Zapata declared the revolutionary Plan of Ayala, which called for the return of land to Indian pueblos (villages). Tens of thousands of impoverished peasants followed him, heeding his cry of "Tierra y Libertad" ("Land and Liberty") and accepting his view that it was "Better to die on one's feet than to live on one's knees." Zapata's supporters seized large sugar estates, haciendas with which they had been in conflict for years. By including previously scorned groups and attending to their agendas, the revolution became more radical and agrarian.

Mexican revolutionaries. General Francisco "Pancho" Villa and Emiliano Zapata (*right*), sporting his flamboyant moustache, sit together with their Mexican revolutionary army, men who had come from many different occupations and walks of life to join the ranks. The radical leaders hailed from different parts of the country, Zapata from south of Mexico City and Villa from the northern border, but they shared common goals.

Diego Rivera, *The Conquest of Mexico* (detail), **1929–30.** Rivera transformed the tradition of painting in Mexico by creating huge murals that tell the history of Mexico in often brutal scenes.

With Díaz in exile, Madero became president, but he was removed by a coup and then assassinated in 1913. General Víctoriano Huerta (1854–1916) attempted to take over and to reestablish a repressive government like that of Díaz. Opposed by all the other major leaders, and also by President Woodrow Wilson of the United States, who sent American troops into Veracruz to express his displeasure with Huerta, the general was forced from power in March 1914. Alvaro Obregón (1880–1928), another general, who made free use of the machine gun, won out militarily, but he agreed to serve under Venustiano Carranza (1859–1920), who had himself installed as provisional president.

The civil war continued, and control of Mexico City changed hands several times, but ultimately the more conservative leaders, Carranza and Obregón, forced out Villa and Zapata. Carranza became president in 1916 and convened a constituent assembly that produced the Mexican Constitution of 1917, promising land reform and imposing restrictions on foreign economic control. It protected Mexican workers by passing a labor code including minimum salaries and maximum hours, accident insurance, pensions, social benefits, and the right to unionize and strike. It placed severe restrictions on the church and clergy, denying them the rights to own property and to provide primary education. (Most of the revolutionaries were anti-clerical. Zapata was an exception in this, as the peasantry who followed him were extremely devoted to the church.) The constitution also decreed that no foreigner could be a minister or priest, vote, hold office, or criticize the government.

Enacting the new laws was easier than implementing them, but having the new constitution in place set a standard of accountability for government and served as a beacon for the continuing revolution. On the material level, not much changed at first. In 1920, Obregón deposed Carranza and became president. He distributed 3 million acres of land to peasants, 10 percent of whom benefited. This redistribution helped to establish the principles of the revolution, demonstrating good faith on the part of the state and putting new land into production, although the state did not provide the technical assistance needed to improve productivity. Politically, Obregón began to include new constituencies in his government, including the labor movement, represented by a Labor Party, and the peasants, represented by a National Agrarian Party. The institutionalization of their presence in government promised new stability through wider

Diego Rivera, *Man at the Crossroads* (detail), **1934.** Rivera's fame spread and he was invited to create a mural for the Rockefeller Center in New York. When John D. Rockefeller saw Rivera's tribute to Karl Marx and communism, he had the mural destroyed. Rivera recreated it at the Palace of Fine Arts in Mexico City.

representation. The representation, everyone recognized, was not only by social class but also by ethnicity and culture. Mestizos and even indigenous Indians achieved a place in government. Mexico's struggle against the threefold problems of racial discrimination against Indians, economic discrimination against the poor, and the denial of both problems behind a façade of political rhetoric was an inspiration throughout Latin America. It had come at a high price: one million killed out of a total population of about 15 million.

The Ottoman Empire

Unlike Mexico, which was generally dependent on European powers for its economic investment capital and initiatives, the Ottoman Empire retained its economic autonomy, although French capital was used to construct its major technological achievement, the Suez Canal. Unlike India, the empire did not lose its sovereignty, but like China, it lost many of the attributes of self-rule, while remaining formally independent. The Ottoman Empire fell behind the industrial and political developments in western Europe and America, and it slowly disintegrated. The process by which the Ottoman Empire became "the Sick Man of Europe" took more than a century. We have already reviewed the first stages.

In 1798, Napoleon successfully invaded Ottoman Egypt. He was expelled not by the Ottomans but by his European enemy, the British. Then the Albanian general dispatched by the Ottomans in 1805 to control Egypt, Muhammad Ali, established Egypt's virtual independence of the Ottomans. In 1830, after an eight-year civil war, in which it gained the military support of Britain, France, and, especially, Russia, Greece won its independence from the Ottomans. One year earlier, as a result of the same struggles, three Balkan states—Serbia, Wallachia, and Moldavia—had also gained their autonomy from the Ottomans. Despite the *Tanzimat* (reorganization) reforms of its administration and army, leading to a parliamentary constitution in 1876, Turkey was defeated by Russia in war the next year, and the year after that, Serbia, Montenegro, and Romania became independent. In 1881, European bankers declared that the Ottoman Empire was not properly managing its finances and was defaulting on its debts. The Europeans demanded and got official representation in the offices of the Ottoman treasury. European powers also claimed rights to intervene in internal Ottoman affairs in order to defend the rights of Christian communities living in the Islamic Ottoman Empire. They stationed representatives of various Christian denominations in Constantinople to assert and represent those rights. Nevertheless, fearing continuing revolt from the restless community of Armenian Christians in Anatolia, the Ottoman government supported a series of attacks on them, killing about 200,000 in 1895.

In 1908, a group of progressive army officers and liberal professionals—collectively called "Young Turks"—seized control of the government under the sultan. During these years, however, the dismemberment of the empire continued. Almost all of its remaining European and North African holdings were stripped away. Bulgaria declared its independence (1908) and Bosnia was annexed by Austria-Hungary (1908). Italy seized the North African territories of Libya and the offshore Dodecanese Islands. Bulgaria, Serbia, and Greece aided Albania in gaining its independence in 1912.

A second Balkan war in the next year concerned the appropriate size of Bulgaria and control over Albania. Serbians, Greeks, Austrians, and even Italians were involved. The decision, favored by Austria, to make Albania an independent kingdom infuriated the Serbians, who wanted to control the region for its access to the sea, and agitated the Russians, who had backed the Serbians as brother Slavs. The economic and military competition among the great powers was embedded in these still larger

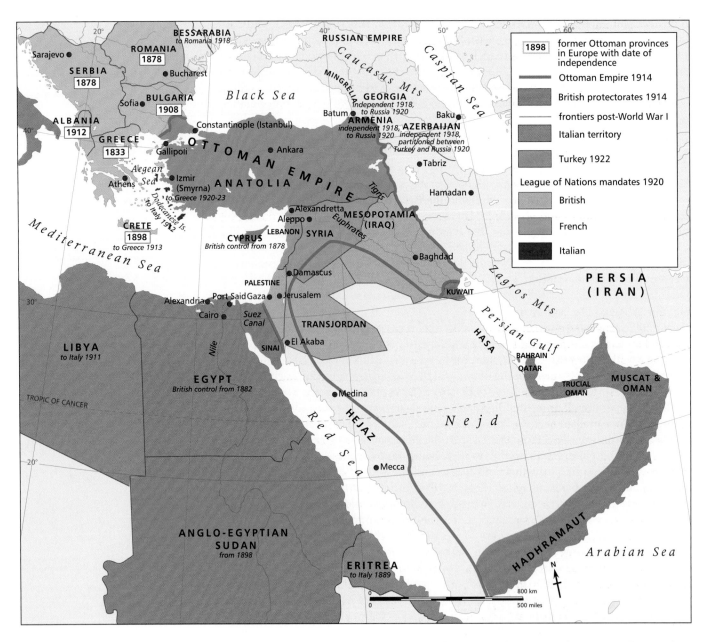

The end of the Ottoman Empire. The last decades of the nineteenth century saw the Ottoman presence in Europe decline as Austria–Hungary, Russia, and several aspiring new nations challenged its power. Arab revolt and internal dissent, combined with the Turkish defeat in World War I, brought to an end 600 years of Ottoman domination. Turkey was the core residual state, while several other regions were mandated to British and French control.

issues of nationalism, a very powerful force in early twentieth-century Europe (see Chapter 18).

People's reverence for their nation-states, and for their shared language, history, ethnicity, and aspirations within those states, had grown so passionate that they were willing to fight and die for them. Cynics argued that the masses of the population were being manipulated into battle by industrialists in each country who stood to profit from war production, but the national feelings were powerful in themselves. Nationalism evoked just as much emotional commitment among the citizens of smaller, newer states with little economic base in military production—like the states in the Balkans—as it did among the great empires.

By 1914, the dismemberment of the Ottoman Empire, the power struggle in the Balkans created by this collapse, and the constant warfare over control of this area created one of the most dangerous regions of the world. Having fallen behind the industrial and military advances of its European rivals, the Ottoman Empire could no longer keep the peace in its region. Without effective Ottoman rule, the multitude of rival ethnic and religious groups encouraged strife and invited the intervention of the major powers of Europe. These powers were already deeply involved in competition for arms, markets, and prestige, and they were committed to mutually antagonistic military alliances, which, for decades, had preserved the peace through a balance of power.

On the one hand, peace and progress appeared to be the hallmarks of the era. On the other hand, international relations were tense and in a state of flux. Peripheral areas had become central. Historically great powers had become colonies and pawns in the hands of relative newcomers. Ethnic tensions and nationalisms of various sorts seemed to appear everywhere, especially in the Balkans. From one point of view, the status of world politics and economics appeared rosy and optimistic; from another, it was tense and potentially explosive.

WORLD WAR I, 1914–18

On June 28, 1914, a Serbian nationalist assassinated Archduke Franz Ferdinand, heir to the Austro-Hungarian throne, and his wife. The assassin was outraged because the Austro-Hungarian Empire had seized Balkan territories with heavily Serbian populations. His bullets were the matches that lit the spark of World War I (called the Great War until World War II surpassed it in magnitude). One month after the murder, at the end of July, Austria-Hungary declared war on Serbia, triggering a domino effect. Under the system of alliances that had been built up over the preceding three decades, countries now came to the aid of one another. Russia mobilized its armies to defend Serbia and to take up positions on the borders of Germany. Fearing attack, Germany declared war on Russia and its ally, France. Intending to strike France quickly and decisively, Germany took the most direct route, invading and crossing Belgium, thus violating an international treaty guaranteeing Belgian neutrality. Britain declared war on Germany on August 4, as did Britain's geographically remote ally, Japan. The alliance system, which had been expected to prevent war among the highly competitive and nationalistic states of Europe, had instead drawn all the major powers into what had begun as a regional conflict in the Balkans. The lack of any organized system for preserving international order was clearly exposed. Within one week, all the major powers of Europe were at war. In November, the Ottoman Empire joined Germany and the Austro-Hungarian Empire in an alliance called the Central Powers. On the other side the British, French, and Russians, joined by the Italians in 1915, formed an alliance called the Allied Powers (the Allies).

Europe had not faced continent-wide warfare since the end of the Napoleonic wars a century earlier. Despite all their armaments, neither side was prepared militarily or psychologically for the years of devastating trench warfare of the Western Front. Germany, attacking France through Belgium, expected a quick victory, but the French response was powerful, and meanwhile the Russians opened an Eastern Front with unexpected speed, forcing the Germans to divide their troop strengths. Military leaders seemed to lack an understanding of how new technology had changed the face of war. The Battle of the Marne River, in northeastern France, fought to a draw between September 5 and 12, set the pattern for the next four years. Each side continuously extended its battle lines outward until the enemies faced each other over a 400-mile front that extended from the North Sea to Switzerland. Each side hunkered down in trenches for a kind of siege warfare, armed with machine guns and artillery, and protected by barbed wire. Attacks by either side, going "over the top" of the trenches,

World War I. European rivalries for political and economic superiority, within Europe and throughout its imperial holdings, erupted in 1914. A fragile system of alliances designed to contain the ambitions of Germany and Austria-Hungary (the Central Powers) collapsed, resulting in a conflict of horrific proportions. Turkey joined the Central Powers. In France and Belgium a stalemate war of attrition developed. In the east a war of thrust and counter-thrust caused enormous popular dissent and exhaustion, eventually bringing the collapse of the Turkish, Russian, and Austrian empires alike. In all, 20 million people died.

were met by withering machine-gun fire. In addition, Germany later introduced poison gas, leading to subsequent international bans against its use (although many nations still continue to store poison gas in their armories). In the first month alone, each side suffered more than a quarter-million casualties and used up ammunition that they thought would last for any future war. Erich Maria Remarque captured the horrors of this trench warfare in his 1929 novel *All Quiet on the Western Front*. Soldiers lived in mud and knew that it could be deadly to leave their trenches. Disease killed many. Altogether millions were killed and millions more were wounded, often with horrendous injuries. An entirely new industry developed to replace absent faces and lost limbs. Generals grasped any new weapon they thought might change the course of war, but the results of experiments generally involved more loss of life.

Major campaigns to overwhelm the opponent by sheer numbers in direct infantry charges resulted in catastrophic losses. In February 1916, the Germans attacked at Verdun, near the confluence of the borders of France, Belgium, and Germany. The battle ground on for six months, with casualties of about 350,000 on each side, before the Germans gave up their attack. In July 1916, the French opened their own attack at

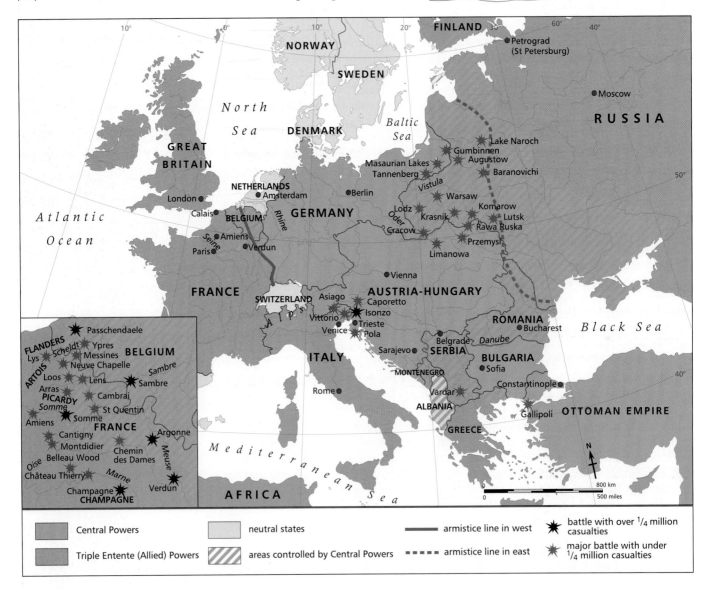

the Somme River, some 50 miles to the north. By this time the British had joined the French in force, bringing in heavy artillery and even some of their new tanks, which could penetrate the barbed wire and the trenches to knock out enemy machine guns. There were, however, few tanks, and the main strategy of the generals on both sides was simply to throw waves of attacking men at one another, directly into the machine-gun fire of the enemy. The costs in lives were almost unbelievable. In four months, the Germans lost a half-million men, the British 400,000, and the French 200,000. On the Western Front the war was essentially a stalemate from this time until the end.

In the east, the Germans defeated the Russians repeatedly, yet the ill-equipped, ill-fed, ill-commanded Russians continued to fight. In 1914, in the first months of the war, 225,000 Russian troops were captured by the Germans at the Battles of Tannenberg and the Masurian Lakes. In 1915, the Germans and Austro-Hungarians launched major offensives against Russia, killing, wounding, or taking captive 2 million Russians, many of whom fought with their bare hands. To send relief to Russia through the Black Sea, the British and French landed some 450,000 troops on the Gallipoli peninsula, at the entrance to the Dardanelles and the Black Sea. In the course of almost a year of fighting, 145,000 of these men were killed or wounded, and the operation was terminated.

In June 1916, Russia launched its own counteroffensive, but by 1917 the war had alienated the Russian people almost entirely. In March 1917, troops in St. Petersburg mutinied. The Russian **Duma** (Parliament) pushed for reforms and the tsar abdicated. The new provisional Russian government attempted to continue the war, but the armies collapsed. In November a Bolshevik communist revolutionary government, headed by V.I. Lenin—whom the Germans had helped to return to Russia—captured power and sued for peace, withdrawing Russia from the war. (The Russian Revolution, one of the most significant events connected with the war, is discussed below.)

Life in the trenches. World War I became notorious for its trench warfare, in which combatants dug themselves into positions but made few territorial gains. The horrifying drudgery, the cold, the wet, the shelling, the machine gun fire, the nervous tension, the smell of corpses and mustard gas lasted for years. By 1918, the end of the conflict, around 8.5 million soldiers had lost their lives.

The British opened another front against the Ottoman Empire by siding with the Arabs of Arabia and Palestine in their struggles against Ottoman imperial rule. British Colonel T.E. Lawrence, "Lawrence of Arabia," took charge of this insurrection and, with his support, the emir Husayn of Hejaz (the west coast of Arabia, including Mecca) declared himself king of the Arabs. Thanks to this pressure of Arabs against Turks, General Edmund Allenby was able to push through Turkish lines and capture Jerusalem, Baghdad, and, finally, Damascus, in October 1918, in a series of battles remembered for their tactical brilliance and for their use of armed cavalry and air support. Faced with this combination of Arab revolt and British military victories, the Ottomans sued for peace in October 1918.

Farther away, in the colonies, British and French forces seized the German colonies in Africa—in Togo, Cameroon, South West Africa, and Tanganyika (now Tanzania)—vowing that the Germans should never come back. Similarly, in East Asia and the Pacific, Japan, an ally of Britain, declared war on Germany in 1914 and quickly took over the German concessions in China and the German-held Marshall and Caroline Islands. In 1915 it presented China with a list of "Twenty-One Demands" to which the

Duma The Russian parliament established by Nicholas II in response to the Revolution of 1905. Its powers were largely restricted to the judicial and administrative areas; the tsar retained control over the franchise.

Chinese had to accede, against their wishes. China felt it was being turned into a colony of Japan.

In the Atlantic, both Britain and Germany disregarded the accepted law of the sea permitting the shipment of cargo not related to military equipment and supplies. The British, whose navy was by far the most powerful, regularly stopped all ships bound for Germany and other enemy states, and confiscated their cargo. The Germans, with a smaller navy, were less able to carry out such a policy. Instead, they directly attacked shipping headed for England and France, torpedoing and sinking ships, especially in the waters surrounding the British Isles. The biggest of these ships, the *Lusitania*, was torpedoed off the Irish coast in May 1915, and 1,200 passengers, including 118 Americans, drowned as the ship sank. America had been slow to enter the war, both because it preferred the peace of neutrality and because it saw no overriding virtue in one side over the other in this war of contending imperial powers. The sinking of the *Lusitania* inclined the Americans to the side of the Allies—reaffirming also a basic preference for more democratic Britain and France over more autocratic Germany and Austria-Hungary—but America joined in the conflict only after another two years and additional provocations.

In January 1917, Arthur Zimmerman, Germany's foreign minister, sent a secret telegram instructing the German ambassador in Mexico City to offer the president of Mexico "an understanding on our part that Mexico is to reconquer her lost territory in Texas, New Mexico, and Arizona," if Mexico joined in an alliance with Germany against the United States. The telegram was intercepted, translated, and published in the United States, astonishing and inflaming public opinion against Germany. At about the same time, at the end of January 1917, Germany announced to the Americans that they would begin unrestricted submarine warfare, sinking on sight all merchant ships around the British Isles or in the Mediterranean.

The United States, which had remained neutral, declared war against Germany and the Central Powers in April 1917. This decision sealed the fate of the combatants, all of whom were thoroughly exhausted by four years of relentless, enervating, disastrous warfare. The American contribution was smaller, and much briefer—only about four months of actual combat—than that of the major European countries, but it came at a decisive time when the Europeans were exhausted. By the end of the war, a year and

HOW DO WE KNOW?

War Experiences Subvert Colonialism

Colonial powers employed their colonial armies in fighting both world wars, transporting them from one battle front to another. Military service overseas often transformed the soldiers, making them skeptical of the advantages of European civilization. Some European soldiers came to realize that at least some of the people they colonized did not respect them but rather feared and hated them. A young journalist from India, Indulal Yagnik, serving briefly as a World War I correspondent in Iraq, wrote of his growing realization of the resentment

Arabs felt for British colonization. He saw Arab women in particular transmitting their resentment by asserting their religious and cultural conventions. He began to understand more fully the opposition to colonialism shared by Indians and Arabs:

We understood ... that in the entire region Arabs regarded the English as their enemies. Bitter antagonism dripped from their eyes. They moved about like lost undertakers, joking among themselves but stopping the moment they saw the British. They talked with the foreigners mechanically, speaking only when it was completely unavoidable. They took their few cents in pay, and otherwise behaved like defeated and dependent enemies. Their dignified women

hid themselves in burkhas, which covered them from head to foot. The white soldiers must have sensed their independent temper, however, and therefore their military superiors issued strict orders not to talk with the local women. (Yagnik, p. 262, translated from the Gujarati by Devavrat Pathak and Howard Spodek.)

- How did Yagnik's experiences in Arabia strengthen his anti-colonial viewpoint?
- How important was Arab women's behavior in convincing Yagnik and the British that the Arabs were anti-colonial?
- Does the evidence suggest that Arab women were more anti-colonial than the men?

a half later, the United States had 4 million soldiers and sailors under arms—two million of them in France and another million on the way—had lent $10 billion in military and civilian assistance, and had set its farms and factories to producing record amounts of food and supplies. Shipping capacity multiplied from one million tons before the war to 10 million by the end. Consumer production facilities in the United States were restructured to provide military equipment and supplies. Sugar and other consumer commodities were rationed. Eight thousand tons of steel were saved in the manufacture of women's corsets.

Once the United States began providing its abundant supplies and fresh troops, the Allied victory was secure. In the spring and summer of 1918, the German high command made a last attempt at an offensive, but they could not withstand the Allied counterattack. Germany sought an armistice. It took effect at 11 a.m. on November 11—11/11/11. As Austria-Hungary, Turkey, and Bulgaria had already withdrawn from battle, the war was over.

The cost in life defied imagining. Some 70 million armed forces were mobilized. Most, of course, were European, but there were also 1.4 million from India who served in the Middle East, East Africa, and France; 1.3 million from the "white" dominions; and 134,000 from other British colonies. The French recruited 600,000 men from their colonies as soldiers and another 200,000 to work in factories in France. Almost 10 million soldiers had been killed and 20 million wounded. England lost one million; France one and one-half, Germany almost two million, Russia one and three-quarters, the Austro-Hungarian Empire somewhat more than one million, Italy half a million, the Ottoman Empire 325,000, and the United States 115,000.

Post-war Expectations and Results

After the bloodshed, destruction, and chaos of the war, it was clear that the world was in for major changes. Defeat in the war forced the end of three historic empires: the Ottoman, the Austro-Hungarian, and the Russian. The British Empire survived, but it had made wartime promises to India of increasing self-government that might limit Britain's imperial power. Internal revolution had brought the 2,000-year-old Chinese Empire to an end shortly before the war began, and Japanese wartime conquests in China suggested that Chinese sovereignty might also be in danger.

In addition, promises had been made during wartime that raised aspirations around the globe. Perhaps the most utopian and most celebrated of all these promises issued from Woodrow Wilson. The American president had declared that the goal of the Allies was to "make the world safe for democracy." Allied war aims, as expressed by Wilson in his Fourteen Points, called for:

> A free, open-minded, and absolutely impartial adjustment of all colonial claims, based upon a strict observance of the principle that in determining all such questions of sovereignty the interests of the population concerned must have equal weight with the equitable claims of the Government whose title is to be determined. (cited in Hofstadter, pp. 224–5)

As leader of the country that had swayed the balance of victory, and as an intellectual in politics, Wilson commanded attention. Minority groups within many different nations, and colonized peoples responded to his apparent message that all peoples should have a voice in their own governments. In addition, millions of people in the colonies had contributed to the war effort of their colonizers. They expected—and sometimes they were explicitly promised—political rewards after the war.

The Arab regions of the Ottoman Empire, for example, understood Wilson's agenda to include independent states for them. They had fought alongside the British against

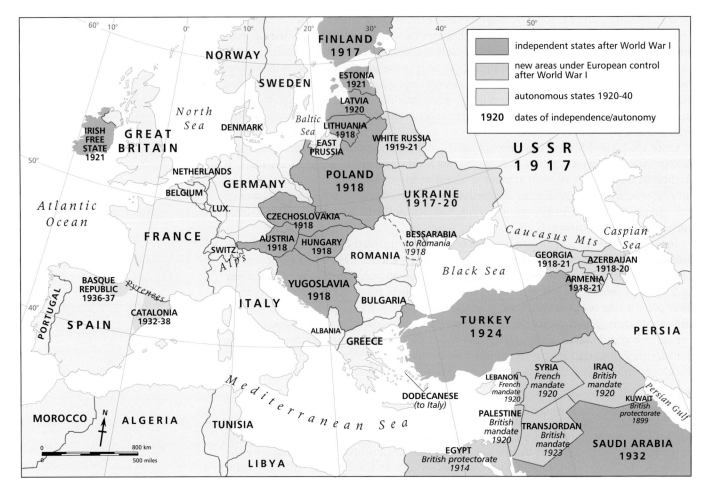

The new post-war nations. In the wake of World War I, old empires fell and new states and colonies (euphemistically called mandates and protectorates) were created. The Austro-Hungarian and Ottoman Empires were eradicated. A belt of nation-states was established throughout Central and Eastern Europe; some had brief lives and were soon annexed by Russia. The core of the Ottoman Empire became Turkey, while other segments were mandated to Britain and France as quasi-colonies.

the Ottoman Empire, and they expected that this wartime contribution would be rewarded. Moreover, in 1915, the British high commissioner (ambassador) in Egypt had privately told Mecca's leading official, Sharif Husayn, that Arabs would receive some kind of independence if they fought against the Ottoman Turks. In addition, and just before the Armistice was signed in 1918, Britain and France declared as their goal: "the complete and definitive liberation of the peoples so long oppressed by the Turks and the establishment of national governments and administrations drawing their authority from the initiative and free choice of indigenous populations."

Jews also looked forward to important changes. Had not the British government promised them "the establishment in Palestine of a national home for the Jewish people" if the Ottoman Empire was conquered? This declaration, issued by Britain's foreign secretary, Lord Balfour, in 1917, may have been issued primarily to enlist Jewish support for Britain against the Ottoman Empire, which held Palestine at the time. It captured the imagination of Jews around the world, especially those who had already emigrated from eastern Europe to settle in Palestine and those left behind in conditions of discrimination and persecution. The Arabs, however, noted that the same Balfour Declaration promised that "nothing shall be done which may prejudice the civil and religious rights of existing non-Jewish communities in Palestine." They believed these two promises to be incompatible.

India, which had contributed not only 1.4 million men, but had also paid £100 million in 1917 and some £20–30 million each year towards Britain's wartime debts, had also received a promise in 1917. The secretary of state for India, Edwin Montagu, declared

Britain's goal to be "the increasing association of Indians in every branch of government, and the gradual development of self-governing institutions, with a view to the progressive realization of responsible government in India as an integral part of the Empire."

Many linguistic and ethnic minorities scattered among the nations of eastern and central Europe, in particular Czechs, Slavs, Estonians, Latvians, and Lithuanians, also looked forward to gaining independent states of their own. The Chinese looked forward to the return of some colonial territories to them, at least those of Germany, which had been seized during the war by the Japanese. Africans in Africa, almost entirely under colonial rule, and in the diaspora, often suffering from crippling discrimination, also took heart. Wilson's pledges appealed, for example, to the brilliant African-American scholar and activist, W.E.B. DuBois, and the Pan-African movement that he headed. DuBois and his movement demanded equality for all people, an end to a kind of internal colonization of blacks in the United States and the colonization of Africa by European powers.

Before the war, only a few nations and regions had granted women the right to vote: Norway, New Zealand, and some of the states in Australia and in the western United States. The suffrage movements elsewhere had not won their objectives. With the end of the war, however, populations and their legislatures, grateful for the contributions of women to the war effort—in the armed services, in factories, and at home—reconsidered. In 1918, Britain granted the vote to women over the age of thirty and, in 1928 extended the right to women over the age of twenty-one. Germany granted women's suffrage in 1918, and the United States in 1920.

The Paris Peace Settlements, 1919

The peace conference convened in Paris in 1919 amid optimistic hopes and high expectations. Thirty-two states were invited, but not the defeated powers nor Russia. Many of their agendas, however, were in conflict with one another. In the redrawing of postwar national borders and the settling of financial accounts, each major power sought its own benefit. Japan, for example, sought to maintain control over the East Asian possessions of Germany that it had captured during the war. Since some of these colonial possessions were in China, the Chinese naturally protested. Prince Faisal represented the Arabs who had contributed to victory over the Ottoman Empire and now sought the creation of new, independent states. Representatives of colonies and of subnational ethnic groups, encouraged by Wilson's doctrine of self-determination of nationalities, sought recognition and some measure of independence and sovereignty. W.E.B. DuBois called for racial justice on behalf of the Pan-African Congress, a group of fifty-eight delegates from Africa and the African diaspora who convened in Paris at the time of the conference. In the end, despite all of the participants who attended—whether officially or unofficially—the American, British, and French delegations were most critical to the negotiations.

Political borders across Europe and the Middle East were redrawn, punishing the states that had lost the war or, in the case of Russia, had withdrawn from it. The Austro-Hungarian and Ottoman Empires were dissolved. Austria-Hungary was reduced and divided into two separate states. Czechoslovakia and Yugoslavia were created from its former territories. The Ottoman Empire disappeared; its core region in Anatolia and the city of Istanbul became the new nation of Turkey. Romania and Greece were expanded from the remainder of the empire's European territories. From its Middle Eastern regions, four new nations were created and then mandated for tutelage to European powers until they would be considered ready for independence. Although the term "mandate" was used, most observers understood these nations to be colonies under a new name. Syria and Lebanon were mandated to France, Palestine

The signing of the Treaty of Versailles, 1919. The French Premier Georges Clemenceau speaks at the signing of the Treaty of Versailles. Woodrow Wilson, the American president, is seated to his right.

and Iraq to Britain. During the war, the Russian Empire had also collapsed and withdrawn from the fighting. A communist government, which seemed threatening to the Allies, had replaced its ruling Romanov dynasty. From territories of the former empire, the new states of Poland, Finland, Estonia, Latvia, and Lithuania were created.

All three of these great empires had held vastly diverse ethnic, religious, and cultural minorities within their borders. The Paris negotiators intended that the new states and new borders that they carved out would give some of the larger minorities their own states and protect hostile ethnic groups from each other and from external domination. Minority rights and legal safeguards were also legislated into the constitutions of the new states and the remaining cores of the old empires.

Germany lost Alsace-Lorraine to France, large areas in the east to Poland, and small areas to Lithuania, Belgium, and Denmark. Germany was ordered to pay heavy reparations for the cost of the war, although in practice not much was paid. Most gallingly for Germany, it was forced officially to accept total responsibility for causing the loss and damage of the war. Germany signed the Treaty of Versailles, which concluded the war, and left Paris humiliated, resentful, but, despite the loss of lands and the financial reparations, potentially still powerful.

The League of Nations

The negotiators in Paris generally agreed on the need for some form of organization to provide for international cooperation, to adjudicate disputes among nations, and, it was hoped, to prevent future warfare. To this end they created the League of Nations in 1920, but disillusionment soon followed. The league was crippled by three congenital defects. First, its principal sponsor, the United States, refused to join because of congressional opposition. The world's most powerful technological, industrial, financial, and military power, the United States withdrew back into the isolation of its ocean defenses. Germany was admitted to membership in 1926; the USSR joined in 1934.

Second, the League failed to resolve the complex issues of national identities and increasing anti-colonialism. In accord with the principle of national self-determination, ten new states were born, or reborn, as a result of the Paris accords, and fourteen states were specifically charged with protecting racial, religious, and linguistic minorities within their borders, assuring those minorities of equal rights with all citizens, including the right to primary school instruction in their mother tongue. In central Europe, however, nationality groups were widely dispersed, and many minorities continued to feel aggrieved.

The antagonism of colonized peoples towards their colonial rulers also intensified as the powerful nations of the world soon returned to business-as-usual. Despite their many wartime promises of self-rule, the League had neither the will nor the power to intervene. For example, even as France and Britain had been promising independence to Arab regions of the Middle East during the war, they had actually signed the Sykes–Picot Agreement in 1916 to divide these regions among themselves. The grant of mandatory powers to Britain over Iraq and Palestine and to France over Syria and Lebanon broke the promise while carrying out the agreement.

Turkey itself was marked for further dismemberment into spheres controlled by France, Italy, and, most provocatively, by Greece, the centuries-old Christian enemy of the Muslim Turks. An independent Armenian state was to be established in eastern Turkey on the shores of the Black Sea, and an independent Kurdistan just to the south of it. Only the armed resistance of Turkish forces led by General Mustafa Kemal (1881–1938) prevented implementation. Musafa Kemal, later called Atatürk, Father of the Turks, drove out the foreign troops stationed in Turkey and preserved the geographical and political independence of his state until Turkey's full sovereignty was recognized by the 1923 Treaty of Lausanne.

In East Asia, the peace treaties assigned Germany's holdings in the Shandong Peninsula of north China to Japan rather than returning them to China. In Paris, Chinese protestors physically blocked the nation's delegates from attending the signing ceremonies, and thus China never did sign the peace agreements. Within China, protests against the treaties by students and others began on May 4, 1919, engendering a continuing critique of China's international humiliation, the apparent bankruptcy of its historical traditions, and the value of its cultural links to the West. This "May Fourth Movement" also helped to sow the seeds of the Chinese Communist Party (CCP), which came to fruition in 1921 following discussions between Chinese revolutionaries and representatives of the newly formed Comintern (Communist International) of the USSR.

In India, Britain fell short of its wartime promise to expand the institutions of self-government; on the contrary, it passed the Rowlatt Acts, which restricted freedoms of the press and assembly. In addition, India faced an inflation that doubled the prices of basic commodities between 1914 and 1920, and an influenza epidemic that killed 12 million people in India alone (of a world total of about 20 million), twice as many people as had been killed in the war. Going into the war, most Indians seem to have trusted that Britain would bring self-government back to India, even if the process seemed very slow. Mohandas Karamchand Gandhi (1869–1948), who was becoming the leader of the Indian national movement, had even recruited troops, unsuccessfully, for the British war effort. All this changed after the war as the British cracked down and the Indians protested. In Amritsar, Punjab, a British general, Reginald Dyer, ordered his troops to fire on an unarmed protest rally. Blocking the only exit, the soldiers turned the outdoor meeting-place of Jalianwala Bagh into a gruesome shooting gallery, killing 379 people and wounding 1,100. The government forced the general to resign, but a popular outpouring of support for him in Britain thoroughly alienated Indian moderates. World War I had already exposed a murderous brutality within European civilization; now it appeared in India as well, thoroughly laced with racism. From this point onward in the eyes of even moderate Indians, British colonial rule had forfeited its legitimacy.

In 1919, Gandhi began to reorganize the Congress around India's peasantry, broadening and deepening a movement that had been based on urban and upper middle classes. In 1920, he began the first of his non-cooperation campaigns, and in 1930 he led the Salt March, a protest movement that mobilized the country and reached media attention throughout the world.

In Africa, Europeans continued to administer the colonies they had seized in the late nineteenth century. British settlers began to move into new settlements, especially in the highlands of Kenya and in Southern Rhodesia (today's Zimbabwe). Especially in the British colonies, African tribal leaders were incorporated into the ruling structures, following some of the policies of indirect rule first evolved in India.

The existence of the League of Nations and its mandate system did, however, begin to suggest that colonialism might be limited over time. In Egypt, the Wafd Party began demonstrations and riots that persuaded the British to grant Egypt nominal independence while still controlling its foreign policy and defense, and the Suez Canal. In 1921, Britain granted dominion status to a new state in southern Ireland, ending centuries of colonial oppression (but leaving Northern Ireland still a part of Great Britain). It granted Iraq nominal independence in 1932.

The League itself, however, had no armed forces. This limited its willingness to intervene in disputes, and made it impossible to back up even the decisions that it was willing to take. The great powers signed the Kellogg–Briand Pact in 1928, agreeing to settle their disputes without warfare, but the pact proved meaningless. The League effectively died when it failed to counter Japan's invasion of China in 1931; Italy's invasion of Ethiopia in 1935, which turned one of only two independent countries in Africa (Liberia was the other) into a colony; Germany's rearmament through the 1930s; and the outbreak of the Spanish Civil War in 1936 (see Chapter 20).

Poster commemorating "The Internationale," the rallying anthem of the Communist movement. Karl Marx (*left*) and Friedrich Engels (*right*), who appear at the top of this poster, collaborated in developing the theoretical principles underlying "scientific socialism" and in organizing a working-class movement dedicated to revolting against capitalism.

THE RUSSIAN REVOLUTION

The war broke the back of the Russian government and brought to power a new form of government that most western European nations and the United States found dangerous and threatening. Others, including some Americans, found it an interesting alternative to the decadence of the West. They saw it as a dream for a better world. The Russian Revolution of 1917 challenged the capitalist order by instituting communism. As we noted in Chapter 17, communism advocated the abolition of private property and the control of a country's economic resources by the state, at least temporarily. It argued that the Communist Party should spearhead this system, by the use of violence if necessary. Leaders of the party believed that Russia could telescope the development process and catapult itself quickly into the ranks of the wealthy and powerful nations. The Bolshevik Party, renamed the Communist Party in 1918, asserted its own dominance over the politics, economy, and society of Russia. Through the worldwide organization of the Communist International, it proposed itself as a model for, and leader of, colonized and backward countries in overthrowing foreign control and capitalist economic development. It argued that poor nations had been intentionally "underdeveloped" by, and for, the rich. The new communist system established by the Russian Revolution endured through years of hardship and of war, both civil and international.

The Build-up to Revolution, 1914–17

Geographically and politically Russia has one foot in Europe, another in Asia. As we have seen, Peter the Great (r. 1682–1725) turned westward, founding St. Petersburg as his capital, port, and window on the west. Catherine II, the Great (r. 1762–96), further nurtured the European Enlightenment at the Russian court. Stunned by his defeat in the Crimean War (1853–6) at the hands of Britain and France in alliance with Turkey, Tsar Alexander II (r. 1855–81) adopted a more liberal policy. He freed Russia's serfs in 1861, instituted the **zemstvo** system of local self-government in 1864, reduced censorship of the press, reformed the legal system, encouraged industrialization, and promoted the construction of a nationwide railway system. Tsar Nicholas II (r. 1894–1917) furthered heavy industrialization under two progressive ministers, Count Sergei Witte (1849–1915) and Peter Stolypin (1862–1911), and allowed the birth of some representative political institutions, but he rejected the democratic reforms demanded by intellectuals, workers, and political organizers.

zemstvo A rural council in the Russian Empire, established by Tsar Alexander II in 1864 and abolished in 1917.

Despite the industrialization introduced under Nicholas II, on the eve of World War I Russia lagged far behind the western European countries economically and industrially. Its population of 175 million was about 75 percent more than that of the United States, more than two and a half times that of Germany, and four times that of Britain; its energy consumption was one-tenth that of the United States, 30 percent that of Germany, and one-fourth that of Britain. Its share of world manufacturing was 8 percent compared with the United States' 32 percent, Germany's 15 percent, and Britain's 14 percent.

Nicholas II had made great strides in increasing industrial production. Energy consumption had increased from 4.6 metric tons equivalent in 1890 to 23 million in 1913; railway mileage from about 22,000 miles in 1890 to 31,000 miles in 1900 to 46,000 miles in 1913; and the per capita level of industrialization doubled from 1880 to 1913. But during that same period, 1880–1913, the United States's per capita level of industrialization quadrupled, Germany's rose three and one-half times, and France's, Italy's, Austria's, and Japan's all slightly more than doubled. In a rapidly industrializing world, Russia had to race much faster just to keep up. To obtain the capital to build its industries Russia invited foreign investment, but this opened the nation to foreign control. In 1917 foreigners held nearly 50 percent of the Russian national debt. Russia was Europe's largest debtor.

Russia's agriculture was unproductive and its technology was primitive. A wealthy elite held enormous power over the land and the peasants who worked it. An exploited peasantry living in **mirs** (village collectives) had neither the economic incentive nor the technical training to produce more. The small parcels of land they farmed privately were subdivided into tiny plots, as sons in each generation shared equally in the inheritance of their fathers. Finally, the government forbade the sale of village land to outsiders. This prevented exploitation by absentee landlords, but it blocked the investment from outside the village that might have funded agricultural improvement through new technology. Productivity stagnated. The sharp class divisions between the peasants and the gentry persisted, marked by differences not only in wealth and education, but also in dress and manners. Moreover, the costs of industrialization and the repayment of foreign loans had to be squeezed out of the agricultural sector. The result was a mass of peasants impoverished, technologically backward, despised by the wealthy elite, and suffering under the weight of a national program of industrialization for which they were made to pay.

mir A self-governing community of peasants in pre-revolutionary Russia having control over local forests, fisheries, and hunting grounds; land was allocated to each family according to size, in return for a fixed sum.

Lenin and the Bolshevik Revolution

Several revolutionary groups protested these conditions, each offering a different plan. The Social Democrats followed George Plekhanov (1857–1918), who saw the need for more capitalist development in Russia to create new urban working and middle classes, which Plekhanov's party would then organize to overthrow the bourgeoisie.

Plekhanov was actually an orthodox Marxist thinker who believed that before a communist revolution could emerge, capitalism would first have to lay the foundations of industry and industrial laborers. A lawyer, Vladimir Ilyich Ulyanov (1870–1924), later calling himself Lenin, advocated a far more immediate and abrupt communist revolution, and he stressed the need for the communist party to provide its leadership.

> Not a single class in history has reached power without thrusting forward its political leaders, without advancing leading representatives capable of directing and organizing the movement. We must train people who will dedicate to the revolution, not a spare evening but the whole of their lives. (Kochan and Abraham, p. 240)

In 1902, in a pamphlet entitled *What Is to Be Done?* Lenin again underlined the need for an absolutely dedicated core of leaders to carry out the revolution: "Give us an organization of revolutionaries and we will overturn Russia!" In January 1905, with revolutionary feelings running high, some 200,000 factory workers and others in St. Petersburg, led by a priest, Father Gapon, assembled peacefully and respectfully to deliver to the tsar a petition for better working conditions, higher pay, and representative government. On that "Bloody Sunday," January 22, the tsar was not actually in the city but his troops fired on the demonstrators, killing several hundred and wounding perhaps a thousand. The government's lack of moral authority was unmasked. By the end of the month almost 500,000 workers were on strike, joined by peasant revolts, mutinies of soldiers, and protests by the intelligentsia of doctors, lawyers, professors, teachers, and engineers.

Before this domestic turmoil erupted, the tsar had committed Russia to war with Japan, but defeats at sea and on land further revealed Russia's inadequacies in both technology and government organization. The defeat in the Russo-Japanese War, domestic tax revolts in the countryside, and strikes in the industrializing cities forced the tsar to respond. Yielding as little as possible, he established the first Duma, or Parliament, representing peasants and landlords, but allowing workers only scant representation. The tsar limited the powers of the dumas, frequently dismissed them, sometimes jailed their members, and chose their class composition selectively to divide the principal revolutionary constituencies, workers and bourgeoisie. The dumas endured as a focus for democratic organization and aspiration, but they were unable to work cooperatively, and the tsar was able to stave off revolution for a decade.

Unable to match the new technological warfare of other European countries, Russia suffered 2 million casualties in World War I. These losses finally united the many forces of opposition and brought down the monarchy. In the midst of revolutionary ferment, in February 1917, 10,000 women in St. Petersburg marched to protest the rationing of bread and demanded the tsar's abdication. Despite government orders, the army refused to fire on them.

In the first revolution of March 1917, the duma forced the tsar to abdicate and established a new provisional government under Aleksandr Kerensky (1881–1970). But the war persisted. The turmoil of mutiny and desertion in the army, food shortages, farm revolts, and factory strikes ground on. More radical groups sought to seize control. Lenin, with the assistance of the German government, which wished to sow discord in Russia, returned from exile in Switzerland. With the

Looters, St. Petersburg, 1905. Small pockets of revolutionary fervor flared up prior to 1917. In 1905, the year these peasants are depicted looting bosses' houses, twenty officers and 230 guards were arrested in St. Petersburg when a plot to assassinate the tsar was uncovered.

motto "Peace, Land, Bread," he called for an immediate withdrawal from the war, land for the peasants, and a government-run food distribution system. Lenin organized an armed takeover of the government headquarters, the railway stations, power plants, post offices, and telephone exchanges. On November 7 (October 25 on the old, Julian calendar), this revolutionary coup succeeded, and the communists seized power. Confounding Marxist doctrine, the revolution had occurred not in one of Europe's most capitalistic and industrialized countries, but in one of the most industrially backward. In March 1918, by signing the Treaty of Brest–Litovsk with Germany the communist government took Russia out of the war.

Civil war between communist revolutionary "Red" and anti-revolutionary "White" forces enveloped the country. Contingents of troops from fourteen countries (including a small number of Americans in the Baltic and 8,000 at Vladivostok on the Pacific) joined the Whites. The Bolshevik government took over ownership of land, banks, the merchant marine, and all industrial enterprises. It confiscated all holdings of the church and forbade religious teaching in the schools. It established the **Cheka** (security police) and instituted a reign of "Red Terror" against its opponents' "White Terror." In Yekaterinburg, the local soviet executed the tsar, his wife, and their children. By 1920, the communists, as the Bolsheviks now called themselves, were victorious in the civil war. In 1921, they banned all opposition, even dissenting voices within the party, and made the central committee, now under Lenin's control, the binding authority in the government. Lenin began the pattern of imprisoning his opponents in labor camps—a policy that was later expanded under his successors into a huge network of camps for political opponents of the government. Millions of citizens were ultimately imprisoned in this **gulag** or prison system.

World war and civil war, which were followed by even more devastating drought, famine, and economic dislocation, convinced Lenin of the need for economic stability and an incentive to produce. In 1921, he implemented the New Economic Policy (NEP), which allowed peasants to sell their products on the open market and middlemen to buy and sell consumer goods at a profit. The central government, however, controlled the "commanding heights" of the economy: finance, banking, international trade, power generation, and heavy industry.

State Planning in Soviet Russia

Lenin sought the industrial transformation of Russia. In 1920, as he established the State Commission for Electrification, he declared: "Communism is Soviet power, plus electrification of the whole country." Lenin invited German and American technicians to Russia to improve productivity by harnessing capitalist means to communist goals. He took special interest in the system of scientific management and time studies in the workplace that had been introduced in America by Frederick Taylor.

Lenin's death in 1924 ushered in a bitter power struggle from which Joseph Stalin (1879–1953) emerged triumphant over Leon Trotsky (1879–1940). Trotsky, a brilliant, ruthless man, who had organized the Red Army, had argued that through careful but

Lenin and Joseph Stalin at Gorki, Russia, 1922. After Lenin's premature death two years after this photograph was taken, Stalin battled to eliminate his rivals (Leon Trotsky was banished abroad and eventually assassinated in Mexico) before emerging as supreme dictator of the Communist Party in 1929. He soon abandoned Lenin's New Economic Policy in favor of a series of brutal five-year plans to enforce the collectivization of agriculture and industry.

Cheka The secret police of early Soviet Russia, established by the Bolsheviks after the revolution of 1917 to defend the regime against dissidents. Criticized for its severe brutality, the agency was reorganized in 1922.

gulag The acronym of Glavnoye, Upravleniye Ispravitelno Trudovykh Lagerey, the "Chief Administration of Corrective Labor Camps," a department of the Soviet secret police founded in 1934 . It ran a vast network of forced labor camps throughout the USSR to which millions of citizens accused of "crimes against the state" were sent for punishment.

bold planning a technologically backward country could leapfrog stages of growth and, through the "law of combined development," quickly catch up to the more advanced. Having defeated Trotsky, Stalin now implemented Trotsky's program. He declared his driving nationalist passion that Russia must no longer lag behind the more developed nations.

> those who fall behind get beaten. But we do not want to be beaten. No, we refuse to be beaten! One feature of the history of old Russia was the continual beatings she suffered for falling behind, for her backwardness. She was beaten by the Mongol Khans. She was beaten by the Turkish beys. She was beaten by the Swedish feudal lords. She was beaten by the Polish and Lithuanian gentry. She was beaten by the British and French capitalists. She was beaten by the Japanese barons. All beat her—for her backwardness: for military backwardness, for cultural backwardness, for political backwardness, for industrial backwardness, for agricultural backwardness. She was beaten because to do so was profitable and could be done with impunity. …
>
> That is why we must no longer lag behind. (Andrea and Overfield, p. 398)

Stalin's rhetoric appealed not only to his immediate audience in Russia, but also to a more global audience of poorer states and colonies beginning to protest against their subordination and to seek independence and development.

To achieve "combined development," in 1928 Stalin instituted nationwide, state-directed five-year plans that covered the basic economic structure of the whole country. In place of capitalism, in which market forces of supply and demand determine production goals, wages, profits, and the flow of capital, labor, and resources, Stalin instituted government planning to make those decisions, from the large-scale national macro-level to the small-scale local micro-level.

Where could Russia find capital to invest in industrial development, especially with most world capital markets closed to the communist state? Stalin turned to his own agricultural sector and peasantry. By artificially lowering the prices for agricultural products and raising the prices for agricultural tools and materials, Stalin used his planning apparatus to squeeze capital and labor out of agriculture into industry. But he squeezed so hard that agricultural productivity fell and peasants withheld their crops from the artificially deflated market. State planning was not working.

Nevertheless, in 1929 Stalin increased the role of the state still further. He collectivized agriculture. More than half of all Soviet farmers were compelled to give up their individual fields and to live and work instead on newly formed collective farms of 1,000 acres or more. The communist government increased the use of heavy machinery and large-scale farming operations, stipulated the goods to be produced and their sales prices, encouraged millions of peasants to leave the farms for work on the state's new industrial enterprises, and eliminated wealthier peasants and middlemen.

Although some farmers were living better in 1939 than 1929, many others were not. The most industrious and talented farmers were killed or imprisoned. Hundreds of thousands of better off peasants, **kulaks**, who refused collectivization were murdered; millions were transported to labor camps in Siberia. Peasants who owned animals preferred to slaughter them rather than turn them over to collectives. There had been over 60 million head of cattle in the USSR in 1928; by 1933, there were fewer than 35 million. Initiative shriveled as the more entrepreneurial farmers were turned into a kind of rural proletariat. The government continued to collect high proportions of the agricultural production to pay for the imports of foreign technology and machinery for its industrial programs. Although few developing countries today are willing to reduce private consumption below 80 percent of the national product, Russia reduced it to little over 50 percent. Much of the difference went to industrial development. The government chose guns over butter. The political coercion and chaos introduced by these

kulak A prosperous peasant in late tsarist and early Soviet Russia. The leaders of local agricultural communities, kulaks owned sizeable farms and could afford to hire labor.

policies, combined with bad harvests in southeast Russia, led to the tragic and wasteful deaths of between 2 and 3 million peasants by 1932.

While the peasants suffered enormous hardship, industry flourished as never before. At first, Russia hired foreign technology and imported foreign machinery. Despite ideological differences with the United States, Stalin, like Lenin before him, saw the necessity of importing American materials, machinery, and even some organizational programming. In 1924 Stalin declared:

> American efficiency is that indomitable force which neither knows nor recognizes obstacles; which continues on a task once started until it is finished, even if it is a minor task; and without which serious constructive work is inconceivable. … The combination of Russian revolutionary sweep with American efficiency is the essence of Leninism. (Hughes, p. 251)

Meanwhile, the Russian government was training its own personnel and learning to construct its own massive industrial plants. At the falls of the Dnieper River, the communist state constructed Dnieprostroy, which, when it opened in 1932, was the largest hydroelectric power station in the world. In the early 1920s, the USSR had imported tens of thousands of tractors, most of them Fords and International Harvesters from the United States. By the 1930s, however, Russia constructed a giant plant at Stalingrad to manufacture its own tractors. At Gorki (Nizhny Novgorod) the government built a plant based on the American Ford model at River Rouge, Michigan. At Magnitogorsk, in Siberia, they constructed a steel complex based on US Steel's plant in Gary, Indiana.

From 1928 to 1938, the per capita level of industrialization nearly doubled. From 1928 to 1940, the production of coal increased from 36 to 166 million tons, that of electricity from 5 to 48 billion kilowatt hours, and that of steel from 4 to 18 million tons. Stalin explained: "The independence of our country cannot be upheld unless we have an adequate industrial basis for defense" (Kochan and Abraham, p. 368). The planners began to convert a nation of peasants into a nation of industrial workers, as the urban population of the country increased three and one-half times from 10.7 million in 1928 to 36.5 million in 1938, from 7 percent of the country's population to 20 percent.

Most dramatically, the Soviet increases came when western Europe and North America were reeling under world depression (see Chapter 20). The communist system won new admirers in the West. The American political comedian Will Rogers commented: "Those rascals in Russia, along with their cuckoo stuff have got some mighty good ideas. … Just think of everybody in a country going to work." Journalist Lincoln Steffens wrote: "All roads in our day lead to Moscow." British political critic and historian John Strachey exclaimed: "To travel from the capitalist world into Soviet territory is to pass from death to birth."

Women in the Soviet Union

For women, too, the Soviet system led to great change, but perhaps less than promised. As elsewhere, World War I brought women into factories, fields, and even the armed forces, and the civil war continued the pattern. Over 70,000 women served in the Red Army. In 1921, 65 percent of Petrograd's factory workers were women. In 1917, the first Soviet marriage law constituted marriage as a civil contract and provided for relatively easy divorce and child maintenance procedures.

The government ordered equal pay for equal work, but the provision was not enforced. To bring law into line with practice, and recognizing the lack of availability of effective birth-control methods, abortion on demand was granted as a right; so was maternity leave with full pay. When the men returned from the war, they wanted their

Russian poster for women textile workers, 1930. Despite the government's difficulties in enforcing "equal pay for equal work," women's rights improved markedly under the communist system. This poster appears to idealize full-time employment combined with raising a family.

jobs back and their women at home, but Russian women retained most of the benefits they had won and "legally speaking, Russian women were better off than women anywhere in the world" (Kochan and Abraham, p. 337). Over the next decades women entered professions so rapidly that they became the majority in medicine and teaching—care-giving occupations—and a substantial minority in engineering, technical occupations, and law.

In practice, however, women bore the "double burden" of continuing the major responsibility for running their homes and caring for their families while working full time. With the introduction of state-planned heavy industrialization after 1929, the double burden on women increased. The factories invited their labor, while shortages of foodstuffs forced them to spend more time and energy in ration lines and in the search for food. Abortion became so common that it was once again outlawed for a time after 1936. The struggle to balance the new legal equality and protection with older social and family traditions continued (and continues today).

Many political leaders of countries under European colonial control saw the Russian example—telescoped development, state planning, rapid industrialization, the transformation of the peasantry into an urban labor force, emphasis on education and health services, national enthusiasm in rebuilding a nation along scientific lines—as just what they needed. As a political prisoner in British India in July 1933, Jawaharlal Nehru, future first prime minister of independent India, wrote to his daughter:

People often argue about the Five Year Plan. ... It is easy enough to point out where it has failed. ... [but] One thing is clear: that the Five Year Plan has completely changed the face of Russia. From a feudal country it has suddenly become an advanced industrial country. There has been an amazing cultural advance; and the social services, the system of social, health, and accident insurance, are the most inclusive and advanced in the world. In spite of privation and want, the terrible fear of unemployment and starvation which hangs over workers in other countries has gone. There is a new sense of economic security among the people ... further ... this Plan has impressed itself on the imagination of the world. Everybody talks of "planning" now, and of Five-Year and Ten-Year and Three-Year plans. The Soviets have put magic into the word. (*Glimpses of World History*, pp. 856–7)

POST-WAR AMERICA

America left World War I as the technological and financial leader of the world. The factories that had supplied war goods returned to producing domestic, consumer products that made the American middle and upper classes the envy of many around the world. Automobile registration rose from about a half million in 1910 to over 8 million in 1920 and 23 million in 1930. In addition, in 1930, American farms employed some 920,000 tractors and 900,000 trucks. Even Stalin in Russia invited American technical assistance in establishing some of the gigantic industrial complexes of the Soviet Union.

In 1910, there were 82 phones per thousand Americans; in 1930, 163. Only in the early 1900s did wealthier people begin to introduce indoor flush toilets and cast-iron bathtubs. By 1925, America was producing 5 million enameled bathroom fixtures annually. Thanks to the efforts of labor unions, the work week was being reduced from 60 hours per week to 45. Paid vacations were becoming common, with 40 percent of large companies giving at least one week of paid vacation per year. Diet improved; sales of fresh vegetables increased 45 percent in the decade after World War I. Life expectancy increased by more than a dozen years between 1900 and 1930, from 47 years to 60 years.

Electricity replaced steam as the major source of power. In 1929, 80 percent of all industrial power was produced by electrical generators, and two-thirds of America's homes were electrified. Washing machines, electric irons, vacuum cleaners, electric toasters, and sewing machines became common in urban homes, and standards of household cleanliness were raised. Commercial radio began broadcasting in 1920 and millions of homes soon had receivers. Many people built their own. Movies became the main mass entertainment, with the first "talkie," *The Jazz Singer*, released in 1927. In 1929, 100 million people attended the movies each week. Watching film stars such as Charlie Chaplin, Gloria Swanson, Mae West, Greta Garbo, and Rudolph Valentino gave viewers new ideas—and new fantasies—about what their lives might be. The films gave audiences around the world their own peculiar version of American life.

Women's lives changed, too, in this decade. Although the sale and prescription of the means of birth control was illegal in most states, Margaret Sanger convened the first birth control conference in 1921 and traveled around the world spreading her message. The size of American families dropped from 3.6 children in 1900 to 2.5 in 1930. About one-fourth of all women of working age actually worked outside the home, especially in office jobs, teaching, and nursing. In 1920, American women were constitutionally granted the right to vote, as they were at about the same time in Britain and Germany.

Much of the image of post-war America is of flappers, speakeasies (after prohibition was introduced by the Eighteenth Amendment to the Constitution in 1919), increased recognition of sexuality of women as well as men, and a general flamboyance. This image may have been true for an urban, upper middle class, white population, a small—if conspicuous—minority of the total population. For most of working class and rural America, life was still quite difficult.

Also, fear permeated some corners of America. The United States engaged in international commerce with its great industrial, agricultural, and administrative power. But it refused to join the League of Nations and generally withdrew from participation in international politics outside of Latin America, where it had substantial financial investments and repeatedly intervened with military force. It seemed to fear involvement outside its own hemisphere.

Internally, in the immediate post-war years, many strikes hit industries in the United States. A third of

Civil aviation. A steward serves passengers on board a KLM Fokker F18 in 1932. In the 1920s, the popularity of aerial circuses and flying clubs, run by former World War I pilots, combined with rapid improvements in technology, heralded a new age of civil aviation. By the 1930s a worldwide network of commercial routes had developed. In these early years the high cost of air travel created an aura of glamor and exclusivity.

a million workers struck against US Steel in 1919. In the same year the Boston police force went on strike. The home of the attorney general, A. Mitchell Palmer, was bombed. Coming as they did just after the Communist Party took over the government of Russia, these events gave many Americans a "Red Scare," and Palmer began rounding up, jailing, and deporting thousands of people accused of being communists, anarchists, and radicals. Hundreds of aliens were deported. The Ku Klux Klan was revived to terrorize Catholics, Jews, and African-Americans, especially the black soldiers returning from war who might no longer know their "place." At its height in the early 1920s the Klan enrolled several million members. By the end of the decade, the fears and frenzies had abated, but new, perhaps greater fears were in store, as the stock market crash of October 29, 1929, following years of economic difficulties on America's farms, ushered in the Great Depression.

The Depression

Worldwide economic depression destabilized domestic and international politics worldwide, but especially in Europe. Depression is a severe economic downturn in production and consumption that continues for at least several months. Periods of depression were considered normal in a free-market economy as the forces of supply and demand periodically fell out of step and then came back into line. But the Great Depression was far more extreme in its extent and duration. On October 29, 1929— "Black Tuesday"—the New York stock exchange crashed. The decline continued for years. By 1933, stocks were worth 15 percent of their value in 1929, ending five years of relative prosperity and marking the beginning of a worldwide economic Depression, which would continue until the outbreak of World War II in 1939.

The United States had emerged from World War I as a creditor nation. To pay the reparations from the war, Germany depended on loans from several nations, especially the United States. With the stock market crash of 1929, however, American financiers called in these loans, undercutting the European economy. In addition, farmers who had produced at record levels during the war had difficulty cutting back production, resulting in huge, unsold surpluses and a depression in agriculture. Faced with such economic difficulties, countries closed their borders to imports so that they could sell their own products internally without competition. But as each country raised its barriers, international markets contracted, increasing the Depression.

Mass unemployment swept Britain, America, and Germany; the unemployment rate among industrial workers in Germany was 30 percent in 1932. Latin American countries, notably Argentina, which had been approaching a European standard of living, found their economies devastated, turned away from European markets, and sought to salvage what they could through domestic development. The value of world trade in 1938 was 60 percent below what it was in 1929.

Communist Russia, standing somewhat apart from the world economy, had introduced centralized national planning in 1928, emphasizing heavy industrialization. Its factories flourished, but agriculture was devastated and levels of private consumption plummeted.

In 1921 there were 2 million unemployed in Britain. They collected unemployment insurance in accord with an act that had been passed a decade earlier. The government also implemented an old-age pension system, medical aids, and subsidized housing. But the world Depression increased this unemployment to almost 3 million. Unemployment payments multiplied while tax collections dropped. The welfare state expanded and government remained stable, but the Depression ground on.

America, the country most dedicated to private enterprise and "rugged individualism," and therefore most reluctant to expand government social welfare programs,

SOURCE

How Should We Live?

The Polish poet Wislawa Szymborska, winner of the Nobel Prize for Literature in 1996, reflects upon the disillusionment of the twentieth century and assumes that life should and must go on nevertheless. "How should we live?" she asks at the close of one of her most poignant poems, written in the 1970s. In this poem, however, she offers no answers:

Our twentieth century was going to
    improve on the others.
It will never prove it now,
now that its years are numbered,
its gait is shaky,
its breath is short.

Too many things have happened
that weren't supposed to happen,
and what was supposed to come about
has not.

Happiness and spring, among other things,
were supposed to be getting closer.

Fear was expected to leave the mountains
    and the valleys.
Truth was supposed to hit home
before a lie.

A couple of problems weren't going
to come up anymore:
hunger, for example,
and war, and so forth.

There was going to be respect
for helpless people's helplessness,
trust, that kind of stuff.

Anyone who planned to enjoy the world
is now faced
with a hopeless task.

Stupidity isn't funny.
Wisdom isn't gay.
Hope
isn't that young girl anymore,
et cetera, alas.

God was finally going to believe
in a man both good and strong,
but good and strong
are still two different men.

"How should we live?" someone asked me
    in a letter.
I had meant to ask him
the same question.

Again, and as ever,
as may be seen above,
the most pressing questions
are naive ones.

---

saw national income drop by half between 1929 and 1932. Almost 14 million people were unemployed. Elected in 1932, in the midst of national despair, Democratic President Franklin Delano Roosevelt rallied the nation with charismatic optimism. Declaring that "The only thing we have to fear is fear itself," he instituted social welfare programs as a means of preserving the capitalist foundation. He provided financial relief for the unemployed; public works projects to create construction jobs; subsidies to farmers to reduce production and eliminate surpluses; and federal support for low-cost housing and slum clearance. A Civilian Conservation Corps was established, ostensibly to promote conservation and reforestation, but mostly to provide some 3 million jobs to the young. The Tennessee Valley Authority created an immense hydroelectric program, combining flood control with rural electrification and regional economic development.

Roosevelt increased the regulation of business and promoted unions. The Securities and Exchange Commission, created in 1929, regulated the stock exchange. The National Recovery Administration encouraged regulation of prices and production until it was judged unconstitutional in 1935. The Social Security Act of 1935 introduced unemployment, old age, and disability insurance—policies already in place in parts of Western Europe well before World War I. Child labor was abolished. Forty hours of work was set as the weekly norm. Minimum hourly wages were fixed. Union organization was encouraged and union membership grew from 4 million in 1929 to 9 million in 1940. The most capitalist of the major powers thus accepted the welfare state. Throughout the century, the scope of welfare expanded and contracted with different governments, philosophies of government, and budgetary conditions, but the principle that the state had a major role in protecting and advancing the welfare of its people persisted.

In Germany, the Depression followed on the heels of catastrophic inflation. In the 1920s the Government induced hyperinflation to pay the resented war reparations, thus wiping out the savings of the middle classes and amplifying further resentment over the punitive Versailles Treaty, including its emphasis on German war guilt and insistence on Germany's disarmament. By 1924 industrial production had recovered but then the Depression wiped out the gains. The new government, called the Weimar Republic, was perceived by many as a weak and precarious experiment in constitutional democracy in a nation accustomed to a military monarchy. Exciting new movements in art and architecture that were responsive to a new technological potential for creativity, notably the Bauhaus school of architecture, were threatened and ultimately driven out of the country. Anti-democratic forces and political ideologies, backed by thugs on the streets, triumphed over aesthetic and cultural creativity.

METHODS OF PRODUCTION AND DESTRUCTION WHAT DIFFERENCE DO THEY MAKE?

The early twentieth century taught us skepticism. The greatest triumphs of science and technology could be transformed into instruments of death. Principles of physics that had been accepted as laws for two centuries and more, were found to be only fragments of larger principles. Public health measures and medicine extended lifespans; world warfare cut them down. Nationalism inspired people to work for the betterment of their country and its people, but at the same time to compete with, and make war against, those in neighboring countries, and often to limit freedoms of minorities even at home. Revolutions continued for a decade and more, benefiting many people, but not fulfilling their promises to the masses. Great empires, some of them hundreds of years old, one of them 2,000 years old, toppled and dissolved in civil warfare. World warfare ended, but left clear indications that it would soon resume because the issues that had caused it remained unresolved. Perhaps most frightening of all, totalitarian governments came to power in parts of the world that had been considered among the most civilized, only to challenge and subvert the whole basis of modern civilization, as we shall see in Chapter 20. This chapter ends with stories of warfare, imperialism, economics, science, and technology that were clearly unfinished. Many of them are still unfolding.

Review Questions

- What did the poet Wislawa Szymborska have in mind when she wrote that in the twentieth century, "A couple of problems weren't going to come up anymore: hunger, for example, and war, and so forth"?
- In what way does the Mexican Revolution appear to be a product of the technological developments of the early twentieth century? What other conditions promoted this revolution?
- What were the chief causes of World War I, and why were the Balkans so important in its origins?
- What promises were made by colonial powers during the war that were not kept afterward?
- What were the most important actions of the Soviet Union in the first decade after the Communist Revolution?
- In what ways was the United States a world leader in the decade following World War I? In what ways was it not?

Suggested Readings

Adas, Michael. *Machines as the Measure of Man* (Ithaca, NY: Cornell University Press, 1989).

Andrea, Alfred and James H. Overfield, eds. *The Human Record*, Vol. 2 (Boston: Houghton Mifflin, 3rd ed., 1998).

Bulliet, Richard W., ed. *The Columbia History of the 20th Century* (New York: Columbia University Press, 1998).

Camus, Albert. *The Myth of Sisyphus* (New York: Vintage Books, 1959).

Chafe, William H. and Harvard Sitkoff, eds. *A History of Our Time* (New York: Oxford University Press, 3rd ed., 1991).

Crossley, Pamela Kyle, Lynn Hollen Lees, John W. Servos. *Global Society. The World since 1900* (Boston: Houghton Mifflin, 2004).

Fox, Richard G., ed. *Urban India: Society, Space and Image* (Durham, NC: Duke University Program in Comparative Studies on Southern Asia, 1970).

Freeman, Christopher. "Technology and Invention," in Bulliet, pp. 314–44.

Freud, Sigmund. *Civilization and its Discontents* (New York: W.W. Norton and Co., 1961).

———. *A General Introduction to Psychoanalysis* (New York: Pocket Books, 1952).

Gandhi, Mohandas Karamchand. *Hind Swaraj or Indian Home Rule* (Ahmedabad: Navajivan Press, 1938).

Hemingway, Ernest. *For Whom the Bell Tolls* (New York: Scribner, 1940).

Hofstadter, Richard, ed. *Great Issues in American History: A Documentary Record* (New York: Vintage Books, 1959).

Howard, Michael and William Roger Louis, eds. *The Oxford History of the Twentieth Century* (New York: Oxford University Press, 1998).

Hughes, Thomas. *American Genesis* (New York: Viking, 1989).

Inkster, Ian. *Science and Technology in History. An Approach to Industrialization* (London: Macmillan, 1991).

Johnson, Paul. *Modern Times* (New York: Harper and Row, 1983).

Keegan, John. *A History of Warfare* (New York: Knopf, 1994). Compares and explicates the history of warfare through styles of war rather than strict chronology. Themes are stone, flesh, iron, and fire.

Kennedy, Paul. *The Rise and Fall of the Great Powers* (New York: Random House, 1987).

Kochan, Lionel and Richard Abraham. *The Making of Modern Russia* (London: Penguin Books, 1983).

Kragh, Helge. *Quantum Generations. A History of Physics in the Twentieth Century* (Princeton: Princeton University Press, 1999).

Landes, David S. *The Wealth and Poverty of Nations* (New York: W.W. Norton, 1999).

Lewis, David Levering. *W.E.B. Du Bois: Biography of a Race 1868–1919* (New York: Henry Holt, 1993).

Pacey, Arnold. *Technology in World Civilization* (Cambridge: MIT Press, 1990).

Pickering, Kevin T. and Lewis A. Owen. *An Introduction to Global Environmental Issues* (New York: Routledge, 1994).

Ramanujan, A.K. "Towards an Anthology of City Images," in Fox, pp. 224–42.

Remarque, Erich Maria. *All Quiet on the Western Front*, trans. by A.W. Wheen (Boston: Little, Brown, 1958).

Rosenberg, Rosalind, "The 'Woman' Question," in Bulliet, pp. 53–80.

Szymborska, Wislawa. *View with a Grain of Sand* (San Diego: Harcourt Brace, 1995).

Wilkie, Brian and James Hurt, eds. *Literature of the Western World*, Vol. 2 (New York: Macmillan, 1984).

Williams, Trevor I.A. *Short History of Twentieth-Century Technology c. 1900–c. 1950* (Oxford: Oxford University Press, 1982)

Yagnik, Indulal. *Autobiography*, Vol. 1 (in Gujarati) (Ahmedabad: Ravaani Publishing House, 1955).

World History Documents CD-ROM

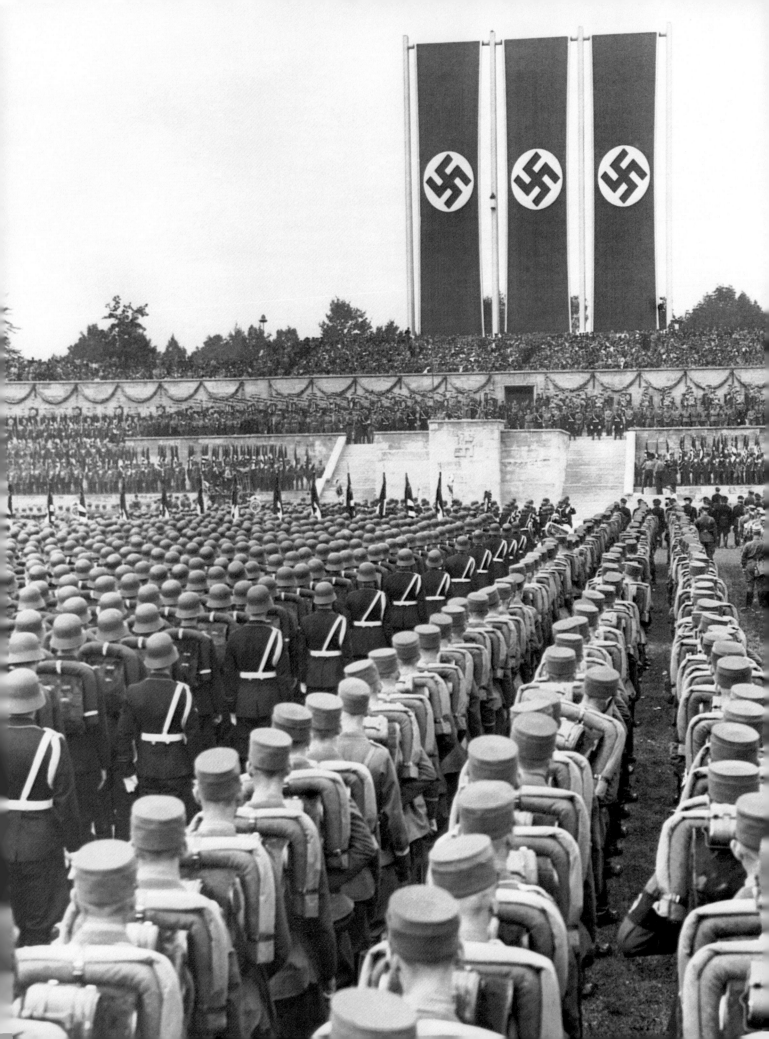

WORLD WAR II AND THE COLD WAR

THE WORLD IN PERIL, 1937–49

KEY TOPICS
- Portents of Disaster
- The Contest of the "isms": Fascism and Communism
- The Descent Toward World War
- World War II
- The Image of Humanity
- The United Nations, Postwar Recovery, and the Origins of the Cold War
- Entering the Second Half of the Twentieth Century:
  What Difference Does it Make?

PORTENTS OF DISASTER

No sooner had the Paris peace treaties been signed than leading economists predicted disaster. In *The Economic Consequences of the Peace*, published in 1920, John Maynard Keynes argued that the treaties would push Germany and Austria into starvation. Like all of Europe, these countries would suffer from the crippling disruption of coal and iron supplies, transport, and imports of food and raw materials. In addition, the treaties stripped Germany of her overseas colonies and investments and her merchant fleet. It imposed on her crushing financial reparations to be paid to the victor nations. Keynes blamed the leaders of Britain, France, Italy, and the United States for their short-sightedness in making these demands, and he warned that starving people "in their distress may overturn the remnants of organization, and submerge civilization itself in their attempts to satisfy desperately the overwhelming needs of the individual."

In the next year, from a very different perspective, the poet William Butler Yeats added his own fears concerning a profound cultural sickness that he saw infecting all of Europe in the wake of the war and the Russian Revolution:

> Things fall apart; the center cannot hold;
> Mere anarchy is loosed upon the world,
> The blood-dimmed tide is loosed, and everywhere
> The ceremony of innocence is drowned;
> The best lack all conviction, while the worst
> Are full of passionate intensity.

Yeats held out no hope in rationality, nor in technological progress, although he professed belief in some mystical religious experience that was yet to come:

> Surely some revelation is at hand;
> Surely the Second Coming is at hand. (cited in Wilkie and Hurt, p. 1655)

A decade later, as worldwide depression confirmed the fears and pessimism of the economist Keynes and the poet Yeats, the psychoanalyst Sigmund Freud, who had pioneered depth studies of the human mind and spirit, wrote of even deeper anxieties. Freud questioned the direction of all civilized, technologically advanced societies and feared that they might all be destroyed:

Opposite **Nazi rally at Nuremberg, 1937.** Nazi Party members fill a stadium at a party meeting in Nuremberg, 1937.

> Men have gained control over the forces of nature to such an extent that with their
> help they would have no difficulty in exterminating one another to the last man. They
> know this, and hence comes a large part of their current unrest, their unhappiness and
> their mood of anxiety. (Freud, pp. 34–5)

The events of the next decade, 1930–39, continued to feed the worst fears of the economist, the poet, and the psychoanalyst. The outbreak of World War II at the end of the decade confirmed their bitter and tragic predictions.

THE CONTEST OF THE "ISMS": FASCISM AND COMMUNISM

fascism A political philosophy, movement, or government that exalts the nation over the individual, the antithesis of liberal democracy. It advocates a centralized, autocratic government led by a disciplined party and headed by a dictatorial, charismatic leader.

Desperate times evoke desperate responses. We have already seen in Chapter 19 one of these desperate responses: the triumph of communism in the Soviet Union. In this chapter we shall see its further development. First, however, we analyze the rise of **fascism** in Italy in the 1920s under Benito Mussolini (1883–1945), in Germany after 1933 under Adolf Hitler (1889–1945), and, to a lesser degree, in Japan, building throughout the 1930s. The term fascism was coined to describe the ideology of Mussolini's movement, party, and government. Fascism exalted the nation over the individual. It called for centralized autocratic government with tight control of the economy and social life of the nation. It demanded the suppression of all opposition through unofficial paramilitary organizations, which often took to the streets and whose members appeared to be thugs. If and when fascists took office, they used the armed forces of the government to suppress opposition. They glorified warfare as a positive virtue. Why people supported fascism is unclear. Some followers must have been attracted by the promise that violence could solve the nation's problems, many more by the promise of a better government and a more prosperous economy than the weak parliamentary governments could deliver. Fascism vested the power of the nation in a supreme leader. In Italy Mussolini, who had himself referred to as *Duce* (pronounced doo-chay), or supreme leader, filled that function.

Italy

Although it had been on the side of the victors, Italy was beset by wartime losses of people and property, economic depression, and the social unrest that beset much of Europe. Labor strikes and peasant unrest in the form of non-payment of rents and occasional seizures of land spread throughout the country. Governments elected in 1919 and again in 1921 were not able to deal with them effectively. Mussolini organized groups of men—mostly thugs—from among the ex-soldiers of the war, calling them *fascio di combattimento*, groups of combatants—derived from the Latin word *fasces* (the bundle of sticks carried by *lectors* of ancient Rome as symbols of power)—and dressed them in uniforms of black shirts. These were his core supporters. When his attempts at winning power through elections in 1921 brought him only about 7 percent of the vote, he turned his men loose on the streets to beat up labor organizers, communists, socialists, and local officials belonging to communist and socialist parties. The fascists claimed that they killed 3,000 opponents in Italy from 1920 to 1922.

Announcing that the nation had descended into chaos, Mussolini declared a "March on Rome" in 1922 and threatened to take over the government. The government capitulated to his threat and asked him to take over for a year as prime minister with full emergency powers. In the next elections, in 1924, Mussolini's party—through the use of violence, intimidation, and fraud—took more than 60 percent of the vote. Seizing control of the state, Mussolini abolished all other parties, took away the right to strike, destroyed labor unions, and sharply censored the press. He instituted his own propaganda wing within the government to indoctrinate Italy into endorsing his programs. He organized the country according to twenty-two major economic categories. For each category he had fascist representatives of labor, employers, and government meet together to decide wages, prices, working conditions, and industrial policies. All of them were assigned to a government minister and brought into the parliament. In fear of Mussolini's power, organised labor toed the line. Mussolini built roads, drained several hundred thousand acres of swamp lands for wheat production and malaria control, and "made the trains run on

Benito Mussolini (*center*) during the Fascist march on Rome, 1922. Mussolini glorified violence and employed armed thugs against his opponents. His methods worked. Even his threat to march his troops into Rome was enough to force the feckless Italian government to hand power over to him.

time". While communists, socialists, liberals, and labor union leaders had little appreciation for either the man or his methods, businessmen and others wanting a society that functioned with little public turmoil gave their approval. They also took patriotic pride in the new colonial war that he led. In 1935, Mussolini attacked Ethiopia, completing his conquest there in 1936. When the League of Nations demanded Italian withdrawal, Mussolini scoffed. The League did nothing of substance to push him, and Mussolini withdrew Italy from the League.

Germany

Mussolini's fascism drew the admiration of the young Adolf Hitler in Germany. Born in Austria, Hitler dropped out of high school at sixteen and went to the national capital, Vienna, at nineteen, supporting himself at odd jobs, especially painting pictures. Much in pre-war Vienna offended him: the wealthy royalty and aristocrats of the court; the prosperous businessmen; the socialist workers; the easy internationalism of the artists and the intellectuals; and, most of all the Jews, who had assimilated into Austrian society and often held high positions in business and the professions. Like many in Vienna, Hitler became a virulent racist, exalting the "pure" German "race" and disparaging all others in a hierarchy that stretched downward from northern Europeans to southern Europeans, to Africans, to Jews at the very bottom.

Moving to Munich in south Germany in 1913, Hitler felt himself more at home. When war broke out, he volunteered for military service—serving as a dispatch runner—and came to value warfare as a blood-stirring and liberating experience. After the war, he began to work against the communist influences that were spreading among workers. In 1919 he joined the anti-communist German Workers' party and became its head. He transformed the party into the National Socialist German Workers' party—abbreviated as "Nazi"—thus launching his political career. Following Mussolini's model, the Nazis built up a group of storm troopers (the SA)—a paramilitary organization that often carried out violence in the streets—and gave them a uniform of brown shirts. The organization of these thugs was just one sign of Hitler's disdain for the democratic German government of his day, usually called the Weimar

Republic for the city in which it met. As in Italy, many people in Germany preferred the order imposed by these paramilitary groups to what they perceived as the weakness of parliament and the street demonstrations of communists and socialists.

The Weimar Republic, an elected government of both working- and middle-class membership, had succeeded the German monarchy which withdrew from power at the end of the war. Both the militant right wing, who wanted a more centralized and powerful government under more autocratic leadership—like the Nazis—and the militant left wing, who wanted a socialist or even communist government and hoped for a revolution like that in Russia, had little respect for Weimar. Both saw the centrist government as too weak.

1923 was an especially difficult year. Germany could not keep up with its payments of war reparations. In response, France seized the highly industrialized Ruhr valley, provoking national outrage in Germany, a good part of it directed against the weakness of the Weimar government itself. In addition, extraordinary inflation completely eroded the value of the German mark, making it hardly worth the paper it was printed on, wiping out the savings of the middle class, impoverishing the lives of workers, and endangering the stability of the government. Among those who further inflamed public opinion against the government, Hitler attempted a *putsch*, a revolt, to overthrow it, in Munich in 1923. Some army officers had already attempted a *putsch* in 1920 but failed. Hitler also failed, and was imprisoned for nine months. But he gained greater popular attention and during his months in jail he wrote *Mein Kampf* (*My Struggle*), his political manifesto, filled with his denunciation of the government, strident nationalism, plans for a Germany restored to—and beyond—her former greatness, the subordination of eastern Europe to Germany, and bitter, all-consuming anti-Semitism. He blamed Jews for being on the left with the communists, on the right with the capitalists, too foreign and exotic, and too assimilated into modern German life. For Hitler, Jews had become the scapegoat whom he could blame for all of Germany's woes.

Recognizing, and frightened by, the dangers of an unstable Germany, the French withdrew from the Ruhr, and the former wartime Allies (excluding the Soviet Union) rescheduled the reparation debts to make them less onerous. For a few years, prosperity returned, but then the international depression of 1929 swept the country back into poverty and renewed humiliation. Germany seethed in anguish. From communists on the left to Hitler on the right, German democracy was held responsible for the nations troubles. Hitler's became the strongest voice. In a series of national elections from 1928 to 1932, his Nazi party's proportion of seats in the German parliament, the Reichstag, went from about 2 percent to about 46 percent, although in the next election, later in 1932, it fell to just below 40 percent. He gained support not only from backers who approved his entire program, but also from many conservatives, including army officers and influential business people, who differed on many points from Hitler's crude nationalism and racism, but who saw him as their chief defense against communism, which they feared even more. In 1933, German political leaders turned to Hitler—the head of the largest single party in the Reichstag—to head a coalition government. Hitler became chancellor of Germany by entirely legal processes. In order to rule without the constraints of a coalition, Hitler called for another election later in the year. In a contest marked by the violence of the SA, suspension of freedoms of speech and press, and a fire in the Reichstag building that Hitler blamed on the communists, the Nazis gained 44 percent of the vote. This was not enough, so Hitler announced a national emergency and, again using his SA thugs to intimidate the opposition, got the votes of a majority of the Reichstag to rule as dictator.

Once in power, Hitler moved swiftly to establish the kind of state that is often called totalitarian—that is, a state in which the individual is subordinated to a centralized administration that controls the national economy, politics, media, and culture, usually under a single dictator or a small council. As Mussolini had himself called *Duce*, so Hitler had himself called **Führer**, leader. In 1925, Hitler had created the SS, another paramilitary organization, dressed in black uniforms. Though initially subordinated to the SA, they rose in prominence. All political parties apart from the Nazis were abolished, and leading Nazis who were viewed as opponents of Hitler were murdered on 30 June, 1934 in an operation carried out by the SS. A secret police force, the *Gestapo*, was established in 1936. Opposition leaders proposing anti-Hitler ideologies were killed or dispatched to concentration camps. Churches were forbidden to criticize the government, and they were encouraged

Nazi Party rally. Over 750,000 Nazi Party workers, soldiers, and civilians greeted Adolf Hitler at the 1934 Nuremberg conference. Against the backdrop of a giant swastika, the German chancellor proclaimed that the Third Reich would last for the next thousand years. Ironically, the trial of Nazi war criminals by the victorious Allied powers would take place in the same city eleven years later.

to cut their ties with overseas branches of their denominations. By contrast, the government encouraged the worship of pre-Christian Teutonic gods. Strikes were forbidden and employers were granted new powers in dealing with workers. Policies were based on "racial science," with Aryans declared to be the most elevated of races, Jews the lowest. Jews were dismissed from public office, including university service and the civil service. In 1935 they were stripped of citizenship.

Why did people tolerate this new order? Some, of course, accepted the new, totalitarian order as appropriate. Others, frightened by the prospect of chaos, impoverishment, and communism, saw it as a severely flawed, but better, alternative. Also, Hitler commanded the use of force in the country, now not only through the SS, but through the legitimate use of the army, police, and secret police. Citizens could protest only at risk to their life and safety. Finally, Hitler's program for rebuilding the country economically and militarily had great appeal. So, too, did his emphasis on the need for *lebensraum*, space for living, an expansion of Germany's territory first into Austria and Czechoslovakia and then through Poland, the Ukraine, and Russia. The Nazi propaganda machine, orchestrated by Joseph Goebbels, indoctrinated the nation, often spreading "the big lie," because, as Hitler said, "in the big lie there is always a certain force of credibility."

Hitler set the nation to work on programs of public works, building housing and superhighways, draining swamps, and reforesting rural areas. In 1936, following the Soviet model, he introduced state planning, although unlike the Russian case, he worked within the framework of private property. He urged Germany to become economically self-sufficient, and its skilled scientists developed many artificial products—such as rubber, plastics, and synthetic fibers—that enabled it to reduce its imports. Germans went back to work. Germany escaped the severe unemployment suffered in most European countries during the Great Depression. The most remarkable dimension of his rebuilding program, however, was the most dangerous and

Führer German for "leader", the title taken by Hitler to assert his total control over Germany.

most threatening: In violation of the Paris peace accords, Hitler began rebuilding Germany's military, and soon he deployed these forces in missions that precipitated world war.

Hitler's Germany shared many characteristics with Mussolini's Italy. Both had developed strong governments that brooked no opposition. Both followed policies of militarism and glorified war. The leaders in both set themselves up as the unchallenged and unchallengeable center of their states. In October 1936, the two governments proclaimed an "axis" that bound them together in international affairs. In the next month, Germany signed an Anti-Comintern Pact with Japan, pledging mutual support against possible attacks from the USSR. The next few years brought these three countries—Germany, Italy, and Japan—together as the axis powers in World War II.

Japan

During the Meiji restoration, Japan had achieved an astonishingly rapid reorganization of government, administration, economy, industry, and finances.

As we saw in Chapter 18, Japan followed Western examples in asserting a sphere of influence in China and seized colonies for itself. It defeated China in Korea in 1895 and became the dominant nation of east Asia, reversing its previous student–teacher relationship with China. Japan made Korea and the island of Taiwan into colonies and defeated Russia by land and sea in East Asia, in 1904–5, after signing a military alliance with Britain in 1902. For the first time in modern history, an Asian country had defeated a European one.

World War I also touched East Asia and profoundly affected its postwar politics. Japan was seated as one of the victorious Five Great Powers at the 1919 peace conference in Paris—the only non-Western nation accepted as an equal at the proceedings. It was assigned control over Germany's Pacific colonies, including the Liaotung Peninsula in north China, which Japan had seized in 1914. This led to the "May Fourth" movement of Chinese students in China, originally a student demonstration that metamorphosed into a broader intellectual movement for Chinese reforms (see Chapter 19). In the end, the Chinese refused to sign the Versailles Treaty.

World War I presented Japan with an unprecedented economic opportunity. While other industrialized countries were occupied with war in Europe, Japan developed its industries relatively free from competition. Between 1914 and 1918 Japan's gross national income rose by 40 percent, and for the first time Japan began to export more than she imported. Heavy industry showed particularly impressive growth. Manufacturing increased by 72 percent while the labor force expanded by only 42 percent, indicating the growing use of machinery to increase productivity. Transport increased by 60 percent. Between 1914 and 1919 Japan's merchant marine almost doubled, to 2.8 million tons. The production and export of consumer goods also advanced. In the first decades of the twentieth century, Japan's most important exports were textiles, primarily silk, 80 percent of which was produced by women.

As a latecomer, Japan could take advantage of technology already developed in the West (the "leapfrogging" path that Trotsky preached in Russia). Japanese industries practiced three different patterns in importing that technology. Some signed agreements with foreign firms to establish branches in Japan; some negotiated for licenses to use the new technologies; and some practiced "reverse engineering," analyzing foreign machinery and reproducing it with adaptations appropriate to Japanese needs. Adaptation produced innovations—for example, in applying chemical research to agricultural and even ceramics production. Private firms imported most of the foreign technology, but the government also encouraged research by funding state universities, laboratories, and the development of military technology.

Japan bridged the "dual economy," the separation between large-scale and cottage industries that has inhibited growth in many countries. In a "dual economy," one sector consists of large, highly capitalized, technically advanced factories employing thousands of workers producing modern products; the other sector includes small-scale workshops, with relatively low capitalization and less up-to-date equipment, often employing fewer than thirty workers, producing traditional goods. In most countries, the small-scale sector tends to shrivel as larger firms achieve economies of scale and put it out of business. Governments, too, often invest their resources in large industries, neglecting the small sector. But in Japan, the smaller factories adopted appropriate scale, new technologies, and began to produce new goods needed by the larger industries. From the early years of the century, Japan evolved systems of sub-contracting between the large and small sectors, which made them interdependent and complementary.

Because of poor harvests in 1918 the price of rice, Japan's staple food, rose sharply. In response, massive riots broke out in hundreds of cities and towns, involving some 700,000 people, lasting fifty days, and resulting in 25,000 arrests and 1000 deaths. The government responded by importing rice and other staples from its colonial territories in Korea and Taiwan. The riots represented the growth of Japan's urban voice as the urban proportion of the population rose from just over 10 percent in 1890 to close to 50 percent in the 1920s (to 78 percent in the 1990s). Labor was increasingly organized and the citizenry politicized. In 1925 all male subjects over the age of twenty-five, 12.5 million people, were given the vote.

The riots also reminded Japan of its increasing dependence on its colonies for daily commodities. In the later 1920s, Taiwan and Korea provided four-fifths of Japan's rice imports and two-thirds of its sugar. For industrial raw materials, such as minerals, metals, petroleum, fertilizers, and lumber, Japan had to look farther afield, and this would lead it into fatal colonial adventures.

In the 1920s, industrial production increased by two-thirds, and the **zaibatsu** (huge holding companies or conglomerates) came to control much of the Japanese economy and were very influential in politics. The four largest—Mitsui, Mitsubishi, Sumitomo, and Yasuda—were controlled by individual families, and each operated a bank and numerous enterprises in a variety of industries, ranging from textiles to shipping and machinery. A Mitsubishi mining company, for example, would extract minerals, which would then be made into a product by one of the Mitsubishi manufacturing companies. Next, this product would be marketed abroad by a Mitsubishi trading firm and transported in ships of another Mitsubishi affiliate. The whole process would be financed through the Mitsubishi bank.

The *zaibatsu* combined large size with an ability to shift production to meet demands. The *zaibatsu* families also held

zaibatsu (Japanese: "wealthy clique") A large Japanese business conglomerate holding many different companies, usually under the control of a single family.

Workers winding induction regulator coils in a Shibaura Engineering Works plant, Tsurumi, Honshu, Japan, 1930. In the 1920s–1930s the Japanese often borrowed from Western models by inviting foreign firms to establish Japanese branches; by obtaining licenses to produce foreign technologies; and by adapting those technologies to Japanese conditions. Their industries consequently "leapfrogged" ahead very rapidly.

Samurai warrior. The ancient and proud warrior class of the samurai worshiped athletic prowess, swordsmanship, and fierce loyalty to the emperor. In 1877 the last 400,000 samurai were pensioned off to become *shizoku*, Japanese gentry, but their virtues lived on in the country's psyche. In times of crisis, the warriors' values turned Japanese nationalism into a potent force.

considerable influence in government, both through the money they controlled and their close family links with prominent politicians. The Major Industries Control Law of 1931, for example, encouraged large companies in key industries to join in cartels to regulate production and prices.

International respect, growing wealth, rising urbanization, increasing industrialization, high rates of literacy, universal male suffrage (1925), and the institutionalization of political parties suggested that Japan was embracing liberal democracy. But the political power of the *zaibatsu* undermined people's faith in democratic practice, and the military held extraordinary power, both under law and in popular opinion. In contrast to most democratic countries, in which the civilian government controls the military, Japanese law specified that the ministers of war and of the navy had to be active generals or admirals. Conversely, the formal powers of the diet were restricted. In theory, the Japanese emperor held the ultimate political authority for the country, and, although he never did govern actively, political leaders speaking in his name dominated public policy at home and abroad. Japan's traditional Shinto religion (see Chapter 9) emphasized the emperor's divinity and asserted the leading role of Japan's samurai warrior ethic.

Many of these military elites began to claim expanded powers for the armed forces. They wished to protect Japan, a resource-poor island nation, especially vulnerable to shifts in international trade and its regulation. The world depression of 1929 shocked the Japanese economy as the value of exports dropped 50 percent between 1929 and 1931. Unemployment rose to 3 million, with rural areas hardest hit. Many civilians seemed to agree with the military: the future would look brighter if Japan could reorganize and control the economy of East Asia for its own benefit. Although the civilian government continued to criticize the military, generals increasingly gained control of the state and turned it toward military goals.

THE DESCENT TOWARD WORLD WAR

The 1920s appeared to usher in a time of peace. The League of Nations had been founded in 1920. The league was not entrusted with peace-keeping missions, but it was expected to be a forum in which international conflicts could be managed through negotiations. It also carried out valuable humanitarian work in fighting epidemic disease in eastern Europe and in resettling political refugees—Russians fleeing the communism of the Soviet Union and Greeks and Armenians expelled from Turkey, for example. The league's Intellectual Cooperation Organization sponsored cultural activities that brought together people from around the world. The organization's annual meetings in Geneva, Switzerland, attracted representatives not only from western European countries and the United States, but also from Mexico, Venezuela, Brazil,

Japan, China, India, Egypt, Poland, Czechoslovakia, and Hungary. They highlighted the increasingly global interaction of the arts and the desire for a free flow of artistic expression.

Individual nations took various steps to prevent war and promote peace. In 1921, a conference was convened in Washington to set limits on competition in naval forces. It achieved agreement on a 5:5:3 ratio in the total tonnage of large ships among Britain, the United States, and Japan, with other World War allies accepting lower limits. In 1925, the major powers, meeting in Locarno, Switzerland, signed a number of agreements designed to relieve some of the burden of guilt that Germany had been forced to accept for World War I and to reintegrate Germany into the European diplomatic world. Germany accepted its western borders with France and Belgium unconditionally and agreed that it would use only diplomacy, and not force, in any attempt to alter its eastern borders with Poland and Czechoslovakia. To reinforce this agreement, France agreed to defend Poland and Czechoslovakia in case of any future attack. (Britain did not sign, arguing that its interests were not involved.) In 1928, sixty-five nations signed the Pact of Paris, known as the Kellogg–Briand Pact for the American secretary of state Frank Kellogg and the French foreign minister Aristide Briand who prepared the groundwork. The signatories to this pact agreed to renounce war as a means of settling international conflicts. By 1928, optimism—and prosperity—had returned to the European world. By 1925, the index of manufacturing in western and central Europe surpassed that of pre-war 1913. (Russia, the worst-hit of all world powers by the war, had returned only to 70 percent, from a low of 13 percent in 1920.) Lasting peace, too, seemed to have been achieved.

And then came the Great Depression and its economic and political pressures. Most remarkably, as the democratic, capitalistic countries of western Europe, the United States, and Latin America struggled with the world depression of the 1930s, the USSR (see Chapter 19), Germany, Italy, and Japan were thriving. Each of the four had adopted dictatorship, national planning, and militarization. Indeed three of them—Germany, Italy, and Japan—launched military campaigns that ultimately resulted in World War II, and the fourth, the USSR, built up a massive military force in anticipation of having to fight them off. The build-up of the militaries and the war campaigns fed on one another. The cost of maintaining the armed forces became so exorbitant that only war victories could pay for them, and to achieve war victories ever-increasing militarization was necessary.

The steps to war unfolded in the 1930s. In 1931, strongly influenced by its wealthy business conglomerates, the *zaibatsu*, and by hyper-nationalist officers in the armed forces, Japan seized Chinese arsenals in Manchuria and began to take over the entire province. Japanese troops had been in place in Manchuria since their victory over the Russians in 1905. As justification for the takeover, they blamed China for the murder of a Japanese officer in Mukden, Manchuria, and for economic boycotts of Japanese goods. In 1932, Japan declared Manchuria an independent state, which it then ruled by establishing the last Chinese emperor, Pu Yi, who had been deposed in 1911, as a puppet head of government. The government was nominally Chinese but the Japanese pulled the strings. China, joined by several small nations, protested to the League of Nations. Japan quit the league, and, in any case, the league took no serious action. None of the other powers felt threatened. They did not want to commit troops, and the western Europeans did not want to alienate Japan at a time when they felt the need for Japan as a partner in a quiet alliance against the Soviet Union. As noted above, many in Japan opposed Japanese militarism, but, as in Germany, violent attacks stifled the opposition. Between 1930 and 1936, two prime ministers, one finance minister, and one important banker were assassinated. Speaking out against militarism in Japan was dangerous.

In 1935, Italy invaded Ethiopia. Once again, the League of Nations imposed no serious response when Ethiopia, a member nation of the league, lodged a protest to the international body.

In 1936, civil war broke out in Spain. The country had been in turmoil as a relatively bloodless revolution deposed the king of Spain in 1931 and established a democratic Spanish republic. For five years, power oscillated between conservative rightists—including members of the clergy, the military, and business elites—and the liberal leftists—including workers, socialists, communists, and anarchists. In elections in 1936, the leftists won, and the rightists, led by General Francisco Franco, began an insurrection that turned into a civil war. Many observers called this a dress rehearsal for World War II because Germany and Italy sent men (Italy sent 50,000 soldiers), money, and weapons to aid Franco and the rightists, while the Soviet Union sent technicians, political advisers, and equipment to bolster the republican government. The major democratic governments of western Europe—including Britain and France—condemned Franco, but sent no support and prohibited the shipment of weapons. The United States declared its neutrality and declared an embargo on the export of arms to Spain. Privately, thousands of volunteers from the democratic nations went to Spain as volunteers to serve with the republican forces. Ernest Hemingway immortalized this International Brigade in his novel *For Whom the Bell Tolls*. Hitler used the war as an opportunity to test the utility of the air force that he was building. Mostly he used them to transport Franco's troops, but on April 28, 1937, German air force squadrons supporting Franco bombed and destroyed the unprotected civilian town of Guernica, the capital of the Basque region of northern Spain. Pablo Picasso, a Spaniard, and probably the most famous painter of his time, immediately painted *Guernica*, perhaps the most famous anti-war painting in history, depicting the anguish, pain, and suffering of men, women, children, and animals. The Spanish Civil War continued on for three years; 600,000 people died. Franco's victory established a right-wing dictatorship that lasted four decades until he died in 1975. The League was not able to resolve the conflicting claims peacefully, and it commanded no armed forces of its own. Armed nationalism triumphed over unarmed internationalism.

Pablo Picasso, *Guernica*, **1937.** Painted as a protest over the German bombing of the little village of Guernica during the Spanish Civil War, this became one of the most famous of all anti-war paintings. Picasso refused to allow it to be moved to Spain from France until after Franco's death in 1975.

On July 7, 1937, Japan invaded China. The pretext was an assault on Japanese troops near Beijing; the goal was the take-over of China. Within months, Japan gained control of most of the densely populated eastern half of the country, although the Chinese withdrew ever deeper into the interior and continued to fight until the very end of World War II. The League of Nations condemned Japan, but took no substantive action. The Japanese refer to this war as the "Pacific War." In global terms, the Japanese invasion of China is usually considered the beginning of World War II, although the war in Europe did not begin until September 1939.

In Europe, after his appointment as chancellor in 1933, Hitler began almost immediately to expand Germany's military position despite the restrictions of the Paris peace treaties. In 1933 he took Germany out of the League of Nations and out of a disarmament conference that was taking place at the time. In 1934, Nazis in neighboring Austria assassinated the prime minister and demanded union with Germany. Hitler's takeover of Austria at this time was prevented only by Mussolini, who declared his opposition to German troops occupying a neighboring country and stationed Italian troops at the Austrian border. In 1935, Nazi intimidation influenced voters in the rich, industrialized Saar region, on the border with France, to vote for annexation to Germany. Most provocatively, in 1935, Hitler began to re-arm Germany. In 1936 he sent his new troops into the Rhineland, German territory just west of the Rhine river, that had been designated a demilitarized zone. No one acted to oppose him. In March 1938, now with Mussolini's consent, German troops moved into Austria, declaring an Anschluss, or union, of the two countries.

Next Hitler focused on Czechoslovakia, and in particular the Sudeten area of that country where some 3 million Germans lived as a minority in the larger Slavic state. He threatened to invade the Sudetenland to annex it to Germany. As fears of war spread, the British prime minister, Neville Chamberlain, and the French premier, Edouard Daladier, flew to Munich to negotiate the fate of Czechoslovakia. They persuaded the Czechs to cede the Sudetenland to Germany, which left the rest of the country open to further German unilateral action. They had persuaded Czechoslovakia to sign its death warrant. They had bought off Hitler by offering up Czechoslovakia, not allowing themselves to realize that they had only delayed the war that was to come. The image of Chamberlain returning from Munich to London proclaiming that he had won "peace for our time" has, ever since, served as a symbol of the folly of appeasing aggressors. The Germans invaded and took over the remainder of Czechoslovakia in March 1939. In the next month, Italy took over Albania.

Russia had agreed to fight against Germany over the issue of Czechoslovakia, if only the French or British would join in, but they would not. Indeed, the British seemed to give more diplomatic attention to Germany, their potential enemy, than to Russia, their potential ally. On August 23, 1939, Russia stunned the

THE MARCH TO WAR

1935–36	Italy conquers Ethiopia
1936–39	Spanish Civil War
July 7, 1937	Japanese troops invade China
Sept 1938	Appeasement in Munich; Germany annexes Sudetenland
Sept 1939	Nazi-Soviet Pact: Germany invades Poland; Britain and France declare war; Poland partitioned between Germany and Russia
Mar–Apr 1940	*Blitzkrieg*: German forces conquer Denmark and Norway
May–June	Italy declares war on Britain and France; German forces conquer France, the Netherlands, and Belgium
June 1940–June 1941	Battle of Britain; Britain holds firm against German bombing attacks
June 21, 1941	German forces invade USSR
Dec 7, 1941	Japanese bomb US Navy, Pearl Harbor
Jan–Mar 1942	Japan conquers Indonesia, Malaya, Burma and the Philippines
June 1942	US Navy defeats Japanese at the Battle of Midway
1942–43	End of Axis resistance in North Africa; Soviet victory in Battle of Stalingrad
1943–44	Red Army slowly pushes Wehrmacht back to Germany
June 6, 1944	Allies land in Normandy (D-Day)
Feb 1945	Yalta conference: Churchill, Roosevelt, and Stalin discuss post-war settlement
March 1945	US planes bomb Tokyo
May 7, 1945	Germany surrenders
August 6, 9, 1945	US drops atom bomb on Hiroshima, and then on Nagasaki
August 14, 1945	Japan surrenders

world by signing a non-aggression pact with Germany, its geopolitical archenemy and ideological rival. A secret protocol of the treaty was an agreement to divide up Poland between them if Poland's territory would ever be conquered. For Hitler, the way was now clear. On September 1, German forces invaded Poland. On September 3, Britain and France finally declared war on Germany. The European theater of World War II had opened.

The early results were ominous. Implementing its strategy of *Blitzkrieg*, lightning war, Germany sent one million troops into Poland, with armored forces in the front and air support above. Poland was not equipped to defend itself, and within a month organized resistance had ended. Germany incorporated western Poland into its new empire. Meanwhile Russia invaded and seized eastern Poland, in accord with its non-aggression pact with Germany. Russia also stationed troops in the Baltic countries of Lithuania, Latvia, and Estonia and attacked Finland militarily to seize part of its land. The League of Nations expelled Russia, but the Russians got the land they wanted from the Finns.

The Early Cost of War Technology

The figures on the military build-up demonstrate the shift from technologies of peace to technologies of war that had occurred throughout the 1930s. The military expenses of the USSR, high even at the outset, multiplied almost eight times; Japan's also multiplied eight times; Germany's, highly restricted by postwar agreements, 46 times.

Defense Expenditures of the Great Powers, 1930–38
(millions of current dollars)

	Japan	Italy	Germany	USSR	UK	France	USA
1930	218	266	162	722	512	498	699
1938	1,740	746	7,415	5,429	1,863	919	1,131

Germany, Japan, and the USSR were all spending about one-fourth of their total national income on defense in 1937, Japan and the USSR slightly more, Germany slightly less. By 1938, Japan's military expenses took up 70 percent of the government's national budget; Germany's 52 percent; Russia's in 1940 reached 33 percent (Kennedy, pp. 300–332). Figures on aircraft production mark the shift to military spending in very specific terms:

Aircraft Production of the Powers, 1932–39

	Japan	Italy	Germany	USSR	UK	France	USA
1932	691	*c.* 500	36	2,595	445	*c.* 600	593
1939	4,467	*c.* 2,000	8,295	10,382	7,940	3,163	2,195

Preparations for war had been going on for a decade.

WORLD WAR II

The War in Europe, 1939–45

After their declaration of war, France and Britain took no immediate military action against Germany and the lull through the winter of 1939–40 is often called the "phony war." In April 1940, however, Hitler resumed his strategy of *blitzkrieg*. Germany invaded Denmark and Norway. On May 10, Germany invaded Belgium, Luxemburg, the Netherlands, and France. Nothing could stop them. The French had prepared an elaborate "Maginot Line" of defended trenches, underground bunkers, minefields, and barbed wire that they thought impregnable. The Germans went around the line to the northwest and penetrated France. German tanks also entered France through Luxemburg and the Ardennes forest, which the French had thought impassable by tanks. Everywhere the Germans scored victories. With Rotterdam under air attack, the Netherlands surrendered. Belgium sued for peace. British, and some French, troops retreated to the French seaport of Dunkirk, and on June 4, leaving their armor behind them, they were hastily evacuated to England. On June 10, Mussolini joined in the attack on France, and soon invaded Greece as well. On June 13, the Germans occupied Paris, and on June 22, France surrendered. The country had been conquered in only one month of fighting. Germany chose to administer the northern two-thirds of France directly. The southern third was administered from the town of Vichy by French officials who collaborated with the Germans. Some French joined General Charles de Gaulle with French forces in exile; some began guerrilla warfare against the Germans. Most acquiesced in the conquest and went about their daily life under German occupation.

World War II in Europe. Fighting began in 1939 with a "blitzkrieg," or lightning war, by Germany and her Italian ally. By late 1942 they controlled most of Europe. But Germany's invasion of Russia in 1941 brought the power of that huge state into opposition and enmeshed Germany into exhausting land war. Britain held out defensively and then began to fight back, especially after the United States entered the war, bringing in air power and material support. By early 1944, the tide had turned.

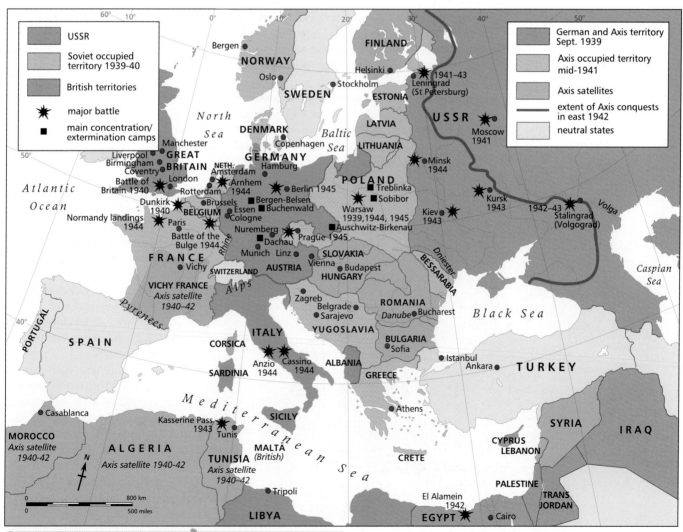

For an interactive version of this map, go to: http://www.prenhall.com/spodek/map20.1

Britain now stood alone against Germany, and Hitler attacked. He launched heavy bombing of London and other strategic cities in Britain throughout the summer and autumn. Prime minister Winston Churchill, who, at the age of sixty-six, had replaced Chamberlain in May 1940, confronted directly the desperation of the situation and addressed his nation in rhetoric that stirred the blood and strengthened the backbone. Within a few days of assuming office, he announced in Parliament: "I have nothing to offer but blood, toil, tears, and sweat!" And a month later:

> We shall go on to the end, we shall fight in France, we shall fight on the seas and oceans, we shall fight with growing confidence and growing strength in the air, we shall defend our island, whatever the cost may be, we shall fight on the beaches, we shall fight on the landing grounds, we shall fight in the fields and in the streets, we shall fight in the hills; we shall never surrender.

Despite heavy losses, including 20,000 dead in London alone, the British held firm, thanks to the Royal Air Force, the invention of radar, and success in cracking German secret codes. By the end of 1940, Germany abandoned the "Battle of Britain" in the air, and gave up plans to invade the island by sea.

To the east, the USSR, operating under cover of the non-aggression pact, had not only seized the eastern half of Poland, and parts of Finland, and incorporated the Baltic States into its empire, it had also seized and incorporated parts of Romania that it had lost in World War I and began to move toward the Balkan states. Hitler moved first. He brought Romania, Bulgaria, and Hungary into the Axis, and occupied Yugoslavia and Greece. Then, in an unexpected, fierce attack, he turned his forces eastward, broke the non-aggression treaty, and invaded Russia on June 22, 1941, a date thereafter viewed in Russia as its Pearl Harbor. A German army of 3 million men and some 3,500 armored vehicles, covered by the air support of the *Luftwaffe* (the Nazi air force), invaded a 2,000-mile front in Russia. The Russians retreated from the central European lands they had taken, and hundreds of miles into the interior of their own country. They transported whole industrial plants deep into the interior. Finally, Stalin, who had been taken completely by surprise by the attack despite his years of preparation for warfare, counter-attacked. The Russian army, under General Georgi Zhukov, pushed the Germans back from their positions around Moscow, relieving that capital city. The Germans, like Napoleon a century and a half earlier, retreated from Moscow in the face of the counter-offensive and the severe winter.

The European war had another front in North Africa. In September 1940, the Italians, who held Libya, invaded Egypt, heading for the Suez Canal. To protect the canal, Churchill diverted troops and supplies from the Battle of Britain to North Africa. The British forces defeated the Italians in Egypt and Libya and even forced them out of Ethiopia. The Germans, however, under General Rommel, entered North Africa and

German soldiers on the Eastern Front, Russia, October 1941. The men moving this field gun into position for the Russian front were Hitler's most elite soldiers, SS Troops of the Police Division. The man in the foreground (*right*) is a "runner" from the cycling troops.

battles raged back and forth between them and the British in 1941 and 1942. British lines, however, held at El Alamein, west of Alexandria, and the Suez Canal remained in British hands. Nevertheless, German submarines in the Mediterranean closed down transportation across the sea, and took a heavy toll on shipping across the Atlantic.

Hitler re-organized his Russian campaign in 1942, directing his troops to the south, in the direction of the rich oil fields of the Caucasus Mountains and the Caspian Sea. By the summer of 1942, Germany had taken all of the western possessions of Russia—the Baltic States, Byelorussia, Poland, and the Ukraine—and stood at the gateway to Leningrad. It held its lines not very far from Moscow, and besieged Stalingrad. Historians sometimes compare Hitler's position to that of Napoleon. Each man held approximately the same areas of Western Europe and each launched an assault into Russia that would devastate the country and force it into deep retreat, but would also leave Germany itself exhausted. To the west, each faced a determined Britain that responded to attacks with unexpected, and ultimately victorious tenacity. The presence of the United States in World War II, however, added a new and additional ingredient into the balance.

From the beginning of the war in Europe, in September 1939, President Roosevelt had supported Britain and the Allies, but his support was limited by the isolationist feelings of many Americans. Roosevelt was able to lift the ban on arms sales in 1939. In 1940, he sent a shipment of arms to England, and later in the same year he added fifty destroyers in exchange for the right to establish military bases in some British possessions in the New World. In 1941, the Congress introduced the Lend–Lease program to provide weapons and supplies to the Allied forces. In 1940 the United States began military conscription, increased the size of its armed forces, and secured bases in Greenland and Iceland in order to protect American and Allied shipping. Still, however, Roosevelt could not commit his country to war—until Japan attacked at Pearl Harbor. To understand this attack, we return to the Pacific theater of warfare.

The War in the Pacific, 1937–42

In 1937, a clash between Chinese and Japanese troops at the Marco Polo Bridge near Beijing triggered a full-scale war with China, which marked the beginning of the Pacific War. The Japanese had not expected the fierce resistance of the Chinese. Planning to end the "China problem" with a single quick victory that would terrify the enemy into suing for peace, the Japanese army launched a full-scale attack on Nanjing, capturing the city in December. Japanese troops murdered, raped, and pillaged in what is now generally known as "the Rape of Nanjing." Twelve thousand noncombatant Chinese were killed in the first two or three days after Nanjing was captured, and about 20,000 cases of rape were reported in the first month. In the first six weeks some 200,000 civilians and prisoners of war were killed in and around the city. The atrocities set an ugly precedent for later Japanese cruelty toward many of the peoples they defeated throughout Asia during the war.

In the face of repeated Japanese advances, the Chinese government retreated to Chongqing, on the upper Yangzi River deep in the interior of the country. The Chinese, like the Russians retreating before the Germans, followed a **scorched-earth** strategy, leaving little in their wake that the enemy could use. The war in China became a stalemate. (Even in 1945, when Japan itself was under attack, about a million Japanese soldiers were still fighting in China, and another 750,000 in Manchuria. China's sheer persistence helped wear out the Japanese.)

In September 1940, Japan signed the Tripartite Pact, formally aligning itself with Germany and Italy as the "Axis Powers." Axis plans, however, were not well coordinated. Japan could have joined in the war against the USSR, opening a second front

scorched earth A strategy of defensive warfare, in which everything that might be of use to an invading army is destroyed by the defending army as it retreats.

from Manchuria, as Germany wished. Instead, it signed a neutrality pact with the Soviet Union in April 1941 and turned southward to capture French Indochina, putting it on a collision course with the USA.

Isolationist pressure in America had thus far kept the USA out of armed warfare, but America did respond to Japanese aggression in China and Southeast Asia by placing an embargo on trade with Japan and by freezing its assets in July 1941. Resource-poor Japan, fearing for its supplies of oil and other raw materials, now had to choose between pulling back from China or confronting the United States in open warfare. Many Japanese resented American resistance to Japan's growing power as just another example of white man's colonialism. On December 7, Japan bombed the American Pacific fleet at Pearl Harbor, Hawaii, with over 300 planes. The Japanese destroyed several battleships and inflicted serious damage on three cruisers, three destroyers, and other ships of various kinds. They also destroyed at least 180 airplanes. Altogether, more than 2,000 people were killed in the attack and over a thousand more were wounded. The attack severely crippled American seapower in the Pacific, though the Navy was able to repair some of the ships. The United States was also extremely fortunate that the three aircraft carriers attached to the Pacific fleet were training elsewhere at the time. America declared war the next day. In Britain, Winston Churchill immediately understood the consequences:

> Hitler's fate was sealed. Mussolini's fate was sealed. As for the Japanese, they would be ground to powder. All the rest was merely the proper application of overwhelming force. (Kennedy, p. 347)

The Japanese leaders who advocated the attacks—and many opposed them—believed that they could defeat America if they struck before American industrial power and troop mobilization could move into high gear. So, on the same day as the attack on Pearl Harbor, Japan also attacked the Philippines, Hong Kong, Malaya, and other bases in Southeast Asia and the Pacific. By the middle of 1942, Japan had conquered the Philippines, the Malay peninsula and Singapore, Indonesia, parts of New Guinea, Indochina, Thailand, and Burma. In the Pacific, it reached almost to Australia. Designating the conquests as the "Greater East Asia Co-Prosperity Sphere," Japan attempted to build an imperial system that would provide raw materials for its industries and markets for its finished products and that would willingly adopt Japanese cultural practices as well.

The plan did not work. The colonial economies could not produce and deliver the supplies that Japan wanted, and, more crucially, Japan could not absorb the agricultural products they could produce. Market structures based on the existing integration of world trade systems were not easily re-organized. Instead of implanting its culture, Japan's occupations generally evoked nationalistic opposition. Japan's treatment of conquered

US servicemen in the Pacific. Landing in Higgins boats from a base in Australia, American troops of the 163rd Infantry Regiment, 41st Division, hit the beach running during the invasion of Wake Island, May 18, 1944. Two months earlier, the United States had begun firebombing Japanese cities.

peoples and prisoners of war was notably harsh and earned it a reputation for cruelty. The brutalizing of thousands of Korean, Chinese, and Filipina women to serve as "sex slaves" for Japanese soldiers came to international attention half a century after the war was over.

Turning the Tide, 1942–5

By the end of 1942 the Allied counter-offensive began. The alliance of Britain, the Free French (an exile government based in London under the leadership of General Charles de Gaulle), the Soviet Union, the United States, and some twenty allied countries slowly evolved. Roosevelt already called them the United Nations. Roosevelt and Churchill, establishing a Combined Chiefs of Staff, decided to concentrate on the western and African fronts, leaving the main fighting against Japan for later.

In the Battle of the Atlantic, British and American navies successfully fought German U-boat (submarine) warfare and opened the ocean to much safer shipping. American troops could now be transported to Europe in relative safety. Under General Eisenhower, Allied forces launched a huge, surprise, amphibious invasion of Algeria and Morocco in November 1942 and pushed eastward. By the spring of 1943 they were met by British forces moving westward from Egypt under General Montgomery, and by May 1943, north Africa was completely recaptured and the sealanes of the Mediterranean were again safe for shipping.

The Russians called on its allies to open a massive, land-based western front that would relieve the German pressure on Russia. The Americans and the British deferred such an attack until they had made more thorough preparations, leaving the Russians to rely on their own resources (and to doubt the commitment of the British and Americans to their Russian allies). Nevertheless, in the winter of 1942–3, the Russians held out successfully against German troops at the Battle of Stalingrad, but at the cost of up to a half-million Russian soldiers killed. More Russians died in the Battle of Stalingrad, between September 1942 and February 1943, than Americans died in the entire war. The Axis powers lost fewer, about 150,000 killed and 90,000 captured. Stalingrad was the turning point in the eastern front. Once the siege was lifted, General Zhukov—already a hero for lifting the siege of Moscow in 1941—opened a Russian counterattack that began to push the Germans steadily westward. By now, also, food, supplies, and material were reaching the Soviet troops under the American Lend–Lease program for the Allies. The millions of Russian troops deployed in these waves of assault tied down millions of Axis troops, as in Operation Bagration, Russia's massive offensive in the summer of 1944. In that year, the Russians recaptured the Ukraine, Byelorussia, the Baltic states, eastern Poland, Romania, and Bulgaria. In early 1945 they entered Germany. These battles on the eastern front also allowed the Allies to open fronts in western Europe with greater safety.

In contrast to the large-scale warfare of the massed armies of the major belligerents, in many countries, partisan, underground resistance also developed—sometimes against the Allies, especially the Russians in eastern Europe, more frequently against the Axis powers. Because warfare had become so mechanized and so overwhelming in its size and scope, the partisans usually had more social and psychological importance than military. In some cases, however, they were quite significant, even militarily.

Yugoslavia presented the most extreme case. It was captured by the Axis powers in April 1941, and partitioned among them, with Germany and Italy taking the largest shares. From one part of the country an independent state of Croatia was created and placed in the charge of the Ustasa party, run by fanatical anti-Serbs. Even the Nazis were shocked at their virulence. Ustasa murdered hundreds of thousands—estimates run as high as 2 million—Serbs and other "undesirables" in 1941. Two groups of

Bombers on a raid. By World War II aircraft of all kinds were poised for aerial combat. Here an SAAF/BAF Beaufighter fires 3-inch RPs during an attack on German positions in the Yugoslavian town of Zuzemberg in 1945. The astronomical cost of bombs and aircraft contributed to the Allies' wartime expenditure of $1,150,000,000,000.

Serbian resistance fighters formed, one led by a Serbian officer in the Yugoslav army, the other by a communist named Josip Broz (1892–1981), who took the name Tito. Tito himself was not a Serb—he had a Croat father and a Slovene mother—but he was willing to work with the Serbs. The two leaders and their groups could not cooperate, so they fought separately against the Axis troops, and sometimes they fought against each other. Tito proved the more effective, and in 1943, after Italy withdrew from the Axis, Britain and America gave him direct support. By the end of the war, Tito commanded some 250,000 men and women and had emerged as the undisputed leader of Yugoslavia.

In the spring of 1943, the American and British air forces, from their bases in Britain, began bombing German cities. Unable to target military positions with accuracy, the air assaults became, in effect, attacks on civilians as well as military objectives. Some officers debated the morality of these attacks, but they continued and increased. Some cities, like Hamburg, were mostly destroyed in fire bombings with far more civilian than military casualties.

On July 10, 1943, the Allies invaded Sicily to begin their Italian campaign, and on July 23, Mussolini's government fell. In September, Italy surrendered and switched sides in the war, joining the Allies. German armies, however, continued to hold Rome. The city was liberated only in June 1944. Finally, the long-awaited land invasion of western Europe began. D-Day, June 6, 1944, brought the largest amphibious military operation in history as Allied forces, American, British, and Canadian troops, under Eisenhower, invaded Normandy and began the push eastward. More than 4,000 ships carried the men; some 10,000 aircraft provided support. On the first day, 130,000 men landed by ship and parachute, one million within a month. Although there were some disagreements over strategy among the Allied generals—the American Eisenhower and the British Montgomery—and some setbacks –as in the Battle of the Bulge in the Ardennes forest of Belgium—the new offensive steadily pushed the Germans back. Paris was liberated in August. Allied troops entered Germany in September.

In the last few months of the war, however, new technologies of destruction were introduced. In September 1944, Germany launched V-2 missiles for the first time against Britain, ushering in an age of missile warfare. In February 1943, the Allies began fire bombing the German city of Dresden, leveling most of it and killing some 50,000 civilians. Since the city had no military or strategic value, the raids were widely condemned as purely punitive. As the Allies finally conquered Germany in bitter combat, the war in Europe finally ended on May 7, 1945 with Germany's surrender. The war in the Pacific continued for another three months.

War in Asia and the Pacific, 1942–5

Even though the War in the Pacific received less Allied attention than the war in Europe, once America committed its industrial and technological strength to fighting Japan, the tide turned. Despite the losses of most of its Pacific fleet, in June 1942 American naval forces won their first battle at Midway Island. Then, from bases in Australia, they moved northwestward, "island hopping," taking Guadalcanal and New Guinea, recapturing the Philippines and the Pacific island chains. During the spring of 1945 they captured Okinawa after three months of brutal fighting. As early as March

1944, the Americans had begun fire bombing Japanese cities. Japan had expected Americans to become tired of the war and negotiate a peace, but instead America demanded unconditional surrender.

The fire bombing intensified. On March 9, 1945, 83,793 people were killed, 40,918 injured, and 267,000 buildings were destroyed in Tokyo alone. Burning and starving— caloric intake had dropped from a daily standard of 2,200 to 1,405 by 1944—Japan fought on. Finally, America dropped the atomic bomb on Hiroshima on August 6, 1945. With the European war won, the USSR invaded Manchuria and Korea on August 8. On August 9, America dropped a second atomic bomb, this time on Nagasaki. On August 15, 1945, Japan offered its unconditional surrender.

Japan lay in ruins. Some 3 million Japanese had died in the war, a fourth of Japan's national assets were destroyed, industrial production was at barely 10 percent of

Summary executions in the Pacific. Japanese soldiers were notoriously brutal in their treatment of prisoners during World War II. British servicemen captured in the Pacific theater were forced to construct the Burma Railway and many died of starvation and disease in the process. Some were murdered in cold blood, as here, the imminent execution of three Allied fighters before open graves.

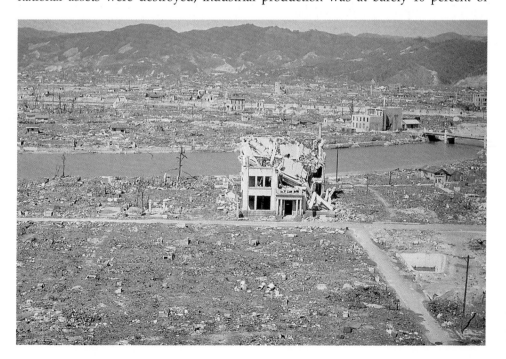

A-bomb devastation. On August 6, 1945, the "Enola Gay" Super-Fortress aircraft released the first atom bomb ever used in warfare over Hiroshima, an important Japanese military base and seaport. Over 130,000 people were killed or injured and the city was largely flattened. The USA took the action—and again, three days later at Nagasaki—in a (successful) bid to end the Pacific War.

World War II in the Pacific. Japan mounted combined operations in 1941 in East Asia, Southeast Asia, and across the Pacific, opening a war front from the borders of India to Hawaii. This supremely aggressive move was meant to secure the resources and markets needed to sustain the "Greater East Asia Co-Prosperity Sphere." It proved impossible to defend: Chinese resistance, a daring US island-hopping campaign in the Pacific—culminating in the explosion of atomic bombs over Hiroshima and Nagasaki—and Soviet assaults on Manchuria defeated Japan completely.

pre-war levels, millions of homes had been destroyed, and Japan had lost all its colonial holdings. Mass starvation was prevented only by food imported by the occupation authorities.

Assessing the Results of the War

World War II is often called a "total war" because it involved the entire populations and economies of the nations that fought it. The distinction between military and civilian disappeared. Non-combatants were bombed and killed on both sides. It is estimated that about 50 million people died—30 million of them civilians. The heaviest fighting was in the Soviet Union, which lost more people than any other country—about 20 million. Japan lost about 2 million people and Germany just over 4 million. Though there are no reliable statistics, China lost at least a million people. Britain and the United States each lost about 400,000. Six million Jews died in Nazi concentration camps along with hundreds of thousands of Poles, gypsies, homosexuals, and handicapped persons.

Japan's early victories over European colonizers provided a double shock. Asians were able to defeat—at least for some time—the most advanced European countries and the United States. As these victories enhanced the image of Japanese power, they undermined the image of the Europeans in Asia. After the war, when the European colonizers attempted to return—the British to Burma and Malaya, the French to Indochina, the Dutch to Indonesia—local nationalist groups rose in protest, sometimes armed, and eventually achieved independence. In this sense, the Japanese victories were responsible for ending European colonialism in the Pacific region.

Technology in the War

World War II witnessed a dramatic increase in the use of technology—tanks, submarines, and aircraft—as well as the number of troops. The sheer costs were staggering, and the forces that could spend more on armaments won the war. The productivity and availability of aircraft on each side represent their overall technological capacity.

Armaments Production of the Powers, 1940–43 (billions of 1944 dollars)		
	1940	1943
Allied combatants		
USA	(1.5)	37.5
USSR	(5.0)	13.9
Britain	3.5	11.1
Axis combatants		
Germany	6.0	13.8
Japan	(1.0)	4.5
Italy	0.75	—
(Source: Kennedy, p. 355)		

Aircraft Production of the Powers, 1939 and 1944		
	1939	1944
Allied combatants		
USA	5,856	96,318
USSR	10,382	40,300
Britain	7,940	26,461
Axis combatants		
Germany	8,295	39,807
Japan	4,467	28,180
Italy	1,800	—
(Source: Kennedy, p. 354)		

Tanks, too, were vital weapons. In 1944, Germany produced 17,800; Russia, 29,000; Britain, 5,000; and the USA, 17,500 (Kennedy, p. 353). In addition to quantitative superiority, the planes, tanks, and other material produced by the Allies were generally qualitatively more modern and sophisticated than those of the Axis powers. No wonder that after the initial shock and advantage of their first attacks, the Axis powers began steadily to fall behind the Allies. The technological and industrial capacity of the Axis powers simply could not keep up.

Women and the War

The military and industrial needs of World War II put new demands on the labor force and women's lives were deeply affected. The demands of keeping factories running at full blast during the war while putting millions of soldiers onto the battlefields required an unprecedented commitment of labor. Even during World War I, millions of women began to work outside the home for pay, and the stereotypes of "men's work" and "women's work" began to erode. This experience contributed to the achievement of women's suffrage in the United States (1920) and in western Europe. Although South American countries were not much involved in World War I, many of them—Brazil, Cuba, Ecuador, El Salvador, and Uruguay—also granted female suffrage between 1929 and 1939 (Rosenberg, p. 67). After World War I, the majority of women did not remain in the workforce, but after World War II, women continued in unprecedented numbers to work in industrial and unconventional jobs.

The mobilization of women was, however, culturally specific. Different combatant countries followed different family and gender policies. German and Japanese women were encouraged to continue to stay at home, despite the exigencies of war. Women served actively in Russian factories. Britain conscripted some women in World War II.

The Allies—the United States, Britain, and the USSR—generally encouraged women to join the wartime workforce. The image of Rosie the Riveter became the recognized symbol of women's contribution to factory work in the Allied countries. The Axis powers, on the other hand, did their best to keep women at home despite the needs of the war. Hitler offered women "emancipation from emancipation." He offered marriage loans to married women who left their jobs, and then cancelled one-fourth of the loan for the birth of each child. The Nazis banned abortion and closed sexual counseling clinics. Mussolini excluded women from government office, doubled the fees of female students in secondary schools and universities, and tried to prevent rural women from relocating in cities. In China, the communists encouraged women to join in the struggle directly; the nationalists kept them at home.

As the troops returned from war to their old jobs, the tendency was for women to return from factory and military service to the home, both by choice and because of social pressure. However, gender relations could not remain unaffected by wartime experience. After the war, feminism found new voices. Simone de Beauvoir published *The Second Sex* in France in 1949, advancing the argument that while sex is biological, gender, the behavioral traits associated with each sex, is learned. As she wrote: "One is not born, but rather becomes, a woman." In the United States, Betty Friedan's *The Feminine Mystique* (1963) challenged women to ask if life as homemaker in suburbia was fulfilling, to consider working outside the home, and to advocate for equal conditions in that work.

In Europe and the United States the new feminism became a powerful, if controversial force. In other parts of the world, the concept of new roles for women outside the home and community was more disputed. Often the very fact that new concepts of gender relations came from the West, from colonial powers, influenced their reception, making them more attractive to some, more suspect to others.

"Rosie the Riveter," symbol of World War II American women workers, on a poster from the War Production Coordinating Committee.

SOURCE

Women as Spoils of War: Japan's Comfort Women

From earliest recorded history, stories of warfare include accounts of soldiers abusing women and of victors seizing women as their reward for victory. The story of Japan's "comfort women" during World War II carries these stories to an unusually cruel extreme. From 1932 to 1945, thousands of women—estimates vary from a few thousand to 200,000—were rounded up and forced into sexual slavery by the Japanese military as "comfort women" serving in "comfort stations"—that is as captive sexual slaves in brothels administered by the Japanese armed forces. Although the situation was widely known in the military and was the subject of a Japanese novel in 1947, later made into a movie, the facts were generally swept under the rug. In 1990, the Korean Council for the Women Drafted for Military Sexual Slavery by Japan began to collect and publish the stories of many Korean women who had been taken by the Japanese and who were willing to talk publicly, forty years after the events.

The Korean women were especially badly treated since the Japanese historically have looked down on Koreans. Subsequently, the Japanese government was called upon to apologize and pay reparations to the women. It has officially refused, although it has encouraged private Japanese donations to the women and it has given some payments without acknowledging official responsibility. The government of Japan has frequently argued that the women were simply sex workers who sold their services to soldiers.

The testimony of Kim Young-shil, interviewed in North Korea in 1992, tells not only of sexual slavery but also of racial cruelty:

There was a girl next to my cubicle. She was younger than I, and her Japanese name was Tokiko. One day an officer overheard her speaking to me and accused her of speaking Korean [which had been forbidden]. He dragged her out to a field and ordered all of us to come out there. We all obeyed. He said, "This girl spoke Korean. So she must die. You will be killed if you do too. Now, watch how she dies." He drew his sword. Horrified, I closed my eyes and turned my face away. When I opened my eyes, I saw her severed head on the ground.

On Sundays we were made especially busy. Soldiers stood in line in front of our cubicles. They got ready for their turn by undoing their puttees from their legs, rolling them up and holding them in their hands. They shamelessly exhibited their lust like animals in heat. Many of them could not control themselves and shouted, "Madaka? Hayaku! Hayaku! [Not finished yet? Hurry! Hurry!] Some even came into my cubicle even before the act was finished.

I was totally exhausted. I could keep neither my sense of humiliation nor my dignity. I felt like a living corpse. When soldiers came to my room and did it to me one after another, it was done to a lifeless body. Again. And again. And again. (Schellstede, pp. 50–51)

Horrors of the War

Two horrors distinguished World War II from all others that came before. Massive warfare had been known before. So too had leaders bent on world conquest, from Alexander the Great and Chingghis Khan to Napoleon. But the decision by the Nazis to obliterate an entire people—the Jews—from the world, without any ostensible economic or territorial goal, and mobilizing the full resources of the state against an unarmed opponent to carry out the task, constituted a new goal, executed by new technology. It was later given a new name, genocide, the extermination of an entire people.

Anti-Semitism was not new in Europe, but the Nazi program was unprecedented. First, it reversed the trend of acceptance and civic equality for Jews advanced a century and a half earlier by the French Revolution. Second, it targeted Jews as an ethnic or racial group rather than as a religious community. This was not a policy for conversion or even for exile. Anyone with a Jewish grandparent was considered Jewish under Nazi laws and marked for death. Third, it put the entire weight of a nation into the task of wiping a people off the face of the earth, using all the technological and organizational skills at its disposal to carry out the mission, and continuing with it even when it was clear that the larger war was lost.

Hitler had made clear his beliefs in racial hierarchy—with Jews at the bottom. Once in power he set out to enslave and later to exterminate these "lesser peoples." He built concentration camps where prisoners were used as slave labor before being gassed and cremated. Millions of Jews were brought to the camps by a railway network

The liberation of Belsen. Shocked British soldiers liberating Belsen concentration camp in 1945 found 40,000 Jews and other victims of the Holocaust dying of starvation, typhus, and tuberculosis. Many prisoners had been used for medical experiments. Framed by an open grave, a Dr Klein is shown speaking to Movietone News. His experiments included injecting benzine into his victims to harden their arteries. He was responsible for thousands of deaths.

Atom bomb test in the Marshall Islands, 1950. The bomb has enormous destruction capability through its sheer explosive power, its radiation, and its ability to plunge the earth's ecology into a "global winter." On the one hand, fear of its power has prevented its use in warfare since 1945. On the other hand, more and more nations have access to the bomb.

specially constructed for this purpose. Even in the closing days of the war, when Germany clearly had been defeated, Hitler ordered the trains and the crematoria to continue operations. By 1945, some 6 million Jews, accompanied by millions from other "inferior" races, especially gypsies and Poles, joined also by homosexuals and handicapped people, had been murdered. The Holocaust, as this butchery was named, made World War II into a conflict of good versus evil even in the eyes of many Germans after the war. The moral crisis and the appalling devastation of the Holocaust are impossible to fully comprehend, but the writing of survivors such as Elie Wiesel helps us to understand them.

The atomic bombs dropped by the United States on Hiroshima and Nagasaki, Japan, introduced a new weapon ultimately capable of destroying all life on earth, changing both the nature of war and peace as well as humanity's conception of itself. At the first test of the bomb, as the fireball rose over the testing grounds at Alamogordo, New Mexico, J. Robert Oppenheimer, architect of the bomb and director of the $2 billion Manhattan Project that produced it, quoted from the Hindu *Bhagavad Gita*: "I am become as death, the destroyer of worlds." Of the 245,000 people living in Hiroshima on August 6, 75,000 died that day, perhaps another 100,000 thereafter, while still others suffered radiation poisoning, cancer, and genetic deformation. Three days later, a second bomb was dropped on Nagasaki, and on August 14, Japan surrendered unconditionally. Today, despite years of continuing efforts toward arms control, there are tens of thousands of nuclear bombs and warheads on missiles,

submarines, and airplanes capable of destroying human life many times over. Most recently, fears have increased that terrorist individuals or groups might gain access to small nuclear devices.

In retrospect, debate has raged over the wisdom and purpose of using the atomic bomb to end the War in the Pacific. Critics see the act as racist, pointing out that this weapon was not used in Europe (although the bomb had not yet been prepared at the time Germany surrendered in May 1945). Cynics suggest that its real purpose had less to do with defeating Japan than with demonstrating United States power to the USSR on the eve of the Cold War. Those who justify the use of the bomb suggest that losses of life on both sides would have been higher had the Allies invaded Japan's home islands. The use of the bomb certainly saved Allied lives, and may even have saved Japanese lives. The casualties in the battles for Pacific islands had been in the hundreds of thousands, and war in Japan itself might have cost a million Allied troops and even more Japanese. Finally, the advocates argue, in a war of such scope and brutality, combatants inevitably use the weapons that are available.

Some of the war technology, however, had by-products of use to civilians. Radar, which Britain developed to protect itself from Germany in the Battle of Britain in 1940, was valuable in commercial aviation. Nuclear energy could be employed under careful supervision for peaceful uses in power generation and medicine. Drugs, such as sulfa

HOW DO WE KNOW?

The Milgram Experiment and The "Final Solution"

How could people carry out acts of such inhumanity as the genocide against the Jews? Perhaps the leaders of Nazi Germany were insane, unrepresentative of normal people. But what about the ordinary Germans who said that they were simply following orders? To what extent do people just follow orders more or less blindly even if they know they are inflicting pain? In 1961, Yale psychologist Stanley Milgram set up an experiment to find out. He solicited volunteers from in and around Yale University. He brought them to a laboratory and explained that the experiment would test the effects of punishment on learning. The volunteer, who was to play the role of "Teacher," was briefly introduced to the "Learner," who was to learn pairs of words read aloud by the Teacher. Each time the Learner failed to learn properly, the experimenter would instruct the Teacher to inflict punishment by delivering an electric shock. The first time, the shock was 15 volts. The second 30, and each successive shock would add 15 additional volts up to a maximum, on the thirtieth failed attempt, of 450 volts.

The Teacher was told that the experiment would test the efficacy of the shocks in promoting learning. In fact, the experiment was to test how much voltage the Teacher would apply to the Learner. Teacher and Learner were sent to separate rooms, but the Teacher could see the Learner through a window. As the Learner made mistakes the experimenter told the Teacher to apply the voltage shocks. At the tenth shock, 150 volts, the Learner—who was an actor playing the role—demanded to be let out of the experiment. But this was not permitted. At this point only ten of the Teachers refused to give any more shocks. Seventy continued applying greater voltage for each wrong answer, in accordance with the experimenter's orders. The Learner continued moaning, shrieking, and demanding to be let out of the experiment. By the time the twentieth shock—300 volts—was administered, the Learner said that he refused to give any more answers. By this point, twenty-one of the volunteers stopped administering shocks despite the commands of the experimenter. At the twenty-first level, the Learner screamed out in sheer pain and gave no answer. Five more volunteers stopped their participation. From the

twenty-third shock onward, the Learner remained silent, perhaps unconscious, perhaps dead. Nevertheless, most Teachers continued applying the shocks on command. Of the eighty volunteers, fifty-one continued to administer the shocks all the way to the top level—450 volts—long after the Learner appeared to be unconscious, if not dead. Milgram concluded that, at least within the confines of this narrowly bounded experiment, "normal" people follow orders in inflicting pain, even to the point of murder, so long as they believe that the person in charge, the experimenter, has the authority and the expertise to give the orders.

- Do you think Milgram's experiment is a valid way to research the question of why apparently normal people followed orders in wartime and the Holocaust? Why or why not?
- If you were the Teacher in the experiment, at what level do you think you would quit? Do you think you are different from the majority here? Why or why not?
- Were you surprised at the results of Milgram's experiment? Why or why not?

and penicillin, entered the civilian pharmacopoeia. But the technology of warfare drew the lion's share of the scientific and technological budgets of many nations, including the largest industrial powers, the United States and the USSR, and of many developing countries, as well.

THE IMAGE OF HUMANITY

Until the eve of World War I, the Western idea of human progress through rationalism, science, and technological progress had been widely accepted. There had been no war between the great European powers since the 1871 conflict between France and Germany, and even that had been relatively small and contained (although 250,000 people died). Democracy seemed both progressive and in the ascendant. Life expectancy and quality seemed to be improving steadily.

The colonial dominance of Europe over ancient Asian and African civilizations had the effect of reaffirming Europeans' belief in the supremacy of their technology and political systems. Students from all over the world were coming to Europe's universities to study Western sciences and arts. If machines were "the measure of man," European civilization measured best of all, and was steadily gaining ground.

Some contrary voices, however, were already breaking through the self-congratulation. Mohandas Gandhi (1869–1948) of India, writing in 1906 in *Hind Swaraj or Indian Home Rule*, caricatured and reevaluated Western accomplishments from a different perspective.

> Formerly when people wanted to fight with one another, they measured between them their bodily strength; now it is possible to take away thousands of lives by one man working behind a gun from a hill. This is civilization. Formerly, men worked in the open air only as much as they liked. Now thousands of workmen meet together and for the sake of maintenance work in factories or mines. Their condition is worse than that of beasts. They are obliged to work, at the risk of their lives, at most dangerous occupations, for the sake of millionaires. Formerly, men were made slaves under physical compulsion. Now they are enslaved by temptations of money and of the luxuries that money can buy. … This civilization takes note neither of morality nor of religion. Its votaries calmly state that their business is not to teach religion. Some even consider it to be a superstitious growth. Others put on the cloak of religion, and prate about morality. … Civilization seeks to increase bodily comforts, and it fails miserably even in doing so. (Gandhi, p.36)

Gandhi concluded: "This civilization is such that one has only to be patient and it will be self-destroyed."

At about the same time in Vienna, in the heart of central Europe, Sigmund Freud's (1856–1939) new art of psychoanalysis ascribed humanity's most profound moving force not to rationality, the pride of European science and technology, but to sexuality. He argued that people did not understand their own deepest drives; these were hidden in the unconscious. He, too, questioned the ability of European civilization to survive:

> There are two tenets of psychoanalysis which offend the whole world and excite its resentment. … The first of these displeasing propositions of psychoanalysis is this: that mental processes are essentially unconscious … [the] next proposition consists in the assertion that … sexual impulses have contributed invaluably to the highest cultural, artistic, and social achievements of the human mind. … Society can conceive of no more powerful menace to its culture than would arise from the liberation of the sexual impulses and a return of them to their original goal. (Freud, pp. 25–7)

New, non-representational, or abstract, art also seemed to question the significance of rationality. The most innovative and honored of its creators, Pablo Picasso, drew from African "primitive" art to create new forms of his own. Through these African-inspired innovations, he demonstrated that the West had much to learn from the naturalism and spirituality of cultures that it dominated politically, economically, and militarily.

Voices of despair multiplied. Even the end of war did not bring renewal. T.S. Eliot's "The Waste Land" (1922) depicts, among its many gloomy scenes, the impending reunion of a wife with her husband, a soldier returning from war. The anticipation is grating and crude, even foreboding, rather than romantic, as the poet tells the wife to prepare:

> Now Albert's coming back, make yourself a bit smart.
> He'll want to know what you done with the money he gave you
> To get yourself some teeth. He did, I was there.
> You have them all out, Lil, and get a nice set.
> He said, I swear, I can't bear to look at you.
> And no more can't I, I said, and think of poor Albert,
> He's been in the army four years, he wants a good time,
> And if you don't give it to him, there's others will, I said.
> Oh is there, she said. Something o' that, I said.
> Then I'll know who to thank, she said, and gave me a straight look.

Eliot (1888–1965), perhaps the most influential English language poet of his generation, captures an arid, spiteful, loveless individual relationship and suggests that the same empty bitterness pervaded the entire society.

With the far greater destruction of World War II and its atomic bombs and genocide, literature reflected humanity at rock bottom, estranged from itself and from the universe. In 1941, at the age of twelve, Elie Wiesel had immersed himself in the practices of Hasidic, orthodox, devotional Judaism in Sighet, Hungary. In reply to the question, "Why do you pray?" he had said, "Why did I pray? A strange question. Why did I live? Why did I breathe?" But in 1944, after three years in a Nazi ghetto, he arrived in Birkenau, the gateway to Auschwitz, the hungriest of the concentration camps.

> Not far from us, flames were leaping up from a ditch, gigantic flames. They were burning something. A lorry drew up at the pit and delivered its load—little children. Babies! Yes, I saw it—saw it with my own eyes … those children in the flames. (Is it surprising that I could not sleep after that? Sleep had fled my eyes.)
>
> So this was where we were going. A little farther on was another and larger ditch for adults. I pinched my face. Was I still alive? Was I awake? I could not believe it. How could it be possible for them to burn people, children, and for the world to keep silent? No, none of this could be true. It was a nightmare. (Wiesel, p. 16)

Wiesel soon becomes aware of someone reciting the Kaddish, the Jewish prayer for the dead.

> For the first time, I felt revolt rise up in me. Why should I bless His name? The Eternal, Lord of the Universe, the All-Powerful and Terrible, was silent. What had I to thank Him for? (Wiesel, p. 22)

The Nobel prize winner Elie Wiesel at the World Economic Forum, 1998. Wiesel survived the Holocaust and devoted his life to alerting the world to its horrors, so that it might never happen again. Unfortunately, other "smaller" Holocausts continue to occur without external intervention.

HOW DO WE KNOW?

The Decision to Drop the Atom Bomb

Because nuclear weapons have so thoroughly changed the nature of war, peace, and diplomacy, and have even changed the way we think about the future of life on earth, attitudes toward them continue to change over time. Since Hiroshima and Nagasaki remain the only wartime deployment of the bomb, the decision to use it has received intense scrutiny. Even as the Manhattan Project was developing the bomb, at least one of the scientists central to its development counseled against using it. Leo Szilard wrote, "A nation which sets the precedent of using these newly liberated forces of nature for purposes of destruction may have to bear the responsibility of opening the door to an era of devastation on an unimaginable scale" (Rhodes, p. 749). President Truman nevertheless chose to drop the bomb, not just once, but twice. In the immediate aftermath of the explosions and Japan's surrender, an overwhelming proportion of Americans approved the decision. Even then, however, "Pacifist groups, a number of atomic scientists, some religious leaders and organizations, and a scattering of political commentators, both liberal and conservative, condemned the atomic attacks because of their indiscriminate killing of civilians and/or the failure of the United States to give Japan an explicit warning about the bomb before Hiroshima (Walker, p. 98).

The United States Strategic Bombing Survey, published in July 1946, concluded that "certainly prior to 31 December 1945, and in all probability prior to 1 November 1945, Japan would have surrendered even if the Atomic bombs had not been dropped" (Walker, p.100). Such a "counterfactual" judgment, however, cannot be proved or disproved.

In 1961, former State Department official Herbert Feis, in his book Japan Subdued, agreed that the Japanese would have surrendered by the end of the year, even without the bomb and even without an invasion, nevertheless "the impelling reason for the decision to use [the bomb] was military—to end the war victoriously as soon as possible (Walker, p. 104). He also noted that had there been an invasion, American casualties would probably have been in the thousands rather than the hundreds of thousands.

Gar Alperovitz, first in his dissertation and then in his book, Atomic Diplomacy, concluded on the basis of diplomatic sources, and especially the diary of Henry Stimson, Secretary of War, that Truman used the bomb more to impress the Russians and improve his bargaining position with them than to subdue the Japanese. Secretary of State James Byrnes, for example, told the American ambassador to the Soviet Union, Joseph E. Davies, that American possession of the bomb "would have some effect [on the Soviets] and induce them to yield and agree to our position" (Walker, p. 64). Through the 1970s and 1980s scholarship responding to new documents tended to confirm a composite account: the bomb had been used both to end the war quickly—although the Japanese would have surrendered even without the bomb and without an invasion—and to intimidate the Russians.

J. Samuel Walker, who summarizes these debates in his book, Prompt and Utter Destruction, adds three more arguments that have been suggested as reasons for the use of the bomb. "Justifying the costs of the Manhattan Project" was one. How could the government spend $2 billion, and employ the efforts of 600,000 workers, and then not employ and demonstrate the results? As Truman's Secretary of War Henry Stimson put it when he heard that the first test bomb had been successful: "I have been responsible for spending two billions of dollars on this atomic venture. Now that it is successful I shall not be sent to prison in Fort Leavenworth" (Rhodes, p. 686). Also, there was a "lack of incentives not to use the bomb." As Stimson wrote, "I believe that no man, in our position and subject to our responsibilities, holding in his hands a weapon of such possibilities for accomplishing this purpose and saving those lives, could have failed to use it and afterwards looked his countrymen in the face." Finally, Truman believed he was dealing with an enemy that was "a beast." Loathing of Japan as a cruel and bitter enemy enabled Truman to use the bomb with a clear conscience. In questioning charges of racism, Walker adds that Truman might have used the bomb against Germany as well, but Germany had surrendered by the time the bomb was ready.

All these arguments came bubbling to the surface in 1995 when the Smithsonian Institution prepared a major display at the National Air and Space Museum in Washington of the Enola Gay, the plane that dropped the bomb on Hiroshima, in commemoration of the fiftieth anniversary. The display was to suggest some of the criticism of the decision that had surfaced since the bombing, but many groups across the United States protested, and the entire exhibit was scaled back and introduced differently. The Enola Gay protest underlined the gap that persisted through a half century between the views of scholars and those of the general public as to the necessity and the morality of the use of the bomb. These questions concerning necessity and morality remain with us. They surround not only the use of the bomb in the past, but also its potential use in the future. Indeed they surround all decisions concerning the use of massive force in warfare.

- In light of these assessments, would you have chosen to use the bomb on August 6, 1945? Would you have used it again on August 9? Why or why not?
- Which reasons would you consider appropriate for using the bomb? Which would you consider inappropriate?
- What have been the bases for different scholars arriving at different conclusions about the reasons for the decision to drop the bomb?

Long-cherished images of humanity and of the gods it had held sacred perished in the Holocaust. Yet Wiesel found the courage to make of his experiences in the death camps the stuff of literature and the basis of a new morality:

> Never shall I forget that night, the first night in camp, which has turned my life into one long night, seven times cursed and seven times sealed. Never shall I forget that smoke. Never shall I forget the little faces of the children, whose bodies I saw turned into wreaths of smoke beneath a silent blue sky.
>
> Never shall I forget those flames which consumed my faith forever.
>
> Never shall I forget that nocturnal silence which deprived me, for all eternity, of the desire to live. Never shall I forget those moments which murdered my God and my soul and turned my dreams to dust. Never shall I forget these things, even if I am condemned to live as long as God Himself. Never. (Wiesel, pp. 41–3)

To transmit this horrible personal history, to warn humanity of its own destructiveness, and to proclaim the need to preserve life became Wiesel's consuming passion. The award of the Nobel Peace Prize in 1986 recognized his mission.

From Japan, which suffered the world's first and only nuclear explosions in warfare, came similar meditations of anguish and despair, followed later by a commitment to prevent such catastrophe in the future. A student in Hiroshima Women's Junior College, Artsuko Tsujioka, remembered the atomic attack on her city in which 75,000 people were killed instantaneously and tens of thousands lingered on to die later or to be misshapen and genetically damaged from the persistent radiation:

> It happened instantaneously. I felt as if my back had been struck with a big hammer, and then as if I had been thrown into boiling oil. … That first night ended. … My friends and the other people were no longer able to move. The skin had peeled off of their burned arms, legs and backs. I wanted to move them, but there was no place on their bodies that I could touch. … I still have the scars from that day; on my head, face, arms, legs and chest. There are reddish black scars on my arms and the face that I see in the mirror does not look as if it belongs to me. It always saddens me to think that I will never look the way I used to. I lost all hope at first. I was obsessed with the idea that I had become a freak and did not want to be seen by anyone. I cried constantly for my good friends and kind teachers who had died in such a terrible way.
>
> My way of thinking became warped and pessimistic. Even my beautiful voice, that my friends had envied, had turned weak and hoarse. When I think of the way it was then, I feel as if I were being strangled. But I have been able to take comfort in the thought that physical beauty is not everything, that a beautiful spirit can do away with physical ugliness. This has given me new hope for the future. (Andrea and Overfield, pp. 417–19)

On a national scale, Japan's peace parks at both Hiroshima and Nagasaki record the nuclear destruction as well as subsequent commitments to seeking international peace. Since World War II, Japan has been committed to keeping nuclear arms out of Japan and has been intensely involved in the efforts of the United Nations to work for peace. Its increased wealth and potential military power in the Pacific, however, put stresses on Japan's anti-militaristic patterns at the turn of the twenty-first century.

The French existentialist author Albert Camus (1913–60), perhaps the most influential voice in European literature in his time, wrote in 1940, the year France fell to Germany: "There is but one truly serious philosophical problem, and that is suicide. Judging whether life is or is not worth living amounts to answering the fundamental question of philosophy." Perhaps, however, rock bottom had been reached, or perhaps hope is part of the human condition, even in conditions of apparent hopelessness, for

Camus answered his own question in *The Myth of Sisyphus* (1942) with an affirmation, which he repeated in 1955:

> This book declares that even within the limits of nihilism it is possible to find the means to proceed beyond nihilism … Although *The Myth of Sisyphus* poses mortal problems, it sums itself up for me as a lucid invitation to live and to create, in the very midst of the desert. (p. 3)

THE UNITED NATIONS, POSTWAR RECOVERY, AND THE ORIGINS OF THE COLD WAR

Out of the rubble of the war, both victors and losers had to restructure new relationships. The creation of the United Nations, "to save the world from the future scourge of war," represented one of their most hopeful responses.

The United Nations

President Roosevelt first used the term "United Nations" publicly in issuing a joint declaration of war aims with Britain, the USSR, China, and twenty-two other countries on New Year's Day, 1942. Planning for a permanent organization began in 1944,

Post-war Europe. Western and eastern bloc competition, following their alliance in crushing Nazi Germany, crystallized in the Cold War. The Soviet Union annexed territories in the Baltic states and eastern Poland and set up a string of puppet communist states later known as the Warsaw Pact alliance, from East Germany to Bulgaria. The Western Allies formed the countervailing NATO alliance. The stalemate continued for forty years.

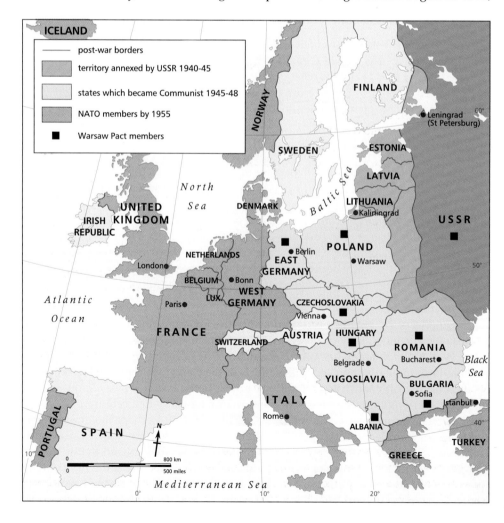

post-war borders

territory annexed by USSR 1940-45

states which became Communist 1945-48

NATO members by 1955

Warsaw Pact members

SOURCE

Preamble to the Charter of the United Nations

We the peoples of the United Nations determined

- to save succeeding generations from the scourge of war. . .
- to reaffirm faith in fundamental human rights, in the dignity and worth of the human person, in the equal rights of men and women and of nations large and small. . .
- to establish conditions under which justice and respect for the obligations arising from treaties and other sources of international law can be maintained. . .
- to promote social progress and better standards of life in larger freedom.

And for these ends

- to practice tolerance and live together in peace with one another as good neighbors . . .
- to unite our strength to maintain international peace and security . . .
- to ensure, by the acceptance of principles and the institution of methods, that armed force shall not be used, save in the common interest . . .
- to employ international machinery for the promotion of the economic and social advancement of all peoples.

Have resolved to combine our efforts to accomplish these aims.

culminating in the Charter of the United Nations, which was signed in San Francisco by fifty countries on June 26, 1945 (and by Poland, also considered a founding member, in October). The main purpose of the organization was "to save succeeding generations from the scourge of war," and its major institutions were designed to respond to threats to the peace. The United Nations' General Assembly, in which every member country was represented and had a vote, provided a forum for the discussion of the major issues threatening world peace. The Security Council, with five permanent members (the United States, the USSR, Britain, France, and China), and several others elected for fixed terms by the General Assembly, could dispatch peace-keeping forces. An International Court of Justice was created to decide disputes among member states. In 1946, the League of Nations was formally dissolved and the United Nations (UN) took on many of its missions, such as promoting public health through the World Health Organization (WHO), and educational, economic, and cultural activities through the United Nations Economic, Scientific, and Cultural Organization (UNESCO). In its early years, the peace-keeping function of the UN was stymied by the mutual hostility of the United States and the Soviet Union. As permanent members of the Security Council, each had the right to veto major policy decisions of the UN, leaving the organization mostly powerless to resolve the key Cold War conflicts between these two postwar superpowers. Nevertheless, its service as a forum for discussions, and its humanitarian activities ensured the place of the UN in the new, emerging international order. Its role increased in significance through the years.

Resettlement

Almost 100 million soldiers served under arms during the war, many of them in foreign lands. Some 15 million of them were killed. Millions more were captured as prisoners of war and required repatriation, resettlement to the areas from which they came. Millions of civilians had also been resettled or imprisoned by conquering armies that feared revolt among their newly subject populations. In addition, Germany and Japan had fought, in part, for *lebensraum,* or more "living space." They had dispatched millions of their civilians to new homes in newly conquered territories. These civilians, too, had to return to their original homes—or, at least, to new homes. Additional millions had been displaced by the warfare, fleeing as best they could from approaching armies. National borders changed as a result of the war, especially in central and eastern Europe, and nationals of various countries often chose, or were forced, to move in accord with the new national geographies. Finally, millions also traveled in the hope of finding lost family members and in search of food.

During the war, for example, millions of Germans had moved, as soldiers or civilians, into eastern Europe and the Baltic countries. The Russians had also exiled about a half million Germans to Siberia. They had similarly deported some 2 million Poles and 180,000 Balts to Siberia, and replaced them with about equal numbers of Russians and Ukranians.

In the years immediately following the war, some 15 million Germans who had been living or fighting in eastern Europe returned to Germany. Four and a half million Poles, most of whom had fled the Nazis or the Communists, or both, returned to Poland. The Russians continued to enforce population exchanges, exiling almost 2 million Ukrainians and central Asian peoples to Siberia, along with some 300,000 Balts to eastern Russia and Siberia. Here, too, they replaced them with about equal numbers of Russians and Ukrainians regarded as loyal to the new communist administration. Some 300,000 Balts fled westward to escape their new Russian masters. Hundreds of thousands of other, smaller groups—Hungarians, Slavs, and Finns—also moved. Also some 320,000 Jews, survivors of the Holocaust in eastern Europe, emigrated to join the effort to create a new Jewish homeland in Palestine.

Similar migrations occurred in East Asia as some 5.5 million Japanese returned home. Most were demobilized soldiers, but hundreds of thousands were civilians who had established homes in Korea and Taiwan over several decades of Japanese colonization. In Manchuria, the Soviet troops, who had entered the war in Asia only in its last few days, seized thousands of Japanese to labor in Siberian labor camps. Other thousands were murdered by Chinese taking revenge.

All these movements were quite different from the return home by millions of victorious American troops. (Some 400,000 had been killed.) The American mainland had been essentially untouched by the war, and the soldiers were repatriated back in more-or-less orderly fashion to their own homes. Moreover, in gratitude for their service and in eagerness to reintegrate the troops peacefully and productively into civilian life, the United States government instituted new programs such as the G.I. Bill of Rights, which enabled millions of the veterans to go to college, an aspiration that otherwise might have been beyond their means. The booming wartime and postwar economy of the United States made these veterans' benefits financially possible, and soon the addition of millions of more highly educated veterans increased the productivity of the country's workforce still further. The postwar period here —and elsewhere—saw a very rapid rise in the birthrate as the country and much of the world recovered from a decade and a half of economic depression and world war. The postwar years brought a baby boom.

Political Reconstruction in Japan and Germany

Following the explosion of atomic bombs on Hiroshima and Nagasaki, Japan signed an unconditional surrender agreement to end the war and came under American occupation and guidance. Germany also surrendered unconditionally to the Allies and was divided into two states that remained separate for forty-five years.

Japan. Japan awaited an uncertain future under American occupation headed by the Supreme Commander for the Allied Powers, General Douglas MacArthur. The occupation lasted until 1952 and focused on four goals: punishing some Japanese leaders as war criminals; establishing democratic institutions and practices; reviving the devastated Japanese economy; and enlisting Japan as an ally in the new Cold War against the USSR. All four goals were achieved.

Some 200,000 wartime leaders were barred from office. Twenty-five of the top leaders were tried for starting the war, and seven were hanged. The emperor was no longer to be regarded as sacred, nor would he wield political power. He would now serve as a constitutional monarch. The preservation of the emperor as a symbol probably made Japanese acceptance of the occupation less difficult.

The colonial empire was dissolved completely, and 5.5 million expatriate Japanese were returned to Japan. The military was completely demobilized. State support for Shinto was ended. Police authority was reduced. Freedom of speech was reintroduced. Political prisoners were freed. A new constitution, issued in 1947, granted universal adult suffrage to everyone over the age of twenty, including women for the first time. The diet became an elected, British-style parliament, with two houses. The judiciary was independent, headed by a supreme court. Guarantees of freedom of assembly, the press, "life, liberty, and the pursuit of happiness," and the "right to maintain the minimum standards of wholesome and cultural living" were also written into the constitution.

Economically, the Occupation Authority pushed ahead on four fronts. First, it redistributed agricultural land. Land held by absentee landlords and land in excess of 10 acres per family had to be sold to the government at low rates. The government, in turn, sold it to small farmers who prospered and felt strong allegiance to the government.

Second, the largest *zaibatsu* were dissolved into their constituent companies and anti-monopoly legislation was passed. Over the next decades, new conglomerates, called **keiretsu**, grew up with many qualities of the *zaibatsu*, but they were less restrictive, and they allowed more scope for the start-up of new companies.

Third, the Occupation Authority encouraged the formation of labor unions, legalizing the right to organize, bargain, and strike. Within three years the unions had grown to several million members and had begun to turn communist. The Occupation Authority then passed new laws to restrict the unions and purge their communist leaders. Unionization and strikes declined, but labor unions, which work closely with management, remained important in Japan's socio-economic life.

Finally, the Occupation Authority restructured the educational system. The contents of school textbooks were dramatically revised to remove much of the emperor-centered, nationalistic wartime ideology. The number of middle school students increased from 2.4 to 4.3 million; high school students from 380,000 to 1.2 million by 1952 to 4.3 million by 1975. By 1995, 90 percent of the appropriate age group graduated from high school. University students increased from 84,000 to 2.5 million in 1995, one-third of the university-age group.

Ironically, within five years of the end of World War II, the United States enlisted Japan as its ally in the Cold War against China and Russia. Japan's postwar

The first meeting of General MacArthur and Emperor Hirohito, September 27, 1945. The seemingly simple news photograph upset Japanese viewers, who thought that General MacArthur insulted the emperor by dressing too casually. The picture reputedly marked the moment when the Japanese recognized that they had been defeated and that the Americans were in charge. Yet the picture also showed that the Americans would support some form of continuing monarchy.

keiretsu Alliances of independent Japanese firms, joining either large corporations in different industries or a large corporation and sub-contractors. They are successors of the pre-war **zaibatsu**.

constitution limited its military commitments, but a United States–Japanese Security Treaty did allow the United States to maintain military bases throughout Japan and to retain Okinawa until 1972. Under this treaty Japan was protected militarily by the United States.

Meanwhile, Japan became a principal supplier of materials and support services to the Americans fighting in neighboring Korea. The Korean War (1950–53) was an economic boon to Japan, providing a jump-start to the new growth. During the war, America bought $4 billion worth of military manufactures and tens of thousands of American troops were stationed in Japan. Between 1950 and 1973, Japan's economy grew at a phenomenal average rate of 10.5 percent a year. The gross national product grew from $24 billion in 1955, to $484 billion in 1975, to $4.3 trillion in 1994.

The American occupation introduced to Japan many management training experts. The most influential was W. Edwards Deming, who brought the concept of quality control systems, or "TQM," Total Quality Management, involving all workers throughout the entire process of production. Japanese businessmen adopted this concept more fully than Americans did. Japanese workers were encouraged to feel themselves a valued part of the production process, their suggestions solicited and taken seriously, their job security ensured to the extent possible, their pay and benefits kept at high levels. Japanese consumer goods, produced through this system of personal dedication combined with the highest technological efficiency, earned a reputation for excellent quality and began to take over large shares of the world market, challenging more established producers, including the Americans.

Germany. At the end of the war, Germany lay devastated. One-fourth of the housing stock was destroyed as was about half of the economic infrastructure. Food supplies, although rationed, left many Germans malnourished, even as millions of refugees were returning. The German state had ceased to exist, and the country was divided by its conquerors into four parts: American, British, French, and Russian. In addition, segments of eastern Germany—East Prussia, Pomerania, and Silesia—were transferred to the Soviet Union and almost 10 million German inhabitants of these lands were forced back into the remainder of Germany.

At first, the Russians, which had suffered horribly during the war, also demanded reparations to be collected from all four zones of Germany, but, beginning in 1946, the Western allies refused to cooperate. The four regions were developing separately and differently. Even on subjects on which they agreed, such as punishing people who had been active officials in the Nazi government, the Russians punished them more severely. All four nations, however, participated in the trial at Nuremberg of twenty-two of the most powerful surviving Nazi leaders for crimes against humanity: mass murder and genocide. Twelve were sentenced to death, seven to lengthy prison terms, and three were acquitted. The Nuremberg Trials have been criticized as "victor's judgment," finding people guilty of crimes that had not been classified at the time they were committed; but other observers hailed them for setting an example of establishing standards of accountability among the highest authorities of government.

The Nuremberg Trials, Nuremberg, October 1945. After the war, the Allies put on trial twenty-two of the most notorious Nazis for crimes against humanity. Some critics called this "victor's judgment", but others thought it established new and better standards of international accountability.

During the first two years of occupation, fundamental differences developed between the zones administered by the Russians and the rest. Free democratic elections took place in the western zones, a free market was restored, and the economy was linked with that of western Europe. Prosperity returned. In the areas controlled by the Russians, elections were rigged, the economy was controlled by the state and it did not quickly recover. In 1948, seeking to gain control of the entire city of Berlin, the Russians instituted a blockade of the city. Although Berlin was also shared by the four powers, it lay deep inside the territory controlled by the Russians. The **Berlin Blockade** was one of the clear opening salvos in the Cold War. President Truman responded with an airlift of supplies that continued for almost a year until the Soviets lifted the blockade.

Berlin Blockade In 1948 the Russians barred the entrance and exit of people and supplies to and from Berlin in an attempt to gain control of the city.

Economic Reconstruction and the Cold War

Europe lay in ruins after six years of the most destructive warfare. Fifty million people were dead, about 20 million of them soldiers in the prime of life. Much of the physical plant was destroyed, including industries and homes. National treasuries were bankrupt. Transportation and communication systems did not work. International trade, which had been disrupted for years, would not revive immediately both because of Europe's inability to pay for imports, and because other nations, both colonies and independent countries like those of Latin America, had developed greater self-sufficiency during the war. They would be in much less need of European exports, even if the exports were available. John Maynard Keynes, the British economist, warned that his nation was facing a "financial Dunkirk."

On the other hand, some of the industrial plant remained operative, and Europeans had not forgotten their skills in managing a flourishing economy. They also received billions of dollars in aid from the United States. The lesson of Germany's retaliation for its feeling of humiliation and impoverishment at the end of World War I would not be repeated. All European nations were eligible for assistance in recovery, and by 1947 recovery had begun, especially in western Europe, but it was fragile.

Communist labor unions, which had at first cooperated with national recovery efforts, began strikes, and communist political parties began winning substantial minorities in national elections. In Greece a civil war that had begun in 1946 pitted communist guerrilla forces against a British-supported government. Tito, in neighboring Yugoslavia, aided the guerrillas. Russian troops on the borders of Turkey threatened to upset the political stability of that country. The United States, fearing that communist Russia would take advantage of European economic weakness and political uncertainty, formulated three new policies. In March 1947, the American President Harry Truman laid down the doctrine that carried his name, describing a polarization that he saw dividing the world between countries with democratic freedoms and majority rule and those based on minority regimes relying upon "terror and oppression, a controlled press, framed elections, and the suppression of personal freedom." The Truman Doctrine offered "to help free people to maintain their institutions and their integrity against aggressive movements that seek to impose upon them totalitarian regimes."

In the same year, the United States began the Marshall Plan, named for the US secretary of state, which offered a total of about $12 billion in financial assistance and equipment to all European nations that wanted it and had appropriate plans for using it. The Marshall Plan expedited Europe's recovery, created new markets for American goods, and reduced the threat of communist takeover. Europe's economic growth reached spectacular levels. By 1950, West Germany's economic production was greater than that of pre-war Germany. By 1958, it outpaced in its national economic product all other European countries, including those that had defeated it in war just a few years before. All western European countries did well, however, in an "economic miracle" that lasted until 1974.

Third, politically and diplomatically the United States implemented a policy of "containment" in regard to the USSR. Formulated by State Department official George Kennan, the containment policy argued that Russia would constantly probe western European and American weakness, but sometime in the future Russia would moderate its aggressiveness. Meanwhile, it could be restrained peacefully. The West should keep up its own economic strength and help others to build theirs; it should use all diplomatic means to limit Russian threats; and it should maintain its military forces at high levels of preparedness.

Both sides feared one another. The Americans saw Russia take over the governments of the countries of eastern Europe, using its armies of post-war occupation to impose communism, in contravention of treaties agreed upon at a wartime conference in Yalta in February 1945. They saw communists attempting to take over the government of Greece in a civil war that lasted from 1946 to 1949. They saw the communists in China under Mao Zedong defeat their opposition and take over that country. They felt that communism might take over the world politically and economically, by fair means or foul. The USSR, on the other hand, as leader of the communist world, feared American capitalist hegemony and military power, especially its sole possession of the A-bomb. It feared the military and economic power that America might bring to bear in any confrontation. It feared encirclement by American allies in Europe and the Pacific.

Russia dominated a wall of allied states in central and eastern Europe and claimed it as a defensive buffer. It moved as quickly as possible to build its own atomic bomb, with nuclear secrets stolen from America. It kept its armed forces extremely strong. In reply, the United States created the North Atlantic Treaty Organization (NATO) in 1949. NATO included democratic countries with capitalist, socialist, and mixed economies: Britain, France (until 1966), Italy, Canada, Denmark, Norway, Iceland, Belgium, the Netherlands, and Luxemburg. Portugal, though not a democracy at first, was also a charter member. In 1952 both Greece and Turkey joined, as did West Germany in 1955. The USSR then formally established the Warsaw Pact among the nations of Bulgaria, Czechoslovakia, East Germany, Hungary, Poland, and Romania, which were communist in their politics and economics. Forty years of Cold War competition had begun.

The wariness of the two sides toward one another led to a polarization of much of the world and a massive arms race. Other American-led pacts included the Organization of American States (1948) and the Southeast Asia Treaty Organization (1954). Defense expenditures of the United States and the Soviet Union mushroomed in an arms race unprecedented in peacetime. In 1948, the United States spent about $10 billion on its military; the USSR about 13. By 1950 these figures had reached 14.5 and 15.5, respectively, and by 1960, 45.3 and 36.9, and they continued to rise. Pessimists lamented these expenditures as wasteful; optimists pointed out that the USA and the USSR actually avoided direct warfare, although some of their allies did not. In the next two decades, from 1945 to 1965, most of the major colonies of the European powers would become independent, and both the USA and USSR would try to win them over to their separate camps. The joining together of these two great movements, the Cold War and decolonization, is a central issue in the next chapter.

ENTERING THE SECOND HALF OF THE 20TH CENTURY WHAT DIFFERENCE DOES IT MAKE?

The first half of the twentieth century ended in horror and hope. Two world wars, holocaust, and nuclear weapons killed some 75 million people. Between the wars economic depression also afflicted most parts of the world, and at their end a new kind of Cold War, waged by two newly risen superpowers, threatened to plunge the world into nuclear destruction that might threaten all human life on earth. These were the greatest horrors.

On the other hand, people around the world joined with Roosevelt in his 1941 statement looking forward "to a world founded upon four essential human freedoms": freedom of speech and expression, freedom to worship God as one chooses, freedom from want, and freedom from fear. They applauded the Atlantic Charter issued by Roosevelt and Churchill, which stated that the two leaders and their countries "respect the right of all peoples to choose the form of government under which they will live; and they wish to see sovereign rights and self-government restored to those who have been forcibly deprived of them." Churchill took this to mean freedom for the countries that had suffered under Axis rule; Roosevelt said that it meant an end to colonialism. People living under colonial rule accepted Roosevelt's reading. Indeed, colonized nations were already gaining independence: Jordan, Lebanon, and Syria in 1946; India and Pakistan in 1947; Ceylon (Sri Lanka), Burma (Myanmar), and Israel in 1948; Indonesia in 1949; and China, completing its communist revolution in 1949, expelled foreign powers from its territories. Racism, especially after the Holocaust, came under attack as never before. Aimé Césaire, the poet and politician from Martinique, wrote caustically:

> At bottom, what . . . the very distinguished, very humanistic, very Christian
> bourgeois of the twentieth century . . . cannot forgive Hitler is not crime in itself,
> the crime against man, it is not the humiliation of man as such, it is the crime
> against the white man, the humiliation of the white man, and the fact that [Hitler]
> applied to Europe colonialist procedures which until then had been reserved
> exclusively for the Arabs of Algeria, the coolies of India, and the blacks of Africa. (Lee,
> p. 145)

Many Europeans agreed with Césaire, although with a different emphasis, that Hitler's racism had shocked them into a new understanding of its viciousness, and to a struggle against it.

The Senegalese poet/statesman Léopold Sédar Senghor held out the promise that Africa, finding its freedom and voice anew, could help Europe to return to health after a generation of destruction:

> The Africa of the empires is dying, see, the agony of a pitiful princess
> And Europe too where we are joined at the navel.
> Fix your unchanging eyes upon your children, who are given orders
> Who give away their lives like the poor their last clothes.
> Let us report present at the rebirth of the World
> Like the yeast which white flour needs.
> For who would teach rhythm to a dead world of machines and guns?
> Who would give the cry of joy to wake the dead and the bereaved at dawn?
> Say, who would give back the memory of life to the man whose hopes are
> smashed?
> They call us men of coffee cotton oil
> They call us men of death.
> We are the men of the dance, whose feet draw new strength pounding the
> hardened earth. (Okpewho, p. 134)

Finally, the formal creation of the United Nations in 1945 offered hope that the peoples of the world could resolve their disputes peacefully and work also for better public health, more fulfilling cultural life, and more fully developed international law.

Review Questions

- How did the depression of 1929–39 affect the recovery from World War I? Please discuss the effects on different countries, such as, Germany, the USA, the USSR, Japan.
- How important were thugs in the rise of fascism in Italy and Germany? What roles did they play? Why did people decide in large numbers to follow them?
- Compare fascism and communism in terms of: (1) power of the state; (2) power of the leader; (3) role of private property; (4) value put on warfare; (5) willingness to enter international, diplomatic relations with other nations as an equal; and (6) individual human rights?
- Warfare had an effect on the role of women, but the effect was different in different countries. Discuss these differences and similarities in the USA, the USSR, Germany, and Japan.
- Elie Wiesel reports losing his faith not only in his fellow humans but also in God as a result of his experiences in the Holocaust. How does this compare with other responses to this disaster and to the atomic bombing of Japan?
- What are the reasons given for the Cold War between the USA and the USSR? Which reason do you think was most significant?

Suggested Readings

PRINCIPAL SOURCES

Dower, John. *Embracing Defeat*. Superb account of Japan under American occupation, 1945–52.

Freud, Sigmund. *Civilization and its Discontents* (New York: W.W. Norton and Co., 1961). Freud explains the battle between love and war. He is not sure which will win out.

Kennedy, Paul. *The Rise and Fall of the Great Powers* (New York: Vintage Books, 1989). Very good on the human and economic costs of war.

Rhodes, Richard. *The Making of the Atomic Bomb* (New York: Simon and Schuster, 1986). A comprehensive study of the Manhattan Project, including the science, administration, and politics of the production of the first nuclear weapon.

Weinberg, Gerhard. *A World at Arms: A Global History of World War II* (Cambridge: Cambridge University Press, 1994). Massive, one-volume history of the war, in all theaters, examining the use of both force and diplomacy.

Wiesel, Elie. *Night* (New York: Bantam Books, 1962). Terrifying personal account of Wiesel's youth in the concentration camps.

Yoshimi, Yoshiaki. *Sexual Slavery in the Japanese Military During World War II*. trans. by Suzanne O'Brien (New York: Columbia University Press, 1995). A comprehensive, academic account of the sexual slavery of the "comfort women" and their relatively recent demands for reparations from the Japanese government.

ADDITIONAL SOURCES

Alperovitz, Gar. *The Decision to Use the Atomic Bomb* (New York: Knopf, 1996). Examines the entire range of debate by both decision makers and later commentators.

Andrea, Alfred and James H. Overfield, eds. *The Human Record*, Vol. 2 (Boston: Houghton Mifflin, 3rd ed., 1998). Excellent collection of primary documents.

Bosworth, R.J.B. *Mussolini* (London: Oxford University Press, 2002). The most recent and important biography of Mussolini.

Browning, Christopher. *Ordinary Men: Reserve Police Battalion 101 and the Final Solution in Poland* (Harper Collins, 1992). An excellent analysis of ordinary people involved in the Holocaust.

——. *The Path to Genocide: Essays on Launching the Final Solution* (Cambridge, England: Cambridge University Press, 1992). An analysis of Nazi Jewish policy.

Bulliet, Richard W., ed. *The Columbia History of the 20th Century* (New York: Columbia University Press, 1998). Excellent selection of academic articles tracing the key themes of the twentieth century.

Cook, Haruko Taya and Theodore F. Cook. *Japan at War: An Oral History* (New York: New Press, 1992). Japanese civilians and soldiers recall their own experiences.

De Grazia, Victoria. *How Fascism Ruled Women: Italy, 1922–1945* (Berkeley, CA: University of California Press, 1992). An examination of the ideas of womanhood under fascism in Italy.

Eliot, T.S. *Collected Poems 1909–1962* (New York: Harcourt, Brace Jovanovich, 1936). Includes "The Waste Land." Eliot's poetry, with its startling imagery, irony, and often despairing search for meaning in the midst of a barren culture, defined modernism in literature.

Friedan, Betty. *The Feminine Mystique* (New York: Dell, 1963).

Gandhi, Mohandas Karamchand. *Hind Swarej or Indian Home Rule* (Ahmedabad: Navajivan Press, 1938). The Mahatma's classic denunciation of the materialism of Western civilization.

Hilberg, Raul. *The Destruction of the European Jews* 3 Vols. (New York: Holmes and Meier, 1984). Comprehensive analysis of the Holocaust.

Keegan, John, ed. *The Times Atlas of the Second World War* (New York: Harper, 1989). Indispensable for following and understanding the unfolding of the war.

Kershaw, Ian. *The 'Hitler Myth': Image and Reality in the Third Reich* (London: Oxford University Press, 2001). A collection of essays attempting to explain why people followed Hitler.

Keynes, John Maynard. *The Economic Consequences of the Peace* (New York: Harcourt Brace Jovanovich, 1920), pp. 211–16. Highly influential critique of the terms of the peace agreements as setting the stage for renewed warfare.

Lee, Lloyd E. *World War II* (Westport, CN: Greenwood Press, 1999). Somewhat sketchy coverage of major issues and campaigns of the war, useful chronology, primary documents, biographies, and bibliography, especially of films and electronic sources.

Marrus, Michael. *The Holocaust in History* (London: Plume Books, 1988). An assessment of literature on the Holocaust.

Morris-Suzuki, Tessa. *The Technological Transformation of Japan.* (Cambridge: Cambridge University Press, 1994).

Okpewho, Isidore, ed. *The Heritage of African Poetry* (Harlow, Essex: Longman Group, 1985). Remarkable anthology with interesting discussions.

Overy, Richard *Why the Allies Won* (New York: W.W. Norton, 1995). An assessment of the economic, strategic, political, and moral balance between the combatants.

Peukert, Detlev, J.K. *The Weimar Republic* (Hill and Wang, 1993). An excellent social and political history of the Weimar Republic and the conditions that led to the rise of Hitler.

Rosenberg, Rosalind, "The 'Woman' Question," in Bulliet, pp. 53–80. Superb, brief survey of the major issues.

Schellstede, Sangmie Choi, ed. *Comfort Women Speak: Testimony by Sex Slaves of the Japanese Military* (New York: Holmes and Meier, 2000). The "comfort women" tell their own stories. Includes photographs of the women today, and a United Nations report on the situation.

Slater, Laura. *Opening Skinner's Box: Great Psychological Experiments of the Twentieth Century* (New York: W.W. Norton, 2004). One of the experiments presented and discussed is Stanley Milgram's.

Speer, Albert. *Inside the Third Reich: Memoirs* (New York: Macmillan, 1970). An insider's account of Nazi administration and wartime operations.

Walker, J. Samuel. *Prompt and Utter Destruction: Truman and the Use of Atomic Bombs against Japan* (Chapel Hill: University of North Carolina Press, 1997) Discusses the pros and cons of the decision to bomb, in light of the knowledge that policy makers had at the time.

Wilkie, Brian and James Hurt, eds. *Literature of the Western World*, Vol. 2 (New York: Macmillan, 1984). Excellent anthology. Gives complete works.

Young, Louise. *Japan's Total Empire: Manchuria and the Culture of Wartime Imperialism* (Berkeley, CA, 1998). An outstanding analysis of Japan's imperial ambitions.

◉ World History Documents CD-ROM

23.4 Nadezhda Mandelstam: *Hope Against Hope*
23.5 The Rise of Benito Mussolini
23.6 Adolf Hitler
24.1 Kita Ikki: *Outline for the Reconstruction of Japan*
24.2 Japanese Imperialism
25.1 Adolf Hitler: *The Obersalzberg Speech*
25.2 *The Atlantic Charter*
25.3 *The Rape of Nanjing*
25.4 Hiroshima and Nagasaki
25.5 Lindsey Parrot: *Tojo Makes Plea of Self Defense*
25.6 *The Charter of the United Nations*

COLD WAR AND NEW NATIONS

REMAKING THE POST-WORLD WAR II WORLD 1945–89

Three issues dominated the first two generations following World War II. The first was the Cold War. Two powers, previously at the periphery of Europe's dominance of global economics and arms, now surpassed Europe, challenging and threatening each other, and insisting that the rest of the peoples of earth choose sides between them. Few political, economic, or cultural events of this period escaped the intense competition of the USSR and the United States. Second, in the twenty years following the war, more than fifty European colonies gained their independence. Each sought its own road to development, many sought to cooperate with like-minded, friendly nations for their mutual support, and almost all were solicited by the two new superpowers to take sides in their global competition. Finally, a variety of strategies and technologies of development resulted from the new competition and the new freedom.

THE COLD WAR, 1945–89: USA VS. USSR

From the middle of the nineteenth century, many leaders of the United States held a belief in its "manifest destiny," a faith that the nation would spread westward from its Atlantic origins, first across the Appalachian mountains, later to the Pacific, and finally overseas. They believed that America had a message to spread about proper governance in the world, first by setting an example, a modern example of the biblical "City upon a Hill," and, second, by actively taking its message to other nations, as Woodrow Wilson had done in his Fourteen Points during World War I and Franklin Roosevelt had done in his "Four Freedoms" address and the Atlantic Charter (with Winston Churchill) during World War II. These extroverted missions often alternated with introverted periods when a policy of isolationism was pursued, but after World War II the extrovert United States prevailed. It emerged from the war victorious and by far the richest, most powerful, and most industrially productive country in the world, and it acted with a vigorous sense of optimism.

In the first years after the war, the United States replaced the Pax Britannica with a **Pax Americana**, a worldwide peace enforced by American arms and wealth. Through its $12 billion investment in the Marshall Plan it encouraged the reconstruction of western Europe along democratic and mixed capitalistic–socialistic patterns. It paid special attention to Germany, attempting to restore its briefly held democracy and to

Pax Americana Literally "American peace," a Latin phrase derived by analogy from Pax Romana (the peace enforced within the boundaries of the Roman Empire by Roman rule) to designate the relative tranquility established within the American sphere of influence after World War II.

Opposite **Zhou Enlai, Bandung Conference, Indonesia, 1955.** Zhou Enlai (center) arrives at the Bandung Conference along with many Third World leaders to articulate a post-colonial world order.

rebuild its economy. It paid even more attention to Japan, which it occupied militarily and politically for seven years. America outlawed the divine status attributed to the emperor, promulgated a democratic constitution and educational system, and introduced new concepts of business management. In part as a result of America's actions, western Europe and Japan became once again two powerhouses of the global economy.

The Soviet Union had a similar sense of mission for extending its power territorially and ideologically. In 1919, just two years after the success of their own revolution, Soviet leaders had established the Third Socialist International, or Comintern (Communist International), to encourage communist parties and revolutionaries throughout the world. Under Stalin, the Comintern continued to dispatch agents around the world to promote communist revolution. To some nations that had been devastated by World War II and to others just emerging from colonialism and seeking a model for rapid modernization, the Soviet Union's government-sponsored industrial successes (see Chapters 19 and 20) appeared attractive. The USSR's ability to survive ferocious punishment in World War II, to fight back, and to triumph, despite untold material damage and the deaths of some 20 million people, earned its people and its government great respect in the world community.

In the closing months of the war, agreements among the Allies signed at Yalta, on the Black Sea, and at Potsdam, Germany, provided some hope that the United States and the USSR would find a way to accommodate their different philosophies and compromise on their aspirations. Unfortunately, this did not happen. Americans interpreted the somewhat vague Yalta agreements as allowing the USSR some dominance among the nations of central and eastern Europe, in its own backyard, but leaving those countries generally independent and free to choose their own governments. Instead, they saw the Soviet Union using armed force to build a central and eastern European empire of its own. Between 1945 and 1948 the USSR imposed communist governments, controlled from Moscow and backed by Soviet troops, on Czechoslovakia, Romania, Bulgaria, Poland, Hungary, and Eastern Germany—adding them to its European empire along with the northern nations of Lithuania, Latvia, and Estonia, which it had annexed in 1940. The USSR then organized the economies of these satellite nations to serve its own, having them produce goods needed by the USSR at artificially low prices. Despite its anti-imperial rhetoric, the Soviet Union had kept control of the tsar's empire and was now adding to it. Observing the Soviet takeover of central Europe, Britain's Winston Churchill observed ruefully, "An iron curtain has descended across the continent." In several western European states, especially Italy, France, and Greece, communist parties were making major inroads in electoral politics.

The Russians interpreted the global political scene quite differently. They saw America's assistance to western Europe and Japan, and its additional support to Turkey and Greece, as an attempt to encircle them. Most of all, the Soviet Union knew that America alone had the atomic bomb, and this made it the most dangerous power on earth.

The Yalta Conference, 1945. At Yalta in February 1945 Stalin (far left), Roosevelt (center), and Churchill (far right) planned their post-war positions in Europe. Misunderstandings between them led later to Cold War tensions and recriminations.

Each side provoked the other, sometimes to the brink of war. The first open test of will came in Germany. Following World War II, the allied victors divided Germany into east and west. The United States, Britain, and France held the western sector, and the USSR held the east. The former capital, Berlin, was divided in the same way, but geographically the city lay deep inside the Russian-held eastern sector, about one hundred miles from the western sectors. In March 1948, the USSR blockaded land access to West Berlin, challenging the ability of the western powers to maintain control over their sectors. Recognizing that Soviet land forces commanded overwhelming power in central Europe, President Truman used the immense air power at his command to airlift supplies and personnel into West Berlin until, almost a year and a half later, in September 1949, Russia lifted the blockade. Nevertheless, Germany remained a divided country, and Berlin a divided city.

Nuclear weapons were the most terrifying arena of competition. Just as the Soviet Union had trembled when the United States exploded the world's first atomic bomb in 1945, so America reverberated in shock when the USSR followed with a bomb of its own in 1949. The American monopoly on nuclear weapons had lasted only four years. (Britain followed in 1952, France in 1960, China in 1964, Israel, unacknowledged, in the 1960s, India in 1974, Pakistan in 1998, and North Korea in 2004). How had Russia managed to crack the monopoly? Spies were suspected—and found—in the government and the scientific community in the United States. In response, Senator Joseph McCarthy unleashed a hunt for spies, communists, and "fellow travelers"—people sympathizing with communist perspectives—in a mixture of serious investigation and paranoia that threatened freedom of expression in the United States for several years. Public proclamations at this time also emphasized the importance of participation in organized religion in American life and contrasted it to the official atheism of the Soviet Union.

In 1952, the USA thought it was once again gaining nuclear supremacy as it exploded the world's first hydrogen bomb, but, to America's consternation, the USSR matched this accomplishment in the very next year. Atomic bombs gain their explosive power when a heavy nucleus splits or fissions into two lighter nuclei. Hydrogen bombs, on the other hand, explode when two lighter nuclei fuse into a heavier nucleus. Hydrogen bombs can be hundreds or thousands of times more powerful than atomic bombs and produce even more deadly radioactive fallout. The "Red scare" and McCarthyism gained renewed strength. Many government bureaucrats, artists, film producers, writers, and university professors suspected of present or past membership in the Communist Party of the United States, or of expressing views considered overly critical of the United States, lost their jobs and were blacklisted. Investigations of such people were carried out by a committee of Congress called the "House Unamerican Activities Committee." This nibbling away at freedom of speech in America was not comparable to the almost complete suppression of it in the Soviet Union, but it did reflect a fear that pervaded America and threatened some of its core values.

The heavens, too, became a field of contest, and here the Russians took an early lead, putting the first space satellite, the *Sputnik*, into orbit in 1957, followed by the first manned satellite in 1961. Embarrassed, President Kennedy vowed that America would be the first to land a man on the moon, within a decade, and in 1969 that mission was accomplished.

The second unnerving shock to the United States was the victory of Mao Zedong's communist People's Liberation Army in China and the expulsion of the nationalist forces to the offshore island of Taiwan. We have touched on the communist revolution in China in Chapter 19, and in the next chapter, Chapter 22, we will give more detail on that revolution and its consequences. Here we note that the communist victory in China—the most populous country in the world, one of its great historic civilizations,

"A great step for mankind ..." Edwin ("Buzz") Aldrin, the second man on the moon, clambers down the ladder of the Apollo II lunar module "Eagle" in July 1969. Neil Armstrong had set foot on the moon moments earlier. The race for supremacy in space between the superpowers was fueled by the Cold War.

and a nation that the United States had helped with military, technical, and food aid for more than a decade—undermined many American beliefs and hopes. Debate raged in the United States about "How We Lost China," revealing the (false) belief that somehow China had once been America's. In any case, the communist camp, with significant help from Russia, now controlled it.

The Korean War, 1950–53

On June 25, 1950, the armed forces of communist North Korea invaded South Korea. The Korean peninsula had been a colony of Japan from 1910 until 1945. At the end of the war, control over the peninsula was divided at the 38th parallel between the Soviets to the north and the USA to the south. The prospect of independence and unification was left for future negotiation. The North Koreans apparently attacked on their own, without Russian or Chinese support. They drove all the way to the southernmost part of the peninsula before American troops, sent as part of a United Nations force, drove them back to North Korea by September, and then kept pushing them farther north toward the border with China. In response, China entered the war, sending in hundreds of thousands of troops in wave after wave of assaults. China crossed the border into the south, capturing the South Korean capital of Seoul for a second time, until additional US and UN forces pushed them back to the 38th parallel, and brought the military and political situation to a stalemate. By war's end in 1953, 115,000 soldiers, including 37,000 Americans, and a million civilians had died in the south. (North Korea did not release statistics.) At least a million Chinese were also killed in the struggle.

The Korean War reconfirmed America's armed opposition to communism but actually increased the American feeling of threat, since now China was also involved. The war strengthened the reputation of the Chinese since they had held the mighty Americans to a military stand-off. Mao had called America a "paper tiger" despite its nuclear weapons. He believed that, after Hiroshima and Nagasaki, America could never again use the arsenal of nuclear weapons that it possessed, and Korea seemed to confirm his view. Ironically, the war poisoned the atmosphere between China and Russia as well, because Stalin had at first offered to support China if it went to war with America, and then withdrew the pledge. Mao made the agonizing decision to proceed alone. In the end, the USSR did lend some support, but Stalin's equivocation left the Chinese leadership feeling betrayed.

The war brought some prosperity to Japan. It made the island nation a manufacturing base for United States war supplies and a prime location for rest-and-relaxation by US troops. It increased the personal contact between Americans and Japanese, especially between GIs and Japanese women. It also led the United States to see Japan as its new ally in the Pacific. The United States terminated its occupation of Japan in 1952, and, reversing its earlier wish that Japan remain unarmed, encouraged that country to create some armed defense forces.

The Korean War tended to drive a wedge between the United States and many of its European allies who had supported the early war effort to repulse the North Korean attack but who felt that the continuing drive into North Korea was unnecessarily belligerent and costly, and provoked the Chinese response. Also in light of this war, America encouraged Germany to grow once again into a major ally with significant armed forces. European nations who had so recently been at war with Germany were apprehensive about a rearmed Germany.

Technologically, helicopters played a major role in the war. US forces in Korea employed them in unprecedented numbers to convoy troops, to stage aerial attacks, and to ferry wounded soldiers to mobile army surgical hospitals (MASH) units. The Chinese threw waves of soldiers into their attacks, compensating with numbers for what they lacked in equipment.

Driven by their mutual hostility, the two superpowers carried "brinksmanship" farther and created militarized organizations of their allies. With its western European allies and Canada, the United States created the North Atlantic Treaty Organization (NATO) in 1949. NATO included democratic countries with capitalist, socialist, and mixed economies: Britain, France, Italy, Canada, Denmark, Norway, Iceland, Belgium, the Netherlands, and Luxembourg. Portugal, though not a democracy at the time, was also a charter member. In 1952, both Greece and Turkey joined, as did West Germany in 1955, only a decade after its defeat in World War II. In response, the USSR formally established the Warsaw Pact in 1955 among the nations of Albania, Bulgaria, Czechoslovakia, East Germany, Hungary, Poland, and Romania, which were communist in their politics and economics, and under the control of the USSR. Four decades of Cold War standoff in Europe had begun. When the USSR crushed democratic revolts in East Germany (1953), Hungary (1956), Czechoslovakia (1968), and Poland (1981), NATO protested but did not intervene.

The Soviet Union after Stalin

Nikita Khrushchev, 1953–64 The USSR itself was changing. After Stalin's death in 1953, Party General Secretary Nikita Khrushchev (1894–1971) began to reveal and reject some of the coercive powers of the communist state. At the Twentieth Party Congress in 1956, Khrushchev exposed the extent of Stalin's tyranny, declaring that:

> Arbitrary behavior by one person encouraged and permitted arbitrariness in others. Mass arrests and deportations of many thousands of people, executions without trial and without normal investigation created conditions of insecurity, fear, and even desperation. (Kochan and Abraham, p. 447)

In 1961, at the Twenty-second Party Congress, Khrushchev denounced Stalin more fully and had his body removed from Lenin's Mausoleum. Khrushchev released a number of political prisoners of conscience, permitted the publication of many politically banned works, and moderated Stalin's plans for heavy industrialization in favor of greater production of consumer goods. The Soviet government itself gradually began to portray Stalin as a political monster, as Khrushchev also began to open more of the record, publicly revealing Stalin's atrocities.

In the new climate of openness, Russian novelist Alexander Solzhenitsyn (b. 1918) was able to publish *A Day in the Life of Ivan Denisovich* (1962), a realistic novel depicting conditions in one of the Soviet prison labor camps. Khrushchev fell from power in 1964, however, and Solzhenitsyn could publish his next two novels—*The First Circle* (1968), set in a prison, and *Cancer Ward* (1968), set in a hospital—only in editions smuggled out of Russia. Internally his writings circulated illegally in **samizdat** ("self-published"), privately copied, formats. In 1970, the novelist was awarded the Nobel

samizdat From the Russian *sam-*, "self-", and *izdatel'stvo*, "publishing house." Literature printed (often in typescript) and circulated secretly to evade official suppression and punishment by the government; also this illegal, underground system of private publication.

gulag The acronym of Glavnoye, Upravleniye Ispravitelno Trudovykh Lagerey, the "Chief Administration of Corrective Labor Camps," a department of the Soviet secret police founded in 1934 under Stalin. It ran a vast network of forced labor camps throughout the USSR to which millions of citizens accused of "crimes against the state" were sent for punishment. The system was exposed by Alexander Solzhenitsyn in *The Gulag Archipelago* (1973).

Prize for Literature. He did not travel to Stockholm to receive the award, however, fearing that he would be denied re-entry to the Russia he loved despite its political problems.

Solzhenitsyn courageously took it upon himself to go beyond *Ivan Denisovich*. In the three volumes of his *Gulag Archipelago* (1973–8), he revealed fully the extent of the **gulag,** the nationwide archipelago of prison labor camps spread throughout the country, most of them in cold, vast, remote Siberia.

> This Archipelago crisscrossed and patterned that other country within which it was located, like a gigantic patchwork, cutting into its cities, hovering over its streets. Yet there were many who did not even guess at its presence and many, many others who had heard something vague. And only those who had been there knew the whole truth. (Solzhenitsyn, p. X)

As many as 8 million citizens were imprisoned at any given time, and some 20 million may have died in the camps. After the publication of the *Gulag Archipelago* in 1973, Solzhenitsyn was stripped of his Russian citizenship and exiled. For about fifteen years he lived in Vermont, USA, until in 1990 a new government in Russia restored his citizenship and he returned in 1994.

Under Khrushchev, the Soviet Union continued to attempt to catch up to the West militarily and economically—and in some competitions even to surpass it, as it did with the *Sputnik* space satellite in 1957. Khrushchev tried, unsuccessfully, to develop agriculturally more of the "virgin lands" of Kazakhstan and Siberia. Agriculture continued to lag and consumer goods continued to be limited, but the USSR seemed on a par with the United States militarily and industrially. But for how long could its relatively backward economy continue to support its investment in heavy military industries? The Soviet government saw no alternative. It felt surrounded and threatened by the United States and its allies, and saw no choice but to continue preparing its defenses—mirroring Stalin's defensive policies in regard to Germany in the 1930s.

In foreign affairs, Khrushchev was as aggressive as Stalin. He maintained Russia's domination of eastern Europe. He crushed the Hungarian uprising of 1956. He stationed nuclear-tipped missiles in Cuba. He allowed the East Germans to build a wall through the heart of divided Berlin in 1961 to close escape routes to the West. The Soviet Party leadership considered Khrushchev reckless and removed him from power in 1964. He was followed by almost two decades of bureaucratic stagnation under Leonid Brezhnev (1906–82).

Leonid Brezhnev, 1964–82 Brezhnev ruled the Soviet Union from 1964 to 1982 as head of the government and general secretary of the Communist Party. In the spring of 1968 Czechoslovakia tried to escape Russian control and establish an independent government. Brezhnev ended the hopes of this "Prague Spring" by declaring that the Soviet Union would intervene in the affairs of its satellites to prevent counter-revolution, a policy later named the "Brezhnev Doctrine." Soviet troops crushed the Czech revolt. In the first years of his administration, Brezhnev built up the armed forces of the USSR, although later he made cutbacks.

Despite the Brezhnev Doctrine, unrest simmered in eastern Europe, most strongly in Poland. Here the Roman Catholic Church remained a powerful voice critical of communist rule, and when Karol Wojtyla, the Polish archbishop of Krakow, was elected pope in 1978, dissidents throughout Poland took heart. Although their country, under communism, was officially atheistic, they now had a symbolic leader at the pinnacle of religious authority in Rome who could address their spiritual longings and provide a beacon of hope for independence from Soviet control. Lech Walesa, a shipyard worker in Gdansk, began to organize what ultimately became Solidarity, an independent trade union federation with a membership of more than 10 million industrial and agricultural workers. Solidarity demanded not only lower prices and higher wages, but also the right to strike, freedom for political prisoners, an end to censorship, and free elections. At Moscow's bidding, the Polish government jailed Walesa and other Solidarity leaders and declared martial law. The pope, however, supported Solidarity, and the United States imposed economic sanctions. In 1982 Brezhnev died, martial law ended, and Walesa was freed. In 1983 he received the Nobel Peace Prize. Demands for more freedom continued to build in Poland and throughout the Soviet Union.

Moscow power parade. At the height of the Cold War, the arms race against the West saw Russian leaders Khrushchev and Brezhnev pouring colossal sums of money into military hardware. This parade shows tanks moving through Red Square, Moscow, to mark the sixty-sixth anniversary of the 1917 October Revolution. Lenin keeps watch.

The USSR suffered its Vietnam in Afghanistan. In 1978, a pro-Soviet coup took over that country. The USSR sent in troops and supplies to put down anti-communist, Islamic revolts against the new government, and sponsored a second coup in favor of an even more pro-Soviet government. More than 100,000 troops helped the new government secure the cities, especially the capital, Kabul, but the Muslim rebels, supported by assistance from the United States, controlled the rural areas. Among the rebels receiving aid from the USA was a group of militant Muslims called the Taliban, and among them was a young Saudi guerrilla fighter named Osama bin Laden. The USSR lost some 15,000 soldiers in eight years of fighting, leading to intense criticism of the Russian government back home. The United Nations brokered a peace agreement in 1988 that called for the withdrawal of all foreign troops, and the Russians went home discredited and in disarray. Afghanistan itself was thoroughly destabilized and descended into continuing civil war, with the Taliban generally taking command, but with no group firmly in control of the entire country.

The American Military-Industrial Complex

The costs of the military-technological competition of the Cold War were astronomical. In 1960, in peacetime, the governments of the world spent nearly $100 billion on military expenses.

In his 1961 farewell address as president of the United States, Dwight Eisenhower, a five-star general who had served as supreme commander of Allied Forces in Europe during World War II, now warned his nation against the dangers of the "military-industrial complex," the combination of military and industrial leaders who might find it in their mutual interests to promote warfare:

We must never let the weight of this combination endanger our liberties or democratic processes. We should take nothing for granted. Only an alert and knowledgeable citizenry can compel the proper meshing of the huge industrial and military machinery of defense with our peaceful methods and goals, so that security and liberty may prosper together.

Defense expenditure. Fueled by the conflict and the Cold War, massive expenditure by the US and USSR on military hardware kept them neck and neck. After 1960, the rapid militarization of the developing nations increased expenditures. After the fall of the Soviet Union, 1989–91, they decreased. Sources: Paul Kennedy, *The Rise and Fall of The Great Powers* and *New York Times 2000 Almanac.*

DEFENSE EXPENDITURE (in billions of current dollars)

	USA	USSR	China	Germany	UK	Japan
1930	.699	.722	–	.162	.512	.218
1938	1.13	5.43	–	7.41	1.86	1.74
1950	14.5	15.5	2.5	–	2.3	–
1970	77.8	72	23.7	6.1	5.8	1.3
1987	293.2	274.7	13.4	34.1	31.5	24.2
1997	273.0	64 (Russia)	36.6	33.4	35.7	40.9

Eisenhower's warning went unheeded. The military build-up continued. So did the direct confrontations with the Soviet Union and its allies. President Kennedy confronted Cuba at the Bay of Pigs and the USSR in the Cuban Missile Crisis. He also committed American advisers to South Vietnam in its conflict with communist North Vietnam. Under President Lyndon Baines Johnson, this assistance mushroomed into a commitment to full-scale warfare with more than a half million US troops fighting in Vietnam.

Most of the armed confrontations were not directly between the Soviet Union and the United States. Despite, or perhaps because of, the destructive power of their arsenals, the European and North American powers exercised restraint. The Cold War never turned hot within their borders. As colonized countries escaped colonialism and became independent—like Korea, Vietnam, and, in a way, China—each of the two superpowers sought to enlist them on its side. In their **client states** (states reliant on them for aid and assistance) in the Middle East, Africa, Asia, and Latin America warfare did break out repeatedly. As a result, many of the wars of the 1950s, 1960s, 1970s, and 1980s were **proxy wars**, wars fought between allies of the US and USSR, as the superpowers usually stood in the background and let others fight and kill on their behalf. In these localized wars the great powers could sell or give away their older weapons systems and test the newer ones in countries whose leaders were only too eager to get them. Many of these proxy wars were fought in Africa—in Congo (Zaire), Nigeria, Ethiopia, Angola, and Mozambique—sometimes with Cuban troops fighting very far from home. In Central American guerrilla wars in Guatemala, Nicaragua, and El Salvador, the United States and the USSR supported opposing parties. In the Middle East, Israel was widely viewed as a client state of the USA, and, in response, many Arab states turned to the USSR for economic aid and military assistance. Some, however, played both sides diplomatically to get whatever benefits they could from the Cold War competition.

client state A state that is economically, politically, or militarily dependent on another state.

proxy war A war waged between dependent, client states of larger, more powerful states that do not become directly involved in the fighting.

The Cuban Missile Crisis

The most frightening moment of the Cold War took place in 1962 in a confrontation over nuclear-tipped missiles deployed in Cuba. Following a revolution in 1959, led by Fidel Castro, Cuba had become a communist country only 90 miles off the coast of Florida, threatening America's self-confidence and its hold over Latin America. Castro, a lawyer who had taken himself into the hills of eastern Cuba to lead a guerrilla war against American-backed dictator Fulgencio Batista, declared a six–point program:

- extensive land redistribution and collectivization, with common use of expensive equipment;
- limits on foreign investment and mobilization of Cuba's own capital through the national bank for investment in industrialization;
- housing policies that would enable each Cuban family to own its own home;
- full employment;
- full literacy in an educational system appropriate to an agrarian country;
- health care facilities for all.

Contrary to promises made before the revolution, Castro did not hold elections, declaring that "the intimate union and identification of the government with the people," made elections unnecessary. Although Castro denied that he was a communist and did, for a time, try to negotiate agreements with the United States, he soon established close military and economic ties with the Soviet bloc. In the Cold War environment of the time, the United States viewed Castro as a communist. When three multinational oil refineries refused to process oil brought to Cuba from the USSR, Castro expropriated the refineries. In response, the United States ended the special quota of sugar that it had guaranteed to purchase from Cuba since the 1930s. In December 1961, Castro openly announced his allegiance to Marxism-Leninism. From that time, Cuba became dependent on the Soviet Union, reversing Batista's earlier dependence on the United States.

Castro then proceeded to carry out his announced program. He expropriated or confiscated foreign assets, including $1 billion in North American property and investments in Cuba. He collectivized farms, which took land away from peasants, and centralized control of the economy in the hands of the government. He took human development issues seriously, and devoted money and energies to health, education, and cultural activities. Education and all medical services were free.

The living standards of most Cubans improved sharply. Most of the elites—hundreds of thousands of people—fled, however, with the acquiescence of the government, which was pleased to have them gone. These exiles were received with open arms in the United States, where they formed a new large community, centered in Miami, which lobbied heavily for the United States to take action against Castro. Meanwhile Castro and his close associate Ernesto "Che" Guevara dispatched advisers throughout Latin America and Africa to promote guerrilla war.

Two confrontations between Cuba and the United States followed. The American government agreed to arm and support a group of about 1,500 Cuban exiles who wanted to invade the island on the assumption that Cuba's people would welcome the opportunity to overthrow Castro. When the exiles did invade, on April 17, 1961, at the Bay of Pigs, they were met not by a popular uprising, but by Cuban armed forces who immediately defeated them. In the next year, Cuba was the focus of the most direct confrontation of the Cold War between the United States and the Soviet Union. The Soviet Union had positioned nuclear missiles in Cuba. They denied the existence of these missiles, but American reconnaissance aircraft obtained photographic evidence. President Kennedy demanded that the missiles be withdrawn, even threatening nuclear war over the

Castro, victorious, en route to Havana. Fidel Castro embraces a child amongst a crowd of well-wishers shortly after taking power. In January 1959, Cuban dictator Fulgencio Batista was ousted by Castro and his popular revolutionary army. The revolutionaries had been hiding in the mountains since December 1956, fighting against Batista's regime. Their fight to overthrow the dictator was called the "26th July Movement," after the date of their first insurrection against Batista.

SOURCE

Guerrilla Warfare

With the success of Mao's communist, agrarian revolution in China and Castro's in Cuba, and continuing peasant uprisings around the world, including Vietnam, the 1960s were especially alive with rural guerrilla warfare. Usually led by young, vigorous, brave, and single-minded revolutionaries, the guerrilla movements had a powerful mystique, and a number of successes. They demonstrated the potential of very simple conflict techniques against the most sophisticated modern weapons. One of the most charismatic of the guerrilla warriors was Ernesto "Che" Guevara, who was born in Argentina in 1928 and who was captured and killed while organizing a guerrilla movement in Bolivia in 1967. He participated in Castro's revolution in Cuba and was later appointed head of the national bank. But Guevara chose life as a full-time revolutionary, helping to establish guerrilla focos, revolutionary outposts, in many locations. His speeches and writings, like Mao's, were a bible to guerrilla warriors.

Nuclei of relatively few persons choose places favorable for guerrilla warfare, sometimes with the intention of launching a counterattack or to weather a storm, and there they begin to take action. But the following must be made clear: At the beginning, the relative weakness of the guerrilla fighters is such that they should endeavor to pay attention only to the terrain, in order to become acquainted with the surroundings, establish connections with the population, and fortify the places that eventually will be converted into bases. The guerrilla unit can survive only if it starts by basing its development on the three following conditions: constant mobility, constant vigilance, constant wariness …

We must carry the war into every corner the enemy happens to carry it—to his home, to his centers of entertainment: a total war. It is necessary to prevent him from having a moment of peace, a quiet moment outside his barracks or even inside; we must attack him wherever he may move …

Our every action is a battle cry against imperialism, and a battle hymn to the people's unity against the great enemy of mankind: the United States of America. Wherever death may surprise us, let it be welcome, provided that this, our battle cry, may have reached some receptive ear and another hand may be extended to wield our weapons and other men be ready to intone the funeral dirge with the staccato singing of the machine gun and new battle cries of war and victory.

(Sigmund, pp. 370, 381)

issue. As the world watched, terrified, in fear of imminent Armageddon, Russian leader Nikita Khrushchev announced that the USSR would remove the missiles in exchange for American promises not to invade Cuba again and to remove its own missiles from Turkey. According to the most recent scholarship, Khrushchev acted here against the wishes of Castro, who was willing to push the nuclear challenge to the Americans even further to the brink. From this point onward, however, the two superpowers pulled back from such direct confrontation.

THE COLD WAR AND THE EMERGENCE OF NEW NATIONS

The Cold War was one of the great postwar reconfigurations. The collapse of colonialism and the emergence of more than eighty new nations from colonial control to independence was another. This process of decolonization was in large part a legacy of the world wars and the global depression, 1914 to 1945. These cataclysms depleted the colonizing powers of manpower, financial resources, and moral status. They no longer had the power to hold on to their colonies, especially as many of the colonies began to assert their right to independence. The colonized peoples, and many of the colonizers themselves, no longer believed in the "White Man's Burden" of civilizing the non-Western world. The almost unimaginable devastation of the wars exploded the myth of the superiority of the civilization of the colonizers.

The allies in World War I had proclaimed the mission of making the world safe for democracy and had promised increased self-government after the war to many of their colonies. Britain had made such promises to its European colony, Ireland, in 1914, and to India in 1917. It promised a new homeland for Jews in Palestine and at the same time promised to do no harm to the existing Arab population of Palestine. At war's end, the smaller ethnic groups in southern and eastern Europe had hoped for new states. Middle Eastern regions, like Lebanon, Syria, Jordan, and Palestine, had looked forward to self-government. Most of these aspirations were quashed. Ireland was given independence, but only after an armed uprising. The Protestant north remained a colony of England. India continued in colonial status. Much of the Middle East was mandated to Britain and France.

As independence movements intensified, Kwame Nkrumah of Ghana wrote:

> I saw that the whole solution to this problem lay in political freedom for our people; for it is only when a people are politically free that other races can give them the respect that is due them. It is impossible to talk of equality of races in any other terms. No people without a government of their own can expect to be treated on the same level as peoples of independent sovereign states. It is far better to be free to govern or misgovern yourself than to be governed by anybody else. (Nkrumah, p.9)

The anti-colonial nationalists gained important new allies as the United States and the Soviet Union both added their voices. The Soviet Union had from its inception under Lenin declared its opposition to overseas colonialism, although its post-World War II holdings in central and eastern Europe and central Asia looked like its own form of colonialism close to home. The United States, too, especially under Franklin Delano Roosevelt and Truman, spoke out for an end of colonialism. These anti-colonial stands had some effect. Churchill, for example, moderated his pro-colonial positions, especially in regard to India, in deference to his wartime colleagues.

In the long run, Churchill's increased moderation wasn't enough. The British voted his party out of office at the end of the war. The people felt that Churchill was the right man for the war, but his was not the right party for the peace. They wanted new directions at home and abroad, including an end to their imperial holdings, which they began to see as economically and militarily costly in the face of renewed colonial resistance, and perhaps as morally inappropriate as well. The combination of increasingly resistant colonized nations and colonizing powers no longer able to repress them led to the conferring of independence.

The British- and French-mandated territories in the Middle East were the first to gain their freedom. Iraq had been granted formal independence from Britain in 1932 as a kingdom. British troops were called in, however, when coups were attempted to overthrow the monarchy. In 1958, a leftist coup did succeed in overthrowing the king, breaking the ties to Britain, and reorienting the country's foreign policy toward the USSR. Jordan gained independence from Britain in 1946, as did Lebanon in 1943 and Syria in 1946 from France.

India, the largest of all the colonies, had begun to organize a modern nationalist political movement from 1885 and finally won its independence from Britain in 1947, although the subcontinent was partitioned on religious grounds into two nations, India and Pakistan. Because of its size and importance, India will be discussed at greater length in the next chapter (Chapter 22).

In the same year the United Nations passed a resolution agreeing to partition the British-mandated land of Palestine between its bitterly antagonistic Jewish and Arab populations. In 1920, only about 60,000 Jews were living in Palestine, about one-tenth the number of Arabs. Jewish immigration and settlement increased between the two world wars, driven in part by the increasing persecution of Jews under the Nazis in Germany and its conquered territories. Arab

Ghana's independence. Prime minister (later president) Kwame Nkrumah waves to a celebrating crowd as the Gold Coast colony becomes the newly independent country of Ghana on March 6, 1957. Nkrumah formed a one-party state in 1964. His regime was ended by a military coup in 1966 during his absence on a trip to China.

resistance to this new stream of immigration from Europe led to repeated armed clashes between the two groups. To reduce the tensions, the British severely restricted Jewish immigration. In the face of the Holocaust, however, the Jewish people felt a desperate need for a safe haven under their own national sovereignty, and they continued to immigrate illegally.

In 1947, as the UN declared its partition plan, the British prepared to leave. Arabs and Jews armed for battle. David Ben-Gurion's declaration of statehood for Israel in 1948 triggered an immediate armed attack by its neighbors. The new state survived the war, even expanding its borders slightly, but no peace treaties were signed, only agreements to cease fire. Since no new government had yet arisen to claim sovereignty over the remaining parts of Palestine, the king of Jordan asserted his country's control of that territory. The area was generally referred to as "the West Bank" of the Jordan River. The entire situation remained volatile.

In China, the communist revolutionaries led by Mao Zedong captured the government in 1949, closed down the foreign holdings in the treaty ports, and asserted China's control over its own destiny. The anti-communist, nationalist Chinese armies fled to the island of Taiwan, leaving China divided as well, although Taiwan was only one third of 1 percent of the size of the mainland in area, and held only about 2 percent of its population. Again, because of China's size and importance, its history of revolution and reconstruction as a communist state will be told in the next chapter.

In Southeast Asia, the Japanese had driven out the European colonial powers during World War II. At the end of the war, the Europeans tried to return but they faced nationalist opponents who wanted no more of colonialism. In Indonesia, the largest of these countries, Achmed Sukarno (1901–70), who had been imprisoned by the Dutch and freed by the Japanese, declared Indonesia's independence in 1945, before the Dutch tried to return. The Dutch did return in 1946 and, with the help of the British, attempted to reestablish their rule through force of arms. In 1949, however, after four years of fighting, and after the United States threatened to cut off Marshall Plan aid to the Dutch, they withdrew, recognizing Indonesian independence.

The Japanese had also seized Vietnam. After World War II, the French attempted to reestablish colonial rule but met armed opposition and guerrilla warfare led by Ho Chi Minh, the leader of the communist Vietminh or Independence League. The Vietminh

Children fleeing from Trang Bang, South Vietnam, June 8, 1972. The children were fleeing from an American napalm attack.

had established themselves in 1939 to fight against French colonialism. Then they had fought against the Japanese occupation. Now they were once again fighting the French. After the French lost the decisive battle of Dienbienphu in May 1954, they signed an armistice agreement with the Vietminh that partitioned the country at the 17th parallel. The Vietminh governed the north. In the south, the French transferred full sovereignty to a new anti-communist government and withdrew their troops. Civil war engulfed the south. The north, under a communist government, called repeatedly for the reunification of the country and supported communist insurgents, the Vietcong, against the government of the south. America, tragically misreading an essentially nationalist civil war as a Cold War battle, and unskilled in fighting guerrilla warfare, committed increasing numbers of its own troops to supporting the government of the south in an ultimately doomed cause. It finally signed a peace agreement in 1973 and evacuated its last troops in ignominious defeat in 1975. More than 58,000 US armed forces died in Vietnam during the war: 200,000 South Vietnamese, 5,000 other allied forces, and more than a million Vietnamese civilians also died. The war displaced more than six and a half million people in South Vietnam alone. The country was reunified in 1976 under the rule and administration of the North Vietnamese.

America evacuating its last personnel from Saigon in defeat, April 30, 1975. More than a decade of warfare in Vietnam convulsed America in bitter disagreements at home, and exposed its inability to understand nationalist guerrilla warfare overseas.

The Vietnam War intruded deeply and divisively into US domestic life. In the 1960s and early 1970s, the civil rights and feminist movements coalesced with the nationwide protest against the war in Vietnam, creating a vibrant, creative, colorful, shrill, and sometimes violent culture conflict that convulsed the country with its excesses on both sides. Publicly and privately, within millions of families, citizens struggled with questions concerning the legitimacy of draft-dodging, the use of drugs, sexual freedom, and the appropriate length of hair. President Johnson (1963–8), buffeted by the anti-Vietnam War movement, declined to run for a second term. The war ended only under President Richard Nixon in 1973. Nixon's opening to communist China marked a turning point in US relations with communist countries as he visited China in 1972, recognized it diplomatically, and finally allowed it to take China's seat on the UN Security Council, replacing the government of Taiwan on that body.

Africa

Although nominally independent since 1922, Egypt gained full sovereignty over the Suez Canal only in 1956. In 1957, Ghana became the first black African country to win its independence, from Britain. Most of the French colonies gained their independence in 1960. Dozens more followed these precedents in the next decade.

Egypt

In 1952, a group of Egyptian army officers, among them Gamal Abdel Nasser (1918–70), overthrew the government of their country, forced King Farouk to abdicate, and asserted their independence from Britain's influence over the country. In 1956, the British withdrew their troops from the Suez Canal and Egypt nationalized the waterway. Israel, which had been suffering from guerrilla attacks across its border from Egypt, reached an agreement with Britain and France jointly to retake the canal, put an end to cross-border attacks, and change the governing policies of Egypt. At the end of

Dismantling of the blockade of the Suez Canal, set up during the Suez Crisis, 1956. The Egyptian frigate *Abukir*, loaded with explosives to form part of an effective blockade of the Suez Canal, is raised between two German salvage ships, the *Energie* and the *Ausdauer*. The *Abukir* was the last of a series of obstructions in the canal, and once it was raised and disposed of, the waterway could be reopened to navigation.

October, Israeli forces attacked Egypt, and a few days later Britain and France bombed Egypt and air-dropped troops to join in the fighting. President Eisenhower, blind-sided and infuriated by this neo-colonial act by his own allies, put pressure on them to withdraw from Egypt and the canal. As a result, Nasser's reputation reached heroic heights throughout the Arab world as a man who had confronted the Western powers, divided them, and got rid of them. In 1967, Nasser concluded an agreement with the Soviet Union accepting its assistance in building the Aswan High Dam on the Nile River, one of the most significant engineering and hydro-electric projects of the day, which went out of its way to preserve ancient Egypt's architectural wonders, despite the problems for the ecology of the region. Nasser died in 1970, and his successor, Anwar Sadat (1918–81), expelled all Soviet advisers, once again demonstrating that third-world politics were mercurial, and could cause problems for both first and second world countries. In 1981, Sadat was assassinated, but his successor, Hosni Mubarak (b. 1928), continued his policies of keeping the Soviets at a distance, and maintaining collegial diplomatic relations with the United States.

Congo

The "Congo crisis" of 1960 demonstrated again the cross-cutting interests of the Cold War superpowers, other international interest groups, and the complex and diverse sub-national units within a newly created nation. The Congo is rich in diamonds, copper, coffee, and crude oil. It has 70 percent of the world's known reserves of cobalt. In earlier days it was also known for its natural rubber, before the general use of its synthetic alternative. For the profits of these products, Leopold II, king of the Belgians, had first taken the Congo as his personal colony in 1885. Because of the extraordinary cruelty of his rule, the Belgian government itself took control in 1908, but violence and autocracy remained characteristic of Belgian rule. Political devolution to limited self-rule began only in 1957. A small group of educated Congolese, who saw the preparations for independence in other African colonies, began to assert national political demands, and the Belgians allowed elections for local self-government. Among the leading contestants, Joseph Kasavubu (c. 1910–69) was an early advocate of independence, but his focus was primarily on his own ethnic Bakongo people. Patrice Lumumba (1925–61) provided a more national and more militant leadership. Anti-government rioting began in January 1959. Belgium began reconsidering its options. In January 1960, it convened a Round Table Conference in Brussels and, with breakneck, unrealistic speed, declared that the Congo would be independent on June 30, 1960.

At the independence celebrations, Lumumba, the newly elected prime minister, delivered a bitter speech revealing his deep-seated, festering rage toward the Belgians:

> We are no longer your monkeys … We have known the back-breaking works exacted from us in exchange for salaries which permit us neither to eat enough to satisfy our hunger, nor to dress and lodge ourselves decently, nor to raise our children as the beloved creatures they are.

HOW DO WE KNOW?

Evaluating the Legacies of Colonialism

As the colonial era ended, historians divided sharply in assessing the impact of colonial rule. Leften Stavrianos, who spent most of his career at the University of California, San Diego, presented a Marxist, primarily economic, critical perspective. Colonial rule created "an unprecedented increase in productivity" in commerce and industry, but no corresponding increase in pay for the workers nor in distribution of wealth to the colony. In many colonies, white settlers and plantation owners seized the best lands. Rural communities were disrupted as

> private property arrangements displaced the former communal ownership and cultivation of land ... Land now became a mere possession, food a mere commodity of exchange, neighbor a mere common property owner and labor a mere means of survival. (Stavrianos, p.9)

As the industrial revolution matured into industrial capitalism, exploitation became more severe. The results were unfortunate and long lasting:

> All these global economic trends combined to produce the present division of the world into the developed West as against the underdeveloped Third World. But underdevelopment did not mean nondevelopment; rather it meant distorted development—development designed to produce only one or two commodities needed by the Western markets rather than overall development to meet local needs. In short, it was the familiar Third World curse of economic growth without economic development. (Stavrianos, p.11)

Theodore Von Laue, who studied Westernization, on the other hand, said very little about economic inequalities. Deeply influenced by Judeo-Christian perspectives, he emphasized the cultural upheavals of colonialism and the paradoxical introduction by force of Western values of freedom:

> The world revolution of Westernization, in short, carried a double thrust. It was freedom, justice, and peace—the best of the European tradition—on the one hand; on the other hand (and rather unconsciously) raw power to reshape the world in one's own image.

The transformation to Western values was not complete, however:

> Underneath the global universals of power and its most visible supporting skills— literacy, science and technology, large-scale organization—the former diversities persist. The traditional cultures, though in mortal peril, linger under the ground floors of life. Rival political ideologies and ambitions clash head on. The world's major religions vie with each other as keenly as ever. Attitudes, values, life-styles from all continents mingle freely in the global marketplace, reducing in the intensified invidious comparison all former absolute truths to questionable hypotheses.

Von Laue looked forward to the day when all people

> Will be ready to fuse their personal egos with the egos of billions of other human beings, even in intimate matters like procreation and family size.

It would appear that the common values on that day would be the Western values of the Enlightenment.

Dipesh Chakrabarty questioned this assumption that Western values would be the governing ones. Born in India after independence, trained in Australia and the United States, and later teaching there as well, Chakrabarty argued that the greatest (self-)deception of the colonizers was to project European values as the appropriate goals for the entire world, and to see history moving in that direction: "First in Europe, then elsewhere." He rejected the idea that the rest of the world exists in Europe's "waiting room." He did appreciate European, Enlightenment values, but he did not think that they were the only valid ones, nor that they ought to or necessarily will become universal. Chakrabarty did not address economic issues. On cultural transformations brought by colonialism, however, he was not prepared to accept Von Laue's celebration of exclusively Western values, nor to look forward to the day when they alone would triumph.

- Which effects of colonialism do you think were more important, the economic and technological effects, or the cultural effects? Please be specific in the effects you are discussing.

- To the extent that the Cold War that lasted from the mid-1940s to the mid-1980s represents in part the values of the West, what values do you think colonized countries learned from the West?

- Do you think it is a good idea that some day the peoples of the world may share a similar set of values? Why or why not? If it is a good idea, then what should those values be? To what extent are they technological values?

We have known the mockery, the insults, the blows submitted to morning, noon, and night because we were *nègres* [blacks]. We have known that our lands were despoiled in the name of supposedly legal text which in reality recognized only the right of the stronger ... And, finally, who will forget the hangings or the firing squads where so many of our brothers perished, or the cells into which were brutally thrown those who escaped the soldiers' bullets—the soldiers whom the colonialists made the instruments of their domination? (Andrea and Overfield, pp. 507–8)

Aerial view of rioting in Leopoldville, Belgian Congo, January 6, 1959. The shot shows Congolese streaming through the streets, pillaging and burning the Belgian shops in the village. Riots raged for two days in the Congolese capital, leaving thirty-five dead.

Within days of independence, the army mutinied; Kasavubu, the new president, dismissed Lumumba, the prime minister; Lumumba, in turn, dismissed Kasavubu; Moise Tshombe (1919–69) declared Katanga, the Congo's richest region, independent under his leadership; the Belgians supported Tshombe's move; both Kasavubu and Lumumba appealed to the United Nations for assistance. Lumumba wanted the UN peacekeeping force that arrived to act with force to bring Katanga, with its rich mineral wealth, back into the Congo, but Kasavubu did not, and ultimately the UN forces did not act. Lumumba called on the USSR for assistance, placing the Congo in the middle of the Cold War struggles. Lumumba was captured by Kasavubu, escaped, was recaptured, turned over to the Katanga secessionists, and murdered, apparently with the complicity of the Belgian government and the assistance of the American Central Intelligence Agency (CIA). UN forces defeated Katanga and its mercenary armed forces only in 1963. By this time, however, other provinces of Congo also revolted against the central government and were subdued with the help of European mercenary troops. Most surprisingly, in the movement to restore the authority of the central government, Moise Tshombe—who had been the leader of secessionist Katanga—became prime minister.

Continuing disputes between Tshombe and President Kasavubu opened the way for a military coup led by Joseph Mobutu (1930–97; later Mobutu Sese Seko). With help from Morocco, France, and the United States, Mobutu held out against invasions and continuing attempts at secession. Mobutu ruled with dictatorial powers, changed the name of the country and of its principal river from Congo to Zaire, and transferred much of the wealth earned by Congo's exports to his own overseas accounts—knowledgeable observers guessed $4 to 5 billion—until he was forced from office and into exile in 1997.

Congo is an especially stark example of the confluence of a weak, poor, new nation, deeply divided among the various ethnic groups within its population, caught in the politics of both the Cold War and the international marketplace, and captured by a kleptomaniac, tyrannical dictator for his own purposes.

Algeria

Algeria, which held a million French settlers, won independence in 1962 after a long and bitter struggle that threatened to plunge France itself into civil war. France had been the colonizing power in Morocco, Algeria, and Tunisia. Independence for Morocco and Tunisia came relatively easily and peacefully in 1956 through negotiations with France. Algeria won its independence, however, only through violence and civil war.

Algeria had the largest European settler community in North Africa. The French in Algeria numbered one million, about 12 percent of the total population, but they held one-third of all the cultivable land. These settlers had become prosperous and comfortable. For them, Algeria was home. By the early 1950s, 80 percent of them had been born in Algeria. Officially, Algeria was not a colony, but an integral part of France with constitutional representation in the French National Assembly. In addition, through the 1930s, the Algerian elite were French-educated and saw themselves as more French than Algerian. By the 1940s, however, reformists were moving to create a more powerful Arab-Islamic nationalism, fostering social unity, a distinct national consciousness, and solidarity with other Arabs against foreign rule.

Charles de Gaulle visits Algiers in June, 1958. Algeria had been agitating for independence since 1954, and in 1956, Ben Bella, one of the main Algerian leaders, was arrested. Two years later a political crisis in France, precipitated by continuing Algerian frustration and pressure for independence, put de Gaulle into office as the new president of the Republic. De Gaulle maintained French rule in Algeria as long as possible, while he prepared the French people for the inevitable shift in power. Finally, in 1962, Algerians achieved independence and the French withdrew.

By the mid-1950s, an Algerian revolution against French rule led by the National Liberation Front (FLN) was met by French repression. The two sides became increasingly entrenched. The violence ratcheted upward and spread not only throughout Algeria, but to France as well. The governmental system of France, the Fourth Republic, was weak, and it fell as civil war seemed to threaten. The hero and leader of the French resistance in World War II, General Charles de Gaulle, was asked to take over as president of France under a new constitution. Despite an apparent mandate to continue the war, de Gaulle chose to negotiate a settlement and finally granted independence in 1962, but only after 300,000 Algerians and 20,000 Frenchmen had been killed. Virtually all the one million European residents, many of whom had lived in the country for generations, left Algeria.

Of the Algerians, only 7,000 were in secondary school, and as of 1954, only seventy living, native Algerians had had a university education. The leaders of the new nation, hardened by their years of guerrilla warfare, and ideologically committed to centralized control, took over the tasks of development. They instituted a four-year plan in 1969, and nationalized the petroleum and natural gas resources that had been discovered in 1956. They devoted much of the new oil revenues to industrialization. They increased education's share of the national budget from 2.2 percent of the gross national product to 10 percent. The birth rate, however, remained very high. Rural migrants streamed toward the cities, and hundreds of thousands of Algerians emigrated to France in search of jobs.

Mozambique, Angola, and Guinea

Portugal held on in Africa longer than any other major colonial power, giving up Mozambique and Angola, and some smaller holdings as well, only after lengthy colonial wars as well as a government coup at home in 1974. Ruled by a dictator, Antonio Salazar, from 1932 to 1968, and then by Marcelo Caetano, Portugal was not about to

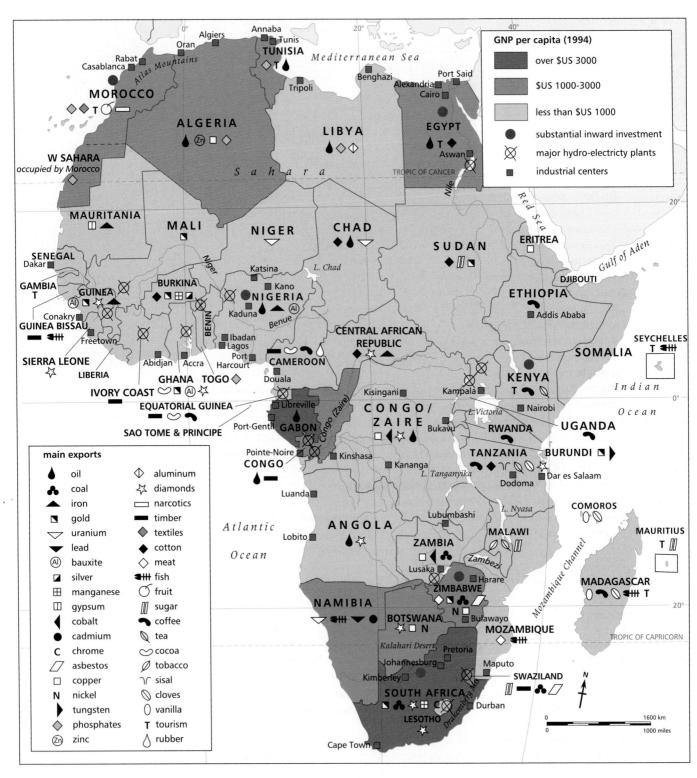

The economic development of Africa. The legacy of European colonialism has determined Africa's economic development, with a persistent reliance upon primary products, mainly mineral wealth and cash crops. Both are widely exploited by multinational franchises, bringing little real economic benefit to local economies. Political instability, corruption, disease, and natural disaster combine with low investment in education and health to create a general condition of underdevelopment. The northern tier of Arab states and South Africa stand out with greater wealth compared with the central part of the continent.

give up control of its large African colonies of Angola and Mozambique, where many Portuguese had settled, and the much smaller colony of Guinea. It governed harshly, with repressive labor policies that forced some 65,000 to 100,000 Mozambiquans to travel each year to work in the mines of South Africa. Each person had to keep an identification passbook at all times. The press was rigidly censored. The police were ruthless. Most of all, alone among the European colonizers Portugal, believed that its own future greatness depended on continuing to control its African colonies. (Portugal was not willing to cede its historic, but tiny, possession of Goa to India until, in 1961, the Indian government dispatched armed forces to seize the enclave.)

In the face of mounting international pressure against colonialism, Portugal maintained that Angola, Mozambique, and Guinea were not colonies, but "overseas provinces." In 1961, revolts broke out in all three colonies. Supported by white-dominated South Africa, Portugal fought fiercely against guerrilla freedom fighters, but the warfare placed great strains on Portugal's economy and armed forces. Moreover, the three colonies were drawn into the Cold War as the USSR and Cuba dispatched troops to aid the guerrillas. Finally, in 1974, a military coup captured the government of Portugal and granted independence to all three colonies. Once again, third-world resistance movements had triumphed over European colonial powers and, in the process, had forced changes in the home government.

In claiming their national independence, individual countries stressed such diverse ideologies as bourgeois democracy, workers' socialism, Islamic resurgence, and indigenous nationalism, often in various combinations. Most African countries obtained independence from 1945 to the 1970s, yet many became unstable countries, in part because when Europeans colonized the countries they drew boundaries for their own convenience regardless of tribal and ethnic differences. These issues of identity will be explored in more depth in Chapters 23 and 24.

Even among the colonizers, colonialism was no longer considered an appropriate form of government, except in rare cases of geographically tiny dependencies, Caribbean or South Pacific islands, for example. As new countries became independent, however, the two contesting blocs of the Cold War tried to win them over and often involved them in proxy wars, as we have seen, and will see further below. One reaction against such interference from the USA and the USSR was the formation of a third bloc, of **non-aligned nations**.

non-aligned nation A newly independent nation that chose not to align itself with either the USA or the USSR in the Cold War.

THE EMERGENCE OF THE THIRD WORLD

As decolonization created new nations in Africa and Asia at the same time that the Cold War divided Europe, many commentators spoke of the emergence of three worlds, or styles of development. The first world consisted of the wealthy, capitalist, democratic countries of western Europe and the United States; the second world was composed of the Communist Party-dominated, middle-income countries of the Soviet Union and its eastern European allies; the third world included the poorer nations, just emerging from colonization and now seeking their appropriate place in the world.

Today the term "third world" is frequently used with a negative, and much resented, connotation to designate poor, technologically backward, inefficiently organized nations. When the term first came to be used in the 1950s, however, it carried more inspirational connotations. In the first wave of decolonization following World War II, newly independent nations faced a world bitterly and expensively polarized into two hostile, belligerent, heavily armed blocs: the North Atlantic Treaty Organization (NATO), led by the United States, and the Warsaw Pact, led by the USSR.

For an interactive version of this map, go to: http://www.prenhall.com/spodek/map21.2

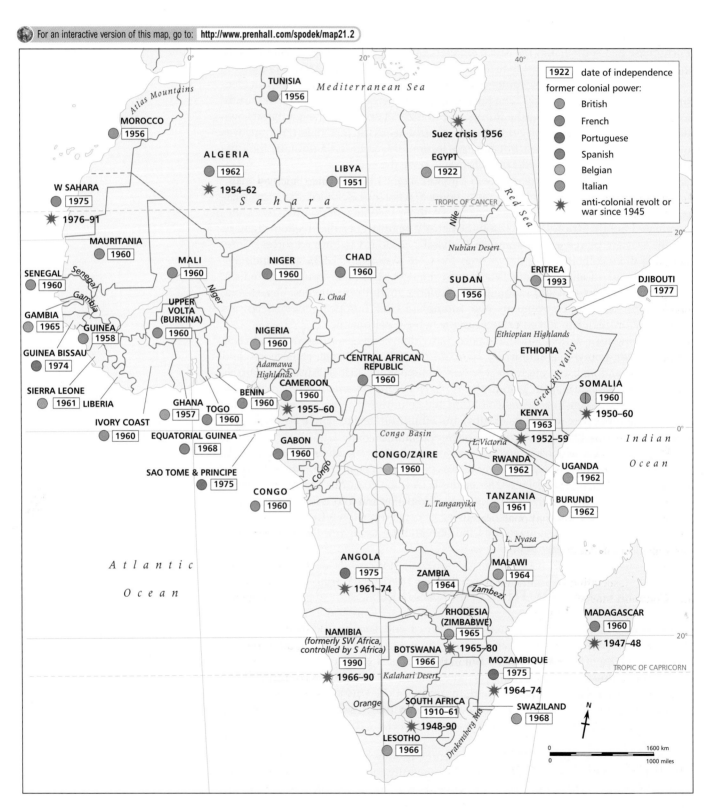

The decolonization of Africa. Ethiopia had been colonized only briefly by Italy, Liberia had been established as an independent state, and Egypt had nominal independence from 1922, but most African states gained their independence after World War II, first those in North Africa, and then, following Ghana in 1957, those of sub-Saharan Africa. Each colonial power had its own pattern for granting independence. The British and French hoped to establish amicable relations, generally, while the Portuguese and Belgians left in more bitter circumstances.

Many of the newly independent nations, advocated a third alternative, a "third world." Many wished to be non-aligned, to avoid taking sides. They felt that Europe and the United States regarded human life as cheap—as two world wars had demonstrated. These new nations urged disarmament, especially nuclear disarmament, at a time when the first two worlds were locked in an arms race to build, first, the atomic bomb, then the hydrogen bomb, and ever more powerful rockets to launch them. They advocated state investment in such basic human needs as food, clothing, shelter, medical care, and small, appropriate-scale technology, often through international assistance, rather than in the purchase of weapons. They reminded the rest of the world that although they were "new nations" politically, many of them, such as India, Egypt, and Ethiopia, were ancient civilizations that took pride in centuries of traditional wisdom.

As they gained independence, these former colonies entered the United Nations, changing the size and complexion of that organization. Although race was not usually mentioned overtly in third-world advocacy, almost all members of the "third world" were peoples of color, while the overwhelming majority of both first and second world groups were white. In 1955, third world representatives convened by Jawaharlal Nehru (1889–1964) of India, Gamal Abdel Nasser (1918–70) of Egypt, and Marshal Tito (1892–1980) of Yugoslavia—who had struggled to set his communist nation free from Soviet control—met at Bandung, Indonesia, to launch their collective entry into international politics. At the Bandung Conference leaders of twenty nations of Africa and Asia articulated a post-colonial agenda. They called for a global reduction in military expenditure and ideological confrontation, and an increase in expenditure for economic development, health, education, welfare, and housing.

The representatives at Bandung were not all from Africa and Asia—Tito, for example, represented Yugoslavia, a European, communist country, that he had set free from Soviet control. Nor were they all non-aligned—Zhou Enlai represented China. Nor did any permanent organization emerge. But for the first time, non-Western leaders assembled to articulate their own vision of a new world order. Many of them also formed regional groups to resolve regional problems and to present a united front in confronting other international organizations, including NATO and the Warsaw Pact. The new regional organizations included the League of Arab States (1945); the Organization of American States (1948), although this organization included the United States and was heavily influenced by it; the Organization of African Unity (1963); the Association of Southeast Asian Nations (1967); the Caribbean Community and Common Market (1973); and the South Asian Association for Regional Cooperation (1983). In 1960, the Organization of Oil Exporting Countries (OPEC) was created primarily by the oil-rich states of the Middle East, but it also came to include oil-producing states in Africa, Indonesia in Southeast Asia, and Venezuela in South America. OPEC's original goals were economic, but in the 1970s it began also to support actively the political goals of its member states in confrontations with Western countries, especially on issues involving Israel and the Arab states. Further meetings of the non-aligned nations took place in Belgrade, Yugoslavia, in 1961; Cairo, Egypt, in 1964; and Lusaka, Zambia, in 1970.

Client States and Proxy Wars

At independence, many of the third world states were unstable politically, impoverished economically, and challenged by their social diversity. Many of them were, nevertheless, rich in natural resources. To prevent instability, to preserve access to natural resources, and for reasons of national and ideological pride, both the Soviet Union and the United States sought these new nations as their allies and clients. The superpowers were often willing to instigate coups to overthrow hostile governments in these new nations and sometimes to involve them in wars against one another.

The internal and external warfare that resulted from this bitter competition was devastating. The warfare usually did not involve the two superpowers directly—although the bloodiest struggles did—but were fought by their proxies. Between 1945 and 1983, perhaps 19 or 20 million people were killed in over one hundred wars and military conflicts, almost all of them in the third world, including: 9 million in East Asia—mostly in the wars in Korea and Vietnam; 3.5 million in Africa; 2.5 million in south Asia; more than a half million in the Middle East, and perhaps another million in the Iran–Iraq war, which lasted from 1980 to 1988 (Hobsbawm, p. 434). Military expansion and the resulting expansion of the state proceeded, proportionately, even more rapidly in the third world than in the first and second. While military expenditures doubled in the developed world of North America and Europe, from $385 billion in 1960 to $789 billion in 1988, in the same period in the developing world they multiplied almost five times, from $28 billion to $134 billion. Between 1960 and 1988, the number of soldiers in the developing nations doubled from 8 million to 16.5 million, in the developed nations it remained stationary at about 10 million. About a third to a half of the wars fought in the third world were, however, guerrilla wars, as peasants and urban workers fought armed struggles in small groups—usually under the leadership of young intellectuals—against their exploitation by the rulers of their country, and against the superpower that backed them.

Despite their poverty and political weakness, third world countries began to have powerful influences in the world, with effects that seriously unsettled the superpowers. In 1948, for example, Marshal Tito of Yugoslavia, who had led his guerrilla forces against the Nazis during World War II, rejected Soviet assistance, even though his country was communist in its politics and economics. He expelled Russian advisers and, in turn, Yugoslavia was expelled from the Comintern.

In 1949, Chinese communist revolutionaries, who had been fighting guerrilla warfare for a generation, successfully took possession of the government of China and forced Chiang Kai-shek and his forces to evacuate to the island of Taiwan. The Chinese communists signed a thirty-year treaty of "friendship, alliance, and mutual assistance" with the Soviet Union. The United States officially chose not to recognize the new government, and within a year China and the US were at war in Korea. China's relations with the USSR also deteriorated. In 1958, the Chinese leader Mao Zedong expressed his frustration with the Russians who seemed far too conservative in spreading communism and who had refused to share their nuclear technology with him. He expelled all his Soviet advisers, accusing them of arrogance. By 1960, the two communist titans were fighting in armed skirmishes over their mutual borders. Russia cancelled its assistance to China, and China began to spread propaganda against the USSR.

Latin America

At about the same time that Congo gained its independence from Belgium, Fidel Castro was completing the revolution in Cuba that overthrew the dictator Fulgencio Batista and soon put Castro on a collision course with the United States. As noted earlier in this chapter, Castro became closely allied with and dependent on the USSR, infuriating the Americans, and especially those new Americans who emigrated from Cuba to escape Castro's revolution. The Americans feared also that Castro's revolutionary rhetoric and example would spread throughout Latin America. It worked actively to isolate the Cuban government from participating in markets, organization, and diplomacy with other governments in the hemisphere.

During the 1960s and the next decades, however, Latin America in general, and especially Central America, was another area of the third world that brought headaches to American policy makers, and embarrassment especially to President Ronald Reagan. Nicaragua, Guatemala, Panama, and Chile were not "new nations." They had become formally independent a century and a half earlier, but they remained poor, divided by social and ethnic differnces, and economically dependent on wealthy, external countries, especially the United States. They identified with the developmental issues of the third world.

Nicaragua Strains in the relationship between the USA and Nicaragua had deep roots. To overthrow a Nicaraguan government, which had begun to grant economic concessions to governments other than the United States, the United States encouraged a revolt in 1909 and dispatched marines to support it. The troops remained, with very few breaks, until 1933, training a Nicaraguan National Guard to join them in defense of US interests. One Nicaraguan army officer, Augusto Cesar Sandino (1893–1934) rejected American hegemony and for seven years fought a guerrilla war against the US marines and the Nicaraguan National Guard until he was deceived during peace negotiations, arrested, and murdered by officers of the guard under Anastasio Somoza Garcia (1896–1956). Somoza subsequently seized control of the national government and, with the support of the United States, turned the presidency into a family dynasty for his two sons after him.

Disgusted with the wretched conditions of the common people at a time when Somoza and his allies were prospering, the editor of *La Prensa* turned his newspaper against the regime in the 1950s. In the 1960s, a revolutionary movement largely composed of students, and naming itself the Sandinista Front for National Liberation in memory of Sandino, initiated an armed guerrilla revolt. As the Somoza government became more rapacious, the resistance expanded and intensified, finally driving the government into exile. By the time the Sandinistas came to power in 1979, however, some 50,000 people had been killed in guerrilla warfare.

United States President Jimmy Carter (1977–80), a liberal in foreign policy, attempted an accommodation with the new Sandinista government, but his successor, Ronald Reagan, pursued a policy of destabilization with almost fanatic zeal. He froze loans that Carter had negotiated. He authorized the creation of a paramilitary force—often referred to as Somocistas or, more commonly, *contras*—to be based in neighboring Honduras for raids across the border into Nicaragua. The US Central Intelligence Agency (CIA) trained and supplied the contras, instructed them in terrorism, and also mined Nicaraguan harbors. These activities violated United States laws and treaties, and were condemned by the World Court, which ordered the United States to end its military and paramilitary actions against Nicaragua. The Reagan administration rejected the authority of the court. When Congress would not sanction further funding for this clandestine war, the Reagan administration arranged for some of the profits of a secret arms sale to Iran—a country generally considered hostile to the United States—to be secretly diverted to financing the contras. The double scandal of the arms sale to Iran and the transfer of funds to the contras embarrassed the Reagan administration and provided a window of opportunity for several Central American

An anti-American poster from the time of the Sandinista revolution, Nicaragua, 1979. Note the various drawings on the figure: military helicopters on the hat; a peace sign ("paz") among the little egghead representations of people massed together demonstrating; an ironic dollar bill with "In God we trust" on the leg. The final touch is the cowboy boot resting firmly on Uncle Sam's hat to keep him in check. Uncle Sam is even a sickly gray color in contrast with the brightly colored cowboy.

governments to negotiate a settlement of the civil war in Nicaragua, including an end to foreign military involvement and a call for honest elections. For his initiative in this effort to negotiate an end to the Nicaraguan conflict, Costa Rican President Oscar Arias was awarded the Nobel Prize for Peace. The nine years of warfare, 1981 to 1990, had cost approximately 60,000 deaths and another 28,000 casualties. Since 1990, Nicaragua has been ruled by democratically elected governments and relationships with the United States have normalized.

Guatemala As we have seen, Latin American critics of United States economic power were often branded communists, and the United States often condemned as communist Latin American attempts to make their societies more egalitarian. In Guatemala, the world's second largest producer of bananas, Colonel Jacobo Arbenz (1913–71) won election as president in an open, free election in 1951. Arbenz proceeded to seize some 400,000 acres of fallow land held by the United Fruit Company, a private company owned mostly by United States citizens. He offered compensation according to the value of the land declared for tax purposes by the Company, but the Company found this insufficient. Arbenz also wanted to build a highway from his capital to the Atlantic Ocean, which would have broken the Company's transportation monopoly. He proposed building a hydroelectric power plant, which would free Guatemala from its dependence on a foreign supply. Finally, fearing an attack by exiles training in neighboring countries, Arbenz sought to buy arms from the United States. When the US turned him down, he bought from Poland, which was then a communist country. Almost immediately a small Guatemalan army-in-exile of some 150 soldiers, equipped by the United States, attacked from Honduras. The Arbenz government fell, virtually without defenders.

Arbenz's successor, Carlos Castillo Armas (1914–57), returned the lands taken from the United Fruit Company, abolished several political parties, disenfranchised all illiterates, about half the adult population, and had those who opposed him jailed, tortured, exiled, or executed. (The term "banana republic" evolved to describe countries like Guatemala that were economically dependent on a single crop that they sold primarily to a superpower, and were helpless in the face of superpower political and military intervention.) Castillo Armas was assassinated in mid-1957, and soon Guatemala plunged into a civil war in which 100,000 people died before a negotiated resolution was achieved in the 1990s. In 1999, President Bill Clinton, speaking in Guatemala, "apologized for US support of right-wing governments that killed tens of thousands of rebels and Mayan Indians in a thirty-six year civil war" (*New York Times Almanac, 2000*, p. 16).

Panama In 1878, a French company, with the permission of the government of Colombia, began to build a canal across Panama, then the most northern region of that nation. The project failed and was put up for sale. The US Congress agreed to pay $40 million for the rights, but the Colombian Congress refused to ratify the new agreement. In 1903, President Theodore Roosevelt encouraged the revolt of a small Panamanian independence movement and ordered American warships to block the arrival of Colombian troops. Three days after the revolt began, he recognized Panama as an independent country. Twelve days later the USA had its treaty, including powerful rights of interference in

Rigoberta Menchu. Menchu, a Guatemalan Indian, won the Nobel Peace Prize in 1992. Her book, *I, Rigoberta Menchu: An Indian Woman in Guatemala*, was published in 1983 and became a bestseller. Although later challenged as exaggerated and "borrowed," this autobiography presents an accurate account of Indian oppression and suffering.

Panama's affairs for the protection of the canal and a 6-mile wide buffer zone along its sides. Panama began its national life as a protectorate of the United States. In 1977 Panama's military government reached an agreement with President Jimmy Carter for the return of the Canal Zone to full Panamanian control in 2000 and that transfer took place calmly, peacefully, and punctually on December 31, 1999.

Chile From 1964 to 1970, Eduardo Frei (1911–81) led a Christian Democratic government in Chile that began a program of agrarian reform and nationalized, with compensation, copper mines owned by United States' private companies. Considered moderate, Frei had good relations with the United States government. In 1970, seeking more radical reform, the voters in Chile elected the socialist Salvador Allende (1908–73). The United States government and major transnational corporations opposed his election and once in office, President Allende confirmed their fears. He increased agrarian reform, purchased control of most banks, and continued the nationalization of the foreign-owned copper industry, which produced three-fourths of Chile's exports. Allende increased the salaries of government workers and expanded medical and housing programs. The usual conflict arose between the desire to improve economic and social benefits, on the one hand, and the problem of finding resources to pay, on the other. Shortages and inflation resulted. The United States government sharply reduced loans and aid to Allende's socialist government, and international banks also cut back on loans. The CIA, with a mandate to overthrow Allende, covertly financed opposition parties and labor strikes. Finally, the middle class, and especially women, who found the resulting chaos and economic instability intolerable, persuaded the military to act. In September 1973, they attacked and bombed the presidential palace, killing Allende.

General Augusto Pinochet (b. 1915), who headed the new government, immediately killed or detained hundreds of thousands of Allende supporters, men and women. He ruled until 1988, feared and hated for his violence toward the opposition, but effective in restoring the economy, with the aid of advisers from the United States. In a plebiscite in 1988, Pinochet was rejected by Chile's voters, and the government passed to the opposition. Chile had returned to democracy.

Iran

In contrast to their apparent victories in Latin America, in Iran, the Americans were humbled. During World War II, the British forced the abdication of Iran's Shah Reza Khan in favor of his son, the pro-British Muhammad Reza Pahlavi. Meanwhile, the increased exploitation of Iran's oil resources had begun to bring new wealth to the kingdom. In 1951, Prime Minister Muhammad Mussadeq (1880–1967) nationalized the Iranian oil industry against the wishes of the shah. In response, Britain and the US conspired with the Iranian army in a coup that supported the shah and overthrew Mussadeq.

Deeply indebted to the West, the shah joined the American-inspired Baghdad Pact, a military alliance directed against the Soviet Union. He invited additional Western oil investment, and proceeded to use Iran's oil wealth to fund deep and massive—but convulsive, erratic, and uneven—Westernization of the country. By the mid-1970s, about 150,000 foreigners had come to Iran to run the new high-technology industries and to live a luxurious lifestyle in secluded "colonies." Rural people were also flooding into the cities, putting great strains on the urban infrastructure. Shortages of foodstuffs and other basic necessities resulted and corruption was everywhere: in the shah's court, the government, the bureaucracy, and within the business community. Opponents of the shah's system of forced modernization—including much of the student community—were pursued, jailed, and often tortured by SAVAK, the shah's secret police.

Opposition to the shah's forced modernization included *ulama*—religious scholars—on the right, who lamented the suppression of traditional religion; students and intellectuals on the left, who were deprived of freedoms of expression; and farmers, who had become urban immigrants, squeezed by inflation, recession, unemployment, and a loosening of what they felt to be the moral foundations of the society. In 1963, a Shiite Muslim religious leader, the Ayatollah Ruhollah Khomeini (1902–89), led an abortive uprising against the shah. The army killed 15,000 rebels and exiled Khomeini. But from Paris the ayatollah kept in contact with dissidents in Iran via tape recordings and telephone, and in 1979 he returned to lead popular demonstrations of as many as 5 million people. Now the shah was forced into exile. Islamic law, the *sharia*, became the law of the land and Islamic government was introduced. Women were ordered to return to draping themselves in the *chador*, or head scarf, and shawl as Iran became a theocracy. Khomeini declared:

> No others, no matter who they may be, have the right to legislate, nor has any person the right to govern on any basis other than the authority that has been conferred by God … It is the religious expert and no one else who should occupy himself with the affairs of the government. (Robinson, p. 171)

The religious fervor of the revolution—especially in the wake of the modernization that had been introduced by the shah—astonished many Western observers.

Strategically located, rich in oil, religiously militant, and internally secure, Khomeini's revolutionary government terrified its neighbors and wreaked havoc on many others more distant. In its first two years, it executed 800 people and exiled thousands. When America offered humanitarian refuge to the exiled shah, who was suffering from cancer, Khomeini seized the American embassy in Tehran and held fifty-two of its staff hostage. President Carter failed to secure their release through negotiations. He then attempted a guerrilla air rescue, which was aborted in humiliating failure. Carter's defeat in the 1980 election was due in part to these failures to cope with Iran. The third world again had powerful effects on Western, superpower politics.

Khomeini's militancy also introduced additional instability into the Middle East. It inspired religious dissidents in Saudi Arabia to attempt to trigger a revolt against the government by attacking the Great Mosque in Mecca during the *hajj* or pilgrimage period in 1979. Three hundred people were killed, and the Saudi government drew closer to the Americans. In Egypt, in 1981, Islamic militants, linked to Iran, assassinated President Anwar Sadat. In 1989, following the publication of the novel *The Satanic Verses*, Iranian clerics proclaimed the Indian-born British author Salman Rushdie a heretic and marked him for execution. A bounty of $5 million was placed on his head, and he was forced into hiding under the protection of the British government. In Beirut and other Middle Eastern centers, Western hostages were seized. Fearing that Iran's Shiite religious revolution would spill across the border, Iraq under Saddam Hussein, with the quiet support of the United States, attacked Iran, precipitating eight years of warfare and hundreds of thousands of deaths.

Legal restrictions on women based on interpretations of religious principles continued, calling for Islamic dress codes and Islamic legal authority over marriage, divorce, child custody, and the right to work. Most Iranian women accepted these restrictions willingly as a stand against Western culture and imperialism. Women's literacy rose to 59 percent, with 95 percent of girls of primary school age attending classes. Birth rates dropped from forty-nine per thousand under the shah to thirty-nine per thousand under Khomeini. The percentage of families using contraception rose from 3 to 23 in

1987 (*World Resources*, 1987, p. 257). Feminism, nationalism, and religion in Iran were intertwined in a unique configuration that did not fit any stereotype.

With Khomeini's death in 1989, more moderate leaders came to power in Iran, seeking more peaceful international relations and limited political moderation at home.

TERRORISM

In addition to the inter-state warfare of the first part of the twentieth century, and the guerrilla warfare of the second half, a third style of warfare became more evident in the 1960s and 1970s: terrorism. Like conventional and guerrilla warfare, terrorism is a style of fighting that can be used by any group. It usually employs violence aimed at civilian non-combatants as a means of creating fear and undermining the enemy's will to fight so that the terrorists may gain aims that they could not otherwise achieve. It is thus normally a weapon of the weak. Nevertheless terrorism can also be used by national governments to force their citizens, or their enemies, to submit to the will of the state. In order to generate the maximum fear, and therefore the greatest gains, terrorist attacks must be high-profile and dramatic. Within recent years they have included airplane hijackings, hostage takings, kidnaps, car bombings, and suicide bombings. They have often targeted geographical locations that will draw the greatest attention. To some degree terrorism and guerrilla warfare may be indistinguishable from one another. The Red Brigades in Italy, the Baader-Meinhof gang or Red Army Faction in Germany, the Sendero Luminoso, or Shining Path in Peru, and the ETA, a Basque separatist group in Spain, were among the most notorious terrorist groups of the 1960s, 1970s, and 1980s. Each of these groups attempted to overthrow a government or, at least, to force major changes in state policy.

The twentieth century has many examples of terrorism. Both Nazi Germany and Communist Russia employed state terrorism—extra-legal detention, imprisonment, torture, and execution—to control their populations. Many of the anti-colonial conflicts included the use of terror, including that of the Irish Republican Army against British rule in Northern Ireland; the FLN revolutionary force against the French in Algiers; the Vietcong against the American presence in Vietnam; the Tamil Tigers, seeking a separate territory under their own control for south Indian Tamils in the predominantly Sinhalese, Buddhist nation of Sri Lanka. Some of the most spectacular acts of terrorism were directed against the government and people of Israel for their occupation of Palestinian land. These included numerous airline hijackings and an assault on the Israeli team at the 1972 Munich Olympic games that left most of the Israeli team dead, and left the Olympic ideal of universal peace in tatters. Palestinians, in turn, asserted that Israel used "state terror" in suppressing them in the West Bank and Gaza Strip.

While the goal of terrorism is to frighten citizens and governments into submission, frequently its effects are the opposite. The public may be inflamed against the terrorists and choose to hunt them down and capture or kill them. Nevertheless, terrorism remains a strategy commonly used by those without substantial armies. Because terrorism has been, and can be, used for a wide variety of causes, the commonly used phrase evolved: "One person's terrorist is another person's freedom fighter."

IN PURSUIT OF PEACE

Perhaps the most amazing outcome of the Cold War was that, for the superpowers, it remained mostly cold. Despite all the saber-rattling, all the expense of weaponry, all

UNITED NATIONS AGENCIES

The primary focus of attention in the United Nations has been on peace and war, but its various programs and agencies, many concerned with technology, have provided forums for the resolution of other issues and the promotion of international welfare. The United Nations' key agencies include:

- International Court of Justice (World Court), has dealt with issues such as territorial rights, territorial waters, rights of individuals to asylum, and territorial sovereignty

- Food and Agricultural Organization (FAO), monitors information for improving food supply and distribution

- World Trade Organization (WTO), oversees international trade, settles trade disputes, and negotiates trade liberalization

- World Bank, provides financial assistance to developing nations

- United Nations Educational, Scientific, and Cultural Organization (UNESCO), sponsors research and publication

- United Nations Children's (Emergency) Fund (UNICEF), establishes programs for family welfare

- World Health Organization (WHO), monitors and researches health conditions

- International Labor Organization (ILO), promotes employment and seeks to improve labor conditions and living standards

- World Intellectual Property Organization, protects the interests of the producers of literary, industrial, scientific, and artistic works

- Commission on Human Rights, gathers information and formulates policy on the rights of persons belonging to national, ethnic, religious, and linguistic minorities, including indigenous peoples

the conniving with client states, despite even the Cuban Missile Crisis, the United States and the Soviet Union pulled back from nuclear war. Although they fought proxy wars, they did not confront each other in direct warfare at all. Some observers speculated that the investment in the threat of nuclear war—in Mutually Assured Destruction, MAD—provided a ritualized pose of macho strength on both sides that allowed the superpowers to avoid actual warfare.

Meanwhile, the United Nations was demonstrating some success as an arena for defusing international tensions, for providing peacekeeping missions to global trouble-spots, and for developing programs for international cooperation.

The United Nations: Growth and New Missions

The membership of the United Nations expanded to 159 sovereign states by the end of 1984, the overwhelming majority of the world's nations. It provided a home in which the newly emerging nations could gain political recognition and representation. The diversity of states brought a diversity of ideologies, and UN decisions and activities were subjected to a constant stream of criticism from one point or another on the political spectrum. Yet within that highly politicized framework the organization went on with its work, providing a forum where nations could meet, discuss common goals, and negotiate agreements. It did not always succeed, but such a forum was invaluable. In the mid-1980s, Soviet leader Gorbachev called the United Nations a "unique instrument without which world politics would be inconceivable today," even though it lacked the sovereignty of a government and commanded only such powers as its members chose to vest in it.

The United Nations began dispatching "peacekeeping" armed forces, with military personnel drawn from many different countries, to police zones of potential conflict. These missions were not designed to fight wars, but to maintain the peace in cases in which antagonistic nations agreed that they did want peace, but feared that without an honest "police force" to maintain that peace war would break out (again). United Nations peacekeeping forces were first sent to the Middle East in 1948 to monitor the ceasefire between Israel and its Arab neighbors. They continue in place even today, with separate but related forces on the Lebanese border and on the Golan Heights in Israeli-occupied Syria. A small force was sent to Cyprus in 1964 to maintain a buffer between the Greek Cypriots and the Turkish Cypriots who had been fighting for control of the entire island. They were also sent to Kashmir in 1972 to monitor the Line of Control between the two countries after peace agreements were signed between India and Pakistan to end their 1971 warfare.

On a third level, asserting its global reach, the United Nations undertook many initiatives in organizing for the general welfare of the globe. These included: coordinating the first global census in 1953; sponsoring the first of a series of meetings of criminologists to establish international principles and standards of criminal justice (1955); helping to negotiate a resolution of the Cuban Missile Crisis (1962), the

A girl vaccinated against smallpox, Nigeria, 1969. By 1979, the World Health Organization declared that smallpox had been eradicated. Every human being on earth had been inoculated against it.

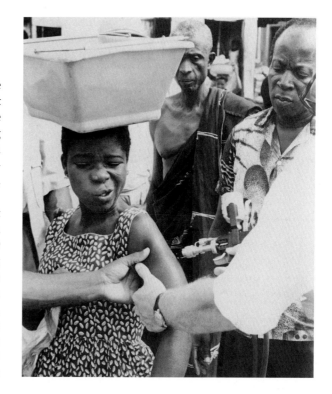

Arab–Israeli war of 1967, and the Iraq–Iran war of 1988. The United Nations also called for the first arms embargo against South Africa (1963) and made it mandatory in 1972. It set up the first rules regulating the laws of the sea, including laws regulating ocean fishing (1970). In 1975, the United Nations sponsored a "Decade for Women," opening with a huge international conference in Mexico City. Later women's conferences followed in Cairo, focusing on reproductive issues, in 1985, and in Beijing in 1995.

In 1979, the World Health Organization (WHO) declared that smallpox had been eradicated by ensuring that every human being on earth had been inoculated against the disease. The WHO was only one of numerous international organizations working officially with the United Nations, many of them created by the UN. Others included: the Food and Agriculture Organization (FAO), which works to increase the productivity of farms, forests, and fisheries; the International Atomic Energy Agency, which monitors the non-proliferation of nuclear weapons and promotes the peaceful use of atomic energy; the International Labor Organization (ILO), which creates labor standards and promotes the

SOURCE

Rachel Carson's Silent Spring

American biologist Rachel Carson's Silent Spring *(1962) exposed the devastating effects on humans, wildlife, and plants caused by the use of toxic chemicals—pesticides, fungicides, and herbicides—in everyday farming and insect control throughout the world. By virtue of its combination of scientific rigor and journalistic vividness,* Silent Spring *is frequently credited as the founding statement of the ecological movement in the twentieth century.*

The most alarming of all man's assaults on the environment is the contamination of air, earth, rivers, and sea with dangerous and even lethal materials. This pollution is for the most part irrecoverable; the chain of evil it initiates not only in the world that must support life but in living tissues is for the most part irreversible. In this now universal contamination of the environment, chemicals are the sinister and little recognized partners of radiation in changing the very nature of the world—the very nature of its life … Chemicals sprayed on croplands or forests or gardens lie long in the soil, entering into living organisms, passing from one to another in a chain of poisoning and death. Or they pass mysteriously by underground streams until they emerge, and through the alchemy of air and sunlight, combine into new forms that kill vegetation, sicken cattle, and work unknown harm on those who drink from once-pure wells. (Carson, pp. 23–4)

Carson's powerful voice evoked responses. For example, after she revealed that DDT, one of the most powerful chemicals used to combat mosquitoes and, thus, malaria, was also poisonous to humans, governments throughout the world generally banned its use. "Green" parties, with strong platforms on ecological issues, began to organize in many countries, especially in western Europe, and more mainstream parties began to adopt some of their programs. Citizens founded organizations such as the World Wildlife Fund and Greenpeace in order to protect the environment. Some farmers began to use natural means of pest control in place of chemicals, and consumers began to seek out "natural" or "organic" foods raised without the use of chemical fertilizers and pesticides.

As Carson pointed out, the political issues, and their implications for the standard of living in each country, were thornier than the technological:

The Earth is one but the world is not. We all depend on one biosphere for sustaining our lives. Yet each community, each country strives for survival and prosperity with little regard for its impact on others. Some consume the Earth's resources at a rate that would leave little for future generations. Others, many more in number, consume far too little and live with the prospect of hunger, squalor, disease, and early death. (Carson, p. 28)

welfare of international workers everywhere; UNESCO, the UN Educational, Scientific, and Cultural Organization, which promotes research and publication; and the World Bank, which extends loans to help poor countries in their development tasks.

Finally, in recognition of the global interdependence of all people in terms of the quality and quantity of air, water, and other basic human necessities found in nature, the UN began its struggle against global ecological destruction with the United Nations Conference on the Human Environment meeting in Stockholm in 1972. Many concerns dominated the agenda, but the main ones were:

- the depletion of the ozone layer through the introduction into the environment of chlorofluorocarbons, formerly a principal chemical in aerosol sprays and in most coolants, such as refrigeration and air-conditioning units;
- global warming, or the greenhouse effect, caused primarily by the introduction into the environment of carbon dioxide, which traps heat in the earth's lower atmosphere, raising temperatures around the globe;
- the destruction of the marine environment through ocean dumping, ship pollution, and the absorption of chemicals into the water table;
- acid rain, the pollution of the atmosphere with chemical pollutants that descend with rainfall;
- deforestation, especially in the tropics, where at least 25 million acres of trees are cut down yearly;
- at a more local level, polluted air, contaminated water, and cigarette smoke are now clearly associated with carcinogens.

In general, more developed countries tended to place the blame for ecological problems on the increase in global population, an increase most marked in the less developed countries. The less developed countries, in response, blamed the more developed as the source of the industries that created the pollution. On the issue of world hunger, the developed countries again pointed to population pressures on food supplies in the less developed countries, while the less developed blamed flaws in the world economy and the food distribution mechanisms, both controlled by the wealthier countries. Agreement was emerging on the need for international cooperation in a stronger UN Environment Program, but the United Nations lacked sovereign power. It could gather information, carry out research, make recommendations, hold conferences, and provide counsel, but it had no powers of enforcement. Implementation depended on the decision of member nations.

Demographics: Health, Migration, Urbanization, and the Green Revolution

Among the first activities of the United Nations was coordinating a global census in 1953. One of the very first specialized agencies that it created was the Food and Agriculture Organization (1945). Soon after came the World Health Organization (1948). The Centre for Human Settlements (Habitat) followed in 1978. All these organizations reflect the importance of the demographic change of the late twentieth century.

The world experienced a population explosion in this period, more than doubling from about 2.5 billion people in 1950 to about 6 billion in 2000. This global population had been only 1.6 billion in 1900, so the growth rate was extraordinary, with the world's population quadrupling in a single century. Alarmed observers spoke of a "population bomb," of a world unable to cope with the population growth, unable to feed the rising population, unable to provide the services needed to sustain them— water, sewerage, public health measures, outdoor resources. The alarm bells clanged even louder as people noted that the population in the less developed, poorer parts of the world was growing much more rapidly than in the wealthier areas, expanding from 1.7 billion in 1950 to 4 billion in 1990. The least developed countries grew fastest of all.

On the other hand, toward the end of the century, birth rates began to decline. Parents exercised family planning. The invention of the birth control pill in 1954 helped in this decision. Among teenagers and young adults the pill was instrumental in altering sexual practices as well as birth rates. In many of the richer countries, especially in Europe, birth rates dropped below replacement levels, that is, more people died than were born.

In the less developed areas birth rates were also decreasing, but much more slowly. China was an exception with a very rapid drop in birth rates as the central government, fearing the results of continuing population growth in their country that already had more than one billion people, implemented a one-family-one-child policy, especially in urban areas. Death rates also decreased almost everywhere, providing for population growth and an increasingly aging population as people lived longer. Japan reached an average expected life span of 80—77 for males, 84 for females.

The surprise, however, was that the world's food supply more than kept pace with the population growth. Per capita food production grew substantially for thirty years from the 1960s, especially as the "green revolution" took root. Under the auspices of the Rockefeller Foundation, agricultural scientists discovered and disseminated new strains of wheat and other grains that increased food productivity by as much as five times. This green revolution saved the world from mass starvation despite continuing population growth. Norman Borlaugh, who directed these efforts, won the Nobel Peace Prize in 1970 for his work.

Many political observers feared, however, that the green revolution would ultimately make the rich richer and the poor poorer, because the new seeds also required

AT A GLANCE : EUROPE AND THE UNITED STATES

DATE	POLITICAL	SOCIAL AND CULTURAL
1950	■ Korean War (1950–53) ■ Egypt nationalizes Suez Canal, establishing independence from Great Britain (1956) ■ Treaties of Rome (1957) lead to establishment of European Community ■ Ghana wins independence from Great Britain (1957)	■ Contraceptive pill becomes available in the late 1950s
1960	■ Cuban Missile Crisis (1962) ■ Algeria wins independence from France (1962) ■ Group of 77 reforms (1964) ■ America involved in Vietnam War (1964–73) ■ Lyndon Johnson sponsors Voting Rights Act (1965) ■ US Defense Department creates internet (1969)	■ Rachel Carson, *Silent Spring* (1962) ■ Betty Friedan, *The Feminine Mystique* (1963) ■ Martin Luther King delivers "I Have a Dream" speech in Washington Mall (1963) ■ Stanley Kubrick, *Dr Strangelove* (1964) ■ Malcolm X assassinated (1965) ■ Apollo II lands on moon (1969)
1970	■ Formation of OPEC (1973) ■ Watergate affair forces resignation of President Nixon (1974)	■ United Nations conference on the Human Environment (1972) ■ Near meltdown of nuclear reactor at Three Mile Island, Penn. (1979)
1980	■ "Star Wars" Strategic Defense Initiative, proposed by President Reagan (1981–8)	■ World Wide Web created (1989)
1990	■ Maastricht Treaty (1991) ■ Bosnian War (1991–5) ■ Russia joins the Group of Seven, forming the G-8 (1997) ■ War in Kosovo (1998–9)	■ United Nations "Earth Summit" in Rio (1992) ■ Around 10 percent of the US population are foreign-born (1997) ■ Internet connection worldwide rises from 3 million people in 1993 to 200 million in 1999 ■ Protests in Seattle, Washington, against the World Trade Organization (1999)

Indian squatter settlement. In the huge cities of the underdeveloped world, shanty towns have sprung up—a makeshift solution to endemic poverty and overcrowding. This squatter settlement in Bombay (population: 11.5 million) might be unsightly, but represents one answer to the acute housing shortage in urban India.

new fertilizers and an abundance of irrigation water and pesticides. Richer farmers could afford to use them, while poorer farmers often lost their land. In addition, over time the chemical fertilizers reduced the fertility of the soil. Finally, because the new seeds were so much more productive than older varieties, farmers began to abandon the multitudes of older seed varieties for the few new ones. Agricultural experts feared that a plant blight affecting even one of these few new seed strains could have catastrophic results. To hold off these frightening prospects, they kept samples of old as well as new crop strains in scientific laboratories where they could be retrieved if necessary.

Population growth was not uniform everywhere. People moved steadily from rural to urban areas and urban growth rates shot up. Estimates suggest that in 1950 about 30 percent of the world's 2.5 billion people, about 750 million people, lived in cities. By 1990, about 45 percent of the world's 6 billion people, about 2.7 billion people, lived in cities. In other words, by 1990, more people lived in the cities of the world than had lived in the entire world in 1900. At the beginning of the century, urbanization was still linked to industrial growth; toward the end of the century, however, the most rapidly growing cities, and, increasingly, the largest of them, were in the poorer, less industrialized areas of the world—for example, São Paulo in Brazil, and Mexico City each with about 15 million in 1990; Mumbai (Bombay) and Kolkata (Calcutta) in India; Buenos Aires in Argentina; Seoul in South Korea; Shanghai and Beijing in China; Lagos in Nigeria; and Rio de Janeiro in Brazil, each with between 10 and 15 million.

Cities strained to provide adequate water, sewerage, electricity, transportation, and public health systems for the newcomers. Many of them lived in slums, and the contrast of slums at the foot of luxury high-rise apartments became a common sight in these third world cities. The images of the slums were sometimes somewhat misleading. Some of the slums were dead-end residential areas. But some were temporary homes of urban immigrants who were trying their best to find a way into jobs that would enable them to improve their conditions. Urban analysts drew a contrast between "slums of despair" and "slums of hope."

Economic Growth

The green revolution helped lead the way to increased economic growth in some of the less developed areas. The great surprise, however, was the extraordinary growth in the "first world," in countries that had been devastated by World War II. The war's biggest losers became the biggest winners in the postwar period.

Western Europe In 1947, Winston Churchill had described Europe as "a rubble heap, a charnel house, a breeding ground for pestilence and hate." But out of the wreckage came several "economic miracles," many of them the result of cooperation between

recent enemies. In 1950, French and West German officials agreed to form the European Coal and Steel
Community and to place these key economic elements under an independent international authority.
The ECSC was born in 1952 with the addition of Italy
and the Benelux countries (Belgium, the Netherlands,
Luxembourg). Its success led to the Treaties of Rome
in 1957 that established the European Economic Community (EEC), or Common Market, to lower, and ultimately remove tariffs among member countries; to
foster the free movement of goods, labor, and capital;
and to establish a single external tariff. The treaties
also established Euratom to create common policies
for the peaceful development of atomic energy.
Agreement on agricultural policy was more difficult
because it involved issues of national self-reliance in
food, the mystique of family farms, and the need to
accommodate rural and urban interests. Nevertheless, in 1962, a Common Agricultural Policy was
also negotiated.

In 1965, the Brussels treaty merged the ECSC, the
EEC, and Euratom, and created the basis of a unified
West European economic administration. Additional
nations were admitted, including Britain, Ireland, and
Denmark in 1973, Greece in 1981, and Spain and Portugal in 1986. Western Europe was moving toward a
"Europe without frontiers," and its economy flourished. Per capita income multiplied. In Germany it
went from $320 in 1949 to over $9,000 in 1978; in Italy
it rose from $638 in 1960 to over $5,000 in 1979. In
West Germany the number of automobiles per 1,000
population rose from 6 in 1948 to 227 in 1970; in
France it rose from 37 to 252.

The recovery of West Germany outpaced the rest of
Europe. Before the war, West Germany had possessed
the most developed infrastructure and a highly trained
professional and technical workforce. With the war over, the country refocused on peaceful production and, with the help of Marshall Plan assistance, rebuilt quickly. By 1960,
it had the highest per capita income in Europe. By the late 1970s, its per capita income
surpassed that of the United States. In tribute to German skills and hard work, the rise
of East Germany, the segment of the country that was incorporated into the Soviet
bloc, was similar. It was the fastest growing economy in eastern and central Europe.

Japan Equally startling was the recovery of Japan. Like Germany, it had an industrial
infrastructure and a highly skilled work force that could shift into production for
peace. The US occupation, 1945–52, improved Japan's competitive position by redistributing land, breaking up the *zaibatsu* holding companies that had controlled the
economy, encouraging the growth of labor unions (until some of them began to
become communist), and restructuring the educational system, opening up high
school and college education for the first time to millions of Japanese students. The
United States also encouraged Japan, as it had Germany, to join it in the Cold War
struggle against the Soviet Union, and Japan benefited both from US investment and

**The Atomium, Euratom headquarters,
Brussels.** As European countries that had
fought each other for centuries began to
forge institutions of cooperation after
1945, collaboration in the peaceful
development of atomic energy took on
both practical and symbolic importance.
The 1957 Treaty of Rome that
established the European Economic
Community (EEC) also created Euratom
to create joint policies. The Atomium at
Euratom headquarters in Brussels
symbolized this new commitment.

from US reliance on the Japanese economy for supplies during the Korean War—and later during the Vietnam War—and for bases for American troops and for their rest-and-relaxation during these wars. Finally, Japan took seriously—more seriously than the United States did at first—the business management advice of the American W. Edwards Deming. Deming called for Total Quality Management (TQM), the highest standards of quality in production, and for including workers from the factory work floor as well as the administrative offices in the planning and evaluation processes for industrial production.

Three events in 1964 symbolized Japan's political reentry into the family of nations and of its resurgent economic power. It was admitted to the Organization for Economic Cooperation and Development (OECD), which until then had included only European and North American nations. The *shinkansen*, or "bullet train," began carrying passengers between Tokyo and Osaka at speeds of 125 miles per hour, the fastest in the world. Tokyo played host to the summer Olympics, winning universal praise for its new architecture, stadiums, hotels, and ability to accommodate and please both the participants and the throngs of spectators. Between 1950 and 1973, Japan's gross domestic product grew at 10.5 percent per year.

In 1973, when the OPEC nations restricted their exports of petroleum and increased the price, creating havoc for most energy reliant countries, Japan replied with the most effective programs for conservation and increased industrial efficiency. It reduced its dependence on oil by 25 percent, it sought oil imports from new sources, and it began to shift into even more knowledge-intensive industries, such as electronics and computers, which are much less energy-dependent. By 1980, Japan's per capita income, at almost $10,000 per year, rivaled America's at $11,400. Economists were beginning to speak of "Japan as Number 1" for the efficiency and quality of its consumer products,

AT A GLANCE: THE SOVIET UNION AND JAPAN

DATE	SOVIET UNION	JAPAN
1950	■ At the 20th Party Congress Nikita Khrushchev officially exposes Stalin's tyranny (1956) ■ Khrushchev crushes Hungarian uprising (1956) ■ Soviet space program puts first rocket, Sputnik, into space (1957)	■ Economic benefits from American participation in the Korean War (1950–53)
1960	■ Alexander Solzhenitsyn, *A Day in the Life of Ivan Denisovich* (1962) ■ Cuban missile crisis (1962) ■ Leonid Brezhnev puts down Czech revolt, or "Prague Spring" (1968)	■ Admitted to Organization for Economic Cooperation and Development (OECD) (1964) ■ Bullet train inaugurated (1964) ■ Hosts Olympics (1964)
1970	■ Lech Walensa begins to organize independent trade union federation, or Solidarity, in Poland (1978) ■ Pope John Paul II visits Poland (1979)	■ Economy hit badly by "oil shocks" (1973)
1980	■ Mikhail Gorbachev institutes policies of glasnost and perestroika on coming to power (1985) ■ Partial meltdown of Chernobyl nuclear power plant (1986)	■ Trade frictions with United States and Europe ■ Equal Employment Opportunity Act (1986) ■ Death of Emperor Hirohito (1989) ■ Hit by recession (1989)
1990	■ Coup attempt against Gorbachev by die-hard communists fails (1991) ■ USSR dissolves into fifteen independent states of which Russia is largest (1991) ■ Boris Yeltsin convenes Constitutional Assembly that produces new constitution for Russia (1993) ■ Russia accorded associate status in NATO (1997) ■ Yeltsin resigns as president (1999)	■ Becomes world's largest donor of foreign aid—$14 billion (1994) ■ East Asian financial collapse (1997)

especially its automobiles, skill in overseas marketing, and prospects for soon surpassing even the United States as the world's leading economy.

Japan's economic success also turned on its ability to bring together government advice and guidance with freely operating private enterprises. Its Ministry for International Trade and Industry (MITI) successfully guided Japanese industries away from "sunset" industries, like steel production, into "sunrise" industries, like automobiles and computers, and helped them find financial investments and marketing opportunities. Several countries of east and Southeast Asia—especially Korea and Taiwan, Japan's former colonies—adopted this model of state guidance and private enterprise with great success. These two nations, along with the city-states of Hong Kong and Singapore, were often referred to as the "Asian tigers" for their aggressive and successful economic development along the Japanese model.

A new model of economic growth was developing, an amalgam of the Russian commitment to planning, the US emphasis on unbridled competition, the wartime experience of national and even international cooperation, and full, guaranteed employment. In the period from the 1950s to the 1980s, the Japanese and their Asian imitators had perhaps gotten it most precisely right, combining free enterprise, state planning and guidance, concern for worker welfare, and a welfare state to provide security. But Japan was not alone in moving toward this model. With different emphases it characterized most of the nations of the industrialized world in these years, often referred to as the "golden years." Even in the face of the "oil shocks" imposed by OPEC in 1973 and again in 1979, these nations could go on building their economies, although somewhat more slowly.

The organization of the economy was not the only change during these years. The goods produced also were new: Private cars and trucks—already very common in America—now became more universal. Plastics and synthetic materials based on polymers replaced conventional materials from cotton and wool in clothing to steel and wood in construction. Television, tape recording, jet engines, radar, transistors and the computers that came from them, nuclear energy—some invented just before World War II, some during the war, some just after—were the new products that helped entice the citizens of wealthier nations, and to some degree even of poorer ones, into a consumer society. Minor differences in product design and quality were the result, and sometimes the goal, of the new competition for the consumer dollar, yen, mark, pound, franc, and lira.

This competition also required that producers—enormous international corporations—invest in research and development in unprecedented volume. Every important company had a division devoted to "R&D" as the value of education and scientific and technological research increased. In conditions of full employment, which became the norm in the wealthier countries in these times, producers also sought labor-saving inventions. Industrial production became more automated everywhere, with Japan leading the way in robotics, the replacement of humans with machines that did relatively detailed and specialized work. More than most countries Japan was driven to robotics by an aging population. As Japan's population had the longest life spans of any nation in the world, its proportion of working age population to the very young and the very old decreased. Robots were part of the answer to this problem.

International Organization

The successes of the "golden years" rested on international cooperation. Part of the institutional base was prepared in 1944 in Bretton Woods, New Hampshire. Representatives of forty nations gathered there to plan a new global economy for the postwar period that would escape the catastrophic depression that had followed World War I.

HOW DO WE KNOW?

The Social Setting of Technology

Even as the developed world created new products, established ever more efficient means for producing them, and designed advertising to convince people that these new products were necessary, a few people raised their voices to ask if this form of economic and technological development was "progress." One of the most prominent of these critics, E.F. Schumacher, declared as the title of his 1973 book: Small Is Beautiful. Schumacher, a British economist, served for twenty years as head of planning at the British Coal Board, but his economic philosophy stressed the small scale rather than the large. He wanted an economics based in nature rather than in the subjugation of nature:

> In the excitement over the unfolding of his scientific and technical powers, modern man has built a system of production that ravishes nature and a type of society that mutilates man ... The development of production and the acquisition of wealth have thus become the highest goals of the modern world in relation to which all other goals, no matter how much lip-service may still be paid to them have come to take second place ... This is the philosophy of materialism, and it is this philosophy—or metaphysic—which is being challenged by events ... It is of little use trying to suppress terrorism if the production of deadly devices continues to be deemed a legitimate employment of man's creative powers ... Equally, the chance of mitigating the rate of resource depletion or of bringing harmony into the relationships between those in possession of wealth and power and those without is non-existent as long as there is no idea anywhere of enough being good and more-than-enough being evil.

Schumacher briefly explored the history of the economics profession to chart its transformation. The first professorship in political economy was endowed at Oxford in 1825, and from the beginning philanthropists and economists alike asked what should be its scope; many, including Schumacher, argued that economics should be subservient to ethics. In 1969, the Nobel Prize for "economic science" was established, suggesting that this discipline would not rank second to any other. Schumacher, however, argued that the earlier evaluation was more appropriate.

Arnold Pacey, a British physicist who became an historian, also argued that technological developments were most effective when they fit the society that was adopting them. Pacey was not directly arguing ethics, as Schumacher was, but his idea that inventions should fit the needs of society, and the society's ability to absorb them, agreed with Schumacher that technological "development" should not proceed for its own sake, but rather for the sake of society. In an era of rapid technological development, when third world nations frequently wanted the same technology for war and for peace as the first world had, the moral principles expressed directly by Schumacher and indirectly by Pacey set up a challenge: What would be the appropriate scale for the technology to be adopted? The argument for appropriate scale technology was made forcefully, in practical terms, by Mahatma Gandhi of India, as we shall see in the next chapter.

- Was Schumacher correct that technological "progress" is pursued, at least some of the time, simply for the purpose of making a profit, whether or not new technology is needed? Please explain with examples.
- Have you examples of technologies that seem appropriate for the people and societies that use them and examples of technologies that seem inappropriate?
- How important do you think it is to ask about the appropriate scale of technology? Can you give an example of such a question in your own life?

They created three new institutions: the International Monetary Fund (IMF), the International Bank for Reconstruction and Development (World Bank), and the General Agreement on Tariffs and Trade (GATT). The IMF provided short-term loans for countries that were having difficulty meeting their balance of payment obligations. These were designed for moments of extreme, but short-term, crisis. The first goal of the World Bank was to provide capital for rebuilding war torn nations. By the late 1960s and 1970s, as European nations had recovered from the economic devastation of the war, the bank increasingly turned to the developmental needs of the third world, although not to their short-term needs for relief. The GATT was designed to promote world trade by bringing down tariffs among all member nations. Until the 1980s all of these organizations were generally praised for their achievements among the capitalist nations of the world. The communist bloc—both the European nations in the Soviet sphere and China after the communist revolution—refused to participate because they did not trust the open market as a means of economic decision making. They rejected the capitalist laws of supply and demand in favor of state planning and therefore could not accept the Bretton Woods principles. In this sense, Bretton Woods helped to divide the world into opposing blocs, even as it proved successful for the West.

Third world nations were not at first much affected by the new international financial agreements, but as they entered more fully into the global economy in the 1980s and 1990s they would raise new issues, as we shall see in Chapter 23. A preview of some of the issues to be raised, however, came with the "oil shocks" created by OPEC in 1973. The Organization of Petroleum Exporting Countries had been formed in 1960, but it first used its economic muscle in international politics during the 1973 Yom Kippur War between Israel and its Arab neighbors. In order to force the West, and especially the United States, to abandon its support for Israel, OPEC embargoed its oil exports to the United States and any other countries that supported Israel. Americans felt the effects personally as they waited in long lines at the pumps for available gasoline. American industry, lacking energy, cut production and laid off workers. Globally the cost of oil quadrupled, forcing similar cutbacks elsewhere. Most third world nations are not oil producers and they were actually hurt most of all, since they could least afford the higher prices and shorter supplies.

To some degree OPEC achieved its political aims. Some companies stopped doing business with Israel, and France agreed to sell advanced weapons to some Arab countries in order to gain assured access to oil supplies. Over time, the industrialized nations learned to cope. Through conservation and the creation and use of more energy-efficient machinery they reduced their oil dependency. To some degree they switched to other fuels. They also found that the Arab oil-rich countries, seeking investment opportunities for their newfound profits, often invested them in first world countries, including the United States. The "oil shocks" demonstrated, however, that at least some third world countries were positioned to demand greater voice in the world economy, and the first world nations would have to listen.

NGOs AND TRANSNATIONALS

Thus far we have mostly discussed governments—making war, making peace, intervening in economies and technologies. The second half of the twentieth century also saw an enormous growth in the number and power of non-governmental organizations (NGOs). They changed the way nations and economies carried out their work.

Normally, the term NGO does not include private businesses, but they too are NGOs, and they created in the later years of the twentieth century not only multinational corporations but even transnational corporations. Multinationals were companies headquartered in one nation but operating in several. By the late twentieth century, America alone had tens of thousands of such corporations. Transnational corporations also operated in many countries, but had no clear headquarters. Sometimes, for financial purposes, often to evade taxes, they placed much of their financial structure in small, relatively unregulated nations, like the Cayman Islands or Curaçao. Regulating and policing the transnationals was not easy. Also, while multinational corporations might finally have to balance their desire for bottom-line profits against the need to live within the laws and values of their home country, transnationals had no other allegiances than profit. Transnational business became more competitive, but less responsive to values other than profit.

At the same time, more conventional non-governmental organizations, much smaller to be sure, also took shape. The World Wildlife Fund, for example, founded in the 1950s, now has more than 5 million members and works in more than one hundred countries. It became the world's largest privately financed conservation organization working to conserve the world's biological diversity, advocate for the use of renewable natural resources in sustainable fashion, and promote the reduction of pollution and wasteful consumption.

Amnesty International grew into a worldwide movement of people with close to 2 million supporters dedicated to the protection and promotion of human rights. Amnesty took as its model the Universal Declaration of Human Rights. It acted to stop grave abuses of the rights of physical and mental integrity, freedom of conscience and expression, and freedom from discrimination. It campaigned to free prisoners of conscience, ensure fair trials for political prisoners, protect refugees, abolish the death penalty, end political killings, and torture. It sought to bring to justice those responsible for human rights violations. It publicized its findings in order to bring public pressure on governments, armed political groups, companies, and others in order to stop the abuses. It worked "within a global community of organizations to ensure broad support and respect for all human rights." In order to maintain its independence of action, Amnesty International accepted no government funding.

Oxfam, originally the Oxford Committee for Famine Relief, traces its origins to a group of Quaker intellectuals, social activists, and Oxford University academics who founded an organization to provide famine relief to Greece during World War II. In the immediate postwar years it directed its attention to European needs, but as early as 1951 it extended famine relief to people in India, and in 1953 to the homeless, hungry, and orphaned at the end of the Korean War. In the 1960s, Oxfam turned primarily to third-world needs. It focused less on famine relief and more on supplying the tools by which people could improve their living standards. Self-help programs emphasized communities improving their own water supplies, farming practices, and health provisions. Oxfam also began to prepare educational materials to explain in the first world the root causes of poverty and suffering, the connections between the first and third worlds, and the role that first world people could play in improving the physical conditions of life in the third world. It began its public lobbying for government and private assistance in development programs throughout the third world and began establishing field offices in the third world to help implement these self-help programs. In 1963, Oxfam Canada was established, the first of several affiliated national Oxfam committees. Oxfam America was established in 1970. Like the other Oxfams, it is a grassroots, broad-based organization that accepts no government funding.

These three well-known organizations are only a few of the thousands of multinational and transnational NGOs. Many of the larger ones are organizations of trade unionists, religious groups, sports enthusiasts, and artists. The Soviet Union dissolved, for example, in part because of international labor support for Lech Walesa's Solidarity Movement and because Cardinal Wojtyla was elevated to the position of pope in the Roman Catholic Church. Many of the same interests that created international governmental and business organizations, and much of the same technology that made them possible, also led to the creation of vast numbers of non-governmental organizations, through which common people created the networks for international contact, cooperation, and action.

Voluntary organizations testified to the importance of grassroots participation in public life and to the ability of small groups of people to affect even the largest of governments and corporations. Through the steady work of NGOs and through the occasional outbursts of public demonstrations, common people expressed their wishes.

LEGACIES OF THE COLD WAR, DECOLONIZATION, ECONOMIC AND SOCIAL DEVELOPMENT WHAT DIFFERENCE DO THEY MAKE?

A healthy skepticism colors the transformations of the twentieth century. "Winners" gained more wealth, power, and convenience than had ever been known. Hundreds of millions of people, long colonized, won their political independence. Yet even the most fortunate often felt insecure, for the wars of the century were the bloodiest ever, the weaponry the most powerful and frightening, carrying the potential to destroy all human life. Governments had shown the power not only to fight wartime enemies but also to attack, imprison, exile, and destroy masses of their own citizens. Transportation and communication meant that almost no area of the world was unaffected by others. Serious questions arose as to the ability of the earth and the seas to withstand the pressures of the new technologies on planetary resources. Even for "winners," this was an age of anxiety.

For those less fortunate, poverty, servitude, ill-health, and hunger remained the common fate. Even though experts declared that new technologies provided the capacity to feed the entire, growing population of the earth, governmental policies, national and international, did not provide the necessary legal and technological means of distribution.

The postwar years, however, seemed to favor the optimists over the pessimists. Global wars stopped. Despite proxy wars, the nuclear weapons of the Cold War remained unused. Almost all colonies gained their independence. The United Nations organization offered a global forum in which the peoples of the world could come together to address their common needs. The purview of the UN was continually extended to include not only conflict resolution, peace keeping, and international law, but also issues of education, child welfare, the condition of women, labor relations, human rights, ecology, settlements patterns, and appropriate technologies. The world's economy—its production of food as well as of consumer goods—expanded more rapidly than its population. Some observers called the postwar years of reconstruction, decolonization, and economic expansion a golden era.

Review Questions

- What were the reasons for the Cold War competition between the USA and the USSR?
- Why did decolonization take place so quickly once the process had begun?
- How did the superpowers and the new nations attempt to use one another for their own benefit? Please give examples.
- What function do voluntary organizations serve in a society? Give examples of how a voluntary organization has changed the policies of a country.
- Why did ecological issues rise to such great importance in the period 1945–85? Give some examples of the issues.

- Many observers have termed the period 1945–73 in western Europe especially a "golden age." Why? Would the same term hold for Africa, Asia, or Latin America in that period? Why or why not?

Suggested Readings

PRINCIPAL SOURCES

Applebaum, Anne. *Gulag. A History* (New York: Doubleday Books, 2003). A comprehensive scholarly account, stressing the economic importance of the Gulag and humman relations inside it. Complements Solzhenitsyn's first-person, fictionalized account.

Bulliet, Richard W., ed. *The Columbia History of the 20th Century* (New York: Columbia University Press, 1998). Comprehensive and thoughtful collection of articles by theme rather than chronology.

Burns, E. Bradford. *Latin America: A Concise Interpretive History* (Englewood Cliffs, NJ, 7th ed., 2001). A standard comprehensive, thematic approach, examines social and political relationships. Especially strong on Brazil.

Carson, Rachel. *Silent Spring* (New York: Penguin Books, 1965). An attack on the chemical and pesticide industries. The most important single book in launching the modern ecological movement.,

Dower, John. *Embracing Defeat* (New York: W.W. Norton, 2000). A comprehensive, wonderfully readable story of America's occupation of Japan, 1945–52. Emphasizes the human contacts more than the institutional changes.

Fieldhouse, D.K. *Black Africa 1945–1980* (London: Allen and Unwin, 1986). An attempt to understand what has gone wrong in independent Africa, and why.

Friedman, Thomas. *From Beirut to Jerusalem* (New York: Farrar, Straus and Giroux, 1989). Presentation of the continuing Israeli-Arab hostility by a leading *New York Times* reporter.

Goncharov, Sergei N., John W. Lewis, and Xue Litai. *Uncertain Partners: Stalin, Mao, and the Korean War* (Stanford: Stanford University Press, 1993). Reveals the bargaining and ultimately the hostility between the communist leaders.

Harden, Blaine. *Dispatches from a Fragile Continent* (Boston: Houghton Mifflin, 1990). *Washington Post* bureau chief in sub-Saharan Africa calls it the way he sees it, and not much is very pleasant or elevating.

Keen, Benjamin. *A History of Latin America*, 2 vols. (Boston: Houghton Mifflin, 7th ed., 2004). Good, standard comprehensive coverage. Now expanded into two volumes.

Kenez, Peter. *A History of the Soviet Union from the Beginning to the End* (Cambridge: Cambridge University Press, 1999). A study and evaluation of principal institutions and their impact. Thoughtful analyses and evaluations.

Kennedy, Paul. *The Rise and Fall of the Great Powers* (New York: Random House, 1987). Kennedy's focus on the balance between economic health and military preparedness among the great powers provides a fascinating theme and an abundance of useful data.

Morris, Benny. *The Birth of the Palestinian Refugee Problem 1947–1949* (Cambridge: Cambridge University Press, 1988). A major revisionist historian indicts the Israelis for driving many Palestinians out of their homes.

Morris, Benny. *Righteous Victims: A History of the Zionist-Arab Conflict, 1881–1999* (New York; Knopf, 1999). Revisionist historian finds plenty of blame to go around for the continuing Arab-Israeli struggle and the inability to resolve it.

Service, Robert. *A History of Twentieth Century Russia* (Cambridge: Harvard University Press, 1997). The story told largely through the actions and statements of Russia's leaders.

Sigmund, Paul, ed. *The Ideologies of the Developing Nations* (New York: Praeger Publishers, 2nd rev. ed., 1972). Excellent selection of observations, analyses, and manifestos by leaders from throughout the third world in its heyday.

Solzhenitsyn, Alexander. *The Gulag Archipelago*, 3 vols. (New York: Harper and Row, 1974–8). The terrifying revelations of the prison system at the base of Soviet government control of its citizens.

Stavrianos, Leften. *Global Rift* (New York: Morrow, 1981). A left-wing interpretation of the divisions between the rich and poor nations of the world, and what caused it.

Vogel, Ezra. *The Four Little Dragons: The Spread of Industrialization in East Asia* (Cambridge: MA: Harvard University Press, 1991). Korea, Taiwan, Singapore, and Hong Kong demonstrated that countries could leap from the third world to the first. Vogel shows how they did it.

ADDITIONAL SOURCES

Andrea, Alfred and James H. Overfield, eds. *The Human Record*, Vol. 2 (Boston: Houghton Mifflin, 3rd ed., 1998).

Avishai, Bernard. *The Tragedy of Zionism* (New York: Farrar Straus and Giroux, 1985). Covers the impact on the Arab world as well as the Jewish.

Black, Maggie. *A Cause for Our Time: Oxfam, the First Fifty Years* (Oxford: Oxford University Press, 1992). Recounts the history of the organization, the tough decisions it has made, and its increasing influence in development planning.

Duus, Peter. *Modern Japan* (Boston: Houghton Mifflin, 2nd ed., 1998). Excellent, comprehensive text.

Fanon, Frantz. *The Wretched of the Earth*, trans. by Constance Farrington (New York: Grove Press, 1963). Classic statement of the psychological wounds of colonialism. Calls for anti-colonial violence as a means of healing.

Gibney, Frank. *Japan: The Fragile Superpower* (Tokyo: Charles E. Tuttle, 3rd rev. ed., 1996). Captures both the strengths, and the surprising weaknesses, of Japan near the end of the twentieth century.

Hobsbawm, Eric. *The Age of Extremes: A History of the World, 1914–1991* (New York: Pantheon Books, 1994). The dean of living historians surveys the scene politically, economically, and culturally. Engagingly written.

International Institute for Environment and Development and the World Resources Institute. *World Resources 1987* (New York: Basic Books, 1987). Basic report with abundant quantitative information.

Johnson, Hazel and Henry Bernstein, eds. *Third World Lives of Struggle* (London: Heinemann Educational Books, 1982). Marvelous and touching selection of biographical and autobiographical sketches of people's lives with some poetry and interpretive articles as well.

Kaufman, Burton I. *The Korean Conflict* (Westport, CN: Greenwood Press, 1999). Brief history and analysis of the war supported by primary documents and biographical sketches.

Kochan, Lionel and Richard Abraham. *The Making of Modern Russia* (London: Penguin Books, 1983). Useful on the Khrushchev and Brezhnev years.

Nkrumah, Kwame. *Ghana: The Autobiography of Kwame Nkrumah* (New York: Thomas Nelson and Sons, 1957). Leader of the first black African country to achieve independence from British rule tells his story, up to 1957.

Nugent, Neill. *The Government and Politics of the European Union* (Durham, NC: Duke University Press, 5th ed., 2003). Dry but comprehensive, thorough examination of the major institutions and their significance.

Power, Jonathan. *Like Water on Stone: The Story of Amnesty International* (Boston: Northeastern University Press, 2001). Recounts the struggles of this pre-eminent international human rights organization.

Robinson, Francis. *Atlas of the Islamic World since 1500* (New York: Facts on File, 1982). Basic reference guide to history as well as geography, with excellent text, maps, and selected topics.

◉ World History Documents CD-ROM

26.1 Joseph Stalin: *The Soviet Victory: Capitalism versus Communism* (February 1946)
26.2 Sir Winston Churchill: *An Iron Curtain Has Descended Across the Continent* (March 1946)
26.3 Harry S. Truman: *The Truman Doctrine* (March 1947)
26.4 George C. Marshall: *The Marshall Plan* (June 1947)
26.5 Korea: The Thirty-eighth Parallel
26.6 General Douglas MacArthur: Report to Congress, April 19, 1951: *Old Soldiers Never Die*
26.7 Henry A. Myers: *East Berliners Rise Up Against Soviet Oppression*, A Personal Account
26.8 Nikita Khrushchev: *The Victory of Communism Is Inevitable!*: Speech to the 22nd Communist Party Congress (1962)
27.1 Mohandas K. Gandhi
27.2 Jawaharlal Nehru: Gandhi and Nehru: *Two Utterly Different Standpoints*
27.3 Frantz Fanon: *The Wretched of the Earth*
27.4 Kwame Nkrumah: *I Speak of Freedom: A Statement of African Ideology*
27.5 Israel's Proclamation of Independence
27.6 Palestinian Declaration of Independence
27.7 Views of a Viet Cong Official
27.8 An American Prisoner of War

CHINA AND INDIA

POSTWAR DEVELOPMENTS, 1914–91

KEY TOPICS
- China, 1925–89
- India, 1914–91
- Comparing China and India: What Difference Does It Make?

Home to some of the world's most ancient and influential civilizations, China and India are almost worlds in themselves. Both are vast and densely populated countries containing, together, some 40 percent of the world's population. Both were subject to European colonial domination in the nineteenth and early twentieth centuries. Both gained full political independence in the middle of the twentieth century and both were, and remain, predominantly agrarian countries. Nevertheless they followed very different paths of development. Because of their sheer size, the similarity of many of their circumstances, and the contrast in their decisions on development, we devote a full chapter to them.

At the turn of the twentieth century China, with 400 million people, contained about one-fourth of the world's population. The India of the British Empire—which included today's Pakistan and Bangladesh—contained about one-sixth, about 285 million people. Both countries were overwhelmingly agricultural, with populations about 80 to 85 percent rural. Both were vast in territory and densely populated.

Politically, India was ruled as a colony of Britain until 1947. China was not administered directly by foreign powers, but Britain, France, Russia, Germany, and Japan had great economic and cultural control over the huge nation and directly ruled small portions of it. Under British rule, India had a single central administration, despite its diverse ethnicities, languages, religions, castes, and local princes. China, on the other hand, was without an effective central government through most of the first half of the century, suffering both civil war and invasion from Japan.

Both countries sought independence from foreign control. Both began these struggles as protest movements from within their modern sectors, envisioning an industrialized, bureaucratized future, led by professional men trained in modern administrative, educational, journalistic, legal, and military skills. As they began to gain success, however, leaders of the struggle for independence in both countries found this urban- and professional-based organization inadequate. They turned instead to mass movements of the peasantry and common people, who were the overwhelming majority of the population.

India and China attained independent statehood at about the same time. India won independence from Britain in 1947. After Japan was defeated in World War II, China continued its nationwide communist revolution that drove out foreign powers and unified almost the entire country in 1949 (except for Taiwan, Hong Kong, and Macao). Then the two countries chose different strategies of development. Influenced by British colonial legacies and by its own heterogeneity, India chose democratic electoral politics and a mixed socialist–capitalist economy, with strong cultural ties to the Western democracies and some military links to the Soviet Union. In China, on the other hand, a victorious communist army asserted strong central control after years of warfare. At first China looked to the Soviet Union for advice and assistance, but soon came into conflict with these mentors on issues of ideology, policy, and national self-interest. Despite the central role of the peasantry in attaining independence, both countries quickly turned toward developing their cities and industries.

Opposite **Jawaharlal Nehru and Zhou Enlai, 1954.** Prime Minister Nehru (right) is cheered by crowds as he arrives on a State Visit to Red China.

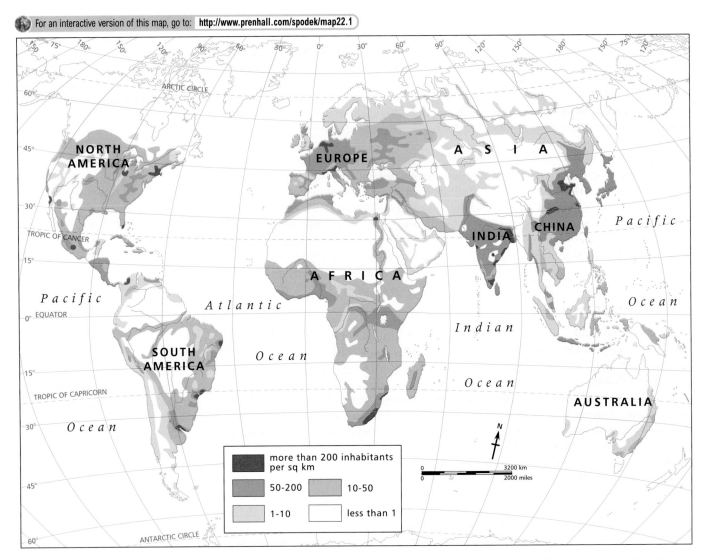

For an interactive version of this map, go to: http://www.prenhall.com/spodek/map22.1

Legend:
- more than 200 inhabitants per sq km
- 50-200
- 10-50
- 1-10
- less than 1

World population distribution today. While the bulk of the world's population lives, as always, in coastal regions or along river valleys, the rapid rise in urbanism over the last century has created enormous imbalances as cities attract economic migrants from their hinterlands and from abroad. Some areas, like Europe, are so urbanized that their entire surface has high densities; others, like China and India, are so packed that even rural areas house urban densities. The only areas with low densities are those ecologically difficult for human life—deserts, mountains, frozen regions.

Both countries also had large rural populations that made industrialization along Western lines, based on smaller populations and urban settings, difficult. They turned to models of technology that were appropriate for their populations and the rural conditions. Often relying on models of development that were different from those used in the West, both countries have become formidable competitors with Europe and the United States in the twenty-first century in spite of their alternate strategies of development.

CHINA, 1925–89

Prelude to Revolution

We have already discussed in Chapter 19 the 1911 revolution that ended China's 2,000-year-old empire, and China's subsequent descent into political and military chaos as local warlords seized control of various regions of the country. We have seen two groups emerging from these divisions as the most powerful and the most likely to subdue the warlords and consolidate a national government: the Guomindang (GMD, National People's Party), led by Chiang Kai-shek (Jiang Jieshi, 1887–1975), and the communists commanded by Mao Zedong (1893–1976). Chiang began as a military commander and later sought to build a government based on his GMD party. Mao began as a Communist Party organizer and later built an army. Both leaders revered Sun Yat-sen (1866–1925) and accepted his "Three People's Principles" as guidelines for their political and economic programs, but they interpreted Sun's teachings quite differently. Where Chiang emphasized the role of businessmen, international alliances, and individual initiative, Mao stressed the peasant farmer, community organization, and indigenous institutions. The two men and their parties fought for control in a bitter civil war that festered for a quarter century following Sun's death in 1925. Both learned that "in a country ruled and plundered by marauding warlord armies, it was naked military power that was crucial in determining the direction of political events" (Meisner, p. 21). In Mao's blunt words: "political power grows out of the barrel of a gun."

Power Struggles, 1925–37

Chiang Kai-shek and the Guomindang Chiang had studied in a Japanese military academy, fought in the 1911 revolution to overthrow the Manchu government, and rose to command China's own new military academy near Guangzhou, established with Soviet financing. After Sun's death, he succeeded to the leadership of the GMD. A staunch advocate of the neo-Confucian New Life movement in the 1930s, Chiang wrote *China's Destiny* in 1943 to reaffirm the conservative virtues of China's indigenous, hierarchical, genteel culture. Yet he also became a Methodist, as Sun had. Also like Sun, Chiang married a Chinese Christian woman (who, also like Sun's wife, was a sister of a wealthy Chinese industrialist), and valued contributions of foreign Christians in China's economic modernization.

Chiang maintained a wide and diverse array of close personal, professional, and financial connections with Shanghai underworld figures, Soviet Comintern agents, Western businessmen, and Christian missionaries. As China dissolved into warlordism, Chiang was named commander-in-chief of the GMD's National Revolutionary Army, and for a quarter of a century he fought to unify China under his own control against three powerful enemies: the warlords; the Japanese, who had invaded Manchuria in 1931 and China itself in 1937; and the communists.

Foreign powers in the treaty ports monitored China's shifting fortunes with considerable self-interest. By 1931, foreigners had invested US$3.25 billion in China, slightly more than double the amount in 1914; which was, in turn, slightly more than double that in 1902. Foreign loans financed Chinese railways and heavy industry, and foreigners held three-fourths of all investments in shipping, almost half of the cotton spindles, and 80–90 percent of the coal mines. Through the early 1920s, the politicization and unionization of industrial workers encouraged many strikes, to which the employers, many of them foreigners, often responded with violence. The employers wanted a compliant government that would help them break the strikes. Most of these employers and foreign investors aided Chiang, hoping to manipulate him as the leader closest to their interests. During the period 1929 to 1937, they lent him much of the money needed to cover the GMD government's annual deficits.

Foreign-based Christian missionaries and educational institutions also supported the GMD, attracted partly by Chiang's own Christian affiliation. The YMCA movement claimed 54,000 members in 1922. In the early 1920s, some 12,000 Christian

AT A GLANCE: CHINA AND INDIA

DATE	CHINA	INDIA
1900	■ Boxer Rebellion against Western influence is suppressed by foreign troops (1900)	■ Mohandas Karamchand Gandhi publishes *Hind Swaraj*, or Indian Home Rule (1909)
1910	■ 1911 Revolution ends Manchu dynasty and 2,000 years of imperial rule ■ Yuan Shihkai elected premier (1911); dies 1916 ■ Warlords battle throughout China ■ May 4th Movement (1919)	■ Gandhi returns from South Africa and establishes new ashram in Ahmedabad (1915) ■ Government of India Act creates dual British/Indian government (1919) ■ British crack down on freedom of the press and assembly in the Rowlatt Acts (1919) ■ Amritsar (Jalianwala Bagh) massacre (1919)
1920	■ Chinese Communist Party formed (1921) ■ Sun Yat-sen dies (1925) ■ Guomindang (GMD) and Communists vie for power (1925–49) ■ Chiang Kai-shek captures Beijing (1927–8); rules from Nanjing ■ Mao's Report on Hunan Peasant Movement (1927)	■ Non-cooperation campaign boycotts British interests (1920–2) ■ Gandhi fasts for twenty-one days to promote Hindu–Muslim unity (1924)
1930	■ Mao Zedong leads Communists on the Long March, from Jiangxi to Yan'an (1934) ■ Japanese seize Manchuria (1931) and go on to invade China proper (1937) ■ Communists kidnap Chiang to gain cooperation in the war against Japan (1936)	■ Salt March campaign (1930–2) ■ Gandhi outflanks socialists by persuading Jawaharlal Nehru to postpone land redistribution ■ Congress appoints National Planning Commission (1938)
1940	■ Japan surrenders; civil war resumes (1945) ■ Foundation of the Communist People's Republic of China (1949) ■ Foreigners expelled (1949)	■ "Quit India" campaign (1942) ■ Independence from Great Britain is followed by partition of the subcontinent (1947)
1950	■ China invades and colonizes Tibet (1950) ■ Korean War (1950–3) ■ "100 Flowers Campaign" briefly permits some freedom of expression (1956–7) ■ Mao initiates "Great Leap Forward" experiment (1958–60)	■ Policy of protective discrimination reserves jobs for untouchable castes (1955) ■ Hindu Marriage Act (1955) and Hindu Succession Act (1956) increase rights for women
1960	■ Diplomatic relations with Russia are severed (1961) ■ Sino-Indian border war (1962) ■ Cultural Revolution initiates party purges and reignites revolutionary zeal; formation of Red Guard (1966)	■ Death of Nehru (1964)
1970	■ China joins United Nations (1971) ■ Groundbreaking visit to China by President Nixon (1972) ■ Mao dies; "Gang of Four" arrested (1976) ■ Deng Xiaoping comes to power; economic liberalization (1979) ■ One family, one child policy (1980)	■ Civil war leads to creation of Bangladesh on land of East Pakistan (1971) ■ Prime Minister Indira Gandhi asserts dictatorial powers during "Emergency Rule" (1975–7) ■ Policy of forced sterilization (1975–7)
1980	■ China joins World Bank and the International Monetary Fund (1980) ■ Students demonstrating in Tiananmen Square are killed by soldiers (1989)	■ Indira Gandhi assassinated (1984)
1990	■ Hong Kong reverts to Chinese sovereignty after 155 years as a British colony (1997) ■ Macao returned to China by Portugal (1999) ■ China voted "most favored nation" trading status by US (2000)	■ Rajiv Gandhi assassinated (1991) ■ Prime Minister P.V. Narasimha Rao lowers tariffs and begins to welcome foreign investments (1991) ■ Pakistan and India test nuclear devices in violation of international treaties (1998) ■ Population reaches 1 billion (1999)

missionaries, slightly more Protestants than Catholics, served in China. Christian and foreign colleges enrolled 4,000 of the 35,000 students in Chinese colleges in 1922, and 9 percent of their students were women. Much Western culture and literature was incorporated in the new curricula of China's universities. Chinese students and intellectuals were eager to hear voices from the West and East, and such luminaries as

Bertrand Russell, John Dewey, Albert Einstein, and Rabindranath Tagore visited and lectured widely.

With the support of Western business and cultural leaders, and of the Soviet Comintern as well, Chiang undertook to defeat the warlords and to reestablish a viable central government. Through the great northern expedition from Guangzhou, Chiang captured Beijing in 1927–8, established his own capital in Nanjing on the lower Yangzi River, and began to consolidate GMD power over China.

Despite these early military victories, Chiang ultimately failed. His government, permeated by corruption, alienated the peasantry by forging alliances with exploitative landlords. High officials sold off provisions intended to feed and clothe China's starving armed forces. When the Japanese invasion of 1937 forced Chiang's retreat into the remote mountainous reaches of Chongqing (Chungking), the communists persuaded the Chinese peasants that they, not the GMD, could best fight off the Japanese and represent peasant interests in a free China.

Mao Zedong, Peasant Revolt, and the Communist Party The communist leader, Mao Zedong (1893–1976), Sun's other principal successor, shared his goals of a strong, united, independent China and the improvement of the people's livelihood, but his background was quite different from Sun's and from Chiang's. First, the 1911 revolution, in which he participated, was over by the time he was eighteen, and was therefore no longer an issue. Second, Mao's personal experience was limited to China. Although he read widely in Western as well as Chinese literature and philosophy, his first travel outside China, a visit to the Soviet Union, came only in 1949. Other Chinese students had traveled to Europe during World War I, and he had helped them. For himself, however, he explained, "I did not want to go to Europe. I felt that I did not know enough about my own country, and that my time could be more profitably spent in China" (Snow, p. 149).

Third, Mao had little experience of the Western business and missionary establishments in China. His own formative experiences were in the countryside and in educational institutions. Compared with both Sun and Chiang, Mao cared little for China's reputation in the West but much for the quality of life of the Chinese peasant. He had grown up on his father's farm in Hunan province, where he learned at first hand of the exploitation of the peasant, in part through the oppressive strategies of his own father, who rose from poverty to become a middle-level farmer and small-scale trader. Mao later recounted that he left this life to become an athletic, serious, politically committed student, reading widely, and consolidating a core group of similarly inclined young men: "My friends and I preferred to talk only of large matters—the nature of men, of human society, of China, the world, and the universe! … We also became ardent physical culturists" (Snow, p. 146).

By 1919, Mao's educational quests had brought him to Beijing (Peking) University, just as China's resentment against foreign imperialism was boiling over. The peace treaties of World War I

Poster from 1960 showing Mao Zedong and supporters of the Cultural Revolution, each holding a copy of Mao's teachings, the "Little Red Book." Mao realized early on that the peasantry could carry forward the ideals of communism, even when the workers' movement was destroyed by Chiang Kai-shek. Mao was determined to eliminate "foreign dogmatism" and was against copying the Soviet blueprint for communism. His unique application of Marxism to China's needs gave rise to a mass following.

assigned Germany's holdings in the Shandong Peninsula of north China to Japan rather than returning them to China. In Paris, indignant Chinese protestors physically blocked their nation's delegates from attending the signing ceremonies, and thus China never did sign the peace agreements. Within China, protests against the treaties by students and others began on May 4, 1919, engendering a continuing critique of China's international humiliation, the apparent bankruptcy of its historical traditions, and the content of its cultural links to the West. The "May Fourth Movement" also helped to sow the seeds of the Chinese Communist Party (CCP), which came to fruition in 1921 following discussions between Chinese revolutionaries and representatives of the newly formed Comintern of the USSR. At that time, Mao was a participant in the study group of Li Dazhao, chief librarian of Beijing University and one of the founders of the CCP. In a statement quite unusual for a Chinese intellectual, Li had already proclaimed the importance of the peasantry and called on the university students to help them to mobilize:

> Our China is a rural nation and most of the laboring class is made up of peasants. If they are not liberated, then our whole nation will not be liberated ... Go out and develop them and cause them to know [that they should] demand liberation, speak out about their sufferings, throw off their ignorance and be people who will themselves plan their own lives. (Spence, p. 308)

Peasant Organization and Guerrilla Warfare When Mao joined the party he began organizing workers in the industrial plants of the Wuhan region, but in 1925 he was reassigned to peasant organization in his native Hunan. Despite the orthodox Marxist doctrines of Comintern advisers, Mao in Hunan came to see the Chinese peasantry, rather than the proletariat, as China's revolutionary vanguard. In terms of technology, he abandoned the emphasis on large-scale industrial planning and sought instead local solutions to local problems through locally developed, appropriate rural technologies. Mao's enthusiastic and influential, but polemical and doctrinaire, 1927 report on the Hunan peasant movement updated Li's rural emphasis:

> the broad peasant masses have risen to fulfill their historic mission ... the democratic forces in the rural areas have risen to overthrow the rural feudal power. The patriarchal-feudal class of local bullies, bad gentry, and lawless landlords has formed the basis of autocratic government for thousands of years, the cornerstone of imperialism, warlordism and corrupt officialdom. To overthrow this feudal power is the real objective of the national revolution ... The leadership of the poor peasants is absolutely necessary. Without the poor peasants there can be no revolution. (de Bary, p. 869)

The peasants had to use their strength to overthrow the authority of the landlords. This revolution required violence.

Mao's enemies had their own tools of violence. While Mao was organizing peasants in the 1920s, Jiang was massacring the core of the revolutionary proletariat. As Chiang completed the northern expedition and consolidated his control over the warlords, he turned, in alliance with the international business community and without excessive objection from the Comintern, to murdering thousands of communist workers in the industrialized cities of Shanghai, Wuhan, and Guangzhou in the spring of 1927. In Changsha, local military leaders joined with the GMD and local landlords to slaughter thousands of peasants who had recently expropriated the land they worked from its legal owners. By the summer of 1928, only 32,000 union members in all of China remained loyal to the Communist Party. By 1929, only 3 percent of party members were proletarians. Mao's peasant alternative was, of necessity, the communists' last resort.

When the GMD put down the Hunan Autumn Harvest Uprising in 1927, Mao's core group retreated to the border area between Hunan and Jiangzi. Other communist leaders, driven from the cities, joined them in this rural area. They built up a **soviet**, a local communist government, redistributing land, introducing improved farming methods, and instituting new educational systems to spread literacy along with political indoctrination. They recruited and trained a guerrilla army. Mao himself formulated its tactics: "The enemy advances, we retreat; the enemy camps, we harass; the enemy tires, we attack; the enemy retreats, we pursue" (Spence, p. 375).

The guerrillas could exist only with the cooperation of the peasantry whom they wished to mobilize. Appropriate, rather revolutionary rules were established to govern soldiers' behavior: "prompt obedience to orders; no confiscations whatever from the poor peasantry; and prompt delivery directly to the Government, for its disposal, of all goods confiscated from the landlords" (Snow, p. 176). These were later elaborated to include: "Be courteous and polite to the people and help them when you can … Be honest in all transactions with the peasants … Pay for all articles purchased" (Snow, p. 176).

soviet A council, the primary unit of government in the Soviet Union at local, regional, and national levels, later adopted by other communist regimes.

Gender Issues under Mao Mao recognized the changes already taking place in women's rights. Feminism had begun to flourish in China by the 1920s with the formation of such organizations as the Women's Suffrage Association and the Women's Rights League. Its constituency was mostly Western-influenced urban intellectuals. *New Youth* magazine, for example, which was often critical of Confucius for his emphasis on patriarchy and obedience to authority, had translated and published Ibsen's *A Doll's House* in 1918. Ba Jinn's novel *Family*, one of the key works of China's reformist New Culture Movement, transplanted Ibsen's advocacy of women's equality and independence into a modern Chinese setting. Margaret Sanger, American feminist and advocate of contraception, toured and lectured throughout China in 1922. There were also some 1,500,000 women working outside their homes for pay in light industrial factories, mostly textiles, in China's cities. Now Mao refocused feminist attention on the countryside and the peasantry:

> the authority of the husband … has always been comparatively weak among the poor peasants, because the poor peasant women, compelled for financial reasons to take more part in manual work than women of the wealthier classes, have obtained more right to speak and more power to make decisions in family affairs. In recent years the rural economy has become even more bankrupt and the basic condition for men's domination over women has already been undermined. And now, with the rise of the peasant movement, women in many places have set out immediately to organize the rural women's association; the opportunity has come for them to lift up their heads, and the authority of the husband is tottering more and more every day. (de Bary, p. 872)

Communist policies took two complementary directions. The first, and more effective, restructured the labor and military

Women of Shanghai with tiny, bound feet working at frames for sorting tea leaves. From the early years of the twentieth century urban women had begun to leave the confines of home to work in light industry. The move from home to workplace gave women more status, which was further strengthened by the reforms of the communist government when it came to power. The abandonment of footbinding in all but the most outlying areas of China did much to enhance the freedom of women.

forces to give more scope and power to women. Building the Chinese soviet and fighting guerrilla battles required the support of every available resource. While women did not usually participate in warfare directly, the increased need for production and personnel brought them out of the house into new jobs, effectively raising their status.

Later, after the revolution had succeeded in 1949, the communists issued a new marriage law forbidding arranged marriages, stopping all purchase and sale in marriage contracts, and encouraging free choice of marriage partners. This law met strong resistance. Men who had already bought their wives objected; so did mothers-in-law, who ruled over each household's domestic labor force. The traditional Chinese family provided for old age security, child-care, medical facilities, and the production and consumption of food, clothing, and shelter. The new communist marriage law seemed to threaten this structure without providing any alternative. The law was not widely enforced. Also, the leadership of the party remained conspicuously male.

The Long March and the Communist Triumph, 1934–49

Chiang sent five successive military expeditions against the Jiangzi soviet, beginning with 100,000 men and leading up to one million. By 1934, the communists could no longer hold out. Mao led some 80,000 men and thirty-five women out of the siege and began the Long March, a 370-day, 6,000-mile strategic retreat, by foot, under constant bombardment and attack from Chiang's forces, across rivers, mountain ranges, marshes, and grasslands, westward to Guizhou and then northward to a final new base camp in Yan'an. Some 20,000 men finally arrived in Yan'an, of whom about half had marched since the beginning, the rest having joined *en route*. The courage, comradeship, commitment, and idealism of this march, in the face of seemingly insurmountable natural obstacles and enemy harassment, were the formative experience of a generation of Chinese communist leaders. At the front, Mao now became the unquestioned leader of the movement, party, and army.

In remote, impoverished Yan'an, Mao established his capital and rebuilt his soviet structure, nurturing his army, inducting its soldiers into agricultural assistance work; redistributing land; encouraging handicrafts; and establishing newspapers and schools, an arts and literature academy, and medical programs for training paramedical "barefoot doctors." The Chinese communist program developed more fully here: a peasant-centered economy, administered and aided by guerrilla soldiers, capped by a dictatorial but comparatively benevolent communist leadership, encouraging literacy accompanied by indoctrination in communist ideology. Tension built up, however, between ideological goals and practical implementation, between being "Red" and being "expert."

Although Yan'an was remote from the main fighting, and was subject to GMD attacks, the communists launched guerrilla action against the Japanese after their invasion of China proper in 1937. By comparison, Jiang seemed less nationalistic. He appeared willing to compromise with the Japanese and more eager to pursue the Chinese communists than to fight the foreign invaders. Mao, on the other hand, wished to join forces with Jiang to unite China against the foreigner. In the "Xian incident," dissident generals arranged the bold kidnap of Jiang in 1936, threatening the life of the GMD leader if he did not join more vigorously in the fight against the Japanese; after this, Jiang moved toward temporary cooperation with the communists.

At first, the Japanese had hoped to rule China with the help of Chinese collaborators, as they had Manchuria, but their cruelty after the capture of Nanjing in December 1937 dashed those hopes. The Chinese vowed to fight back. The communists fought a rearguard guerrilla war from their northern base in Shaanxi, while Jiang led

The legend of the map reads:

- occupied by Japan 1933
- area of Japanese influence 1932-37
- Communist strongholds to 1935
- Long March Oct. 1934-Oct. 1935
- Communist base 1935-45
- occupied by Japan by 1944
- Communist controlled by 1945

a scorched-earth retreat to a new headquarters far up the Yangzi River in Chongqing. Soldiers and civilians suffered catastrophically.

By the early 1940s, nationalist cooperation began to unravel as communists and GMD forces jockeyed for temporary power and future position. After a temporary respite in 1945, full-scale civil war resumed. The USA extended help to Chiang in training his troops, airlifting them to critical military locations, and turning over to them war *matériel*. The Soviet Union, fighting for its life against Germany, stayed out of the conflict against Japan until the last week of the war.

The Communist Revolution in China. Chinese communists and nationalists (GMD) united briefly to subdue the warlord factions which emerged after the collapse of the Manchu (Qing) dynasty, and to consolidate a national government. After 1927 Nationalist repression forced the communists to retreat to remote areas, focussing in the northwest after the Long March of 1934–5, where guerrilla warfare continued. With the Japanese invasion of China proper in 1937, China was torn by both international and civil war. After Japan's defeat in 1945, the communists turned to defeating the GMD as well.

Then it entered Manchuria, carrying off a great deal of that region's military and industrial equipment to the Soviet Union, while turning over some of it to the Chinese communists. As China's civil war continued after 1945, communist forces in many parts of the country, well disciplined and warmly supported by peasants, defeated the ill-disciplined and ill-provisioned GMD forces, whose rations and materials were often sold off for private profit without ever reaching them. By the fall of 1949, the communists had driven the GMD completely out of mainland China to the island of Taiwan. The GMD occupied and took over houses and businesses of Taiwanese who already lived there. They claimed that Taiwan was the true China that should be reunited with what became known as mainland China. The Communist People's Republic of China was born.

Revolutionary Policies, 1949–69

Implementing the Principles of the Long March, 1949–55 For Mao and the guerrilla veterans who dominated the new government, the principal fears were foreign domination, internal chaos, and the lingering power of the wealthy classes and the large-scale landholders. The new rulers modeled much of their new government on their experiences during the Long March and the Yan'an soviet. They returned to these experiences for inspiration in difficult times as long as they lived. Important policies included:

- redistribution of land;
- women's rights to hold land;
- appropriate technology;
- production and equal distribution of basic necessities for everyone;
- universal literacy (actually reaching about 69 percent by 1980, about 60 percent for females, 78 percent for males).

The government mobilized tight-knit, local, social networks not only to suppress such vices as opium addiction and prostitution but also to enforce rigid political indoctrination and conformity, including the informing by one family member against another and coercing personal confessions of political deviance.

Land redistribution was a top priority. During this class revolution, perhaps half the peasantry of China received at least some benefits while as a many as one million landlords were killed. Lacking experience in urban economic affairs, the communist government at first invited the cooperation of businessmen, both Chinese and foreign. But policies changed abruptly as China entered the Korean War in October 1950. Threats, expropriation, and accusations of espionage—sometimes justified—against businessmen and Christian missionaries forced almost all foreigners to leave China by the end of 1950. Numerous campaigns against counter-revolutionaries; the confiscation and redistribution of private property; hundreds and even thousands of executions; intensive public, group pressure to elicit confessions from those perceived as enemies of the revolution; and regular confrontations between workers and owners, now incorporated into the processes of labor relations, destroyed the capitalist sector in China. Pressured by the United States, many countries refused to recognize the new government. The communist Soviet government, on the other hand, maintained a strong alliance and helped to draft and implement China's first five-year plan between 1952 and 1957.

Communist policies on urbanization and industrialization were more ambivalent. The communists had come to power as an anti-urban, peasant movement. The large cities, especially Shanghai, had fostered the foreign enclaves, extraterritorial law, and colonial behavior that flagrantly insulted the Chinese in their own

country, but they also housed
China's industrial base, military technology, administration, and cultural life. As
the communists began to
capture the nation's cities,
Mao began to reevaluate
their potential:

> From 1927 to the present
> the center of gravity of our
> work has been in the
> villages—gathering
> strength in the villages,
> using the villages in order
> to surround the cities, and
> then taking the cities. The
> period for this method of
> work has now ended. The
> period of the city leading
> the village has now begun.
> (Spence, p. 508)

Policies and results, however, were uneven. To restrain urban growth, the government
promulgated severe limitations on internal migration, but movement from the countryside continued steadily, if slowly. China's population, which had been 10.6 percent
urban in 1949, reached 17.4 percent urban in 1976. In sheer numbers this was an
increase from 57 million to 163 million people. As time went by, the cities again challenged communist ideological purity—Guangzhou promoted capitalism; Beijing,
political protest; Shanghai, internationalism. Chinese leaders like Liu Shaoqi and Deng
Xiaoping argued on behalf of urban, bureaucratic, centralized, "expert" industrialization; Mao and Lin Piao wanted rural, grassroots, "Red" populism. Some, like Zhou
Enlai, sought a compromise and synthesis.

Militarily, the communists extolled the spirit of the guerrilla warrior over high-tech
weaponry. They taunted America, the world's most heavily armed country, as a
"paper tiger," unwilling or unable to use its vast arsenal, especially its nuclear
weapons, in combat. Indeed, China itself fought the United States to a draw in Korea,
1950–3, and then saw America withdraw in defeat from Vietnam in 1975. Nevertheless,
China also bought, produced, or purloined up-to-date military technology. In 1964,
China exploded its first atomic bomb; in the mid-1970s it followed with hydrogen
bombs; in 1980 it tested missiles with a range of 7,000 miles; and in 1981, launched
three space satellites.

"Let a Hundred Flowers Bloom," 1956–7 Economically, China adopted a five-year
plan based on the Soviet model. It called for multiplying the value of industrial output
between 1952 and 1957 almost two and one-half times, and claimed at the end to have
overachieved the target by 22 percent. By the end of the plan, even democracy seemed
a possibility. In 1956–7, Mao's call, "Let a hundred flowers bloom, let a hundred
schools of thought contend," opened the gates of public expression and even criticism
of government. In Beijing, students and others posted their thoughts on what became
known as Democracy Wall. By late 1957, however, fearing uncontrolled, growing
protest, the government shifted its policies. It jailed protesters, sent them to labor
camps, and exiled them to remote rural farms.

Trial of a landlord. Most such trials
ended with a confession and a promise
to reform; some with a bullet for the
accused. In its first moves toward
collectivization, the communist
government instituted a number of land
reforms that gave the land to the
peasants who worked it and did away
with the landlords—literally.

HOW DO WE KNOW?

A Journalist–Activist Responds to the "Hundred Flowers" Campaign

When Mao introduced the "Hundred Flowers" campaign, journalist Liu Binyan praised him for his democracy. As he saw the reaction of the party, however, and the subsequent use of the campaign as a means of identifying and punishing critics of the government, he came to see the entire movement as a trap. Liu Binyan became one of the most prominent and most active of the opponents of the communist government of China. Not all historians agree with this assessment of Mao's motives, although the results were clear.

This excerpt is both a primary document, as the record of a participant, and a secondary document, as a later assessment of a previous event.

I do not remember a moment in my life more exhilarating than when Mao Zedong's February 1957 speech to the State Council was released. My estimation of him soared

to sublime heights. At China Youth News the response was equally enthusiastic; it seemed as if we were at the beginning of a new era in China ... In that speech, Mao announced that dogmatism should not be mistaken for Marxism; he reiterated his policy of letting "a hundred flowers bloom and a hundred schools of thought contend"; he advocated open criticism and reiterated that senior party leaders should not be exempt from criticism. As for strikes by workers and students—unprecedented since the founding of the People's Republic and now taken seriously for the first time—he said the right way of dealing with them was not by force or coercion but by overcoming bureaucratism.

These issues were exactly the unspoken ones that had been weighing on me for the last few years—special privileges with party ranks, bureaucratism, and dogmatic tendencies. Now my disquiet had been dispelled as if by magic. The political climate in Beijing cleared up; the mood of intellectuals brightened, everything seemed to take on a rosy hue. Mao was virtually advocating more democracy and liberalization in matters of ideology; as a journalist and writer, I now felt I had a free hand in pursuing my vocation.

[Liu then describes meetings with local party officials that demonstrated that many did not interpret Mao's words as he did. They saw any approval of open expression to be very limited, at most.]

Thirty years later, I reread Mao's speech (the original version, not the one revised for publication) and realized that at the time I had been too preoccupied with his main drift to detect hints of other tendencies hidden between the lines. For instance, he did not mince words over Stalin's dogmatism, but then insisted that Stalin must be assessed on the "three-seven" principle—that is, seven parts merit to three parts fault. Again Mao considered "democracy" as basically a tool to mobilize the people for the Party's own ends. (Liu, pp. 69–70.)

- Which of Liu's points make his document a primary source document? Which of his points make it a secondary source document?
- Why did Liu find Mao's campaign to let a "hundred flowers bloom," surprising?
- What led Liu to change his mind in assessing the purpose of Mao's "hundred flowers bloom" campaign?

Steel furnace, Shiu Shin, China, 1958. Every thirty minutes, some 50 kilos of iron is smelted in the several hundred ovens at this steel furnace.

The "Great Leap Forward," 1957–60 Increasingly threatened by population growth in Chinese cities and an inability to feed urban populations, the government implemented the "Great Leap Forward," grouping almost all of rural China into communes, "sending down" city people to villages, virtually terminating whatever small private enterprises had survived, and attempting to downscale and disperse industry by establishing local, small-scale enterprises, referred to generically as "backyard steel mills." The Great Leap Forward, administered by powerful, distant government officials who attempted to restructure the entire economy of the nation according to communist ideology, led to economic catastrophe, including millions of deaths by starvation.

The Cultural Revolution, 1966–69 Unhappy with what he saw was going on in China, Mao began to silence resistance. The government relaxed for a few years, but then reinstated even more extreme ideological and economic

policies in the Great Proletarian Cultural Revolution in 1966. Mao sought through this revolution to purge the party of time-serving bureaucrats and to reignite revolutionary fervor. Those who responded most enthusiastically were the army and students, who, with Mao's encouragement, organized themselves into the Red Guard. Teachers were denounced by their students and by party officials; professors and intellectuals were exiled to remote villages and forced to undertake hard labor.

The Long March was now thirty years in the past, yet nostalgia for its ideological zeal still motivated China's aging leaders. Mao was venerated as their last hope to restore the intensity of those early days of the revolution. Key quotations from his statements were published in millions of copies of *The Quotations of Chairman Mao*, often called the Little Red Book because of its size and the color of its cover. These were circulated and read publicly throughout the country. Economic chaos and starvation on the one hand and the total stifling and destruction of intellectual and academic life on the other brought China to a standstill. For three years, 1966–9, militant, committed anarchy reigned.

Recovery, 1970–76

As the damage became clearly visible, China reversed its policy in yet another example of *fang–zhou*, loosening up– tightening down. The People's Liberation Army was given the task of suppressing the Red Guards, the youth and student cadres who had wreaked chaos in the name of Mao. New international respectability was sought, most dramatically by the normalization of relations with the United States after President Nixon visited China in 1972. Domestically, attention refocused on the restoration of economic productivity. Imports and exports, which had held roughly flat for several years at slightly over $2 billion each through the late 1960s, rose steadily until, in 1978, each registered $10 billion. One fourth of the imports were machinery and equipment, including complete plants—6,934 of them in 1978—built entirely by foreigners (Spence, p. 641). Almost all of these new factories were in heavy industries, especially petrochemicals and iron and steel. By 1980, China was producing more steel than Britain or France.

"Between 1950 and 1977 industrial output grew at an average annual rate of 13.5 percent ... the highest rate of all developing or developed major nations of the world during the time, and a more rapid pace than achieved by any country during any comparable period of rapid industrialization in modern world history" (Meisner, pp. 436–7). Meanwhile, agriculture was upended, collectivized, and relatively neglected in terms of investment. The agonizingly slow growth of agriculture at 2.3 percent a year from 1952 to 1977 could barely keep pace with population growth of 2 percent a year. By the time Mao died in 1976, China was poised for a dramatic change in leadership and policies.

International Relations

USSR In terms of international relations, also, China had already implemented a series of dramatic turnabouts. In the first decade of communist rule, its chief ally was the USSR, which helped the new communist state

–next pg

Tiananmen Square, June 5, 1989. Tanks traveling down Changan Boulevard, in front of the Beijing Hotel, are confronted by a brave Chinese man who pleads for an end to the killing of demonstrating students. This photograph came to symbolize the struggle of the Chinese people to reassert their dignity and gain democracy in the face of the huge and powerful communist regime.

irredentist An individual or group that seeks to restore territory to the state that once owned it.

design its five-year plan, train and provision its armed forces, and build factories, transportation facilities, urban neighborhoods, and administrative centers. But in the mid-1950s, the USSR under Khrushchev began to moderate its own militant policies both domestically and internationally. China, however, remained more "Red," and the two countries quarreled bitterly over ideology, as they had in 1927. In the summer of 1960, the USSR recalled all of its technical advisers in China, including those working on atomic energy projects. Diplomatic relations were severed in 1961. In China's border disputes with India, which spilled over briefly into warfare in 1962, the USSR backed India's claims and entered into defense alliances with China's opponent.

Armed conflicts with the USSR arose over borders in northern Manchuria and Xinjiang province. Fighting in 1969 led to about 100 Russian and 800 Chinese casualties. At considerable expense, China then concentrated its defense forces in these border areas. Only after 1985, under Gorbachev's new policies of *glasnost* (political and cultural openness) and *perestroika* (economic restructuring) in the Soviet Union, were diplomatic relations between the two countries normalized. Still, the two powers remained wary and armed across thousands of miles of shared borders.

The United States Relations with the United States began in cold hostility. For almost two decades after 1949, America lamented and resented the "loss" of China and continued to support Chiang's **irredentist** forces on Taiwan after 1949, mostly because it wanted to combat communism. Communist policies thoroughly alienated capitalist business people and Christian religious communities, both of which had invested in China. The Chinese government's use of "brainwashing" tactics to convert their internal opponents through unremitting propaganda, group pressure, and official coercion,

President Nixon meets with Communist Party Chairman Mao Zedong in Beijing, during his groundbreaking 1972 visit to China. The Chinese government, clearly worried by aggressive Soviet policy in Czechoslovakia, took steps to improve relations with the United States. Four years after the Sino-Western rapprochement, begun in 1971, foreign trade with China had tripled, and by 1980, China had joined the International Monetary Fund and the World Bank.

China's pingpong team are invited to America by the National Pingpong Association, USA, April 1972. In this friendly match, a Chinese and an American pingpong player are on the same side, a symbol of the new friendship between China and America.

scandalized Americans. China's "liberation" of Tibet in 1950, and the ruthless suppression of the Tibetan Buddhist revolt in 1959, seemed to confirm the militaristic, brutal nature of the government, although no one moved to aid the Tibetan resistance. The Korean War, provoked by North Korea's invasion of the south in 1950, led to the three-year engagement of American and United Nations forces against those of China, ended in a deadlock. Against the advice of its closest overseas allies, the USA lobbied to keep the People's Republic of China out of the United Nations; the government of Taiwan represented the Chinese people.

In the early 1970s, however, the diplomatic scene changed dramatically. Mao and his new advisers, retreating from the economic catastrophe of the Cultural Revolution, sought assistance from abroad. President Nixon and Secretary of State Henry Kissinger also favored more pragmatic policies. In 1971, the USA did not stand in the way of China's joining the United Nations, and in the next year, Nixon visited China, advancing the normalization of relations between the two countries, but at the expense of Taiwan.

East Asia Within its own area of the world, China for 2,000 years has viewed itself as the dominant, central power, and has sought that recognition from its neighbors with mixed success. In many of these countries, China was a feared and resented neighbor, not an uncommon relationship for a regional superpower. China invaded Tibet in 1950 and forced the Dalai Lama to flee and to seek refuge in India in 1959. In Cambodia, it backed the murderous Khmer Rouge Party and its leader Pol Pot in the vicious civil wars through the 1970s, even committing troops briefly to combat.

On the other hand, the astonishing economic recovery of Japan after World War II, challenged China's leadership position and forced the country to reconsider its economic programs. Moreover, in several nearby states, Chinese minorities were viewed with suspicion as possible subversive infiltrators for the Chinese nation and the Communist Party. In anti-Chinese and anti-communist riots in Indonesia in 1965 thousands of Chinese were murdered, and hundreds of thousands more were exiled.

India Finally, China's relationship with India has been complex. When India became independent in 1947 and China completed its revolution in 1949, they chose dramatically different social, political, and economic paths, and both saw themselves as leading the third world in new patterns of development. At the Bandung Conference in 1955 both offered leadership to nations newly emerging from colonialism. China became a model for agrarian guerrilla revolt throughout Southeast Asia and beyond, while India's non-violent path inspired others, especially in Black Africa.

India did not protest China's takeover of Tibet in 1950 and consistently backed China's petition to enter the United Nations. But differences over border demarcations in the mountainous regions of Leh and Ladakh led to open warfare in 1962. The Chinese decisively defeated Indian troops, penetrated through the mountain passes to within striking distance of India's heartland, and then withdrew voluntarily to the borders they had claimed. The war undercut the concept of third world solidarity, and India's first test of nuclear devices in 1974 increased the mutual suspicion.

Post-Revolutionary China

China demonstrated the inevitability of each huge nation of the world finding its own developmental path. China might for a time take guidance from one foreign ideology or another, and it might enter into alliances with various powers at one time or another, but finally it sought a path appropriate to its own size, geography, power, technology, and historical experience. Chinese at home and abroad, including many who disapproved of current government policies, took pride in the newfound unity, power, and independence of the Central Kingdom. China might make mistakes, but they would be its own mistakes. Leaving behind a century of humiliating colonialism and devastating international and civil war, China sought to establish stability and ideological purity. Soon it would seek a larger place in the world.

INDIA, 1914–91

The Independence Struggle, 1914–47

British Policies and Practices Established in 1885 at British initiative as a vent for Indian nationalist criticism, the Indian National Congress led the resistance to British rule in the early twentieth century, usually through constitutional protest. The Congress leadership was concentrated in the hands of men who were educated in British ways, through British-run schools, sometimes in Britain itself. Somewhat more than a third of its members were trained in the legal profession. In 1835, T.B. Macaulay, legal adviser to the British government of India, had declared the intent of the government's educational policies to create a class "Indian in blood and colour, but English in taste, in opinions, in morals, and in intellect" (Hay, p. 31); the Congress leadership reflected the results. By 1906, Muslims began to fear an India under exclusive Hindu control and formed their own organization, the All-India Muslim League.

The British in India claimed to be preparing India for democratic, responsible government and in 1917, the British Secretary of State for India, Edwin Montagu, announced the goal of British policy to be "increasing association of Indians in every branch of the administration, and the gradual development of self-governing institutions, with a view to the progressive realisation of responsible government in India as an integral part of the British Empire." A series of constitutional reforms had already established official councils with substantial Indian membership,

INDIAN INDEPENDENCE—KEY FIGURES	
Rabindranath Tagore (1861–1941)	Indian poet, painter, and musician from Bengal, who translated his own verse into English. He received the Nobel prize for literature in 1913. An ardent nationalist and advocate of social reform, he resigned his knighthood (granted in 1918) in protest against British repression in India.
Mohandas Karamchand Gandhi (1869–1948)	Indian political and spiritual leader, who fought against anti-Indian discrimination in South Africa before returning to India in 1914. He became leader of the Indian National Congress in the 1920s. Gandhi maintained non-violent ideals through civil disobedience campaigns and was imprisoned in 1922, 1932, 1933, and 1942 for anti-British activities. He played a crucial part in the negotiations leading to independence.
Muhammad Ali Jinnah (1876–1948)	The founder of Pakistan. A member of the Indian National Congress, at first he advocated cooperation between Hindus and Muslims. Later, he transformed the Muslim League from a cultural to a political organization. In 1940, Jinnah demanded the partition of British India into separate Muslim and Hindu states. Jinnah achieved his goal, but he had to accept a smaller state than he had demanded. He became governor-general of Pakistan in 1947 and died in office.
Jawaharlal Nehru (1889–1964)	Indian nationalist politician and prime minister, 1947–64. Before partition, he led the socialist wing of the Congress Party and was regarded as second only to Gandhi. Between 1921 and 1945, he was imprisoned by the British nine times for political activities. As prime minister he developed the idea of non-alignment (neutrality toward the major powers), established an industrial base, and sustained a parliamentary democracy based on the rule of law.
Subhas Chandra Bose (1897–1945)	Indian nationalist leader (known as "Netaji"—"RespectedLeader"), who called for outright Indian independence. Frequently imprisoned, he became president of the All-India Congress (1938–9). He supported the Axis powers (Germany, Italy, and Japan) during World War II and became commander-in-chief of the Japanese-sponsored Indian National Army. He was reported killed in a plane crash during his military career, adding to his stature as a martyr for his nation.

elected by very limited elites, to advise the government. The Government of India Act, 1919, expanded provincial and central legislatures and created a dual government, or dyarchy, transferring powers over agriculture, public works, education, local self-government, and education to Indian elected legislators at the provincial level.

This half-way house proved unstable; Britain had trouble deciding whether it wished India to be a democracy or a colony. Each new issue revealed the contradiction. When the post-war years increased the demands for political independence, the government responded with repression. Against the advice of all of the elected Indians in the Imperial Legislative Council, in 1919, the government cracked down on freedom of the press and assembly by passing the Rowlatt Acts. When British troops shot into a protest meeting in Amritsar, Punjab, killing 379 Indians and wounding 1,100 (see Chapter 19), the British government lost its aura of legitimacy. Even Indian moderates could no longer justify British rule.

Gandhi's Innovations and Courage At this juncture Mohandas Karamchand Gandhi—Mahatma Gandhi—emerged as a leader offering new political directions, new moral perspectives, and new programs of internal reform. Gandhi called India to find strength and courage in its own peasant roots and spiritual traditions. His success had limitations, but all political activity until well past independence, almost to the present, would revolve around the Congress, which he now reconstructed into a mass movement.

Gandhi Develops *Satyagraha* in South Africa Gandhi's family had been advisers to local rulers in western India for several generations, and his uncle felt that if Mohandas were to maintain the family tradition under British rule, he must travel to Britain to study law. Gandhi emerged from three years of study in London with a deeply considered reaffirmation of his Indian heritage in Hinduism, in religious openness, and in an appreciation of localized, small-scale organizations. Two days after completing his legal training, one day after being admitted to the bar, Gandhi boarded a steamship returning to India. He practiced law for a year, with no special distinction, and then accepted the case of an Indian emigrant business firm in South Africa. There, apparently for the first time, Gandhi suffered racist persecution personally and repeatedly.

The Indian community in South Africa had mostly come to work as indentured laborers. The South African government wanted them to return home at the end of their service and instituted laws to make their long-term status untenable. Indians were required to carry identification cards at all times and to pay heavy head taxes. Most disturbing of all, in 1913, the government nullified all marriages not performed by Christian clergy, rendering illegitimate the children of almost all the Indian immigrants. Although he had arrived as the lawyer for a wealthy Indian Muslim client, Gandhi identified with the pain and humiliation of his less privileged countrymen and, indeed, suffered along with them. He was physically evicted from public facilities and threatened with beatings and even death for asserting his rights. Until now a rather private person, Gandhi began to organize a protest movement.

Instead of leaving at the end of his year's employment, Gandhi remained in South Africa for twenty-one years, 1893–1914, advancing methods of resistance:

- *Satyagraha*, "truth force," called for self-sacrificing, non-violent mass demonstrations, demanding that the persecutors recognize the immorality of their own position and redress the suffering of the oppressed;
- *Ahimsa*, non-violence, in the face of attack;
- Civil disobedience against unjust laws, with a willingness to suffer the legal consequences, including imprisonment, and frequently the illegal consequences, such as beatings;

SOURCE

Gandhi's First Experience with Racism in South Africa

Mahatma Gandhi published his Autobiography originally as a series of newspaper articles. Many of the episodes also carried a moral message for readers. The story of his first encounter with racism in South Africa implies that he had never experienced such severe discrimination, neither in colonial India nor during his law school days in London.

On the seventh or eighth day after my arrival, I left Durban. A first class seat was booked for me. ... The train reached Maritzburg, the capital of Natal, at about 9 p.m. ... A passenger came next, and looked me up and down. He saw that I was a "colored" man. This disturbed him. Out he went and came in again with one or two officials. They all kept quiet, when another official came to me and said, "Come along, you must go to the van compartment."

"But I have a first class ticket," said I.

"That doesn't matter," rejoined the other. "I tell you, you must go to the van compartment."

"I tell you, I was permitted to travel in this compartment at Durban, and I insist on going on in it."

"No you won't," said the official. "You must leave this compartment, or else I shall have to call a police constable to push you out."

"Yes, you may. I refuse to get out voluntarily."

The constable came. He took me by the hand and pushed me out. My luggage was also taken out. I refused to go to the other compartment and the train steamed away. I went and sat in the waiting room, keeping my hand bag with me, and leaving the other luggage where it was. ...

It was winter, and winter in the higher regions of South Africa is severely cold. Maritzburg being at a high altitude, the cold was extremely bitter. My overcoat was in my luggage, but I did not dare to ask for it lest I should be insulted again, so I sat and shivered. There was no light in the room. A passenger came in at about midnight and possibly wanted to talk to me. But I was in no mood to talk.

I began to think of my duty. Should I fight for my rights or go back to India, or should I go on to Pretoria without minding the insults, and return to India after finishing the case? It would be cowardice to run back to India without fulfilling my obligation. The hardship to which I was subjected was superficial—only a symptom of the deep disease of color prejudice. I should try, if possible, to root out the disease and suffer hardships in the process. (Jack, p. 29–30)

- the establishment of a headquarters, modeled on the Hindu religious *ashram*, providing living and working quarters for himself, his family, and the closest allies in his campaigns;
- the creation of a publishing house for spreading the principles of his movement.

Because he renounced violence, Gandhi called these methods "passive resistance," but there was nothing passive about them; they were actually systems of "militant non-violence." These techniques were later adopted by leaders of resistance movements around the world from Martin Luther King (1929–68) in the USA to Nelson Mandela (b. 1918) in South Africa itself.

In 1909, Gandhi published *Hind Swaraj or Indian Home Rule*. Banned in India, this short book championed India's own civilization, exhorted Indians to conquer the feelings of fear and inferiority inherent in their colonial situation, and forthrightly attacked British hegemony.

We have hitherto said nothing because we have been cowed down ... it is our duty now to speak out boldly. We consider your schools and law courts to be useless. We want our own ancient schools and courts to be restored. The common language of India is not English but Hindi. You should, therefore, learn it. We can hold communication with you only in our national language ...

We cannot tolerate the idea of your spending money on railways and the military. We see no occasion for either ... We do not need any European cloth. We shall manage with articles produced and manufactured at home. You have great military resources ... You may, if you like, cut us to pieces. You may shatter us at the cannon's mouth. If you act contrary to our will, we shall not help you; and without our help, we know that you cannot move one step forward. (Jack, pp. 118–19)

Gandhi's success in South Africa was limited to short-term compromises with the government, but he earned the esteem of his countrymen in both South Africa and India. When he returned home and established a new *ashram* in Ahmedabad in 1915, they eagerly awaited his political initiatives for India itself

Gandhi Returns to India and Leads the Congress Popular discontent with British rule already existed. By 1907, the extremist wing of Congress, led by Bal Gangadhar Tilak (1856–1920), called for the British to leave India immediately. Tilak and the extremists employed the idioms and festivals of Hinduism as the basis for Indian nationalism. Economically, **swadeshi** ("of one's own country") campaigns for the use of indigenous products, especially after 1905, had demonstrated that voluntary boycotts of imports could spur Indian industrial productivity and profits. How much more effective legal control over tariffs could be once the British left! Businessmen and industrialists were especially attracted by these *swadeshi* boycotts. They resented British reluctance to share industrial secrets, restrictions on industrial and infrastructural investment, removal of tax monies from India back to Britain in the form of "home charges," and limits on career advancement for Indians. Gandhi did not create the independence movement in India, rather he gave it new leadership and direction.

Gandhi soon demonstrated this organizational genius. Several peasant movements that Gandhi would come to direct began with their own local organization, as in Champaran in Bihar, 1917; in Kheda, 1917; in Bardoli, 1922; and in Gujarat 1928. Peasants from these areas asked Gandhi to provide more sophisticated and effective leadership to advance their own initial activities. Millworkers in Ahmedabad, too, had already organized themselves (against local employers, not against the British), when they asked Gandhi to take charge of their strike in 1919. As he responded to these requests from local groups, Gandhi recognized India's smoldering grass-roots anger, inflamed by postwar economic hardship and political repression. He reconstituted the Congress into a mass organization with millions of dues-paying members, a standing

swadeshi "Of one's own country," a Hindi word used as a slogan in the Indian boycott of foreign goods, part of the protest against Britain's partition of Bengal in 1905.

Gandhi and Nehru. Mahatma Gandhi, wearing his customary *dhoti*, and Jawaharlal Nehru are deep in conversation at the All-India Congress Committee Meeting in Bombay, July 6, 1946, where Nehru took office as president of the Congress. Gandhi and Nehru were the charismatic figures who led the Indian National Congress, a broad-based political organization which was the vehicle for the nationalist movement for independence.

satyagraha A Hindi expression meaning "truth force," applied to Gandhi's policy of non-violent opposition to British rule in India.

executive committee to keep the organization functioning between annual meetings, and a program of mass civil disobedience, *satyagraha* (truth force).

Gandhi mobilized India's enormous size and diversity by cultivating personal and political alliances with the major regional leaders. His most analytic and thorough biographer, Judith Brown, praises his skill in winning the allegiance of such regional giants as C. Rajagopalachari (1879–1972) in Madras; Rajendra Prasad (1884–1963) in Bihar, later the first president of independent India; Vallabhbhai Patel (*c.* 1873–1933) in Gujarat, who went on to become chairman of the entire Congress Party; and Jawaharlal Nehru (1889–1964) in Uttar Pradesh (then called United Provinces), who became the first prime minister of independent India in 1947, a post he held until his death.

Gandhi was not successful everywhere, however. He did not capture the leadership nor the rank and file of the large eastern state of Bengal. In Calcutta, Subhas Chandra Bose (1847–1945) often opposed Gandhi as too ascetic in his personal life, too narrow in his intellectual interests, too dictatorial in his political authority, and too compromising with business and landlord interests in consolidating his power. Left-wing socialists throughout India also found Gandhi too cozy with big business and landlord interests. When the Congress socialists advocated land redistribution in the 1930s, Gandhi successfully won over the highly respected, usually socialist, Nehru, and the divisive issue was deferred until after independence. Despite valiant efforts, Gandhi failed to capture the most important Muslim leadership. Mohammed Ali Jinnah (1876–1948), leader of the movement for a separate Pakistan, found Gandhi's style both too ascetic and too Hindu. As independence neared, Jinnah did not trust Gandhi's Congress to deal equitably with Muslims.

Hindu–Muslim Unity Gandhi attempted to hold Hindus and Muslims together in a secular, egalitarian India. After World War I, he supported the caliph as the chief religious authority of the Muslims of the Ottoman Empire against British designs, even after the fall of the Ottoman Empire. In 1924, Gandhi fasted for twenty-one days to promote Hindu–Muslim unity. During the partition riots in 1947, he walked through violence-torn areas to advocate peace in Calcutta, Bengal, Bihar, and Delhi. In both Calcutta and Delhi he fasted for several days on behalf of Hindu–Muslim peace. And at least temporarily the antagonists on both sides put down their weapons. The British viceroy referred to Gandhi as a "one man boundary force" and marveled that Gandhi had achieved by moral persuasion what four army divisions might not have been able to accomplish.

Nevertheless, many Muslims doubted that they would receive fair treatment in a majority Hindu country. They regarded even Gandhi's political idiom as excessively Hindu. Gandhi believed that his greatest political failure was the partition of India into two nations, secular India with its Hindu-majority and Muslim Pakistan. He refused to participate in independence celebrations and spent his time trying to bring peace to areas of Hindu–Muslim conflict. In 1948, Gandhi was assassinated by a Hindu fanatic who found him soft on Muslims. The Hindu–Muslim breach remains a problem today, both in tensions across the international border between India and Pakistan, especially in Kashmir, and in domestic conflict between Hindus and Muslims.

Abolition of Untouchability Gandhi worked to end untouchability. He was not opposed to the general concept of the caste system, seeing differences among people, even by birth, as a part of social reality, but he fought the designation of about 15 percent of India's Hindu population as outcastes, humiliated and oppressed. Declaring, "It has always been a mystery to me how men can feel themselves honored by the humiliation of their fellow beings," Gandhi coined for the untouchables a new name, *harijan*, "children of God."

harijan A Hindu term meaning children of God, applied by Mahatma Gandhi to the poorest classes of Indian society, including the untouchables.

Many ex-untouchables saw Gandhi as patronizing. They did not call themselves children of God, but *dalits*, "oppressed peoples". In 1932, a political issue crystallized the differences. In preparing for a new constitution, there was general agreement that a proportion of elective offices should be "reserved" for ex-untouchables. The *dalit* leaders insisted on more: that the voting for these reserved seats be limited only to *dalits*. Gandhi rejected this demand. He wanted all voters to select from among the untouchable candidates. Otherwise the untouchables would form a political nation-within-a-nation, as Muslims were beginning to do. He declared a fast-unto-death on the issue. After a week, the untouchables' leader, B.R. Ambedkar (1893–1956), a lawyer trained in part at Columbia University, acceded to Gandhi's demands. At the same time Hindu leaders, their consciences touched, began to push for an end to restrictions on untouchables and opened many Hindu temples to *dalit* participation.

dalit "oppressed person," a blunt term adopted by ex-untouchables to describe their status.

In 1955, the government began a policy of protective discrimination, reserving a limited percentage of places in government jobs, universities, and elected offices only for the "scheduled castes," those castes that were listed on an official schedule as formerly untouchable. The issue of reservations for scheduled castes has continued as a hot, sometimes violent topic since Independence. Over the years the questions of how many places should be reserved, for whom, under what categories, and for how long have not been resolved.

Cultural Policies Gandhi rejected the use of English in India's public life and schools. He urged instead the development of India's regional languages and literatures. In his first major address after returning to the subcontinent he argued:

> Suppose that we had been receiving, during the past fifty years, education through our vernaculars … we should have today a free India, we should have our educated men, not as if they were foreigners in their own land but speaking to the heart of the nation; they would be working among the poorest of the poor, and whatever they would have gained during the past fifty years would be a heritage for the nation. (Jack, p. 131)

After Independence, Indian vernaculars increasingly displaced English as the language of instruction in India's educational institutions from primary school through university level. The constitution called for two link languages for official communication: English and Hindi. English was to be phased out by 1965, but as the date approached, rioting by opponents assured that both languages would be kept. Widespread knowledge of English among India's high school and university educated classes kept the country more closely in touch with world developments. Parents with aspirations for their children's career prospects usually encouraged them to study English as skills in English continued as one of the markers separating the upper classes from the lower.

Prohibition Gandhi led a temperance movement to ban alcoholic drinks. His argument was based primarily on concern for the effects of alcohol abuse on working-class families, especially when the husband/breadwinner spent his earnings on drink. After Independence, many states of India chose to restrict the use of liquor, but only Gandhi's home state of Gujarat retained almost total prohibition—and this encouraged enormous problems of bootlegging and of collusion between politicians and bootleggers.

Appropriate Technology Because of Gandhi's concern for appropriate technology, the Congress Party made the spinning wheel its emblem; hand-spun, hand-woven cloth its dress; and the production of a daily quota of hand-spun yarn a requirement for

SOURCE

Gandhi and Labor Relations

Most famous for his advocacy of the spinning wheel and his condemnation of mechanized industry, Gandhi was actually very pragmatic in his approach to technology. He recognized that the mechanized Indian textile industry gave jobs to hundreds of thousands of workers and produced yarn and cloth that Indian consumers desperately needed. Cynics added that the millowners were among Gandhi's most generous financial supporters. Gandhi played a pivotal role in founding the Ahmedabad Textile Labour Association, one of India's most powerful labor unions, and he served as an adviser to several others. His advice to labor, and to management as well, reflected his view of the importance of harmony rather than conflict in industrial relationships, as in all human relationships.

Two paths are open before India today, either to introduce the western principle of "Might is right," or to uphold the eastern principle that truth alone conquers, that truth knows no mishap, that the strong and the weak alike have a right to secure justice. The choice is to begin with the laboring class. Should the laborers obtain an increment in their wages by violence? Even if that be possible, they cannot resort to anything like violence, howsoever legitimate may be their claims. To use violence for securing rights may seem an easy path, but it proves to be thorny in the long run. Those who live by the sword die also by the sword …

If, on the other hand, they take their stand on pure justice and suffer in their person to secure it, not only will they always succeed but they will also reform their masters, develop industries and both master and men will be as members of one and the same family. A satisfactory solution of the condition of labor must include the following:

1. The hours of labor must leave the workmen some hours of leisure.
2. They must get facilities for their own education.
3. Provision should be made for an adequate supply of milk, clothing and necessary education for their children.
4. There should be sanitary dwellings for the workmen.
5. They should be in a position to save enough to maintain themselves during their old age.

None of these conditions is satisfied today. For this both the parties are responsible. The masters care only for the service they get. What becomes of the laborer does not concern them … The laborer, on the other hand, tries to hit upon all tricks whereby he can get maximum pay with minimum work.

A third party [the union] has sprung up between these two parties. It has become the laborer's friend. (from *Young India*, June 1, 1921, reprinted in Homer Jack, pp. 157–9)

membership. Gandhi expressed his early denunciation of modern machinery in *Hind Swaraj* in a mystical, religious idiom. Later he demanded small-scale, labor-intensive, alternative technologies for economic and humanitarian reasons:

> Hunger is the argument that is driving India to the spinning wheel … We must think of millions who are today less than animals, who are almost in a dying state. The spinning wheel is the reviving draught for the millions of our dying countrymen and countrywomen … I do want growth. I do want self-determination. I do want freedom, but I want all these for the soul … A plea for the spinning wheel is a plea for recognizing the dignity of labor.

Again, not everyone agreed with Gandhi. His most powerful disciple, Jawaharlal Nehru, advocated modern machinery and technology. Nehru could see both sides of the technological debate. He had been educated in England, but Gandhi had introduced him—as he had introduced a generation of India's leaders—to the reality of India's 500,000 villages, where 85 percent of its population lived a technologically simple, generally impoverished existence:

> He sent us to the villages, and the countryside hummed with the activity of innumerable messengers of the new gospel of action. The peasant was shaken up and he began to emerge from his quiescent shell. The effect on us was different but equally far-reaching, for we saw, for the first time as it were, the villager in the intimacy of his mud-hut, and with the stark shadow of hunger always pursuing him. We learnt our Indian economics more from these visits than from books and learned discourses. (Nehru, p. 365)

In the end, however, Nehru came down unequivocally in favor of large-scale industry. Otherwise India might again become a colony:

> It can hardly be challenged that, in the context of the modern world, no country can be politically and economically independent, even within the framework of international inter-dependence, unless it is highly industrialized and has developed its power resources to the utmost … Thus an attempt to build up a country's economy largely on the basis of cottage and small-scale industries is doomed to failure. It will not solve the basic problems of the country or maintain freedom, nor will it fit in with the world framework, except as a colonial appendage. (Nehru, p. 414)

In his studies in Britain, and in a visit to the Soviet Union in the 1930s, Nehru had become a socialist and an advocate for national economic planning to guide the uses of high technology. In 1938, the Congress appointed its own National Planning Commission, the forerunner of the official planning commission established after Independence.

Congress Campaigns for Independence, 1920–22, 1930–32, 1942 Gandhi led the Congress in three massive, nationwide *satyagraha* campaigns. The non-cooperation campaign of 1920–22 boycotted British colonial schools, law courts, administrative positions, manufactures, and imports. The Congress began to provide internally for these functions, encouraging the creation of a separate school system, facilities for conflict resolution, and *swadeshi*/boycott activities that took the place of a tariff in restricting foreign imports. The Congress was not only opposing the British government, it was also constructing a parallel government. In a few localities, Indians refused to pay taxes.

A decade later, in the Salt March campaign of 1930–32, Gandhi mocked the government's monopoly on the manufacture and sale of salt by marching to the sea and manufacturing salt from seawater. This simple action initiated a nationwide campaign of civil disobedience and law breaking. It focused world attention on the colonial government's lack of authority and respect in the eyes of most Indians. Ten years later, the "Quit India" campaign of 1942 refused Indian political support to Britain's efforts in World War II unless independence was granted. (The Indian army, however, did fight loyally under British command.) Despite these three massive, nationwide campaigns, the British did not finally concede independence until 1947.

Most Indians praise Gandhi as the father of the new nation and many regard him as saintly, but India's transformation into an independent state was not only a moral victory, but also an exercise in *realpolitik*, in the reality and importance of everyday politics. In granting independence to India, Britain was responding not only to Gandhi's politics and moral message, but also to enormous losses in the global economic depression and World War II. Britain had lost both the ideological commitment to maintaining its empire in India and the economic and military power to hold India against its will.

The Salt March. Mahatma Gandhi begins the symbolic 240 mile, 27-day walk from Ahmedabad to Dandi on the coast, where he collected sea salt and thus technically broke the salt law—the government's monopoly on salt production. Civil disobedience did not win independence immediately, but it did discredit the moral and political authority of the colonial government.

Independence, 1947

Pakistan At independence, despite Gandhi's efforts to maintain unity, the subcontinent was partitioned into Hindu-majority India, governed by the officially secular Congress Party, and Muslim-majority Pakistan, under an officially Muslim government. The creation of Pakistan was a response to both cultural–religious claims and to political-economic demands. Muhammad Iqbal had turned his poetry into a persuasive plea for a nation governed according to Islamic principles, while Muhammad Ali Jinnah, Pakistan's first president, argued the political case for an equitable distribution of national positions and patronage between Hindus and Muslims.

Pakistan's peculiar geography, with two "wings," east and west, separated by some 800 miles of hostile Indian territory, reflected the distribution of Muslim majorities in the subcontinent. At partition an estimated 12 million people shifted their homes—6 million Hindus and Sikhs from east and west Pakistan moving to India, 6 million Muslims from India transferring to Pakistan. The transfer of population was bloody; between 200,000 and one million people were murdered. Few Hindus remained in Pakistan, but a sizeable Muslim minority, 10 percent of India's population, remained in India. While Hindus and Muslims mostly cohabited the land peacefully, under a

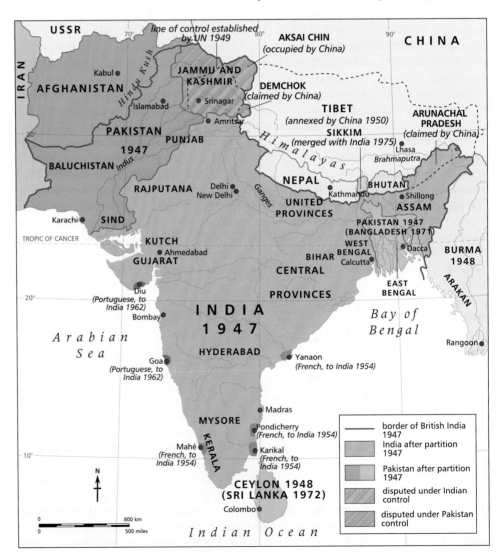

Political change in South Asia after 1947. At independence in 1947, British India was partitioned into secular, but Hindu-majority, India and Muslim Pakistan amid enormous violence and migration. Disputes over Kashmir continue until today. In 1971, the east wing of Pakistan fought, with Indian assistance, a war of independence against the west and became Bangladesh.

secular constitution, tensions between them remained and were sometimes exploited by political leaders.

Kashmir Relations between India and Pakistan remained tense after partition, and exploded into warfare in 1947 and again in 1965 over the issue of Kashmir. Under British rule, partly as a tactic of "divide and rule," about one-third of India's land, with one-fourth of its population, was governed indirectly by local "princes." At the time of independence, the rulers of these local states were officially given the option of joining India or Pakistan or remaining independent.

Mass migration. The partition of India at independence created an unprecedented transfer of population in two directions: Hindus fled Pakistan for the safety of India, and Muslims living in India struggled to get safely over the border into their new homeland. This packed train, groaning with refugees from Pakistan, arrives in Amritsar, just over the Indian border, on October 16, 1947.

Through the craft and coercion of India's home minister, Vallabhbhai Patel, every state finally opted to join India or Pakistan, according to geographical proximity—except Kashmir. The largest of all the princely states geographically, and situated between India and Pakistan, it appeared that Kashmir might choose independence. As the maharaja was considering his options, armed guerrilla fighters invaded from Pakistan. The maharaja asked India to defend him. India agreed, on condition that he bring Kashmir into the Indian union, and he agreed. The decision was contested because the ruler was a Hindu while the overwhelming majority of the population was Muslim.

The wars that broke out in 1947 and 1965 effectively divided Kashmir, with the larger, richer sector held by India, the smaller, poorer sector by Pakistan. The cease-fire line became the *de facto* border between them. Although India promised a plebiscite, it was not held and no one has ever consulted the Kashmiris formally and systematically about their wishes. Relations between India and Pakistan remained hostile and the Kashmir border remained the flashpoint of greatest tension. Sri Lanka, an island off the coast of southern India and also a British possession, gained independence in 1948.

Bangladesh Pakistan and India also fought in 1971. That war was triggered by the break-up of the two wings of Pakistan and the formation of the new nation of Bangladesh in the east. The union of Urdu-speaking, arid, West Pakistan, with Bengali-speaking, marshy, East Pakistan, despite their separation by 800 miles of hostile Indian territory, had been peculiar and unstable from its creation. India, which had officially declared itself a secular democracy, had always maintained that religion alone could not be the basis of a state. When East Pakistan challenged the dominance of West Pakistan, India saw its own philosophy validated, and its arch-rival divided in two. In 1971, East Pakistan declared its independence and India fought alongside the newly emerging nation of Bangladesh, an impoverished, densely populated country of 125 million people.

Problems of the New Government of India

Unifying and Consolidating the Nation Despite Gandhi's quixotic vision of transforming the Congress from a political lobby into a non-official, social service institution, the Congress members quickly transformed the organization into a formal political party and took over the new government of India. Swift action by the independent government quickly consolidated the country. Home Minister Vallabhbhai Patel convinced and coerced India's 562 "princes" to declare their merger with India, ending the fear of a break-up of the subcontinent into numerous, separate, small states. Dispute over the legitimacy of Kashmir's accession was the sole exception.

Other threatened fragmentation was also averted. Gandhi had organized the Congress by linguistic regions, different from the administrative units employed by the British. After independence, following several regional disputes, the Congress government drew up the new state borders in accordance with these linguistic borders.

Strong separatist movements emerged in Punjab, based on discontent within the Sikh religious community; in Muslim-majority Kashmir; and in the far distant and ethnically Mongoloid northeast Himalayan regions of Assam. Separatism also simmered in the southern state of Madras based on linguistic and cultural differences from the north. The state was later renamed Tamil Nadu, in recognition of its Tamil-speaking population. A combination of political bargaining and armed force has kept the country together.

Democracy and its Challenges Gandhi's Congress generally respected constitutional process, and the democracy proposed by British rulers became a reality in India after Independence. Except for two years of "Emergency Rule," 1975–7, during which Prime Minister Indira Gandhi (1917–84) asserted dictatorial powers, India has functioned democratically and constitutionally as a union of some thirty states and territories, with universal adult franchise and guaranteed freedoms of press, assembly, speech, religion, and an independent judiciary. Despite imperfections, India prided itself on being the world's largest democracy. Within its democratic framework, communist governments have also been freely elected in individual states, first in Kerala in 1957—the first freely elected communist government in the world—and later in West Bengal.

In the 1950s, small groups of revolutionary guerrillas, named Naxalites, for the village of Naxalbari in Bihar where they began their activities, have attacked government authorities in local areas, but Indians have not given strong support to militant communism. The reasons may be India's generally religious orientation, skepticism about a philosophy and organization tied to foreign governments, recognition of communism's origin as a proletarian rather than a peasant movement, and state repression of revolutionary organizations.

Until 1991, laissez-faire capitalism fared even less well. Only one party ever directly espoused a capitalist philosophy of development, and it had limited success and a short life. Indians, including much of the business community, seemed to view capitalism as excessively individualistic and materialistic, based on a philosophy of self-interest often seen as greed, and associated with colonialism in the past and the return of a neo-colonial economic dominance in the present. Despite a large free-enterprise sector in the economy, especially in agriculture, most major Indian parties have advocated socialism, on the grounds of its stated concern for the common good. Nehru, in particular, espoused "a socialist pattern of development." His policy continued in force for a generation after his death, despite widespread criticism that it led to excessive power—and corruption—concentrated in the state and in the bureaucrats who controlled access to business licenses and investment capital. Many of these views changed in 1991 when India was forced by regulations of the International Monetary Fund to move towards a more free-market economy (Chapters 23 and 24).

Through the first four decades of Independence, India's democracy was dominated by one party, the Congress, and the party's leadership was dominated by one family, the Nehru dynasty. Jawaharlal Nehru, prime minister from Independence until his death in 1964, was soon succeeded by his daughter, Indira Gandhi, who was prime minister in 1967–77 and from 1980 until her assassination in 1984. She was followed by her son, Rajiv, 1984–9. When Rajiv was also assassinated while seeking reelection in 1991, many Congress leaders asked his widow, Italian-born Sonia Gandhi, to take up the family political mantle. At the time, she declined.

Gender Issues The struggle for independence recruited women, and after independence India instituted universal adult suffrage. In each national election approximately 55 percent of women voted, compared with about 60 percent of men. In 1988, women held forty-six seats out of 537 in the lower house of Parliament, twenty-eight out of 245 in the upper, indicating a slowly increasing proportion from 1950. State government ratios were similar. With Mrs. Gandhi serving as prime minister (1966–77, 1980–84), a woman reached and held the pinnacle of political power. Although first nominated and elected to office on the strength of her father's reputation, later on Mrs. Gandhi was elected on her own merits.

Prime Minister Indira Gandhi Of course, not all women are feminists, including Mrs. Gandhi. Her father introduced her to politics from childhood. When he became prime minister, he asked her to preside over his official residence, since his wife, Indira's mother, had died ten years earlier. At Nehru's death in 1964, Indira was named minister of information and broadcasting, and two years later the Congress High Command named her prime minister, under the mistaken assumption that they could control her. Instead she split the party in a bitter struggle, and gained control of the majority. Declaring her motto of "Down with Poverty," she followed socialist policies, for example, nationalizing India's major banks, and ending the special annual financial allotments to India's former princely rulers. Her reputation as a tough, determined leader grew when she ordered Indian troops into East Pakistan in the 1971 civil war; her support facilitated the creation of Bangladesh. In 1974, she ordered India's first underground test of an atomic bomb.

Mrs. Gandhi's political manipulations partially undermined India's democratic system. In 1975, facing the likely loss of political power, she had the president of India declare an "Emergency." She jailed the leaders of the opposition, curtailed freedom of speech and of the press, and set quotas of people to be rounded up for forcible repro-

Indira Gandhi, prime minister of India (1966–77; 1980–84), inspects the guard at an Independence Day celebration, August 23, 1967. Mahatma Gandhi did much to encourage women's participation in public life during the years leading to Independence. Although many women are well-educated, overall the literacy rate among females is only 38 percent (66 percent for males).

ductive sterilization, largely in response to India's large population. For these dictatorial excesses she was voted out of office when she restored elections in 1977.

Voted back to power in 1980, after a brief period in jail for election irregularities, Mrs. Gandhi once again used her popularity to manipulate the Congress Party, especially at the state levels, to ensure that the major regional leaders were dependent on her. One of these leaders, a Sikh extremist who was for a time her ally, escaped her control and mobilized an armed opposition, centered in the most important Sikh shrine, the Golden Temple in Amritsar. Mrs. Gandhi finally ordered the army to capture and secure the temple. Thousands died in the confrontation and sacred shrines were destroyed. Four months later, in 1984, two Sikh members of her personal bodyguard assassinated her.

As prime minister, Mrs. Gandhi relied on her sons for advice, a common relationship between widows and their sons, especially in India. Sanjay, the younger, was widely regarded as unprincipled in his actions, and many of the excesses of the Emergency were a result of his advice. When Sanjay died in the crash of the stunt airplane he was flying, Indira prevailed upon his older brother Rajiv, a pilot with Indian Airlines, to fill in as her chief adviser. When Mrs. Gandhi was assassinated, Rajiv was chosen by the party as prime minister. Both of the sons counseled a greater concern with modern technology, and began to guide India in that direction.

Legal Changes The 1955 Hindu Marriage Act raised the age of marriage for Hindu women to fifteen (eighteen for men) and assured Hindu women the right of divorce. The Hindu Succession Act of 1956 gave daughters equal rights with sons in inheriting their father's property. On the other hand, parliament did not legislate new personal law for non-Hindus, so other religious communities continued under their traditional laws. The issue disturbed many feminists but they trod lightly here because many Muslims, even feminist Muslims, did not want the secular state to interfere in the religious law of their community.

patrilineal The tracing of ancestry, kinship, and inheritance through the male line.

patrilocal Residence by a couple in or near the home of the male's family or group.

Social Changes Because family structures in India, especially north India, are both **patrilineal** and **patrilocal**—that is, inheritance and residence patterns follow the family of the male—the birth of a female child is often regarded as a financial and even emotional burden. Years of childcare and expense culminate in the girl's leaving home for marriage into another family, often somewhat distant and with limited ties to the family of origin.

The sex ratio in India in 1991, about 927 women to 1,000 men, is one of the lowest in the world. It suggests the systematic neglect of females, especially young girls. As amniocentesis and sonograms become more widely available, allowing parents to know the sex of unborn children, abortion of females may result. Suicide rates for Indian women are high, and isolated cases of *sati* (*suttee*), in which a widow immolates herself on her husband's funeral pyre, continue. In 1987, the literacy rate among females was 29 percent as compared with 57 percent for males; but this was up from 8 percent and 25 percent, respectively, in 1951. South India's treatment of women is widely regarded as more egalitarian, perhaps because of different local traditions, including some influence of matrilineal systems that follow the females line in inheritance and residence.

sati (suttee) An ancient Hindu custom that requires widows to be burned on the funeral pyre of their husbands, or soon afterward.

Economic Changes Disconcerting results from a 1984 anthropological study of a village near Delhi suggest that the position of poor, rural women was actually deteriorating as a result of increasing general prosperity in the new economic system and of increasing urbanization.

There were several factors affecting women's work, all producing a marked decline in women's employment opportunities. First, women who had worked in agriculture alongside their male kin were displaced when their husbands left field work to seek jobs in the cities. Second, women who traditionally worked in caste-based occupations as servants through *jajmani* (family patronage systems) could no longer find such jobs. Third, mechanization had replaced female labor in a variety of arenas. Finally, changes in cropping patterns had made female help in the fields less necessary. These factors all contributed to the marginalization of poor women, giving them less voice in their families and ultimately devaluing them (Wadley, in Wiser and Wiser, p. 287).

An encouraging contrary development was the organization of working women into effective unions that provide both economic opportunity and political representation. In cities such as Mumbai (Bombay), Madras, and Ahmedabad, voluntary organizations of tens of thousands of working women have begun to gain access to capital for working-class women who carry on their own small businesses; to form cooperatives, which help them secure raw materials and market finished products; to lobby government for workers' safety, health, insurance, maternity, and job protection in non-unionized, small-scale shops; to develop new educational models for job training; and to create new systems of health delivery, especially for women. One of the most important of these organizations is the Self-Employed Women's Association (SEWA) in Ahmedabad, a daughter organization of the Textile Labour Union, which had been founded with the help of Mahatma Gandhi.

Economic and Technological Change after Independence

The Green Revolution Economically and technologically, India has accomplished the once seemingly impossible feat of producing enough food to feed its growing population. At independence, India had 361 million people; by the mid-1980s, the population had more than doubled to three-quarters of a billion people. During droughts in 1964–6 mass-starvation was averted only by the importation of 12 million tons of food grains each year, primarily from the United States. Then, in the late 1960s, the "green revolution" took root in India. New strains of wheat, developed in Mexico under the auspices of the Rockefeller Foundation, were introduced. They increased India's productivity even faster than her population. India, almost miraculously, proved able to feed itself. Between the early 1960s and the late 1970s, rice production rose by more than 50 percent; wheat production tripled. Total grain production rose from about 50 million tons per year at independence to about 150 million tons in the mid-1980s.

Meanwhile, a "white revolution" in dairy production and distribution was also taking place. Dairy cooperatives were formed throughout India, enabling village farmers to pool and ship their highly perishable products to urban markets—as fresh milk in refrigerated train cars, and as processed cheese and dairy products in conventional shipping—thus providing incentives for increasing production.

These revolutions in agriculture were not without their problems. First, ecologically, questions were raised about relying so exclusively on so few new strains of "miracle wheat." Were too many seeds coming from too few genetic baskets? Would the massive new quantities of chemical fertilizers needed to support the new seeds ultimately ruin the ecology? Second, economic growth increased disparities and tensions between haves and have-nots and between those who worked more entrepreneurially and those who did not. The new productivity benefited most those who already had the economic resources to afford the new seeds, fertilizers, pesticides, and irrigation water. The rich were getting richer—although the poor did not seem to be getting poorer—and social

New technology crosses gender lines. Power tillers provide a new technology more appropriate economically than either bullock-drawn plows or tractors in some areas of India. They are available through collaboration with Japan (Mitsubishi). In entering her new occupation, the driver has received financial and technical assistance from SEWA, the Self-Employed Women's Association in Ahmedabad.

tensions increased. Similarly, disparities between rich and poor states grew. The Punjab, in particular, progressed dramatically in transforming both its agriculture and small industries. The small northern state became the richest in India, the country's breadbasket.

Land Redistribution Control of land and its redistribution was a matter for each state in India, and different states enacted different policies. In general, redistribution was accompanied by compensation paid by the new owners, and the process has been peaceful but slow.

Family Planning, Life Expectancy, and the Condition of Children Government implementation of family planning, rejected overwhelmingly in the wake of Indira Gandhi's program of forced sterilization in 1975–7, has been soft-pedaled ever since. Nevertheless birth rates fell to about 33 per thousand in 1985, down from about 44 per thousand at independence, indicating great general interest in smaller, planned families. Life expectancy at birth rose from about 30 years at independence in 1947 to 56 in 1985. On the other hand, at the outset of the 1990s, the World Bank reported that 66 percent of India's children under age five were malnourished.

Industrialization and its Consequences Industrial productivity increased, but the structure of the workforce did not change—exactly the process Gandhi had feared. New machinery produced more goods more efficiently, but it did not provide proportionately more jobs. The business and industrial sectors contributed only 5 percent to the nation's income in 1947; slightly more than 30 percent by the mid-1980s. Industrial production multiplied almost five times between 1951 and 1980. In the 1980s it was increasing almost 8 percent a year. Urbanization increased to 27 percent, up from 17 percent at independence. On the other hand, the percentage of workers in industry essentially stagnated: about 10 percent in 1951; about 13 percent in 1980. Unemployment was reported steady at 8 percent.

Until the 1980s, industrial policy derived from Gandhi's and Nehru's conflicting philosophies. Gandhi had urged austere consumption levels, handicraft production, spinning wheels, and national self-sufficiency through import substitution. Nehru implemented socialism, central planning, industrialization, government control and development of the "commanding heights" of the economy—energy, steel, petroleum, banking—and regulation of the large-scale capitalist sector. Despite their strong differences on the importance of large-scale industry and modern technology, both Gandhi and Nehru stressed internal self-sufficiency in production.

These policies were increasingly challenged by a new international political-economic wisdom in the 1980s based on the economic successes of the East Asian countries and the political policies of President Reagan in the USA and Prime Minister Margaret Thatcher in Britain. Increased consumption spurred increased productivity, and a consumer society began to appear in India.

High-tech innovation for both home and foreign markets increased productivity, and India began to manufacture submarines, computer software (of which it had become a world center) and hardware, and machine tools, and even prepared to export nuclear power plants adapted to third world conditions. Its impressive scientific and technological establishment had the capacity to adopt and adapt the newest technological advances.

In part, these technological successes were possible because of an extraordinary imbalance in India's educational expenditures. The government strongly favored higher education while starving the primary schools. These policies, rooted in traditional hierarchical attitudes and interests, produced a skewed society in which the

HOW DO WE KNOW?

Technological Hazards and Questionable Accountability

Indian attitudes toward modern technology have fallen between the skepticism of Gandhi and the enthusiasm of Nehru. Some of the most biting critiques of India's technological policies on development came from a "modern intellectual," Ashis Nandy, who criticized the government for giving excessive power to the scientific-technological establishment. In particular he focused on India's nuclear establishment in the mid-1980s:

Nuclear scientists were freed from all financial constraints. The budget of the nuclear program ... was routinely pushed through parliament without any scrutiny whatsoever. And the expenditures ... were never publicly audited. All data on performance ... failures, unsafe technology and insufficient regard for human rights ... were protected by law from the public gaze. And all enquiries made from outside the nuclear establishment were pre-empted with the help of a special act that made it impossible to mount any informed, focused, data-based criticism of India's nuclear programme. (Nandy, p. 5)

Further skepticism concerning winners and losers in the quest for industrial modernization resulted from a tragedy of poison gas leakage in a Union Carbide insecticide plant in Bhopal in 1984, the worst industrial accident of its kind in the world up to that date. Compounding the tragedy for the victims, the American-owned corporation resisted payment of compensation:

Dreadful tragedy struck central India's Bhopal ... in December 1984 ... Deadly invisible gas from Union Carbide's insecticide storage tanks had escaped through defective valves to be blown by ill-winds over the slumbering bodies of thousands of poor innocents outside that giant plant's walls, less than 400 miles south of New Delhi. Within hours, 2,000 people were dead and hundreds of thousands of others had been injured by the worst industrial accident of recent history. Union Carbide was still American owned, one of the few multinationals in India that had not been taken over by a majority of Indian shareholders and management ...

Though hundreds of billions of dollars in damages were quickly claimed in thousands of lawsuits filed both in India and America, virtually nothing was paid to any of the actual victims for seven full years after the tragedy devastated Bhopal. Legal snares and questions of jurisdiction plagued the process, serving to thwart justice instead of expediting its realization. (Wolpert, pp. 421–2)

- Why do you think that India's nuclear development program had such independence of action without public political supervision? Do you approve of such secrecy in India? In the nuclear development programs in the USA? Why or why not?
- On what basis do you think Union Carbide resisted paying compensation to most of the victims of the leak? After you have made your guesses, you may wish to check Bhopal and Union Carbide on the Web to see what answers you can find.
- In an overwhelmingly agrarian, poor, rural society such as India, what do you think is the proper place for modern industry, such as nuclear weapons? Peaceful use of atomic energy? Chemical insecticides?

highly educated elites compared with the best anywhere in the world, but overall basic literacy was only 43 percent. Again, Gandhi's fears were coming true.

International Relations

India was the first major colony to win independence after World War II, and it served as a leader to other newly emerging countries. Nehru, in particular, provided articulate, innovative direction, and after independence India remained a model of democratic political stability and gradual economic growth in a society of unparalleled heterogeneity. Its international role, however, declined. India's border war with, and defeat by, China in 1962 crippled its claim to third world harmony and leadership. In the wake of this war, India began to spend more on its armed forces. Military expenditures rose from US$ 1.7 billion in 1960 to US$ 9.8 billion in 1987 (in constant dollars).

Decolonization throughout the world was virtually complete by the 1980s, and political colonialism was no longer a major global issue. The attention of new nations shifted to economic development. Japan and the highly successful "tigers" of East and Southeast Asia, with their more open, more liberalized, and more expansive economies attracted them. In a world concerned with economic growth, the persistence of poverty and illiteracy made India a questionable model for others. Its progress seemed too slow. It remained, however, the dominant power in the South Asia region.

COMPARING CHINA AND INDIA
WHAT DIFFERENCE DOES IT MAKE?

At the end of World War I, India's demand for independence ignited a mass movement that bore many similarities to China's. With the vast majority of its population in rural areas, India, like China, was rooted in agriculture and its peasantry. Like China's Mao, India's Mahatma Gandhi mobilized this rural constituency. Both leaders created new social and economic institutions for greater equity and also emphasized the need for new, simple technologies appropriate to their agrarian, impoverished societies. Both regarded their methods and solutions as models for others to copy.

The differences between the two mammoth countries were at least equally significant. Unlike China, which had no functioning central government between 1912 and 1949 and had been carved into numerous European and Japanese spheres of influence, India had a central government, which was under British colonial control until independence in 1947. While China suffered decades of civil warfare, political disputes in India were addressed through generally peaceful, constitutional processes. India's nationalist leaders, unlike those of China, welcomed businessmen and professionals along with the peasantry in their independence struggle. Unlike China, in its independence movement India pursued an extraordinary strategy of non-violent mass civil resistance. It fought no civil war nor did the battles of World War II significantly touch its borders. When independence came, relations with colonial Britain continued harmonious, and India retained membership in the Commonwealth of Nations. Even the partition of the subcontinent into India and Pakistan in 1947 followed constitutional processes, although the subsequent transfers of population were enormously violent. The 1971 creation of the independent country of Bangladesh on the land of East Pakistan was the product of civil war, in which India aided Bangladesh against West Pakistan. Naxalite movements brought outbursts of guerrilla warfare in localized regions. Hindu–Muslim and high caste–low caste tensions sometimes also burst into violence, but the open violence of these confrontations was usually confined to local areas and short periods of time.

A generation after ending colonialism, both countries could point to significant accomplishments including: cumulative and growing economic expansion, more rapid in China, slower in India; political cohesion; and social transformation in accord with their differing agendas. Both countries had moved from concentration on rural areas, a promise of their colonial struggles, to concern also with their cities and their industries. They shared a similar challenge: How to maintain a coherent national agenda after the unifying enemy of colonialism had been defeated?

After 1949, China continued to live out its revolutionary, agrarian heritage. Soon after taking power, it expelled foreigners—capitalist, communist, and Christian—and sought to develop internally, with its own resources. With the Korean War it immediately signaled its willingness to assert leadership in third-world armed struggle. Periodically, it created development plans modeled on the experience of the Long March and the Chinese soviet in Yan'an: the Great Leap Forward, with its backyard steel furnaces, and the Great Proletarian Cultural Revolution, with its exile of urban bureaucrats and intellectuals to forced labor in rural China. The new government also turned to developing its cities and industries. Through it all, the Communist Party remained in control. When policy disputes threatened to pull the party apart, Chairman Mao reasserted his control. He rewarded the "Red" rather than the "Expert" among his colleagues, and lost power only as he neared his death in 1976.

After 1947, as an independent country, India chose a pattern of political democracy and a mixed economy, balancing a "socialist pattern of society," with considerable allowance for private ventures. India confronted enormous, persistent challenges from both its own social structure and the colonial heritage: hierarchical caste divisions, especially discrimination against ex-untouchables; conflict between religious communities, especially Hindus and Muslims, but Sikhs as well in and around the Punjab; tensions among regional and linguistic groups; renewed oppression of women; an economy of scarcity with widespread, persistent hunger and poverty; and continuing massive population growth. In these struggles, India followed policies of political stability for development, including technological policies of great diversity.

Both China and India were aware of the technological and economic progress of Japan and the Asian tigers. For China this represented a galling challenge since the Japanese powerhouse dominated the economics of east Asia, displacing China from her historic position. India did not see itself in competition with Japan, but it recognized that the smaller countries of Southeast Asia, which had previously trailed India, had now surpassed it economically and in consumer technology. India, too, saw this as a model and a challenge.

Review Questions

- Compare Mao and Gandhi in terms of both their personal experience with agrarian issues and their policies for dealing with them.
- Compare Mao and Gandhi in terms of their policies on the use of violence and non-violence in attaining their political objectives. To what extent are the differences in their philosophies a result of differences in the political context in which they lived and worked?
- Compare the status of women in the philosophies of Mao and Gandhi.
- To what degree did the experiences of the Long March and the guerrilla war of the Chinese communist revolution provide good guidelines for government policy in governing China after 1949?
- To what degree did the experiences of the Indian independence movement provide good guidelines for government policy in governing India after 1947?
- In the debate over the technology to be used in modern India, what do you think are the strong and weak points of Gandhi's position and of Nehru's position?

Suggested Readings

CHINA

Andors, Phyllis. *The Unfinished Liberation of Chinese Women 1949–1980* (Bloomington: University of Indiana Press, 1983). Feminist, anti-patriarchal ideology was central to the Chinese communist program. Andors captures the ideology and the degree of implementation.

Blunden, Caroline and Mark Elvin. *Cultural Atlas of China* (New York: Facts on File, 1983). Another in the excellent Facts on File series. More than an atlas, it is a comprehensive approach to China, scholarly yet very accessible.

de Bary, W. Theodore, *et al. Sources of Chinese Tradition*, Vol. 2 (New York: Columbia University Press, 1999). An outstanding anthology of statements by China's intellectual and political leaders. The 1999 revision doubled the number of selections.

Ebrey, Patricia Buckley, ed. *Chinese Civilization: A*

Sourcebook (New York: The Free Press, 1993). A very different selection from de Bary's. Ebrey's selections capture the lives of common people. Illuminating and excellent.

Meisner, Maurice. *Mao's China and After* (New York: The Free Press, 1986). A thoughtful, rather pro-Mao account of the revolution. A scholarly, accessible standard.

Schell, Orville, ed. *The China Reader*, 4 vols. (New York: Random House, 1967–74). These volumes tell the story of China's revolution from the end of the colonial era through the end of Mao's years through an exceptional array of documents.

Snow, Edgar. *Red Star over China* (London: Victor Gollancz, 1968). Journalist Snow visited Mao in Yan'an and brought back to the West the first detailed knowledge of the man and the movement. Inspiring from a very pro-Maoist viewpoint.

Spence, Jonathan D. *The Search for Modern China* (New York: W.W. Norton & Company, 1990). Clearly written, detailed yet highly accessible, excellent as an introduction to the subject and to further scholarly investigation. Reissued in paperback in 2000.

INDIA

Bayly, Susan. *Caste, Society, and Politics in India from the Eighteenth Century to the Modern Age* (Cambridge: Cambridge University Press, 1999). Accessible, highly scholarly introduction to the phenomenon of caste, the changing meaning of caste, and the changing economic and political significance of caste.

Brown, Judith M. *Modern India: The Origins of an Asian Democracy* (New York: Oxford University Press, 1984). Stresses the constitutional processes in achieving independence, and in the negotiations between the British and the Congress. Brown sees India's post-independence democracy as a result of that process.

Chandra, Bipan. *India's Struggle for Independence, 1857–1947* (New York: Penguin Books, 1989). Chandra stresses the popular, revolutionary side of the independence struggle, and sees Gandhi as the integrative force who encouraged it to take democratic directions.

Dalton, Dennis. *Mahatma Gandhi: Non-Violent Power in Action* (New York: Columbia University Press, 1993). Remarkably lucid account of Gandhi's theory and practice of *satyagraha*, especially good on his fast in Calcutta, 1947.

Forbes, Geraldine. *Women in Modern India* (Cambridge: Cambridge University Press, 1998). Useful survey of women in education, cultural and social life, and reform, the nationalist movement, the economy, and recent political action. Especially interesting for shift from elite issues to the masses.

Hay, Stephen, ed. *Sources of Indian Tradition*, Vol. 2 (New York: Columbia University Press, 2nd ed., 1988). Excellent selection of statements by Indian political and cultural leaders. Stresses the elites.

Nehru, Jawaharlal. *The Discovery of India* (Bombay: Asia Publishing House, 1960). A personal history, Marxist in orientation, written from jail by the prime minister of India, illuminating both of the nation's history and of Nehru's understanding of that history.

Rothermund, Dietmar. *An Economic History of India: From Pre-Colonial Times to 1991* (London: Routledge, 1993). Clearly written, succinct introduction to the subject.

Rudolph, Lloyd I. and Susanne Hoeber Rudolph. *The Modernity of Tradition* (Chicago: University of Chicago Press, 1967). Still the clearest introduction to the idea that tradition and modernity are not opposites, but interact in the hands of creative leaders—like Gandhi, and like later caste leaders.

Wiser, William H. and Charlotte Viall Wiser, *Behind Mud Walls 1930–1960* (including Susan Wadley, "The Village in 1984," "The Village in 1998")

(Berkeley: University of California Press, 2000). The Wisers kept revisiting a north Indian village and writing down their observations. A fascinating, very readable review. Make sure to get the latest edition, as Susan Wadley continues to update the Wisers' work.

ADDITIONAL SOURCES

Bouton, Marshall M. and Philip Oldenburg, eds. *India Briefing: A Transformative Fifty Years* (Armonk, NY: M.E. Sharpe, 1999). Every year or two, Oldenburg and a co-editor bring together an excellent, scholarly set of interpretive essays on current events in India under the title *India Briefing*. This edition covered the entire period from independence.

Brass, Paul. *The Politics of India since Independence* (Cambridge: Cambridge University Press, 2nd ed., 1994). Another in the Cambridge series of comprehensive introductions to India. Brass is comprehensive, thoughtful, and, appropriately, quite skeptical of official rhetoric.

Drèze, Jean and Amartya Sen. *India's Economic Development and Social Opportunity* (Delhi: Oxford University Press, 1998). Sen won the 1998 Nobel prize for economics for his stress on the importance of education and health in development economics. Here he and Drèze bring that perspective to an analysis of India's record.

Fairbank, John King. *The Great Chinese Revolution: 1800–1985* (New York: Harper & Row, 1986). Until his death, Fairbank was one of the masters of Chinese history. This book is now dated, but very useful and interesting.

Frankel, Francine. *India's Political Economy, 1947–1977* (Princeton: Princeton University Press, 1978). To know how India said it was doing, and how it was actually doing in economic and political development after independence, this is a good place to begin.

Goldman, Merle and Roderick MacFarquhar, eds. *The Paradox of China's Post-Mao Reforms* (Cambridge: Harvard University Press, 1999). Although focused on China after Mao, the contrast is illuminating.

Hardgrave, Robert L. and Stanley Kochanek. *India: Government and Politics in a Developing Nation* (Stamford, CT: Harcourt College Publishers, 1999). A standard, introductory text, continuously revised for three decades.

Jack, Homer, ed. *The Gandhi Reader* (New York: Grove Press, 1956). A comprehensive source book covering Gandhi's philosophies and activities in politics, economics, and moral life, mostly by Gandhi, some about him.

Jayakar, Pupul. *Indira Gandhi* (New York: Viking, 1992). A friendly, but critical biography by a friend and colleague.

Karlekar, Hiranmay, ed. *Independent India: The First Fifty Years* (Delhi: Oxford University Press and the Indian Council for Cultural Relations, 1998). A set of assessments of uneven quality, but many quite fascinating of many aspects of India since independence. Written in India for Indians, may be somewhat dense for foreign readers.

Kennedy, Paul. *The Rise and Fall of the Great Powers* (New York: Random House, 1987). Kennedy looks at the great powers since 1500. He introduces China only in recent times. India doesn't make it. Interesting for his view of what counts in national greatness.

Liang, Heng and Judith Shapiro. *Son of the Revolution* (New York: Vintage Books, 1983). Liang's biography as a young man who survived the Cultural Revolution, but saw it destroy his parents, their marriage, his schooling, and his earlier belief that the revolution was benign.

Liu Binyan. *A Higher Kind of Loyalty* (New York: Pantheon, 1990). Exiled from China, journalist Liu Binyan writes from America incisive, angry criticism of the actions of the government of the country that he loves.

MacFarquhar, Roderick Timothy Cheek, and Eugene Wu, eds. *The Secret Speeches of Chairman Mao* (Cambridge, MA: Council on East Asian Studies, 1989).

Nandy, Ashis, ed. *Science, Hegemony and Violence* (Delhi: Oxford University Press, 1988). Nandy is an oddity, a prominent, Western-educated intellectual who is quite skeptical of Western influences in India, including scientific and technological influences.

Pa Chin. *Family* (Garden City, N.Y.: Doubleday & Company, 1972). This novel of the 1910s and 1920s presented a new, feminist vision of what a family might be in modern China.

Ramusack, Barbara, *et al. Women in Asia: Restoring Women to History* (Bloomington: Indiana University Press, 1999). Product of a decade-long project of the Organization of American Historians to provide perspectives and bibliographies on the study of women in the non-Western world. Other volumes treat sub-Saharan Africa, the Middle East, and Latin America.

Schell, Orville and David Shambaugh, eds. *The China Reader: The Reform Era* (New York: Vintage Books, 1999). An excellent selection of essays and observations on the changes in China after Mao's death. Updates the earlier four volumes of *China Reader* noted above.

Weiner, Myron. *The Child and the State in India* (Princeton: Princeton University Press, 1991). In a very critical, down-to-earth assessment, Weiner asks why literacy rates and school attendance are so low, and child labor so extensive. Hierarchical values are a major culprit.

Wolf, Eric R. *Peasant Wars of the Twentieth Century* (New York: Harper & Row, 1969). A classic comparative study of the philosophies and strategies of modern guerrilla warfare. China figures prominently.

Wolpert, Stanley. *A New History of India* (New York: Oxford University Press, 7th ed., 2004). A useful, standard, sometimes rambling, highly readable text.

Wu, Harry. *Bitter Winds* (New York: John Wiley, 1994). One of the most bitter attacks on political repression in contemporary China.

World History Documents CD-ROM

24.3 Mao Zedong: *Report of an Investigation into the Peasant Movement in Hunan*
24.4 Li Shaoqi: *How to Be a Good Communist* (1939)
24.5 The New Communist State (1940-1950)
24.6 Mao Zedong: *From the Countryside to the City* (May 1949)
24.7 The Failure of the Nationalist Government: The American Assessment (1949)
27.1 Mohandas K. Gandhi
27.2 Jawaharlal Nehru: Gandhi and Nehru: *Two Utterly Different Standpoints*

Into a New Century

During the last decades of the twentieth century many people felt that they were living through the end of an old era and the birth of a new one. The Cold War ended, the process of decolonization was complete, free-market economics gained ground, the computer revolution was underway, feminism continued to make great strides. All of these transformations forced people to rethink their identities. Where did they stand on the great issues of the day? How were their lives changed by them? To what degree could they live lives of their own choosing?

The women's movement now reached out to include global constituencies and concerns. In Mexico City in 1975 the United Nations sponsored the first World Conference on women's issues. Here and in subsequent related meetings in Copenhagen (1980), Cairo (1994), and Beijing (1995) women learned about the concerns of one another across national borders and political systems. Often they came away surprised at the differences in their perspectives. Westerners stressed access to better jobs, for example, while women from poorer countries sought changes in the power structures of international politics and economics that left them impoverished. Despite these glaring differences, participants also came away with new strategies and renewed appreciation for women's power in collective action.

The ecological devastation of the earth also evoked international action, also not always successfully. The logging of the Brazilian rainforest continued, and some of the activists working to preserve the forest were shot to death. Scientific evidence of global warming continued to accumulate, and progress was made in assembling a global response to cut back on the production of toxic chemicals and gases. The United States, however, refused to sign the Kyoto Agreement on global warming, nor did it offer feasible alternatives. Since the USA was the largest producer of toxic substances, the refusal partially undermined the movement. Many nations and localities did introduce effective conservation and anti-pollution programs locally, within their own borders.

In the face of hunger and starvation in Africa, a number of internationally renowned popular musicians banded together to give a series of concerts (Live Aid) in 1985 in London and around the world, raising awareness of global poverty and contributing the proceeds to alleviate the hunger in Africa.

The 2001 strikes on the World Trade Center in New York City and the Pentagon outside of Washington shocked America, and the rest of the

Above Leah Rabin, wife of the Israeli Prime Minister Yitzhak Rabin (later assassinated), at the World Conference on International Women, Mexico City, 1975.

Right The Brazilian rainforest after logging and burning, 1985.

Live Aid concert finale, London, 1985. From left are George Michael, Paul McCartney, Andrew Ridgeley, Freddie Mercury, David Bowie, and Bob Geldof.

world, by demonstrating the worldwide reach of the militant Islamic organization al-Qaeda. Unlike other terrorist organizations, which usually had specific, negotiable goals, al-Qaeda seemed to target US power and interests in an attempt to frighten America out of its involvement in the Middle East or even to undermine the entire capitalist-military structure of the Western world. American President Bush declared war on terrorism, identifying militant, terrorist elements in the Islamic world as America's new chief enemy.

The attack on the World Trade Center, New York, September 11, 2001.

The 2004 meeting of the World Social Forum in Mumbai (Bombay), India, brought together some 100,000 people, representing many of the identities contesting for recognition in the early twenty-first century. The Forum began as an alternative to the

meetings of the G-8, the leading industrialized powers of the world. It has continued to grow as it has added to its agenda concerns for gender relations—including not only women but also gays, lesbians, bisexuals, and transgendered people; global ecology; and the dramatically unequal distribution of political and economic power. The contrast between the elite G-8 and the populist Forum made clear some of the alternative identities that clamored for recognition in the first years of the new century.

More than 100,000 demonstrators take to the streets to protest at the World Social Forum, Bombay, 2004.

QUESTIONS

1. In what ways were the issues of Western middle-class women different from the issues of the women of the Third World?
2. Why has it been difficult to create an international consensus on a program to preserve the ecology of the globe?
3. Do you think that the musicians who performed in the Live Aid concerts would have been comfortable attending the World Social Forum? Why or why not?

PART 8

Evolving Identities

1979–Present

We have chosen "identities" as the theme for this Part. Everyone acts out of a sense of identity, our understanding of who or what we are, have been, and wish to become. Beyond the individual, a sense of identity is important also to groups, institutions, and nations. In large part identities are based on historical experiences. Through them the past has a strong influence on the future. At the same time, identities are flexible. To some degree they change as we change and as circumstances change. Some parts of our identities change with our changing age and status.

Nations, too, have complex identities. Consider the United States. It is a relatively new nation, born in 1776, yet it is one of the very oldest of the world's constitutional democracies. It has protected private property, yet it has enacted important laws restricting the freedom of businesses in favor of a larger public good. It proclaims democracy and freedom for all, yet it held slavery as legal until 1865, practiced Jim Crow policies formally and informally for another century, and it continues to show significant levels of racial discrimination in practice even today.

Religions, as well, have diverse aspects to their identities. Sometimes they emphasize the literal, historic teachings of their founders and sometimes they emphasize the need for flexibility in interpreting those teachings. Sometimes they seek greater centralization and conformity, at other times they may promote greater individual freedom of conscience and action. Economic systems also undergo changes in their identity, from an emphasis on private enterprise to an emphasis on government control—to one on cooperative enterprise.

The formation of identity in recent years has been subject to more diverse and more intense influences than ever before. Transportation, travel, communication, and, most especially the World Wide Web have multiplied the influences on our sense of individual and collective identity.

In this Part we shall be examining the end of the Cold War; the collapse of the Soviet Union; the realignment of Third-World countries; the renewed infusion of religion into politics; the rise of global terrorism; the expansion of illegal trafficking—of drugs most of all, but also of weapons, women and children, and human organs; women's issues; the spread of new, fearsome, formerly unknown epidemic diseases such as AIDS; the rise of East Asian economic power; the emergence of the United States as the unrivalled master of large-scale military power; the damage being done to the world's ecology. In Chapter 23 we shall consider some of the major challenges to established identities that have arisen in the recent past. In Chapter 24 we shall examine several case studies of responses to those challenges.

UN World Conference on Women, Great Hall of the People, Beijing, China, 1995.

MITRA KASIH
POS LSM
KOMPAS
Gunung Slamet Terbakar
Dephut Alokasikan Dana

NEW PUBLIC IDENTITIES

1979–PRESENT

KEY TOPICS
- Political Identities
- Religious and Cultural Identities
- Globalization: New Economic and Cultural Identities
- Ecological Issues
- Public Identities: What Difference Do They Make?

This chapter explores four central elements of individual, group, national, and global identities. It begins with political identities, addressing especially the disintegration of the Soviet Union and the end of the Cold War. It continues with a discussion of the increasing importance of religion in public life in many different ways and in many different parts of the world. It next considers the phenomenon of economic and cultural globalization—that is, the increased importance of global markets and the international exchange of commodities and culture. Finally, it will examine the changes in global ecology over the past two to three decades.

POLITICAL IDENTITIES

The Soviet Union Dissolves

The collapse and disintegration of the Soviet Union, and of the Communist Party that created and administered it, shocked the political and cultural world of the late twentieth century. The entire process unfolded in just two years, 1989–91, and transformed identities around the globe. From the time of its establishment in 1917, the Soviet Union had offered alternative models to the capitalism and individualism of western Europe and the United States. Through the global depression, it had demonstrated that state planning could keep an economy—at least its industrial sectors—humming. It alone had responded vigorously to the dangers posed by the rise of Nazism by building up a strong military defense, and throughout World War II it held the Eastern Front at enormous cost in lives and specie. During the Cold War, the Soviet Union alone provided a balance against the overwhelming military power of the United States, and offered support and an alternative path for newly independent nations emerging from colonialism. At the same time, the totalitarian power of the communist government and the gulag of prison camps through which it enforced that power were crucial ingredients in Soviet identity. Its occupation of central and eastern Europe from 1945 made it an imperial, and dreaded, neighbor.

Individuals, institutions, states, and governments had looked to the Soviet Union as a model for seven decades—some with hope, others with fear and apprehension. With its collapse they lost a pole star in their map of the political universe. Political identities everywhere were reshuffled. Two men guided the process that brought the Soviet Union to its end, Mikhail Gorbachev and Boris Yeltsin.

Mikhail Gorbachev, 1985–91 Mikhail Gorbachev (b. 1931) came to power in the USSR in 1985. He assessed the problems of the Soviet Union directly and bluntly. Its

Opposite **Protest against global warming, Pontianak, Indonesia, 2000.** Due to forest fires that rage on unchecked, and to urban congestion, Indonesia is one of the most polluted places on earth.

economy was neither producing nor distributing goods effectively. Its bureaucracy was bloated with Party officials, while the growing professional classes protested restrictions on freedom. The Churches continued to seek greater freedom of expression. In the satellite countries of eastern Europe and in the non-Russian states of the USSR itself—especially the Baltic states and in the states of Central Asia, which were culturally, linguistically, and religiously different from Russia—nationalist groups sought greater independence. In its haste to industrialize, the USSR had allowed technology to get out of control, as evident in the massive pollution of air and sea, most frighteningly in the Aral Sea, which was drying up. In addition, the ongoing war in Afghanistan was bleeding the country of lives, treasure, and spirit. Finally, the Soviet Union was engaged in an arms race with the United States that it could no longer afford.

glasnost A Russian word meaning "openness," adopted as a political slogan by the Soviet leader Mikhail Gorbachev in 1986. It encouraged greater freedom of expression and genuine debate in social, political, and cultural affairs; with **perestroika**, it heralded greater democracy and improved relations with the West.

perestroika A Russian word meaning "restructuring," used, like **glasnost**, to describe the reforms introduced by the Soviet leader Mikhail Gorbachev after 1985. It marked the development of a more flexible socio-economic system, distinguished by a move to a market-oriented economy, increased private ownership, and decentralization.

In response to these problems, Gorbachev introduced his policies of **glasnost** (political and cultural openness) and **perestroika** (economic restructuring). Glasnost meant, first of all, telling the truth about communist Russia, and this included the truth about the past. Khrushchev had already revealed many of Stalin's atrocities. Under Gorbachev historians revealed even more: some 20 million people killed under Stalin and a similar number oppressed. Glasnost also extended to the present. Russians, who would have agreed with novelist Alexander Solzhenitsyn's 1973 statement, "It has always been impossible to learn the truth about anything in our country," now heard directly about the depth of their nation's problems.

Glasnost revealed the problems. Perestroika looked for solutions. Gorbachev tried to reduce the size of the bureaucracy, to increase the efficiency of agriculture and industry, and to trim the military budget. He appointed reformers like himself to important government offices. He planned and began a more competitive economic system, but still under the general direction of state planning. The competition was among state-owned firms rather than among private companies, which did not exist. Gorbachev was somewhat trapped by his own promises, for soon the reformers were criticizing him for moving too slowly and for an unwillingness to cut free of discredited communist economics. Neither the bureaucracy nor the economy responded adequately to his reforms. The nuclear explosion at Chernobyl in the Ukraine in 1986, the worst industrial accident in history in terms of short- and long-term damage, and a gas pipeline fire that killed hundreds in 1989 exemplified and added to his woes.

In terms of political reforms, Gorbachev moved more boldly, and this paradoxically proved his downfall. Under glasnost, ethnic groups throughout the length and breadth of the highly diverse Soviet Union began to voice their grievances. Riots between ethnic groups broke out in Kazakhstan, Tajikistan, Kyrgyzstan, and Uzbekistan. Gorbachev could restore order only with difficulty. He was unable to stop the fighting in Nagorno-Karabakh, an enclave within Muslim Azerbaijan but with a majority of Christian Armenians. Full-scale independence movements began in the Baltic states of Lithuania, Latvia, and Estonia, as well as in Georgia. Others soon followed.

Meanwhile, the war in Afghanistan that Brezhnev had initiated in 1979 ground on, with about 2000 Russian soldiers dying every year and no evidence of Soviet gains. In 1988, Gorbachev allowed multi-candidate elections and began to give the Supreme Soviet increased powers. In February 1990, he announced that non-Party candidates could stand for office. The monopoly of the Communist Party over the government ended. Gorbachev was willing to see the Soviet empire and the Communist Party disintegrate, and they did. His spokesman announced that he was replacing the Brezhnev Doctrine of massive intervention in rebellious satellite countries with the (Frank) Sinatra Doctrine of "My way," allowing them to break free of the Soviet Union however they chose. The fervor of their response was most clearly demonstrated when Germans tore down the Berlin Wall on November 9, 1989. Gorbachev continued his

negotiations for arms reductions with US Presidents Reagan and Bush, and in December 1989, Gorbachev and Bush formally announced the end of the Cold War.

With the removal of Soviet armies, all six satellite nations in eastern and central Europe became independent: East Germany, Poland, Hungary, Czechoslovakia (which, in 1993, divided into the Czech and Slovak Republics), Bulgaria, and Romania. Divided at the end of World War II, East and West Germany re-united after tearing down the Berlin Wall that had most conspicuously marked their division. Gorbachev at first resisted the right of constituent republics of the USSR to declare their independence and leave the union, but many now defied his wishes: the Baltic states of Estonia, Latvia, and Lithuania; the eastern European Slavic states of Belarus, Ukraine, and Moldova; the Caspian Sea states of Armenia, Georgia, and Azerbaijan; and the Muslim majority states in Central Asia: Turkmenistan, Uzbekistan, Tajikistan, Kyrgyzstan, and Kazakhstan. With government control uncertain, historic national and ethnic identities re-emerged within and between these states. These identities were sometimes hostile to one another, and violent clashes, as well as celebration, marked the end of the Soviet empire.

Reformers criticized Gorbachev for moving too slowly, but in August 1991 diehard communists mounted a coup against him because they felt he had moved too quickly. While Gorbachev was vacationing in the Crimea, a group of anti-reform members of his government, with the support of a number of military officers, placed Gorbachev under house arrest and assumed control of his Kremlin offices. The coup failed largely because Boris Yeltsin, one of the reformers and the elected president of the Russian Federation, opposed it. He turned his headquarters in the Russian parliament building into the center of public resistance to the coup, contacted political leaders across Russia and around the world to gain support, and courageously went out to the streets and climbed atop an armored troop carrier to make his position clear. When the army refused to attack Yeltsin and his headquarters, the coup was finished. Gorbachev returned from the Crimea, but Yeltsin was the hero of the moment.

The break-up of the Soviet Union. The Soviet experiment with Marxist ideology crumbled, after seventy years, at the end of the 1980s. President Gorbachev's policy of *glasnost* (1985) allowed the nations of eastern Europe to move, largely bloodlessly, toward independence and economic reform, but in the Caucasus mountains and Central Asia reform was often accompanied by an insurgence of nationalism, organized crime, and power struggles. In 1991 these nations also became independent—except for Chechnya, where fighting continued for years.

SOURCE

Gorbachev at the United Nations, December 7, 1988

Gorbachev left two contrasting legacies. At home, he failed in his practical attempts to bring perestroika, the restructuring of the Russian economy, politics, and society. On the other hand, his vision of the future for the world inspired people everywhere. It underpinned his dismantling of the Soviet Union, its Communist Party, and its control over the satellite countries of central and eastern Europe. The vision seemed utopian yet, somehow, perhaps, achievable. Gorbachev's speech at the United Nations General Assembly in New York City on December 7, 1988, summarized his goals and aspirations. It called for global cooperation, tolerance for diverse social and political systems, protection for the globe's ecology, assistance for development in the poorer nations, and disarmament, which he pledged to begin immediately in the Soviet Union on his own initiative. This was quite a new agenda for the Soviet Union, and for the world. The speech drew enthusiastic, even ecstatic praise from statesmen and common people around the world.

Further world progress is now possible only through the search for a consensus of all mankind, in movement toward a new world order . . . It is a question of cooperation that could be more accurately called "co-creation" and "co-development." The formula of development "at another's expense" is becoming outdated. In light of present realities, genuine progress by infringing upon the rights and liberties of man and peoples, or at the expense of nature, is impossible . . .

It is evident, for example, that force and the threat of force can no longer be, and should not be instruments of foreign policy . . .

The variety of sociopolitical structures which has grown over the last decades from national liberation movements also demonstrates this. This objective fact presupposes respect for other people's views and stands, tolerance, a preparedness to see phenomena that are different as not necessarily bad or hostile, and an ability to learn to live side by side while remaining different and not agreeing with one another on every issue . . .

In the course of such sharing, each should prove the advantages of his own system, his own way of life and values, but not through words or propaganda alone, but through real deeds as well . . . Otherwise we simply will not be able to solve a single world problem; arrange broad, mutually advantageous and equitable cooperation between peoples; manage rationally the achievements of the scientific and technical revolution; transform world economic relations; protect the environment; overcome underdevelopment; or put an end to hunger, disease, illiteracy, and other mass ills. Finally, in that case, we will not manage to eliminate the nuclear threat and militarism.

Now about the most important topic, without which no problem of the coming century can be resolved: disarmament . . .

Today I can inform you of the following: The Soviet Union has made a decision on reducing its armed forces. In the next two years, their numerical strength will be reduced by 500,000 persons . . . The Soviet forces situated in those countries [of central and eastern Europe] will be cut by 50,000 persons, and their arms by 5000 tanks.

We would also like to draw the attention of the world community to another topical problem, the problem of changing over from an economy of armament to an economy of disarmament. Is the conversion of military production realistic? . . . We believe that it is, indeed, realistic . . . It is desirable that all states, primarily the major military powers, submit their national plans on this issue to the United Nations.

We are talking first and foremost about consistent progress toward concluding a treaty [with the United States] on a 50 percent reduction in strategic offensive weapons . . . about elaborating a convention on the elimination of chemical weapons—here, it seems to us, we have the preconditions for making 1989 the decisive year; and about talks on reducing conventional weapons and armed forces in Europe. We are also talking about economic, ecological and humanitarian problems in the widest possible sense . . .

One would like to believe that our joint efforts to put an end to the era of wars, confrontation and regional conflicts, aggression against nature, the terror of hunger and poverty, as well as political terrorism, will be comparable with our hopes. This is our common goal, and it is only by acting together that we may attain it. Thank you.

http://www.cnn.com/SPECIALS/cold.war/episodes/23/documents/gorbachev

Since most of the leaders of the coup attempt were diehard members of the Communist Party, Yeltsin outlawed the activities of the Party in Russia. A few days later Gorbachev resigned as general secretary of the Party and moved to dissolve it altogether. On December 24, 1991, the USSR recognized the legitimacy of the claims to independent national identity of its constituent states and formally dissolved itself into fifteen independent states. The new states joined in a loose Commonwealth of

Independent States (CIS) as a mechanism for continuing cooperation. The
USSR was no more; the Communist
Party was reduced to a shell; the
global political landscape was transformed. The nation that Gorbachev
had ruled no longer existed. Yeltsin's
Russia was by far its largest surviving
state.

Boris Yeltsin, 1991–9 One of the first
problems facing Boris Yeltsin (b. 1931)
was disposing of the nuclear arsenal
of the former USSR. Eighty percent of
these weapons were on Russian soil
and under Russian control. Yeltsin
reopened discussions with the USA
concerning arms reductions and
signed treaties to carry them out. He
achieved an agreement with Belarus
to control its weapons, but others of

Mikhail Gorbachev, 1991. President
Gorbachev speaks at a press conference
during a peace summit in Moscow.

the new states kept at least limited control over the weapons on their soil. The rest of
the world worried about the final disposal of the enormous nuclear arsenals that
remained in the states of the CIS, including Russia, which were poor and of questionable stability. The fear was not so much that the weapons would be used by these
states but that they might be sold off, in whole or in parts, to other nations eager to
gain access to nuclear weapons and technology.

Yeltsin convened a constitutional assembly, which produced a new constitution
in 1993. The Russian economy continued to lag, however, and Yeltsin and the parliament came into direct, violent conflict. Following armed battles in which about 150
people were killed, Yeltsin reasserted his power as president. He was re-elected in
nationwide multiparty elections in 1996 that reaffirmed Russia's commitment to
democracy.

In its first post-communist years, Russia suffered grievously. In the decade 1991 to
2000, the gross domestic product dropped by 50 percent, the lifespan of citizens fell by
two and a half years, the birthrate dropped by a third, and the mortality rate rose
by a quarter, while a small class of entrepreneurs made great profits. The government
privatized its economic holdings, selling them off at bargain rates to its supporters,
who became very wealthy overnight. In a face-off with government, "robber capitalists," wielding huge economic power, refused to pay taxes, bringing the nation to near
bankruptcy. Petty crime also became commonplace, and organized criminal gangs
flourished.

Internationally, Yeltsin's greatest success may have been winning the confidence
and support of foreign financial institutions and governments, which kept Russia's
floundering economy afloat through investments, loans, and debt rescheduling. In
1997, Russia was accorded associate status in NATO, its former arch-enemy, while the
Czech Republic, Poland, and Hungary were invited as full members, an astonishing
turnaround after four decades of cold war.

Yeltsin's greatest embarrassment was the continuing war in the breakaway province
of Chechnya, an Islamic-majority region near the Caspian Sea. Chechnya was not
given its independence from Russia along with the other states of the former USSR. It
therefore declared its independence and secession from Russia in 1994 and began a

A Russian woman with a photo of her son killed during the assault by Russian special forces on the Moscow Theater, Moscow, 2002. Russian special forces stormed the Moscow Theater after Chechen rebels had taken hundreds of hostages in their demands for the release from captivity of leading Chechen separatists.

guerrilla war. All the technology of the once proud Russian army could not permanently defeat the nationalist rebels, although there were periods of relative calm, nor could the Russian government negotiate a graceful retreat. On December 31, 1999, in the face of continuing economic difficulties, charges of corruption, war in Chechnya, and concerns about his health and drinking problems, Yeltsin resigned as president of Russia, naming Vladimir Putin acting president.

Vladimir Putin, from 2000 Vladimir Putin (b. 1952) was subsequently elected Yeltsin's successor. He continued the war in Chechnya and it drags on, with occasional terrorist attacks in Moscow, as probably the greatest drain on his presidency. Under Yeltsin, and continuing under Putin, the economy has been on a roller-coaster, which at present seems to be moving stably, if slowly, upward. Putin has not, however, moved toward political and economic liberalization. Formerly head of Russia's secret police, he has brought into his government people of similar background. He has jailed prominent leaders who seemed to threaten to expand freedom of the press, to build personal economic fortunes, and to challenge him politically. Putin's methods appear popular and his government stable. He was re-elected president in March 2004, with 72 percent of the vote, although most observers questioned the fairness of the election, citing manipulation of the state media and stuffing of ballot boxes. Russia has moved from its former identity as a totalitarian state, but it has not (yet) become a liberal democracy. The highly respected *Economist* magazine of London remarked that, despite its new orientation, "Russia has a corrupt legal system, a monstrous bureaucracy, and laws like thick mud" (*Economist*, 22 May 2004).

European Identity

While nationalism was growing among the states and satellites of the former Soviet Union—many of them in Europe—so too was a new sense of European identity. The definition of Europe has always been contested. Sometimes it has referred to the entire continent—a geographical peninsula, really—from the Ural mountains in the east to the Atlantic Ocean in the west; sometimes it has been used as a shorthand for the industrialized, mostly democratic nations of western Europe; sometimes it has designated the areas of the peninsula where Christianity, and especially Roman Catholicism and Protestantism, have flourished. The rise of the Soviet Union and the Cold War had introduced an East–West political–military division into Europe. The breakdown of the USSR also began to break down that division and identity. In 1990, East and West Germany were reunited amid great jubilation. In 2004, Hungary, the Czech Republic, Slovakia, Poland, Lithuania, Latvia, and Estonia—along with Malta, Cyprus, and Slovenia—joined the European Union, an economic and political union that already included 15 nations of western Europe. Other nations waited in the wings, having already submitted, or beginning to prepare, their applications for membership: Romania, Bulgaria, Croatia, Serbia, Macedonia, and, largest of all, Islamic Turkey.

The USA as the Lone Superpower

The disintegration of the Soviet Union left the United States as the only country in the world able to project massive military, economic, and cultural power everywhere on the globe. The USA had become the only "superpower." This level of unparalleled political, military, and economic power created a new identity for the USA and for the world. For centuries, world politics had turned on a balance of power among the major nations. This was true even during the Cold War, when the two superpowers balanced one another.

In the 1990s, however, America's position was confirmed economically as well as politically, as Japan, America's number one economic competitor globally, sank into a recession from which it has still not fully recovered. Until the end of the 1980s, Japan's economy continued to outperform that of any other major nation (see Chapter 19), but in 1989 an economic "bubble" burst in Japan and the country slipped into an unexpected recession. Land values plummeted by two-thirds. (The total land of Japan had been valued at four times the total value of land in the United States.) The Nikkei stock market index followed, dropping by 60 percent from 1989 to 1992. Billions of dollars in paper wealth were wiped out, and Japan fell into a long-term depression. The Japanese government that had been credited with masterminding forty years of continuous growth was now blamed for economic recession. By contrast, in the early 1990s, the American economy entered into a new phase of growth, one of the longest and steepest in the history of the country, led by innovations in communications technology.

In 1992 Francis Fukuyama published *The End of History*, building on over a decade and a half of research and argumentation. He argued, triumphally, that the fall of Russian communism had left just one viable political-economic system in the world, the capitalist-democratic system of the United States, western Europe, and a few other countries. This system had won, he argued, because it was the best.

There were some outstanding examples that seemed to support his point. In 1991, India, which was already democratic, began a set of policy changes crafted to reduce the role of the state in the national economy and to convert to greater reliance on free markets both at home and in international trade and investment. In addition, without the Soviet Union as an alternative, many nations turned toward America for assistance or advice. Almost all the former satellites of the USSR chose to move toward free-market economic policies, and the Czech Republic, Hungary, and Poland joined NATO, with Russia's full consent. Middle Eastern nations had no alternative to aligning their foreign policies toward America and to relying on America to mediate the Arab–Israeli dispute. In the Caribbean, Cuba's economy, which was already weak, virtually collapsed as the Soviet Union could no longer buy its sugar crop nor supply subsidies. Economically crippled, the Caribbean island no longer had the strength to send guerrilla troops to other parts of Latin America nor to parts of Africa where it had been deeply enmeshed: Angola, Mozambique, and Ethiopia.

Despite the examples that seemed to support Fukuyama's thesis, there were more examples that contradicted it. Triumphalism, it turned out, was not justified. Nationalism remained a powerful force, often without regard for economic or even military consequences. For example, going from west to east across Afro-Eurasia:

Osama bin Laden appears on Al-Jazeera television, October 17, 2001. Bin Laden here praises the attacks of September 11 and defies the US in its threats to attack Afghanistan's Taliban government. The US overthrew the Taliban some days later.

Northern Ireland continued to gain in its struggle against Britain for self-government, but periodic armed guerrilla attacks by the Irish Republican Army impeded the process. Yugoslavia, as we shall see in Chapter 24, shattered into separate states that went to war against each other for reasons of ethnicity and religion more than economics. Fighting to determine the borders between Ethiopia and Somalia and Ethiopia and Eritrea continued for years, long after Soviet intervention in the area ended. Tens of thousands of people in each of the three countries died in the warfare. North Korea pursued a policy of isolation from the rest of the world under the rigid dictatorship of Kim Il Sung (r. 1972–94) followed by his son Kim Jong Il (r. 1994–). Since 1993, North Korea has been working on a program for developing nuclear weapons and is now believed to have such weapons, adding an element of instability in East Asia and beyond. North Korea pursued its program of nuclear development despite poverty to the point of starvation among its people.

Most dramatically, terrorist attacks on the United States and its interests at home and overseas exploded any illusions that American values were prevailing globally or that there was a single unified American identity. One attack was from within as Timothy McVeigh blew up the federal building in Oklahoma City in 1995, in retaliation for the government's 1993 armed assault on the Branch Davidians, a small religious sect based in Waco, Texas. More typically these attacks occurred overseas and were part of a violent dialogue with Islamic militancy. In 1983, a suicide car-bomb destroyed the US embassy in Beirut, Lebanon, killing 63. Later in the same year suicide bombers exploded a truck-bomb at US Marine headquarters at the international airport in Beirut, killing 241 US Marines and sailors. (Minutes later another bomb killed 58 French paratroopers in their barracks also in Beirut.) In 1993, a bomb delivered by Muslim terrorists exploded in the garage under the World Trade Center in New York, killing six. In Saudi Arabia, a bomb killed seven Americans at a military training installation in 1995, and another exploded at an American air force barracks in 1996, killing 19. In 1998 almost simultaneous explosions at US embassies in Kenya and Tanzania killed 220 people. In 2000 a small boat sailed alongside the USS *Cole*, a US Navy destroyer, in the harbor at Aden, Yemen, and bombed the ship, killing seventeen sailors. Most spectacularly, on September 11, 2001, representatives of the Islamic militant group al-Qaeda hijacked four American commercial jet airliners and used them as suicide bombers in exploding and destroying the two buildings of the World Trade Center in New York, killing some 2800 people, a wing of the Pentagon outside of Washington, D.C., and crashing one, apparently targeted for a major government installation in Washington, in western Pennsylvania.

Shocked out of a sense of its own invulnerability, America declared war on terrorism. Terrorism is usually defined as a form of guerrilla warfare. It is a strategy employed by the weak against the strong. It attacks civilian non-combatants, in civilian locations, to terrify a general population into conceding political benefits. Although the strike on September 11, 2001 against America was extraordinary in its daring, scale, and spectacle, and in not having a specific political goal, in principle, terrorism was not a new method of fighting. According to statistics compiled by the US Department of State, there had been hundreds of terrorist attacks around the world annually. From 1981 to 1991, counting all attacks against all victims in all places, they averaged more than 500 a year. From 1991 to 2001 there were never fewer than the 274 in 1998. When America proclaimed a "war on terrorism," many wondered what form would such a war take, how would it be fought, and how would one know when victory was achieved?

In addition to terrorist attacks by enemies of US interests, American actions on the international stage were isolating the superpower from its allies. America's penchant for acting unilaterally frequently appeared arrogant and alienated friends as well as enemies. America imposed sanctions on Iran and Cuba and forced others to comply. It

SOURCE

Osama bin Laden, leader of al-Qaeda

Osama bin Laden was born in Saudi Arabia in 1957, the seventeenth child and seventh son of a devout Sunni Muslim family that had become extremely wealthy in the construction business. He grew up in an atmosphere of militant Wahabi puritan interpretations of Sunni Islam, at a time when Islamic nationalism was growing, and earned a degree in public administration in Jeddah in 1981. He went to Afghanistan to join in the struggle against Soviet occupation and created al-Qaeda ("the base") to obtain and organize war supplies and to lead troops in the field. When the Soviets withdrew, bin Laden returned to Saudi Arabia committed to a militant, politicized vision of Islam. When the USA invaded Iraq in 1991, he offered to help the Saudi government in case of attack. Bin Laden was enraged as the government turned to the Americans for their defense, invited US troops onto Saudi lands, and put him under government surveillance. He returned to Afghanistan, only to find that it had collapsed into civil war. He went to Sudan, then led by a militant Islamic government. In 1994, the government of Saudi Arabia revoked his citizenship and froze his assets in Saudi Arabia. Under pressure from Saudi Arabia and the United States, Sudan expelled bin Laden in 1996 and he returned to Afghanistan, which had come under the government of the Taliban, a group of seminary students with military experience who had unified the country after eighteen years of warfare. Here bin Laden established the World Islamic Front for the Jihad against Jews and Crusaders, a headquarters for radical Muslim movements. He issued a fatwa stating that it was the duty of Muslims to kill US citizens and their allies. In his camps he trained jihadis for these tasks.

Shortly after the attacks on the United States on September 11, 2001, bin Laden broadcast the following message on the Arabic news channel al-Jazeera:

What the United States tastes today is a very small thing compared to what we have tasted for tens of years. Our nation has been tasting this humiliation and contempt for more than 80 years. Its sons are being killed, its blood is being shed, its holy places are being attacked, and it is not being ruled according to what God has decreed. Despite this, nobody cares.

When Almighty God rendered successful a convoy of Muslims, the vanguards of Islam, He allowed them to destroy the United States.

I ask God Almighty to elevate their status and grant them Paradise. He is the one who is capable to do so.

When these defended their oppressed sons, brothers, and sisters in Palestine and in many Islamic countries, the world at large shouted. The infidels shouted, followed by the hypocrites. One million Iraqi children have thus far died in Iraq although they did not do anything wrong. Despite this, we heard no denunciation by anyone in the world or a *fatwa* by the rulers' *ulema* [body of Muslim scholars].

Israeli tanks and tracked vehicles also enter to wreak havoc in Palestine, in Jenin, Ramallah, Rafah, Beit Jala, and other Islamic areas and we hear no voices raised or moves made. But if the sword falls on the United States after 80 years, hypocrisy raises its head lamenting the deaths of these killers who tampered with the blood, honor, and holy places of the Muslims.

The least that one can describe these people is that they are morally depraved. They champion falsehood, support the butcher against the victim, the oppressor against the innocent child. May God mete them the punishment they deserve.

They came out in arrogance with their men and horses and instigated even those countries that belong to Islam against us. They came out to fight this group of people who declared their faith in God and refused to abandon their religion. They came out to fight Islam in the name of terrorism.

Hundreds of thousands of people, young and old, were killed in the farthest point on earth in Japan. [For them] this is not a crime, but rather a debatable issue. They bombed Iraq and considered that a debatable issue.

But when a dozen people of them were killed in Nairobi and Dar es Salaam, Afghanistan and Iraq were bombed and all hypocrite ones stood behind the head of the world's infidelity—behind the Hubal [an idol worshipped by pagans before the advent of Islam] of the age—namely, America and its supporters. These incidents divided the entire world into two regions—one of faith where there is no hypocrisy and another of infidelity, from which we hope God will protect us . . .

As for the United States, I tell it and its people these few words: I swear by Almighty God who raised the heavens without pillars that neither the United States nor he who lives in the United States will enjoy security before we can see it as a reality in Palestine and before all the infidel armies leave the land of Mohammed, may God's peace and blessing be upon him.

God is great and glory to Islam.

May God's peace, mercy, and blessings be upon you.

http://news.bbc.co.uk/1/hi/world/south_asia/1585636.stm

refused to ratify international treaties, cut foreign aid, withheld dues to the United Nations and other international agencies, cut State Department funding, and abolished the United States Information Agency. In declining to sign the Kyoto Protocol on

Anti-war protesters march through the streets of Piccadilly, central London, 2004. Up to 100,000 people from across the UK attended the march and rally, calling for troops to be removed from Iraq. The Campaign for Nuclear Disarmament, Stop The War Coalition, and the Muslim Association of Britain organized the event. Hundreds of thousands also marched in Rome, New York, and other major cities worldwide.

the reduction of greenhouse gases, a bill signed by 178 nations and recommended by all the major advocates of a healthy global ecology, and by offering no alternative vision, America was perceived as flouting world opinion. In supporting Israel's assassination attacks on Palestinian guerrilla leaders, which often also killed innocent civilians, America differed from most of the rest of the world.

Most of all, in going to war against Iraq in March, 2003, America stood blatantly—advocates would say boldly—against most of world opinion. On February 15, 2003, as American leaders threatened to attack Iraq, street demonstrations were held in cities in the United States (again demonstrating the lack of a homogeneous "American identity) and around the world, many of them attracting hundreds of thousands of participants. In both London and Rome up to a million demonstrated against the coming war. Most of the rest of the world wished to investigate America's claims that Iraq might have weapons of mass destruction, but they were willing to trust United Nations weapons inspectors to find them and to allow international sanctions to keep Iraq under control. If further military action was necessary, they wished it to be under UN auspices. They called America's actions unilateral and arrogant, and America found itself isolated in many of its foreign policy decisions.

In the form of its fight against terrorism, America also evoked some criticism. At the time of the September 11 attacks, America had received the sympathy of the world, but questions arose as it responded by attacking Afghanistan unilaterally, killing thousands of civilians as well as some Taliban members, and then withdrawing before a new government capable of administering the entire country had been established. Questions increased as America attacked Iraq in 2003, without any credible proof that Iraq had been involved in the earlier attacks.

Defending free and open societies from terrorism presents enormous challenges: to maintain the openness of the society, to track down and prosecute the terrorists, and not to provoke others into joining them. Would America be able to do it? Was America's response appropriate to and commensurate with the attacks? Would America's responses not actually provoke more terrorists to attack? Was America losing perspective both at home and abroad in this war against terrorism? These were questions echoing around the world and in the 2004 presidential election in the United States itself.

RELIGIOUS AND CULTURAL IDENTITIES

The past twenty to thirty years have provided abundant evidence of the power of religious faith to motivate public as well as private action, in all major religions and regions. The 1979 revolution in Iran provides a good example and is a good place to begin a global survey. That revolution, led by the Ayatollah Khomeini, not only over-threw the shah of Iran, but also successfully challenged the power of the United States that stood behind the throne. The resistance of the Islamic militant Taliban in Afghanistan, successfully repelling the Soviet invasion of its country through the 1980s, further extended that message. Organized religious groups were capable of inflicting great punishment on even the most powerful nations. In Iran and Afghanistan resurgent Islam had confronted and repelled both of the world's super-powers.

Islamic identity was not, however, easy to define. Among the 1.3 billion Muslim faithful and the dozens of Islamic-majority nations, there are many different group-ings, sects, and perspectives. As we saw in Chapter 22, Iraq felt threatened by its neigh-bor Iran. The new Iranian leadership aggressively proclaimed its Shi'a identity, while Iraq was ruled by a more-or-less secular dictator who nevertheless identified with his own Sunni sect, which dominated over a 60 percent Shia majority. In addition, both nations claimed control over the Shatt al-Arab waterway at the entrance to the Persian Gulf. Scattered fighting between them escalated into full-scale warfare that dragged on for eight years at the cost of up to a million lives. Saudi Arabia, also Sunni, felt threat-ened by potential Iranian subversion, especially after Iranians set off a bomb in Mecca, near the sacred Ka'aba, in 1987. The Saudis, at least briefly, drew closer to the United States.

In several countries with overwhelmingly Muslim populations, struggles broke out between forces that wished to keep the country secular and those that wanted Islamic principles and practices to be institutionalized as official public policy. In Turkey and Algeria secular armed forces intervened in elections throughout the 1990s to keep Islamic political parties from coming to power. In 1981, in Egypt, members of the Islamic Brotherhood assassinated the relatively secular President Anwar Sadat, who had jailed many of their members and had made peace with Israel. They also attempted to assassinate his successor, Hosni Mubarak, who followed similar policies.

In Africa, south of the Sahara, where Islam, Christianity, and indigenous African religions had usually coexisted peacefully, armed struggle broke out among them. In Chad, which is about 50 percent Muslim, mostly in the north, and 25 percent each Christian and followers of indigenous religions, mostly in the south, civil war broke out in 1966 and has continued on-and-off, with the occasional intervention of French troops, at the request of the government, and of Libyan troops, sometimes at the request of the government of Chad and sometimes in order to claim parts of the war-torn country for themselves.

Neighboring Sudan has experienced similar instability in government, with ineffec-tive parliaments and unstable military governments alternating in power through a series of coups. In addition, the people of the north, home to the 70 percent of the pop-ulation that is Sunni and mostly Arab, have repeatedly attempted to impose Islamic law on the south, which is mostly black and mostly practices indigenous religions. The result has been a series of civil wars in a country that is overwhelmingly poor and prone to famine. As many as 2 million people died in wars and famines—mostly southerners—and millions more, mostly southerners, have been displaced from their homes. In 1993, Amnesty International charged that the government was carrying out ethnic cleansing against the southerners. In 2004, forces in the north and south appeared poised to reach accommodations that might allow peace and stability, but forces in the Darfur region of the western part of the country, claiming oppression, were still at war with the central government and with local armed groups, the Jan-jaweed, which were backed by the government. In Darfur, however, the issue seemed to be ethnic rather than religious, northern Arabs against western black Africans. Both groups were Muslim by religion. The United Nations and several individual nations extended relief aid and considered military intervention to protect the inhabitants of Darfur and impose peace on the region.

Nigeria, by far the most populous African country, with 130 million people, has been beset by many cross-cutting struggles, of which the attempt to impose Islamic law has been only one. But in this country whose population is about 45 percent Muslim, 45 percent Christian, and 10 percent followers of indigenous religions, this issue has led to rioting. In early 2000, some 2000 people were killed in northern Nigeria when Shari'a law was instituted in Kaduna State. In retaliation, several hundred Muslims were killed in the east and south, and many more began to migrate to areas where their religious group was dominant. In May 2004, in the central Nigerian Plateau State, Christians attacked the Muslim market town of Yelwa, leaving an estimated 67 to 670 people dead. Muslims and Christians fled areas in which they were minorities and resettled in areas of their own majorities. In the north around the town of Jos, Muslims retaliated, leaving 20,000 Christians homeless. President Obasanjo put the area under military command, bringing, on the one hand, relief from the violence but, on the other, fear for Nigeria's fragile democracy. Despite the hostility it engendered among non-Muslims, several additional northern states instituted Islamic law as the basis of their official legal codes.

Although perhaps not significant in internal politics, issues of Islam and women have brought unwanted international attention to Nigeria. In 2002, a young woman accused of adultery was to be stoned to death, but she appealed the case, and its disposition is not yet clear. In 2002, the Miss World Pageant was scheduled for Nigeria until Muslim leaders decried the spectacle as incompatible with Islam. Riots broke out killing one hundred people, and the Pageant was moved to London, where such exhibitions of attractive young women in competition are considered acceptable.

One of the worst examples of religious strife occurred in eastern Europe, in the Balkans, where civil war raged from 1992 to 1995 and continued to sputter afterward as well. Hundreds of thousands of people died and many more were made at least temporarily homeless in the worst warfare in Europe since World War II. The Balkans are a region of divisive nationalisms, and although religion was not the only issue in the war, it was important. The ethnic diversity of the Balkans was most clear in the multi-ethnic new state of Yugoslavia that was created after World War I. After World War II, ethnic hostilities were suppressed by the nation's leader Marshal Tito, and even after his death the communist government of the country continued his policies.

After communism collapsed along with the Soviet Union in 1989, however, Yugoslavia splintered into three major regions, and religion was one of the key elements in the division. Serbia's population was about 65 percent Orthodox Christian, 19 percent Muslim; Croatia's was 77 percent Roman Catholic, 11 percent Orthodox; and Bosnia-Herzegovina's was 40 percent Muslim, 31 percent Orthodox, and 15 percent Catholic. The country was divided into three, and war broke out among the three new states, as well as within them. As fighting intensified, many observers noted that religious identity became increasingly important. People who had not identified strongly with any religious group found that they had to choose sides. Religious identity seemed to inspire the worst violence, murder, rape, and torture. In Chapter 24 we shall look more closely at the case of the breakdown of Yugoslavia into these constituent units in 1991–2, noting here only that religion was one of the key factors.

Hinduism and Islam in South Asia

As India approached independence in 1947, many Muslim leaders held out for a Muslim homeland, and finally this demand led to the partition of India into India and Pakistan (see Chapter 22). As these events unfolded, most attention focused on Muslim religious identity. The Congress Party asserted that it was not a Hindu organization, but a secular political party. This was the basis for its claim that there was no need for a separate Muslim country; everyone could live under a secular government in a secular state. This was Gandhi's claim, and Jawaharlal Nehru, first prime minister of India, 1947–64, sustained India's official secularism. He governed India as a "composite," or multicultural, society. If anything, he tended to favor Muslims as a minority in need of protection.

Even during the Independence struggle, however, there was a strong Hindu movement that did not welcome secularism nor the equality of non-Hindus, and especially Muslims, in India. The Hindu Mahasabha (Great Assembly) was largely eclipsed by the Congress, but it represented a powerful group within India. The Mahasabha's cultural organization, the RSS (Rashtriya Swayamsevak Sangh, National Volunteer Organization) was temporarily banished from public life in India because one of its members assassinated Gandhi for being too accommodating toward Muslim demands.

In the 1980s Hindu militants resurfaced as a significant political voice in India, reconstituted as the Bharatiya Janata Parishad (Indian People's Party), or BJP. At first the BJP drew little attention and few votes, but then its leadership began to stress its Hindu nature. They scorned Muslims as not being true Indians, but rather descendants of military invaders, or converts to their foreign religion, and more loyal to the world community of Muslims, and in particular to Pakistan, than to India.

L.K. Advani, the chief organizer of the BJP, organized a tour across north India in 1990, riding in a van decorated as a war chariot of Lord Rama. To add to the religious symbolism, Advani began his tour from the west coast town of Dwarka, the home of the Somnath Temple, destroyed by Muslim, Mughal invaders when they entered India in 1296, and rebuilt immediately after India became independent. To complete the symbolism, Advani ended his tour at the north Indian town of Ayodhaya, the home of a mosque built by the first Mughal emperor allegedly on the grounds of a Hindu temple that he destroyed and that was said to mark the earthly birthplace of the Hindu Lord Rama. Actually Advani himself did not complete the pilgrimage. He was arrested by the chief minister of the state in which Ayodhaya is located on the grounds of inciting to riot. The pilgrimage had instigated rioting between Hindus and Muslims throughout its journey.

Two years later, in defiance of the government of India and in violation of a pledge that he had made, Advani instigated the destruction of the Ayodhaya mosque. In response, riots broke out throughout India. In Mumbai (Bombay) 2000 people were killed and bombs exploded in the city's stock exchange. Nevertheless, the BJP's electoral totals continued to climb from one election to the next. By the end of the decade, the BJP won enough votes to achieve a governing coalition.

In office, the BJP leadership stressed "Hindutva," or "Hinduness" as the basis of their political identity. "Hindutva" was to some degree a call for greater piety in religion, but it was far more a political rallying call to make Hindu identity the basis of national identity, and thus to exclude non-Hindus from full membership in the Indian nation. In 2002, a group of militant Hindus were returning from a pilgrimage to Ayodhaya. They apparently heckled some Muslim vendors on a train platform in one of the towns of Gujarat State. In response, Muslims burned part of the train, killing 59 pilgrims. Across Gujarat State, attacks against Muslims followed, killing at least 1000 people and leaving some 100,000 homeless, in refugee camps. The attacks seemed organized, and the state police did little to stop them, bringing charges against the state government of complicity in the killing.

This called attention to one of the most important elements in civil riots. Riots and attacks may break out at any time, but the key question is: What does the government

Militant Hindus atop and around Babri Mosque, Ayodhaya, India, 1992. In December 1992 many thousands of Hindu extremists destroyed the 430-year-old Muslim mosque, claiming that it had been built on ground originally sacred to Hindus as the birthplace of the Lord Rama.

do about them? If the police and government act immediately to stop them, the damage is minimal; if they do not, the damage increases; if the police and government actually help in the attacks, the situation is called a pogrom, an attack on a specific ethnic, racial, or religious group, that has the backing, or a least the complicity, of the state.

In the next state elections, the ruling BJP party won a landslide victory, gaining its biggest majorities in areas where the attacks had been most deadly, and suggesting that the call of Hindutva and the attacks on Muslims were politically effective. Meanwhile, throughout India, wherever the BJP held power, school textbooks were being rewritten to give prominence to stories of Hindu power and to show Muslims as foreigners and unpatriotic. Muslims seemed to be under siege.

On the other hand, in the national elections of 2004, the BJP was badly defeated. Mostly the vote seemed to be, once again, an anti-incumbency response of the lower middle classes and the poor, based at least as much on opposition to economic policies that favored the wealthy, as it was a vote against Hindutva. To complicate the analysis of the election, the BJP party had actually reduced its emphasis on Hindutva and had begun attempting some rapprochement with Muslim Pakistan. Some more militant members of the party argued that the BJP had not emphasized Hindutva enough to win the election!

To add to the complication that is Indian identity, the head of the triumphant Congress Party was Sonia Gandhi, the widow of the assassinated former prime minister, Rajiv Gandhi, and the daughter-in-law of his mother, the assassinated former prime minister Indira Gandhi. Sonia was Italian by birth, and the BJP had derided her Indian political credentials throughout the election. As it came time for the Congress to select a new prime minister, she voluntarily stepped aside, apparently to allow a native-born Indian to take the position, perhaps also to reduce the threat of further assassinations in her family. Manmohan Singh became the new prime minister. For the first time a Sikh rather than a Hindu was prime minister. And the president of India, filling a largely ceremonial position, was a Muslim! Despite the emotional appeal of Hindutva, most Indians seemed to appreciate the virtues of a composite identity.

Confucianism

As the "Asian tiger" nations in East and Southeast Asia—especially Taiwan, Korea, Singapore, and Hong Kong—began to improve their economies, a reassessment of the virtues of Confucian philosophy took place. Economists and sociologists who had earlier argued that an emphasis on family solidarity and social integration were inhibiting growth, now began to argue that these were among the most significant cultural characteristics promoting growth! (We have discussed in Chapter 22 some of these attempts by academics to evaluate the significance of cultural identity in economic and political development.)

In China, the communist government had forbidden the teaching and practice of Confucianism for decades, rejecting its elitism and hierarchy. In the 1990s the government began to change course, allowing some degree of cultural liberalization along with economic liberalization. Confucianism has had a limited rebirth in China that may also facilitate better relationships with overseas Chinese who also accept

Confucianism. In 1999, the government celebrated lavishly the 2550th anniversary of the birth of Confucius, praising him for his exemplary humanity and benevolence.

Judaism

Religious identities in Judaism also underwent enormous change. After almost 2000 years of living as minorities in diaspora communities, Jews gained a (small) state of their own in Israel. They were, however, surrounded by hostile neighbors. With some, Egypt and Jordan, they could achieve political settlements and peace treaties. But with others, like Syria and Lebanon, they could not. The greatest hostility appeared between them and the Palestinians whom they had conquered in warfare. As a result of their changed status, Jewish political philosophy seemed to change. Previously, as weak and dependent people, they emphasized the biblical concept that they would live "not by might and not by power," but by God's spirit. Now, surrounded by hostility, many of them came to believe that only might and power would enable them to survive. In control of their own state, they built the most powerful armed force in the Middle East, and used it in ways that appeared necessary to the Israeli government but excessively brutal to many others.

Through immigration, the United States had become the home of about 5 to 6 million Jews, about 40 percent of the world's total (about a million more than in Israel). Here unprecedented freedom for this minority group served to loosen the bonds of group solidarity. Many chose not to affiliate. Slightly more than 50 percent of American Jews intermarried with their Christian neighbors, and various studies arrived at different predictions as to what might be the religious identity, if any, of their children. On the other hand, a new, very liberal, branch of Judaism, Reconstructionism, joined the Orthodox, Conservative, and Reform movements, and all four labored intensely to ensure that their sense of Jewish identity would continue.

Christianity

Christianity, by far the world's largest religion, with two billion people professing the faith, found itself no longer predominantly European. By the year 2000, somewhat more than one half billion Christians lived in Europe, somewhat less than a half billion in Latin America, somewhat more than a third of a billion in Africa, somewhat less than a third of a billion in Asia, somewhat more than a quarter of a billion in North America, and about 25 million in Oceania. All the years of missionary proselytizing throughout the colonies of Europe reaped an abundant harvest.

Half of this Christian population were Roman Catholics, and half of these lived in Latin America. The election of Polish Cardinal Karol Josef Wojtyla as Pope John Paul II (b. 1920) in 1978 reflected the international diversity of the Roman Church, for he was the first non-Italian Pope since 1523. His career highlighted some of the identity issues in the Catholic Church at the turn of the twenty-first century. First, by selecting a cardinal from behind the "Iron Curtain" the Church was directly giving moral support to the people under the control of the Soviet Union. The communist government was officially atheistic and suppressed religious freedom both in Russia, where Orthodox Christianity had been dominant for a thousand years, and in the eastern and central European countries where Roman Catholicism had been more prominent. The Church, and many others, saw the Cold War not only as a struggle between economic and political systems, but also as a struggle between atheism and religious faith. In his first overseas trip, to Mexico in 1978, John Paul II stressed this theme to a crowd that some estimated at 5 million people, the largest crowd in human history. (In 1995, in Manila, 4 million are estimated to have attended the pope's mass.) In the year after his elevation to the papacy, John Paul II visited Poland to the enthusiastic welcome of millions of his countrymen who saw him as a beacon of hope for greater freedom. Throughout the 1980s, as Lech Walesa organized the Solidarity labor movement in Poland against the government, the pope offered moral support. He began his many travels abroad stressing human rights and the importance of religious and national freedom everywhere. As communism collapsed by the end of the decade, many felt that John Paul II was giving a belated reply to Stalin's sarcastic question about the power of the pope, "How many divisions has *he* got?"

Poland itself had suffered grievously during his lifetime. During World War II the young Karol Wojtyla had been forced to work as a manual laborer, interrupting his university education, and developing a lifelong concern for the welfare of the laboring poor. In his 1987 encyclical *Sollicitudo rei socialis* (On Social Concern) John Paul II pointed to the danger of the ever-widening gap between the rich and poor in all countries. He preached "the right of every individual to the full use of the benefits offered by science and technology" for the good of all people. (In a belated rapprochement with science, in 1984 the Vatican announced that the Church had erred in prosecuting Galileo.) "The voice of the Church, echoing the voice of human conscience . . . deserves and needs to be heard in our time when the growing wealth of a few parallels the growing poverty of the masses" (Lernoux, p. 409). While he was an enemy of atheism and communism, he was no friend of capitalism, which he saw as exploitative of workers. In 1979, at Yankee Stadium in New York City, he denounced the rich of the United States, and of other wealthy countries, for neglecting their poor.

In terms of ecumenical relationships, John Paul II demonstrated his openness to the world by his remarkable record of world travels—to Mexico, the United States, Turkey, India, China, Cuba, Africa, the Philippines, Haiti, Egypt, Israel, and many others—about 100 overseas trips in all, traveling a greater distance than all previous popes combined. He reached out to non-Catholics and non-Christians, especially Jews and Muslims in his trip to the Holy Land in March 2000, and in his meeting with the chief Sunni cleric, the Sheikh al-Azhar in Cairo. He called anti-Semitism a sin and referred to Jews as "our older brothers in faith." He visited Canterbury Cathedral in England, the most important cathedral in the Anglican faith, and Lutheran churches in Germany and Sweden.

The pope's positions were, however, quite complex. His conservative orientation of the Church had already appeared in his rulings on personal, family, and sexual issues. During the meetings of the Second Vatican Council, convened in Rome in 1962 by the much beloved Pope John XXIII (r. 1958–63) to update several of the Church's teachings, the future John Paul II articulated his more conservative positions: opposition to abortion, birth control, the ordination of women as priests, and homosexual practices, and in favor of clerical celibacy. Nevertheless, Catholics around the world practiced birth control to about the same extent as their non-Catholic neighbors, ignoring the Church's teachings on this issue. Meanwhile many other Christian groups were liberalizing their attitudes toward gender differences. For example, the Church of England, founded in part because of King Henry VIII's wish to divorce his first wife, voted to ordain women as priests in 1994. The Episcopalian Church in the United States ordained a female bishop for the first time in 1988 and the first openly gay male bishop in 2003.

John Paul II also took a conservative position on the means of combating poverty. In the late 1960s and 1970s a new school of thought, called liberation theology, was taking shape in Latin America. Identifying with Jesus' ministry to the poor, it began to establish grassroots organizations in poor neighborhoods of cities and in rural pockets of poverty. These *communidades de base* combined study, prayer, and active efforts to identify, define, and solve the problems of their localities by directly confronting them. They challenged local leaders to effect needed change. By the late 1970s, some observers estimated 80,000 *com-munidades de base* in Brazil alone.

As liberation theology threatened the state and the wealthy, it confronted powerful opposition forces that were willing to engage in violence if necessary. In March 1980, Archbishop Oscar Romero of El Salvador was assassinated as he was officiating at mass in a San Salvador chapel. The right-wing assassin had opposed the archbishop's message: "When all peaceful means have been exhausted, the church considers insurrection moral and justified" (Keen, p. 595). Romero, who had also advised soldiers that it was morally just to refuse to follow unjust orders, was only one of about 850 Church leaders who had been assassinated since the assassination of Camilo Torres, a priest and sociologist in Colombia. An outstanding scholar and teacher, Torres gave up on peaceful reform and joined Colombia's communist-led guerrillas. He was killed in a battle with government forces in February 1966. In December 1980, three American nuns and a lay missionary who had gone to work with poor refugees in El Salvador were also murdered by security officers of the state.

Radical religion. A priest holds hands with members of the Base Christian Community in Panama. Proponents of liberation theology, which originated in Latin America in the 1960s, typically aligned themselves with left-wing, revolutionary movements, such as the Sandinistas in Nicaragua. When influential priests and bishops espoused a Marxist view of society and argued that the Church's role was to assist the oppressed, they came into conflict with established Catholic authorities as well as political leaders.

The advocates of liberation theology claimed to combine Christian ethics with Marxist politics, and Pope John Paul II, raised in communist Poland, rejected this confrontational Marxist orientation toward class struggle. As new posts opened, he appointed mostly conservative clergy, and as a result the clergy in Latin America were deeply split. About 20 percent aligned themselves with liberation theology, but the overwhelming majority, especially in Brazil, aligned themselves with the new orientation of Rome and rejected this level of activism. Some critics claim that the pope's opposition to liberation theology helped open the door to the rapid growth of Protestant evangelical Christianity in Latin America.

Evangelical Christianity

Evangelical Christianity was giving a new face to the world's largest religion especially in the Americas. In 1940 there were barely a million Protestants in all of Latin America; by 2004 there were some 50 million, one-tenth of the total population. About half of them live in Brazil. About 80 to 90 percent of the Protestants are Pentecostals, appealing usually to the very poorest groups in society, and often to those who have been uprooted from rural areas to the growing cities of the continent. Pentecostals differ from more mainstream Protestants in their emphasis on direct, personal experience of God and revelation, rather than on the authority of scripture or of the Church hierarchy. Many of these Pentecostal groups are allied with North American churches and often receive assistance from them. Pentecostal religion seems to appeal most to women in Latin America. It often refers to Jesus as Divine Husband and Father, emphasizes male responsibility and chastity, and calls for a "reformation of machismo" in family relationships. Poor women see Pentecostalism improving their lives and the lives of their family.

The Church of Jesus Christ of Latter Day Saints, the Mormon Church, is another North American denomination—although not an evangelical denomination—with growing representation in Latin America. Today, somewhat fewer than half of all Mormons live in the United States, about 5.2 million people, where the faith was founded in the nineteenth century. About a third live in Latin America.

The new Protestant religious groups provide the same kind of support in Latin America that early Christianity did in the Roman Empire: community, cooperation, material assistance, along with spiritual fulfillment, emotional spontaneity, enthusiasm, and even ecstasy. The God of the Pentecostals, like the God of the born-again Christians in the United States, is very near and very personal.

Religion in the United States

Throughout our period, America has been the most formally religious of all industrialized countries, as measured by the proportion of the population who are members of churches and attend them regularly. In the years of the Cold War, Americans proclaimed their religious belief as one of the characteristics that set them in opposition to "godless Communism." By 1960, 95 percent of Americans identified with some religious denomination. In 1954, Congress added the words "under God" to the pledge of allegiance to the flag, and in 1955 required the words "In God we trust" to be included on all American currency. President Eisenhower declared, "our government makes no sense unless it is founded in a deeply felt religious faith—and I don't care what it is." The center of gravity of American religion rested with the "mainline" Churches—Baptists, Episcopalians, Lutherans, Methodists, Presbyterians—each with membership numbering in the millions, and established, formal organizational structures and forms of prayer. That center was expanding to include Roman Catholics, symbolized by the election of John Kennedy as President in 1960. Although generally associated with conservative, status quo politics, much of the American "mainline" religious community was also open enough to support the Reverend Martin Luther King, the African-American Baptist minister, who led the fight for equal rights for blacks and minorities in the 1950s and 1960s.

As American culture began to move in new directions in the 1960s and 1970s, the mainline religious groups were often willing to modify their conservative positions, to become more relativistic, and embrace, accept, or at least tolerate these changes: the anti-Vietnam War protests, the Civil Rights movement, the women's movement, the increased immigration of Latin Americans and Asians, the revolution in sexual mores, the public expression of gay and lesbian lifestyles, and the development of a "counterculture," which embraced drugs, folk and protest music, provocative styles of dress and self-presentation, and freer sexual expression.

Many believing Christians, however, saw the social and cultural habits of America changing beyond recognition. They (re)turned to their Bibles to rediscover the fundamentals of their faith, and decided that America was moving in the wrong direction. These **fundamentalists** began creating more of their own organizations and institutions.

They certainly had the numbers to do it. A Gallup poll in 1979 showed that one out of three American adults reported a "born-again" conversion, an experience of being touched and changed by a personal encounter with Jesus. 50 percent believed that the Bible was an accurate account of history. 130 million people reported listening to and watching 1300 evangelical Christian radio and television stations.

American demographics enhanced the power of the fundamentalists. Northerners and Midwesterners were moving to the south and southwest. These migrants brought

fundamentalist a person who believes in the literal truth of the bible as a revelation from God. Sometimes, more loosely, people of any religion who express intense devotion to their faith.

more liberal views into these areas, but at the same time they also absorbed more conservative values. The south began once again to provide Presidents: Carter of Georgia in 1976, Clinton of Arkansas in 1992 and 1996, and Bush of Texas (although he had been born and raised in New England) in 2000. For Carter and Bush, "born-again" experiences figured prominently in their understanding of the world. Bush stated that Jesus Christ was the philosopher most important in formulating his own thinking. A gap of incomprehension was growing between northeastern and west coast religious and cultural liberals on the one hand and southern, southwestern, and midwestern religious fundamentalists and cultural conservatives on the other.

With incomprehension came fear and some confrontation on both sides. The US government besieged for 51 days and finally assaulted the small Branch Davidian religious enclave, an illegally-armed splinter group of the Seventh Day Adventists, directed by David Koresh in Waco, Texas, in 1993, leading to the deaths of four federal agents and more than seventy people inside the compound. Some more violent vigilante groups, including white supremacist groups, began to see the US government as the enemy of individualism and freedom of religion. In Oklahoma City, Timothy McVeigh bombed the federal building in April 1995, killing 168 people.

Sexuality and family relations resurfaced as bitterly contested religious issues. The Supreme Court's Roe vs. Wade decision (1973) legalized abortion, but abortion clinics were attacked and burned by people who viewed abortion as murder. Some doctors who performed abortions were murdered, and across the country Planned Parenthood offices and clinics hired armed security personnel for their safety. Feminists like Congresswoman Patricia Schroeder pushed for legal rights through the Equal Rights Amendment. They were opposed, successfully, by anti-feminists like Phyllis Schlafly, who organized within the "Moral Majority" movement of the Reverend Jerry Falwell. Falwell had become the most famous of the evangelists of the 1970s and 1980s. His home congregation in Lynchburg, Virginia, grew to 18,000 members with sixty associate pastors. Its religious services were broadcast on 392 television channels and 600 radio stations.

A few of the leading televangelists were disgraced in public sex scandals involving adultery, consorting with a prostitute without regard to public scrutiny, and accusations of participating in homosexual relationships that they themselves had condemned as sinful. In the early 2000s, the Roman Catholic Church was severely embarrassed by public revelations of the sexual exploitation of children by priests. In dioceses throughout the country, the Church attempted to resolve these issues through increased training, monitoring, and disciplining of its clergy, by public apologies, and by cash payments of restitution to past victims. Sex scandals enveloped President Clinton, who carried on a sexual affair with a young White House intern but publicly denied it for several months. Clinton survived an impeachment trial for perjury, but the serious business of governing the country was neglected during these long proceedings. Clinton's defenders charged that conservatives in the opposition party had fastened on his private behavior in order to cripple him politically.

Pornography became a multi-billion dollar industry involving some of the nation's most reputable companies, distributors like Time Warner and Comcast for home video, and major chains like Marriott and Hilton for hotel distribution. For many Americans, viewing pornography was simply a form of recreation, but to counter the perceived exploitation and degradation of sex, Tim LaHaye, co-founder of the Moral Majority, published *How to Be Happy Though Married* (1968), *Understanding the Male Temperment* (1977), *The Battle for the Family* (1982), and *Sex Education in the Family* (1985). His wife Beverley published *The Spirit-Controlled Woman* (1976), *I Am a Woman by*

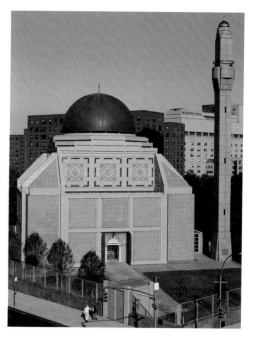

Islamic Cultural Center, New York City. Religions from around the world were finding new homes in America, often transplanted by new groups of immigrants and supplemented by native-born American converts.

HOW DO WE KNOW?

Perspectives on Religious Identity in the United States

Two recent studies of religious identity in the United States have painted contrasting pictures. Diana Eck celebrates an ever-increasing array of new and different religious communities. After noting the increasing diversity of their congregations and services in her Cambridge neighborhood, Eck sent her Harvard students to explore more systematically, first around Boston and then in their hometowns across America. In her book, A New Religious America, she reports the results of this Pluralism Project, exploring the extent to which "new" religions—especially Hinduism, Buddhism, and Islam, are appearing in America. She links her findings directly to the recent global migrations that are bringing about a million new immigrants to America every year:

> The immigrants of the last three decades . . . have expanded the diversity of our religious life dramatically, exponentially. Buddhists have come from Thailand, Vietnam, Cambodia, China, and Korea; Hindus from India, East Africa, and Trinidad; Muslims from Indonesia, Bangladesh, Pakistan, the Middle East, and Nigeria, Sikhs and Jains from India; and Zoroastrians from both India and Iran. Immigrants from Haiti and Cuba have brought Afro-Caribbean traditions, blending both African and Catholic symbols and images. New Jewish immigrants have come from Russia and the Ukraine, and the internal diversity of American Judaism is greater than ever before. The face of American Christianity has also changed with large Latino, Filipino, and Vietnamese Catholic communities; Chinese, Haitian, and Brazilian Pentecostal communities; Korean Presbyterians, Indian Mar Thomas, and Egyptian Copts. In every city in the land church signboards display the meeting times of Korean or Latino congregations that nest within the walls of old urban Protestant and Catholic churches.

Karen Armstrong's cross-cultural study of militant fundamentalist movements in Islam in Egypt and Iran, in Judaism in Israel, and in Christianity in the United States, paints a very different picture. Armstrong spent seven years as a nun, then became a college professor, and during the past two decades has become one of the most respected writers on religious history, especially on Christianity, Islam, and Judaism and their relations to one another. Her reflections on fundamentalist Christianity in the United States suggest very little flexibility, compromise, or openness to new religious groups:

> Fundamentalism is not going to disappear. In America, religion has long shaped opposition to government. Its rise and fall has always been cyclical, and events of the last few years indicate that there is still a state of incipient warfare between conservatives and liberals which has occasionally become frighteningly explicit. In 1992, Jerry Falwell, who still adheres to the old-style fundamentalism, announced that with the election of Bill Clinton to the presidency, Satan had been let loose in the United States. Clinton, Falwell thundered, was about to destroy the military and the nation by letting "the gays" take over. Executive orders permitting abortion in federally funded clinics, research on fetal tissue, the official endorsement of homosexual rights, were all signs that America "had declared war on God."

How can we reconcile these very different perspectives on religious identity in contemporary America? Philip Jenkins, in his study of the global expansion of Christianity suggests that we consider the demographics:

> The number of adherents of non-Christian religions in the United States is strikingly small. If we combine the plausible estimates for the numbers of American Jews, Buddhists, Muslims, and Hindus, then we are speaking of about 4 or 5 percent of the total population.

This proportion is not so different from western Europe where non-Christians form about 10 percent of the population of France, 4 percent of Britain, and 5 percent of Germany and the Netherlands. In many African and Asian nations, religious minorities make up 10 to 20 percent of the population, and in some cases even more. The same questions that attend religious diversity in many other countries of the world appear also in the USA.

So Eck's celebratory report is restricted to a very small, and perhaps not quite so remarkable, proportion of the population. On the other hand, Armstrong's fundamentalists also do not make up an American majority. In a 1984 poll, only 9, percent of Americans identified themselves as "fundamentalists," although "44 percent believed that salvation comes only through Jesus Christ."

Religious identity is important to most people in America. Both new immigration and "old time religion" are having their effects on shaping it. The results of this amalgam are not yet clear. As Eck remarks, "diversity alone does not constitute pluralism . . . whether we are able to work together across the lines of religious difference to create a society in which we actually know one another remains to be seen."

- What other historical examples can you give of national religious identity changing under the influence of new immigrant groups?
- What other historical examples can you give of new religious identities clashing with older established ones?
- Do you think that demographics is the main reason for the differences in perception about American religious life as represented by Eck and Armstrong? What other reasons can you suggest?

God's Design (1980), and The Restless Woman (1984). Together they published The Act of Marriage: The Beauty of Sexual Love (1976). For these fundamentalist religious authors, same-sex marriage, approved in Massachusetts in 2004 (and legal in the Netherlands since 2000), was unthinkable.

Fundamentalist books and films captured huge audiences. From 1995 to 2004, Tim LaHaye and Jerry B. Jenkins published twelve volumes in the "Left Behind" series, which describes the last days on earth before the second coming of Jesus Christ. According to *Newsweek Magazine*, the books sold a total of 62 million copies. Mel Gibson's film *The Passion of the Christ* (2004) touched a chord among believers, grossing $368 million in the first three months following its release in February 2004, although no major studio had been willing to distribute it and most major film reviewers criticized the film for excessive violence in depicting Jesus' crucifixion.

Despite the continuing power of the mainline Churches and of the rising visibility of the "born-again" fundamentalists, secularism and non-affiliation also increased in the period 1990 to 2001. The percentage of adults who reported their religious identity as Christian dropped from 86 to 76. The number of adults who did not subscribe to any religion doubled from 14.3 million to 29.4 million, from 8 percent to 14 percent of the total population. Another 5 percent were unwilling to answer survey questions about their religious identity posed by the American Religious Identification Survey of the Graduate Center of the City University of New York, in 2001, up from 2 percent in 1990. While 80 percent of the population did claim some religious identity, only 54 percent reported that they lived in a household where at least one member belonged to a formal religious institution of worship. This quiet decline in religious affiliation, quite different from the very public pronouncements of the religious evangelists, suggested that perhaps, beneath the surface, America was moving in the direction of European countries, with their much lower proportions of religious affiliation.

New immigrants brought yet another, international, dimension to American religious identity, increasing its diversity and cosmopolitanism. As Hindus and Sikhs immigrated from India; Muslims from the Middle East and Pakistan; Buddhists from Southeast Asia; and other religious groups from elsewhere, American religious identity broadened. The new immigrants and their native born children sometimes encountered xenophobia, but they enriched and extended religious identity and ethnic identity in the United States. They made up only about 7 to 8 percent of the total population, but with their mosques, temples, sanctuaries, and church announcement boards in non-European languages, they added an extremely visible new dimension to American religious identity. That identity continues in flux.

GLOBALIZATION: NEW ECONOMIC AND CULTURAL IDENTITIES

Increasing communication technology, free market capitalism, and decreasing government regulation made "globalization" the buzzword of the turn of the twenty-first century. Technologies, markets, and nations were being brought together:

> in a way that is enabling individuals, corporations and nation-states to reach around the world farther, faster, deeper and cheaper than ever before, and in a way that is also producing a powerful backlash from those brutalized or left behind by this new system. (Friedman, 1999, pp. 7–8)

Economically, globalization thrives on inexpensive transportation and communication. Politically, it requires freedom of movement of goods, services, capital, knowledge, and people across borders, although the freedom of people to move is more restricted than the other categories. It functions with little regard to international borders, rules, and regulations; it creates new institutions for working independently of them. It increases the level of interaction of peoples, producing new and different social and cultural forms. It brings increased travel and tourism, brings more world music and literature, as well as new dimensions of international economic investment. It allows billions of dollars of investment capital to move across the globe at the stroke of a computer keypad. The sums are staggering, and increasing. In 1990, total private capital for investment going from the United States, Japan, and the European Union totaled $43.9 billion; in 1997, $299 billion. In 2001, the US alone invested a total of $114 billion overseas. According to the World Trade Organization, total exports of merchandise and commercial services worldwide reached $6.5 trillion in 1997. US trade alone in 2000 reached $2.7 trillion.

Globalization evokes passionate responses both pro and con. Under its umbrella, local and global identities meet and interact with one another and both identities are modified in the process. Usually both become more flexible, but sometimes, people and groups resist modification and change. They insist on keeping their identity as "pure" as possible. We have seen examples of both of these reactions at the beginning of this chapter. Pessimists argue that globalization threatens to homogenize the world's cultures into a single "McDonald's" culture and to replace its many languages with a single, dominant global language, English. Optimists assert that globalization provides communication networks that allow small, niche cultures, languages, and organizations to flourish. At the international level, globalization may appear uniform and corporate, but at the local level it may encourage the evolution of enriched economic and cultural patterns.

Although many advocates of globalization claim that its home is the entire world and its benefits are equally accessible to everyone, more critical observers see it headquartered in the United States, and spread not only by America's businesses but also by its effective control over the World Bank and related global financial institutions. They see globalization as just one more measure of the superpower status of the United States.

The Internet and the World Wide Web

The technologies of globalization are computerization, satellite communication, the internet, and the world wide web. The growth of these communication networks is astounding. The first modern, practical computers were created during and immediately after World War II, at first based on vacuum tubes and then in the late 1950s on transistors. The first integrated-circuit based computer was marketed by IBM in 1965. The internet was created by the United States Defense Department in 1969 as an intricate web of tens of thousands of computer networks linked by telephone lines to expedite communication within the government and related agencies, and to provide emergency backup in case other communication means failed. Commercial service began in the 1980s when the US National Science Foundation created facilities for connecting private computer networks to government networks. The first computer virus was created by a Cornell University graduate student in 1988. In 1989 Tim Berners-Lee, a British scientist working in a nuclear energy laboratory in Geneva, posted a message to an internet newsgroup announcing the "World Wide Web (www) Project," a kind of electronic public access bulletin board. In 1993 an American, Marc Andreeson, developed a new form of browser that made the WWW accessible to the general public. Both of these inventors allowed their inventions to be used without charge, making the WWW essentially a free service.

In 1994, some 3 million people were connected to the internet worldwide; by mid-1999, 200 million. By 2002, the number of users had risen to 650 million worldwide, including 166 million Americans. About 35 percent of the users claimed English as their native tongue; about 12 percent Chinese. The internet became "the fastest growing form of media in history" (*New York Times Almanac*, 2000, p. 816).

HOW DO WE KNOW?

Evaluating Globalization

Globalization—in the sense of global networks of economic, political, and cultural exchange—is not new. We have seen examples throughout this text going back thousands of years. The increasing sophistication of transportation and communication, especially the computer, the internet, and the world wide web, however, have given globalization far greater scope in the last two decades than ever before. As the power of globalization has increased over the past fifteen years, its evaluations have become more careful and more nuanced.

Thomas Friedman, chief foreign political correspondent for the New York Times, introduced his highly influential The Lexus and the Olive Tree *with a sense of the inevitability of globalization:*

> I feel about globalization a lot like I feel about the dawn. Generally speaking, I think it's a good thing that the sun comes up every morning. It does more good than harm. But even if I didn't much care for the dawn there isn't much I could do about it. I didn't start globalization. I can't stop it—except at a huge cost to human development—and I'm not going to waste time trying. All I want to think about is how I can get the best out of this new system, and cushion the worst, for the most people. (p. xviii)

Joseph Stiglitz, Nobel Prize winner in Economics, served for a number of years as vice president and chief economist of the World Bank. Stiglitz came away from the experience appalled by the failures of globalization and the hardships it often inflicted, especially on the poor. His *powerful critique,* Globalization and its Discontents, *differs sharply from Friedman's general acceptance of the system:*

> I have written this book because while I was at the World Bank, I saw firsthand the devastating effect that globalization can have on developing countries, and especially the poor within those countries. I believe that globalization—the removal of the barriers to free trade and the closer integration of national economies—can be a force for good and that it has the potential to enrich everyone in the world, particularly the poor. But I also believe that if this is to be the case, the way globalization has been managed, including the international trade agreements that have played such a large role in removing those barriers and the policies that have been imposed on developing countries in the process of globalization, need to be radically rethought. (pp. ix–x)
>
> Today, few—apart from those with vested interests who benefit from keeping out the goods produced by the poor countries—defend the hypocrisy of pretending to help developing countries by forcing them to open up their markets to the goods of the advanced industrial countries while keeping their own markets protected, policies that make the rich richer and the poor more impoverished—and increasingly angry. (p. xv)

Professor of politics Manfred Steger introduces Rethinking Globalism *by denying the inevitability of globalization—despite Friedman's assertions—and arguing for his own* vision of an egalitarian, peaceful world order as a guideline for world economic planning:

> The contributors to this volume are united in their conviction that globalization is an incipient process, slowly giving rise to new forms of globality whose eventual qualities and properties are far from being determined. Globalization is neither inevitable nor irreversible; it does not necessarily have to mean or to be what globalists say it means or is . . . The central task for scholars committed to a study of the ideological dimensions of globalization lies in offering both the general public and the academic community thoughtful analyses and critiques of globalism, the dominant ideology of our time . . . Hence, a "critical theory of globalization" is explicitly guided by a normative vision—the ideal of a more egalitarian and less violent global order. (pp. 10–11)

- *What experience has each author had in defining, evaluating, and implementing globalization?*
- *To what degree is each author dogmatic in his evaluation of globalization? What dogmas does he seem to accept or to reject?*
- *To what extent can you begin, on the bases of these authors' suggestions, to formulate your own values in evaluating globalization? On the bases of these introductions, which of the three books do you think you would find most interesting? Most useful?*
- *How do the ideas of George Soros, discussed in our text above, compare with those of these authors?*

In 1999, the file-sharing service Napster became available, allowing users to exchange files, including music, without need of copyright. Millions used this service until a court ruled Napster illegal in 2001. Users shifted to other file-sharing services, but the courts continued to investigate them for breach of copyright. Within the computer and the music industries fierce battles were underway to determine how copyrights would or would not be implemented when technology had created such new means of access to materials virtually without cost. By April 2002, one billion personal computers had been manufactured since the first one in 1975. Among the ten wealthiest Americans in 2003, according to *Forbes Magazine*, four had amassed their fortunes in the computer industry, led by Bill Gates with $46 billion. (Four others were heirs of Sam Walton of Walmart.) With the internet and world wide web, shopping, research, and accessing documents could all be done while sitting in front of a computer at home or in an

Before the silicon chip. Immediately after World War II, when the first practical computers were constructed, advances in information theory and the invention of the transistor gave birth to such hulking monsters as ENIAC, developed at the University of Pennsylvania in 1946. It weighed 50 tons and occupied 2000 square feet of floor space.

office, or even from a portable computer while traveling. E-mail, another facility of the internet, made instantaneous global communication available at nominal cost.

Many people lost their jobs to more efficient and cost-effective technology-based organizations, and many with less education were threatened by economic organizations that required ever more training. In the United States and globally, the new technologies increased the gap between rich and poor, as those who access and guide the technological transformation did well, but many others were left behind. Poor nations are also left farther behind as the rich nations, notably the United States, were richer. Moreover, because the new technologies were dependent on research laboratories, these facilities, especially in the United States, continued to attract talented, skilled persons, draining them from less technologically sophisticated nations. To some degree this was offset by new employment opportunities. New, communications-related jobs are foot-loose, and many highly skilled jobs were being outsourced to third-world countries, where salaries were lower. For example, Bangalore and Hyderabad, cities in India, became miniature "Silicon Valleys" through the investments of multinational companies like IBM, Texas Instruments, and Microsoft, and through the entrepreneurship of local information technology experts. Here, highly skilled personnel earned salaries far higher than most local salaries, yet substantially below those of the US, the European Union, and Japan. These salary differentials helped drive the constant flow of investment capital, goods, and labor around the globe.

Disparities, Disruptions, and Crises: A Cautionary Tale from Asia

Average living standards around the world have been improving. During the 1990s the proportion of people suffering from extreme poverty fell from 30 to 23 percent (*Human Development Report*, p. 5), in large part thanks to the improvements in China's economy. The disparities between rich and poor are increasing, however, as often happens when new sources of wealth become available for private development. In 1996, the poorest 20 percent of the world's population received only 1.4 percent of the world's income, down from 2.3 percent in 1966; the richest 20 percent received 85 percent, up from 70 percent (statistics from *United Nations Development Report*, p. 80). Poverty can increase even in conditions that are improving overall. "Over the past two decades [1983–2003] income inequality worsened in 33 of 66 developing countries with data" (*Human Development Report*, p. 5).

Whole regions of the world could rise and fall economically by abrupt shifts in global investment patterns as the countries of East and Southeast Asia discovered at the turn of the twenty-first century. Following Japan's model of development (see Chapter 21), the countries of East and Southeast Asia experienced extraordinary growth. Between 1965 and 1996, the average annual growth of the GNP for the world as a whole was 3.1 percent. For South Korea it was 8.9 percent; Singapore, 8.3; Hong Kong, 7.5; Thailand, 7.3; Indonesia, 6.7; Malaysia, 6.8; the Philippines, 3.5. Japan's growth had slowed after its 1989 recession, but still averaged 4.5 percent. China, although it followed different models, grew at 8.5 percent. "Before July 2, 1997 the Asian Pacific was considered, rightly, to be the world's success story of economic development and technological modernization of the past half-century" (Castells, Vol. 3, p. 206).

Then the currency of Thailand fell sharply, as investors recognized that the national economy was not expanding as rapidly as incoming investment and loans, and the country had a mounting trade deficit. The values of land and industry on which the loans and investments had been based were artificially inflated, and they collapsed, as did the value of Thai currency. Investments stopped abruptly and loans were recalled, first from Thailand and then from neighboring countries with similar financial problems. South Korea, Thailand, Indonesia, Malaysia, and the Philippines, which had seen $93 billion in net investments enter their countries in 1996, saw $12 billion leave in 1997. In the space of a few months entire national economies collapsed and others went into a deep recession. Japan, the world's second largest economy, suffered financial bankruptcies and the devaluation of its stocks and bonds.

What had happened? The Asian economies had been doing many things right. They had budget surpluses, low inflation, high rates of savings, and substantial exports. But they had taken on more loans, especially short-term loans, than their productivity justified, and as collateral they had presented real estate, which was dramatically and unrealistically overpriced. Beyond this, their internal financial systems were not "transparent"—that is, not open to external analysis and evaluation. Presumably they were hiding some important information. (Similar problems had surfaced in Japan after the 1989 "bubble" burst.) Corrupt politicians, bureaucrats, bankers, and organized crime leaders were guiding investments inappropriately, for their own benefit, and covering up their actions. Meanwhile investment money and loans poured in from overseas. The monies were misused, pocketed, or poorly invested in speculation, until finally the economies collapsed.

The governments, which had been so helpful as their economies had grown, were now not strong enough to bail out the failing banks and industries. (In the United States, in the 1980s, the government had spent $250 billion bailing out savings and loans associations that had made bad investments.) The system of government direction, which had produced economic miracles, now left a wake of recession and depression. Those that had relied less on international funds and that had paid more attention to basic business fundamentals—like Taiwan and Singapore—had fewer troubles; those that had taken in the most foreign loans and investments and had invested least prudently—like South Korea, Indonesia, and Thailand—were most affected.

The International Monetary Fund came to the rescue in some of these countries with massive loans, but the very arrival of the IMF frightened off other investors, who saw this as a sign of economic insolvency. Also the IMF was more concerned with recovering its loans and investments than with the economic health of the defaulting country. It implemented the "Washington consensus": opening the borders to international investment (although this was already in place and had caused some of the problems), lowering or removing tariffs against imports, privatizing (selling off) government businesses, reducing government welfare programs, laying off government employees, and devaluing local currency. All these measures are the instruments of classical, conservative economic theory, although many economists argued that these measures had never been rigidly enforced in the economies of wealthy countries. The IMF virtually took over control of the economy of the defaulting country. It demanded a regimen of economic austerity so severe that it jeopardized the health and welfare of the citizens of the country. This was the experience in South Korea in 1997, which accepted a bailout loan of $58 billion, the largest ever in the history of the IMF.

Some international bankers, like billionaire George Soros, saw the need for countries to be more honest and more transparent. They argued that state guidance and regulations should be cut back as national economies grew and that private enterprise should be given more scope. But they also argued that some regulation was needed at the international level. Trillions of dollars in investment funds were swirling around the globe without guidance or tracking or common purpose, battering the economies of all but the largest states. As Soros argued:

> The world has entered a period of profound imbalance in which no individual state can resist the power of global financial markets and there are practically no institutions for rule-making on an international scale. Collective decision-making mechanisms for the global economy simply do not exist . . . In short we need a global society to support our global economy. A global society does not mean a global state. To abolish the existence of states is neither feasible nor desirable; but insofar as there are collective interests that transcend state boundaries, the sovereignty of states must be subordinated to international law and international institutions.

Capital markets had become global, but the national and international institutions for keeping them honest and transparent had not. This was the great institutional deficiency now exposed by the experience of East and Southeast Asia. After several years of suffering and of economic restructuring, these countries have mostly recovered their former economic health, and some like Korea and Singapore have pushed far ahead. Their experience, however, highlights the dangers of global capital movements and of wishful thinking.

Opposition to Globalization

In December 1999, the World Trade Organization (WTO), the United Nations' agency for setting the terms of international trade, met in Seattle, Washington. Protestors blocked the streets of this normally tranquil city and demonstrated dramatically their apprehensions at the increasing tempo of world trade and their demands for more regulation by national governments and by the United Nations. Many of the protestors argued that they favored world trade, but with some regulations to provide protection for the environment, human rights, labor, and children's welfare. They feared that the demands for profits would overrun these humanitarian concerns. Similarly, many national and religious groups feared that the spread of powerful global communications systems would overwhelm their unique cultures. Few such groups wished to stop globalization entirely, but they sought limits and restraints that would protect their cherished identities and interests.

Similar protests have stalked subsequent meetings of the WTO and of other groups promoting globalization in Davos, Switzerland, Salzburg, Austria, Bangkok, Thailand, Melbourne, Australia, Quebec City, Canada, Gothenburg, Sweden, and elsewhere. In August 2001, over 100,000 gathered in Genoa, Italy, to protest at the meeting of the G-8, the leaders of the eight most prominent economically advanced countries. The meeting was protected by 16,000 police and military police. In a tense confrontation, one of the protestors was shot to death.

In 2001, a new umbrella organization of protestors took form as the World Social Forum. They held their first meeting in Porto Alegre, Brazil, in January 2001, attracting thousands of delegates. The 2002 meeting took place in Florence, Italy; 2003 in Paris, France; 2004 in Mumbai (Bombay), India. At first, many of the costs of the meetings were underwritten by major international foundations, but both the foundations and the participants came to believe that this funding undercut the populist nature of the sessions. Although many groups gathered to protest a wide array of perceived injustices, the main goal of the Forum was to find alternative political and economic models to those that dominate the world today. The Forum seeks new paradigms, new policies, and new identities for world development.

At the dawn of the twenty-first century, we are witnessing a global balancing act between rapidly expanding technological capabilities, the desire for economic profits, the need to protect human rights, a passion to preserve group identities, and the uncertain power of the state to intervene on behalf of those contentious interests. The balancing act in itself is not new, but its global pervasiveness is.

The Global Criminal Economy

Just as the global economy is part of our reality and identity, so transnational, organized crime is also part of that reality and identity. For transnational organized crime is big business. Although carried out against the law, and therefore requiring special under-the-table arrangements with law officers and government officials, transnational crime employs many of the same information networks as does legal business.

The scale and scope of the illegal economy is staggering. Drugs are the largest segment, nuclear weapons perhaps the newest and most frightening. Because these activities are illegal, estimates of their size varies. "The 1994 United Nations Conference on Global Organized Crime estimated that global trade in drugs amounted to about $500 billion a year; that is, it was larger than the global trade in oil" (Castells, Vol. 3, p. 172). The leader of the Medellin drug cartel in Colombia, Pablo Escobar, was a billionaire, listed in *Forbes Magazine* as the world's seventh richest man (although he was killed by Colombian security forces in 1993). Overall profits from all kinds of organized international criminal activities were estimated at between $750 billion and $1 trillion a year. Sociologist Manuel Castells lists some of the leading participants in this vast global market place:

> Crime is as old as humankind. But global crime, the networking of powerful criminal organizations, and their associates, in shared activities throughout the planet, is a new phenomenon that profoundly affects international and national economies, politics, security, and ultimately, societies at large. The Sicilian Cosa Nostra (and its associates, La Camorra, Ndrangheta, and Sacra Corona Unita), the American Mafia, the Colombian cartels, the Mexican cartels, the Nigerian criminal networks, the Japanese Mafiyas, the Turkish heroin traffickers, the Jamaican Posses, and a myriad of regional and local criminal groupings in all countries [including the Chinese Triads and the Japanese Yakuza whom he discusses later], have come together in a global, diversified network that permeates boundaries and links up ventures of all sorts. While drugs traffic is the most important segment of this worldwide industry, arms deals also represent a high-value market. (Castells, Vol. 3, pp. 166–7)

The 1994 United Nations Conference cited seven major forms of international organized crime.

Drugs The most widespread and the largest of all illicit international businesses in terms of volume of business and profits are drugs of various kinds. Their major sources include Colombia and Mexico in Latin America, Thailand and Myanmar in Southeast Asia, and Afghanistan in Central Asia. In some of these countries, notably Colombia and Afghanistan, control of the drug trade has given regional warlords the power to challenge and sometimes to control the central government. Synthetic drugs,

Colombian anti-narcotics police in a poppy field, El Silencio, Colombia, 2002. This area was once the safe haven of rebels from the Revolutionary Armed Forces of Columbia (FARC). They controlled the area from 1998 until 2002 during failed attempts to find a peaceful settlement between them and the government.

such as LSD and Ecstasy, are more commonly made in the United States and Europe.

Smuggling of Illegal Immigrants In 2000, this "human cargo" was estimated at 4 million people per year, and its profits at $5 to $7 billion. It represents a new form of slavery. Estimates of illegal migrants from Latin America—especially Mexico—into the United States are about one million each year. Through the 1990s, illegal immigration into the European Union rose to an estimated half-million persons per year.

Trafficking in Women and Children Most of this illegal commerce is for sexual slavery, mostly from Southeast Asia, but with an increasing number of women coming from Russia and eastern Europe after the fall of the Soviet Union. Some of the women travel voluntarily, but many are abducted or deceived or deeply in debt and are then sold. Because they are watched closely so that they cannot escape their condition and their debts, their position is different from that of a sex worker who works voluntarily for payment. A report in the *New York Times Magazine* in early 2004 asserts the existence of a very significant trade in women being brought either by force or through false promises from Russia and eastern Europe via Mexico into the United States. A growing traffic in children for adoption has also arisen, especially from Latin America to the United States. The babies and children are often sold with the consent of their parents, but sometimes they are kidnapped.

Trafficking in Body Parts The modern medical miracle of organ transplants has also inspired a new criminal industry: trafficking in body parts. Sometimes these parts are taken from corpses, without permission from the family. Some of these may be unclaimed bodies in morgues. Particularly extensive practices have been reported from Russia. The Chinese government apparently routinely harvests the organs of criminals who have been executed and keeps the profits for the government. In Japan, loan sharks are reported to have demanded body organs in repayment of overdue debts. Less commonly, and more clearly criminal, the organs may be stolen in surgical operations performed without consent—as the recent film *Dirty Pretty Things* portrayed graphically.

The greatest problem has been the harvesting of the organs—kidneys, for example—of the living poor for the benefit of transplant recipients who can afford to pay for them. In this "organ bazaar," the "donors" may sell their organs to pay their way out of debt. "Transplant tourism" has emerged. "Affluent transplant tourists can travel to select medical sites in Turkey, eastern Europe, Cuba, Germany and the United States in search of transplants that they cannot arrange quickly or safely enough at home" (Scheper-Hughes, p. 3). To "explore the social and economic context of organ transplantation, focusing on the human rights implications of the desperate, worldwide search for organs," a team of anthropologists, human rights activists, physicians, and social medicine specialists has founded "Organs Watch" at the University of California, Berkeley. Its reports chart recent developments.

Money Laundering In 1999, the International Monetary Fund estimated global money laundering between $.5 trillion and $1.5 trillion. The range, as well as the amount, give some sense of the size of the business. "Laundering" is the process by which illegal profits are disguised as legal. The first step is to deposit them in banks or other financial institutions that do not inquire as to their source. Such banks are located in small countries—for example, Panama, Aruba, the Cayman Islands, and the Bahamas—that do little to control banking procedures. Once in these banks, the funds can be transferred electronically to other financial institutions and invested in legitimate businesses. This network link between the worlds of illegal and legal business gives the world of illegal business its power and viability. Launderers may earn up to 25 percent of the total value of the transaction.

Weapons Trafficking Most weapons sales are legal, but sales to nations under international embargo—for example, Iran, Iraq, and Libya—are not. Nor are sales to guerrilla groups, partisans in civil wars, and terrorist groups. Some of the weapons for sale are remnants of Cold War stocks first supplied to their clients by the United States and Russia. Others are newly produced weapons. As in illegal transactions generally, these illicit arms sales earn great profits because of the need for secrecy and pay-offs.

Trafficking in Nuclear Materials From the early 1990s this threat was especially severe from the stocks of nuclear materials in the Soviet Union and its eastern European allies. Enormous stockpiles were in storage. Security was light. Demand was great. And some one hundred thousand workers connected with nuclear production and storage were receiving very inadequate pay, and sometimes were not paid at all, as the economies of eastern Europe collapsed. As disarmament continued, more material was likely to be available and the risks have probably increased. After the 9/11 terror attack in the United States, fears also increased that nuclear materials might pass not only to the hands of states, but also to the hands of terrorist organizations.

As additional nations have entered into the "nuclear club," illegal sales of weapons-grade nuclear materials are increasing. In February 2004, Dr. Abdul Qadeer Khan, the "father" of Pakistan's nuclear bomb, announced publicly that he had personally been operating an international black market in weapons-grade nuclear materials. This confession made public what had been an open secret for almost two decades, that Pakistan had been involved in such nuclear transfers. Although both Khan and Pakistan's president, Pervez Musharraf, denied that the government of Pakistan was involved in the nuclear materials sales, no serious observer believed that such operations could be carried out by a single individual.

The illegal trafficking of women, Xiamen, China, 2003. A Chinese man is here detained in a police van with women whom he has been accused of trying to smuggle to Taiwan.

Pakistan's activities in the nuclear market place suggested that countries like Libya and Iran would be able to acquire and assemble nuclear weapons—although Libya offered to give up its quest for nuclear weaponry in early 2004. Perhaps Islamic nations—and perhaps private armies—would benefit most from Pakistan's technology and sales, but more comprehensively, the entire network of nuclear transactions around the world would be encouraged. A Pakistani weapons expert, disturbed by his country's entry into the international bazaar, described the nuclear marketplace: "Once they had the bomb, they had a shopping list of what to buy and where. A.Q. Khan can bring a plain piece of paper and show me how to get it done—the countries, people, and telephone numbers. 'This is the guy in Russia who can get you small quantities of enriched uranium. You in Malaysia will manufacture the stuff. Here's who will miniaturize the warhead. And then go to North Korea and get the damn missile.' … This is not a few scientists pocketing money and getting rich. It's a state policy."

International networks played an increasingly important role in the global criminal economy. Through the 1960s, 1970s, and 1980s, and even into the 1990s, specific criminal groups worked through their own localized networks. The most famous perhaps were the two drug cartels based in Colombia—one in Cali, the other in Medellin, each with its own leaders and policies—and the Russian mafia, much of it Jewish, seizing new opportunities offered by the breakdown of Communist Party control over the Russian economy. By 1997, Russian and Colombian criminal organizations were forging alliances in the Caribbean. The Russians offered access to new drug markets in eastern Europe to the Colombians, who sought, in exchange, heavy equipment that would enable them to protect and deliver their drugs, including a submarine, armored helicopters, surface-to-air missiles that would let them attack government helicopters, and small arms. The Russians also opened banks in the Caribbean and strip clubs in south Florida that would facilitate money laundering. Each of the groups retained a high degree of internal secrecy and cohesion, but networked to take advantage of the opportunities offered by the other.

In 2000 the United Nations adopted a "Convention against Transnational Organized Crime," the first legally binding UN instrument in the field of crime. The convention suggests ways of improving international cooperation against crime that crosses national borders and legal systems. It considers the laws of extradition, provides for witness protection and for shielding legal businesses from investments by illegal businesses. Signatories to the convention are required to establish domestic criminal laws against: participating in an organized criminal group; money laundering; corruption; and obstruction of justice. Additional protocols were adopted to combat the smuggling of migrants, and the buying and selling of women and children for sexual exploitation or sweatshop labor. Another protocol under consideration would address the illicit manufacture of and traffic in firearms that supported civilian, terrorism, and organized crime. The battles between the forces of law and order and the organizations of internationally organized crime were, however, far from over. As a senior American enforcement official told a *Washington Post* reporter, "American law enforcement is not organized to fight this threat. We are in for a long, long battle, and we are sort of outnumbered at this point." The law enforcement agencies of other nations were no better equipped for the international battleground.

Medicine, Science, and Global Ecology

People are living longer. Many factors contribute: more and better food for many (but not all); better public sanitation and health; cleaner cities and streets; more focused and effective medicines; more thorough medical care. Globally, the average life expectancy for females rose from 52 in 1960 to 65 in 1980, to 68.5 in 2000. Male life expectancy also rose steadily, although it lagged behind female: 49 in 1960 to 61 in 1980 to 65 in 2000. In this forty-year period, people in low-income countries gained about sixteen years of life expectancy, those in high-income countries gained about nine years, because they started from a higher base. In 1960, people in low-income countries had lived about twenty-six years less than those in high-income countries; in 2000, only about eighteen years less. In 2003, Japan had reached the highest average longevity rates in the world: 77.6 for males; 84.4 for females. These increasingly high rates of longevity, combined with declining birth rates, especially in wealthy countries, meant that as people reached old age, they would constitute a large proportion of the population, and they would require care from the decreasing proportion of younger people. The way in which younger and older people estimated their mutual rights and obligations was undergoing a change, although no one knew how it would work out.

In countries where parents had a preference of one sex over another in their children—usually preferring males over females—new medical procedures such as amniocentesis and sonograms were used to determine the sex of fetuses, and females were often aborted. In addition, boy children received better care—more and better quality food, medical care, and education—than girls. As a result, sex ratios in such countries as China and India began to shift. No one knew what would be the ultimate effect of having an adult population that had substantially more men than women nor how this would affect men's and women's identities.

Access to medicine and medical care was also becoming an issue, especially in the struggle to bring the global AIDS epidemic under control. When AIDS first appeared as a health threat in the late 1970s, no drugs were available for treatment, and the disease was deemed to be fatal. By the end of 2002, approximately 28 million people had died of the disease and 42 million more were infected. By 1996, various drugs were found to be effective in inhibiting the development of the disease, but the drugs were very expensive. In the third world, where 95 percent of the cases occur—70 percent in sub-Saharan Africa—the drugs are prohibitively expensive.

Several issues are emerging from this situation. First, from a humanitarian point of view, AIDS is a dreadful killer, and the search is on for more effective ways of preventing, inhibiting, and curing it. Second, in the face of such pervasive death, especially concentrated in sub-Saharan Africa, where as much as 25 percent of the population is infected in some states, fear is increasing that the social fabric of the society will unravel. Third, negotiations have been taking place between political and humanitarian leaders and drug companies to manufacture the appropriate antiretroviral drugs and make them available at low cost in low-income countries.

Finally, some nations of the world have begun to see the political as well as humanitarian implications of the widespread AIDS epidemic and have pledged their support to fighting it. For example, in May 2003 the United States Congress voted to spend $15 billion to fight AIDS globally, and especially in Africa, although actual allocation of the money has been slow. The question of the cost of drugs will continue to surface in a wide array of contexts—in addition to AIDS—as drug companies discover and create ever newer and more effective drugs, and people live longer and become more reliant on the drugs. How can prices be set high enough to satisfy the needs of drug companies to carry on their business and research with a reasonable profit, and yet low enough so that people can afford the drugs they need? How will the drug companies, drug users, and governments view their obligations to one another?

The biology of human identity came to the center of world attention in 1997 when scientists in Scotland succeeded in cloning a sheep and were experimenting with producing blood in the bodies of animals that could be used for human transfusions. The long-term consequences of such genetic engineering are as yet unknown, but they are permanent, transmitted to every subsequent generation of their recipients, so the procedures are the subject of intense scrutiny and debate. In 1990 the United States government initiated the Human Genome Project to identify all the approximately 100,000 genes in human DNA, and to "map" the sequences of the 3 billion chemical bases that make it up. In June 2000, it announced success, as did a private research laboratory. The next task was to understand the functioning of each component. Here, too, private laboratories were also working aggressively on these puzzles for the new technology promises great wealth to its masters, although the costs to consumers are not yet known. In 2003 the government announced completion of the project as they had

Dolly, the cloned sheep, 1997. Genetic engineering offered great hopes for increasing longevity, health, and food supplies, but it enters a new, unknown world of biological transformation that cannot be reversed.

found up to 99 percent of the structure of the human genome. The project had taken thirteen years and cost $2.7 billion.

Biologists and biochemists have learned how to substitute one gene for another, yielding astonishing new hybrids of grains that have multiplied food productivity and of animals that are more productive of meat, milk, and even certain chemicals useful in medicine. Genetic engineering in humans promises to cure certain genetically based illnesses like cystic fibrosis, muscular dystrophy, and Huntington's chorea—although this has not yet been accomplished. The science carries the promise, and the threat, of creating humans who are taller or shorter, heavier or lighter, blue eyed or brown. The ethical issues involved in genetic manipulation are as significant as the scientific ones.

ECOLOGICAL ISSUES

In 1990, the United Nations became involved in organizing against global ecological destruction. Many concerns filled the agenda. The main ones were:

- The depletion of the ozone layer through the introduction into the environment of chlorofluorocarbons, a principal chemical in aerosol sprays and in most coolants, such as refrigeration and air-conditioning units;
- Global warming, or the greenhouse effect, caused primarily by the introduction into the environment of carbon dioxide, which traps heat in the earth's lower atmosphere, raising temperatures around the globe;
- The destruction of the marine environment through ocean dumping, ship pollution, and the absorption of chemicals into the water table;
- Acid rain, the pollution of the atmosphere with industrial chemicals that descend with rainfall;
- Deforestation, especially in the tropics, where at least 25 million acres of trees are cut down yearly;
- At a more local level, polluted air, contaminated water, and cigarette smoke that were clearly associated with carcinogens.

Trees destroyed by acid rain, Sebestiana, Czech Republic, 1997. Acid rain is one of several pollutants produced by industry that threaten life and health on our planet.

In general, more developed countries tended to place the blame for ecological problems on the increase in global population, an increase most marked in the less developed countries. The less developed countries, in response, blamed the more developed as the source of the industries that create the pollution. On the issue of world hunger, the developed countries again pointed to population pressures on food supplies in the less developed countries, while the less developed blamed flaws in the world economy and food distribution mechanisms, both controlled by the wealthier countries. Agreement is emerging on the need for international cooperation in a stronger UN environment program, but for the present the United Nations lacks sovereign power. It can gather information, carry out research, make recommendations, hold conferences, and provide counsel, but it has no powers of enforcement. Implementation depends upon the decision of member nations. Local and global identities have not yet merged. Nor have the peoples of the earth yet accepted their obligations to future generations.

PUBLIC IDENTITIES
WHAT DIFFERENCE DO THEY MAKE?

With this chapter we can no longer assess the messages that may be deciphered from the past for the future, for here we are studying contemporary history. We do not have closure. We do not know how events will unfold. We do not know their consequences. As we assess the significance of changing human identities in regard to politics, religion, economics, culture, and the natural world, we use the tools that the study of history has taught us. We learn to weigh evidence, evaluate sources, find appropriate contexts, reckon what seems to us believable on the basis of our understanding of how people and systems work. We use our own identities as touchstones to understand the identities of others. Not that ours and theirs are alike. They are not. But the better we understand our own identities and how they have been formed, the better able we are to understand others. With self-knowledge, with historical tools, with the best evidence we can assemble, we do our best to understand current trends in order to make our way into the future.

Review Questions

- To what extent would you classify the broadcast of the Olympics or World Cup soccer or a Cricket Test Match series or the Baseball World Series as an example of globalization? You may wish to consider political, economic, social, and cultural issues concerning the broadcast.
- What is the nature of religious beliefs that lead some people to claim that their religious belief is their principal identity?
- What is the nature of nationalism that leads some people to claim that their national identity is their principal identity?
- What is the nature of economic systems that leads some people to claim that their economic identity is their principal identity? Please give an example from this text of a person or a group that has proclaimed such an economic identity. How does the economic identity interact with the global identity?
- How do ecological concerns build a global identity? How do they interfere with a global identity?
- In your own life, what do you see as the relationship between local identities and global identities?

Suggested Readings

Appadurai, Arjun. *Modernity at Large* (Minneapolis: University of Minnesota Press, 1996). Global thinking on the cultural implications of modernization, especially on the impact from lesser developed countries to more developed.

Arab Human Development Report 2003: Building a Knowledge Society (New York: United Nations Press, 2003). In this volume, in an annual series, 26 Arab scholars examine the development and dissemination of knowledge in the Arab world and find it lagging. Makes suggestions for improvement. Abundant statistical tables along with qualitative assessments.

Armstrong, Karen. *The Battle for God* (New York: Knopf, 2000). A thoughtful, thorough assessment of religious militancy in Egyptian and Iranian Islam, Israeli Judaism, and American Christian fundamentalism.

Bulliet, Richard W., ed. *The Columbia History of the 20th Century* (New York: Columbia University Press, 1998).

Castells, Manuel. *The Information Age: Economy, Society and Culture*, 3 vols. (Malden, MA: Blackwell, 1996–2000). An amazingly comprehensive assessment of the contemporary global scene, including universal perspectives and local case studies from a wide range of locations.

Chomsky, Noam. *Hegemony or Survival: America's Quest for Global Dominance* (New York: Henry Holt, 2003). A blistering attack on US foreign policy as excessively violent and self-interested, by a foremost American critic.

Duus, Peter. *Modern Japan* (Boston: Houghton Mifflin, 2nd ed., 1998). Summary narrative and interpretation, highly accessible, by a scholarly expert.

Enwezor, Okwui. *The Short Century. Independence and Liberation Movements in Africa 1945–1994* (Munich: Prestel, 2001). History told through art, cloth, posters, photography, architecture, music, theater, literature, and film—as well as a relevant selection of primary documents in politics, ideology, and ethics. The lavish catalogue of a blockbuster museum show. Emphasizes the interweaving of African and Western forms.

Esposito, John. *Unholy War: Terror in the Name of Islam* (New York: Oxford University Press, 2002). Masterful explanation of the role of jihad in Islam historically, and most of all, today. Sees the issue in context, and explains what is and is not Islamic about holy war.

Farah, Douglas, "Russian Mob, Drug Cartels Joining Forces," *Washington Post*, September 29, 1997, A-1. Reports their alliance for mutual business profits and protection. http://www.washingtonpost.com/wp-srv/inatl/longterm/russiagov/stoiries/mafia0902997.html

Freeman, Christopher. "Technology and Invention," in Bulliet, pp. 314–44.

French, Howard. *A Continent for the Taking. The Tragedy and Hope of Africa* (New York: Knopf, 2004). Outstanding journalistic account primarily of west and central Africa. Tragic in its perspective, with lots of responsibility placed on outsiders—Europeans, Americans—as well as on Africans.

Friedman, Robert I. "Land of the Stupid: When You Need a Used Russian Submarine," *New Yorker*. Recounts the career in crime of Ludwig Fainberg, key member of the Russian mafia.

Friedman, Thomas L. *The Lexus and the Olive Tree* (New York: Farrar, Straus, Giroux, 1999). Highly influential, generally favorable, assessment of globalization by the principal foreign affairs correspondent of the *New York Times*.

——. *Longitudes and Attitudes* (New York: Anchor Books, 2003). Selection of articles, mostly on global terrorism and its effects after 9/11, still optimistic, but much more cautious about the direction of globalization.

Fukuyama, Francis. "The End of History?" *National Interest*, Summer 1989, pp. 3–18. An early, highly influential, presentation of the thesis later developed in his book of the same name.

Fukuyama, Francis. *The End of History and the Last Man* (New York: Free Press, 1992). Argues that the combination of democracy and capitalism is proving to be the best system ever devised. Very self-congratulatory concerning the system.

Gibney, Frank. *Japan: The Fragile Superpower* (Tokyo: Charles E. Tuttle, 3rd rev. ed., 1996). Widely read, highly controversial prediction of future armed clashes between religions and ideologies, especially between Christianity and Islam unless increased cross-cultural dialogue takes place. Sees hostility prevailing over accommodation.

Hersh, Seymour M. "Annals of National Security," *The New Yorker*, March 8, 2004. http://newyorker.com/fact/content/?040308fa_fact. Analysis of the nuclear sales conducted by Pakistani nuclear scientist A.Q. Khan and the role of his government and the US government in the process.

Human Development Report 2003: Millennium Development Goals: A Compact among Nations to End Poverty (New York: Oxford University Press, 2003). Published for the United Nations Development Program, looks especially at issues of reducing poverty. Excellent qualitative essays and useful array of statistical tables.

Jenkins, Philip. *The Next Christendom: The Coming of Global Christianity* (New York: Oxford, 2002). Charts the transformation of Christianity from a European to a global religion and speculates on its future.

Keen, Benjamin. *A History of Latin America* (Boston: Houghton Mifflin, 6th ed., 2000).

Khalidi, Rashid. *Resurrecting Empire* (Boston: Beacon Press, 2004). Head of Columbia University's Middle Eastern Institute examines new suggestions that an American imperial policy would be good for the world, and argues that they are incorrect.

Kosmin, Barry and Egon Mayer, "American Religion Identification Survey," Graduate Center of the City University of New York, 2001. http://www.gc.cuny.edu/studies/aris_index.htm

Landesman, Peter, "The Girls Next Door," *New York Times Magazine*, January 5, 2004. Exposes trafficking in women bought and sold as sex slaves, some of them from Russia and eastern Europe, coming via Mexico and ending up in the United States.

Lernoux, Penny. *Cry of the People* (New York: Penguin, 1982). A personal and scholarly account of liberation theology and its effects in Latin America.

Maalouf, Amin. *In the Name of Identity: Violence and the Need to Belong*, trans. from the French by Barbara Bray (New York: Arcade Publishing, 2001). An essay both scholarly and personal on identities that divide and separate people and other identities that provide solidarities, with many historical examples.

McGrath. Alister. *The Future of Christianity* (Oxford: Blackwell, 2002). A personal overview of Christian religious trends worldwide. Emphasizes the increasingly non-European nature of Christianity.

Nash, Gary, *et al. The American People* (New York: Harper Collins, 3rd ed. 1994).

Newsweek Magazine. May 24, 2004, "Religion: The Pop Prophets."

Nye, Joseph S., Jr. *The Paradox of American Power* (New York: Oxford University Press, 2002). International power can be manifest in military, economic, and cultural terms. America at the turn of the century is emphasizing the first two, but losing out in the third.

Scheper-Hughes, Nancy, "The Organ of Last Resort," *The UNESCO Courier* (July/August) 2001.

Soros, George. *The Crisis of Global Capitalism* (New York: Public Affairs, 1998). Soros is a billionaire capitalist who had great respect for the potentials of the system, but also sees the dangers of unregulated behavior. He surveys the system and proposes rules and regulations.

Speth, Gustave. *Red Sky at Morning: America and the Crisis of the Global Environment* (New Haven: Yale University Press, 2004). A sobering assessment of the state of the world's ecology, and of our responsibilities, by a former environmental adviser to Presidents Carter and Clinton.

Steger, Manfred. *Rethinking Globalism* (Lanham, MD: Rowman & Littlefield, 2004). A collection of academic essays generally critical of globalization because of its social and cultural effects as well as its economic effects. Several articles bring third-world perspectives.

Stiglitz, Joseph. *Globalization and its Discontents* (New York: W.W. Norton, 2002). A devastating attack on the IMF and World Bank by a Nobel Prize winner who has served as a high official in them.

Watson, William E. *The Collapse of Communism in the Soviet Union* (Westport, CN: Greenwood Press, 1998). Brief introduction with narrative and analysis of key events, chronology, biographies, and primary source documents, from the 1950s to 1991.

World Development Report 2003: Sustainable Development in a Dynamic World: Transforming Institutions, Growth, and Quality of Life (New York: World Bank and Oxford University Press, 2003). Annual World Bank assessment of the condition of economic and social development worldwide. This volume reflects the Bank's greater concern with issues of poverty and sustainability.

DOCUMENTS

United Nations Office on Drugs and Crime. "The United Nations Convention against Transnational Organized Crime and its Protocols." http://www.unodc.org/unodc/crime_cicp_convention.html http://www.unodc.org/adhoc/palermo/theconvention.html

"Organs Watch" http://sunsite.berkeley.edu/biotech/organswatch/pages/about.html

JOURNALS

The Journal of Contemporary Criminal Justice contains frequent articles on international crime.

FILMS

Dirty Pretty Things produced by Stephen Frears, 2003. Focuses on immigrants, many of them illegal, struggling to get by in London, evading the police, exploited by employers, and some of them involved in trafficking in human organs. Shocking, moving, and believable.

Maria Full of Grace, written and directed by Joshua Marston, 2004. Maria rejects her dead-end life in Colombia to sign on as a "mule," carrying cocaine illegally to the United States. Suggests the contrast between the legitimate and illegitimate opportunities in a drug-based economy that includes Colombia and the USA.

◎ World History Documents CD-ROM

29.1 Helmut Kohl, "A United Germany in a United Europe" (June 5, 1990)

29.2 François Mitterrand: The Reconciliation of France and Germany (September 24, 1990)

29.5 Pope John Paul II, *Centesimus Annus*

29.6 Saddam's Invasion of Kuwait: Two Rationales

29.7 George W. Bush, "We Wage War to Save Civilization Itself" (2001)

REGIONAL IDENTITIES AND THE TWENTY-FIRST CENTURY

KEY TOPICS
- Europe
- Africa
- Latin America
- China and India
- Israel and Palestine: Jews and Arabs

In Chapter 23 we examined the development of new identities around the globe. We explored these new identities in politics, religion, economics, culture, and ecology. In this final chapter, we examine a series of case studies of new identities being formed, encouraged, and sometimes resisted. In two regions of the world—Europe and Africa—we will look at contrasting uses of identity. Western and central Europe have made great progress toward forging a common European identity among nations that had been enemies and had fought to exhaustion in long and bitter warfare. In south-eastern Europe, in sharp contrast, nationalist-ethnic-religious divisions—manipulated by ruthless political leaders—carved up Yugoslavia into warring states. In Africa, South Africa broke out of its apartheid past and forged a new multiracial identity, while Rwanda and Congo collapsed into ethnic warfare that killed millions. The two largest nations of Latin America, Brazil and Mexico, moved toward achieving identities as democratic countries in which the voices of the poor would be taken seriously. Powerful, wealthy interests at home and abroad introduced challenges to these goals, but promising negotiations moved ahead. China and India, the world's two most populous countries, were each moving toward new identities as capitalistic economies, although at different tempos. China moved aggressively to leave behind its recent history of economic communism and embrace capitalism. India moved more tentatively from a less doctrinaire socialism to a less fervent capitalism. Finally, the conflict in the Middle East between Israel and the Palestinians demonstrated the enormous, continuing influence of identity on religious, ethnic, and international relations.

EUROPE

Western and Central Europe

In the aftermath of the devastation of the world wars, western Europe turned itself around and set an example of regional cooperation and even unification. After the end of the Cold War, the countries of central Europe also joined in. The resulting European Union (EU) brought to the region a half-century of peace, rapid economic reconstruction and growth, a more prominent voice in international affairs, and restored cultural creativity.

In 1947, Britain's wartime leader Winston Churchill described Europe as "a rubble heap, a charnel house, a breeding ground for pestilence and hate." Many of Europe's leading statesmen agreed with this brooding assessment and sought to create new institutions that would transform the continent from a killing field into a zone of

Opposite **Israeli-Palestinian relations on the West Bank, 2000.** An Israeli soldier is seen in discussion with two Palestinian women.

peace. Many of them, including Germans, believed that, after the wars, they had to reintegrate and restrain Germany within the framework of European civilization. They saw economic cooperation as a means of achieving these goals. In 1950, the French foreign minister, Robert Schuman, and the West German Chancellor, Konrad Adenauer, agreed to form the European Coal and Steel Community (ECSC) to place these key industries under an independent international authority. Its first president was the French administrator Jean Monnet (1888–1979), who is often called "The Father of Europe." The ECSC expanded as a multinational organization in 1952 with the addition of Italy and the Benelux countries (Belgium, the Netherlands, and Luxembourg).

The political and economic success of the ECSC encouraged further moves toward west European integration. The Treaties of Rome in 1957 established a customs union, the European Economic Community (EEC), or Common Market, to lower and, ultimately, remove tariffs among member countries; to foster the free movement of goods, labor, and capital; and to establish a single external tariff. The treaties also established Euratom to create common policies for the peaceful development of atomic energy. Agreement on agricultural policy was more difficult because it involved issues of national self-reliance on food, the mystique of family farms, and the need to accommodate rural and urban interests. Nevertheless, in 1962, a Common Agricultural Policy was also negotiated, although it remains one of the most contested and controversial of European policies. European nations often accuse one another of seeking special privileges for their own agriculture, and third-world countries charge, correctly, that Europe's subsidies to its own agriculture give it special and unfair advantages in global, competitive markets. Until the early 1980s, "agriculture took up 80 percent of the Community's budget and the rows provoked by the costs of agricultural policy absorbed (it sometimes seemed) 99 percent of its energies" (Gilbert, p. 7).

In 1965, the Brussels Treaty merged the ECSC, the EEC, and Euratom, and created the basis of a west European economic administration with a commission, council, parliament, and court. From 1972, the heads of the governments of the EEC nations began to meet on a regular basis in an assembly soon known as the European Council. Additional nations were admitted: Britain, the Republic of Ireland, and Denmark in 1973, Greece in 1981, and Spain and Portugal in 1986.

In 1986, the leaders of the twelve members of the EEC of that date signed the Single European Act, committing themselves to the creation by the end of 1992 of "an area without internal frontiers in which the free movement of goods, persons and capital is ensured" (Gilbert, p. 175). Also in 1986, the flag of the European Community, twelve gold stars arranged in a circle on a light blue background, was flown for the first time. The EEC adopted Beethoven's Ninth Symphony, with its chorus of Schiller's *Ode to Joy*, as its anthem. Western Europe was moving well beyond a free-trade common market toward a "Europe without frontiers."

In 1991, the Treaty of Maastricht proposed a monetary union and paved the way to the creation of a European Central Bank (ECB) and a single European currency, the Euro, introduced in 1999 and fully operational in 2002. Maastricht also called for the creation of common policies in foreign and security matters, and cooperation in issues of justice and internal affairs, but these initiatives have not yet been implemented. When ratified in 1993, the treaty converted the EEC into the European Union (EU). In 1995, Austria, Finland, and Sweden joined, creating in western Europe the world's largest integrated market with over 370 million people in fifteen nations.

Following the collapse of the USSR in 1991, many of the nations of central Europe, freed from Soviet control, began to submit their applications for membership of the EU. In 2004, seven of them were admitted as new members—Lithuania, Latvia, Estonia, the Czech Republic, Slovakia, Hungary, and Poland—along with the two island nations of Cyprus and Malta, and Slovenia, newly independent from the former

SOURCE

The Continuing Rationale for European Integration

In 1995, François Mitterrand (1916–96), past president of France and an elder statesman both of his own country and of the European Union, spoke passionately to the parliament of the EU, summarizing its great accomplishments in binding up the physical, emotional, and economic wounds of war-devastated Europe. He looked forward to even greater achievements in formulating and enhancing its collective cultural identity. Mitterrand asserted that the success of the EU as a whole would also enhance the cultural identity and creativity of each of its member states, just as the collective success of its economic policies had benefited the economies of the individual member nations.

Our Europe must be embodied in something more than simply balance sheets and freight tonnages. I would go as far as to say ... that it needs a soul, so that it can give expression ... to its culture, its ways of thinking, the intellectual make-up of its peoples, the fruits of the centuries of civilization of which we are the heirs. The expressions of Europe's many forms of genius are rich and diverse; and, as in the past, we must share with the whole world—while not seeking to impose them, somewhat differently from in the past—our ideas, our dreams, and, to the extent that they are of the right kind, our passions. ...

The cultural identity of nations is reinforced by the process of European integration. The Europe of cultures, ladies and gentlemen, is a Europe of nations as opposed to a Europe of nationalism. ...

I was born during the First World War and fought in the Second. I therefore spent my childhood in the surroundings of families torn apart, all of them mourning loved ones and feeling great

bitterness, if not hatred, towards the recent enemy, the traditional enemy. ...

My generation has almost completed its work; it is carrying out its last public acts, and this will be one of my last. It is therefore vital for us to pass on our experience. Many of you will remember the teaching of your parents ... will have felt the suffering of your countries, will have experienced the grief, the pain of separation, the presence of death—all as a result of the mutual enmity of the peoples of Europe. It is vital to pass on not this hatred but, on the contrary, the opportunity for reconciliation which we have, thanks—it must be said—to those who, after 1944–1945, themselves bloodstained and with their personal lives destroyed, had the courage to envisage a more radiant future which would be based on peace and reconciliation. That is what we have done.

(*Official Journal of the European Communities: Debates of the European Parliament*, 1994–5 Session No 4–456, pp. 45–51, excerpted in Hunt, p. 343)

Yugoslavia. These states added another 75 million people to the EU. The dream of a unified, peaceful, prosperous, democratic Europe seemed in large part fulfilled in most of the territory from the Atlantic to the borders of Russia. Europeans shared a common market, without internal tariffs, and a common currency regulated by the ECB. They could travel throughout the EU with only a basic identity card, for the most part encountering no customs formalities, and they could live wherever they chose within the EU. Although the EU recognizes twenty official languages, English has become the most common language for commercial, political, and cultural exchange throughout the continent, as it has throughout the world.

The increased regional and economic diversity of the EU, however, raised new challenges. In 2004, the text of a new constitution for the organization was under consideration, and the members jockeyed for power as between larger states and smaller, richer and poorer, those with long-standing membership and the newcomers, and those more friendly toward the foreign policies of the United States and those less. As always, some nations were more jealous of their national culture and identity and more resistant to entering more deeply into the EU and to giving it more powers. Others were more willing to see the EU play a larger role in their national lives and in setting international foreign policy. The European Union has become far more than a loose association but is less than a unified state. It provides neither welfare nor basic educational functions to its inhabitants. It does, however, finance programs in science and technology, culture, and the environment, and it supports efforts to raise the economic status of its poorer member states to that of the wealthier. It sets standards for health and safety regulations, social security and working conditions, and agriculture.

Many questions about the further significance of the EU remain. Elections to the European parliament in 2004, the fifth of the every-five-year elections, saw the lowest turnout of voters ever. Only about 45 percent of eligible voters turned out, suggesting that the EU is of greater significance to its political and economic elites, who generally promote it, than to its rank-and-file, whose voting has been unenthusiastic.

One of the most significant sets of questions still facing the EU concerns its reception of new applicants. Several new nations in the Balkans wished to enter, and the EU continues to consider—and to postpone—the application of Turkey to join. What would be the geographic and cultural limits of the new integrated Europe? Should the EU add a nation that is geographically mostly not in Europe, and religiously and culturally Islamic, although constitutionally secular? How far is the EU willing to push the envelope of "European" identity?

Euro-pessimists also note the inability of the EU to respond effectively to warfare and genocide in the former Yugoslavia. The European Union was slow to react during the initial warfare, 1992–5, and again in 1998 during the warfare and "ethnic cleansing" in Kosovo.

Yugoslavia

While western and central Europe were creating a new, integrated identity, Yugoslavia, in the Balkan region of southeastern Europe, moved in the opposite direction. The Balkans are home to diverse religions and nationalisms, although the peoples of the region are ethnically similar to one another, mostly descendants of groups that immigrated some 1400 years ago. Throughout most of their history, these peoples have lived together in relative harmony, but external political pressures and internal political leaders have sometimes inflamed fault lines among the population to create bitter warfare. The last century has seen examples of both harmony and lethal conflict.

The new state of Yugoslavia ("land of the South Slavs") that was created after World War I contained a wide variety of national groups, somewhat uneasily. During World War II, the different groups fought against one another, some siding with Germany, others with Russia. Marshal Josip Broz Tito led the pro-Russian guerrilla forces. After the war, Tito became leader of the devastated country. He suppressed ethnic hostilities and enforced policies of Yugoslavian national integration and identity, maintaining political control through the Communist Party. However, he allowed individual ownership of most of the agricultural economy and decentralization of industry. Remarkably, he was able to break free from Russia's control to chart a separate Yugoslav path. The economy grew at an average pace of 7 percent per year, and Yugoslavia seemed to be developing an integrated nationalism that subsumed all of its diverse groups. This integration continued for another decade after Tito's death in 1980.

After communism collapsed in the Soviet Union in 1989, and the Soviet Union itself dissolved in 1991, Yugoslavs, too, voted to break up their union. Four of the six political regions declared their independence, leaving Serbia and Montenegro as the rump Yugoslavia. Three of the regions found separation especially difficult because they were composed of different national groupings internally. To some degree these national identities were also religious

Josip Broz Tito with troops, 1951. Tito salutes as he reviews troops of the Yugoslav army.

identities, although Yugoslavs were not especially zealous in their religious observance, especially after a half-century of communist rule. Serbians were generally Orthodox, while most Croatians were Roman Catholic. Bosnians were the most mixed, but with a plurality Muslim. Intermarriage between religious and national groups was not uncommon.

Serbia's president, Slobodan Milosevic, and the head of his military, Radovan Karadzic, rejected the new national divisions of Yugoslavia. They attempted to keep Croatia and Bosnia-Herzegovina (the complete name of the state including all its regions), and especially their regions with large Serbian populations, under Serbia's control. Civil war raged for three years, 1992–5, during which Serbia undertook a policy of "ethnic cleansing," a euphemism for genocide, attempting to kill or drive out the Muslim and Croat populations, especially from Bosnia. Milosevic employed rape and torture as instruments of policy. Hundreds of thousands of people died and many more were made homeless in the most devastating warfare in Europe since World War II. The United Nations attempted repeatedly to broker a peace agreement, but each attempt was rejected or broken. Many observers faulted the European Union, the United States, and the United Nations for indifference to the warfare, in part because they were unwilling or unable to commit the military forces necessary to impose peace. In 1995, however, US diplomat Richard Holbrooke succeeded in brokering a peace agreement that was initiated in Dayton, Ohio, in November 1995 and signed in Paris in December by the presidents of Bosnia-Herzegovina, Croatia, and Serbia. To oversee the agreements, the United Nations dispatched 60,000 peacekeeping troops.

Former Yugoslavian president Slobodan Milosevic talks to the judges at the UN Tribunal in The Hague, 2001. With a guard at his side, and as seen on a video screen at the press center, this is the second court appearance of Milosevic, accused of war crimes in the former Yugoslavia.

None of the three new states was, however, internally homogeneous. Within the newly created nation of Serbia, one province, Kosovo, had a majority of people who were Albanian by ethnicity and Muslim by religion. Kosovo also had enormous historical significance. In 1389, the conquest of Kosovo by the Muslim Ottoman Turks marked their triumph over Serbia and the destruction of the Serbian state for 600 years. Political leaders of both Bosnians and Serbs could stoke lingering historical memories of this battle in order to inflame current-day antagonisms, if they chose. For example, on June 28, 1989, the 600th anniversary of the Battle of Kosovo, one million Serbs assembled to hear Milosevic recall the glories of Serbia's past.

In 1998, when the Albanian Muslims of Kosovo declared their intention to secede from Serbia and launched a guerrilla war, Milosevic responded with fury, driving some 700,000 ethnic Albanians from their homes in Kosovo and resuming his policies of ethnic cleansing. As Kosovars were murdered, tortured, and raped, the UN and NATO debated whether they should intervene in the internal affairs of a sovereign state. Many observers saw this debate as a legalistic evasion of humanitarian responsibility. Finally, NATO began a seventy-two-day campaign of bombing that led Serbia to surrender and give up its claims. Milosevic accepted 50,000 UN troops as peacekeepers. Before the UN soldiers arrived, however, the remaining Albanian Muslim Kosovars and the returning refugees drove out the Serbian residents of Kosovo, implementing reverse ethnic cleansing. Hatreds and revenge flowed in both directions. As peace was established and enforced, the Serbs were also invited to return.

In 1993, the UN Security Council established an ad hoc International War Crimes Tribunal at The Hague to rule on the atrocities that emerged during the warfare. In

2000, Milosevic was defeated in Serbian elections and the new government turned him over to this tribunal for trial as a war criminal for his actions in Kosovo, the first European invocation of such a trial since World War II. Nevertheless, even from his position under trial in The Hague, Milosevic continues to be influential in Serbian politics. Many consider him an ardent patriot and his party remains powerful. When the Serbian prime minister, Zoran Djindjic, was assassinated in 2003, Milosevic, in The Hague, was suspected as one of the planners, although Serbian drug dealers were also under suspicion. Also in 2003, a Bosnian Serb leader, Biljana Plavsic, was sentenced to eleven years in prison by the International War Crimes Tribunal in The Hague. Known as "the Iron Lady," she surrendered voluntarily and pleaded guilty to war crimes during the 1992–5 civil war, the first high-ranking official actually to be punished by the tribunal.

The tribunal also indicted eight men for sexual assault, the first time that the systematic practice of rape had been condemned and prosecuted as a weapon of war and a "crime against humanity," and not just overlooked as "something that happens" during the stress of warfare. Thus another identity—sexual identity—was partly redefined, and legally protected, as a result of the 1992–5 warfare.

AFRICA

The Nigerian Nobel Laureate author Wole Soyinka said in the 1990s, "South Africa is our dream, Rwanda our nightmare." South Africa became the model of a nation forsaking an apartheid identity of racial separation for a new identity as a multiracial, multi-ethnic democracy. At the same time Congo, Rwanda, and Burundi broke down into internal civil warfare and international conflict as well.

South Africa

Wole Soyinka at UNESCO, Paris, October 16, 1986. Soyinka is here seen celebrating his Nobel Prize for Literature.

The first major group of European settlers in Africa came from the Netherlands in 1652 and established themselves around the Cape of Good Hope. A century and a half later, during the Napoleonic wars, British settlers arrived and took possession of this colony. As the British Anglicized the government and freed the slaves, the Dutch settlers, called Afrikaners or Boers, felt alienated and left in a "great trek" that took them north of the Orange River. The discovery of diamonds in 1867 and of gold in 1876 increased the value of South African land and brought the two groups into conflict. The South Africans of British descent defeated the Boers in three years of warfare, 1899–1902, but the two groups finally came together to form the Union of South Africa (USA) in 1910.

The new Union adopted the Afrikaners' harsh policies toward the black majority. Wages and conditions in the European mines were so abysmal that Africans would not work them, and Chinese contract laborers were imported. The 1913 Native Land Acts restricted African residence and purchase of land to only 13 percent of the surface of the country, effectively forcing black Africans into service as landless laborers in white-controlled farming and industry. The labor market had two impermeable tiers, the top with better conditions and pay for whites, the bottom for blacks. Non-whites had no political rights.

Still more restrictive laws after 1948 established apartheid (segregation of the races). Blacks working in the cities could not legally establish residence but had to commute long distances each day from black residential areas or to stay in dormitory settings, leaving their families behind in the village areas.

Black African frustration, resentment, and anger at first expressed itself principally through independent Ethiopian Churches as early as the 1870s and 1880s. The African

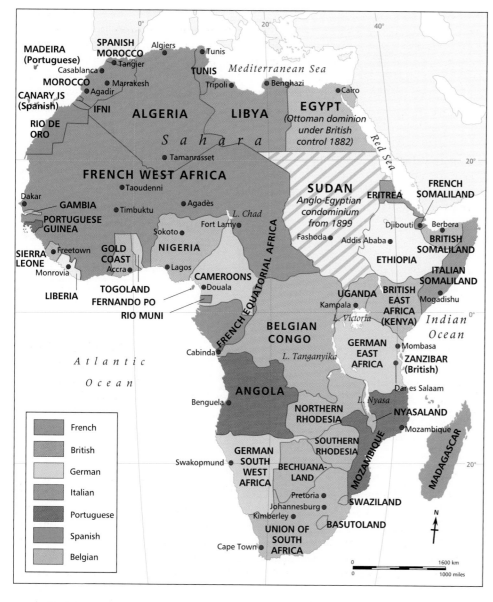

Africa in 1914. By the end of the nineteenth century, Africa presented European imperialists with their last chance to claim a "place in the sun." In a scramble for territory, Belgium, Germany, and Italy joined Spain, Portugal, Britain, and France in carving up the continent, riding roughshod over native concerns with brutal insensitivity. Conflict between the colonists was common, the war between the British and Dutch in South Africa being the most bloody.

National Congress (ANC) formed in 1913 as a constitutional party of protest and grew steadily over several decades. In the 1950s, as other African nations began to win independence, Europeans urged South Africa to liberalize its racial policies, but the government of South Africa stubbornly resisted. It confronted unarmed political protest in March 1960 at Sharpeville with a massacre in which sixty-nine black Africans were killed and many were wounded. The ANC shifted to strikes and armed protest, renouncing attacks on people and limiting itself to sabotage of property. The South African government continued to crack down, maintaining its apartheid policies and sentencing ANC leader Nelson Mandela (b. 1918), a brilliant and charismatic forty-six-year-old lawyer, to life imprisonment. At his trial in 1964, Mandela expressed his frustration with the white government of South Africa and its apartheid rule, his own commitment to his country, and his vision for its future:

> I have fought against white domination. I have cherished the ideal of a democratic and free society in which all persons live together in harmony and with equal

Ethnic groups in Africa. The insensitivity to local conditions of many European colonial administrators created territorial boundaries which failed to match the underlying cultural map of Africa and its peoples. The results of this were seen in post-independence internecine conflicts between ethnic groups hemmed into artificial national territories: Congo (Zaire), Nigeria, Uganda, Angola, Zimbabwe, Sudan, and, more recently, Rwanda and Burundi are among those that have reaped this bitter harvest.

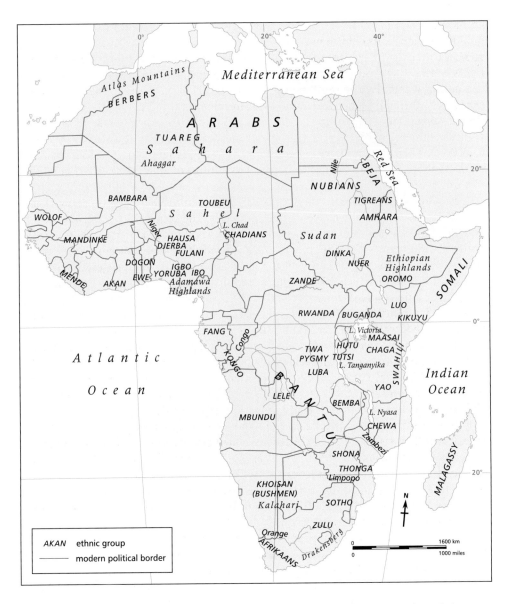

opportunities. It is an ideal which I hope to live for and to achieve. But if needs be, it is an ideal for which I am prepared to die. (Edelstein, p. 73)

The ANC and the general movement for racial justice were crippled but not killed off by the government's repression. As Zambia and Zimbabwe, Angola and Mozambique won independence and majority rule in the 1960s and 1970s, world attention focused on South Africa as the last remaining center of white, minority rule. In addition, the newly independent, "frontline" nations bordering South Africa sheltered members of the ANC and other movements for majority rule, including some dedicated to guerrilla warfare. Through the United Nations as well as through unilateral actions, many nations adopted sanctions against South Africa, restricting or stopping trade; "disinvesting" or withdrawing economic investments; and ending diplomatic, cultural, and sports exchanges. South Africa was to be treated as a pariah nation, cut off from intercourse with much of the rest of the world until it moved toward racial equality.

Enforcing the sanctions proved difficult. South Africa was a regional economic powerhouse, with rich resources: 85 percent of the world's platinum; two-thirds of its chromium; half its gold; half its manganese; and substantial proportions of its gem-quality diamonds. Its GNP, which had been 30 percent of all of sub-Saharan Africa's in 1960, increased to 35 percent by 1987. Geopolitically, 90 percent of Europe's oil passed by its waters. Many large and powerful nations saw sanctions as self-destructive and did not fully comply. The frontline states had tens of thousands of workers who subsisted only through jobs in the South African mines and industries; these states continued surreptitious trade and diplomatic relationships. In addition, to withstand guerrilla threats, South Africa increased its military personnel from 24,000 in 1960 to 97,000 in 1987, and its military expenditures from US$243 million to US$3,292 million, equal to about 50 percent of the military expenditures of all of black Africa combined (Sivard, p. 53).

Nevertheless, the sanctions did gradually exact their toll; isolation was painful, culturally and diplomatically as well as economically. The continuing expansion of independence among the African states brought black rule ever closer to South Africa's borders, and unrest within the country continued. In 1976 protests against government educational policies began in Soweto, a black township outside Pretoria, and led to nationwide riots in which 600 people were killed. Some liberalization was granted: black labor unions were legalized, the prohibition of interracial sex was abolished, segregation in public transportation ended. Finally, in 1990, the new government of President F.W. de Klerk (b. 1936) lifted its ban against the ANC and freed Nelson Mandela after he had spent twenty-seven years in prison. It repealed apartheid laws and began wary and difficult negotiations with the ANC for transition to majority rule. In 1993, de Klerk's National Party and the ANC under Mandela's leadership agreed on the principle of a new constitution. In 1994 elections, open equally to all races on the principle of one person-one vote, the ANC won 62 percent of the vote.

South Africans confronted the problem of establishing a new political and cultural identity for themselves after the collapse of apartheid government. For the first time in their history, the blacks of South Africa counted as political equals to the whites. But unlike many other colonial situations in which most white colonizers left the newly independent colony, in South Africa, the whites had been residents of the country for centuries. This was their home. They viewed themselves as Africans, and most of them had no intention of leaving. Even if they did, they had no other home to which to go. Thus 32 million mostly impoverished and until-recently suppressed and persecuted blacks and 8 million mostly wealthy and highly privileged whites had to find new ways of getting along together. One of their highly imaginative solutions was a Truth and Reconciliation Commission, which functioned from 1996 to 1998 in an effort to clear the air for further interracial cooperation in the future.

The commission was initiated by President Nelson Mandela and headed by Archbishop Desmond Tutu, the recently retired Archbishop of Cape Town and head of the Anglican Church in South Africa. Its goal was to bring the peoples of South Africa together by exposing the bitter and violent realities of the past and, through that exposure, enabling all of its peoples to see themselves as part of a single nation. The commission heard cases of some 20,000 people who suffered gross human rights violations from the Sharpeville massacre in 1960 until the first democratic election in 1994. They discovered horrifying documents, such as the minutes of the State Security Council directing undercover operations in the 1980s seeking "the identification and elimination of revolutionary leaders, particularly those with charisma"; "to make the rotten areas clean before they become too infected. To establish that requires a lot of violence from our side, regardless of the international reaction" (Edelstein, p. 178).

Thousands of people from all corners of the country stepped forward to testify. Thousands were granted some measure of reparations from the state treasury. Most

Seaside segregation. South African apartheid manifests itself on a beach in Durban, in 1985. The sign, written in English and Afrikaans, proclaims that the beach "is reserved for the sole use of the members of the white race group." Apartheid (Afrikaans for "apartness"), the policy of separate development and segregation of the races of South Africa, was supported and encouraged by the Nationalist Party when it came to power in 1948. With the African National Congress in power in South Africa, the country is emerging from the constraints of its racial policies and building a more united nation.

A new and democratic dawn for South Africa. South African president Nelson Mandela and second deputy president F.W. de Klerk address a huge crowd in front of the Union Building in Pretoria, after the inauguration ceremony on May 10, 1994. Only a few years earlier it would have been inconceivable that the imprisoned Nelson Mandela could ever attain high office in a country so firmly wedded to the policies of apartheid.

whites, unable to state publicly that they had benefited from apartheid, did not initiate the act of admitting their crimes. Some, however, did step forward, helping in the process of reconciliation. Many others came because of accusations of criminal activity brought against them. The proceedings of the commission were not equivalent to criminal trials, and amnesty could be granted to those who could demonstrate that they were carrying out the political policies of the state, rather than their own agendas, and were acting without sadism. In his concluding remarks, Archbishop Tutu proclaimed the exemplary success of the commission in healing South Africa's racial wounds and facilitating the emotional unification of the country and a new national identity:

> We have been privileged to help to heal a wounded people ... When we look around us at some of the conflict areas of the world, it becomes increasingly clear that there is not much of a future for them without forgiveness, without reconciliation. God has blessed us richly so that we might be a blessing to others. Quite improbably, we as South Africans have become a beacon of hope to others locked in deadly conflict that peace, that a just resolution, is possible. If it could happen in South Africa, then it can certainly happen anywhere else. Such is the exquisite divine sense of humor.
>
> Truth and Reconciliation Commission of South Africa Report
> http://www.info.gov.za/reports/2003/trc/

Rwanda and Congo

While South Africans of different ethnic origins were learning to live together, the Hutus and Tutsis were committing mutual genocide that ripped apart Rwanda and then helped accelerate Congo's descent

HOW DO WE KNOW?

South Africa's Truth and Reconciliation Commission

Many observers of the commission's proceedings raised serious criticisms. Some felt that the granting of amnesty came too easily to defendants in these non-criminal proceedings. Defendants could plead that they were simply following orders of the government and that they had not acted sadistically, and receive amnesty. Dirk Coetzee, first commander of a counter-insurgency unit, and his team, were convicted in criminal court for the murder of Griffiths Mxenge, a civil rights lawyer, but subsequently the commission granted them amnesty because they were simply carrying out their duties as policemen engaged in the government's struggle against the liberation movement. Griffiths's brother was disgusted with this decision for amnesty:

My main objection is that amnesty promotes the interests of the perpetrators, as once they are granted amnesty they are not criminally liable and no civil action can be instituted against [them], and that is totally against the interests of the victims. It is totally unjust. (Edelstein, p. 113)

On the other hand, Josephine Msweli was more forgiving of the men who killed her sons:

I want the people who killed my sons to come forward because this is a time for reconciliation. I want to forgive them and I also have a bit of my mind to tell them. I would be happy if they could come before me because I don't have [my] sons today ... I want to speak to them before I forgive them. I want them to tell me who sent them to come and kill my sons. Maybe they are

my enemies, maybe they are not. So I want to establish as to who they are and why they did what they did. (Edelstein, p. 154)

One member of the commission, Pumla Gobodo-Madikizela, a clinical psychologist, reaffirmed the healing power of public disclosure by victim and perpetrator alike: "If a memory is kept alive in order to transcend hateful emotions, to free oneself or one's society from the burden of hatred, then remembering has the power to heal" (Edelstein, p. 30). She lamented, however, the inability of most whites, despite the commission, to recognize that they had benefited from the general violence of the system of inequality imposed by apartheid.

Despite its shortcomings, the commission brought truth to light, and most commentators believed that this truth allowed purification of the body politic. It allowed the true identity of the old state to be exposed so that a new identity could be formed. Michael Ignatieff, director of the Carr Center for Human Rights Policy at the Kennedy School of Government, Harvard University, wrote:

Any society that allows its torturers to retire with medals and pensions inevitably pays the price. The price of lies is immobilized nostalgia for tyranny ... you cannot create a culture of freedom unless you eliminate a specific range of impermissible lies ... The Truth Commission had rendered some lies about the past simply impossible to repeat. (Edelstein, pp. 20–21)

Ignatieff concluded that the Truth and Reconciliation Commission made it impossible for white South Africans to deny the violence of their society. They

could no longer deflect blame by saying that any problems were caused only by

a few rotten apples, but those were the exceptions rather than the rule. What the TRC uncovered was something very different indeed: not a few bad apples, not a few bad cops ... but a system, a culture, a way of life that was organized around contempt and violence for other human beings. The truth, the cold core, of apartheid was the Sanlam building in Port Elizabeth where they threw you against radiators and beat you with wet towels. Every South African citizen was contaminated by the degradation, that deadness, that offence against the spirit. (Edelstein, p. 21)

Knowing the painful truth, however, would ultimately set the society free.

- President Mandela inspired the creation of the commission and Bishop Tutu was its chairman. Based on the concept and workings of the commission, how would you characterize the politics and ethics of these two men?
- How would you interpret the key goals of the commission? Were they realistic? Do you think they correspond to human nature as you understand it?
- Ignatieff argues that torture and violence against citizens were not an aberration caused by "a few rotten apples," but by "a system, a culture, a way of life that was organized around contempt and violence for other human beings." To what extent do you think his rhetoric and his description of consequences mirror the debate about the actions of Americans in the Abu Ghraib prison scandal in Iraq in 2004?

into civil war. The origins of the hostility between Hutus and Tutsis confounds easy understanding. On the one hand they appear to be age-old enemies, with often distinct physical and psychological attributes. On the other, they have often gotten along well together. This mixture of alternating antagonism and cordiality—so reminiscent of the Balkans—defies simple definition. In a prize-winning and influential book on the Rwandan genocide, *We Wish to Inform You that Tomorrow We will be Killed with Our Families: Stories from Rwanda*, Philip Gourevitch discusses the complexity:

First-time voters, South Africa, 1994. Residents of the Western Transvaal queue to vote for the first time in South Africa's multiracial elections in 1994. After years of apartheid and oppression, black South Africans showed a respect and devotion to their new democracy that inspired citizens of democracies around the world who often took for granted their own right to vote and to participate in governance.

While convention holds that Hutus are a Bantu people who settled Rwanda first, coming from the south and west, and that Tutsis are a Nilotic people who migrated from the north and east, these theories draw more on legend than on documentable fact. With time, Hutus and Tutsis spoke the same language, followed the same religion, intermarried, and lived intermingled, without territorial distinctions, on the same hills, sharing the same social and political culture in small chiefdoms. The chiefs were called Mwamis, and some of them were Hutus, some Tutsis; Hutus and Tutsis fought together in the Mwamis' armies; through marriage and clientage, Hutus could become hereditary Tutsis, and Tutsis could become hereditary Hutus. Because of all this mixing, ethnographers and historians have lately come to agree that Hutus and Tutsis cannot properly be called distinct ethnic groups. (Gourevitch, pp. 47–8)

The groups, nevertheless, have developed separate identities. The **Hutus** were originally cultivators, the **Tutsis** pastoral herdsmen, in a society where possession of cattle outranked farming. Although in many cases the two groups are physically indistinguishable, in general the Tutsis are "lanky and long-faced, not so dark-skinned, flat-nosed, thick-lipped, and square-jawed," while the Hutus are "stocky and round faced, dark-skinned, flat-nosed, thick-lipped, and square-jawed" (Gourevitch, p. 50). Rwandans have no written records of their history before the appearance of Europeans, so there is no further clear explanation of the evolution of the relationships between the groups.

As in other parts of the world, however, emerging ethnic identity became the basis of power. After 1860, a Tutsi became king of a small region and expanded it to about the size of present-day Rwanda. He favored Tutsis in his government and reduced the status of Hutus. European rulers—Germans before World War I and Belgians afterward—reinforced these ethnic identities by making them official. Both favored the Tutsis. In 1933–4, the Belgians took a census of Rwanda and issued identification cards that categorized each Rwandan as either Hutu or Tutsi. (Only about 1 percent of the population was of a different group, mostly Twa, or Pygmy.) Belgians were carrying out the same sorts of policies that the British had established with the caste system in

India, in making official and formal the distinctions that until now had been unofficial and informal. They were imposing on the people of Rwanda the same sort of separate identity that divided Belgians at home between the French-speaking Walloon minority to the south and the Flemish-speaking majority in the north. Further, the Belgians forced the Hutus into work on plantations and in construction, and set up the Tutsis as their taskmasters. In the public schools they instructed students in the official hierarchy between the elevated Tutsis and the diminished Hutus. Identities that had formerly been porous took on new, powerful reality. Many Hutus left Rwanda for Congo and Uganda in order to escape this system of degradation.

As independence approached, Hutus, who made up 85 percent of the population, seized on the concept of majority rule and on their identification as the earlier arrivals in Rwanda to claim that they should rule Rwanda, publishing the *Hutu Manifesto* in 1957 to make this argument. In 1959, a Hutu activist was attacked and beaten nearly to death by Tutsi activists, and Hutus responded by attacking Tutsi homes throughout Rwanda. This was the first recorded actual physical attack by one group on the other.

In 1962, Rwanda became an independent country with the Hutu majority in control. Battles broke out regularly between Hutus and Tutsis. About a quarter-million Tutsis fled Rwanda itself, some of them conducting guerrilla attacks back across the border. The patterns of violence depended on the political leadership. Under the first president, Grégoire Kayibanda (1962–73), violence against the Tutsi increased; the second president, Juvénal Habyarimana (1973–94), otherwise a dictatorial military ruler, ordered an end to violence against the Tutsis, and it stopped.

In 1990, a Tutsi-led army, the Rwandan Patriotic Front (FPR), led by Paul Kagame, invaded from Uganda. In 1991 a ceasefire was negotiated and the constitution was amended to allow multiparty participation in the government. In 1993 the government and the FPR agreed to a broad-based transitional government that would include the FPR. Many Hutus believed that Habyarimana was too accommodating to the Tutsis, and when his plane was shot down and he was killed in April 1994, popular belief held that extremist Hutus were responsible. An immediate—and apparently planned—genocide was unleashed against the Tutsi minority. About 800,000 Tutsis were murdered in less than four months. The United Nations, the United States, and world opinion responded with horror, but no action. The genocide ended only when a Tutsi army, made up of men who had taken refuge in Uganda, returned to Rwanda, captured the capital and established a new government.

The warfare spilled over into Congo (Zaire as it was then called), where about 2 million Hutus had taken refuge. Many of the refugees were armed, and they conducted border raids back into Rwanda, attempting to destabilize the Tutsi-led government. In response, the Rwandan government attacked the Hutus in Congo, making no distinction between guerrilla fighters and

Rwandan refugees at Rusomo, Tanzania, May 1, 1994. Some 250,000 refugees from civil war in Rwanda crossed the border into Tanzania in 1994.

simple refugees. The government of Congo was in a very weakened state as its dictator for the past quarter-century, Mobutu, was dying of cancer. The Rwandans easily fought off the Congolese troops sent to protect the Hutu refugees. The Rwandans then entered into an alliance with Laurent Kabila, a rebel determined to overthrow Mobutu's government. The Hutu–Tutsi wars now expanded into the international arena. Within months, in May 1997, Kabila, with his Rwandan Tutsi allies, plus allies from Uganda, had conquered Congo, and Mobutu fled. As they marched across the country the Tutsis killed Hutus wherever they found them.

Kabila's new government was unstable, and his opponents accused him of selling out to the Rwandans and the Ugandans. So he terminated those alliances and made new ones with Angola, Zimbabwe, and the Hutu people, who had been his enemies. Congo is extremely rich in diamonds, oil, and metals, including gold, copper, cobalt, and tantalum, an important component in miniaturized electronics, and other nations were eager to enter the fighting in order to claim a part of this wealth for themselves. By 2000, soldiers from Rwanda, Uganda, Angola, Zimbabwe, Namibia, and perhaps Chad, along with many independent rebel groups, were involved in the fighting, in which about 300,000 people were killed, while another 3 million died of starvation and disease. Some called it the First African World War.

Laurent Kabila was assassinated in 2001. His son Joseph succeeded him and began to reach peace agreements among the warring parties. But Congo is both rich and weak, so fighting over its natural wealth continues, although at lower levels of intensity. Periodic attacks between Hutus and Tutsis also continue, both in Congo and in Rwanda. Major powers from outside Africa, notably the United States, have been reluctant to enter the warfare, but do act behind the scenes, backing whichever local forces seem most likely to help them gain access to Congo's resources.

LATIN AMERICA

Approaching the last quarter of the twentieth century, Latin America had to cope with fundamental demographic problems while trying to mark out its place in the global economy. In addition, as it observed cultures changing everywhere, it had to determine what its own cultures might become. The thirty-three countries of Latin America that had held 38 million people in 1900 and 166 million in 1950 had grown to just under a half billion in 2000. In that last half century, the population of the countryside had remained approximately stable, at about 100 million, but the urban population soared from 40 percent of the population to 75 percent, from about 66 million to about 375 million. The giant metropolises of Mexico City and São Paulo, Brazil, testified to the urban transformation. Each had between 15 and 20 million people and was still growing rapidly.

The older, rural-based systems of caudillo (strong-man ruler) and rural hacienda estates, worked by largely illiterate peasantry, were giving way to urban life, higher levels of education, some industrialization and an industrial labor base, and telecommunications, which kept Latin Americans up-to-date participants in the latest shifts of global economics and culture. A general movement after the 1970s away from military rule and toward democratization was part of the result. In some countries, notably Colombia and Mexico, the illegal drug trade was also a mark of Latin America's integration into the global economy (see Chapter 23). No single country in Latin America is representative of the whole, but two stand out by reason of their size, Mexico, with a population of slightly more than 100 million, and Brazil, with about 175 million. Together they represent more than half the population of the entire region. Their quests for new identities deserve special attention.

Mexico

The Mexican revolution beginning in 1910 brought Mexico more stable government, some commitment to improving the life of common people, concern for bringing together the varied population strands of this ethnically diverse country, and, in 1929, the seeds of the Institutional Revolutionary Party (PRI). This party was founded to bring democracy to Mexico, and to some degree it did. By 2000, when it was defeated in a presidential election for the first time, it had become the longest-ruling party in the world. That longevity was marked, inevitably, by corruption and a growing desire to enjoy the perquisites of office without responding to the needs of the people. The PRI hold on power began to diminish in the 1980s as it lost substantial numbers of elections for regional officials. Even in elections that it did win, its percentage of the vote declined sharply, and in 1997 it lost control of the Chamber of Deputies, Mexico's parliament. In 2000, when Vicente Fox of the National Action Party (PAN) was elected president, the PRI was finally removed from power. Political and cultural observers attributed Fox's victory in part to a general disgust with the PRI's abuses of power over a very long time, but they also wrote of a shift in Mexico's identity.

In 1968, student protests against the abuses of power of the government and its lack of support for effective economic development—similar to student movements around the world in that tumultuous year—sparked much larger demonstrations of hundreds of thousands of Mexicans. President Díaz Ordaz put down these riots with a massive show of force that led to the murder of several hundred protestors. The demonstrations and the government's use of force alerted the world to problems in Mexico that could not be covered over even by the Olympic summer games, which Mexico hosted for the first time just a few days later.

The 1970s brought improvement in Mexico's economy as the world price of oil escalated and Mexico became a major exporter. The country spent its profits and went into debt, which others were happy to fund. When oil prices fell in 1986, Mexico needed a loan from the International Monetary Fund (IMF) and was required to accept belt-tightening measures. Investment in Mexico declined, and people of means left the country. The PRI barely won the presidential election of 1988, even though it was widely thought to be rigged.

Mexico's transformation was continuing quietly behind the scenes as well as publicly. New election procedures were put in place to ensure fairer and freer elections. The Chamber of Deputies began to take on real powers to limit and counterbalance presidential powers. Various grassroots groups were growing up to protect the environment and to demand that criminal gangs be prosecuted. Journalists were increasingly active in investigating corruption. Businessmen, who once supported the PRI for its protection, began to find that its corruption weighed heavily on the national economy. With increasing urbanization, and through the years of the oil boom, these business interests became larger and better connected with world markets and thinking.

In 1994, Mexico, the United States, and Canada established the North American Free Trade Association (NAFTA), an agreement to end all tariffs and trade barriers among them. By opening the markets of Mexico and the United States to competition, NAFTA challenged Mexico to compete against the greater productivity of US industrial technology and challenged the United States to compete against the lower wages of Mexican labor. Both sides feared a loss of jobs and markets. The value of the Mexican peso dropped sharply, and once again an international consortium of lenders came to the rescue, but also imposed austerity measures that compromised Mexico's financial independence in the short run and brought cries of protest against the World Bank and the IMF.

The economic development of Latin America. Following the Great Depression and World War II, the nations of Latin America sought to move beyond their dependence upon the export of primary goods—minerals, timber, and food. Investment from North America and Europe allowed some industrial development in Chile, Argentina, Brazil, and Mexico, but was often undermined by political instability. Development throughout the region is diverse as are economic policies.

On January 1, 1994, the very day NAFTA took effect, Maya Indians in the economically backward Chiapas state rose in armed confrontation against the policies of the central government, leaving forty-five dead. The incident called into question the cultural accomplishments of the Mexican revolution in uniting the people. Academic and journalistic analyses of the Chiapas uprising begin with the intense poverty of this most southern state of Mexico. The state is rich in oil, coffee plantations, and sugar, but in the mountainous regions, where most of its Maya Indians live, the soil is poor and quickly exhausted by the meager corn crop. Second, although a minority of the population of the state, the Maya dominate the mountain regions and had historically resisted the Spanish takeover of the land. As remote, mountain Indians, they were scorned and persecuted both by the Spanish and by their mestizo successors. The Maya revolt was quite complicated, for it turned not only against the government but also pitted Maya against Maya, more revolutionary groups against those seeking a negotiated solution, Catholics against Protestants, and rival families against one another seeking vengeance in ongoing feuds. The breach between mestizos and Indians, however, continued to fester as another fault line in Mexican national identity.

Vicente Fox on the campaign trail, 2000. Presidential candidate Fox greets supporters at a rally in Sinaloa City, Mexico.

In urban areas, too, culture was undergoing profound change. Two *New York Times* journalists captured the changes:

> Patterns of everyday life were changing. Businessmen were forgoing their traditional three-hour tequila lunch, and the Veracruz cigar and game of dominoes that followed it. Now young executives were gobbling a sandwich at their desks and washing it down with a diet Coke. The bittersweet November 2 Day of the Dead celebrations— when Mexicans traditionally stream into cemeteries with baskets of food for graveside picnics with the spirits of their departed—were giving way to the trick-or-treat processions of Halloween. (Preston and Dillon, p. 477)

Many Mexicans were ready for the political change that removed the PRI from power, at least temporarily, and brought in Vicente Fox, a former Coca-Cola executive, to office. Fox has had a difficult time governing this country in transition. As a man of wealth and education he did not fully identify with the majority of his nation, although he did better than many previous PRI presidents. He lived a lavish life, as did his advisers; he did not carefully supervise financial transactions of his government; the economy lost 500,000 jobs in his first year in office (including some that moved to China, where labor was even cheaper than in Mexico); he failed to solve the standoff with the Maya in Chiapas; and agreements that he hoped to reach with President Bush to legalize the status of a substantial proportion of the millions of Mexicans living illegally in the United States fell through when Bush turned his attention elsewhere after the attacks of 9/11. By 2004, Fox was a much weakened president. Nevertheless, with his victory in 2000 Mexico had turned a corner in moving toward a new identity with fuller democracy and representation of the common person. Perhaps Fox would not be the man to bring the process to fruition, but that process seemed larger than the man himself, and careful observers believed that it would continue.

Brazil

As Brazil sorts out its identity, it moves between several key contradictions created by its history. Brazil remained a slave-holding country until 1888, and for decades after emancipation Brazilian authorities attempted to "whiten" the country by barring immigration of blacks while promoting immigration from Europe and East and West Asia.

Economic inequality is more severe in Brazil than in any other major nation. The top 10 percent of the population earns 50 percent of the wealth, and the bottom 10 percent less than 1 percent. About 1.7 percent of the landowners hold nearly half the arable land. The so-called "Brazilian economic miracle," especially from 1969–74, did little to change these ratios. The country became richer, but the vast majority of the people did not. Urbanization has not helped very much. In 1950, Brazil was one-third urban, two-thirds rural. By 1980, those proportions were reversed. The cities, however, are ill-equipped to service the needs of their vast new populations.

Culturally, Brazil has preserved and extended two traditions that have earned international praise, but they are also problematic in terms of the nation's identity. One is soccer, the national sport, which virtually everyone plays and in which Brazil excels. Brazil is the only country to have won five World Cups in the sport, from their first in 1958 to their most recent in 2002. Their most outstanding players—Pele, probably the most famous ever; Ronaldo, named the world's best player in 1996 and 1997; and, more recently, Roberto Carlos—are the world's best. Many of them, however, play for Brazil only during the World Cup games. Otherwise they play for other teams in other countries that pay higher salaries. Brazilian teams cannot afford them.

Another area of excellence is the samba dance form and especially its annual representation in Rio's great pre-Lenten celebration of Carnival, the festival of dance, song, revelry, and sexual and class role-reversal for which the city is world famous. Here, too, however, contradictions abound. The samba grew up among the poor, black people of Rio's slums, or *favelas*. In the 1920s, the government attempted to outlaw this dance and other expressions of African-based culture. Then, in the 1930s and 1940s, the government reversed course and sponsored samba exhibitions and the Carnival celebration itself as a means of proclaiming Brazilian cultural authenticity and racial integration. In most recent years, however, the rich people of Rio celebrate Carnival in designated parade grounds in downtown Rio, while the poor and common people of the city continue to dance in the *favelas*. The two groups do not often meet during Carnival.

The divisions between rich and poor have also created a climate of violence in the major cities and in rural areas as well. By the end of the twentieth century, Brazil was averaging an annual homicide rate of 25 per 100,000, somewhat more than double the very high rate of the United States. Important leaders of reform have been assassinated, including leaders of the ecology movement in Brazil, such as Chico Mendes Filho (1944–88), who organized inhabitants of the rainforest into a union to gain benefits in education, health care, and to defend the forest itself against loggers and immigrants, and Ademir "Dema" Federicci (1959–2001), who struggled to stop the illegal logging on Indian reserves and to stop the construction of a dam that would help big landholders at the expense of small farmers.

From 1964 to 1988 Brazil was ruled by a military dictatorship—usually endorsed by the United States—which exercised widespread political repression and drove its enemies to exile, prison, and death. In 1979, however, political parties were allowed to form, and, after 1984, elections were permitted. In 1994, Fernando Henrique Cardoso was elected president, and he initiated some legislation to protect the rainforest and reduce disparities in wealth.

In 2002, the election of Luis Inacio Lula da Silva (Lula) promised a possible turning point in Brazilian public life. Lula had been born into extreme poverty and hunger, the seventh child of a working-class woman whose husband walked out on her shortly after Lula was born. From a teenage job as a factory worker he grew over the years to become one of the nation's most militant and effective union leaders. On the basis of the union, he helped to found the Workers' Party (PT). On his fourth attempt in 2002, he was elected president.

In office, however, Lula trimmed his rhetoric and actions as he discovered that big business interests could not easily be defied. On the one hand, he introduced a program called *bolsa familia*, which gives $25 per month to the poorest families, with the hope of expanding it to some 50 million people. He also moved to settle some 500,000 poor, landless families on land of their own, but by mid-2004 he had accommodated only one-tenth that number. In the eyes of the poor this seems a small return on their expectations. The $25 monthly dole is helpful, but jobs would be better, and they are not forthcoming. Beyond the tens of thousands who have received land, millions more still clamor for their share.

Lula has continued Brazil's policies of borrowing from the IMF and even exceeding the belt-tightening measures called for by these loans. At the end of 2003, interest payments on Brazil's debt required about 40 percent of the nation's gross domestic product. Worse, in the first year of Lula's presidency, Brazil's economy shrank slightly and the number of jobs declined. Street crime as well as white-collar corruption continued as major problems. Loggers and settlers continued to encroach on the Amazon rainforest. Brazil's bankers and capitalistic businessmen have been pleased with Lula's conservatism in office, but his constituency of the impoverished has grown disillusioned.

Brazilian fans celebrate as their soccer team parades in triumph in Brasilia, 2002. Brazil captured their unprecedented fifth World Cup title in Japan by defeating Germany 2–0 in the final.

Lula has traveled extensively and has begun to help build a coalition of nations that are relatively poor, but whose size guarantees them a voice in world affairs, including India, South Africa, and, perhaps, China. He has argued successfully in the World Trade Organization (WTO) against the subsidies that richer nations have given their agricultural producers to give them an unfair advantage in world trade. He hopes to force the rich countries to fulfill their part of international bargains and to recognize that poverty and inequalities are unhealthy for everyone.

Lula's Brazil is searching for new identities that respond to the internal tensions between rich and poor, races and ethnicities, geographic regions, and, externally, to the power of the global economy, the possibility of forming new international coalitions, and the despair and dynamism of the poor.

CHINA AND INDIA

Again, because of their enormous size, we devote a section to China and India. Each is in the process of developing a new sense of the relationship between government and civil society, between government and the economy, and the nation's place in world affairs. China's new identity represents a sharper break with its communist past. India, which was less radical to begin with, also changes more slowly.

China after Mao: An Era of Reform

On September 9, 1976 Mao died. By the end of the year, the "Gang of Four," the four leaders who claimed to be closest to Mao, including his wife Jiang Qing, were under arrest. They had been among the most militant of the high-level officials responsible for the Cultural Revolution of 1966. China was in the midst of a struggle for succession. By December 1978 it became apparent that Deng Xiaoping (1904–97) and his allies had achieved control of the party and its agenda. They remained in control for the next two decades.

Born in Sichuan Province, Deng spent his formative years, from the age of sixteen to twenty-one, studying, doing factory work, and organizing on behalf of the Communist Party among the expatriate Chinese. After a few months' visit in Moscow, he returned to China as a political and military organizer of soviets in southwest China. On the Long March he became a close companion of Mao. As an army officer, he shared the military command of as many as 300,000 troops. In 1952 Mao called him back to Beijing, and his star continued to rise until 1966 when he appeared too moderate for the leaders of the Cultural Revolution. He was stripped of his offices and exiled to a tractor repair factory in southern China. Deng was recalled to Beijing by Mao only in 1973.

Deng advocated economic liberalism, but within a state firmly controlled by the Communist Party. By the time of his death, Deng and his colleagues had sold off about half of the state's economic holdings leaving only 18 percent of the workforce in state employment, down from 90 percent in 1978. He welcomed foreign investment, which reached $42 billion in 1997, and loans, reaching a total of $130 billion in foreign debt. Exports rose to account for 25 percent of total production. Per capita income quadrupled. Deng also shifted more investment to agriculture, ended collectivization, and introduced a "private responsibility system," unleashing enormous productivity gains of 9 percent a year in the early 1980s. The growth in China's total gross domestic product (GDP) led the world, averaging 11.2 percent per year, 1986–97. Health standards improved. Life expectancy reached seventy.

As its population topped one billion, China acted aggressively, and successfully, to limit population growth. Government programs for "small family happiness," beginning in 1974, culminated in the 1980 policy of one family, one child. The party set birth quotas for each county and city, established a nationwide system for distributing contraceptive devices, enforced regulations against early marriage, provided incentives for having only one child and disincentives for having more. The bureaucracy monitored pregnancies and births carefully and abortions were frequently coerced if necessary (Rosenberg, p. 70). Fertility rates dropped to 2.3 per hundred women in the 1980s, indicating considerable success. The policy evoked massive unrest, evasion—more easily accomplished in rural areas—and, in some case, female infanticide, as couples preferred their one child to be male. The smaller families, however, led to a dramatic reduction in the responsibilities of child care and encouraged greater freedom for women in the home and greater equality and participation in work and public life outside. In a society accustomed to having large families, many observers thought it also produced spoiled only-children. By the year 2000, the birth rate had dropped so low that the government began considering relaxation of the policy. In 2004 they introduced a change: If both parents were themselves only children, products of the one-family-one-child policy, they were permitted to have two children.

HOW DO WE KNOW?

The Force behind China's Economic Growth: Capitalism or Socialism?

As Chinese productivity grew at record rates in the 1980s, and even faster in the 1990s, almost all commentators attributed the economic expansion to the capitalistic reforms promoted by Deng Xiaoping. They usually contrasted Deng's success to the failed communist policies that he discarded. See, for example, the very representative point of view presented in a fine, new history of the twentieth century:

> The Chinese state had established a Soviet-style command economy in the 1950s by nationalizing industry and foreign trade, setting prices and collectivizing agriculture; inefficiency and low growth resulted ... Living standards remained low, and most people lived in cramped, unmodernized housing ...
>
> After Mao's death in 1976, reformers gained more power and began more active restructuring of the economy. Deng Xiaoping, a masterly politician who became head of the Central Advisory Commission, slowly moved the party toward economic reform. Once they were allowed to contract out of their agricultural communes, peasants deserted them in droves, working as family units and selling their surpluses in private markets. Output and rural incomes rose, stimulating rural industry. As trading companies under local control multiplied, foreign contacts expanded and foreign investment poured into the country. Overseas Chinese returned to invest.

> ... a new private sector boomed in southern coastal areas ... Wages rose and so did demand for consumer goods. (Crossley et al., p. 476)

Nobel Prize-winning economist Amartya Sen might not disagree with the analysis of Deng's reforms, but he gives much more credit to the accomplishments of Mao's communist government in paving the way. His analysis of China's success comes as part of a discussion of the market-based economic policies that India began to adopt in 1991. Sen uses China's example to caution against the transition to capitalism before appropriate social policies have been set in place:

> While pre-reform China was deeply skeptical of markets, it was not skeptical of basic education and widely shared health care. When China turned to marketization in 1979, it already had a highly literate people, especially the young, with good schooling facilities across the bulk of the country. In this respect, China was not very far from the basic educational situation in South Korea or Taiwan, where too an educated population had played a major role in seizing the economic opportunities offered by a supportive market system. In contrast, India had a half-illiterate adult population when it turned to marketization in 1991, and the situation is not much improved today [1999].
>
> The health conditions in China were also much better than in India because of the social commitment of the pre-reform regime to health care as well as education. Oddly enough, that commitment, while totally unrelated to its helpful role in

market-oriented economic growth, created social opportunities that could be brought into dynamic use after the country moved toward marketization ... But the relevance of the radically different levels of social preparedness in China and India for widespread market-oriented development is worth noting even at this preliminary stage of the analysis. (Sen pp. 42–3)

Sen does credit Indian democracy with other advantages for development that are lacking under China's communist government. In general, however, he seems to turn upside-down Marx's view of the triumph of communism arising out of a base constructed by capitalists. In China he sees capitalism arising out of a base constructed by communists.

- Is Sen's account of the achievements of Chinese communism inaccurate, or is he simply giving credit to a human-welfare achievement that others are overlooking? Why is he giving this emphasis? Is he right to stress the importance of human welfare measures in economic development?
- According to Sen, why should Indian leaders be cautious in adopting for their own country the free-market policies that seem to work for China?
- To what degree should human welfare be considered in the assessment of the success of an economic system? Can an economic system be considered successful if education, health, and welfare standards of the general population are not rising?

After Deng's death, the transition of power occurred smoothly, with Jiang Zemin succeeding him as China's most important political leader. China moved to liberalize the economy even further, especially by selling off state-run enterprises to private ownership. By 2003, the United Nations Development Programme reported that

> China has enjoyed the fastest sustained economic advance in human history, averaging real per capita growth of 8% a year over the past decade. Its per capita income is now $3,976 in purchasing power parity terms. ... According to World Bank estimates based on consumption surveys, the proportion of people living on less than $1 a day declined in China from 33% in 1990 to 16% in 2000. ... China's exceptional growth is partly explained by its market-based reforms that started in 1978 ... These reforms have enabled China to integrate with the global economy at a phenomenal pace. Today it is the largest recipient of foreign direct investment among developing countries

rising from almost zero in 1978 to about $52 billion in 2002 (nearly 5% of GDP) … Manufactured exports accounted for … 90% [of all of Chinese exports] in 2001. … telecommunications equipment and computers now account for a quarter of its exports … Literacy stands at 84%. (*Human Development Report 2003*, p. 73)

After fifteen years of debate, China was admitted to the World Trade Organization in November 2001, recognizing its full participation in the world of global trade on capitalist principles.

The evident successes of China's combination of communist government with capitalist economics nevertheless left the country with many problems. Despite the rise in overall national wealth, distribution of the wealth was a problem. There are still some 220 million people living in abject poverty on less than $1 per day. Although even the poor are becoming richer, the divisions between rich and poor are growing. These divisions are largely regional. The economy of the coastal and southern regions of China, with their manufacturing industries and export trade, grew through the 1990s at 13 percent per year, five times the rate of the inland and northern regions.

China's "floating population," rural people who shifted to China's cities, and from inland areas to the coast, in search of jobs, grew to more than 100 million. Previously, government regulations had forbidden such internal migration. Now these new urbanites, still without legal permits for long-time residence, formed up to one-third of the population of some of China's cities. They were blamed for increases in crime and social unrest. Of course they also provided low-cost labor for China's growing economy—when they could find jobs.

Environmental degradation, including the pollution of air and water, has increased with China's industrialization. The rise of factories and cars and the use of artificial fertilizer increased dramatically the level of pollution of land, air, and water in China. Some of the most colossal projects were the largest offenders. The Three Gorges Dam on the upper Yangzi River, the largest hydro-electric project in the world, not only displaces more than one million residents, flooded out by the reservoir that forms behind the dam, but also mixes the industrial wastes that have been emptied into the river through the years into that reservoir of water that will be drunk downstream throughout central China. The cost of the dam, to be opened in 2009, is about $30 billion. The government justifies the dam as a project befitting China's status as one of the great powers of the world, and one whose electricity generation will in fact save China's air from the pollution that would otherwise have come through coal generation of electricity.

More recently, China's use of high-sulfur gasoline as a means of fueling its ever-increasing engines is drawing enormous criticism. Sulfur levels in fuels are tightly regulated in the United States and Europe because of their high toxicity. China feels it cannot be so picky. Despite the fact that the sulfur pollutes the air, ruins the catalytic converters that have been designed to cut down on other pollutants, and burns at very low efficiency, it is cheap and available. China feels that this is a necessary alternative for a relatively poor, rapidly developing country.

At higher levels of the economy, white-collar crime and corruption became major problems. As in Russia, as the government liberalized, state assets were often sold to the Party faithful at bargain prices. Meanwhile, the lure of new profits, a relaxation in law enforcement, and a rise in bribery created a new class of privately wealthy moguls. China witnessed a rapid recrudescence of quasi-illegal night spots, gangsterism, drug dealing, secret societies, prostitution, and gambling, much of it owned and run by the police and military.

Deng's government could speak proudly of its accomplishments in the "four modernizations" of agriculture, science and technology, industry, and defense. Critics, however, called for the "fifth modernization"—democracy. In 1989, tens of thousands of demonstrators, mostly students, assembled in Tiananmen Square, demanding democracy as the antidote to a government ruled by old men, infested with corruption, and no longer in touch with the grass roots. The government called in the army to clear the square. In the process, several hundred (some say as many as 5000) demonstrators were killed, and more injured. The students' protests were tragically validated, but their proposed solution would have to wait.

Also in 1999 the government arrested thousands of members of the Falun Gong religious movement. Falun Gong combined elements of Buddhism, Taoism, and the martial arts. The group declared itself apolitical, but the government of China feared that any group of such size had potential political implications. Its membership surpassed that of the Communist Party. In 1999 after the Falun Gong staged the largest unauthorized demonstration in Beijing since 1989, the government banned the sect entirely. No potential challenge to the government would be tolerated.

The Three Gorges Dam, Hubei Province, China, 2003. By 10 a.m. each morning at the dam site, the Yangtze River rises 114 meters above sea level. Despite the criticism of the dam's impact on the ecology and residents of its region, the Chinese government views this as one of its most beneficial and spectacular technological accomplishments.

The government's public statements on the SARS health epidemic of 2002 reflected its ambiguous relationship with transparency. The epidemic of this previously unknown disease that killed some 350 people in China was, at first, not reported. The Chinese understood, correctly, that news of the epidemic would cut into its international business and travel. As news did emerge, however, the World Health Organization and others censured China for covering up news that could have enabled faster health responses throughout the world. From then on, China released news about the epidemic promptly and widely.

China also permitted and even encouraged the growth of Non-Governmental Organizations, as long as they did not appear to threaten government control. NGOs are the heartbeat of democracy, since they encourage the participation of the people in public affairs, and frequently involve foreign participation as well. NGOs work in China, for example, in rural education and development, biodiversity, drug control, family planning, environment and science, and women's and children's development. They are the backbone of civil society and are beginning to flourish, expanding in numbers of participants, areas of activity, and foreign involvement. (Americans tend to take NGOs, usually referred to as voluntary organizations in the USA, for granted since they are so widespread and so active throughout the country. In many other nations, like China, they are a relatively new phenomenon, and must constantly negotiate their status with the government, which usually regulates them lest they challenge government authority.)

In terms of international relations, also, China implemented a series of dramatic turnabouts. Within its own area of the world, China for 2000 years has viewed itself as the dominant, central power, and has sought that recognition from its neighbors with mixed success. The startling economic success of South Korea and Taiwan, not to mention that of Japan, at first challenged both China's regional supremacy and its communist path of development. As the Chinese economy grew at unprecedented rates after 1979, however, China began to regain some of its historic pre-eminence in the region. In 1997 the island of Hong Kong, and the tiny strip of adjacent territories on the mainland, which had been a British colony since 1842, reverted to Chinese sovereignty. (Two years later tiny Macao was returned to China by Portugal.) Commercial and political observers, as well as the people of Hong Kong themselves, wait and watch to see the policies that China implements in this historic outpost of capitalism. Political demonstrations in favor of continuing democratic institutions have become commonplace in Hong Kong. In July 2003, for example, an estimated 500,000 people demonstrated in Hong Kong against proposed laws that would have curtailed civil rights—and the laws were abandoned.

In many neighboring countries, China was feared and resented, not an uncommon relationship for a regional superpower. Even internally, it was viewed as an invading and conquering power. In its own Xinjiang Autonomous Region, the Central Asian Muslim Uighur population resented Chinese rule and waged low-intensity guerrilla war against it. The Tibet Autonomous Region similarly opposed Chinese rule. China invaded and colonized Tibet in 1959, driving Tibet's religious-political leader, the Dalai Lama, into exile. From his home in exile in India, and during his frequent world travels, the Lama spoke out for more freedom, especially religious freedom for Tibetans. China backed the murderous Khmer Rouge Party and its leader Pol Pot in the vicious civil wars in Cambodia in the late 1970s and 1980s, even committing troops briefly to combat.

In several nearby states, Chinese minorities were viewed with suspicion as possible fifth-column infiltrators, for both the Chinese nation and the Communist Party. In anti-Chinese and anti-communist riots in Indonesia in 1965, thousands of Chinese were murdered, and hundreds of thousands more were exiled.

After early cooperation, misunderstandings and even armed border conflicts had marked China's relations with the USSR. The two nations argued over ideology. In the 1980s, however, both countries softened their positions. With Gorbachev promoting glasnost (political and cultural openess) and perestroika (economic restructuring) in the USSR, and Deng advocating greater economic openness and diplomatic pragmatism in China, relations between the two countries normalized. In July 2002, they signed a twenty-year friendship agreement.

Relations with the United States also warmed. After decades of conflict—armed in Korea, diplomatic over issues like the fate of Tibet and its exiled leader, the Dalai Lama—in the early 1970s the diplomatic scene changed dramatically. Mao and his new advisers, retreating from the economic catastrophe of the Cultural Revolution, sought assistance from abroad. President Nixon and his Secretary of State, Henry Kissinger, also favored more pragmatic policies. In 1971, the USA did not stand in the way of China's joining the United Nations, and in the next year, Nixon visited China, advancing the normalization of relations between the two countries. In 1979 formal diplomatic relations were resumed. While the USA still formally protests the 1989 Tiananmen Square crackdown on democracy, relations are improving and top-ranking American government officials visit Beijing regularly, albeit on Chinese terms. In 1997, the United States Congress voted to continue China's permanent "most favored nation" trade status, and further bilateral trade agreements followed, despite opposition to China's persistent and extreme human rights abuses. One-fifth of all China's exports go to the USA and these form 9 percent of all US imports. In 2002, the USA imported $125 billion of goods and services from China while exporting only $22 billion, leaving a trade surplus for China of $103 billion. In 2001 China was welcomed into the WTO.

China's identity shifts over the past thirty years have been astonishing: from inward looking to full participant in global affairs, from communist economy to capitalist, from economic catastrophe to the fastest growing of all the major world economies. And while the government remains thoroughly vigilant against any direct challenge to its authority and control of power, much within this formerly closed society has opened up with more consumer goods and a rampant desire for them: fashionable clothes, more open expressions of sexuality, Western and world music, new telecommunications, including internet connections and access to the broadcasts of the BBC, the Voice of America, and CNN. How long and how deeply the economic boom can continue, how the authoritarian government can coexist with a broadening band of civic activism and consumer expression, are critical questions that will absorb China's attention, and the world's.

India after Congress Dominance: A Quiet Revolution in Caste and Politics

In the first years of India's Independence, the Congress Party under Jawaharlal Nehru represented the public face of India's identity. The government was committed politically to democratic institutions and processes; socially to a composite society that had a place for all of India's religious and ethnic groups; and economically to a mixed economy that maintained private property rights and freedom for private entrepreneurs, but with government control of major industries, financial institutions, and access to the permits and licenses needed to create or expand businesses. The Congress itself was largely an upper-middle-class institution, although its rank-and-file membership included millions of peasants and workers. The Nehru family embodied the Congress system. Two years after Nehru died in 1964, his daughter, Indira Gandhi, became prime minister and ruled for most of the years until her assassination in 1984. Then her son, Rajiv, became prime minister and governed until 1989. The Congress did not die at this point, nor did the Nehru dynasty pass away. To some degree these identities remained remarkably stable through more than a half century. In 2004, the Congress Party returned to its position as India's largest, although not so dominant as before, and Rajiv's widow, Sonia, is today its head. But new parties, some of them national, many more of them existing only within individual states, grew up to challenge Congress rule and reduce its power. Even in 2004, when it recaptured the central government, Congress did so only through alliances with other parties.

As parties have multiplied in number, India has become far less centralized than it was at Independence. Three issues have dominated public life, often referred to as the three Ms: Mosque, Mandal, and Markets. In Chapter 23 we discussed at some length the public attacks on the Muslim role in India's public life—symbolized by the destruction of the Babri Mosque at Ayodhaya and the rise of the BJP political party. Here we will discuss Mandal and Markets.

The Mandal Commission B.P. Mandal was appointed by the prime minister of India to deal with an economic and social problem that had bedeviled Indian politics for decades. Even under the British in 1935, untouchables, called scheduled castes (SCs) because they were listed on an official government schedule, were given special "reservations" or minimum quotas in public life. This affirmative action program in the fields of government jobs, elected positions, and education covered 15 percent of the population. But what of the next levels up, usually referred to as the Other Back-ward Classes (OBCs)? Some additional 50 percent of the population—more in some areas—had also suffered severe discrimination on the basis of caste, although perhaps not quite so extreme as the SCs. In south India, where the proportion of Brahmins and other high castes is very low—perhaps 3 percent Brahmins, for example—and where these Brahmins are often referred to as colonialists, reservations had begun a century before, in 1870, under the British. A regional party, the Justice Party, arose to represent the lower castes and oppose Brahmin control. In 1920, it won the elections for the limited government positions then available. In the south, the upper castes were already being displaced from power.

In north India, where Brahmins formed about 10 percent of the population and other higher castes another 10 to 15 percent, government had postponed confronting the issue. The Mandal Commission was the second formal attempt to address it. In

AT A GLANCE: NEW IDENTITIES

DATE	ISRAEL	E./CENTRAL AFRICA	S. AFRICA	MEXICO	BRAZIL
1970	■ Arab terrorists attack Israeli athletes at Munich Olympics (1972)	■ Uganda: Under Idi Amin's regime, 300,000 killed in ethnic war; Asians expelled from the country (1971–9) ■ Rwanda: tensions between rival Tutsi and Hutu tribes erupt in repeated warfare and massacres (from 1972)	■ Portugal's dictatorship overthrown; Mozambique and Angola (1974) ■ South Africa: Protests in Soweto against apartheid education policies lead to nationwide riots (1976)	■ Steady economic growth, 1950s–1980s, based largely on oil	■ Military dictatorship in power (1964–88) ■ Political parties form (1979)
1980	■ Palestinians begin *intifada* against Israeli control (1987)	■ Tanzania's Julius Nyerere retires (1985)	■ South Africa only white-ruled country south of the Sahara (after 1980) ■ Commonwealth and US sanctions (1986)	■ Collapse of oil price forces Mexico to turn to IMF and other international lenders (1980s)	■ Elections permitted (1984)
1990	■ Jordan signs peace treaty with Israel (1995) ■ Assassination of President Yitzhak Rabin cripples peace process (1995)	■ Somalia dissolves into severe civil warfare (1991) ■ Eritrea achieves independence from Ethiopia (1993) ■ Zaire (renamed Republic of Congo): Laurent Kabila seizes power (1997); civil war continues	■ South Africa: President F.W. de Klerk lifts ban against ANC; Mandela freed (1990) ■ National Truth Commission investigating abuses under apartheid (1995)	■ North American Free Trade Association (NAFTA) (1994) ■ Peso collapses ■ 145 Maya Indians killed in riots in Chiapas state (1994)	■ President Fernando Collor de Mello driven from power on corruption charges (1992) ■ International Monetary Fund loans give the IMF influence over Brazilian policy ■ MERCOSUR, free-trade zone (1995)
2000	■ Failed Camp David negotiations between Ehud Barak, Yasser Arafat, and Bill Clinton (2000) ■ World Court condemns Sharon's wall separating Jews and Palestinians (2004)	■ Laurent Kabila assassinated (2001) ■ Joseph Kabila takes power (2001)	■ First democratic elections in South Africa; Nelson Mandela as President (1994–2003)	■ Vicente Fox elected President of Mexico (2000)	■ Lula da Silva elected President of Brazil (2002)

1980 the commission made its report public, arguing that OBCs constituted about 52 percent of the nation's population and recommended that 27 percent of the positions in the central administration and in the public sector should be reserved for them. Although the "C" in OBC officially referred to class rather than caste, the Mandal Commission argued that caste was the most significant indicator of class and identified some 3743 castes as OBCs.

Congress Party leaders at first chose to do nothing, but by the mid-1980s other parties, some representing primarily OBC constituents, began to clamor for implementation of the commission's report. The road was rocky. The Congress government of Gujarat State, led by an OBC in 1985, attempted to implement the principles of the Mandal Commission report and was forced from office by mass protests and riots from the upper castes. (Americans, accustomed to class-based public protests coming from below and attacking elites, may be surprised that such protests may also come from above. Backlash protests against racial desegregation in the 1960s, however, were also of this nature.) New parties, however, began to form around the issue of reservations, sometimes led by OBCs themselves, particularly at the state level, and sometimes by upper-caste members committed to concepts of equality, or seeking additional votes, or both.

In 1990, the prime minister, V.P. Singh brought the issue to a head nationally by implementing the Mandal Commission recommendations. This and other of his reformist programs alienated many upper-class and upper-caste people, and he was forced from power in 1991 when new elections brought the Congress Party back to power. Nevertheless, a transformation was taking place. In the major north Indian states, from 1984 to 1999 the percentage of upper castes elected to the national parliament dropped by a third, from 47 to 31, while the percentage of OBCs doubled, from 11 to 22. India's two largest states, Uttar Pradesh and Bihar, were ruled by OBC parties headed by OBC leaders. Singh explained the overall significance of the shift that was taking place:

> Now that every party is wooing the deprived classes, with every round of elections more and more representatives of the deprived sections will be elected. This will ultimately be reflected in the social composition of the local bodies, state governments, and the central government. A silent transfer of power is taking place in social terms. (Jaffrelot, p. 139)

Many predictable problems have occurred. When caste alone was the criterion for affirmative action, the beneficiaries were often the wealthiest and best educated members within the lowest castes, the so called "creamy layer," rather than the poorest and least educated. Antagonism between castes was common as the new reservation policies were put into place, challenging old hierarchies. Upper-caste people scoffed at the SCs and OBCs in public office, claiming that standards were dropping. Lower-caste groups resented the oppression and scorn of the upper. Parties formed very odd coalitions for election purposes. SCs and OBCs, who might have made common cause against the upper castes, chose instead to form separate coalitions with them. Old hierarchies were giving way to a new fluidity in political relationships. New identities were being formed as voters began to see that they had unprecedented powers if they could take advantage of new opportunities for organization. Caste identity itself was being transformed from a ritual and economic category to a political identity that required coalition-building among groups that previously had seen each other as separate and unequal.

Attempts to redress gender discrimination arose from somewhat different motivations than the system of caste reservations. Nevertheless, the 73rd amendment to the Constitution, passed in 1992, did set aside specific reservations for women. It guaranteed to women one-third of the seats in elected bodies in both urban and rural local government. By 2003, an estimated one million women across India filled these seats. On the other hand, the powers of local government are quite limited, and attempts to extend the reservation policy for women to state-wide and national government offices have not gone beyond the talking stages. The percentage of women voting in national elections rose from 37 in 1952 to 58 in 1998. The number of women members of the Lok Sabha, the lower house of parliament, has increased from 22, about 4.5 percent, in 1952 to 45, about 9 percent, in 2004. Women have served as chief ministers in several states throughout the country, but the percentage of women voting in many state assemblies has actually gone down. Women are beginning to organize effectively as they understand the power of the vote, but they have not created the collective power that the lowest castes have managed to develop.

Markets, the IMF, and Capitalist Economics As upper-caste groups have lost some of their political powers, they have moved more actively into business careers, and the growth of private economic markets is the third area in which Indian identity is taking on new forms. In 1991, under pressure from the IMF, India began to move away from the state-guided, socialistic, and red-tape-laden economy of the early days of Independence toward a free-market economy. It was not India's choice to move in this direction, however, and the transformation has not been whole-hearted. A shortage of foreign exchange funds forced the nation to turn to the IMF for a loan. In exchange, the IMF insisted that India follow the IMF prescription of "the Washington consensus": fire excess government workers, cut subsidies to the poor, privatize government-owned businesses, devalue the currency, eliminate government controls over business, open domestic markets to international investment and trade. In short, accept a free-market economy.

To some extent, India did accept this new economic dispensation. Many politicians and economists who had been devotees of socialism and state control of the development of the country changed their minds, and for the first time since Independence, many people spoke favorably of capitalism. Not everyone, to be sure. Many believed capitalism to be rapacious, interested only in profit and not in human welfare. But others admitted that the government had become a drag on economic development. India's policy of "permit raj"—of requiring government permits to open new businesses or expand old ones, or to import capital goods—had stifled investment and promoted the corruption of government officials. They admitted that keeping India's domestic markets relatively closed to foreign imports and investments raised the price of Indian goods for consumers and enabled Indian business to operate inefficiently, and to charge high prices for shoddy products. They admitted that the government hired far too many workers where few were needed, and subsidized some poor people who were, as a result, working less hard than they might. Many industrialists feared that India could not compete in world markets once tariffs and subsidies were removed, but many others welcomed opportunity and the challenge.

India's economic growth rate rose to about 6.5 percent per year in the 1990s, and even a little higher in the early 2000s. Foreign direct investment rose to about $3 billion per year, much higher than the $200 million in the years before 1991, although this was only a small fraction of China's rate of foreign direct investment. India's holdings of foreign currency rose from a crisis level of only about $1 billion in 1991 to about $40 billion a decade later. Firms became more efficient and more profitable. Stocks sold on the Indian stock exchange multiplied in value 500 percent between 1990 and 1999.

As is common in a capitalist economy, some sectors and regions began to move ahead much faster than others, increasing inequalities. For example, the state of Gujarat, the fastest growing state in India at the time, saw its per capita gross development product increase at 7.6 percent per year from 1991 to 1997. Gujarat began to compare its growth rate with that of the East Asian tigers. In the same period, however, India's slowest growing states economically—and largest in terms of population—Bihar and Uttar Pradesh, grew by only about 1.2 percent per year. Previously, the central government had tried to compensate for these kinds of disparities by giving higher levels of assistance to poorer states. Now the richer states, embracing capitalist doctrine, protested this allocation of assistance, arguing that it rewarded economic incompetence and punished economic accomplishment.

The information technology (IT) sector has been a leader in growth domestically and internationally, while some older, declining, "sunset" industries, like jute, lag far behind. IT has become a leader not only in producing software, but in serving as a "backoffice" for international businesses, creating hundreds of thousands of jobs. The excellence of India's upper levels of education in technology has also made it possible for many Indians, skilled in IT, to find jobs elsewhere. Silicon Valley in the USA has been a prime destination. Here, too, there has been a change in Indian identity: as India becomes a recognized leader in IT research and productivity, the Indians who relocate to Silicon Valley are no longer seen as a "brain drain," depleting India's supply of trained manpower, but rather as valuable contributors to India's development. The accusation that Indians who go overseas to earn a living are deserters has changed as they obviously keep closely in touch with family and friends back in India, remit money to them, and establish new outposts of Indian culture in their new homes. Indian Americans are the first or second most wealthy ethnic community in the United States, and their influence in America, and their assistance to India in the form of remittances and investments, gives them a respected position in the eyes of most Indians. Indian enterprise appears ready for further export growth. A new area ready for expansion appears to be pharmaceuticals and perhaps the film industry, known as "Bollywood," a merger of the styles of Bombay and Hollywood, will follow.

The new economic identity, based on free markets, is far from dominant in India. First, government still acts as a drag on business. It has not withdrawn completely from the processes of regulating Indian business, nor has it privatized some of the biggest state-run enterprises, nor has it removed all subsidies. Its policies of providing subsidies to economically less successful states has drawn the opposition of stronger states that believe that their hard work goes unrewarded. It is also widely viewed as corrupt in using its powers to extort money from businessmen to the extent that business suffers. Also, the benefits of the new economy have gone especially to those who are already skilled and experienced, like the IT elites, while they leave out the common, relatively poor citizens.

The 2004 national election seemed to echo the resentment of the poor for the rich, as voters defeated the incumbent BJP party and gave a surprising victory to the Congress, nowadays considered more "pro-poor" than the BJP, and to Prime Minister Man Mohan Singh. One of the most prominent advocates of the importance of information technology in India's development, Chandrababu Naidu, the chief minister of the south Indian state of Andhra Pradesh, was one of the candidates most severely routed in the election. The opposition charged that while a relative few were benefiting from IT,

Man Mohan Singh, 2004. Man Mohan Singh, an expert in economics, presided over the restructuring of India's economy after 1991 and became prime minister in the Congress Party-dominated government in 2004. He is here flanked by the Congress Party chief Sonia Gandhi, widow of the assassinated Prime Minister Rajiv Gandhi.

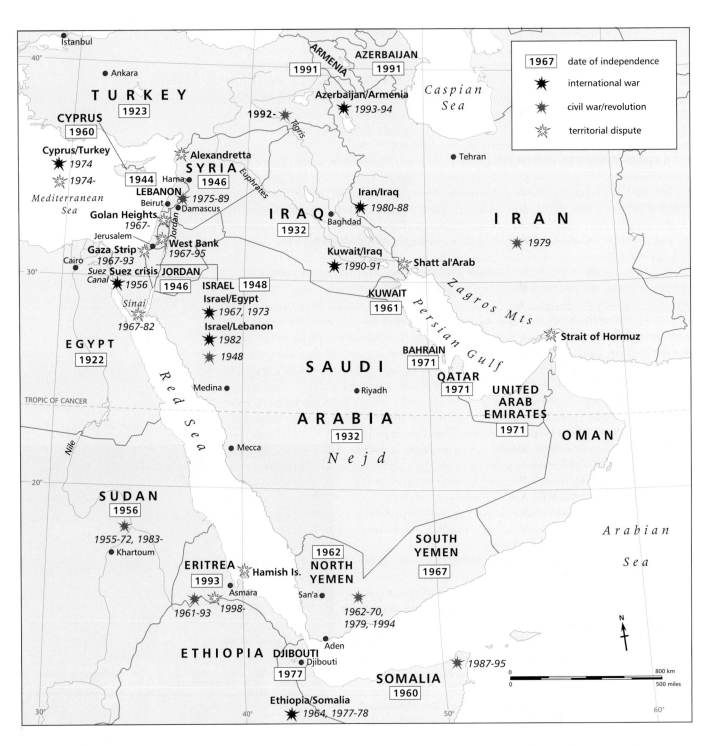

The Middle East since 1945. The presence of oil and gas reserves, the establishment of a Jewish homeland state of Israel in Palestine (1948), and the intervention of outside states have dominated the the region. In addition to Arab–Israeli confrontations, an eight-year conflict between Iran and Iraq, a war over Iraq's invasion of Kuwait, the American invasion of Iraq in 2003, and civil wars and revolutions have kept the region in turmoil.

millions of simple peasants were still going hungry, and a conspicuous number were committing suicide as a result of their poverty. Naidu's defeat carried an important lesson. India was moving to open its economy to capitalism far more cautiously than China, in large part because India was a democracy and had to take popular opinion into consideration. This democracy had become firmly rooted since Independence, and it, too, was part of India's identity.

ISRAEL AND PALESTINE: JEWS AND ARABS

The relationships between Israelis and Arabs combine so many compelling issues and tell so many intertwined stories that collectively they have touched the imagination of much of the world. Of all issues in the modern Middle East, Israeli–Arab relations have been the most contentious and the most discussed by historians. At their heart are multiple, intertwined conflicts of identity: religious, political, territorial, economic, colonial, and generational. Although this case study will focus on events of the past two decades, in order to understand them, we must go back about a century in terms of politics, and two millennia in terms of religion.

The conflict of religious identities between Jew and Muslim seems, at first glance, to be the most important. Ever since 135 C.E., when the Romans exiled the Jews from Judaea (Israel), they sought to return. They believed that God had promised this land to them, as recorded in the Bible, and their prayers regularly included a reminder to God of his promise.

After the Jewish exile, other peoples occupied the land. After its conquest by Muslim empires, at the end of the seventh century, the overwhelming majority of the residents of Palestine (the generally accepted geographical name of the area through the centuries after the Romans departed) were Muslims. When Jews actually did begin to return to Palestine in significant numbers, toward the end of the nineteenth century, the hundreds of thousands of Arabs resident there saw that return as a challenge to their own religious supremacy. In some ways, then, the Israel–Arab conflict is based on a religious conflict that dates back at least 1300 years.

Politics, however, was perhaps even more important. The Jews who began to return to Palestine were motivated less by a religious quest than by the perceived need for a political homeland and refuge. Europe, where most Jews lived, was permeated by nationalism in the nineteenth century, and Jews absorbed this spirit. At first, the goal was expressed in national-cultural terms: to restore Hebrew as a living language of everyday national life; to work the land again after centuries of urban ghettoization; to live as a "normal" people with a land and culture of its own. Then, as pogroms against Jews resumed with unprecedented ferocity under Russian Czar Alexander III after 1881, the movement of Jewish nationalism became far more urgent and far more political. Persecuted Jews needed a refuge.

Assimilated Jews, living more contentedly in the USA and western European countries, at first discounted this argument. Even the Jews fleeing Russian pogroms headed mostly to the USA; only a comparative handful chose the more difficult, nationalistic route to Palestine. But then anti-Semitism resurfaced strongly in the 1890s in France. Assimilated Jews of western Europe were shocked. The Austrian-Jewish journalist Theodor Herzl (1860–1904) founded the modern political Zionist movement—"Zion" is a biblical designation for Jerusalem—to restore to Jews a political homeland in their ancestral land of Palestine.

Now a third identity—a colonial identity—entered the conflict. In 1917, during World War I, the British government issued the Balfour Declaration, proposing to redistribute the lands of the Ottoman Empire if Britain could conquer them:

> His Majesty's Government view with favour the establishment in Palestine of a national home for the Jewish people, and will use their best endeavours to facilitate the achievement of this objective, it being clearly understood that nothing shall be done which may prejudice the civil and religious rights of existing non-Jewish communities in Palestine.

Intentionally or not, this declaration inserted a colonial voice of divide-and-rule into the middle of the Middle East. Arabs and Jews simply followed through, playing their

The Camp David peace accords. In Maryland, September 1978, Israeli prime minister Menachem Begin, President Jimmy Carter, and Egyptian president Anwar Sadat relax during the historic Camp David peace talks that resulted in the 1979 treaty between Israel and Egypt. The Camp David Accords, documents signed by the leaders of Israel and Egypt, were a preliminary to the signing of the formal peace treaty between the two nations. The treaty returned the Sinai to Egypt.

assigned, antagonistic roles. As a result of the war, the end of Ottoman rule, and the beginning of British and French colonialism in the region, Arab nationalism took root. The two nascent nationalisms, Arab and Zionist, grew up together, and were soon fighting for control of the same land. Their numbers were, however, quite unequal. In 1920 there were only about 60,000 Jews and ten times that number of Arabs living in the area.

The Jewish immigrants—"pioneers" as they called themselves—came mostly from cities and small towns in eastern and central Europe. They had European educations, philosophies, technologies, and attitudes, and they usually viewed the Arabs among whom they settled as educationally backward and technologically primitive nomadic and farming peoples. Many of the Jewish settlers built egalitarian collective farms, kibbutzim, to maximize agricultural efficiency, achieve a social vision, and provide for their common defense. The Zionists argued, with a kind of colonial paternalism, that they could help reform and modernize the land and the people, but they took little account of the displacement of local society caused by their arrival and the anger it evoked. Armed Arab uprisings attempted unsuccessfully to halt and drive out Jewish immigration from the 1920s onward, with particularly severe attacks in 1929 and 1936.

The Holocaust marked the turning point. For Jews, that catastrophe re-affirmed the desperate need for a political state and refuge. They tended to (mis)identify the efforts of Arabs to block the creation of Israel, not as a struggle over control of land, but as a new Nazism, intent on root-and-branch destruction. This portrayal increased Jewish fear of, and opposition to, Arab concerns. Some Jewish immigrants also argued that their own suffering and desperation created the need for a small area to call their own that far outweighed any claims of the Arab inhabitants, who had, in any case, far more territory to call their own. The Jews did not seek armed conflict, but neither would they retreat in the face of armed opposition. Meanwhile Arabs asked pointedly: Why should Christian guilt over a Holocaust in Europe be expiated by assigning to Jews lands held by Muslims in the eastern Mediterranean? In Arab eyes, this was European colonialism parading as humanitarianism at Arab expense.

With United Nations' approval, Israel declared itself a state in 1948 in about one-half of the land of Palestine. Arab armies immediately attacked, but the state survived and even won some additional territory. Many Palestinians fled the new state, becoming the "wandering Jews" of the Middle East. Palestinians generally argue that they were forced out by armed intimidation; Jews claim that Palestinians followed their leaders' advice that they leave temporarily in order to return later in armed triumph. A great outpouring of revisionist historical writing by Israeli authors such as Benny Morris has provided documentary evidence that gave support to both claims. Whatever the immediate cause, some 600,000 Palestinians fled the borders of Israel at the time of the establishment of the state and the 1948 war. Another million stayed on as citizens, although many would say as second-class citizens, inside the borders of Israel.

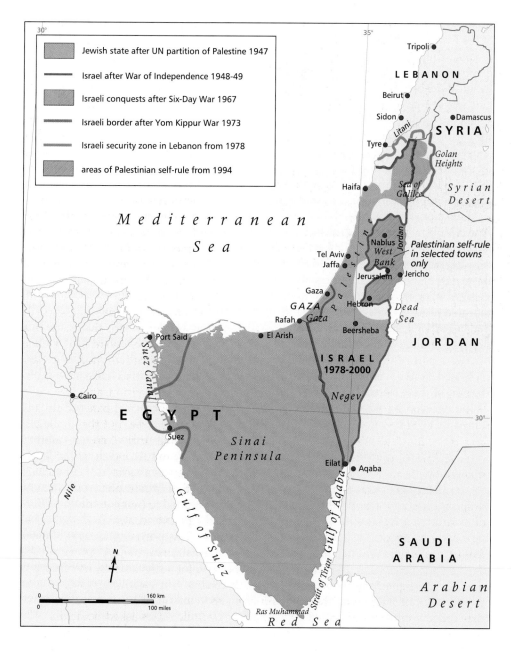

Israel and its neighbors. The creation, with Western support, of a Jewish homeland in Palestine in 1947 occurred at a time of increasing Arab nationalism. Israel's birth in 1948 was attended by a war and more followed in 1956, 1967, 1973, and 1982. Peace treaties exist only with Egypt, which regained the Sinai peninsula, and Jordan (1994). Beginning in 1987, an *intifada* (uprising) by Palestinians forced more attention on Israeli–Palestinian relations—an extremely vexed issue. In 1993, the Palestinian Liberation Organization and Israel began negotiations that would return land to Palestinian control and perhaps lead to a Palestinian state, while recognizing Israel's right to exist. So far these negotiations have proved fruitless and a second *intifada* began in 2000.

Map legend:
- Jewish state after UN partition of Palestine 1947
- Israel after War of Independence 1948-49
- Israeli conquests after Six-Day War 1967
- Israeli border after Yom Kippur War 1973
- Israeli security zone in Lebanon from 1978
- areas of Palestinian self-rule from 1994

Israelis believed that the neighboring Arab states would—and should—absorb the exiles. After all, Israel had absorbed more than a million Jews who immigrated from Arab states after 1948, either pulled by the attraction of a Jewish homeland or pushed by fear of future reprisals by Arabs. But the Arab states chose to leave the Palestinians in refugee status, living in refugee camps, or seeking employment in the oil fields of the Persian Gulf region, or leaving the area entirely. The result has been a bitter irridentism, a desire to reclaim their homeland, represented among Palestinians primarily by the Palestine Liberation Organization (after 1996 the Palestine National Authority); militant hostility toward Israel; and unsettled refugee groups that threaten the stability of neighboring states.

Israel's 1967 conquest of the West Bank and Gaza Strip left one and a half million Palestinians under an increasingly harsh military occupation. Israel opened the lands conquered in 1967 to Jewish settlement, and about 400,000 Jews, under the protection of the Israeli army, came to settle among the 2 million Arabs of these areas. The Palestinians wanted to establish a state of their own in this land. Rejecting these territorial ambitions for a Palestinian state, the Israelis tightened the occupation. The Israeli–Arab conflict had two inter-related dimensions. The first was the internal struggle between two nations—Israel and a Palestine-striving-to-be-born—inhabiting a single geographical land. The second was the international strife between Israel and the surrounding Arab states. Through the 1970s and early 1980s, Arabs expressed their anger through violent attacks within Israeli borders as well as terrorist attacks against international travelers, especially in airports and airplanes, and against the Israeli athletes participating in the 1972 Munich Olympics. Israeli bombings of refugee camps were a common response.

The Israeli–Palestinian–Arab conflict had global implications. It inflamed the entire Arab world, which was the location of the world's greatest oil reserves. In 1973, when Israel and its neighbors fought another war, the oil-rich Arab countries, acting through the Organization of Petroleum Exporting Countries (OPEC) rationed and embargoed the export of oil to the United States and western Europe to demonstrate their anger at Western support for Israel and their power over the world's oil resources. OPEC repeated its restrictions through the 1970s, and the world economy went into a decline that lasted for several years. In addition, with the United States usually taking the side of Israel, and the USSR usually siding with the Arab nations, the Middle East conflict became a part of the global Cold War confrontation. Finally, militant Islamic groups pressured Arab governments to take a more active role in the conflict, threatening the stability of these states.

Children of the *intifada*, 2001. This wall separates Israelis and Palestinians in the Gaza quarter of Rafah.

The decision by Anwar Sadat of Egypt to seek a peace treaty with Israel, finally signed in 1979, therefore signaled a significant breakthrough. Egypt was the largest and most powerful of the frontline states bordering Israel, so the treaty sharply diminished the likelihood that the local conflict would spread beyond its home region. When Palestinians in the West Bank and Gaza regions began an *intifada* (uprising) in 1987, employing both civil disobedience and low-intensity violence in a pattern of continuous demonstrations to disrupt Israeli control, the rest of the Arab world gave little practical assistance. Israel cracked down and hardened its positions.

Some renewed possibilities for peace opened in the early 1990s as the Soviet Union dissolved, ending the superpower rivalries that had helped militarize the Middle East. Also, the 1991 Gulf War in Iraq led to divisions and re-alignments among Arab states. New openings toward Israel appeared possible. Many observers looked to the USA to broker, or to impose, a peace agree-

ment in the region, but the United States, despite a great deal of public diplomacy, remained unwilling to assert itself, and when it did, it supported Israeli positions so strongly that it was seen more as an ally of Israel than as an "honest broker" between the two sides. US support for Israel seemed to be a product of historical sentiment toward the nation and its origins as well as of political lobbying both by Jewish voters and by many fundamentalist Christian groups, who saw the rebirth of Israel as part of God's plan for ultimately converting the Jews to Christianity. Religious as well as political identities in the United States had their influence on identities in the Middle East, and vice versa.

A breakthrough in the internal Israeli–Palestinian conflict appeared in 1993, when the government of Israel and the Palestine Liberation Organization signed an agreement—called the "Oslo accords" for the Norwegian city in which the agreements had been reached—to recognize each other, to cease fighting, and to extend at least limited self-rule to the Palestinians in Gaza and the West Bank. For the first time, each of the two combatants agreed publicly and in principle to recognize the identity and existence of one another. Until this point, the Palestinians had refused to recognize the legitimacy of the Jewish state and Israel had refused to recognize the legitimacy of the Palestinians' claim to their own state. Peace accords between Israel and the Palestinians opened the way for other Arab nations to normalize their relations with Israel. Jordan, under King Hussein, signed a peace treaty in 1994.

The euphoria did not last. A Jewish extremist assassinated Israeli prime minister Yitzhak Rabin, a sponsor of the peace agreement, in 1995. Later in the year Arab militants bombed several Israeli buses. The advocates for renewed violence on both sides were overwhelming the advocates for peace. The election of Ehud Barak as Israel's

SOURCE

The Geneva Accords: A Non-Governmental Plan for Peace

Intense peace negotiations between Israelis and Palestinians at Camp David in the United States in 2000 and in Taba, Egypt, in 2001 failed to produce peace agreements. Nevertheless, some of the representatives decided to continue to pursue a detailed framework for a peace agreement as a model of what might be achieved and to prove that responsible leaders on both sides could be partners in the search for peace. At the end of 2003, the Israeli Yossi Beilin and the Palestinian Abed Rabbo unveiled the agreements they had reached in their secret meetings in Geneva. They distributed copies throughout Israel and the Palestinian territories, claiming that at least 40 percent of each population accepted their framework for peace. Meanwhile the second Palestinian intifada *and Israel's harsh repression continued all around them, on the one hand mocking their efforts as utopian and, on the other, demonstrating dramatically the need for peace.*

We, the undersigned, a group of Palestinians and Israelis, endorse, on this day, October 12, 2003, a model draft framework final status agreement between the two peoples. At this point in time, after the Palestinian government and the Israeli government have accepted the Road Map [an international plan especially favored by the Americans], which includes reaching a final status settlement by 2005, based on a two-state solution, we consider it to be of utmost importance to present to the two peoples and the entire world an example of what such a final status agreement could include. This is proof that despite all the pain entailed in concessions, it is possible to reach an historical compromise which meets the vital national interests of each side. We present this model agreement as a package—which stands together as an integral whole.

In the near future we will launch a campaign whose goal is to convince both sides of the value of such an historical compromise in the spirit of this model framework agreement, designed to put an end to the protracted conflict …

The decision to complete and later present this model draft agreement was not easy for any of us, however, we have decided to pursue this path since we believe that action of this type can serve as a source of hope after a long period of suffering, killing, and mutual accusations, that it can help build trust and facilitate the removal of the walls between our nations. In the context of the Road Map process, this draft agreement signifies a mutually acceptable and realizable endgame—to be reached by 2005, and as an answer to the skeptics and supporters of endless interim agreements. This agreement will bring about the creation of a sovereign Palestinian State alongside Israel, put an end to the occupation, terminate conflict and bloodshed, and end all mutual claims.

prime minister in 1999 seemed to favor peace agreements once more. Hopes were high that negotiations between him and the Palestinian leader, Yasir Arafat, sponsored by President Clinton at Camp David in 2000, would bring peace, but the dialogues broke down. Israelis lost heart. Even the "peace camp" lamented that Arafat did not want peace, that there was no "partner for peace" on the side of the Palestinians, that nothing short of the destruction of the Israeli state and identity would satisfy the Arabs. Arafat claimed that the proposed agreements simply did not meet his minimum demands for the creation of the new state of Palestine.

Leadership on both sides became more militant. Among the Palestinians, organizations dedicated to guerrilla warfare and terrorism against civilians gained increasing power and inspired a second *intifada* beginning in September 2000. Israel elected Ariel Sharon and his militant Likud Party over Barak and his more moderate Labor Party in 2001, symbolizing the return to hard-line militance rather than negotiated peace. Palestinian militants increasingly invoked the concept of Islamic *jihad*, or religious warfare. They recruited suicide bombers—people who are willing to die as they deliver bombs hidden on their bodies to explode in enemy locations—to attack Israeli military and civilian targets that they could not otherwise penetrate. Israeli leaders invoked ancient biblical references to Jewish control over the conquered territories and recent memories of the Holocaust, and they defended themselves with overwhelming, brutal power, including the use of assassination against specific militants. Between the beginning of the second *intifada* and mid-2004, approximately 1000 Israelis and 2500 Palestinians were killed. The Israeli occupation of the West Bank and Gaza continued harsh and disruptive of daily life. In return, the Palestinian *intifada* made it impossible for Israelis to rest in peace and security. Even efforts proclaimed to limit violence created antagonisms. Sharon began building a huge physical barrier to separate Jews from Palestinians, but the barrier ate deeply into land that Palestinians expected to be part of their state. The World Court condemned it totally, and the Israeli Supreme Court ruled that it had to be rerouted to be less disruptive to everyday Palestinian life. Palestinians selected new prime ministers thought to be more amenable to peace negotiations than Arafat, but Arafat remained the power behind the throne, and Israelis did not trust his intentions. The continuing conflict also introduced tensions into the relationships between the United States and the European Union. The United States generally supported Israeli positions, while the Europeans were more sympathetic to the Palestinians.

Ironically, and sadly, everyone seemed to know the basic outlines of what was needed for a peace agreement: mutual recognition of Israel and Palestine; an end of violence; national borders corresponding generally to the borders before the 1967 war, with minor territorial adjustments; and the dismantling of Israeli settlements in Palestinian territories. Indeed political leaders of the Israelis and the Palestinians, meeting as private individuals in Geneva intermittently between 2001 and 2003, drew up a plan for peace that expressed these basic principles. They claimed that a majority on both sides would accept them, but that political leadership on both sides would not allow it. In mid-2004 it appeared that everyone knew what might bring peace, but that not everyone wanted it, nor did they trust the other side to keep its agreements. Militant, oppositional, fierce, and fearful identities stood in the way.

Review Questions

- Literary critic Edward Said wrote that "the major contest in most modern cultures concerns the definition or interpretation of each culture." To what extent do the case studies of this chapter support Said's assertion?

- What are the means by which political leaders inflame, or tamp down, potential ethnic, religious, and cultural confrontations? Please give examples.
- Does this chapter seem to suggest that history repeats itself, or that historical change is often surprising because we never know what is coming next?
- To what extent does change in identity seem a natural phenomenon, in part because each new generation will have its own new way of looking at the past?
- What changes in political, economic, social, or cultural identities in the United States and the world currently seem to be most directly affecting your life?

Suggested Readings

With this chapter we are moving into contemporary times, and even into current events. In addition to television and radio news, and newspapers and the popular newsmagazines like *Time*, *Newsweek*, and *U.S. News and World Report*, two publications, serving an educated but not specialized readership, that are especially useful in tracking these events are:

Economist, a weekly review published in London and with extensive coverage of the United States and the entire world. Edited from a traditional liberal perspective—that is, favoring free markets and human rights as developed over the past centuries in Europe and the USA—the *Economist* covers the globe each week. Whatever one may think of its philosophical and political bias, the comprehensiveness and accessibility of its coverage cannot be matched in the English language.

New York Review of Books, published bi-weekly, takes the form of a tabloid of book reviews, but its reviews are lengthy and extensive explorations of subject areas. The particular book or books under assessment serve as a springboard for wide-ranging, thoughtful, and careful discussions of the subject matter. The authors are leading scholars in their fields.

BOOKS AND ARTICLES

Ayres, Alyssa and Philip Oldenburg, eds. *India Briefing: Quickening the Pace of Change* (Armonk, NY: M.E. Sharpe, 2002). The most recent, as of 2004, of a series published every year or two, of outstanding summary articles on developments in contemporary India. Various articles on politics, economics, social life, the arts, and culture.

Bearak, Barry, "Poor Man's Burden," *New York Times Magazine*, June 27, 2004. Descriptive analysis of Lula, as man and leader, and the problems he is encountering as president of Brazil.

China Development Brief. *250 Chinese NGOs: Civil Society in the Making* (Unpublished Report: China Development Brief, 2001). Underlines the importance of NGOs to China's progress—economic as well as political—and outlines the mission and accomplishments of 250 of them.

Chomsky, Noam. *Middle East Illusions* (Lanham, MD: Rowman and Littlefield, 2004). Chomsky takes to task everyone for failures in Middle East policy. He is especially critical of the United States for its uncritical support of Israel.

Crossley, Pamela Kyle, Lynn Hollen Lees, and John W. Servos. *Global Society: The World since 1900* (Boston: Houghton Mifflin, 2004). A fine, well-written history of the twentieth century, organized thematically rather than by nations or regions. Special emphasis on technology and useful references to websites for further research.

Das, Gurcharan. *India Unbound* (New York: Random House, 2000). A newspaper columnist and successful businessman reports on, and relishes, the opening of the Indian economy since 1991.

Edelstein, Jillian. *Truth and Lies: Stories from the Truth and Reconciliation Commission in South Africa* (New York: The New Press, 2001). Portraits and testimony—often quite moving—from individuals who spoke to the commission.

French, Howard. *A Continent for the Taking. The Tragedy and Hope of Africa* (New York: Knopf, 2004). A senior writer for the *New York Times* places the blame for Africa's current difficulties on self-interested political leaders in both Africa and the West, showing that there is plenty of blame to go around.

Gilbert, Mark and Jonathan T. Reynolds. *Africa in World History: From Prehistory to the Present* (Upper Saddle River, NJ: Prentice Hall, 2004). A useful survey. Up to date.

Gilbert, Mark. *Surpassing Realism: The Politics of European Integration since 1945* (Lanham, MD: Rowman and Littlefield, 2003). Step-by-step account of the building of the European Union with fascinating contemporary commentaries along the way.

Glenny, Misha. *The Balkans: Nationalism, War, and the Great Powers, 1804–1999* (New York: Viking, 2000). Comprehensive account of the Balkans and their somewhat unfortunate fate in the hands of the great powers, sometimes because of intervention, sometimes because of lack of intervention.

Gourevitch, Philip. *We Wish to Inform You that Tomorrow We will be Killed with Our Families: Stories from Rwanda* (New York: Farrar, Straus and Giroux, 1998). Brilliant journalistic reporting from the killing fields of Rwanda. Attempts to understand and explain the differences between Tutsis and Hutus.

Guillermoprieto, Alma, "Mexico City: 'The Morning Quickie,'" *New York Review of Books*, August 12, 2004, 40–43. Journalistic account of a Mexico not yet past the corruption of the PRI, not yet committed to a clean, functioning democracy, but able to mock, and therefore perhaps improve, its leadership.

Hughes, Neil C. *China's Economic Challenge: Smashing the Iron Rice Bowl* (Armonk, NY: M.E. Sharpe, 2002). Credits China with enormous, positive change economically and also politically, but argues that for China to continue to march forward she will have to introduce greater personal, political democracy.

Human Development Report 2003: Millennium Development Goals: A Compact among Nations to End Human Poverty (New York: Oxford University Press for the United Nations Development Programme, 2003). A survey of the nations of the world with an abundance of statistical tables and numerous, brief, specific topical discussions.

Hunt, Michael H. *The World Transformed: 1945 to the Present: A Documentary Reader* (Boston: Bedford/St. Martin's, 2004). An outstanding selection of primary documents with global scope and thematic breadth.

Jaffrelot, Christophe, "The Subordinate Caste Revolution," in Ayres and Oldenburg, pp. 121–58. Excellent, brief discussion of the rise of the lower castes in a silent, relatively peaceful revolution.

Kishwar, Madhu. *Off the Beaten Track: Rethinking Gender Justice for Indian Women* (New Delhi: Oxford University Press, 1999). The editor of one of India's leading feminist journals, Manushi, discusses the evolution of her thought in light of the possible and the ideal.

Meade, Teresa. *A Brief History of Brazil* (New York: Checkmark Books, 2004). Brief incisive account, with many insights presented through sidebars. Especially interesting on culture, music, and sports. Well-chosen illustrations.

Mishra, Pankaj, "India: The Neglected Majority Wins!" *New York Review of Books*, August 12, 2004, 30–37. A thoughtful report on the victory of the Congress and failure of the BJP in India's 2004 national election, taking great pleasure in poorer people asserting their political wishes.

Mukherji, Joydeep, "The Indian Economy: Pushing Ahead and Pulling Apart," in Ayres and Oldenburg. A professional economist's thoughtful, comprehensive, but brief assessment of the state of India's economy, about 1991–2002.

Nugent, Neill. *The Government and Politics of the European Union* (Durham, NC: Duke University Press, 5th ed., 2003). Detailed exposition of the institutional workings of the EU, with very useful historical prelude and concluding perspectives on the future.

Preston, Julia and Samuel Dillon. *Opening Mexico. The Making of a Democracy* (New York: Farrar, Straus and Giroux, 2004). Two *New York Times* reporters narrate the events that marked the contemporary "Opening of Mexico" from about 1968 to 2004. Readable, thoughtful, and engaged.

Rogel, Carole. *The Breakup of Yugoslavia and the War in Bosnia* (Westport, CN: Greenwood Press, 1998). Basic narrative supported by detailed chronology and primary documents to 1997. Critical of almost all participants and of NATO and the USA for years of appeasement.

Rosenberg, Rosalind, "The 'Woman Question,'" in Richard W. Bulliet, ed. *The Columbia History of the 20th Century* (New York: Columbia University Press, 1998).

Sen, Amartya. *Development as Freedom* (New York: Random House, 1999). Nobel Prize-winning economist stresses the significance of human development—health, education, and welfare—as the key issue in economic development, both as its cause and its result. Clearly and persuasively argued.

Sivard, Ruth Leger. *World Military and Social Expenditures 1996* (Washington: World Priorities, 16th ed., 1996). A useful compilation of statistical data revealing the colossal amounts spent by many nations of the world for military purposes, especially as compared with relatively smaller amounts for health, education, and other social purposes.

Tully, Mark and Gillian Wright. *India in Slow Motion* (New Delhi: Viking Penguin, 2002). Tully was the BBC's revered and respected correspondent from New Delhi for 25 years, and here continues to report with his partner. He is perceptive and direct about his observations, especially the toll that political corruption takes on Indian development.

Ullman, Richard H. ed. *The World and Yugoslavia's Wars* (New York: Council on Foreign Relations, 1996). Explores not only the wars but also the (lack of) responses by the European Community, the United States, and the United Nations.

World History Documents CD-ROM

28.4 Keith B. Richburg, "A Black Man Confronts Africa"
28.5 Alain Destexhe, "Rwanda and Genocide in the Twentieth Century"
29.3 Ethnic Cleansing in Northwestern Bosnia: Three Witnesses
29.4 Deng Xiaoping, "A Market Economy for Socialist Goals"
29.8 Henry A. Myers, "Now, in the Twenty-First Century"

GLOSSARY

Abhidhamma (Ub-ih-DUM-eh) One of the three principal divisions of the Buddhist scriptures, or Tripitaka, the others being the **Sutta** and the **Vinaya**. It comprises a logical analysis of the Buddha's teachings, arranged systematically, and is more impersonal and abstract than the Sutta. Its aim is meditational, and an important element involves an examination of states of consciousness.

agora (AG-o-rah) A central feature of ancient Greek town planning. Its chief function, like the Roman forum, was as a town market, but it also became the main social and political meeting place. Together with the acropolis, it normally housed the most important buildings of the town.

anthropology The scientific study of human beings in their social and physical aspects. Physical anthropologists study fossil remains to explain the origins and biological evolution of humans and the distinctive features of different races. Cultural anthropologists are concerned with the evolution of human society and cultures, especially through language. Social anthropologists have typically confined their work to "primitive" societies; they seek to analyze social norms, customs, belief, and ritual.

asiento (a-SEE-en-toe) A contract between the Spanish crown and a private individual or sovereign power, by which the latter was granted exclusive rights to import a stipulated number of slaves into the Spanish American colonies in exchange for a fee. The British South Sea Company was granted a monopoly at the Treaty of Utrecht of 1713, a privilege that was relinquished for a lump sum in 1750.

assimilation The process by which different ethnic groups lose their distinctive cultural identity through contact with the dominant culture of a society, and gradually become absorbed and integrated into it.

balance of power In international relations, a policy that aims to secure peace by preventing any one state or alignment of states from becoming too dominant. Alliances are formed in order to build up a force equal or superior to that of the potential enemy. Such a policy was practiced in the ancient world, for example by the Greek city-states.

bas relief (bah reh-LEEF) In sculpture, relief is a term for any work in which the forms stand out from the background, whether a plane or a curved surface. In bas (or low) relief, the design projects only slightly from the background and the outlines are not undercut.

Berlin Blockade In 1948 the Russians barred the entrance and exit of people and supplies to and from Berlin in an attempt to gain control of the city.

Bible From the Greek *biblia*, books. The Jewish bible, written in Hebrew, comprises the thirty-nine books of the Old Testament (a Christian designation), the canon of which was probably established by 100 C.E. Regarded as divinely inspired, these scriptures are made up of three parts: the Torah (Law), the first five books— Genesis to Deuteronomy—whose authorship is attributed to Moses; the Prophets; and the Writings (the Psalms, etc.). The Christian Church incorporated these books, together with the Apocrypha (supplementary books written in Greek) and the **New Testament** writings, into its bible, the form of which was fixed by the end of the fourth century C.E.

bourgeoisie (boor-ZHWA-zee) A French word that originally applied to the inhabitants of walled towns, who occupied a socio-economic position between the rural peasantry and the feudal aristocracy. With the development of industry, it became identified more with employers, as well as with other members of the "middle class," including professionals, artisans, and shopkeepers. (In Marxist theory, the word refers to those who own the tools of production and do not live by the sale of their labor, as opposed to the **proletariat**.)

bourse stock exchange.

caliph (KAY-lif) The spiritual head and temporal ruler of the Muslim community. As successor to the prophet Muhammad, the caliph is invested with absolute civil and religious authority, providing that he rules in conformity with the law of the Quran and the **hadith**.

capitalism An economic system characterized by private or corporate ownership of the means of production and by private control over decisions on prices, production, and distribution of goods in a free, competitive market of **supply and demand**.

cartel An association of independent producers or businessmen whose aim is to control the supply of a particular commodity or group of commodities in order to regulate or push up prices.

caste (KAST) An element in a hierarchical social system in which the ranks are strictly defined, usually according to descent, marriage, and occupation. In more rigorous caste systems, such as that of Hinduism in India, mobility from one caste (Sanskrit: *varna*) to another is prohibited, and traditions and ritual dictate rules for social intercourse as well as such matters as education, diet, and occupation.

centuries The smallest units of the Roman army, each composed of some 100 foot-soldiers and commanded by a centurion. A legion was made up of 60 centuries. Centuries also formed political divisions of Roman citizens; they met in assembly to elect the chief magistrates and had some judicial powers.

Cheka (CHECK-a) The secret police of early Soviet Russia, established by the Bolsheviks after the Revolution of 1917 to defend the regime against dissidents. Criticized for its severe brutality, the agency was reorganized in 1922.

chonin City merchants and their collective class. During the Tokugawa shogunate this class grew in wealth, power, and sophistication.

Christmas The Christian feast celebrating the birth of Jesus Christ. The day of his actual birth is unknown, but the early Church probably chose this date because it coincided with pagan festivals of sun worship associated with the winter solstice. Pagan cults seem to have been the source of some popular customs connected with Christmas.

client state A state that is economically, politically, or militarily dependent on another state. During the Cold War, states such as Cuba and Guatemala supported the policies of the USSR and the USA, respectively, while receiving extensive assistance from them.

collectivization A policy that aims to transfer land from private to state or communal ownership. It was adopted by the Soviet government in the 1920s and implemented with increasing brutality; by 1936 almost all the peasants had joined the *kolkhozy* (large collective farms), although many resisted violently. The integration of agriculture into the state-controlled economy helped to supply the capital required for industrialization.

comprador (kahm-prah-DOOR) (Portuguese: "buyer") A Chinese merchant hired by Western traders to assist with their dealings in China. The comprador provided interpreters, workers, guards, and help over currency exchange.

concordat (kahn-KOR-dat) A public agreement, subject to international law, between the Pope as head of the Roman Catholic church and a temporal ruler regulating the status, rights, and liberties of the church within the country concerned.

consul (KON-sul) Under the Roman Republic, one of the two magistrates holding supreme civil and military authority. Nominated by the Senate and elected by citizens in the Comita Centuriata (popular assembly), the consuls held office for one year and each had power of veto over the other. Their power was much restricted after the collapse of the Republic in 27 B.C.E., when the office fell under the control of the emperors.

contract labor Labor provided by workers under binding, legally enforceable contract, usually for a lengthy period, sometimes years, sometimes in organized gangs of laborers, and often for projects in distant locations. Compare **indentured labor**.

conurbation An enormous, complex city, made up of many parts, each of which is a small town or city by itself—a megalopolis.

creole (KREE-ol) In the sixteenth to eighteenth centuries, a white person born in Spanish America of Spanish parents. Excluded from the highest offices under the Spanish colonial administration, the creoles became the leaders of revolution, and then the ruling class of the new independent nations. The term creole is also used more loosely, with a wide range of applications.

cuneiform (kyoo-NEE-uh-form) A writing system in use in the ancient Near East from around the end of the fourth millennium to the first century B.C.E. It was used for a number of languages in the area, but the earliest examples, on clay tablets, are in Sumerian. The name derives from the wedge-shaped marks (Latin: *cuneus*, a wedge) made by pressing the slanted edge of a stylus into soft clay. The signs were abstract versions of the earlier **pictograms**, and represented whole words or the sounds of syllables.

daimyo (DIH-my-oh) The feudal lords of Japan, who by the sixteenth century controlled almost the entire country. Their constant warfare was finally ended in 1603 under the Tokugawa **shogunate**; they subsequently served as local rulers, joined to the **shogun** by oath. In 1868, when imperial rule was restored, their domains or **han** were surrendered to the emperor; in 1871 they were given titles and pensioned off.

dalit "oppressed person," a blunt term adopted by ex-untouchables to describe their status.

Daoism (Taoism) (DAO-iz-um) A religio-philosophical system of ancient China, which emerged in the sixth century B.C.E. Daoism rejected the activism of Confucianism, the other great Chinese philosophical tradition. It emphasized spontaneity and individual freedom, a *laissez-faire* attitude to life and government, simplicity, and the importance of mystical experience. True happiness could be attained only by surrendering to the Way or principle (Chinese: *dao*) of Nature. The principle texts of Daoism are the *Laozi* or *Classic of the Way and Its Power*, traditionally attributed to the philosopher Laozi, and the *Zhuangzi* of Zhuang Zou.

Dar al-Islam (DAHR ahl-is-LAHM) The literal meaning of the Arabic words is "the abode of peace." The term refers to the land of Islam, or the territories in which Islam and its religious laws (**shari'a**) may be freely practiced.

deme (DEEM) A rural district or village in ancient Greece, or its members or inhabitants. The demes were a constituent part of the **polis** but had their own corporations with police powers, and their own cults, officials, and property. Membership of the deme was open only to adult males, and was hereditary; it also guaranteed membership of the polis itself.

developed world Those countries that enjoy considerable wealth, derived largely from sophisticated industrialization, and characterized by high standards of living, healthcare, and literacy, advanced technological development, democratic constitutions, and world influence, as well as high labor costs and energy consumption. They comprise most of Europe, the United States, Canada, Japan, Australia, and New Zealand, the first areas to be industrialized.

developing world Those countries lacking advanced industrial development and money for investment, and with a low *per capita* income. Their economies are largely agrarian, often relying on one crop, with low yields. Labor is plentiful, cheap, and unskilled; levels of literacy are low; poverty, disease, and famine have not been eliminated. They include most Asian countries, as well as Africa and Latin America. (*See* **third world**.)

dhimmi (dim-MEE) A person who belongs to the class of "protected people" in the Islamic state, who could not be forcibly converted to Islam. They originally comprised the followers of the monotheistic religions cited in the Quran, the "People of the Book" (e.g., Jews and Christians), to whom scriptures had been revealed, and the principle has in some instances been extended to followers of other religions.

diaspora (die-AS-pur-uh) A dispersion of peoples. Most commonly used to refer to the dispersion of Jews among the Gentiles, which began with the Babylonian captivity of the sixth century B.C.E.; the Hebrew term for diaspora is *Galut*, "exile." Because of the special relationship between the Jews and the land of Israel, the term refers not only to their physical dispersion but also has religious, philosophical, and political connotations. The African diaspora refers to the settlement of people of African origin to new locations around the world. "Trade diaspora" has been used to refer to centers of trade in which traders from many different countries live and work.

diffusion The spread of ideas, objects, or traits from one culture to another. Diffusionism is an anthropological theory that cultural similarities among different groups can be explained by diffusion rather than **innovation**, and, in its most radical form, that they derive from a common source.

divine right of kings A political doctrine influential in the sixteenth and seventeenth centuries. It held that the monarch derived his or her authority from God and was therefore not accountable to earthly authority. James I of England (1603–25) was a foremost exponent.

dominance The imposition of alien government through force, as opposed to **hegemony**.

Duma (DOO-ma) The Russian parliament established by Nicholas II in response to the Revolution of 1905. Its powers were largely restricted to the judicial and administrative areas; the czar retained control over the franchise. The first two dumas (1906, 1907) were radical and soon dissolved; the third (1907–12) was conservative; the fourth (1912–17) became a focus of opposition to the czarist regime, particularly over its conduct of World War I, and enforced Nicholas's abdication in 1917.

Easter The principal feast of the Christian calendar celebrating the resurrection of Christ. It is preceded by the penitential season of Lent, which culminates in the solemnities of Holy Week and Good Friday, commemorating Jesus' crucifixion. The date varies, and can fall on any Sunday between March 22 and April 25. The feast was associated by the early Christians with the Jewish Passover, and in some Churches a vigil is held on the night of Holy Saturday.

econometrics The use of statistical techniques and mathematical models to analyze economic relationships. Econometrics may be applied by a government or private business to test the validity of an economic theory or to forecast future trends.

ecumene (EK-yoo-MEEN) A Greek word referring to the inhabited world and designating a distinct cultural-historical community.

empiricism (em-PEER-eh-cism) The theory that all knowledge originates in experience; the practice of relying on direct observation of events and experience for determining reality. Often contrasted with rationalism on the one hand and with mysticism on the other.

enclosure acts Laws passed in England in the late 1700s to 1800s that converted public lands held in common into parcels of land to be sold to private owners.

encomienda (en-co-me-EN-da) A concession from the Spanish crown to a Spanish American colonist, giving him permission to exact tribute —in gold, in kind, or in labor—from a specified number of Indians living in a certain area; in return he was to care for their welfare and instruct them in the Catholic faith. The system was designed to supply labor for the mines, but it was severely abused and later abolished.

enlightened despotism A benevolent form of absolutism, a system of government in which the ruler has absolute rights over his or her subjects. It implies that the ruler acts for the good of the people, not in self-interest.

epigraphy (eh-PIG-reh-fee) Inscriptions, usually on stone or metal, or the science of interpreting them.

Eucharist (YOO-kah-rist) From the Greek *eucharistia*, thanksgiving. The central **sacrament** and act of worship of the Christian Church, commemorating the Last Supper of Christ with his disciples, his sacrifice on the cross, and the redemption of mankind, and culminating in Holy Communion, when his Body and Blood in the form of water and wine are conveyed to the believer.

exogamy (adj. exogamous) The practice by which a person is compelled to choose a marital partner from outside his or her own group or clan, the opposite of endogamy, the choice of partner from within the group. Sometimes the outside group from which the partner is to be chosen is specified.

extraterritoriality In international law, the immunities enjoyed by the official representatives of a sovereign state or international organization within a host country; they are in effect "foreign islands," and thus exempt from prosecution, interference, or constraint.

fascism (FASH-ism) A political philosophy, movement, or government that exalts the nation over the individual, the antithesis of liberal democracy. It advocates a centralized, autocratic government led by a disciplined party and headed by a dictatorial, charismatic leader. The term fascism was first introduced by Benito Mussolini in Italy in 1919 and takes its name from the Latin word *fasces*, the ancient symbol of state authority, a bundle of rods bound around an ax.

feudal (FEW-dull) Refers to both a social, military, and political system organized on the basis of land tenure and the manorial system of production. Property (the fief) was granted to a tenant (vassal) by a lord in exchange for an oath of allegiance and a promise to fulfill certain obligations, including military service, aid, and advice; in return, the lord offered protection and justice. Originally bestowed by investiture, the fief later became hereditary. Within the system, each person was bound to the others by a web of mutual responsibilities, from the king or emperor down to the **serfs**. Feudalism is particularly associated with medieval Europe, and with China and Japan. (*See* **manorial economy**.)

first world The advanced capitalist nations of the **developed world**, as opposed to the second world (countries with socialist state systems, particularly the former Soviet bloc) and the **third world**.

free market economy An economic system in which the means of production are largely privately owned and there is little or no government control over the markets, which operate according to **supply and demand**. The primary aim is to maximize profits, which are distributed to private individuals who have invested capital in an enterprise. The system is also known as a free enterprise economy or capitalism.

Führer German for "leader", the title taken by Hitler to assert his total control over Germany.

fundamentalist a person who believes in the literal truth of the bible as a revelation from God. Sometimes, more loosely, people of any religion who express intense devotion to their faith.

garden city A planned town combining work, residential, agricultural, and recreational facilities, and surrounded by a rural belt. This influential idea was the British planner Ebenezer Howard's solution to rural depopulation and the urban overcrowding of the industrial age. Letchworth (1903) in southeast England was the first example.

gazi (GAH-zee) A warrior or war leader in Islam, sometimes used as a military title among the Turks.

Girondins (juh-RAHN-dins) A French revolutionary group formed largely from the middle classes, many of them originally from the Gironde region. They were prominent in the Legislative Assembly (1791), urged war against Austria (1792), opposed the more radical **Montagnards**, and were overthrown in 1793.

glasnost (GLAZ-nohst) A Russian word meaning "openness," adopted as a political slogan by the Soviet leader Mikhail Gorbachev in 1986. It encouraged greater freedom of expression and genuine debate in social, political, and cultural affairs; with **perestroika**, it heralded greater democracy and improved relations with the West.

guild (GILD) A sworn association of people who gather for some common purpose. In the towns of medieval Europe, guilds of craftsmen or merchants were formed in order to protect and further the members' professional interests and for mutual aid. Merchant guilds organized trade in their locality and had important influence on local government. Craft guilds were confined to specific crafts or trades; they set and maintained standards of quality, regulated production and controlled recruitment through the apprenticeship system; they also had important social and religious functions. In India the guilds were associations of businessmen and producers who regulated weights and measures and prices and enforced quality control.

gulag (GOO-lahg) The acronym of Glavnoye, Upravleniye Ispravitelno Trudovykh Lagerey, the "Chief Administration of Corrective Labor Camps," a department of the Soviet secret police founded in 1934 under Stalin. It ran a vast network of forced labor camps throughout the USSR to which millions of citizens accused of "crimes against the state" were sent for punishment. The system was exposed by Alexandr Solzhenitsyn in *The Gulag Archipelago* (1973).

hacienda (ah-thee-EN-da) A large rural estate in Spanish America, originating with Spanish colonialization in the sixteenth century. The laborers, usually Indians, were in theory free wage earners, but in practice many became bound to the land through indebtedness to the owner. The owners (*haciendados*) controlled local and sometimes national government.

hadith (huh-DETH) Traditional records of the deeds and utterances of the prophet Muhammad, and the basis, after the Quran, for Islamic theology and law. The hadith provide commentaries on the Quran and give guidance for social and religious life and everyday conduct.

han In Japan, the territory or feudal estate controlled by a **daimyo** under the Tokugawa shogunate (1603–1868). Although legally subject to the central government, each *han* formed an autonomous and self-sufficient economic unit, with its own military forces. They were abolished in 1871.

harijan (har-YAH-jahn) A Hindu term meaning children of God, applied by Mahatma Gandhi to the poorest classes of Indian society, including the **untouchables**.

hegemony (hih-JEM-o-nee) The predominance of one unit over the others in a group, for example one state in a confederation. It can also apply to the rule of an empire over its subject peoples, when the foreign government is exercised with their substantial consent. Hegemony usually implies exploitation but, more positively, it may connote leadership (*see* **dominance**).

heliocentric A system in which the sun is assumed to be at the center of the solar system—or of the universe—while Earth and the planets move around it. Ptolemy of Alexandria's geocentric or Earth-centered system dominated scientific thought in the Western world from the second century C.E. until the publication of Copernicus's *De revolutionibus orbium coelestium* in 1543. There was much religious and scientific controversy before his thesis was shown to be essentially correct.

hieroglyphs (HIGH-ur-o-glifs) The characters in a writing system based on the use of **pictograms** or **ideograms**. In ancient Egypt, hieroglyphics were largely used for monumental inscriptions. The symbols depict people, animals, and objects, which represent words, syllables, or sounds.

hijra (HIJ-reh) The "migration" or flight of Muhammad from Mecca, where his life was in danger, to Medina (then called Yathrib) in 622 C.E. The Islamic era (A.H.: After Hijra) is calculated from this date, which coincides with the establishment of the first Islamic state.

historiography The writing of history, or the theory and history of historical writing.

Homo erectus The most widespread of all prehistoric hominids, and the most similar to humans. Evolved about 2 million years ago and became extinct 100,000 years ago.

hoplite A heavily armed foot soldier of ancient Greece, whose function was to fight in close formation, usually in ranks of eight men. Hoplites were citizens with sufficient property to equip themselves with full personal armor, which consisted of a helmet with nasal and cheek pieces, a breastplate and greaves of bronze. Each soldier carried a heavy bronze shield, a short iron sword, and a long spear for thrusting.

Huguenot Any protestants in France in the sixteenth and seventeenth centuries. Their legal status changed according to the wishes of the monarch on the throne at the time.

humanism A term applied to the intellectual movement initiated in Western Europe in the fourteenth century by such men as Petrarch and Boccaccio and deriving from the rediscovery and study of Classical, particularly Latin, literary texts. The humanist program of studies included rhetoric, grammar, history, poetry, and moral philosophy (the humanities); the humanist scholar aimed to emulate Classical literary achievements. The examination of Classical civilization formed the inspiration for the **Renaissance**. Although humanism attached prime importance to human qualities and values, unlike its twentieth-century counterpart it in no way involved the rejection of Christianity.

icon (I-kon) A representation of Christ, the Virgin Mary, or other sacred personage or saint, usually a painted image on wood but also wrought in mosaic, ivory, and other materials. The term is usually applied to the sacred images of Eastern, particularly Byzantine and Orthodox, Christianity, where they are regarded as channels of grace. (*See also* **iconoclast**.)

iconoclast (I-kon-o-klast) An image-breaker, or a person who rejects the veneration of **icons**, on the grounds that the practice is idolatrous. Strong disagreements over the cult of images in the Byzantine Empire led to attacks on the images themselves, and the use of icons was forbidden during the Iconoclastic Controversy (726–843 C.E.), when many were destroyed.

ideogram (ID-ee-o-gram) (alternative: ideograph) A character or figure in a writing system in which the idea of a thing is represented rather than its name. Languages such as Chinese use ideograms, but they cannot easily represent new or foreign words and huge numbers of symbols may be required to convey even basic information.

imam (ih-MAHM) In Islam, a title for a person whose leadership or example is to be followed, with several levels of meaning. In a general sense, it can refer to a leader of prayer in a mosque, or the head of a community or group. Among Shi'a Muslims, the title has special significance as applying to the successors of Muhammad, who were regarded as infallible and exercised absolute authority in both temporal and spiritual spheres (*see* **caliph**).

indentured labor Labor performed under signed indenture, or contract, which binds the laborer to work for a specific employer, for a specified time, usually years, often in a distant place, in exchange for transportation and maintenance. The indenture is usually very restrictive and its conditions harsh. After the abolition of slavery in the nineteenth century, in many regions like the Caribbean, imported, indentured labor (from Asia) was employed extensively. Compare **contract labor**.

Indo-Aryan (in-DOH-AIR-ee-un) A sub-group of the Indo-Iranian branch of the Indo-European group of languages, also called Indic and spoken in India, Sri Lanka, Bangladesh, and Pakistan. The

Indo-Aryan languages descend from Sanskrit, the sacred language of Hinduism; they include Hindi, a literary language, the more colloquial Hindustani, and the widely spoken Sindhi, Bengali, Gujarati, Punabi, and Sinhalese.

Indo-European The largest family of languages, believed to be descended from a single unrecorded language spoken more than 5000 years ago in the steppe regions around the Black Sea, which later split into a number of dialects. The languages were carried into Europe and Asia by migrating peoples, who also transmitted their cultural heritage. The family includes the following sub-groups: Anatolian (the earliest recorded language, now extinct), Indo-Iranian, Armenian, Greek, Albanian, Tocharian, Celtic, Italic, Germanic, Baltic, and Slavic.

indulgences In the Roman Catholic church, the remission from the temporal penalty of an absolved sin, obtainable through good works or special prayers and granted by the church through the merits of Christ and the saints. The financial value often attached to indulgences in the late medieval church led to widespread abuse.

infitah An Arabic term meaning liberality and receptiveness to new ideas and arguments. In commerce, it implies expansion and freedom from restrictive rules and regulations.

innovation The explanation that similar cultural traits, techniques, or objects found among different groups of people were invented independently rather than spreading from one group to another, as in **diffusion**.

interregnum An interval between reigns (Latin: "between reigns"). The term may refer to the period of time between the death of a monarch and the accession of his successor, to a suspension of the usual government, or to the period of rule of an usurper.

irredentist An individual or group that seeks to restore territory to the state that once owned it.

Jacobins (jak-uh-bins) A French revolutionary party founded in 1789; the word derives from the popular name for the former Dominican convent in Paris, where meetings were held. It later became the most radical party of the Revolution, responsible, under Robespierre, for implementing the Reign of Terror and the execution of the king (1793).

janapada (juh-nah-pah-dah) A Sanskrit word that occurs in ancient texts with reference to a large political district.

janissary (JAN-ah-ser-ee) A member of the elite corps of Ottoman footsoldiers. Originally, in the late fourteenth century, they were Christian conscripts from the conquered Balkans who were forcibly converted to Islam and subjected to strict rules, including celibacy. Highly trained, they later became very powerful, frequently engineering palace coups; they were massacred after their insurrection in 1826.

jizya A tax levied on non-Muslims who were considered monotheistic people-of-the-book and therefore to be protected: Jews, Christians, and, later, Zoroastrians and Hindus.

keiretsu (kay-re-tsoo) Alliances of independent Japanese firms, either between large corporations in different industries or between a large corporation and sub-contractors. They are successors of the pre-war **zaibatsu**.

kulak (koo-LAK) A prosperous peasant in late czarist and early Soviet Russia. The leaders of local agricultural communities, kulaks owned sizeable farms and could afford to hire labor. They vigorously opposed Stalin's **collectivization** policy and were regarded as class enemies; large numbers were deported or executed, and their property confiscated.

laissez-faire (les-ay-FAIR) An economic policy of non-interference by government in the working of the market and the economic affairs of individuals. Proponents of the theory, which was developed in the eighteenth century, argued that an unregulated economy would work "naturally" at maximum efficiency and that the pursuit of self-interest would ultimately benefit society as a whole.

lateen (lah-TEEN) A triangular sail affixed to a long yard or crossbar at an angle of about 45 degrees to the mast, with the free corner secured near the stern. The sail was capable of taking the wind on either side. The rig, which was developed by the Arabs, revolutionized navigation because it enabled vessels to tack into the wind and thus to sail in almost any direction; with a square sail, ships could only sail with the wind behind them.

Legalism A school of Chinese philosophy that came into prominence during the period of the Warring States (481–422 B.C.E.) and had great influence on the policies of the Qin dynasty (221–207 B.C.E.). Legalists took a pessimistic view of human nature and believed that social harmony could only be attained through strong government control and the imposition of strict laws, enforced absolutely. The brutal application of this political theory under the Qin led to the fall of the dynasty, and Legalist philosophy was permanently discredited in Confucian philosophy.

libido, id In Freudian psychology, the aggressive force in humans largely representing the drive for sex and power.

madrasa (mah-DRASS-ah) A traditional Islamic school of higher education, principally of theology and law, literally a "place of study." The madrasa usually comprised a central courtyard surrounded by rooms in which the students resided and with a prayer room or mosque, where instruction took place. Tuition, board, and lodging were free. Studies could last for several years and primarily consisted of memorizing textbooks and lectures.

mahdi (MAH-dee) An Arabic word meaning "the right-guided one." According to Islamic tradition, a messianic leader will appear to restore justice, truth, and religion for a brief period before the Day of Judgment. Some Shi'a Muslims believe that the twelfth **imam** (ninth century C.E.) will reappear as the Mahdi. Several impostors have claimed the title.

mandala (MUN-dull-eh) A symbolic circular diagram of complex geometric design used as an instrument of meditation or in the performance of sacred rites in Hinduism and Buddhism.

Mandalas can be drawn, painted, wrought in metal, or traced on the ground. Buddhist examples are usually characterized by a series of concentric circles, representing universal harmony and containing religious figures, with the Buddha in the center.

manorial economy An economic system based on the manor, or the lord's landed estate, the most common unit of agrarian organization in medieval Europe. The manor comprised the lord's own farm (the demesne) and the land farmed by peasant tenants or **serfs** who were legally dependent on the lord and owed him or her **feudal** service on the demesne. The manor was not completely self-contained but it aimed more at self-sufficiency than at the market and supported a steady increase in population up to the fourteenth century.

mantra (MUN-tra) A formula of utterances of words and sounds that are believed to possess spiritual power, a practice of both Hinduism and Buddhism. The efficacy of the mantra largely depends on the exacting mental discipline involved in uttering it correctly. Repetition or meditation on a particular mantra can induce a trancelike state, leading to a higher level of spiritual consciousness.

maroonage A situation of slaves in the West Indian islands in the early eighteenth century. They organized their escape and sometimes lived in communities in inaccessible mountainous regions or forests.

mazombo A direct descendant of Portuguese settlers in the Americas.

medieval A term coined in fifteenth-century Italy to describe the "middle ages," the period between antiquity and the contemporary Renaissance. It originally had negative connotations, for the Middle Ages were regarded as a period of artistic and cultural decline as compared to the lost glories of ancient Rome and the Renaissance attempts to emulate and surpass those achievements.

Meiji restoration The reforms effected in Japan in the name of the emperor Mutsuhito (r. 1867–1912), who was known as the Meiji emperor. During his reign constitutional changes restored the emperor to full power, displacing the militarily powerful shogun, and Japan adopted many western innovations as it became a modern industrial state.

mercantilism An economic policy pursued by many European nations between the sixteenth and eighteenth centuries. It aimed to strengthen an individual nation's economic power at the expense of its rivals by stockpiling reserves of bullion, which involved government regulation of trade. Measures included tariffs on imports, the passing of sumptuary laws to keep demand for imported goods low, the promotion of thrift, and the search for new colonies, both as a source for raw materials and as a market for the export of finished goods.

mestizo (mis-TEE-zo) A person of mixed race. In Central and South America it usually denotes a person of combined Indian and European descent.

mir (MEER) A self-governing community of peasants in pre-revolutionary Russia having control over local forests, fisheries, and hunting grounds; arable land was allocated to each family according to size, in return for a fixed sum. The communes had elected officials and were responsible for the payment of taxes.

mita (MEE-tah) A system of forced labor in Peru, begun under Inca rule and continued by the Spanish colonists, by which Indian communities were required to contribute a set number of laborers for public works for a given period. Conditions were appalling, particularly in the mines, and many Indians perished. The system was abolished in 1821. (*See* **repartimiento**.)

Monophysites (moh-NOF-ih-sites) The supporters of a doctrine in the early Christian Church that held that the incarnate Christ possessed a single, wholly divine nature. They opposed the orthodox view that Christ had a double nature, one divine and one human, and emphasized his divinity at the expense of his capacity to experience real human suffering. The doctrine survived in the Coptic and some other Eastern Churches.

monopoly The exclusive control over the production or supply of a particular commodity or service for which there is no substitute. Because there is no competition, the supplier can fix the price of the product and maximize profits.

Montagnards (MAHN-ton-yards) Members of a radical French revolutionary party, closely associated with the **Jacobins** and supported by the artisans, shopkeepers, and **sansculottes**. They opposed the more moderate **Girondins** and controlled the Legislative Assembly and National Convention during the climax of the Revolution in 1793–4.

mulatto (mah-LAHT-oh) In the Americas, a person of mixed race, usually with parents of European and African origin.

myth An interpretive story of the past that cannot be verified historically but has a deep moral message.

nabob (NAY-bahb) A British employee of the East India Company who made a huge fortune in India, often through corruption, in the eighteenth century.

neo-colonialism The control exercised by a state or group of states of the **developed world** over the economies and societies of the **developing world**. Although the latter countries may be legally independent, investment and economic control are often accompanied by political manipulation.

Neolithic (NEE-o-lith-ick) "New Stone Age"—the last division of the Stone Age, immediately preceding the development of metallurgy and corresponding to the ninth–fifth millennia B.C.E. It was characterized by the increasing domestication of animals and cultivation of crops, established agricultural communities, and the appearance of such crafts as pottery and weaving. Although tools and weapons were still made of stone, technological improvements enabled these to be ground and polished rather than flaked and chipped.

Neoplatonic (nee-o-PLAH-ton-ick) A philo-sophical system founded by Plotinus (205–270 C.E.) and influenced by Plato's theory of ideas. It emphasizes the transcendent, impersonal, and indefinable "One" as the ground of all existence and the source of an eternal world of goodness, beauty, and order, of which material existence is but a feeble copy. By cultivating the intellect and rejecting the material world, humans may become mystically united with the One. Neoplatonism, the last school of Greek philosophy, influenced both Christian theology and Islamic philosophy.

New Testament The second part of the Christian bible, written in Greek and containing the writings attributed to the first followers of Jesus. The twenty-seven books fall into four parts: the four Gospels, dealing with life of Christ; the Acts of the Apostles, concerning the early life of the Church; the Epistles (or letters), written mainly by St Paul; and the Book of Revelation. The canon was established by the end of the fourth century C.E.; the title indicates the Christian belief that Christ's life, death, and resurrection fulfilled prophecies in the Hebrew scriptures, the Old Testament.

ninety-five theses Luther's exposition of his beliefs and his differences with the Catholic Church, posted publicly as a challenge to Church authority.

non-aligned nation A newly independent nation that chose not to align itself with either the USA or the USSR in the Cold War.

paleoanthropologist A student of the earliest humans and the setting in which they lived.

Paleolithic (PAY-lee-o-lith-ick) "Old Stone Age"—the first division of the Stone Age (the earliest phase in a system devised in the nineteenth century to classify human technological development). The Paleolithic (*c.* 1.5 million B.C.E.–10,000 B.C.E.) extends to the end of the last Ice Age and is associated with the emergence of humans, the use of rudimentary tools of chipped stone or bone, and the practice of hunting and gathering. Evidence of painting and sculpture survives from the later, or Upper Paleolithic, period.

paradigm A model of reality representing one viewpoint.

paterfamilias (pay-ter-fuh-MILL-ee-us) The head of a family or household in Roman law—always a male—and the only member to have full legal rights. The *paterfamilias* had absolute power over his family, which extended to life and death. The family included not only direct descendants of the *paterfamilias* through the male line, unless emancipated by him, but also adopted members and, in certain cases, wives. On his death, each son would become a *paterfamilias* in his own right.

patrician (puh-TRISH-un) A member of the elite class of ancient Roman citizens. In the early days of the Republic, patricians held a monopoly of state and religious offices, but this privileged position was gradually eroded with the admission of other social classes to office (see **plebeian**).

patrilineal The tracing of ancestry and kinship through the male line only.

patrilocal Residence by a couple in or near the home of the male's family or group.

Pax Americana Literally "American peace," a Latin phrase derived by analogy from Pax Romana (the peace enforced within the boundaries of the Roman empire by Roman rule) to designate the relative tranquility established within the American sphere of influence after World War II.

Pax Romana (PAKS roh-MAHN-uh) The "Roman Peace," that is, the state of comparative concord prevailing within the boundaries of the Roman Empire from the reign of Augustus (27 B.C.E.–14 C.E.) to that of Marcus Aurelius (161–180 C.E.), enforced by Roman rule and military control.

Pentecost The Greek name for a Jewish festival that falls on the fiftieth day after Passover. The name was adopted by the Christian Church to commemorate the descent of the Holy Spirit on the Apostles of Christ and the beginning of their preaching mission on the fiftieth day after the resurrection of Christ at **Easter**.

perestroika (pair-es-TROY-ka) A Russian word meaning "restructuring," used, like **glasnost**, to describe the reforms introduced by the Soviet leader Mikhail Gorbachev after 1985. It marked the development of a more flexible socio-economic system, distinguished by a move to a market-oriented economy, increased private ownership, and decentralization.

philology The study of languages, or comparative linguistics. Philologists identify common characteristics in languages, study their relationships and trace their origins.

philosophes (fee-luh-ZAWFS) A group of eighteenth-century French writers and philosophers who emphasized the supremacy of human reason and advocated freedom of expression and social, economic, and political reform. They included Voltaire, Montesquieu, Rousseau, and Diderot, editor of the *Encyclopédie* (1751–72), which manifested their ideas. The *philosophes* influenced the ideals of the French Revolution and the American Declaration of Independence.

pictogram (alternative: pictograph) A pictorial symbol or sign representing an object or concept. Prehistoric examples have been found all over the world. Because of the difficulty of representing words other than concrete nouns, writing systems using pictograms generally evolved into those using **ideograms**.

plebeian (plih-BEE-un) A citizen of ancient Rome who was not a member of the privileged patrician class. Plebeians were originally excluded from state and religious offices and forbidden to marry patricians, but from the early fifth century B.C.E. they gradually achieved political equality, gaining admission to all Roman offices. From the later Republican period, the term *plebeian* implied low social class.

polis (POE-lis) The city-state of ancient Greece. It comprised not only the town, which was usually walled with a citadel (acropolis) and a market place (agora), but also the surrounding countryside. Ideally, the *polis* comprised the citizens, who could reside in either town or country; they participated in the government of the state and its religious affairs, contributed to its defense and economic welfare, and obeyed its laws.

praetor (PREE-tor) In ancient Rome, the name was originally applied to the consul as leader of an army. In 366 B.C.E. a further praetor was elected with special responsibility for the administration of justice in Rome, with the right of military command. Around 242 B.C.E. another praetor was created to deal with lawsuits involving foreigners. Further praetors were subsequently appointed to administer the increasing number of provinces. Under the Empire, the position eventually became an honorary appointment.

pre-history The period of time before written records began, which varied from place to place. In this period the study of human development is dependent on the evidence of material remains, such as stone tools or pottery.

primary source Original evidence for an event or fact, as opposed to reported evidence (*see* secondary source).

proletariat In Marxist theory, those who live solely by the sale of their labor, as opposed to the bourgeoisie. The term is usually applied to the wage workers engaged in industrial production.

proxy war A war waged between dependent, client states of larger, more powerful states that do not become directly involved in the fighting; for example the wars among Ethiopia, Somalia, and Eritrea, backed at different times in the 1970s and 1980s by the USSR and the USA. Civil wars between armed factions within a country, each backed by a different foreign power, as in the Congo in the 1960s, are also referred to as proxy wars.

Puranas (poo-RAH-nuz) A collection of poetic tales in Sanskrit, relating the myths and legends of Hinduism. The Puranas expound such topics as the destruction and creation of the world, the genealogy of the gods and patriarchs, the reigns and times of the heroes, and the history of royal dynasties.

quaestor (KWESS-ter) A junior official in ancient Rome. There were originally two, elected annually, but more were appointed as the empire expanded. Most were financial officials. The minimum age was twenty-five, and on completion of the tenure membership of the Senate was automatically conveyed.

Quran (koo-RAHN) The holy book of Islam, believed to contain the direct and authentic word of God as communicated to his prophet Muhammad in a series of revelations by the angel Gabriel. According to tradition, these were collected in the Quran under the caliph Uthman (d. 656) after Muhammad's death. Written in classical Arabic, the Quran is regarded as infallible and is the principal source of Islamic doctrine and law.

radiocarbon dating A method of estimating the age of organic matter, also known as Carbon-14 dating. Carbon dioxide contains a small proportion of the radioactive isotope carbon-14, which is produced in the upper atmosphere by cosmic rays. It is absorbed by green plants, and passes to animals via the food chain. When the organism dies, the amount of carbon-14 in its tissues steadily decreases, at a known rate. The date of death can thus be estimated by measuring the level of radioactivity. The method is mostly used for dating wood, peat, seeds, hair, textiles, skin, and leather.

realpolitik (ray-AHL-poe-lee-teek) A German term meaning practical politics, that is, a policy determined by expediency rather than by ethical or ideological considerations.

Renaissance (REN-ay-sahnz) Literally "rebirth," a French term applied to the cultural and intellectual movement that spread throughout Europe from the fourteenth century. It was characterized by a new interest in Classical civilization, stimulated by the Italian poet Petrarch, and a response to the challenge of its models, which led to pride in contemporary achievement and renewed vigor in the arts and sciences. The new concept of human dignity found its inspiration in **humanism**.

repartimiento (ray-par-tee-mee-EN-toh) A system by which the Spanish crown allowed Spanish American colonists to employ Indians for forced labor, whether in agriculture or the mines. This had to be for the production of essential food or goods, and was for limited periods, but there was much abuse. (*See* mita.)

republic A state that is not ruled by a hereditary leader (a monarchy) but by a person or persons appointed under the constitution. The head of state may be elected and may or may not play a political role.

sacrament In Christian theology, a rite or ritual that is an outward sign of a spiritual grace conveyed on the believer by Christ through the ministry of the Church. In the Orthodox and Roman Catholic Churches seven sacraments are recognized: baptism, confirmation, penance, the Eucharist, marriage, ordination, and anointing of the sick. The two most important of these, baptism and the **Eucharist**, are the only sacraments recognized by most Protestant Churches.

sahel (sah-HAYL) "Shore"—the northern and southern edges of the Sahara Desert. A semi-arid region of Africa, extending from Senegal eastwards to the Sudan and forming a transitional zone between the Sahara desert to the north and the belt of **savanna** to the south. The area is dry for most of the year, with a short and unreliable rainy season, and is subject to long periods of drought. Low-growing grasses provide pasture for camels, pack oxen, cattle and sheep.

samizdat (SAHM-is-DAHT) From the Russian *sam-*, "self-", and *izdatel'stvo*, "publishing house." Literature printed (often in typescript) and circulated secretly to evade official suppression and punishment by the government; also this illegal, underground system of private publication.

samurai A member of the warrior class of feudal Japan, who became vassals of the **daimyo**. Characterized by their military skills and stoical pride, they valued personal loyalty, bravery, and honor more than life. During the peaceful years of the Tokugawa **shogunate** (1603–1867) they became scholars, bureaucrats, and merchants. The class was officially abolished in 1871.

sansculottes (sanz-koo-LAHT) (French: "without knee-breeches") In the French Revolution, members of the militant, generally poorer classes of Paris, so-called because they wore trousers rather than the knee-breeches of affluent society. The dress was also adopted by political activists. The name was proscribed after the fall of Robespierre in 1794.

sati (suttee) (sah-TEE) An ancient Hindu custom that requires widows to be burned on the funeral pyre of their husbands, or soon afterwards. The practice of self-immolation was officially abolished in British India in 1829.

satrapy (SAY-truh-pee) A province or colony in the Achaemenid or Persian Empire ruled by a satrap or governor. Darius I completed the division of the Empire into provinces, and established 20 satrapies with their annual tributes. The term satrapy can also refer to the period of rule of a satrap.

satyagraha (sut-yah-grah-hah) A Hindi expression meaning "truth force," applied to Gandhi's policy of non-violent opposition to British rule in India.

savanna (sah-VAN-ah) The grassland areas of the tropics and sub-tropics adjacent to the equatorial rain forests in each hemisphere and bordered by arid regions of desert. Savannas cover extensive parts of Africa, South America, and northern Australia. The natural vegetation is mainly grass with scattered shrubs and trees, the latter low and often flat-topped. The land is particularly suitable for cattle rearing.

scorched earth A strategy of defensive warfare, in which everything that might be of use to an invading army is destroyed by the defending army as it retreats. Practiced by Russia in its retreat before the armies of Napoleon and, later, of Nazi Germany; also practiced by the Chinese in the face of Japanese invasion in the 1930s and 1940s.

serf An agricultural worker or peasant bound to the land and legally dependent on the lord, characteristic of the **manorial economy** and the **feudal** system. Serfs had their own homes, plots, and livestock but they owed the lord labor, dues, and services. These services could be commuted to rent, but serfs remained chattels of the lord unless they were emancipated by him or her, or escaped. Serfdom declined in western Europe in the late medieval period, but persisted in parts of eastern Europe until the nineteenth century.

shaman (SHAH-men) In the religious beliefs of some Asian and American tribal societies, a person capable of entering into trances and believed to be endowed with supernatural powers, with the ability to cure the sick, find lost or stolen property, predict the future, and protect the community from evil spirits. A shaman may act as judge or ruler, and as a priest a shaman directs communal sacrifices and escorts the souls of the dead to the next world.

shari'a (SHAR-ee-ah) The "road" or sacred revealed law of Islam, based on the Quran and the traditional teachings of Muhammad. Since Islam does not distinguish between the religious and the secular spheres, Islamic law applies to every aspect of life. It covers such matters as marriage, divorce, inheritance, diet, and civil and criminal law.

shogun (SHOW-gun) The military dictator of Japan, a hereditary title held by three families between 1192 and 1867. Although they were legally subservient to the emperor, their military power gave them effective control of the country, and they also took on judicial and administrative functions. The Tokugawa Shogunate (1603–1867) established a powerful centralized government at Edo (Tokyo). Imperial rule was restored in 1868.

shogunate The government of the **shogun**.

soviet A council, the primary unit of government in the Soviet Union at local, regional, and national levels, also adopted by other Communist regimes. Committees of workers' elected deputies first appeared in 1905 to coordinate revolutionary activities; they sprang up throughout the Russian Empire and were a crucial agent in the Revolution of 1917, forming the basis of Soviet administration thereafter.

signares (SEEN-yahr-es) African concubines of French traders in the Senegambia.

Sikhs Members of a religious community founded in the Punjab region of North India by Guru Nanak in the sixteenth century. Sikhism combines *bhakti*, devotional Hinduism with Islamic Sufism. In the face of the militant opposition of its neighbors, Sikhs also became a militant armed group.

sinicization (sigh-ne-sigh-ZAY-shen) The adoption and absorption by foreign peoples of Chinese language, customs and culture.

social contract A mythical, underwritten agreement made at an early stage of human development among citizens in creating a government, or between citizens and a ruler, which defines the rights and obligations of each party to the contract. The citizens accept the authority of the state; and the state agrees to act only with the consent of the governed. The idea goes back to Plato and became influential in seventeenth- and eighteenth-century western Europe through the writings of Hobbes, Locke, and Rousseau.

sophist (SOF-ist) An itinerant professor of higher education in ancient Greece, who gave instruction for a fee. The subjects taught, which included oratory, grammar, ethics, mathematics, and literature, had the practical aim of equipping pupils for successful careers. The sophists were criticized for their ability to argue for any point of view regardless of its truth and for their emphasis on material success. They were prominent in the fifth and early fourth centuries B.C.E.

Sufi (SOO-fee) In Islam, a member of one of the orders practicing mystical forms of worship that first arose in the eighth and ninth centuries C.E. Sufis interpret the words of Muhammad in a spiritual rather than a literal sense. Their goal is direct personal experience of God, achieved by fervent worship (*see* tariqa).

supply and demand In economics, the relationship between the amount of a commodity that producers are able and willing to sell (supply), and the quantity that consumers can afford and wish to buy (demand). The price fluctuates according to a product's availability and its desirability. Supply and demand thus controls a **free market economy**. In practice it is usually subject to some degree of regulation.

Sutta (SOOT-eh) The second section of the Buddhist scriptures or **Tripitaka**, the others being the **Abhidhamma** and the Vinaya. It contains the basic teachings of Buddhism, attributed to the

Buddha himself, and expounded in a series of discourses in a lively and engaging style, employing allegories and parables. It also includes birth stories of the Buddha and other material.

swadeshi (svah-day-shee) "Of one's own country," a Hindi word used as a slogan in the Indian boycott of foreign goods, part of the protest against Britain's partition of Bengal in 1905. The Indian people were urged to use indigenous goods and to wear garments of *khadi*, homemade cloth.

swaraj (svah-raj) A Hindi word meaning "self-government" or "home rule," used as a slogan by Indian nationalists in their campaign for independence from British rule.

syllabary (SIL-eh-ber-ee) A writing system in which each symbol represents the syllable of a word (cf. ideogram). The system appears to have been used for some ancient Near Eastern languages, but Japanese is the only modern-day language to use a syllabary.

syncretism (SING-kri-tiz-ehm) The attempt to combine or harmonize doctrines and practices from different philosophical schools or religious traditions, or the absorption of foreign elements into one particular religion. The term is also used to refer to hybridity in other areas, such as art and culture.

TaNaKh (tah-NAKH) A Hebrew term for the books of the Bible that are written in Hebrew. The word is composed of the initial letters of the words Torah (first five books of the Bible, traditionally attributed to Moses), Nevi'im (the books of the Prophets) and the Ketuvim (additional historical, poetic, and philosophic writings). This threefold division of the Bible is commonly found in the Talmud.

tariqa (tah-REE-cah) In Islam a generic term meaning "path," referring to the doctrines and methods of mysticism and esoterism. The word also refers to schools or brotherhoods of mystics, which were often situated at a mosque or the tomb of a Muslim saint.

teleology (tay-lee-OHL-o-gee) From the Greek word *telos*, "end," the philosophical study of final causes or purposes. A "final cause" is an event in the future for the sake of which an occurrence takes place. Teleology refers especially to any system that interprets nature or the universe as having design or purpose. It has been used to provide evidence for the existence of God.

themes A theme was originally a military unit stationed in one of the provinces of the Byzantine empire, but it later applied to the large military districts that formed buffer zones in the areas most vulnerable to Muslim invasion. By the ninth century the system was extended throughout the empire. Soldiers were given farms in the themes in exchange for military service, but they were later able to commute this for tax, which led to the decline of the system.

thermoluminescence A dating technique used for pottery or other fired material. Electrons produced by radiation will be trapped in the flaws of a crystal lattice, but will be liberated in the form of light when heated. The light emissions occur at a

constant rate and can be measured when the substance is reheated, and correlated to the duration of exposure to radiation. The period of time that has elapsed since the crystal was last heated can then be estimated.

third world The countries outside the **first world** and the **second world** (countries with socialist state systems); more loosely, the **developing world**, which contains more than 70 percent of world population. The twenty-five least developed countries are sometimes characterized as "fourth world."

transhumance (trans-YOO-menz) A form of pastoralism or nomadism organized around the seasonal migration of livestock, practiced in areas that are too cold or wet for winter grazing. The animals are moved to mountain pastures in warm seasons and to lowland ones in winter, or between lower and upper latitudes, or between wet- and dry-season grazing areas.

trebuchet (TRAY-boo-shay) A military engine for hurling heavy missiles, operated by counterpoise, on the principle of the seesaw. Developed in China, the trebuchet first appeared in Europe in the twelfth century.

tribals The aboriginal peoples of the Indian sub-continent, who are outside the **caste** system and live quite separately from the rest of society, generally in remote places. They are thought to have migrated to India in pre-historic times, probably before the emergence of Hinduism.

tribune (TRIB-yoon) In ancient Rome, a **plebeian** officer elected by the plebeians and charged to protect their lives and properties, with a right of veto against legislative proposals of the Senate. The office was instituted during the fifth century B.C.E. and had great political influence under the Republic, but it lost its independence and most practical functions in the time of Augustus (27 B.C.E.–14 C.E.). Military tribunes were senior officers of the legions, elected by the people.

triumvirate (try-UM-vihr-ate) In ancient Rome a board of three men appointed for special administrative duties. An unofficial coalition between Julius Caesar, Pompey, and Crassus was formed in 60 B.C.E. After Caesar's murder in 44 B.C.E., a triumvirate that included his heir Octavian (later Augustus), Mark Antony, and Marcus Lepidus was appointed to maintain public order; it held almost absolute powers and lasted until 36 B.C.E.

ulama (OO-leh-ma) The theologians and legal experts of Islam. The *ulama* form a body of scholars who are competent to decide on religious matters. They include the imams of important mosques, teachers in religious faculties in universities, and judges.

umma (UM-ma) The community of believers in Islam, which transcends ethnic and political boundaries.

untouchables Members of the lowest castes of traditional Indian society or those outside the caste system; the "untouchable" groups were those engaged in "polluting" activities.

Vedas (VAY-duz) Sacred Hindu hymns or verses composed in Sanskrit around 1500–1000 B.C.E.

Many Vedas were recited or chanted during rituals; they are largely concerned with the sacrificial worship of gods representing natural and cosmic forces. The foremost collection is the *Rigveda*, followed by the *Samaveda*, *Yajurveda*, and *Atharvaveda*; the *Brahmanas*, *Aranyakas*, and *Upanishads* are later commentaries but are also considered canonical.

Vinaya (VIN-eh-yeh) The first part of the Buddhist scriptures, or **Tripitaka**. It concerns the early history, regulations, and discipline of Buddhism, focusing in particular on rules for monks and nuns and on such practical subjects as ordination, holy days, dress, food, and medicine.

vodoun The popular religious cult of Haiti, as well as other areas of the Caribbean. It combines ritual elements from Roman Catholicism with theological and magical elements of West African origin. Vodoun ritual centers on animal sacrifice, drumming, and dance, and contact with a populous spirit world through trance.

Yurts (YOORTZ) A portable dwelling used by the nomadic people of Central Asia, consisting of a tentlike structure of skin, felt or hand-woven textiles arranged over wooden poles, simply furnished with brightly colored rugs.

zaibatsu (zai-ba-tsoo) (Japanese: "wealthy clique") A large Japanese business corporation, usually under the control of a single family. A *zaibatsu* was a form of **cartel**, engaging in all important areas of economic activity and funded by its own bank. They emerged under the modernizing Meiji government (1867–1912) and were dissolved by the Allies in 1946 after World War II.

zemstvo (ZEMPST-voh) A rural council in the Russian Empire, established by Tsar Alexander II in 1864 and abolished in 1917. The assemblies, which operated at both district and provincial level, comprised the representatives of individual landed proprietors and village communes (**mir**). They were concerned with such matters as primary education, road building, agricultural development, and public health.

ziggurat (ZIG-gu-rat) A temple tower of ancient Mesopotamia, constructed of square or rectangular terraces of diminishing size, usually with a shrine on top built of blue enamel bricks, the color of the sky. They were constructed of mud brick, often with a baked brick covering, and ascended by flights of steps or a spiral ramp. The sloping sides and terraces were sometimes planted with shrubs and trees. There were ziggurats in every important Sumerian, Babylonian, and Assyrian center.

zimbabwes (zim-BAHB-ways) Stone-walled enclosures or buildings built during the African Iron Age in the region of modern Zimbabwe and Mozambique. The structures were the courts of local rulers. They have been associated with foreign trade, integrated farming and animal husbandry, and gold production. The Great Zimbabwe is the ruins of the former capital of the Monomatapa Empire, situated in Zimbabwe and occupied from around the thirteenth to the sixteenth century C.E.

INDEX

Bold page numbers refer to captions of pictures and of maps.

spearthrower tool **28**
Spencer, Christopher: rifle 572
Spencer, Herbert 607, 636
Spengler, Oswald 590
Spice Islands *see* Moluccas
spinning jenny 562, 565, **565**, 568
Spivak, Gayatri Chakravorty 626
Spring and Autumn Annals 209
Sri Lanka (Ceylon) 244, 250, 257, 267, 286, 401, 408, 721
Srivijaya Empire 258, 259, 285, 406
St. Catherine's Monastery **334**
St. Petersburg (Petrograd/Leningrad) 455, 474–5, **475**, 665, 673, 674
Stalin, Joseph **675**, 675–7, 695, 698, 726, 808
Stalingrad, battle of 701
Stanley, Henry Morton 627
Stanton, Elizabeth Cady 582
Starley, John Kemp 572
Stavrianos, Leften 739
steam power 562, 566–7, 568, 593
steel industry 562, 571, 572, 574, 612, 651, 652, 677, 680, **778**, 779
Steffens, Lincoln 677
Steger, Manfred 829
stelae: Egyptian **71**; Mayan 106, **106**, 107; Sumarian **58**, **59**
Stephen II, Pope 338
Stephens, John Lloyd 107
Stephenson, George 562, 568, **568**
steppe nomads 191, 193–4, 194, **195**
stirrups 207
Stoicism 166, 188–9, 235
Stolypin, Peter 673
Stonehenge, Salisbury Plain **269**
Stopes, Marie 653
Strachey, John 677
Struggle of the Orders 173
stupas 243, 249, 288, **288**
suburbs, growth of 588, 592
subway systems 592
Sucré, Antonio José de 551
Sudan 598, 817–18
Suevi 196
Suez Canal 571, 598, 620, 621, 698, 699, 737, **738**, 755
suffragettes **580**, 581, **581**, 582
Sufis/Sufism 363, 365, 368–70, 378, 501, 504, 506
sugar plantations 455, 457, 460–1, 469, 480, 481, 496–7, 498, 586–7
Sui dynasty 208, 223, 224–5, 229, 230, 294
Sukarno, Achmed 736
Suleiman (Süleyman) I ("the Magnificent") 501, 502
Sulla, Lucius 166, 178, 179
Sullivan, Louis Henry **592**
Sumatra 258, 259, 406
Sumer/Sumerians 118, 127, 128; ale 51, 53, 56; art 54; city-states 48–9, 50, 60, 61–2; cylinder seals 48, 52, **53**; key events 58; king lists 56; religion 51–2, **54**; trade **52**, 53–4; women 53, 60; writing 48, 54–5, 56; ziggurats **41**, 51
Sumitomo 691
Summa Theologica (Aquinas) 442
Sun Yat-sen 617, **657**, 657–8, 769, 770, 771
Sundiata, King of Mali 365
Sunga dynasty 243, 250
Sungir 268
Sunnis 355, 357, 358, 506, 815, 817
Surat 610
Surya (Hindu deity) 275
Susa 118, 128, 138, 140, 156, 159

Sutta 289
Sutton, William 572
Swahili, the 460
Swahilis 111, 367, 400
Sweden 426, 430, 470, 474, 475, 844
Sweezy, Paul 626
Sweyn Forkbeard **426**
Swinton, Ernest 573
Switzerland 181, 192
Sykes-Picot agreement 671
Syracuse 143, 166
Syria 78, 129, 130, 131, 140, 156, 166, 168, 170, 195, 199, 200, 359, 505, 506, 621, 669, 671, 721, 735, 752 *see also* Damascus
Szilard, Leo 712
Szymborska, Wislawa: "How Should We Live?" 646, 681

Tabriz 418, 506
Tacitus, Emperor 163, 167, 171, 184, 189, 192, 323, 328
Tagore, Rabindranath 771, 782
Taiping Rebellion 598, 616
Taiwan 613, 633, 638, 690, 691, 736, 746, 759, 776, 781, 820
Taj Mahal 374, **375**
Tajikistan 808, 809
Takshasila *see* Taxila
Talas River, battle of 208, 229, 230, 236, 296, 358
Talbot, William Henry Fox 573
Tale of Genji (Lady Murasaki) 301
Taliban, the 731, 815, 817
Talmuds 308, 318
Tamerlane/Tamberlane *see* Timur the Lame
Tamil culture **255**, 256, 284
Tamil Nadu *see* Madras
TaNaKh 308, 309–10, 312–15, 319
Tang dynasty 92, 208, 224–9, **226**, **227**, 230, 236, 294, 295, 297, 408, 479
Tanganyika 627, 628 *see also* Tanzania
Tange, Kenzo 645, **645**
tanks 573, 705
Tantric Buddhism 296–7
Tanzania 13, 14, **14**, 29, 620, 814, 868 *see also* Tanganyika
Tanzimat 608, 661
Tarentum 166
tariqas 370
Tartars 417, 419
Tashkent 418
Tasman, Abel 447, 491, 493
Tasmania **25**, 447
Tatars 408
Tawney, R. H. 465
taxation 126; China 219, 221; Inca 110; Muslim 355; Persia 138; Roman 175
Taxila 159, 250, 253, 290, 293
Tbilisi 418
tea 222, 412, 421
technology 646–7, 649, 650–2; and domestic change 650–1; and gender relations 653–4; and globalization 828–30; social setting 760; and urbanization 654; and war 654, 696, 702, **702**, 705–6, 708–10, 731–2 *see also* computers/information technology; Industrial Revolution; inventions; science
Tegaste 331
telegraphs 572, 573, 593, 650, 651
teleology 9
telephones 572, 593, 650, 651, 678
telescopes 526, 527, 529

temple mounds, Mississippi 111
Ten Commandments 265, 312
Tendai Buddhism 299
Tenochtitlán 103, 396, 454, 455
Teotihuacán 55, 97, **101**, 101–2, **102**, 108, 115
Tertiary period 11
Tertullian 171
Teshik-Tash 268
Tesla, Nikola 572, 573
Texas 538, 553
textile industry: Britain 562, 563, 564–7, **565**, 568, 575, 624; India 468, **469**, **477**, 562, 565, 567, 586, 604, 611–12, 787–8; Netherlands 466 *see also* cotton/cotton industry; silk; wool industry
Thailand 257, 258, 286, 700, 831
Thatcher, Margaret 796
Thebes, Egypt 66, 73, 77, 78
Thebes, Greece 143, 155, 158
Theodora, Empress **336**
Theodosius I, Emperor 196
Theodosius II, Emperor 198
Theravada Buddhism 231, 289, 301
thermoluminescence 22
Thermopylae, battle of 146
Thessaly 155
Third World 743–5, 761
Thodosius, Emperor 329
Thomas Aquinas, St. 442
Thompson, E. P. 532, 581
Thoth (Egyptian deity) 70
Thousand and One Nights, The 407
Thrace 135, 155, 200
Thucydides 147, 148, 152, 153
Thutmosis I, of Egypt 131
Tiananmen Square massacre 557, 770, **779**, 865, 866
Tiantai Buddhism 299
Tiber River 163
Tibet 218, 225, 286, 288, 302, 507, 513, 613, 781, 866
Tigris River 53
Tikal 103–4, **104**, 106
Tilak, Bal Gangadhar 656, 785
Timbuktu 111, 114, 365–6, 374
Timgad **186**
Timur the Lame (Tamerlane/Tamberlane) **362**, 363, 374, 379, 419, 505, 506
Tito, Josif Broz 702, 719, 745, 746, 818, 846, **846**
Titus, Arch of **319**
Tivoli: Hadrian's Villa **174**
Tiwanaku 97, 109
Toba Wei 223, 294
tobacco 455, 457, 481, 489, 624
Tocqueville, Alexis de 600
Todaiji complexes 299
Todar Mal 503
Toji Temple 300
Tokugawa Ieyasu 480
Tokugawa shogunate 455, 480, 633, 635
Tokyo 480, 632, 634, 635, 636, 703, 758
Toltecs 97, 98, 103, 108, 397
Tomyris 135
tool-making, prehistoric 22, **27**, 27–9, **28**, 36–7, **38**, 39, 45
Torah, the 308, 309, 310, 311, 315–16, 317, 318
Torquemada, Tomás de 380
Torres, Camilo 823
Tou Wan, Princess: burial suit **215**
"Toumai" skull 14–15, 19, **19**
Toure, Samori 623, 628
Tournai 432
Tours, battle of 336, 357